# THEIR SPORTING LEGACY

## THE PARTICIPATION
## OF CANADIANS
## OF UKRAINIAN DESCENT
## IN SPORT, 1891-1991

*To Mary + Eli*

*George + Barbara*

# THEIR SPORTING LEGACY

## THE PARTICIPATION
## OF CANADIANS
## OF UKRAINIAN DESCENT
## IN SPORT, 1891-1991

### K. W. SOKOLYK

*With best wishes*

*K. W. Sokolyk*

The Basilian Press
Toronto, Ontario, Canada

𝕿𝖍𝖊 𝕭𝖆𝖘𝖎𝖑𝖎𝖆𝖓 𝕻𝖗𝖊𝖘𝖘

265 Bering Avenue, Toronto, Ontario M8Z 3A5

Printed in Canada

---

National Library of Canada Cataloguing in Publication Data

Sokolyk, K. W., 1958-
         Their sporting legacy: the participation of Canadians of
Ukrainian descent in sport, 1891-1991

Includes bibliographical references and index.
ISBN  0-921537-44-1


         1. Ukrainian Canadians--Sports--History.  2. Ukrainian
Canadians--Sports--Societies, etc.--History  3. Ukrainian--
Canadian athletes--Biography.  I. Title.

GV585.S565 2002      796'.089'91791071      C2002-900164-1

---

Front cover photo:  Lakehead Ukrainian Athletic Club *Ukes* juvenile
hockey team, c.1938

Back cover photos (clockwise from left):  Evelyn Wawryshyn, Steve
Oneschuk, Sylvia Fedoruk, Mike Bossy (courtesy of the New York
Islanders), and George Bossy.

For my parents, Yaroslav and Oksana Sokolyk,
without whose encouragement and support
this book would not have been possible.

# ACKNOWLEDGEMENTS

The author would like to acknowledge and thank the great number of people who contributed information and/or photographs, or assisted in the research process.

Those individuals who submitted material about their own careers or about the clubs they organized, coached or managed are not listed here. Their names and their contribution to sport are part of the main text.

There are individuals, though, that should to be mentioned: Michael Czuboka, Phil Drackett, Bo Fodchuk, Martin Harris, Peter Kolaski, Roman Kucil, Vince Leah, Glynn Leyshon, Ph.D., Russell Luch, Michael Marunchak, Ph.D., Vern May, Jim McAuley, William B. McNulty, Eugene Oryszczyn, Bohdan Pauk, Roman Petryshyn, Ph.D., George Romanovych, Dr. Roman Romanovych, Ostap Steckiw, Frances Swyripa, Ph.D., A. W. Taylor, Ph.D., Jim Trifunov, Omelan Twardowsky, Walter Williams, Olha Woycenko and Gary Zeman. Their assistance is appreciated.

A very special thank you to Diane Imrie and Kate Dwyer of the Northwestern Ontario Sports Hall of Fame in Thunder Bay, Tony Techko of the Windsor/Essex County Sports Hall of Fame, Ed Sweeney of the Manitoba Hockey Hall of Fame and Louise Froggett of the Canadian Football Hall of Fame and Museum in Hamilton. They always came through with the requested material.

In addition, the following organizations, represented by the mentioned individuals, also provided information and/or photographs, or assisted in the research process:

David Allen, Saskatchewan Sports Hall of Fame, Regina
Budd Bailey, Buffalo Sabres
Martin Blake, World Professional Billiards & Snooker Association, Bristol, England
Darren Boyko, Hockey Hall of Fame, Toronto
William Chmiliar, Norwood Legion, Edmonton
Diane Darlington, Alberta Sports Hall of Fame, Calgary
Thomas Fisher, Curling Hall of Fame and Museum of Canada, Baie d'Urfe
Richard Gabruch, Ukrainian Canadian Committee Saskatchewan Provincial Council, Saskatoon
Philip Gimbarzhewsky, Ukrainian Canadian Cultural Society of Vancouver Island, Victoria
William Harasym, Association of United Ukrainian Canadians, Toronto
Julie Hensley, Washington Capitals
Zenon Hluszok, Ukrainian Cultural and Educational Centre, Winnipeg
Joe Horrigan, Pro Football Hall of Fame, Canton, Ohio
Lois Howard, Manitoba Sports Hall of Fame, Winnipeg

C. Fred Johnson, Canadian Canoe Association
Mark Kelly, Salt Lake Golden Eagles Hockey Club
Bud Knight, Manitoba 5 Pin Bowling Association, Winnipeg
Sylvie Korim, Athlete Information Bureau, Ottawa
Peter Kwasny, St. Nicholas Parish Men's Club, Winnipeg
Walter Kuz, The New Pathway Publication, Toronto
Steve McCarthy, Manitoba Sports Hall of Fame and Museum, Winnipeg
Archie Miller, Canadian Lacrosse Hall of Fame, New Westminster
Myron Momryk, National Archives of Canada, Ottawa
George Moskal, Association of United Ukrainian Canadians, Toronto
Wolodymyr Okipniuk, Homin Ukrainy Publication, Toronto
Dave Parkes, Curl Canada, Ottawa
Lt.-Col. G. W. Pearson, National Defence Headquarters, Ottawa
Philip Pritchard, Hockey Hall of Fame, Toronto
Janice Smith, Alberta Sports Hall of Fame and Museum, Calgary
Allan Stewart, Canada's Sports Hall of Fame, Toronto
Toni Stokes, Canadian Amateur Wrestling Association, Ottawa
Randy Undercofler, Philadelphia Flyers
Donna Wilk, St. Vladimir Institute Library, Toronto
Leon Wowk, Ukrainian Canadian Committee Saskatchewan Provincial Council, Saskatoon
Tony Unitas, Canadian Boxing Hall of Fame, Toronto

As did the following organizations and institutions:

| | |
|---|---|
| Canadian Volleyball Association | Quebec Nordiques |
| Hartford Whalers | St. Michael's College School |
| Los Angeles Kings | Toronto Maple Leafs |
| New Jersey Devils | Vancouver Canucks |
| New York Islanders | Washington Capitals |
| Pittsburgh Steelers | Winnipeg Jets |

The hockey and football cards illustrated in the book have been reproduced with the kind permission of the O-Pee-Chee Company Limited of London, Ontario.

Finally, a sincere thanks to Luba Butska, Andrew Gregorovich, John B. Gregorovich, Lesya Jones, Dr. Michael Kondracki, George Tracz, Ph.D., Oksana Vatseba and my parents for their valuable suggestions.

My apologies for any omissions.

The publication of this work was facilitated by the
financial assistance of the
Ukrainian Canadian Foundation of Taras Shevchenko (Winnipeg).

The Ukrainian Canadian Centennial Commission, appointed
by the Ukrainian Canadian Congress, provided
a grant which assisted in the research process.

# TABLE OF CONTENTS

# FOREWORD

The year 1951 was memorable for me. I was elected to the Ontario Provincial Parliament for the first time. I also became captivated by the Toronto Maple Leafs' challenge for the Stanley Cup, the championship series against Montreal, Bill Barilko's overtime Stanley Cup winning goal, and the apprehension and sadness of a nation when the plane Barilko was on board disappeared over Ontario's North.

*Their Sporting Legacy: The Participation of Canadians of Ukrainian Descent in Sport, 1891-1991* profiles the sporting career of Bill Barilko and some 300 other Canadian athletes, coaches and sports administrators of Ukrainian descent. With strong spirit, determination and courage they made a lasting imprint on Canadian sport.

In 1951, I continued to witness the growth of organized Ukrainian sport in Toronto. I welcomed this development because sport, while providing physical training, emphasizes self-discipline and fair play - two fundamental elements in the upbringing of youth, and key characteristics of community and nation building.

*Their Sporting Legacy: The Participation of Canadians of Ukrainian Descent in Sport, 1891-1991* presents historical surveys of some 70 Ukrainian volunteer-based sports clubs, leagues and teams that operated in more than 20 Canadian towns and cities. By providing their members with physical training, these organizations helped shape youth into today's citizens and leaders. Their impact on Canadian sport and society is therefore important.

In summary, the participation of Canadians of Ukrainian descent in sport is a significant accomplishment whose story should be told.

*John Yaremko, Q.C., LL.D.*
*Toronto*

# PREFACE

This book documents the participation of Canadians of Ukrainian descent in sport. The first part surveys sports clubs, leagues and teams. The second part explores the careers of individuals.

The clubs and teams chronicled were all organized and operated by Canadians of Ukrainian descent. In addition, all the clubs and teams participated in competitive Canadian leagues. The Ukrainian sport leagues were also organized and operated by Canadians of Ukrainian descent. Participation in the leagues was usually open only to Ukrainian teams. In-house sports programs operated by non-sporting Ukrainian organizations are not discussed unless the organization in question had at least one team in a structured Canadian league.

No attempt is made to evaluate the clubs, leagues and teams. The fact that they existed and flourished suggests that they played an important role in the history of the Ukrainian community in Canada, and in the history of sport in Canada.

The athletes, coaches and sports administrators profiled are of Ukrainian descent. All either competed or coached in the professional ranks, represented Canada in amateur or professional competitions, or distinguished themselves in Canadian sport.

Extensive research was conducted for this work. More than 250 books and periodicals were consulted. Most Ukrainian language newspapers published in Canada were surveyed, as were numerous Canadian dailies. In addition, more than 450 letters, most accompanied by questionnaires, were sent to athletes, sports pioneers, and sports activists requesting information. Personal interviews were conducted with sports pioneers and sports activists in Montreal, Oshawa, Ottawa, Toronto, Hamilton, Niagara Falls, Windsor, Sudbury, Thunder Bay, Kenora, Winnipeg, Roblyn and Saskatoon. Telephone interviews were conducted with organizers across Canada.

With a few minor exceptions, the research and writing were completed in the summer of 1993, five and a half years after beginning the work.

Unfortunately, at the club level some of the sport activists and organizers could not be located while others had already passed away. Of those located and contacted, only some responded to requests for information and interviews.

Sport activists and organizers who agreed to interviews provided a wealth of information. They often tried to recall events from decades ago. At times their recollections were vague. Nevertheless, in some instances, personal recollections were the only known source of information available at the time of writing.

Newspapers and journals were also a good source of information about the clubs, leagues, and teams.

The Ukrainian language press intermittently reported on the operations of the Ukrainian clubs, relying almost fully on unsolicited contributions from volunteers within the community. This coverage peaked in the 1950s.

Prior to about 1960, in most cities the local press reported daily on community sports, with Ukrainian clubs receiving their share of coverage. Much information was gathered from the pages of these dailies, particularly about clubs in Hamilton, Sudbury, Winnipeg, Montreal, Oshawa, Saskatoon, and Port Arthur - Fort William (now Thunder Bay). This information usually highlighted the athletic accomplishments of a club and very rarely delved into administrative aspects.

Subsequently, however, the popularization of professional sports through the broadcast media resulted in an almost complete removal of community sports from the sports pages.

There are omissions and gaps in information about athletes, coaches and sports administrators. In some instances, neither individuals nor their families could be located. In other instances, the contacted individuals did not respond to requests for information. It was possible, though, to gather sufficient information from various sources to profile some 300 individuals. Unfortunately, for many individuals there was insufficient information to draft a profile.

The inclusion of an athlete, coach or administrator in this book does not in any way suggest that the information incorporated into the profile is complete. Aside from professional hockey leagues, only a few sport bodies have maintained a historical statistical profile of their respective sport over an extended period of time. In some cases, sport bodies did not respond to requests for official records and statistics.

All statistical data were compiled from newspapers, periodicals, media guides, completed questionnaires or competition results. The data are provided in the form given at the time of publication (please see Appendix VII for a more detailed discussion about statistical data).

Great care was taken to verify and ensure that the information presented in this book is accurate, and to acknowledge use of photographs. The author will gladly receive information that will enable him to rectify, in future editions, any inadvertent errors or omissions.

In some instances, information that was available did not make it to the pages of this book. Junior or collegiate statistics were omitted unless a record was established, or a major championship won. In amateur and professional competition, generally only the results of major meets or accomplishments were included.

Many of the sources used in this book are in Ukrainian. Where accepted transliterations of names could not be obtained, a literary transliteration was made.

The rules of English orthography, particularly their application to sports in Canada, have not followed a consistent pattern. In some sports, the traditional British English spelling has been superseded by American. While it may appear inconsistent, to avoid confusion, the spelling used in this book attempts to parallel the accepted usage in each sport. For example, the Canadian Football League utilizes the British form of "centre" to denote a position of a player while the National Hockey League uses the American "center," and so on.

The clubs, leagues and teams surveyed in this book are referred to throughout as being Ukrainian. This usage is a matter of convenience. More appropriately, the term Ukrainian-Canadian or Canadian-Ukrainian should be used.

It is hoped that this work on the participation of Canadians of Ukrainian descent in sport will inspire enthusiasts to examine the subject matter more thoroughly in the future. I urge the reader to assist in preserving the history of these clubs, teams and leagues by depositing any available archival materials, scrap books, memorabilia, uniforms, etc. with the Ukrainian Cultural and Educational Centre, 184 Alexander Avenue East, Winnipeg, Manitoba, R3B 0L6.

*K. W. Sokolyk,*
*Toronto - Durham, Ontario,*
*July, 1993.*

# INTRODUCTION

"The role of sports and games in Canadian life has, strangely, lacked chroniclers . . . The history of sport is a neglected field. Historical works usually consider wars, government, religion, social change, trade, and so on,"[1] wrote Nancy and Maxwell Howell in the introduction to their book *Sports and Games in Canadian Life: 1700 to the Present*. The Howells reiterated what British historian A. Lunn wrote in his 1927 book *A History of Skiing*: "The historian . . . is apt to forget that sport in some form or another is the main object of most lives, that most men work in order to play, and that games which bulk so largely in the life of individuals cannot be neglected in studying the life of a nation."[2] In 1985, former athlete turned historian Bruce Kidd expanded on the Lunn and Howell thesis by suggesting that historians should also look at the role of ethnic sports. Kidd argued that "ethnic sport studies [are] necessary for a full understanding of the immigrant experience in Canada."[3]

In Canada, numerous popular and academic books on the subject of sport have appeared. Some have endeavoured to study sport in a particular period of time, others a particular sport, while still others focused on a particular league, team or personality. Within this body of literature, however, the role that immigrants have played in the development of sport in Canada has been documented only marginally. The only major English-language works in this field that come to mind are Leible Hirshfield's *The Jewish Athlete: A Nostalgic View* (1980), Gerald Redmond's *The Sporting Scots of Nineteenth-Century Canada* (1982), and a collection of essays, *Sport Pioneers: A History of the Finnish-Canadian Amateur Sports Federation* (c.1986), edited by Jim Tester.

Among Canadians of Ukrainian descent, the awareness of their sports heritage and its contribution to the development of their ethnic community is remarkably limited. The history of Ukrainian sports clubs, leagues, and teams has been almost completely overlooked, as has been the history of the participation of athletes of Ukrainian descent in organized Canadian sport.

The only books fully dedicated to this subject are *Beyond the Uke Line: Ukrainians in the National Hockey League* by George Tatomyr (1990) and *"Ukraina" Sport Association - Toronto* co-authored by Jaroslaw Chorostil and Roman Kostriuk (1983). The two books, while pioneer works in their field, present very specific topics.

Partially broaching the subject of Ukrainians and sport in Canada are Michael Czuboka's *Ukrainian Canadian, Eh?* (1983) and Oleksander Skocen's Ukrainian-language autobiography *With Soccer into the World* (1985).

*Their Sporting Legacy: The Participation of Canadians of Ukrainian Descent in Sport, 1891-1991* intends to provide a more general survey of the participation in sport by Ukrainian immigrants in Canada and their heirs during their first century of settlement in Canada.

# IMMIGRATION TO CANADA

H istorically, mass Ukrainian immigration to Canada has been viewed as having occurred in three distinct waves. The reasons for leaving Ukraine and the socioeconomic background of each wave differed. This uniqueness resulted in somewhat different aspirations of each arriving group. Imbedded in these aspirations was a particular disposition or a conceived role for sport.

The first wave of immigration began in 1891 with the arrival of Wasyl Eleniak and Ivan Pylypiv. The wave lasted through the outbreak of World War I in 1914. In those years some 170,000 Ukrainians, largely of peasant background, arrived in Canada. The majority settled on the uninhabited expanses of the virgin Canadian prairies. The Canadian government induced the immigrants to come to Canada and to settle on the prairies by offering them 160 acre (64.8 hectare) homesteads for ten dollars.

The second wave of Ukrainian immigration occurred between the two World Wars and brought 68,000 settlers to Canada. The rural parts of the Prairie Provinces once again absorbed most of the immigrants. In general, this group was better educated and occupationally more diverse than the previous one.

The third wave of immigration occurred in the years 1947 to 1954 when 34,000 Ukrainians were admitted into Canada. These individuals were predominantly refugees uprooted by World War II who had resided in displaced persons (DP) camps of Western Europe since the cessation of hostilities. This group had a very diverse educational and socioeconomic background. Most of these immigrants settled in the urban centres of Ontario.[4]

# ORGANIZED SPORT

## THE EARLY YEARS

The earliest documented evidence of organized Ukrainian sports life in Canada dates back to 1907 at the Ruthenian Training (Normal) School in Brandon, Manitoba. The school was established by the provincial government to meet the need for trained Ukrainian bilingual teachers, as had been done in St. Boniface for French teachers in 1899.[5] The school had two instructors in charge of physical training. In addition, the students attended a physical education course twice weekly in the evenings at the YMCA. In 1910, the students organized a soccer team. Considering the economic hardships of the era and Brandon's relative isolation, the team was well outfitted in matching uniforms and soccer shoes with cleats. The school operated until 1916.[6]

*Photo courtesy of M. Marunchak*

*The first soccer club of Ukrainian students of the Normal School in Brandon, 1910*

The first documented participation of a Ukrainian sports club in a public display occurred in Winnipeg on September 14, 1914. On that day, children attending the community school *Ridna Shkola*[7] at Sts. Vladimir and Olga Church put on a show of athletic exercises for a community audience. The exercises were reminiscent of those performed in Lviv, Ukraine, by members of the sport association Sokil Batko. The *Ridna Shkola* participants even had smart matching uniforms that were similar to those used by Sokil Batko. In Winnipeg, under the guidance of sport enthusiast and teacher Konstantin Zalitach, the *Ridna Shkola* group practised and performed on a regular basis.[8]

It is not a coincidence that the earliest evidence of organized Ukrainian sport life occurred in the *ridna shkolas*. In fact, this phenomenon was common in Canada at the time; schools and other institutions of learning were the cradle of sport in the country.[9] Sport was encouraged by individuals in charge of the Canadian school systems and the public playgrounds to solve a perceived urban crisis caused by rural-urban migration and "foreign" (that is, non-British) immigration. In particular, it was believed that sport "Canadianized" the foreign child and emphasized British qualities "such as self-discipline and moral will-power, devotion to fair play, justice and equality and above all, the sense of loyalty and duty to one's side that, in a larger context, was the essence of patriotism."[10]

Aspiring Canadian public school teachers, during their training in normal schools (teacher training schools), were given instruction in traditional British and North American sports. They were encouraged to use sport as a cornerstone of character building. As a result, almost every school in the country had a sports program of some sort.

Some of the teachers instructing in Ukrainian evening or Saturday schools brought the sporting tradition of their occupied homeland to Canada. These traditions, to a great extent, were cultivated in Ukraine by two chains of sport associations bearing the names Sitch and Sokil Batko. Both associations argued that sport developed discipline, order, character, healthy bodies and healthy minds. These characteristics, the two associations believed, were necessary to train cadres of nationally conscious youth.

*Konstantin Zalitach and the Ridna Shkola group in Winnipeg, 1914*

During the formative years before World War I, sport outside the school system was not an important factor in the daily lives of Ukrainians. The immigrants were foremost interested in economic stability. Isolated on the homesteads or in rural communities, the newcomers were occupied in a struggle for subsistence. Forests and bush had to be uprooted and transformed into fields, crops had to be planted and winterized shelters constructed. Money was scarce and chores had to be done.

Consequently, parents did not appreciate their children abandoning household responsibilities or a possible supplementary income to pursue "frivolous" pastimes. Sport, if at all practised in the area of settlement, was seen as a non-productive activity or a luxury that the household could not afford. It was also something the immigrants did not understand. Primarily of a rural peasant background, they were not exposed to sport during their upbringing.

Economic stability, while the major objective of Ukrainians, was not the only aspiration. Canadian historian W. Morton wrote that the early Ukrainian immigrants, more than any other group, brought with them ". . . a sense of nationalism, born at once of oppression and the teaching of their leaders."[11] This nationalism, a longing for ethno-cultural survival, resulted in a massive effort to establish a Ukrainian community within their newly adopted community. The immigrants contributed time, money and resources to build Ukrainian schools and churches, and to organize Ukrainian political, social, and cultural associations.

Prior to the outbreak of World War I, though, sport was not part of the community agenda of Ukrainians in Canada and was only rarely pursued on an individual basis. The participation of Ukrainians in organized Canadian sport, such as that of O. Holinsky on the Creighton Mine baseball team in 1911, was a unique exception.[12] However, in Canadian institutions of learning it was a different matter; sport was part of the curriculum and parents accepted it as being an appropriate component of the schooling experience.

## BETWEEN THE WARS

World War I and the prosperity that followed brought about major socioeconomic changes in the lives of Canadians, including those of Ukrainian descent. To a large extent, economic stability had been attained by those settlers remaining on the farms and those migrating to urban centres.

In the cities and towns after World War I, the industrial jobs were such that an individual had more leisure time. More important, though, with leisure time on their hands, the first Canadian-born generation of Ukrainians had an opportunity for learning and pursuing the leisure interests of other longer-established Canadians. Sport, which gained much popularity after the war, was one of these interests.

At first, Ukrainians played pick-up sports on vacant lots, streets and in parks. Subsequently, they began to join community-based sports clubs. In a few years, Ukrainian sports enthusiasts started to organize their own teams, clubs and leagues.

The formation of "ethnic" sports clubs in Canada, at the time, was fairly popular and not innovative. One sports historian has argued that "the ethnic rivalry which naturally exists in a multicultural society, in many fields, has been continuously reflected in Canadian sport. Since earlier times, when British and French competed in various athletic contests with Indians and Eskimos, as well as each other, sports has gradually developed to involve nearly all the ethnic groups in Canada within its competitive embrace."[13]

The Montreal Curling Club was the first chartered sports club in Canada. It was founded by Scottish immigrants in 1807, although it did not become a permanent fixture until 1820. The first Finnish sports club was formed in 1906. By 1934, more than forty Finnish clubs existed in Canada.[14] The Winnipeg Falcons hockey club that won the 1920 world amateur championship was an Icelandic club. German, Jewish, Polish, and other ethnic clubs were also organized in Canada at the turn of the century.

The first Ukrainian "sports" group to be formed outside the school setting was organized in the mid-1920s as an integral part of the framework of the Ukrainian Boy Scout and Sporting "Sitch" Association. Founded by Volodymyr Bossy, the grandfather of hockey star Michael Bossy, and other post-war immigrants, Sitch was a monarchist movement which supported the claims of the Ukrainian monarch-in-exile, Pavlo Skoropadsky, to head an independent Ukraine.[15]

One of the organization's objectives was to "encourage and promote lawful amateur games and exercises."[16] Despite its name, the organization was more of a paramilitary outfit open to boys, girls and adults. It conducted regular drill training, competed in drills against other Canadian and American military and paramilitary units, and partook in military type manoeuvres.[17]

The fundamental reason for practising drills was to train men and women for the liberation of Ukraine.[18] Sitch was a Ukrainian nationalistic organization and the paramilitary training included advocacy of a desirable patriotism. In addition, the drills were practised to train the members for the defence of Canada and the British Empire, to instil respect for the flag, monarch and country, and to sharpen the physical and mental skills of the participants.

Nevertheless, at the time, drills were considered a sport. They provided the participants with strenuous physical training, discipline, an appreciation of teamwork and a respect for rules.

Sitch gained much popularity among Ukrainians in the 1920s. Its success can be attributed to two major reasons. First, Sitch was a Ukrainian nationalistic organization. Secondly, Sitch emulated the popular Canadian paramilitary organizations of the era. It was affiliated with the Canadian General Council of the Boy Scouts Association and it was regularly invited by the government and military establishments to partake in civic, military and patriotic functions. Many Ukrainians believed that association with an organization possessing such loyalist characteristics would make them model citizens in the eyes of the British majority.

In the 1920s and 1930s, only a small number of Sitch branches across Canada participated in organized sport as we know it today. In Toronto, Oshawa and some Western Canada locations, baseball teams were established.

At the time, additional established Ukrainian organizations began advocating the formation of sport clubs within their organizations' structures.

The Ukrainian Labour-Farmer Temple Association (ULFTA), a pro-communist organization, was the first major association to advocate the formation of in-house sport groups for youth. The organizers believed that these sport clubs would be an ideal vehicle to keep youth within the ranks of the parent association. In 1926, the national executive published manuals outlining routines for physical fitness and group exercises, and circulated them to all the branches. Editorials appeared as early as December 1927 in *Youths' World*, the official publication of the Youth Section of the ULFTA, calling for mass participation in organized sports.

Even with such support, the establishment of sustainable sport programs at the branches was not a given. The older membership of the ULFTA was opposed to sport, claiming that it was no more than horseplay or undesirable Americanism.[19] By 1930, though, the bloc supporting sport exerted enough influence to see the establishment of programs in Montreal, Port Arthur, Timmins, Toronto, and Winnipeg. Other locations soon followed.

*Ukrainian Branch of the Workers' Sports Association of Toronto, 1928*

The ULFTA sport movement was affiliated with the Workers' Sports Association of Canada (WSA). Established by the Young Communist League (YCL), the WSA was "intended to be one of the most powerful of the Communist Party of Canada's 'mass organizations,' designed to win both sympathetic and uncommitted non-party members to the communist cause. WSA members were not required to be communists; the organization was successfully controlled by a 'faction' of YCL members acting under party discipline."[20]

Both the WSA and ULFTA sport groups were as much interested in sport as in using sport for political propaganda and gains. They actively opposed events such as the Olympic Games, but at the same time, they lauded Spartakiades for "workers" and glorified Soviet sport. In organizing sport clubs, they argued, "that just as the YMCAs can be used by the bosses for drawing youth away from the Labour movement, the Workers' Sports is a force drawing youth to the Labour movement."[21]

In 1931 a baseball club was formed by the youth of the ULFTA in Calgary. One of its members wrote to the newspaper, *The Young Worker*: "We played several games with the WSA teams in Drumheller, Edmonton, and succeeded in getting quite a number of members. But the most important work carried on by our team is the work in breaking up some fascist teams and winning the members for the WSA. We noticed some difference in the team of the Ukrainian fascist organization. We took advantage of this by calling them to a conference and asking them to unite with us in a Workers sports team. They agreed, despite the fact that their fathers are in the executive of the Ukrainian fascist organization."[22]

The organization branded "fascist" by the ULFTA and WSA was probably the non-communist Narodnyi Dim (People's Home).

By the mid-1930s, the workers' sport clubs became less militant. Sport was pursued for the sake of sport. Some of the more radical activists criticized this development, claiming it distracted members from revolutionary work.[23] In 1937, ULFTA took a further step in orienting its sport clubs into the mainstream. A resolution of the XVIth ULFTA national convention, based on a recommendation of the WSA, encouraged the sport clubs to enter into agreements with the YMCAs and YWCAs for the use of their facilities.[24] One-time ideological foes were now acceptable. There is no evidence, though, to suggest that any of the ULFTA sport clubs pursued this proposal.

The sport activities of the ULFTA differed significantly from those of other Ukrainian clubs. Besides baseball, the labour sport movement encouraged participation in sports that were popular in the Soviet Union. Gymnastics, distance running, and human pyramid building were the mainstay of the ULFTA clubs. In addition, the ULFTA sport clubs in general did not join mainstream Canadian sports leagues. They competed in leagues organized by the Workers' Sports Association. These leagues consisted of sport clubs affiliated with other socialist or communist organizations and with trade union clubs.

In 1935, the Workers' Sports Association sent a team to participate in exhibition competitions in the USSR. It was the first Canadian sport delegation ever to visit the Soviet Union. Stops on the tour included Kharkiv, Ukraine. Members of the Canadian team included all-round track and field athlete Billy Philipovich of Myrnam, Alberta, and gymnast Walter Kaczor of Winnipeg, Manitoba.

In the mid-1930s, the national executive of the Ukrainian National Youth Federation (UNYF) took an active role in encouraging branches to form clubs. In addition, many Ukrainian churches formed softball and/or basketball teams that competed in church leagues. Even cultural and educational societies, such as Prosvita, formed sports clubs. As with the ULFTA, the primary objective was to attract and keep Ukrainian youth within the framework of the organization or the church.

These clubs were affiliated with youth, political, cultural or church groups, and the sports program was an in-house activity for the members. To participate in the sport program, one usually had to be a member of the parent organization. The mainstream Canadian clubs and clubs formed by other non-Ukrainian ethnic groups were therefore the only alternative venues for organized sport. Ukrainian youth for the most part shied away from these clubs. Ethnicity, language, and religion made them outsiders. As a result, they preferred to group together and play pick-up sports.

Those who ventured into the world of organized sport were sometimes disappointed. Discrimination, exclusion, and religious indoctrination persisted among some Canadian clubs, and membership in the other ethnic clubs was very much restricted. In the Lakehead area, for instance, many talented athletes were turned away by established clubs because of the athletes' ethnicity. Those that were admitted were often excluded from spontaneous or organized social outings or functions of the club.[25] In the north end of Winnipeg, where most Ukrainians lived, a fine sports program was operated by the United Church. To be able to participate, one had to sit in on Sunday Bible School. With nowhere else to go, many Ukrainians did just that.[26]

On February 6, 1926, the *Winnipeg Evening Tribune* carried a story about the sport team Vics of the Sutherland Mission church in North Winnipeg. The Vics had just captured, for the second consecutive year, the national athletic championship of the Canada Standard Efficiency Test by defeating 18,000 entrants from across Canada. In describing the Vics team, the newspaper reported "all the boys comprising this group are new Canadians." Born in Canada of immigrant parents, the team included Z. Rybka, S. Masarick, Alex Netchuk, Slaw Rebchuk, Adam Romaniuk, Peter Dobush, and Isadore Rybka. The team was coached by the Reverends Harry Atkinson and J. M. Shaver.

By 1925, sports-minded Ukrainian community activists came to the conclusion that the established Canadian sport clubs and other ethnic clubs did not adequately meet the sporting needs of Ukrainian youth. Besides the previously mentioned concerns of discrimination, exclusion, and indoctrination, the activists also believed that once Ukrainian youth joined the established clubs they would be lost to the Ukrainian community. Ukrainian sport clubs, they argued, would not only retain a large segment of youth within the Ukrainian community, but would also attract those youthful Ukrainians who had never considered themselves a part of it. In 1928, V. H. Koman, the president of the Canadian Ukrainian Athletic Club of Winnipeg, wrote: "To ensure that our [Ukrainian] youth will want to be part of our organizations, we have to offer them that which attracts them. Our organizations must foster all aspects of sport."[27]

Several additional factors contributed to the founding of the independent Ukrainian clubs after World War I. The organizers were aware that Ukrainian youth was very much interested in sport. They envisaged involvement in organized sport as an ideal way to prevent juvenile delinquency. They believed it was beneficial to the well-being of the participants and would be readily accepted by the participants and parents. Albert Slivinski, the organizer of the Lakehead Ukrainian Athletic Club (LUAC) in 1936, believed that physical fitness was a fundamental building block during a youth's formative years. Convinced that there were simply too many Ukrainian youth with nothing to do, he proposed to occupy them in a Ukrainian setting while providing them with proper sports training.[28] Sixteen-year-old Michael Starr (Starchevsky) launched the Ukrainian Athletic Club in Oshawa in 1927 to keep Ukrainian youth out of pool halls and out of trouble.[29] Starr would later serve as Labour Minister of Canada.

Lastly, most organizers believed that sport was an ideal vehicle through which Ukrainian youth could participate as equals in the life of a town or city. They argued that when two teams met on a playing field, the only determining factor was athletic ability.

Most of the organizers of the independent Ukrainian sport clubs were Canadian-educated or Canadian-born. As a result, their understanding of sport was based on the "British" sport influence instilled in them in schools. This understanding, though, was not analogous with experience in establishing or operating sport clubs. The individuals were enthusiasts willing to implement their ideas.

The organization of Ukrainian sport clubs in the inter-war years, therefore, naturally progressed past the in-house programs of the youth, political, cultural or church groups. Independent Ukrainian sport clubs began forming across Canada in the mid-1920s. To a large extent, they were modeled on existing Canadian amateur athletic clubs and the sports that they offered - baseball, softball, basketball, football, curling, and bowling - were typically Canadian. Once these clubs were organized, they entered teams into local community, church or YMCA leagues.

In the fall of 1925, the Canadian Ukrainian Athletic Club (CUAC) was founded in Winnipeg.

At the time, nobody envisioned that the club would leave a significant mark on Canadian sport. Over the years, hundreds would compete at various levels on CUAC baseball, softball, hockey, soccer, basketball, lacrosse, and football teams in Winnipeg leagues. Many of the teams won championships, but the record of the senior girls' softball is unmatched. The team won the Manitoba championship on twenty-two occasions, with a string of 17 consecutive titles between the years 1957 and 1973. In 1965, the team won the inaugural national championship. In addition, the CUAC offered house league curling and 5 pin bowling. The club had its own home grounds - a field covering two city blocks. On those grounds were a club house, hockey rink, soccer and football field, baseball diamonds, basketball and tennis courts.

*The first Canadian Ukrainian Athletic Club girls' softball team, 1932*

As with most Ukrainian clubs at the time, the CUAC did not exclusively cater to Ukrainian youth. From the club's inception, anyone could join it and participate in its activities. The CUAC's fifteenth anniversary yearbook states that the club's "chief object and purpose has been the fostering and furtherance of sport and athletics amongst the youth of Greater Winnipeg."[30] In the early years, though, the club was comprised primarily of Ukrainian youth. It was unproven, laboured under an ethnic label, and offered only boys' hardball, so the more status-conscious individuals and those seeking greater sporting diversity preferred to associate with Winnipeg's more established athletic clubs. However, once the CUAC expanded its program and started winning championships, the club gained recognition outside the Ukrainian community. Prospective stars of all backgrounds were now eager to play for its teams, and were welcomed.

The vigour that went into organizing sport clubs at this time was no less than the vigour used in organizing other facets of community life. The Lakehead club, for instance, was able to attract three hundred individuals before any teams were formed.[31] Financial and moral support for the clubs was now generally good. Ukrainian community businessmen sponsored the teams, bought jerseys, and provided transportation.

Fan support was also growing in the late 1920s and in the 1930s, with hundreds and sometimes thousands of fans attending an event. The fans came out to the games for a number of reasons. First, there was the element of curiosity - what in the world are our children doing? Very few, if any, of the parents had ever participated in or watched sport. Second, at the time there was no television. Watching community sport events was considered an appropriate way of spending an evening or a Saturday afternoon. The Ukrainians, of course, would go and watch Ukrainian teams compete.[32] With time, many Ukrainians became great fans of the teams. They felt that it was their moral duty to provide the teams with the encouragements necessary to win games. It was also their duty to protect a team, the name of the sponsoring organization and by extension the entire Ukrainian community, from dishonour. On more than one occasion, Ukrainian fans jousted with opposing teams and their fans.

In the winter of 1939, under the heading "Riotous Scene is Witnessed," *The Fort William Daily Times-Journal* described one incident at a hockey game: "The puck had been barely faced when Brown of the Maroons and Kalynuk of the Ukes tangled, precipitating one of the most riotous scenes to be seen in a lakehead arena this season. Spectators leaped over the boards and joined with players in the general melee. Lights were doused in an effort to subdue the rowdying."[33]

Some clubs, to instill a sense of Ukrainian patriotism and to raise much needed funds, involved their members in cultural or political events. Plays and musicals were staged; recitation of poetry, folk dancing, and caroling were all part of the milieu of the clubs. These events were well supported by the Ukrainian public. As non-Ukrainians began to join the clubs, however, these activities began to decline and eventually ceased.

Across Canada in the 1930s, inter-urban sports competitions grew in popularity as more and more people acquired access to the automobile and travel grew easier. This new trend did not bypass the Ukrainian sports clubs. In fact, it helped to weld local Ukrainians not only into a larger Ukrainian Canadian community, but also into a continental Ukrainian community. Winnipeg's Canadian Ukrainian Athletic Club, for instance, visited Ontario at the invitation of the Kenora Ukrainian Athletic Club, while members of the Toronto Ukrainian Softball League travelled to the United States to take part in sports tournaments hosted by the Ukrainian Youth League of North America.

Travel also gave rise to the greater interaction between various branches of Ukrainian organizations. One of the first organizations to actively pursue branch fraternization was the Canadian Ukrainian Youth Association (SUMK) which was affiliated with the Ukrainian Orthodox Church. In 1933, the association held its first jamboree at Smokey Lake, Alberta. Part of the program was an exhibition of pyramid building. Subsequent local and regional jamborees held at various locations in Western Canada had sport programs that included inter-branch competitions or exhibitions. Initially, the young men from the branches participated in pyramid building while the young women took part in group exercises. In 1936, a men's softball tournament was added to the program of the jamborees. A women's tournament followed two years later.

In 1923, the first Ukrainian "Sports Day" was organized in Winnipeg.[34] Eleven years later, on July 1, the Ukrainian community of Winnipeg decided to copy the Dominion Day tradition of the other sport clubs in the city by organizing a Ukrainian Field Day. The Ukrainian event also became a Dominion Day tradition and continued for several years. Competitions were held in softball and track and field.

*Petro Mohyla Institute hockey team, 1919*

During the inter-war years, two Ukrainian leagues were organized. In 1932, the Ukrainian Softball League was founded in Toronto. Six teams representing Ukrainian organizations and churches in Toronto participated. According to founder Dr. Elias Wachna, "these were the depression days and this was the thing to do. It was good for them [Ukrainian youth], it was good for their health, morale and keep them off bars and dances and things like that . . ."[35] Two years later, the Ukrainian Diamond Ball League was organized in Winnipeg. Eight teams competed in men's baseball. The league was organized to promote sport and to give fledgling sport groups affiliated with various Winnipeg organizations a venue where they could comfortably compete.

In the schools, sport continued to flourish in the years between the two World Wars. Ukrainian bursas (residences) such as the Taras Shevchenko Institute and the Mykhailo Hrushevsky Institute of Edmonton, the Petro Mohyla Institute of Saskatoon, and St. Joseph's College of Yorkton all had organized competitive sport programs. The two big sports were hockey and baseball. Football, basketball, soccer and volleyball were encouraged but had less of an appeal.

As early as 1924, Ukrainian language teachers in Canada acknowledged the need for organized sport. That summer, the Association of Ukrainian Teachers of Canada conducted a four-week course at the University of Manitoba aimed at Ukrainianizing Ukrainian teachers.[36] Professor Ivan Bobersky, an organizer of the Sokil sport movement in Western Ukraine at the turn of the century, was the director of the course. In addition to the expected lectures on Ukrainian language, literature, history, geography, and music, the curriculum included instruction in physical education. Dr. Manoly Mihaychuk was provided with four hours of lecture time to examine the historical development of Ukrainian sport and physical education. Mykhailo Kumka conducted five two-hour workshops at which the teachers were exposed to and given the opportunity to practise group exercises and drills.[37]

The inclusion of instruction in physical education at the 1924 course for teachers appears to have been a unique happening. More than likely, credit for it can be attributed solely to Bobersky. There appears to be no evidence that would suggest that any subsequent course for Ukrainian teachers included instruction in physical education.

By the start of World War II, sport had become an integral component of Ukrainian community life. It was fostered by churches, and cultural, social and political organizations, as well as youth associations, and independent sport clubs. In some instances, the clubs were organized on an ad hoc basis by individuals wishing to participate in sport. With time, these clubs gained formal structure. In other instances, clubs were formally organized by community activists and the idea of sport was then propagated among the membership of an organization or the community at large. Regardless of their roots, once operational and registered with local leagues, the Ukrainian clubs and teams became an integral component of Canadian sport.

# WORLD WAR II

World War II put a damper on sports right across Canada. Most clubs reduced or ceased their programs because of a shortage of young men. More than 60 members of the Canadian Ukrainian Athletic Club served in the various branches of the Canadian armed forces, while some 40 members of the Ukrainian Softball League of Toronto were in the service. The large number of Ukrainian volunteers was in part a reflection of the role sport played in their lives. The sense of "loyalty and duty to one's side that, in a larger context, was the essence of patriotism" committed 35,000 to 50,000 to the war effort. Even at the lower figure, 14.4 per cent of the Ukrainian population was in uniform.[38]

The Ukrainian soldier, however, did not abandon sport. In London, England, members of the Ukrainian Canadian Servicemen's Association (UCSA) organized a softball team of Air Force personnel and another made up of Army personnel. The Ukrainian Canadian Committee (UCC) provided the teams with uniforms and games were played every Sunday during the summer of 1945 in Hyde Park.[39]

On the home front, men's and women's CUAC teams played in many fund-raising games for the war effort under the auspices of the Athletic Patriotic Association (APA). The women's auxiliary of CUAC wholeheartedly committed itself to the war effort assisting the Red Cross and the St. John's Ambulance Society. Part of the Toronto Ukrainian Softball League's itinerary at the time included sponsoring farewell parties for soldiers being sent overseas and sending parcels to the troops.

# THE POST-WAR ERA

The end of the war saw the rejuvenation of some of the established Ukrainian sport clubs in Canada and the start-up of many new teams and clubs. The returning veterans, bound by camaraderie, organized sport teams within the framework of the veterans' associations. The newly arrived immigrants, bound by their own shared experiences, also began forming their clubs.

The interest of the new immigrants in sport was transplanted with them from Europe to Canada. Prior to World War II, the lands they left behind had well-established sport programs at the community and the "professional" level. In Eastern Ukraine, which had been under Soviet rule, mass participation in sport had been encouraged. In Western Ukraine, which had been under Polish rule, community sport was a popular vehicle for training cadres of nationally conscious youth. In both Eastern and Western Ukraine, strong "professional" first division soccer clubs had existed.

Towards the end of World War II, with the onslaught of the Red Army, many Ukrainians fled from their homeland to seek refuge in the Western Allied sectors of post-war Europe. These refugees were assigned to the displaced persons (DP) camps. In addition, many Ukrainians who toiled in German forced labour camps made their way to the DP camps after the surrender of Germany. At these camps, there were a sufficient number of sport enthusiasts to organize an intricate network of sport clubs and competitions. When these individuals immigrated to Canada, they almost immediately renewed their involvement in sport.

The new immigrants organized their own clubs, rather than join the established Ukrainian or Canadian clubs, for a number of reasons. They were inexperienced or unfamiliar with baseball and basketball, the two sports that were the mainstay of the Ukrainian sport clubs in Canada. It appears that of the more than 25 sport clubs founded by the new immigrants, only one, the Sts. Peter and Paul hockey club of St. Boniface, committed itself to a popular and established Canadian sport.

*Members of the Lakehead Ukrainian Athletic Club Ukes football team, c.1948*

There was also a language barrier. The language of the Canadian clubs was of course English, but by that time English had also become the language of the existing Ukrainian sport clubs.

In addition, many newcomers believed that they would return to Ukraine in the near future. As a result, while in Canada they wanted to preserve the legacy of their European clubs, their sports, and their achievements.[40]

Many of the immigrants arriving in Canada from the DP camps were assigned to menial physical jobs for a period of one year. After that they were free to pursue an education or any line of work for which they were qualified. Nevertheless, many of the older professionals did not have the opportunity to renew their careers due to a language barrier. This was particularly traumatic for those who had vibrant, productive and respected professional careers in Europe. As a result, many of these individuals channelled their expertise into community work, which in a very short period of time became their raison d'etre. In the Ukrainian community, they were respected by their fellow immigrants for their past achievements and positions, not for their current occupations. Many of these individuals were sport enthusiasts. They had volunteer or professional organizational experience from Ukraine and the DP camps. The obvious place for them to channel their expertise was in sports clubs.

Identified with the post-war immigrant-founded Sport Association Ukraina in Toronto, for example, were numerous eminent sport activists from Europe. They included Myroslaw Welyhorskyj - professor of physical education, Evhen Chuchman - manager of the first division soccer team Ukraina in Lviv, Karlo Mulkewytch - editor of the newspaper *Sportowi Wisti*, Evhen Spolsky - president of the Sport Club Tryzub in Lviv, Jaroslaw Chorostil - executive with the Sport Club Syan in Przemysl, and others.

There were also accomplished athletes, some with professional European experience, who were eager to compete. Among the professional soccer stars arriving from Europe to play for Ukrainian community clubs were Oleksander Skocen - Dynamo Kyiv and l'O.G.C. Nice; Ostap Steckiw - USVA Valenciennes and Olympique Lyonnais; Walter Zakaluzny - FC Jahn Regensburg and Shwaben Augsburg, and others.

Starting in 1948, the new immigrants organized clubs across Canada, from Vancouver to Montreal. Once these clubs became operational, they entered teams into local leagues.

At times leagues did not exist into which a team could be entered. This led Ukrainian sport activists to participate in the creation of such bodies. The founders of the Strila soccer club of Oshawa, for example, were also co-founders of a soccer league in that city. The founders of Ukrainian volleyball teams in the Toronto area assisted their counterparts from the Baltic communities to organize a volleyball league. In this manner, the sports of the recent European immigrants were woven into the fabric of organized Canadian sport in several parts of Canada.

*Ukrainian Sports Association Strila soccer team of Oshawa, 1956*

The formation of a strong soccer team was the primary objective of all the post-war immigrant-organized clubs. The choice of sport was thoroughly consistent with the European experience of the organizers, as was their mode of operating the clubs. In cities with large Ukrainian populations such as Edmonton, Montreal, Sudbury, and Toronto, the executives administered these clubs as if they were semi-professional enterprises rather than community clubs. The athletes were financially rewarded for their services. The teams were trained by professionals. The calibre of play was high, and the clubs were well marketed in the community.

The major objective of the clubs was to win championships. No effort was spared to secure the finest players. Stars arriving from Europe or transferring from other clubs were guaranteed jobs and compensation for their services. Non-Ukrainian athletes were widely recruited. Much emphasis was placed on the minor league system, with Sport Association (SA) Ukraina - Toronto, for example, operating as many as seven teams in one year. The minor league system was usually restricted to Ukrainian youth.

The new immigrants attended the games of these new clubs in masses. It was common, during the 1950s, to have thousands of fans cheering the SA Ukraina soccer club in Toronto. During the years 1952-1960, more than 1.1 million fans attended the team's games.

The avid interest of the recent immigrants in their sport teams in Canada was, at the time, in some respects unique and in others similar to that of the Hungarians, Poles and others from Eastern Europe. The uniqueness was in part the result of their non-relationship with Soviet Ukraine. The similarity was the desire of the immigrants to preserve and build on some of their European sports experiences.

The Ukrainians who fled their homeland during World War II, and subsequently settled in Canada, severed most ties to sport in Soviet Ukraine. Most of the refugee sport fans did not want to support clubs in Soviet Ukraine which were used by the communist regime for political gains. In addition, the local Ukrainian press only sporadically reported scores and other sports news from Ukraine. The Canadian press did not at all. This lack of coverage was in sharp contrast to the experience of other groups that settled in Canada. The newspapers in Canada, for example, regularly carried features such as Old Country Cricket or Football Scores which had the latest sports information from the British Isles. For many years, the Canadian Broadcasting Corporation radio service regularly carried soccer results from Britain. The community press of the other immigrant groups usually had fairly good sport coverage from their homelands. As other groups settled in Canada, their local press extensively covered the sports back home. With the popularization of television one could regularly watch sport from many foreign countries.

The regular coverage of sports from the "old country" provided these immigrants with an opportunity to maintain their attachment to their favourite clubs overseas. This attachment often overrode every effort by local organizers to have these individuals support clubs in Canada bearing the names of their favourite overseas teams or their land of birth. The Ukrainian fans, though, were hindered in maintaining an attachment to their favourite clubs in Ukraine because of the country's political situation and the limited coverage of its sports in the press. As a result, they full-heartedly supported the Canadian version of the home team.

At the stadium, they saw players that they once cheered in Ukraine or the DP camps. These players wore the colours of their favourite Ukrainian clubs from Europe. Even the names of the teams had their first use on the European continent. For the Ukrainian immigrants, this continuum of their European experience was a splendid respite from the daily toil for subsistence.

The massive community involvement in the sporting experience eased the process of adaption to the new land. This involvement also helped create a cohesive community. Just as cities and towns around the world had local or regional teams to rally around, the Ukrainian community in Canada rallied around its teams. Many believed that the vitality of the community was judged by the success of its teams.[41]

In 1965, the Toronto Plast Vedmedyky junior girls' volleyball team competed in Ottawa and Vancouver for the Eastern Canada and Canadian volleyball championships respectively. The warmhearted reception the Vedmedyky were privy to in Ottawa and Vancouver, and the fervent fan support generated for the Toronto team astonished competitors, coaches and officials participating in the events. In both cities, the local Ukrainian community's support for a visiting Ukrainian team, such as the Vedmedyky, was an act of solidarity which groups or communities with shared characteristics can experience. Vedmedyky team member Christine Tomkiw reminisced about the experience: "In Ottawa and in Vancouver we realized that our supporters were not happy for us, but that they were happy with us as one big Ukrainian family."[42]

Unfortunately, the clubs did not always serve as a cohesive force in the community. In Vancouver, Edmonton, Sudbury, Montreal, and Toronto, clubs splintered. In some years, competing Ukrainian clubs existed. In Edmonton, for example, three unassociated Ukrainian soccer clubs operated in 1951. Each had problems fielding a full complement at games. While the rivalry may have been healthy in principle, it often discouraged the athletes and fans, and led to the premature demise of some of the clubs.

The success of the community in organizing the post-war clubs and leagues and the success of many of the clubs and leagues themselves cannot be overlooked. By the mid-1950s, these clubs achieved some of their greatest successes, both on the field of play and with their work with youth.

By 1960, however, there was a general demise in the activities of most of the Ukrainian sport clubs. This demise, though, was not unique to Ukrainian clubs. Many sports clubs at the time began experiencing declining participation rates. In part, this was caused by the expansion of highly competitive extracurricular sport programs at secondary and post-secondary institutions which drew many athletes from the clubs. In addition, television was blamed by community sport activists for the decline in participation.[43]

There were also other reasons. Some were particular to Ukrainian clubs in general, while others were specific to individual clubs.

For the second and third generation of Ukrainians, language was no longer a barrier to joining Canadian clubs. There was also much less parental pressure to join Ukrainian clubs. In addition, the Ukrainian community was migrating from its "ghettos" to the more affluent neighbourhoods. The sport clubs did not follow, opting to remain at their established sites in the older parts of the cities. Travel time to practices and competitions now became a factor in determining the club of choice. Perhaps most important, the Ukrainian clubs did not offer sports such as hockey, football and baseball which were coveted by contemporary youth. The clubs were still devoted to soccer, a sport that was losing its appeal among the first generation born in Canada. As a result, in the cities that operated Ukrainian sport clubs, young Ukrainians increasingly opted for the Canadian community clubs.

*Plast Vedmedyky volleyball team, 1965 Canadian Junior Champions*

Some Ukrainian sport activists took their expertise to Ukrainian youth organizations. There they established vibrant sport programs primarily in the area of volleyball. Toronto's youth organizations Plast and the Ukrainian Youth Association (SUM), for instance, dominated junior women's volleyball in Canada for close to a decade. Also, from the ranks of these organizations came national team members Christine Eliashewsky, Julia Kucharchuk-Andruchiw, Walter Rosocha, Andrew Stanko, Halya Stefaniuk and Peter Stefaniuk.

By 1960, all the clubs organized by the armed forces veterans folded. Age and family responsibilities took their toll. The Labour Temple clubs also folded. After World War II, there had been a great interest among the Labour Temple clubs to organize and participate in Pan-Slavic leagues. In 1948, for instance, the Toronto Slav Softball League included a Polish, Macedonian, Russian, Yugoslav, and three Ukrainian teams. A new generation of youth, though, did not carry on with the tradition. Of the pre-war clubs, the Canadian Ukrainian Athletic Club and the Institute Prosvita Athletic Club were the only two still active at the time.

In 1979, the Ukrainian Slo-Pitch League was established in Toronto. League co-founder Paul Kulchisky stated his reason for organizing the league was that, in his opinion, no Ukrainian-Canadian organization or church was providing activities for Ukrainian teens and young adults of Toronto in a Canadian context.[44] The success of the league was manifested by its rapid growth. By 1988, a total of 267 players competed on 15 teams.

In the spring of 1982, the Ukrainian Youth Soccer Association league was formed in Toronto for children. Parents called for an organized summer league after their children had participated in weekly practice sessions at a Ukrainian-language immersion school in the city. By 1987, the league had more than 300 participants.

The Ukrainian Slo-Pitch League and the Ukrainian Youth Soccer Association were two successful sport programs that evolved out of demand in the 1980s.

\* \* \*

During the first 100 years of Ukrainian settlement in Canada, the number of Ukrainian community based sports clubs, leagues and teams was significant. Organized sport activity, in addition to the independent clubs, was fostered by the churches, and cultural, social, and political institutions, and the youth organizations. Some forms of organized sport activity existed for some time in Brantford, Brooklands, Calgary, Edmonton, Espanola, Hamilton, Kenora, Kingston, Kirkland Lake, Kitchener, Lethbridge, Model Farm, Montreal, Moose Jaw, Mundare, Oshawa, Port Arthur - Fort William, Preston, Saskatoon, St. Catharines, Shandro, Sudbury, Toronto, Vancouver, Windsor, Winnipeg, and Yorkton. In many cities, more than one club, league or team existed. In addition, in the United States, Canadians from Manitoba formed the Adanacs baseball club in Detroit in 1928, while Canadian servicemen in England formed their own baseball teams during World War II.

# FUNDING THE SPORTS PROGRAMS

From the earliest days, Ukrainian sport clubs, leagues and teams were established and operated on a non-profit basis by devoted volunteers. These devotees contributed a great deal of time to administer the clubs and to provide enthusiastic athletes with sound sporting programs. In 1955, for example, each of the ten executive officers of Toronto's SA Ukraina contributed on average 250 hours of volunteer work for the club.[45]

A critical task for the volunteers was to ensure a solid financial base for their club. Operating costs were generally significant, and may have included such items as uniforms, equipment, referee fees, league fees, transportation, insurance, rental of facilities, player stipends and other. Funds generated by membership dues were never sufficient to cover costs. Perhaps, therefore, the most arduous task facing the volunteers was raising funds, seeking sponsorships and securing donors.

The most extensive fund raising was likely conducted by Winnipeg's CUAC. The club sold memberships, operated a canteen, held dances, draws, carnivals, staged concerts and plays. A Ladies Auxiliaries was organized to assist in the raising of funds. Activities included teas, socials, banquets and raffles. And at games, a hat was passed around. Other clubs used similar fund-raising techniques, and also may have held bingos, stags, variety shows, "*Malankas*" - Ukrainian New Year's Balls, or went caroling.

Privately owned Ukrainian businesses, over the years, sponsored Ukrainian sporting entities. For some businesses, sponsorship was part of their good corporate citizen image, both in the Ukrainian community and outside. For others, sponsorship was a sentimental decision. More recently, Ukrainian community businesses, such as the credit unions, have become involved. The private and community businesses have sponsored teams, bought jerseys, and provided services such as transportation, dry cleaning and advertising. Sponsorship by non-Ukrainian businesses has not been significant.

While substantial amounts were generated through fund raising and sponsorship, at the end of the day, many a hat came back with not enough to pay the umpire or the referee. Members would then dip into their own pockets to make up the difference. No club was unique in this aspect. Members of most clubs contributed funds in excess of their dues to sustain the operations of their clubs.

# COORDINATING THE SPORT ACTIVITIES

Since the establishment of the first Ukrainian sport clubs in the 1920s, a desire of many of the participants was to develop and foster sporting ties with their counterparts in other cities. As the automobile made travel easy in the 1930s, inter-urban sport competitions among Ukrainian clubs became popular. At first, clubs would travel to another community and play the local team. The games were often held in conjunction with a picnic or a festival. In August of 1932, the Ukrainian Softball League of Toronto hosted its inaugural Ukrainian Field Day. For the first time, Ukrainian clubs from a number of communities participated. The event attracted softball teams from St. Catharines, Hamilton, Toronto and Oshawa.

In 1936, the Ukrainian Softball League of Toronto participated in the Ukrainian Olympiad held in Philadelphia. The event was hosted by the Ukrainian Youth League of North America (UYLNA). One of the objectives of this coordinating body of Ukrainian youth organizations was the popularization of sport. It had a General Sports Director and divisional attaches. Peter Wasylyk of Toronto served as an attache representing the Canadian Division.

World War II and internal organizational problems put a temporary stop to the UYLNA sports program in 1942. After the war the program was revived. Annual sport rallies held at alternating sites became the focal point of the sports program. For many years teams from Toronto travelled to the venues in the United States. Toronto hosted the 1950 and 1953 rallies. The last of these UYLNA rallies was held in the mid-1960s. At one time or another, competition was held in athletics, basketball, bowling, golf, softball and volleyball.

In 1936, the Catholic Youth League of America held its inaugural track and field meet in Philadelphia. Athletes from Canada probably did not compete at the event. In the subsequent two years they did, with Hamilton sprinter William Murmylyk winning the 100-yard dash in a game's record time of ten seconds flat at the 1938 meet held at Pittsburgh.

The desire of the post-war immigrants to preserve their European sports experience included the call for a council that would coordinate sport activity in North America. This council would be modeled after two now defunct bodies the activists were familiar with - the Ukrainian Sport Association from pre-war Ukraine, and its successor in the DP camps, the Council of Physical Culture.

Representatives of nine clubs from the United States and four from Canada attended a meeting in Toronto on December 24, 1955, at which the Association of Ukrainian Sport Clubs of North America (USCAK) came into being. Among the proposed objectives of the association was the organization of annual Ukrainian inter-club tournaments in various sports. As well, the association called for mass participation in physical activity by Ukrainian youth organizations. Those participants attaining a certain prescribed norm would be awarded with a pin of physical fitness.

On May 15, 1956, the Canadian division of USCAK was formed. Ten clubs from across Canada were invited to participate at the founding meeting. Of the ten, only the Institute Prosvita Athletic Club of Winnipeg had been organized prior to the war, but by 1956 it also served post-war immigrants. There appears to be no evidence to suggest that the Canadian promoters of USCAK considered approaching the established pre-war clubs or those post-war clubs organized by Canadian forces war veterans. The intent of Canadian division of USCAK, it seems, was to only embrace the post-war immigrant-established clubs. The meeting proceeded to elect Jaroslaw Chorostil of Toronto the division's first chairman and to set an agenda for action.

*Souvenir programme of the XIth USCAK Track and Field Championships at Grafton, 1969*

In 1957, the Canadian division of USCAK organized the first North American inter-club championship held under the auspices of the association. The event was the men's volleyball championship. In subsequent years, USCAK Canada organized inter-club championships in track and field, volleyball, table tennis, and chess. These championships were a major attraction in the Ukrainian sports community. At the 1965 track and field championships held at the Plast Camp *Sitch* at Grafton, Ontario, 219 athletes representing 11 clubs participated. At the same venue, three years later, the championship attracted a record 229 athletes, although the number of clubs fell to nine. (Please see Appendix VI for a list of host sites.)

In addition to organizing inter-club championships, USCAK Canada cooperated with Baltic sport federations and councils to stage track and field, soccer, and volleyball competitions. These competitions were popular in the 1960s and the early 1970s. Athletes who represented "Ukraine" in these competitions were selected by the USCAK executive with the assistance of the USCAK-appointed coaching staff. The selection committee, though, did not restrict the selection process to individuals competing with USCAK member clubs. Athletes of Ukrainian descent were recruited to participate in the meets and tournaments.

The Canadian division of USCAK ceased to operate in the early 1980s. The death of Chorostil and other USCAK activists created a void that no one wanted to fill. After some encouragements from USCAK headquarters in the United States and Canadian sport activists, USCAK Canada was revived in December of 1989. Yaroslaw Kowal of Toronto was elected president. Five months later, the Canadian division of USCAK sponsored the 33rd annual Ukrainian inter-club volleyball championships which were hosted by Toronto.

Along the way, the Association of Ukrainian Sport Clubs of North America (USCAK) was renamed in English to the Ukrainian Sports Federation of USA and Canada (USCAK). Its Ukrainian name remained unchanged.


# ETHNIC SELF-PRESERVATION, PATRIOTISM AND SPORTS


Over time, more than 90 Ukrainian sport clubs, leagues and independent teams were organized in Canada. The organizers of these entities maintained that in addition to their athletic value, the clubs were meant to serve as vehicles for ethnic self-preservation and for fostering patriotism. Others suggested that the popularization of the Ukrainian name and of the plight of Ukraine could be advanced in Canada through the successes of the clubs.

It appears, though, that in many instances these patriotic objectives were overdramatized to boost participation in the clubs and community support for the clubs or, in other words, to ensure the clubs' continued viability.

In the 1929 almanac *Klenovyi Lystok - Maple Leaf* - V. H. Koman, president of CUAC wrote, that only through activities that youth enjoyed, such as sport, would the Ukrainian community be able to attract and maintain youth within its ranks.[46]

The CUAC did not exclusively cater to Ukrainian youth. From its inception, anyone could join the club or participate in its activities. A non-discriminatory membership policy was practised by CUAC and other Ukrainian unaffiliated sport clubs organized prior to World War II. While at first the number of non-Ukrainians participating on the teams was low, it increased significantly as the clubs gained popularity. Even the sport clubs affiliated with Ukrainian youth or other organizations did permit non-Ukrainians to join, though at times with reservations.

After World War II, the newspaper *Novyi Shliakh - New Pathway*, in analyzing the performance of the post-war immigrant organized SA Ukraina - Montreal soccer team, noted that "the Ukrainian community of Montreal thanks our players for their contribution to the popularization of the Ukrainian name in the area of sport."[47]

In 1954, publisher-editor Karlo Mulkewytch wrote in the editorial of the first issue of *Sportowi Wisti - Sport's News* that: "The increase in the number of Ukrainian youth in this land necessitates that we take greater control over their sport upbringing. The youth should not only be provided with proper physical training, but also should be educated in nation building. The youth should serve the interest of the Ukrainian nation, propagate the good name of Ukraine with its victories and championships . . ."[48]

The pursuit of the popularization of the Ukrainian name and the championing of the Ukrainian cause through sport logically required competitive or championship teams. At the time, it was believed by some managers and athletes that the Ukrainian clubs could not fill their rosters with quality Ukrainian players. As a result, the clubs recruited non-Ukrainians.

The recruitment of non-Ukrainian players to foster the popularization of the Ukrainian name did not appear to trouble the executives of the clubs and only rarely were the consequences of this action questioned. By recruiting non-Ukrainians, the clubs were depriving Ukrainians of participation. This of course was in total contradiction to the clubs' stated objectives of providing Ukrainian youth with a venue for sport.

Jaroslaw Chorostil, co-author of the book *"Ukraina" Sport Association - Toronto* analyzed this predicament: "The youth, having experienced discriminatory exclusion by its own coaches began to lose faith in its abilities, which led to indifference and disillusionment. The door to improving their potential was firmly shut. And thus, in full view of the club's executive, our youth began to abandon sport."[49]

Thus, while the pre-war and post-war organizers of sport clubs had tenets of ethnic self-preservation and of fostering patriotism, the sport clubs may in fact have been vehicles of integration and assimilation. The use of non-Ukrainian players on the teams contributed to the greater use of the English language. The participation in Canadian leagues required interaction with other Canadians. Playing games at various stadiums across the city required the players to leave the confines of their ethnic ghetto. Even surveying local newspapers for results or stories about their teams made the athletes more aware of the mainstream non-immigrant issues, thus furthering integration.

# SPORT CONTACTS WITH UKRAINE

The first sport contact with Ukraine occurred in 1935 when Ukrainian athletes from Canada were selected to the Workers' Sports Association team that competed in exhibition meets in the USSR. One of the stops on the tour was Kharkiv, Ukraine.

After World War II, the Soviet Union requested membership in the International Olympic Committee. Membership was granted and Soviet athletes, among them Ukrainians, were soon participating in international sport. For many years, the only sport contact was between athletes representing Canada and athletes representing the USSR at international competitions. The Soviets, though, tried to keep contacts at an individual level to the minimum.

Jennifer Diachun, a star member of Canada's gymnastics team, requested permission in 1973 to train in the USSR. The Soviet authorities denied her the request because of her Ukrainian roots.[50]

*Toronto's Yurko Parubchak (right) holds training session*
*with Ukrainian players in Lviv, 1989*

At the 1973 Canada-USSR track meet in Saskatoon, Canadian athletes John Konihowski and Gayle Olinek wore T-shirts during one of the warm-ups that had "Molson's Ukrainian" printed on them. A member of the Soviet sport delegation noticed Konihowski wearing the shirt. The meet was halted and the athlete was ordered to remove the offending shirt.[51] Only after Konihowski had removed the shirt did the meet resume. Officially, the Soviets did not want the Canadian mistakenly identified as belonging to the Soviet team. Unofficially, the Soviets may not have wanted Konihowski to wear the shirt for it identified him as being of Ukrainian descent. With two-thirds of the Soviet team being from Ukraine, the overseers were probably concerned that their athletes would make contact with Konihowski and Olinek.

The first direct sport contact between a Ukrainian community team from Canada and one from Ukraine occurred in 1989. At the time, Paul Kulchisky organized a softball team consisting of Toronto area youth. The team spent two weeks in Ukraine playing against Ukrainian clubs and holding clinics in Kyiv, Lviv, Chernivtsi and Khmelnytskyi. The following year, the Lviv Lions, a team made up of students of the Lviv Institute of Forestry and Wood Technology, travelled to Toronto to complete the exchange.

The declaration of sovereignty by Ukraine in August of 1991 brought about a myriad of political, social, and economic changes to the country. Changes also began to take hold in the realm of sport.

During the weekend of November 30 - December 1, 1991, Montreal hosted the first leg of the World Cup series in swimming. The event marked the first time that a team from Ukraine participated independently, albeit unofficially, in an international sport competition. The Ukrainian team of six athletes and three officials had their return air fare paid to Montreal by the Ukrainian Sports Federation of USA and Canada (USCAK). In Montreal the Ukrainian team was overwhelmed by the reception accorded to them by the Ukrainian community. The team was greeted at the airport, cheered wildly by flag-waving fans at the pool, and feted at receptions. The Ukrainian swimmers responded by winning three gold, three silver, and three bronze medals.

A new era of sport contacts between Canada and Ukraine had begun.

# THE OLYMPIC GAMES

The Olympic Games were for many years a preoccupation of many Ukrainian sport clubs and various Ukrainian community-based organizations.

In 1928, the Workers' Sports Association of Canada called for the boycott of the bourgeois Olympics that were to be held in Amsterdam. It also supported a call for an alternative counter-Olympics in Moscow. The Ukrainian Workers' Sports Association, which by that time had affiliated itself with the WSA, supported this position. The anti-Olympic rhetoric recurred prior to the 1932 and the 1936 Olympics. The youth wing of the Ukrainian Labour-Farmer Temple Association used its publication *Militant Youth* to actively campaign against the Olympic movement. To what extent the general membership participated in the campaign is difficult to determine.

After World War II, the USSR gained admission into the Olympic movement and the anti-Olympic campaign ceased. The Ukrainian socialist press in Canada now celebrated the accomplishments of Soviet sport.

The admittance of the USSR into the Olympic movement brought about immediate criticism of the International Olympic Committee (IOC) by the nationally conscious Ukrainians in Canada and elsewhere. Soviet Ukraine, a founding member of the United Nations, was denied the right to participate independently at the Olympic Games. The United States-based Ukrainian World Committee for Sport Affairs under the leadership of Bohdan Shebunchak, MD, and Smoloskyp Information Service under the long-time leadership of Osyp Zinkewych were at the forefront of lobbying the IOC and drawing public attention to this injustice. Both of these organizations had active Canadian members and were morally and financially supported by the Ukrainian community in Canada.

A year prior to the 1976 Montreal Olympics, Jaroslaw Pryszlak recommended to the Montreal branch of the Ukrainian Canadian Committee (UCC) that a committee be formed which would bring attention to Moscow's practice of colonialism and national discrimination in sport. The committee would also lobby for the independent participation of Ukraine in the Olympic movement. The Montreal branch of the UCC agreed and the Ukrainian Olympic Committee came into being with Pryszlak as chairman.

During the 1976 Olympic Games, the Ukrainian Olympic Committee disseminated information about Ukrainian athletes at the Olympic Media Centre. Included in the information were press releases, brochures, and a booklet, *Olympic Team of Ukraine*, which listed the Ukrainian athletes at the Olympics. The committee also initiated and assisted in preparing a daily radio show which was broadcast in English, French and Ukrainian, and held two widely attended press conferences. The defection of Ivan Charalambij, a Ukrainian from Romania, undoubtedly made the press conferences popular.

For the duration of the Olympic Games, the Ukrainian Olympic Committee was augmented by representatives of Smoloskyp and the World Congress of Free Ukrainians (WCFU). In addition, Ukrainian youth from many parts of North America assisted the committee in its activities.[52]

When the Olympic Games returned to Canada in 1988, members of the Ukrainian Youth Association (SUM) from around the world gathered at an "Olympic Camp" on the outskirts of Calgary. The group disseminated information about Ukraine and Ukrainian athletes to the thousands of fans attending the Calgary Olympic Winter Games.

In 1989, Yuri Shymko, president of the World Congress of Free Ukrainians which had its headquarters in Toronto, asked K. W. Sokolyk to head up an Olympic Commission within the framework of the WCFU. The mandate of the commission was to lobby the international sport federations and the International Olympic Committee for Ukraine's right to independent participation in sport. In 1990, the commission began assisting Valery Choutiy, chairman of the Olympic Commission of "Rukh." Rukh at the time was the unofficial opposition movement to the communist government in Ukraine. In October, the Olympic Commission of Rukh was restructured into the Ukrainian National Olympic Committee. A short time later, the Ministry of Sport of Ukraine responded with its own National Olympic Committee (NOC) of Ukraine. The former committee called for Ukraine's independent participation in sport while the latter preferred the status quo.[53] As a result, the Olympic Commission in Toronto supported the objectives of the former committee.

Ukraine's proclamation of independence in 1991 drastically changed the mandate of the Olympic Commission of the WCFU. In Ukraine, Valery Choutiy disbanded his committee while the National Olympic Committee of Ukraine under president Valery Borzov gained International Olympic Committee recognition in March of 1992. Opposition turned to cooperation. Early in 1992, the WCFU Olympic Commission offered to publish a Barcelona '92 media guide for the NOC of Ukraine. A member of the Commission, Osyp Zinkewych, served as co-editor. The cost of publishing was covered by the WCFU with the assistance of the Ukrainian Sports Federation of USA and Canada (USCAK). Thousands of copies of the media guide and of a brief history of Ukrainian participation in the Olympic Games, *Olympic Ukraine,* were distributed to the media at the 1992 Barcelona Olympics.

Of the many activities undertaken over the years to promote Ukraine's independent participation in international sport, not all were of an administrative nature. During the 1960s and early 1970s, Ukrainian sport activists, in conjunction with the Baltic sports federations, cooperated to stage sport competitions. Volleyball and basketball tournaments and track meets were part of this milieu. The events emphasized the plight of athletes and sport in the homelands of the immigrants. These events were popular among Canadian athletes with such past, present or future Canadian national team members or future professionals as Zenon Andrusyshyn, Peter Buniak (Jerome Drayton), Borys Chambul, Julia Kucharchuk, Walter Rosocha, Halya

Stefaniuk, Peter Stefaniuk, and Morris Zubkewych representing "Ukraine."

Another vehicle used to promote the independent participation of Ukraine and other Eastern European countries in sport was the Free Olympiad. Organized by Ukrainian, Estonian, Latvian, Lithuanian, and Armenian sports activists, the first such event was held in Toronto in 1980. It attracted 300 competitors from all over North America. Canadian national team members Borys Chambul and Leo Rautins were among the athletes competing. Brigadier General Denis Whitaker was the Honourary Chairman of the event. The patrons included Ontario premier the Hon. William G. Davis and a host of other provincial and federal politicians, including the Rt. Hon. Joe Clark, MP; Ed Broadbent, MP; Bernard Newman, MPP; and Nicholas Leluk, MPP. The Free Olympiad was held again in Toronto in 1984.

*Souvenir programme of the 1984 Free Olympiad*

# THE SPORT PRESS

During the first 100 years of Ukrainian settlement in Canada, the Ukrainian immigrant community developed an extensive press to serve its needs. The first Ukrainian newspaper in Canada appeared in 1903. Since that time, dozens of different Ukrainian and English language newspapers and periodicals were published by the Ukrainian community.

It was not until the early 1920s, though, that the first reports of sporting events were published. Through the end of World War II, the Ukrainian press intermittently reported on the operations of Ukrainian clubs and the success of Ukrainian athletes. The press relied almost completely on unsolicited contributions from volunteers within the community.

After the war, sports coverage in Ukrainian media increased significantly. Most English language Ukrainian newspapers and periodicals featured some sports. The Ukrainian language press also increased the scope of its press coverage. The post-World War II immigration was sports news-hungry and the media responded. In terms of column space, sports coverage peaked in the 1950s.

At the same time, two short-lived Ukrainian language newspapers fully devoted to sports appeared. Both newspapers were published in Toronto.

*Sportowi Wisti, 1954*

*Sportowi Wisti* (Sport's News) first appeared on May 12, 1954. It was privately published and edited by Karlo Mulkewytch (the sports enthusiast published a newspaper by the same name in Lviv, Ukraine, between 1930-33). *Sportowi Wisti* consisted of four pages and cost 10 cents. The newspaper included sports news and feature articles. More than a half of each issue was dedicated to soccer. *Sportowi Wisti* folded after less than a year of publication because of a lack of paid subscriptions.

*Sport, 1955*

On May 7, 1955, a second attempt to establish a Ukrainian sports newspaper occurred with the first issue of *Sport*. The newspaper was published by Ukrainian Echo Publishing Co. Ltd. and edited by an editorial board. It also featured sports news and feature articles. Again, most of each issue was dedicated to soccer. A copy of the eight-page *Sport* cost 10 cents. The last issue of the paper appeared on July 14, 1956. Once again, a lack of subscribers terminated the paper.

One of the most prolific Ukrainian language sports writers in Canada was Dr. Roman Romanovych of Winnipeg. His reports appeared in Ukrainian newspapers for more than two decades. The editor of *Forum*, Andrew Gregorovich of Toronto, authored numerous articles in English about Ukrainian athletes and sports in general.

# THE ATHLETES

The history of the participation of Ukrainians in Canadian sport would be incomplete without reference to the individuals who made an impact on sport in Canada.

The first documented participation of a Ukrainian in Canadian sport was that of O. Holinsky on the Creighton Mine baseball team in 1911. In 1914, Manoly Mihaychuk competed in an officially sanctioned international sport event when he placed third in the pole vault at a Manitoba versus North Dakota Intervarsity track meet. According to the 1915 *Kalendar Ukrainskoho Holosu - Ukrainian Voice Almanac*, Mihaychuk also won a Canadian title in a "jumping" event. Unfortunately, this latter result could not be verified.

The first known athletes of Ukrainian descent who attained national recognition were Nick Wasnie - National Hockey League (1927-35), Mike Chepesuik - British Empire Games gold medallist in wrestling (1930) and Toronto Argonauts (1930-34), John Garuik - Saskatchewan Roughriders (1930-43) and Bronko Nagurski - Chicago Bears (1930-37 and 1943) and the world professional wrestling champion (1937-38 and 1939-40).

Since those initial successes of Ukrainian athletes, hundreds more have distinguished themselves in amateur and professional sport. Many factors probably have contributed to the success of Ukrainian athletes. In speculating why so many Ukrainian players have made it to the NHL, for instance, former "Uke Line" member John Bucyk wrote: ". . . our ancestry and upbringing produces a mighty fine work ethic. We Ukrainians have good breeding and are known for our Strong-Like-Bull reputations and longevity."[54] And Tony Unitas, founder of the Canadian Boxing Hall of Fame, in a profile written in conjunction with the induction of boxer Peter Kolaski into the Hall, reiterated on the theme: ". . . Pete's a hard worker. He was a hard fighter. Well, he's Ukrainian, isn't he???"[55]

*Photo courtesy of the Canadian Football Hall of Fame and Museum*

*Mike Chepesuik*

For many athletes, sport was "a ladder of social and economic mobility,"[56] whether by outcome or design. Hockey player Eric Nesterenko stated: "I was looking to be somebody and the game was my way. It was my life."[57] Another hockey player Eddie Shack declared that if not for hockey ". . . I'd be an absolute rotten loser. Oh, I wanted out, and Junior hockey did it for me . . ."[58]

The pursuit of sport and its corollary of social and economic mobility was not without its impediments. Top level sport was not, as many have suggested, "an arena for true meritocracy, a world where raw talent rather than accent, surname, or appearance define the individual."[59] Numerous Ukrainian athletes were instructed to change, or voluntarily changed, their names in the hope that this would improve their chances in sport and life. Boxer Al Delaney was told by his handlers that he would never succeed competing under his given name Alex Borshuk. Long distance runner Peter Buniak changed his name to Jerome Drayton. The name Buniak "marked him as an immigrant, something less than a full member of society."[60]

Appearance also mattered. In describing the Soviet hockey team's arrival in a hotel lobby at the 1963 World Championship, author Mordecai Richler wrote: "Suddenly the Russian team, off to a game, emerged from the elevators, already in playing uniforms and carrying sticks. A Canadian journalist whispered to me, 'Don't they look sinister?' As a matter of fact, if you overlooked the absence of facial stitches, they closely resembled the many Canadians of Ukrainian origin who play in the National Hockey League."[61]

In 1956, George Kusyj won the Canadian wrestling championship in the 174-pound division. The competition was also considered an Olympic selection trial. Kusyj, though, did not make the Olympic team. According to Canadian Olympic officials, there was not enough money to send all the athletes who won titles to the Melbourne Olympics. The Ukrainian community was incensed. This anger was expressed in the Toronto published newspaper *Homin Ukrainy*

- *Ukrainian Echo*: "The question stands, why was George Kusyj not named to the national team. Could it be, because he is Kusyj?"[62] Two years later, prior to the Canadian Commonwealth Games trials, the Ukrainian community began a fund raiser to pay for Kusyj's way to the Commonwealth Games at Cardiff, Wales, in the event he made the team. Kusyj, though, did not win the trials.

As late as the 1970s, various forms of alleged bias persisted. Gayle Olinek placed second in the 800-metre event at the 1971 Pan American Games Trials. The selection committee overlooked her and sent the third place finisher to the Games instead. At the 1972 Olympic Trials, sprinter Joyce Sadowick-Yakubowich won the 200-metre dash, yet she was not named to the team in that event. In some instances, such decisions made the athletes work harder. Joyce Yakubowich recalled: ". . . it made me even more determined in my sport. I wanted to help prove that Ukrainian Canadians were tough, were winners . . ."[63]

The number of different individuals involved in incidents where accent, surname or appearance seem to have been a factor suggests that the incidents were more than just sporadic occurrences. Nevertheless, some incidents may have been honest mistakes, unpopular decisions, or perceived injustices. In almost every situation, though, the sports-minded members of the Ukrainian community viewed these occurrences as a form of prejudice.

In the past quarter century, gender discrimination has been viewed as another form of prejudice or bias that has permeated sport. When Canadian sports historians or activists discuss this issue, the Abigail Hoffman incident is usually recounted. In the mid-1950s, Hoffman played hockey incognito on a boys' team. Eventually "Ab" was discovered to be Abigail. Overnight she became a media sensation and subsequently a symbol of gender injustice in sport.

At the start of the 1947-48 season, twelve-year-old Phyllis Chorney was banned from playing hockey on a boys' team in Winnipeg. She had played on the team the previous two seasons, scoring 14 goals in her second year. Chorney, though, did not get the attention accorded to Hoffman. Yet Chorney was a pioneer of sorts. Her desire to take part in sport, whether on a girls' team or not, was in part indicative of a movement occurring at the time. The era shortly after World War II saw a substantial increase in the participation of women in sport. Ukrainian women, particularly in Western Canada, took an active part in this movement. Among the pioneers of Ukrainian women in sport were Sylvia Fedoruk - an outstanding all-round athlete (1946-62), and Evelyn Wawryshyn - a professional baseball player (1946-51) and a member of the 1950 Canadian Championship women's ice hockey team. Joining Wawryshyn on that victorious hockey team was Phyllis Chorney.

*Evelyn Wawryshyn*

The determination of Ukrainian athletes, both female and male, has led many to be selected to Canada's national teams. The first documented athlete to attain the honour was Mike Chepesuik who was named to the 1930 British Empire Games team. The first documented world champion was Paul Kozak, a member of the 1937 Kimberley Dynamiters hockey team. Two years later, Dick Kowcinak duplicated the feat with the Trail Smoke Eaters hockey team. For most athletes, representing Canada at the international level was an unforgettable experience. Fourteen-year-old Jennifer Diachun was overcome with excitement and started to cry with joy upon marching into Mexico City's Olympic Stadium during the opening ceremonies of the 1968 Olympic Games. In the same stadium a few years later, Joyce Yakubowich wept openly during the playing of *O Canada* after her victory in the 400-metre sprint at the Pan American Games. "Something just stirs you deep inside," stated Yakubowich. "I guess I'm pretty nationalistic. I was really proud of what I had and what I had done."[64]

Even for three post-World War II Ukrainian immigrants to Canada, Myron Bereza, Ostap Steckiw, and Walter Zakaluzny, the honour of being selected to represent Canada in the qualifying matches of the 1958 World Cup was an unforgettable experience. Years later, Steckiw recalled: "My most memorable moment [in sport] was when the late Bill Simpson, president of the Canadian Soccer Association, informed me by telephone that I had been selected to represent Canada." Bereza reminisced: "I played in the National Soccer League for Ukraina in those days and had never left the borders of Canada. Then, suddenly I'm in Mexico City, playing for my country. It's something one has to experience before realizing how much it really means to a person."[65]

An athlete's success in sport, whether as a member of the national team or in the professional ranks, brought about the inevitable exposure and scrutiny in the media and the community. Between the two World Wars, the phrase "credit to his race" was frequently used in describing the "ethnic" sport stars. This phrase had its roots in the liberal assimilationist philosophy regarding minorities that placed "emphasis on individual rather than group ethnicity, on social mobility through sport as through other mainstreaming activities, on acculturation through the intermediary of role models . . ."[66]

The Anglo-Protestant majority, by accentuating a minority individual's success in mainstream Canadian society made it clearly understood that success was not to be looked for in the confines of the ethnic ghettos. Only those minority individuals who succeeded in the mainstream were accorded recognition by their peers and in the media. Thus, to succeed and be recognized, members of the minorities had to participate in the mainstream, and in doing so they acquired qualities that were considered to be Canadian or British. These qualities provided them with social and economic mobility and paved the way to their acceptance as citizens. In the minority immigrant communities, the success of individuals, therefore, was viewed with admiration and envy. Overnight, successful individuals became role models, prompting many others to set out to duplicate or surpass the feats of their idols.

The assimilationist philosophy that stressed individual ethnicity and the concept of being a "credit to one's race" was presented time and again in the sports pages of the mainstream Canadian media. Many Black, Italian, Jewish and other successful minority athletes were identified by their ethnicity. It was a Black Sam Richardson, an Italian Tony Lazerri, or a Jew Goody Rosen that starred on the sporting fields of North America. In addition, nicknames were given to athletes and clubs which accentuated their ethnicity. American sprinter Eddie Tolan was the "Negro Flash," Calgary football great Normie Kwong was the "China Clipper," Winnipeg Blue Bomber quarterback Jack Jacobs was "Indian Jack," Toronto Argonaut quarterback Annis Stukus was the "Loquacious Lithuanian," Sudbury distance runner Dave Komonen was the "Flying Finn," while the Montreal Canadiens hockey club was referred to as the "Flying Frenchmen."

In contrast, Ukrainian athletes, with a few minor exceptions such as the famed "Uke Line" of the Boston Bruins or hockey great Terry "Uke" Sawchuk, were not singled out for their Ukrainian ancestry. A number of possible explanations exist for this phenomenon. For most of the era covered in this book, Ukraine was not independent.[67] Ukrainian immigrants, therefore, were generally considered to have emigrated from the political territories that were defined as the Austro-Hungarian Empire, Poland, Russia, or Romania. Consequently, the media either ignored the ethnicity of the athletes, or to explain their Slavic names, labelled them as Russians or Poles. In addition, many young, promising athletes believed that being a "credit to one's race" only applied to proven athletes. Some struggling to succeed chose not to publicize their ethnic roots or to correct misnomers.

Nevertheless, many Ukrainians in Canada themselves took the philosophy of identifying with those that were a "credit to their race" to heart. Ukrainian newspapers at times reported on the accomplishments of the Ukrainian athletes. When Ukrainian sport fans met, more often than not, they discussed the latest feats of Ukrainian athletes. To Ukrainians throughout the country, these athletes represented not only sporting success, but also success in Canadian life. They were ideal role models.

The post-war proliferation and accomplishments of "ethnic" athletes made archaic, by the mid-1960s, the once popular liberal position of identifying ethnic stars in mainstream society. Ukrainians, though, continued to follow the careers of Ukrainian athletes and take pride in their accomplishments both in amateur and professional sport.

To recognize the accomplishment of Canadian athletes of Ukrainian descent, the Canadian Ukrainian Sports Hall of Fame was founded in 1992. The Hall's inaugural dinner was held on August 12, 1992, at Vancouver's Park Royal Hotel. The guest speakers at the event were former athletes, the Honourable Justice Mr. John Sopinka and Joyce Yakubowich. Although no inductions were made, the aforementioned speakers and Mike Chepesuik were recognized as honourary members of the Hall of Fame. The driving force behind the ambitious project was Vancouver resident Boris "Bo" Fodchuk.

# THE LEGACY

In 1991, the year Ukrainians celebrated a century of their settlement in Canada, an arena in Winnipeg was named after hockey legend Terry Sawchuk. That same year, brothers John and Stan Shaley, who guided the Canadian Ukrainian Athletic Club senior girls' softball team to 17 consecutive provincial titles and a national championship in 1965, were inducted into the Softball Canada Hall of Fame.

To the vast majority of Canadians, the fact that at some time in the past Sawchuk and the Shaleys may have been described as being a "credit to their race" was inconsequential. The three were being honoured because of their contribution to sport in Canada. They were a credit to their home town and to their sport. For Canadians of Ukrainian descent, however, the recognition had an added meaning. It showed that with effort, determination, and commitment, Ukrainian athletes, coaches, and administrators had made a lasting imprint on Canadian sport history.

In 1992, the 1965 national championship Canadian Ukrainian Athletic Club senior girls' softball team was inducted into the Manitoba Sports Hall of Fame. It was the first time that a team operated by a Ukrainian community club was thus recognized. The recognition not only celebrated the achievement of one team but also affirmed the high level of sport that was offered to the general community by Ukrainian sport clubs, leagues, and teams.

*Brooklands Ukrainian Athletic Club hockey team, c.1935*

This then is the story of those who were a credit to their sport and who were bound by a common thread, their ethnic heritage. It is a story of athletes, of their triumphs and failures. It is also a story of the volunteers, of those who worked with great devotion to establish and operate community sport clubs.

This story is their sporting legacy.

# THE CLUBS, LEAGUES AND TEAMS

The clubs, leagues and teams are profiled by city in alphabetical order. In some cases, they had more than one name. They are listed by the name used for the longest period of time. For a complete cross-reference, please see page 840.

# BROOKLANDS, MANITOBA

## BROOKLANDS UKRAINIAN ATHLETIC CLUB

In the early 1930s, the community of Brooklands was a separate political jurisdiction located on the outskirts of Winnipeg. It was home to about 260 Ukrainian families. For those families, the community life was centred around the T. H. Shevchenko Ukrainian Institute. In 1932, Nick Shaley, John Moroz and Peter Susky of the Canadian Ukrainian Athletic Club (CUAC) of Winnipeg helped Harry Klymkiw of Brooklands organize the sons and daughters of the Shevchenko Institute members into the Brooklands Ukrainian Athletic Club (BUAC). While the Institute provided the nucleus for the club, the formal establishment of BUAC in 1932 resulted in an open membership policy.

After BUAC gained some exposure in Brooklands and Winnipeg, in some circles it became known affectionately as the "Buicks."

In 1934, BUAC entered a team in the newly formed men's Ukrainian Diamond Ball League. The team played in the league for just one year.

During the 1934-35 season, a BUAC team competed in the Weston Hockey League. The club performed admirably and won the league championship.

BUAC entered a team into the Greater Winnipeg Intermediate Girls' Softball League in 1936. The team had a respectable first season, making the playoffs but bowing out in two straight games to West Kildonan in the opening round.

In 1938, the BUAC girls' ball team dominated the Greater Winnipeg Intermediate Softball

League. The club, which had a run of thirteen consecutive victories, finished at the top of the standings and received a bye into the finals. BUAC then went on to defeat Fort Rouge Aces for the championship.

*Brooklands Ukrainian Athletic Club girls' softball team, c.1938*

During the summer of 1940, the BUAC girls' softball team played in the Greater Winnipeg Senior Softball League. BUAC had a very difficult time competing in this league because of the high calibre of play. The team won but a handful of games and failed to make the play-offs.

The following year BUAC ceased operations.

In late 1947, the Brooklands Ukrainian Athletic Club was revived, and a new executive was elected at a "reorganizational" meeting. In addition, Harry Klymkiw and Nick Soliljak were honoured with life memberships for their outstanding contribution to the club.

After the reorganization, it appears that the only activity the club was able to establish was an in-house mixed bowling league. The club continued operating this league for a number of years.

# CALGARY, ALBERTA

## RED ACES

E arly in 1931, the youth section of the Ukrainian Labour-Farmer Temple Association (ULFTA) organized a young men's softball team. Shortly afterwards, the team challenged the softball team of the (Ukrainian) People's Home to a game. The challenge was accepted. The game attracted a wide audience, and ended in a 9-9 tie. Afterwards, the executive of the ULFTA agreed to sponsor the softball team of their youth section. A meeting was called, an executive was elected, and the Red Stars softball team was officially established. In addition, a team of younger boys was organized.

During the summer of 1931, the Red Stars competed against Workers' Sport Association (WSA) aligned teams in Canmore, Drumheller, Edmonton, and other locations. The team also challenged non-WSA teams to games in Calgary and in nearby farming communities. The intent was to break up existing teams and to replace them with WSA teams. The Red Stars succeeded in accomplishing this in Forest Lawn. The Red Stars also succeeded in breaking up a Ukrainian "fascist" softball team and recruiting some of its members.[1] The team branded "fascist" by the Red Stars was probably that of the (Ukrainian) People's Home, a literary-cultural non-communist organization.

In June, the Red Stars travelled to Edmonton to partake in a picnic sponsored by the Communist Party of Canada. There they played a game against the Red Brigade, an Edmonton WSA team. The Calgary team lost the encounter.

In the spring of 1932, the Red Stars were reorganized and renamed the Red Aces. The team was also outfitted in new uniforms. This was financially possible after a number of fund raising dances during the winter. The team of younger boys inherited the uniforms of the Red Aces. The youth section also expanded its sports program that spring by organizing a girls' softball team.

*Red Aces, 1932*

In addition to competing against WSA teams in the summer of 1932, the Red Aces played games against "bourgeois" teams, some of which were affiliated with the YMCA and against a team sponsored by a Ukrainian non-communist organization. Playing manager of the Red Aces was Mykhailo Danylyshyn.

It is not known how long the Reds Aces existed. The fate of the other two teams sponsored by the Calgary branch of the ULFTA is similarly unknown.

# EDMONTON, ALBERTA

## LIONS

The collapse of the Ukrainian Sports Club of Edmonton after the 1953 season created a vacuum for Ukrainian soccer enthusiasts, particularly for those who wanted to play for a
Ukrainian club. With so many other ethnic groups fielding teams, it was expected that the
Ukrainian community of Edmonton could also. Two years would pass, though, before a new
team was organized.

In the spring of 1956, Ivan Tymchyshyn concluded that it was time to organize a soccer team.
Tymchyshyn had previous experience in this area, having founded the Ukrainian Sports Club
Sitch in 1951. Sitch later merged with the Canadian Sports Association Ukraina to form the
Ukrainian Sports Club of Edmonton.

The new club was formally established in May and named the Lions. Tymchyshyn was elected president, M. Dwornyk secretary, and Kril treasurer. Mykola Senyk, who helped in the
organization of the club, was appointed coach of the team.

The Lions were one of eight teams fielded in the second division of the Edmonton District
Soccer Association League. The club was competitive during its debut season, winning 8
games, drawing 2 and losing 4 to place third in the standings. It was captained by Wolodymyr
Shwetz. Towards the end of the season, coach Senyk was replaced by Wolodymyr Stebelsky
who had recently arrived from Toronto.

During the off-season, the Lions absorbed players from a defunct Hungarian club. The league
was also reorganized at that time and the Lions were promoted to the first division. Coach

Stebelsky spent the off-season strengthening the club. His prize acquisition was Paul Dezman, captain of the Alberta Selects.

At first, the Ukrainian-Hungarian combination did not play well. The club had problems in the offensive zone and was not scoring goals. Stebelsky changed tactics and the team began to steadily improve. By mid-August, the Lions had climbed from the basement of the 11-team league into third place.

On September 1, the Lions faced Edmonton Scottish. Three Ukrainian players refused to play, protesting the use of eight Hungarian players in the starting line-up of the team. The Ukrainians argued that the Lions were a Ukrainian team and that at least half of the starters should be Ukrainian.

No information about the club subsequent to that September date was uncovered.

# TARAS SHEVCHENKO INSTITUTE *SHEVS*

In 1917, Ukrainian Catholics in the Edmonton area organized the Taras Shevchenko Institute, which became operational in 1918. The institute was a residence for Ukrainian students attending schools in Edmonton. It also offered compulsory lessons in Ukrainian subject matters, and voice and choral studies. The institute was unable to raise sufficient funds to pay for the building that it purchased and had to cease operations in 1922. In 1925, it was re-established at a leased facility, that included an athletic field.

It appears that sport became an integral component of the institute's extracurricular activities in the second phase of the institute's existence. In the winter of 1927-28, a hockey team was iced and competed in a three-team league. The Shevs won the most games in league play. That spring, a baseball team was formed which also played in a three-team league that included the Ukrainian M. Hrushevsky Institute. The Shevs triumphed once again.

During the 1928-29 hockey season, the Taras Shevchenko Institute competed in a league against a German and a French institute. The season culminated with playoffs at the famed Edmonton Arena where the Shevs prevailed. In 1930, the Shevs won the Edmonton College League.

In addition, the institute had active basketball, soccer, and rugby teams.

Brother Volodymyr and brother Methodius were active in organizing and coaching the sport teams at the institute.

*Taras Shevchenko Institute Shevs hockey team, 1930*

# UKRAINIAN SPORTS ASSOCIATION *SITCH*

The Ukrainian Sports Association Sitch was organized in 1951 by Ivan Tymchyshyn within the framework of the Ukrainian Youth Association (SUM), Edmonton branch. At the time, the unaffiliated Canadian Sports Association Ukraina operated in Edmonton. Tymchyshyn was convinced, though, that the independent CSA Ukraina did not serve the needs of the community well, particularly the element that belonged to SUM.

The Sitch team that was assembled in 1951 consisted mostly of SUM members with a few former Ukraina players switching allegiances. The team was entered in the Edmonton league and played with some success.

During the two seasons that Sitch existed, games played against Ukraina were particularly hard-fought. There was some bitterness between the two clubs and emotions ran high. The rivalry, though, created a greater interest in the two teams and brought out more than an average number of fans.

Prior to the start of the 1952 season, the Edmonton Soccer Association changed the format of league play. The regular season would comprise two parts. Those clubs finishing the first half of the schedule at the top half of the standings would be grouped in the first division for the remainder of the year. Those at the bottom half would make up the second division. In the second half, there would be no inter-division play.

Sitch played well and after the first half of the season was assigned to the first division. In the second half of the schedule, the club placed last in the first division and was demoted to the second division for the 1953 season.

On December 21, 1952, the Ukrainian Sports Club Sitch ceased to exist. The executives of Sitch and Ukraina came to the conclusion that the Ukrainian community of Edmonton was too small to sustain two competitive soccer clubs. As a result, they merged into the Ukrainian Sports Club of Edmonton.

# UKRAINIAN SPORTS ASSOCIATION *UKRAINA*

In 1948, members of the Edmonton branch of the Ukrainian National Youth Federation (UNYF) organized an informal sport club. Volleyball was the primary sport, and exhibition matches were played against Plast, YMCA, RCMP and others. The club became popular and non-UNYF members began to join. At the same time, the Ukrainian Youth Association (SUM) attempted to organize its own volleyball club. This failed and SUM turned its efforts to organizing a soccer club. Mykola Senyk was retained as the coach of the soccer team and practices began. The team known as Sport Club Ukraina never played a game because it lacked players. The club fell apart after Senyk left, shortly after its creation.

The Ukrainian National Youth Federation seized this opportunity, and at a public meeting on June 12, 1949, formally re-organized the ad hoc sport club into the Ukrainian Sports Association Ukraina (USA Ukraina). The first executive of the association included Hryhoriy Bratkiw - chairman, Michael Bayrak - vice-chairman and Peter Formensky - secretary. Mykhailo Lysko, who played a leading role in organizing the club, did not seek a position on the executive. Strong opposition to the formation of the club came from SUM and from within the ranks of the Ukrainian National Federation (UNF). SUM objected to the sport club being affiliated with UNYF. Even some UNF members questioned whether sport should be part of the organization's program. Other UNF members questioned the legality, from the organization's perspective, of establishing a sport club without the prior approval of the National Executive.

USA Ukraina overcame these difficulties to field a soccer team in 1949. The team had, in fact, been organized some time before the formal establishment of the sport club, and had been practising since April. The performance of the team in its debut season was respectable. At the conclusion of the schedule, the team was awarded with the title "Gentlemen's Team."

During the Labour Day weekend, USA Ukraina and UNYF hosted the Ukrainian Youth Festival. Exhibition matches were held in volleyball and soccer against the Lethbridge Ukrainian Sports Association Orlyk. The visitors won the soccer game 6-0 and the volleyball match 15-3 and 15-8.

In November, the executive of the club unexpectedly resigned and a new one headed by Hryhoriy Dmytriw was elected.

During the winter of 1949-50, the club offered table tennis and chess. Club members Paul Dezman and Morris Iwasykiw advanced to the semi-finals of the Edmonton table tennis championships while Iwasykiw was a finalist in the singles.

In 1950, USA Ukraina fielded two soccer teams, a senior and a junior. The senior team was augmented by players transferring from the Lethbridge Orlyk. In the early part of the season, the team played well, recording a string of victories. This success substantially increased interest in the club in the Ukrainian community and a group was formed to raise funds. Reverend Marko Dyrda was the chairman, and the group included many prominent citizens of Edmonton's Ukrainian community.

The group believed that a sound financial base was required to ensure the success of the club. Funds were needed to recruit impact players who would lead the team to championships. Some players expected remuneration, others accommodations, and still others wanted guarantees of employment. The financial base could only come from the economically established "old immigrants," rather than from the soccer-oriented newcomers. To access this base, it was argued that USA Ukraina would have to break its ties with the UNYF.

The executive of USA Ukraina agreed with the recommendations. At a public meeting attended by more than 200 people on July 9, 1950, the club severed its ties with UNYF and was restructured to become an independent entity. Reverend Dyrda was elected president, former member of parliament Michael Luchkovich was named manager of the soccer team, and another former member of parliament, Anthony (Antin) Hlynka assisted with the management and administration of the club. Oleksander Skocen, an established European professional who had recently immigrated to Canada, was offered the position of playing coach which he accepted. To reflect the wider base of the club, the name was changed to the Canadian Sports Association Ukraina.

*Ukrainian Sports Association Ukraina soccer team, c.1950*

CSA Ukraina completed the 1950 regular schedule in second place. The club was invited to compete for the Alberta Cup. After winning its opening match, play in the Cup competition was suspended.

In September, CSA Ukraina organized a two-day youth sports festival in Edmonton. Participants in the event included members of the local branches of Plast, SUM and UNYF, Lethbridge USA Orlyk, and CSA Ukraina. Competition was held in soccer, track and field, and volleyball.

During the winter of 1950-51, competition in table tennis continued. A women's volleyball team was fielded which finished second in league play. The club also acknowledged a substantial debt and a number of the soccer players still had claims on honorariums. Oleksander Skocen left for Toronto, as did a number of other players who had transferred to Ukraina from Orlyk the previous year. CSA Ukraina was rapidly losing its prestige in the community. In addition, the club lost its monopoly on soccer in the organized Ukrainian community with the formation of the Ukrainian Sports Association Sitch in the spring of 1951.

During the winter, a general meeting was held at which Wolodymyr Batytsky was elected club president. Batytsky and his executive eliminated the fanfare of the past year and scaled down the expectations. This had positive impact on a team still feeling the turmoil of the past year and reeling from the loss of a number of veteran players. During the 1951 season, Ukraina members played good soccer without putting pressure on themselves. The club began the year by winning the Dragoon's Cup, a competition held prior to the start of the regular schedule. Ukraina finished the regular season in second place and won another cup at a mini-tournament in Edmonton organized by the German Football Club.

Prior to the start of the 1952 season, the Edmonton Soccer Association changed the format of league play. The regular season would comprise two parts. Those clubs finishing the first half of the schedule at the top half of the standings would be grouped in the first division for the remainder of the year. Those at the bottom half would make up the second division. There would be no inter-division play in the second half. After the first half of the season Ukraina was relegated to the second division. The club won the second division and was promoted to the first division for the 1953 season. The team was captained by W. Kyrylo.

On December 21, 1952, the Canadian Sports Association Ukraina ceased to exist. The executives of Ukraina and Sitch came to the conclusion that the Ukrainian community of Edmonton was too small to sustain two competitive soccer clubs. As a result, they merged into the Ukrainian Sports Club of Edmonton.

The new unified club fielded a team under the name Lions in the Edmonton soccer league in 1953. The team, though, lacked strong management, and some of the players took advantage of this by missing practices and games. The Lions sometimes played with as few as eight players, and the team barely completed the season.

# UKRAINIAN SPORTS ASSOCIATION *UKRAINA*

In the early 1980s, Fedir Petrychkovych, a soccer enthusiast and a recent immigrant from Lviv, Ukraine, promoted the idea of a Ukrainian soccer club in Edmonton. Orest Windyk, Michael Swystun, John Parubay, Nick Chaschiwsky, and Bohdan Krawchenko supported the idea and joined forces with Petrychkovych in 1982 to organize the Ukrainian Sports Association Ukraina. Orest Windyk was elected the club's first president. Commencing that year, the sports association fielded teams bearing the name Karpaty in various city leagues.

The debut Karpaty team was registered in the under-21 Edmonton District Soccer Association league in 1982. The club did not start practising till shortly before the start of the season. When it entered competition, it obviously was not prepared for the challenge and was outplayed on almost every occasion. In addition, the club had just enough players for a regular line-up. This meant that players had to be on the field for the duration of a game as there were no available substitutes. Nevertheless, under the guidance of coach David Marples, the team began to jell towards the end of the season.

To improve on the previous year's performance, practices in 1983 began in February. In addition, an over-21 team was organized.

During the winter of 1985-86, the senior Karpaty soccer team played in the Edmonton District Soccer Association indoor soccer league. The team placed second in the second division and was promoted to the first division for the 1986-87 indoor season. It was also recognized with a trophy as the best disciplined team in the league. Elected president of the association that winter was Michael Slipchuk, the Canadian junior men's figure skating champion.

During the summer of 1986, Karpaty finished in second place in league play and the team was promoted to the second division for the 1987 outdoor season. The club was coached by Todd Mulyk. The under-21 team finished its season in third place. It also participated in a tournament in Kelowna. The club was coached by Chris Cahill.

Karpaty played well during the 1988 outdoor season and the team was promoted to the league's premier division.

During the winter of 1988-89, the team placed first in the standings in the first division. The victory promoted Karpaty to the premier division for the following indoor season. The team was led on offence by Barton Pawluski, on defence by John Latezek, and in goal by John Mancini.

During the 1989 and 1990 outdoor seasons, Karpaty played in the premier division. The team was coached by Dennis Larmour.


## PRESIDENTS OF THE UKRAINIAN SPORTS ASSOCIATION UKRAINA

| | |
|---|---|
| Orest Windyk | (1982-86) |
| Michael Slipchuk | (1986-89) |
| Barton Pawluski | (1989-  ) |

# HAMILTON, ONTARIO

## ST. VLADIMIR SOFTBALL TEAM

In 1950, the Hamilton branch of the Canadian Ukrainian Youth Association (SUMK), operating under the auspices of St. Vladimir Ukrainian Orthodox Church, organized a softball team and entered it in the Hamilton Church Fastball League. It was believed that a softball team would help diversify the activities of the association. Diversity would make the association's program more interesting for the existing members and would attract new members.

In its initial year of operation, the team consisted exclusively of SUMK members. Among those who contributed to organizing the team, and subsequently played on it, were E. Kuchma, V. Kuchma, J. Maraschuk, E. Panchesyn, T. Poloreski, P. Popiel, T. Radchuk, B. Sorokowski, B. Stasiuk, S. Stasiuk, W. Ukrainitz, B. Yacashyn and Jim Blaschuk, the team's playing coach. The manager was M. Serwatuk while R. Hewak helped out as the assistant manager. Financially, the team was sponsored by the owner-operator of Master Cleaners and congregation member P. Iwaskiw. His sponsorship allowed the team to purchase uniforms. In subsequent years, additional sponsors provided assistance.

In 1951, the Hamilton Church Fastball League revised the rules pertaining to club rosters. Each club was now entitled to have three imports or non-members of their church play on the team. St. Vladimir responded to the rule change by recruiting three imports. The new players had an immediate impact on the team. Play improved significantly, and the team completed the season in third place.

The following year, with much the same line-up, St. Vladimir continued to improve its game and finished the regular season in second spot. In the first round of the playoffs the team was eliminated by St. Enoch.

In 1953, St. Vladimir won the league pennant with a record of 10 wins and 5 losses, and received a bye into the championship final. It then swept St. Thomas in three straight games to win the championship. In the first round of the Ontario Intermediate AA Softball playoffs, St. Vladimir defeated a team from St. Catharines. In the second round or the semi-finals, St. Vladimir lost the best-of-five series in the deciding fifth game.

During the 1954 season, St. Vladimir played inconsistently but nevertheless qualified for the playoffs. The club defeated New Westminster in the semi-finals. In the championship series against Cavalry, St. Vladimir lost.

The following season, St. Vladimir posted a winning record with 11 victories in 16 starts. The club qualified for a round robin playoff but failed to advance to the championship final.

In addition to competing in the church league, the St. Vladimir softball team provided the Hamilton Branch of SUMK with a novel vehicle for inter-branch fraternization and cama-raderie. A number of SUMK branches in southern Ontario had softball teams, and friendly games among the branches became popular. The games were usually held on weekends and in conjunction with branch picnics. Among those SUMK branches that Hamilton played matches against were Grimsby, Waterford, Long Branch and Oshawa.

During the summer of 1956 and 1957, St. Vladimir continued to play in the Intermediate Church League.

St. Vladimir opened the 1958 season slowly. After 13 games, the SUMK team only had one win to its credit. Subsequently, it won a number of games in a row and qualified for post-season play. The club carried the momentum of the latter part of the season into the playoffs, winning its semi-final against Legatts. In the best-of-five final against Wentworth Baptist, St. Vladimir was defeated in four games.

The St. Vladimir team folded after the 1958 season. The team had difficulty replenishing its ranks, as some of the players left the Hamilton area while others found age catching up to them. In addition, work and family responsibilities were making it more difficult for the individuals to play in a regularly scheduled league.

# UKRAINIAN SPORTS CLUB *DNIPRO*

In 1953, Stephen Telepchuk was appointed sport coordinator at the Hamilton branch of the Ukrainian Youth Association (SUM). Telepchuk decided that the position required action and, as a result, he set out, with the assistance of Nykola Shmahun, to organize a sport program for the youth group. Soccer was the obvious sport to start with, as most male members of the branch had pursued the sport in Ukraine or in the displaced persons (DP) camps of post-war Europe. Telepchuk presented the plan to the SUM executive and it was endorsed.

An application to enter a team, to be known as the Ukrainian Sports Club Dnipro, was submitted to the Southern Ontario Soccer League. The league's executive bypassed the standard procedure of assigning a new team to the weaker Second Division by placing Dnipro in the ten-team First Division. The special privilege was extended to the club as a result of the league's very high regard for Ukrainian soccer players at the time. The assessment was based primarily on the performance of Toronto's SA Ukraina.

Dnipro played well in its inaugural season to finish in sixth place in the league standings. In competition for the Hamilton Spectator Trophy, emblematic of the city championship, Dnipro defeated Hamilton United 2-1 in the quarter-finals and Slovakia 3-1 in the semi-finals to gain a berth in the final. Westinghouse, which was competing in the much tougher National League in Toronto, was Dnipro's opponent. The game was barely two minutes old when a Dnipro player deflected the ball into his own net. That was the only goal scored against Dnipro goaltender and captain Steve Telepchuk. For the remainder of the game he tended the team's net brilliantly. Mykhailo Malaniuk, Nykola Witkowsky, and Taras Brezdenj scored for Dnipro as the novice club defeated Westinghouse 3-1 and won the Spectator Trophy, the oldest contested Cup in Canada.

In 1954, the Ukrainian Sports Club Dnipro, or as it was more commonly called, the Ukes, added an under-16 juvenile soccer team to its program. The team was entered in the Hamilton Minor Soccer Association league where it played to a fourth place in the standings. It was coached by Walter Turyk and Jaroslaw Klun. The senior team fared poorly, finishing the season in tenth place out of 12 teams. It was unsuccessful in its defence of the Spectator Trophy.

The following year, the juvenile Dnipro Ukes placed second in league standings. In the play-offs, the club won the Doyle Cup, emblematic of the city championship. The juveniles were coached by Turyk and captained by Nick Strembicky. The senior club continued to experience difficulties on the soccer pitch. It tried to resolve some of them by borrowing players from the reserve teams of Toronto's SA Ukraina, but the move did not improve the on-field fortunes of the club.

*Ukrainian Sports Club Dnipro, 1953*

In 1956, the juvenile soccer team was dropped as many of the players were called up to fill voids on the senior team. Even then, according to some observers, almost everything went wrong for the senior team. Training camp began late, with many veterans deciding not to attend. Consequently, in the early part of the season, play was below par. Frustrated, the team continued its losing ways during the season. Dnipro won one game and lost 11 to finish in last place. The team, though, had potential; the *Hamilton Spectator* reported, "How can a team like Dnipro be at the bottom of the Senior League? They have tremendous power, yet fail to get on the victory trail."[2]

In 1957, the Ukrainian Youth Association (SUM) lost interest in Dnipro. A local sports enthusiast and member of SUM, Wolodymyr Harbuzinski, decided to continue operating the club independently. Harbuzinski immediately renamed the club Sport Association Ukraina. The team and the new management had a difficult time that year. The club nevertheless improved on the previous year's record by winning three games. In 1958, after losing its first six games (during which the club was outscored 23 to 3), Ukraina pulled out of the league and folded. Lack of interest led to the demise of the club. It was difficult to recruit players, it was difficult to get fan support, and it was difficult to get sponsors.

*Ukrainian Sports Club Dnipro logo*

# UKRAINIAN VETS

In the spring of 1948, members of the Canadian Legion General Orlick Branch 522 in Hamilton formed a softball team. A number of good ball players were members of the legion and they decided to continue their camaraderie through sport. To round out the roster, a few non-legion members were recruited. The recruits were usually friends of the legion members. The Ukrainian Vets softball club was sponsored by the legion and competed under its name.

In May of 1948, the team was entered into the intermediate AA Mountain Fastball League. The Vets made an immediate impact on the league. En route to winning the pennant, the club did not lose one game in its inaugural season. The Vets then swept the semi-finals against the Tates. In the best-of-three final, the Vets lost their first game of the season. Nevertheless, they defeated the Porcelains to win the league championship. The title qualified the Vets to the provincial Sr. "B" playdowns, where the team failed to advance past the opening round, losing a close series to the Dundas Graftons.

The following year, the Vets continued to play in the Mountain Fastball League. The club made the playoffs, but with the improved competition, the Vets failed to duplicate the previous year's undefeated record. In the playoffs, the club swept the Porcelains to win the league title. The Vets then faced the Beaches club in a best-of-five final for the Hamilton intermediate "A" championship. It took the Vets four games to dispose of their opponents and win the Hamilton title.

The victory qualified the Vets to vie for the Ontario title. In the opening round, a best-of-three series against Guelph, the Vets lost the first game but came back to win the next two. In the second round, Niagara Falls fell to the Vets in two straight games in a series that determined the zone championship. The Vets then faced Toronto Fairbank Memorial in a three-game series. In the opening game, the Vets dropped a 5-4 decision in ten innings. In the second game, the Vets were trailing 4-2 in the ninth but came back to tie the game on a Johnny Olejnik home run. The game was settled in the 12th inning when the Vets brought a runner across the plate on an error. In the final and deciding game, the Vets were blasted 12-5 by their Toronto opponent.

One of the most prominent players on the Vets in their first two years of existence and in subsequent years was Nick Pidsodny. The colourful all-round athlete was an outstanding pitcher, hurling numerous no-hitters. He was also a power hitter. During the winter months, Pidsodny tended goal for minor pro hockey clubs: among others, Buffalo of the AHL, Dallas and Houston of the USHL, Vancouver and Oakland of the PCHL, and Sydney of the MMHL. Pidsodny was also a fine lacrosse goaltender.

In 1950, the Vets defended their Mountain League pennant. League playoffs were set aside that year as the schedule required an immediate start of the city championship. The Vets, having won the pennant, faced the Polish White Eagles in a best-of-five final. The Vets swept the White Eagles in three straight games. The club then defeated Erie House of Niagara Falls to win the intermediate "A" zone championship. Chatham fell next to the Vets as they qualified for the best-of-three Southern Ontario intermediate "A" softball final against Evans Motors of Toronto. In the first game, the Vets defeated Toronto 4-2. Evans Motors came back to win the second game by a 7-1 count. The deciding game turned out to be a nail biter as both teams played outstanding defensive ball. In the end, Toronto won the game 1-0.

In the spring of 1951, the Vets decided to move up to a higher calibre league. After dominating the Mountain League for three seasons, they sought a more challenging competitive environment. In May, the team joined the Big Four Senior Softball League. The competition was indeed tougher and it took the Vets a full month to win their first game. Subsequently, they won a handful of games and finished the season in last place in a four-team league.

In 1952, the team continued to struggle in the Big Four League winning only three games during the season. The Vets were managed by Mike Stasiuk and coached by F. Wolkowski.

The following year the Vets entered their team in the Woodlands Intermediate "A" Softball League. After a poor start, the team ended the season with seven consecutive victories to place second in the standings. In the opening round of the playoffs, the Ukrainian Vets defeated the Polish Vets.

During the 1954 season, the Vets continued to play in the Woodlands Intermediate "A" Softball League. Johnny Olejnik was the club's playing manager while Frank Smith handled the coaching duties. The club had a record of 9 wins and 7 losses to place second in the league standings. Three weeks of continuous rain washed out the opening round of the playoffs. In late September the league folded because of financial woes.

The General Orlick Legion Branch 522 sponsored the team during its eleven-year existence. Stag parties were popular fund raisers. Refreshments, food, games, and prizes were on the program. Proceeds were used to purchase uniforms and equipment and for other necessary expenses.

In 1955, the Woodlands League was restructured and the Vets entered a team once again. Johnny Olejnik continued managing the club. Stan Wolkowski, former quarterback with the Hamilton Tiger-Cats, joined the Vets at the shortstop position. The Vets once again finished in second place with a record of 12 wins, 8 losses and 2 ties. The team won the opening game of the semi-finals against Stoney Creek. The series was then cancelled because Stoney Creek had to move on to the provincial playoffs. As a result, the Vets faced Moosehead for the league title. In a closely fought series, the Vets lost the championship in the fifth and deciding game.

In 1956, the Vets won the Woodlands Major Fastball League pennant with a record of 16 wins, 8 losses and a tie. During an exhibition game that season, Bill Shugan, a nine-year pitching veteran with the Ukrainian Vets, was honoured for his 25-year contribution to the game of baseball. Shugan received a silver plate and fishing gear. Finishing first in the regular season gave the Vets a bye into the final. After winning the first two games of a best-of-five series, the Vets lost three in a row to UEW. The club was once again managed by John Olejnik.

The Vets repeated as pennant winners of the Woodlands league in 1957. Their record included 17 wins, 6 losses and a tie. The Vets' Herb Mushie won the league batting title with a .348 average. Nick Pidsodny won all nine games he pitched that season, posting a 1.34 ERA. In the best-of-five final for the league championship, the Vets collapsed and were beaten in three straight games by UEW.

During the 1958 season, the Vets continued playing in the Woodlands league. The schedule included games against teams in the Big Four League which would count in the final standing. The season concluded with the Vets tied for second spot with a record of 8 wins and 11 loses. In a best-of-three sudden death to determine the finalist, the Vets lost out to their perennial nemesis UEW.

The Ukrainian Vets team folded after the 1958 season. For a few years, the team had difficulty replenishing its ranks as some of the players left the Hamilton area while others found age catching up to them. In addition, family responsibilities and the pressures of shift work were making it more difficult for the individuals to play in a regularly scheduled league.

# KENORA, ONTARIO

## KENORA UKRAINIAN ATHLETIC CLUB

The Kenora Ukrainian Athletic Club (KUAC) evolved out of a youth club that was organized at the Prosvita Literary Society in Kenora in 1932. Steve Weslak (Wasyluk), the youth club's first president, introduced badminton to the club members. After some initial training and in-house tournaments, the club began competing against other youth and sport clubs of Kenora. The badminton program lasted through about 1936.

In the late 1930s, Karl Lozinski, president of the youth club, spearheaded a drive to organize a hockey team. A juvenile team was put together and entered into league play. The team was operated by Prosvita with the assistance of the women's auxiliary, the Olha Kobylanska Society. For a number of years, the team was sponsored by Mykola Kochaida and Wasyl Melnyk, the owners and operators of the Dalmor Hotel.

At the time, the hockey team and the sport program offered by Prosvita became known as the Kenora Ukrainian Athletic Club. Evidence suggests that a softball team was also organized prior to World War II.

In 1939, the juvenile KUAC hockey team won the Chappel Cup. The hockey team continued to operate in the early 1940s. At that time, Karl Lozinski managed the club, while John Zibinski, Sr. handled the coaching duties. The hockey team folded after an internal disagreement. During its existence, the team was outfitted with blue jerseys with yellow trim. The letters KUAC were emblazoned on the front.

*Kenora Ukrainian Athletic Club juvenile hockey team*

In the 1950s, a bantam hockey team was iced by KUAC. Billy Ratuski coached it for a number of years. The boys eventually moved into the juvenile age bracket where they played under the watchful eye of coach Don Sawchuk. The team won the Chappel Cup in 1958.

# KINGSTON, ONTARIO

## UKRAINIAN SPORTS CLUB OF KINGSTON

The Ukrainian Sports Club of Kingston (also known as the Ukrainian Athletic Association of Kingston) was founded on June 3, 1956. The first executive of the club included Ihor Szkrumelak, president; Wasyl Janischewskyj, vice-president; M. Andrijowych, treasurer; and Paul Paliyenko, secretary. The club was organized to promote physical fitness among its members and to publicize the Ukrainian community and its aspirations: "We represented Kingston in other towns where we went but we were most interested in representing ourselves as a group of Ukrainians."[3] Since it was unaffiliated, the club also served as a social entity where individuals of different political convictions could fraternize.

Most of the members of the Ukrainian Sports Club of Kingston were post-World War II immigrants. Many were transients in Kingston, either post-secondary students attending Queen's University or young professionals. At its peak, the club had at most some 25 members.

*Membership Card of the Ukrainian Sports Club of Kingston*

The European connection of the members undoubtedly influenced the choice of sports the club pursued. A volleyball team was organized immediately and membership was sought in a local league. Subsequently, club members participated in basketball, chess and soccer.

The Ukrainian Sports Club of Kingston operated irregularly for a number of years. Scholastic and professional responsibilities superseded participation in sport, making it difficult to have a continuous program. With time, most students and professionals returned to their home towns and the club ceased operations.

# KIRKLAND LAKE, ONTARIO

## UKRAINIAN SPORTS ASSOCIATION *DNIPRO*

On April 24, 1950, a meeting was held in Kirkland Lake with the intent of organizing a sport club. The meeting was called by Wasyl Didiuk, a teacher with the local Ukrainian Catholic Church. Most of those attending the meeting were young men who had immigrated to Canada from the displaced persons camps of Germany. These individuals, to fulfil their immigration obligations, were assigned to work in the mines of the Kirkland Lake area. At the meeting, Didiuk argued that sport would be a worthwhile respite from the grind at the mines. He also argued that through sport Ukrainians could enhance their presence in the town.

The meeting concluded with the founding of the Ukrainian Sports Association Dnipro. The club's first executive included W. Didiuk, president; P. Woycyshyn, vice-president; M. Bey, secretary; M. Weselyj, treasurer; and M. Hrab, sports activity co-ordinator. Although the club was affiliated with the local Ukrainian Catholic Church, anyone could join.

Most of the fledgling club's members had European soccer experience, either from Ukraine or from the DP camps. As a result, soccer was the first sport organized. Within a short period of time Dnipro made its debut. The club's first victory came in mid-July in an exhibition match against a Polish soccer team from Noranda. Dnipro won the encounter 4-0.

The Dnipro soccer team was not registered in a league. For a number of years it played exhibition matches against local Canadian clubs and against clubs organized by other recently arrived groups.

In addition to soccer, USA Dnipro fielded a men's volleyball team. The team competed against clubs from Northern Ontario and Quebec. Dnipro did not have enough female members to field a women's team. The women that did belong to the club trained and scrimmaged with the men's volleyball team.

*Ukrainian Sports Association Dnipro volleyball team, 1952*

The USA Dnipro was well-supported by the Ukrainian community and by the Ukrainian organizations of Kirkland Lake. The older immigrants, in particular, were taken by the enthusiasm of the club and enjoyed attending its practices and games. The club was assisted financially by the church, the League for the Liberation of Ukraine, and by P. Woycyshyn, an established local bakery owner-operator.

The Ukrainian Sports Association Dnipro ceased to operate in 1954. By that time, most of the club members had fulfilled their immigration obligations and had left the area to resettle elsewhere.

# KITCHENER, ONTARIO

## UKRAINIAN CATHOLIC CHURCH
## OF THE TRANSFIGURATION HOCKEY TEAM

A passion for hockey prompted group of young men who attended the Ukrainian Catholic Church of the Transfiguration or lived in its vicinity to organize a team in 1960. The drive was spearheaded by three Grygaski brothers. Upon formation, the team approached George Yaremy for adult guidance. He readily agreed to coach the enthusiasts. Subsequently, his brother Michael Yaremy joined the team as manager.

*Church of the Transfiguration hockey team, c.1960*

The Church of the Transfiguration sponsored the team and it was registered in the local Catholic church hockey league for young adults (late teens and early twenties). The team competed in the league for three years posting a nearly perfect record: it won the league title in each of the years and it won every game it played with the exception of one which ended in a tie.

The Transfiguration Church hockey team folded after three seasons - work and family responsibilities made it difficult to ice a sufficient number for skaters for games.

# LETHBRIDGE, ALBERTA

## UKRAINIAN SPORTS ASSOCIATION *ORLYK*

In mid-1948, a large group of Ukrainian refugees arrived in the Lethbridge area from the Orlyk Displaced Persons (DP) Camp at Berchtesgaden, West Germany. Most of the group members had been assigned to work on beet farms in the area as part of their resettlement agreement. After the fall harvest, a substantial number relocated to Lethbridge for the winter. Immediately, they set out to establish Ukrainian community organizations. The small local Ukrainian population was sceptical of the capability of the new immigrants to establish such organizations.

In early 1949, a group of sport enthusiasts, among them Yaroslaw Baziuk and Dmytro Pysch, organized the Ukrainian Sports Association Orlyk. It was an independent and self-sustained entity. Almost all of those that joined the club had European volleyball and soccer experience and were eager to participate in organized sport.

Only a short time later, on March 10, Orlyk fielded its first team in competition. The Lethbridge YMCA was the opponent in an exhibition volleyball match. At the end of the month, Orlyk challenged the Baltic DPs to matches in volleyball and basketball. Orlyk won the volleyball game while the Baltic all-stars were victorious in basketball. That day, Orlyk's junior basketball team made its debut by defeating a local high school team.

On April 24, some 1,500 enthusiasts came out to watch USA Orlyk play its first soccer game. The event was a major community happening in Lethbridge, attracting both recent immigrants and long-time members of the community. In addition, the sceptical Ukrainian residents came out to determine the viability of the new club. For the record, Orlyk won the exhibition match

4-1 over the area's top team, the Miners. The local press was impressed with Orlyk's play and referred to the club as "classy Orlyk." Throughout the summer, the Orlyk soccer team played exhibition matches. Playing coaches of the team were W. Stebelsky and D. Pysch.

*Ukrainian Sports Association Orlyk soccer team*

In September, Orlyk travelled to Edmonton to participate in that city's Ukrainian Youth Festival. Exhibition matches were held in volleyball and soccer against Edmonton's SA Ukraina. Orlyk won the soccer game 6-0 and the volleyball match 15-3 and 15-8. The following year, SA Ukraina organized a two-day youth sports festival in Edmonton. Participating in the event were members of the local branches of the youth associations Plast, SUM, and UNYF and sport clubs Ukraina and Orlyk. Competition was held in soccer, track and field, and volleyball. Orlyk proved to be the best Ukrainian sport club in Alberta by winning most of the events.

During the summer of 1950, Orlyk once again played exhibition matches against local and area teams. The president of the club that year was W. Radyo.

After the 1950 soccer season, the Ukrainian Sports Association Orlyk dissolved. Almost all of the club members had left Lethbridge for Edmonton or Toronto after fulfilling their immigration obligations.

# LONDON, ENGLAND

## UKRAINIAN CANADIAN SERVICEMEN'S ASSOCIATION

In early 1943, the Ukrainian Canadian Servicemen's Association (UCSA) was formally founded in England. Initiated and organized by Corporal Bohdan Panchuk, the association served Canadian servicemen and women of Ukrainian descent stationed in England. The association's club house in the heart of London was the focal point for those interested in having contact with their fellow Ukrainian soldiers. In addition, the association organized social and cultural events, and religious celebrations. Once the liberation of Western Europe began, association members in the field were at the forefront in assisting Ukrainian forced labourers and refugees. UCSA's priority was to prevent these individuals from being repatriated to the USSR. The club house became the administrative centre of this work which carried on past the conclusion of the war.

*Ukrainian Canadian Servicemen's Association logo*

When the hostilities ceased, the servicemen in England awaiting demobilization and repatriation suddenly had time on their hands. On July 29, 1945, Air Force personnel challenged the Army to a game of softball at London's Hyde Park. The challenge was accepted. A high-scoring but closely contested game was played, with Army winning 21-19. Curious English spectators watched the game with bewilderment. Most had never seen the game played before and when some players started chanting "kill the umpire," bewilderment turned into disbelief. The spectators were assured that what they were hearing was just Canadian hyperbole, an aggrandizement associated with poor refereeing.

The Sunday baseball games between Air Force and Army at Hyde Park became regular fare. There was never a shortage of players as most wanted to participate. The servicemen found the games to be a good pastime, one that in many ways reminded them of life back home. It was also an unconscious celebration of survival, since it helped them forget about the war. Londoners found it inspiring to watch the teams play their hearts out, and they flocked to the games. It did not matter that they did not understand the game, it was, like the end of the war, a breath of fresh air.

*Ukrainian Canadian Servicemen's Association softball team, 1945*

The National Executive of the Ukrainian Canadian Committee located in Winnipeg provided the Ukrainian Canadian Servicemen's Association with two sets of game jerseys. One set was yellow with blue trimmings while the other was blue with yellow trimmings. Both sets had a large UCSA crest on the front.

The games in Hyde Park continued through the summer. Eventually, the soldiers all returned to Canada and the baseball teams and the Ukrainian Canadian Servicemen's Association ceased to exist. Many servicemen joined veteran's organizations and participated in organizing sports clubs within their framework.

# MONTREAL, QUEBEC

## SPORT ASSOCIATION *UKRAINA*

On April 4, 1949, a number of sports-minded individuals, among them J. Serbyn, J. Sklar, J. Kulba, I. Pluwak and Chobych gathered in Montreal with the idea of forming a soccer team and establishing a sport club. The result was the formation of the Ukrainian Sport Club Dnipro. In their desire to field a soccer team that season (which was just days from starting), the club organizers were willing to commence work without a club constitution and with an ad hoc executive that included representatives from various Ukrainian youth organizations of the city. The organizers realized the risk of this approach but felt it necessary to get off the ground quickly.

During the 1949 season, Dnipro played in the Montreal "B" League with relative success for a first-year team. Off the field, discontent was fermenting in the ranks of the ad hoc executive. In fact, one observer noted that Dnipro completed the season only because of the determination of its players. As a result, a new ad hoc committee was put together by J. Serbyn, J. Kulba, J. Buchatsky, B. Denisewich and W. Cap with the intent of organizing a new sport club in Montreal that would be structured and have by-laws. An advertisement was placed in the Ukrainian press, advising that at a meeting on November 20, 1949, a new sport club would be formed. Those attending would also be briefed on the activities of Dnipro.

The founding meeting concluded with the formation of the Sport Association Ukraina. Its first executive, which was elected for a "temporary" duration, included J. Serbyn, president; J. Kulba, vice-president; O. Buchatsky, secretary; E. Oryschuk, treasurer; J. Buchatsky, coordinator of men's sports; and I. Shumsky, coordinator of women's sports. Those gathered also approved the club objective - to promote all aspects of sport among the Ukrainian community of Montreal.

SA Ukraina and its predecessor SC Dnipro were organized by the recently arrived immigrants from Europe. The driving force behind the clubs was Jaroslaw Serbyn, one-time president of the Sport Club Skala in Stryi, Ukraine, and later of the Sport Club Sitch in the displaced persons camp at Regensburg, West Germany. The selection of the name Ukraina and of team colours red and black represented the desire of the organizers to continue their European sporting heritage; the name and the colours were those used by the most popular team in Lviv, Ukraine. In addition, the organizers believed that the incorporation of Ukraine in the name of the club would publicize the Ukrainian community and further its aspirations.

Some years later, Montreal soccer league officials requested that all clubs remove reference of ethnicity from their names. SA Ukraina refused.

The charter of SA Ukraina established the club as an unaffiliated and non-partisan entity. Membership was open to Ukrainians and non-Ukrainians alike. The club operated on a non-profit basis. Funds were raised via donations, by organizing dances and through caroling.

The Dnipro club did not cease to exist with the founding of SA Ukraina. The Ukrainian National Federation tried to keep it alive. Most of the original Dnipro athletes, though, joined the new SA Ukraina, and Dnipro faded into obscurity.

Within a few weeks, SA Ukraina commenced operations with an intramural chess tournament. The event was held at a house which the club leased at 3951 City Hall Avenue. Efforts were made to establish a volleyball and table tennis team that winter, but these did not materialize.

In the spring of 1950, SA Ukraina organized its first soccer team which was then entered in the Montreal City League. The team played 24 league games, won 21, tied 1 and lost 2. It scored 79 goals and had only 18 scored against. It finished in first place, leaving behind 12 teams in the standings. Based on this stellar performance, the team was promoted to the senior first division. SA Ukraina's Bohdan Kluchnyk was the league's scoring champion.

SA Ukraina's debut in the first division was more than challenging. In the off-season, the team lost a number of older veterans through retirement. Their younger replacements lacked experience. This, coupled with a much higher calibre of play in the first division, resulted in a seventh-place finish.

In the winter of 1951-52, Ukraina entered a foursome into the Montreal class "A" team chess championships.

In 1952, the SA Ukraina soccer team finished the season in fifth place among ten teams. When first place finisher Italia withdrew from the playoffs, Ukraina, the best of the non-playoff bound teams, was given the opportunity to play. SA Ukraina readily accepted. In a semi-final match, Ukraina lost 2-0 to Stelco.

*Sport Association Ukraina logo*

During the 1953 soccer campaign, Ukraina's game improved significantly. The club finished the eighteen-game season in third place with 11 wins and 7 losses. It competed for and won the Steve McKellar Memorial Trophy, or as it was commonly known, the Charity Cup. Ukraina also partook in its first ever competition for the Quebec Trophy, advancing to the semi-finals of this competition for the Quebec championship. The play of the Ukraina soccer team during that summer was so inspiring that the *Montreal Star* soccer columnist Doug Campbell began referring to the players as the "Whiz Kids."

During the winter of 1953-54, the SA Ukraina chess club partook in both individual and team competition in the Montreal Chess League. Among the ten clubs registered, SA Ukraina placed in the top five both in individual and team competition. The association also expanded its sport program that winter by introducing a men's volleyball team. The rookie team played a number of exhibition matches.

In 1953, SA Ukraina pooled its resources with the Ukrainian Youth Association SUM and the League for the Liberation of Ukraine to purchase a property at 51 Bagg Rue. The facility became the association's permanent administrative centre and clubhouse.

SA Ukraina completed the 1954 regular soccer season play, as it had the previous year, in third spot. In Cup play, Ukraina advanced to the Quebec Trophy final by defeating United 4-1 in a preliminary round, Stelco 3-2 in the quarter-finals, and the Kickers 2-0 in the semi-finals. It lost in the final 3-0 to Vickers. Competing for the first time for the Dominion Cup, emblematic of the national championship, Ukraina lost in the opening round to the Kickers. The team was coached by Kislinger.

When Professor Mykola Andruchiw took over as SA Ukraina president in 1953, he immediately started promoting the idea of friendly matches among Ukrainian clubs in Canada and the United States. The first such exhibition match occurred in the summer of 1954 when SA Ukraina hosted the soccer club Sitch from Elizabeth, New Jersey. In subsequent years, friendly matches were contested in soccer and also table tennis and volleyball.

During Andruchiw's reign as president, SA Ukraina also began to actively recruit star players. Dmytro "Pete" Waskiw, the league's scoring champion in 1954, rejoined SA Ukraina in 1955 after an absence of two years. Andruchiw, though, did not limit his area of search to Montreal. Players from Toronto and the United States at various times wore the uniform of SA Ukraina. Some players travelled to Montreal just for the games. Others were billeted by the club for the duration of the season. Among those Andruchiw recruited were American Olympian Zenon "Red" Snylyk, future American Olympic and national team coach Eugene Chyzowych, and Canadian internationals Ostap Steckiw and Walter Zakaluznyj of Toronto. Ukrainian players were also brought over from Western Europe.

In the fall of 1954, SA Ukraina sport coordinator Zenon Duda augmented the club's winter sport activities by adding a volleyball program. The program operated out of a rented school. Two men's teams, a senior "A" and a senior "B," and two women's teams, a senior and a junior, were organized. During the winter of 1954-55, both men's teams and the senior women's team were fielded in Montreal volleyball leagues. To gain experience, the Plast girls' volleyball team trained with SA Ukraina. The table tennis team, in addition to a regular schedule of events, hosted the Sokil club from New York City. The visitors won this friendly match. The chess team once again participated in league play.

In early 1955, SA Ukraina expanded its recruiting process for soccer players. According to the *Montreal Star*, SA Ukraina "management changed its nationalistic policy over the winter and went about rounding up such well-known stars as Sammy Martin and Bill Drake of Hakoah, Jimmy MacAuley from St. Paul and grabbing Cammie Buchanan, just off the boat from the Big Time in England."

The recruitment of both Ukrainian and non-Ukrainian stars began paying dividends in 1955. That year, SA Ukraina won four team trophies. In addition, Bill Drake was named the recipient of the McLagan Cup as the National League's MVP.

Competing for the Quebec Trophy, SA Ukraina blasted the Swiss 8-0 in the opening round, defeated Stelco 3-0 in the quarter-finals, and the Kickers 3-0 in the semi-finals. In the title match, SA Ukraina easily disposed of the Vickers 5-0 to win the Quebec championship.

Ukraina now faced Ontario Champion Ulster of Toronto in a best-of-three final for the title of Eastern Canada. Just before the start of the first game, two Ukraina stars who were set to return after disqualifications had their suspensions extended. This threw the club into turmoil, and Ulster won the opening match 1-0. In the second game, Ukraina came back to tie the series at one win apiece by downing Ulster 3-1. During that game, Ukraina had three goals called back. In the third and deciding game, played in as many days, the players showed signs of fatigue. Both clubs failed to score as they battled to a scoreless draw during regulation time.

Confusion ensued about how to decide the championship. The decision arrived from a Dominion League representative: thirty minutes of overtime were to be played. The referee called the players out on the pitch to begin the overtime. As soon as play began, the Ulster players walked off the field. They wanted to play a fourth game to decide the championship. League representatives tried to convince Ulster to return but to no avail. The officials then agreed to have the game replayed. The Ulster team, though, had already boarded a train for Toronto. As a result, Ukraina won the game by default and advanced to the Canadian championship.

SA Ukraina faced the New Westminster Royals for the national championship. The Royals had defeated the Institute Prosvita Athletic Club (IPAC) of Winnipeg in the Western Canada final. The format of the championship required a team to accumulate four points to be declared a winner. All of the games were played in Toronto.

More than six thousand fans, most of them Ukrainians, crowded into the Fred Hamilton Stadium to watch the opener. The organizers, recognizing the significance of the Ukrainian crowd, made the public address announcements in English and Ukrainian.

After taking a 1-0 lead in the first half of the first game on a goal by captain Pete Waskiw, the Ukrainians had three unanswered goals scored against them in the second half to lose the match 3-1. The second game ended in a 1-1 draw with both teams failing to capitalize on excellent scoring opportunities. Once again, Waskiw tallied for SA Ukraina. For the Royals, a win or a tie in the third game would assure the club of the national championship. A victory by Ukraina would force a deciding game. Ukraina had nothing to lose, and the Royals did not want to prolong the series: as a result, both teams came out on the field playing aggressive end-to-end soccer. The game ended in a 2-2 draw with the championship going to the New Westminster Royals. Scoring for SA Ukraina were Waskiw and Stan Palinsky.

During the summer of 1955, SA Ukraina also contested the Charity Cup. In the semi-finals, Ukraina was held to a 3-3 tie by Vickers. Scoring all three goals for Vickers was hockey goal-tender Lorne "Gump" Worsley. The league then decided that the semi-final should be replayed. A few weeks later, Ukraina defeated Vickers 6-1. In the Charity Cup final, Cantalia and SA Ukraina played to a scoreless draw which included thirty minutes of overtime. As a result, SA Ukraina and Cantalia were declared joint holders of the Cup.

Friendly matches against Ukrainian clubs continued that year with SA Ukraina travelling to Elizabeth, New Jersey, to play Sitch, and Philadelphia to play Tryzub. In the summer, Ukraina hosted Philadelphia's Tryzub. Some 2,000 fans witnessed the match between the two Ukrainian clubs in Montreal.

SA Ukraina also expanded its soccer program in 1955 when it organized a bantam team that entered play in the Montreal Bantam Football League. This move was undertaken to promote sport among Ukrainian youngsters and to develop a potential feeder system for the senior soccer club. In its first year of operation, the bantam club, under coach J. Buchatsky, won the league championship.

In June of 1955, SA Ukraina hosted a sports festival which was referred to as the Ukrainian Olympic Games. One hundred and ninety-nine athletes representing seven Ukrainian organizations of Montreal participated in the one-day event at Westmount Stadium. Competition was held in track and field, soccer, and volleyball. Bohdan Kowaluk, J. Buchatsky and Zenon Duda were the prime organizers of the event.

During the winter of 1955-56, the men's volleyball team placed fourth in the senior class "A" league. The women's team placed in third spot. The junior girls entered league competition for the first time that year. SA Ukraina expanded its sport program that winter when it introduced boys' basketball. Coached by P. Kozub and managed by Reverend T. Harasymchuk, the team played in a local league.

*Sport Association Ukraina women's volleyball team, 1956-57*

In 1956, the SA Ukraina soccer team won the Carling Red Cap Trophy, emblematic of the National League championship. The team also won the Charity Cup. Personal trophies were awarded to Dmytro "Pete" Waskiw, the National League scoring champion; James MacAuley, the top goalkeeper; and Bill Drake repeated as league MVP. The bantams, under the tutelage of M. Kozulak and Z. Bandura, once again had a good year and repeated as champions. In addition, the midget team won its league championship. The midgets were coached by I. Tomko.

During the winter of 1956-57, the boys' basketball team won the Montreal championship. The junior girls' volleyball team, coached by Z. Duda, placed third out of six teams. The men's team suffered setbacks all season and finished at the bottom of the standings.

The 1957 soccer season was the most memorable in the history of SA Ukraina. In Quebec Trophy competition, SA Ukraina strutted its powerful offence by blasting Ottawa in the second round 6-1. In the final, it appeared that Ukraina ran out of steam. Game one saw Sparta tie SA Ukraina in the dying seconds. The second game ended in a scoreless draw even after 30 minutes of overtime. In the third game, Ukraina scored twice in the last 15 minutes to defeat Sparta 2-0 and win the Quebec Trophy.

Once again SA Ukraina was challenging for the national title. In Halifax, the club proceeded to defeat the Nova Scotia champions, the Halifax Shipyards, 8-2. It then disposed of the Ontario champions, the Corinthians of Windsor, 2-0 to win the Eastern Canada Championship.

On Sunday September 22, SA Ukraina faced the North Shore United FC from Vancouver for the Canadian title. More than 5,000 fans, the largest crowd to watch a soccer game that year in Montreal, witnessed SA Ukraina become the first Ukrainian club in Canada to win a national senior championship. Playing on a soggy field in intermittent rain, Ukraina fell behind 1-0 after only 16 minutes of play. Pete Waskiw tied the game nine minutes later. Joe Feeney scored the winner for Ukraina in the 68th minute of play after heading a pass from Waskiw into the Vancouver net. The enthusiastic Ukrainian fans kept screaming *slava - hurrah* as time wound down.

*Sport Association Ukraina soccer team, 1957 Canadian Champions*

The line-up of the winning team included playing coach Zenon Snylyk, Myron Hrycyn, Joseph Feeney, Ostap Steckiw, James MacAuley, Dmytro Waskiw, John Pollock, Anatol Shapka, Alexander O'Neill, John Ursika and John McVicar. The substitutes were Robert Resch and Jack Sim. Also seeing action with the club that year were Mykhailo Senyk, Stefan Szylo, Joseph Shneider, Walter Korolus, Mykhailo Polonskyj, Wolodymyr Golash, Stefan Janyk, Bert Nathan, Osyp Horobiowskyj and John Neilson.

The national championship generated much excitement in the Ukrainian community. Soccer enthusiasts and sports fans celebrated the victory. Newspapers hailed the accomplishment. One newspaper highlighted the significance of the event by stating: "SA Ukraina Montreal having won the championship on the soccer pitch, has realized a great moral and propaganda victory and in doing this, it has fulfilled its mandate 100 per cent."[4]

At the conclusion of the soccer season, playing coach Snylyk was selected the league's MVP and was awarded the McLagan Cup.

During the winter of 1957-58, SA Ukraina fielded three different age group basketball teams. The teams were primarily made up of members of the midget and junior soccer teams. The midget basketball team won the city championship in 1958. The volleyball program experienced major setbacks that winter. The men's team was unable to field a full team at games and as a result it suspended operations part-way through the season.

In 1958, SA Ukraina repeated as the National League champions. The defence of the Canadian title was quickly terminated when Celtic defeated Ukraina 1-0 in the semi-finals of the Quebec Trophy competition.

In January of 1959, SA Ukraina's application for acceptance in the National Football League was approved. The league, which represented the highest level of soccer in Ontario and Quebec, included Toronto's Sport Association Ukraina and the Ukrainian Sport Club Trident. Montreal's debut year in this league was not particularly inspiring. They played 26 games, winning 9, tying 2, and losing 15 to place tenth in league standings.

The 1960 National Football League season for SA Ukraina was no better. The club finished in 11th place among 13 league members, winning 5 games in 24 starts.

In the winter of 1960-61, SA Ukraina did a lot of soul searching. In three short years it had fallen from the pinnacle of Canadian soccer to the basement of the National Football League. Club management decided to rejuvenate the club by concentrating on programs for youth. After an absence of a few years, the volleyball, table tennis and basketball programs were reactivated. An attempt was also made to organize a ski group.

When summer came around, SA Ukraina entered three soccer teams into junior age leagues, two in Montreal, and one in neighbouring Lachine. The senior club left the National Football League to play in the less competitive Montreal National League. The Montreal league, though, was not prepared to operate that summer as there was a shortage of clubs. The management of SA Ukraina, with its counterparts at some of the other clubs, worked feverishly to put together an operational league for the summer. The administrative efforts were successful and play began. The SA Ukraina team played well during the season to finish in third place among six teams. In the playoffs, Ukraina defeated Cantalia to win the Labatt's Trophy.

During the 1962 season, Ukraina finished second in the East division of the National League. In the semi-finals it defeated the Kickers 2-1. The club then defaulted the championship final; a day before the competition, Ukraina executives notified the league that the team would be unable to play the match as it was scheduled on a Ukrainian feast day. SA Ukraina striker Mike (Kopa) Noha was the co-scoring leader in the league. The junior team enjoyed a very successful season, winning the Quebec championship.

In 1963, SA Ukraina registered its senior soccer team with the Eastern Canada Professional Soccer League. SA Ukraina had difficulty keeping pace with most of the teams in this league, finishing the season with 5 wins, 5 ties, and 15 losses. The club placed fifth in the standings, just three points from the league cellar. The team was coached by former SA Ukraina star S. Szylo.

In mid-September, the senior soccer club left Canada for a goodwill tour of the Caribbean Islands and Central America. The team played in Puerto Rico, Guadeloupe, Suriname, Aruba and Curacao. Ukraina did not win one game on the trip, but that mattered little as the touring players and the host clubs had an opportunity to observe and learn different soccer styles from each other. The trip, though, created a major repercussion for SA Ukraina in Canada as the Quebec governing body of soccer did not sanction the five matches. According to the international governing body of soccer FIFA, approval for any international matches was required from the governing body in whose jurisdiction the club was operating. SA Ukraina was fined $500 and suspended from operations subject to a review. The fine was paid, and, at a meeting of the provincial executive in April of the following year, SA Ukraina was reinstated.

The disappointing result in the Eastern Canada Professional Soccer League, the lack of good players, and particularly the lack of funds resulted in the club's rejoining the National Interprovincial Football League for the 1964 season. The club also decided to "Ukrainianize" its senior soccer team. To a large extent, members of the 1962 junior championship team found starting positions on the senior squad. The team finished in seventh place out of eight. In other years, such a result would not have been encouraging for club management, but in this rebuilding year it was.

In 1965, the SA Ukraina soccer team transferred to the newly created Quebec National Football League - Major Division. The team finished the regular season in fourth place. In the playoffs Ukraina won its semi-final game. In the final, Ukraina lost 2-1 to Kalena. The rebuilding process was showing signs of success.

During the winter of 1965-66, the SA Ukraina junior soccer team won the Montreal Junior "A" indoor soccer championship.

The senior soccer team experienced a downfall in 1966. It lost more games than it won, finishing the season with 16 points in 20 games. The club failed to generate any offence, recording a total of 23 goals while ceding 43. SA Ukraina, though, sneaked into the playoffs as one of three teams tied for sixth spot in the league standings. It was eliminated from further play by SC Hungaria in the opening round of the playoffs. Ukraina also fielded a "B" team in the second division that year.

*Sport Association Ukraina junior soccer team, 1967 Quebec Junior Champions*

The senior soccer team continued to perform poorly in 1967. It finished near the bottom of the 14-team leagues and did not qualify for post-season play. In contrast, the SA Ukraina junior soccer team dominated competition in Quebec. The club won the provincial championship. Junior players S. Yanick and D. Zelman gained all-star berths.

In 1968, the play of SA Ukraina improved marginally. The club completed the season in eighth position with a record of 7 wins, 3 ties and 10 losses. It qualified for the playoffs but was eliminated in the quarter-final round.

In the spring of 1969, SA Ukraina began its 20th anniversary celebrations with a friendly match against Toronto's SA Ukraina. Other friendly matches and social events followed.

The 20th anniversary season saw an unexpected resurgence of the senior soccer team. SA Ukraina was once again exhibiting form that won it major championships in the past. The team won the Quebec Trophy; in competition for the Canadian title, Ukraina defeated the Ontario champion the Polish White Eagles of Sudbury in a bitterly fought contest. Regulation time ended in a scoreless draw. Thirty minutes of overtime did not provide a winner as both sides scored once. To decide the game, the referee ordered a shootout. Ukraina scored four times on six free kicks. White Eagles only managed one goal. Ukraina thus stayed alive in its quest for the national championship.

The next hurdle, the Eastern Canada championship, was contested in Newfoundland. SA Ukraina's opponent was the Maritime champion St. John's Feildians. The game was played in a howling gale; strong winds sweeping off the Atlantic Ocean blew diagonally across the soccer field, creating havoc to which neither side could adjust. Ukraina managed to take a 2-0 lead in the first half on goals by Tony Stipersky and Mike Kutic. In the second half, the Feildians controlled the game but only managed to score once. Ukraina thus advanced to the national championship for the third time in its 20-year history.

In Vancouver, SA Ukraina faced the local Italian club Columbus. After the first half, Ukraina was down 1-0. At the start of the second half, Ukraina's goaltender was knocked out. Somewhat groggy, he nevertheless remained in the game. Columbus seized the opportunity and scored two quick goals. Ukraina management responded by replacing the goaltender. By this time, the club was discouraged and played without heart. Columbus scored seven more unanswered goals to defeat Ukraina 10-0.

In regular season play, Ukraina placed atop the Montreal Major League with a record of 13 wins, 5 ties, and 4 losses. The team led the league with most goals for and the fewest against. When the season concluded, coach Silla Sandrin was rewarded with the Coach of the Year Award by the league, and netminder Andy Regina won the Goalkeeper of the Year Award.

The 1969 SA Ukraina reserve team competed in the fourth division. The club finished the season in first place, led by division scoring leader Dmytro Zelman's 26 goals.

After four years in operation, SA Ukraina's broomball team won the playoff championship in 1970. The team was organized and coached by D. Zelman.

The first division soccer team of SA Ukraina was unable to repeat as league champions in 1970. The team won 11, tied 5 and lost 6 to place fourth in the standings. Nevertheless, Ukraina qualified for the eight-team playoffs. The team won its quarter-final and semi-final matches. In the playoff final, Ukraina was defeated 1-0 in overtime by the league leaders Kelena. The reserve fourth division team placed third in its league while the pee-wee team was fifth.

One of the major concerns of SA Ukraina in 1970 was financial stability. Operating costs of the senior soccer team amounted to $5,577 while gate receipts totalled $959. At the association's general meeting, various cost-saving measures and fund-raising ventures were discussed. It was argued that the association should limit itself in the recruitment of non-Ukrainian players. The roster of the team could be filled by Ukrainians who would play to uphold the honour of the sport association rather than financial compensation. Among the fund-raising ventures that appealed to the executive were caroling and the organization of a Ukrainian New Year's Dance - "*Malanka*."

The 1971 senior soccer team placed fifth in league standings just six points back of the league leader. The team played 20 matches, winning 8, tying 8 and losing 4. In the opening round of competition for the Quebec Trophy, Ukraina defeated a Greek team 3-0. In the second round, Ukraina lost 3-0 to the Rangers. The club was coached by S. Palinsky. Dave Cooper was awarded the McLagan Trophy as the league's MVP. The reserve team, coached by Lucien Kulyk, placed fourth in its league. A pee-wee team, coached by D. Zelman placed second in the East Division of the Montreal League, winning 7, tying 5 and losing but once.

During the winter of 1971-72, a broomball team competed in a Montreal league finishing the season in second place. The club then won the playoffs for the Montreal championship.

In 1972, SA Ukraina soccer team won the Quebec Trophy for the fourth time in its history. The club defeated Luso Sport in the championship final 3-1 in front of some 2,500 fans at Jarry Stadium. During the regular season, the club placed fourth in league play. In the playoffs, it was eliminated in the semi-final round. SA Ukraina also operated a reserve and a pee-wee team that season. Club nominee Donna Humeniuk was crowned Miss Quebec Soccer that year. The following year the senior soccer club once again finished in fourth place. Ray Dawe was named the league's MVP.

A booklet published in conjunction with the 25th anniversary of SA Ukraina in 1974 provided a critical analysis of the club's history: "Without a doubt, our sport association has had fantastic achievements, particularly in soccer, even though they were fleeting. In addition, we have had no less significant results in women's and men's volleyball, broomball and chess. Some of these teams were also champions; nevertheless, they were treated as second class citizens, with scant attention accorded to them. The results of this are catastrophic . . . There is no inflow of new members, the participation of the older members is minimal . . . We have been unable to provide physical training to legions of youth . . . The results of our 25 years of work are mediocre."[5]

There was a call for the restructuring of the association with emphasis placed on grassroots participation in many different sports. Pee-wee and junior teams were encouraged. The association, though, did not follow through on the suggestions. The status quo remained.

In the years 1974 to 1978, SA Ukraina fielded three soccer teams - a Major League team, a Fourth Division reserve team and a Junior team. In 1975 the junior team won the Quebec championship. The team was coached by E. Palinsky.

The association's 30th anniversary celebrations in 1979 were highlighted by the senior soccer team capturing the Quebec Trophy for the fifth time. During the regular season, the club competed in the Andrews division of the Quebec Pre-Excellence Division, winning 14 and losing 3 to take first place. Ukraina then faced Barrabas, the champion of the league's other division for the Pre-Excellence Cup. Regulation time ended with both teams having scored twice. Two ten-minute overtime periods were then played. Barrabas scored two goals in the first minute to take a commanding lead. Ukraina did not give up, scoring three unanswered goals to take the championship. The victory promoted the club to the Excellence league for the following season. Pera Mikhailovitch, with 26 goals, was the league's leading scorer. The team was coached by S. Palinsky. The association continued the operation of the fourth division and junior teams that year.

The promotion to the Excellence League was short-lived for SA Ukraina. The club finished the 1980 season in last place with a record of 3 wins, 4 ties, and 7 losses in 14 starts and was demoted back to the Pre-Excellence league. Due to a lack of interested players and a lack of interest in the team by the Ukrainian community, the senior club folded after the 1980 season.

In the fall of 1980, a women's volleyball team was organized by John Bezpalok. The team was operational for only one season.

In the spring of 1982, SA Ukraina decided once again to go back to the grass roots and offer a soccer program at the minor level. A pee-wee "B" and a midget "B" teams were formed and entered into local leagues.

During the winter of 1982-83 and 1983-84, SA Ukraina fielded a men's soccer team in the Montreal Recreational Indoor League. The club won the league title in 1983.

For many former SA Ukraina soccer players, the absence of competitive outdoor sport created a void in their lives. As a result, a number of them decided to resurrect the senior soccer team in 1984. With the average age of the team members being nearly 35, the club was registered in the recreational league - Amicale de l'ouest. The team was coached by Gary Grosko.

It did not take long for the players to regain their form and play competitive soccer. The inaugural season concluded with the team capturing the league championship. The SA Ukraina recreational soccer club was still operational in 1991 with newly arriving Ukrainian immigrants from Poland and Ukraine succeeding the aging veterans.

## PRESIDENTS OF THE SPORT ASSOCIATION UKRAINA

| | |
|---|---|
| Jaroslaw Serbyn | (1949-51) |
| Evhen Oryschuk | (1952) |
| Mykola Andruchiw | (1953-57, 1960-61) |
| Jaroslaw Pryszlak | (1958) |
| Ivan Kucharsky | (1959) |
| Ivan Tseyko | (1962-63) |
| Yarema Sawka | (1964-66) |
| Sviatoslav Tomiuk, MD | (1967-69, 1971-87) |
| Mykhailo Zwonok | (1970) |
| Lucien (Luka) Kulyk | (1987- ) |

# UKRAINIAN NATIONAL ATHLETIC CLUB

In January of 1939, the Montreal Branch of the UNYF informed the UNYF National Executive that it was planning to establish a sports program for its members. That summer, a young men's softball team was organized. It was coached by Ihor Tomiuk.

Information about the club's activities during the war years is sketchy. Plans were made to expand the sport program to include boxing and table tennis. In 1944, branch members participated in organized badminton, bowling and table tennis.

After the war, the UNYF sport club was reorganized and named Ukrainian National Athletic Club. The first executive included Taras Batiuk, chairman; M. Bilous, secretary; and Halya Kondzolka, treasurer. During the winter of 1945-46, the club operated a bowling league in which four teams competed.

It is not known how long the Ukrainian National Athletic Club existed.

# UKRAINIAN YOUTH ASSOCIATION

The involvement of a youth association in sport depends primarily on the enthusiasm of the organization's sports co-ordinator. In Montreal, the Ukrainian Youth Association (SUM) became active in sport when Fedir Bezpalok assumed that post. A veteran of Montreal's SA Ukraina soccer club, Bezpalok proceeded to organize a soccer program for the youth of SUM.

In 1967, three soccer teams were fielded in the Kiwanis Club sponsored league of Maisonneuve. The teams played inconsistent soccer during the first half of the season as many of the boys were new to the game. Subsequently, the teams gained enough experience, technical skills and confidence to become competitive. The pee-wee team finished the season in first place, capturing the Kiwanis Club Cup with a record of 11 wins, 1 tie and 4 losses. The team was coached by R. Hupaliwsky. The bantam team, coached by P. Dziuba, placed second in its division. To celebrate the centennial of Canada's Confederation, the bantams played a match against the Western Canada champions from Saskatchewan. SUM lost the closely played game 4-3. The mosquito team also placed second in its division. The club was coached by W. Hirniak.

In the fall of 1967, a men's volleyball team was organized and entered into a local league. The team was coached by Mykola Chobych and Myron Figol. A women's basketball team was also organized that fall. It was coached by F. Bezpalok.

*Ukrainian Youth Association (SUM) bantam soccer team, 1967*

During the summer of 1968, the three soccer teams were once again registered for competition by SUM. The bantam team won the Challenge Cup.

In the mid-1970s, SUM fielded a soccer team under the name Strila. The association prided the fact that the team had an all-Ukrainian roster. A girls' volleyball team operated at the same time period and was coached by Ivan Bezpalok.

In 1960, a chess club was organized at SUM by W. Antoniv, S. Harasymovych and P. Hrycak. The club hosted irregular championships for Ukrainians of Montreal and also a tournament at the SUM camp *Verkhovyna*. In 1960, the chess club organized a simultaneous chess tournament. Well-respected Ukrainian chess player and American master Stephen Popel tested his skills against forty Montreal chess enthusiasts. The event proved to be very successful and the club organized three more such tournaments in subsequent years. Area masters (non-Ukrainians) provided competition to the members of the chess club.

In addition, for many years the chess club organized workshops and tournaments for SUM youth at their summer camps.

# MOOSE JAW, SASKATCHEWAN

## UKRAINIAN NATIONAL YOUTH FEDERATION

In the spring of 1950, a baseball club was organized by the members of the Moose Jaw Branch of the Ukrainian National Youth Federation (UNYF). The team was registered under the name UNYF in the local Senior "B" league. It completed the season by qualifying for the playoffs but was eliminated in the first round. The team was coached by A. Bechtold.

During the summer of 1951, the UNYF team once again played in the senior "B" loop. At the conclusion of the season, the softball program was discontinued. It was successfully argued that the cost of operating the team was beyond the financial means of the Moose Jaw Branch of the UNYF.

# OSHAWA, ONTARIO

## ST. GEORGE'S

St. George's Ukrainian Athletic Club of Oshawa was probably organized in 1929. At that time, a team bearing that name was entered into the men's Oshawa City Industrial Softball League at the juvenile level. The St. George's Ukes were never competitive during their inaugural season; they lost by scores as great as 32-9. With no hope of making the playoffs, the players became discouraged and started to miss games. After defaulting a number of games, the team withdrew from the league prior to the conclusion of the season. A year later there was no evidence of a baseball team affiliated with the St. George's Catholic church operating in any Oshawa league.

In 1931, a team by the name of St. George's Ukrainians was registered in the Oshawa Sunday School Softball League.

In 1932, St. George's competed in the Oshawa Sunday School Softball League. The team's play was erratic and it failed to make the playoffs.

In August of that year, St. George's travelled to Toronto to participate in the inaugural Ukrainian Field Day. The event was hosted by the Ukrainian Softball League of Toronto with teams participating from St. Catharines, Hamilton, Toronto and Oshawa. The softball tournament ended with St. George's and the Ukrainian Nationals of Oshawa having an identical record of two wins apiece. It was determined that St. George's would face the Nationals in Oshawa to determine the Ukrainian Ontario softball champion. St. George's lost the game 25-15.

It is not known whether the St. George's baseball team continued to operate in subsequent years.

# ST. JOHN'S

In the early 1950s, the Canadian Ukrainian Youth Association (SUMK) regularly held picnics and get togethers in southern Ontario. Quite often at these events, pick-up softball games were played between the branches. The popularity of the inter-branch games led the organizers to schedule them in the program of such events. Some branches began to take the games seriously and started to hold practices beforehand. Eventually, the camaraderie and the excitement of sport resulted in the registering of some of the softball teams in organized leagues.

The Oshawa branch of SUMK, which was affiliated with St. John's Ukrainian Orthodox Church, registered its team in the Oshawa Church Softball League in 1951. The team competed in the league under the name St. John's. It was sponsored by Anne and Michael Starr, the owners and operators of Maple Cleaners in Oshawa. At the time, Michael Starr was mayor of Oshawa. Later he would serve as Minister of Labour of Canada.

*St. John's softball team, 1953 Oshawa Church League Champions*
*(Michael Starr, MP, middle row third from right)*

During the first two seasons St. John's experienced mixed results. In 1953, the team played well all year and qualified for the playoffs. The best-of-five final saw St. John's defeat St. Gertrude's in the deciding game to win the championship. Pitcher John Masiewich led the team during the season. The St. John's team existed only for a short time thereafter. The team had difficulty in replenishing its ranks. In addition, family responsibilities and shift work made it difficult for the individuals to play in a regularly scheduled league.

During the early 1950s, the Oshawa branch of SUMK also participated in mixed bowling.

# SPORTS ASSOCIATION *UKRAINA*

At the conclusion of the 1961 season the Ukrainian Sports Club Strila of Oshawa ceased operations. Dr. Mykola Ostafiychuk, one of the prime sponsors of Strila, pushed for the disassociation of Strila from the Ukrainian National Federation. This occurred and Strila was restructured as an independent club operating out of the Dnipro Hall under the name Sports Association Ukraina. The club's first executive consisted of Hryhoriy Dolishny, president; I. Perun, secretary; and D. Maykut, manager of a yet to be organized soccer team.

Ukraina had at its disposal many of the players that competed for Strila the previous year. These individuals wanted to play for a Ukrainian team and Maykut provided them with an opportunity to do so. When the team opened the 1962 season, most considered SA Ukraina a returning club under new management and with a new name, rather than a novice entry.

After placing first in the standings with a record of 8 wins, 2 ties, and 2 losses, Ukraina was crowned champion of the Oshawa and District Soccer League. En route to the first-place finish, the club scored 32 goals and gave up just 14. At the conclusion of the season, Ukraina's goalkeeper Joe Burchowych was presented with an award for being the best goalie in league competition. Striker Charles Smith was the co-winner of the scoring title with 11 goals. The team was coached by Frank Malawy.

*Sports Association Ukraina soccer team, 1962*

Ukraina lost the 1962 playoff final to Polonia, a team with which Ukraina developed a tremendous rivalry.

For the 1963 season, Leonid Choloniuk assumed the coaching duties of Ukraina. The veteran athlete also continued to play with the team. When the regular schedule concluded, Ukraina occupied third place in the standings. Ukraina also marked its "10th anniversary" that year. To celebrate the occasion, a friendly match was played with Toronto's SA Ukraina which ended in a 2-2 draw. A banquet and dancing followed the game.

During the 1964 soccer season, SA Ukraina fielded two teams. The senior team continued playing in the First Division. Its record of 5 wins, 1 tie, and 9 losses placed it in fifth position among six teams. A reserve team was registered in the Second Division. This team completed the season with 6 wins, 2 ties, and no losses to tie for first place on points. The club, though, lost out the championship honour on a goal differential.

The fortunes of the senior Ukraina soccer team fell even further in 1965. The team won 4 games and was on the losing end 10 times. In the standings the team placed sixth among eight teams.

The following year, Ukraina played average soccer. It finished the season in fourth place out of six teams. The result qualified Ukraina for the playoffs. The club won the semi-finals and then upset league leader Italia 4-3 in the final to win the Lancaster Cup, emblematic of the Oshawa championship.

SA Ukraina played average soccer once again in 1967 and finished the season in the middle of the standings. In the final of the Carling Cup competition, the team lost 2-0 to Italia.

# TRIDENTS

In 1985, a group of sports enthusiasts who knew each other through the Ukrainian Youth Association (SUM) organized a soccer team. The club operated out of the Ukrainian Cultural Centre Dnipro and was under the control of its sports administrator. Practices were held on the centre's soccer field. The centre was the primary benefactor of the team, supplying it with uniforms and other equipment. Additional sponsorship was provided by members of the community. The team, known as the Tridents, was entered in the senior division of the Motor City Soccer League located in Durham Region.

Among those who helped establish the club, and subsequently played on the team and filled administrative positions, were Andy Kadayklo, Greg Polityka, captain Steven Dobby, and Boghdan Postolan. For a number of years, the team was coached by Roy Dobby and managed by Steve Laschuk.

Tridents played with varied success during their existence.  On the soccer pitch they were capable of matching any team in the league.  Defensively, Tridents were strong, but unfortunately, lacked a concentrated offence.  As a result, they did not get into the win column often.  An indication of the team's defensive strength was the awarding of the 1986 most valuable defenceman in the league honours to Greg Polityka.

*Ukraina soccer team, 1989*

In 1988, Tridents changed their name to Ukraina.  This was done to make the team visibly identifiable with the Ukrainian community.

A few years later, the Ukraina soccer team folded.

# UKRAINIAN ATHLETIC CLUB

In the summer of 1927, the established Ukrainian organizations of Oshawa did not offer sport as part of their programs.  Sixteen-year-old Michael Starr viewed this as a void in the structure of community life.  Starr believed that sports was an excellent vehicle for character building and that youth should participate in it.  To see young Ukrainians lingering idly or spending their time in pool halls dejected Starr.  As a result, he organized a softball club for Ukrainian youth, named the Ukrainian Athletic Club (UAC).  The M. Hrushevsky Prosvita Hall sponsored the club.  Michael Starr would later serve as mayor of Oshawa and subsequently as Minister of Labour of Canada.

In 1928, the club was entered in the Oshawa City Industrial League at the juvenile level. The games were all high-scoring and error prone which made them unpredictable and exciting. At mid-point in the season, UAC was tied for second place in the six-team league. In the second half, it faltered and failed to make the playoffs.

In 1929, the UAC moved up to the junior division. Once again it failed to make the playoffs. Michael Starr continued to be the team's inspiration, playing at three positions: pitcher, first base, and outfield, as well as doing most of the coaching, managing, and organizational work.

St. George's Ukrainian Catholic church assumed the sponsorship of the team in 1931. The team competed in the eight-team Oshawa Sunday School Softball League under the name Ukrainian St. George's or simply the Ukrainians or Ukes. The club played well, qualifying for a best-of-three playoff to determine which team would face the league pennant winner in the final. Playing against Trinity, the Ukrainians won the opener 18-15. Trinity came back to take the second game 13-4. In the deciding game, the Ukrainians were down 6-5 entering the eighth inning. They then scored 5 unanswered runs to win the game and advance into the final. The Ukrainians upset pennant winner Tuxis in the opening game 12-11. Tuxis came back to take the next two games, 12-7 and 12-5, to claim the championship.

In 1932, the team was reorganized and once again became affiliated with the local branch of Prosvita. It also was renamed the Ukrainian National. The Nats competed in the Oshawa Sunday School League which had expanded to ten teams. After losing their first two games of the season, the Nats won seven straight. At the half-way point in the schedule they were tied for second place with a 7 and 2 record. The club was then involved in a fracas with Tuxis which forced the executive of the league to temporarily ban all games at Cowan Park, site of the melee.

In August of 1932, the Ukrainian Nationals travelled to Toronto to participate in the inaugural Ukrainian Field Day. The event was hosted by the Ukrainian Softball League of Toronto with teams participating from St. Catharines, Hamilton, Toronto and Oshawa. The softball tournament ended with the Nats and St. George's of Oshawa having an identical record of two wins apiece. It was determined that the Nats would face St. George's in Oshawa to determine the Ukrainian Ontario softball champion. The Nats won the game 25-15.

After returning to the regular schedule, the club continued to play consistently and once again qualified for the playoffs. They won their semi-final, defeating the Anglican Young Mens Club. In the final they faced their old nemesis, the Tuxis club. This series was a repeat of the previous year's. The Nats won the first game, but lost the next two and with that the championship.

To raise funds for the team, members organized dances at the Prosvita Hall. In addition, during the summer of 1932, the Ukrainian Nationals held a lottery.

In 1933, after only five years of existence, the Nats won the Oshawa city championship.

The following year, the club once again was reorganized, this time becoming affiliated with the local branch of the Ukrainian Boy Scout and Sporting Sitch Association. The team was also renamed Ukrainian Sitch. The club's line-up, though, was only slightly different from that of the Young Nationals of the previous year. The team continued to play well, but was unable to defend the city championship.

From 1927 through 1934, a group of young Ukrainian men played softball in Oshawa under various team names. They moved about from one Ukrainian organization to another. Their affiliation with these organizations was at arm's length; all they were seeking was sponsorship for their team.

The Ukrainian community of Oshawa accepted these teams with reservation at first. Most had no idea why the group of young men would pursue this economically unproductive activity. Most also did not understand the game itself. Those fans that came at first were there because of curiosity. After a while, attending the games became social event with upwards of 2,000 people in the park.

Many years later, Michael Starr hypothesized that the Ukrainian community accepted sport for its entertainment value. During the summer months, most Ukrainian organizations scaled down their activities. Other forms of entertainment, such as the big screen or radio, were out of reach to many because of a language barrier. With nothing better to do, the people headed for the ball park.

# UKRAINIAN SPORTS ASSOCIATION *STRILA*

In early 1954, a series of meetings was held in Oshawa at which the details relevant to the creation of the Ontario County Soccer Association league were finalized. At about the same time, a group of recently immigrated Ukrainian soccer enthusiasts concluded that a number of ethnic groups in the area had or were organizing soccer teams. The enthusiasts, among them Stephen Chaban, Bohdan Dulak and Peter Senyk called a meeting in March to organize a Ukrainian soccer club. They did not want the Ukrainian community to be left behind.

At the meeting, the first executive of the club was elected: K. Prushynsky, president; B. Dulak, vice-president; S. Chaban, secretary; and Ivan Guzyliak, treasurer. Dulak was also appointed coach of the not yet organized team. The name chosen for the club was the Ukrainian Sports Association Strila, after the sports club Strila in Zhovkva, Ukraine. The majority of the organizers were members of the Oshawa branch of the Ukrainian Youth Association (SUM), and as a result, the sports club became affiliated with the youth group.

The spring of 1954 was an extremely busy time for the executive members of USA Strila. In addition to assembling a soccer team for the upcoming season, they took an active part in the organizational work leading to the establishment of a soccer league in Oshawa.

In a short period of time, a soccer team was put together and registered in the Ontario County Soccer Association league. The team was one of seven charter teams in the league. The players signed by the team were recent arrivals from Europe and mostly members of SUM. The majority had European soccer experience, but not as much as management believed was necessary to have for a competitive team. On May 15, Strila played its first game, tying the Scottish club 2-2. For Strila this was a great morale booster, as the Scottish were considered one of the strongest clubs in the seven-team league.

Strila finished its inaugural season gaining the respect of its opponents and fans. In league play the club placed second; in the playoffs, Strila defeated a team from Claremont in the final to win the Lancaster Playoff Cup. Strila also participated in two tournaments, winning both. In August, it won the Labatt's Cup at a tournament of local teams, and in September it won the Arthur Latcher Cup at an invitational event in Stouffville. During the year, the club had good fan support with up to 2,000 people showing up for some matches.

In the early days the club was financially strapped. It had no permanent office space, much less a club house. For a good period of time, Chaban and Dulak operated the club out of their homes. Once the construction of the Ukrainian Cultural Centre Dnipro was completed, the club moved its operations there. The club also relied on the community for support. Dmytro Hentosh, a local businessman sponsored uniforms for the team, and Anne and Michael Starr, MP, the owners and operators of Maple Cleaners in Oshawa, provided the club with free laundry service for uniforms.

The lack of funds, though, did not hinder the recruitment of players by Strila. The club was able to entice proven athletes with full-time jobs at General Motors in Oshawa. Such deals were arranged by a great fan of the club, Dr. John Chmara, who at the time was employed by the automaker.

During the first year, attempts were made to expand the club's program by organizing volleyball, table tennis and chess groups. These attempts failed; there was a lack of interest among club members and in the Ukrainian community.

*Ukrainian Sports Association Strila soccer team, 1954 Oshawa Champions*

In 1955, USA Strila was reorganized and strengthened with the acquisition of a number of new players. The club finished first among nine teams in league competition, winning 15 and losing once. It was an overall team effort, offensively and defensively. Strila scored 64 goals and was scored upon 19 times. In the playoffs, the club once again won the Lancaster Cup.

After the conclusion of the season, Strila's affiliation with the Ukrainian Youth Association (SUM) was terminated. SUM and their Dnipro Hall partner, the League for Liberation of Ukraine, deemed that the affiliation with a sport club was not part of their mandate. The two organizations asked Strila to disassociate itself; Strila left to become an independent club. Within a short period of time, Strila loosely affiliated itself with the Ukrainian National Federation.

During the 1956 and 1957 seasons, the competitive level of the club fell and it finished in fourth and third place respectively.

The 1958 season began with Strila losing four straight games. This resulted in a complete reorganization. In addition, a deal was made with Toronto's SA Ukraina which would allow its junior and reserve players to compete with Strila. This arrangement benefited both clubs; Strila became more competitive while the Toronto players acquired game experience. Leonid Choloniuk, an SA Ukraina player on loan to Strila, scored six goals in a game against Uxbridge to establish a provincial record for most goals in a match.

In the spring of 1959, the Sports Association Strila expanded its activity by fielding a junior soccer team. The juniors were organized by B. Dulak and Dmytro Kocan. They were coached by

Ivan Baluta. The team was not entered in a league and played only exhibition matches. It faced both local teams and those from the neighbouring communities of Ajax, Bowmanville, Lindsay, etc.

The senior Strila completed the 1959 schedule in second place among 12 teams. During the season the club scored 90 goals to establish a league record for most goals in a season. That year, Strila was augmented by players from Toronto's Ukrainian Sports Club Trident.

Strila began the 1960 season outfitted in new uniforms, a gift to the team from Dr. Mykola Ostafiychuk. On defence, the club played well allowing only 26 goals against. However, the offence sputtered all season scoring only 46 goals, half of the previous year's total. In the standings, Strila fell one notch to third place.

The collapse of Toronto's Trident resulted in many of its players searching for new teams to play with. Some of them joined Strila for the 1961 season. As in the previous year, Strila played well defensively and had outstanding goalkeeping. Joe Burchowych allowed only 13 goals in 14 games. The club, though, had no offence and its players managed to score only 21 goals. Strila finished the season in fourth place. In the playoffs, the team was eliminated in the semi-finals.

At the conclusion of the 1961 season the Ukrainian Sports Association Strila ceased operations. Dr. Ostafiychuk, one of the prime sponsors of Strila, pushed for the disassociation of Strila from the Ukrainian National Federation. This occurred and Strila was restructured as a new independent club operating out of the Dnipro Hall under the name Sport Association Ukraina. Most of the Strila players went on to play for the new Ukraina team.

# YOUNG UKRAINIAN NATIONALS

In 1935, the members of the Oshawa branch of the Ukrainian National Youth Federation organized a softball team and entered it in the Oshawa and District Softball Association league. Known as the Ukrainians, the team was coached by Peter Hercia, Boris Shelenkoff and Michael Starr. All three were veterans of Sitch, Ukrainian Nationals, and Ukrainian Athletic Club teams of the past decade. Mike Petryshyn managed the club while Paul Cherewatyj handled the administrative tasks.

In the first year of operation, the Ukrainians competed at the junior level. The team played well, winning the Oshawa and the Eastern Ontario championships.

*Ukrainians softball team, 1935 Oshawa Champions*
*(Michael Starr far right)*

In 1936, the national executive of the Ukrainian National Youth Federation began urging its branches to organize sport clubs. The members of the Oshawa branch were already playing on a team which was not, though, officially affiliated with the UNYF. To fulfil the request of the national executive, the club became affiliated with the UNYF and was renamed the Young Ukrainian Nationals (YUN).

The Young Ukrainian Nationals was a junior age team that played in a junior league and in the senior Industrial League. At the junior level, the team was undefeated, sweeping the regular schedule and the playoffs to win the city championship. At the senior level it lost only once in ten starts. The club was led by its captain Bill Yourkevich.

The victory at the junior level qualified YUN to represent Oshawa at the provincial championships. The team opened the playoffs with a series against the Peterborough champions in Peterborough. The YUN team was met in Peterborough with astonishment; an "ethnic" club was the Oshawa champion. In addition, very few in Peterborough had ever heard of Ukrainians or tried to pronounce their names. This made for a very exciting series for the fans; YUN swept the series, 17-4 and 16-4. The next series against Trenton would determine the Eastern Ontario champions and the region's representative in the provincial semi-finals. Without much difficulty, YUN defeated Trenton, 20-9 and 13-7, and was crowned Eastern Ontario champions.

The club then travelled west to play Toronto Lakeshore in one of the two provincial semi-finals. The Oshawa YUN was on the losing end of two games, 5-2 and 15-14, and its hopes of a berth in the final were dashed.

In 1937, the YUN club once again won the Oshawa championship. In the Eastern Ontario final it defeated Belleville in three games; it lost the opener 5-4 in extra innings and then won two straight, 8-7 and 15-8, to take the title. In the provincial best-of-three semi-finals, YUN faced the Toronto Rideaus. Home ground made the difference as YUN won in Oshawa and lost both games in Toronto. Boris Shelenkoff and O. Pereyma handled the managerial duties.

During the summer of 1938, the UNYF operated a junior softball team.

The Young Ukrainian Nationals club was well-supported by the Ukrainian community. Regular season games were attended by hundreds of fans. Once the club advanced to the play-offs, it was not uncommon to have more than a thousand ardent fans at the games. The fans were completely absorbed by the events on the softball diamond and by the actions of the fans of opposing teams. Emotions often ran high, particularly in games against the Polish club.

The local business community provided the team with sponsorship. In any given year, a number of businesses would sponsor a player or two on the team. The name of the sponsoring business often appeared on the team jerseys: Glizuk Grocery, Poloz Ladies Wear, Muzyka Shoes, etc. Harry Lysak, who operated a coal delivery service, would place wooden benches on the back of his truck and transport both players and fans to and from games.

In 1939, a junior team was not fielded as there was lack of athletes of that age group. Enough, though, were available to form a juvenile team and one was put together and entered in the Oshawa and District Juvenile Softball League. The team finished the regular season with a 10 and 4 record which qualified it for the playoffs. The Young Ukrainians Nationals won the semi-finals but lost the city final to the Hobos. The team was captained by George Pavlenchuk, coached by John Hraynyk, and managed by Alex Shestokowsky.

The Young Ukrainian Nationals started to play ball in the 1940 season, but towards the end of the schedule the club dropped out of the league. It had lost too many young men to the war effort and was unable to fill its ranks with newcomers.

After the war, efforts were made to revive the baseball team but they were unsuccessful.

During the winter of 1954-55, a hockey team was organized by the Ukrainian National Youth Federation. Outfitted in flashy blue and yellow jerseys, it competed in the Oshawa Mercantile League.

# ST. CATHARINES, ONTARIO

## UKRAINIAN SPORT CLUB TRIDENT

In the early 1960s, Ukrainian soccer enthusiasts in St. Catharines were perplexed by the lack of a Ukrainian sports club in the city. Other groups such as the Poles, Germans, etc. operated clubs that catered to their youth. As a result, in 1963, a group led by John Fedoryshyn established the Ukrainian Sport Club Trident. The sport club was organized as an affiliate of the St. Catharines branch of the Ukrainian Democratic Youth Association (ODUM), of which Fedoryshyn was president. Membership in the sport club, though, was open to any Ukrainian.

The club executive immediately set out to organize a soccer team. Wrestler George Kusyj, a member of Canada's 1954 Commonwealth Games team, was retained as coach and trainer. Fedir Martiniuk and J. Fedoryshyn helped out with the training and coaching tasks. During the summer of 1963, a team of young boys (under-15) was registered in a local youth league.

The Ukrainian Sport Club Trident was active for three years. During that time it operated the youth team with varied success. In 1966, the club was unable to fill the roster of the team with Ukrainian players. Rather than recruit non-Ukrainians, the club suspended operations.

# SASKATOON, SASKATCHEWAN

## ST. GEORGE'S SOFTBALL TEAM

In 1948, Harry Dyrda and John Melnyk approached Reverend Michael Pelech of St. George's Parish in Saskatoon and requested that the church sponsor a softball team organized by the young men of the congregation. Reverend Pelech passed the request to the church committee, which agreed to buy jerseys, bats, balls, and other necessary equipment on the condition that after each season all of it would be returned to the church. The jerseys were blue and gold with St. George's emblazoned on the front.

That year, St. George's registered its team in the Saskatoon Commercial Softball League. It was one of about six teams assigned to the West Side Division. In assembling the team, manager John Melnyk and coach Harry Dyrda also recruited Ukrainian players from outside the congregation. St. George's played well in its inaugural season. Starting pitcher Patrick Bobyn was the club's leader, posting an undefeated record. Playing at shortstop was Mike Shabaga, who some years later would represent Canada at the World Ice Hockey Championship.

St. George's won its division and advanced to play YMHA in a best-of-five final for the city championship. The church club won the playoff opener. In the second game, YMHA launched a protest against pitcher Bobyn, alleging that he was pitching illegally. The league had a rule whereby "the pitcher prior to delivery shall present (show) the ball for one second." According to the YMHA, Bobyn was not doing this; the umpire agreed. As a result, Bobyn had to change his delivery and it threw his game off stride. St. George's lost the second game, came back to take the third, but lost the fourth. The fifth and deciding game and the city championship went to YMHA.

Indications are that the club folded after that one season. The departure of Harry Dyrda and of some of the other members precluded another summer of baseball.

# SPORTS TOURNAMENT

In the 1960s, Reverend Wolodymyr Iwaszko, a priest with St. George's Ukrainian Catholic Cathedral, was also the chairman of the Ukrainian Youth Association Plast in Saskatoon. As a priest, he had access to the parish's youth centre which housed a regulation-size gym. Plast members were encouraged to use the facilities. Nevertheless, Reverend Iwaszko was not satisfied. He strongly believed that it was time to make sport an integral component of all of the Ukrainian youth organizations in Saskatoon. As a result, Reverend Iwaszko and the members of the St. George's Cathedral Church executive organized a sports tournament in 1966.

Four organizations entered teams into the inaugural tournament: Plast, Ukrainian Catholic Youth of St. George's Cathedral, Ukrainian Catholic Youth of Sts. Peter and Paul, and the Ukrainian Catholic Students Club Obnova. Competition was held in men's badminton, basketball, table tennis and volleyball, and in women's volleyball. In subsequent years, the program was expanded to include all of the aforementioned sports for women. Competition in badminton and table tennis included singles, doubles, and mixed doubles events.

The Sports Tournament grew to league size and scope in a very short time. For instance, during the winter of 1968-69 the Sports Tournament was contested over two months and in 1974-75 it was contested over four months: December - table tennis, January - volleyball, February - basketball, and March - badminton. During the 1970-71 and 1971-72 seasons, competition in floor hockey was also held. This competition was restricted to 10 to 12-year-old boys.

*Sports Tournament competitors, 1968*

Over the years, eight Ukrainian youth organizations from Saskatoon competed at various times in the Sports Tournament. In addition to the four that fielded teams at the inaugural event, the Ukrainian National Youth Federation, Ukrainian Youth Association (SUM), Sheptytsky Institute Students and St. George's Cathedral Athletic Men's Club also participated. During the 1968-69 tournament, the only year for which data on participants was found, 134 young men and women partook in the event.

At the conclusion of the tournament, the winner of each of the 14 events contested received a trophy. Commencing in 1971, a trophy was presented to the overall team champion. Winning the team trophy were the Ukrainian National Youth Federation, 1971; Plast, 1972-73-74; and St. George's Cathedral Ukrainian Catholic Youth, 1975. In 1972, the tournament organizers initiated a trophy for the best all-round male and female competitor. All of the trophies were donated to the tournament by private individuals and by Ukrainian organizations.

The Sports Tournament continued on a regular basis through 1978. Subsequently it was organized occasionally, since Reverend Iwaszko, the driving force behind the tournament, no longer had the strength to continue. Among those of the younger generation, not too many were interested in this added responsibility.

# UKRAINIAN SPORTS CLUB

In the winter of 1954-55, a group of Saskatoon sports enthusiasts that included Theodore Baran, Reverend Wolodymyr Iwaszko, John Melnyk, Walter Sharko and Dr. Stephen Worobetz concluded that the established Ukrainian associations of the city lacked organized sports activities; those Ukrainians who wanted to participate in sport had to join local community clubs. As a result, the group decided to organize a sports club for Ukrainian youth. They called a meeting for May 15, 1955, at which the Ukrainian Sports Club (USC) was formally launched. Reverend Iwaszko, who in addition to his priestly duties had refereed soccer games in Ukraine, was elected the club's first president. The remainder of the executive included Frank Oryschak, vice-president; Ted Pasichniak, secretary; I. Bedzyk, treasurer; and Dr. Stephen Worobetz, club physician. At the meeting it was also announced that an under-15 soccer team had already been organized and entered in the Saskatoon Bantam Football League.

When the season began, coach T. Baran had 22 players on his roster and was able to substitute freely. The USC bantam Eagles finished the regular season in second place out of five teams with a record of 5 wins, 3 ties, and 4 losses. Two of its members, Emile "Ted" Baran at goal and Bill Repchinski at full back, were named to the city all-star team for a match against Winnipeg.

In 1956, the Ukrainian Sports Club fielded two soccer teams but its attempt to organize a girls' softball team did not succeed. John Melnyk coached the bantam team that year. The team finished the season tied for first place with Westmount. Both teams earned 20 points in the 16-game schedule. USC won one more game than Westmount but that was not the criterion used to award first place. Westmount was declared the winner based on a better (by one) goals for and against average. The USC bantam team then swept the playoffs and won the A. A. Murphy Trophy.

*Ukrainian Sports Club bantam and junior soccer teams, 1956*

The newly organized juvenile under-18 team was coached by Ted Pasichniak. The team finished the season in second place with 12 points, 12 back of league-leading Westmount. In the best-of-three playoffs, Westmount faced USC. Westmount won the opener and tied the next two games to win the playoff trophy.

The formation of the Association of Ukrainian Sport Clubs of North America (USCAK) in December of 1955, a council that would coordinate sport activity in North America, received the moral support of the Ukrainian Sport Club. Subsequently, USC joined the Canadian Division of the council. Nevertheless, the distance separating Saskatoon from other USCAK club member cities precluded any sport contacts.

The Ukrainian Sports Club was always short of operating funds. To alleviate the problem, a monthly bingo night was organized. Commencing in 1956, the club's executive and the Ladies' Auxiliary worked hard to make these fund raisers successful. In 1957, the club raised $522 in this manner. USC was also helped out financially by St. George's Ukrainian Catholic Church.

During the winter of 1956-57, the Ukrainian Sports Club organized a table tennis league in Saskatoon. Competing in the league were teams from the Sheptytsky Institute, the Ukrainian Catholic Youth of Saskatoon and of Nutana and others. Dr. Worobetz, the club's physician and the future Lieutenant-Governor of the province (1970-76), donated a trophy to the men's winner.

During the winter months, a small group of chess enthusiasts sharpened their skills. In addition, volleyball was encouraged but never gathered much of a following.

In 1957, the juvenile division of the Saskatoon District Minor Soccer association suspended operations. Players were available; unfortunately, there were no volunteers to coach and or manage them. In the bantam division, USC qualified for the playoffs. It won the semi-final game 4-2 over Nutana Legion.

The Saskatoon school system introduced soccer as part of its extracurricular activities in 1958 and as a result most of the local soccer clubs folded. The Ukrainian Sports Club also suspended operation. Table tennis and chess were not popular enough at the time to warrant the club's existence.

# SHANDRO, ALBERTA

## SHANDRO BASKETBALL TEAM

In the early 1930s, the village of Shandro featured a men's basketball team comprising members of two Shandro families. The team played in exhibition games.

A number of men on the team were the sons of Andrew Shandro. In 1913, the farmer turned politician became the first Ukrainian in Canada elected to a provincial parliament.

It could not be determined how long the Shandro family basketball team existed.

*Shandro basketball team, 1930*

# SUDBURY, ONTARIO

## UKRAINIAN SOCCER CLUB TRIDENTS

In 1963, Mike Kolomyjec and Walter Rohatyn organized a junior soccer team in Sudbury and named it the Ukrainian Soccer Club Tridents. The two fathers wanted to provide their boys and other youngsters with an activity which would constructively occupy their summer months. They also wanted an activity in a Ukrainian setting. Aside from summer camps, there was no organized activity for Ukrainian youths in the city during the vacations.

From their inception, the Tridents were affiliated with the Ukrainian National Federation (UNF). The federation sponsored the club and provided it with facilities. Initially, most of the players were drawn from the membership of the federation. With time, Ukrainians affiliated with other organizations joined, as did non-Ukrainians.

For a number of years, the team competed in the Sudbury Junior Soccer League, and in 1969 in the Junior "A" division of the Sudbury Football Association. In the latter year, the team was coached by Moe Marunchak, a veteran goaltender.

By the 1970 season, a number of players were no longer eligible to compete in the junior ranks. As a result, an application was submitted to enter the team in the senior league of the Sudbury and District Football Association. In the spring, the Tridents were one of two teams which gained membership in the expanded seven-team league. The club finished its inaugural regular season in sixth place with a record of 1 win, 3 ties and 7 losses. Coach Moe Marunchak, who also tended goal for his club, was not discouraged by the results of the first year. With the exception of two players, the team's average age was just under 18. He believed that with maturity and experience the club would become competitive.

The following year the club improved on its record but still finished out of the playoffs.

During the 1972 season, the play of the Tridents improved significantly. The team finished the regular season in third place with a record of 7 wins, 3 ties and 2 loses. In a sudden-death semi-final playoff, Tridents held the league leaders Croatia Andria to a 2-2 draw after regulation play. Two fifteen-minute overtime periods did not settle the outcome as both teams scored once. The game was decided on penalty kicks with Croatia outscoring Tridents 3-2. The Tridents were coached by Graziano Usic and managed by P. Panas. Centre half George Krauss won the league's scoring title. He would repeat in 1973 and 1975.

Tridents made a breakthrough in Cup play in 1972 as they won the Charity Cup and the Sudbury Star Cup, emblematic of the Northern Ontario championship. In competition for the Ontario Cup, Tridents defeated Ottawa Centennial 2-0 and Kingston International 1-0 before losing 3-0 in a semi-final match to a Toronto team.

Tridents also travelled to Oshawa to play an exhibition game against that city's Ukrainian-sponsored Tridents soccer team and against a Croatian team. The visitors defeated the Oshawa Tridents 5-3 and tied Croatia 2-2.

In 1973, after only four years of play at the senior level, Tridents won their first league title by finishing on top of the standings with a record of 10 wins, 1 tie and 1 loss.

The team continued to improve, and a year later Tridents registered what would eventually prove to be their most successful season in history; the team was undefeated during the regular season winning 8 and tying 2, to once again place first in league standings.

In Cup play, Tridents won the locally contested Charity Cup and the Canadiana Festival Cup. In competition for the Ontario Cup, Tridents defeated the Sudbury Flyers and Aurora. The team then defeated Thunder Bay to win the Northern Ontario title and the Sudbury Star Cup. The victory advanced the Tridents to the provincial semi-finals against the previously undefeated Ottawa Royals. The Sudbury side defeated Ottawa 2-0 to advance to the Ontario Cup two-game total-goal series against Windsor Italia. Tridents lost the opener at home 1-0. Playing in Windsor, the team lost its second successive game by a one goal margin, 3-2. A large number of Ukrainians from Windsor and area attended the match and cheered the Sudbury team.

For his efforts in guiding the Tridents to the Ontario Cup final, coach Greg Zorbas was nominated for the 1974 Sudbury Sportsman of the Year award. Zorbas concurrently coached the Laurentian University soccer team.

While competing with the Tridents in the early 1970s, most players were enrolled at Laurentian University. For example, in 1973, seven Ukrainian players from the Tridents played on the university soccer team. The Laurentian team was considered one of the strongest in Canada at the time.

In 1975, the Tridents registered their second consecutive undefeated season. Their record of 9 wins and 1 tie was good for first place in the standings. In the semi-final round of the play-offs, Tridents defeated United 2-1. The first game of a two-game total-goal final against Croatia-Andria ended in a scoreless draw. Tridents then claimed the championship Cup by winning the second game 1-0 in overtime. Five Tridents players were named to the league all-star team that year.

In the opening round of Ontario Cup play, the Tridents were stunned 4-1 by Sudbury United. Coach Fulio Stepancich conceded that the defending finalists were overconfident during most matches that season. The loss "woke the team up" according to the coach and made them work harder. Subsequently, the team won the Labatt's Cup Tournament, the Charity Cup and Canadiana Festival Cup.

The senior Tridents team folded early in the 1976 season. At that time a new semi-professional team was formed in Sudbury. Twelve Tridents players left for the Sudbury Cyclones, leaving the team with just four players.

# UKRAINIAN SPORTS CLUB LIONS

On May 18, 1952, members of the Ukrainian National Youth Federation (UNYF) Sudbury branch organized the Ukrainian Sports Club Lions. The first executive consisted of Terry Kozemchuk, president; Konstantin Bayus, secretary; and Mykola Petrucha, treasurer. On May 21, Kozemchuk submitted an application to enter a team in the Sudbury District Football Association (SDFA) league. Kozemchuk argued that there was room for a second Ukrainian team in the league (the Ukrainian Sports Club Sitch was a member since 1950), because of the great number of experienced Ukrainian soccer players in the area; one team could not absorb them all. The league agreed and approved the application.

The emergence of sport activities within the UNYF branch predates the founding of the Lions club by a number of years. In 1943, and shortly after the end of the war, volleyball clubs existed, but in a house league capacity.

In its inaugural season, the roster of the Lions was made up of players who at one time or another played for Sitch. The most prominent among these was Lions' newly appointed captain Walter Hirnyj. In July, the Lions faced for the first time the established Ukrainian Sports Club Sitch. The game was emotionally charged as both clubs tried to please their respective fans. The Lions won 3-1. Although some viewed this and other Lions' victories as upsets, the club played consistent and competitive soccer to finish the season in the middle of the standings. Forward Oreste Kocijan was the club's leading scorer with 14 goals in 15 games. He was also named to the city all-star team.

*Ukrainian Sports Club Lions soccer team, 1952*

The Lions pulled out of the SDFA league prior to the start of the 1953 season and its players were dispersed among the league teams.

At the time, the Lions also organized a juvenile soccer team. The club would eventually also sponsor a junior team. The two teams competed in Sudbury leagues for a number of years.

The Lions rejoined the SDFA league in 1955. The team comprised some veteran players of the now defunct Sitch and young players that came up through the junior ranks of the Lions. The Lions finished the season in third place out of five teams with a record of 2 wins, 4 ties and 2 losses. The team was matched with the Italia Flyers in a two-game total-goal semi-final. The Lions upset Italia in the opening game 1-0. The Italians came back to win the second game by an identical score. This necessitated a sudden-death playoff which was won by Italia.

The Lions suspended operation of the senior team once again after the 1955 season.

The following year, a junior Lions team participated in a three-team Sudbury league.

# UKRAINIAN SPORTS CLUB *SITCH*

S port enthusiasts among the members of the Sudbury branch of the Ukrainian Youth Association (SUM) decided to organize a sport club in 1949. They believed that sport would be a good diversion from their daily routines. They also believed that the name Ukraine was not propagated in Sudbury sports; other ethnic groups had their sport clubs, but not the Ukrainians. As a result, the Ukrainian Sports Club Sitch came into being that year. The club was autonomous and had its own executive. The founders and early organizers of the club were B. Borys, W. Dejczakiwsky, M. Klid, W. Lubinsky, Maluha, and M. Zawerucha.

For Sitch, soccer was the obvious sport to pursue, since almost all of the members of SUM were recent immigrants from Europe and those organizing the sport club had European soccer experience.

During the summer of 1949, Sitch only played exhibition matches as the team was organized well past the start of the regular season. Myron Chayka was the playing coach of the team.

Once the cold weather set in, members participated in a house-league chess tournament.

In the spring of 1950, Sitch played its first regular season game in the Sudbury District Football Association (SDFA) losing 5-0 to the Polish White Eagles. Sitch, more commonly known as Ukrainians or Ukes, improved its play substantially over the course of the schedule to finish in third place out of eight teams. In the playoffs for the Evans Cup, Sitch lost in the opening round 3-2 to Caruso. The team was managed by Nick Waller.

The SDFA All-Star game in 1950 matched a "British" team against a "European" team. The British team comprised players of British extraction, while the European team comprised those athletes who once called mainland Europe their home. Named to the European team were six players from Sitch: Myron Chayka, Nestor Chytra, Alf Galins, Walter Hirnyj, Myron Kobryn, and Nick Lidow.

During the summer of 1951, Sitch dominated soccer in Sudbury. It was a fast team that specialized in low long passes executed with speed and great accuracy. The club finished the regular season undefeated, recording 9 wins and 3 ties to place first in league standings. It had the best goals for (34) and goals against (16) record in the league. Six of its players were among the league's top-ten scorers.

Sitch contested two Cups in 1951. In competition for the Charity Cup, Sitch won its quarter-final and semi-final matches. In the final, Sitch was to face the Polish White Eagles who won the Cup the previous year. The White Eagles, though, withdrew from the league, citing a problem with the "attitude" of the referees and officials towards the team. Sitch was therefore awarded the Charity Cup by default.

In competition for the Star Cup, emblematic of the Northern Ontario Championship, Sitch won its semi-final match against Ryans 2-1. In the Cup final against Caruso, the two teams ended regulation play in a scoreless deadlock; a further thirty minutes of overtime did not produce a winner. The game was called and a replay ordered. In the second final, Caruso opened the scoring in the second half. Sitch captain and league MVP runner-up M. Chayka scored on a penalty kick with four minutes remaining to tie the game. With no winner at the end of regulation play, the game went into overtime. Forward Heino Saare rifled a shot past the Caruso goaltender in the second half of overtime to give Sitch the victory. Goaltender Alf Galins kept Sitch in the game, making 17 stops, some of them described as "brilliant" by the local media.

*Ukrainian Sports Club Sitch soccer team, c.1952*

At one point in the game, emotional Sitch fans charged onto the field when one of their favourite players was kicked. The referee and the police subdued the infuriated spectators before anything serious happened. The scene was reflective of the dedicated and passionate fan support which the club had during the season.

The 1951 All-Star game matched Sitch against the Sudbury All-Stars. The game ended in a 2-2 draw. Part of the revenue raised from the game was apportioned to Bill Magur of Sitch, who had severely injured his knee at the start of the season. The injury caused Magur to miss more than two months of work. Neither the club nor the league had insurance.

Sitch manager and coach Nick Waller was pleased with his team's performance in 1951, but promised to field an even stronger team in 1952. Waller stated that his objective was to have a Dominion contender. During the off-season he recruited players, bringing in three from England and one from Toronto.

The 1952 season began with great expectations. More than 2,000 fans attended an exhibition game. People were interested in seeing the team Waller put together. The regular season opener against Polish White Eagles brought out 2,500 fans. Sitch lost that encounter 3-1. The season was two games old when it was discovered that the player Sitch signed from Toronto had previously signed with another team for the season. Hoping to avoid a suspension, he left Sitch for his original club.

In mid-July, Sitch faced, for the first time, the Ukrainian Sport Club Lions, a new entry in the league. The roster of Lions included a number of players who played for Sitch the previous year. The game was emotionally charged as both clubs tried to please their respective fans. The Lions upset Sitch 3-1.

Sitch ended the season tied for first place in the league with the White Eagles. Playmaking centre Ujeko Masina, who led the league in scoring with 28 goals in 16 games, was primarily responsible for the team's success. Masina also established a league record when he scored seven goals in one game. Andy Semeniuk of Sitch was the league's top goaltender, surrendering 12 goals in 9 games. Five Sitch players and coach Waller were named to the city All-Star team.

The tie for first place in the league standings resulted in the league arranging a two-game total-goal playoff to determine the champion and winner of the Anderson Cup. The first game ended in a 1-1 draw. In the second game, Sitch was down 2-0 when manager Waller ordered his club off the field in protest over allegedly poor officiating. At a league hearing, Sitch was fined $200 for the incident; at the same time, Sitch filed a protest that one of the White Eagles players was ineligible because of a previously signed contract. The league reviewed the evidence and concurred with Sitch. Since the player in question played one regular season game which the White Eagles won, the club was stripped of the two points that they were awarded for the victory. With that decision, Sitch won the Anderson Cup in a boardroom. On the playing field, Sitch won the Charity Cup that year.

In competition for the right to represent Ontario in the Dominion Cup playoffs, Sitch met Toronto's Italo-Canadians. The game, played on a rain soaked field in Sudbury, saw the two teams draw at one at the end of regulation play. The Italians scored in overtime to win the Ontario championship.

Stephen Charko was appointed manager of Sitch for the 1953 season and outside left Walter Lesiuk was named playing coach. The withdrawal of the Lions from the league saw a number of the defunct team's players return to Sitch. Once again, the club brought in players from England. The team finished the season in second place. In the playoffs, Sitch defeated Garson in the semi-finals and the White Eagles in the final to win the Evans Cup, emblematic of the league's playoff champion.

Sitch won the Charity Cup in 1953 for the third consecutive year. In competition for the Star Cup, Sitch did not advance past the semi-finals.

In 1954, Sitch finished in last place out of six teams. It did not advance to any Cup finals. The frustration of not playing well, coupled with the high expectations of the fans, resulted in many players feeling emotionally sapped. In addition, the players were starting to feel their age. Most were employed in the mines or mine-related industries and the physical demands of their shift jobs were substantial. Every day, it was more difficult to work a shift and then play an entire match.

A number of Sitch players decided not to return for the 1955 season. The club also lost some players to Toronto's SA Ukraina. Unable to fill its depleted roster from within SUM or from the general population, the Ukrainian Sports Club Sitch folded.

# THUNDER BAY, ONTARIO

(once Port Arthur and Fort William)


## FOOTBALL CLUB *SICZ*


I n May of 1949, the Port Arthur Football Association admitted a sixth team into its league. Interestingly, the admission occurred one week into the season and a revision of the 1949 schedule had to be made. The sixth entry into the league was the Football Club Sicz. On May 20, *The Port Arthur News-Chronicle* reported: "Little at present is known about the new entry excepting that the Sicz Club will operate from Fort William and is comprised largely of displaced persons from Europe. The entry was made by Dr. Gwozdecky."

Dr. George Gwozdecky, an immigrant from Ukraine, was the driving force behind the club. He gathered a small group of enthusiasts, among them individuals who had soccer experience from Ukraine and/or from the displaced persons camps of Europe, and organized them into a soccer club. Dr. Gwozdecky coached the club and served as its president as well.

In its opening game on March 27, 1949, Sicz was crushed 5-0 by Brent Park. A few day later, Walter Hirnyj led Sicz to its first victory by scoring three goals in a 4-1 win. During the season, the club had, on occasion problems fielding a complete team. Sometimes Sicz played with as few as nine players, while at other times it defaulted games. In League Cup play Sicz failed to make the playoffs. In addition, the team failed to make the playoffs in Legion Cup play, a ten-game tournament during the season, finishing fifth out of the six teams.

Prior to the start of the 1950 season, the Football Club Sicz changed its name to Ukrainian Sports Klub (Club) - USK. When competition began, USK defaulted the first game because three of its players unexpectedly left the Lakehead area. The league, not wishing to lose a team, encouraged USK to fill its depleting ranks with Japanese-Canadians who had soccer experience and were settling in the area. This never materialized, and USK failed to field a team for its second scheduled match. In the first game that it played, USK was routed 8-0 by Brent Park. Nevertheless, the press reported on this match favourably: "Despite the lopsided score, the Ukrainian Sports Club impressed with their hustle and clever passing plays. They never let up during the entire game even though it was quite apparent in the last half that theirs was a lost cause."

Three days later, on June 7, 1950, the Ukrainian Sports Klub cancelled its entry in the league. Lack of players and the difficulty of fielding a team were cited as reasons for the withdrawal. A number of USK players went on to compete for other teams.

# LAKEHEAD UKRAINIAN ATHLETIC CLUB

S ituated on the north shore of Lake Superior, the adjacent towns of Port Arthur and Fort William (later renamed Thunder Bay) were gripped by the depression in 1934. For a group of young unemployed Ukrainian men, the prospect of passing the time idly was appalling. They had boundless energy and nowhere to expend it. On the urging of two sport enthusiasts and brothers, Martin and Maurice Chepesiuk, a football team was organized. Pete Patraniuk, Alex Pupeza, Jim Chepesiuk, and Morris Yemchuk also played a role in the formation of the club. While some of the team members had high school football experience, many had none at all. Nevertheless, they all eagerly participated in practices and scrimmages.

Known as the Ukes, the group submitted an application for membership in the local rugby-football league but was denied admission. As a result, the Ukes played exhibition matches against teams that were part of the established city leagues. The teams accepted games against the Ukes because it gave them an opportunity to test new plays and player combinations. In addition, a basketball team was organized by the Ukes at the time. That team was also refused membership in the local league. An attempt to organize a hockey team failed.

The Ukes had no formal structure and no funding at the time. The athletes did not have equipment, uniforms or even a basketball. After much pleading, a local high school lent the Ukes equipment and uniforms. Martin Chepesiuk, the only member of the team to own a car, would pack twelve players with their football gear into his vehicle and drive them to games.

In 1936, the Ukes approached Albert Slivinski, a sport enthusiast and an active member of the Prosvita Reading Hall of Fort William, and requested that he formally establish a structured sport club from the loosely knit group. Slivinski agreed.

In early September of 1936, Slivinski formally established the Lakehead Ukrainian Athletic Club (LUAC). He successfully inspired a group of sport enthusiasts to mobilize the Ukrainian youth attached to the three Prosvita organizations in the area (Fort William, Port Arthur, and Westfort) and merged them with the initial core group to form the club.

Albert Slivinski believed that physical fitness was a fundamental building block during formative years. Convinced that there were just too many Ukrainian youths running around with nothing to do, he proposed to occupy them in a Ukrainian setting while providing them with proper sports training. The idea of partaking in sports in a Ukrainian club was enthusiastically accepted, and within weeks, *The Port Arthur News-Chronicle* reported that the club had more than 300 members. Initially, membership was restricted to those who had at least one Ukrainian parent.

The first executive of the Lakehead Ukrainian Athletic Club included Albert Slivinski, president; Nick Kozak, vice-president and team representative on the executive of the Lakehead Rugby Union (LRU); Eugene Hlady, recording secretary; Nettie Urick, treasurer; and Zeon Fedori, financial secretary. Future senator Paul Yuzyk, who was in the area doing organizational work for the Ukrainian National Youth Federation of Canada, was made honourary president. Although no formal affiliation with a Ukrainian organization appears to have existed, the LUAC had very close ties to Prosvita, which could be referred to as LUAC's parent organization, and in its early years, to the Ukrainian National Youth Federation.

The Lakehead Ukrainian Athletic Club formally began its sports program on September 15, 1936. The event was a rugby (football) practice. The club had entered a team into the Lakehead Rugby Union and the first game was less than two weeks later. The Lakehead Ukrainian Athletic Club Ukes opened the season, decked in blue jerseys with a big yellow U on the front, by taking a 27-0 beating at the hands of the Flamingoes. The team went through its first season winless, scoring but 4 points and having 79 scored against them. They finished in last place in the three team league. The team was coached by Martin Chepesiuk with the assistance of Maurice Chepesiuk.

In November of 1936, the LUAC put in an application for admittance into the Thunder Bay Junior Hockey League. Admittance was denied. While in principle the league was willing to accommodate the request, in practice it could not because of lack of ice space in the area's two indoor arenas. The league issued a statement in which their position was outlined, ". . .it is the opinion of the Thunder Bay Hockey Association and of the junior clubs at present comprising the circuit that the team cannot be admitted owing to the admission of the respective Fort William and Port Arthur rink company managements that the same could not be accommodated. Although the association and the teams feel that they would be a welcome addition. . ."[6] For the Lakehead Ukrainian Athletic Club, this was a major blow. With hockey teams being organized at the juvenile, midget, and bantam levels, a junior club would have been a natural progression for the players.  In addition, it would have enhanced the LUAC's presence in the area.

When the LUAC submitted an application for admittance of three teams (bantam, juvenile and midget) with the Fort William Midget Hockey Association, the request was not denied.  All bantam, juvenile and midget games at the time were played on outdoor rinks and there was no lack of ice space on them.  While severe cold, snow and blizzards often forced the postponement of games, only rarely did this keep the teens from heading out to the rinks.  During the season, the three teams competed with minor success and failed to make the playoffs.  Making his hockey start with the LUAC Ukes that year was Steve Hrymnak, later of the Chicago Black Hawks.

In November of 1936, LUAC also entered a team in the intermediate division of the local basketball league.  After an undefeated first half of the season, which gave it an automatic bye into the playoffs, the team dropped a couple of games.  In a best-of-three playoff, the Ukes defeated Collegiate in two straight  to win the Ellis Memorial Trophy, emblematic of the Ft. William City Intermediate Basketball Championship.  The Ukes then "travelled" to Port Arthur to take on that city's champions in a best-of-three final for the Thunder Bay basketball title.  The Ukes lost two in a row.  During the year and in the playoffs, the team was led by N. Yemchuk.  The coaching duties were shared by William Bodnar and playing coach John Dowhosza.

*Lakehead Ukrainian Athletic Club intermediate basketball team, 1936-37 Fort William Champions*

That winter, a juvenile basketball loop was formed and the LUAC entered a team.  The juveniles failed to impress, ending up in the middle of the standing.

During the early years of the club, to instill a sense of Ukrainian patriotism and to raise much needed funds, LUAC members put on plays and variety shows which were well accepted by the local Ukrainian community. On one occasion, the club raised $82.25, a formidable amount in those days. After a while this practice ceased, as with every year more and more non-Ukrainians joined the ranks of LUAC.

In the summer of 1937, LUAC entered two teams into the YMCA juvenile softball league. The league comprised 12 teams divided into two division. Ukes West Enders played in division "A" while Ukes East Enders in division "B." Both teams failed to win one game of the five-game schedule.

Wishing to improve on the previous year's disappointing rugby season, new coach N. Yemchuk started practices well before the season opener. The team, though, lost four straight before withdrawing from further play with two games remaining. Mathematically eliminated from the playoffs, LUAC management saw no reason to continue the season. Alex Horbow was the Uke's most valuable player during that campaign.

In December, the hockey and basketball seasons began. This time, only one hockey team was iced by the LUAC - the juvenile Ukes. This team had a respectable season, qualifying for the Fort William Championship. In a two-game total-goal series against the Chapple Wolverines, the Ukes lost the first game 2-1 and tied the second 3-3. In basketball, LUAC entered a senior team into the YMCA City Basketball League. This team was forced to withdraw from the league because of a player shortage. A juvenile team fared much better; it finished in first place in a six-team league. In a two-game total-point final, the Ukes won the first game from the West Fort Red Indians 16-10. In the second game, at the end of regulation time, the Ukes were down by 6 points. On total points, the teams were tied. The Ukes lost the championship in sudden-death overtime.

In the summer of 1938, efforts were made to have the LUAC Ukes join the Big Four baseball league but nothing materialized. In late August, the Thunder Bay branch of the Canadian Amateur Athletic Association organized a track and field meet for the Lakehead area athletes. Representing LUAC and winning medals were M. Chichka, with a gold in the javelin, and M. Yemchuk, with a silver in the javelin.

The Ukes football team secured the services of playing coach Barney Taylor for the 1938 season. Taylor brought with him a knowledge of the game that previous coaches lacked, as well as proper training methods. He had gained much experience playing for the Winnipeg Victorias, forerunners of the Blue Bombers, during the 1926 and 1927 seasons. As a result, the team finally made it into the win column, but still finished out of the playoffs.

In the late 1930s, the football team secured its own clubhouse. The facility was a shack between the CNR and CPR tracks. It was a popular hangout for the players and many beer parties were held there after games.

The 1938-39 basketball season saw the Ukes once again competing in the intermediate league. They finished the regular season undefeated. In the final, a two-game total-point affair, the Ukes demolished their opponents in both encounters to once again win the Ellis Memorial trophy. The team was led by Yemchuk.

In juvenile hockey, as in the previous year, the team qualified for the two-game total-goal final. The first game ended in a 4-4 tie but it brought about a scene which was discussed for a long time in the area: "The puck had been barely faced when Brown of the Maroons and Kalynuk of the Ukes tangled, precipitating one of the most riotous scenes to be seen in a lakehead arena this season. Spectators leaped over the boards and joined with the players in the general melee. Lights were doused in an effort to subdue the rowdying. . ."[7] The Ukes lost the second game 5-2.

In 1939, the Uke rugby team was coached by Bill Christie. Captain and quarterback of the team was Alex Horbow. For the first time, the Ukes won more games than they lost and made the playoffs. In a best-of-three final, the Ukes lost the first game in a tightly fought defensive battle 3-2. In the second game, they lost 20-14. Horbow was the stand-out for the Ukes throughout the season and in the playoffs. As a result of his performance, he was slated for a try-out with the Winnipeg Blue Bombers the following season. World War II precluded that opportunity, as Horbow committed himself to the war effort.

World War II also impacted on the sport programs of the Lakehead Ukrainian Athletic Club. During the war years, LUAC only managed to field two teams, both in basketball. The 1939-40 Ukes basketball team competed in the senior league winning but one game. The following season, the Ukes secured the services of two former western senior stars, "Cowboy" Chikowski and Steve O'Gradnick. The club finished at the top of the senior standings. In the playoffs, with Chikowski out of the line-up, they were upset and lost the championship.

The Lakehead Ukrainian Athletic Club resumed activity in the fall of 1946 when it entered a team in the Thunder Bay Senior Basketball League. At mid-point in the season, the league almost folded, not because of a lack of players or teams, but because of a lack of referees. Nevertheless, the league overcame this crisis and the season was completed. The Ukes finished tied for third spot in the six-team league and qualified for post-season play, but were swept in two straight games by the Aces.

In January of 1947, two hockey teams, a bantam and a juvenile, were entered into the Fort William Minor Hockey Association circuit. A few weeks into the season, the Ukes bantam team was caught using an overage player. All games through that date were forfeited and as a result the team did not make the playoffs. The juvenile club, on the other hand, made the play-offs but bowed out in the semi-finals in three straight games.

In the fall, after a six year absence, the Ukes once again entered a team in the Lakehead Rugby Football Union. Under the guidance of playing coach Alex Horbow, the Ukes finished the regular season in last place in the three team league, with 1 win and 3 losses to their credit. Because of the structure of the playoffs, they qualified for a sudden-death semi-final against the second place Mustangs, whom they defeated.

In a two-game total-point final, the Ukes faced the previously undefeated Redskins. The first encounter was won by the Redskins by the smallest of margins: 12-11. In the second game, the Ukes handed the Redskins their first defeat of the season in a hard-fought, bruising defensive contest. The final score was Ukes 5, Redskins 1. The Lakehead Ukrainian Athletic Club Ukes, for the first time in their history, had won the Phil Asseff Memorial Trophy and were champions of the Lakehead Rugby Football Union. Gaining personal recognition was Tom Beda of the Ukes, who won the Dr. A. T. Gillespie Trophy as the most valuable backfielder in the league that season.

*Lakehead Ukrainian Athletic Club rugby-football team, 1947 Lakehead Champions*

Rugby-football had barely ended when play began in the seven-team Ellis Memorial Basketball League. The Ukes played good basketball to finish the season in second place with 9 wins and 3 losses. The club was just two points back of the league-leading Aces. In a best-of-three semi-final, the Ukes faced the Aces, against whom they lost twice during the regular season. The Ukes lost the opening game. They came back to win the second game comfortably and in the third game, in a squeaker, defeated the Aces 25-24. The upset victory advanced the team to the best-of-five final against Navy. The series was a see-saw affair going the distance. The Ukes lost the opener, won the next two, then lost the fourth. They wrapped up the championship with a 32-29 win in the fifth and deciding game. Nevertheless, there were some very anxious moments; with one minute and 45 seconds remaining, two Uke players fouled out and the team had to play shorthanded for the duration.

The victory advanced the Lakehead Ukrainian Athletic Club Ukes, as the representatives of the Thunder Bay District, to the Manitoba Amateur Basketball Association's intermediate playdowns. The Ukes hosted the Brandon Crocks in a best-of-three semi-final, with the winner advancing to the Manitoba final. The opening game, which saw the lead change hands several times, was won by the visitors 54-48. In the second game, the Ukes were outclassed by the Crocks, losing 65-53. During the season and in the playoffs, the Ukes were led by Johnny Hancharek.

In 1948, the Ukes defended the Phil Asseff Memorial Trophy. They finished the regular season in first place, winning 3 and losing 1. In a best-of-three final, they defeated the Mustangs in the first game 10-9, tied the second game 6-6, and came from behind to win the third game 17-6. The Ukes scored 16 points in the fourth quarter, including a 55-yard touchdown by Boris Chepesiuk on an interception in the dying minutes of the game. The team was coached by Eddie Gayoski. Bob Stewart, halfback with the Ukes, won the Dr. Gillespie Trophy.

The basketball Ukes finished the 1948-49 schedule in second place, amassing 10 points in 8 games. In the first game of the semi-finals, the Ukes, in one of the biggest upsets of the season, lost to Lakehead Technical Institute 34-31. They came back to win the second game 44-34. Without the services of their scoring leader Hancharek, the team lost the third game 42-28.

The 1949 rugby football season opened on a humiliating note. The defending champion Ukes were beaten 14-0 before a crowd of more than 3,000 spectators that had braved intermittent rain to see the game. The team went on to finish the season in third place with 1 victory and 3 losses. The club qualified for the playoffs but lost 7-0 to the Redskins in a semi-final game. A poor showing by the team that year was expected by club management, as only 11 players from the previous year's championship team returned. As a result, the Ukes had many new faces in their line-up. The team was once again coached by Gayoski.

During the off-season, the Lakehead Ukrainian Athletic Club dropped sponsorship of the rugby-football team. The desire to carry on prompted the players to take over the management of the team for the 1950 season. Managing the club and competing proved to be more than a challenge and the season could only be described as disappointing. The team was outscored

59 to 19 and lost all four games it played. Often, the team failed to reach the 25 man limit and, as a result, lacked depth. The Ukes were coached by Harry Franchi.

In 1951, the club was reorganized once again. Eleven players and staunch supporters joined forces to share ownership and management. In 1951, the Ukes also changed their name to the Roughriders.

An expected affiliation with Regina Roughriders of the Western Canada Football Union was the reason for the switch in name for the Ukes. ". . .We're expecting word of formal affiliation any day from Regina" said coach Harry Franchi, "But whether it becomes official or not, we're going to carry on as the Fort William Roughriders."[8]

The desired affiliation never materialized, although a few years later a deal was signed with the Ottawa Rough Riders.

The Ukes/Roughriders opened the season on a losing note. Several days later, Franchi resigned, citing a difference of opinion. Assistant coach Orval Penner took over but could not change the fortunes of the club. They ended the season in last place with 1 win, 1 tie and 6 losses.

The Roughriders continued to operate as a community club for a number of years. Contributing to the club's success were, among other, former Uke stalwarts such Bob Babin, Alex Horbow and others.

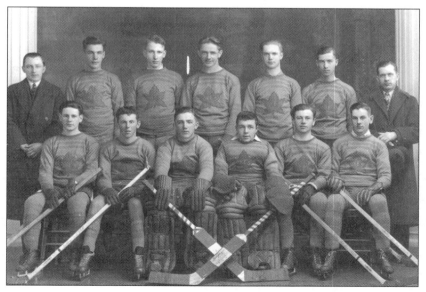

*Lakehead Ukrainian Athletic Club Ukes juvenile hockey team, c.1938*

# TORONTO

## CARPATHIAN SKI CLUB

In the spring of 1955, Bohdan Jaciw gathered a group of skiing enthusiasts at his home in Toronto with the intent of organizing a ski club. Most of those attending were experienced skiers. Many could trace their skiing roots to the Carpathian mountains of Ukraine or to the Alps of Germany. Most were also at some point in time associated with the Carpathian Ski Club (KLK), either in Ukraine, or while interned in the displaced persons camps in post-war Germany. (The acronym "KLK," by which the club has been popularly known not only in Europe but also in North America, reflects its Ukrainian name - Karpatskyi Leschetarskyi Klub.) It is not surprising, therefore, that the club organized that day in 1955 became known as the Carpathian Ski Club - Toronto. Bohdan Jaciw was elected its first president.

*Carpathian Ski Club logo*

The original Carpathian Ski Club was founded in 1926 in the city of Lviv. While alpine skiing was the primary pursuit of the club, members were also very active in track and field, swimming, and tennis. After the end of World War II, many members of the Carpathian Ski

Club found themselves scattered throughout the displaced persons camps of Germany. In a very short period of time, they rejuvenated their club and began organizing sport activities. With the majestic and challenging Alps adjacent to many of the camps, skiing became ever more popular. In addition, some became interested in mountain climbing. On September 1, 1947, KLK members Ihor Suchowersky and Bohdan Jaciw became the first Ukrainians to scale France's Mont Blanc, at 4,807 metres, the highest mountain in the Alps. Towards the end of that turbulent decade, club members once again embarked towards the unknown. Canada, United States, and Australia were but some of the destinations. Those that settled in North America revived the Carpathian Ski Club in New York City in 1953 and two years later in Toronto.

*Bohdan Jaciw (left) and Ihor Suchowersky (right) at the summit of Mt. Blanc, 1947*

The Carpathian Ski Club of Toronto began its outdoor activities during the winter of 1955-56. Almost every weekend, club members would seek out the ski runs of southern Ontario. There they worked on the technical aspect of the sport and also partook in recreational skiing. In January of 1956, club members B. Jaciw, S. Maziar, and G. Hoshowatiuk took part in the second annual inter-club ski championships of the Association of Ukrainian Sport Clubs of North America (USCAK) at Whiteface Mountain in New York State. S. Maziar was the club's top skier, winning two medals - a gold and a silver. In March, the Carpathian Ski Club of Toronto organized its first club championship. Competition was held in the slalom, downhill, and the combined event, at both the junior and senior levels.

For a number of years, the Carpathian Ski Club of New York organized an "Autumn" social at the Ukrainian resort *Soyuzivka* in the Catskill Mountains of New York State. One of the features of the event was a target shooting competition. Participants tested their skills in archery and small calibre shooting. Toronto KLK member Lidia Palij won the women's small calibre event in 1957 and 1959. She placed second in 1956 and 1958.

Under the enthusiastic guidance of club president S. Maziar, the 1956-57 season began with a ten-day skiing trip to Mont Tremblant in Quebec. In January, the club held its championships. That year the championships had an added significance. A short while earlier, the Carpathian Ski Club had become a member of the Canadian Amateur Ski Association and its members became eligible to compete in regional, provincial and national championships. As a result, winners of the club championship would advance to the class "C" Southern Ontario Championships. Competing in the junior division at his first Southern Ontario Championships, Steve Bukojemsky had a top-ten finish. In the senior division Maziar had a top-twenty finish.

The following winter, the club once again headed to Mont Tremblant. Unfortunately, there was no snow on the mountain. This prompted the participants to travel to Lac Beuport where good snow conditions existed. A number of skiers from Montreal and New York City joined the group. The Toronto KLK partook in its first competition of the season in January when it travelled to Whiteface Mountain. There it met the Carpathian Ski Club of New York in a friendly competition. The event was significant because it was the first Association of Ukrainian Sport Clubs of North America (USCAK) sanctioned ski meet that offered competition for women. Five KLK members took part in the Southern Ontario Championships that spring at Collingwood. The best result was S. Maziar's seventh-place finish in the slalom. Before the snow melted, club members once again travelled to Whiteface Mountain. Competing in the USCAK inter-club championships, the skiers from Toronto placed second in the overall team standings. G. Hoshowatiuk won the only gold medal for the club.

Carpathian Ski Club members also partook in kayaking, although they did not represent the club in sanctioned competition. In the summer of 1958, Steve Maziar and Steve Bukojemsky placed second in a pairs event on the Hudson River in New York State.

The primary interest of the club was skiing and most of the club's resources were committed to that end. In the early years, experienced skiers coached the beginners. Later a number of members attended instructors' courses sponsored by the Canadian Amateur Ski Association. The expertise they acquired was appreciated for many years. During the week, clinics were organized, films were shown, and plans were made. At one point in time, the club entertained the idea of purchasing a ski resort. The plan, though, never materialized. A number of other plans also did not materialize, among them organizing groups dedicated to water skiing and fishing.

The 1958-59 season included a trip to Whiteface Mountain, Sugarbush, and Stowe. A friendly competition with the club's New York counterpart was held at Lake Placid. A few weeks later, at the USCAK inter-club championships held at Lake Placid, KLK duplicated its second-place finish from the previous year. Lucy Drunewych led the medal parade with two gold and a silver. The season concluded with a trip to Mont Tremblant and Mont Plante.

At the 1960 Southern Ontario Championships, Lucy Drunewych won the women's combined trophy. Drunewych, who started to ski only four years earlier, placed second in both the slalom and the downhill to accumulate enough points for the overall title. In the men's class "C" competition, Steve Bukojemsky placed fourth in the downhill and fifth in the slalom. At the Ukrainian inter-club championships, the Carpathian Ski Club of Toronto finally won its first overall title. The club was led by L. Drunewych, who won the overall individual women's crown.

The 1960-61 season began with an expedition to Sugarbush in Vermont. About 40 members of KLK Toronto and New York took part in the skiing activities.

The 1962-63 season included a trip to the Laurentians and to Whiteface Mountain. The club championships were held at Owen Sound.

*Carpathian Ski Club, 1959*

The Carpathian Ski Club of Toronto welcomed all those interested in skiing, regardless of skill, age, or competitive experience. It was primarily a family-oriented sports club. In particular, the major ski outings to the Laurentians and the American northeast, as well as the weekend jaunts in Ontario, provided families with an ideal opportunity to enjoy the outdoors together with other Ukrainians. Member families treasured this characteristic of the club, and even though the club did not have a formal summer program, they embarked on many camping trips together.

The 1964 Ukrainian inter-club championships at Whiteface Mountain were cut short by bad weather. On the first day of competition, the slalom events were successfully completed. Overnight rain washed away the snow and all further competition was cancelled. Lucy Drunewych won the slalom in a time of 44.9 seconds. The overall club trophy was not awarded that year.

During the club's tenth season of operation in 1964-65, membership swelled to more than 80. The club partook in the 1965 USCAK inter-club championships at Mont Blanc in Quebec as the defending title holder. Once again, L. Drunewych was the club's star performer, placing first in the slalom and second in the combined. The club, though, ceded the championship trophy to New York. That year, club members entertained the idea of amalgamating with the Ukrainian Tennis Club Lviv as many belonged to both clubs. A merger did not occur.

The 1965-66 season began with a masquerade ball at *Watra* resort in Durham, Ontario. During the Christmas break, the club skied at Mont Tremblant and Mont Blanc. The club championships were held at Beaver Valley, with Borys Hul and Lucy Drunewych winning the men's and women's titles respectively. In February, the annual inter-club championships were held at Mont Blanc. Competing in adverse conditions with the temperature dropping to -32°C (-25°F), KLK Toronto won back the overall club title. The season concluded with a poorly attended trip to Mt. Sutton in the Eastern Townships of Quebec.

During the 1966-67 ski season, the camaraderie that banded the KLK members started to dissipate. More often than not, club members went skiing on their own or in small groups. Only a few individuals attended the Mont Ste-Anne trip. Nevertheless, the Association of Ukrainian Sport Clubs of North America (USCAK) inter-club championships held at St. Jovite were well-attended, since, for the first time since their inception, a junior category was contested. Many KLK members who had children of junior age were particularly pleased with this development. The conditions for competition were even more adverse than in the previous year, with temperatures dropping to -41°C (-41°F) on the wind-swept mountain. The Carpathian Ski Club of Toronto overcame the cold and repeated as club champions.

The 1968 USCAK inter-club championships were held in Easton, New York. The event was almost cancelled as rain washed away most of the snow. The organizers nevertheless decided to proceed with the competition. KLK Toronto fared poorly, placing fifth in the overall club standings. The club wrapped up the season with a very successful trip to Mont Ste-Anne.

As in previous years, the 1968-69 season began with a traditional outing during the Christmas break to the Laurentians. Record snow falls made the skiing most enjoyable. Club members also journeyed to Killington, Vermont, to partake in the Ukrainian inter-club championships.

Reliable Lucy Drunewych was Toronto's best performer, winning the overall women's title. The other club members did not fare as well, and the club placed fourth in the standings. The season ended with a trip to Mont Tremblant in March and to Mont Ste-Anne in April.

In the early 1970s, the Carpathian Ski Club of Toronto changed its role. Group outings and trips were discontinued, as were most social events. The club became a loose federation of individuals, each pursuing one's own goals in sport and in organized Ukrainian community life. They were, though, tied to the club by tradition and a sense of history. Those KLK members who were also members of Plast began organizing ski camps for Plast youth. Many Plast members and others who wanted to compete in the Ukrainian inter-club competitions would do so now under the name of Carpathian Ski Club of Toronto. In this format, the Carpathian Ski Club of Toronto placed third at the 1972 and 1975 USCAK inter-club championships, and second in 1976 and 1980. In similar fashion, George Tatarsky won the USCAK junior inter-club tennis championship in 1976.

# ST. JOSAPHAT'S

B uilt in 1910, St. Josaphat's Church was the centre of Ukrainian spiritual and community life during the early years of Ukrainian settlement in Toronto. Activities included choir and drama groups, Ukrainian language courses, secular and ecclesiastic associations, and a Prosvita.

In 1932, St. Josaphat's expanded its activities into sport when it became one of two founding members of the Ukrainian Softball League.

In the fall of 1934, fourteen-year-old Sonny Wilson (born Myroslaw Woloshinski) organized a hockey team of Ukrainian youngsters, members of the St. Josaphat's congregation. Wilson also coached and played on the team. In its inaugural year, the St. Josaphat's Ukes won the Toronto Minor Bantam Championship.

At the conclusion of the hockey season, Wilson organized and managed a softball team that competed in a Toronto church league. "Sonny made it a rule to organize only young men of Ukrainian descent for either hockey or baseball teams, for in that way he was able to publicize their heritage."[9] By 19, Sonny Wilson was playing hockey for the New York Stock Exchange, refereeing hockey, and umpiring Class B baseball. His ambition to officiate major league professional hockey and baseball never materialized. He died in his twenties during a hockey practice.

In 1938, the title of the Ukrainian Softball Leagues was won by St. Josaphat's. Peter Doros managed the club while Peter Wasylyk was the club's president.

# ST. VLADIMIR'S / SUMK / ODUM

Sport at St. Vladimir's Ukrainian Orthodox Cathedral was most often associated with two youth groups that operated under the auspices of the church - the Canadian Ukrainian Youth Association (SUMK) and the Ukrainian National Democratic League (ODUM).

In 1932, the Ukrainian Softball League was organized in Toronto. The founding members immediately set out to assist the established Ukrainian organizations and churches to organize softball teams. SUMK responded by establishing a team and entering it into competition. The team competed for a number of years in the league.

In 1949, the St. Vladimir's softball team, which competed in the Bellwoods Park League, won the District Toronto Softball League Championship. The team was managed by D. Sadowy, coached by P. Yellow and captained by P. Szoldra.

During the winter of 1950-51, a St. Vlad's basketball team played in a city league.

For a number of years in the late 1950s, a men's volleyball team competed in the senior "B" division of the Ontario Volleyball Association league in Toronto. After the 1960-61 season, ODUM terminated its sponsorship of the team citing rising costs. Team members Paul Kelembet and Valentin Polakiwsky decided to keep the team together and sought out new sponsorship. In the fall of 1961 the club became affiliated with the University Settlement House Community Centre.

In the early 1960s, a junior men's basketball team competed in the TREC church league. The team was organized by T. Ilenchuk.

In the fall of 1966, the general meeting of the Association of Ukrainian Sport Clubs of North America (USCAK) - Canadian division recommended that a volleyball league be formed in Toronto. ODUM was one of the city's youth groups that entered teams in men's and women's competition. The men's team placed third in the inaugural season of competition.

In the 1970s, ODUM operated a team in the Ukrainian Floor Hockey League, while in the

1980s, a men's team competed in the Ukrainian Slo-Pitch Softball League and a women's team played in the Ukrainian-Canadian Girls Slo-Pitch League.

*ODUM softball team, 1987*

In the late 1970s, to instill an enthusiasm for sport and competition, to provide basic instruction, and to get its young members into shape, ODUM often organized two-week "sports" camps during the summer. Sports such as basketball, golf, soccer, swimming, tennis, track and field, volleyball and water polo were practised. The camps were widely attended and well-liked by the participants.

# SPORT ASSOCIATION *UKRAINA*

After the end of World War II, Toronto became one of the prime destinations for Ukrainians from the displaced persons (DP) camps of Europe. Among those arriving in the city were athletes, coaches, and sports administrators from pre-war Ukraine. Many of these individuals had organized a network of sport clubs in the displaced persons camps of post-war Europe.

On May 16, 1948, a group of the recently arrived sport enthusiasts met at the Prosvita Society Hall in Toronto to organize a sport club. These individuals had the desire to continue their European sporting experience in Canada; they longed for organized soccer and volleyball. Joining established clubs was out of the question. The Ukrainians were unfamiliar with the language of these clubs, and many believed that their stay in Canada was temporary and that in a short period of time, they would return to an independent Ukraine.

On that day, the Ukrainian Sport Club Skala came into being. William Boytchuk, the initiator of the meeting, assumed the presidency. Assisting him were Stephen Boytchuk, Oleksander Derzhko, Peter Chaplynsky, Ivan Mocherniak, Stephen Yarema, and Oleksander Zeltway. At the time, no one even envisioned that the club would leave a significant mark on sport in Toronto and Canada. Over the years, hundreds of aspirants and athletes competed on the club's soccer, volleyball, basketball, softball, hockey, table tennis, and chess teams. The success of the club's soccer teams peaked in the 1950s, while the men's volleyball team won the 1975 national championship. Participating in the activities of the association, and contributing to its success almost entirely, were post-war immigrants and their descendants.

On May 30, 1948, a subsequent meeting was held at which the club was formally established. Skala's name was changed to Sport Association Ukraina in honour of the most eminent sports club in Western Ukraine prior to the war, the Sport Association Ukraina of Lviv. William Boytchuk was elected president. The remainder of the executive included Oleksander Derzhko, vice-president; Volodymyr Stoyko, secretary; Ivan Chaykiwsky, treasurer; and Mykhailo Kopach, manager. Semen Mackevych, an established immigrant, sport enthusiast, and an individual who tirelessly devoted his time to help the new immigrants, was named the club's honourary president. Steadfast administrative and organizational support during the club's formative years was provided by Alexander Chykalo.

During the summer of 1948 a soccer team was assembled. The team played 5 exhibition matches, winning 3 and losing 2. In addition, a volleyball and basketball team competed in exhibition matches. The club also organized house league table tennis and chess tournaments. Twenty-nine club members organized and partook in these activities. In the fall of 1948, a second general meeting was held at which the association accepted the constitution of the Council of Physical Culture. This council was established by Ukrainian refugees in the DP camps of Germany. Its mandate was to coordinate the activities of Ukrainian sports club in the free world.

*Sport Association Ukraina logo*

In early 1949, SA Ukraina had a fallout with the executive of the Prosvita Society. The sports club considered itself an independent entity while Prosvita considered the club an affiliate. As a result, SA Ukraina left Prosvita Society Hall and rented "club house" facilities at the Ukrainian-owned Duke of Connaught Hotel. During the first half of 1949, the number of members in the sports association increased rapidly to 149, necessitating yet another move in the summer to more spacious premises rented on Bathurst Street. All of the aforementioned locations were used primarily for administrative purposes; they lacked athletic facilities. During the winter months, the club operated its sport program at a gymnasium rented from the United Church.

The strong showing of the soccer club in 1948 and avid fan support expedited the club's admission into the Ontario Football Association in May of 1949. The SA Ukraina team was assigned to the second division of the Toronto and District Football Association. It finished the 1949 regular season in first place with a record 25 wins, 4 ties, and 4 losses, and was awarded the Daily Star Cup. SA Ukraina also won the Loblaws Cup in the playoffs. The team represented Toronto in an inter-city competition with Hamilton, winning the Halliwell Cup. On the soccer pitch, the team was led by Roman Panczyszyn. The striker scored 42 goals - one third of SA Ukraina's total output.

SA Ukraina also fielded a junior and a bantam team in 1949. The junior club placed fifth out of nine teams in a junior league. The team's centre and captain, Yaroslaw Sokolyk, became the first Ukrainian of the post-war migration to gain an all-star berth when he was selected to represent Ontario. The bantams, coached by O. Zeltway, played exhibition matches during the summer.

During the winter of 1948-49, SA Ukraina entered a team in the newly formed four-team Ukrainian Basketball League of Toronto. Ukraina placed first in league play. It then won the playoffs and the right to represent Canada at the Ukrainian Youth League of North America (UYLNA) Sports Rally at Rochester, New York. SA Ukraina, though, did not compete at the rally. The newly elected management of the club concluded that it was inappropriate to send a team primarily consisting of Lithuanian ringers to a Ukrainian youth rally.

The use of recruited non-Ukrainians on SA Ukraina's basketball team was a precedent that would be repeated many times. For many years, the major objective of the club's management was to field the strongest possible teams, particularly in soccer, teams that would win championships. Successful teams would market the club and attract fans. More important, successful clubs would promote and foster the recognition of Ukraine and Ukrainians in the community.

To win championships, no effort was spared to secure the finest players. Stars arriving from

Europe or transferring from other clubs were guaranteed jobs and compensation for their services. Non-Ukrainian athletes were recruited. Much emphasis was also placed on setting up a minor league system that in the future would feed the senior club. One year, SA Ukraina operated seven such clubs. The minor league system was usually restricted to Ukrainian youth. In a fortnight, the management of SA Ukraina began operating the association as if it was a semi-professional enterprise, rather than a community club.

Not all of the club's non-Ukrainian athletes were recruited. Some joined the ranks of SA Ukraina because of Slavic roots. Only a few of the ethnic communities in Toronto had sport clubs that were capable of fielding soccer teams. Some of the Slavic athletes from communities that did not have their own teams often preferred to join a club such as Ukraina rather than an Italian, Irish, or Canadian community club.

During the winter of 1949-50, SA Ukraina also fielded a men's volleyball team that won the Toronto Intermediate League title. At the provincial championship, SA Ukraina was undefeated in five starts to win the Dr. R. Brooke Championship Cup. A women's volleyball club was organized but only played exhibition matches as at the time there was no organized women's league. The chess club, numbering some 30 enthusiasts, placed second in team competition at the Toronto championships, while Ivan Teodorovych-Suk placed third in individual competition. The club's table tennis team placed second in the intermediate team competition at the city championships.

The success of the senior SA Ukraina soccer club in 1949 resulted in a promotion to the premier National Soccer League for the 1950 season. At about that time, SA Ukraina entered negotiations with the Ukrainian Youth Association SUM, Prosvita Society, the League for Liberation of Ukraine, and the Homin Ukrainy Publishing Co. to jointly purchase a building.

The debut in the National Soccer League proved to be a difficult one. The final standings confirmed that SA Ukraina was not yet on par with the stronger clubs in the league. Ukraina placed sixth out of eight teams with a record of 4 wins, 1 tie and 9 losses. Roman Panczyszyn continued to lead the team in scoring in 1950. Three years later, a severe knee injury prematurely terminated the star's soccer career.

The year 1950 came to an end with SA Ukraina and its partners purchasing a building on Bathurst Street. This alleviated a major problem for the association as membership had swelled to 471 and it was becoming extremely difficult to operate out of a leased facility. At the same time, SA Ukraina expanded its activities beyond sport. The club organized socials and dances. It participated in Ukrainian cultural and political activities in the city and it invited guest speakers to lecture on varied topics. It raised funds for the less fortunate immigrants in Canada and for Ukrainian war invalids in Europe. Member Roman Kostiuk was particularly active in this charitable work.

During the winter of 1950-51, the men's table tennis team, consisting of M. Trofymovych, V. Bilous, and E. Stepko, won the city team championship. In individual competition Bilous placed second, while the team of Trofymovych and Bilous won the doubles event. The women's table tennis team advanced to the city final but lost to Firebanks. The women's volleyball team, anticipating the formation of a league, continued to play exhibition matches. One of the men's volleyball teams placed second in a senior league while the other club placed third in the intermediate league. A boxing team was organized. It competed in one exhibition match, losing to Central YMCA 6-4.

The chess club entered two teams in the city club championships. The senior level team won their championship and the intermediate team placed second in their division.

During the 1951 soccer season, SA Ukraina improved its game considerably, finishing the schedule in third place with 13 wins, 3 ties and 8 losses. In the playoffs for the National Soccer League Cup, SA Ukraina won its opening game. The other two semi-finalists chose not to play their match as it was very late in the fall. As a result, SA Ukraina won its first National League Cup, albeit by default.

The junior SA Ukraina soccer team won the league championship and the Ontarion Cup. It registered 14 wins in 17 starts. The bantam team also had a winning season, with a record of 7 wins, 1 tie and 2 losses.

During the winter of 1951-52, SA Ukraina continued to operate table tennis, volleyball and chess programs. The men's table tennis team competed in the top "major" division; they finished the season in third place. The team of Trofymovych and Bilous won the doubles event. The intermediate men's team and the women's team competed sporadically. The intermediate men's volleyball team placed second, while the senior team failed to win one game. The intermediate chess club placed second in its division while the senior club settled for third place.

For the senior SA Ukraina soccer team, the 1952 season was a trying one, as 29 players at one time or another played with the club. The schedule concluded with SA Ukraina sitting in fifth place out of ten teams with a record of 9 wins, 3 ties and 6 losses. The club's only success came when it won the Arnold Cup.

The reserve team, which competed under the name Ukrainian Falcons, folded mid-way through the season. Too many of its players were called up by the senior team. Conversely, the junior and bantam teams won their respective league championships and Cups.

The departure of some SA Ukraina athletes resulted in the partial collapse of the association's winter program. The senior volleyball team not only failed to win a game, but often defaulted because of a lack of players. The intermediate team played with some success, but the club was without a coach or a manager. The table tennis team placed second in league competition but failed to win any individual or doubles trophies. Only the intermediate chess club, led by Dmytro Kulyk, won the city championship.

During the 1953 soccer season the team played well, finishing the regular schedule in first place with a record of 11 wins, 3 ties and 2 losses. The club then won the playoffs. SA Ukraina was the first club created by the post-war immigration to attain the double success.

The success of Toronto's SA Ukraina and that of Montreal Italia (which won 42 games of the 43 it contested) prompted the Canadian Soccer Association to match these two teams in an exhibition game. SA Ukraina won the encounter 3-1 and was thereby recognized as the best team in Eastern Canada, and by some as the best team in the country. Midfielder Ostap Steckiw was SA Ukraina's playing coach during the year while Nick Waller, former manager of Sudbury Sitch, handled the managerial duties.

The junior soccer team captured the Toronto Cup by winning the Toronto city championship. The bantams and juveniles played only exhibition matches.

As part of the club's fifth anniversary celebrations, SA Ukraina played an exhibition match against the Ukrainian Levy (Lions) club of Chicago. Thousands of fans watched Ukraina defeat the Lions 6-1. The season concluded with the blessing of the association's flag and a banquet at which the guest speaker was Danylo Skoropadsky, the heir to hetman Pavlo Skoropadsky, head of a short-lived Ukrainian monarchist government in 1918.

By 1953, SA Ukraina senior soccer club had become a significant community entity. The Ukrainian population of Toronto rallied around its team. If one could not help the team on the field, then one would from the spectator stands. At times, some spectators even found it necessary to help out on the field by tangling with opposing players or referees. During the 1950s, it was common to have thousands of fans cheering SA Ukraina at games. In the years 1952-1960, more than 1.1 million fans attended SA Ukraina soccer games.

During the winter of 1953-54, the men's volleyball team placed second while the women's team under the leadership of Iryna Shumsky, finished in fourth spot. The table tennis team failed to complete the season because of a lack of players.

During the 1954 season, the soccer team finished in first place with a record of 11 wins, 3 ties and 2 losses. Lev Dyczkowsky led the team in scoring with 26 goals. The club, though, failed in its bid to win the playoffs. During the year SA Ukraina played several exhibition matches with Ukrainian and non-Ukrainian clubs in Canada and the United States. Some of the clubs that Ukraina faced were the Manitoba Selects, Institute Prosvita Athletic Club of Winnipeg, Slovak from Chicago, Plast-Pryat from Philadelphia, Chernyk from Detroit, Ukraina from Montreal, and Sitch from Elizabeth, New Jersey. The club was once again coached by O. Steckiw and managed by N. Waller.

*Photo courtesy Wolodymyr Tracz, Anne Photo Studios*

*Sport Association Ukraina soccer team,1953 National League Champions*

SA Ukraina also fielded two junior teams and a bantam team in 1954. Not one of these teams completed the season. The teams lacked coaches and managers.

During the winter of 1954-55, the men's and the women's volleyball teams finished in fourth position. The table tennis team was relegated to exhibition games because it failed to submit its registration papers on time. The chess team placed third in the city club competition. In individual play, Ivan Teodorovych-Suk won the provincial title and placed third at the national championship.

SA Ukraina repeated as National Soccer League champions in 1955. The club's record was 11 wins, 5 ties and 2 losses. Once again, though, the club failed to win the playoffs. Myron Bereza led the team in scoring with 23 goals. Ostap Steckiw was the club's playing coach. The reserve team also won its division with a record of 10 wins, 3 ties and 1 loss. The junior team placed second while the bantams won their division. The reserve and the junior team were coached by Walter Zakaluzny. Representing SA Ukraina on the board of the National Soccer League was John Luczkiw. The former vice-president of the association held the post for a number of years.

The association organized a soccer school for youth that year with members S. Romanec, O. Steckiw, and W. Zakaluzny providing the instructions. The school was short-lived as few enrolled.

One of the mandates of the SA Ukraina executive elected in late 1955 was to expand the activities of the youth soccer teams and of the volleyball and chess clubs. The executive was aware that this would cost money but decided to proceed by reducing outlays on the senior soccer team. In 1955 for instance, SA Ukraina's revenue was $27,002 from gate receipts, caroling, dances, socials, festivals, sponsorships, donations, and membership dues from some 500 individuals. Expenditures amounted to $26,949, of which $9,812 was allocated for the compensation of players on the senior team, $6,507 for league dues and field rentals for the senior team, $735 for the operation of the reserve and the junior teams and $9,895 for other expenses.

The new executive succeeded in attaining its objective. In cooperation with the Ukrainian Youth Association SUM, SA Ukraina organized two bantam soccer teams that competed under the names of Strila and Chayka. Both teams won their respective leagues. The junior SA Ukraina team also won its championship.

On December 24, 1955, SA Ukraina hosted a meeting at which the Association of Ukrainian Sport Clubs of North America (USCAK) was established. Among the proposed objectives of the association was the coordination of sport activity in North America. SA Ukraina became a charter member of USCAK, and also of the Canadian division of USCAK that was launched in May of 1956 with the help of the Toronto sport club. Over the years, SA Ukraina members served on the executives of USCAK and its Canadian division.

The senior soccer club lost a number of star players to transfers during the winter of 1955-56. As a result, the roster of the first team in 1956 was filled with players from the reserve team. Most of the replacements had much enthusiasm but little experience. The year also saw Oleksander Skocen return to SA Ukraina in the capacity of coach to replace Ostap Steckiw who left to coach Trident and play for the Ukrainian American Sports Club (UASC) of Rochester.

Stephen Sohuyko, a member of the sports association, passed a series of exams in 1956 that qualified him to referee games in the National Soccer League. Some 15 years later he would be promoted to Referee-in-Chief of the league.

Another major task faced by the executive that year was the question of facilities. The executive was convinced that without a club house with a gymnasium and the required equipment and amenities, the sports club could not expect to maintain or increase its youth membership. SA Ukraina wanted to build its own facilities while the other co-owners of the structure on

Bathurst Street wanted to build a multi-purpose cultural and sports centre. They argued that should SA Ukraina proceed on its own, the plans of the Ukrainian Youth Association SUM and others may not be realized. The sport association eventually settled on the proposal of its partners. A short time later, a large property at 83-85 Christie Street was jointly purchased, with SA Ukraina being a minor shareholder. When the sport association moved into the new facilities in 1957, it was obligated to pay on a monthly basis a $250 rental and renovation fee.

During the winter of 1956-57, SA Ukraina fielded five volleyball teams: two men's, two women's and a junior men's. With the exception of the junior team that won the provincial championship, the remaining teams did not enjoy success on the courts. Walter Stochansky, a future international referee, coached the two men's teams. The table tennis team existed in name only.

In April, member of the chess club organized an open championship for Ukrainians in the Toronto area. Intended as an annual event, it was contested irregularly over the next 20 years. Andrij Usyp won the inaugural tournament while Dmytro Kulyk, a member of the association's chess club, won the Toronto city championship that year.

The soccer season was, as in the previous years, controversial; compensation was once again a source of disagreement between the management and the players. To compound the problem, five players threatened to walk out on the team unless a stronger roster was assembled. The fans were also demanding a more competitive team. Management eventually capitulated and three former stars returned to the club midway through the season. Having lost its authority over the soccer club, the executive resigned shortly afterwards. The soccer team finished the season with a record of 8 wins, 5 ties and 14 losses.

That summer, youth development co-ordinator Myroslaw Osadchuk organized two bantam and two juvenile soccer teams. He also expanded much effort to organize a bantam league within the auspices of the National Soccer League. Some 70 youngsters participated in this program which was run by O. Skocen. M. Osadchuk resigned later in the year after vociferously objecting to the decisions of the executive with regards to the senior team.

In 1957, SA Ukraina members Myron Bereza and Walter Zakaluzny and former member Ostap Steckiw were selected to represent Canada at the World Cup qualifying matches. The threesome played in games against Mexico and the United States. The selection of the three to the national team was a good indication of the level of soccer played by the club. In addition, over the years M. Bereza, L. Dyczkowsky, W. Dyczkowsky, H. Rygailo, A. Shapka, O. Steckiw and W. Zakaluzny were named to the Ontario all-star team for matches against touring European clubs. In 1956, O. Skocen was named coach of the provincial All-stars for a game against Aberdeen of Scotland, while O. Steckiw coached the provincial All-stars in games against

Mexico in 1958 and Rapid of Vienna a year later.

The new club house facilities at Christie Street became operational in 1957 and quickly became popular with SA Ukraina members, fans and athletes. A tradition evolved to gather after senior soccer team games and discuss the course of events over snacks and refreshments. In addition, the club house had two pool tables and card tables which were used on a regular basis by club members. The high rental cost of the facilities resulted in SA Ukraina returning to 140 Bathurst Street in 1962.

In the fall of 1957, university student Borys Sorokiwsky organized a basketball team at SA Ukraina which consisted of a number of players who previously saw action with Trident. The team was one of 58 that competed at the intermediate "A" level during the winter of 1957-58. Led by captain John Dacyshyn, future member of Canada's Olympic team, the club surprised everyone by winning the city championship. In the opening round of the provincial playoffs, SA Ukraina won its opening game against Niagara Falls. In the second game the club walked off the court after a series of questionable calls by the referees. For its action, the team was suspended from further play.

On the volleyball courts, five teams were once again fielded. The men's team, competing at the Senior "B" level, completed the schedule undefeated and as a result was promoted to the "A" division for the next season. Both the junior and intermediate men's teams won their respective league championships, but failed to advance past the opening rounds of the provincial championship. The senior women's team placed third in league play and at the provincial championship. Competing in Chicago, the team won the inaugural Ukrainian inter-club championship of North America sanctioned by the Association of Ukrainian Sport Clubs of North America (USCAK).

During the summer of 1958, SA Ukraina fielded six soccer teams. In addition to the first division team, a reserve, junior, two bantam and a midget team represented the association. Ostap Steckiw coached the senior and the reserve teams while W. Zakaluzny handled the other clubs.

The senior soccer club competed in the expanded 15-team inter-provincial National Soccer League. It placed fifth in the standings with a record of 17 wins, 3 ties and 8 losses. The club qualified for the playoffs but failed to make an impression. In conjunction with SA Ukraina's tenth anniversary celebrations, a friendly match was played against the touring Admira FC Vienna. The visitors won the game 3-0. The play of SA Ukraina impressed an official of the Austrian sports federation and he proposed to arrange a tour of the Far East for the SA Ukraina soccer team. The executive of SA Ukraina agreed to the proposal and the Canadian Soccer Association sanctioned the tour. The trip, though, never materialized; the athletes could not afford to take an extended period of time from work to partake in the trip.

The senior soccer team also participated in the fifth anniversary celebrations of the Ukrainian Sports Association Strila of Oshawa.

During the winter of 1958-59, the intermediate "A" basketball team played well and qualified for the playoffs. It won the semi-final round but lost in the city final. The senior women's volleyball team finished the season in third place while the intermediate club folded after a string of defeats. The senior men's team found play at the "A" level extremely competitive. The team won 2 of 14 starts and was relegated back to the "B" division for the following year. The intermediate volleyball team qualified for the playoffs. The chess club continued to hold house league tournaments during the winter months.

From the perspective of SA Ukraina fans, the 1959 soccer season was extremely interesting because the outcome of games could never be predicted. The club defeated all the top teams in the league but, unexplainably, it lost to all the weak teams. As a result, Ukraina had to settle for third place, 4 points back of league leading Cantalia, with a record of 14 wins, 5 ties and 7 losses. At the conclusion of the season, private entrepreneurs formed an indoor league featuring six players a side. The organizers promised each team $1,500 per game. SA Ukraina played four games before the venture failed because of financial difficulties.

The senior soccer team played two exhibition matches in the United States in 1959. In New York, SA Ukraina defeated the professional champion of the United States, the Jewish club Hakoah. The following day SA Ukraina lost to Philadelphia's Trident.

The bantam "A" team won its division and then defeated Barrie to win the Globe and Mail Cup.

During the winter of 1959-60 Ivan Teodorovych-Suk won the provincial chess title. The chess club held a number of in-house tournaments. The volleyball teams did not register any significant results, with the exception of the senior women's club that repeated as the Ukrainian inter-club champion of North America. In March, the association organized a volleyball tournament which attracted seven clubs, five men's and two women's, from Toronto and St. Catharines. Trident won the men's competition while SA Ukraina won the women's.

Playing coach O. Steckiw attempted to strengthen the senior soccer club in 1960 by recruiting a number of key players. Among these were Herbert Pohl, a former junior all-star goalkeeper in Poland, forward Leonid Dowhaluk, a former Austrian junior all-star, and defenceman Sean Burke formerly of Shamrock Rovers and an Irish international. Also playing on the team were three loans from Philadelphia's Trident: Andy Racz, Alex Czayka and Mike Noha.

The anticipated arrival of the Soviet club Leningrad Zenit to play an exhibition match against an Ontario All-Star team resulted in a major conflict between the executive of SA Ukraina and William Simpson, president of the Ontario Soccer Federation.

*Sport Association Ukraina soccer team in action*

Ukraina playing coach Ostap Steckiw was appointed coach of the Ontario All-Star team for the match against the visiting Soviet club. At first, the management of SA Ukraina agreed with the appointment. A few days before the match, though, the executive changed its mind. As a result, Steckiw resigned from the appointment and from SA Ukraina. Four additional SA Ukraina players named to the all-star team were also denied permission to play the Soviet team.

The senior soccer team completed the 1960 season in sixth place, recording 12 wins, 4 ties and 10 losses.

A track and field team was assembled that summer for competition at the inaugural Ukrainian inter-club championship of North America sanctioned by the Association of Ukrainian Sport Clubs of North America (USCAK). SA Ukraina athletes amassed 89 points to place sixth in the overall point tally.

In the fall of 1960, Ostap Wynnyckyj organized a juvenile (under-18) hockey team and had it registered with the Toronto Hockey League. The club played a number of games representing SA Ukraina. The club left Ukraina after it was discovered that over half of its roster was made up of non-Ukrainian athletes.

The men's volleyball team once again won the "B" division and was promoted to the "A" division. The women's volleyball team was reorganized with an emphasis placed on youth. As a result the team struggled all season. The women nevertheless managed to place second at the Ukrainian inter-club competition.

Nineteen sixty-one was one of the most difficult years in the club's history. The association was $5,000 in debt and had not yet signed any soccer players for the coming season. Unable to find a sufficient number of quality players, the club sent coach Owen Willoghby to the British Isles to recruit players; Willoghby came back with five. During the season, accusations of favouritism were levelled at the coach which resulted in his departure. Some players refused to play while others demanded their immediate transfer. By the time the season was over, 24 players appeared in games for SA Ukraina.

In addition to the club's internal problems, the viability of the National Soccer League was tested when a number of its teams jumped to the new Eastern Canada Professional Soccer League. The new league significantly reduced the number of fans attending NSL games, and reduced revenues for the clubs. By the end of the year, Ukraina's debt increased to $13,000. To alleviate this predicament, the club embarked on a major membership drive. In a short period of time, 180 new paying members were signed.

The senior soccer team, in the midst of these controversies and difficulties, finished the season in fifth place and qualified for the playoffs. In the semi-finals, SA Ukraina defeated the White Eagles 2-0 and 3-2. In the championship final, SA Ukraina defeated Hungaria twice by an identical 1-0 score to win the Labatt's Cup.

The financial woes of the association resulted in the under-funding of the bantam and midget soccer teams, and the poor performance of the teams was in part blamed on this. The bantams and midgets were coached and managed by W. Boytchuk, B. Hul, W. Rybak, O. Skocen and N. Waller.

During the winter of 1961-62 both the men's and the women's volleyball teams won the Ukrainian inter-club championship. In Toronto league play, the women placed fourth as did the men.

In the spring of 1962, SA Ukraina attempted to join the Eastern Canada Professional Soccer League; participation in the stronger league would increase gate revenues and make the club more viable. SA Ukraina even co-opted Member of Provincial Parliament John Yaremko and *Toronto Telegram* publisher John Basset to lobby on its behalf. The efforts were in vain. The league admitted four new members but not SA Ukraina. As a result, the club continued to play in the National Soccer League.

SA Ukraina finished the 1962 soccer season in second place with a record of 14 wins, 6 ties and 2 losses. The club scored 45 goals and was scored against 9 times. It was coached by W. Zakaluzny and managed by O. Zeltway and M. Shmotolocha. The association fielded two minor teams which were coached and managed by W. Trutiak, B. Hul and G. Nasadiuk.

During the winter of 1962-63, the women's volleyball team competed at the senior level and placed fifth out of six teams. It was coached by Taras Bidiak. The senior men's team finished the regular season in fourth place out of eight teams and qualified for the national championship. There Ukraina played to a fourth place finish. The team was coached and managed by Walter Stochansky.

In the spring, SA Ukraina organized and hosted the 1963 Ukrainian inter-club volleyball championships. Teams participated from New York, Passaic, Chicago, Winnipeg and Toronto. SA Ukraina women won the championship while the men placed second.

Prior to the start of the soccer season, the executive concluded that it was no longer capable of recruiting and paying for top players. Nevertheless, it persisted unsuccessfully to gain membership in the professional league.

The 1963 soccer team included a few carryovers from the previous year and also a number of inexperienced newcomers. Coach O. Skocen was given the task of moulding the group into a respectable team. After a number of early disappointments, the club jelled and finished in third place. It won 11 games, tied 2 and lost 5. In the playoffs, SA Ukraina defeated FC Virtus-Italia in the semi-finals 1-0 and 1-0 and Hakoah in the final 1-0 and 3-2 to win the O'Keefe Cup. The trophy was presented to Ivan Ihnatowych, the captain of SA Ukraina, by William Boytchuk, the recently elected president of the National Soccer League and a former president of the club. Among the players competing for SA Ukraina that year was 18-year-old Gerry Organ who would later gain fame as a placekicker with the Ottawa Rough Riders of the Canadian Football League.

During the summer, SA Ukraina played a number of exhibition matches with Ukrainian clubs both in Canada and the United States. Twice they played against Strila of Oshawa in matches celebrating that club's tenth anniversary. In Rochester, SA Ukraina faced the Ukrainian Sports Club. The Toronto team also played a home and away series with Kryla of Chicago. These matches were widely attended by Ukrainian fans.

The junior soccer team also had a successful season, winning 10 matches, drawing 4 and losing 2 to place second in the standings. In the playoffs, the team played with a partial roster and consequently fared poorly. A number of SA Ukraina players disqualified themselves from post-season play when they were called up to the senior club.

During the winter of 1963-64, SA Ukraina continued its chess and volleyball programs. The men's volleyball team placed second at the Ontario championship and thus qualified for the national championship. In Winnipeg SA Ukraina was assigned to the second pool of the qualifying round robin tournament. It placed second with a 9-3 record and advanced to the tournament semi-finals where it met Hamilton YMCA which finished with a 12-0 record in the first pool. SA Ukraina won the opening set 15-11, lost the second 15-5, and extended Hamilton to 18-16 in the final set. Hamilton YMCA subsequently won the championship while SA Ukraina was awarded third place. At the Ukrainian inter-club championship contested in Detroit, the team placed second. Playing coach of the volleyball team was Ivan Ihnatowych.

The women's volleyball team, also coached by I. Ihnatowych, won the Ukrainian inter-club championship for the third consecutive year. In Toronto league play at the senior level, the team finished fourth.

As the 1964 soccer season approached, the senior soccer club's application to the Eastern Canada Professional Soccer League was once again rejected. As a result, preparation got under way to field a team in the National Soccer League. Coach Skocen was provided with only a slightly changed roster from the previous year. The players knew each other and this resulted in a strong and disciplined game. The team finished the season in first place winning 12, tying 7 and losing 2. In the best-of-three semi-finals, SA Ukraina defeated Olympia 1-1, 1-0 and 3-0. In the final against FC Abruzzi, the club won 1-0 and 4-1. SA Ukraina's captain that year was Leonid Dowhaluk.

The junior soccer club also had a successful season and won the Toronto championship. The team's strength was highlighted when eight members were named to the provincial all-star team. Playing on the team was Zenon Andrusyshyn, future national track and field team member and professional football star. The juniors were coached by M. Sochaniwsky and managed by G. Nasadiuk and B. Hul.

In 1964, Sport Association Ukraina was granted a charter by the provincial government. The club also sold its share of the building at 140 Bathurst Street for $20,000. Part of the money was used to pay off the club's debt which amounted to $15,773. The remainder was designated for the club's commitment to the facilities at Christie. SA Ukraina continued to have a "club house" facility at Bathurst for two more years where they operated a very successful buffet. This enterprise provided the sports association with a steady income, $6,133 in 1965, and $4,586 in 1966.

During the 1964-65 season, the senior men's volleyball team played inconsistently and did not duplicate its successes in open competition of the previous year. At the Ukrainian inter-club championships, the team won first place. The women's volleyball team did not register any successes.

The senior soccer team, coached by O. Steckiw, completed the 1965 regular schedule in the National Soccer League once again in first place. The team had a record of 15 wins, 4 ties and

3 losses. In the playoffs the club faltered. The junior team folded part-way through the season after a misunderstanding among the club's management. The youth team coached by W. Borecky competed in the Etobicoke League and won the Etobicoke Guardian Cup.

During the winter of 1965-66, the men's and the women's volleyball teams won the Ukrainian inter-club championship. In Toronto league play, the men placed third while the women settled for fifth position. The men's club also participated at an Open Tournament of the Ontario Volleyball Association and placed sixth out of 15 teams. The men were coached by W. Bukata while B. Hul directed the women's team. Member of the volleyball team Ivan Ihnatowych gained personal recognition when he was named to the Ontario All-Star team that year. The chess club met sporadically that winter. Its member I. Teodorovych-Suk was co-winner of the Greater New York Open chess championship which was contested by 115 masters.

One of the executive's primary goals for the 1966 soccer season was to "Ukrainianize" the senior soccer team. The executive believed that by recruiting non-Ukrainians for the team, it was discouraging Ukrainian youth whose skills they were trying to cultivate at the bantam and junior level. The disillusionment, they argued, would lead youth to abandon the club and possibly sport.

During the season, the senior soccer club's roster reflected the objective of the executive. Nine of the eleven starters were Ukrainians. Most were young and only a few had experience at the premier level. The team's performance was beyond the executive's expectations. They finished the regular season in third place with 39 points, only three back of the league leading Sudbury Italia. The team also played exhibition matches in Rochester and Buffalo. The senior team was once again coached by O. Steckiw.

The bantam team, coached by W. Borecky and managed by B. Hul, played in the York Town League, finishing the schedule in third place. An old-timer team, the Old-Boys, was organized that year. The Old-Boys hosted a team from Chicago.

In 1966 William Boytchuk was re-elected for the fourth time as president of the National Soccer League while another club member, Ostap Wynnyckyj, was elected vice-president.

During the winter of 1966-67, SA Ukraina was informed that it had to vacate the facilities on Bathurst Street. The credit union that had bought out SA Ukraina's shares in the building two years earlier was in the process of expanding its operations. This directive created a major problem for the club. It had to nominate and elect an executive that was willing to assume the added responsibilities. In particular, members believed that SA Ukraina required its own building "club house" to operate successfully. To purchase a property, the association required money. At the end of 1967, the club was still looking for money and for a building while operating out of the business premises of members Markian Kohut and later Iryna Moroz.

In addition to play in a Toronto league during the 1966-67 season, the men's volleyball team competed in the Ukrainian Volleyball League. The team did not have a successful campaign in the Toronto OVA league but won the championship of the Ukrainian Volleyball League. The team also won the Ukrainian inter-club championship held at the Ukrainian resort *Soyuzivka* at Kerkhonkson, New York. Team member Walter Rosocha was selected to represent Canada at the 1967 Pan American Games.

The 1967 senior soccer team, with a relatively unchanged roster from the previous year, plummeted in the standings to sixth place. Its record was 8 wins, 2 ties and 8 losses. The "Ukrainianization" of the team and its success the previous year had little impact on the club's status within the Ukrainian community of Toronto. Even the most loyal fans were disillusioned and the number attending games dropped to a handful.

W. Borecky once again operated the bantam soccer team.

The association's general meeting at the end of 1967 brought about an unexpected result. For the first time since the club's inception, a number of former soccer players offered their services in various administrative capacities. In addition, SA Ukraina's founder William Boytchuk was named the club's honourary president in recognition of his twenty years of service for the club.

Fund-raising for a club house was one of the association's main activities during 1968. Caroling and a "*Malanka*" - Ukrainian New Year's dance brought in $2,500. The *Malanka* New Year's dance became an annual event

The lack of a club house resulted in the demise of SA Ukraina's chess club. Most members transferred to other clubs. Ivan Teodorovych-Suk, competing individually but as a member of SA Ukraina, placed second at the Toronto championship and won the Ontario title in 1968.

Prior to start of the soccer season, the new executive was in a quandary with regards to the senior soccer team. None of the players were signed and the club's fiscal status was poor. Some members of the executive suggested that the team's operation be suspended for a year. This was countered by arguments that should this option be taken, SA Ukraina would not be able to regroup and would fold. Eventually it was agreed to raise the necessary funds and field a team given that it was the association's 20th anniversary.

The senior SA Ukraina team completed the season with a record of 11 wins, 6 ties an 1 loss to place second in the league standings. The club qualified for the playoffs but was eliminated in the opening round by Olympia. During the course of the season, SA Ukraina's goalkeeper Orest Lysak had the lowest goals against average in the league. The senior team was coached by O. Skocen and managed by O. Steckiw.

The junior soccer team also placed second in the junior division of the NSL. It won 9 games, tied 2 and lost 3. The club was managed by W. Borecky. The bantam team placed fourth in league play. The team was managed by W. Zakaluzny and A. Horsky.

During the summer, D. Melnyk organized a group of tennis enthusiasts within the club. The club participated at the Ukrainian inter-club championships and member Catherine Zakaluzny won the junior ladies' title.

In early 1969, SA Ukraina hosted the Association of Ukrainian Sport Clubs of North America (USCAK) inter-club chess tournament. The tournament was organized by B. Nazarko who had just recently reactivated the SA Ukraina chess club. Twenty-eight players competed in the tournament. Dr. Orest Popovych, representing the Chornomorska Sitch of New Jersey, won the event. A short time later, Toronto also hosted the Ukrainian inter-club volleyball championship. SA Ukraina did not have either a men's or a women's team to enter in the event.

In May 1969, SA Ukraina realized one of its primary objectives when it purchased a property at 186 Wallace Street in Toronto. Over a number of years, the site was converted into a functional club house.

The 1969 soccer season saw a radical departure from the "Ukrainianization" process begun a few years earlier. More than 80 per cent of the senior team's roster was non-Ukrainian. SA Ukraina finished the season in eight place among 14 teams. It was coached by A. Horsky and managed by J. Kowal.

SA Ukraina's reserve team in 1969 was made up of the members of the previous year's junior team. The club was entered in the reserve league even though many of the players were still of junior age. It was believed that play in a more competitive environment would allow players to adjust more readily to the senior game in the event that they were called up. The team was coached by W. Borecky and managed by I. Kerkush.

At the general meeting of the National Soccer League in 1969, SA Ukraina founder and member William Boytchuk was once again elected president. He served in that capacity through 1981. Subsequently, he was named Honourary Life President of the league.

During the winter of 1969-70, the chess club competed at a Toronto club tournament where it placed second. At the Ontario championship, I. Teodorovych-Suk placed third. An attempt was made to revive the association's volleyball program in winter but it failed.

The senior soccer team was fully "Ukrainianized" for the 1970 season. A number of less experienced youths were given an opportunity to prove themselves. The performance of the club was below expectations. The team only won four games during the season. It was trained by A. Horsky and later by W. Zakaluzny.

During the summer of 1970, SA Ukraina co-sponsored an under-17 soccer team with the Ukrainian Youth Association SUM. The team competed at the junior "B" level, placing second in the standings and in the playoffs. It won a tournament hosted by the Association of Ukrainian Sport Clubs of North America (USCAK). The team competed under the name Ukrainian Youth and was coached by Mykhailo (Mike) Harapyn.

In 1971, the senior soccer team placed fourth out of 14 teams in the National Soccer League. In the playoffs, the team won the opener over Heidelberg but was eliminated in the subsequent game by Portugalia. The playing coach of the team was Leonid Dowhaluk. The Ukrainian Youth soccer team was still formally co-sponsored by SA Ukraina but the association's involvement in the operations of the team was negligible.

During the winter of 1971-72 only the chess club operated. Bohdan Nazarko organized a tournament for the Ukrainian championship of Toronto. In addition, a team was sent to Glen Spey, New York, where the Ukrainian inter-club championship was held. Victor Dzera was the club's top performer placing third.

The 1972 soccer season was considered by many one of the most disappointing in the sport association's history. The senior team began the season with only two Ukrainian players on its roster. One of Toronto's Ukrainian weeklies immediately criticized this development with a stinging attack: "With the upcoming game of SA Ukraina, the question arises about its roster. Why only the Dowhaluk brothers? Where have all the Ukrainian players that were with the team the previous year disappeared to?. . . Who is responsible for this - the association executive, the team manager or the coach? This question has to be positively resolved, otherwise the club's executive will have no moral basis to call upon Ukrainian soccer fans to financially support the team."[10] While 4,500 fans watched the opener, only 300 came out for the subsequent game.

After this charge, SA Ukraina signed two additional Ukrainian players but that did little to appease the disgruntled fans. On the soccer pitch the senior team had an average season, placing sixth out of 14 teams with a record of 13 wins, 6 ties and 9 losses.

In 1973, Sports Association Ukraina celebrated its silver jubilee. The election of Borys Hul as

SA Ukraina's president marked the first time in history that the association elected a former club athlete to the position. Borys Hul had played with the club's junior teams.

Amid protests from some who wanted a competitive senior team in the jubilee season regardless of the cost or the players' ethnic backgrounds, the executive decided to partially "Ukrainianize" the team. The season concluded with SA Ukraina occupying the eleventh position out of 16 spots. The team recorded 9 wins, 5 ties and 16 losses. At the conclusion of the season, SA Ukraina was awarded with a trophy for being the most disciplined and gentlemanly team in the league. SA Ukraina also fielded an under-23 team that year.

Part of the jubilee celebrations included exhibition matches played by the Old-Boys against clubs from Toronto and Rochester.

In early 1974, the Ukrainian Volleyball Club of Toronto folded after the death of its founder and manager Yaroslaw Krywonis. The volleyball club's three teams, two men's and a women's, transferred to SA Ukraina, reactivating the association's volleyball program.

The men's team completed the season winning the league and provincial championships. It defeated all opponents to win the Ontario Open, and was invited to compete in a specially organized Tournament of Four that included Canada's national team, and the top teams from Quebec and the United States. SA Ukraina defeated the clubs from Quebec and the United States. In the final, SA Ukraina almost upset Canada's national team, losing by the smallest of margins, 15-13, 16-14 and 17-15.

The second men's team faltered throughout the season while the women finished third in league play.

The chess club participated at the Ukrainian inter-club championships at Detroit. SA Ukraina players swept the first three places. Victor Dzera won the tournament. Pavlo Bezkachko took second place while Bohdan Nazarko settled for third.

Four soccer teams were fielded by SA Ukraina in the summer of 1974. The senior men's team completed the season in 16th position out of 19 teams in the league. The team won 6 games, tied 5 and lost 25. Leonid Dowhaluk was the team's playing coach while Wolodymyr Skocen was captain. The under-23 team and the bantam team had losing seasons. The Old-Boys team challenged the under-23 to a set of friendly matches.

During the winter of 1974-75, the men's volleyball team played consistently to win the Senior "AA" league of the Ontario Volleyball Association. At the provincial championship, the club lost only one game in the qualifying round and advanced to the playoffs. In the semi-finals, SA

Ukraina disposed of the Tartars 15-8 and 15-11. In the final, SA Ukraina defeated Ottawa Onion Patch 15-8 and 15-12 to win the provincial title and qualify for the national championship.

*Sport Association Ukraina men's volleyball team, 1975 Canadian Champions*

At Quebec City, eight provincial champions gathered to determine the national champion. SA Ukraina played through the qualifying round without losing one game. In the semi-finals, SA Ukraina was extended to three games by Sherbrooke, 4-15, 15-6 and 15-12. In the final, SA Ukraina met the defending Canadian champion Manitoba Goats. The Goats won the first three points of the first game but after that SA Ukraina - Toronto regained its composure and began to control the game. The club from Toronto won the first game and the championship, 15-12, 15-8 and 15-3.

The Canadian championship team included captain Peter Stefaniuk, John Eliashevsky, Mstyslaw "Misty" Fedak, Roman Geley, George Ihnatowycz, Ihor Kushper, Ihor Lotocky, Walter Safranchuk, Andrew Stanko, Orest Stanko and George Zajac. The team was coached by Mel Holick and managed by Borys Hul. It was the first all-Ukrainian team to win a national championship of Canada. The team also won the Ukrainian inter-club championship contested at Rochester, New York, that year.

The women's volleyball team placed second in league play, two points back of the leader. At the Ukrainian inter-club tournament, the team finished fourth. The women's team was coached by Roman Komorowsky. The sports association also organized a junior girl's volleyball team which was trained by Marika Pawlychko-Skocen.

Prior to the 1975 season, the National Soccer League established two divisions. SA Ukraina, based on its poor performance of the previous year, was assigned to the second division.

Competing against weaker teams, SA Ukraina nevertheless could not improve its record. It won 4 games, tied 6 and lost 20. A new junior team was organized that spring by L. Dyczkowsky and H. Rygailo which competed in a junior "B" league. The Old-Boys expanded their activities by playing nine matches.

In the fall, the chess club organized two tournaments. It also sent a team to the Ukrainian inter-club championship at which member Bohdan Myndiuk placed second.

In 1975, Sports Association Ukraina applied for and was granted membership in the Ukrainian Canadian Committee, an umbrella organization coordinating the activities of the Ukrainian community in the city. Association members also helped in the campaigns of two Ukrainian candidates running for provincial office.

The senior men's team repeated as champions of the Senior "AA" league of the Ontario Volleyball Association. The club also won the Ontario Open tournament which was contested by 15 entrants. At the provincial championship the club was eliminated by the previous year's finalist Onion Patch. The women's team competed at the Senior "A" level and placed fourth in league play. It was trained by Halya Stefaniuk. The junior girls' team was not yet entered in league play. Later in the year, the three volleyball teams competed at the Ukrainian inter-club championship at Rochester. All three placed second.

In June, the chess club hosted the Ukrainian inter-club championship. The three-day event attracted 21 players. SA Ukraina members V. Dzera and I. Teodorovych-Suk placed second and third respectively.

In 1976, SA Ukraina temporarily suspended operations of its senior soccer team. The team's poor performance, the high cost of operating it and the lack of Ukrainian players resulted in the decision. So as not to lose the team's membership in the National Soccer League, SA Ukraina paid the required entry fee. During the summer the association fielded a junior "B" team which placed fourth in its league and a bantam team which won the Minor League championship of the NSL. The juniors were coached and managed by O. Steckiw and L. Dyczkowsky while S. Haba and H. Rygailo handled the bantams.

During the 1976-77 volleyball season, the senior men's club maintained its dominance of the "AA" league by once again placing first. At the provincial championship, the club lost its opening match and was eliminated. SA Ukraina entered four teams, two men's, a women's, and a junior women's, in the Ukrainian inter-club volleyball championship. The men's "A" team and the women's team placed first. The men's "B" team placed second while the junior ladies placed third.

The chess club hosted the 11th championship for Ukrainians of Toronto and participated at the

Ukrainian inter-club championship at Philadelphia. Pavlo Bezkachko won the Toronto event while SA Ukraina contenders did not place at the Philadelphia tournament.

SA Ukraina's soccer program in 1977 included an under-23 team, a junior team and the Old-Boys team. The under-23 team placed tenth while the juniors finished the season in third spot. The "leave of absence" of the senior soccer team was extended for one more year after the payment of a registration fee and a guarantee that a team would be fielded in the following year.

The departure of a number of volleyball players resulted in the reorganization of both the men's and women's teams in the fall of 1977. Paul Kelembet was the playing coach of the men's team that placed third in the Senior "A" Interlock League. The women's team, coached by Roman Struhanyk, was not entered in a competitive league. Both teams competed at the Ukrainian inter-club championship in Cleveland without success.

In the winter, SA Ukraina entered a team in a new indoor soccer league. The non-competitive league was organized to provide teams with a venue where they could develop strategies and cultivate skills during the winter months.

In 1978, the chess club once again hosted the Ukrainian inter-club championship. Borys Bachynsky of Philadelphia won the event.

The return of the senior soccer club to the National Soccer League was accomplished by transferring most of the under-23 team to the new senior team. With this action, the under-23 team ceased to exist. The senior team competed in the second division, posting a record of 4 wins, 2 ties and 6 losses. SA Ukraina also fielded a bantam team which folded after most of its members departed for summer camps.

The senior men's volleyball team began the 1978-79 season playing at the senior "A" level. The club was then promoted to the senior "AA" division where it completed the season. At the Ukrainian inter-club championship held at St. Catharines, the team placed third. The women's team was entered in the OVA league without much success.

During the 1979 season, the senior soccer team won 7, tied 7 and lost 10. The team was coached by M. Harapyn. The juniors competed in the North York League where they placed second in league standings. In the playoffs, the team lost the championship final. The juniors were coached by Roman Lenko.

In the fall, the chess club sent a team to participate at the Ukrainian inter-club championship at Philadelphia. Club member A. Lupyniak placed third.

Competing at the senior "AA" level, the men's volleyball team completed the 1979-80 season in sixth place. The team was coached by Paul Kelembet. The senior women's team placed second out of nine teams. The club was coached by Yaroslaw Loyowsky.

In 1980, Toronto hosted the Free Olympiad. SA Ukraina played an integral role in the organization of the Olympiad and was responsible for the soccer competition.

The Ukrainian soccer team, predominantly composed of SA Ukraina athletes, won the gold medal at the Olympiad. The team was managed by SA Ukraina's Evstakhii (Stan) Haba and coached by SA Ukraina's Taras Bidiak and Leonid Dowhaluk. The Ukrainian men's volleyball team was coached by SA Ukraina's Paul Kelembet and included four athletes from the sport association. The volleyball team won the silver medal.

During the regular soccer season, the senior club won 5, tied 3 and lost 14 to place ninth in league standings. The junior team completed the schedule of the North York League without losing a game. The juniors placed first in the standings and won the playoffs. The cost of operating the two soccer clubs during the 1980 season was $17,529.

Jerry Dyczkowsky, who came up through the SA Ukraina minor soccer program, was named captain of the senior soccer team in 1980. He still held the position in 1992, the longest serving captain in the sport association's history.

SA Ukraina operated two volleyball teams during the winter of 1980-81. The men's team played at the senior "AA" level and finished the season in fifth place. The women competed in the OVA intermediate league where they placed fourth.

Victor Dzera, a member of the association's chess club, won the Ukrainian inter-club championship contested over three days at Chicago. The chess club also hosted the Toronto open championship for Ukrainians at which Oleksander Charchenko won his second consecutive title.

The senior soccer club was unable to generate any offence and as a result, finished the 1981 season in last place with a record of 2 wins, 4 ties and 14 losses. The club participated in competition for the National Soccer League Cup and surprised everyone by advancing to the final. In a two-game total-goal final for the Cup, SA Ukraina lost the opener to the Hamilton Steelers 3-0 at Hamilton. Playing in Toronto, the club won the second game 3-2. The previous year's junior team had aged and was now entered in the under-23 league. The team participated at an international tournament in Dallas where they drew with Germany 0-0 and lost to Mexico 1-0 and to Dallas 1-0.

Celebrations marking the 70th anniversary of SA Ukraina of Lviv were held in Philadelphia in 1981. Members of Toronto's SA Ukraina executive were actively involved in the organization of the celebrations. In addition, the Toronto association sent three teams to partake in the event. The men's volleyball team won its tournament while the women placed second. The Old-Boys soccer team lost in the final to a team from Philadelphia.

During the 1981-82 volleyball season, the men's team played at the senior "AA" level and finished the schedule in seventh place out of eight teams. As a result, the team was demoted to the senior "A" division. Paul Kelembet coached and managed the team. The women's volleyball team won the intermediate division and was promoted for the following season.

In 1982, SA Ukraina did not field a senior soccer team. The club had a falling out with the National Soccer League the previous year and the misunderstanding was still unresolved. That year, the association's involvement in soccer was limited to sponsoring a team of 6 to 9-year-olds in the newly organized Ukrainian Youth Soccer Association league. Borys Hul coached the youngsters.

At the 1982 Ukrainian inter-club chess championship, SA Ukraina members B. Nazarko and B. Stepanenko tied for second place.

The men's volleyball team won the senior "A" division during the 1982-83 season. Playing coach of the team was George Ihnatowycz. The women's team did not experience the same success on the court. Playing coach of the team was Darka Horyn-Sergio.

In 1983, Sports Association Ukraina celebrated its 35th anniversary. In conjunction with the celebrations, SA Ukraina hosted the Ukrainian inter-club volleyball and chess championships. Eleven men's and eight women's teams, representing nine cities in Canada and the United States, participated in the volleyball championship. The men's side was won by the host club while Cleveland Lviv won the women's division. The chess tournament attracted a record number of entries with 32 and was won by the association's Victor Dzera.

In conjunction with the celebrations, a 427-page chronological history of the club titled *"Ukraina" Sport Association - Toronto,* was published by the association. Jaroslaw Chorostil worked on the book until his passing in 1980. Roman Kostiuk completed the manuscript.

In 1983, the men's senior soccer team was entered in the West Division of the Toronto and District Soccer League. SA Ukraina recorded 5 wins, 3 ties and 12 losses to place tenth in an 11-team league. Ihor Prokipchuk was the team's playing coach.

In 1983, a group of young Ukrainian men approached SA Ukraina seeking sponsorship for their fastball team. The association agreed and the team was registered in the Kismet League. It finished the season in fifth place.

The women's volleyball team, coached by D. Horyn-Sergio, captured first place in the senior "B" league during the 1983-84 season. The men's team played at the senior "A" level. It was coached by P. Kelembet. Victor Dzera repeated as the USCAK inter-club chess champion.

In 1984, Toronto once again hosted the Free Olympiad. Athletes of Ukrainian, Latvian, Estonian and Lithuanian descent competed in athletics, basketball, ice hockey, shooting, soccer, swimming, tennis and volleyball. SA Ukraina provided assistance in the organization of the event. In addition, SA Ukraina contributed athletes, trainers and coaches to the Ukrainian team.

The Ukrainian soccer team was managed by SA Ukraina's Stan Haba and Hryhoriy Rygailo. Haba also managed the Ukrainian hockey team. The Ukrainian men's volleyball team was coached by SA Ukraina's Paul Kelembet and included four athletes from the sport association. The basketball team was managed by SA Ukraina's Taras Bidiak.

The record of the senior soccer team improved to 6 wins, 6 ties and 10 losses during the 1984 season. The team, coached by A. Fil and managed by S. Haba and Z. Zwarych, also improved its position in the standings by placing eighth among 12 teams.

During the 1980s, attendance at SA Ukraina soccer games dropped to an average of about 50 to 100 per game. For the club executive, the lack of interest and fan support in the association had a somewhat demoralizing effect. However, there was never a shortage of eager athletes to form teams.

In the fall of 1984, the Plast Hrim (Thunder) volleyball team transferred to SA Ukraina. For Plast, the cost of sponsorship had become excessive. At the same time, SA Ukraina was looking at ways to revitalize its volleyball program. The team competed under the name SA Ukraina Hrim. Paul Kelembet coached the team. The women's volleyball team, after its promotion into the senior "A" league, continued to play well placing second in the standings. Darka Horyn-Sergio was the team's coach.

For the 1985 soccer season, SA Ukraina retained the coaching staff and management from the previous year. It was believed that continuity would aid in the team's development. The team, though, did not responded as expected. Its record of 5 wins, 5 ties and 10 losses just barely kept the team out of the league's basement. SA Ukraina placed tenth in a 13-team league.

The women's volleyball team completed the 1985-86 season in sixth and last place at the senior "A" level and was demoted. The men's team playing at the senior "A" level was coached by Paul Kelembet and managed by Alex Sochaniwsky.

In 1986, Stan Haba assumed the coaching duties with the senior SA Ukraina soccer club. The team recorded 8 wins, 8 ties and 8 losses to place seventh in the 13 team league.

During the 1986-87 season, the women's volleyball team played at the senior "B" level while the men continued to play at the "A" level. The 30th USCAK inter-club championship was held in May of that year at Maplewood, New Jersey. SA Ukraina women's team placed third at the event.

Also during the winter, the senior soccer team was registered in an indoor soccer league. The games and practices provided the players with an opportunity to work on their physical conditioning and soccer skills.

In the summer of 1987, the senior soccer team continued to play in the first division of the Toronto and District Soccer League. Coached by former SA Ukraina soccer player Taras Bidiak, the team duplicated its placing of the previous year on 8 wins, 2 ties and 10 losses.

During the winter of 1987-88, SA Ukraina operated two senior men's volleyball teams. Paul Kelembet coached one team to fifth place in the senior "A" league while Alex Sochaniwsky guided the other to sixth place in the senior "B" league. An effort was made to field a women's team; unfortunately, there was not a sufficient number of interested individuals to form a team. As a resulted, SA Ukraina suspended its women's volleyball program. Also that winter, SA Ukraina's Myron Moskal won the Toronto chess championship among Ukrainians.

In May of 1988, the city of Philadelphia hosted the Ukrainian Olympiad and Youth Rally. Some 700 athletes representing 12 sports and youth associations participated in the three-day event. Borys Wrzesnewskyj was SA Ukraina's only medal winner at the Olympiad. He won four medals in track and field competition: a gold, two silver and a bronze. The two volleyball teams that SA Ukraina entered in the competition failed to place in the top three.

Stan Haba took over as coach of the senior soccer team for the 1988 season. Zenon Zwarych remained as manager. The team placed sixth in the 10-team league with a record of 4 wins, 4 ties and 6 losses.

As in the previous year, SA Ukraina operated senior "A" and senior "B" men's volleyball teams during the winter of 1988-89. The teams placed fourth and fifth in their respective divisions. At the USCAK inter-club championship held at Maplewood, New Jersey, both SA Ukraina teams qualified for the playoffs by winning their respective division. The SA Ukraina I team won pool "A" while SA Ukraina Hrim won pool "B". In the playoffs, SA Ukraina I lost in the final to place second at the championship while SA Ukraina Hrim placed fourth. Ten teams participated in the tournament.

The duo of Haba and Zwarych continued to operate the senior soccer team in 1989. Captain Jerry Dyczkowsky assisted in the coaching. The team did not show much improvement over the last year, finishing the season with a record of 7 wins, 2 ties and 9 losses to place seventh in an expanded 11-team league.

In the spring of 1990, SA Ukraina hosted the 33rd annual Ukrainian inter-club volleyball championships. Twelve men's teams and five women's teams, representing nine cities in Canada and the United States, participated in the event at York University. The Chornomortsi Club of New Jersey won the men's title, SA Ukraina placed second for the third year in a row, and the Ukrainian Volleyball Club of Minnesota captured the bronze medal. In the women's division, the Lviv Sport Club of Cleveland took first place honours.

The sport association also hosted the Ukrainian inter-club chess championship. M. Moskal placed third at this event.

The senior soccer team completed the 1990 schedule with a record of 3 wins, 4 ties and 10 losses to place last among ten teams. As a result it was demoted. The team was coached by B. Fil and managed by S. Haba and Z. Zwarych.

In the late 1980s and early 1990s, the SA Ukraina senior soccer club was augmented by Ukrainian refugees and immigrants arriving from Poland and Ukraine. Most of these individuals had considerable European soccer experience and were a welcome addition to the soccer team.

During the winter of 1990-91, the men's volleyball team played in the OVA Sr. "B" league. It completed the season in 13th place among 16 teams. Paul Kelembet continued to coach the team.

The SA Ukraina senior soccer team won the championship of the Metro Toronto Association League in 1991. The club finished the season undefeated with a record of 13 wins and 4 ties. The goals for and against were 50 and 13 respectively. Zbigniew Kondziak won the best goalkeeper award while Stan Haba was honoured as coach of the year. The victory promoted SA Ukraina to the Second Division of the Toronto and District Soccer League.

That year, members of SA Ukraina - Toronto assisted the Ukrainian Sports Federation of USA and Canada - USCAK (formerly the Association of Ukrainian Sport Clubs of North America) to organize a sport tour of Ukraine in conjunction with the celebrations honouring the 80th anniversary of the Sports Association Ukraina of Lviv. Participating in the celebrations from Toronto's SA Ukraina were members of the executive, the Old-Boys team, four athletes selected to the USCAK men's volleyball team, and chess player M. Moskal.

The cinderella team of the 1992 soccer season in Toronto was SA Ukraina. Just promoted to the tougher second division, the team surprised everyone by placing first in league standings and capturing the championship. The title assured SA Ukraina of its second promotion in as many years. The team's record included 18 wins, 2 ties and 2 losses. Playing coach and captain of the team was Jerry Dyczkowsky. Stan Haba and Zenon Zwarych handled the managerial duties.

Although at times embroiled in turmoil and often in pursuit of conflicting objectives, SA Ukraina evolved into the most dynamic Ukrainian sport club organized in Canada by the postwar immigration. Hundreds of aspirants, athletes and veterans, from pee-wees to the Old-Boys, competed on the club's teams. Some participated at a recreational level while others embraced the competitive spirit and strove to improve their athletic skills. The large number individuals that participated in the club's programs since 1948 attests to the club's outreach into the community. The success of the club's teams and of individual club members in Canadian sport attests to the quality of the sport programs operated by the club.

## PRESIDENTS OF THE SPORT ASSOCIATION UKRAINA

| | |
|---|---|
| William Boytchuk | (1948, 1953, 1956-57, 1962) |
| Myroslaw Welyhorskyj | (1949) |
| Stephen Romanec | (1950) |
| Jaroslaw Chorostil | (1950, 1961, 1963, 1967) |
| Evhen Chuchman | (1951) |
| Stephen Pawliuk | (1951-52) |
| Karlo Mulkewytch | (1954) |
| Nicholas Waller | (1955) |
| Mykhailo Brygadyr-Wrubelsky | (1958-60) |
| Onufriy Petryshyn | (1964) |
| Roman Kostiuk | (1964-65, 1978) |
| Wolodymyr Rybak | (1966, 1971) |
| Mykhailo Shmotolocha | (1968-70, 1972) |
| Borys Hul | (1973-74) |
| Wolodymyr Ihnatowycz | (1975-77, 1983-88) |
| Yaroslaw Fenyn | (1979-82, 1989- ) |

# UKRAINIAN BASKETBALL LEAGUE

In the fall of 1949, sport enthusiast Jean Harasym, representing the Ukrainian Youth League of North America (UYLNA), met with representatives of SA Ukraina, UNYF Toronto - Tridents, UNYF - Toronto West, and the Canadian Ukrainian Youth Association (SUMK) to discuss the possibility of forming a basketball league. Harasym, whose sports experience included serving with the Toronto Sports Service League for Canadian soldiers during World War II, believed that a basketball league would offer Ukrainian youth of Toronto an opportunity to develop their basketball skills. In addition, Harasym wanted the league champion to represent Canada at the Sports Rallies organized by UYLNA. The meeting concluded with the formation of the Ukrainian Basketball league.

In its first season of operation, the league comprised four teams representing the aforementioned clubs. Six games were scheduled for each team, followed by a playoff. At the conclusion of the season, the league found itself in a major predicament: all four teams won 3 and lost 3 games. To determine the winner, it was decide to play a round robin tournament followed by a playoff. This proved to be a good decision for the fans who were following the league in ever-increasing numbers. In the round robin tournament, SA Ukraina swept all three opponents to claim first place. In the opener of a two-game total-point playoff, SA Ukraina defeated second place SUMK 45-37. SUMK won the second game 64-61 but did not score enough points to offset the deficit of the first game. SA Ukraina thus became the first champion of the Ukrainian Basketball League.

SA Ukraina, though, did not represent Canada at the UYLNA Sports Rally that was held that year in Rochester, New York. The newly elected management of SA Ukraina concluded that it was inappropriate to send a team primarily consisting of Lithuanian ringers to a Ukrainian youth rally. As a result, an all-star team was selected from the remaining clubs to compete in Rochester.

No information about the league during the 1950-51 season was uncovered.

The following year, the "international" Bathurst-College Community Basketball League began operations with the UNYF Tridents representing the Ukrainian community. The new league's championship trophy was inherited from the Ukrainian Basketball League.

# UKRAINIAN-CANADIAN GIRLS
# SLO-PITCH LEAGUE

For a number of years, sisters, girlfriends, and wives watched men play softball in the Ukrainian Slo-Pitch Softball League (USPSL) of Toronto. In 1985, a group of them decided that they too wanted to play organized softball. Enthusiasts Marta Lewitski and Sandy Nimchuk met with Myron Tymochko, one of the founders of the men's league, and Dominic Chiaromonte, a supporter of the men's league, to discuss the logistics of setting up a league. A short time later, on June 17, 1985, the first meeting of the Ukrainian-Canadian Girls Slo-Pitch League (UCGSPL) was held. At the meeting, an executive was elected that included Marta Lewitski, president; Chris Kowalsky, vice-president; Sandy Nimchuk, treasurer; and Chris Hamiwka and Lesia Horochowskyj, secretaries. It was decided that the league would start play in 1986.

*Ukrainian-Canadian Girls Slo-Pitch League logo*

In the summer of 1985, the executive organized three teams that competed in exhibition games against each other. The three teams, Caravan, Caravan Video, and Sir Dukes were joined in 1986 by Artex and ODUM to inaugurate league play. The number of teams in the league peaked in 1988 with six. In 1991, the number fell to four.

Initially, membership in the Ukrainian-Canadian Girls Slo-Pitch League was open to women 16 years of age or older who were of Ukrainian descent or married to an individual of Ukrainian descent. In addition, each club was allowed four "imports" or non-Ukrainians on its 18-player roster. Subsequently, the import rule was changed, reducing the number of imports to three per team.

In the late 1980s, a typical season for the league consisted of a regular schedule that had teams play each other four times. At the conclusion of the regular schedule, playoffs were held.

Every June, the league hosted a one day tournament open to any women's team in the city. During the year, UCGSPL teams were free to compete in tournaments organized by other clubs or leagues.

In 1987, UCGSBL and USPSL put together a mixed team which was fielded at mixed tournaments. In 1987 and 1988, the team qualified for the provincial playoffs. The first year, the team declined as the dates coincided with the men's provincial tournament, while in the latter year it fared poorly. Cooperation between USPSL and UCGSPL continued when in 1991 the women's league began running its tournament concurrent with the men's at the Ukrainian National Federation's Camp *Sokil* at Hawkestone, on beautiful Lake Simcoe.

In 1990, the league organized an all-star team that competed under the name Awesome Chicks. The team won two Toronto tournaments and thereby qualified for the Ontario championship. At the provincials, the Awesome Chicks were eliminated from competition early in the tournament.

*Ukrainian-Canadian Girls Slo-Pitch League team Muddies, c.1986*

From its beginnings, the Ukrainian-Canadian Girls Slo-Pitch League operated as a social sports club. For the women, the games were a night out away from the daily routine of city life.

The principal benefactor of the league was the Ukrainian Caravan Restaurant. The restaurant sponsored a team and the pennant trophy. It also supplied the league with office facilities free of charge. After games, Caravan often provided the teams with a complimentary buffet.

## PRESIDENTS OF THE UKRAINIAN-CANADIAN GIRLS SLO-PITCH LEAGUE

Marta Lewitski                    (1985-87)
Lida Derbish                      (1988-89)
Rosie Parubchak                   (1990-91)


# UKRAINIAN LABOUR-FARMER TEMPLE ASSOCIATION / ASSOCIATION OF UNITED UKRAINIAN CANADIANS

The first documented evidence of sport at the Toronto branch of Ukrainian Labour-Farmer Temple Association (ULFTA), renamed the Association of United Ukrainian Canadians (AUUC) in 1946, dates back to 1925. The *Young Worker* reported that some members "had started a weekly 5 mile run for fitness."[11] Later that year, the publication reported the "Ukrainian branch has bought equipment and has challenged the other three branches to play them."[12]

In early 1927, the Toronto branch organized a gym class. Every Monday night, enthusiasts participated in group exercises, pyramid building, and classical gymnastics training. In later years, the program was expanded with the introduction of new routines such as tumbling, Swedish drills, and novelty acrobatics.

The organizers and supporters of the gym class believed that these activities instilled a sense of discipline in the participant and provided the individual with sound physical training.

That fall, the Toronto branch of the ULFTA became affiliated with the Workers' Sport City Council and a short time later with the Workers' Sports Association of Canada (WSA). The two umbrella groups encouraged the formation of sport clubs among pro-communist and socialist organizations and coordinated their activities. The organizers believed that these sport clubs would be an ideal vehicle to keep youth within the ranks of the parent association. In addition, the clubs could serve as a means of recruiting unaligned youth into the sphere of the parent association.[13]

With the opening of the Toronto Labour Temple in 1927, considerable growth occurred in the sport program. It was reported, but could not be verified, that the national executive of the ULFTA in Winnipeg provided the Toronto sport group with the substantial sum of $2,500 for the purchase of gymnastics equipment in 1928.[14]

During the winter of 1928-29, 41 individuals participated in the gym classes. The following year, the club had about 70 members. The first public exhibition occurred in January of 1929. In April, the first competition was held when the branch hosted a meet against a Finnish and a Jewish club. The Ukrainian group was trained by Semko Berketa and P. Kryskiw.

In 1937, the gymnastics club introduced report cards. In a letter to the parents, instructor Florence Kaczor explained: "We are starting this system so parents will take a greater interest in their children's programs."

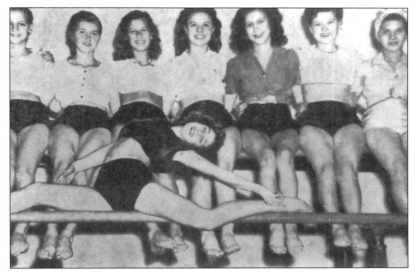

*Association of United Ukrainian Canadians gymnastics group, c.1948*

Over the years the gymnastics club maintained its popularity with branch members. It operated through the mid-1980s. Individuals such as Florence Kaczor, Fred Kaczor, Tony Kay (Kobyliansky), Jerry Prociw and Marie Prociw were largely responsible for the popularity and resulting longevity of the club.

To encourage the establishment of similar clubs, the Toronto branch visited many nearby towns, putting on shows and displays. The Oshawa, West Toronto and Windsor branches responded by pursuing a sports program.

In the summer of 1930, two softball teams were fielded by the Toronto branch. In 1934, a ULFTA softball team competed in the WSA affiliated Central Baseball League of Toronto.

After World War II, there was great interest among socialist and pro-communist organizations to establish and participate in Pan-Slavic sport leagues. In 1947, sport enthusiasts at the AUUC helped found the Toronto Slav Softball League (TSSL). The league included teams organized by Polish, Macedonian, Russian, Yugoslav, and Ukrainian groups. The president of the league in its inaugural year was Tony Daschuk of the East Toronto branch of the AUUC. Most of the members competing on the two Ukrainian teams in the league were World War II veterans.

The East Toronto branch was the inaugural winner of the league's championship. East Toronto eliminated AUUC Club 323 in the semi-finals and the Yugoslav team in the final. The championship team was managed by Harry Pasiak. The following year the league operated with eight teams. Steve Pruski, a member of the 1945 Toronto Argonauts Grey Cup championship team, coached the West Toronto AUUC entry. Toronto Club 323 branch defeated East Toronto in the playoff final to take the championship. The Toronto branch was coached by Mike Rawlyk and managed by Joe "Hopper" Peiluk. Member of the Toronto team Walter Chernysh was named president of the league.

The number of teams in the Toronto Slav Softball League decreased to five for the 1950 season. The two Ukrainian teams finished the season tied for third place. Both teams won their semi-final series. In the championship final, Branch 323 overcame the stubborn Branch 340 in the deciding fifth game to capture the title.

The TSSL folded in the early 1950s. Family responsibilities and the pressures of shift work were making it more difficult for the individuals to play in a regularly scheduled league.

In October 1951, the International Sports League was organized in Toronto. The Toronto AUUC, through its newly formed Dynamo Youth Club, entered a volleyball and a basketball team into competition. The Dynamos were also challenged to a floor hockey game by a sports group of "Carpatho-Russian" youth.

During the summer of 1952, the Dynamo club organized the first Eastern Canada AUUC Track and Field meet at the Ukrainian Camp Palermo outside of Toronto. A total of 41 competitors from 9 locales participated in the event. The Toronto branch won the overall championship. Montreal held down second place while Dunville placed third. Bill Morris of Toronto headed the committee that promoted and organized the event.

In 1953, the meet expanded to include softball and tug-of-war.

In 1955, Camp Palermo hosted the 2nd Ontario Youth Festival. Sports were included in the program and the Toronto branch won the women's basketball tournament.

Vera Pauk and Florence Kaczor organized a boxing group in the fall of 1956. One-time middleweight boxer Russ Barko trained the young fighters.

A basketball team was also organized in the fall of 1956. It was registered in the Toronto Intermediate Basketball League. The team was managed by Bill McCulla and sponsored by the bookstore *Ukrainska Knyha*. The team won 9 and lost 9 to place fifth in the 10-team league. The following year the team entered the Toronto Junior Basketball League.

The Toronto branch of Ukrainian Labour-Farmer Temple Association and its successor, the Association of United Ukrainian Canadians, also offered an intramural sport program for its members.

In 1935, members of the youth section of the downtown Labour Temple decided to try bowling. The group got hooked, and bowled regularly but informally through 1946 with the exception of a few years during the war. In 1947, the group established the Club 323 Bowling League. Four teams competed initially, with the number expanding to six in 1950.

Members of the West Toronto Ukrainian Labour Temple began bowling in 1946. A year later, the group formalized the activity by establishing the Club 340 AUUC Bowling League.

In November of 1952, Club 323 Bowling League merged with the Club 340 Bowling League to make a larger and more competitive league. That year the league operated with eight teams. The number peaked in the mid-1960s when some 20 teams participated in competition. For many years, bowling enthusiast Vic Mihay and Walter Chernysh were largely responsible for the growth and success of the league.

When the league celebrated its 45th anniversary in 1992, it was acknowledged as being one of the longest continuous intramural programs operated by a non-sporting Ukrainian organization. In 1953, Club 340 hosted an Inter-city Bowling championship. AUUC teams from Toronto and Hamilton participated. The event proved to be popular and was organized intermittently through 1972, with AUUC bowling teams from Toronto, Hamilton, and Montreal participating. After the collapse of bowling programs in Hamilton and Montreal, Toronto began participating in AUUC-WBA Western (Canada) Bowling tournaments. The tournament eventually became a national affair when Sudbury hosted it in 1984. Three years later, Club 340 hosted the tournament in Toronto.

# UKRAINIAN ORIENTEERING CLUB *LYSIACHYJ BIH*

In the late 1960s and the early 1970s, as the sport of orienteering started to gain popularity in Canada, a number of Ukrainians joined the ranks of the participants. In 1967, in the Toronto area, Vera Malanczyj heard a lecture by orienteering enthusiast Sass Peepre. Malanczyj, who at the time was a physical education student and a Ukrainian Youth Association Plast leader, tried the sport and was soon advocating it among her colleagues in Plast.

In a short period of time, Malanczyj assembled a small group of enthusiasts that regularly participated in orienteering meets. Most were members, or former members, of Plast. For these individuals, orienteering was a natural progression of their scouting activities. They all enjoyed the outdoors, physical activity, and the challenge of orienteering. The sport provided a test in endurance, map and compass reading skills, decision making, and moving through terrain. Once competition concluded, they enjoyed themselves among friends in the outdoors. An outing to an orienteering meet was both a competitive challenge and a social event.

*Ukrainian Orienteering Club Lysiachyj Bih logo*

In 1975, Orienteering Ontario passed a by-law which stated that all participants in orienteering meets must be members of orienteering clubs. The Ukrainian participants, who at the time did not belong to any club, decided to form their own. For club organizers Bohdan Kolos, Walter Kuz, Vera Malanczyj and Alex Slywynskyj, the task was not difficult. Most of the prospective club members were already good friends and had previously attended orienteering meets together.

In its inaugural year, the Ukrainian Orienteering Club Lysiachyj Bih (Fox Run) had about ten members. With time, its numbers increased and membership peaked at about 40 in the early 1980s. Towards the end of the decade membership dropped off to 20.

One of the requirements of each member club of Orienteering Ontario is the hosting of an annual class "A" competition. This is a top level competition recognized by the Canadian Orienteering Federation for point scoring towards the national championship. Each class "A" competition must have up to eight courses of different lengths, from two to ten kilometres. The duties of each host club include the selection of a site, laying out of courses, preparation of topographical competition maps and vetting the courses. Once competition commences, it is the club's responsibility to do the starts and timing, man the water and check points, verify the results, score the competition and perform all other required administrative work.

Over the years, the Ukrainian Orienteering Club annually hosted one-day class "A" meets which went under the name "Fox Trot." The name for the meet was derived from the club's logo - a fox trotting through the forest. The Fox Trot competitions have been held in the Ganaraska Forest north of Port Hope, on the Vivian tracks in the vicinity of the Ukrainian Recreational Club *Howerla*, in a forest north of Kelso Conservation area, and at other locales in Ontario. The best-attended competition attracted more than 175 competitors. Subsequently, the Ukrainian Orienteering Club teamed up with the Toronto Orienteering Club to host a two-day meet. This event, known as the "Turkey Trot," quickly became one of the favoured competitions among orienteers.

Commencing in 1985, individual club members became actively involved in organizing Wednesday night meets in Toronto parks. These weekly events during the summer months offered the avid orienteer a choice of two or three courses which could be easily completed after work before the sun set.

Through the years, members of the Ukrainian Orienteering Club did not forget their Plast roots as they pursued the sport of orienteering. They hosted clinics for Plast members in Toronto. They also visited summer camps to organize or help organize orienteering meets for Plast youth.

Since 1975, club members have regularly competed at various competitions in Canada and abroad. The most prolific competitors have been Vera Malanczyj, Eugene Mlynczyk and Walter Kuz. On many occasions they won their age group championships, particularly Walter Kuz who was, at the time, one of the oldest competitors in Canada. In 1970, Vera Malanczyj competed at the famed O-Ringen in Sweden and in 1990 she became the first Ukrainian from Canada to compete in an orienteering meet in Ukraine. The competition, called "Kyivski Kashtany" (the Chestnuts of Kyiv), was organized by the Ozor Club of Kyiv in the vicinity of the Ukrainian capital.

After Ukraine gained independence in 1991, the Ukrainian Orienteering Club paid the initiation and membership dues for the Orienteering Federation of Ukraine with the International

Orienteering Federation. In 1992, the seventh and eighth stages of the World Cup in orienteering were held in Canada and the United States respectively. With the financial support of the Ukrainian Orienteering Club, two competitors from Ukraine were able to take part in the North American component of the competition. The club's financial assistance also allowed some ten Ukrainian orienteers to compete in the European stages of the World Cup. This was a first for Ukrainian orienteers.

*Ukrainian Orienteering Club, c.1980*

Ukrainian Orienteering Club members have also contributed to the development of orienteering in Ontario. In 1981-82, Vera Malanczyj served as secretary and president of Orienteering Ontario and stayed on the board of directors the following year as past president. Eugene Mlynczyk produced the illustrations for the book *Orienteering*, which was co-authored by Ron Lowry and Ken Sidney. The book was published by Orienteering Ontario in 1985.

Over the years, the activities of the Ukrainian Orienteering Club have not all been conventional. Club members have organized "practice meets" on the streets of Toronto and Etobicoke. These events more often than not astonished passers-by. The practice meets concluded with friendly get-togethers.

# UKRAINIAN SLO-PITCH SOFTBALL LEAGUE

I n the summer of 1978, Paul Kulchisky was asked to organize a softball tournament as part of the annual Sports Day at the Ukrainian National Federation's Camp *Sokil* at Hawkestone, Ontario. Eight teams, some of them hastily put together, entered the tournament. Afterwards, a number of participants, enthusiastic about the success of the tournament, called for the formation of a Ukrainian softball league. Kulchisky readily agreed with the request. He was of the opinion that no Ukrainian Canadian organization or church provided activities for Ukrainian youth of Toronto in a Canadian context. This was an opportunity to change that.

*Ukrainian Slo-Pitch Softball League logo*

Kulchisky co-opted Myron Tymochko to help, and the two laid the ground work for a league during the winter of 1978-79. Various Ukrainian churches and organizations were approached and encouraged to organize and register softball teams with the league. The league also accepted teams which were unaffiliated, as it believed that there were many Ukrainians who were not tied to any organization. When spring arrived, the season opened with eight teams - Royce Boys, Hawkestone Hawks, Colt 45, Mucha Machinery, MUNO 1, MUNO Induks, Muno Oldtimers, and St. Demetrius Church.

The Ukrainian Slo-Pitch Softball League (USPSL) formally came into existence in 1979. It was established as an independent member-run organization. The league's presidency was accepted by Walter Turylo while Paul Kulchisky assumed the posts of executive secretary and treasurer. For the first three years of its existence the league operated out of Kulchisky's home.

Membership in the league was open to any male who had at least one parent of Ukrainian descent. Each team was also allowed three "imports" or non-Ukrainians. In 1988, this by-law was augmented to grant non-Ukrainians an opportunity to request Ukrainian status. In particular, this was done to suit those non-Ukrainians who were married to Ukrainians and whose sons were eligible to play in the league as Ukrainians. Individuals had to write the league requesting this status. They also had to explain their contribution to the league and their involvement in the community.

During the summer of 1979, the league organized the first official Hawkestone Summer Tournament for teams competing in the league. Some 150 people attended the event. In 1981, the tournament was expanded to two days. The Hawkestone tournament continued to gain popularity and within a few years was recognized as one of the most popular athletic and social events in the Toronto area. When the tournament celebrated its tenth anniversary in 1989, more than 1,000 people were in attendance.

*USPSL season opener c.1985, league commissioner P. Kulchisky (forefront left) and Metro Toronto Chairman Dennis Flynn (forefront right).*

In 1988, the Hawkestone tournament was recognized by Slo-Pitch Ontario as a provincial qualifying event with the winner advancing to the provincial championship tournament. As a result, the competitive level of the tournament was high. The greatest success that a USPSL team had at an Ontario championship was in 1986, when the Dukes placed second in the province at the "C" level.

Over the years the Ukrainian Slo-Pitch Softball League grew as more teams joined in. The number peaked in 1986 when 16 registered for competition. The total number of players, coaches and managers was 240 that year. This number increased to 267 in 1988, even though the number of teams dropped to 15. In 1991, the league consisted of 12 teams.

Initially, the USPSL comprised one division with each team playing about 20 games. Subsequently, it expanded to two divisions and the number of games played by each team increased to 32. Expansion resulted in a two-tier league with the Tier A "Kiev" Division being stronger and more competitive than the Tier B "Lviv" Division. At the conclusion of the season, the winner of tier B was promoted to tier A while the last place finisher in Tier A dropped back to tier B.

The league's regular season has usually lasted from mid-May to late August with the playoffs following. League games have been played at parks located in Etobicoke and Mississauga.

The evolution of the league has included numerous innovations. In 1983, the office of the Commissioner was created and the first Banquet and Presentation Night was held. In 1984, the league approved its constitution, mandated that all teams have full uniforms, and began utilizing registered paid umpires. In 1985, the league introduced Opening Day Ceremonies. This event has included balloons, drinks, choirs, a band and dignitaries, among them Mississauga mayor Hazel McCallion, Metro Toronto Chairman Dennis Flynn, Yuri Shymko, MPP, and Andrew Witer, MP.

In 1985, USPSL co-founder Myron Tymochko helped softball enthusiasts Marta Lewitski and Sandy Nimchuk organize the Ukrainian-Canadian Girls Slo-Pitch League (UCGSPL). Shortly thereafter the two leagues put together a mixed team which was fielded at mixed tournaments. In 1987 and 1988, the team qualified for the provincial playoffs. The first year the team declined as the dates coincided with the men's provincial tournament while in the latter year it fared poorly. Cooperation between the USPSL and UCGSPL continued when in 1991, the women's league began running its tournament concurrent with the men's at Hawkestone.

USPSL teams have also participated in various other tournaments primarily in southern Ontario. In the late 1980s, the Kozaks team made the first of what would become an annual appearance at a tournament held in conjunction with the Ukrainian festival at the resort *Verkhovyna* in New York State.

From its inception, the Ukrainian Slo-Pitch Softball League has been almost entirely sponsored by the Ukrainian business community of Toronto and supported by its organizations. Team uniforms, trophies and prizes were purchased by the businesses. In particular, Cardinal Funeral Homes, Newediuk Funeral Home, Ukrainian (Toronto) Credit Union, Blue Goose Tavern, Ukrainian Caravan Restaurant, Humber Sports, ODUM and John Saychuk had a long lasting sponsorship commitment. In addition, St. Mary's, St. Josaphat's and Holy Eucharist Churches provided their halls for meetings and banquets while the Ukrainian National Federation provided and expanded the facilities at Camp *Sokil* for the annual tournament.

In the course of its existence, the Ukrainian Slo-Pitch Softball League has also provided donations to community and cultural groups. Among the recipients have been the Barrie Tornado Relief Fund, Free Olympiad, Kalyna Girls' Choir, Annette Recreation Centre, and the *Toronto Sun* Christmas Fund. After Ukraine gained membership in the International Olympic Committee in early 1992, the league provided a donation to the National Olympic Committee of Ukraine and the Ukrainian Baseball Federation. Part of the donation paid for the initiation dues of the Ukrainian Baseball Federation with the International Baseball Federation.

**PRESIDENTS OF THE UKRAINIAN SLO-PITCH SOFTBALL LEAGUE**

| | |
|---|---|
| Walter Turylo | (1979) |
| Roman Serkies | (1980) |
| Roman Turenko | (1981) |
| Bob Bardyn | (1982-83) |
| Roman Mamalyga | (1984) |
| Myron Tymochko | (1985) |
| George Humeniuk | (1986-87) |
| Paul Kulchisky | (1988) |
| Bob Nosyk | (1989-90) |
| Wasyl Saluchok | (1991) |

# UKRAINIAN SOFTBALL LEAGUE

On April 10, 1932, Dr. Elias Wachna gathered a group of young sports enthusiasts for the purpose of encouraging and organizing softball among Ukrainians in Toronto. The meeting ended with the founding of the Ukrainian Softball League. The Ukrainian Softball League was at times referred to as the Ukrainian Athletic League or the Ukrainian Athletic Club. Dr. Wachna was elected president and Bill Dzurman the secretary-treasurer. Helping out were John Korchinski, Steven Sukmanowski, and John Kobin. Membership was open to those whose father was of Ukrainian descent. The stated purpose of the league was "to foster and improve amateur softball, to promote and protect the members' mutual interests, to institute and regulate competition for the Ukrainian championship."[15] Years later, Dr. Wachna added "These were the depression days and this was the thing to do. It was good for them, it was good for their health, morale and [to] keep them off bars and dances and things like that. . ."[16]

The Ukrainian Softball League in April of 1932 existed in name only; there were no teams. The founding members immediately set out to assist the established Ukrainian organizations and churches to organize softball teams. The Ukrainian People's Home on Lippincott Street was the first to form a team, with St. Josaphat's Church on Franklin Avenue a close second. Four more teams were organized prior to the start of the inaugural season. Winners of the championship in the first year were the Cossacks, a team representing the Ukrainian Boy Scouts and Sporting Sitch Association. The team was managed by S. Sawick.

*Ukrainian People's Home (Toronto) softball team that competed in the Ukrainian Softball League, c.1935*

In August of 1932, the Ukrainian Softball League organized the inaugural Ukrainian Field Day. The event was held at Toronto, with teams participating from St. Catharines, Hamilton, Toronto, and Oshawa. The softball tournament ended with the Nats and St. George's of Oshawa having an identical record of two wins apiece. It was determined that the Nats would face St. George's in Oshawa at a later day to determine the Ukrainian Ontario softball champion.

In 1933, the Cossacks repeated as champions. The following year the title went to the National AC. Managerial duties were shared by T. Janicky and D. Sadoway. In 1935, the Ukrainian People's Home from New Toronto won the General V. Sikevich Trophy, emblematic of the league championship. The team was managed by William Pawlak. The championship was regained by the National AC in 1936 under manager William Smith.

Over the years, the Ukrainian Softball League hosted a number of track and field days in

Toronto. The league's track team participated in two track meets against Ukrainian clubs in the United States. Several softball teams also travelled to the United States to compete against Ukrainian teams. To reciprocate, the league hosted softball teams from Auburn, Buffalo, New York, Rochester and other American locations. Games were also played against Ukrainian clubs from southern Ontario.

In 1936, the Ukrainian Softball League sent a team to Philadelphia to compete at the First Ukrainian Olympiad. The spectacle was organized by the Ukrainian Youth League of North America (UYLNA) and drew participants from eastern United States and Canada. The Ukrainian Softball League of Toronto won the softball contest and placed third in track and field after clubs from Palmerton and Detroit. Toronto's Fred Pechaluk won the 220-yard dash in a time of 25.2 (which was recognized as a Ukrainian North American record), and Walter Diak tied for first place in the 440-yard run. Dr. Elias Wachna led the Toronto delegation to Philadelphia.

In 1937, the Brotherhood of Ukrainian Catholics won the league championship. M. Millar was president of the club while J. Janowski handled the managerial duties. The following year the title went to St. Josaphat's AC. P. Doros managed the club while Peter Wasylyk was the club's president. A year later, the championship was won by the National AC. C. Kachkowski was club president while T. Jaworski managed it.

In 1939, Dr. Wachna and Fred Pechaluk started to organize a women's softball league. They were unable to find a sufficient number of interested Ukrainian women. As a result, they organized the Ukrainian Ladies' Softball Team and entered it into an existing league. The all-Ukrainian team was made up of women from 18 to 20 years of age. In its inaugural season, the team competed in the Toronto Church League and won that league's championship. The following year, the club was registered in the Earlscourt Park League. The women also won that league's championship. In 1941, the team played in the St. Clair League. The following year, the league folded. Efforts to register with another league were unsuccessful as the league's compliment was full. As a result, a number of the women transferred to teams which were registered. This led to the demise of the Ukrainian team. During its existence, the women's team was managed by Fred and Gus Pechaluk.

World War II had a major impact on the Ukrainian Softball League. By 1942, more than forty members were serving in the various branches of Canada's armed forces. The shortage of men forced the league to downsize to four teams. Part of the league's itinerary at the time included sponsoring farewell parties for soldiers being sent overseas and sending parcels to the troops. Peter Wasylyk and Jean Harasym played leading roles in administering the club in those years.

The Ukrainian Softball League operated a bowling league during the winter months for a number of years. The league was mixed, and about 50 individuals, mostly young professionals, participated in the activity each year. Dr. Michael Lucyk played a leading role in the operations of the bowling league.

## PRESIDENTS OF THE UKRAINIAN SOFTBALL LEAGUE

Elias Wachna, MD                    (1932)
Peter Wasylyk                      (1940-42)

# UKRAINIAN SPORTS CLUB TRIDENT

The history of the sport club which eventually would bear the name Ukrainian Sports Club Trident dates to the fall of 1937. At that time, Ostap Bedriy organized a men's softball team from the Toronto members of the Ukrainian National Youth Federation (UNYF). Over the years, members of the branch fielded various sport teams that competed under the names UNYF, UNF and MYH. It 1944, the name Tryzub (Trident) became affiliated with a UNYF team for the first time. Some time later, the club became known as the Ukrainian National Sports Club Trident. In 1952, after "absorbing" the Ukrainian Canadian Athletic Club Trident, the name Ukrainian Sports Club Trident came into use.

In its early years, the club was an intrinsic component of UNYF, the youth element of the Ukrainian National Federation (UNF). Sport enthusiasts at UNYF organized and operated athletic activities for their fellow members. With time, to fill gaps on the rosters of teams, non-UNYF members were recruited. When the two Trident sports clubs amalgamated in 1952, the new club became an independent entity affiliated with the UNF. It had its own constitution and executive. Membership in the club was open to anyone with athletic ability. Nevertheless, USC Trident was, for the duration of its existence, a club of the Ukrainian National Federation of Toronto.

In 1938, competing under the name of UNF in the St. Clair Softball League, the team won the championship by defeating LeMans in the final 5-3. The following year the team competed in the Ukrainian Softball League. In 1940, UNYF, managed by Marko Topolnicki, was once again registered in the Ukrainian Softball League.

*Ukrainian Sports Club Trident logo*

Towards the end of 1941, UNYF member Paul Fedun organized a junior age hockey team.  The team competed in the Toronto Hockey League (THL).

The 1942, the UNYF softball team was entered in the Ukrainian Softball League.  It was managed by O. Bedriy.

In the fall of 1942, Michael Rebryk took over the coaching duties of the hockey team.

Information about the sport activities at UNYF during the war years is rather sketchy.  Evidence, though, suggests that a softball and a hockey program operated.

*UNYF softball team, c.1940*

In the fall of 1944, a badminton team was formed.  The team nicknamed itself the Tridents.  The popularity of the name soon resulted in it being adopted by the club.  That winter, club members also partook in fencing, table tennis and boxing.

In the fall of 1945, a hockey team by the name of Ukrainian Nationals was entered in the Toronto Hockey League Junior "B" Division.  The team won its first two games but then experienced many setbacks.

Information about the sport activities at UNYF in the immediate post-war years is also lacking. Evidence, though, does suggest that a softball and a hockey program operated.

At the 1949 Ukrainian Youth League of North America (UYLNA) sports rally in Detroit, the men's baseball team placed second. One of the objectives of this coordinating body of Ukrainian youth organizations was the popularization of sport. Jean Harasym of Toronto was a great advocate of the UYLNA and its sport rallies. She encouraged Toronto-area Ukrainian teams to participate in the events.

In the fall of 1949, Michael Rebryk organized a basketball team. The team was one of four entered in the Ukrainian Basketball League. At the end of the season, all four teams had the same number of points. To determine a winner, a round robin series was played. The UNYF team placed third.

During the winter of 1949-50, UNYF fielded two hockey teams in the Toronto Hockey League, an intermediate and a minor-midget.

On July 18, 1951, after a fallout with SA Ukraina, a number of athletes and administrators organized a new sports club. They named it the Ukrainian Canadian Athletic Club Trident. Semen Mackevych, the initiator of the new club, was elected president; Julian Konotopsky, vice-president; Mykhailo Bardyn, secretary; and Michael Rebryk, treasurer. At first the club operated out of private homes. Subsequently, the Ukrainian People's Home at 191 Lippincott Street provided the club with two rooms free of charge. Nevertheless, the club had financial difficulties. In addition to membership dues, the club had to generate funds by hosting a dance and taking out a loan.

A soccer team was formed immediately and Oleksander Skocen, an established European professional who recently played for SA Ukraina, was named its coach. On the team's roster were other former SA Ukraina players. However, it was too late to enter the team into a local soccer league as the regular season was in progress. The team managed to play two exhibition matches that season.

In the fall, the Ukrainian Canadian Athletic Club Trident began negotiations with the Toronto branch of the UNF for a merger with its Ukrainian National Sports Club Trident. The publication *Ukrainian Trend* reported in its sports notes that the "Ukrainian Canadian Athletic Club Trident has emphatically stated its desire to be incorporated by the Ukrainian National Youth Federation Athletic Club."[17] The new Trident required a sound financial base which it believed the UNF could provide.

The Toronto Branch of the UNF saw the merger of the two clubs as a potential to create championship teams and thus increase its prestige in the community, particularly among the recently arrived displaced persons. The club UNF was negotiating with was predominantly made up of recent arrivals from Europe.

Not surprisingly, a merger occurred in January of 1952. The new Ukrainian Sport Club Trident (popularly referred to as the Tridents) retained the colours of the Trident club formed the previous year and its by-laws. Dr. Stepan Rosocha, a member of the UNF executive and an ardent supporter of the merger, was elected president. The executive included Dr. S. Lucyk, first vice-president; Walter Marko, second vice-president; Onufriy Maksymiv, secretary; and S. Olesnycky, treasurer. The Ukrainian National Federation Hall at College and Spadina became the club's home.

The original Trident club, although part of the negotiations, fared poorly in the deal. By the end of 1952, two of the three sports that it had operated were dropped from the program by the new executive of the merged club. Neither softball, with a history of twelve years, nor hockey, with ten, survived. The recently formed basketball team was retained, in part due to its success on the courts.

The Ukrainian Sport Club Trident, with the exception of the basketball program, effectively became a sport club for the post-World War II immigrants. The club promoted and placed much emphasis on sports fostered in Ukraine and later in the displaced persons camps, such as soccer, table tennis, and volleyball.

During the 1951-52 season, the Tridents played excellent basketball to qualify for the two-game total-point final of the Bathurst College Community Basketball League. Competing against the Japanese team the Mustangs, the Tridents won the first game 51-43 and the second game 72-60 to capture the league title. At the UYLNA sports tournament, the Tridents upset some of the powerful American teams to win the championship.

In 1952, Wolodymyr Iwanyk organized a boxing program. In his youth, Iwanyk boxed with the Sokil club in Lviv, Ukraine. While in the Munich DP camp, Iwanyk trained boxers. At the UNF Hall, eight to ten boxers trained regularly under his watchful eye. Their first competition was against the YMCA club at the UNF Hall. The Trident boxers performed well; an established local boxing promoter in attendance was impressed with the proficiency of Walter Haba and Ernie Smigelski and snatched the two for his club. The departure demoralized the remaining boxers and Iwanyk. Shortly thereafter the boxing program ceased to exist.

For a number of years in the 1950s, boxing promoters used the gymnasium of the Ukrainian National Federation Hall to stage amateur bouts. In particular, the Oakwood Boxing Club, with which Haba and Smigelski competed, staged regular Monday night shows at the hall.

In 1952, USC Trident gained membership in the National Soccer League and was assigned to its second division. The club had a very successful debut season, winning 17 and tying 1 in an 18-game campaign. Tridents then defeated Mahers in a two-game total-goal final to take the Play Off Cup of the Metro League. Personal trophies were awarded to Skocen, the league's top scorer, and to Mariano Angelucci, the league's top goalie. The club was managed by Mykhailo Bardyn and Yuri Karmanin. At the end of the year, the Tridents gained membership in the first division National League.

The 1952-53 Tridents basketball team once again dominated the Bathurst College Community Basketball League. The team, managed by Jean Harasym and coached by M. Rebryk, lost only one game during the entire regular season. In the semi-finals, the team had no problem disposing of its opponent. In a two-game total-point final, USC Trident came up against a tough Polish Vets club dropping the opener 76-69. USC Trident won the second game 73-70, but was unable to overcome the deficit.

The debut of the Tridents soccer club in the National League was encouraging as it won its opener 2-0 against the Polish club the White Eagles. The team completed the season tied for third place in the nine-team league, winning 7, tying 3 and losing 5. Playing coach Skocen was awarded the Holland Trophy by the league for his sportsmanship and gentlemanly conduct.

The 1953-54 basketball team won the championship of the Bathurst College Community Basketball League. The club then captured the provincial championship.

The calibre of basketball exhibited by the Tridents over the years was exceptionally high, and can be attested by the fact that among others, the team defeated the University of Toronto in an exhibition match. During his tenure as coach, Mike Rebryk managed to recruit some of the area's finest basketball stars to compete for the Tridents. Many of them had extensive basketball experience at the university or senior league level. Some competed simultaneously for other teams. In particular, Mike Baida, Vic Kurdyak, future professional football star Steve Oneschuk, and future Olympian John Dacyshyn were all members of the University of Toronto Varsity Blues' basketball team when they played for the Tridents.

During the winter of 1953-54, the men's volleyball team, coached by O. Kuchkuda, competed at the Senior "B" level and won the provincial championship.

During the 1954 soccer season, the club showed little consistency and completed the 20-game schedule with 7 wins, 6 ties and 7 losses.

In the fall of 1954, a chess section was formed, and in its first friendly match it drew against a Hungarian Club.

Michael Rebryk's basketball Tridents could not repeat the success of the previous year. They finished second in league standings behind eventual Canadian senior "B" champion Andy's AC. Tridents also competed in the basketball championships of the UYLNA placing second. In the course of the season, the team won all eight exhibition games that it contested, defeating, among others, the University of Western Ontario.

On the volleyball courts, a new junior entry placed a respectable third in the provincial championships. The men's team, competing for the first time in the more competitive senior league, experienced numerous setbacks. The club was coached by O. Pavliw.

In table tennis, the Tridents team placed fifth in a Toronto senior league. A "multinational" table tennis tournament saw Tridents and SA Ukraina combine their talents to form a Ukrainian team. The Ukrainian Selects placed fourth.

The 1955 soccer season was one of reorganization for the first division Tridents. In the off-season, a number of veterans retired, including playing coach Skocen. The club engaged Alex Arangelovic, a veteran of European and Australian soccer, to guide the team in the capacity of playing coach. Arangelovic was given only a few proven athletes to work with. As a result, the club experienced a continuous turnover of players as the coach searched for a winning combination. The team completed the regular schedule with a record of 7 wins, 2 ties and 9 losses to place seventh. In addition, USC Trident fielded a reserve and a junior team.

On December 24, 1955, representatives of the USC Trident attended a meeting at which the Association of Ukrainian Sport Clubs of North America (USCAK) was established. Among the proposed objectives of the association was the coordination of sport activity in North American. Tridents became a charter member of USCAK and also of the Canadian division of USCAK that was launched in May of 1956 with the help of the Toronto sport club. Over the years, USC Trident members, among them M. Bardyn, O. Skocen, M. Synyshyn and M. Tsar, served on the executives of USCAK and/or its Canadian division.

Hoping to gain additional experience, the Tridents basketball team joined a summer league in 1955. The experience proved to be helpful as the club finished a tough 1955-56 season in second place in the eight-team Bathurst College League. In the semi-finals, Tridents eliminated the Latvians and then dethroned defending champions Andy's AC in a two-game final. The championship team was coached by M. Rebryk and led on the court by J. Dacyshyn, M. Baida, V. Kurdyak, and E. Boguski.

*Ukrainian Sports Club Trident soccer team, 1952 Metro Soccer League Champions*

During the winter of 1955-56, a junior and senior volleyball team were fielded by the sport club.

In 1956, Ostap Steckiw took over as coach of the senior USC Trident soccer team. The team improved its fortunes from the previous year by winning 12, drawing 5 and losing 7 to place fourth in league standings. In the first round of the playoffs, the club was eliminated from further competition by Italia.

The Tridents basketball team completed the 1956-57 season without a defeat. It then swept both semi-final games against ABCPA. In the best-of-three final against the Mustangs, the Tridents won the first game 82-61. The team then lost two in a row. In men's volleyball, the Tridents had a disappointing season in the senior league placing eighth. The team, though, won the inaugural championship of the Association of Ukrainian Sport Clubs of North America (USCAK). The junior volleyball team competed in the intermediate "B" league with little success. The Tridents men's table tennis team also gained success at the USCAK championship by placing first in the team competition.

The senior soccer team under coach O. Steckiw played inconsistently throughout the 1957 season. Many believed that the team's primary weakness was the lack of experienced players. The team won 12, lost 12 and tied 3 to finish the season in sixth spot. When the league awards were announced, the Tridents were the inaugural winner of a new award for the most gentle-manly team. That summer, a reserve team and three junior age teams were also operated by USC Trident. Club management placed special emphasis on the junior teams. It was hoped that within a couple of years, players developed through the Trident system would crack the line-up of the senior soccer team.

The 1957-58 basketball team once again won the Bathurst College Community Basketball League championship. The Tridents contested the championship final against a Lithuanian team, and won the opener 83-69. In the second game, at the end of regulation time, the two teams were tied 91-91. In overtime, the Tridents dominated the court to capture the game 105-97 and the championship. The team then competed at the UYLNA championship in Scranton, Pennsylvania. In the semi-finals, the Toronto team defeated host Scranton 91-85. In the final, after being down by five points at the end of the second quarter to Johnson City, the Tridents turned the game around to win the championship 102-87. Ed Boguski was a standout for the team all year. For coach Rebryk, it was his ninth season with the team.

In senior volleyball, USC Trident once again competed in the OVA senior "A" league. The team finished in last place and as a result was demoted to the senior "B" league. Competing in a tournament organized by the Royal Military College in Kingston, the Tridents defeated all entrants to take top honours. The team also defended its USCAK championship, defeating the Lions of Chicago in the final. The reserve men's volleyball team competed in the intermedi-ate "B" division. The team played inconsistently and completed the season in the middle of the standings. In addition, a women's intermediate volleyball team was organized. Not yet ready to face the challenges of league play, the team limited itself to training and exhibition matches.

In table tennis, competing for the first time in the first division of the Toronto table tennis league, USC Trident placed fourth in team competition. In the semi-finals, the Tridents were eliminated from further play by the league-leading Masaryk Hall.

During the 1958 soccer competition, USC Trident once again had a problem fielding a first rate team. Coached by S. Huminilowycz, the team placed ninth in the 15-team National League winning 11, losing 15 and tying 2 games. While it had difficulty winning games, the team con-tinued to play good clean soccer and was once again awarded the trophy for the most gentle-manly team. The Tridents reserve team qualified for post-season play in the reserve league and went on to win the playoffs. Three junior age teams were once again operated by the club.

During the winter of 1958-59, the Tridents basketball team completed yet another undefeated season in the Bathurst College Community Basketball League. In the semi-finals, the Tridents defeated the Latvians. In the best-of-three final, the Tridents faced the Japanese club Yamada. In the final opener, Tridents easily handled their opponent 78-43. In the second game, Yamada fought back to tie the series with a 68-63 victory. In the final game, the Tridents blasted Yamada 88-46 to win the championship.

The Tridents women's volleyball team saw league action for the first time that winter. Entered in the intermediate league, the team played with relative success in its first campaign. The senior men's team once again competed in the "A" league when the assigned demotion to the "B" league was reversed. The team once again played poorly, avoiding last place and demotion by a whisker. The intermediate team that competed in the "B" league had a lacklustre season.

In table tennis, USC Trident competitors made a major breakthrough when team member O. Melaschenko won the "B" division of the Ontario championship. A few weeks later, Melaschenko won the Ontario Open table tennis championship.

During 1959, the Tridents soccer club failed to register a winning season. It placed 11th out of 14 teams in the National League with a record of 7 wins, 2 ties and 13 losses. The team was coached by Frank Pike. The Tridents reserve team showed only marginal success during this period. The failure of the Tridents on the field was starting to reflect in the number of fans attending games. For the players it was becoming ever more demoralizing.

The 1959-60 basketball team once again triumphed in the Bathurst College Community Basketball League. The title was the sixth for the Tridents in ten years. As in many of the previous years, the team was led by Ed Boguski.

The men's volleyball team, competing in the Senior "A" League, finished the season in fifth place out of eight clubs. Tridents' record of 4 wins and 10 losses was an indication of the competition encountered. The intermediate women's team improved tremendously from the previous year to finish the season tied for first. Because of set differentials, the team was awarded second place.

The 1960 soccer season was Tridents' most disappointing. After experimenting for two years with players from Europe, Trident manager Nick Waller and coach Oleksander Skocen decided to recruit players from South America. Six players from Argentina joined the club, among them Juan Wareckij and Gregory Budko of the Argentine First Division. Nevertheless, the soccer club continued its losing ways. The team finished in last place among the 13 teams with a record of 2 wins, 3 ties and 19 losses.

The disappointing season on the soccer pitch and subsequent internal difficulties within the club resulted in the cancellation of the senior level soccer program.

The 1960-61 basketball season saw the Tridents place second in league standings. On the volleyball courts, USC Trident men's team competed in the OVA senior "A" league. The team occupied the basement of league standings all year. At the Ukrainian inter-club championships held at Toronto, the Tridents defeated the Lions of Chicago in the final to capture the title. An intermediate women's team was also fielded that year.

Even though there was no senior soccer team, the sport club decided not to drop its junior age soccer program. As a result, in the summer of 1961, two midget and one junior team were entered into league competition.

During the winter of 1966-67, USC Trident fielded two basketball teams in the Bathurst College Community Basketball League. The junior team won the championship of its division.

That winter, two Tridents volleyball teams competed in the inaugural season of the Ukrainian Volleyball League. The women placed third among four entrants while the men failed to win a game and finished in seventh and last place. Both teams were primarily made up of UNYF members. The women's club was coached by Paul Kelembet.

In the fall of 1967, the senior men's SA Ukraina volleyball team transferred in almost its entirety to USC Trident. Among those who transferred were national team member Walter Rosocha, future national team member Andrew Stanko and veteran playing coach Paul Kelembet. This move immediately made the Tridents men's volleyball team competitive. Most members of the previous year's team were relegated to the "B" squad. The two teams, though, trained and practised together. Kelembet continued to coach the women's team.

The senior men's volleyball team played well during the 1967-68 season, qualifying for the Canadian championship contested in Hamilton. The Tridents completed the preliminary round with a record of 3 wins and 9 losses to place fifth in their pool. The team did not qualify for the championship playoffs. At the USCAK Ukrainian inter-club championship held at Rochester, the Tridents men's team won the gold medal. The club's playing coach Paul Kelembet was named the tournament's outstanding competitor.

During the winter of 1967-68, the Tridents once again participated in the Ukrainian Volleyball League. The men's "A" team won the championship while the "B" team placed third. The women placed third.

In the spring of 1969, USC Trident hosted the 12th annual Association of Ukrainian Sport Clubs of North America (USCAK) volleyball championship. USC Trident teams fared well in their respective divisions at the tournament. The men's team won the championship while the women placed third.

In the summer of 1969, the Tridents bantam soccer team that competed in the Borough of York League made it to the playoffs. In the deciding game, after two overtime periods the game was still tied at 0-0. A shoot out followed, with one player taking all of his team's three shots. USC Trident named goalkeeper Muzychka to take the shots. He scored three times. At the same time, he stopped one of the opponent's shots to secure the championship for his team.

The USC Trident expanded its operations in the fall of 1969 when a tennis program was introduced. Twice a week, young members had the opportunity to train indoors under the watchful eye of D. Melnyk.

During the winter of 1969-70, USC Trident operated four volleyball teams. The senior men's team and women's teams were coached by Paul Kelembet and managed by Theodore Ilenchuk. The two junior teams were trained by Orest Lysak and Chester Cherniawski.

At the 1970 USCAK championship, the men's volleyball team won the title for the third consecutive year. Walter Rosocha of the Tridents was named the tournament's outstanding competitor.

As for most of the 1960s, during the summer of 1971 and 1972, USC Trident also fielded a junior soccer team.

It appears that the Ukrainian Sports Club Trident ceased operating in late 1972.


## PRESIDENTS OF THE UKRAINIAN SPORTS CLUB TRIDENT

| | |
|---|---|
| Sam Mackevych | (1951) |
| Stepan Rosocha | (1952, 1955) |
| Walter Marko | (1956) |
| Michael Rebryk | (1957) |
| Mykhailo Tsar | (1958) |
| Mykhailo Bardyn | (1959) |
| O. Surkalo | (1960) |
| Robert Dnieper | (1961) |
| Julian Polika | (1969, 1970) |

# UKRAINIAN TENNIS CLUB *LVIV*

Among Ukrainian tennis enthusiasts who settled in Toronto after World War II, the idea of establishing a tennis club began to formulate during the winter of 1953-54. At that time, an attempt was made to organize a tennis group within the Ukrainian Sports Club Trident. During the winter of 1954-55, indoor tennis training occurred at the Ukrainian National Federation Hall under the watchful eye of John Banko, a former Yugoslav Davis Cup player. In the summer of 1955, former members of pre-World War II tennis clubs of Lviv, Roman Dzerowych, M. Horban, B. Kalba and Y. Terlecki, as well as recent enthusiasts W. Iwanyk, S. Maziar and J. Moroz, came to the conclusion that an independent tennis club would serve the needs of Toronto's Ukrainian tennis enthusiasts best.

As a result, newspaper ads appeared in Ukrainian language newspapers announcing the formation of the Ukrainian Tennis Club Lviv (UTC Lviv). The ads informed the public of the club's intent: to instil a love for tennis among Ukrainian youth. Experienced club members would help out in the coaching and training of the youth. The club would also serve as a training and a competitive base for adults of varied tennis experience. An informative meeting was held on July 10 and a month later, on August 16, the first formal meeting of the club was held. Roman Dzerowych was elected president; Y. Terlecki, vice-president; Stephen Maziar, secretary; Orysia Haras, treasurer; and Walter Iwanyk, organizational chairman.

*Ukrainian Tennis Club Lviv logo*

The club began its activities immediately. Three times a week members practised on tennis courts secured free of charge from the City of Toronto at Landsdowne Park and later Christie Pits. Club members, numbering about thirty in the first year of operation, eagerly began honing their tennis skills. Inter-club matches were organized with a Lithuanian tennis club and the Polish White Eagles Club. The summer season concluded with play for the club championship. Walter Iwanyk won the men's title while Lucy Drunewych captured the women's.

The following year the club expanded its operations by including an "international" match. It went down in defeat to the Levy Sport Club of Chicago. Once again inter-club competitions were held with local clubs. Iwanyk and Drunewych repeated as club champions. They were the first winners of trophies sponsored by local businessman Dr. Boyko.

In 1957, the men's club title was won by Z. Drach, while in the women's division I. Stecyk triumphed. Friendly matches were held with numerous Toronto clubs. During the Labour Day weekend, club representatives travelled to Chicago to compete at the Ukrainian North American Championships sanctioned by the Ukrainian Sports Federation of the United States and Canada (USCAK). Unfortunately, Lviv-Toronto was the only club to appear for the championship and as a result the women's competition was cancelled and the men's diluted. In tournament play, W. Iwanyk placed third. That year, Lviv began organizing an Ontario championship for Ukrainians. The competition was cancelled due to a lack of interest.

*Ukrainian Tennis Club Lviv team at the Ukrainian inter-club championship, 1958*

In 1958, representatives of the UTC Lviv competed in a tournament at the Ukrainian resort *Soyuzivka* in the Catskill Mountains of New York State. The tournament was organized by the Carpathian Ski Club of New York and was recognized as the official North American championship among Ukrainians by the Ukrainian Sports Federation of the United States and Canada. The championship quickly gained popularity as the location was easily accessible, the facilities ideal, and the organizational structure ensured that the tournaments ran efficiently. The championship, which has been successfully contested through 1991, attracted more than 150 competitors in some years.

Winning the women's title in 1958 was Lviv's Iryna Stecyk. Toronto also won the women's club championship. Stecyk's victory was a start of a dynasty that would finally end in 1966. For nine consecutive years, Lviv players won the women's singles title. In addition to her 1958 victory, I. Stecyk also won in 1959, 1960 and 1962. Lucy Drunewych was the winner in the years 1961 and 1963-66. She also won the title in 1969. Drunewych's six titles established a championship record.

In 1960, the Ukrainian Tennis Club Lviv introduced competitive tennis for junior age players. Junior age categories were included in the club championships and junior players participated in inter-club competitions. Competing in junior age group categories, Y. Stecyk and R. Melnyk captured Ukrainian Sports Federation of the United States and Canada sanctioned titles.

The Ukrainian Tennis Club Lviv was an independent sports club. Financially it was self-sustained. Dues were collected from members. The award night socials raised nominal funds for the club. Those travelling to tournaments paid their own way. The club did not have enough members or resources to operate in any other manner. Membership in the UTC Lviv peaked in the early 1960s when some 50 individuals participated in the club's tennis program.

Over the years, UTC Lviv played numerous exhibition matches against many of the tennis clubs of Toronto. Among them were such traditional Canadian clubs as the Old Mill Tennis Club and others such as those organized by Japanese, Lithuanian, Polish, and other emigre groups. Almost every year, the club would host or travel to tournaments to compete against other Ukrainian tennis clubs of North America. Competition was held against Chernyk of Detroit, Lviv of Cleveland, the Carpathian Ski Club of New York and the Levy Sport Club of Chicago.

In March of 1964, the Ukrainian Tennis Club Lviv lost its driving force when Roman Dzerowych passed away. The passing created a vacuum in the club which could not be filled. As a result, the club slowly disintegrated. Competition against other Ukrainian clubs of North America ceased as did the competition against clubs in Toronto. The only activities retained were the internal club championships and the yearly trek to *Soyuzivka*. As a result, many members became disillusioned with the Ukrainian Tennis Club Lviv and left for other clubs.

In 1965, an attempt was made to revive all of the club's previous activities. The attempt failed. An effort was made to amalgamate with the Carpathian Ski Club - KLK but this also did not materialize.

# UKRAINIAN VOLLEYBALL CLUB TORONTO

For more than eight years, a group of boys, all members of the Ukrainian Youth Association Plast, represented Plast in volleyball competition. By 1972, most of them had left the youth association but continued to play volleyball on its team. The hierarchy of Plast expressed their dissatisfaction with that arrangement; they believed that representatives of Plast in athletic competition should be active members of the association. In addition, the cost of operating the team was becoming excessive. As a result, Plast cancelled its sponsorship of the team.

The desire of the teammates to continue to play together resulted in the team leaving Plast in the spring of 1972 and forming the Ukrainian Volleyball Club (UVC) Toronto. Yaroslaw Krywonis, the manager of the team while it was with Plast, was the driving force behind the formation of the UVC. Once the club became operational, he almost single handedly ran it. One of Krywonis' stipulations was that membership on the teams be restricted to athletes of Ukrainian descent.

The first major test for the UVC occurred a few weeks after the formation of the club, at the 1972 Canadian Championship. The team played well in the qualifying matches and advanced to the quarter-finals where it disposed of the Winnipeg Wesmen in two games, 15-13 and 15-4. In the semi-finals, the Ukrainian Volleyball Club met the Volleyball Club of Vancouver which had three national team members on its roster. It was expected that the UVC, with two former national team members in its line-up - Andrew Stanko and captain Walter Rosocha, would keep the game close. The Vancouver club, though, easily defeated the UVC in two games, 15-9 and 15-4. The defeat placed the Ukrainian Volleyball Club in fourth place at the national championship. The team was coached by Mel Holick, a former coach of the Canadian men's national team.

The senior men's UVC strengthened itself for the 1972-73 season with the addition of future national team member and professional Peter Stefaniuk. Expectations were high and the team did not disappoint. The Ukrainian Volleyball Club registered an undefeated season in league play, winning all 16 games to place first in the Senior "AA" league of the Ontario Volleyball Association and capture the provincial championship. At the national championship, the UVC had a good preliminary round but lost in the quarter-finals to the Volleyball Club of Vancouver, 15-6 and 15-13. Competing in the Ontario Open that season, the UVC advanced to the semi-finals before bowing out to a powerful Michigan club. At the Association of Ukrainian Sport Clubs of North America (USCAK) championship, UVC decimated the opposition to capture the top prize.

In the fall of 1973, the UVC entered two men's teams in league play. In addition, a women's volleyball team was organized and registered in the OVA intermediate league. The women's team was organized and coached by Roman Komorowsky. Part way through the 1973-74 season, Yaroslaw Krywonis passed away and the club found itself in a void. After some soul searching, the athletes and coaches decided to disband the Ukrainian Volleyball Club Toronto and join the Sport Association Ukraina. Three teams, two men's and a women's, transferred to Ukraina, revitalizing that club's volleyball program.

The senior men's "AA" team completed the season by winning the league and provincial championship. It defeated all opponents to win the Ontario Open and was invited to compete in a specially organized "Tournament of Four" that included Canada's national team and the top teams from Quebec and the United States. Ukraina defeated the clubs from Quebec and the United States. In the final, Ukraina almost upset Canada's national team, losing by the smallest of margins, 15-13, 16-14 and 17-15. The club was coached by Mel Holick.

The women's team completed the 1973-74 season by placing second in the intermediate league. The second men's team lacked consistency throughout the season and fared poorly.


# UKRAINIAN VOLLEYBALL LEAGUE


In the fall of 1966, the general meeting of the Association of Ukrainian Sport Clubs of North America (USCAK) - Canadian division recommended that a volleyball league be formed in Toronto. Attending the meeting were delegates from the city's youth and sports organizations, and they agreed to register teams should a league be formed. The meeting concluded with the founding of the Ukrainian Volleyball League of Toronto. Wolodymyr Ihnatowycz was elected the league's president and was given the mandate to organize the league and to make it operational.

W. Ihnatowycz spent two months conceptualizing, planning and laying the ground work. On January 21, 1967, the league began operations.

The league was not a league in the general sense of the word. Rather, it was a series of one-day tournaments held during the winter months, with the points accumulated in each tournament totalled at the conclusion to determine the winner. This approach was necessary because some of the clubs were already committed to playing in city leagues and many of the athletes were also playing for their respective schools. It was feared that these multiple allegiances could result in conflicting obligations. In addition, it was believed that the one-day tournaments would provide the youths with a broader forum for fraternization.

*Women's teams participating in the UkrainianVolleyball League, 1966-67*

There were two such tournaments in the league's inaugural season. The third one was cancelled due to club commitments to city league and tournament play. Participating in the league were seven men's clubs - SA Ukraina, Plast, ODUM, SUM, UNYF, USC Trident and St. Basil's College and four women's - SUM, Plast, USC Trident and ODUM. SA Ukraina won the overall league title in the men's division while SUM won the women's.

A number of clubs failed to register for the 1967-68 season. To compensate for this, the league requested the participating clubs to field two teams if possible. Six men's teams and four women's subsequently took part in the competition. The women from SUM repeated as league champions while the men's title was won the by USC Trident.

*Men's teams participating in the Ukrainian Volleyball League, 1966-67*

A shortage of entries resulted in the demise of the Ukrainian Volleyball League after the 1967-

68 season. Some of the clubs ceased operations while others opted out due to their commitments to city league and tournament play.

# UKRAINIAN YOUTH ASSOCIATION *PLAST*

Ukrainian immigrants arriving in Toronto from the displaced persons camps of Europe established the Ukrainian Youth Association Plast - Toronto Branch in 1948. The organizers of the branch were at one time all active Plast members in Ukraine and/or Western Europe and wanted to re-establish the association in Canada. Plast itself was a youth organization modelled on the scouting principles of Lord Baden-Powell.

Many in Plast believed that sport was a solid building block of the ideals of scouting. As a result, Plast incorporated sport in its program from the earliest days. Nevertheless, it would take a few years before Plast began to organize teams that would compete in Ukrainian inter-club championships and in Canadian leagues.

By the mid-1960s, Plast had a vibrant sport program. To facilitate its coordination and to develop it further, the Toronto branch included the position of sport coordinator on its executive. Among those who served in that capacity commencing in 1964 were Wolodymyr Komisar, Walter Kuz, Yaroslaw Krywonis, Zenon Duda, Oleksander Zeltway, Orest Haras, Petro Jacyk, Bohdan Suszko, and Slavko Lawryshyn. The position was suspended in the early 1980s.

After the founding of the Association of Ukrainian Sport Clubs of North America (USCAK) in December of 1955, Plast embraced the association's objective that called for the mass participation in physical activity by Ukrainian youth organizations. Those participants attaining a certain prescribed level would be awarded with a pin of physical fitness. Fulfilling the requirements for the pin became a prerequisite for Plast's badge program.

In the 1950s, the women's fraternity (kurin), "Ti scho hrebli rvut" became the first group to regularly participate in sport activities by training in the various disciplines of track and field. In preparation for the 1957 International Plast Jamboree that was to be hosted by the Toronto branch at its summer camp *Plastova Sitch* at Grafton, Walter Kuz spent a year training the members in aspects of sports officiating. At the jamboree, the group formed the core of the sports officials. To a great extent, it was also responsible for encouraging sports among the younger Plast members of the Toronto branch.

In the late 1950s, Oleksander Zeltway organized a men's volleyball team from Plast members. The team was registered with the OVA intermediate league for 1958-59 season. In a short period of time, the team members developed a sporting bond that lasted for over a quarter of a century. With a few minor changes in its personnel, the team played together through the year 1985. In addition to league play, the team also competed at USCAK championships.

In 1960, Plast entered a team at the inaugural Ukrainian inter-club track and field championships sponsored by the Association of Ukrainian Sport Clubs of North America. The team placed third in the overall competition.

These track and field meets became an annual event and were held through the year 1979. The meets were hosted by numerous sports clubs and youth organizations in Canada and the United States. Plast Toronto hosted the event four times at its summer camp *Plastova Sitch* at Grafton. In 1965, 219 athletes from 11 clubs participated, in 1968, 229 athletes from 9 clubs, in 1969, 175 athletes from 6 clubs, and in 1971, 214 athletes from 5 clubs participated. Athletes from Plast placed first in the overall standings at these track and field meets in the years 1963 through 1969 and from 1976 to 1979.

The meets became very popular and a keen rivalry developed among the leading clubs. To instill an enthusiasm for sport and competition, to provide basic instruction and to get its competitors into shape, Plast often organized a two week "sports" camp prior to the track meets. The camps were widely attended and well liked by the participants.

In the late 1950s, Walter Kuz organized a girls' sport group from the membership of Plast. Kuz was a great advocate of an organized sport curriculum for Plast and a staunch supporter of USCAK's physical fitness pin program. Initially, the girls practised various routines, did exercises and participated in intramural competitions.

To pass the winter months, Plast sport enthusiast Borys Hul, who at the time was also associated with the Sport Association Ukraina, encouraged the girls to come out to Ukraina's pick-up volleyball sessions. During the winter of 1960-61, the girls began to develop volleyball skills and quickly mastered the basic elements of the game. In the fall of 1961, the team was entered by SA Ukraina into the competitive Ontario Volleyball Association (OVA) intermediate league.

Plast became concerned when it found out that a team made up of its members was representing another organization in sport competition. The team was allowed to finish the 1961-62 season with SA Ukraina but the following year the team was entered into league play as a representative of Plast. At about this time, the girls named themselves *Vedmedyky* (Teddy Bears). The first major success of the Vedmedyky in volleyball competition occurred in the spring of

1963 when the team placed third at the Ukrainian inter-club championship sponsored by USCAK.

In 1963 and 1964, Vedmedyky participated in the USCAK track and field championships, winning the overall title for Plast on both occasions.

On the volleyball courts, Vedmedyky won the 1963-64 Intermediate Level championship of the Ontario Volleyball Association. The victory advanced the team to the senior loop. In the fall of 1964, Walter Stochansky took on the coaching duties of the Vedmedyky volleyball team, and Kuz remained as trainer. The two became an ideal tandem; on and off the court they complemented each other. More importantly though, both were innovators. Kuz introduced then unheard of warm-ups and calisthenics prior to training sessions and games. Stochansky spent hours studying and evaluating new training techniques and game strategies developed by the great Japanese women's teams of the 1960s. Many of these training techniques and strategies were incorporated by the Vedmedyky.

The administrative organizer and chaperon of the Vedmedyky team was Chrystyna Wolycka. She accompanied the girls on many of their travels and was responsible for maintaining Plast mores.

During the 1964-65 season, the Vedmedyky played well in the senior OVA loop to place fourth. Because the girls were all still of junior age, the team entered competition for the provincial title at the junior level. At the Ontario junior championship, the club won the provincial title. Subsequently, the Vedmedyky won the Eastern Canada championship.

*Plast Vedmedyky volleyball team, 1965 Canadian Junior Champions*

At the Canadian championship in Vancouver, the team was granted permission to compete at both the junior and the senior level. The Vedmedyky placed second in their pool in the senior championship to qualify for the final four. The team eventually finished in fourth place.

In the final of the junior championship, Vedmedyky defeated the B.C. Mainland Stars 15-4 and 15-8 to win the national title.

Captain Christine Tomkiw was honoured as the tournament's MVP and was named to the all-star team. Joining her on the all-star team were four other Vedmedyky - Lida Barchynsky, Christine Eliashevsky, Vera Malanczyj and Lida Syrotynsky. Also playing on the championship team were Lida Eliashevsky, Maria Tarnawskyj and Nadia Zubyk.

During the winter of 1964-65, Zenon Duda began organizing a sport program for boys. The group's first activity was the formation of a volleyball team which held practices and played two exhibition matches.

The Vedmedyky continued their high calibre of play during the 1965-66 volleyball season. The team advanced to the quarter-finals of the Ontario Open Championship, placed fourth at the Toronto Invitational, and was runner-up in the OVA senior league play. The team then captured the provincial junior championship and the Eastern Canada Junior Championship. The season culminated with the Vedmedyky defending their national junior championship in Calgary. At the senior national championship the junior team once again placed fourth. The championship team included captain and national junior championship MVP Christine Eliashevsky, Lida Barchynsky, Lida Eliashevsky, Luba Olesnycky, Roma Panczyszyn, Maria Tarnawskyj, Christine Tomkiw and Nadia Zubyk.

The boys' volleyball team was entered in the Toronto Senior "B" for the 1965-66 season. The team completed its inaugural season in a respectable sixth spot among 12 teams. Because the boys were all still of junior age, the team entered competition for the provincial title at the junior level. The team placed fourth out of four teams. The boys' team completed the season with a sixth-place finish at the Eastern Canada championship. One of the problems experienced by the team that year was the lack of a permanent coach. At one time or another Lubomyr Iwashko, Walter Kuz and Vera Malanczyj tried to fill the void by coaching the team.

After winning the second national championship, a number of the Vedmedyky starters left the team for other clubs. Their positions were filled by rookies from within the ranks of Plast. The team played well during the 1966-67 season and qualified for the 1967 national senior championship. There they finished in sixth place with a record of 3 wins, 2 ties and 3 losses.

During the winter of 1966-67, the Vedmedyky also competed in the inaugural season of the

Ukrainian Volleyball League. The team placed second. Plast also fielded a men's team in the league which also placed second.

In 1967, the inaugural Canada Winter Games were held. Selected to Ontario's volleyball team were three members of the Vedmedyky: Luba Olesnycky, Lida Syrotynsky and Christine Tomkiw. Also joining the team were three former members: Christine Eliashevsky, Lida Eliashevsky and Maria Tarnawskyj. At the Canada Winter Games, the Ontario team, consisting predominantly of the Vedmedyky and its alumnae, battled its way to the gold medal. Christine Eliashevsky also gained personal recognition in 1967 when she was named to Canada's Pan American Games team.

On the senior OVA circuit the Vedmedyky placed third during the 1967-68 season. At the 1968 Canadian championship at Hamilton, the team played in pool B. The club's record of 4 wins and 6 losses failed to qualify it for the championship playoffs. At the Ukrainian inter-club championship held at Rochester, the Vedmedyky placed second. The club was coached by W. Kuz. At the provincial junior championships, the junior Vedmedyky placed second. At the Eastern Canada championship Plast lost in the final 5-15, 15-10 and 6-15 to the Ukrainian Youth Association (SUM) of Toronto. The girls were coached by Vera Malanczyj and Lida Syrotynsky.

During the winter of 1967-68, Plast also operated a volleyball program for midget girls. The major objective of the program was to teach youngsters the fundamentals of volleyball. In addition, a senior ladies recreational team was organized that year.

Plast fielded two men's volleyball teams during the 1967-68 season in the OVA league. The team competing in the intermediate league placed first. Subsequently, the team competed at the provincial junior championships placing fourth.

In addition to participating in OVA league play during the 1967-68 season, Plast once again entered teams for competition in the Ukrainian Volleyball League. The women placed second, the men's "A" team placed fourth, and the men's "B" team placed sixth.

In the summer, Plast participated at a shooting meet hosted by the Ukrainian recreational club *Howerla*. George Harapa of Plast won the individual title while Plast placed second in the team competition.

In the late 1960s and early 1970s, Vera Malanczyj served as national sports coordinator for Plast. During her tenure she actively encouraged Plast branches to incorporate the USCAK physical fitness pin program into their curriculum. With the help of her Vedmedyky teammates, Malanczyj was able to administer the pin program at most Plast summer camps across

Canada. It was a major achievement, as by that time other Ukrainian organizations in Canada had completely neglected the program. Plast honoured Malanczyj for her work in promoting the pin program. She was also one of a very few individuals to have met the requirements for the silver pin at the time.

In the fall of 1968, two Vedmedyky teams started play on the OVA circuit. Only one completed the schedule. The senior women's team suspended operations prior to the conclusion of the season; team members left after becoming disenchanted with the changed direction of the Plast sport program and their team's role within it. The junior Vedmedyky team, unaffected by the turmoil, won the championship of the senior "B" league. At the provincial junior championship, Plast lost in the final to SUM 15-11 and 15-3. The juniors also represented Plast at the Ukrainian inter-club championships placing second.

The Vedmedyky sport group formally disbanded in August of 1969. The existence of the group within Plast was a unique phenomenon. In addition to participating in the regular Plast program and fulfilling its requirements, the girls were at the forefront of Plast's sport program for a decade. They competed at the highest level of organized volleyball in Canada. They participated in Ukrainian volleyball and track and field championships, they coached junior boys' and girls' volleyball teams, organized and conducted sport camps, and implemented USCAK's physical fitness pin program. Most also found time to represent their secondary and/or post-secondary schools in volleyball competition.

Plast once again fielded two men's teams, an intermediate and a senior "B," during the 1968-69 season in the OVA league. At the USCAK inter-club championship the men's team placed second.

During the summer of 1969, the shooting club trained under the guidance of Andrij Rohowsky. *Howerla* was once again the site of a shooting tournament at which Plast participated.

In the late 1960s and the early 1970s, as the sport of orienteering started to gain popularity in Canada, devotee Vera Malanczyj began advocating the sport among her colleagues in Plast. In a short period of time, she assembled a small group of enthusiasts who regularly participated in orienteering meets, often under the auspices of Plast. In 1975, this group founded the Ukrainian Orienteering Club.

Four Plast teams competed in OVA leagues during the 1969-70 volleyball season. The junior men placed fourth in the league's intermediate division. At the Ontario championship the team won the silver medal and an invitation to the Canadian championships. Playing in Calgary for the national title, the club placed sixth with a record of 4 wins and 6 losses. The senior men's team won the senior "B" championship and was promoted to the senior "A" division for the following season. Future national team member Andrew Stanko coached the junior team and was playing coach of the senior team. The junior women's team, coached by Lida Barchynsky, placed third in the senior "B" division. A lack of interest resulted in the women's senior "A" team folding midway through the season. At the USCAK championship held at Detroit, the men's and women's teams both placed third.

The appointment of Yaroslaw Krywonis to the position of sport coordinator saw the expansion of Plast's sport program in the winter of 1969-70. In December of 1969, ice was acquired at a Toronto park and a hockey program commenced. Nine to eleven-year-olds were instructed in the basics of the game by a staff headed by Zenon Tatarsky. The youngsters also had an opportunity to scrimmage. In January of 1970, Jaroslaw Moroz, a member of the Carpathian Ski Club (KLK), introduced a ski program to Plast. The ski group partook in three trips in its inaugural season. The teenage skiers were coached by KLK members. KLK also organized a ski school for Plast at Toronto's Centennial Park. Lack of interest resulted in the cancelling of this program. In addition, an extensive intramural program was launched which saw competition between troops.

At the 1970 shooting meet at the recreational club *Howerla*, Plast won the team championship title while member George Komorowsky won the individual title. Andrij Rohowsky continued to coach the members of the shooting club.

Plast fielded a junior and a senior men's team in the OVA league during the 1970-71 season. The men's team played at the senior "A" level. It won the USCAK inter-club volleyball championship. At the 1971 Ontario Games, the men's volleyball team met SUM in the championship game. Plast lost the closely contested final. Andrew Stanko coached both men's teams while the junior women's team was coached by O. Haras.

The hockey program was expanded during the winter of 1970-71 to include older boys. Close to seventy youngsters participated in the program, which, as in the previous year, included training and games.

During the 1970 Christmas break, Plast held its first ski camp. Some 100 participants spent six days skiing at St. Donat in the Laurentian Mountains of Quebec. The participants were taught skiing techniques by 11 instructors whose services were provided by the federal government free of charge. Bohdan Jaciw, a member of Plast and the Carpathian Ski Club, organized the camp for Plast. The ski camp was a big success and the activity became an integral component of Plast's curriculum. For many years, members of the Carpathian Ski Club helped organize the camps for Plast which were held at St. Donat, St. Jovite, Mont Tremblant, and other locations in the Laurentians.

A senior "A" volleyball team was once again fielded by Plast during the 1971-72 season. By early 1972 most team members had left Plast but continued to play volleyball on its team. This did not sit well with the Plast executive. The general consensus was that a team bearing Plast's name should have at least a number of athletes active in the organization. In addition, the cost of operating the team was becoming excessive for Plast. As a result, Plast cancelled its sponsorship of the club. The team and its manager, Y. Krywonis, left Plast in the spring of 1972 to form the Ukrainian Volleyball Club Toronto. A short time later, the team competed at the national championship, losing in a quarter-final match.

When Yaroslaw Krywonis departed with the volleyball team, he also resigned from his sport coordinator post with Plast. The resignation led to a decline in the association's sport program. In particular, teams were no longer entered into the Ontario Volleyball Association leagues.

The hockey program folded in the early 1970s because of difficulties in securing ice time. The intramural sports program folded in 1977 because of a lack of interest. A year later Plast ran its last summer sports camp. The camps were scheduled to precede the Ukrainian inter-club track and field championships sponsored by the Association of Ukrainian Sport Clubs of North America (USCAK), and when the championships were suspended, Plast discontinued organizing the camps. Of all the sports activities, only the ski camps survived the 1970s and continued to enjoy great popularity through 1991.

In the spring of 1979, Plast members Roman Kocur, Andrij Kos, and Alex Sochaniwsky organized a volleyball team. Since most of the team members were from Plast, the team asked the youth association for sponsorship. After a year of training, the team named Plast Hrim (Thunder), entered the OVA qualification tournament. The team qualified and began play in the OVA league at the senior "B" level in the fall of 1980. Walter Stochansky coached the team. Eventually the cost of sponsorship became excessive for Plast and in 1984, the team transferred to SA Ukraina.

*Plast Thunder jersey crest, c.1980*

# UKRAINIAN YOUTH ASSOCIATION

O ver the years, members of the Toronto branch of the Ukrainian Youth Association (SUM) had the opportunity to represent their organization in a number of competitive sports, among them track and field, floor hockey, hockey, soccer, and volleyball. The level of sport activity in any one year varied, depending primarily on the enthusiasm of the association's sport coordinator and individual counsellors.

Sport at SUM was an extension (on a voluntary basis) of the association's curriculum for youth. To ensure that the sport program complied with the objectives of the association, it was placed under the direct control of a sport coordinator who reported to the executive of the branch. The primary objective of the sport program was to provide the members with a venue where they could collectively participate in sport in a Ukrainian and concurrently a SUM environment. The rosters of the teams that SUM fielded, to a very large extent, were filled by SUM members. At times, non-SUM members were recruited from other Ukrainian youth organizations. On very rare occasions, non-Ukrainians were permitted to compete on SUM teams. In return, the youth association assumed the operating costs of the sport program.

In the early 1950s, SUM organized a men's volleyball team that competed at the Intermediate "A" level with varied success. Prior to the start of the 1956-57 season, the club was strengthened by the addition of a number of SA Ukraina players. The team jelled quickly and played well during the season, qualifying for the provincial championship. In a round robin tournament, SUM defeated a Polish club from Windsor and a Lithuanian club from Toronto, but lost to an Estonian club from Toronto. SUM's record qualified it for the championship final against the Lithuanians, which it won in two straight sets. At the national championships at Ottawa, SUM was ousted in a double elimination match. The club was coached by T. Kuryluk.

In 1960, SUM entered a team at the inaugural Ukrainian inter-club track and field championships sponsored by the Ukrainian Sports Federation of USA and Canada (USCAK). The SUM team placed third in the overall competition.

From the organizers' perspective, the track and field meet was a success and it became an annual event held through the year 1979. The meets were hosted by numerous sport clubs and youth organizations in Canada and the United States. SUM Toronto hosted the event three times at its summer camp *Veselka* in Acton. In 1961, 169 athletes from ten clubs competed, in 1962, 113 athletes from 9 clubs, and in 1973, 175 athletes from six clubs participated. The Ukrainian Youth Association SUM placed first in the overall standings at these meets in the years 1970 through 1975.

The track meets became very popular among the participants and a keen rivalry developed between the leading clubs. SUM often organized a two or three week "sports" camp prior to the meets to prepare its athletes for competition. These camps were widely attended and well liked by the participants. Canadian national team members Zenon Andrusyshyn, Borys Chambul and Lubomyr Chambul all had their start in track and field at the SUM camps or the track and field meets.

In the fall of 1960, youth counsellor Alex Chumak organized a hockey team from members of his troop the Lions. To fill the roster, Chumak recruited a number of 10 to 12-year-old boys from other troops in SUM. Known as the Ukrainian Lions, the team began workouts under the watchful eye of Alex Chumak and his brother Paul. During the winter of 1960-61, the Chumaks restricted the team's activity to practices. The Lions were still too inexperienced to enter a competitive league.

A year later, the Lions were registered in the Catholic Youth League. The team played for a number of seasons, winning the league championship in the 1965-66 season. The team folded after Alex Chumak enrolled at university.

Shortly after arriving in Canada, international gymnastics coach and judge Eugene Oryszczyn became associated with SUM's sport program. In the years 1961-67, he held clinics for members of the association at which youngsters were introduced to various sports. During the summer, he attended camps and advocated sport. Oryszczyn also organized and coordinated massive group drills. Among the more memorable performances were at the unveiling of monuments of Ukrainian poet Taras Shevchenko in Winnipeg in 1961 and Washington, D.C. in 1964, and at Expo '67 in Montreal. The Winnipeg and Washington performances were held in darkened arenas with the participants carrying small illuminating devices. Oryszczyn also produced the group drills at SUM jamborees at Acton, Ontario, and Ellenville, New York. Some of the performances included more than 800 participants.

During the 1964-65 season, the SUM women's volleyball team won the championship of the OVA senior "B" league.

In the mid-1960s, Wolodymyr Ihnatowycz assumed the post of sport coordinator for the branch. He held the position for a number of years. During those years, sport activity flourished at the association and, in retrospect, the period was undoubtedly the most challenging and fruitful in the association's history.

SUM operated out of the Ukrainian Cultural Centre at 83 Christie Street and had the use of the centre's indoor sport facilities. According to Ihnatowycz, the facilities were under-utilized by SUM members. As a result, his first objective was to organize an activity that would put the facility into regular use. A volleyball program was his choice.

Wolodymyr Ihnatowycz led by example. He personally organized and began coaching a junior girls' volleyball team. In three short years, he moulded the Ukrainian Youth girls into one of Canada's finest volleyball clubs. In 1967 and in 1968, the girls won the championship of the Ukrainian Volleyball League. In the latter year, the club won the Ontario junior title defeating Plast Toronto in the final match 5-15, 15-10 and 15-6. A few days later, the juniors won the Eastern Canada Championship at Montreal. At the national championship, Ukrainian Youth placed second after losing in the final 15-9 and 15-11 to the Manitoba Bisonettes. The team was led by its captain and future national team member Julia Kucharchuk and by another future national team member Halya Stefaniuk.

In 1968, the SUM girls also won the first of eight consecutive North American championships for Ukrainian clubs sponsored by the Ukrainian Sports Federation of USA and Canada (USCAK). On six of these occasions, Julia Kucharchuk was named the tournament's outstanding female competitor.

After the establishment of a girls' volleyball team at SUM, a boys' team was organized. The boys made their competitive debut in the Ukrainian Volleyball League part-way through the 1966-67 season. Among those getting his start in volleyball with the SUM team was future national team member and professional Peter Stefaniuk. The team was organized and coached by Roman Kuzmyn.

*Ukrainian Youth Association (SUM) volleyball team, 1970 Ontario Junior Champions*

In 1969, Ukrainian Youth girls repeated as provincial junior champion defeating Plast Toronto 15-11 and 15-3. At the national championship, Ukrainian Youth duplicated its second-place finish of the previous year.

For the 1969-70 volleyball season, the junior girls' team of the past year was entered in the Senior "A" division. This was necessitated when a number of girls exceeded or were soon to exceed the age ceiling for juniors. Competing for the first time at the senior "A" level, Ukrainian Youth won the Ontario championship. A short time later, at the national championship the club played to a third-place finish. During the 1969-70 season, SUM also fielded a junior volleyball team. This team continued the tradition of its predecessor by winning the third consecutive provincial title for the organization. The junior club failed in its bid to win the national title, placing third. SUM also fielded a junior boys' team that year which placed fourth at the Ontario championship.

During the summer of 1970, Ukrainian Youth co-sponsored an under-17 soccer team with SA Ukraina. The team competed at the junior "B" level, placing second in the standings and in the playoffs. It won a tournament hosted by the Ukrainian Sports Federation of USA and Canada. The club was coached by Mike (Mykhailo) Harapyn.

The women's senior " B" volleyball team was revitalized for the 1970-71 season. It responded by winning the city championship in its division. The club was coached by members of the senior "A" team Julia Kucharchuk and Marika Pawlychko. The two veterans also trained two groups of aspiring beginners. The women's senior "A" team played with varying results. It was coached by W. Ihnatowycz. At the 1971 Ontario Games, the men's volleyball team met Plast in the championship game. SUM overcame its stubborn opponent to win the gold medal. The team was coached by R. Kuzmyn.

In the fall of 1970, Bohdan Chmyliwsky organized a hockey team and registered it for competition with the Catholic Youth Organization League. The minor bantam team of 14 and 15-year-old youngsters completed the regular season in second place with a record of 11 wins, 1 tie and 3 losses. Defenceman and captain Roman Moroz led SUM by scoring 34 of the club's 61 goals. In the playoffs, the team won six straight games to take the league championship trophy. The team was coached by Bohdan Chmyliwsky and trained by Yaroslaw Rozeliuk and Bohdan Kopanyshyn. A number of private sponsors helped the team to secure uniforms.

The Ukrainian Youth soccer team was entered in the Junior "A" division for the 1971 season. It placed fifth among 11 teams, winning 10, drawing 5 and losing 10. Formally, the team was still co-sponsored, but SA Ukraina's involvement in its operations was negligible.

During the winter of 1971-72, the bantam hockey team continued playing in the league sponsored by the Catholic Youth Organization.

In late October, the senior "B" men's volleyball team, coached by Roman Kuzmyn, won a qualifying tournament and was promoted to the senior "A" league for the 1971-72 season. Three women's competitive teams operated that year. The senior women's team won the provincial title and advanced to the national championship. There they were stopped in the semi-finals by the Calgary Cals. The women's provincial championship team was coached by Andy Andruchiw and Julia Kucharchuk. The senior "B" team was coached by M. Pawlychko while W. Ihnatowycz handled the intermediate team. In addition, SUM operated three non-competitive volleyball teams.

During the 1972-73 season, the Ukrainian Youth boys' and girls' junior volleyball teams played well. Both clubs captured the provincial championship. The junior girls' team, coached by Andy Andruchiw, defeated Toronto Baby Blues in the final match, while the boys, coached by R. Kuzmyn and R. Struhanyk, defeated Hamilton. At the national championship played at Quebec City, the girls were eliminated in the quarter-finals. The boys' team advanced to the final where they met Winnipeg East Caledonia, the five-time defending Canadian champion. Ukrainian Youth put up a strong fight but lost the title match in two sets, 15-13 and 15-9. The senior women won the Quebec Open Tournament in the fall of 1972. The team was coached by Eli Drakich and included two former national team members, Julia Kucharchuk and Rozika Sulaticki.

During the summer of 1975, Mykhailo Muzychka organized two soccer teams of SUM youngsters. The pee-wee Skala team, which was generally referred to as the Ukes, played in the North York Minor Soccer League. After posting a record of 10 wins, 2 ties and 5 losses, the team qualified for the playoffs, only to lose in the opening round. A mosquito team saw limited action.

In the mid-1970s, members of SUM were instrumental in organizing the Ukrainian Floor Hockey League. Games were played at the Ukrainian Cultural Centre at Christie Street. The league operated for a few years and included about six teams which were sponsored by Ukrainian youth organizations and churches.

# UKRAINIAN YOUTH SOCCER ASSOCIATION

During the winter of 1980-81 and 1981-82, students attending the primary Ukrainian immersion St. Josaphat Catholic School in Toronto had an opportunity to partake in weekly soccer clinics, training sessions, and pick-up games. Dr. Walter Medwidskyj, a parent, organized the activity. Mike (Mykhailo) Harapyn, a former soccer player with Toronto's SA Ukraina, directed the sessions. The weekly sessions quickly gained popularity and soon both participants and parents called for an organized summer soccer league.

In response to the demand, Mike Harapyn, Roman Maksymiv, Dr. Walter Medwidskyj, and Stephen Yakymiv organized the Ukrainian Youth Soccer Association (UYSA) in the spring of 1982. Dr. Medwidskyj became the association's first president while most of the logistics and administrative work were performed by M. Harapyn. In its first year, the league operated with two divisions, an under-10 and under-12. Four teams played in each of the divisions. With 12 players to a team, nearly 100 children of Ukrainian descent participated.

*Ukrainian Youth Soccer Association logo*

The fundamental objective of the Ukrainian Youth Soccer Association was to provide every child who wished to play soccer with an opportunity to do so. Membership in the association was on an individual basis subject to an age criterion. That is, those individuals who wished to play soccer were registered with the league and assigned to teams, rather than organized teams gaining membership in the league. Initially, teams were fielded in two age group divisions. Subsequently, the number of categories increased and aspiring stars from age 5 to 18 could join. Through the age of 15, all teams could be mixed. No set gender ratios existed.

In the league's first few years of existence, parents played an integral role in the operations of the teams. Individuals such as Ihor Kurok, Wasyl Nykoluk, Vera Lykhach, Emile Lubinsky, Bohdan Shklarenko, Roman Wynnyckyj, and the four original organizers all coached or managed clubs. The league used its own referees. Most were retired soccer players.

In 1983, the UYSA selected an under-12 all-star team from the four house league teams competing in that age group. The all-star team travelled to Ellenville, New York, where it partook in the age group soccer championship organized by the Ukrainian Sports Federation of USA and Canada (USCAK). Led on the soccer pitch by S. Bandera, M. Metelsky, and S. Zaraska, and coached by M. Harapyn, the UYSA all-star team captured first place in its division.

The UYSA put together all-star teams on an ad hoc basis for five years. The teams represented the association at various tournaments. In 1988, the UYSA organized three all-star teams to compete at the Metro All-Star Tournament. All three teams, the under-10, under-12, and under-14, won their respective divisions.

In 1984, the executives decided to form "rep" teams which would play in the competitive city leagues. This decision was taken to allow the gifted athletes a better opportunity to develop their skills. At first the rep teams were overwhelmed by the competition, losing by double digit scores. It did not take long, though, for the rep teams to become competitive. In 1987, the first year the rep teams competed as the Islington Rangers in the Metro League, the under-10 team, coached by former national team member Myron Bereza, won the Metro Cup. That same year, the under-16 club, coached by Dennis Metelsky, placed second in the Metro Cup. A year later, Bereza led the under-11 team to the Metropolitan Toronto Soccer Association league championship.

*Ukrainian Youth Soccer Association under-10 "rep" team, 1985*

In 1989, Metelsky coached the under-15 rep team to the Metro Cup championship. Metelsky was with the club in 1990 as it won the under-16 Metro Cup championship and the Metro playoffs. A year later, he saw his club win the under-17 Metro Cup. Also winning the Metro Cup that year was the under-11 team coached by Steve Rozak and Paul Woloshansky.

In 1986, the rep teams were made open to all comers. A Ukrainian background was no longer a requirement. Most rep teams, though, have maintained a high number of players of Ukrainian descent. At the time, the house league did not change its membership policy.

Since its inception in 1982, the Ukrainian Youth Soccer Association house league grew by more than one team a year. By 1987, the league had 21 house league teams and three rep teams with some 300 players of Ukrainian descent competing in the ranks. The number of players dropped to about 200 by the end of the decade.

As the league expanded, the need for trained coaches and referees increased. To encourage high standards, the UYSA paid the registration for those individuals who enrolled in coaching and or refereeing certification programs. The league also started encouraging older players to try their hand at refereeing. This initiative gave the players an opportunity to experience the game from a different perspective.

To operate a house league and rep teams required significant finances. In the late 1980s, each player upon registration received a shirt, shorts, socks, and insurance coverage. At the end of the season, each player was presented with a participant's trophy and a team picture, and hosted at a team dinner. In addition, tournament costs were covered. While the players payed a nominal registration fee, the UYSA could not do without business sponsorship. More than 20 Ukrainian enterprises sponsored teams. To give the sponsoring business recognition, the name of the sponsor was emblazoned on the game jerseys.

Towards the end of the decade, age excluded many of the initial UYSA members from further competition. As a result, the association formed a pick-up league composed of alumni, coaches, managers and referees. The group played on a regular basis and entered a team at a tournament at Camp *Sokil* at Hawkestone, Ontario, in 1990 and 1991.

The Ukrainian Youth Soccer Association has, over the years, provided many with an opportunity to participate in organized soccer regardless of skill. It has also provided those seeking a competitive environment with an opportunity to develop their skills. In its short existence, two UYSA alumni, Orest Bereza and Roman Harapyn, have gone on to play for the junior Toronto Blizzards of the Metro Toronto Soccer Association, while Peter Blazenko and Mike Fedoruk were named to the Ontario all-star team.

In 1991, six members of the UYSA were selected to the North American Ukrainian all-star team. The team was organized by the Ukrainian Sports Federation of USA and Canada (USCAK) for the purpose of touring Ukraine in conjunction with the celebrations honouring the 80th anniversary of the Sports Association Ukraina of Lviv. The all-star team was co-coached by UYSA's Mike Harapyn. The team played exhibition matches in Vynnyky, Komarno, Dobrohostiv and Boryslav in Ukraine.

# UNIVERSITY SETTLEMENT UKRAINIANS

For a number of years the Ukrainian Democratic Youth Association (ODUM) sponsored a volleyball team that competed in the senior "B" division of the Ontario Volleyball Association league in Toronto. After the 1960-61 season, ODUM terminated its sponsorship of the team, citing rising costs. Team members Paul Kelembet and Valentin Polakiwsky decided to keep the team together and sought out new sponsorship. In the fall of 1961, the club became affiliated with the University Settlement House Community Centre.

*University Settlement Ukrainians, 1961-62*

The University Settlement Ukrainians were registered in the OVA Senior "B" League for the 1961-62 season. In its inaugural year, the team won the championship of the league. A short time later, the team won the provincial championship. The following year, the team fell back to third place in league standings.

A lack of players to start the 1963-64 season resulted in the merger of the University Settlement

Ukrainians with a Polish volleyball team. The team finished the season in second place. At the end of the year the team folded.

Paul Kelembet was the playing coach of the University Settlement Ukrainians during the club's three year existence.

# VANCOUVER

## UKRAINIAN SPORTS CLUB *BERKUT*

On February 13, 1950, the Ukrainian National Youth Federation (UNYF) held a meeting to organize a sports club. The Federation's first attempt in 1949 resulted in the formation of the Ukrainian Sports Club Sokil. The club, though, severed its relationship with UNYF after only a month and a half and became independent. Yaroslaw Bilak rallied the UNYF members to form a new club. It was argued that Sokil had become an inactive sports club. It was also argued that an organization such as the UNYF should have a sports club within its framework.

Those attending the meeting agreed that the UNYF should form a new sports club, and on that date the Ukrainian Sports Club Berkut came into being. A. Kuliak was elected president; L. Trach, vice-president; R. Kozoris, secretary; and O. Kasiuchnych, treasurer. Individuals volunteered to organize sections in badminton, baseball, basketball, calisthenics, chess, soccer, swimming, table tennis and volleyball. In team sports such as baseball, basketball and volleyball, both men's and women's teams were planned. Initiation fees were set at 50 cents and the monthly dues were 25 cents. In addition, the UNYF agreed to provide the club with financial assistance.

The formation of Berkut resulted in a number of Sokil members returning to a UNYF-sponsored club. This left Sokil without sufficient personnel and it folded.

The ambitious plans of Berkut were not realized. In 1950, the club only managed to organize activities in badminton, chess and table tennis. On paper, the club had some 40 members but only about 20 actively participated.

During the winter of 1950-51, the club played two exhibition table tennis matches against the Polish club Polonia. With the arrival of warm weather, tennis was pursued. During the year the club also held a house league chess tournament.

# UKRAINIAN SPORTS CLUB *SOKIL*

I n 1949, members of the Ukrainian National Youth Federation (UNYF), Vancouver Branch, organized a soccer team and entered it in the North Division of the city soccer league at the intermediate level. They named the team Sokil. Subsequently, a sports club bearing the name Ukrainian Sports Club Sokil was formally established by the UNYF branch. The initiators of the soccer club and the sports club were Walter Klymkiw, a university student from Winnipeg, S. Chomnytsky, who assumed the club's presidency; and W. Boretsky and the Soltys brothers, soccer enthusiasts with European experience.

Just a month and half after its founding, Sokil left UNYF to become an independent entity. The decision to leave was reached at a general meeting with a majority of the members opting for the proposal. After leaving the UNYF, the club operated out of a Ukrainian Catholic church. In February 1950, the independent Sokil club organized a table tennis tournament with the Polish club Zgoda. The Ukrainian side won the event 10-6.

The Ukrainian Sports Club Sokil ceased to operate shortly after that tournament. The UNYF had, at the time, organized a new sports club which attracted a number of Sokil members. This left Sokil with an insufficient membership to warrant continuation of activities.

# WINDSOR

## CANADIAN UKRAINIAN YOUTH ASSOCIATION - ST. VLADIMIR

The Canadian Ukrainian Youth Association (SUMK), Windsor Branch, participated in sport on a varied basis. At certain times in its history the association had a strong sports program. At other times, it was nearly non-existent. The emphasis placed on sport depended on the executive.

In the 1950s, SUMK sponsored a basketball team called St. Vladimir. The team competed in the Windsor Church Basketball Association league. During the 1954-55 season, St. Vladimir placed first in the standings. The club was led by Ed Mularchyk, who would join the Ottawa Rough Riders Football club that year.

In March, St. Vladimir defeated Cavalry United in a two-game total-point playoff 141-115 to win the Intermediate "B" championship of the Windsor Church Basketball Association. Mularchyk scored 32 of his team's 63 points in the second game. The victory advanced St. Vladimir to the provincial playdowns. In the opening two-game total-point series, St. Vladimir defeated St. Paul's United of Sarnia 116-80. St. Vladimir subsequently defeated Hamilton Melrose United 138-111 to win the provincial semi-final. In the championship series against Brampton St. Paul's, St. Vladimir won 64-40 in Windsor and 62-50 in Brampton to win the title. The team was coached by Nick Petruk and managed by Walter Wachna.

During the 1955-56 season, St. Vladimir played in a combined Senior-Intermediate Windsor Church Association Basketball League. The team failed in its bid to win the league championship, going down in defeat to Central United 62-54 and 68-64. The club nevertheless qualified for the provincial Intermediate "A" Playdowns. It defeated Sarnia St. Paul's in the opening round. In the second round, St. Vladimir was eliminated by Toronto North Parkdale United.

*Canadian Ukrainian Youth Association (SUMK) basketball team, 1955*

Ten years later, SUMK once again had a strong basketball program. The club won the 1966-67 Intermediate "B" provincial championship of the Ontario Church League. In 1968 and 1970, the club won the Eastern Canada SUMK basketball championship.

# SPORT ASSOCIATION UKRAINE

In the summer of 1950, members of the Windsor Branch of the Ukrainian Youth Association (SUM) organized the Ukrainian Sport Association Sitch. Among those that played a role in the founding of the club were Peter Bubela, Steve Fenkanyn, John Leskiw, Fred Luciw, Walter Marchenkowsky, Bill Nimylowych and Jaroslaw (Jerry) Sweryda. Most of these individuals had been actively involved with sport in Ukraine and later in the displaced persons camps of Europe. Upon arriving in Canada, the organizers desired to continue their European sporting heritage.

During its existence, Sitch was a club operated by the Ukrainian Youth Association SUM. Osyp Dorosh, in his capacity as sports coordinator for the youth association, administered the club. Membership in the club, though, was not restricted to those belonging to SUM.

Ukrainians from other organizations and non-Ukrainians were allowed to join.

The youth association did not have the financial resources to support the club. As a result, team members purchased their own athletic equipment.

*Sport Association Ukraine soccer team, 1951*

During the summer of 1950, Sitch members played pick-up volleyball in city parks. Both men's and women's teams were organized. Sitch also fielded a soccer team that summer. The team limited itself to exhibition matches. A home-and-away series against the Ukrainian Sports Association Levy (Lions) of Detroit proved to be extremely popular with the Ukrainian community. Some 500 fans watched Sitch win the second match 6-2 in Windsor after dropping the opener 3-1. The team was coached by A. Georgevich.

In 1951, Sitch was registered in the ten-team Essex County Football Association. The club was referred to as Ukrainian Sitch, or simply as Ukrainians by the media and the soccer establishment. As a result, the executive of Sitch changed the name of the club to Sport Association Ukraine. In addition, the executive believed that the name Sitch was meaningless to the general populous while the name Ukraine publicized the Ukrainian community and its aspirations.

During the 1951 season, the soccer team played 13 games, winning 3, tying 1 and losing 9. After defaulting a game in late October, the team disbanded without completing the season. Shift work and family responsibilities led to the demise of the soccer team. Without its primary objective, Sport Association Ukraine folded.

# UKRAINIAN NATIONALS

In the spring of 1946, the Windsor branch of the Ukrainian National Youth Federation (UNYF) organized a softball team which competed under the name Ukrainian Nationals. Sport enthusiast John Yanush inspired the branch to form the team. Oleksa Kocikowsky, president of the Windsor branch of the Ukrainian National Federation, agreed to manage the club. He was also instrumental in raising funds necessary to purchase uniforms for the club. The team was coached by Nicholas Patrick.

During the summer of 1946, the Ukrainian Nationals played 13 games in the city league, of which they won 10. The team was captained by J. Yanush. Michael Patrick, future mayor of Windsor, was the club's pitcher. A number of the team members were recently demobilized army veterans. Their presence added a "joie de vivre" which made the game most enjoyable for all team members.

The highlight of that summer was a road trip to Thorold where the Ukrainian Nationals met the Toronto UNYF softball team in a challenge game as part of a provincial UNYF festival. The Windsor team won the hotly contested match 11-9.

The Ukrainian Nationals softball team operated only that one year.

During winter of 1946, the Windsor branch offered its members a bowling program.

# WINNIPEG

## CANADIAN UKRAINIAN ATHLETIC CLUB

In the fall of 1925, a group of sports enthusiasts gathered at the Institute Prosvita Hall, corner of Arlington and Pritchard in Winnipeg, with the idea of organizing an athletic club. The meeting ended with the formation of the Canadian Ukrainian Athletic Club (CUAC). The name, though, would not come into use until the following year. The first executive consisted of Nick Shaley, president; Michael Leslie, vice-president; John Moroz, secretary; Basil Baleshta, treasurer; Harry Gushe, manager and trainer; and Paul Barycki, assistant manager. Lawyer Joseph Dyk was named honourary president.

At the time, nobody envisioned that the club would leave a significant mark on Canadian sport. Over the years, baseball, softball, hockey, soccer, basketball, lacrosse and football teams sponsored by CUAC competed in Winnipeg leagues at various levels. Many of the teams won championships, but the record of the senior girls' softball is unmatched. The team won the Manitoba championship on twenty-two occasions, with a string of 17 consecutive titles between the years 1957 and 1973. In addition, CUAC offered house league curling and 5 pin bowling. The club had its own home grounds - a field covering two city blocks. On those grounds were a club house, hockey rink, soccer and football fields, baseball diamonds, and basketball and tennis courts.

The motives of the founding individuals for organizing an athletic club were essentially the same; they wanted to promote sport among the Ukrainian youth of Winnipeg and to provide those wishing to participate with an opportunity to develop their athletic skills. In 1928, V. H. Koman, the president of CUAC wrote: "To ensure that our [Ukrainian] youth will want to be part of our organizations, we have to offer them that which attracts them. Our organizations must foster all aspects of sport."[18] CUAC, though, was not a club exclusively catering to

Ukrainians. From its inception, anyone could join the club or participate in its activities. In fact, the CUAC's fifteenth anniversary yearbook states that the club's "chief object and purpose has been the fostering and furtherance of sport and athletics amongst the youth of Greater Winnipeg."[19] The club's motto was "Sound of body - sound of mind."

In the early years the club consisted primarily of Ukrainian youth. As it was unproven and offered only boys' hardball, others preferred to play with the more established athletic clubs of Winnipeg. However, once CUAC expanded its program and started winning championships, the club gained recognition. Prospective stars of all backgrounds were now eager to play for the Blues. After the club acquired a field for its home grounds in the late 1930s, it effectively became a community sports club with a slight majority of members being of Ukrainian extraction. The CUAC executive, though, remained primarily of Ukrainian background. In fact, right through 1991, most of the executive could trace their roots in the CUAC to the very early years of the club.

In the spring of 1926, the club was reorganized. John Moroz assumed the presidency. In 1927, when the Institute Prosvita decided to charge rent, CUAC moved out. The club was an independent entity with no formal ties to Prosvita. It spent some time operating out of private residences and businesses before establishing itself at the Ukrainian Reading Association Prosvita Hall in 1928.

For the CUAC executive, the choice of sport in which to make the club's debut was not difficult to make. There were many Ukrainian boys playing pick-up baseball in the neighbourhood who were eager to compete in organized ball. As a result, CUAC entered a team in the city Boys' Juvenile Baseball League. The team finished the season in a respectable third place. The following year, the club entered a junior team in the Winnipeg District Baseball League. This club also finished third in the standings.

Spurred by the success of the previous two years, in 1928 the club decided to enter a baseball team in the men's Intermediate League. The application was rejected. The league believed that CUAC would be weak and not competitive. As a result, the league feared that CUAC would drop out of competition before the finish of the season. CUAC appealed and the league reversed its decision. Not only did CUAC finish that season, but it remained part of the league through the league's last year. During the 1928 season, the team was managed by Edward Johnson. It finished the 19-game season out of the playoffs with 10 wins, 8 losses and a tie.

In 1929, the intermediate men's team qualified for the playoffs. They lost in the semi-finals to Elmwood. The team was once again coached by Johnson. M. Karahan was selected to the league all star-team. In 1930-31, the team played with minor success. Of note was a 1930 roadtrip to Tyndall, Manitoba, where CUAC faced a local team. This trip was the first of many that CUAC would take throughout its history. In the fall of that year, CUAC organized an in house 5 pin mixed bowling league.

In the spring of 1932, CUAC entered a girls' team in the City Intermediate League. This development is the first known example of organized sport for girls among the Ukrainian Canadian sports clubs in Canada. Managed by Paul Sikorski and coached by Slaw Rebchuk and Mike Hradoway, the team started off slowly, losing the opener 34-0. Nevertheless, as the season progressed so did the skills of the girls, and towards the end of the season they were very competitive. In intermediate boys' competition, the team qualified for the playoffs but was eliminated in the semi-finals. The team was under the guidance of Nick Shaley. During that year, members of the CUAC helped organize the Brooklands Ukrainian Athletic Club.

In 1933, the Canadian Ukrainian Athletic Club published its first yearbook. The tradition carried on through 1951. The yearbooks, some reaching 80 pages, included reports of the club's activities, schedules for the upcoming season, profiles of the players and teams, and advertisements. These yearbooks were a major source of revenue for the continuously cash-starved CUAC.

*Canadian Ukrainian Athletic Club yearbook, 1941*

On the playing fields of Winnipeg, the 1933 version of the CUAC boys' baseball team failed to impress and finished out of the playoffs. The girls' softball team did not fare any better. The respective clubs were managed by J. Memrick and P. Sikorski. In the fall of that year, in order to keep the girls together during the winter months, a basketball team was organized and entered into the Intermediate Girls' League. The club was undefeated in regular season play. It won its division and advanced to the city championship, thus becoming the first CUAC team to vie for a city title. Competing in a two-game total-point series against the winner of the other division, the Dominion Business College, CUAC won the first game by eight points. In the second, its hopes for a championship were dashed as it lost by ten. The club was coached by John Nitchuk.

In 1934, the CUAC executive organized the Ukrainian Diamond Ball League. They assisted in the organization of a sports club at the Ukrainian Canadian Society *Kobzar* in Fort Rouge. They co-organized and were responsible for all sports events and competitions at the first Ukrainian Field Day held on July 1, at the Old Exhibition Grounds. The field day became a Dominion Day tradition and continued for a number of years. Events were held in softball and track and field. To raise funds, the club staged a concert that included music, dance and a one act comedy at the Reading Hall Prosvita. The event was a sell out.

With respect to club sports, CUAC once again fielded a boys' baseball team and a girls' softball team. Both teams failed to make the playoffs. The girls' team managed some success when it placed second at the Winnipeg Beach Softball Tournament. In the fall, the intermediate girls' basketball team set out to challenge for the city championship. It placed second in its division.

The years 1935 and 1936 were very difficult for the Canadian Ukrainian Athletic Club. The country was in a depression and sport became a luxury. "Money was hard to come by. Funds for the various activities were raised through selling memberships, holding dances, draws, carnivals and passing the hat around at their baseball games. Many a hat came back with not enough to pay the umpire. The members would dip into their own pockets to make up the difference. . ."[20] CUAC had to vacate the facilities it had leased on Selkirk Avenue. The girls' basketball program was cancelled. Still, the CUAC managed to operate two teams; the intermediate girls' softball team played only fairly as did the intermediate boys' baseball team. In 1936, the boys' Intermediate League ceased to exist. CUAC then joined the existing Greater Winnipeg Senior Baseball League. The girls also joined a senior league that year.

In 1937, both the men's baseball and the girls' softball teams showed great poise in qualifying for the playoffs. The men's senior team finished the regular season tied for second with Norwood. They faced the Norwood club in the playoffs and lost out after a thrilling series. The club was managed by Bill Maslak. The senior girls' team finished the season fourth out of nine teams. They knocked out Transcona in the opening round of the playoffs. In the second round they lost to the St. Boniface Athletic Club. The club was managed by F. Parnell. The two teams travelled to Grand Forks, North Dakota, during the summer. There, the CUAC girls' team defeated the state champions in the two games that they played. The men did not fare as well.

In the fall, a Ladies Auxiliary was organized. The group largely comprised wives of members of the parent body. Its primary function was to assist in the raising of funds, to contribute to the financing of the club's sports and community activities and to otherwise support the projects of the parent body. Fund raising activities included teas, socials, banquets, and raffles. "After the club house was built and all the CUAC activities became centred there, the auxiliary became extremely active. They equipped and manned the canteen, donated trophies to youth and sport activities at the Isaac Newton School, and they also gave financial aid to the North End YMCA Swimming Pool and the St. Nicholas School Fund as well as donating two High School Scholarships for Annual Competition to Sisler High."[21] During World War II, the auxiliary wholeheartedly committed itself to the war effort, assisting the Red Cross and the St. John's Ambulance Society. Other philanthropic projects were also supported by the group.

The year 1937 was one of the most significant in the history of the Canadian Ukrainian Athletic Club. Slaw Rebchuk, who at the time was the president of the club, spearheaded the executive and club members in a drive to secure "home grounds" for the CUAC teams. After a lengthy search and extensive negotiations, the City of Winnipeg gave CUAC the use of an empty lot on the corner of Arlington Street and Church Avenue in the northern part of Winnipeg. A committee headed by V. H. Koman then solicited funds from the Ukrainian community for baseball stands, which were built by the members themselves. An old railway boxcar was transported to the site and it served as a club house for many years. The official opening of the grounds occurred on May 28, 1937.

In 1938, the Canadian Ukrainian Athletic Club won its first provincial title when the girls' team defeated St. Boniface in three games to secure the Manitoba Senior Softball Championship. In the final game, the CUAC Blues outscored their opponents 21-7. During the regular season the club played well and finished in a four-way tie for first place. The girls swept through the playoff rounds without any problem. The team was once again managed by F. Parnell. The senior men's team was competitive but did not make the playoffs.

During the 1939 baseball and softball seasons, CUAC teams failed to bring a championship home. In senior men's play, the team advanced to the playoffs but was trounced by Transcona in four straight games. The girls' team completed the season without securing a playoff berth. In the fall, after two years of discussion and feasibility studies, a junior hockey club was entered into the North Division of the Winnipeg junior league. More than 125 individuals responded to ads in the papers inviting players for a tryout with the club. In its inaugural season the team was coached by S. McCallum. It won 10 games, lost 7 and tied 1 to finish in second place. The team failed to win the opening round of the playoffs, losing to the St. James Canadians in a hard-fought series.

In the summer of 1940, the senior girls' team finished in third place in the regular season, winning 15 games while losing 10. It went on a very successful goodwill road trip to play in towns in western Manitoba. Winnipeg alderman William Scraba and mayor John Queen were members of the entourage. The men's team finished in second spot after setting a city record of nine straight wins. Their won-loss record was 19-12. Hockey almost did not materialize that fall, as the league battled with the Manitoba Amateur Hockey Association (MAHA) and Olympic Rink. The differences were finally resolved and play began in December. Expectations were high, but the club could not meet them. A number of players were called up for active military service, while a few were lost to injuries. The result was a mediocre third-place finish in a four-team division. The team was coached by Mike Kryschuk and was led by Johnny Arondeus and Ted Plouffe who gained all-star berths.

The 1941 season witnessed CUAC teams winning two city and one provincial championship. The senior girls won the Greater Winnipeg and Manitoba Championship. The run for the two championships included a twelve-game winning streak and two personal pitching accomplishments of note. Anne Minerch stymied the opposition by pitching 37 consecutive scoreless innings while Sylvia Maxwell pitched a no-hitter. The city championship series was unfortunately anticlimactic, as the opponents withdrew from play citing an eligibility infringement by one of the CUAC athletes. Thereafter, the CUAC Blues contested the unofficial championship of Western Canada when they met the visiting Saskatchewan title holders, the Regina Army and Navy Bombers. CUAC lost two straight games. In a game to determine the provincial softball champion, CUAC blasted the intermediate title holders, St. Vital 23-5. The girls' team was coached by John Shaley and managed by John Nitchuk.

The senior men's club overcame the loss of three pitchers to the armed forces to place third in league standings. In the semi-finals it defeated St. Boniface. In the championship series, which saw both teams lead, CUAC eventually defeated Transcona to capture the Baldy Northcott Trophy, emblematic of the league championship. The team was co-managed by Steve Gunter and Stan Shaley and coached by Nick Shaley. That summer, CUAC also sponsored a midget baseball team. An existing team was looking for a sponsor, and CUAC readily agreed.

During World War II, more than 60 members of CUAC saw service in the various branches of the Canadian armed forces and the Merchant Marine. Bill Manson, captain of the first CUAC junior hockey team, perished during an air operation over Europe.

In the fall, a juvenile hockey team was added. In previous years, the junior club always had difficulty in finding replacements for injured players. CUAC management believed that a juvenile entry would serve as a "farm" team for the junior squad. The juvenile team was coached by Vince Leah, a Winnipeg sports writer and a future inductee into the Manitoba Sports Hall of Fame. Both the juvenile and junior teams failed to make the playoffs. Cal Gardner, a future professional, initially played on the juvenile team and in mid-season was moved up to the junior club.

In 1942, all three ball teams entered in league play by CUAC won championships. The midget boys' team managed by W. Kormylo won the city championship. The girls' senior softball team repeated as provincial champions. After finishing in second place in league play, the CUAC Blues won the semi-finals three games to one. In the final, the Blues were down three games to none when they staged a brilliant comeback to win four straight and the Winnipeg Championship. Subsequently they defeated St. Vital Tigerettes to win the Manitoba title. As in the previous year, J. Nitchuk and J. Shaley worked with the team. The men's team finished the season in first place with a 17 win and 7 loss record. In the semi-finals they dumped St. Boniface and in the final they defeated Transcona. Stan Shaley led the team with 40 home runs and a .460 batting average. The Blues were managed by Harry Barchuk and coached by Nick Shaley.

The 1942-43 hockey season saw the junior team go through three coaches. S. McCallum resigned midway through the season. Pete Langelle replaced him. Unable to get time off from the Air Force and the Air Force hockey team, Langelle resigned just before the start of the playoffs. Club manager John Mirus assumed the coaching duties in the playoffs. The team lacked consistency all year. Nevertheless, it made the playoffs in the North Division but was eliminated in the first round. Harry Mosienko was the team leader. In juvenile hockey, the team finished in fifth position and out of the playoffs. It was coached by Joe Popiel.

In 1943, the men's senior baseball team once again repeated in winning the Northcott Trophy. Managed by H. Barchuk and coached by S. Shaley, the team qualified for the playoffs. In the semi-finals, they barely pulled through to defeat St. Boniface in eight games (one game was called because of darkness while another ended in a tie). The final also went the distance, with the Blues clinching the championship with a 6-2 win in the deciding game. The girls' team failed in its bid to repeat as Winnipeg champions, losing to St. Vital in the seventh game of the final.

In the fall of 1943, CUAC decided to expand its hockey program by adding a midget hockey team. Club management viewed this step as an opportunity to give the 13 to 16-year-old boys a chance to play organized hockey. It would also create a pool of experienced players upon which the juvenile and junior clubs could draw. Coached by John Hawryluk, the midgets played surprisingly good hockey, winning 6, tying 1 and losing 3. They won a sudden-death semi-final but lost the two-game championship series. The junior hockey team once again lost a number of players to the war effort but still managed to place second in its division. In the semi-finals the juniors lost to St. Boniface. The team was coached by W. Monson. The juvenile squad, coached by Parnell, played average hockey and did not make the playoffs.

On the baseball diamond, the senior men won the Greater Winnipeg Senior Baseball Championship in 1944 for the fourth straight time. As in previous years, the club lost good players to the armed forces. Nevertheless, a number of new players were recruited by playing manager S. Shaley and coach N. Shaley, who then did a fine job moulding the newcomers with the veterans. The club finished the season in first place with a 16 and 7 won-loss record. In the first round of the post-season play, the CUAC Blues swept St. Boniface in four straight. It took the Blues five games to dispose of Transcona and win the city title. The senior girls' team placed first in the league by winning 12 games and losing only 4. As a result, the girls received a bye into the final which they lost in seven games. The team was managed by Stephen Mykytyn and co-coached by H. Martin and J. Shaley. On the field it was led by Minnie Pieluck.

The junior hockey team, after only three practices, embarked on what was to become their best and last season. A new scheduling format introduced by the league that year opened the door for inter-division play. Against teams in its own division, CUAC players held their own. In games against the much stronger South Division, CUAC ended up taking a beating. The Manitoba junior champions Winnipeg Monarchs, for instance, pounded CUAC 16-3 (The following season, former CUAC junior coach W. Monson would lead the Monarchs to the Memorial Cup, emblematic of junior hockey supremacy in Canada). Unfortunately, not every team in the North Division had to face every team from the south. The powerful Monarchs did not play once against St. Boniface. This probably had an impact on the final standings. CUAC, though, made the playoffs. They defeated St. Boniface in two straight semi-final games. Playing in the North Division final for the first time, the Blues lost two in a row to the Esquires.

The juvenile hockey club, under the guidance of F. Hnatowich and J. Hawryluk, failed to meet expectations and played inconsistent hockey throughout the season. According to some, the team failed to get much-needed breaks, and thus finished out of the playoffs. The midgets, competing in a very tough 14-team league, also missed the playoffs. Having three hockey teams on its program was evidently not enough for the CUAC, as it added a bantam team in the fall of that year. Under the guidance of Eugene Slipetz, the team made a fine showing in a season that was marred by the postponement and cancellation of games due to poor ice conditions on the outdoor rinks. The team impressed CUAC management to the extent that it decided to organize a second bantam team for the following season.

In 1945, the senior men's baseball team was dethroned after a four-year championship reign. The club made the playoffs, but failed to get past Transcona in the semi-finals. Stan and Nick Shaley once again managed and coached. The girls' softball team finished the regular season tied for first place with St. Boniface. In a sudden death-game to determine the league champion, the CUAC Blues dropped a 7-3 decision. The Blues' losing streak continued in the semi-finals. Their season ended when they dropped two straight semi-final games much to the disappointment of manager Mykytyn and coaches J. Shaley and S. Rebchuk. Evelyn Wawryshyn, who would later star in the All-American Girls Professional Baseball League, was the team's MVP.

During World War II, a great number of young American men, including many professional baseball players, served in the armed forces. As a result, major and minor professional leagues struggled. To maintain fan interest in the game, bubblegum magnate and Chicago Cubs owner Philip Wrigley founded the All-American Girls Professional Baseball League in 1943. The league operated through the 1954 season. Sixty-four women from Canada saw action in the league. Four of those were CUAC alumnae: Olive Bend (1943-45), Mary Shastel (1944), Doris Shero (1950) and Evelyn Wawryshyn (1946-51).

In the fall of 1945, the Canadian Ukrainian Athletic Club, and two other clubs sponsoring hockey teams in the Junior North Division, put forth a set of demands to the Manitoba Amateur Hockey Association. The demands of the clubs included that all teams play an equal number of home and away games, that clubs playing exhibition games be paid a reasonable amount for expenses, with the remainder of the revenue being split equally between all the other teams in the league, that all teams be treated equally with regards to the availability of practice ice time, and that the dressing room facilities in the Olympic Rink be improved. The demands of the North League teams were primarily in response to their tight financial position. Playing teams from the South League would ensure a greater cash flow as those teams had a much wider following.

"It was mutually agreed that the three North Division Clubs would drop out of hockey should some favourable action not be taken on these recommendations. . . As there was no worthwhile action on the part of the MAHA, the North Division clubs had no alternative but to discontinue hockey operations."[22] Not only did the three clubs pull out their junior teams, but operations of the juvenile, midget, and bantam teams were also suspended. In total, 21 teams comprising approximately 300 players were withdrawn.

In the summer of 1946, the Canadian Ukrainian Athletic Club added soccer and lacrosse to its program. Midget and bantam teams were organized in both sports. The bantam soccer team, coached by Red Kowalski, showed much ability and determination in reaching the playoffs in its first season. The midgets were coached by Bill and Mike Kuzik and did not fare as well. The lacrosse program was only marginally competitive, as most of the players were new to the game. Nevertheless, coaches Roberts and Ulliot believed that the teams made remarkable progress over the duration of the season.

CUAC also expanded its baseball program when it entered a junior boys' team into the city league. The team failed to win a game. Stephen Bilinsky was responsible for organizing the team. The senior men's baseball club placed third in regular season play, won the semi-finals against St. Boniface, but ran out of steam in the final against Transcona. The girls' softball team played well all season to place second in the league standings. In the semi-finals they were eliminated by St. Vital.

In the fall of 1946, the Canadian Ukrainian Athletic Club took one more step towards realising its dream of having an all-round sports complex on the grounds at Arlington and Church. The club built an outdoor skating rink and purchased a railway boxcar for shelter. The official opening of the rink occurred on February 27, 1947. An Ice Carnival was organized in conjunction with this event, featuring the crowning of a Carnival Queen, various races, and a skating exhibition. The carnival became an annual CUAC event for a number of years. The ice rink quickly became popular and the club executive was soon considering a house league and a bantam hockey team for the next season.

After a number of years of disappointments, the men's baseball and girls' softball teams once again won championships. The men's team, which was still managed and coached by the Shaley duo of Stan and Nick, finished the season in second place. The semi-final series against St. James went to seven games. In the final, a best-of-five affair, the Blues once again went the distance before securing the championship. The girls' softball team placed second in the league. It then won the Manitoba Championship, and advanced to the Western Canada Senior Softball Championship. CUAC faced the Saskatoon Ramblers for the title in a best-of-five series. The Blues lost the first game 3-0, won the second 6-3, lost the third 6-0 and, playing their eleventh game in eleven nights, lost the fourth game in 13 innings by a score of 2-1. The team was managed by S. Mykytyn and coached by J. Nitchuk and J. Shaley. The junior boys' team once again had a disappointing season.

*Canadian Ukrainian Athletic Club senior men's softball team, 1947*

Soccer continued during the summer of 1947. It was a season of heavy rains which often turned fields into mud bowls, putting a damper on the game.

In the fall of 1947, CUAC entered a team in the Winnipeg Men's Senior Basketball League. Coached by Alex Nitchuk, the team finished in second place, winning 7 of the 12 regular season games. In a sudden-death semi-final, the team was eliminated from further play. That fall, CUAC also organized a girls' junior basketball team which was entered in the Winnipeg Junior Girls' Basketball League. The team completed the 13-game regular season without losing once. The team then won the city championship sweeping Dominion Knit in a best-of-three final. Pitted against the Brandon Y Kings in a two-game total-point semi-final for the provincial championship, the Blues easily handled their opponent, both in Winnipeg and in Brandon. The team then travelled to Flin Flon to play the local Legionettes for the Manitoba Championship. Once again it was a two-game total-point series. The Blues lost twice, the first game by three points and the second by two. On the court, during the regular season and play-offs, the team was led by petite Elva Waslyk. It was managed by J. Shaley and coached by Mike Daski and Harold Mauthe.

That fall, CUAC also reintroduced its hockey program. This time around, the program was limited to bantam hockey. At the time, bantam hockey was played primarily outdoors while higher level clubs such as the juniors used indoor facilities. CUAC had its own rink where the bantam team could practise and play. As a result, it was no longer burdened with arena rental costs.

With hockey and basketball seasons barely over, softball and baseball practices once again signalled the return of summer in 1948. The men's senior baseball team lost most of its players during the off-season to a newly organized league. As a result, the Shaley brothers had a difficult task in putting together a team which could defend the 1947 championship. They and the team fell short. Placing third in regular season play, the Blues managed to win the semi-finals against St. James. In the final they were swept in four straight games by Transcona. The girls' softball team finished tied for first in the league with 13 wins and 5 losses. A sudden-death playoff loss dropped them into second place. In the semi-finals they were eliminated from further play by St. Boniface. John Shaley managed the team while John Nitchuk handled the coaching duties. The boys' junior team improved greatly from the previous years and almost had a winning season by winning 11 and losing 13. For the first time the juniors managed to squeak into the playoffs but bowed out in the opening round.

Major changes occurred at the CUAC grounds in 1948. The railway boxcar was finally replaced by a modern club house. The four bare walls and a roof were financed by the Winnipeg City Parks and Recreation Board as part of their expanding community program in city parks. CUAC was to operate the facility which was to be known as the CUAC Community Centre Club House. This was in sharp contrast to the other community centres of Winnipeg which were operated by the city and named after city streets. In addition, CUAC funds and manpower were utilized to fully equip and furnish the facilities and to build a 500-seat baseball stadium. Winnipeg Mayor Garnet Coulter officially opened the club house during the third annual Ice Carnival on February 26, 1948.

During the fall and winter months of 1948-49, CUAC operated three hockey teams and two basketball teams. The previous year's junior girls' basketball team matured to the senior ranks. They had an excellent season, winning all 12 regular season games. They encountered no great difficulty in sweeping the city championship in two games. Competing against Brandon Y Queens for the provincial championship, the Blues won the game played in Winnipeg 26-20. In Brandon, they outscored their opponents 45-25 to capture the Manitoba title. The undefeated team then travelled to Alberta to face the Edmonton Mortons for the Western Canada Senior Girls' Basketball Championship. In the first game of a two-game total-point series, the Blues were trounced 44-17. In the second game, the team made a valiant comeback winning 43-31. It was not enough, though, to overcome the 27-point deficit from the first game. The club was managed by J. Shaley and coached by H. Mauthe, M. Daski and P. Kazan. On the court, the team was led by Lesia Dowhanyk, Elva Waslyk and Doris Shero.

Comprising new recruits, the junior girls' basketball team did not match the success of the senior team. The Blues won 7, lost 7, and tied 1 to qualify for the playoffs with a third place finish. The club won once and lost once in a two-game total-point series but lost on aggregate 37-33. The team was handled by E. Levinsky, H. Mauthe and M. Daski. There was a desire to continue the fledgling senior men's basketball program. CUAC, though, could not find the funds to do so. The hockey program included a midget and two bantam teams.

The 1949 senior men's baseball team experienced difficulties throughout the season. They did manage to squeak into the playoffs, but were eliminated from further play in four straight games in the opening round. Stan Shaley continued to manage the team while J. Raleigh took on the coaching duties. The senior girls' softball club played consistently to finish second in league standings. They had little trouble sweeping St. Boniface in the semi-finals. In the final, their fortunes dissipated and they lost four straight to St. Vital. Doris Shero gained personal recognition when the league honoured her with the Gibson Trophy for being the best outfielder in the league. J. Nitchuk and J. Shaley continued to coach and manage the girls. The junior boys' team led by pitcher W. Kanuiga played .500 ball for the first time in its history. They made the playoffs but were eliminated in the semi-finals.

For the second year in a row, CUAC had to drop a basketball team from its activities. After only two years in existence, the junior girls' program was cancelled. The senior girls' basketball team continued to operate and it had another stellar season. Once again the club finished the regular season undefeated. Once again it won the city and provincial championships. In play against the Vancouver Eilers for the Western Canada title, CUAC lost the opener 61-42. In the second game, the senior girls managed to hold Vancouver to 54 points, but they themselves could only muster 43.

The summer of 1950 saw the men's senior team win its sixth Winnipeg championship. The club played good ball all season for coach Raleigh and manager S. Shaley. In the final, they dropped the opener to Transcona 8-5 but came back to win four straight. The bid of the girls' softball team to win the championship was once again put on hold by a tough St. Vital team. The boys' junior baseball club made the playoffs, but was eliminated in the opening round.

In the fall, the senior girls' basketball team once again embarked on a path which the girls hoped would finally reward them with a Western Canada title. After completing their third consecutive regular season in the senior league without losing a game, the Blues ran into a shortage of players in the playoffs and were left at the short end of a series with the Dominos. During the regular season, Blues' stars E. Waslyk and L. Dowhanyk were the league scoring leaders for the third year in a row. John Shaley continued managing the team while H. Mauthe did the coaching.

One of the bantam hockey teams that CUAC sponsored won the city championship that winter. The team then travelled to Brandon to vie for the provincial title. Due to a long layoff, the team was rusty and did not succeed in bringing the championship home.

*Canadian Ukrainian Athletic Club bantam lacrosse team, 1950*

For the 1951 baseball season, playing manager S. Shaley had to partially rebuild the previous year's championship team. From the start, it was obvious that the team lacked the strength of its predecessor. It did make the finals but fell short against St. Boniface. After a slow start, John Shaley's senior girls' softball team surprised everyone as it charged up the league standings to place first. It then proceeded to lose three straight to West Kildonan in the league championship series. The junior boys' baseball team, because of new uniforms, was nicknamed the "Flashy Blues." The team, though, was not that flashy on the diamond, as it finished the regular season in third place and was eliminated from further competition in the opening round of the playoffs.

The summer of 1951 also saw the demise of the CUAC soccer program. Lack of finances and waning interest were but some of the reasons why soccer ceased to be sponsored.

The 1952 senior girls' CUAC Blues finished second in their league, playing a little better than .500 ball. In the semi-finals they upset the pennant winner St. Boniface Athletics. The final, a best-of-seven affair against the West Kildonan Tigerettes, went the distance before CUAC settled the championship in its favour. Peggy Walchuk, Olga Uszy, and future Olympian Dorothy "Dot" Kozak were but some of the stars that carried CUAC to the title.

The senior men's team also won the city title that year. In the final against the Transcona Railroaders, CUAC was able to subdue one of the hottest hitters in Winnipeg - hockey great Terry Sawchuk. Home from Detroit for the summer, the goalie terrorized pitchers in the Winnipeg Senior Men's Baseball League with his hitting power. The junior men's team was not as successful as it did not make it past the semi-finals. The team nevertheless found some consolation in their second place finish at the Greater Winnipeg Junior Baseball Tournament.

In 1953, manager John Shaley's CUAC senior girls finished the season in second place with 10 wins and 8 losses. The team disposed of the third place Ramblers in the semi-finals. In the final, CUAC once again faced the Tigerettes. This time, the Blues needed only six games to capture the city championship. In the provincial championship, CUAC overpowered Brandon Curly's 8-2 and 10-2 to take the title. The senior men played average ball all season. They finished in the middle of the standings, qualifying for post-season play. The semi-final series against Transcona was a see-saw affair going the full seven games. In the seventh and deciding game, CUAC lost a heartbreaker 7-6. The junior men's baseball team lost more games than it won and did not make the playoffs.

1954 brought CUAC its last senior men's city baseball title. The Blues, coached by Stan Shaley, completed the regular season with a record of 15 wins, 11 losses and 1 tie. In the semi-finals, the team required all seven games to dispose of Transcona and advance to the championship against St. Boniface Native Sons. In the final, the Blues were out-hit and out-scored, yet managed to defeat St. Boniface in six games to win their eighth Winnipeg Championship. The pitching arm of Walter Kanuiga was a major factor in the team's success.

The senior girls' team completed the regular season tied for first place with the Ramblers. Unfortunately, the team could not carry the momentum into the sudden-death playoff to determine the pennant winner and later into the playoffs. In the sudden-death playoff, CUAC lost 2-1 to the Ramblers in 12 innings. The game, though, was protested by manager John Shaley who alleged that a Rambler pitcher used the illegal spit ball. The protest was upheld and the game replayed. This time CUAC lost 6-3. In the subsequent semi-finals, CUAC went down in defeat to the West Kildonan Tigerettes.

The junior men's team did not have a particularly good season in 1954. Outplayed at just about every position, the junior Blues were the most error prone team in the league. They were credited, for instance, with committing 25 errors during a double header which they lost on aggregate 33-3 to Columbus Club. As a result, the media referred to them as the "hapless CUAC." During the season manager Bill Konyk was replaced by Aggie Kukulowicz. The change, though, did not turn the team's fortunes around.

In 1955, three CUAC baseball teams made it to the final round of the playoffs. The midget club, though, was the only one able to win a championship. After finishing first in league play, the midgets had little problem in sweeping the opposition in the playoffs to take the title. The senior men's team came very close to winning the city title. In one of the most exciting finals to be played in Winnipeg in a long time, crowds of up to 3,000 witnessed CUAC battle St. Boniface, with the latter winning the championship in the seventh game.

The Greater Winnipeg Senior Girls' Softball League was reduced to three teams in 1955 as St. Boniface dropped out of the circuit. CUAC completed the reduced regular season by winning the pennant and getting a bye into the final. There the Blues were upset by the Ramblers in five games. The junior Blues showed even less poise than in the previous year. They lost 12 straight games before finally winning their first. The victory, though, did very little for the Blues as they went right back to their losing ways.

In July of 1956, the CUAC senior girls' team became the first Ukrainian Canadian sports club to have one of its games broadcast live over television. During the game, both teams hustled in front of the cameras, with CUAC winning the game 7-6. The calibre of play was good, and the teams made a positive impression on the viewing audience. As a result, attendance at league games increased. During the season, the Blues lost more games than they won, finishing the schedule in second place, eight games behind the pennant winner. They had little difficulty in defeating the Ramblers in the semi-finals but were unable to defeat the Tigerettes in the final.

The men's senior team led the league at mid-season but faltered towards the end to finish in third place. Advancing to the final, CUAC could not upset the defending champions St. Boniface Native Sons. Showing some improvement over the past year, the junior squad won 5 and lost 25 to finish 18 games behind the pennant winner. Although the juniors won but five games, they did not finish in last place as there was a more hapless team.

1957 was a memorable year for the CUAC senior girls' team. It won the league pennant on the last day of the season, posting a record of 13 wins and 7 losses. Down three games to two in the city final, CUAC stormed back to win the Winnipeg Championship. CUAC then swept the best-of-five provincial final against Holy Ghost, outscoring its opponent 60-9. The victory began one of the longest streaks in Canadian sport history. For seventeen consecutive years, the girls of the Canadian Ukrainian Athletic Club would win the Manitoba championship.

CUAC was able to maintain its explosive hitting and steady pitching as it opened a best-of-seven series against the Edmonton Truckettes for the Western Canada Softball Championship. The Winnipeg team swept Edmonton in four straight games to become the first team from Manitoba to win the Eiler Memorial Trophy. For manager John Shaley, it was a dream come true; after sixteen years of coaching and managing, he won his first Western title.

*Canadian Ukrainian Athletic Club senior girls' softball team, 1957 Western Canada Champions*

Neither the CUAC senior men's team nor the junior men's team won championships that year. The senior team was eliminated from further play in the semi-final round, while the junior team showed improvement over the previous year by qualifying for the playoffs. In the opening round the juniors lost to the pennant winner Elmwood.

In 1958, the CUAC senior girls improved their winning percentage to .866 and once again won the league pennant. In the playoffs for the Winnipeg title the club defeated West Kildonan Tigerettes. As in the previous year, Holy Ghost provided the opposition in the provincial championship. CUAC won three straight games to easily capture the Manitoba crown. The defence of the Western Canada Softball Championship was unsuccessful as CUAC was eliminated in a best-of-three semi-final by Regina.

The junior men's team finished the season with a losing record, yet placed second in league standings. The team was not a factor in the playoffs. The senior men's team also lost more games than it won in what was to be its last season. The following year, the senior men's league ceased operations as there was a shortage of entries.

The CUAC senior girls' team failed to win the pennant in 1959. Nevertheless, the players fought back in the playoffs to win their seventh straight city title. The junior men's team continued to improve finishing second in league standings with a record of eight wins, seven losses and three ties. In the semi-finals, the juniors defeated third place Columbus Club. In a closely fought final, the team bowed out to the league pennant winner Elmwood.

In 1960, the CUAC Blues senior softball team placed first in league standings with a 15 and 2 record. The team proceeded to win the Manitoba title by taking West Kildonan four games to two. The Blues then travelled to Regina to compete in the Western Canada Championship. First they disposed of Regina 10-7, then they clobbered Calgary twice, 22-0 and 14-4, to win the Western Canada Championship. When Winnipeg Senior Girls' Softball League announced its all-star team, six CUAC starters were on it. The championship team was managed by J. Shaley and coached by S. Shaley and H. Martin.

The junior men did not fare well that year. They qualified for the playoffs by placing fourth in league play but were quickly eliminated in the opening round by Columbus Club.

The following year, the senior girls easily repeated as city and provincial champions. Plans were drawn up to have CUAC defend its Western Canada title, but the high cost of staging the event prevented this from happening. The junior men completed the regular season in second place. At times, the club showed flashes of brilliance. Pitcher Wayne Sorbey, for instance, hurled a no-hitter. Unfortunately, the club lacked consistency and did not make it past the first round of the playoffs.

Led by Bev Sawchuk and Dot Rose, the 1962 edition of the CUAC girls' softball team, finished league play in first place with a record of 15 wins and 2 losses. Once again, the club had little difficulty in repeating as Winnipeg and Manitoba champions. In Regina, the Blues were unsuccessful in defending their Western Canada Championship. The junior men's team qualified for the playoffs but once again could not overcome the semi-final hurdle.

While many clubs in 1963 would have been more than happy to match CUAC's record from the previous year, not so the girls from CUAC. The senior Blues set out to improve. They lost only one regular season game of the 16 they played. The team continued its winning ways in the playoffs by sweeping the Canadian Polish Athletic Club in four games. When the softball season was finally over and the Winnipeg and Manitoba championships won, CUAC boasted a record of 23 wins and 2 losses in regular season, playoff, and exhibition games. On the other hand, the junior men played lacklustre ball all summer, compiling a record of only five wins in 15 starts.

The year 1964 brought about the demise of the CUAC junior men's team. The club completed its schedule tied for third and last place with a record of 3 wins and 12 losses, 12 games behind the undefeated league leading Orioles. Even with this poor record, the Blues made the playoffs. Lack of players and poor hitting and fielding led to the quick elimination of the team. Some time later, with the core of the team reaching senior age, CUAC decided to fold the junior team and revive the senior club.

The senior girls continued their winning ways that year. The club easily clinched the league pennant. Utilizing its great depth, the team stormed through the playoffs, winning yet another provincial title.

*Canadian Ukrainian Athletic Club senior girls' softball team, 1965 Canadian Champions*

During the 1965 regular season, the senior girls' team played with its now-expected consistency, losing only 3 times in 18 starts to win the pennant. In the playoffs, it had little difficulty in winning the city championship. As Manitoba's representative to the first-ever Canadian Softball Championship, CUAC qualified for the national final with preliminary round victories over Ontario's Port Arthur Nor-Shors and British Columbia's Victoria Vicettes. Down by four runs in the championship game, CUAC came back to score eight unanswered runs to win the national title. After 24 years of coaching and managing, manager John Shaley remarked: "This has to be the best of all the championships we have won." The Canadian Ukrainian Athletic Club championship roster included Dot Rose, Frankie Little, Joan Ingram, Laurie Bradawaski, Bev Sawchuk, Darlene Kellsey, Rita Woodlands, Grace Bouchard, Judy

Cochrane, Heather Hextall, Jo-Anne Bedrich, Alda Tait, Joyce Tully, Joanne Vincelette, Gail Roberts, Helen McFarlane and Diane Martin. The club was coached by Stan Shaley.

The inaugural season for the revived CUAC senior men's team was quite disappointing. The team won only 4 games of the 20 it played to finish in last place in the Eastern Division of the Manitoba Senior Baseball League.

In the spring of 1966, the CUAC midget boys' hockey team won the Manitoba Championship.

During the summer of 1966, the CUAC senior girls swept through the regular season and the playoffs without losing a game. Full of optimism, the girls embarked to Toronto to defend their Canadian title. They dearly wanted to win the championship because the victorious club would represent Canada at the Pan American Games which were to be held in the home town of the Blues the following year. It was not to be. John Shaley's club was eliminated from the title hunt when it lost 2-0 to Toronto in a semi-final game.

In only their second year in the senior league, the men's team improved its record to 9 and 7 to place third in league standings, just $2\frac{1}{2}$ games out of first place. The club qualified for the playoffs but could not overcome St. Boniface.

In February of 1967, CUAC softball veterans Dot Rose, Joan Ingram, and Laurie Bradawaski won the Canadian curling championship playing on Betty Duguid's Fort Garry rink.

That year, the senior girls competed in their third consecutive Canadian Championship. Once again, it was Ontario's representative Toronto that stopped the Blues' bid for their second national title. During the Pan American Games, the club was invited to play an exhibition game. The senior men's team returned to its losing ways that year, winning but 3 games of the 14 they contested to finish in last place.

During the summer of 1968, the senior girls' team played in some of the most interesting games ever featured in girls' softball in Canada. The club finished the regular season by winning the pennant. It then took time off to play in the national championship which was held in Winnipeg that year. In their opening game, CUAC defeated the Edmonton Pats 10-0. Then the rains came. Ed Corbett, president of the Canadian Amateur Softball Association, decided to play the series indoors in the Winnipeg Arena. The teams found it difficult to adjust to this new environment and the games were often marred by confusion. CUAC was unable to cope with indoor softball and the opposition, losing 5-0 to Carpetland of Toronto and 9-6 to the Saskatoon Imperials to be eliminated from further play.

The Blues then proceeded to win the provincial championship and qualified to represent

Manitoba at the Canada Games in Halifax the following year. CUAC was unable to field a men's team in 1968 and as a result took a temporary leave of absence from the league.

For the CUAC girls, the highlight of the summer of 1969 was their participation in the Canada Games. In the opening game, CUAC players committed eight errors as they lost 14-9 to Alberta. The poor play and the resulting rout prompted manager John Shaley to state that he had "never seen this club play so bad." Shaley regrouped his charges and they proceeded to win the next three games, defeating Nova Scotia 3-2, Quebec 10-1 and the Northwest Territories 9-4. CUAC then dropped a close 3-2 decision to the two-time defending Canadian champion Toronto Carpetland. The girls completed the tournament with an 11-3 victory over Prince Edward Island and a 4-3 loss to British Columbia. Although CUAC finished the tournament with a winning record, it was not good enough to qualify for the playoff round.

After returning to Winnipeg, the club defended its Manitoba title by defeating the West End Tigerettes in the final. After an absence of one year, the men's senior team made a comeback in 1969. The club finished the regular season in seventh place, $10\frac{1}{2}$ games out of first, with a record of 8 wins and 14 losses.

The following year, the senior men's team could only put together 4 wins in 13 starts to finish in seventh place, 8 games behind the pennant winner. The season was the team's last in the league. The senior girls' team continued its winning ways in 1970 as it captured yet another provincial title by defeating CPAC in the playoff final.

In 1971, CUAC once again tangled with CPAC for the provincial title. The CUAC girls, led by Bobbi Janoway, Lynn Andrews, and Carol Sykra, were unstoppable as they chalked up yet another championship. The club then travelled to Regina to represent Manitoba in a softball tournament but was unsuccessful.

In 1972, the CUAC senior girls won the provincial championship by defeating the Tigerettes in the final. This advanced them to the Canadian championships at the Canadian National Exhibition in Toronto. Competing in the "B" pool, the club only managed one win in four starts.

In December of 1972, the Canadian Ukrainian Athletic Club's 45 years of association with the grounds at Church and Arlington came to an end.

Earlier in the year, the city had commissioned a report on the reorganization of the city's public works, engineering, and parks and recreation services. The private consultant's report, submitted to the city in November, recommended centralized control of public parks and recreation operations, and that the "city should own and support community clubs on a standardized financial and program basis, and consider getting ownership of clubs owned by other parties."[23]

In addition, according to the CUAC executive, a number of community leaders in Winnipeg expressed their displeasure that the name Canadian Ukrainian Athletic Club was used in a city park.[24]

Shortly thereafter, the city essentially took over all aspects of the centre and the sports facilities at the park that club members had spent time and money developing and fostering for nearly half a century. To reflect the change, the name CUAC Community Club was replaced with the name Sinclair Park Community Centre.

While CUAC was able to retain control of its sport programs, the loss of facilities effectively terminated most of them. The club stopped operating all its minor league programs - little league baseball and minor hockey. House league bowling and curling were retained as they never operated out of Sinclair Park.

In 1973, CUAC wanted to use the Sinclair Park baseball field for its senior girls' softball program but was told that there was no room. Not wanting to fold the team, the club began searching for an alternate site. The Old Exhibition Grounds became home to the Blues that year. Most of the games the club played were exhibition as the lack of interest and shortage of entries reduced the schedule of the Winnipeg Girls' Softball League significantly. It was in these trying and confusing times that CUAC won its last provincial championship. This was the 17th consecutive year that the girls' softball team won the Manitoba title after other victories in 1938, 1941, 1942, 1947 and 1953.

In 1974, the league folded, and with it the CUAC senior girls' team. The demise of this CUAC team, just a year short of the club's 50th anniversary, ended CUAC's operating teams in Winnipeg leagues. It was the end of an era for one of the finest sports clubs that ever existed in Canada. CUAC, though, did not fold that year. The parent body continued to operate as a social and philanthropic organization. For example, CUAC sponsored blind athlete Doris Choptain who won five gold medals at the 1976 Olympiad for the Physically Disabled. The house league programs still attracted good turnouts and as a result were continued.

In 1930, CUAC formed a house league Five Pin Mixed Bowling League. The creation of the league was in part to provide club members with a regular activity in the winter months. At the time, CUAC was not sponsoring any teams in the winter and club members readily accepted this new venture. Gaining popularity through the years, this league continued operating until 1988, when a decrease in bowling members resulted in the cessation of its operations. Until that time, however, CUAC bowling league enthusiasts often participated in various tournaments organized by the Winnipeg 5 Pin Bowling Association. In 1958, the CUAC Ladies' Auxiliary formed an afternoon recreational 5 pin bowling league. The league was still in operation in 1991.

In 1942, CUAC formed a mixed curling league with six teams. Of the 24 players, 22 had never curled before. Nevertheless, curling proved to be very popular and was still being enthusiastically pursued in 1991 with a total of ten rinks in action. The curling league underwent two major changes in the years of its existence. In 1946, the league became a men's league, and in 1983, it reverted back to the mixed concept. As with bowling, CUAC curling rinks were often entered in city or provincial bonspiels.

In its 65 years of operation, the Canadian Ukrainian Athletic Club provided an opportunity for hundreds of boys, girls, men and women reflecting the ethnic diversity of Winnipeg to participate in one of the most varied sports and community programs ever offered by a single volunteer organization. Its founders in 1925 could not have envisioned that their efforts would yield such spectacular results. And it is noteworthy that these results were achieved by a core group of dedicated volunteers that in any one year rarely exceeded twenty-five in number. It was this parent body of the CUAC, supported by its Ladies' Auxiliary, that organized, sponsored, and financed the many teams and activities that brought the club to such prominence over so many years.

In 1991, John and Stan Shaley were inducted into the Softball Canada Hall of Fame. They thus became the first Canadians of Ukrainian descent to be inducted into a hall of fame for their work with a Ukrainian community sports club. The following year, the 1965 Canadian champion CUAC Blues girls' softball team was inducted into the Manitoba Sports Hall of Fame. This was the first induction of a team operated by a Ukrainian community sports club into a hall of fame.

## PRESIDENTS OF THE CANADIAN UKRAINIAN ATHLETIC CLUB

| Nick Shaley | (1925) |
| John Moroz | (1926, 1930-33, 1952-54) |
| V. H. Koman | (1927-30, 1934) |
| Slaw Rebchuk | (1935, 1937-39) |
| Walter Lewicki | (1936) |
| Steve Mykytyn | (1940-42) |
| John Shaley | (1943-45, 1957-64, 1967-92) |
| John Mirus | (1946-47) |
| Fred James (Gniazdowsky) | (1948-51) |
| Joe Miskie | (1955-56) |
| John Mushey | (1965-66) |

# CANADIAN UKRAINIAN FOOTBALL CLUB

On December 26, 1949, after a few months of organizational work, twenty-six sports enthusiasts gathered at the Markian Shashkewych Hall to launch a sports club that would cater exclusively to Ukrainian youth. The organizers believed that the existing Ukrainian sports clubs in Winnipeg were unable to meet the needs of the post-World War II immigration. The initiatory group, headed by Michael Borowyk, had the support of the Winnipeg branches of four Ukrainian youth organizations: Plast, Canadian Ukrainian Youth Association (SUMK), Ukrainian National Youth Federation (UNYF), and Ukrainian Youth Association (SUM). Representatives from these organization took an active part in the preliminary organizational work of the club.

At the meeting, the Ukrainian Sports Club of Winnipeg was formally established. The first executive included Mykhailo Worobetz, president; M. Borowyk, vice-president; Ivan Hewryk, secretary; and Ihor Welyhorskyj, treasurer. The coordinators of men's and women's sport programs were Mykola Hnatiw and Tamara Kosach respectively. The club also selected its colours at the meeting; teams representing the Ukrainian Sports Club of Winnipeg would be attired in red and green jerseys.

The Ukrainian Sports Club had been barely established when eight club members were entered in the Winnipeg Chess Championship. Two club members, L. Drebotij and Roman Wrzesnewskyj, showed good results.

Attempts were made to organize basketball and volleyball teams that winter but nothing materialized. In the spring of 1950, a soccer team was entered into the second division of the Winnipeg and District Football League of the Manitoba Football Association.

On April 22, 1951, the Ukrainian Sports Club was reorganized and renamed Canadian Ukrainian Football Club (CUFC). Many of the club members and executive were departing Winnipeg for Eastern Canada, and as a result constant turmoil existed. With renewed optimism, the club once again entered a team in the second division of the Winnipeg and District Football League. It won its opening exhibition game against the Germania Football Club 5-1 but thereafter, the fortunes of CUFC varied.

To raise funds (which the club was always short of), members held dances, went caroling, and in one year organized a concert in memory of poet Taras Shevchenko. Nevertheless, in the spring of 1952, CUFC was unable to continue leasing a club house and moved its centre of operation to the hall of the Ukrainian Reading Association Prosvita, with which it became formally affiliated.

On the soccer pitch in 1952, the club played 12 regular season games, winning 3, drawing 2 and losing 7. The eight points placed the club in fourth place in league standings. In addition, the club contested seven Cup games, gaining only minimal success. It managed to hold the 1951 league champion Weston Bread to a 3-3 draw in the opening round of the John Queen Cup play. In the second round, CUFC was blasted 6-1 by the Germania Football Club and eliminated from further competition.

In 1953, the soccer team continued to play in the second division. In the fall, the CUFC volleyball team lost in the final of a Manitoba tournament to the Winnipeg Businessmen's Club. In December, competing in a Manitoba table tennis tournament, P. Burdz and O. Melnyk placed second in the men's doubles, M. Bukatyj won the women's singles, and R. Korol won the men's consolation title.

In 1954, the Canadian Ukrainian Football Club experienced yet another disappointing soccer season. It won only 2 games while dropping 10 in a 12-game season. One of the highlights of the 1954 season was the arrival of Toronto SA Ukraina to play a Winnipeg all-star team comprising CUFC and Institute Prosvita Athletic Club aces. The Ukrainian all-stars from Winnipeg lost a close 2-1 contest to Toronto. At a Winnipeg table tennis tournament, club members Korol, Derkach and Pankewych swept the top three prizes.

*Canadian Ukrainian Football Club, 1956*

The CUFC soccer team continued to play in the second division in 1955 without much success. The club challenged the Ukrainian Sports Club Kyiv from Minneapolis to a friendly match. Playing in Winnipeg, the visitors defeated the hosts 2-0.

In 1956, the roster of the Canadian Ukrainian Football Club was completely shaken. Club management decided to go with youth, and when the season began, the average age of the team members was 20 years, with the oldest but 24. Only five players from the previous year's team were on the roster. The team was managed by Dr. Roman Romanovych. An effort was made to organize a junior team but it never materialized.

In 1957, the Canadian Ukrainian Football Club registered a team for competition in the second division. The club folded, though, before the season began. An all-round lack of interest led to the demise of the club. It was difficult to field teams, it was difficult to raise funds, and there was little fan support. The youth organizations that had played a fundamental role in the founding of CUFC had by then distanced themselves from the club. In an effort to salvage its program, the club tried to make an arrangement with the Institute Prosvita Athletic Club so that it would serve as a feeder for the first division IPAC soccer team. IPAC, though, was not interested in the arrangement.

While the Canadian Ukrainian Football Club folded in the spring of 1957, former members and supporters used the name to organize social functions for a number of years. In addition, in the fall of 1960, a soccer team was organized and entered into a Winnipeg indoor league using the original CUFC name, the Ukrainian Sports Club. Individuals previously associated with the USC and the CUFC did not play a role in the founding of the new club which operated for only one year.

ПРОГРАМКА

С. Т. Київ — К. У. Ф. К.

(Мінеаполіс, ЗДА)          (Вінніпег, Канада)

3-го ВЕРЕСНЯ, 1955
год. 5.00 пополудні

*CUFC versus Kyiv (Minneapolis) programme, 1955*

PRESIDENTS OF THE CANADIAN UKRAINIAN FOOTBALL CLUB

Mykhailo Worobetz            (1950)
Volodymyr Bilynskyj, MD      (1950 - 1951)
Roman Korol                  (1951, 1953)
Stephen Kechko               (1952)
Mykhailo Muzychenko          (1953)
Wasyl Cap                    (1954 - 1957)

# INSTITUTE PROSVITA ATHLETIC CLUB

The Canadian Ukrainian Institute Prosvita was established in Winnipeg in 1916. The institute was modeled on the Prosvita Society of Lviv, a cultural-educational organization that had hundreds of branches and affiliates throughout Ukraine. In 1918, the Winnipeg organizers purchased a lot at the corner of Pritchard and Arlington. Three years later the construction of a building commenced. Upon completion, Prosvita began to operate a library, choir, youth group, theatre company, women's club and a Ukrainian school - *Ridna Shkola* at the facility.

Sport activity, at the home of the Canadian Ukrainian Institute Prosvita, predates the institute's direct sponsorship of sport by a number of years. In particular, the Ukrainian Gymnastics and Sports Association Sitch operated out of the Institute in the 1920s as did the Canadian Ukrainian Athletic Club (CUAC) in 1925. A few years later a sports club affiliated with the institute, the Institute Prosvita Athletic Club (IPAC), came into being. Sport enthusiasts such as Mike Moskal, William Ewaskiw, Mike Yaremko and William Harrow all figured in the founding of IPAC in 1932.

In 1934, IPAC was one of the eight men's clubs entered into the Ukrainian Diamond Ball League organized by the Canadian Ukrainian Athletic Club. The league was established to promote sport and to give fledgling Ukrainian sport groups in the Winnipeg area a venue where they could comfortably compete. The league was in operation for four years. In 1935 and in again 1937, IPAC won the Hon. W. J. Major Trophy, emblematic of the league championship. On both occasions it defeated the Markian Shashkewych school in the final. The 1937 team was captained by M. Yaremko and managed by B. Kulchycky.

In 1939, IPAC entered an intermediate girls' softball team into the Greater Winnipeg Intermediate Girls' Softball League. For many years, the IPAC team, often referred to as the "gold and blue" served as a feeder for the CUAC senior girls' softball teams. In its inaugural

season, IPAC placed second in league standings.  In a best-of-three semi-final, IPAC was eliminated from further play by the Brooklands Ukrainian Athletic Club.

*Institute Prosvita Athletic Club softball team, 1937 Ukrainian Diamond Ball League Champions*

In 1940, the intermediate girls' softball team, led by pitching ace "Caper" Caparewich, had a
stellar season.  The club won 17 and lost but 1 to place first in league standings.  Unfortunately
the club failed to carry its momentum into playoffs, bowing out to St. Vital in the opening round.

The following year, the IPAC intermediate girls' softball team was reorganized.  The team consisted of girls who had never before played organized ball.  The novices played erratically all
season, winning by margins as great as 24-8 and losing by similar counts.  The club finished
second in the league standings, but won only half the number of games of the league leading
St. Vital Tigerettes.  In the semi-finals, even without the services of its two disabled pitchers,
IPAC managed to squeeze by the Border Athletic Club.  In the final, IPAC was swept by St.
Vital in four straight games.  The team was managed by Mike Yaremko.

The 1942 season saw Minnie Pieluck and Mary Shastel lead the IPAC intermediate team to a
first-place finish in league competition.  In the semi-finals, IPAC easily defeated its opponent.
In the final, St. Vital once again disposed of IPAC's hopes for a championship.  IPAC won the
first game of a best-of-five series but was then was out-pitched and out-hit by the Tigerettes to
lose the championship.

After a year's absence from the Greater Winnipeg Intermediate Softball League, IPAC once
again fielded a team in 1944.  The season began slowly with the club consistently losing
games.  In mid-season, the players turned their fortunes around and embarked on an extended
winning streak which culminated in the club securing a playoff spot.  In a best-of-three series,
IPAC bowed out in two straight to the St. James Canucks.

IPAC opened the 1945 season winning a number of games in a row. The team then began to falter. Nevertheless, it managed to scrap enough wins together to place third in the league standings. In the opening round of the playoffs, IPAC was blown out in three straight games by the Fort Rouge Cardinals.

In 1946, the IPAC intermediate girls' softball team swept through the regular season by winning 16 and losing only 2. In the semi-final opener the girls were shocked by St. Vital. They came back to take the next two games and advance to the final. Playing against St. James Canucks in a best-of-five series, IPAC jumped to a two game lead. The Canucks fought back to take the third and fourth games. In the deciding game, IPAC squeezed by 10-9 to win the Winnipeg Intermediate Girls' Softball Championship in an exciting nail-biter. The team was managed by Steve Koniuk.

The following year, the girls' softball team continued to play championship ball. It finished the regular season by winning 13 games and losing 5 to place second in the standings. IPAC then went on to sweep the Canucks in a best-of-three semi-final, relying on the outstanding pitching of Nadia Baydack. In the best-of-seven final, IPAC faced the league pennant winner Kurl E Q. IPAC dropped the first two games but then fought back, winning four straight to take the championship. Nadia Baydack and captain Lesia Dowhanyk contributed greatly to the success of the team on the field.

For the 1948 season, the Intermediate Girls' Softball League was restructured into the Girls' Senior "B" Softball League. IPAC, which lost a number of its star players to CUAC, struggled most of the season. The team finished third in the standings, winning nine and losing just as many. In the semi-finals, it was eliminated by the fourth place St. James Canucks.

The following year, the team once again failed to play with any consistency. Nevertheless, it made the playoffs. In the semi-final opener, IPAC was blasted 20-1 by the IMCO Cardinals. The team came back to take the second game in a squeaker by a 3-2 count. IMCO then won two to eliminate IPAC from further post-season play.

In the late 1940s, Stanley Zedd, owner of the Margaret Rose Tearooms, sponsored minor soccer teams which carried the name Margaret Rose Rovers. Zedd, an advocate of organized Ukrainian sport, was for many years associated with the Canadian Ukrainian Athletic Club. In 1950, he asked the Institute Prosvita Athletic Club management whether they would be interested in assuming the sponsorship of the Rovers. As many of the boys on the teams were Ukrainian, IPAC readily brought the clubs into its fold. That summer, midget, juvenile and junior soccer teams known as the IPAC Rovers were fielded. Frank "Finky" Moski (Moskal), soccer player and sport enthusiast, managed and coached the teams. Led by Leo Konyk, the midget team won the city championship. The junior Rovers also won the city title. Goalie J.

Sedun, who had a string of seven consecutive shutouts during the season, contributed greatly to the team's undefeated season.

Of the clubs established before the war, IPAC was the only one that successfully operated a soccer program for an extended period of time. The Canadian Ukrainian Athletic Club made an effort but it was short lived. Another unique feature of the soccer program was that for many years it attracted the offspring of the old immigrants, a group that was generally not interested in the game. Only after the soccer program at IPAC became well established did the new immigrants sign up.

The 1950 IPAC girls' softball team did not show any improvement from the previous year. The club finished in fourth place. In the opening round of the playoffs against Transcona, IPAC was blasted in three straight games. In September, IPAC was one of twelve teams that took part in the inaugural Greater Winnipeg Softball Tournament. The club placed fourth.

The fortunes of the IPAC senior "B" girls' team in 1951 hit rock bottom. The club lost almost every game it played. It did not qualify for post-season play.

On the soccer pitch, all three IPAC Rover teams continued to excel. Even though the junior team's winning streak, dating back to the previous season, was snapped, it still won the city championship. The juvenile team also dominated its division.

In the summer of 1952, for the third year in a row, the IPAC Rovers junior soccer team won the Greater Winnipeg Junior Soccer Championship. In a sudden-death game, the club proceeded to win the Manitoba junior title by defeating United Weston 2-0. The club then travelled to Saskatoon to vie for the Western Canada title against Saskatoon Mayfair Rangers. At the last moment, though, the series was designated as the Canadian Championship. In a two-game total-goal final, IPAC defeated the Rangers 4-1 and 2-0 to culminate its season-long unbeaten string with the national championship.

The championship IPAC Rovers junior soccer team was coached by Frank Moski. Playing on the team were Fred Ingaldson, Bernie Krill, Ivan Symchyck, Jim Hilderman, Gordie Chem, Dave McMullan, Ed Solarz, Stan Drozda, Will Wagner, Joe Krutish, Mike Koncur, Ian Richardson, Syd Bercovich, Bob Daski, Ron Heindl and captain Sam Dolhun.

A midget and junior soccer team also saw action that summer.

In 1952, a senior soccer team was entered into the second division of the Manitoba Football Association league. Competing under the name Institute Prosvita Ukrainians (IPU), the club included individuals with European soccer experience. IPU had a relatively successful inaugural season, winning more than half of the games played and placing second in league stand-ings. Frank Moski was the playing coach of the team.

On the baseball diamond, the 1952 IPAC senior "B" girls' team showed improvement over the previous year by qualifying for the playoffs. In the semi-finals, they defeated St. James Legionettes. In the championship series, IPAC extended Wecos to six games before bowing out.

While club management celebrated the success of its teams, it was the range and scope of the sports program and its broad community outreach that management took pride in. By 1952, more than 200 neighbourhood youngsters participated in the IPAC sports program. While the majority were Ukrainian, ethnicity was not a prerequisite.

The Institute Prosvita Ukrainians soccer team continued to play in the second division in 1953. The team played well but had problems in winning games. Some maintain that this was the result of the players spending too much time passing the ball around and not shooting often enough. Towards the end of the season, the team took time out to play in a tournament at Saskatoon where it defeated the local all-star team 3-1 and tied a club from Edmonton.

The IPAC soccer club made its debut in the first division in 1954. The club had a lacklustre regular season, ending up tied for last place in the league standings. On the other hand, its record was very successful in Cup play. In competition for the John Queen Cup, emblematic of the city championship, IPAC defeated United Weston in the semi-finals 3-2. In the final, IPAC lost 5-1 to Army and Navy Scottish. In competition for the Manitoba championship - the Manitoba Cup, IPAC defeated the Scottish in the quarter-finals, FC Germania in the semi-finals, and Weston Bread in the best-of-three final. The IPAC soccer club was managed by Steve Kechko.

Among Ukrainian soccer fans, the highlight of the 1954 Winnipeg soccer season was the visit of SA Ukraina from Toronto. The visitors played an exhibition match against the Ukrainian Winnipeg all-stars representing IPAC and the Canadian Ukrainian Football Club (CUFC). SA Ukraina won the match 2-1 in front a large number of spectators.

In August of 1955, in a three-game final to determine Manitoba's representative to the Dominion Cup - national championship, the IPAC soccer team defeated FC Germania. In the Western Canada semi-finals, IPAC hosted Saskatoon United. In the opener, IPAC did not have much problem in taking the visitors 4-1 after scoring three goals in a span of five minutes. The second game was played the following day, and for IPAC it was the fourth in five days. The Winnipeg side succeeded by squeaking through with a 1-0 win after a Saskatoon player put the ball into his own net. The victory advanced IPAC to the Western Canada championship.

*Institute Prosvita Athletic Club soccer team, 1955 Manitoba Champions*

Royal Westminster, the 1953 Canadian Champion, was IPAC's opponent for the Western Canada title. In the first half of the first game, IPAC was thoroughly outplayed but nevertheless managed to hold New Westminster to a 1-1 draw. In the second half, IPAC lost four players to serious injuries. Royal Westminster capitalized on this misfortune by scoring three unanswered goals en route to a 4-1 victory. In the second game, played the following day, IPAC was forced to use four reserve players. New Westminster was unstoppable as it rolled to a 7-0 victory.

The run for the national title behind them, IPAC players returned to defend the Manitoba Cup. They did this by defeating the Army and Navy Scottish club in the final. In league play, IPAC once again was not as successful as it was in the various Cup competitions. The team won 5 and lost 5 to place fourth. At the end of the 1955 season, the Manitoba Football Association selected IPAC defender Sam Dolhun as the year's outstanding player in Manitoba.

In the mid-1950s, IPAC soccer team members, coaches, medical staff and club management were all fitted for navy blue blazers bearing a club logo on the breast pocket, grey flannels, and white shirts. Not only did this garb nurture solidarity among club members, it was also an excellent promotional medium.

During the winter months, IPAC offered a number of sports programs, among them table tennis. In the spring of 1956, IPAC placed second in the Winnipeg team table tennis championships. The IPAC team was strengthened by athletes from the CUFC.

The 1956 soccer season brought about a marked improvement in performance of IPAC during league play. The club won 5, tied 2 and lost 2 to place first in league standings. In a best-of-three playoff for the National League Cup, IPAC lost twice to Germania. That summer, IPAC once again won the John Queen Cup by defeating arch rival Germania 1-0. In early fall, an all-star team comprising IPAC and CUFC players travelled to Minneapolis to play a friendly match against the Ukrainian Sports Club Kyiv. The hosts defeated the Winnipeg Ukrainian all-stars. During the season, the team was led by F. Moski, B. Daski, S. Dolhun, F. Baranyk, L. Konyk, J. Symchyshyn, Wagner and goalie F. Ingaldson.

An interesting half-time spectacle that year was the performance of the Forester Prosvita Drum Majorettes.

In the fall of 1956, Steve Kechko, manager of the IPAC senior soccer team, was elected vice-president of the Manitoba Football Association.

The 1957 soccer season was marred by tragedy, disappointing play, and an undeserved playoff berth. IPAC lost one of its own when team member Johnny Hunt was killed in a tragic rail-road accident. On the soccer pitch, the club could not put back-to-back wins together and, as a result, finished out of the playoffs. The suspension of the Scottish resulted in IPAC being offered a playoff berth. When opponent United Weston defaulted the playoff match, IPAC advanced to the final. In a best-of-three series for the league championship, IPAC was blasted twice by Germania. It was very obvious that the club should not have been in the playoffs.

In the winter of 1957-58, an indoor soccer league was organized featuring two twenty-minute halves and six men on the field. IPAC was one of eight teams to enter the league.

In the spring of 1958, IPAC secured the coaching services of E. Goedel, who at one time toiled in the premier Austrian league and spent the previous season playing for IPAC. Goedel's task of regrouping was difficult due to the number of players who had left IPAC in the off-season, among them star goaltender F. Ingaldson. As a result, Goedel went on a recruiting spree, signing both proven and unproven players. The club fared poorly during the regular season, losing 11 and tying 1 in 12 games. As a result, there were calls for changes in the club's structure. Some believed that the coach had too much authority to recruit players. Others believed that players, particularly non-Ukrainian, should not be recruited at all; rather, prospective starters should be brought up through the IPAC junior program.

In the fall of 1958, Sam Dolhun brought the Winnipeg Buffaloes, a junior basketball team he had coached the previous year, into the IPAC fold. Dolhun, who at one time played soccer for IPAC, also had a strong basketball background. He won the Canadian basketball championship with the Paulins club in 1954.

In their inaugural season with IPAC, the Buffaloes won the Manitoba title and then reached the semi-finals of the Canadian junior basketball championship. IPAC lost the best-of-five semi-final series against Vancouver YMCA in the dying seconds of the fifth game. The two teams were tied at two victories apiece, and with five seconds to go in game five, IPAC led by a single point. An IPAC foul resulted in two YMCA free throws. Both were sunk and YMCA went on to win the game 69-68. The IPAC Buffaloes were led by captain Bob Seepish that year.

The 1959 version of the IPAC senior soccer club played poor soccer. The club finished the season with 2 victories, 3 ties and 10 losses. The players scored but 14 goals and had 50 scored against them. Fortunately for IPAC, there was a weaker club in the league. As a result, IPAC did not finish at the bottom of the standings. After a winter of soul searching, IPAC cancelled its soccer program in the spring of 1960.

For coach Sam Dolhun and manager Harvey Lipkin, the 1959-60 basketball season was most challenging and particularly rewarding. As only four players returned from the previous year's team, a major drive was organized to recruit players. The success of the team exceeded most expectations. The junior IPAC Buffaloes lost only one game during the regular season. In the Manitoba final, they had some difficulty with the Canadian Polish Athletic Club but eventually won the best-of-five series in five games. The club then blasted the Fort William Spud Canucks to win the Manitoba-Thunder Bay title and advance to the junior Western Canada playdowns. In the semi-finals, IPAC rolled over the Moose Jaw Jesters. In the final, IPAC came up against its previous year's nemesis, the Vancouver YMCA. Once again the YMCA club defeated IPAC. Kenneth Galanchuk, a future member of Canada's national basketball team, was one of the new recruits responsible for IPAC's success that year.

In the spring of 1960, IPAC's volleyball team competed in a one-day tournament for the Manitoba Championship. The club finished in fifth spot among six teams.

During the 1960-61 season, the junior basketball team continued to play exceptionally well. It finished tied for first place in league play with 14 wins and 2 losses. It then won a sudden-death playoff to determine first place. In the playoffs, IPAC lost its momentum. The club was eliminated from further play after a ten-point lead evaporated with seven minutes remaining in the fifth and deciding game. Once again, the team was coached by Sam Dolhun.

In 1961, IPAC re-entered a team into the first division of the National Soccer League. Sam Dolhun, after an absence of four years, returned to the soccer club, as did Fred Ingaldson. The return of the two stars did not do much to improve IPAC's fortunes. The club finished the season tied for last place. IPAC, though, managed to avoid the basement on the basis of goal differentials.

Fred Ingaldson's return to IPAC was also of great significance to the basketball program. Ingaldson, who competed in the sport at the 1960 Olympics, agreed to be the playing coach of a newly formed senior IPAC basketball team. The team primarily comprised players from the previous year's Carling team (on which Ingaldson had played) and of IPAC juniors. The senior Buffalos finished the 20-game 1961-62 regular season undefeated. After winning the league and provincial titles, IPAC faced Lethbridge in a best-of-five Western Canada Championship. The Lethbridge side, having a substantial height advantage, handled the IPAC team in four games without much difficulty. During the playoffs, IPAC was led by Ingaldson and Kenneth Galanchuk. The IPAC junior team finished the playoffs in second spot after dropping a best-of-five final in four games to the Canadian Polish Athletic Club.

In the spring of 1962, the IPAC volleyball team was one of twenty-seven clubs entered in the Manitoba Volleyball Championships. IPAC failed to advance past the opening round robin play.

As spring made way for summer, the IPAC soccer team began its season. The club exhibited a higher level of play than in the previous year but still failed to qualify for the playoffs. It finished the twelve game season in fourth place with nine points. The setbacks on the field were a prelude to the cancelation of the senior soccer program in the off-season. Not only was there a shortage of players, but most organizational and administrative positions were unfilled. It was also decided that IPAC should now concentrate its scarce resources on developing a strong youth soccer program. As a result, over the next few years, midget, bantam, juvenile and/or junior teams were entered for play in Winnipeg leagues.

The 1962-63 senior basketball team placed first in the Greater Winnipeg Senior Basketball League with 17 wins in 20 starts. The playoffs were an interesting affair. Only two of the four teams that qualified would have been eligible for competition in the national championship had they won. The Blues were ineligible because the team consisted of professional football players from the Winnipeg Blue Bombers, while the Voodoos were a United States Air Force team from Grand Forks. IPAC lost the league playoffs to the Blues. It then defeated St. Andrew's in a series which determined Manitoba's representation at the national final.

At a four-team tournament played at Lethbridge to decide the Canadian champion, IPAC lost to Montreal's Yvon Coutu Huskies 109-72, and to the host team and eventual champion Lethbridge Nationals 77-53. In the consolation final, IPAC defeated British Columbia Harlem 105-62 to take the bronze medal.

The junior IPAC basketball team had a poor record that season. It won 7 of 12 games and placed third in league standings. The club never made it past the opening round of the playoffs.

On the volleyball courts, the 1962-63 senior IPAC team placed second at the YMCA

Invitational Tournament. At the Manitoba Championship, IPAC was eliminated in the early rounds. The team was coached and managed by Ben Kussy.

The 1963-64 senior basketball team won the league title and Manitoba Championship. Fred Ingaldson was the league's top scorer with 492 points in 18 games, a whopping 207 points more than his nearest rival. In the semi-finals of the national championship, IPAC upset three-time defending Canadian champion Lethbridge in three straight games. The Western champions then travelled to Toronto to play against the Eastern champions, the Toronto Dow Kings. IPAC could not keep pace with the much faster Toronto team and lost in its bid for a national title in three straight games. Fred Ingaldson, the top scorer during the championship tournament, impressed with his game and, as a result, was selected to Canada's 1964 Olympic team.

The 1963-64 junior basketball team, not to be outdone, advanced to the Western Canada championship by winning the Manitoba title. Winning the provincial title was not a significant accomplishment as the lack of interest resulted in the collapse of the junior league. As a result, the IPAC junior club was entered into the senior "B" league, while the other surviving junior team, the University of Manitoba Cougars, played exhibition matches. Nevertheless, a Manitoba junior "final" was played at which IPAC defeated the Cougars.

The club then travelled to Calgary to compete in a best-of-three Western Canada semi-final against the local Mount Royal College. IPAC needed all three games to advance. Playing in Vancouver for the Western championship, IPAC lost three straight games to the Vancouver CYO Saints in a best-of-five final. Upon returning to Winnipeg, the team finished the senior "B" schedule in first place with a record 16 wins and 4 losses. The club was coached by Martin Terry.

The 1964-65 senior basketball season commenced without playing coach Ingaldson who was in Japan for the Olympics. Upon his return he left IPAC to play for the St. Andrews Dunlop team. A month later, Kenneth Galanchuk transferred to the University of Manitoba Bisons. The greatly weakened and demoralized IPAC club nevertheless managed to complete the season in second place. In the final, the undefeated Dunlops easily overpowered IPAC. At the junior level, IPAC posted a formidable record of 28 wins in 30 games. The club won the Manitoba title by defeating St. Andrews. At the national championship played in Hamilton, IPAC lost 65-40 to tournament favourite Victoria Chinooks and 89-64 to the Calgary Cougars.

To gain experience, the IPAC basketball team was entered into the Winnipeg YMCA summer league during the summer of 1965. The team played relatively well, tying for first place. In the playoffs, it was defeated by arch-rival St. Andrews. The summer experience though was of no consequence to the IPAC club as in the fall the basketball program was dropped.

Prior to the start of the 1966-67 volleyball season, the unaffiliated Winnipeg Ukraina team, after failing to secure sponsorship, transferred to the Institute Prosvita Athletic Club.

During the winter of 1967-68, the IPAC volleyball team played well, qualifying for the Canadian championship. At the tournament in Hamilton, IPAC placed third in its pool in the preliminary round. Its record of 8 wins and 4 losses failed to qualify the team for the championship playoffs.

In the summer of 1968, IPAC fielded two soccer teams, a juvenile and a playground "A." After a solid season, the juvenile team captured the Manitoba juvenile championship. The club spotted its opponent a one goal lead. With seven minutes remaining, IPAC scored the tying goal, and just two minutes later Zenon Hluszok popped the winner for IPAC. The team then lost 5-1 to Ft. Rouge in a game to determine Manitoba's representative to the Western Canada Championship. The team was coached by Mike Sribnyj. The little leaguers, coached by M. Hawryshko, won three age group cups.

In 1969, both teams moved into higher divisions. The juniors completed the regular season with an almost flawless record. Out of 22 games, they won 20, tied 1 and lost 1. The juveniles also had a good season, winning 29 and losing 3. The juniors began their quest for the Manitoba title by defeating St. Vital 1-0 in the semi-finals. In the final, IPAC lost 3-1 to United Weston. The game was marred by questionable officiating, which saw, among other incidents, an IPAC goal disallowed by the referee. IPAC's protest was supported by the linesman to no avail.

In 1972, the Institute Prosvita Athletic Club came under new management. Osyp Stech assumed the presidency while P. Lushczyk took on the task of sport coordinator. One of the first decisions of the new executive was to rename the IPAC Rovers soccer team the IPAC Ukraina. Competing in the third division of the Manitoba Central Soccer League, the club placed third in league standings. It was coached by B. Byhold.

In 1973, coach Byhold guided IPAC Ukraina to the third division title. As a result it was promoted to the second division.

Michael Sribnyj assumed the coaching duties for the 1974 season. The team, though, was not prepared for the higher calibre of play required in the second division. The season concluded with IPAC placing a distant sixth in the standings.

In 1975, under the guidance of new coach I. Werhun, IPAC Ukraina regained its winning ways to place second in league standings. After this success, the team was promoted to the first division.

The IPAC - Ukraina's inaugural season in the first division in 1976 proved to be far too challenging for the athletes and coach Werhun. The team finished in last spot and was demoted back to the second division.

*Institute Prosvita Athletic Club logo*

In the spring of 1976, IPAC formed a second soccer club made up of juniors. Coached by Z. Hluszok the team Lviw was entered into the fourth division of the Manitoba Central Soccer League. Lviw's debut season was successful as the club placed second and was promoted to the third division at the end of the season.

In 1977, IPAC Ukraina and IPAC Lviw experienced numerous setbacks in the regular season. As a result, it was decided to fold the Lviw club in mid-season so that the Ukraina club could be strengthened. This tactic did not succeed as Ukraina finished in last spot. Only a reorganization of the league prevented IPAC Ukraina from being demoted to the third division. A. Ganter had the task of coaching Ukraina during this difficult year.

In 1978, it was hoped that yet another coaching change would turn fortunes around for IPAC Ukraina. Z. Hluszok, though, had more difficulties than could be imagined, as the team finished last in the nine-team division. A demotion to the third division was not avoidable at season's end.

Wasyl Kucharsky assumed the presidency of IPAC in 1979. He and executive members Bohdan Bochna and Evhenia Kucharsky had the unenviable task of halting IPAC's slide into obscurity. That year, it did not appear as if the soccer team was destined for better times as it placed eighth in the weak third division. Coach J. Hrineky had his arms full, as did Hluszok the previous year.

In 1980, IPAC Ukraina secured the coaching services of T. Capone, who would be with the team for three years, longer than any other coach in the past decade. Capone showed his resolve by leading the team out of the third division's cellar into a respectable third spot.

In 1981, goaltender George Romanovych returned to IPAC after a six-year absence. The 23-year-old played brilliantly, registering 10 shutouts in 16 games and conceding only 10 goals. His goals against average of 0.625 was the lowest among all goaltenders playing in the 47-team Manitoba Central League. The average also established a record that still stood in 1992. Romanovych was the impact player the team needed to help vault it into first place in the third division with a record of 10 wins, 5 ties and 1 loss. The result assured the team of a promotion into the second division. Offensively the team was led by long time captain I. Pecuh.

For IPAC president Kucharsky, the result was gratifying. The club was once again capable of challenging Winnipeg's finer teams. Nevertheless, concern was expressed over the fact that more than half of the team was non-Ukrainian.

At the end of the 1981 season, IPAC awarded George Romanovych the MVP trophy. In addition, Zenon Hluszok was recognized for his ten years of service with the club.

Play in the second division during the 1982 season proved to be tougher than most expected. The team placed seventh.

In 1983, IPAC Ukraina moved up a few notches to place fifth. In competition for the provincial cup, the club was eliminated in the quarter-finals. The club competed under the watchful eye of coach F. Hohel.

In 1984, the soccer team showed a marked improvement to place second in its division. As a result, it was promoted to the first division from which it fell unceremoniously nine years earlier.

Under new coach J. Varnaus, the 1985 team had difficulty competing against the much stronger clubs of this division and could only muster a ninth place finish.

In 1986, IPAC Ukraina surprised everyone by placing second in league standings. As a result of growing popularity, the Central Soccer League was restructured and IPAC Ukraina was assigned to the premier division.

In 1987, playing coach I. Smerkal led the team to a sixth-place finish. At season's end, Smerkal, the league's leading scorer, was honoured by the league for his scoring prowess. Contesting the Manitoba Cup, IPAC Ukraina was eliminated in the semi-finals.

The Institute Prosvita Athletic Club folded at the end of the season; it had become too costly to operate the club.

In the winter of 1991, recently arrived Ukrainian immigrants from Poland and Ukraine convinced the management of the Institute Prosvita to re-activate its defunct sport program. Prosvita president Peter Manastyrsky was enthralled by the request and was instrumental in the organizational work. In the spring, the Institute Prosvita bought the third division Britannia Lions franchise of Manitoba Central Soccer League for $400 and with it the right to enter a team into play. In its inaugural year, the club that represented the Institute was required by league rules to retain the name Britannia Lions. Nevertheless, in soccer circles the club was referred to by its proper name - IPAC Ukraine. The new team played well, winning the championship of the third division and qualifying for a promotion to the second division. The club was captained by goaltender Slawomir Karhut, coached by Myroslaw Benko, and managed by former IPAC player Ihor Pidhirnyj.

The following year, IPAC expanded its soccer program by acquiring the rights to the first division Winnipeg Bari. Once again, a new team was assembled and prepared for competition. In its inaugural season, Winnipeg Bari-IPAC won the championship of the ten-team First Division and was promoted to the Premiere Division. En route, the team registered 12 wins, 2 ties, and 4 losses. Winnipeg Bari-IPAC was managed by Reverend Protodeacon Taras Maluzynsky and coached by former IPAC stalwart Ben Kussy. George Romanovych, a former star goaltender with IPAC, also rejoined the team and was named its captain.

The second division IPAC Ukraine team, mainly comprising junior age players, completed its season in sixth place with a record of 4 wins, 5 ties, and 9 losses. The team was coached by Oleh Boukailo.

An IPAC Selects team competed at the 25th annual Labatt's International Soccer Tournament at Thunder Bay. The team lost the championship final of the Kyle Division in overtime. While in Thunder Bay, IPAC was hosted at a welcoming reception by the city's Institute Prosvita.

For almost 60 uninterrupted years, the Canadian Ukrainian Institute Prosvita of Winnipeg sponsored the Institute Prosvita Athletic Club. While the primary objective of the Institute was cultural-educational enlightenment, the notable sport program that it operated is a reminder of the diverse role that the organization played in serving its members and the community.

| | |
|---|---|
| William Ewaskiw | (1952) |
| Michael Sribny | (1954) |
| Osyp Stech | (1972-74) |
| P. Luszczyk | (1975) |
| Zenon Hluszok | (1976-78) |
| Wasyl Kucharsky | (1979-87) |
| club inactive | (1988-90) |
| Peter Manastryrsky | (1991) |

# STS. PETER AND PAUL

In the fall of 1951, recent immigrant to Canada and sports enthusiast Reverend Konstantin Hawryliw organized a hockey team from the members of his parish, the newly established Sts. Peter and Paul Church in St. Boniface, on the outskirts of Winnipeg. The team, known as Sts. Peter and Paul, was registered in the Catholic Inter-Parish Hockey League of Winnipeg. The 1951-52 inaugural season of the Sts. Peter and Paul hockey team was trying. While most of the players had hockey experience, much work was required to mould them into a cohesive unit. The team improved progressively and gained confidence. The following season, John Kozoriz became manager of the team and he added a few experienced players to the roster. The team responded by playing well and placing second in league standings.

Throughout the club's existence, the roster of the team was almost exclusively filled by Ukrainian athletes. These individuals were of various ages, from teens to thirties. They also had differing hockey experience. The team was coached at various times by Jim Mosienko, the brother of Bill Mosienko, and by Peter Petrow. John Kozoriz remained manager of the team for the remainder of its existence.

Sts. Peter and Paul completed the 1953-54 season with a record 7 wins, 2 ties and 1 loss to place first in league standings. In the semi-finals, Sts. Peter and Paul won over the defending champion St. Joseph. In the final, Sts. Peter and Paul defeated the Flying Frenchmen of St. Boniface Cathedral to win the Knights of Columbus Trophy. The third game of the best-of-three final went into overtime with Jim Mosienko securing the championships on a long shot with 15 seconds remaining. Team member W. Petrow gained personal recognition when he was honoured as the league's most gentlemanly player. The coach of the championship team was P. Petrow.

At the conclusion of the season, a number of individuals, among them priests, called for the creation of similar hockey teams at the other Ukrainian Catholic churches. These individuals viewed the Sts. Peter and Paul team as an exemplary vehicle for promoting the church and the Ukrainian community. In addition, it was argued that such teams offered individuals the opportunity to play sports in a Ukrainian environment. Only the Church of the Blessed Virgin Mary responded and registered a team with the league at the start of the 1954 season.

*Sts. Peter and Paul hockey team, 1955*

Sts. Peter and Paul repeated as champions of the church league in 1954-55 and 1955-56, thus becoming the first team to win three consecutive championships. The latter championship final was particularly interesting as the two Ukrainian teams faced off for the Knights of Columbus Trophy. The experienced Sts. Peter and Paul had little difficulty in sweeping the Blessed Virgin Mary hockey team in three straight games.

During the off-season the Catholic Inter-Parish Hockey League folded and with it the Sts. Peter and Paul hockey team.

# STS. VLADIMIR AND OLGA

In the fall of 1927, Reverend Petro Oleksiw organized a young men's basketball team from the members of Sts. Vladimir and Olga Church in Winnipeg. The team was entered in a seven-team Catholic Church basketball league sponsored by the Knights of Columbus. Sts. Vladimir and Olga completed the 30-game schedule by qualifying for the playoffs. The team then won a best of three final against St. Paul's College to capture the Knights of Columbus Cup. The team was captained by Mykhailo Faryna.

During the summer of 1928, members pursued baseball on an organized level.

It could not be determined how long the church of Sts. Vladimir and Olga maintained a sport program.

# TRIDENT GOLF CLUB

In early 1940, Dr. Paul Huculak founded the Trident Golf Club in Winnipeg. During the summer months the members made regular outings to the city's golf links. On August 15, the club championship was contested at Pine Ridge Golf Course. Dr. V. F. Bachynski won the event. The season concluded with a stag banquet attended by more than 50 members and friends. At the banquet, Dr. Bachynski was presented with the Empire Drug Trophy, emblematic of the club championship. The trophy was donated by the Empire Drug Stores Limited.

*Trident Golf Club awards night, 1940*

In 1941, the golf club re-elected Dr. Huculak as its president. The club scheduled its golf outings for the second Sunday and the last Wednesday of each month. The club championship in 1941 was once again won by Dr. Bachynski. Shortly after the club's 1941 fall banquet, Dr.

Huculak left for Toronto. The Trident Golf Club faded into obscurity after his departure.

# UKRAINIAN CANADIAN VETERANS BRANCH 141

The end of World War II brought about the demobilization and repatriation of Canadian soldiers serving overseas. Those who returned to their home town of Winnipeg were invited to attend a meeting on June 14, 1945, sponsored by the Ukrainian Canadian Committee and the Rehabilitation Committee. At the meeting, John Solomon, MLA, Rev. Capt. S. W. Sawchuk, Rev. O. Pelech, Ivan Gulay and Dr. B. Dyma urged those veterans in attendance to organize a Ukrainian Canadian veterans' association. This association would be a spin-off of the Ukrainian Canadian Servicemen's Association (UCSA) that operated during the war in England. Those in attendance agreed, and on that day the Ukrainian Canadian Veterans' Association was founded. The initial primary objective of the association was to encourage and help organize Ukrainian legion branches across Canada.

One of the first cities to respond was Winnipeg, where in November of 1945, the Ukrainian Canadian Veterans Branch 141 was formed. In the spring of the following year, Peter Okrainec, a bustling sport enthusiast, helped organize a fastball team of legion members. The team was entered in the Canadian Legion Fastball League and was assigned to play in the "B" division. Okrainec was the team's coach and catcher, while W. Melnyk was the manager, later replaced by first baseman Mike Chalenda. The team was sponsored by the Spitfire Service, a messenger and delivery service owned and operated by veterans and members of Branch 141. On the diamonds, the Branch 141 team had a good first year. It qualified for the playoffs but lost the best-of-three series in four games (the second game, which Branch 141 was leading by five runs, was called because of darkness).

The Branch 141 softball team of 1946 was a modest start to what would be, in time, an ambitious sports program. The branch, through its sports committee, organized a three-tier sports program, with all three tiers not necessarily operating every year. The first tier included teams that were made up of branch members and entered into competitive leagues. The second tier was a house league program for branch members and their spouses. The third tier was the sponsorship of community sports.

During the early years, most of the emphasis was placed on fielding a competitive men's softball team. In 1947, the team placed third in the Canadian Legion Fastball League. In the years 1948 to 1951, the team played with varied success.

*Branch 141 softball team, 1946*

In 1952, Branch 141 placed third in league competition and qualified for the playoffs. In the semi-finals the team defeated Weston. In the best-of-seven final, Branch 141 defeated Army-Navy-Air Force (ANAF) in five games to win the league championship. The club then met the Canadian Pacific Railway Club for the Senior Men's Manitoba Championship. Branch 141 won the best-of-seven series in six games.

The Edmonton Dittrichs provided the opposition in the Western Canada Senior Championship. The best-of-five series was played in Winnipeg. The games were scheduled on five successive days.

Edmonton won the opening game 9-6. Branch 141 came back to take the second game 2-0 in a marathon 17-inning game. Righthand pitcher Lou Lucki went the distance to record the shutout. Game three was won by the Dittrichs 6-1. Lucki started game four for Branch 141. He pitched a 3-0 no-hitter, the first to be recorded in a Western Canada playoff game. With the series tied at two games, both teams planned strategy for the deciding game. Branch 141 manager Metro Semotiuk decided to go with pitcher Lucki again, his third start in four days. The decision proved to be a good one, as Lucki pitched nine innings of shutout ball to extend his scoreless streak to 35 innings and help Branch 141 wallop the Dittrichs 16-0.

Ken Yost, president of the Western Canada Softball Association, subsequently initiated talks aimed at organizing a Canadian championship. A playoff against the Eastern Canada champions never materialized.

In 1953, Branch 141 repeated as the Legion League champions. The team then won the Manitoba Senior Championship, defeating Brandon ANAF. The Western Canada championship was not contested that year.

In 1954 Lou Lucki rejoined the club, ending a one year retirement. This led many to believe that the Branch 141 team would be a contender for the national title. The team showed its strength by winning the Canadian Legion Fastball League pennant. The playoffs barely commenced when Branch 141 took time off to travel to Calgary to defend its Western Canada championship. In a best-of-three semi-final against Baysel-Ashdowns, the veterans lost the first game 9-8, won the second 2-1, and lost the third 3-1. The team returned to Winnipeg and resumed the league's championship playoff which it won. The Branch 141 team was managed by Met Simenik.

In 1955, Branch 141 once again fielded a team in the Legion league. The team qualified for the playoffs and advanced to the final for the fifth year in a row. The club did not have the necessary pitching and hitting to repeat as champions. It lost the final in six games to the Fort Rouge Legion.

The mid-1950s saw the end of the Branch 141 fastball team. The veterans were starting to age. Some retired to participate in house league sports or to help foster community sports through the branch. Those who continued to play found it increasingly difficult to remain competitive.

House league sport was first introduced at Branch 141 in 1949 when a mixed bowling league was formed. The bowling league was still in operation in 1991. There was also a Ladies Auxiliary Bowling League.

In the 1950s, golf, curling and fishing clubs were organized. Members of the golf and curling clubs represented the branch in competitions sponsored by the Royal Canadian Legion. The curlers also participated in open competitions. In 1954, the Branch 141 rink won the Northern Manitoba Curling Championship. The fishing club held regular outings for its members and was still operational in the late 1980s. For many years, one of the most talked about events organized by the fishing club was the 1954 fishing derby. It was the first one day derby in Canada that offered a car for the best catch. Shoal Lake was the setting for the 270 fishermen who vied for the car. Spike Chapley and Alex Fedun played a key role in the success of the fishing club.

Under the presidency of Peter Okrainec, Branch 141 started to sponsor community sport teams. The first such attempt was in 1954 when the branch agreed to salvage the defunct Elmwood Bombers football franchise. The team operated as the Ukrainian Vets for two seasons in the Manitoba Intermediate Football League. For the team's debut, the branch chartered buses to transport fans from the branch club house to the stadium. Booster buttons, pennants and team colours were sold at the games. The team won only one game in eight starts during its first season. The second season saw the Ukrainian Vets qualify for the playoffs. They lost the best-of-three final in four games. One of the games ended in a tie even after overtime.

Subsequently, Branch 141 started to sponsor softball teams from the pee-wee through the junior level. In any year, three or four branch-sponsored teams competed in Winnipeg leagues. A number of them won city championships and some the provincial titles. In many instances, branch members coached and or managed the teams. Individuals such as Gus Beitz, Eddie Kaye, Steve Melnyk, Peter Okrainec, William Pesclovitch, Walter Proutt and Thomas Zaharia were integral to the branch's sports program.

The devotion of the Ukrainian Canadian Veterans Branch 141 to sport was significant when one considers that sport was never the association's main objective. It was not even the primary youth-oriented activity. Commencing in 1953, the branch expanded much effort and resources to sponsor Air Cadets. Sport was just one element of a broad community program.

The magnitude of the branch's involvement in sports can be viewed from another perspective. In the mid-1950s, Winnipeg Blue Bomber great Dick Huffman, a veteran of the US Marines, joined the branch. He stated that he liked the branch because of its enthusiasm for sports. At the same time, Jack Matheson, a Navy veteran and one of Western Canada's top sports writers, also joined the branch. He too was impressed with the work the branch was doing in sports. In 1967, branch member of Polish descent Joe Zaleski was named head coach of the Winnipeg Blue Bombers Football Club.

# UKRAINIAN CHESS CLUB

On January 12, 1928, a group of chess enthusiasts gathered at the office of Dr. Boryslaw Dyma with the intent of organizing a chess club. Most of those attending were young professionals who had an interest in the game. The meeting concluded with the founding of the Ukrainian Chess Club. The club's first executive included Dr. Paul Huculak, president; L. Sikevych, vice-president; Mykola Karabut, secretary; and Mykola Zalozetsky, treasurer. Eighteen members were signed up at the time.

The chess club began operating immediately. Initially, the members gathered every Thursday at the pharmacy of M. Zalozetsky to test their skills. Subsequently, the club relocated to the office of Dr. Huculak. The Ukrainian Chess Club's first tournament was won by M. Karabut with Zyhmont Bychynsky placing second. Both were awarded with silver trophies.

It could not be determined how long the Ukrainian Chess Club operated.

# UKRAINIAN DIAMOND BALL LEAGUE

In 1934, the Canadian Ukrainian Athletic Club (CUAC) organized the Ukrainian Diamond Ball League. Eight teams, the Brooklands Ukrainian Athletic Club (BUAC), Trident YMC, Ukrainian National Home, Institute Prosvita Athletic Club, Ukrainian Reading Association Prosvita, Kobzar Fort Rouge, St. Ivan's Athletic Club, and the Markian Shashkewych School from Point Douglas competed in men's baseball for a trophy donated by the Honourable W. L. Majors, K.C. The league was organized to promote sport and to give fledgling sport groups in the aforementioned organizations a venue where they could comfortably compete. According to one observer, the games, or as he referred to them, the battles "were knock-down drag-out affairs, every one."[25]

In 1935, the league was reorganized with the following clubs partaking in competition: Institute Prosvita, Reading Association Prosvita, Taras Shevchenko Reading Association of East Kildonan, and Markian Shashkewych School. The Institute Prosvita Athletic Club won the championship trophy, defeating the Markian Shashkewych School in the final.

The teams that competed in the league in 1936 were the Canadian Ukrainian Institute Prosvita, Markian Shashkewych School, Ukrainian National Home, and the Ukrainian Athletic Club operating out of the Ukrainian Prosvita Association at St. Boniface.

In 1937, the Institute Prosvita club once again won the title. The league folded after the completion of the season that year. The City of Winnipeg Diamond League was formed, largely with teams that were commercially sponsored. Most of those who played in the Ukrainian Diamond League joined teams in the new league.

# UKRAINIAN STUDENTS' CLUB *KOZAKS*

In the mid-1970s, University of Manitoba students Nestor Budyk and Myroslav Zatwarnicky began entertaining the idea of organizing a hockey team from members of the Ukrainian

Students' Club. At the start of the 1974-75 season, a team named Kozaks was registered by the students' club with the university intramural league. The Kozaks, coached by the Reverend Michael Wiwchar and managed by Peter Melnycky, won the league championship that year.

During the 1975-76 hockey season, the Kozaks failed in their bid to repeat as league champions. In February, the Kozaks travelled to Newark, New Jersey, to face the Chornomorska Sitch all-star hockey team and to make history. It was the first time that a Ukrainian hockey team from Canada faced a Ukrainian hockey team from the United States. Led by captain Roman Hrabowych, the Kozaks defeated their hosts 5-2 and 9-0 in the two-game series. Some 1,000 fans watched the two games.

*Ukrainian Students' Club Kozaks, 1975*

The student team once again won the league championship in the winter of 1976-77. During the 1979-80 season, the Kozaks captured first place in league standings. In post-season play, the club was eliminated in the semi-finals by Science. The team was coached by Ihor Holowczynski.

# UKRAINIAN TENNIS CLUB

O ne day in early 1928, after spending a substantial amount of time waiting for a public tennis court at Kildonan Park, Stephen Bilinsky and Volodymyr Kisilewsky concluded that a way to alleviate the problem would be to organize a tennis club. A short while later, the

Ukrainian Tennis Club was established.  The first executive included the two aforementioned individuals.  Most of those who registered with the club were university students or young professionals.

The old grounds of the YMCA acquired by St. Paul's collegium had an idle and unkept tennis court.  The Ukrainian Tennis Club approached the collegium with regard to using it and was granted permission.  In a very short period of time, the tennis enthusiasts restored the facility.  Throughout the summer of 1928, club members honed their skills and competed in friendly matches.  On occasion they were provided with coaching by a more advanced player.

It could not be determined how long the Ukrainian Tennis Club existed.


# WINNIPEG *UKRAINA*


O n September 24, 1964, the Winnipeg media reported that a new team by the name of Winnipeg Ukraina had been registered in the  Winnipeg Senior "A" Volleyball League.  The team was organized by a group of young men who had recently graduated from university.  Harry Dmytryshyn, a four time Manitoba all-star, played a leading role in the establishment of the team.

The response to the new club was positive and the number of athletes that registered also allowed the organizers to field a reserve team in the senior "B" league.

The Winnipeg Ukraina senior "A" team completed its inaugural season in first place with a record of 34 wins and 14 losses.  The club had an 18-point margin over the second place team.  In the opening round of the playoffs, Winnipeg Ukraina was upset by the Winnipeg Kids who completed the season in fourth place.  At the Manitoba closed championship, Winnipeg Ukraina was eliminated in the semi-finals.  The team eventually won the Manitoba Open Championship and thus qualified for the national tournament.

At the Canadian Championships at Vancouver, Winnipeg Ukraina competed in pool "A," placing sixth with 5 wins and 9 losses.  The record failed to qualify the team for the playoffs.

The following season, Winnipeg Ukraina continued to play well and once again the team advanced to the Canadian Championships at Calgary.  There the team won 2, split 2, and lost 1 to place second in its pool.  As at the previous national championship, the team came up short in 1966 and did not qualify for the championship playoffs.

A unique experience for the Winnipeg Ukraina team members, at both national championships, was the encounter with the Plast Vedmedyky team from Toronto. The two Ukrainian teams enjoyed fraternizing at the events.

During its first two years of operation, Winnipeg Ukraina was unable to secure sponsorship. As a result, the team transferred to the Institute Prosvita Athletic Club (IPAC) for the 1966-67 season.

Shortly after the founding of Winnipeg Ukraina in 1964, team member John Baluta was elected president of the Winnipeg Senior Men's Volleyball League. In 1965, William Swystun, also a member of the volleyball team, was named chairman of the 1967 Pan American Games Society Volleyball Committee. Joining him on the committee was John Baluta in the capacity of Meet Director.

# YORKTON

## ST. JOSEPH'S COLLEGE

St. Joseph's College at Yorkton was founded by Bishop Budka in 1919 and began operations a year later. It was a private school with a residence on site that could accommodate more than 100 students. Outdoor sport facilities included a baseball diamond, an ice rink, and volleyball and tennis courts. The students also had an indoor gymnasium at their disposal. The college was operated by the monastic Brothers of Christian Schools.

In the mid-1920s, Volodymyr Bossy arrived at the college to assume the responsibility of teaching Ukrainian subjects. Bossy, a co-founder of the Sitch movement in Canada, immediately organized a branch at the college. Twice a week, member students participated in group exercises and drill training. Bossy also organized a baseball team that competed against other schools in the city and teams from other towns. In winter the students played hockey against local teams.

In the early 1940s, future Chicago Black Hawk Metro Prystai received his basic hockey training while attending St. Joseph's College at Yorkton.

# THE ATHLETES, COACHES
# AND ADMINISTRATORS

The athletes, coaches and administrators are listed in alphabetical order.  For a complete cross-reference of individuals by sport, please see page 845.

## A NOTE ON THE STATISTICAL DATA

The statistics presented reflect the style of data accumulation particular to each sport and league.  As a result, inconsistencies exist.  In addition, statistical compilation of sporting results over time has undergone major revision.  Revisions have also occurred in the interpretation of criteria by which records are verified.

Please see Appendix VII for a more detailed discussion about statistical data.

An asterisk (*) indicates that the athlete won the league championship in the particular year, i.e. Grey Cup, Stanley Cup, etc.

# ACHTYMICHUK, GENE

"Acky"

| | |
|---|---|
| sport: | hockey |
| given name: | Achtymichuk, Eugene Edward |
| born: | Lamont, Alberta |
| | September 7, 1932 |
| height: | 1.80 m / 5'11" |
| weight: | 77 kg / 170 lbs |
| position: | center |
| shoots: | left |

Gene Achtymichuk was a high scoring all-star center with the junior Crow's Nest Coalers in the Western Canada Hockey League. After turning professional, Achtymichuk spent much of his career in the minor pro leagues. While with the Montreal Canadiens organization, he was predominantly engaged by a variety of clubs in the WHL and the QHL, making only brief appearances with the parent club. During the summer of 1958, Achtymichuk was drafted by the Red Wings and assigned to their affiliate, the Edmonton Flyers. He was called up briefly by the Red Wings in the winter of 1958-59 before heading back to the minor pro leagues. During the 1962-63 season, Achtymichuk established an EHL record by registering 96 assists in the regular season. The following year he was the runner-up in the EHL's scoring race with 118 points.

Gene Achtymichuk led the Long Island Ducks to the EHL championship in 1965. The following year he was the top scorer in the EHL playoffs. In the summer of 1966, he was named playing coach of the Ducks. The team qualified for post-season play with a fourth-place finish in its division. It was then eliminated in the opening round of the playoffs. Subsequently, Achtymichuk assumed the role of playing coach of the Edmonton Monarchs. In the years 1977 to 1981, Achtymichuk coached the Fort Saskatchewan Traders Junior A hockey club.

Gene Achtymichuk captained the Edmonton Old Timers hockey club on its tour of the USSR in 1984. Included in the itinerary was a game in Kyiv.

## ALL-STAR SELECTIONS

| 1963-64 | center | EHL | Second Team |
|---|---|---|---|
| 1964-65 | center | EHL | First Team (North Division) |
| 1965-66 | center | EHL | First Team (North Division) |

# RECORD

| year | team | league | regular season GP | G | A | PTS | PIM | playoffs GP | G | A | PTS | PIM |
|------|------|--------|----|----|----|-----|-----|----|----|----|-----|-----|
| 1951-52 | Montreal | NHL | 1 | 0 | 0 | 0 | 0 | | | | | |
| 1952-53 | Buffalo | AHL | 50 | 7 | 4 | 11 | 18 | | | | | |
| 1953-54 | Victoria | WHL | 65 | 11 | 21 | 32 | 25 | 5 | 1 | 0 | 1 | 0 |
| 1954-55 | Victoria | WHL | 69 | 18 | 19 | 37 | 18 | 5 | 0 | 1 | 1 | 2 |
| 1955-56 | Quebec | QHL | 64 | 22 | 28 | 50 | 34 | 7 | 0 | 5 | 5 | 2 |
| 1956-57 | Montreal | NHL | 3 | 0 | 0 | 0 | 0 | | | | | |
| | Quebec | QHL | 62 | 16 | 41 | 57 | 40 | 10 | 2 | 4 | 6 | 4 |
| 1957-58 | Montreal | NHL | 16 | 3 | 5 | 8 | 2 | | | | | |
| | Montreal | QHL | 54 | 14 | 38 | 52 | 28 | | | | | |
| 1958-59 | Detroit | NHL | 12 | 0 | 0 | 0 | 0 | | | | | |
| | Edmonton | WHL | 39 | 16 | 17 | 33 | 30 | 3 | 0 | 1 | 1 | 6 |
| 1959-60 | Edmonton | WHL | 67 | 20 | 51 | 71 | 44 | 4 | 1 | 3 | 4 | 4 |
| 1960-61 | Sudbury | EPH | 37 | 5 | 28 | 33 | 16 | | | | | |
| | Edmonton | WHL | 25 | 6 | 14 | 20 | 2 | | | | | |
| 1961-62 | Portland | WHL | 69 | 17 | 56 | 73 | 10 | 3 | 0 | 0 | 0 | 0 |
| 1962-63 | Knoxville | EHL | 68 | 30 | 96 | 126 | 29 | 5 | 1 | 5 | 6 | 4 |
| 1963-64 | Knoxville | EHL | 72 | 30 | 88 | 118 | 42 | 8 | 4 | 4 | 8 | 4 |
| 1964-65* | Long Island | EHL | 71 | 30 | 83 | 113 | 28 | 15 | 3 | 9 | 12 | 8 |
| 1965-66 | Long Island | EHL | 72 | 34 | 83 | 117 | 62 | 12 | 6 | 10 | 16 | 8 |
| | Portland | WHL | | | | | | 2 | 0 | 0 | 0 | 0 |
| 1966-67 | Long Island | EHL | 71 | 13 | 45 | 58 | 82 | 3 | 0 | 0 | 0 | 2 |
| 1967-68 | Long Island | EHL | 35 | 6 | 12 | 18 | 24 | | | | | |

# ALEXIUK, ED

sport:      volleyball
born:       Winnipeg, Manitoba
            May 17, 1952
height:     1.91 m / 6'3"
weight:     93 kg  / 205 lbs

Ed Alexiuk began playing competitive volleyball at the age of 13. In his senior year of high school in 1970, he led his Dakota Collegiate team to the Manitoba provincial title. That same year, he won the Canadian junior volleyball championship while competing for the Manitoba Junior Nomads. In his teens, Alexiuk also excelled in baseball, basketball, football and hockey. For a few years he played senior baseball for the Canadian Ukrainian Athletic Club (CUAC).

Upon enrolling at the University of Manitoba, Ed Alexiuk joined the school's volleyball team. In his first three seasons with the team, Alexiuk contributed greatly to its success. During that time, the University of Manitoba won three consecutive CIAU national championships. In 1973, Alexiuk was selected to represent Canada at the World University Games. A year later, he was named to Canada's national team. Alexiuk retired from the national team in 1977, after having competed at the 1975 Pan American Games and the 1976 Montreal Olympics. A ninth-place finish at the Montreal Games was the best ever by a Canadian men's volleyball team at an Olympiad.

After his retirement from the national team, Alexiuk played for Bonaire Amstel. The club placed second at the 1978 Canadian Championships. A year later, he won the national title while playing for the Winnipeg Volleyball Club.

Ed Alexiuk, a physical education instructor, successfully coached volleyball at the junior and senior high school levels. In addition, he initiated and encouraged volleyball programs and clinics. In 1983, Alexiuk began playing "old-timers" volleyball with the Winnipeg Tigers.

AWARDS

| 1973 | Order of the Buffalo Hunt  -  Province of Manitoba |
| 1976 | Gold Cup  -  Province of Manitoba |

RECORD

| year | competition | team | placing |
|------|-------------|------|---------|
| 1970 | Canadian Junior Championships | Manitoba Junior Nomads | 1 |
| 1971 | CIAU Championships | University of Winnipeg Wesmen | 1 |
| 1972 | CIAU Championships | University of Winnipeg Wesmen | 1 |
| 1973 | CIAU Championships | University of Winnipeg Wesmen | 1 |
|      | World University Games | Canada | 16 |
| 1974 | Canadian Championships | Grand Beach Goats | 2 |
|      | World Championships | Canada | 20 |
| 1975 | Montreal Pre-Olympic Tournament | Canada | 3 |
|      | Brazilian Tournament | Canada | 3 |
|      | Pan American Games | Canada | 5 |
| 1976 | Olympic Games | Canada | 9 |
| 1977 | NORCECA Zone Championships | Canada | 3 |
| 1978 | Canadian Championships | Bonaire Amstel | 2 |
| 1979 | Canadian Championships | Winnipeg Volleyball Club | 1 |

# AMBROSIE, RANDY

| sport: | football |
| born: | Winnipeg, Manitoba |
|       | March 16, 1963 |
| height: | 1.93 m / 6'4" |
| weight: | 113.5 kg / 250 lbs |
| position: | offensive tackle |

Randy Ambrosie began playing organized football in 1978 with the East Side Eagles of the

Winnipeg Bantam Football League. That year, he made the all-star team and was named the league's Most Valuable Player. Subsequently, Ambrosie played with the East Kildonan Lions and St. Vital Mustangs before joining the University of Manitoba Bisons in 1981. He was the Bisons' outstanding lineman in the years 1982-84. In 1983 and 1984, he was named to the Western Inter-Collegiate Football League All-Star team and in 1984 he gained All-Canadian honours.

Randy Ambrosie was selected second overall in the 1985 CFL College Draft by the Calgary Stampeders. He won a regular starting position with the Stampeders at the 1985 training camp. When the season concluded, Ambrosie was the club's nominee for the Schenley Most Outstanding Rookie Award. Ambrosie played with Calgary for another full season before being traded to Toronto part way through the 1987 schedule. His arrival was timely, since the Argos advanced to the Grey Cup game that year. In 1989, Randy Ambrosie was traded to the Edmonton Eskimos.

# ANDREYCHUK, DAVE

| | |
|---|---|
| sport: | hockey |
| given name: | Andreychuk, David |
| born: | Hamilton, Ontario |
| | September 29, 1963 |
| height: | 1.91 m / 6'3" |
| weight: | 97.5 kg / 215 lbs |
| position: | left wing / center |
| shoots: | right |

*Photo courtesy of the Buffalo Sabres*

Dave Andreychuk began playing hockey at the age of six, in part influenced by his father who enjoyed playing the game himself. At age 16, Andreychuk was drafted by the Oshawa Generals of the OHA. In his final season of junior hockey, he registered 57 goals and 43 assists and was named the league's Most Improved Player. He was then selected 16th overall in the 1982 NHL Entry Draft by the Buffalo Sabres. His first year of pro hockey included play for the Sabres, reassignment to Oshawa, and being named to Team Canada for the World Junior Championship. At the tournament, Andreychuk excelled, scoring 11 points in seven games to lead Canada to the bronze medal.

The following year, in his first full season with the Sabres, Andreychuk established himself as a starting center and led the team in goals scored with 38. During the 1985-86 season, Andreychuk played on Buffalo's fourth line. It was a checking line and did not receive much ice time. Nevertheless, one of Andreychuk's most memorable offensive scoring feats occurred that season. In a game against the Bruins, he scored five goals and assisted on a sixth as Buffalo defeated Boston 8-6.

A natural goal scorer, Andreychuk has a reputation for positioning himself in front of the opponent's net and waiting for the puck. With his extremely long arm reach he is able to scoop up rebounds or deflect point shots. His size and strength make it difficult for defenders to clear him from the spot. An excellent stick handler, he also mastered the art of winning face-offs. By his third year in professional hockey, he was winning 70 per cent of his draws.

## AWARDS

1982        Most Improved Player  -  OHL

## RECORD

| year | team | league | regular season GP | G | A | PTS | PIM | playoffs GP | G | A | PTS | PIM |
|------|------|--------|-----|----|----|-----|-----|-----|----|----|-----|-----|
| 1982-83 | Buffalo | NHL | 43 | 14 | 23 | 37 | 16 | 4 | 1 | 0 | 1 | 4 |
| 1983-84 | Buffalo | NHL | 78 | 38 | 42 | 80 | 42 | 2 | 0 | 1 | 1 | 2 |
| 1984-85 | Buffalo | NHL | 64 | 31 | 30 | 61 | 54 | 5 | 4 | 2 | 6 | 4 |
| 1985-86 | Buffalo | NHL | 80 | 36 | 51 | 87 | 61 | | | | | |
| 1986-87 | Buffalo | NHL | 77 | 25 | 48 | 73 | 46 | | | | | |
| 1987-88 | Buffalo | NHL | 80 | 30 | 48 | 78 | 112 | 6 | 2 | 4 | 6 | 0 |
| 1988-89 | Buffalo | NHL | 56 | 28 | 24 | 52 | 40 | 5 | 0 | 3 | 3 | 0 |
| 1989-90 | Buffalo | NHL | 73 | 40 | 42 | 82 | 42 | 6 | 2 | 5 | 7 | 2 |
| 1990-91 | Buffalo | NHL | 80 | 36 | 33 | 69 | 32 | 6 | 2 | 2 | 4 | 8 |

international

| year | team | competition | GP | G | A | PTS | PIM | Place |
|------|------|-------------|----|----|----|-----|-----|-------|
| 1983 | Canada | World Junior Championship | 7 | 6 | 5 | 11 | 14 | 3 |
| 1986 | Canada | World Championship | 10 | 3 | 2 | 5 | 18 | 3 |

# ANDRUSYSHYN, ZENON

"Big Zee"

| | |
|---|---|
| sport: | athletics, football |
| born: | Gunzberg, Germany |
| | February 25, 1947 |
| height: | 1.88 m / 6'2" |
| weight: | 95 kg / 210 lbs |
| position: | punter and kicker |

In his early teens, Zenon Andrusyshyn starred on a number of soccer teams, among them Toronto's Ukraina. In 1961, he was named to the center position of an Ontario age group all-star team. In the mid-1960s, Andrusyshyn established Canadian junior records in the discus and javelin. In 1966, he was named the outstanding performer at the Canadian Junior Track and Field Championships; he won the javelin in a junior record toss of 242 feet 1½ inches, and placed second in the discus and shot put. At the 1966 Commonwealth Games, Andrusyshyn competed in the three throwing events. His best result was a seventh-place finish in the javelin. Andrusyshyn's prowess in the javelin led to a track and field scholarship from the University of California at Los Angeles (UCLA). During a practice, he broke the American college record. However, after elbow surgery, Andrusyshyn was released from the team.

Andrusyshyn's departure from the track team, though, did not have any bearing on his status with the UCLA football team with which he had a successful tryout. The lack of football experience (only three games in high school) did not worry the coaches, since they were impressed with his ability to kick 50-yard field goals with consistency. Andrusyshyn's tenure as the UCLA punter and placekicker was colourful; he quickly became the darling of the UCLA fans. He met movie stars, took bit parts in television and movies, drove a red Porsche and subjected his coaches to pranks, such as requesting permission to wear golden shoes. In his first year with the team, he led the nation in punting with an average of 44.17 yards. After three years, with his college career at an end, Andrusyshyn left UCLA as their fourth highest scorer in history with 146 points. In addition, his punting average of more than 42 yards was the second highest in the university's history.

Zenon Andrusyshyn's professional football career as a punter and placekicker included play in three leagues and spanned more than fifteen years. Drafted by the Dallas Cowboys of the National Football League in the 9th round (231st overall), he was cut before he made the team. He then pursued a career with the Canadian Football League. Play in Canada was interrupted on two occasions when he joined the Kansas City Chiefs of the NFL for the 1978 season and the Tampa Bay Bandits of the USFL in 1983 for three seasons. In 1986, once again playing in the CFL, Andrusyshyn scored his 1,000th point, and became only the eighth player in league history to attain the milestone. He established the CFL record for the longest punt of 108 yards in 1977, and the third longest field goal of 57 yards in 1980.

In the mid-1970s, Andrusyshyn became active with Athletes in Action, a Christian movement whose members work with youth.

## AWARDS

| 1984 | USFL | Special Teams Player of the Year |

## ALL-STAR SELECTIONS

| 1967 | punter | All-American |
| 1969 | punter | All-American |
| 1980 | punter | CFL All-Eastern |
| 1981 | punter | CFL All-Eastern |

## RECORD

athletics

| year | competition | event | placing | result | | | |
|------|-------------|-------|---------|--------|---|---|---|
| 1965 | Oakville Trafalgar Meet | javelin | 1 | 220 ft | 5 | in | nhs |
| 1966 | Waterloo Warrior Invitational | discus | 1 | 177 ft | 3 | in | nhs & njr |
| | Ukrainians vs Lithuanians | javelin | 1 | 236 ft | 8 | in | njr |
| | Canadian Jr. Championships | javelin | 1 | 247 ft | 1½ | in | njr |
| | | shot put | 2 | | | | |
| | | discus | 2 | | | | |
| | Canadian Championships | javelin | 1 | 235 ft | 8 | in | nr |
| | Commonwealth Games | javelin | 7 | 210 ft | 7 | in | |
| | | discus | 14 | 144 ft | 7 | in | |
| | | shot put | 10 | 47 ft | 5 | in | |
| 1968 | Canadian Championships | javelin | 7 | 217 ft | 0 | in | |

nhs   Canadian high school record

njr   Canadian junior record

nr   Canadian record

---

308

| scoring | | | regular season | | | | | | playoffs | | | | | | Grey Cup game | | | | | |
|---|---|---|---|---|---|---|---|---|---|---|---|---|---|---|---|---|---|---|---|---|
| year | team | league | GP | TD | C | FG | S | PTS | GP | TD | C | FG | S | PTS | GP | TD | C | FG | S | PTS |
| 1971 | Toronto | CFL | 14 | 0 | 1 | 0 | 8 | 9 | 2 | 0 | 0 | 0 | 1 | 1 | 1 | 0 | 0 | 0 | 0 | 0 |
| 1972 | Toronto | CFL | 14 | 0 | 3 | 6 | 14 | 35 | | | | | | | | | | | | |
| 1973 | Toronto | CFL | 14 | 0 | 25 | 19 | 18 | 100 | 1 | 0 | 0 | 3 | 1 | 10 | | | | | | |
| 1974 | Toronto | CFL | 16 | 0 | 22 | 32 | 16 | 134 | | | | | | | | | | | | |
| 1975 | Toronto | CFL | 16 | 0 | 20 | 30 | 11 | 121 | | | | | | | | | | | | |
| 1976 | Toronto | CFL | 16 | 0 | 29 | 22 | 7 | 102 | | | | | | | | | | | | |
| 1977 | Toronto | CFL | 16 | 0 | 22 | 23 | 15 | 106 | 1 | 0 | 2 | 0 | 2 | 4 | | | | | | |
| 1978 | Kansas City | NFL | ... | 0 | 0 | 0 | - | 0 | | | | | | | | | | | | |
| 1979 | Hamilton | CFL | 8 | 0 | 15 | 10 | 10 | 55 | 1 | 0 | 1 | 1 | 0 | 4 | | | | | | |
| 1980 | Toronto | CFL | 16 | 0 | 31 | 30 | 15 | 136 | | | | | | | | | | | | |
| 1981 | Toronto | CFL | 16 | 0 | 21 | 18 | 16 | 91 | | | | | | | | | | | | |
| 1982 | Toronto | CFL | 9 | 0 | 24 | 11 | 8 | 65 | | | | | | | | | | | | |
| | Edmonton | CFL | 2 | 0 | 0 | 0 | 1 | 1 | | | | | | | | | | | | |
| 1983 | Tampa | USFL | ... | 0 | 32 | 23 | - | 101 | | | | | | | | | | | | |
| 1984 | Tampa | USFL | ... | 0 | 55 | 17 | - | 106 | | | | | | | | | | | | |
| 1985 | Tampa | USFL | ... | 0 | 51 | 14 | - | 93 | | | | | | | | | | | | |
| 1986 | Montreal | CFL | 6 | 0 | 9 | 14 | 4 | 55 | | | | | | | | | | | | |

| regular season | | | field goals | | | | | punting | | | | kickoffs | | | |
|---|---|---|---|---|---|---|---|---|---|---|---|---|---|---|---|
| year | team | league | GP | ATT | GD | AVE | LK | NO | YDS | AVE | LP | NO | YDS | AVE | LK |
| 1971 | Toronto | CFL | 14 | 1 | 0 | 0.0 | 0 | | | | | | | | |
| 1972 | Toronto | CFL | 14 | 16 | 6 | 32.2 | 45 | 125 | 5,626 | 45.0 | 75 | 40 | 2,276 | 56.9 | 65 |
| 1973 | Toronto | CFL | 14 | 37 | 19 | 34.3 | 52 | 121 | 5,521 | 45.6 | 67 | 40 | 2,252 | 56.3 | 81 |
| 1974 | Toronto | CFL | 16 | 54 | 32 | 30.1 | 52 | 142 | 6,653 | 46.9 | 85 | 42 | 2,312 | 55.0 | 81 |
| 1975 | Toronto | CFL | 16 | 56 | 30 | 30.4 | 54 | 126 | 5,432 | 43.1 | 69 | 59 | 3,705 | 62.8 | 90 |
| 1976 | Toronto | CFL | 16 | 38 | 22 | 32.6 | 46 | 132 | 5,772 | 43.7 | 63 | 45 | 2,463 | 54.7 | 75 |
| 1977 | Toronto | CFL | 16 | 37 | 23 | 30.5 | 50 | 128 | 5,788 | 45.2 | 108 | 43 | 2,360 | 54.9 | 85 |
| 1978 | Kansas City | NFL | ... | 0 | 0 | 0.0 | 0 | 79 | 3,247 | 41.1 | 61 | 0 | 0 | 0.0 | 0 |
| 1979 | Hamilton | CFL | 8 | 20 | 10 | 24.2 | 43 | 51 | 2,205 | 43.2 | 66 | 27 | 1,686 | 62.4 | 90 |
| 1980 | Toronto | CFL | 16 | 42 | 30 | 32.8 | 57 | 122 | 5,524 | 45.3 | 85 | 55 | 3,136 | 57.0 | 90 |
| 1981 | Toronto | CFL | 16 | 25 | 18 | 27.3 | 54 | 149 | 7,037 | 47.2 | 74 | 44 | 2,406 | 54.7 | 85 |
| 1982 | Toronto | CFL | 9 | 21 | 11 | 27.1 | 48 | 82 | 3,759 | 45.8 | 70 | 39 | 2,285 | 58.6 | 76 |
| | Edmonton | CFL | 2 | 0 | 0 | 0.0 | 0 | 16 | 670 | 41.9 | 55 | 0 | 0 | 0.0 | 0 |

| regular season | | | | field goals | | | | | punting | | | | kickoffs | | | |
|---|---|---|---|---|---|---|---|---|---|---|---|---|---|---|---|---|
| year | team | league | GP | ATT | GD | AVE | LK | NO | YDS | AVE | LP | NO | YDS | AVE | LK |
| 1983 | Tampa | USFL | ... | 31 | 23 | | | 90 | 3,583 | 39.8 | | | | | |
| 1984 | Tampa | USFL | ... | 25 | 17 | | | 65 | 2,672 | 41.1 | | | | | |
| 1985 | Tampa | USFL | ... | 20 | 14 | | | 52 | 2,026 | 39.0 | | | | | |
| 1986 | Montreal | CFL | 6 | 18 | 14 | 35.0 | 46 | 51 | 2,009 | 39.4 | 53 | 19 | 1,110 | 58.4 | 69 |

| playoffs | | | | field goals | | | | | punting | | | | kickoffs | | | |
|---|---|---|---|---|---|---|---|---|---|---|---|---|---|---|---|---|
| year | team | league | GP | ATT | GD | AVE | LK | NO | YDS | AVE | LP | NO | YDS | AVE | LK |
| 1971 | Toronto | CFL | 2 | 0 | 0 | 0.0 | 0 | 19 | 747 | 39.3 | 56 | 7 | 392 | 56.0 | 65 |
| 1973 | Toronto | CFL | 1 | 6 | 3 | 23.7 | 35 | 13 | 543 | 41.8 | 65 | 3 | 129 | 43.0 | 62 |
| 1977 | Toronto | CFL | 1 | 2 | 0 | 0.0 | 0 | 11 | 467 | 42.5 | 66 | 4 | 332 | 58.0 | 68 |
| 1979 | Hamilton | CFL | 1 | 1 | 1 | 37.0 | 37 | 6 | 202 | 33.7 | 46 | 4 | 232 | 58.0 | 64 |

| Grey Cup game | | | | field goals | | | | | punting | | | | kickoffs | | | |
|---|---|---|---|---|---|---|---|---|---|---|---|---|---|---|---|---|
| year | team | league | GP | ATT | GD | AVE | LK | NO | YDS | AVE | LP | NO | YDS | AVE | LK |
| 1971 | Toronto | CFL | 1 | 0 | 0 | 0.0 | 0 | 11 | 466 | 42.4 | 59 | 2 | 77 | 38.5 | 42 |

# BABY, JOHN

"Butch"

| | |
|---|---|
| sport: | hockey |
| given name: | Baby, John George |
| born: | Sudbury, Ontario |
| | May 18, 1957 |
| height: | 1.83 m / 6'0" |
| weight: | 88.5 kg / 195 lbs |
| position: | defense |
| shoots: | right |

Card reproduced courtesy of O-Pee-Chee Co.

John Baby played junior hockey for his home-town Sudbury Wolves. During the 1977-78 season, he made a brief appearance with the Cleveland Barons of the NHL. When the Cleveland franchise merged with the Minnesota North Stars in the summer of 1978, Baby was put on Minnesota's reserve list. In the 1979 expansion draft, Baby was claimed by the Quebec Nordiques. He failed to make the team and finished his career playing in the minor leagues.

| year | team | league | regular season | | | | | playoffs | | | | |
|------|------|--------|----|----|----|-----|-----|----|----|----|-----|-----|
| | | | GP | G | A | PTS | PIM | GP | G | A | PTS | PIM |
| 1977-78 | Cleveland | NHL | 24 | 2 | 7 | 9 | 26 | | | | | |
| | Binghamton | AHL | 25 | 3 | 1 | 4 | 16 | | | | | |
| | Phoenix | CHL | 16 | 3 | 3 | 6 | 25 | | | | | |
| 1978-79 | Minnesota | NHL | 2 | 0 | 1 | 1 | 0 | | | | | |
| | Oklahoma City | CHL | 76 | 18 | 22 | 40 | 114 | | | | | |
| 1979-80 | Syracuse | AHL | 73 | 3 | 24 | 27 | 73 | | | | | |
| 1980-81 | Binghamton | AHL | 66 | 9 | 25 | 34 | 80 | 2 | 0 | 0 | 0 | 2 |

*Photo courtesy of the Hartford Whalers*

# BABYCH, DAVE

"Slug"

| | |
|---|---|
| sport: | hockey |
| given name: | Babych, David Michael |
| born: | Edmonton, Alberta |
| | May 23, 1961 |
| height: | 1.88 m / 6'2" |
| weight: | 75 kg / 215 lbs |
| position: | defense |
| shoots: | left |

When the Winnipeg Jets selected Dave Babych second overall in the 1980 NHL Entry Draft, they believed that he was just the type of player who would form the foundation of their team. The Jets' belief was based on his outstanding record in junior hockey; in successive years and in two different leagues, he was named the Top Defenseman. The Jets did not hesitate to select him as an underage junior and resisted offers from several teams that were interested in him. In Winnipeg, Babych became an immediate impact player and was often referred to as "the franchise." An exceptionally powerful skater with great endurance, Babych was regarded by many as one of the strongest players in the league. While he did not advocate fighting, when provoked he would convincingly decimate his opponents.

During the 1985-86 season Babych was traded to the Hartford Whalers. In his first four seasons there, he led all club defensemen in scoring and was twice voted by the media as the Whalers' top defenseman. In May of 1991, Babych was claimed by Minnesota in the NHL Expansion Draft. Some two weeks later he was traded to Vancouver. Dave Babych is the brother of hockey player Wayne Babych.

## AWARDS

| 1978 | Rookie of the Year Trophy  -  AJHL |
| 1978 | Top Defenseman Trophy  -  AJHL |
| 1980 | Top Defenseman Trophy  -  WHL |
| 1986 | Top Defenseman  -  Hartford Whalers |
| 1989 | Top Defenseman  -  Hartford Whalers |

## RECORD

| | | | regular season | | | | | playoffs | | | | |
| year | team | league | GP | G | A | PTS | PIM | GP | G | A | PTS | PIM |
|---|---|---|---|---|---|---|---|---|---|---|---|---|
| 1980-81 | Winnipeg | NHL | 69 | 6 | 38 | 44 | 90 | | | | | |
| 1981-82 | Winnipeg | NHL | 79 | 19 | 49 | 68 | 92 | 4 | 1 | 2 | 3 | 29 |
| 1982-83 | Winnipeg | NHL | 79 | 13 | 61 | 74 | 56 | 3 | 0 | 0 | 0 | 0 |
| 1983-84 | Winnipeg | NHL | 66 | 18 | 39 | 57 | 62 | 3 | 1 | 1 | 2 | 0 |
| 1984-85 | Winnipeg | NHL | 78 | 13 | 49 | 62 | 78 | 8 | 2 | 7 | 9 | 6 |
| 1985-86 | Winnipeg | NHL | 19 | 4 | 12 | 16 | 14 | | | | | |
| | Hartford | NHL | 62 | 10 | 43 | 53 | 36 | 8 | 1 | 3 | 4 | 14 |
| 1986-87 | Hartford | NHL | 66 | 8 | 33 | 41 | 44 | 6 | 1 | 1 | 2 | 14 |
| 1987-88 | Hartford | NHL | 71 | 14 | 36 | 50 | 54 | 6 | 3 | 2 | 5 | 2 |
| 1988-89 | Hartford | NHL | 70 | 6 | 41 | 47 | 54 | 4 | 1 | 5 | 6 | 2 |
| 1989-90 | Hartford | NHL | 72 | 6 | 37 | 43 | 62 | 7 | 1 | 2 | 3 | 0 |
| 1990-91 | Hartford | NHL | 8 | 0 | 6 | 6 | 4 | | | | | |

international

| year | team | competition | GP | G | A | PTS | PIM | Place |
|---|---|---|---|---|---|---|---|---|
| 1981 | Canada | World Championship | 7 | 0 | 2 | 2 | 8 | 4 |
| 1989 | Canada | World Championship | 10 | 2 | 0 | 2 | 4 | 2 |

# BABYCH, WAYNE

| | |
|---|---|
| sport: | hockey |
| given name: | Babych, Wayne Joseph |
| born: | Edmonton, Alberta |
| | June 6, 1958 |
| height: | 1.80 m / 5'11" |
| weight: | 86.5 kg / 191 lbs |
| position: | right wing |
| shoots: | right |

*Card reproduced courtesy of O-Pee-Chee Co.*

As a youth, Wayne Babych aspired to be a baseball pitcher. His father, who years earlier turned down an opportunity to play professional baseball for the Washington Senators, was the inspiration. By age 17, Wayne was an outstanding prospect and the Montreal Expos wanted him to pitch for their affiliate at Quebec City. Babych, though, did not want to leave home and declined the offer. Shortly afterwards, he hurt his pitching arm, and so effectively terminated his pitching aspirations. As a result, he turned to hockey.

Babych spent five years playing junior hockey in the WCHL, three with the Edmonton Oil Kings, and two with the Portland Winter Hawks. With Portland he had consecutive 50-goal seasons and first team all-star selections. As a result of his scoring prowess, Babych was a much sought-after player; he was picked third overall in the 1978 NHL Entry Draft by St. Louis Blues. In his first professional season, Babych was considered a shoo-in for the rookie of the year honours. Unfortunately, a fractured ankle sidelined him for 13 games and effectively ended his chances for the award.

A very strong player with great endurance, Babych liked to play a punishing game, particularly when hitting in the corners. He was nevertheless a clean player, with a good shot and good passing skills.

Babych spent five seasons with St. Louis. The 1980-81 season was the most successful: he registered 54 goals, a team record, and 42 assists for 96 points. That season, the Blues established a club record for wins (45) and points (107) to place first in the Smythe Division. In the playoffs, the team was upset in the quarter-finals. After a disappointing 1983-84 season, St. Louis conditionally traded Babych to Edmonton. Within days, the Oilers returned him to St. Louis to cancel the trade. He was then picked up by Pittsburgh in the waiver draft. Babych played with Pittsburgh for a season before being traded to Quebec. Two months later, he was acquired by the Hartford Whalers with whom he played sparingly.  In the fall of 1987, when Hartford assigned him to the farm team, Babych decided to retire from the game of hockey.  Wayne Babych is the brother of hockey player Dave Babych.

## RECORD

| year | team | league | regular season | | | | | playoffs | | | | |
|------|------|--------|----|----|----|-----|-----|----|----|----|-----|-----|
| | | | GP | G | A | PTS | PIM | GP | G | A | PTS | PIM |
| 1978-79 | St. Louis | NHL | 67 | 27 | 36 | 63 | 75 | | | | | |
| 1979-80 | St. Louis | NHL | 59 | 26 | 35 | 61 | 49 | 3 | 1 | 2 | 3 | 2 |
| 1980-81 | St. Louis | NHL | 78 | 54 | 42 | 96 | 93 | 11 | 2 | 0 | 2 | 8 |
| 1981-82 | St. Louis | NHL | 51 | 19 | 25 | 44 | 51 | 7 | 3 | 2 | 5 | 8 |
| 1982-83 | St. Louis | NHL | 71 | 16 | 23 | 39 | 62 | | | | | |
| 1983-84 | St. Louis | NHL | 70 | 13 | 29 | 42 | 52 | 10 | 1 | 4 | 5 | 4 |
| 1984-85 | Pittsburgh | NHL | 65 | 20 | 34 | 54 | 35 | | | | | |
| 1985-86 | Pittsburgh | NHL | 2 | 0 | 0 | 0 | 0 | | | | | |
| | Quebec | NHL | 15 | 6 | 5 | 11 | 18 | | | | | |
| | Hartford | NHL | 37 | 11 | 17 | 28 | 59 | 10 | 0 | 1 | 1 | 2 |
| 1986-87 | Hartford | NHL | 4 | 0 | 0 | 0 | 4 | | | | | |
| | Binghamton | AHL | 6 | 2 | 5 | 7 | 6 | | | | | |

international

| year | team | competition | GP | G | A | PTS | PIM | Place |
|------|------|-------------|----|----|----|-----|-----|-------|
| 1978 | Canada | World Junior Championship | 6 | 5 | 5 | 10 | 4 | 3 |
| 1979 | Canada | World Championship | 7 | 1 | 2 | 3 | 0 | 4 |

# BAHNUIK, DON

sport:      football
born:       Canora, Saskatchewan
            . . .
height:     1.88 m / 6'2"
weight:     113.5 kg / 250 lbs
position:   defensive tackle

*Photo courtesy of the Canadian Football Hall of Fame and Museum*

Don Bahnuik first played organized football, albeit six-man sandlot, in his home town of

Canora, Saskatchewan. Subsequently, he joined the junior Regina Rams playing both offensive and defensive tackle. He was with the club for three years, was a league all-star in each of the three years, and in 1964 was the club's MVP.

In 1966, Don Bahnuik made the active roster of the Saskatchewan Roughriders, and in the fall of that year, he helped the team win the Grey Cup. After a couple of seasons spent acquiring knowledge and technique during practices and games, he became a regular starter with the Roughriders in 1969 and was with the club through the end of 1974 season. The hard working solid defensive tackle utilized his size and raw strength to help contain the offensive game of the opponents. In addition to the 1966 Grey Cup game, Bahnuik also played in the 1967, 1969 and 1974 fall classics, but was on the winning side only in the first encounter.

## BALON, DAVE

| | |
|---|---|
| sport: | hockey |
| given name: | Balon, David Alexander |
| born: | Wakaw, Saskatchewan |
| | August 2, 1937 |
| height: | 1.78 m / 5'10" |
| weight: | 78 kg / 172 lbs |
| position: | left wing |
| shoots: | left |

Dave Balon was one of three brothers who played junior hockey for Prince Albert Mintos of the SJHL. Dave, though, was the only one who made it to the NHL. He played for three clubs in the big league. He also played with one WHA and six minor pro teams during a career that spanned 17 seasons. In his time, one of the faster skaters in hockey, Balon played a robust game. In particular, he liked to check opposing goalies who wandered out of their crease.

Balon began his NHL career with the New York Rangers. At the end of the 1963 season he was part of a blockbuster trade with Montreal - which saw the likes of J. Plante, L. Worsley, P. Goyette and three others change uniforms. With Montreal, he won the Stanley Cup in 1965 and 1966. When the NHL expanded in 1967, Balon was left unprotected and the Minnesota North Stars drafted him. A year later he was back in New York.

Dave Balon was not known as a great goal scorer. Before returning to New York in 1968, his personal high was 24 goals and he averaged only about 18 goals per year during his whole

NHL career. In New York, Balon was placed on a line centered by Walt Tkaczuk. The combination clicked, and Balon found the net 33 times during the 1969-70 campaign and 36 times the following season. This scoring prowess was a surprise, especially when one considers that the line was used primarily for checking. For its tenacity, the line was nicknamed the "Bulldog Line."

In the early 1970s, Balon started to slow down. His play deteriorated and he spent much time sitting on the bench. This frustrated Balon and his reaction was to work harder. Unfortunately, this was counterproductive. By 1974, he was too weak to do anything and he left the game. Some years later, Dave Balon was diagnosed with Multiple Sclerosis. During the 1980s, despite his illness, he operated a number of businesses and coached old-timer hockey in Prince Albert.

## RECORD

| year | team | league | regular season | | | | | playoffs | | | | |
|------|------|--------|----|----|----|-----|-----|----|----|----|-----|-----|
| | | | GP | G | A | PTS | PIM | GP | G | A | PTS | PIM |
| 1957-58 | Vancouver | WHL | 4 | 0 | 2 | 2 | 8 | | | | | |
| 1958-59 | Saskatoon | WHL | 57 | 12 | 25 | 37 | 80 | | | | | |
| 1959-60 | NY Rangers | NHL | 3 | 0 | 0 | 0 | 0 | | | | | |
| | Vancouver | WHL | 3 | 1 | 1 | 2 | 2 | | | | | |
| | Trois-Rivieres | EPHL | 61 | 28 | 42 | 70 | 104 | 7 | 2 | 2 | 4 | 19 |
| 1960-61 | NY Rangers | NHL | 13 | 1 | 2 | 3 | 8 | | | | | |
| | Kitchener | EPHL | 55 | 15 | 26 | 41 | 77 | 7 | 1 | 1 | 2 | 12 |
| 1961-62 | NY Rangers | NHL | 30 | 4 | 11 | 15 | 11 | 6 | 2 | 3 | 5 | 2 |
| | Kitchener | EPHL | 37 | 24 | 18 | 42 | 87 | | | | | |
| 1962-63 | NY Rangers | NHL | 70 | 11 | 13 | 24 | 72 | | | | | |
| 1963-64 | Montreal | NHL | 70 | 24 | 18 | 42 | 80 | 7 | 1 | 1 | 2 | 25 |
| 1964-65* | Montreal | NHL | 63 | 18 | 23 | 41 | 61 | 10 | 0 | 0 | 0 | 10 |
| 1965-66* | Montreal | NHL | 45 | 3 | 7 | 10 | 24 | 9 | 2 | 3 | 5 | 16 |
| | Houston | CPHL | 9 | 6 | 6 | 12 | 0 | | | | | |
| 1966-67 | Montreal | NHL | 48 | 11 | 8 | 19 | 31 | 9 | 0 | 2 | 2 | 6 |
| 1967-68 | Minnesota | NHL | 73 | 15 | 32 | 47 | 84 | 14 | 4 | 9 | 13 | 14 |
| 1968-69 | NY Rangers | NHL | 75 | 10 | 21 | 31 | 57 | 4 | 1 | 0 | 1 | 0 |
| 1969-70 | NY Rangers | NHL | 76 | 33 | 37 | 70 | 100 | 6 | 1 | 1 | 2 | 32 |
| 1970-71 | NY Rangers | NHL | 78 | 36 | 24 | 60 | 34 | 13 | 3 | 2 | 5 | 4 |
| 1971-72 | NY Rangers | NHL | 16 | 4 | 5 | 9 | 2 | | | | | |
| | Vancouver | NHL | 59 | 19 | 19 | 38 | 21 | | | | | |
| 1972-73 | Vancouver | NHL | 57 | 3 | 2 | 5 | 22 | | | | | |
| 1973-74 | Quebec | WHA | 9 | 0 | 0 | 0 | 2 | | | | | |
| | Binghamton | AHL | 7 | 0 | 1 | 1 | 0 | | | | | |

# BALUIK, STAN

| | |
|---|---|
| sport: | hockey, golf |
| given name: | Baluik, Stanley |
| born: | Port Arthur, Ontario |
| | (now Thunder Bay) |
| | October 5, 1935 |
| height: | 1.73 m / 5'8" |
| weight: | 72.5 kg / 160 lbs |
| position: | center |
| shoots: | left |

*Photo courtesy of the Northwestern Ontario Sports Hall of Fame*

Sports kept Stan Baluik busy during his teen-age years. In winter he played hockey for the Fort William Canadians. During the 1953-54 season, his last with the club, Baluik led the league in scoring with 35 goals and 51 assists. In the summer Baluik played golf. He competed in his first Canadian Open in 1951, at the age of 15. In 1954 he won the Ontario Junior Golf Championship, shooting rounds of 75 and 74. That same year he was signed by the Kitchener Canucks of the OHL. During the 1955-56 season, he led the league in scoring.

Baluik played professional hockey with Victoria Cougars of the WHL, Providence Reds and Springfield of the AHL, and Chicoutimi and Montreal of the QHL. During the 1959-60 season he made a brief appearance with the Boston Bruins of the NHL. In 1956, Baluik entered the world of professional golf when he accepted the position of club professional with the Fort William Golf and Country Club. He held it for seven years. In 1964 he moved to Lincoln, Rhode Island, to become head pro at the Kirkbrea Country Club. He remained with the club for 25 years. In addition to his duties with the clubs, Baluik entered many tournaments. Some of the tournaments that he won include the Thunder Bay Pro-Am in 1963, the Vermont Open in 1965, the Rhode Island Open in 1971 and the New England Pro-Am in 1973 and 1975.

## AWARDS

| | |
|---|---|
| 1956 | Eddie Powers Scoring Trophy - OHL Scoring Leader Scorer |
| 1960 | Dudley "Red" Garrett Memorial Trophy - AHL Rookie of the Year |

# RECORD

| year | team | league | regular season | | | | | playoffs | | | | |
|------|------|--------|----|----|----|-----|-----|----|----|----|-----|-----|
| | | | GP | G | A | PTS | PIM | GP | G | A | PTS | PIM |
| 1954-55 | Montreal | QHL | 2 | 0 | 0 | 0 | 0 | | | | | |
| 1956-57 | Chicoutimi | QHL | 68 | 16 | 20 | 36 | 36 | 10 | 1 | 3 | 4 | 12 |
| 1957-58 | Victoria | WHL | 32 | 13 | 15 | 28 | 45 | | | | | |
| | Springfield | AHL | 5 | 2 | 0 | 2 | 8 | | | | | |
| 1958-59 | Victoria | WHL | 55 | 28 | 26 | 54 | 57 | 3 | 1 | 1 | 2 | 0 |
| 1959-60 | Boston | NHL | 7 | 0 | 0 | 0 | 2 | | | | | |
| | Providence | AHL | 65 | 23 | 57 | 80 | 60 | 5 | 2 | 3 | 5 | 2 |
| 1960-61 | Providence | AHL | 71 | 26 | 37 | 63 | 67 | | | | | |
| 1961-62 | Providence | AHL | 69 | 25 | 56 | 81 | 55 | 3 | 1 | 0 | 1 | 6 |
| 1962-63 | Providence | AHL | 72 | 23 | 58 | 81 | 52 | 6 | 2 | 3 | 5 | 4 |
| 1963-64 | Providence | AHL | 65 | 27 | 41 | 68 | 55 | 3 | 1 | 2 | 3 | 4 |

# BARANIUK, CHRIS

| | |
|---|---|
| sport: | gymnastics |
| born: | Selkirk, Manitoba |
| | September 21, 1967 |
| height: | 1.70 m / 5'7" |
| weight: | 58 kg / 128 lbs |

In 1979, Chris Baraniuk tested his gymnastic skills for the first time, winning the overall title at the Manitoba midget championships.  In 1985, he won the all-around novice titles of Manitoba and Western Canada. A year later, he won his first Manitoba open title.  In the fall of 1985, Baraniuk enrolled at the University of Saskatchewan.  He represented the university in competition for five years winning the intercollegiate all-around title in 1990 and gaining three All-Canadian selections.

Baraniuk was a talented all-round gymnast.  His best performances were in the vault.  He was also known for good routines on the high and parallel bars.

Chris Baraniuk competed at numerous provincial, regional and national championships. One of his strongest performances was at the Western Canada Championship in 1989 where he won five gold medals. For the effort he was named Manitoba Male Gymnast of the Year. Baraniuk's best performance at a national championship was a fifth place in the vault in 1990.

AWARDS

1989        Manitoba Male Gymnast of the Year

RECORD

| year | competition | event | placing |
|---|---|---|---|
| 1987 | Western Canada Championships | all-around | 3 |
| | | high bar | 1 |
| | Canadian Championships | vault | 6 |
| 1988 | Western Canada Championships | all-around | 3 |
| | National University Cup | all-around | 4 |
| | | rings | 2 |
| 1989 | Richmond Invitational | all-around | 1 |
| | National University Cup | all-around | 2 |
| | | vault | 1 |
| | | high bar | 1 |
| | Western Canada Championships | all-around | 1 |
| | | vault | 1 |
| | | pommel horse | 1 |
| | | rings | 1 |
| | | parallel bars | 1 |
| | Canadian Championships | all-around | 11 |
| | | vault | 6 |
| 1990 | National University Cup | all-around | 6 |
| | | vault | 1 |
| | Western Canada Championships | all-around | 1 |
| | | parallel bars | 1 |
| | Canadian Championships | vault | 5 |

## BARILKO, BILL

"Billy the Kid," "Bashin' Bill"

| | |
|---|---|
| sport: | hockey |
| given name: | Barilko, William |
| born: | Timmins, Ontario |
| | March 25, 1927 |
| died: | McAlpine Township, Ontario |
| | August 26, 1951 |
| height: | 1.80 m / 5'11" |
| weight: | 83.5 kg / 184 lbs |
| position: | defense |
| shoots: | left |

In the spring of 1945, while playing for the Porcupine Junior A Combines, Bill Barilko was noticed by Toronto Maple Leafs general manager Conn Smythe. That fall, Barilko tried out unsuccessfully with Toronto's senior affiliate, the Pittsburgh Hornets, and was assigned to the Hollywood Wolves of the Pacific Coast Hockey League for more seasoning. In Hollywood he quickly made a name for himself. His devastating hip checks had the town buzzing and "Billy the Kid" soon became a favourite of the film stars. When Bill Barilko joined the Leafs midway through the 1946-47 season, the club was anguishing in disarray. Barilko's feisty play and eternal optimism, however, turned the season quickly around. Barilko was with the Leafs to stay.

A rushing defenseman, Barilko was one of the toughest players of the game at the time. He was also fearless, perfecting the art of blocking shots long before the days of good protective equipment. His hard accurate shot was dreaded by goaltenders. Although he never made an all-star team nor did he establish any records, except for leading the league in penalty minutes during the 1947-48 season, Barilko was an integral component of the high-flying Leafs. During his five years with the team, the Leafs won the Stanley Cup four times. The most memorable victory, in the spring of 1951, was to be Barilko's last. That year, the Leafs opened a three-games-to-one lead in the Cup final. The fifth game went into overtime. Two minutes into extra time, after a heated skirmish in front of the Montreal net, Barilko found a loose puck near the left face-off circle. A powerful shot sailed past the sprawling Montreal goalie. The Leafs and Bill Barilko were at the pinnacle of the hockey world.

That summer, Barilko and Timmins dentist-pilot Dr. Hudson went fishing by floatplane to a remote area near James Bay. On the return trip, Dr. Hudson landed the Fairchild 24 aircraft for fuel at Rupert House. With inclement weather quickly settling in, the twosome was discouraged from continuing their journey. Sadly though, they set out. The residents of Rupert House watched as the plane cumbersomely and just barely cleared the tree-line. When the aircraft failed to arrive in Timmins an alarm was raised. An air search was immediately launched.

Two days later, the Royal Canadian Air Force joined in the search, making it the largest combined operation on record, but to no avail. Eleven years later, the wreckage was spotted by chance. When investigators arrived, they found the remains of the pilot and Bill Barilko still strapped in their seats.

As a final honour, the Toronto Maple Leafs retired Bill Barilko's number 5 sweater from play.

RECORD

| year | team | league | regular season | | | | | playoffs | | | | |
|---|---|---|---|---|---|---|---|---|---|---|---|---|
| | | | GP | G | A | PTS | PIM | GP | G | A | PTS | PIM |
| 1945-46 | Hollywood | PCHL | 38 | 4 | 5 | 9 | 103 | 12 | 2 | 3 | 5 | 8 |
| 1946-47 | Hollywood | PCHL | 47 | 9 | 2 | 11 | 69 | | | | | |
| * | Toronto | NHL | 18 | 3 | 7 | 10 | 33 | 11 | 0 | 3 | 3 | 18 |
| 1947-48* | Toronto | NHL | 57 | 5 | 9 | 14 | 147 | 9 | 1 | 0 | 1 | 17 |
| 1948-49* | Toronto | NHL | 60 | 5 | 4 | 9 | 95 | 9 | 0 | 1 | 1 | 20 |
| 1949-50 | Toronto | NHL | 59 | 7 | 10 | 17 | 85 | 7 | 1 | 1 | 2 | 18 |
| 1950-51* | Toronto | NHL | 58 | 6 | 6 | 12 | 96 | 11 | 3 | 2 | 5 | 31 |

# BARYLUK, MITCH

| | |
|---|---|
| sport: | basketball |
| born: | Winnipeg, Manitoba |
| | June 20, 1931 |
| height: | . . . |
| weight: | . . . |

When Mitch Baryluk moved to Port Arthur (now Thunder Bay) in 1952, organized basketball in the area was in a poor state. Baryluk set out to rebuild it. As a player, coach, and administrator, he sought out and introduced innovative ideas which he believed would make the sport more popular. Baryluk started and promoted Basketball Booster Nights, often bringing in teams from out of town. He introduced senior women's basketball and a summer basketball league. He also organized the first basketball clinics for high school coaches and players.

For many years, Mitch Baryluk coached both at the high school level and in the senior league of the Thunder Bay Basketball Association (TBBA). He also served on the executive of the association for 15 years, including two terms as president. In 1973 Baryluk retired. Five years later he came out of retirement to join the Oldtimers as a playing coach. The club had much success in northern Ontario including victories in the Geraldton Invitational Tournament (1981-84) and the 1986 Manitoba Amateur Basketball Association's Master Hoop Classic in Winnipeg.

## INDUCTIONS

1986        Northwestern Ontario Sports Hall of Fame

## RECORD

basketball

| year | competition | team | placing |
|------|-------------|------|---------|
| 1950 | Canadian Junior Championship | Winnipeg Stellars | 1 |
| 1951 | Canadian Junior Championship | Winnipeg Stellars | 1 |
| 1986 | Manitoba Master Hoop | Classic Oldtimers | 1 |

administration

| year | position |
|------|----------|
| 1953-68 | executive, Thunder Bay Basketball Association |

# BAYDOCK, DONNA

| | |
|---|---|
| sport: | volleyball |
| given name: | Baydock, Donna Anne |
| born: | Winnipeg, Manitoba |
| | August 28, 1957 |
| height: | 1.83 m / 6'0" |
| weight: | 79.5 kg / 175 lbs |

Donna Baydock was a star on the University of Manitoba's volleyball team in the years 1975 to 1977. She captained the team, was twice named its MVP and in 1977 was honoured with the University of Manitoba Female Athlete of the Year award. During that period, she also was a member of Canada's junior volleyball team, won a silver medal at the 1975 Canada Games - representing Manitoba - and won the national junior championship competing for the Bisonettes.

From 1977 to 1982, Donna Baydock was a member of Canada's national team. The power hitter competed at the 1978 World Championships and the 1979 Pan American Games. In 1980 she was appointed captain of the national team. As a result of the Olympic boycott, the team competed in the Olympic Boycott Tour in West Germany.

After graduating from the University of British Columbia with a Master's degree in physical education, Baydock coached volleyball at the University of Manitoba in the years 1981-82 to 1985-86. She led the team to the silver medal at the 1986 CIAU championships. In the fall of 1986 she was named coach of the University of British Columbia Thunderbirds. Through the completion of the 1991-92 season, she consistently led the team to a top-ten ranking in the country. Donna Baydock has also held numerous administrative functions, amongst them the presidency of the CIAU Women's Volleyball Coaches Association.

## AWARDS

| 1977 | University of Manitoba Female Athlete of the Year |
| 1989 | CIAU Coach of the Year |

## RECORD

competitive

| year | competition | team | placing |
| --- | --- | --- | --- |
| 1975 | Canada Games | Manitoba | 2 |
| 1976 | Canadian Junior Championships | Bisonettes | 1 |
| | Junior NORCECA Championships | Canada | 2 |
| 1977 | World Junior Championships | Canada | 7 |
| 1978 | World Championships | Canada | 13 |
| 1979 | NORCECA Championships | Canada | 4 |
| | Pan American Games | Canada | |
| 1980 | Canadian Championships | Vancouver Old Time Ladies | 1 |

coaching

| year | competition | capacity | team | placing |
|------|-------------|----------|------|---------|
| 1988 | Junior NORCECA | assistant coach | Canada | 2 |
| 1989 | Canada Games | coach | British Columbia | 4 |

administrative

| | |
|---|---|
| 1981-85 | Secretary - Manitoba Volleyball Association |
| 1990- | Vice-President - British Columbia Volleyball Association |
| 1991- | President - CIAU Women's Volleyball Coaches Association |
| 1991- | Chairperson - Ethics Committee, British Columbia Women's Coaches Committee |

# BELLOWS, BRIAN

| | |
|---|---|
| sport: | hockey |
| born: | St. Catharines, Ontario |
| | September 1, 1964 |
| height: | 1.80 m / 5'11" |
| weight: | 90.5 kg / 200 lbs |
| position: | right wing |
| shoots: | right |

*Card reproduced courtesy of O-Pee-Chee Co.*

Brian Bellows started playing hockey at the rather late age of nine. He rapidly developed his skills and at 16 he was playing junior hockey for the Kitchener Rangers. In 1982, he was instrumental in leading the Rangers to the Memorial Cup Championship. For his effort during that season he was honoured with a first team all-star selection. At the Memorial Cup tournament he was honoured with the Most Sportsmanlike Player award. While playing for the Rangers, Bellows entered the OHL record books as the youngest coach in league history. He coached the Rangers for two games while recovering from an injury. At the time he was 17 years old.

Brian Bellows was the second overall pick in the 1982 NHL Entry Draft. He was selected as an underage junior by the Minnesota North Stars and earned himself a starting position at his first training camp. In his rookie season, Bellows scored 35 goals and added 30 assists. He immediately became a team leader and in January 1984 he became the youngest captain in the club's history.

During the latter part of the 1980s, Bellows played inconsistent hockey scoring as few as 23 and as many as 40 goals in a season. During the 1989-90 season Bellows silenced his critics with a 55-goal season. During the playoffs that year he led the Stars in scoring with seven points in seven games. A year later, Bellows' goal production declined during the regular season. In the playoffs, Bellows caught fire and led all Minnesota shooters with 29 points. His play was instrumental in leading the North Stars to an unexpected appearance in the Stanley Cup final that year.

Bellows represented Canada at the 1984 Canada Cup and at three World Championships. At the 1989 event, he led all players with eight goals and was the tournament scoring co-leader with 14 points. The International Ice Hockey Federation recognized Bellows by naming him the best forward of the championship.

Brian Bellows has over the years contributed many hours to volunteer work with youth. In 1986, he was honoured by American First Lady Nancy Reagan for the establishment of the Brian Bellows Chemical Abuse Awareness Program.

## AWARDS

| 1982 | George Parsons Trophy  -  Memorial Cup Tournament Most Sportsmanlike Player |
| 1989 | Best Forward  -  World Hockey Championship |

## ALL-STAR SELECTIONS

| 1981 | right wing | Memorial Cup | All-Star Team |
| 1989-90 | left wing | NHL | Second Team |

## RECORD

| | | | regular season | | | | | playoffs | | | | |
|---|---|---|---|---|---|---|---|---|---|---|---|---|
| year | team | league | GP | G | A | PTS | PIM | GP | G | A | PTS | PIM |
| 1982-83 | Minnesota | NHL | 78 | 35 | 30 | 65 | 27 | 9 | 5 | 4 | 9 | 18 |
| 1983-84 | Minnesota | NHL | 78 | 41 | 42 | 83 | 66 | 16 | 2 | 12 | 14 | 6 |
| 1984-85 | Minnesota | NHL | 78 | 26 | 36 | 62 | 72 | 9 | 2 | 4 | 6 | 9 |
| 1985-86 | Minnesota | NHL | 77 | 31 | 48 | 79 | 46 | 5 | 5 | 0 | 5 | 16 |

| year | team | league | regular season | | | | | playoffs | | | | |
|------|------|--------|----|---|---|-----|-----|----|---|---|-----|-----|
| | | | GP | G | A | PTS | PIM | GP | G | A | PTS | PIM |
| 1986-87 | Minnesota | NHL | 65 | 26 | 27 | 53 | 34 | | | | | |
| 1987-88 | Minnesota | NHL | 77 | 40 | 41 | 82 | 81 | | | | | |
| 1988-89 | Minnesota | NHL | 60 | 23 | 27 | 50 | 55 | 5 | 2 | 3 | 5 | 8 |
| 1989-90 | Minnesota | NHL | 80 | 55 | 44 | 99 | 72 | 7 | 4 | 3 | 7 | 10 |
| 1990-91 | Minnesota | NHL | 80 | 35 | 40 | 75 | 43 | 23 | 10 | 19 | 29 | 30 |

international

| year | team | competition | GP | G | A | PTS | PIM | Place |
|------|------|-------------|----|---|---|-----|-----|-------|
| 1984 | Canada | Canada Cup | 5 | 0 | 1 | 1 | 0 | 1 |
| 1987 | Canada | World Championship | 10 | 1 | 3 | 4 | 8 | 4 |
| 1989 | Canada | World Championship | 10 | 8 | 6 | 14 | 2 | 2 |
| 1990 | Canada | World Championship | 8 | 3 | 6 | 9 | 8 | 4 |

# BEREHOWSKY, DRAKE

| | |
|---|---|
| sport: | hockey |
| born: | Toronto, Ontario |
| | January 3, 1972 |
| height: | 1.85 m / 6'1" |
| weight: | 95 kg / 210 lbs |
| position: | defense |
| shoots: | right |

*Photo courtesy of the Toronto Maple Leafs*

The Toronto Maple Leafs took a considerable risk when they made Drake Berehowsky their first choice, 10th overall, in the 1990 NHL Entry Draft. Less than a year earlier, Berehowsky tore ligaments in his knee. The injury required surgery and he missed the remainder of the season. The Leafs, though, were impressed with his credentials and had faith that Berehowsky would completely recover. Berehowsky's performance at his rookie training camp was stellar and he started the season. After a few games, to gain seasoning, he was reassigned to junior hockey. He played for both Kingston and North Bay. A major disappointment that year was his unsuccessful tryout for Canada's national junior hockey team.

As a youngster, Berehowsky was highly touted, being picked first overall in the OHL midget priority selections. A strong skater with a good shot, Drake Berehowsky was also recognized for his ability to handle the puck.

## AWARDS

| | |
|---|---|
| 1992 | Max Kaminsky Trophy - OHL Outstanding Defenseman |
| 1992 | Outstanding Junior Defenseman in Canada |

## RECORD

| year | team | league | regular season | | | | | playoffs | | | | |
|---|---|---|---|---|---|---|---|---|---|---|---|---|
| | | | GP | G | A | PTS | PIM | GP | G | A | PTS | PIM |
| 1988-89 | Canada | | 1 | 0 | 0 | 0 | 0 | | | | | |
| 1990-91 | Toronto | NHL | 8 | 0 | 1 | 1 | 25 | | | | | |

# BEREZA, MYRON

| | |
|---|---|
| sport: | soccer |
| born: | Ternopil, Ukraine |
| | August 24, 1936 |
| height: | 1.70 m / 5'7" |
| weight: | 68 kg / 150 lbs |
| position: | left wing |

Myron Bereza began his soccer career in Belgium in 1950 with the junior club Seraieng. The following year, he arrived in Canada and joined the junior SA Ukraina - Toronto soccer team. Bereza led the team to the Toronto junior championship, scoring a team-leading 19 goals. In the spring of 1952, fifteen-year-old Bereza made the roster of the senior SA Ukraina team. The following year, he helped the club win the first of three consecutive National League championships.

In 1956, Bereza joined the Ukrainian American Sports Club (UASC) of Rochester. The club advanced to the semi-finals of the American championship. In 1957, UASC won the Eastern

US championship and advanced to the final of the US championship. That series concluded, Bereza joined the Canadian national team in the preliminary round of the 1958 World Cup playdowns. Canada defeated the United States twice, 5-1 and 3-2. Against Mexico, Canada lost twice and was eliminated from further play. In 1958, Bereza returned to SA Ukraina with which he played until his retirement in 1966.

Myron Bereza, a diminutive left wing forward, was extremely dangerous with the ball in the offensive zone. He was a consistent goal scorer who was also effective in setting up goals.

From 1984 to 1990, Myron Bereza coached teams competing in the Ukrainian Youth Soccer Association (UYSA) league. In 1987 he led the under-10 rep team to the Metro Cup. A year later, Bereza led the under-11 rep team to the Metropolitan Toronto Soccer Association league championship.

## RECORD

competitive

| year | team |
|------|------|
| 1950 | FC Seraieng (junior) - Belgium |
| 1951 | SA Ukraina (junior) - Toronto |
| 1952-56 | SA Ukraina - Toronto |
| 1956-57 | Ukrainian American Sports Club - Rochester, USA |
| 1958-66 | SA Ukraina - Toronto |

international

| year | team | competition | GP | G | Place |
|------|------|-------------|----|---|-------|
| 1957 | Canada | World Cup Qualifying | 4 | 0 | eliminated |

# BEVERLEY, NICK

"Slick Nick"

| | |
|---|---|
| sport: | hockey |
| given name: | Beverley, Nicholas Gerald |
| born: | Toronto, Ontario |
| | April 21, 1947 |
| height: | 1.88 m / 6'2" |
| weight: | 84 kg / 185 lbs |
| position: | defense |
| shoots: | right |

*Card reproduced courtesy of O-Pee-Chee Co.*

Nick Beverley (the family had earlier anglicized the surname from Bezverchney) learned to skate and play hockey on a pond in a rural area of Scarborough not far from the family home. At 17, the tall and rangy defenseman joined the Oshawa Generals of the OHA and for a while played on a shift with Bobby Orr. In his last year of junior hockey, Beverley was named the Generals' captain.

Nick Beverley spent five years in the minor pro leagues before getting a regular job in the NHL in 1972 when he cracked the starting line-up of the Boston Bruins. A year later he was traded to Pittsburgh. Beverley would change teams four more times - playing for the New York Rangers, Minnesota North Stars where he served as captain, Los Angeles Kings and Colorado Rockies - before retiring in 1980. During his career, Beverley was known for his steady play, poke checks and good lead passes. He was a positional player who made few mistakes.

Immediately upon retirement, Nick Beverley joined the coaching fraternity when he agreed to take on the responsibilities with the Houston Apollos of the CHL, an affiliate of the Los Angeles Kings. George Maguire, general manager of the Kings, stated: "Throughout his career, Nick has had the reputation of being a class guy and a leader. . . Even in his short time with the Kings (seven games), one could see that he could communicate with the younger players. . ."[1] The Apollos, though, folded before the season ended. The following season, the Kings assigned Beverley to the position of assistant coach of the New Haven Nighthawks of the AHL.

In early 1982, Nick Beverley was promoted to head coach of the Nighthawks. During his tenure, he showed leadership both off and on the ice. When one game day in 1984 the team had only 13 available skaters due to injuries, suspensions and call-ups by the parent club, Beverley suited up for the game. While he played only two shifts assisting on a shorthanded goal, the gesture inspired the team to victory.

The Kings fired Nick Beverley as coach of the Nighthawks in 1985, but retained his services as a scout with the parent club in Los Angeles. With the Kings, he worked his way up to director of player personnel, assistant general manager, and by 1992, general manager.

## RECORD

| year | team | league | regular season | | | | | playoffs | | | | |
|------|------|--------|----|----|----|-----|-----|----|----|----|-----|-----|
| | | | GP | G | A | PTS | PIM | GP | G | A | PTS | PIM |
| 1966-67 | Boston | NHL | 2 | 0 | 0 | 0 | 0 | | | | | |
| 1967-68 | Oklahoma City | CPHL | 70 | 7 | 20 | 27 | 60 | 4 | 0 | 0 | 0 | 17 |
| 1968-69 | Oklahoma City | CHL | 62 | 3 | 22 | 25 | 32 | 12 | 0 | 4 | 4 | 4 |
| 1969-70 | Boston | NHL | 2 | 0 | 0 | 0 | 2 | | | | | |
| | Oklahoma City | CHL | 58 | 6 | 24 | 30 | 26 | | | | | |
| 1970-71 | Hershey | AHL | 70 | 3 | 23 | 26 | 46 | 4 | 0 | 0 | 0 | 2 |
| 1971-72 | Boston | NHL | 1 | 0 | 0 | 0 | 0 | | | | | |
| | Boston | AHL | 73 | 9 | 31 | 40 | 36 | 9 | 0 | 5 | 5 | 2 |
| 1972-73 | Boston | NHL | 76 | 1 | 10 | 11 | 26 | 4 | 0 | 0 | 0 | 0 |
| 1973-74 | Boston | NHL | 1 | 0 | 0 | 0 | 0 | | | | | |
| | Pittsburgh | NHL | 67 | 2 | 14 | 16 | 21 | | | | | |
| 1974-75 | NY Rangers | NHL | 67 | 3 | 15 | 18 | 19 | 3 | 0 | 1 | 1 | 0 |
| 1975-76 | NY Rangers | NHL | 63 | 1 | 8 | 9 | 46 | | | | | |
| 1976-77 | NY Rangers | NHL | 9 | 0 | 0 | 0 | 2 | | | | | |
| | Minnesota | NHL | 52 | 2 | 17 | 19 | 6 | | | | | |
| 1977-78 | Minnesota | NHL | 57 | 7 | 14 | 21 | 18 | | | | | |
| 1978-79 | Los Angeles | NHL | 7 | 0 | 3 | 3 | 0 | | | | | |
| | Colorado | NHL | 52 | 2 | 4 | 6 | 6 | | | | | |
| 1979-80 | Colorado | NHL | 46 | 0 | 9 | 9 | 10 | | | | | |
| | Fort Worth | CHL | 12 | 0 | 6 | 6 | 4 | | | | | |
| 1983-84 | New Haven | AHL | 1 | 0 | 1 | 1 | 0 | | | | | |

# BEZRUCHKA, STEPHEN

sport:      mountaineering
born:       Toronto, Ontario
            May 9, 1943
height:     1.96 m / 6'5"
weight:     93 kg / 205 lbs

For many years, Steven Bezruchka, a medical doctor specializing in Third World medicine and high altitude problems, combined his professional expertise with his passion for mountain climbing. In 1981, Dr. Bezruchka successfully scaled the difficult East Ridge of Mount Logan, Canada's highest mountain. A few months later, he was in China challenging Muztagh Ata in the Pamir Range. The expedition was part of a series of high altitude training climbs in preparation for the following year's planned ascent of Mount Everest by a Canadian team.

Dr. Bezruchka and his colleagues set a number of firsts during the training expedition. They were the first ever Canadian alpinist team to climb in China and the September ascent was the latest in the season that an attempt had been made to reach the peak of Muztagh Ata. Despite severe weather conditions, heavy snow and temperature dropping to -30°C, Dr. Bezruchka was one of three climbers to reach the 7,546-metre summit.

In 1982, Dr. Bezruchka was one of eleven members of Canada's first successful conquest of Mt. Everest. He was the high altitude doctor with the expedition and did not challenge the summit. Numerous injuries and four tragic deaths due to an avalanche and an ice fall kept Dr. Bezruchka extremely busy.

In 1969 and 1970, Dr. Bezruchka and his wife spent time exploring Nepal. The experience resulted in the writing of *A Guide to Trekking in Nepal*. Experts have called the book "excellent. . . Indispensable for anyone going to Nepal."[2] Subsequently, Dr. Bezruchka wrote *Pocket Doctor: Your Ticket to Good Health while Travelling* and *Nepali for Trekkers*. In addition, Dr. Stephen Bezruchka has served in various administrative positions with the Alpine Club of Canada of which he became a member in 1965.

| year | peak | country | height reached | |
|------|------|---------|---------|---|
| 1967 | Mt. New Brunswick | Canada | 11,115 ft | 3,388 m* |
| 1978 | Mt. Robson | Canada | 12,972 ft | 3,954 m* |
| 1981 | Mt. Logan | Canada | 19,850 ft | 6,050 m* |
| 1981 | Muztagh Ata | China | 24,758 ft | 7,546 m* |
| 1982 | Mt. Everest | Nepal | 20,000 ft | 6,100 m |
| 1983 | Mt. Steele | Canada | 16,644 ft | 5,073 m* |
| 1983 | Mt. Lucania | Canada | 17,147 ft | 5,226 m* |

\*   summit

# BILINSKI, MIKE

| | |
|---|---|
| sport: | professional wrestling |
| born: | . . . |
| | . . . |
| height: | 1.80 m / 5'11" |
| weight: | 86 kg / 190 lbs |

Mike Bilinski's wrestling career probably began in the early 1920s. In the years 1923-29, he was billed as the Western Canadian Middleweight champion.  In 1927, he likely first challenged for the Canadian professional middleweight title.

In April 1923, Bilinski participated in the first boxer versus wrestler match in Manitoba defeating "Fats" Salter.  Mike Bilinski, a native of Winnipeg, operated a wrestling club in Edmonton in the early 1930s.

# BLACK, STEPHEN

| | |
|---|---|
| sport: | hockey |
| given name: | Chorney, Stephen |
| born: | Fort William, Ontario |
| | (now Thunder Bay) |
| | March 31, 1927 |
| height: | 1.83 m / 6'0" |
| weight: | 84 kg / 185 lbs |
| position: | left wing |
| shoots: | left |

*Photo courtesy of the Northwestern Ontario Sports Hall of Fame*

After playing for a number of seasons in the minor pro leagues for Oakland and St. Louis, Stephen Black cracked the starting line-up of the Detroit Red Wings in 1949. That year the Wings won the Stanley Cup. The following season, after playing a few games for Detroit, he was traded to Chicago with L. Fogolin for B. Olmstead and V. Stasiuk. Failing to make the Hawks for the 1951-52 season, Black was assigned to the St. Louis Flyers. A year later he signed on with Calgary of the WHL. Stephen Black was a member of the 1954 Calgary WHL championship team. The club then won the Edinburgh Cup by defeating Quebec.

## RECORD

| year | team | league | regular season | | | | | playoffs | | | | |
|---|---|---|---|---|---|---|---|---|---|---|---|---|
| | | | GP | G | A | PTS | PIM | GP | G | A | PTS | PIM |
| 1946-47 | Oakland | PCHL | 60 | 43 | 36 | 79 | 79 | | | | | |
| 1947-48 | St. Louis | AHL | 58 | 11 | 18 | 29 | 29 | | | | | |
| 1948-49 | St. Louis | AHL | 62 | 24 | 47 | 71 | 59 | 7 | 0 | 5 | 5 | 12 |
| 1949-50* | Detroit | NHL | 69 | 7 | 14 | 21 | 53 | 13 | 0 | 0 | 0 | 13 |
| 1950-51 | Detroit | NHL | 5 | 0 | 0 | 0 | 2 | | | | | |
| | Chicago | NHL | 39 | 4 | 6 | 10 | 22 | | | | | |
| | Indianapolis | AHL | 8 | 1 | 2 | 3 | 13 | | | | | |
| | Milwaukee | USHL | 9 | 4 | 6 | 10 | 11 | | | | | |
| 1951-52 | St. Louis | AHL | 37 | 9 | 21 | 30 | 34 | | | | | |
| 1952-53 | Calgary | WHL | 45 | 21 | 16 | 37 | 61 | 5 | 4 | 3 | 7 | 2 |
| 1953-54* | Calgary | WHL | 43 | 21 | 33 | 54 | 29 | 18 | 2 | 4 | 6 | 6 |

# BODNAR, GUS

| | |
|---|---|
| sport: | hockey |
| given name: | Bodnarchuk, August |
| born: | Fort William, Ontario |
| | (now Thunder Bay) |
| | August 24, 1925 |
| height: | 1.78 m / 5'10" |
| weight: | 72.5 kg / 160 lbs |
| position: | center |
| shoots: | right |

*Photo courtesy of the Northwestern Ontario Sports Hall of Fame*

For a number of years Gus Bodnar played hockey on open-air rinks he and his friends made on an empty lot behind the family home in Fort William. The hockey enthusiasts would open up a city hydrant and flood the lot. Eventually, Bodnar worked his way up through minor hockey to play indoors with the Fort William Canadians junior club. During the 1942-43 season he led the club in scoring and was instrumental in the club's advance to the semi-finals of the Memorial Cup tournament. In the fall, Bodnar made news when he became one of only a few first-year players to crack the starting line-up of the Toronto Maple Leafs.

Gus Bodnar did not disappoint the Leafs' brass that year. Just 15 seconds into his first professional game, Bodnar scored a goal, establishing a record for the fastest goal from the start of a game by a rookie. Bodnar ended the season with 22 goals and 40 assists, second best on the Leafs and tenth best in the league. He was the NHL's rookie of the year and was awarded the Calder Trophy. In 1945 and 1947 he won the Stanley Cup with the Leafs. After the 1947 playoffs, Bodnar was traded to Chicago. During the 1948-49 campaign he accounted for 45 points, ninth best in the league. On March 23, 1952, Bodnar established an NHL record for the three fastest assists. He assisted on all three goals that Bill Mosienko scored in a span of 21 seconds. In February of 1954, Bodnar was traded to Boston where he finished his career the following season.

For close to 15 years Bodnar coached junior hockey teams in Ontario. He was a no-nonsense coach, a strict disciplinarian off the ice. He preached education: "The day has long gone when you could get away with just being a hockey player." General tom-foolery on game trips was replaced by books. The only acceptable excuse for missing a practice was school.

During the 1960-61 season, Bodnar coached the St. Catharines Teepees Junior A team. Later he formed, coached, and managed the Lindsay Junior C team. In 1966, he was appointed coach of the Toronto Marlboros and in the spring of 1967, he led them to the Memorial Cup, defeating home-town Port Arthur Marrs in the final. During the 1970-71 season, as a favour to Punch Imlach, he managed and coached the Salt Lake Golden Eagles of the WHL. He returned to Canada the following year to take up the coaching and managerial duties with the Oshawa Generals of the OHA. He held the joint position until 1975. During the 1976-77 season, he was co-coach of Canada's junior hockey team.

## INDUCTIONS

1983        Northwestern Ontario Sports Hall of Fame

## AWARDS

1944        Calder Trophy  -  NHL Rookie of the Year
1972        Matt Layden Trophy  -  OHA Coach of the Year

## RECORD

| year | team | league | regular season | | | | | playoffs | | | | |
|------|------|--------|----|----|----|-----|-----|----|----|----|-----|-----|
| | | | GP | G | A | PTS | PIM | GP | G | A | PTS | PIM |
| 1943-44 | Toronto | NHL | 50 | 22 | 40 | 62 | 18 | 5 | 0 | 0 | 0 | 0 |
| 1944-45* | Toronto | NHL | 49 | 8 | 36 | 44 | 18 | 13 | 3 | 1 | 4 | 4 |
| 1945-46 | Toronto | NHL | 49 | 14 | 23 | 37 | 14 | | | | | |
| 1946-47* | Toronto | NHL | 39 | 4 | 6 | 10 | 10 | 1 | 0 | 0 | 0 | 0 |
| | Pittsburgh | AHL | 15 | 10 | 9 | 19 | 10 | 9 | 2 | 2 | 4 | 4 |
| 1947-48 | Chicago | NHL | 46 | 13 | 22 | 35 | 23 | | | | | |
| | Pittsburgh | AHL | 6 | 2 | 3 | 5 | 0 | | | | | |
| 1948-49 | Chicago | NHL | 59 | 19 | 26 | 45 | 14 | | | | | |
| 1949-50 | Chicago | NHL | 70 | 11 | 28 | 39 | 6 | | | | | |
| 1950-51 | Chicago | NHL | 44 | 8 | 12 | 20 | 8 | | | | | |
| 1951-52 | Chicago | NHL | 69 | 14 | 26 | 40 | 26 | | | | | |
| 1952-53 | Chicago | NHL | 66 | 16 | 13 | 29 | 26 | 7 | 1 | 1 | 2 | 2 |
| 1953-54 | Chicago | NHL | 45 | 6 | 15 | 21 | 20 | | | | | |
| | Boston | NHL | 14 | 3 | 3 | 6 | 10 | 1 | 0 | 0 | 0 | 0 |
| 1954-55 | Boston | NHL | 67 | 4 | 4 | 8 | 14 | 5 | 0 | 1 | 1 | 4 |

| coaching record | | | regular season | | | | | playoffs | | | |
|------|------|--------|----|----|----|----|----------|----|----|----|----|
| year | team | league | G | W | L | T | Standing | G | W | L | T |
| 1970-71 | Salt Lake City | WHL | 72 | 18 | 49 | 5 | 6 | | | | |

# BOIMISTRUCK, FRED

sport:      hockey
born:       Sudbury, Ontario
            November 4, 1962
height:     1.80 m / 5'11"
weight:     86.5 kg / 191 lbs
position:   defense
shoots:     right

Fred Boimistruck, a third round pick in the 1980 NHL Entry Draft, joined the Toronto Maple Leafs in 1981 after being a member of two successive Memorial Cup champions with the Cornwall Royals. Boimistruck came to the Leafs with high expectations, having won the Emile Bouchard Trophy as the top defenseman in the QMJHL. He played most of the 1981-82 season with the Leafs. The following season he spent primarily in the Toronto farm system. At the end of the 1983-84 season, Boimistruck was picked up by the Los Angeles Kings and assigned to the Fort Wayne Komets. In October 1984, he was released by the Kings.

## AWARDS

1981        Emile Bouchard Trophy  -  QMJHL Top Defenseman

## RECORD

| year | team | league | regular season | | | | | playoffs | | | | |
|------|------|--------|------|------|------|------|------|------|------|------|------|------|
| | | | GP | G | A | PTS | PIM | GP | G | A | PTS | PIM |
| 1981-82 | Toronto | NHL | 57 | 2 | 11 | 13 | 32 | | | | | |
| 1982-83 | Toronto | NHL | 26 | 2 | 3 | 5 | 13 | | | | | |
| | St. Catharines | AHL | 50 | 6 | 23 | 29 | 32 | | | | | |
| 1983-84 | St. Catharines | AHL | 80 | 2 | 28 | 30 | 68 | 7 | 1 | 0 | 1 | 19 |
| 1984-85 | Fort Wayne | IHL | 2 | 0 | 1 | 1 | 5 | | | | | |
| 1985-86 | Langnau | Swiss | 6 | 1 | 2 | 3 | | | | | | |

international

| year | team | competition | GP | G | A | PTS | PIM | Place |
|------|------|-------------|------|------|------|------|------|-------|
| 1981 | Cornwall | World Junior Championship | 5 | 3 | 0 | 3 | 8 | 7 |

# BOLONCHUK, LARRY

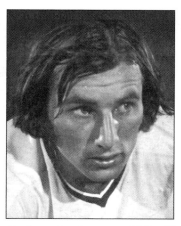

| | |
|---|---|
| sport: | hockey |
| born: | Winnipeg, Manitoba |
| | February 26, 1952 |
| height: | 1.78 m / 5'10" |
| weight: | 86 kg / 190 lbs |
| position: | defense |
| shoots: | right |

*Card reproduced courtesy of O-Pee-Chee Co.*

Larry Bolonchuk played junior hockey with the Winnipeg Jets of the WCHL. In 1972, he was drafted by the Vancouver Canucks of the NHL and the Winnipeg Jets of the WHA. Bolonchuk opted for the Canucks. At his rookie NHL training camp, Bolonchuk impressed coach Vic Stasiuk and earned a spot on the team. After about a dozen games, Bolonchuk was sent to the farm club for more seasoning. He played in the minor pro leagues for a number of years, winning the IHL championship with the Des Moines Capitals in 1974 and with the Dayton Gems two years later.

In the 1974 NHL Expansion Draft, the Washington Capitals selected Bolonchuk from Vancouver. He was with the Capitals organization for five seasons alternating between the parent club and farm system. In one of those seasons, the 1977-78 campaign, he played regularly in the NHL.

Larry Bolonchuk, a non-rushing defensive defenseman, always liked to be involved in the action. Coach Stasiuk stated: "I liked the way he stuck his nose in there. . . went right into the center of the action."

## ALL-STAR SELECTIONS

1976-77    defense  IHL  Second Team

## RECORD

| year | team | league | regular season | | | | | playoffs | | | | |
|---|---|---|---|---|---|---|---|---|---|---|---|---|
| | | | GP | G | A | PTS | PIM | GP | G | A | PTS | PIM |
| 1972-73 | Vancouver | NHL | 15 | 0 | 0 | 0 | 6 | | | | | |

| | | | regular season | | | | | playoffs | | | | |
|---|---|---|---|---|---|---|---|---|---|---|---|---|
| year | team | league | GP | G | A | PTS | PIM | GP | G | A | PTS | PIM |
| 1972-73 | Seattle | WHL | 59 | 2 | 9 | 11 | 97 | | | | | |
| 1973-74 | Seattle | WHL | 3 | 0 | 2 | 2 | 4 | | | | | |
| * | Des Moines | IHL | 71 | 6 | 27 | 33 | 166 | 10 | 2 | 4 | 6 | 42 |
| 1974-75 | Dayton | IHL | 58 | 9 | 21 | 30 | 139 | 14 | 0 | 13 | 13 | 31 |
| 1975-76 | Washington | NHL | 1 | 0 | 1 | 1 | 0 | | | | | |
| | Dayton | IHL | 77 | 4 | 39 | 43 | 174 | 15 | 0 | 11 | 11 | 59 |
| 1976-77 | Washington | NHL | 9 | 0 | 0 | 0 | 12 | | | | | |
| | Dayton | IHL | 71 | 2 | 21 | 23 | 124 | 4 | 0 | 2 | 2 | 6 |
| 1977-78 | Washington | NHL | 49 | 3 | 8 | 11 | 79 | | | | | |
| | Hampton | AHL | 14 | 1 | 1 | 2 | 38 | | | | | |
| | Hershey | AHL | 19 | 0 | 7 | 7 | 12 | | | | | |
| 1978-79 | Binghamton | AHL | 75 | 2 | 28 | 30 | 108 | 10 | 0 | 1 | 1 | 18 |

# BOROWIK, ALEXANDRA

"Alex"

| | |
|---|---|
| sport: | gymnastics |
| born: | Toronto, Ontario |
| | November 3, 1970 |
| height: | 1.68 m / 5'6" |
| weight: | 52 kg / 115 lbs |

Alexandra Borowik was a member of Canada's gymnastics team for three years. During that time, she competed in many international tournaments and partook in a team training camp in Beijing, China. In 1987, after placing seventh in the Canadian trials, she was named as an alternate to Canada's team for the World Championships. The team placed eighth.

A good all-round gymnast, Borowik was comfortable on all the apparatuses. As a result of solid training and coaching, she was relaxed during competition, and her presentation was crisp and very disciplined. To the observer, the presentation was also very elegant, since Borowik was taller than most female gymnasts.

Upon enrolling at the University of Toronto, Borowik joined the school's varsity gymnastics team. Alexandra Borowik's gymnastic skills also helped her land a role in the Canadian-made movie *Flying*; as a stunt double, she did various tumbling passes and a back tuck somersault over a car.

## RECORD

| year | competition | event | placing | result |
|------|-------------|-------|---------|--------|
| 1985 | Canadian Junior Championships | all-around | 2 | 70.58 |
|      |             | beam | 2 | 17.68 |
|      |             | uneven bars | 3 | 17.98 |
|      | Pre-World International | all-around | 8 | |
| 1986 | Elite Canada | all-around | 11 | 71.08 |
|      | Hungarian Invitational | all-around | 13 | 73.50 |
|      | Canadian Championships | all-around | 7 | 73.22 |
|      |             | beam | 6 (tie) | 18.08 |
|      |             | floor | 11 | 18.08 |
|      |             | uneven bars | 8 | 18.66 |
|      |             | vault | 8 (tie) | 18.40 |
|      | Pacific Alliance Championships | all-around | 16 | 36.10 |
|      |             | team | 3 | 113.10 |
| 1987 | Avignon Invitational | all-around | 13 (tie) | 36.05 |
|      |             | vault | 5 | 18.75 |
|      | Canadian Championships | all-around | 11 | 73.30 |
|      | World Trials | all-around | 7 | 148.80 |
|      | World Championships | alternate | | |
|      | Elite Canada | all-around | 3 | 73.40 |
|      |             | floor | 2 | |
|      |             | beam | 3 | |
| 1988 | Australian Invitational | all-around | 6 | 36.90 |
|      |             | beam | 6 | 18.50 |
|      |             | floor | 6 | 18.20 |
|      |             | uneven bars | 7 | 18.55 |
|      |             | vault | 6 | 18.725 |
|      | Canadian Championships | all-around | 25 | 35.95 |
|      | Olympic Trials | all-around | 10 | |
| 1991 | National University Cup | all-around | 2 | 36.26 |

# BOSSY, DAN

| | |
|---|---|
| sport: | canoeing |
| given name: | Bossy, Daniel Paul |
| born: | Montreal, Quebec |
| | August 4, 1938 |
| height: | 1.83 m / 6'0" |
| weight: | 99 kg / 220 lbs |

Between the years 1955 and 1963, Dan Bossy participated and won or placed in more than 100 canoeing events in North America. In 1960, he placed second in the 1000-metre C-1 event at the Olympic trials in Ottawa. Unfortunately, because of a lack of funds, Bossy's Olympic hopes did not materialize. That year Bossy competed at the North American Championships. He placed second in the half-mile C-1 and C-2 events. In winter, Dan Bossy played hockey. In 1957, he was with the Jr. "A" St. Laurent Jets. The next ten years he played intermediate "A" hockey in St. Lambert. Subsequently, Dan Bossy joined an old-timer hockey team and competed in such far away exotic places as Hawaii. Dan Bossy is the brother of paddler George Bossy and hockey coach Leo Bossy and the uncle of paddler Don Bossy and hockey player Mike Bossy.

## RECORD

| year | competition | event | | placing | result |
|---|---|---|---|---|---|
| 1958 | Canadian Junior Championships | C-1 | 1000 m | 3 | |
| 1960 | Canadian Championships | C-1 | 1000 m | 2 | |
| | | C-4 | 1000 m | 1 | 4:41.4 |
| | North American Championships | C-1 | ½ mile | 2 | |
| | | C-2 | ½ mile | 2 | |
| | | C-4 | 1000 m | 3 | |
| 1961 | Canadian Championships | C-1 | 1000 m | 3 | |
| | | C-4 | 1000 m | 3 | |

# BOSSY, DON

"Dode"

sport:          canoeing
given name:     Bossy, Donald
born:           Hamilton, Ontario
                February 13, 1948
height:         1.75 m / 5'9"
weight:         72.5 kg / 160 lbs

Don Bossy trained and competed with the Cartierville Boating Club from 1957 to 1968. At the 1965 Canadian Canoe Championships, he won three medals in junior competition and one in the open. The following year, at the national championships, Bossy along with B. Norris won the 10,000-metre C-2 event. He placed second in the 1000-metre C-1. The former result qualified Bossy and Norris for the North American Championships, which they won. At the 1967 Pan American Games, the duo won a gold medal in the 10,000-metre C-2 and a silver in the 1000-metre C-2.

During the winter months, Bossy played hockey. In 1967, he was drafted by the Detroit Red Wings to play for their farm team, the Hamilton Red Wings of the OHA. That same year, while playing hockey, he separated his shoulder. The injury required an implant and it terminated a promising career in sports for Don Bossy at the age of twenty. Don Bossy is the brother of hockey player Mike Bossy and the nephew of paddlers George and Daniel Bossy and hockey coach Leo Bossy.

## RECORD

| year | competition | event | | placing | result |
|------|-------------|-------|--|---------|--------|
| 1965 | Canadian Junior Championships | C-2 | 1000 m | 1 | 4:43.4 |
|      |             | C-4 | 1000 m | 3 | |
|      |             | war canoe | | 1 | 3:55.8 |
|      | Canadian Championships | war canoe | | 1 | 3:53.2 |
| 1966 | Canadian Championships | C-2 | 1000 m | 2 | |
|      |             | C-2 | 10,000 m | 1 | |
|      |             | C-4 | 1000 m | 3 | |
|      | North American Championships | C-2 | 10,000 m | 1 | 55:56.9 |
|      |             | C-4 | 1000 m | 2 | |

| year | competition | event | | placing | result |
|------|-------------|-------|--|---------|--------|
| 1967 | Canadian Junior Championships | C-1 | 1000 m | 1 | 4:57.2 |
| | Canadian Championships | C-2 | 1000 m | 2 | |
| | | C-2 | 10,000 m | 1 | 51:38.5 |
| | | war canoe | | 1 | 3:58.4 |
| | Pan American Games | C-2 | 1000 m | 2 | 5:04.8 |
| | | C-2 | 10,000 m | 1 | 48:17.1 |
| | North American Championships | C-2 | 10,000 m | 1 | 45:59.8 |
| | | C-2 | 1000 m | 3 | |
| | Olympic Trials | C-2 | 1000 m | 2 | |
| 1968 | Canadian Championships | C-2 | 1000 m | 2 | |
| | | C-2 | 10,000 m | 1 | 47:19.4 |
| | | C-4 | 1000 m | 1 | |
| | | war canoe | | 1 | 3:51.7 |
| | North American Championships | C-2 | 1000 m | 2 | |
| | | C-2 | 10,000 m | 3 | |
| | | C-4 | 1000 m | 1 | 4:57.6 |

# BOSSY, GEORGE

| | |
|--|--|
| sport: | canoeing, football |
| given name: | Bossy, George Walter |
| born: | . . . |
| | . . . |
| height: | 1.85 m / 6'1" |
| weight: | 86 kg / 190 lbs |

George Bossy was the first member of the Bossy clan to gain recognition in sport when in 1951 he won the national championship in the half-mile C-1 event. The self-coached Bossy repeated as national champion in the event, now converted to the metric 1000 metres, at the 1956 championship and in the subsequent three championships. Bossy also competed at the 10,000-metre distance, winning the national title in 1954. That same year he teamed up with brother Leo to win the national junior C-2 championship. Bossy paddled out of the Cartierville Boating Club through the entire 1950s and for a time coached the club.

In 1952, George Bossy competed at the Olympics. He did not advance to the final, finishing fifth in a semi-final heat. Four years later Bossy once again competed at the Olympics, finishing eighth in the final. Bossy also represented Canada at a number of North American Championships, consistently placing in the top three.

In 1952, Bossy also saw limited action with the Montreal Alouettes of the Canadian Football League. He had previously played football at the end position with McGill University. George Bossy is the brother of paddler Dan Bossy and hockey coach Leo Bossy, and the uncle of paddler Don Bossy and hockey player Mike Bossy.

## RECORD

| year | competition | event | | placing | result |
|------|-------------|-------|---|---------|--------|
| 1951 | Canadian Championships | C-1 | $\frac{1}{2}$ mile | 1 | 4:42.3 |
| 1952 | Olympic Games | C-1 | 1000 m | 5 H | 5:25.8 |
| 1953 | Canadian Championships | C-1 | $\frac{1}{2}$ mile | 2 | |
| | Canadian Junior Championships | C-2 | $\frac{1}{2}$ mile | 3 | |
| | North American Championships | C-1 | 1000 m | 3 | |
| 1954 | Canadian Junior Championships | C-2 | $\frac{1}{2}$ mile | 1 | 4:23.8 |
| | Canadian Championships | C-1 | $\frac{1}{2}$ mile | 2 | |
| | | C-1 | 10,000 m | 1 | 1:01:13.3 |
| | North American Championships | C-1 | 1000 m | 3 | |
| 1955 | Canadian Championships | C-1 | $\frac{1}{2}$ mile | 2 | |
| | | C-1 | 10,000 m | 2 | |
| | | C-2 | 10,000 m | 2 | |
| 1956 | Canadian Championships | C-1 | 1000 m | 1 | 5:19.8 |
| | North American Championships | C-1 | 1000 m | 3 | |
| | Olympic Games | C-1 | 1000 m | 8 | 5:39.4 |
| 1957 | Canadian Championships | C-1 | 1000 m | 1 | 5:17.0 |
| | | C-1 | 10,000 m | 2 | |
| | | war canoe | | 2 | |
| | North American Championships | C-1 | 1000 m | 2 | |
| 1958 | Canadian Championships | C-1 | 1000 m | 1 | 5:17.6 |
| | North American Championships | C-1 | $\frac{1}{2}$ mile | 1 | 4:50.0 |
| 1959 | Canadian Championships | C-1 | 1000 m | 1 | 6:00.0 |

# BOSSY, LEO

"Lion"

| | |
|---|---|
| sport: | hockey, canoeing |
| born: | . . . |
| | . . . |
| height: | . . . |
| weight: | . . . |

An avid paddler in his youth, Leo Bossy, along with his brother George, won the gold medal in the junior half-mile C-2 event at the 1954 Canadian Championships. Subsequently, Leo Bossy won silver medals at the 1956 and 1957 Canadian Championships in the junior C-1 event.

In 1966, Leo Bossy was appointed coach of the Montreal Junior Canadiens hockey team for the 1966-67 season. His tenure with the club was short-lived. Bossy later coached the Halifax Canadiens of the Maritime Junior A Hockey League. In January of 1969, after receiving a four-game suspension, Bossy was released. The club at the time was in first place. During the 1969-70 season, Bossy made a brief coaching appearance with the Laval Saints of the QMJHL and a year later with Rosemount of the same league.

Leo Bossy is the brother of paddlers George and Daniel Bossy and the uncle of paddler Don Bossy and hockey player Mike Bossy.

# BOSSY, MIKE

"Boss"

| | |
|---|---|
| sport: | hockey |
| given name: | Bossy, Michael |
| born: | Montreal, Quebec |
| | January 22, 1957 |
| height: | 1.83 m / 6'0" |
| weight: | 84.5 kg / 186 lbs |
| position: | right wing |
| shoots: | right |

*Photo courtesy of the New York Islanders*

Mike Bossy began playing hockey at the age of three on a rink his father made by flooding the backyard. He quickly developed into a scoring machine. As a pee-wee, he registered 170 goals in a forty-game season. When Bossy became eligible for the NHL Entry Draft in 1977, he had just completed playing his fourth season with the Laval Nationals of the QJHL. During those four years he scored 309 goals and tallied 221 assists. Nevertheless, his scoring prowess was disregarded in the draft. In the first round, fourteen teams overlooked him, concerned about his ability to play a physical game. The New York Islanders, drafting 15th, decided to take a chance on the right winger after their scout, who knew Bossy personally, assured the club that Bossy would make it in the big league.

Bossy arrived at the New York Islanders training camp full of enthusiasm. He was a skinny kid with the desire not only to prove his detractors wrong but to show that he was the best. He worked hard and was rewarded with a regular spot on the team roster. The season ended with Bossy establishing an NHL rookie scoring record with 53 goals. He was named to the league's second all-star team and was awarded the Calder Trophy as rookie of the year. The following year he tallied a career-high 69 goals which established a league record for right wingers. During the 1980-81 season, Bossy scored 50 goals in his club's first 50 games to tie Rocket Richard's legendary record from 1944-45. He finished the season with a league-leading 68 goals. In the playoffs, he led the Islanders to their second Stanley Cup with a playoff record 35 points.

Mike Bossy's effectiveness on the ice was a result of a number of factors. He was an extremely fast skater who appeared to be drifting lazily. This allowed him to elude defenders and find a good scoring position. He relied on the flick shot, wrist shot and backhand and they were arguably the most accurate in hockey. He also had an extremely quick puck release. Many goalies swore that he shot the puck before he got it.

During the 1981 Canada Cup, Bossy scored seven goals in eight games. He was selected to the tournament all-star team and was named Canada's MVP. Canada though was humiliated in the final. The disappointment of losing the Canada Cup was not reflected in Bossy's play during that NHL season. He scored a career-high 147 points. His 83 assists established a new record for a right wing. That year he was the playoff MVP leading the Islanders to their third straight Stanley Cup and scoring the Cup-winning goal himself. The following season he led the Islanders to their fourth Stanley Cup. Once again he scored the Cup winning goal, the first player ever to score two consecutive Cup-winning goals. That season he also won the Lady Byng Trophy for his clean game. During the summer of 1984, Bossy once again represented Canada at the Canada Cup tournament. Here he scored perhaps the most important goal of his life. In the semi-final game, in overtime, he deflected the puck into the Soviet net. This advanced Canada to the tournament final which Canada won.

During the 1985-86 season, Bossy scored his 500th career goal and his 1,000th career point.

For the ninth consecutive time, he scored at least 50 goals in a season, an NHL record. The following year Bossy played with lower back pains. His fragile body was showing signs of the physical abuse he endured over the years. While his play slowed down, his crusade for clean hockey intensified. When the season ended, for the first time in his career, Bossy failed to score at least 50 goals. He decided to sit out the following season and rest his back. Rest, though, did not help. In the fall of 1988, at age 31, Mike Bossy announced his retirement. In 1991, Bossy was honoured with an induction into the Hockey Hall of Fame and the following year his jersey number 22 was retired by the Islanders. Mike Bossy is the nephew of hockey coach Leo Bossy, and paddlers George and Daniel Bossy as well as the cousin of paddler Don Bossy.

## INDUCTIONS

1991        Hockey Hall of Fame

## AWARDS

| | |
|---|---|
| 1974 | Top Rookie Trophy  -  QJHL |
| 1977 | Frank Selke Trophy  -  QJHL Most Gentlemanly Player |
| 1978 | Calder Trophy  -  NHL Rookie of the Year |
| 1982 | Conn Smythe Trophy  -  NHL Playoff MVP |
| 1983 | Lady Byng Trophy  -  NHL Most Gentlemanly Player |
| 1984 | Lady Byng Trophy  -  NHL Most Gentlemanly Player |
| 1986 | Lady Byng Trophy  -  NHL Most Gentlemanly Player |

## ALL-STAR SELECTIONS

| | | | |
|---|---|---|---|
| 1977-78 | right wing | NHL | Second Team |
| 1978-79 | right wing | NHL | Second Team |
| 1980-81 | right wing | NHL | First Team |
| 1981 | right wing | Canada Cup | First Team |
| 1981-82 | right wing | NHL | First Team |
| 1982-83 | right wing | NHL | First Team |
| 1983-84 | right wing | NHL | First Team |
| 1984-85 | right wing | NHL | Second Team |
| 1985-86 | right wing | NHL | First Team |

| year | team | league | regular season | | | | | playoffs | | | | |
|------|------|--------|-----|----|----|-----|-----|-----|----|----|-----|-----|
| | | | GP | G | A | PTS | PIM | GP | G | A | PTS | PIM |
| 1977-78 | NY Islanders | NHL | 73 | 53 | 38 | 91 | 6 | 7 | 2 | 2 | 4 | 2 |
| 1978-79 | NY Islanders | NHL | 80 | 69 | 57 | 126 | 25 | 10 | 6 | 2 | 8 | 2 |
| 1979-80* | NY Islanders | NHL | 75 | 51 | 41 | 92 | 12 | 16 | 10 | 13 | 23 | 8 |
| 1980-81* | NY Islanders | NHL | 79 | 68 | 51 | 119 | 32 | 18 | 17 | 18 | 35 | 4 |
| 1981-82* | NY Islanders | NHL | 80 | 64 | 83 | 147 | 22 | 19 | 17 | 10 | 27 | 0 |
| 1982-83* | NY Islanders | NHL | 79 | 60 | 58 | 118 | 20 | 19 | 17 | 9 | 26 | 10 |
| 1983-84 | NY Islanders | NHL | 67 | 51 | 67 | 118 | 8 | 21 | 8 | 10 | 18 | 4 |
| 1984-85 | NY Islanders | NHL | 76 | 58 | 59 | 117 | 38 | 10 | 5 | 6 | 11 | 4 |
| 1985-86 | NY Islanders | NHL | 80 | 61 | 62 | 123 | 14 | 3 | 1 | 2 | 3 | 4 |
| 1986-87 | NY Islanders | NHL | 63 | 38 | 37 | 75 | 33 | 6 | 2 | 3 | 5 | 0 |

international

| year | team | competition | GP | G | A | PTS | PIM | Place |
|------|------|-------------|----|---|---|-----|-----|-------|
| 1981 | Canada | Canada Cup | 7 | 8 | 3 | 11 | 2 | 2 |
| 1984 | Canada | Canada Cup | 8 | 5 | 4 | 9 | 2 | 1 |

# BOWER, JOHNNY

"China Wall"

| | |
|---|---|
| sport: | hockey |
| given name: | Bower, John William |
| born: | Prince Albert, Saskatchewan<br>November 8, 1924 |
| height: | 1.80 m / 5'11" |
| weight: | 85.5 kg / 189 lbs |
| position: | goal |
| shoots: | left |

Like many boys who grew up on the prairies during the depression, Johnny Bower started playing hockey on frozen ponds. His family was poor but that did not stop him from pursuing the game he loved. Goal pads were crafted out of old mattresses, sticks were made of branches, and skates were passed down from one boy to another. Bower's goaltending skills developed quickly and he was soon playing junior hockey with the Prince Albert Black Hawks. In

1939, at the age of 15, Bower enlisted in the Canadian Army. He served for three and a half years, two of which were overseas. In 1943, he received a medical discharge, returned to Canada and rejoined the Prince Albert Black Hawks. The other teams in the league protested Bower's presence arguing that someone who had just served more than three years in the army could not still be of junior age. Bower's birth certificate could not be located and the league allowed him to finish the season.

In 1945, Bower joined the Cleveland Barons of the AHL. With the exception of the 1953-54 season, when he was with the New York Rangers, Bower played for 13 seasons in the minor pro leagues. His record there was exceptional. In 592 AHL games he recorded 45 shutouts and during the 1957-58 season he was not scored against in five consecutive games. He gained numerous all-star berths, was named the league's top goalie three times, and was the league's MVP for three consecutive seasons.

In the summer of 1958, the Toronto Maple Leafs drafted Bower from the New York Rangers organization. The 33-year-old goaltender was not interested in going to Toronto or the NHL. His attitude towards the big league had soured somewhat a few years earlier. During the 1953-54 season he played well for the Rangers, posting a 2.60 goals against average and recording five shutouts. The following year, though, the Rangers reassigned Bower to the minors. The Leafs, however, persuaded Bower with a lucrative two-year contract to join their team. At an age when most hockey players retire, Bower was about to establish himself as one of the finest goaltenders in the history of professional hockey.

Johnny Bower played for the Toronto Maple Leafs for 12 seasons. He won the Vezina Trophy as the league's top goalie in 1960-61. He shared the trophy with teammate Terry Sawchuk in 1964-65. Bower led the Leafs to four Stanley Cup titles. He played in five All-Star games, posting an incredible 0.60 goals against average and was named to the first all-star team in 1961. Bower was a superb competitor who gave it his all during both practices and games. He was fearless in protecting his goal, sprawling with acrobatic abandon to stop shots. He was also known for the speed with which he used his goal stick to poke the puck away from challenging shooters. The amiable goaltender also tried his hand at singing. He recorded "Honky the Christmas Goose" for Capitol Records in 1965.

Johnny Bower, the "ageless wonder," retired from the game after the 1969-70 season. Earlier, he had become the first player eligible to collect his NHL pension while still playing the game. He and his wife also celebrated their 25th wedding anniversary while he was an active player. Bower remained with the Toronto organization for another 20 years. He was the club's goaltending coach and scout. At times, when the Leafs needed a practice goalie, Bower would put on his skates and pads and astound the young players with his vigour.

# INDUCTIONS

| . . . | Providence Hockey Hall of Fame |
| . . . | Cleveland Barons Hockey Hall of Fame |
| 1976 | Hockey Hall of Fame |
| 1988 | Saskatchewan Sports Hall of Fame |

# AWARDS

| 1952 | Harry "Hap" Holmes Memorial Trophy  -  AHL Top Goaltender |
| 1955 | WHL Outstanding Goaltender Award |
| 1956 | Rhode Island Athlete of the Year |
| 1956 | Les Cunningham Trophy  -  AHL Most Valuable Player |
| 1957 | Harry "Hap" Holmes Memorial Trophy  -  AHL Top Goaltender |
| 1957 | Les Cunningham Trophy  -  AHL Most Valuable Player |
| 1958 | Harry "Hap" Holmes Memorial Trophy  -  AHL Top Goaltender |
| 1958 | Les Cunningham Trophy  -  AHL Most Valuable Player |
| 1961 | Vezina Trophy  -  NHL Top Goaltender |
| 1965 | Vezina Trophy  -  NHL Top Goaltender |

# ALL-STAR SELECTIONS

| 1950-51 | goal | AHL | Second Team |
| 1951-52 | goal | AHL | First Team |
| 1952-53 | goal | AHL | First Team |
| 1954-55 | goal | WHL | Second Team |
| 1955-56 | goal | AHL | First Team |
| 1956-57 | goal | AHL | First Team |
| 1957-58 | goal | AHL | First Team |
| 1960-61 | goal | NHL | First Team |

# RECORD

| | | | regular season | | | | | | | | playoffs | | | | | | | |
| year | team | league | GP | MIN | W | L | T | GA | AVE | SO | GP | MIN | W | L | T | GA | AVE | SO |
|---|---|---|---|---|---|---|---|---|---|---|---|---|---|---|---|---|---|---|
| 1945-46 | Cleveland | AHL | 41 | 2,460 | 18 | 17 | 6 | 160 | 3.90 | 4 | | | | | | | | |
| | Providence | AHL | 1 | 48 | 0 | 1 | 0 | 4 | 5.00 | 0 | | | | | | | | |
| 1946-47 | Cleveland | AHL | 40 | 2,400 | 22 | 11 | 7 | 124 | 3.10 | 3 | | | | | | | | |

| | | | regular season | | | | | | | | playoffs | | | | | | | |
|---|---|---|---|---|---|---|---|---|---|---|---|---|---|---|---|---|---|---|
| year | team | league | GP | MIN | W | L | T | GA | AVE | SO | GP | MIN | W | L | T | GA | AVE | SO |
| 1947-48 | Cleveland | AHL | 31 | 1,880 | 18 | 6 | 6 | 83 | 2.65 | 1 | | | | | | | | |
| 1948-49 | Cleveland | AHL | 37 | 2,200 | 23 | 9 | 5 | 127 | 3.43 | 3 | 5 | 329 | 2 | 3 | 0 | 23 | 4.19 | 0 |
| 1949-50 | Cleveland | AHL | 61 | 3,660 | 38 | 15 | 8 | 201 | 3.30 | 5 | 9 | 548 | 4 | 5 | 0 | 27 | 2.96 | 0 |
| 1950-51* | Cleveland | AHL | 70 | 4,280 | 44 | 21 | 5 | 213 | 2.99 | 5 | 11 | 703 | 8 | 3 | 0 | 32 | 2.73 | 0 |
| 1951-52 | Cleveland | AHL | 68 | 4,110 | 44 | 19 | 5 | 165 | 2.41 | 3 | 5 | 300 | 2 | 3 | 0 | 17 | 3.40 | 0 |
| 1952-53* | Cleveland | AHL | 61 | 3,680 | 40 | 19 | 2 | 155 | 2.53 | 6 | 11 | 745 | 7 | 4 | 0 | 21 | 1.69 | 4 |
| 1953-54 | NY Rangers | NHL | 70 | 4,200 | 29 | 31 | 10 | 182 | 2.60 | 5 | | | | | | | | |
| 1954-55 | Vancouver | WHL | 63 | 3,780 | 30 | 25 | 8 | 171 | 2.71 | 7 | 5 | 300 | 1 | 4 | 0 | 16 | 3.20 | 0 |
| | NY Rangers | NHL | 5 | 300 | 2 | 2 | 1 | 13 | 2.60 | 0 | | | | | | | | |
| 1955-56* | Providence | AHL | 61 | 3,710 | 45 | 14 | 2 | 174 | 2.81 | 3 | 9 | 540 | 7 | 2 | 0 | 23 | 2.56 | 0 |
| 1956-57 | Providence | AHL | 57 | 3,501 | 30 | 19 | 8 | 138 | 2.37 | 4 | 5 | 300 | 1 | 4 | 0 | 15 | 3.00 | 0 |
| | NY Rangers | NHL | 2 | 120 | 0 | 2 | 0 | 7 | 3.50 | 0 | | | | | | | | |
| 1957-58 | Cleveland | AHL | 64 | 3,870 | 37 | 23 | 3 | 140 | 2.17 | 8 | | | | | | | | |
| 1958-59 | Toronto | NHL | 39 | 2,340 | 15 | 17 | 7 | 107 | 2.74 | 3 | 12 | 746 | 5 | 7 | 0 | 39 | 3.14 | 0 |
| 1959-60 | Toronto | NHL | 66 | 3,960 | 34 | 24 | 8 | 180 | 2.73 | 5 | 10 | 645 | 4 | 6 | 0 | 31 | 2.88 | 0 |
| 1960-61 | Toronto | NHL | 58 | 3,480 | 33 | 15 | 10 | 145 | 2.50 | | 3 | 180 | 0 | 3 | 0 | 9 | 3.00 | 0 |
| 1961-62* | Toronto | NHL | 59 | 3,540 | 31 | 18 | 10 | 152 | 2.58 | 2 | 10 | 579 | 6 | 3 | 0 | 22 | 2.28 | 0 |
| 1962-63* | Toronto | NHL | 42 | 2,520 | 20 | 15 | 7 | 110 | 2.62 | 1 | 10 | 600 | 8 | 2 | 0 | 16 | 1.60 | 2 |
| 1963-64* | Toronto | NHL | 51 | 3,009 | 24 | 16 | 11 | 106 | 2.11 | 5 | 14 | 850 | 8 | 6 | 0 | 30 | 2.12 | 2 |
| 1964-65 | Toronto | NHL | 34 | 2,040 | 13 | 13 | 8 | 81 | 2.38 | 3 | 5 | 321 | 2 | 3 | 0 | 13 | 2.43 | 0 |
| 1965-66 | Toronto | NHL | 35 | 1,998 | 18 | 12 | 5 | 75 | 2.25 | 3 | 2 | 120 | 0 | 2 | 0 | 8 | 4.00 | 0 |
| 1966-67* | Toronto | NHL | 24 | 1,431 | 12 | 9 | 3 | 63 | 2.64 | 2 | 4 | 183 | 2 | 0 | 0 | 5 | 1.64 | 1 |
| 1967-68 | Toronto | NHL | 43 | 2,239 | 14 | 18 | 7 | 84 | 2.25 | 4 | | | | | | | | |
| 1968-69 | Toronto | NHL | 20 | 779 | 5 | 4 | 3 | 37 | 2.85 | 2 | 4 | 154 | 0 | 2 | 0 | 11 | 4.29 | 0 |
| 1969-70 | Toronto | NHL | 1 | 60 | 0 | 1 | 0 | 5 | 5.00 | 0 | | | | | | | | |

# BOYCHUK, ANDY

| | |
|---|---|
| sport: | athletics |
| given name: | Boychuk, Andrew Harry |
| born: | Orono, Ontario |
| | May 17, 1941 |
| height: | . . . |
| weight: | . . . |

*Photo courtesy of Canada's Sports Hall of Fame*

Andy Boychuk developed into one of Canada's top distance runners in the mid-1960s. He competed in distances from 5,000 metres to the marathon, being most successful in the latter event. Boychuk won his first national marathon title in 1966. He competed at the Commonwealth Games that year, placing tenth. In 1967, Boychuk placed sixth in the Boston Marathon in a Canadian record time of 2:18.17. That year he also defended his Canadian title and was named to the Pan American Games team. At the Games, Boychuk won the gold medal in a Pan American Games record time of 2:23.02. He crossed the finish line about 500 metres ahead of the second place finisher. For his fine performances in 1967, Andy Boychuk was honoured with the Jack W. Davies Trophy, awarded annually to the outstanding Canadian athlete in track and field.

In 1968, Boychuk won his third consecutive national marathon title. That same year, at the Motor City Marathon, Boychuk placed second to Jerome Drayton who was running the distance for the first time. Ironically, it was Boychuk who urged Drayton to try the marathon just a short time earlier. Both men represented Canada in the marathon at the 1968 Olympics, with Boychuk placing tenth in the rarefied air of Mexico City. Andy Boychuk won his fourth and last national marathon title in 1970.

## AWARDS

| | |
|---|---|
| 1967 | Jack W. Davies Trophy - Outstanding Canadian Athlete in Track and Field |
| 1967 | Sarnia Observer Citizen of 1967 |
| 1967 | Sarnia Area Outstanding Man of the Year |

| year | competition | event | placing | result | |
|------|-------------|-------|---------|--------|---|
| 1965 | Canadian Championships | 6 miles | 3 | | |
| | Hamilton | 10 miles | 3 | 56:17 .0 | |
| 1966 | Boston Marathon | marathon | 13 | 2:27:20 | |
| | Hamilton Around the Bay Race | 19.1 miles | 1 | 1:37:29 | |
| | Canadian Championships | marathon | 1 | 2:35:24 | |
| | Commonwealth Games | marathon | 10 | 2:58:45 .2 | |
| | | 6 miles | 8 | 29:54 .0 | |
| 1967 | Boston Marathon | marathon | 6 | 2:18:17 | cb |
| | Canadian Championships | marathon | 1 | 2:26:22 | |
| | | 10,000 m | 2 | 31:02 .0 | |
| | Pan American Games | marathon | 1 | 2:23:02 .4 | @ |
| 1968 | Canadian Championships | 10,000 m | 3 | 30:09 .6 | |
| | | marathon | 1 | 2:29:21 | |
| | Motor City Marathon | marathon | 2 | 2:24:19 | |
| | Olympic Marathon Trials-1 | marathon | 1 | 2:17:50 .0 | |
| | Olympic Games | marathon | 10 | 2:28:40 .2 | |
| 1969 | Dominion Day Meet | 6 miles | 1 | 28:50 .2 | |
| 1970 | Canadian Championships | marathon | 1 | 2:32:21 .0 | |
| | Boston Marathon | marathon | 8 | 2:21:06 | |
| | Commonwealth Games Trials | 5,000 m | 4 | 14:26 .6 | |
| | | 10,000 m | 3 | 29:41 .8 | |
| | Commonwealth Games | marathon | 10 | 2:18:45 .0 | |
| 1971 | Weribee | marathon | 1 | 2:18:34 .0 | |
| 1975 | Boston Marathon | marathon | 10 | 2:16:13 .0 | |
| | Bermuda International | marathon | 1 | 2:25:14 | |
| | Hamilton Around the Bay Race | 19.1 miles | 1 | 1:41:16 | |

cb   Canadian best

@   Pan American Games record

# BOYKO, BRUCE

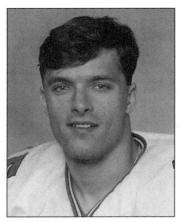

sport:        football
born:         Hamilton, Ontario
                March 2, 1967
height:       1.91 m / 6'3"
weight:       94.5 kg / 208 lbs
position:     slot back

*Photo courtesy of Royal Studios*

Bruce Boyko was a starter on the Western Michigan University football team for three years. In his junior year, he earned an honourable mention on the All-Mid-Atlantic Conference team after catching 44 passes. In his senior year, he caught 26 passes averaging 11.3 yards per reception. In total, Boyko caught 106 passes for 1,306 yards and scored 8 touchdowns. His college career numbers placed him fourth on the university's all-time list for receptions and total yards. During his college career, Boyko also had a streak of 23 consecutive games with at least one catch.

Bruce Boyko was selected by the Saskatchewan Roughriders in the second round, 9th overall, of the 1990 CFL Collegiate Draft. During the 1990 season, Boyko was used at the slot back position. The following year he played primarily on special teams.

## RECORD

| regular season | | | | scoring | | | | | | pass receiving | | | | |
|---|---|---|---|---|---|---|---|---|---|---|---|---|---|---|
| year | team | league | GP | TD | C | FG | S | PTS | | NO | YDS | AVE | LG | TD |
| 1990 | Saskatchewan | CFL | 18 | 0 | 0 | 0 | 0 | 0 | | 18 | 259 | 14.4 | 24 | 0 |
| 1991 | Saskatchewan | CFL | 18 | 0 | 0 | 0 | 0 | 0 | | 5 | 44 | 8.8 | 12 | 0 |

# BOYKO, DARREN

| | |
|---|---|
| sport: | hockey |
| born: | Winnipeg, Manitoba |
| | January 16, 1964 |
| height: | 1.75 m / 5'9" |
| weight: | 77 kg / 170 lbs |
| position: | center |
| shoots: | right |

Darren Boyko's first season of junior hockey was memorable. He helped the St. Boniface Saints capture the 1981 Manitoba junior hockey championship. En route, he won the Manitoba Junior Hockey League's scoring title, was named the league's MVP and Rookie of the Year, and was honoured with a First All-star team selection. The following two seasons he played junior hockey with the Winnipeg Warriors of the WHL.

Upon enrolling at the University of Toronto in the fall of 1983, Boyko joined its hockey team. He played an instrumental role in helping the Varsity Blues capture the national championship that season. The following year he served as captain of the team. In the mid-1980s, Boyko also played on Canada's national team.

In 1985, Boyko joined HIFK Helsinki of the Finnish league. A few years later, the Winnipeg Jets signed him as a free agent and his only appearance in the NHL occurred during the 1988-89 season. Subsequently, Darren Boyko returned to Finland, rejoined HIFK Helsinki and in time established himself as the top non-Finnish born point scorer in Finnish hockey.

## AWARDS

| | |
|---|---|
| 1980-81 | MVP - MJHL |
| 1980-81 | Rookie of the Year - MJHL |
| 1980-81 | Scoring Leader - MJHL |
| 1982-83 | Most Sportsman Like Player - WHL |

## ALL-STAR SELECTIONS

| | | | |
|---|---|---|---|
| 1980-81 | center | MJHL | First Team |

# RECORD

| year | team | league | regular season | | | | | playoffs | | | | |
|------|------|--------|-----|-----|-----|-----|-----|-----|-----|-----|-----|-----|
| | | | GP | G | A | PTS | PIM | GP | G | A | PTS | PIM |
| 1985-86 | Canada | | 4 | 1 | 1 | 2 | 0 | | | | | |
| | Helsinki | Finnish | 36 | 18 | 26 | 44 | 8 | 8 | 1 | 3 | 4 | 2 |
| 1986-87 | Helsinki | Finnish | 44 | 22 | 13 | 35 | 44 | | | | | |
| 1987-88 | Helsinki | Finnish | 44 | 14 | 40 | 54 | 16 | | | | | |
| 1988-89 | Winnipeg | NHL | 1 | 0 | 0 | 0 | 0 | | | | | |
| | Moncton | AHL | 18 | 3 | 7 | 10 | 2 | 4 | 0 | 0 | 0 | 0 |
| | Helsinki | Finnish | 34 | 15 | 15 | 30 | 10 | 2 | 0 | 0 | 0 | 0 |
| 1989-90 | Helsinki | Finnish | 42 | 12 | 20 | 32 | 36 | 2 | 1 | 0 | 1 | 2 |
| 1990-91 | Helsinki | Finnish | 42 | 16 | 22 | 38 | 20 | 3 | 0 | 3 | 3 | 4 |

# BOYTCHUK, WILLIAM

| | |
|---|---|
| sport: | soccer |
| born: | Dzuriv, Ukraine |
| | April 27, 1922 |
| height: | 1.75 m / 5'9" |
| weight: | 80.5 kg / 178 lbs |

William Boytchuk played soccer in post-World War II Europe while studying at the Ludwig Maximillian University in Munich. Upon immigrating to Toronto, he immediately set out to establish a Ukrainian sport club. In April 1948, the Ukrainian Sport Club Skala came into being. Boytchuk assumed the presidency of the club. At a subsequent meeting a few weeks later, the club was formally established and the name was changed to Sport Association Ukraina in honour of the most eminent sports club in Western Ukraine prior to the war, the Sport Association Ukraina of Lviv. Boytchuk was elected the association's first president, and served five one-year terms. During his first term, he saw the club grow from a handful of members to more than 100. In 1953 and 1956, Boytchuk was elected president when the club was in turmoil. Boytchuk's no-nonsense approach allowed him to overcome most obstacles and ensure the club's viability. Boytchuk, though, did not restrict himself to administrative work; he also coached and managed bantam and midget soccer teams.

In 1963, Boytchuk was elected President of the National Soccer League (NSL). He oversaw the merger of the NSL with the Eastern Canada Professional Soccer League into the National Soccer League of Eastern Canada in 1967 and was elected its president. He served in that capacity for over a decade. Among his accomplishments of that time period was the initiation of the building of Lamport Stadium in Toronto's west end.

In 1969, William Boytchuk was elected to the Toronto City Council. Apart from a two-year hiatus from 1976 to 1978, he was re-elected through the 1991 municipal election. While in office, Boytchuk was at the forefront of assisting community sport clubs and organizations. He was an ardent supporter of Toronto's bid for the 1996 Olympics and served on the City of Toronto's 1996 Olympic Committee.

In 1968, SA Ukraina's founder William Boytchuk was named the club's honourary life president in recognition of his twenty years of service for the club. During those years, SA Ukraina evolved into the most dynamic Ukrainian sport club organized in Canada by post-war immigrants. Subsequently, the National Soccer League also recognized Boytchuk for his service by naming him Honourary Life President.

## RECORD

administration

| year | position |
|------|----------|
| 1948 | President, Sport Association Ukraina |
| 1953 | President, Sport Association Ukraina |
| 1956-57 | President, Sport Association Ukraina |
| 1962 | President, Sport Association Ukraina |
| 1963-67 | President, National Soccer League |
| 1967-81 | President, National Soccer League of Eastern Canada |
| 1986-90 | member, City of Toronto's 1996 Olympic Committee |

# BRODA, TURK

| | |
|---|---|
| sport: | hockey |
| given name: | Broda, Walter Edward |
| born: | Brandon, Manitoba |
| | May 15, 1914 |
| died: | Toronto, Ontario |
| | October 17, 1972 |
| height: | 1.75 m / 5'9" |
| weight: | 81.5 kg / 180 lbs |
| position: | goal |
| shoots: | left |

Walter "Turk" Broda became a goalie by default. As a youngster he was somewhat overweight and his skating was poor. When he decided to play organized hockey, tending the net was an obvious assignment. Broda took the task seriously and his play improved progressively. During his early teens, one of his major disappointments was failing to make the Brandon Native Sons junior club. In the spring of 1933, when the Native Sons goalie was ruled ineligible, Broda was given an opportunity to play. He excelled in the nets as the Native Sons battled it out in the Memorial Cup playoffs. He then played for a season with the Winnipeg Monarchs before joining the Detroit Olympics of the International League.

After the 1935-36 season, Toronto Maple Leafs' general manager Conn Smythe purchased Turk Broda for a then record price of $8,000. Smythe believed that Broda would be the ideal goaltender for the Leafs. Broda did not disappoint; in 14 seasons, he led the club to eight Stanley Cup finals, of which the club won five, including an unprecedented three consecutive championships. During those years Broda won the Vezina trophy on two occasions and was twice named to the first all-star team and once to the second. Squeezed in among those accomplishments were two years of service with the Canadian Army during World War II. Overseas, Broda played catcher on the championship softball team in the Canadian Army.

One of the most jovial and relaxed goaltenders of all time, Broda had an unflappable disposition. Nevertheless, he was a fierce competitor and the higher the stakes, the better he played. As the Leafs vied for their third consecutive Stanley Cup in the spring of 1949, Broda posted a 1.57 goals against average. Two years later, his average of 1.06 in the playoffs once again helped the Leafs capture the Cup.

Broda remained chubby all his life and in November of 1949 his waistline and that of a few other Leafs became the target of Conn Smythe. Broda was ordered to lose seven pounds in five days or be taken out of the nets. To give Broda an added incentive, Smythe called up the club's reserve goalie from the farm team. The "antifat edict" was soon referred to as the "Battle of the Bulge" by the media and millions of Canadians waited to see whether Broda would succeed. After five days of dieting, Broda achieved the weight by less than a pound.

After hanging up his skates, Broda embarked on a coaching career. He guided the Weston Dukes to the Ontario Junior B championship in his first year of coaching. He then moved to Ottawa where he coached the Senators of the QHL for a year. Commencing with the 1954-55 season, he was behind the Toronto Marlboro bench for ten years. During that period, the Marlies won three league titles and two Memorial Cups, in 1955 and again in 1956. He later coached Charlotte of the EHL, Moncton of the Maritime junior circuit, the London Nationals of the OHA and the Quebec Aces of the AHL. During the off-season Turk Broda excelled in golf and enjoyed thoroughbred horse racing.

## INDUCTIONS

| 1967 | Hockey Hall of Fame |
| 1983 | Manitoba Sports Hall of Fame |

## AWARDS

| 1941 | Vezina Trophy - NHL Top Goaltender |
| 1948 | Vezina Trophy - NHL Top Goaltender |

## ALL-STAR SELECTIONS

| 1940-41 | goal | NHL | First Team |
| 1941-42 | goal | NHL | Second Team |
| 1947-48 | goal | NHL | First Team |

## RECORD

| | | | regular season | | | | | | | | playoffs | | | | | | | |
|---|---|---|---|---|---|---|---|---|---|---|---|---|---|---|---|---|---|---|
| year | team | league | GP | MIN | W | L | T | GA | AVE | SO | GP | MIN | W | L | T | GA | AVE | SO |
| 1935-36* | Detroit | IHL | 44 | 2,820 | 26 | 18 | 3 | 101 | 2.14 | 6 | 6 | 360 | 6 | 0 | 0 | 8 | 1.33 | 1 |
| 1936-37 | Toronto | NHL | 45 | 2,770 | 22 | 19 | 4 | 106 | 2.30 | 3 | 2 | 133 | 0 | 2 | 0 | 5 | 2.26 | 0 |
| 1937-38 | Toronto | NHL | 48 | 2,980 | 24 | 15 | 9 | 127 | 2.56 | 6 | 7 | 452 | 4 | 3 | 0 | 13 | 1.73 | 1 |
| 1938-39 | Toronto | NHL | 48 | 2,990 | 19 | 20 | 9 | 107 | 2.15 | 8 | 10 | 617 | 5 | 5 | 0 | 20 | 1.94 | 2 |
| 1939-40 | Toronto | NHL | 47 | 2,900 | 25 | 17 | 5 | 108 | 2.23 | 4 | 10 | 657 | 6 | 4 | 0 | 19 | 1.74 | 1 |
| 1940-41 | Toronto | NHL | 48 | 2,970 | 28 | 14 | 6 | 99 | 2.00 | 5 | 7 | 438 | 3 | 4 | 0 | 15 | 2.05 | 0 |
| 1941-42* | Toronto | NHL | 48 | 2,960 | 27 | 18 | 3 | 136 | 2.76 | 6 | 13 | 780 | 8 | 5 | 0 | 31 | 2.38 | 1 |
| 1942-43 | Toronto | NHL | 50 | 3,000 | 22 | 19 | 9 | 159 | 3.18 | 1 | 6 | 439 | 2 | 4 | 0 | 20 | 2.73 | 0 |

| | | | regular season | | | | | | | | playoffs | | | | | | | |
|---|---|---|---|---|---|---|---|---|---|---|---|---|---|---|---|---|---|---|
| year | team | league | GP | MIN | W | L | T | GA | AVE | SO | GP | MIN | W | L | T | GA | AVE | SO |
| 1945-46 | Toronto | NHL | 15 | 900 | 6 | 6 | 3 | 53 | 3.53 | 0 | | | | | | | | |
| 1946-47* | Toronto | NHL | 60 | 3,600 | 31 | 19 | 10 | 172 | 2.87 | 4 | 11 | 680 | 8 | 3 | 0 | 27 | 2.38 | 1 |
| 1947-48* | Toronto | NHL | 60 | 3,600 | 32 | 15 | 13 | 143 | 2.38 | 5 | 9 | 557 | 8 | 1 | 0 | 20 | 2.15 | 1 |
| 1948-49* | Toronto | NHL | 60 | 3,600 | 22 | 25 | 13 | 161 | 2.68 | 5 | 9 | 574 | 8 | 1 | 0 | 15 | 1.57 | 1 |
| 1949-50 | Toronto | NHL | 68 | 4,040 | 30 | 25 | 12 | 167 | 2.48 | 9 | 7 | 450 | 3 | 4 | 0 | 10 | 1.33 | 3 |
| 1950-51* | Toronto | NHL | 31 | 1,827 | 14 | 11 | 5 | 68 | 2.23 | 6 | 8 | 492 | 5 | 1 | 0 | 9 | 1.10 | 2 |
| 1951-52 | Toronto | NHL | 1 | 30 | 0 | 1 | 0 | 3 | 6.00 | 0 | 2 | 120 | 0 | 2 | 0 | 7 | 3.50 | 0 |

# BUCYK, JOHNNY

"Chief"

| | |
|---|---|
| sport: | hockey |
| given name: | Bucyk, John Paul |
| born: | Edmonton, Alberta |
| | May 12, 1935 |
| height: | 1.83 m / 6'0" |
| weight: | 98 kg / 215 lbs |
| position: | left wing |
| shoots: | left |

Johnny Bucyk first began to play hockey on a rink in his back yard. The rink's creation was unintentional. His mother dumped dirty laundry water out into the back and it froze quickly in the bitter Edmonton winters. Johnny, his brother Billy, and all the neighbourhood kids would spend endless hours chasing the puck on that rink. Many years later Bill Bucyk recalled: "We didn't have any hockey sticks so we'd use old broomsticks, and for pucks we'd use old tennis balls or stones or frozen balls of manure from the milkwagon horse. . . We didn't have any pads so we'd use old magazines stuck under our socks, old Eaton's catalogues. We used to put Johnny in goal a lot because he was the smallest. And he was good too."[3]

Johnny Bucyk, though, started to grow. At age ten, while playing pee-wee he switched to defense. Later he became a forward. At 14, Bucyk was noticed by a Detroit Red Wing scout and put on the team's negotiation list. Upon joining the Edmonton Oil Kings Junior A team, Bucyk showed his determination to become a star. Unfortunately, his skating ability lacked sorely. As a result, the Oil Kings sent him to a figure skating school for a whole summer. The experience helped Bucyk tremendously. After completing his junior tenure, he was assigned to Detroit's affiliate the Edmonton Flyers of the WHL. With the club, he won the league's rookie of the year honour in 1954-55 after establishing a league record for assists and points. The following season he made his NHL debut with the Red Wings. Detroit, though, did not have Bucyk in its plans and he was traded to Boston in July of 1957 for Terry Sawchuk.

Over the next 21 seasons, Bucyk became a fixture with the Boston club. For a number of years he played on a line with Vic Stasiuk and Bronco Horvath. The high scoring threesome was referred to as the "Uke Line." Twice he savoured champagne from the Stanley Cup and on two occasions he was named to an all-star team. One of his greatest individual achievements was scoring 51 goals during the 1970-71 season.

A cool and calm athlete, Bucyk twice won the Lady Byng Trophy as the most gentlemanly player in the league. He was a model of consistency, able to perform solidly every game. Bucyk was also a natural leader; he had a way of inspiring teammates. In particular, Bucyk did everything possible to make rookies feel welcome. As a result of his leadership, on two occasions he was entrusted with the captaincy of the Bruins.

Upon retiring, the Bruins retained Johnny Bucyk as an administrative assistant. He also made his way into the press booth, doing colour commentary on the Bruins' radio network. For his contribution to the club, the Bruins honoured Bucyk by retiring his number 9 sweater in 1980. A year later he was enshrined in the Hockey Hall of Fame. Johnny Bucyk is the uncle of hockey player Randy Bucyk.

## INDUCTIONS

1981        Hockey Hall of Fame

## AWARDS

1955        Rookie of the Year  -  WHL
1963        E. Dufresne Trophy  -  Outstanding Boston Player in Home Games
1966        E. Dufresne Trophy  -  Outstanding Boston Player in Home Games
1971        Lady Byng Trophy  -  NHL Most Gentlemanly Player
1974        Lady Byng Trophy  -  NHL Most Gentlemanly Player
1977        Lester Patrick Trophy  -  NHL for Contributions to American Hockey

## ALL-STAR SELECTIONS

| 1954-55 | left wing | WHL | Second Team |
| 1967-68 | left wing | NHL | Second Team |
| 1970-71 | left wing | NHL | First Team |

# RECORD

| year | team | league | regular season GP | G | A | PTS | PIM | playoffs GP | G | A | PTS | PIM |
|------|------|--------|----|----|----|-----|-----|----|----|----|-----|-----|
| 1953-54 | Edmonton | WHL | 2 | 2 | 0 | 2 | 2 | | | | | |
| 1954-55* | Edmonton | WHL | 70 | 30 | 58 | 88 | 57 | 9 | 1 | 6 | 7 | 7 |
| 1955-56 | Detroit | NHL | 38 | 1 | 8 | 9 | 20 | 10 | 1 | 1 | 2 | 8 |
| | Edmonton | WHL | 6 | 0 | 0 | 0 | 0 | | | | | |
| 1956-57 | Detroit | NHL | 66 | 10 | 11 | 21 | 41 | 5 | 0 | 1 | 1 | 0 |
| 1957-58 | Boston | NHL | 68 | 21 | 31 | 52 | 57 | 12 | 0 | 4 | 4 | 16 |
| 1958-59 | Boston | NHL | 69 | 24 | 36 | 60 | 36 | 7 | 2 | 4 | 6 | 6 |
| 1959-60 | Boston | NHL | 56 | 16 | 36 | 52 | 26 | | | | | |
| 1960-61 | Boston | NHL | 70 | 19 | 20 | 39 | 48 | | | | | |
| 1961-62 | Boston | NHL | 67 | 20 | 40 | 60 | 32 | | | | | |
| 1962-63 | Boston | NHL | 69 | 27 | 39 | 66 | 36 | | | | | |
| 1963-64 | Boston | NHL | 62 | 18 | 36 | 54 | 36 | | | | | |
| 1964-65 | Boston | NHL | 68 | 26 | 29 | 55 | 24 | | | | | |
| 1965-66 | Boston | NHL | 63 | 27 | 30 | 57 | 12 | | | | | |
| 1966-67 | Boston | NHL | 59 | 18 | 30 | 48 | 12 | | | | | |
| 1967-68 | Boston | NHL | 72 | 30 | 39 | 69 | 8 | 3 | 0 | 2 | 2 | 0 |
| 1968-69 | Boston | NHL | 70 | 24 | 42 | 66 | 18 | 10 | 5 | 6 | 11 | 0 |
| 1969-70* | Boston | NHL | 76 | 31 | 38 | 69 | 13 | 14 | 11 | 8 | 19 | 2 |
| 1970-71 | Boston | NHL | 78 | 51 | 65 | 116 | 8 | 7 | 2 | 5 | 7 | 0 |
| 1971-72* | Boston | NHL | 78 | 32 | 51 | 83 | 4 | 15 | 9 | 11 | 20 | 6 |
| 1972-73 | Boston | NHL | 78 | 40 | 53 | 93 | 12 | 5 | 0 | 3 | 3 | 0 |
| 1973-74 | Boston | NHL | 76 | 31 | 44 | 75 | 8 | 16 | 8 | 10 | 18 | 4 |
| 1974-75 | Boston | NHL | 78 | 29 | 52 | 81 | 10 | 3 | 1 | 0 | 1 | 0 |
| 1975-76 | Boston | NHL | 77 | 36 | 47 | 83 | 20 | 12 | 2 | 7 | 9 | 0 |
| 1976-77 | Boston | NHL | 49 | 20 | 23 | 43 | 12 | 5 | 0 | 0 | 0 | 0 |
| 1977-78 | Boston | NHL | 53 | 5 | 13 | 18 | 4 | | | | | |

# BUCYK, RANDY

| | |
|---|---|
| sport: | hockey |
| born: | Edmonton, Alberta |
| | November 9, 1962 |
| height: | 1.80 m / 5'11" |
| weight: | 84 kg / 185 lbs |
| position: | center |
| shoots: | left |

*Photo courtesy of the Salt Lake Golden Eagles*

Randy Bucyk played five years of varsity hockey while pursuing a civil engineering degree at Boston's Northeastern University. He then played for a season and a half with Sherbrooke of the AHL. In January of 1986, Bucyk was signed as a free agent by the Montreal Canadiens. He appeared in 19 games with the Canadiens. The following season he was once again with Sherbrooke. In the summer of 1987, Bucyk signed as a free agent with the Calgary Flames. He made two starts with the club before being shipped to Salt Lake City of the IHL. Randy Bucyk is the nephew of hockey player Johnny Bucyk.

## RECORD

| year | team | league | regular season | | | | | playoffs | | | | |
|------|------|--------|----|----|----|-----|-----|----|----|----|-----|-----|
| | | | GP | G | A | PTS | PIM | GP | G | A | PTS | PIM |
| 1984-85* | Sherbrooke | AHL | 62 | 21 | 26 | 47 | 20 | 8 | 0 | 0 | 0 | 20 |
| 1985-86 | Montreal | NHL | 17 | 4 | 2 | 6 | 8 | 2 | 0 | 0 | 0 | 0 |
| | Sherbrooke | AHL | 43 | 18 | 33 | 51 | 22 | | | | | |
| 1986-87 | Sherbrooke | AHL | 70 | 24 | 39 | 63 | 28 | 17 | 3 | 11 | 14 | 2 |
| 1987-88 | Calgary | NHL | 2 | 0 | 0 | 0 | 0 | | | | | |
| | Salt Lake City | IHL | 75 | 37 | 45 | 82 | 68 | 19 | 7 | 8 | 15 | 12 |
| 1988-89 | Salt Lake City | IHL | 79 | 28 | 59 | 87 | 24 | 14 | 5 | 5 | 10 | 4 |
| | Canada | | 4 | 0 | 0 | 0 | 2 | | | | | |
| 1989-90 | Salt Lake City | IHL | 67 | 22 | 41 | 63 | 16 | 11 | 2 | 6 | 8 | 10 |
| 1990-91 | Salt Lake City | IHL | 18 | 4 | 4 | 8 | 2 | | | | | |

# BUDY, TIM

sport:          hockey
given name:     Budy, Timothy
born:           Selkirk, Manitoba
                February 14, 1967
height:         1.83 m / 6'0"
weight:         86 kg / 190 lbs
position:       left wing
shoots:         left

Tim Budy played three years of junior hockey for the Notre Dame Varsity Hounds. In his last season he registered 40 goals, added 48 assists and was named the team's MVP. His proficiency in hockey and his outstanding academic standing resulted in a full scholarship to Colorado College. Of the four years Budy played collegiate hockey, two were as team captain. In his senior year he led the team with 23 goals and 23 assists. For his academic and athletic achievements, Budy was named WCHA athlete of the year and was nominated for the Hober Baker Award which honours the outstanding player in collegiate hockey. Budy was the New Jersey Devils' first draft choice, 17th overall, in the 1988 NHL Supplemental Draft. He made his professional debut with Utica of the AHL.

## AWARDS

1989    Manitoba Ukrainian Sportsman of the Year (co-winner)
1989    Athlete of the Year  -  WCHL

## RECORD

| year | team | league | regular season | | | | | playoffs | | | | |
|------|------|--------|----|---|---|-----|-----|----|---|---|-----|-----|
|      |      |        | GP | G | A | PTS | PIM | GP | G | A | PTS | PIM |
| 1988-89 | Utica | AHL | 3 | 0 | 0 | 0 | 2 | | | | | |

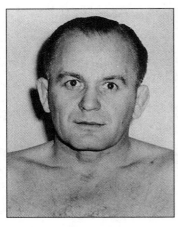

# BUNKA, GEORGE

| | |
|---|---|
| sport: | wrestling, professional wrestling |
| born: | St. Julien, Saskatchewan |
| | April 22, 1912 |
| height: | 1.73 m / 5'8" |
| weight: | 71.5 kg / 158 lbs |

When George Bunka was a youngster living in rural Saskatchewan, his uncle Alex Boytzun, a prominent Alberta wrestler, came to visit. Bunka immediately took a liking to his uncle and decided then and there to become a wrestler. In the spring of 1934, Bunka joined his uncle at his home at Leduc, Alberta, and started to train under his guidance. Only days into his workouts, Bunka cracked a rib and was immobilized. He resumed training in the fall of 1935. A few months later, in the spring of 1936, Bunka won the Northern Alberta championship in the 158 pound category. He followed that by winning the Alberta championship and a ticket to the 1936 Olympic trials. Unfortunately, he failed to make the team.

In 1937, Bunka turned professional and after a couple of bouts in Edmonton he moved to Vancouver. There he became a crowd favourite, competing in hundreds of matches. In 1945, he won the Western Canada middleweight championship. In 1946, Bunka sailed to England, where he was based while working on a professional circuit that operated in France, Switzerland, and Holland. He fought as often as five or six times a week. In 1948 Bunka travelled to Mexico where he wrestled for six months. He left the country after having bullets thrown at him during a match by fans of an opponent. Upon returning to Canada, he continued to wrestle out of Vancouver. A knee injury terminated Bunka's wrestling career in 1952.

In the ring Bunka was an exciting wrestler to watch. "Keep 'em guessing!" was his motto since he never wrestled the same way twice. Once, after being thrown from the ring, he slipped beneath the ring, rose from the other side, and surprised his opponent by pinning him from the back. He was a fighter who went all out on every occasion to entertain his fans.

George Bunka was also an outstanding classical wrestling coach. In 1939, after coaching for only a year, he trained an unprecedented six winners at the British Columbia championship. At the 1940 national championship, four of his proteges won titles. Some years later, he coached Nick Mohammed to the Canadian title and a berth on the 1952 Canadian Olympic team.

# BURCHUK, MIKE

| | |
|---|---|
| sport: | volleyball |
| born: | Ste Rose du Lac, Manitoba |
| | October 18, 1949 |
| height: | 1.80 m / 5'11" |
| weight: | 84 kg / 184 lbs |

*Photo courtesy of Volleyball Canada*

Mike Burchuk began his volleyball coaching career with the Lord Selkirk High School in Winnipeg, which he led to back-to-back provincial titles in 1977 and 1978. In 1978, he also coached Manitoba's provincial team to a third-place finish in the national championship and, a year later, to the gold medal at the Canada Games.

These early successes resulted in Burchuk being hired prior to the 1980-81 season by the University of Winnipeg to coach the women's volleyball team. In his first season with the team, Burchuk's club won 45 games, lost 23, and tied 2 to place second in the GPAC conference. The following year, the club placed fifth in the nation. It was quickly becoming evident that a national championship team was in the making. It came sooner than most expected. The following season, the club did not lose once as it powered its way to a Canadian championship. It was the first of six consecutive national titles for perhaps the most powerful dynasty in the history of Canadian women's volleyball. In those six years the club lost only 11 games in 365 starts. It posted two undefeated seasons and won 33 of 36 tournaments that it entered.

Before Mike Burchuk left the University of Winnipeg in the spring of 1989, the teams that he coached played a total of 539 games in nine seasons, winning 478, tying 5 and losing 56 for a winning percentage of 89.4. In addition, the teams won 43 of the 56 tournaments they entered.

During the University of Winnipeg days, Burchuk also coached the Wesmen Volleyball Club to two national juvenile titles in 1983 and 1988, and the Prairie Blue Volleyball Club to the national championship in 1984.

In 1980, Mike Burchuk made his international coaching debut when he was named assistant coach of Canada's team to the NORCECA Junior Championships. Thereafter, he served as an assistant coach of Canada's senior team at a World Championship, a World University Games and the 1984 Olympics.  In 1986 he was named coach of Canada's junior team and in the spring of 1989, Mike Burchuk was named head coach of Canada's national volleyball team.

## AWARDS

| | |
|---|---|
| 1981 | CIAU Coach of the Year |
| 1982 | CIAU Coach of the Year |
| 1983 | CIAU Coach of the Year |
| 1983 | Manitoba Ukrainian Sportsman of the Year |

## RECORD

| year | competition | capacity | team | placing |
|---|---|---|---|---|
| 1979 | Canada Games | coach | Manitoba | 1 |
| 1980 | Canadian Junior Championships | coach | Skinners VB Club | 4 |
| | NORCECA Junior Championships | assistant | Canada | |
| 1981 | GPAC League | coach | University of Winnipeg | 2 |
| | Canadian Junior Championships | coach | Wesmen VB Club | 2 |
| 1982 | World Championships | assistant | Canada | 11 |
| | CIAU Championships | coach | University of Winnipeg | 5 |
| 1983 | NORCECA Championships | assistant | Canada | |
| | World University Games | assistant | Canada | 4 |
| | Canadian Juvenile Championships | coach | Wesmen VB Club | 1 |
| | CIAU Championships | coach | University of Winnipeg | 1 |
| 1984 | Olympic Games | assistant | Canada | |
| | Canadian Championships | coach | Prairie Blue VB Club | 1 |
| | CIAU Championships | coach | University of Winnipeg | 1 |
| 1985 | Canada Cup | assistant | Canada | |
| | World University Games | assistant | Canada | |
| | CIAU Championships | coach | University of Winnipeg | 1 |
| 1986 | NORCECA Junior Championships | coach | Canada | |
| | CIAU Championships | coach | University of Winnipeg | 1 |
| 1987 | World Junior Championships | coach | Canada | |
| | CIAU Championships | coach | University of Winnipeg | 1 |
| 1988 | Canadian Juvenile Championships | coach | Wesmen VB Club | 1 |
| | CIAU Championships | coach | University of Winnipeg | 1 |
| 1989 | CIAU Championships | coach | University of Winnipeg | 4 |
| | NORCECA Championships | coach | Canada | 2 |
| | World Cup | coach | Canada | 8 |
| 1990 | Goodwill Games | coach | Canada | 7 |

| year | competition | capacity | team | placing |
|------|-------------|----------|------|---------|
| 1990 | World Championships | coach | Canada | 14 |
| 1991 | Pan American Games | coach | Canada | |

# BUREGA, BILL

"Wild Bill"

| | |
|---|---|
| sport: | hockey |
| given name: | Burega, William |
| born: | Winnipeg, Manitoba |
| | March 13, 1932 |
| height: | 1.85 m / 6'1" |
| weight: | 91 kg / 200 lbs |
| position: | defense |
| shoots: | left |

Bill Burega finished his junior hockey career in 1952 on a winning note. His club, the Winnipeg Monarchs, won the junior championship of Western Canada. Subsequently, Burega played professional hockey for over a decade. He skated for 13 teams in six leagues. During the 1955-56 season he made a brief appearance with the Toronto Maple Leafs of the NHL. An extremely hard-hitting blue liner, Burega forced opponents to keep their heads up. He also liked to mix it up.

## RECORD

| year | team | league | regular season | | | | | playoffs | | | | |
|------|------|--------|----|----|----|-----|-----|----|----|----|-----|-----|
| | | | GP | G | A | PTS | PIM | GP | G | A | PTS | PIM |
| 1952-53 | Glace Bay | MMHL | 72 | 6 | 10 | 16 | 163 | 11 | 0 | 1 | 1 | 15 |
| 1953-54 | Ottawa/Quebec | QHL | 41 | 0 | 5 | 5 | 115 | 7 | 0 | 0 | 0 | 8 |
| 1954-55* | Pittsburgh | AHL | 57 | 2 | 5 | 7 | 140 | 10 | 0 | 2 | 2 | 24 |
| 1955-56 | Toronto | NHL | 4 | 0 | 1 | 1 | 4 | | | | | |
| | Winnipeg | WHL | 67 | 2 | 18 | 20 | 151 | 14 | 2 | 4 | 6 | 33 |
| 1956-57 | Winnipeg | WHL | 70 | 1 | 14 | 15 | 197 | | | | | |
| 1957-58 | Buffalo | AHL | 56 | 0 | 7 | 7 | 136 | | | | | |
| 1958-59 | Saskatoon | WHL | 62 | 2 | 10 | 12 | 104 | | | | | |
| 1959-60 | Sault Ste. Marie | EPHL | 2 | 0 | 0 | 0 | 6 | | | | | |
| | Spokane | WHL | 65 | 4 | 14 | 18 | 162 | | | | | |

| | | | regular season | | | | | playoffs | | | | |
| --- | --- | --- | --- | --- | --- | --- | --- | --- | --- | --- | --- | --- |
| year | team | league | GP | G | A | PTS | PIM | GP | G | A | PTS | PIM |
| 1960-61 | Calgary | WHL | 67 | 3 | 32 | 35 | 73 | 5 | 1 | 1 | 2 | 6 |
| 1961-62 | Los Angeles | WHL | 70 | 1 | 14 | 15 | 142 | | | | | |
| 1962-63 | Los Angeles | WHL | 70 | 1 | 11 | 12 | 142 | 3 | 0 | 2 | 2 | 6 |
| 1963-64 | Los Angeles | WHL | 51 | 0 | 7 | 7 | 75 | 12 | 0 | 3 | 3 | 31 |
| 1964-65 | Vancouver | WHL | 70 | 3 | 10 | 13 | 161 | 5 | 0 | 0 | 0 | 10 |

# BURTNYK, KERRY

"Bubba"

sport:     curling

born:     Reston, Manitoba
November 24, 1958

height:     1.83 m / 6'0"

weight:     81.5 kg / 180 lbs

*Photo courtesy of the Western Canada Pictorial Index*

Kerry Burtnyk's rise to the pinnacle of Canadian curling was meteoric. At the age of 19, he was the winner of the 1978 Manitoba Junior Championship. A year later, he won the gold medal at the Canada Games. In the spring of 1981, Burtnyk skipped his rink to the Manitoba title. Competing in the Canadian Championship, he curled consistently to advance to the final. In the championship game, the Burtnyk rink scored one of the most stunning victories in the history of the championship. Down by two points in the last end, Burtnyk scored three to secure a 5-4 victory. Not only did the victory advance him to the World Championship where the team placed third, but it also rewrote the Canadian curling record book. At the age of 22, Burtnyk became the youngest skip ever to win the Canadian championship. The success of the 1980-81 curling season did not end there. Burtnyk was also the top money winner in cash bonspiels across the nation that year.

In subsequent years, stockbroker Burtnyk was unable to duplicate the successes of 1980-81 season, winning but a number of cash bonspiels. In 1987, he declined an invitation to participate in the Olympic trials. A year later, Kerry Burtnyk once again won the Manitoba title but was unsuccessful in his attempt to capture the Canadian championship.

| 1981 | Manitoba Ukrainian Sportsman of the Year |
| --- | --- |

RECORD

| year | competition | position | placing | result |
| --- | --- | --- | --- | --- |
| 1978 | Manitoba Junior Championship | skip | 1 | |
| 1979 | Canada Winter Games | skip | 1 | |
| 1981 | Manitoba Championship | skip | 1 | |
| | Canadian Championship | skip | 1 | 10-3 |
| | World Championship | skip | 3 | 8-2 |
| 1988 | Manitoba Championship | skip | 1 | |
| | Canadian Championship | skip | 4 | 7-4 |

*Photo courtesy of the Philadelphia Flyers*

# BUSNIUK, MIKE

| sport: | hockey |
| --- | --- |
| given name: | Busniuk, Michael |
| born: | Fort William, Ontario (now Thunder Bay) December 13, 1951 |
| height: | 1.91 m / 6'3" |
| weight: | 91 kg / 200 lbs |
| position: | defense |
| shoots: | right |

Mike Busniuk was drafted out of the University of Denver in the 5th round of the 1971 draft by the Montreal Canadiens. After completing his collegiate tenure in 1974, he was assigned to Montreal's farm team, the Nova Scotia Voyageurs. Busniuk was on two AHL championship Calder Cup teams with Nova Scotia, in 1976 and 1977. In the fall of 1977, he signed as a free agent with the Philadelphia Flyers. Failing to make the team, he was assigned to the Maine Mariners of the AHL. Busniuk drank champagne from the Calder Cup for the third time as the Mariners won the AHL championship that season. The following year, the Mariners repeated as champions and Busniuk entered the record books as the first player to be on four consecutive Calder Cup teams. In the fall of 1979, Busniuk won a starting position with the Flyers which he held for two seasons.

Mike Busniuk is the brother of hockey player Ron Busniuk.

RECORD

| year | team | league | regular season | | | | | playoffs | | | | |
|---|---|---|---|---|---|---|---|---|---|---|---|---|
| | | | GP | G | A | PTS | PIM | GP | G | A | PTS | PIM |
| 1974-75 | Nova Scotia | AHL | 69 | 15 | 17 | 32 | 94 | 6 | 1 | 0 | 1 | 2 |
| 1975-76 | Beauce | NAHL | 65 | 14 | 52 | 66 | 179 | 14 | 1 | 12 | 13 | 61 |
| * | Nova Scotia | AHL | | | | | | 1 | 0 | 0 | 0 | 4 |
| 1976-77* | Nova Scotia | AHL | 80 | 1 | 15 | 16 | 160 | 12 | 0 | 0 | 0 | 4 |
| 1977-78* | Maine | AHL | 76 | 5 | 15 | 20 | 72 | 12 | 0 | 1 | 1 | 44 |
| 1978-79* | Maine | AHL | 79 | 10 | 34 | 44 | 215 | 10 | 0 | 5 | 5 | 4 |
| 1979-80 | Philadelphia | NHL | 71 | 2 | 18 | 20 | 93 | 19 | 2 | 4 | 6 | 23 |
| | Maine | AHL | 3 | 2 | 1 | 3 | 7 | | | | | |
| 1980-81 | Philadelphia | NHL | 72 | 1 | 5 | 6 | 204 | 6 | 0 | 1 | 1 | 11 |
| 1981-82 | Maine | AHL | 78 | 12 | 26 | 38 | 203 | 4 | 1 | 0 | 1 | 20 |
| 1982-83 | Maine | AHL | 11 | 0 | 5 | 5 | 14 | 17 | 1 | 5 | 6 | 105 |
| 1983-84* | Maine | AHL | 2 | 0 | 1 | 1 | 2 | 16 | 1 | 1 | 2 | 2 |

*Photo courtesy of the Buffalo Sabres*

# BUSNIUK, RON

"Buzzy"

| | |
|---|---|
| sport: | hockey |
| given name: | Busniuk, Ronald Edward |
| born: | Fort William, Ontario |
| | (now Thunder Bay) |
| | August 13, 1948 |
| height: | 1.80 m / 5'11" |
| weight: | 81.5 kg / 180 lbs |
| position: | right wing |
| shoots: | right |

Ron Busniuk won the rookie of the year honours while playing for the Fort William Canadians of the TBJHL.  Subsequently he played for the University of Minnesota at Deluth.  Property of the Montreal Canadiens, Busniuk did not make the team and was assigned to the farm system.  In the summer of 1972, he was sold to the Buffalo Sabres.  During the next two seasons he made brief appearances with the club.  In the 1974 Intra-League Draft, he was picked up by the Detroit Red Wings.  The fast skating playmaker, though, jumped to the rival WHA.  He played for Minneapolis, New England and Edmonton.

In 1984 and once again in 1985, Busniuk coached the Thunder Bay Twins to the Allan Cup championship.  Ron Busniuk is the brother of hockey player Mike Busniuk.

## ALL-STAR SELECTIONS

1973-74    defense  AHL   First Team

## RECORD

| year | team | league | regular season | | | | | playoffs | | | | |
|------|------|--------|-----|---|---|-----|-----|-----|---|---|-----|-----|
|      |      |        | GP  | G | A | PTS | PIM | GP  | G | A | PTS | PIM |
| 1970-71 | Montreal | AHL | 59 | 11 | 9 | 20 | 136 | 3 | 0 | 1 | 1 | 10 |
| 1971-72* | Nova Scotia | AHL | 67 | 13 | 13 | 26 | 133 | 15 | 3 | 5 | 8 | 74 |
| 1972-73 | Buffalo | NHL | 1 | 0 | 0 | 0 | 0 | | | | | |
| * | Cincinnati | AHL | 71 | 5 | 34 | 39 | 205 | 15 | 1 | 7 | 8 | 39 |
| 1973-74 | Buffalo | NHL | 5 | 0 | 3 | 3 | 4 | | | | | |
| | Cincinnati | AHL | 68 | 7 | 24 | 31 | 146 | 5 | 1 | 1 | 2 | 8 |
| 1974-75 | Minnesota | WHA | 73 | 2 | 21 | 23 | 176 | 12 | 2 | 1 | 3 | 63 |
| 1975-76 | Minnesota | WHA | 60 | 2 | 11 | 13 | 150 | | | | | |
| | New England | WHA | 11 | 0 | 3 | 3 | 55 | 17 | 0 | 2 | 2 | 14 |
| 1976-77 | New England | WHA | 55 | 1 | 9 | 10 | 141 | | | | | |
| | Edmonton | WHA | 29 | 2 | 2 | 4 | 83 | 5 | 0 | 2 | 2 | 37 |
| 1977-78 | Edmonton | WHA | 58 | 2 | 18 | 20 | 157 | 5 | 0 | 0 | 0 | 18 |

# CHAMBUL, BORYS

| | |
|---|---|
| sport: | athletics |
| born: | Toronto, Ontario |
| | February 17, 1953 |
| height: | 1.94 m / 6'4" |
| weight: | 112 kg / 246 lbs |

Borys Chambul began competing in the discus throw at the age of fourteen for the Ukrainian Youth Association (SUM) at the annual track and field meets organized by the Association of Ukrainian Sport Clubs of North America (USCAK). By the age of 16, he was competing at the national senior level. After graduating from high school, Chambul accepted an athletic scholarship to the University of Washington, in Seattle. In 1975, he represented Canada at the World University Games placing fifth with a toss of 55.60 metres. Chambul was in top form the following year. He won the NCAA championship and the Canadian championship. Shortly before the start of the 1976 Olympics, at a Pre-Olympic meet in the United States, Chambul hurled the discus 65.40 metres to break the NCAA, Canadian and Commonwealth records.

At the Olympics, Chambul succumbed to pressure and failed to qualify for the final. "My big mistake was trying to go for the gold medal in the preliminary round instead of taking it calmly to assure myself of a spot in the final."[4] In 1978, Chambul in part redeemed himself when he won the gold medal at the Commonwealth Games. He then set his sights on the Moscow Olympics and took a year off from work to train. Canada, though, joined the boycott of the Olympics. "I was in the best shape of my life in 1980. . . I was throwing the discus further than the record distance I had set in 1976."[5] Boris Chambul is the brother of shot putter Lubomyr Chambul.

## RECORD

| year | competition | event | placing | result |
|---|---|---|---|---|
| 1972 | North American Baltic Chmps | discus | 2 | 54.17 m |
| 1974 | NCAA Championships | discus | 6 | 182 ft 6 in |
| 1975 | Canadian Championships | discus | 2 | 54.18 m |
| | World University Games | discus | 5 | 55.38 m |

| year | competition | event | placing | result |
|------|-------------|-------|---------|--------|
| 1976 | NCAA Championships | discus | 1 | 61.64 m |
|      | Canadian Championships | discus | 1 | 56.30 m |
|      | Olympic Trials | discus | 1 | 60.46 m |
|      | Pre-Olympic Meet | discus | 1 | 65.40 m* |
|      | Olympic Games | discus | qr | 55.86 m |
| 1977 | Canadian Championships | discus | 1 | 54.08 m |
|      | World Cup Trials | discus | 2 | 57.46 m |
|      | United States Championships | discus | 7 | 198 ft 6 in |
| 1978 | Canadian Championships | discus | 1 | 59.82 m |
|      | United States Championships | discus | 7 | 197 ft 9 in |
|      | Commonwealth Games | discus | 1 | 59.70 m |
| 1979 | Pan American Games Trials | discus | 1 | 61.26 m |
|      | Pan American Games | discus | 5 | 59.42 m |
|      | World Cup Trials | discus | 4 | 57.88 m |
| 1980 | Canadian Championships | discus | 1 | 64.32 m |
|      | Olympic Alternative (Norway) | discus | 4 | 60.68 m |
|      | Free Olympiad | discus | 1 | 62.78 m |
| 1981 | Canadian Championships | discus | 3 | 55.28 m |
| 1982 | Canadian Championships | discus | 1 | 58.76 m |
| 1984 | Free Olympiad | discus | 2 | 55.50 m |
| 1987 | Ontario Championships | discus | 2 | 53.14 m |
| 1988 | Ontario Championships | discus | 3 | 53.90 m |

\* Canadian, Commonwealth and NCAA record

qr qualifying round

# CHAMBUL, LUBOMYR

"Luby"

| | |
|---|---|
| sport: | athletics |
| born: | Toronto, Ontario |
| | October 29, 1958 |
| height: | 1.86 m / 6'1" |
| weight: | 106.5 kg / 235 lbs |

Lubomyr Chambul began competing in field events in 1972 for the Ukrainian Youth

Association (SUM) at the annual track and field meets organized by the Association of Ukrainian Sport Clubs of North America (USCAK). Eventually, Chambul became a shot put specialist. At the 1976 Olympic trials, he placed sixth in the event. Some years later, while attending the Western Kentucky University, Chambul was consistently ranked as one of the top shot putters in the United States collegiate ranks. At the 1982 NCAA indoor championships, Chambul placed fifth with a personal best toss of 19.24 metres. In 1984, he won the national shot put title.

Chambul represented Canada at the 1983 World University Games and the 1982 and 1986 Commonwealth Games, winning a bronze medal at the former with a toss of 17.46 metres. Lubomyr Chambul is the brother of discus thrower Borys Chambul.

## RECORD

| year | competition | event | placing | result |
|------|-------------|-------|---------|--------|
| 1976 | Olympic Trials | shot put | 6 | 14.01 m |
| | Canadian Junior Championships | shot put | 4 | 14.05 m |
| 1978 | Canadian Championships | shot put | 5 | 15.21 m |
| 1980 | Canadian Championships | shot put | 4 | 17.53 m |
| | Free Olympiad | shot put | 1 | 17.48 m |
| 1981 | NCAA Championships | shot put | 7 | 19.08 m |
| | Canadian Championships | shot put | 2 | 18.17 m |
| 1982 | NCAA Indoor Championships | shot put | 5 | 19.24 m |
| | Canadian Championships | shot put | 4 | 17.90 m |
| | Commonwealth Games | shot put | 3 | 17.46 m |
| 1983 | Canadian Championships | shot put | 3 | 18.70 m |
| | World University Games | shot put | 7 | 17.61 m |
| 1984 | Canadian Championships | shot put | 1 | 18.45 m |
| 1985 | Canadian Championships | shot put | 2 | 17.54 m |
| | World Cup Trials | shot put | 4 | 16.72 m |
| 1986 | Canadian Indoor Championships | shot put | 1 | 17.73 m |
| | Canadian Championships | shot put | 2 | 17.94 m |
| | Commonwealth Games | shot put | 7 | 16.86 m |
| 1987 | Ontario Championships | shot put | 2 | 15.92 m |

# CHARALAMBIJ, IVAN

sport:     canoeing
born:      Mila 23, Romania
           July 28, 1955
height:    1.65 m / 5'5"
weight:    59 kg / 130 lbs

Ivan Charalambij was a child when he was initiated into the art of paddling by his father who was a fisherman on the Danube River. The young Charalambij immediately took a liking to paddling and at the age of 12 he started to compete. In the early 1970s, Charalambij was recognized as one of Romania's top junior paddlers with Olympic potential. At the 1971 Romanian Championships, he won two events in junior C-2 competition and was named to the star-studded national team. He would be developed into a pairs specialist. Charalambij graduated to the senior level in 1973 placing second in two events. In 1975 and 1976, Charalambij won two medals at each of the national championships.

Ivan Charalambij and his partner arrived in Montreal for the 1976 Olympics as the heavy favourites to win medals in both the 500 and 1000-metre C-2 events. The duo had just won the 1000-metre event at the Moscow Pre-Olympic Regatta, defeating all the East-European favourites. In Montreal, Ivan Charalambij decided to forgo Olympic glory by defecting to Canada a day prior to his first event.

After settling in Canada, Charalambij set his sights on the 1980 Olympics. For four years he trained and competed with the Rideau and Carlton Place Canoe Clubs. He dominated the Canadian Championships and represented Canada at numerous international competitions. Unfortunately, Ivan Charalambij's dream of paddling at the Olympics was not realised since initially Canada could not guarantee his safety in the USSR and subsequently Canada joined the boycott of the Moscow Olympics.

## RECORD

| year | competition | event | | placing | result |
|------|-------------|-------|---|---------|--------|
| 1971 | Romanian Junior Championships | C-2 | 500 m | 1 | |
| | | C-2 | 5,000 m | 1 | |

| year | competition | event | | placing | result |
|------|-------------|-------|---|---------|--------|
| 1972 | Romanian Junior Championships | C-2 | 500 m | 1 | |
| | | C-2 | 1000 m | 1 | |
| | Kyiv International Junior Regatta | C-2 | 500 m | 3 | |
| | | C-2 | 1000 m | 2 | |
| | World Junior Championships | C-7 | 500 m | 3 | |
| 1973 | Romanian Championships | C-2 | 1000 m | 2 | |
| | | C-2 | 10,000 m | 2 | |
| 1974 | Romanian Championships | C-2 | 1000 m | 2 | |
| | | C-2 | 10,000 m | 2 | |
| 1975 | Romanian Championships | C-2 | 1000 m | 1 | |
| | | C-2 | 10,000 m | 1 | |
| 1976 | Romanian Championships | C-2 | 500 m | 1 | |
| | | C-2 | 1000 m | 1 | |
| | Moscow Pre-Olympic Regatta | C-2 | 1000 m | 1 | |
| 1977 | Canadian Championships | C-1 | 500 m | 1 | 2:15.9 |
| | | C-2 | 500 m | 1 | 2:10.1 |
| | | C-2 | 1000 m | 1 | 4:34.3 |
| | North American Championships | C-1 | 500 m | 2 | |
| | | C-1 | 1000 m | 1 | |
| | | C-1 | 10,000 m | 1 | |
| 1978 | Canada Cup | C-1 | 500 m | 1 | |
| | | C-1 | 1000 m | 1 | |
| | Canadian Championships | C-2 | 500 m | 1 | 2:04.4 |
| | | C-4 | 1000 m | 1 | 4:42.9 |
| | Pan American Championships | C-2 | 500 m | 2 | |
| | | C-2 | 1000 m | 2 | |
| 1979 | Pan American Championships | C-2 | 500 m | 2 | 2:03.5 |
| | | C-2 | 1000 m | 2 | 4:05.1 |
| | Copenhagen International Regatta | C-2 | 500 m | 2 | 1:47.3 |
| | | C-2 | 10,000 m | 2 | 45:27.7 |
| | Milan International Regatta | C-1 | 500 m | 4 | |
| | | C-1 | 1000 m | 3 | 4:19.38 |
| | | C-1 | 10,000 m | 7 | |
| | Nottinghamshire Regatta | C-1 | 1000 m | 7 | 4:50.43 |
| | | C-2 | 10,000 m | 7 | 45:51.1 |
| | World Championships | C-1 | 10,000 m | 12 | 53:06.5 |
| | | C-2 | 1000 m | 9 | 4:09.5 |

# CHEPESUIK, MIKE

| | |
|---|---|
| sport: | wrestling, football |
| given name: | Chepesuik, Michael William |
| born: | Fort William, Ontario |
| | (now Thunder Bay) |
| | April 25, 1908 |
| height: | 1.83 m / 6'0" |
| weight: | 77-91 kg / 170-200 lbs |

*Photo courtesy of the Canadian Football Hall of Fame and Museum*

Growing up in Fort William, Mike Chepesuik excelled in soccer and rowing. In 1924, as a member of the Westfort Wanderers, he won the local junior soccer championship. While at the Ontario Agricultural College (forerunner of the University of Guelph), Chepesuik was regarded as an outstanding all-round athlete. The Hall of Fame plaque which enshrines his career at Guelph reads: "In his unassuming way, he soon found a place on almost every college team. Wrestling was his forte, although rugby, soccer and track and field, basketball and baseball found him ready. . ."

After graduation, Chepesuik moved to Toronto and joined the Toronto Argonaut Rowing Club. He played football with the Argos at the guard position in the years 1930-34, winning the Grey Cup in 1933. A year later he was named to the league's all-star team. In addition, Mike Chepesuik rowed with the club and was a member of the foursome that won the prestigious Fourth of July race in Detroit in 1930.

Mike Chepesuik also wrestled. In 1930, he won the Canadian 174 pound wrestling title and was named to represent Canada at the British Empire Games (forerunner of the Commonwealth Games). There he won the gold medal in his weight class. Unfortunately, his name was misspelled at the pre-game registration and to this day all records suggest that a Mike Chepewick rather than Mike Chepesuik won the title. In 1932, Chepesuik failed in his bid to compete at the Los Angeles Olympics when he lost, by a decision, in the final of the Canadian Olympic trials. Most in attendance, though, were of the opinion that Chepesuik out-wrestled his opponent. Discouraged, he retired from the sport with a record of never having been pinned in competition.

Mike Chepesuik remained a physical fitness buff for life. In his eighties, he was still doing 400 push-ups a day. In 1992, at the inaugural dinner of the Canadian Ukrainian Sports Hall of

Fame, he was recognized as an honourary member. Mike Chepesuik is the uncle of William Chepesiuk of Toronto, who maintained the family's rowing tradition by winning the Canadian junior straight fours title in 1971.

## INDUCTIONS

1984    University of Guelph Sports Hall of Fame

## ALL-STAR SELECTIONS

1934    guard    Canadian Rugby Union

## RECORD

wrestling

| year | competition | event | placing |
|------|-------------|-------|---------|
| 1930 | Intercollegiate Championships | heavyweight | 1 |
|      |             | light-heavyweight | 1 |
|      | Canadian Championships | 174 lbs | 1 |
|      | British Empire Games | 174 lbs | 1 |
| 1932 | Olympic Trials | 174 lbs | 2 |

# CHERKAS, RON

| | |
|---|---|
| sport: | football |
| born: | Kamsack, Saskatchewan |
| | December 30, 1953 |
| height: | 1.93 m / 6'4" |
| weight: | 109 kg / 240 lbs |
| position: | defensive tackle |

*Photo courtesy of the Canadian Football Hall of Fame and Museum*

Ron Cherkas played collegiate football while on a scholarship at Utah State. In 1976, he joined the Saskatchewan Roughriders as the club's territorial exemption. During his rookie season, the big, strapping Cherkas saw limited action as the clubs's backup defensive tackle and end.

He also appeared in his first Grey Cup game that year, albeit in a backup capacity. The following year Cherkas won a starting position with the Roughriders.

Prior to the start of the 1980 season, Ron Cherkas was traded to the Hamilton Tiger-Cats. A few weeks later he was traded to the Winnipeg Blue Bombers. He returned to Saskatchewan part way through the 1982 season. During the 1983 training camp, Cherkas was traded to the British Columbia Lions. He failed to make the team and was released. That season he became a journeyman player, appearing in three games with the Montreal Concordes and five with the Winnipeg Blue Bombers, before returning to finish the year with the Lions. For Cherkas the return to Lions was timely; the team advanced to the Grey Cup game only to lose the fall classic by one point. Ron Cherkas finished his football career with the Lions in 1984.

# CHOMYC, LANCE

| | |
|---|---|
| sport: | football |
| born: | Edmonton, Alberta |
| | March 2, 1963 |
| height: | 1.83 m / 6'0" |
| weight: | 88.5 kg / 195 lbs |
| position: | kicker |

Lance Chomyc, a punter and a placekicker, joined the University of Toronto Varsity Blues football club in 1983 after having played for two years with the junior Edmonton Wildcats. In his first year of varsity football, Chomyc was named to the OUAA All-Star team after leading the nation in punting and scoring. In 1984, he was second in scoring. Chomyc was selected in the sixth round, 46th overall, in the 1985 CFL College Draft by the Ottawa Rough Riders. Prior to the start of his rookie season, Chomyc was released by Ottawa and picked up on a 21-day trial by the Saskatchewan Roughriders. The western Roughriders also released him and he joined the Toronto Argonauts on another 21-day trial. This time he made the team and contributed 72 points during the year.

In 1986, Chomyc established a team record when he made all six field goal attempts in a single game. He was named to the CFL All-Star team after leading the Eastern Division in scoring with 157 points. It was the first of three consecutive Eastern Division scoring titles.

During the 1988 season, Chomyc established a club record for field goals in a game with seven. He did it on two occasions. The season concluded with Chomyc scoring 207 points, only the third player in league history to surpass the 200 point mark.

In 1990, Chomyc established a league record for most converts in a season with 76. He also became the Argos' all-time scoring leader when he surpassed Zenon Andrusyshyn's record of 899 points. The following year, after testing the free-agent market in the United States, Chomyc re-signed with the Argos. It was a year that Argo fans will not forget. The club acquired Notre Dame star Raghid "Rocket" Ismail. The club won all its home games and it won the Grey Cup. In the process, Chomyc broke the club's single season scoring record when he eclipsed the 207 point mark. Then with two seconds remaining in the final game of the season, Chomyc kicked a 35-yard field goal to establish a CFL single season scoring record with 236 points.

Chomyc participated in two Grey Cup games. En route to the 1987 fall classic, he tied the league record for most field goals in a playoff game with six. In the final, the Argos lost 38-36. After the record-breaking 1991 season, Chomyc and the Argos rolled through the playoffs and won the Grey Cup on an icy field in Winnipeg.

## AWARDS

1991        Lew Hayman Trophy  -  CFL Outstanding Canadian, Eastern Division

## ALL-STAR SELECTIONS

| 1986 | kicker | CFL | All-Eastern |
| 1986 | kicker | CFL | |
| 1988 | kicker | CFL | All-Eastern |
| 1991 | kicker | CFL | All-Eastern |
| 1991 | kicker | CFL | |

## RECORD

| scoring | | | regular season | | | | | | playoffs | | | | | | Grey Cup game | | | | | |
|---|---|---|---|---|---|---|---|---|---|---|---|---|---|---|---|---|---|---|---|---|
| year | team | league | GP | TD | C | FG | S | PTS | GP | TD | C | FG | S | PTS | GP | TD | C | FG | S | PTS |
| 1985 | Toronto | CFL | 12 | 0 | 21 | 14 | 9 | 72 | | | | | | | | | | | | |
| 1986 | Toronto | CFL | 18 | 0 | 38 | 37 | 8 | 157 | 2 | 0 | 6 | 4 | 0 | 18 | | | | | | |
| 1987 | Toronto | CFL | 18 | 0 | 44 | 47 | 8 | 193 | 2 | 0 | 3 | 7 | 1 | 25 | 1 | 0 | 3 | 3 | 0 | 12 |
| 1988 | Toronto | CFL | 18 | 0 | 58 | 48 | 5 | 207 | 1 | 0 | 1 | 1 | 0 | 4 | | | | | | |
| 1989 | Toronto | CFL | 18 | 0 | 35 | 33 | 10 | 144 | 1 | 0 | 1 | 0 | 0 | 1 | | | | | | |
| 1990 | Toronto | CFL | 18 | 0 | 76 | 38 | 10 | 200 | 2 | 0 | 5 | 5 | 1 | 21 | | | | | | |
| 1991* | Toronto | CFL | 18 | 0 | 64 | 55 | 7 | 236 | 1 | 0 | 5 | 1 | 0 | 8 | 1 | 0 | 4 | 2 | 2 | 12 |

| regular season | | | field goals | | | | | punting | | | | kickoffs | | | |
|---|---|---|---|---|---|---|---|---|---|---|---|---|---|---|---|
| year | team | league | GP | ATT | GD | AVE | LK | NO | YDS | AVE | LP | NO | YDS | AVE | LK |
| 1985 | Toronto | CFL | 12 | 26 | 14 | 30.2 | 47 | 1 | 37 | 37.0 | 37 | 9 | 457 | 50.8 | 61 |
| 1986 | Toronto | CFL | 18 | 48 | 37 | 32.3 | 49 | 0 | 0 | 0.0 | 0 | 19 | 1,059 | 49.5 | 83 |
| 1987 | Toronto | CFL | 18 | 64 | 47 | 36.2 | 55 | 1 | 45 | 45.0 | 45 | 65 | 3,807 | 58.6 | 95 |
| 1988 | Toronto | CFL | 18 | 59 | 49 | 30.6 | 57 | 0 | 0 | 0.0 | 0 | 0 | 0 | 0.0 | 0 |
| 1989 | Toronto | CFL | 18 | 55 | 33 | 31.2 | 50 | 17 | 691 | 40.6 | 54 | 48 | 2,688 | 56.0 | 90 |
| 1990 | Toronto | CFL | 18 | 52 | 38 | 28.8 | 52 | 0 | 0 | 0 | 0 | 110 | 5,688 | 51.7 | 68 |
| 1991* | Toronto | CFL | 18 | 65 | 55 | 29.7 | 53 | 13 | 434 | 33.4 | 48 | 50 | 2,574 | 51.5 | 73 |

| playoffs | | | field goals | | | | | punting | | | | kickoffs | | | |
|---|---|---|---|---|---|---|---|---|---|---|---|---|---|---|---|
| year | team | league | GP | ATT | GD | AVE | LK | NO | YDS | AVE | LP | NO | YDS | AVE | LK |
| 1986 | Toronto | CFL | 2 | 5 | 4 | 31.5 | 43 | 0 | 0 | 0.0 | 0 | 4 | 198 | 49.5 | 53 |
| 1987 | Toronto | CFL | 2 | 8 | 7 | 24.3 | 34 | 0 | 0 | 0.0 | 0 | 0 | 0 | 0.0 | 0 |
| 1988 | Toronto | CFL | 1 | 1 | 1 | 39.0 | 39 | 0 | 0 | 0.0 | 0 | 0 | 0 | 0.0 | 0 |
| 1989 | Toronto | CFL | 1 | 0 | 0 | 0.0 | 0 | 0 | 0 | 0.0 | 0 | 2 | 109 | 54.5 | 70 |
| 1990 | Toronto | CFL | 2 | 6 | 5 | 31.0 | 38 | 0 | 0 | 0.0 | 0 | 0 | 0 | 0.0 | 0 |
| 1991* | Toronto | CFL | 1 | 1 | 1 | 24.0 | 24 | 1 | 42 | 42.0 | 42 | 0 | 0 | 0.0 | 0 |

| Grey Cup game | | | field goals | | | | | punting | | | | kickoffs | | | |
|---|---|---|---|---|---|---|---|---|---|---|---|---|---|---|---|
| year | team | league | GP | ATT | GD | AVE | LK | NO | YDS | AVE | LP | NO | YDS | AVE | LK |
| 1987 | Toronto | CFL | 1 | 5 | 3 | 38.7 | 50 | | | | | | | | |
| 1991* | Toronto | CFL | 1 | 4 | 2 | 23.0 | 27 | | | | | | | | |

# CHORNEY, MARC

| | |
|---|---|
| sport: | hockey |
| born: | Sudbury, Ontario |
| | November 8, 1959 |
| height: | 1.83 m / 6'0" |
| weight: | 89 kg / 196 lbs |
| position: | defense |
| shoots: | left |

After an outstanding career with the University of North Dakota that included an All-American selection, Marc Chorney joined the Pittsburgh Penguins who had selected him in the sixth round, 115th overall in the 1979 NHL Entry Draft. After two years with Pittsburgh, he was traded to Los Angeles at the start of the 1983-84 season. In the summer of 1984, Chorney was signed by the Washington Capitals as a free agent. He failed to make the team and was demoted to the AHL. Marc Chorney eventually returned to Northern Ontario where he helped the senior Thunder Bay Twins capture the Allan Cup in 1988.

## RECORD

| year | team | league | regular season | | | | | playoffs | | | | |
| | | | GP | G | A | PTS | PIM | GP | G | A | PTS | PIM |
|---|---|---|---|---|---|---|---|---|---|---|---|---|
| 1980-81 | Pittsburgh | NHL | 8 | 1 | 6 | 7 | 14 | 2 | 0 | 1 | 1 | 2 |
| 1981-82 | Pittsburgh | NHL | 60 | 1 | 6 | 7 | 63 | 5 | 0 | 0 | 0 | 0 |
| | Erie | AHL | 6 | 1 | 3 | 4 | 4 | | | | | |
| 1982-83 | Pittsburgh | NHL | 67 | 3 | 5 | 8 | 66 | | | | | |
| 1983-84 | Pittsburgh | NHL | 4 | 0 | 1 | 1 | 8 | | | | | |
| | Los Angeles | NHL | 71 | 3 | 9 | 12 | 58 | | | | | |
| 1984-85 | Binghamton | AHL | 48 | 4 | 25 | 29 | 38 | 7 | 0 | 4 | 4 | 9 |

# CHORNEY, TERRIS

| sport: | football |
|---|---|
| born: | Iterna, Saskatchewan |
| | November 11, 1969 |
| height: | 1.88 m / 6'2" |
| weight: | 121 kg / 267 lbs |
| position: | centre |

In high school Terris Chorney excelled in hockey and football. He played six-man football in his home town of Iterna but moved to Saskatoon in grade 12 in order to play a higher calibre of game. As co-captain, and playing both offence and defence, he led the Holy Cross Crusaders of Saskatoon to the 1986 Provincial 5A Football Championship. His talents were recognized when he was selected to the North Team for the Provincial Senior Bowl. Chorney was named team captain and contributed to the team's victory in the Bowl game. In winter,

Chorney was an imposing defenseman playing in Melville. He was recruited widely by both junior football and hockey clubs.

Chorney chose to devote his training to football. In 1987, he joined the Regina Rams football club of the Prairie Junior Football Conference and won a starting position at the right guard. That year the Rams won their conference and the Canadian championship. Chorney was named the club's Rookie of the Year. In 1988, Chorney enrolled at the University of Nebraska in the civil engineering program. He became a walk-on with University of Nebraska Cornhuskers football club where he played at the centre position. In February of 1992, the Edmonton Eskimos selected Terris Chorney in the fourth round, 26th overall, of the CFL draft.

# CHYCHRUN, JEFF

| | |
|---|---|
| sport: | hockey |
| born: | LaSalle, Quebec |
| | May 3, 1966 |
| height: | 1.93 m / 6'4" |
| weight: | 96 kg / 212 lbs |
| position: | defense |
| shoots: | right |

Photo courtesy of the Philadelphia Flyers

A native of LaSalle, Quebec, Jeff Chychrun grew up and played minor hockey in Ottawa. In the fall of 1983, he began his junior tenure with the Kingston Canadians of the OHL. He played a tough and an aggressive game. This impressed the Philadelphia Flyers and they drafted him as an underage junior in the second round, 37th overall of the 1984 NHL Entry Draft. Chychrun played two more years of junior hockey before moving up into the professional ranks.

During the 1986-87 season, Chychrun made his professional debut. He played mostly with the Hershey Bears of the AHL. The following season, Chychrun was once again playing for Hershey. The club won the Calder Cup, emblematic of the league championship. Chychrun earned himself a starting position with the Flyers during the 1988 training camp. For the next three seasons he was part of the tough, high intensity Philadelphia blueline corps. He paid a price for the aggressiveness, spending the equivalent of ten games in the penalty box. In the summer of 1991, Chychrun was traded to the Los Angeles Kings.

## RECORD

| year | team | league | regular season | | | | | playoffs | | | | |
|------|------|--------|----|---|---|-----|-----|----|---|---|-----|-----|
| | | | GP | G | A | PTS | PIM | GP | G | A | PTS | PIM |
| 1985-86 | Hershey | AHL | | | | | | 4 | 0 | 1 | 1 | 9 |
| | Kalamazoo | IHL | | | | | | 3 | 1 | 0 | 1 | 0 |
| 1986-87 | Philadelphia | NHL | 1 | 0 | 0 | 0 | 4 | | | | | |
| | Hershey | AHL | 74 | 1 | 17 | 18 | 239 | 4 | 0 | 0 | 0 | 10 |
| 1987-88 | Philadelphia | NHL | 3 | 0 | 0 | 0 | 4 | | | | | |
| | Hershey | AHL | 55 | 0 | 5 | 5 | 210 | 12 | 0 | 2 | 2 | 44 |
| 1988-89 | Philadelphia | NHL | 80 | 1 | 4 | 5 | 245 | 19 | 0 | 2 | 2 | 65 |
| 1989-90 | Philadelphia | NHL | 79 | 2 | 7 | 9 | 250 | | | | | |
| 1990-91 | Philadelphia | NHL | 36 | 0 | 6 | 6 | 105 | | | | | |

# CHUMAK, VALENTIN

sport:          athletics
born:           . . ., Ukraine
                July 2, 1949
height:         . . .
weight:         . . .

*Photo courtesy of the Ontario Track & Field Association*

Valentin Chumak is probably the only athlete in the world who can claim title to both a Canadian and Ukrainian Championship. In 1977, he won the Ukrainian Championship in the hammer throw and was ranked tenth in the world with a best throw of more than 77 metres. For reasons unknown, he was not selected to the Ukrainian team for the USSR championships. Chumak went at his own expense. Emotionally exhausted, he fared poorly. Upset with the selection committee and with his own performance, he quit training.

In 1982, Chumak moved to Egypt to be with his Egyptian wife. There he coached for a while before moving on to Turkey and finally settling in Canada. To gain exposure in the track community, something that was necessary to gain a coaching position, Chumak started to throw the hammer again. In 1985, he won the Canadian Championship and went on to pursue a coaching career at the National Sports Centre in Downsview, Ontario.

## RECORD

| year | competition | event | placing | result |
|---|---|---|---|---|
| 1971 | Ukrainian Spartakiade | shot put | 2 | |
| 1975 | Znamensky Memorial | hammer | 2 | |
| 1977 | Ukrainian Championships | hammer | 1 | 75.86 m |
| 1985 | . . . | hammer | 1 | 65.46 m |
| | Canadian Championships | hammer | 1 | 60.40 m |

# CHYZOWSKI, DAVE

| | |
|---|---|
| sport: | hockey |
| born: | Edmonton, Alberta |
| | July 11, 1971 |
| height: | 1.85 m / 6'1" |
| weight: | 86 kg / 190 lbs |
| position: | left wing |
| shoots: | left |

*Photo courtesy of the New York Islanders*

The New York Islanders made Dave Chyzowski their number one pick, second overall, in the 1989 NHL Entry Draft. The Islanders were looking for a scorer and the scouting reports suggested that Chyzowski was a good one. The season preceding the draft, while playing junior hockey for the Kamploops Blazers, he scored 56 goals in 68 games. His slap shot was timed at more than 145 km/h (90 mph). It was quickly released and extremely accurate.

Dave Chyzowski cracked the Islanders' line-up in the fall of 1989 and played impressively. In December, he was named to Canada's national team for the 1990 World Junior Championship.

The Islanders gave Chyzowski permission to join the team. At the world championship in Finland, Chyzowski led Canada to the gold medal by scoring a team-leading nine goals and four assists. He was named Canada's MVP and was honoured with a berth on the World Junior first All-Star team. Upon returning to the Islanders, Chyzowski's play was plagued by inconsistency. To regain confidence he was reassigned back to Kamploops. The following season, Dave Chyzowski was once again playing with the Islanders.

## ALL-STAR SELECTIONS

| 1990 | left wing | World Junior All-Stars | First Team |

## RECORD

| | | | regular season | | | | | playoffs | | | | |
|---|---|---|---|---|---|---|---|---|---|---|---|---|
| year | team | league | GP | G | A | PTS | PIM | GP | G | A | PTS | PIM |
| 1989-90 | NY Islanders | NHL | 34 | 8 | 6 | 14 | 45 | | | | | |
| | Springfield | AHL | 4 | 0 | 0 | 0 | 7 | | | | | |
| 1990-91 | NY Islanders | NHL | 56 | 5 | 9 | 14 | 61 | | | | | |
| | Capital District | AHL | 7 | 3 | 6 | 9 | 22 | | | | | |

| international | | | | | | | | |
|---|---|---|---|---|---|---|---|---|
| year | team | competition | | GP | G | A | PTS | PIM | Place |
| 1990 | Canada | World Junior Championship | | 7 | 9 | 4 | 13 | 2 | 1 |

# COOPER, JOE

| sport: | hockey |
|---|---|
| given name: | Krupiak, Joseph |
| born: | Winnipeg, Manitoba |
| | December 14, 1914 |
| died: | Tifton, Georgia, USA |
| | March 30, 1979 |
| height: | 1.88 m / 6'2" |
| weight: | 91 kg / 200 lbs |
| position: | defense |
| shoots: | right |

As a youngster, Joe Cooper enjoyed playing hockey. His immigrant parents, though, did not share their son's enthusiasm for the game. In fact, they were very much against his playing hockey. As a result, he had to hide his skates from them for quite some time. Cooper managed to overcome that hurdle, and in a short period of time developed into a fine prospect with a reputation for his bruising bodychecks and scoring ability. He played junior hockey with the Winnipeg Knights of Columbus and the Selkirk Fishermen.

In 1934, Cooper signed with the New York (Brooklyn) Crescent of the EHL for $50 a week. It was more money than he had ever seen. A year later he was playing with the Philadelphia Ramblers of the Canadian-American Hockey League for an annual salary of $1,700. He also had his first taste of the NHL that year appearing in one game with the New York Rangers. In the fall of 1936, Cooper won a regular starting position with the Rangers. In 1938, he was dealt to the Chicago Black Hawks. He played with the club through to the end of the 1945-46 season only taking time to serve in the Canadian armed forces in 1942 and 1943. While stationed in Ottawa, he played hockey with the Ottawa Commandos of the QSHL. The team won the Allan Cup in 1943. After the 1945-46 season, Cooper was traded back to New York where he concluded his NHL career.

Joe Cooper was not a flashy or a spectacular defenseman. He was, though, competent, reliable, and hard working. His longevity in the NHL is a testament to his abilities. Although generally regarded as a quiet athlete who did not like to mix it up, Cooper in his time was credited with the hardest punch in professional hockey. During an all-out melee, Cooper punched an opponent, sending him over the boards into the timekeeper's booth. The newspapers, though, reported that Cooper sent his victim flying into the press box. Those familiar with Madison Square Garden, the site of the incident, knew that the press box was actually 50 feet above the ice. Until the story was straightened out, opposing players were in awe of Cooper's strength.

Joe Cooper and his wife Oksana died accidently while returning home from a Florida vacation in 1979.

## INDUCTIONS

1986        Manitoba Hockey Hall of Fame

## ALL-STAR SELECTIONS

| 1934-35 | defense | EHL | First Team |
| 1935-36 | defense | CHL | First Team |

| year | team | league | regular season | | | | | playoffs | | | | |
|------|------|--------|-----|-----|-----|-----|-----|-----|-----|-----|-----|-----|
| | | | GP | G | A | PTS | PIM | GP | G | A | PTS | PIM |
| 1934-35* | New York | EHL | 21 | 5 | 14 | 19 | 70 | 7 | 5 | 0 | 5 | 16 |
| 1935-36* | Philadelphia | CHL | 48 | 5 | 10 | 15 | 86 | 4 | 1 | 0 | 1 | 6 |
| | NY Rangers | NHL | 1 | 0 | 0 | 0 | 0 | | | | | |
| 1936-37 | NY Rangers | NHL | 48 | 0 | 3 | 3 | 42 | 9 | 1 | 1 | 2 | 12 |
| 1937-38 | NY Rangers | NHL | 46 | 3 | 2 | 5 | 56 | 3 | 0 | 0 | 0 | 4 |
| 1938-39 | Chicago | NHL | 17 | 3 | 3 | 6 | 10 | | | | | |
| | Philadelphia | AHL | 35 | 8 | 15 | 23 | 50 | | | | | |
| 1939-40 | Chicago | NHL | 44 | 4 | 7 | 11 | 59 | 2 | 0 | 0 | 0 | 6 |
| 1940-41 | Chicago | NHL | 45 | 5 | 5 | 10 | 66 | 5 | 1 | 0 | 1 | 8 |
| 1941-42 | Chicago | NHL | 47 | 6 | 14 | 20 | 58 | 3 | 0 | 2 | 2 | 2 |
| 1942-43* | Ottawa | QSHL | 16 | 1 | 5 | 6 | 26 | 12 | 4 | 6 | 10 | 18 |
| 1943-44 | Chicago | NHL | 13 | 1 | 0 | 1 | 17 | 9 | 1 | 1 | 2 | 18 |
| | Ottawa | QSHL | 10 | 0 | 1 | 1 | 18 | | | | | |
| 1944-45 | Chicago | NHL | 50 | 4 | 17 | 21 | 50 | | | | | |
| 1945-46 | Chicago | NHL | 50 | 2 | 7 | 9 | 46 | 4 | 0 | 1 | 1 | 14 |
| 1946-47 | NY Rangers | NHL | 59 | 2 | 8 | 10 | 38 | | | | | |

# COPOT, MURRAY

| | |
|---|---|
| sport: | hockey |
| given name: | Copot, Murray Taras |
| born: | Bladworth, Saskatchewan |
| | September 17, 1923 |
| height: | 1.80 m / 5'11" |
| weight: | 86 kg / 190 lbs |

Murray Copot was serving aboard HMCS *Alberni* when it was sent to the bottom of the Bay of Biscay by a torpedo from a German U-boat during World War II. Of the 105 crew members only 19 survived. A wounded Murray Copot was one of them, having been rescued from the choppy Atlantic five and one-half hours after the ship went down. "After the war was over,

I didn't think about it for a few years. Then I began to wonder: Why pick me? We lost so many young men in the navy. But I was a survivor. Maybe that's why I thought I had to do something with young people." That, and his own five children.

Prior to enlistment, Copot played Junior "B" hockey in Teulon, Manitoba (1938-41). It was natural then, that some years after settling in Calgary in 1948, he took up coaching hockey. In 1970, he coached the Triwood juveniles to the provincial title. The greatest satisfaction he got from coaching, though, was watching children come off the ice with smiles on their faces. Copot's support of young hockey players even made its way to the family residence. He and his wife Mary boarded many young hockey players, some on their way to the NHL, such as Zarley Zalapski, Jim Paek and Adrien Plavsic.

In 1963, Copot joined the ranks of hockey administrators. Over the years, he held numerous posts culminating with the presidency of the Alberta Amateur Hockey Association and serving as a director of the Canadian Amateur Hockey Association. One of the initiatives Copot advocated and worked on was the banning of bodychecks in the younger age groups. Copot also worked with the Organizing Committee of the 1988 Olympic Winter Games.

In 1991, the city of Calgary renamed Thornhill Arena the Murray Copot Arena. That same year he was honoured as Volunteer of the Year by the Canadian Amateur Hockey Association.

## INDUCTIONS

1993        Alberta Amateur Hockey Hall of Fame

## AWARDS

1980        Award of Merit  -  Calgary Minor Hockey
1981        Honoured Athletic Leader  -  Calgary Booster Club
1981        Recognition Award  -  Calgary Minor Hockey
1985        Recognition Award  -  Canadian Amateur Hockey Association
1988        Volunteer 88 Club  -  1988 Olympic Winter Games Organizing Committee
1991        Volunteer of the Year  -  Canadian Amateur Hockey Association

## RECORD

administration

| year | position |
|---|---|
| 1963-73 | Director, Tiny Mite Division League - Minor Hockey Association of Calgary |
| 1963-78 | Board of Directors, Minor Hockey Association of Calgary |

| 1975-77 | President, Minor Hockey Association of Calgary |
| 1977- | Board of Directors, Alberta Amateur Hockey Association |
| 1978-86 | Vice President, Alberta Amateur Hockey Association |
| 1986-88 | President, Alberta Amateur Hockey Association |
| 1986-88 | Director, Canadian Amateur Hockey Association |

# CYNCAR, MARCO

| | |
| --- | --- |
| sport: | football |
| born: | Edmonton, Alberta |
| | April 13, 1958 |
| height: | 1.83 m / 6'0" |
| weight: | 85 kg / 187 lbs |
| position: | wide receiver |

*Photo courtesy of the Canadian Football Hall of Fame and Museum*

While attending the University of Alberta, Marco Cyncar played on its football team. In 1979, the Edmonton Eskimos made him their first choice in the Territorial Exemptions. Edmonton then traded Cyncar to Hamilton where he made his CFL debut. The Tiger-Cats used the versatile Cyncar in numerous roles. He caught passes, punted, kicked, ran back punts and kick-offs. In 1981, Edmonton re-acquired Cyncar. He played with the team through the end of 1991 season.

The Eskimos used Cyncar almost exclusively at the wide receiver position. During his career he averaged less than two receptions per game. His best year statistically was in 1987 when he caught 43 passes for 710 yards and three touchdowns. In a 1989 playoff game, Cyncar showed his versatility by running back four kickoffs for 204 yards, the longest being 58 yards. A member of three Grey Cup winning teams with Edmonton, one of Marco Cyncar's most memorable moments in sport was catching a crucial touchdown pass in the 1987 Grey Cup game.

# RECORD

## scoring

| year | team | league | GP | TD | C | FG | S | PTS | GP | TD | C | FG | S | PTS | GP | TD | C | FG | S | PTS |
|---|---|---|---|---|---|---|---|---|---|---|---|---|---|---|---|---|---|---|---|---|
| | | | regular season | | | | | | playoffs | | | | | | Grey Cup game | | | | | |
| 1980 | Hamilton | CFL | 16 | 0 | 2 | 0 | 0 | 2 | 1 | 0 | 0 | 0 | 0 | 0 | 1 | 0 | 0 | 0 | 0 | 0 |
| 1981* | Edmonton | CFL | 16 | 1 | 0 | 0 | 0 | 6 | 1 | 0 | 0 | 0 | 0 | 0 | 1 | 0 | X1 | 0 | 0 | 2 |
| 1982* | Edmonton | CFL | 8 | 0 | 0 | 0 | 0 | 0 | 1 | 0 | 0 | 0 | 0 | 0 | 1 | 0 | 0 | 0 | 0 | 0 |
| 1983 | Edmonton | CFL | 15 | 1 | 0 | 0 | 0 | 6 | 1 | 0 | 0 | 0 | 0 | 0 | | | | | | |
| 1984 | Edmonton | CFL | 16 | 0 | 0 | 0 | 0 | 0 | 1 | 0 | 0 | 0 | 0 | 0 | | | | | | |
| 1985 | Edmonton | CFL | 16 | 1 | 0 | 0 | 0 | 6 | 1 | 0 | 0 | 0 | 0 | 0 | | | | | | |
| 1986 | Edmonton | CFL | 18 | 3 | 0 | 0 | 0 | 18 | 2 | 1 | 0 | 0 | 0 | 6 | 1 | 0 | 0 | 0 | 0 | 0 |
| 1987* | Edmonton | CFL | 18 | 3 | 0 | 0 | 0 | 18 | 2 | 0 | 0 | 0 | 0 | 0 | 1 | 1 | 0 | 0 | 0 | 6 |
| 1988 | Edmonton | CFL | 18 | 0 | X1 | 0 | 0 | 2 | 1 | 0 | 0 | 0 | 0 | 0 | | | | | | |
| 1989 | Edmonton | CFL | 17 | 1 | 0 | 0 | 0 | 6 | 1 | 0 | 0 | 0 | 0 | 0 | | | | | | |
| 1990 | Edmonton | CFL | 18 | 0 | 0 | 0 | 0 | 0 | 2 | 0 | 0 | 0 | 0 | 0 | 1 | 0 | 0 | 0 | 0 | 0 |
| 1991 | Edmonton | CFL | 14 | 0 | 0 | 0 | 0 | 0 | 1 | 0 | 0 | 0 | 0 | 0 | | | | | | |

X    two point convert

## pass receiving

| year | team | league | GP | NO | YDS | AVE | LG | TD | GP | NO | YDS | AVE | LG | TD | GP | NO | YDS | AVE | LG | TD |
|---|---|---|---|---|---|---|---|---|---|---|---|---|---|---|---|---|---|---|---|---|
| | | | regular season | | | | | | playoffs | | | | | | Grey Cup game | | | | | |
| 1980 | Hamilton | CFL | 16 | 13 | 180 | 13.8 | 27 | 0 | 1 | 0 | 0 | 0.0 | 0 | 0 | 1 | 2 | 37 | 18.5 | 23 | 0 |
| 1981* | Edmonton | CFL | 16 | 40 | 541 | 13.5 | 28 | 1 | 1 | 3 | 58 | 19.3 | 27 | 0 | 1 | 7 | 61 | 8.7 | 16 | 0 |
| 1982* | Edmonton | CFL | 8 | 6 | 87 | 14.5 | 38 | 0 | 1 | 0 | 0 | 0.0 | 0 | 0 | 1 | 0 | 0 | 0.0 | 0 | 0 |
| 1983 | Edmonton | CFL | 15 | 16 | 298 | 18.6 | 30 | 1 | 1 | 3 | 38 | 12.7 | 14 | 0 | | | | | | |
| 1984 | Edmonton | CFL | 16 | 26 | 460 | 17.7 | 48 | 0 | 1 | 4 | 51 | 12.8 | 19 | 0 | | | | | | |
| 1985 | Edmonton | CFL | 16 | 27 | 372 | 13.8 | 41 | 1 | 1 | 2 | 27 | 13.5 | 15 | 0 | | | | | | |
| 1986 | Edmonton | CFL | 18 | 37 | 522 | 14.1 | 34 | 3 | 2 | 9 | 85 | 9.4 | 25 | 1 | 1 | 1 | 6 | 6.0 | 6 | 0 |
| 1987* | Edmonton | CFL | 18 | 43 | 710 | 16.5 | 58 | 3 | 2 | 3 | 54 | 18.0 | 24 | 0 | 1 | 1 | 6 | 6.0 | 6 | 1 |
| 1988 | Edmonton | CFL | 18 | 31 | 419 | 13.5 | 32 | 0 | 1 | 1 | 10 | 10.0 | 10 | 0 | | | | | | |
| 1989 | Edmonton | CFL | 17 | 11 | 193 | 17.5 | 46 | 1 | 1 | 0 | 0 | 0.0 | 0 | 0 | | | | | | |
| 1990 | Edmonton | CFL | 18 | 26 | 385 | 14.8 | 34 | 0 | 2 | 4 | 66 | 16.5 | 25 | 0 | 1 | 2 | 24 | 12.0 | 22 | 0 |
| 1991 | Edmonton | CFL | 14 | 13 | 178 | 13.7 | 35 | 0 | 1 | 0 | 0 | 0.0 | 0 | 0 | | | | | | |

# CZICH, JOHN

sport: badminton
given name: Czich, John Mironko
born: Renfrew, Ontario
January 17, 1953
height: . . .
weight: . . .

In 1972, John Czich won the Ontario junior badminton title. A year later, he participated in his first national championship. While attending the Royal Military College, Czich excelled in boxing and badminton. He continued competing in badminton after joining the Canadian Forces as an air engineer officer.

In 1976, as a member of the Thomas Cup team, Czich won the North American Division, advancing to the quarter-finals of the International Division. The following year he won the gold medal in the doubles event at the Pan American Badminton Championships. At the 1978 Commonwealth Games in Edmonton, John Czich won the silver medal in doubles competition. In 1979, he was once again a member of the Canadian Thomas Cup team which won the North American title and advanced to the quarter-finals of the International Division.

## INDUCTIONS

1980    Canadian Forces Sports Hall of Fame

## AWARDS

. . .    Royal Military College Outstanding Athlete

## RECORD

| year | competition | event | placing |
|------|-------------|-------|---------|
| 1976 | Canadian Badminton Championships | singles | 2 |
|      | Thomas Cup North American Division | team | 1 |
|      | Thomas Cup International Division | team | |
| 1977 | Pan-Am Championships | doubles | 1 |
| 1978 | Commonwealth Games | team | 2 |

| year | competition | event | placing |
|------|-------------|-------|---------|
| 1978 | North of Scotland Open | singles | 1 |
|      |             | doubles | 1 |
| 1979 | Canadian Badminton Championships | singles | 1 |
|      | Thomas Cup North American Division | team | 1 |
|      | Thomas Cup International Division | team | |
|      | AM-CAN International Mixed Team | singles | 1 |
|      |             | doubles | 1 |
|      | Mexican Open | doubles | 1 |

# DACYSHYN, ANNA

| | |
|---|---|
| sport: | diving |
| born: | Edmonton, Alberta |
| | October 7, 1969 |
| height: | 1.62 m / 5'4" |
| weight: | 50 kg / 110 lbs |

*Photo courtesy of the Athlete Information Bureau*

Anna Dacyshyn was only twelve years old when she was selected to represent Canada at an international junior meet, on the basis of a third place finish at the Canadian Age Group Diving Championships. She placed a strong second in the 10-metre tower event, an event that, over time, became her specialty. In 1985, she placed second in the 10-metre event at the World Age Group Championships (15-17 years) and a year later, she won her first national title at the Canadian Winter Championships.

After taking a year off, Dacyshyn returned to competition in 1988, with the hope of qualifying for the Olympics. She did not make the team. Not discouraged, she set new goals for herself. In 1989, she placed third in the 10-metre tower event at the FINA World Cup and had fine results in international meets. A year later, at the Commonwealth Games in Auckland, New Zealand, Anna Dacyshyn won the gold medal in her specialty - the 10-metre tower.

| year | competition | event | placing | result |
|------|-------------|-------|---------|--------|
| 1985 | Canadian Championships | 1 m | 10 | 366.77 |
| | | 3 m | 8 | 565.32 |
| | | 10 m | 3 | 584.60 |
| | World Age Group Championships | 10 m | 2 | 348.48 |
| 1986 | Canadian Winter Championships | 10 m | 1 | 592.11 |
| | Dive Canada | 10 m | 3 | 420.63 |
| | Canadian Championships | 3 m | 5 | 624.41 |
| | | 10 m | 5 | 547.76 |
| 1988 | Pan Am Invitational | 3 m | 11 | 352.55 |
| | | 10 m | 1 | 396.50 |
| | Rostock International | 10 m | 5 | 403.65 |
| | Dive Canada | 10 m | 5 | 380.88 |
| | Olympic Trials | 10 m | 3 | 764.97 |
| 1989 | China Open | 10 m | 4 | 376.08 |
| | FINA World Cup | 10 m | 3 | 393.33 |
| | Canadian Championships | 10 m | 1 | 589.00 |
| | Volksbank International | 10 m | 2 | 217.23 |
| | Bolzano International | 10 m | 3 | 204.84 |
| 1990 | Commonwealth Games | 10 m | 1 | 391.68 |
| | Goodwill Games | 10 m | 6 | 379.80 |
| 1991 | Canadian Championships | 10 m | 2 | 422.10 |
| | World Championships | 10 m | 4 | 210.33 |

# DACYSHYN, JOHN

"Jumpin' John," "Shony"

| | |
|---|---|
| sport: | basketball |
| born: | Toronto, Ontario |
| | March 9, 1935 |
| height: | 1.91 m / 6'3" |
| weight: | 100 kg / 220 lbs |
| position: | center |

While playing high school basketball, John Dacyshyn's name appeared on the sports pages of

Toronto newspapers often in greater regularity than the names of some of the city's established professionals. "Dacyshyn, a brilliant six-foot-three forward. . ." or "John Dacyshyn, undoubtedly the best player. . ." was how the sport scribes portrayed the young basketball star. In 1954, while competing for the Bathurst Heights senior team, Dacyshyn netted 50 points in one game to establish a city record. Dacyshyn was also a star with the University of Toronto Varsity Blues team in the years 1955-59.

Blessed with great natural ability, and with a body built up through physically demanding summer jobs, "Jumpin' John" Dacyshyn consistently out-rebounded much taller opponents. His vertical jump under the basket was something wonderful to behold.

Upon graduation, John Dacyshyn played for the Dow Kings in a senior men's league in Toronto. The team won the 1962-63 Ontario Championship and the Canadian Championship a year later. At the Black Ball Tournament held in Aurora in 1963, Dacyshyn scored a record 50 points in a 32-minute game. Thirty years later, the record still stood unbroken. In 1964, John Dacyshyn was selected to Canada's national team at the center position. The team paid its own way to the Olympic qualifying tournament in Yokohama, Japan, with the knowledge that should they advance to the Olympic Games, the Canadian Olympic Association (COA) would reimburse their expenses. The Canadian team played its heart out posting a 7-2 record to qualify for the Games. Dacyshyn, though, would not compete at the Olympics. During the qualifying tournament his mother passed away and he returned home for the funeral. Dacyshyn wanted to rejoin his teammates in Tokyo but the COA did not have funds for the airfare.

During his high school and university days, John Dacyshyn also competed for St. Vlads and the Tridents, two Ukrainian community-based teams competing in the Bathurst-College Community Basketball League.

## RECORD

| year | team | competition | results |
|------|------|-------------|---------|
| 1963 | Toronto Dow Kings | Ontario Championship | 1 |
| 1964 | Toronto Dow Kings | Canadian Championship | 1 |
| 1964 | Canada | Olympic Games | dnc |

# DANEYKO, KEN

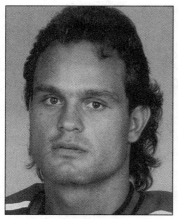

| | |
|---|---|
| sport: | hockey |
| given name: | Daneyko, Kenneth |
| born: | Windsor, Ontario |
| | April 17, 1964 |
| height: | 1.83 m / 6'0" |
| weight: | 95.3 kg / 210 lbs |
| position: | defense |
| shoots: | left |

*Photo courtesy of the New Jersey Devils*

The New Jersey Devils made Ken Daneyko their second pick and the 18th player to be selected overall in the 1982 NHL Entry Draft. Daneyko played one more season with Seattle of the WHL before securing a starting job with the Devils in the fall of 1983. A few weeks into the rookie season he broke his right leg. The injury severely hindered his early development and he failed to make the team the following season. A year later, after a disappointing training camp, he was once again reassigned to the farm system. Midway through the season Daneyko was called up by the Devils to replace an injured player. His play impressed and he became a regular.

With seasoning, Daneyko became a dependable defenseman, and was twice rewarded with a selection to the national team competing at the World Championships, in 1986 and 1989. A good skater and puck handler, he played an intense and physical game. During the 1986-87 season, his first complete season with the Devils, Daneyko established a team record for penalty minutes with 183. In the next two seasons, Daneyko kept rewriting the club's record book as the amount of time he spent in the penalty box continued to increase significantly.

## RECORD

| year | team | league | regular season | | | | | playoffs | | | | |
|---|---|---|---|---|---|---|---|---|---|---|---|---|
| | | | GP | G | A | PTS | PIM | GP | G | A | PTS | PIM |
| 1983-84 | New Jersey | NHL | 11 | 1 | 4 | 5 | 17 | | | | | |
| 1984-85 | New Jersey | NHL | 1 | 0 | 0 | 0 | 10 | | | | | |
| | Maine | AHL | 80 | 4 | 9 | 13 | 206 | 11 | 1 | 3 | 4 | 36 |
| 1985-86 | New Jersey | NHL | 44 | 0 | 10 | 10 | 100 | | | | | |
| | Maine | AHL | 21 | 3 | 2 | 5 | 75 | | | | | |
| 1986-87 | New Jersey | NHL | 79 | 2 | 12 | 14 | 183 | | | | | |
| 1987-88 | New Jersey | NHL | 80 | 5 | 7 | 12 | 239 | 20 | 1 | 6 | 7 | 83 |

| | | | regular season | | | | | playoffs | | | | |
|------|------|--------|-----|-----|-----|-----|-----|-----|-----|-----|-----|-----|
| year | team | league | GP | G | A | PTS | PIM | GP | G | A | PTS | PIM |
| 1988-89 | New Jersey | NHL | 80 | 5 | 5 | 10 | 283 | | | | | |
| 1989-90 | New Jersey | NHL | 74 | 6 | 15 | 21 | 219 | 6 | 2 | 0 | 2 | 21 |
| 1990-91 | New Jersey | NHL | 80 | 4 | 16 | 20 | 249 | 7 | 0 | 1 | 1 | 10 |

international

| year | team | competition | GP | G | A | PTS | PIM | Place |
|------|------|-------------|-----|-----|-----|-----|-----|-------|
| 1986 | Canada | World Championship | 7 | 0 | 0 | 0 | 0 | 3 |
| 1989 | Canada | World Championship | 8 | 0 | 0 | 0 | 4 | 2 |

# DANYCHUK, BILL

| | |
|---|---|
| sport: | football |
| given name: | Danychuk, William D'Arcy |
| born: | Timmins, Ontario |
| | August 29, 1940 |
| height: | 1.91 m / 6'3" |
| weight: | 109 kg / 240 lbs |
| position: | tackle, offensive guard |

*Photo courtesy of the Canadian Football Hall of Fame and Museum*

An all-star athlete while attending the Niagara District Secondary School at Niagara-on-the-Lake, Bill Danychuk excelled in basketball, football, and track. In 1960, he received an athletic scholarship from the University of Tennessee. He was a starter on the university's football team in his last two years there. In 1965, Danychuk joined the Hamilton Tiger-Cats football club and earned a starting job at the tackle position in his rookie season. He was later switched to the offensive guard position at which he excelled for a number of years.

Danychuk, a member of three Grey Cup championship teams, believed that offensive linemen were the "unsung heroes of a football team," whose talents were rarely appreciated by the fans. Nevertheless, football experts did notice Danychuk's exceptional talent and for four consecutive years, 1968 to 1971, he was the Tiger-Cats' nominee for the Most Outstanding Canadian Schenley Award. In 1971, he was also the nominee for the Outstanding Lineman Schenley Award. In the years 1967 and 1970, he was named to the CFL all-star team.

During the 1971 season, Danychuk was switched back to the offensive tackle position. At that position he also gained all-star recognition when he was named to the All-Eastern team in 1972 and 1973. After playing for 11 seasons, Bill Danychuk retired from the game in 1976. His talent was once again recognized when Hamilton's Best Team of the Century was compiled; he was on its roster. In addition to playing football, Danychuk served as vice-president of the CFL Players' Association for seven years. He also served as director of the World Bingo League for a number of years.

AWARDS

| 1968 | Hamilton Tiger-Cats MVP |
|---|---|

ALL-STAR SELECTIONS

| 1967 | guard | CFL | All-Eastern |
|---|---|---|---|
| | guard | CFL | |
| 1968 | guard | CFL | All-Eastern |
| 1970 | guard | CFL | All-Eastern |
| | guard | CFL | |
| 1972 | offensive tackle | CFL | All-Eastern |
| 1973 | offensive tackle | CFL | All-Eastern |

# DANYLUK, TERRY

| sport: | volleyball |
|---|---|
| born: | Tofield, Alberta |
| | March 22, 1960 |
| height: | 1.88 m / 6'2" |
| weight: | 86 kg / 190 lbs |

*Photo courtesy of the Athlete Information Bureau*

Some of Canada's national volleyball team's best results in international competition were attained while Terry Danyluk played in its ranks. Used as a setter, Danyluk was always part of the action on the court. At the 1983 World University Games, the team and Danyluk won the silver medal. It was the first time in history that a Canadian team won a volleyball medal at the competition organized for university students. A year later, at the Los Angeles Olympics, the Canadian team placed fourth. Although it failed to win a medal, the result was a best ever by a Canadian squad at the Olympics. While a student of physical education at the University of Calgary, Terry Danyluk also competed for the university volleyball club.

## RECORD

| year | competition | team | placing |
|------|-------------|------|---------|
| 1981 | World University Games | Canada | 6 |
| 1983 | World University Games | Canada | 2 |
| | Pan American Games | Canada | 5 |
| 1984 | Olympic Games | Canada | 4 |
| 1985 | World University Games | Canada | 5 |

# DASKI, MIKE

| | |
|---|---|
| sport: | hockey |
| born: | Winnipeg, Manitoba |
| | May 24, 1929 |
| height: | 1.73 m / 5'8" |
| weight: | 75 kg / 165 lbs |
| position: | center |
| shoots: | left |

In the late 1940s, Mike Daski was regarded as one of Winnipeg's finest young all-round athletes. He played competitive baseball, basketball, football, hockey, and soccer with great enthusiasm. In 1948, he was a member of the junior Winnipeg Light Infantry basketball club which was acknowledged national champion. A year later he coached the Canadian Ukrainian Athletic Club (CUAC) basketball team to the provincial senior girls' championship. In 1952, he was a member of the Institute Prosvita Athletic Club (IPAC) provincial championship soccer team.

Unfortunately, Mike Daski's compact size prevented him from pursuing football or hockey professionally in North America. On the advice of a hockey man, Daski left for Europe in 1949 to gain "good pay and hockey experience." He thus embarked on a hockey odyssey that saw him play and/or coach in Austria, Canada, England, Germany, Holland, Italy, Scotland and the United States, winning major championships in four of the countries. He was also the Detroit Red Wings' head scout for Europe in the years 1967-70.

In the fall of 1953, Daski assumed the duties of playing coach with the Red and Black Devils of Milan. The club had an exceptional season losing only once in 48 starts and capturing the Italian championship. Daski's line contributed for some 300 goals, tops in Europe. The following year, Mike Daski was back in Canada playing for the Brandon Wheat Kings. The team won the Western Canada championship while Daski led in playoff scoring. He returned to Europe in 1955 as playing coach of Bad Tolz in Bavaria. The club won the German championship that season.

The Winnipeg Maroons signed Daski in 1962. He helped the club to the 1963 Western Canada Championship, and the following year, the Allan Cup. Daski returned to coach Bad Tolz in the fall of 1964. He was with the team for four seasons, winning the German championship in 1965-66. Often, at the conclusion of the relatively short German season, he would join a British team and play out the year. In this fashion, he saw action with Paisley, Brighton and Wembley, retiring as a player in 1968. His popularity with players and fans, though, continued to secure him hockey jobs on the continent where he was still successfully coaching in 1991. During his coaching career, Daski had only two losing seasons. Mike Daski has been credited with developing the "Daski Box," a rigorous training routine that includes jumps over boxes, slaloms and other demanding elements.

## AWARDS

1984        Coach of the Year - Italian Hockey League

## ALL-STAR SELECTIONS

1954-55     center     MHL Sr.     First Team

## PLAYING RECORD

| | | | regular season | | | | | playoffs | | | | |
|---|---|---|---|---|---|---|---|---|---|---|---|---|
| year | team | league | GP | G | A | PTS | PIM | GP | G | A | PTS | PIM |
| 1949-50 | Harringay | English | ... | | | | | | | | | |
| | Ayr | Scottish | ... | | | | | | | | | |
| 1950-51 | Kelowna | MOAHL | ... | | | | | | | | | |
| 1951-52 | Philadelphia | EHL | 25 | 5 | 10 | 15 | 20 | | | | | |

| year | team | league | regular season GP | G | A | PTS | PIM | playoffs GP | G | A | PTS | PIM |
|------|------|--------|------|---|---|-----|-----|------|---|---|-----|-----|
| 1952-53 | Sydney | MMHL | 1 | 0 | 0 | 0 | 0 | | | | | |
| | St. John | NBSHL | ... | | | | | | | | | |
| 1953-54* | Milan | Italian | 48 | 52 | | | | | | | | |
| 1954-55 | Brandon | MHL Sr. | ... | | | | | | | | | |
| 1962-63 | Winnipeg | SSHL | ... | | | | | | | | | |
| 1963-64* | Winnipeg | SSHL | ... | | | | | | | | | |

# COACHING RECORD

regular season

| year | team | league |
|------|------|--------|
| 1953-54+* | Milan | Italian |
| 1955-56+* | Bad Tolz | German Division I |
| 1956-57 | Bad Tolz | German Division I |
| 1957-59+ | Montana-Vermala | Swiss Division II |
| 1964-65 | Bad Tolz | German Division I |
| 1965-66* | Bad Tolz | German Division I |
| 1966-67 | Bad Tolz | German Division I |
| 1967-68 | Bad Tolz | German Division I |
| 1968-69* | Holzkirchen | German Division III |
| 1969-70* | Rosenheim | German Division II |
| 1970-71 | Augsburg | German Division I |
| 1971-72 | Garmisch | German Division I |
| 1972-73 | Landshut | German Division I |
| 1973-74 | Garmisch | German Division I |
| 1975-77 | Bad Tolz | German Division I |
| 1977-78 | Salzburg | Austrian Division I |
| 1978-79 | Munich | German Division II |
| 1979-80 | Nurnberg | German Division II |
| | Kloten | Swiss Division I |
| 1980-81 | Kaufbeuern | German Division I |
| 1981-82 | Berlin | German Division I |
| 1982-83 | Straubing | German Division II |
| | Tillburg | Dutch Division I |
| 1983-85 | Merano | Italian Division I |
| 1985-86 | Bayreuth | German Division I |
| 1986-88 | Geleen | Dutch Division I |
| 1990-92 | Selb | German |

+ playing coach

# DELANEY, AL

| | |
|---|---|
| sport: | boxing |
| given name: | Borshuk, Alexander |
| born: | Oshawa, Ontario |
| | June 14, 1916 |
| height: | 1.88 m / 6'2" |
| weight: | 86 kg / 190 lbs |

*Photo courtesy of the Windsor/Essex County Sports Hall of Fame and Museum*

The year was 1934. Boxer Joe Louis' handlers were looking for an untried opponent so that their pugilist could make a triumphant professional home-town debut in Detroit after five successful fights in Chicago. The opponent they found was one Alex Borshuk of Windsor, an eighteen-year-old who also turned professional that year.

"That fistic struggle on September 11, 1934, at the Detroit Naval Armouries brought Joe Louis to the brink of defeat. Borshuk hit him so hard that one of his molars was chipped. Experiencing excruciating pain and with defeat imminent, Louis stalked Borshuk with his famed killer-instinct and stopped him in the fourth round. 'They never knew how close I came to losing' the Brown Bomber later reminisced."[6]

Alex Borshuk, who for the better part of his career fought under the name of Al Delaney, quickly became recognized as one of the finest heavyweights in the world. He fought with the best of them: Joe Louis, Tommy Loughran, Buddy Baer, George Nichols, Gus Lesnevich, Freddie Mills and other. In total, he entered the ring on 84 occasions, winning 48 fights, losing 29 and drawing 7. Among his victories was the Canadian Heavyweight Championship in May 1941, when he beat Tiger Warrington. In October, he defended the title by defeating Eddie Wenstob. Proceeds from the latter bout were donated to the war effort's Spitfire Fund. Soon afterwards Borshuk himself enlisted in the Canadian Army.

Alex Borshuk - Al Delaney fought most of his professional fights during the great depression, a time when prize money was rather scarce. Nevertheless, he managed to win over a quarter of a million dollars. With the money, he embarked on a life style that would ultimately destroy his career. Champagne and women became the order of the day. At first he would miss workouts and enter the ring out of shape; later he would miss fights all together. Many years later, Borshuk assessed his career: "The only way to make it in this business is to live like a priest, and I ain't no priest. . . I could have been the heavyweight champion of the world. I had the ability. I just wasn't serious."[7]

## RECORD

| year | opponent | result | round |
|------|----------|--------|-------|
| 1934 | Chuck Doris | W | 6 |
|      | Bud Creed | W | 8 |
|      | Mitzi Minikel | KO | 2 |
|      | Chet Reynor | W | 4 |
|      | Flash Fiser | W | 6 |
|      | Tiny Groves | KO | 2 |
|      | Bert Paxton | KO | 3 |
|      | Tiger McClelland | W | 6 |
|      | Roscoe Toles | W | 8 |
|      | Joe Louis | KO by | 4 |
| 1935 | Bill Fogarty | KO | 1 |
|      | Young Hippo | KO | 1 |
|      | Johnny Vorce | W | 8 |
|      | Frank Wojack | KO | 3 |
|      | Larry Johnson | W | 6 |
|      | Buddy Baer | KO by | 4 |
|      | Tommy Loughran | D | 6 |
|      | Johnny Freeman | W | 6 |
|      | George Nichols | D | 6 |
|      | Bob Godwin | KO | 2 |
|      | Terry Mitchell | W | 8 |
| 1936 | Steve Dudas | L | 6 |
|      | Bob Pastor | D | 6 |
|      | Joe Lipps | W | 8 |
|      | Billy Ketchel | W | 8 |
|      | Tony Gelento | W | 6 |
|      | Billy Nichy | W | 8 |
|      | Charley Massera | W | 8 |
|      | Tony Galento | D | 8 |
|      | Buck Everett | L | 8 |
|      | Izzy Singer | D | 10 |
|      | ? Winston | W | 10 |
|      | Ralph Barbara | KO | 5 |
| 1937 | Jim Howell | W | 6 |

| year | opponent | result | round |
|------|----------|--------|-------|
| 1937 | Harry Stably | KO | 7 |
|      | Norman Baines | W | 10 |
|      | Maurice Strickland | L | 10 |
| 1938 | Max Zona | KO | 7 |
|      | Jack London | WF | 4 |
|      | Jack London | L | 10 |
|      | Merio Preciso | KO | 9 |
|      | Arno Kroblein | W | 10 |
|      | Pancho Villar | KO | 7 |
| 1939 | Tony Arpino | KO | 2 |
|      | Merio Preciso | W | 10 |
|      | Jack London | KO by | 8 |
|      | Walter Neusel | L | 10 |
|      | Chuck Crowell | KO by | 4 |
|      | Harold Blackshear | KO by | 6 |
|      | Newsboy Millich | W | 10 |
| 1940 | ?  Winston | W | 10 |
|      | Newsboy Millich | KO | 5 |
|      | Ernie McDonald | W | 10 |
|      | Junior Munsell | L | 10 |
|      | Stan Savold | W | 10 |
|      | Tiger Jack Fox | L | 10 |
|      | Tiger Jack Fox | KO by | 9 |
|      | Eddie Mader | KO | 7 |
|      | Freddy Fiducia | L | 10 |
|      | Bill Poland | D | 10 |
|      | Patsy Perroni | L | 10 |
|      | Willie Reddish | L | 10 |
|      | Gus Lesnevich | W | 8 |
|      | Willie Pavlovich | W | 6 |
|      | Abe Simon | L | 10 |
| 1941 | Bill Poland | L | 10 |
|      | Buddy Walker | L | 10 |
|      | Harry Bobo | KO by | 8 |
|      | Wally Cross | W | 8 |
|      | Erv Sarlin | L | 10 |
|      | Wallace Cross | W | 8 |
|      | Clarence Jones | L | 10 |
|      | Wally Cross | L | 8 |

| year | opponent | result | round |
|---|---|---|---|
| 1941 | Tiger Warrington | W | 10 + |
| | Roscoe Toles | KO by | 3 |
| | Eddie Wenstob | W | 12 + |
| | Bob Pastor | KO by | 6 |
| 1942 | Al Robinson | W | 10 |
| 1944 | Ken Shaw | D | 8 |
| | Freddie Mills | KO by | 5 |
| | Bruce Woodcock | KO by | 5 |
| | Al Robinson | W | 8 |
| | Ken Shaw | L | 8 |

+    Canadian Professional Championship

# DEMCHUK, JOHN

| | |
|---|---|
| sport: | professional wrestling |
| born: | Stoyaniv, Ukraine |
| | December 22, 1909 |
| died: | Victoria, British Columbia |
| | June 16, 1962 |
| height: | 1.75 m / 5'9" |
| weight: | 81.5 kg / 180 lbs |

John Demchuk began his professional wrestling career in 1932, in Edmonton, the city to which he immigrated three years earlier. After many successful bouts in Canada he was engaged in 1936 by a British promoter to wrestle in Europe. Competing out of London, Demchuk twice won the European light-heavyweight titles. He toured Europe widely and once competed in Palestine. With war clouds gathering on the continent, Demchuk returned to Canada in 1939. In the 1940s, he competed mostly in southern Ontario. In 1951, he moved to Los Angeles, California, from where he won two American titles. John Demchuk died in 1962 while competing in a wrestling match.

# DERLAGO, BILL

sport:          hockey
given name:  Derlago, William Anthony
born:         Birtle, Manitoba
                August 25, 1958
height:         1.78 m / 5'10"
weight:        88 kg  / 194 lbs
position:       center
shoots:        left

*Photo courtesy of the Winnipeg Jets*

In his third season of junior hockey, Bill Derlago of the Brandon Wheat Kings established a WCHL record of 96 goals. He added 82 assists for a league-leading 182 points. The following year, he registered 89 goals and at the end of the season the Vancouver Canucks made him their first pick, fourth overall in the 1978 NHL Entry Draft. Derlago missed most of his first NHL season after he severed his knee ligaments. After surgery and rehabilitation, Derlago returned to the Canucks but his play suffered. As a result, Vancouver traded him to the Leafs. In Toronto, Derlago proved to be a steady performer with four thirty-goal seasons in spite of being plagued by injuries. In 1982, he tore his knee ligaments and in 1985, he had surgery to repair a dislocated shoulder.

Bill Derlago's heavy thighs and a powerful build made him appear to be a slow skater. He was, though, deceptively fast and his upper-body strength allowed him to stave off defenders. Derlago finished his NHL career as a travelling utility player. In his last two seasons he played for four NHL teams.

## AWARDS

1977      Bob Brownridge Memorial Trophy  -  WCHL Scoring Leader

## RECORD

| year | team | league | regular season | | | | | playoffs | | | | |
|------|------|--------|----|----|----|-----|-----|----|----|----|-----|-----|
| | | | GP | G | A | PTS | PIM | GP | G | A | PTS | PIM |
| 1978-79 | Vancouver | NHL | 9 | 4 | 4 | 8 | 2 | | | | | |
| | Dallas | CHL | 11 | 5 | 8 | 13 | 9 | | | | | |
| 1979-80 | Vancouver | NHL | 54 | 11 | 15 | 26 | 27 | | | | | |
| | Toronto | NHL | 23 | 5 | 12 | 17 | 13 | 3 | 0 | 0 | 0 | 4 |

| | | | regular season | | | | | playoffs | | | | |
|---|---|---|---|---|---|---|---|---|---|---|---|---|
| year | team | league | GP | G | A | PTS | PIM | GP | G | A | PTS | PIM |
| 1980-81 | Toronto | NHL | 80 | 35 | 39 | 74 | 26 | 3 | 1 | 0 | 1 | 2 |
| 1981-82 | Toronto | NHL | 75 | 34 | 50 | 84 | 42 | | | | | |
| 1982-83 | Toronto | NHL | 58 | 13 | 24 | 37 | 27 | 4 | 3 | 0 | 3 | 2 |
| 1983-84 | Toronto | NHL | 79 | 40 | 20 | 60 | 50 | | | | | |
| 1984-85 | Toronto | NHL | 62 | 31 | 31 | 62 | 21 | | | | | |
| 1985-86 | Toronto | NHL | 1 | 0 | 0 | 0 | 0 | | | | | |
| | Boston | NHL | 39 | 5 | 16 | 21 | 15 | | | | | |
| | Winnipeg | NHL | 27 | 5 | 5 | 10 | 6 | 3 | 1 | 0 | 1 | 0 |
| 1986-87 | Winnipeg | NHL | 30 | 3 | 6 | 9 | 12 | | | | | |
| | Quebec | NHL | 18 | 3 | 5 | 8 | 6 | | | | | |
| | Fredericton | AHL | 16 | 7 | 8 | 15 | 2 | | | | | |

# DIACHUN, JENNIFER

"Spider"

| | |
|---|---|
| sport: | gymnastics |
| given name: | Diachun, Eugenia Marie |
| born: | Toronto, Ontario |
| | August 14, 1953 |
| height: | 1.65 m / 5'5" |
| weight: | 59 kg / 130 lbs |

When Jenny Diachun was ten years old, she had excess energy which drove her mother crazy. To expend some of the energy, she was enrolled in a recreational non-competitive gymnastics class. An extremely quick learner, she was soon invited to train with a team of competitive gymnasts. Under the guidance of coach Elizabeth Austin of the Harmony Club, Diachun entered competition for the first time and started scoring successes at the provincial novice level. Diachun quickly outgrew the Harmony Club and in 1967 transferred to the Scarborough Winsonnete club which was coached by national team coach Marilyn Savage. That year she won four gold medals at the Canadian junior championships.

In 1968, coach Savage suggested that the 14-year-old Diachun enter the Canadian Olympic trials to gain competitive experience. Diachun stunned everyone by placing second overall on the basis of her performance at the three trials. The result qualified her for the Olympic team. Although Diachun did not place in the medals at the Mexico Olympics, she was Canada's youngest team member and top performer in the gymnastics competition. For Diachun, the Mexico Games were the highlight of an exciting career. Particularly rewarding was being selected as one of five athletes from Canada to march in the closing ceremonies.

Jennifer Diachun was an extremely hard working and disciplined athlete. Even though she was a quick learner (it only took her two weeks, for instance, to master the difficult back somer-sault on the beam), Diachun trained diligently. She refused to puppet moves but would rather analyse and rationalize each component of a routine. This gave her confidence and eliminat-ed nervousness.

In 1969, Diachun won her first national all-around championship. Judges always favoured the incumbent champion and only after Diachun defeated her main rival at an international com-petition in Mexico, did the Canadian judges give her recognition. Subsequently Diachun won four more national all-around championships, the last two under the guidance of coach Brian McVey of the Seneca Gymnastics Club. A member of the national team for a number of years, Diachun represented Canada at the 1971 Pan American Games where she won two bronze medals, at the 1970 and 1974 World University Games and at the 1968 and 1972 Olympics.

After retiring from competitive gymnastics in late 1974, Jennifer Diachun-Palmer embarked on a career in physiotherapy and rehabilitative medicine. She has also coached and choreo-graphed gymnastics. In 1987 and 1988, she was the manager of the Ontario team to the nation-al championships.

During her competitive days, Diachun was one of Canada's top gymnasts. Her true potential may never have been realized since coaching in Canada was somewhat behind its European counterparts at the time. Slava Rostrovski, the Soviet coach of Olga Korbut, was once quoted as saying: "Give me Diachun for a year and I'll give you an Olympic champion." After the 1973 World University Games in Moscow, Diachun did try to stay in the USSR for additional training but the Soviets refused because of her Ukrainian roots.

## RECORD

| year | competition | event | placing | result |
|------|-------------|-------|---------|--------|
| 1967 | Canada Games | all-around | 2 | |
| | | uneven bars | 1 | |
| | | floor | 2 | |
| | | balance bar | 2 | |
| 1968 | Olympic Trials | all-around | 2 | 70.20 |

| year | competition | event | placing | result |
|------|-------------|-------|---------|--------|
| 1968 | Olympic Games | all-around | 51 | 70.45 |
|      |             | team | 16 | |
| 1969 | Canadian Championships | all-around | 1 | |
|      |             | vault | 1 | |
|      |             | uneven bars | 1 | |
|      |             | beam | 1 | |
|      |             | floor | 1 | |
|      | Copa de las Americas | all-around | 4 | 35.05 |
|      |             | vault | 1 | |
| 1970 | Canadian Championships | all-around | 1 | |
|      |             | vault | 1 | 17.90 |
|      |             | uneven bars | 1 | 18.15 |
|      |             | beam | 2 | |
|      |             | floor | 1 | 18.10 |
|      | World University Games | uneven bars | 4 | |
|      |             | team | 5 | |
| 1971 | Canadian Championships | all-around | 1 | |
|      | Pan American Games | all-around | 6 | 71.30 |
|      |             | uneven bars | 5 | 17.67 |
|      |             | floor | 3 | 18.55 |
|      |             | team | 3 | 351.35 |
| 1972 | Canadian Championships | all-around | 1 | |
|      | Olympic Games | all-around | 50 | 70.87 |
|      |             | team | 11 | |
| 1973 | Canadian Championships | all-around | 2 | |
|      | Intercollegiate Championships | all-around | 1 | |
|      | World University Games | uneven bars | 4 | |
| 1974 | Canadian Championships | all-around | 1 | 73.40 |

# DIDUCK, GERALD

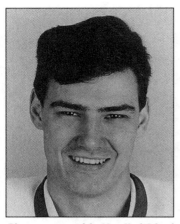

| sport: | hockey |
| --- | --- |
| born: | Edmonton, Alberta |
| | April 6, 1965 |
| height: | 1.88 m / 6'2" |
| weight: | 94 kg / 207 lbs |
| position: | defense |
| shoots: | right |

*Photo courtesy of the New York Islanders*

After a fine junior career with the Lethbridge Broncos, Gerald Diduck, a first round pick in the 1983 NHL Entry Draft, joined the New York Islanders for the 1984-85 season. He played well in his rookie year, gaining confidence and respect. The following year his play was not up to his potential and he was assigned to the Islanders' farm team in Springfield. Two seasons later, Diduck once again had a regular starting position with New York. In addition to a regular shift, he was often used on the power play and in a penalty killing role. In September of 1990, Diduck was acquired by the Montreal Canadiens. He played with them for half a season before moving on to the Vancouver Canucks. Gerald Diduck is the brother of hockey player Judy Diduck.

## RECORD

| year | team | league | regular season | | | | | playoffs | | | | |
| --- | --- | --- | --- | --- | --- | --- | --- | --- | --- | --- | --- | --- |
| | | | GP | G | A | PTS | PIM | GP | G | A | PTS | PIM |
| 1983-84 | Indianapolis | IHL | | | | | | 10 | 1 | 6 | 7 | 19 |
| 1984-85 | NY Islanders | NHL | 65 | 2 | 8 | 10 | 80 | | | | | |
| 1985-86 | NY Islanders | NHL | 10 | 1 | 2 | 3 | 2 | | | | | |
| | Springfield | AHL | 61 | 6 | 14 | 20 | 173 | | | | | |
| 1986-87 | NY Islanders | NHL | 30 | 2 | 3 | 5 | 67 | 14 | 0 | 1 | 1 | 35 |
| | Springfield | AHL | 45 | 6 | 8 | 14 | 120 | | | | | |
| 1987-88 | NY Islanders | NHL | 68 | 7 | 12 | 19 | 113 | 6 | 1 | 0 | 1 | 42 |
| 1988-89 | NY Islanders | NHL | 65 | 11 | 21 | 32 | 155 | | | | | |
| 1989-90 | NY Islanders | NHL | 76 | 3 | 17 | 20 | 163 | 5 | 0 | 0 | 0 | 12 |
| 1990-91 | Montreal | NHL | 32 | 1 | 2 | 3 | 39 | | | | | |
| | Vancouver | NHL | 31 | 3 | 7 | 10 | 66 | 6 | 1 | 0 | 1 | 11 |

| year | team | competition | GP | G | A | PTS | PIM | Place |
|------|------|-------------|----|----|----|-----|-----|-------|
| 1984 | Canada | World Junior Championship | 7 | 0 | 0 | 0 | 4 | 4 |

# DIDUCK, JUDY

| | |
|---|---|
| sport: | hockey, ringette |
| born: | Edmonton, Alberta |
| | April 21, 1966 |
| height: | 1.68 m / 5'6" |
| weight: | 65 kg / 152 lbs |
| position: | defense |
| shoots: | left |

*Photo courtesy of the Canadian Amateur Hockey Association*

For Judy Diduck, 1990 was a memorable year. She won two gold medals at two world championships in two different sports. Both tournaments were contested in Ottawa just a month apart. In February, she was a member of the Alberta Selects that won the gold medal at the inaugural World Ringette Championship. In March, she was a member of Team Canada that won the gold medal at the inaugural Women's World Ice Hockey Championship. At the hockey championship, Diduck scored only one goal but it was undoubtedly the most important of her life. In the championship final against the Americans, Team Canada fell behind 2-0. The Canadians fought back to score one. Then, on a Canadian power play, Judy Diduck broke in all alone on the American goalie and neatly tucked the puck in to tie the game. The goal swung the momentum to Team Canada and the club proceeded to score three unanswered goals.

An all-round athlete, Judy Diduck began playing ringette at age ten. Nine years later, she began to play hockey on a regular basis. Upon joining the Edmonton Chimos hockey club, ringette took a back seat to hockey because of time. When the opportunity arose to play at the 1990 world ringette and hockey championships, Judy Diduck put everything aside to train and compete in both sports. The many months of hard work were capped by two world titles. In early 1992, Diduck was once again a member of Canada's gold medal team at the world hockey championship. Judy Diduck is the sister of hockey player Gerald Diduck.

international

| year | team | competition | GP | G | A | PTS | PIM | Place |
|------|------|-------------|-----|---|---|-----|-----|-------|
| 1990 | Canada | World Championship | 5 | 1 | 0 | 1 | 6 | 1 |
| 1992 | Canada | World Championship | 5 | 0 | 1 | 1 | 2 | 1 |

# DOMANSKY, DON

| | |
|---|---|
| sport: | athletics |
| given name: | Domansky, Bohdan |
| born: | Ulm, Germany |
| | August 11, 1946 |
| height: | 1.80 m / 5'11" |
| weight: | 79.5 kg / 175 lbs |

*Photo courtesy of the Northwestern Ontario Sports Hall of Fame*

A versatile sprinter, Don Domansky first gained recognition while a teen-ager by establishing numerous age group records in distances through 400 metres. In high school, he ran the 100 yards in 9.8 seconds, the 220 in 21.2, and the 440 in 48.4. He enrolled at the University of California at Los Angeles (UCLA) on a track scholarship. In 1966, he helped UCLA to a gold medal in the 4x440-yard relay and the overall NCAA championship. At the Commonwealth Games that year he won a bronze medal in the 440 yards in a Canadian record time of 46.4 seconds. He was a member of the Canadian silver medal relay team that also established a national record. Domansky's 44.4 split was the second fastest in track history.

In 1967, Domansky was a member of the UCLA 4x110-yard relay team that equalled the world record of 39.6 seconds. At the NCAA championships he placed fifth in the 440 yards. Shortly afterwards he established a Canadian record of 45.8 seconds in the 400 metres at the USA versus British Commonwealth meet. Named captain of the Canadian track team to the 1967 Pan American Games, Domansky inspired by example, winning the bronze medal in the 400 metres and equalling his Canadian record of 45.8 seconds. In the world rankings announced at the end of the year, Domansky held down the fourth spot at the 400-metre distance. His time of 45.8 was the third fastest in the world that year.

Don Domansky was voted captain of the UCLA track team in 1968. A hamstring injury at the California Relays kept him out of the NCAA championships. The injury also kept Domansky from realizing his potential at the 1968 Olympics. Early in the year, track experts had predicted that he would make the final of the 400-metre sprint. Domansky, though, did not make it past the opening heats.

After the 1970 Commonwealth Games, Don Domansky retired from competition. At that time, he began to coach the Thunder Bay Olympic Club. He also served as president of the North Western Track and Field Association and vice-president of the Ontario Track and Field Association. In 1975, Domansky made a successful comeback to competitive track. He ran the 400 metres in 45.9 seconds, the fastest time by a Canadian since 1967. The following year, Don Domansky won a spot on Canada's Olympic 4x400-metre relay team. In Montreal the Canadian foursome placed fourth in a Canadian record time of 3:02.64.

## INDUCTIONS

1985        Northwestern Ontario Sports Hall of Fame

## AWARDS

1966        Thunder Bay Athlete of the Year
1968        Thunder Bay Athlete of the Year

## ALL-STAR SELECTIONS

1966        track and field        All-American

## RECORD

| year | competition | event | placing | result |
|------|-------------|-------|---------|--------|
| 1964 | Canadian Junior Championships | 220 y | 1 | 22.1 |
| | | 440 y | 1 | 48.8 |
| | Olympic Trials | 200 m | 3 | |
| | | 400 m | 5 | |
| 1966 | NCAA Championships | 4 x 440 y | 1 | 3:07.5 |
| | Commonwealth Games | 220 y | 5 | 20.9 |
| | | 440 y | 3 | 46.4  nr |
| | | 4 x 110 y | 5 | 40.4  nr |
| | | 4 x 440 y | 2 | 3:04.9  nr |

| year | competition | event | placing | result | |
|------|-------------|-------|---------|--------|---|
| 1967 | UCLA vs USC | 4 x 110 y | 1 | 39.6 | = wr |
| | NCAA Championships | 440 y | 5 | 46.4 | |
| | | 4 x 440 y | 5 | 3:08.8 | |
| | Canadian Championships | 200 m | 1 | 21.5 | |
| | | 400 m | 1 | 46.6 | |
| | USA vs British Commonwealth | 400 m | 3 | 45.8 | nr |
| | | 4 x 400 m | 2 | 3:01.7 | |
| | Pan American Games | 200 m | 4 SF | 20.9 | |
| | | 400 m | 3 | 45.8 | = nr |
| 1968 | Canadian Championships | 400 m | 1 | 46.6 | |
| | Olympic Games | 400 m | 5 H | 46.4 | |
| | Canada vs Norway | 400 m | 1 | 46.0 | |
| 1969 | Canada vs Czechoslovakia | 100 m | 2 | 10.4 | |
| | | 200 m | 2 | 20.9 | |
| 1970 | Commonwealth Games Trials | 200 m | 1 | 20.9 | |
| | | 400 m | 2 | 47.4 | |
| | Commonwealth Games | 100 m | 4 H | 10.6 | |
| | | 200 m | 5 H | 21.5 | |
| 1975 | Pre Pan Am Meet | 400 m | 1 | 45.9 | |
| | Pan American Games | 4 x 400 m | 3 | 3:03.92 | nr |
| 1976 | Canadian Indoor Championships | 400 m | 3 | 48.8 | |
| | Olympic Trials | 400 m | 2 | 46.86 | |
| | Olympic Games | 400 m | 6 H | 47.24 | |
| | | 4 x 400 m | 4 | 3:02.64 | nr |

wr   World record

nr   Canadian record

# DOROHOY, EDDIE

"The Great Gabbo," "Pistol"

| | |
|---|---|
| sport: | hockey |
| given name: | Dorohoy, Edward |
| born: | Medicine Hat, Alberta |
| | March 13, 1929 |
| height: | 1.75 m / 5'9" |
| weight: | 68 kg / 150 lbs |
| position: | center |
| shoots: | left |

Eddie Dorohoy played junior hockey with the Lethbridge Native Sons. In 1948, he led the club to the Western Canada final. A knee injury prevented Dorohoy from playing in the final which was won by Port Arthur, the eventual Memorial Cup champions. The following year Dorohoy was invited to the Montreal Canadiens' training camp. The stocky and tough-looking rookie became an immediate hit with the veterans because of his fun-loving comic approach to the game. At the first full practice that he attended, Dorohoy was put on a line with Rocket Richard and Elmer Lach. Soon he was instructing his all-star line mates on how to play their positions: "You take this guy over here, Elmer. And you can look after that guy, Rocket. I'll look after the rest of these punks by myself."[8] Before training camp concluded, the non-stop talking Dorohoy became known as the "Great Gabbo."

The only action Dorohoy saw in the NHL was in his rookie year with the Canadiens. Even then, he spent most of the season playing for Dallas of the USHL. The following season Dorohoy made his way to the west coast playing for Victoria Cougars of the PCHL and later of the WHL. He won the league scoring title during the 1950-51 season with 87 points, 28 of which were scored in the last ten games of the schedule. The following year, he finished in a tie for second. Prior to the start of the 1952-53 season, Lester Patrick appointed Dorohoy playing coach of the Cougars. At 25, Dorohoy was probably the youngest coach in professional hockey at the time.

Eddie Dorohoy played minor pro hockey for over a decade. In 1959 he set a league record for registering an assist in 15 consecutive games. He also established a WHL all-time mark with 421 assists. Upon retiring Dorohoy pursued a coaching career. The Brandon Wheat Kings of the MJHL and the Winnipeg Jets of the WCHL were among the teams under his guidance in the 1960s.

# AWARDS

1959       Leader Cup  -  WHL Most Valuable Player

## ALL-STAR SELECTIONS

| | | | |
|---|---|---|---|
| 1951-52 | center | PCHL | Second Team |
| 1953-54 | center | WHL | Second Team |
| 1958-59 | center | WHL | First Team (Prairie Division) |

## RECORD

| year | team | league | regular season | | | | | playoffs | | | | |
|---|---|---|---|---|---|---|---|---|---|---|---|---|
| | | | GP | G | A | PTS | PIM | GP | G | A | PTS | PIM |
| 1948-49 | Montreal | NHL | 16 | 0 | 0 | 0 | 6 | | | | | |
| | Dallas | USHL | 34 | 19 | 21 | 40 | 76 | 4 | 2 | 2 | 4 | 0 |
| 1949-50 | Cincinnati | AHL | 6 | 0 | 0 | 0 | 2 | | | | | |
| | Victoria | PCHL | 31 | 15 | 16 | 31 | 25 | | | | | |
| 1950-51* | Victoria | PCHL | 68 | 29 | 58 | 87 | 64 | 12 | 6 | 8 | 14 | 8 |
| 1951-52 | Victoria | PCHL | 68 | 29 | 56 | 85 | 66 | 13 | 3 | 4 | 7 | 12 |
| 1952-53 | Victoria | WHL | 70 | 24 | 54 | 78 | 97 | | | | | |
| 1953-54 | Victoria | WHL | 70 | 26 | 53 | 79 | 46 | 5 | 1 | 2 | 3 | 4 |
| 1954-55 | Victoria | WHL | 68 | 33 | 52 | 85 | 41 | 5 | 2 | 2 | 4 | 10 |
| 1955-56 | Seattle | WHL | 69 | 18 | 41 | 59 | 131 | | | | | |
| 1956-57 | Seattle | WHL | 70 | 31 | 55 | 86 | 70 | 6 | 2 | 6 | 8 | 4 |
| 1957-58 | Victoria | WHL | 58 | 34 | 41 | 75 | 51 | | | | | |
| 1958-59 | Calgary | WHL | 64 | 35 | 74 | 109 | 56 | 8 | 2 | 4 | 6 | 6 |
| 1959-60 | Vancouver | WHL | 33 | 17 | 21 | 38 | 30 | | | | | |
| 1960-61 | Vancouver | WHL | 2 | 0 | 0 | 0 | 0 | | | | | |
| 1961-62 | LA/Vancouver | WHL | 37 | 6 | 10 | 16 | 14 | | | | | |
| 1962-63 | Vancouver | WHL | 6 | 0 | 2 | 2 | 0 | | | | | |
| | Knoxville | EHL | 20 | 7 | 20 | 27 | 2 | 5 | 1 | 2 | 3 | 0 |
| 1963-64 | New Haven | EHL | 18 | 11 | 18 | 29 | 6 | 5 | 2 | 3 | 5 | 2 |
| 1964-65 | Spokane | WHL | 47 | 20 | 50 | 70 | 118 | | | | | |

# DRAYTON, JEROME

| | |
|---|---|
| sport: | athletics |
| given name: | Buniak, Peter |
| born: | Kolbermoor, Germany |
| | January 10, 1945 |
| height: | 1.75 m / 5'9" |
| weight: | 58 kg / 127 lbs |

*Photo courtesy of the Ontario Track & Field Association*

Jerome Drayton was Canada's top distance runner for fifteen years. He established one world and five Canadian records. He won almost every major marathon: Boston, Fukuoka, and others. In 1969, Drayton was ranked the number one marathoner in the world by *Track and Field News*, a result of winning two fast marathons and establishing two Canadian records. His time of 2:10:08.4 in winning the 1975 Fukuoka was the world's fifth best ever in a marathon. In 1977, he was named Canada's Male Athlete of the Year. A year later, he was inducted into Canada's Sport Hall of Fame.

Jerome Drayton's career, though, was full of trials and tribulations. After winning the 1968 Olympic 10,000-metre trials within 1.5 seconds of the Canadian record, the selection committee refused to name him to the Olympic team. Instead, Dave Ellis, who established the Canadian record earlier in the season, was selected. A major controversy followed which resulted in the selection committee giving Drayton another chance to prove himself. Running all by himself, he broke Ellis' record only to discover that the distance was short by less than 10 metres. The committee refused to budge. In the marathon, Drayton also had to prove himself again. The second time around he convinced the committee that he was Olympic calibre by setting a new Canadian record by more than two minutes. At the 1968 Olympics, Drayton had to drop out of the marathon because of dysentery.

In the Ukrainian community, it was widely believed that Drayton, who was then competing under his given name Peter Buniak, was being discriminated against because of his ethnicity. Drayton himself viewed his name as a liability. It labelled him as an immigrant. As a result he had his name changed.

In 1972, Drayton failed to qualify for the Olympics, or so he thought. His time in the marathon trial exceeded the required standard. Later it was discovered that the course was a kilometre too long. The track officials refused to accept the results and send Drayton to Munich. A second trial was arranged, just weeks before the Olympics. Drayton, realizing that he would completely drain himself, declined to compete.

Four years later, at the Montreal Olympics, Drayton was favoured to win a medal based on the sizzling 2:10:08.4 he had run the previous year. Injuries, though, forced him to ease his training regiment. Nevertheless, Drayton was able to reach peak form for the Olympics, but just five days before the race he caught a head cold which, in his words, "destroyed me." Drayton placed sixth - more than two minutes out of the medals - and wept. Later that year, a healthy Drayton defeated the Montreal Olympic champion at the Fukuoka marathon, the unofficial world championship.

Jerome Drayton retired from competitive racing in the early 1980s, an Olympic medal having eluded him. "If I could plan the perfect ending to my career, I would run into the Olympic Stadium at the head of the marathon. My mother would be sitting in the stands and I would win the gold medal."[9] It was not to be.

## INDUCTIONS

| 1978 | Canada's Sports Hall of Fame |
| 1991 | Canadian Road Running Hall of Fame |

## AWARDS

| 1969 | Fred Begley Memorial Trophy - Outstanding Marathoner in Canada |
| 1970 | Fred Begley Memorial Trophy - Outstanding Marathoner in Canada |
| 1973 | Fred Begley Memorial Trophy - Outstanding Marathoner in Canada |
| 1975 | Ontario Athlete of the Year |
| 1976 | Fred Begley Memorial Trophy - Outstanding Marathoner in Canada |
| 1977 | Norton Crowe Award - Canadian Male Athlete of the Year |
| 1977 | Fred Begley Memorial Trophy - Outstanding Marathoner in Canada |
| 1979 | Fred Begley Memorial Trophy - Outstanding Marathoner in Canada |

## RECORD

| year | competition | event | placing | result |
|------|-------------|-------|---------|--------|
| 1965 | Hamilton | 10 miles | 2 | 55:47.0 |
| 1967 | Waterloo | 2 miles | 1 | 9:33.2 |
| 1968 | Canadian Championships | 5,000 m | 3 | 14:20.2 |
| | | 10,000 m | 1 | 29:19.4 |

| year | competition | event | placing | result | |
|------|-------------|-------|---------|--------|---|
| 1968 | Motor City Marathon | marathon | 1 | 2:23:57 | |
| | Olympic Marathon Trials-2 | marathon | 1 | 2:16:11 | cb |
| | Ukrainians vs Lithuanians | 1,500 m | 1 | 4:01 .6 | |
| | | 3,000 m | 1 | 8:31 .9 | |
| | Olympic Games | marathon | dnf | | |
| 1969 | Boston Marathon | marathon | dnf | | |
| | Canadian Championships | 10,000 m | 1 | 30:04 .6 | |
| | Canadian Cross Country C'ships | | 1 | 37:46 .8 | |
| | Tokyo | 10,000 m | 6 | 29:08 .0 | nr |
| | Motor City Marathon | marathon | 1 | 2:12:00 | cb |
| | Fukuoka Marathon | marathon | 1 | 2:11:12 .8 | cb |
| 1970 | Boston Marathon | marathon | dnf | | |
| | Canadian Championships | 5,000 m | 1 | 14:14 .8 | |
| | | 10,000 m | 1 | 29:37 .0 | |
| | Commonwealth Games Trials | 5,000 m | 1 | 13:50 .8 | |
| | | 10,000 m | 1 | 28:25 .8 | nr |
| | CNE Track Meet | 10 miles | 1 | 46:37 .6 | wr |
| | Commonwealth Games | 10,000 m | 10 | 28:45 .0 | |
| | | marathon | dnf | | |
| | Motor City Marathon | marathon | 1 | 2:23:13 | |
| 1971 | Canadian Championships | 10,000 m | 1 | 30:28 .6 | |
| 1972 | Canadian Championships | 10,000 m | 2 | 30:35 .6 | |
| | | marathon | 1 | 2:23:13 .0 | |
| 1973 | Hamilton Around the Bay Race | 19.1 miles | 1 | 1:37:53 | |
| | Canadian Championships | 10,000 m | 3 | 29:48 .53 | |
| | | marathon | 1 | 2:13:26 .8 | |
| 1974 | Boston Marathon | marathon | 3 | 2:15:40 .0 | |
| | Hamilton Around the Bay Race | 19.1 miles | 1 | 1:39:40 | |
| | Commonwealth Games | marathon | 17 | 2:29:20 .0 | |
| 1975 | Fukuoka Marathon | marathon | 1 | 2:10:08 .4 | cb |
| | Canadian Championships | 10,000 m | 1 | 28:39 .6 | |
| | Helsinki | 5,000 m | 5 | 13:34 .92 | |
| 1976 | Canadian Championships | 5,000 m | 2 | 14:46 .6 | |
| | Olympic Games | marathon | 6 | 2:13:30 .0 | |
| | Fukuoka Marathon | marathon | 1 | 2:12:35 .0 | |
| 1977 | Boston Marathon | marathon | 1 | 2:14:46 .0 | |
| | New York Marathon | marathon | 2 | 2:13:52 .0 | |
| 1978 | Canadian Championships | 10,000 m | 1 | 29:57 .5 | |
| | Commonwealth Games | marathon | 2 | 2:16:13 .46 | |

| year | competition | event | placing | result |
|------|-------------|-------|---------|--------|
| 1978 | Toronto Marathon | marathon | 2 | 2:18:07 .4 |
| 1979 | Boston Marathon | marathon | 11 | 2:14:47 .0 |
|      | National Capital Marathon | marathon | 1 | 2:18:05 .0 |
| 1980 | New York Marathon | marathon | 21 | 2:17:58 .74 |
|      | Maryland International Marathon | marathon | 1 | 2:19:45 |
| 1981 | Boston Marathon | marathon | 250 | 2:28:49 |

cb    Canadian best

nr    Canadian record

wr    World record

# DYZANDRA, PAUL

| | |
|---|---|
| sport: | boxing |
| given name: | Dzyndra, Paul |
| born: | Transcona, Manitoba |
| | March 25, 1917 |
| height: | 1.78 m / 5'10" |
| weight: | 71 kg / 156 lbs |

Paul Dyzandra started to work out at a local CNR Athletic Club gym in Winnipeg in 1935. The following year, he entered into the field of amateur boxing. After only a few months of boxing, Dyzandra surprised the veterans by winning the Manitoba title in the welterweight division. Since it was an Olympic year, the victory assured him of a trip to the Olympic Games Trials. There, Dyzandra lost in a preliminary round to M. Holm of New Brunswick.

Paul Dyzandra successfully moved up to the middleweight division in 1938 by winning the Manitoba title. In 1939, Dyzandra capped his amateur career by winning the Dominion of Canada Middleweight championship. The following year he turned professional and won the Western Canada title. As a professional, Dyzandra fought mostly in the United States. He entered the ring on 25 occasions, winning the vast majority of his fights.

World War II brought Paul Dyzandra back to Winnipeg where he enlisted with the Royal Canadian Air Force. During his years of service, Dyzandra had very little opportunity to compete. As a result, he retired from the sport. After the cessation of hostilities and his discharge from the Air Force, Paul Dyzandra was honoured by the Sports Association of Winnipeg in the Hall of Fame in the Winnipeg Arena.

Paul Dyzandra was coached and trained by George "Scotty" Thompson. In the professional ranks he was managed by Harry Ronebie.

## INDUCTIONS

1945        Sport Association of Winnipeg Hall of Fame

## RECORD

| year | competition | division | result |
|------|-------------|----------|--------|
| 1936 | Manitoba Championships | welterweight | 1 |
|  | Olympic Trials | welterweight |  |
| 1938 | Manitoba Championships | middleweight | 1 |
| 1939 | Dominion of Canada Championships | middleweight | 1 |

# ELIASHEVSKY, CHRISTINE

| | |
|---|---|
| sport: | volleyball |
| born: | Munich, Germany |
| | March 1, 1947 |
| height: | 1.68 m / 5'6" |
| weight: | 50 kg / 110 lbs |

Christine Eliashevsky's volleyball career began in the early 1960s with the Vedmedyky sports club of the Ukrainian Youth Association Plast in Toronto. With the Vedmedyky, she won back-to-back Canadian junior volleyball championships in 1965 and 1966. In the latter championship, she captained the team and was selected as the tournament MVP. In 1967, as a member of team Ontario, she won the gold medal in volleyball at the inaugural Canada Winter Games. Later that year she represented Canada at the Pan American Games.

While enrolled at the University of Toronto in the late 1960s, Eliashevsky starred on the school's volleyball team. After graduating with a Master's degree in linguistics from the University of Strasbourg, Christine Eliashevsky made Basel, Switzerland, her home. For many years, she competed at the local club level in Switzerland.

AWARDS

1966        Canadian Junior Championship MVP

RECORD

| year | competition | team | placing |
|------|-------------|------|---------|
| 1965 | Canadian Junior Championships | Plast Vedmedyky | 1 |
|      | Canadian Championships | Plast Vedmedyky | 4 |
| 1966 | Canadian Junior Championships | Plast Vedmedyky | 1 |
|      | Canadian Championships | Plast Vedmedyky | 4 |
| 1967 | Canada Games | Ontario | 1 |
|      | Pan American Games | Canada | 6 |

# ELYNUIK, PAT

| | |
|---|---|
| sport: | hockey |
| born: | Foam Lake, Saskatchewan |
| | October 30, 1967 |
| height: | 1.83 m / 6'0" |
| weight: | 84 kg / 185 lbs |
| position: | right wing |
| shoots: | right |

*Photo courtesy of the Winnipeg Jets*

Pat Elynuik's first year of junior hockey was memorable; his team, the Prince Albert Raiders, won the Memorial Cup. In the process, he established himself as a solid winger, and a year later he was selected by the Winnipeg Jets in the first round, seventh overall in the 1986 NHL Entry Draft. That fall, Elynuik was named to Canada's team for the 1987 World Junior Championship. The team played well but after a bench-clearing brawl with the Soviets it was disqualified from the tournament.  After graduating from junior hockey, Elynuik spent the first two seasons of his professional career alternating between Winnipeg and its AHL affiliate in Moncton.

During the 1989-90 season, his first complete season in the NHL, Elynuik tied for the team lead in goals with 32.  His 74 points that season were second-best on the team.  A year later, the quiet, polite and unassuming Elynuik led the Jets in scoring with 31 goals.  His shooting percentage of 20.7 was best among the Jets and ninth best in the league.  That season he also tied a club record by registering five points in one period.

## RECORD

| year | team | league | | regular season | | | | | | playoffs | | | | |
|------|------|--------|---|----|---|---|-----|-----|---|----|---|---|-----|-----|
| | | | GP | G | A | PTS | PIM | | GP | G | A | PTS | PIM |
| 1987-88 | Winnipeg | NHL | 13 | 1 | 3 | 4 | 12 | | | | | | |
| | Moncton | AHL | 30 | 11 | 18 | 29 | 35 | | | | | | |
| 1988-89 | Winnipeg | NHL | 56 | 26 | 25 | 51 | 29 | | | | | | |
| | Moncton | AHL | 7 | 8 | 2 | 10 | 2 | | | | | | |
| 1989-90 | Winnipeg | NHL | 80 | 32 | 42 | 74 | 83 | | 7 | 2 | 4 | 6 | 2 |
| 1990-91 | Winnipeg | NHL | 80 | 31 | 34 | 65 | 73 | | | | | | |

international

| year | team | competition | GP | G | A | PTS | PIM | Place |
|------|------|-------------|----|---|---|-----|-----|-------|
| 1987 | Canada | World Junior Championship | 7 | 6 | 5 | 11 | 2 | DSQ |

# EURCHUK, MIKE

| | |
|---|---|
| sport: | wrestling |
| born: | Vegreville, Alberta |
| | October 30, 1938 |
| height: | 1.78 m / 5'10" |
| weight: | 100 kg / 220 lbs |

Mike Eurchuk started wrestling in his late twenties.  In his early thirties, he won the Alberta

Championship in the heavyweight division. Realizing that his age was starting to become a drawback, Eurchuk retired from competitive wrestling to concentrate on coaching, officiating, and administration. He coached for thirteen years at the local club level and two years at the University of Alberta. As an administrator, Eurchuk was involved in some capacity with nearly every wrestling association and wrestling officials' governing body in Alberta and Canada. In addition, he worked on special projects - bid committees for various championships, organizational committees, and the presidencies of championships.

It was in the field of officiating that Mike Eurchuk contributed most to Canadian wrestling. Before retiring in 1984, he had officiated at 46 national level tournaments, including 16 national, 12 junior, and 8 university championships, five national team trials, four Canada Winter Games, and the National Junior Olympics. In addition, he was involved in the officiating of more than 1,500 individual matches at thirty international tournaments, among them the World Championships, and the Pan American, Commonwealth, and Olympic Games. An outstanding official, he was one of very few elevated from Level III directly to Level I, without ever being in Level II. He was also among an elite group of wrestling officials, whose number did not exceed 25, that had been honoured by the International Amateur Wrestling Federation (FILA) with the Honorary International Exceptionelle Official in Perpetuity.

An educator by profession, Mike Eurchuk was widely used by FILA to evaluate wrestling officials. In addition, he has written several papers on wrestling. Titles include "Bending vs Breaking the Rules", and "Skills of an Effective Mat Chairman," both of which appeared in the *Canadian Wrestler* and "International Wrestling Rules Simplified," published by the Edmonton Public School Board.

## INDUCTIONS

| | |
|---|---|
| 1979 | Edmonton Boxing and Wrestling Hall of Fame |
| 1984 | Alberta Sports Hall of Fame |

## AWARDS

| | |
|---|---|
| 1970 | Presidents Award - Alberta Amateur Athletic Union |
| 1974 | Wrestling Official of the Year - Alberta |
| 1975 | Wrestling Contributor of the Year - Alberta |
| 1977 | Wrestling Official of the Year - Alberta |
| 1977 | Contributor of the Year - Canadian Amateur Wrestling Association |
| 1980 | Amateur Sports Official of the Year - Canada |
| 1982 | Administrator of the Year - Canadian Amateur Wrestling Association |
| 1982 | FILA Gold Star - International Amateur Wrestling Federation |

1985      Honourary International Exceptionelle Official in Perpetuity
- International Amateur Wrestling Federation (FILA)

## RECORD

coaching

. . .      University of Alberta - wrestling

officiating

| year | competition | |
| --- | --- | --- |
| 1969 | World Junior Championships | Referee |
| 1970 | World Championships | Referee |
| 1971 | World Junior Championships | Referee and Manager |
| 1973 | World Junior Championships | Referee |
| 1974 | European Championships | Referee |
| 1975 | FILA Invitational | Mat Chairman and Evaluator |
| | World Junior Championships | Referee |
| | Pan American Games | Mat Chairman |
| 1976 | Olympic Games | Referee |
| 1977 | World Cup | Referee |
| | World Junior Championships | Mat Chairman |
| | Pan American Championships | Mat Chairman and Evaluator |
| 1978 | Commonwealth Games | Referee |
| 1979 | Pan American Games | Mat Chairman and Evaluator |
| | World Espoir Championships | Mat Chairman and Evaluator |
| | FILA Invitational | Mat Chairman and Evaluator |
| 1980 | Pan-Am Junior Championships | Mat Chairman and Evaluator |
| 1981 | World Espoir Championships | Mat Chairman |
| | World Championships | Referee |
| 1982 | World Championships | Referee |
| | Commonwealth Games | Referee |
| 1983 | World Cadet Championships | Mat Chairman |
| 1984 | World Cup | Mat Chairman |
| 1984 | European Championships | Referee |

# EVANSHEN, TERRY

"The Flea"

| | |
|---|---|
| sport: | football |
| given name: | Evanshen, Terrance Anthony |
| born: | Montreal, Quebec |
| | June 13, 1944 |
| height: | 1.78 m / 5'10" |
| weight: | 84 kg / 185 lbs |
| position: | wide receiver |

*Photo courtesy of the Canadian Football Hall of Fame and Museum*

Terry Evanshen's outstanding play at the wide receiver position on the D'Arcy McGee High School football team in Montreal earned him an athletic scholarship to Utah State University in 1962. In 1964, Evanshen played semi-professional football in the Atlantic Coast League. The following year, the Montreal Alouettes brought Evanshen back to Canada as a defensive back. The club, though, was in need of a receiver, and Evanshen was used in that capacity in his first season, catching an Eastern Conference-leading 37 passes for 631 yards and three touchdowns. For his fine play he was named the 1965 Gruen Trophy winner - the outstanding Canadian rookie in the Eastern Conference. Montreal, though, believed that Evanshen was too small to be an effective receiver, and during the off-season he was traded to the Calgary Stampeders.

Terry Evanshen set the Stampeders offence on fire in 1966. He led the CFL with 67 receptions for 1,200 yards. One of the receptions was for 109 yards, which equalled the league record. He was named to the Western All-Star team and was the runner-up for the Schenley Most Outstanding Canadian Player award. The following year, Evanshen once again led the CFL with 96 receptions for 1,662 yards. His 17 touchdowns equalled a league record. In addition to a Western All-Star selection, Evanshen was named to the CFL All-Star team. His season culminated with the Schenley Most Outstanding Canadian Player award. In a best-of-three Western final, misfortune struck. The Stampeders won the first game and were leading the second when Evanshen slipped and fell, breaking his leg. The Stamps lost the game and the series.

Evanshen had two more successful seasons in Calgary before a trade in 1970 placed him back with the Montreal Alouettes. He adjusted quickly to his new club, helping them win the Grey Cup that year. In 1971, he led the East in receptions with 50 for 825 yards, and was once again honoured with the Schenley Most Outstanding Canadian Player award. Prior to the 1974 season, Evanshen signed with the Hamilton Tiger-Cats. He finished his playing days with the

Toronto Argonauts in 1978.

During a 14-year career in the Canadian Football League, Terry Evanshen played in 198 games and caught a pass in a league-record 181 games. In total, his "sure pair of hands" caught 600 passes for 9,697 yards and 80 touchdowns. During that time he committed only three fumbles. In the playoffs, Evanshen caught 66 passes for 1,040 yards and 12 touchdowns. The outstanding achievements of Terry Evanshen were recognized in 1984 when he was inducted into the Canadian Football Hall of Fame.

## INDUCTIONS

1984        Canadian Football Hall of Fame

## AWARDS

1965        Gruen Trophy  -  CFL Outstanding Canadian Rookie in East
1967        Dave Dryburgh Memorial Trophy  -  CFL Western Division  Scoring Leader
1967        Schenley Award  -  CFL Most Outstanding Canadian
1971        Schenley Award  -  CFL Most Outstanding Canadian

## ALL-STAR SELECTIONS

| 1965 | wide receiver | CFL | All-Eastern |
|------|---------------|-----|-------------|
| 1966 | wide receiver | CFL | All-Western |
| 1967 | wide receiver | CFL | All-Western |
|      | wide receiver | CFL |             |
| 1968 | wide receiver | CFL | All-Western |
| 1969 | wide receiver | CFL | All-Western |
| 1971 | wide receiver | CFL | All-Eastern |
| 1975 | wide receiver | CFL | All-Eastern |

## RECORD

| | | | regular season | | | | | | | | playoffs | | | Grey Cup game | | |
| | | | scoring | | | pass receiving | | | | | scoring | | | scoring | | |
| year | team | league | GP | TD | PTS | NO | YDS | AVE | LG | TD | GP | TD | PTS | GP | TD | PTS |
|------|------|--------|----|----|-----|----|-----|-----|----|----|----|----|-----|----|----|-----|
| 1965 | Montreal | CFL | 14 | 3 | 18 | 37 | 631 | 17.1 | 85 | 3 | 1 | 1 | 6 | | | |
| 1966 | Calgary | CFL | 16 | 9 | 54 | 67 | 1,200 | 17.9 | 109 | 9 | | | | | | |
| 1967 | Calgary | CFL | 16 | 17 | 102 | 96 | 1,662 | 17.3 | 63 | 17 | 2 | 2 | 12 | | | |
| 1968 | Calgary | CFL | 16 | 9 | 54 | 63 | 1,002 | 15.9 | 43 | 9 | 3 | 2 | 12 | 1 | 2 | 12 |
| 1969 | Calgary | CFL | 16 | 8 | 48 | 65 | 951 | 14.6 | 45 | 8 | 3 | 1 | 6 | | | |

| | | | regular season | | | | | | | | | playoffs | | | Grey Cup game | | |
|---|---|---|---|---|---|---|---|---|---|---|---|---|---|---|---|---|---|
| | | | scoring | | | pass receiving | | | | | | scoring | | | scoring | | |
| year | team | league | GP | TD | PTS | NO | YDS | AVE | LG | TD | | GP | TD | PTS | GP | TD | PTS |
| 1970* | Montreal | CFL | 14 | 7 | 42 | 37 | 625 | 16.9 | 48 | 7 | | 3 | 1 | 6 | 1 | 0 | 0 |
| 1971 | Montreal | CFL | 14 | 5 | 30 | 50 | 825 | 16.5 | 65 | 5 | | | | | | | |
| 1972 | Montreal | CFL | 14 | 3 | 18 | 33 | 407 | 12.3 | 35 | 3 | | 1 | 0 | 0 | | | |
| 1973 | Montreal | CFL | 14 | 1 | 6 | 18 | 278 | 15.4 | 64 | 1 | | 2 | 0 | 0 | | | |
| 1974 | Hamilton | CFL | 14 | 1 | 6 | 29 | 431 | 14.9 | 33 | 1 | | 1 | 0 | 0 | | | |
| 1975 | Hamilton | CFL | 16 | 13 | 78 | 55 | 970 | 17.6 | 81 | 13 | | 1 | 1 | 6 | | | |
| 1976 | Hamilton | CFL | 14 | 3 | 18 | 20 | 307 | 15.4 | 26 | 3 | | 2 | 3 | 18 | | | |
| 1977 | Hamilton | CFL | 12 | 0 | 0 | 19 | 245 | 12.9 | 39 | 0 | | | | | | | |
| 1978 | Toronto | CFL | 8 | 1 | 6 | 11 | 136 | 12.4 | 30 | 1 | | | | | | | |

# EZINICKI, BILL

"Wild Bill"

| | |
|---|---|
| sport: | hockey, golf |
| born: | Winnipeg, Manitoba |
| | March 11, 1924 |
| height: | 1.78 m / 5'10" |
| weight: | 77 kg / 170 lbs |
| position: | right wing |
| shoots: | right |

Bill Ezinicki always had a passion for sport. He began to play organized hockey at ten, and at twelve he shot a 99 at the Manitoba Amateur Golf Championship. He also found time to compete in football and soccer. At seventeen he was recruited by the Oshawa Generals hockey club. He was a member of the team that won the Memorial Cup in 1944. Upon graduation from junior hockey, Ezinicki played a few games with the Toronto Maple Leafs before serving 18 months in the army. While stationed at Camp Shilo, he starred on the base's soccer club.

After demobilization, Bill Ezinicki resumed his professional hockey career with the Toronto farm club at Pittsburgh. During the 1946-47 season, he cracked the starting line-up of the Leafs. He played regularly with Toronto for four seasons and was a member of three Stanley Cup teams. After a fallout with club management over golf, he was traded to Boston in 1950. Before the start of the 1952-53 season, he was sold to Toronto but did not make the club. In February of 1955 he was sold to New York where he finished his NHL career.

A free skating defenseman, Ezinicki is best remembered for his bruising bodychecks which he worked hard at to perfect. Not naturally big in stature, Ezinicki developed his body by weightlifting regularly. In addition, he studied the skating habits of his opponents from the bench to determine when they were most vulnerable. Once on the ice, Ezinicki would locate the puck carrier, execute a wide deceptive turn, and hit him head-on with his upper body. The result was devastating. He was loved by the fans of the teams that he played for and loathed by all others. "Kill Ezinicki" rival fans chanted once during a junior game in Montreal; some years later an angry female Rangers' fan stabbed him with a hatpin as he skated by. Although his bodychecks were generally considered legal, Ezinicki liked altercations. He led the league in penalties with 145 minutes during the 1948-49 season and 144 minutes a year later.

Ezinicki's passion for hockey was only surpassed by his passion for golf. He did everything possible to prolong the golf season, reporting to training camp on time only twice in eight years of professional hockey. As an amateur he won the 1941 Manitoba Open. He was the runner-up at the 1941 and 1943 Manitoba Amateur Championship, and the 1947 Canadian Amateur Championship. In 1948, he made his professional debut at the Philadelphia Invitational shooting 311, 30 strokes behind the winner. Over the years, Ezinicki played part-time on the PGA tour, winning a number of lesser tournaments, among them the 1956 New England PGA and the Open titles in Rhode Island, Massachusetts, Maine, and Vermont in 1960, and the Maritime Open in 1965. He also had a second place finish at a Bob Hope Classic. Ezinicki's best year on the PGA tour was in 1960.

In 1949, Bill Ezinicki became the pro at Toronto's New Uplands course. After being traded to the Boston Bruins, he worked as a pro in Cape Cod. Later he took the job of club pro at the exclusive International Golf Club, the longest course in America measuring 8,325 yards. He held the position through the 1980s.

## INDUCTIONS

1986        Manitoba Hockey Hall of Fame

## AWARDS

1966        Boston Sportsman of the Year

## RECORD

| year | team | league | regular season | | | | | playoffs | | | | |
|------|------|--------|----|---|---|-----|-----|----|---|---|-----|-----|
| | | | GP | G | A | PTS | PIM | GP | G | A | PTS | PIM |
| 1944-45 | Toronto | NHL | 8 | 1 | 4 | 5 | 17 | | | | | |
| 1945-46 | Toronto | NHL | 24 | 4 | 8 | 12 | 29 | | | | | |

| year | team | league | regular season | | | | | playoffs | | | | |
|------|------|--------|----|---|---|-----|-----|----|---|---|-----|-----|
|      |      |        | GP | G | A | PTS | PIM | GP | G | A | PTS | PIM |
| 1945-46 | Pittsburgh | AHL | 27 | 9 | 12 | 21 | 23 | | | | | |
| 1946-47* | Toronto | NHL | 60 | 17 | 20 | 37 | 93 | 11 | 0 | 2 | 2 | 30 |
| 1947-48* | Toronto | NHL | 60 | 11 | 20 | 31 | 97 | 9 | 3 | 1 | 4 | 6 |
| 1948-49* | Toronto | NHL | 52 | 13 | 15 | 28 | 145 | 9 | 1 | 4 | 5 | 20 |
| 1949-50 | Toronto | NHL | 67 | 10 | 12 | 22 | 144 | 5 | 0 | 0 | 0 | 13 |
| 1950-51 | Boston | NHL | 53 | 16 | 19 | 35 | 119 | 6 | 1 | 1 | 2 | 18 |
|  | Pittsburgh | AHL | 13 | 6 | 3 | 9 | 24 | | | | | |
| 1951-52 | Boston | NHL | 28 | 5 | 5 | 10 | 47 | | | | | |
|  | Pittsburgh | AHL | 16 | 4 | 9 | 13 | 53 | 11 | 3 | 1 | 4 | 67 |
| 1952-53 | Pittsburgh | AHL | 41 | 15 | 13 | 28 | 115 | 7 | 0 | 3 | 3 | 8 |
| 1954-55 | NY Rangers | NHL | 16 | 2 | 2 | 4 | 22 | | | | | |
|  | Ottawa | QHL | 18 | 5 | 6 | 11 | 39 | | | | | |
|  | Vancouver | WHL | 15 | 5 | 2 | 7 | 50 | | | | | |

# FEDERKO, BERNIE

| | |
|---|---|
| sport: | hockey |
| given name: | Federko, Bernard Allan |
| born: | Foam Lake, Saskatchewan May 12, 1956 |
| height: | 1.83 m / 6'0" |
| weight: | 88 kg / 178 lbs |
| position: | center |
| shoots: | left |

Bernie Federko was born in Foam Lake, a town that has produced many outstanding hockey players. As a youngster he played endless hours of hockey with his neighbour Dennis Polonich. While he also excelled in volleyball and basketball, Federko dreamed of a professional hockey career in the NHL. The first step in the realization of the dream occurred when he joined the junior Saskatoon Blades of the WCHL. At the conclusion of the 1975-76 season, his last in junior hockey, Federko was named the league's MVP. That season he led the league with assists (115) and points (187). His point total surpassed Bobby Clarke's league record. He was drafted in the first round, seventh overall, by the St. Louis Blues of the NHL, and sixth overall by the Edmonton Oilers of the WHA.

Bernie Federko opted for the NHL and a dream came true. A superb stickhandler and play-maker, Federko had the patience to develop countless scoring opportunities. More often than not, Federko would forgo shooting on net to set up his wingers. According to one of his coach-es, Federko's unselfish play kept his goal totals down. Nevertheless, in 1986 Federko became the Blues' all-time scoring leader when he netted his 293rd goal. In 1988, he was named team captain and a year later, after 13 seasons with St. Louis, he was traded to Detroit. Federko was stunned by the trade. He felt unwanted in Detroit, since the Wings had given up a fan favourite to secure his service. In the summer of 1990, the Red Wings bought out the remaining year of his contract. Rather than try out with another team, Bernie Federko retired.

## AWARDS

| 1976 | MVP Trophy - WCHL |
|------|-------------------|
| 1976 | Bob Brownridge Memorial Trophy - WCHL scoring leader |
| 1977 | Ken McKenzie Trophy - CHL Rookie of the Year |

## ALL-STAR SELECTIONS

1976-77    centre    CHL    Second Team

## RECORD

| year | team | league | regular season | | | | | playoffs | | | | |
|------|------|--------|----|----|----|-----|-----|----|----|----|-----|-----|
| | | | GP | G | A | PTS | PIM | GP | G | A | PTS | PIM |
| 1976-77 | St. Louis | NHL | 31 | 14 | 9 | 23 | 15 | 4 | 1 | 1 | 2 | 2 |
| | Kansas City | CHL | 42 | 30 | 39 | 69 | 41 | | | | | |
| 1977-78 | St. Louis | NHL | 72 | 17 | 24 | 41 | 27 | | | | | |
| 1978-79 | St. Louis | NHL | 74 | 31 | 64 | 95 | 14 | | | | | |
| 1979-80 | St. Louis | NHL | 79 | 38 | 56 | 94 | 24 | 3 | 1 | 0 | 1 | 2 |
| 1980-81 | St. Louis | NHL | 78 | 31 | 73 | 104 | 47 | 11 | 8 | 10 | 18 | 2 |
| 1981-82 | St. Louis | NHL | 74 | 30 | 62 | 92 | 70 | 10 | 3 | 15 | 18 | 10 |
| 1982-83 | St. Louis | NHL | 75 | 24 | 60 | 84 | 24 | 4 | 2 | 3 | 5 | 0 |
| 1983-84 | St. Louis | NHL | 79 | 41 | 66 | 107 | 43 | 11 | 4 | 4 | 8 | 10 |
| 1984-85 | St. Louis | NHL | 76 | 30 | 73 | 103 | 27 | 3 | 0 | 2 | 2 | 4 |
| 1985-86 | St. Louis | NHL | 80 | 34 | 68 | 102 | 34 | 19 | 7 | 14 | 21 | 17 |
| 1986-87 | St. Louis | NHL | 64 | 20 | 52 | 72 | 32 | 6 | 3 | 3 | 6 | 18 |
| 1987-88 | St. Louis | NHL | 79 | 20 | 69 | 89 | 52 | 10 | 2 | 6 | 8 | 18 |
| 1988-89 | St. Louis | NHL | 66 | 22 | 45 | 67 | 54 | 10 | 4 | 8 | 12 | 0 |
| 1989-90 | Detroit | NHL | 73 | 17 | 40 | 57 | 24 | | | | | |

# FEDKO, ALEX

| | |
|---|---|
| sport: | swimming |
| born: | Bensheim, Germany |
| | April 30, 1949 |
| height: | 1.83 m / 6'0" |
| weight: | 84 kg / 185 lbs |

In 1961, when Alex Fedko was 11 years old, his parents enrolled him at the University Settlement House Community Centre in Toronto. The young Fedko had excess energy and his parents wanted him to expend it by participating in organized sport. At the Centre, Fedko learned to swim. One of the instructors saw that Fedko had potential and convinced him to join the University Settlement Aquatic Club (USAC). The evaluation was accurate; the following year Fedko had the second fastest time in Canada among 11 and 12-year-olds in the 50-yard backstroke. In 1963, two years after learning how to swim, Fedko competed at his first national senior championship.

While attending Toronto's Harbord Collegiate, Fedko won numerous city and provincial high school titles. Concurrently, he swam with USAC and competed at the senior level at the national championships. In 1966, Fedko was selected to Canada's Commonwealth Games team. His best result at the Games was a sixth place finish in the 110-yard backstroke.

Upon graduating from high school in 1967, Fedko enrolled at Simon Fraser University on a swimming scholarship. At the time, the university's swim team competed on the National Association of Inter-Collegiate Athletics (NAIA) circuit in the United States. Fedko won the 100-yard backstroke at the NAIA championships in 1969, establishing an American collegiate record of 55.8 seconds. He also won a silver medal in the 200-yard backstroke. The following year, Fedko won three silver medals at the NAIA championships. In both years he was the captain of the swim team and was named All-American.

Alex Fedko's career peaked in 1969. That year he won the Canadian championship in the 100-metre backstroke and established the American collegiate record in the 100-yard backstroke. He captained the Canadian swim team that toured Canada, competing against the New Zealand national team. He also captained the Ontario swim team at the inaugural Canada Games.

In 1971, Alex Fedko switched to water polo.  He competed at a forward position with the Toronto Waterpolo Club at University Settlement.  In 1974, Fedko was invited to the national team training camp to prepare for the upcoming Olympics.  He declined because of his school workload and an injured rotator cuff.  A broken leg terminated his water polo career in 1985.

Alex Fedko also coached swimming.  Commencing in 1972, he coached for ten years in the Toronto area.

## RECORD

| year | competition | event | placing | result |
|------|-------------|-------|---------|--------|
| 1965 | Canadian Championships | 4 x 100 m freestyle | 3 | 4:00.1 |
| | | 4 x 200 m freestyle | 3 | 9:17.0 |
| 1966 | Canadian Championships | 110 y backstroke | 3 | 1:04.5 |
| | | 220 y backstroke | 4 | 2:21.0 |
| | | 110 y butterfly | 4 | 1:02.9 |
| | | 4 x 110 y medley | 2 | 4:21.8 |
| | | 4 x 110 y freestyle | 1 | 3:52.8 nr |
| | Commonwealth Games | 110 y freestyle | 3 H | 58.3 |
| | | 110 y backstroke | 6 | 1:05.2 |
| | | 220 y backstroke | 3 H | 2:27.7 |
| 1967 | Canadian Championships | 100 m backstroke | 6 | 1:05.4 |
| | | 200 m backstroke | 7 | 2:24.4 |
| | | 100 m butterfly | 6 | 1:02.2 |
| | | 200 m butterfly | 4 | 2:26.6 |
| | | 4 x 100 m freestyle | 1 | 3:52.1 |
| | | 4 x 100 m medley | 1 | 4:14.1 |
| | | 4 x 200 m freestyle | 1 | 8:43.9 |
| 1968 | Canadian Championships | 100 m freestyle | 5 | 56.5 |
| | | 100 m backstroke | 3 | 1:03.5 |
| | | 100 m butterfly | 5 | 1:01.2 |
| | | 200 m backstroke | 5 | 2:19.8 |
| | | 200 m IM | 6 | 2:23.7 |
| | | 4 x 100 m medley | 1 | 4:10.7 |
| | | 4 x 100 m freestyle | 1 | 3:48.3 nr |
| 1969 | Canadian Winter Championships | 100 m backstroke | 1 | 1:02.4 |
| | NAIA Championships | 100 y backstroke | 1 | 55.8 cr |
| | | 100 y butterfly | 4 | |
| | | 200 y backstroke | 2 | |
| | | 200 y IM | 4 | |

| year | competition | event | placing | result |
|------|-------------|-------|---------|--------|
| 1969 | Canada Summer Games | 100 m freestyle | 3 | 56.5 |
| | | 100 m butterfly | 3 | 1:01.0 |
| | | 100 m backstroke | 4 | 1:04.8 |
| | | 4 x 100 m medley | 3 | |
| | | 4 x 100 m freestyle | 1 | 3:48.0 |
| | | 4 x 200 m freestyle | 3 | |
| | Canadian Championships | 100 m freestyle | 6 | 57.8 |
| 1970 | Canadian Winter Championships | | | |
| | & Commonwealth Games Trials | 100 m freestyle | 4 | 56.2 |
| | | 100 m backstroke | 8 | 1:04.5 |
| | | 100 m butterfly | 5 | 59.5 |
| | | 200 m IM | 7 | 2:26.8 |
| | NAIA Championships | 100 y backstroke | 2 | |
| | | 100 y butterfly | 2 | |
| | | 200 y backstroke | 2 | |
| | | 200 y IM | 4 | |
| | CIAU Championships | 200 y IM | 2 | |
| 1971 | Pan American Games Trials | 100 m freestyle | 6 | 56.4 |
| | | 100 m butterfly | 4 | 1:00 |
| | | 200 m IM | 7 | 2:23.5 |

cr    American collegiate record

nr    Canadian record

H    in qualifying heat, does not advance to final

# FEDORICK, WALTER

| | |
|------|------|
| sport: | athletics |
| born: | Montreal, Quebec |
| | January 30, 1918 |
| died: | Hamilton, Ontario |
| | March 18, 1979 |
| height: | 1.75 m / 5'9" |
| weight: | 70.5 kg / 155 lbs |

When Walter Fedorick was twelve years old, he lost the sight in his left eye after being hit by a thrown stone. A few years later Fedorick took up boxing. He was quickly dissuaded from this activity by his older brother John, who feared that Walter could lose the other eye. John also suggested that Walter try road racing to expend his boundless energy. In the spring of 1935, after some convincing, the young Fedorick started to train. Afraid of being seen, he trained at night. Two months later, Fedorick entered his first competition, the Hamilton Spectator 2.5 mile road race, and won.

Walter Fedorick quickly established himself as one of the top road runners in Canada as well as a excellent track competitor. He was touted as a fine prospect for the 1940 Olympic Games. Because of the war, the Games were cancelled, as were most of the track competitions in Canada. Fedorick ran in road races before retiring in 1941.

The desire to run, though, was overwhelming, and in 1944, Fedorick returned to competition. In 1946, he re-established himself as one of the nation's top distance runners after winning the national championship in the 5-mile event and posting the best times in Canada at the 5 and 15-mile distances. He entered 15 races of which he won 13. He also had a second and a third place finish. The following year, the powerfully built Fedorick ran his first marathon.

In the spring of 1948, Walter Fedorick ran his first Boston Marathon and placed seventh. Subsequently, at the Canadian marathon championship and Olympic trials, Fedorick placed second and was named to the Olympic team. The Olympic marathon course was the roughest he had ever run. By the time he crossed the finish line in 23rd place, his toes and feet were blood-blistered and his legs were numb. He was forced to give up running for four months while his feet and legs healed.

After the Olympics, Fedorick switched to shorter distances because of his persistently sore feet. Most experts believed, though, that the 30-year-old runner's career was over. Fedorick surprised everyone in 1949 by winning the Canadian championship in the six-mile event and establishing two Canadian native records at the distance within a month. The following year, Fedorick earned a spot on the Commonwealth Games team with a second place finish in the six-mile race at the national championships. At the Commonwealth Games Fedorick placed eighth. He also entered the marathon without training for the distance and finished the race in tenth position.

Walter Fedorick's fascination with the marathon was overwhelming and he once again began to train for the event. He made a spectacular comeback at the distance in 1951 by winning the Canadian championship and placing third at the American. Unfortunately, the comeback was short-lived. Fedorick was forced to retire from competitive running, due to a medical disor-der, while training for the Helsinki Olympics in early 1952. Ironically, during a competitive career that spanned 14 years, Walter Fedorick did not once drop out of a race.

# RECORD

track

| year | competition | event | placing | result | |
|------|-------------|-------|---------|--------|---|
| 1938 | United States Jr. Championships | 5,000 m | 3 | | |
| | Ontario Championships | 6 miles | 2 | | |
| 1946 | Canadian Championships | 5 miles | 1 | 27:39.2 | |
| | Canada vs United States | 5 miles | 3 | | |
| 1947 | Canadian Championship | marathon | 3 | 2:52:41 | |
| | Montreal Marathon | marathon | 2 | 2:40:20 | |
| 1948 | Boston Marathon | marathon | 7 | 2:41:23 | |
| | Canadian Championship | marathon | 3 | 2:46:29.0 | |
| | Olympic Games | marathon | 23 | 2:52:12 | |
| 1949 | Ontario Championships | 6 miles | 1 | 32:58.6 | nr |
| | Canadian Championships | 6 miles | 1 | 32:44.0 | nr |
| | Toronto Police Games | 5 miles | 1 | 27:04.4 | |
| | CNE Athletic Meet | 10 miles | 1 | 57:06.9 | |
| 1950 | Commonwealth Games | 6 miles | 8 | 32:42 | * |
| | | marathon | 10 | | |
| | Canadian Championships | 6 miles | 2 | 32:39 | |
| | Toronto Police Games | 5 miles | 1 | 26:48.4 | |
| | CNE Athletic Meet | 10 miles | 1 | 56:56 | |
| 1951 | Maine Marathon | marathon | 5 | 2:40:29.2 | |
| | Canadian Championship | marathon | 1 | 2:58:42 | |
| | United States Championship | marathon | 3 | 2:40:02 | |

road racing

| year | competition | event | placing | result |
|------|-------------|-------|---------|--------|
| 1935 | Spectator Trophy Race (jr.) | 2.5 miles | 1 | 14:17.8 |
| 1936 | Berwick (Pennsylvania) | 9.3 miles | 12 | |
| | Berwick (Pennsylvania) | 9.3 miles | 13 | 50:55 |
| 1938 | Hamilton New Year's Day Race | 10 miles | 1 | 57:50 |
| 1941 | Hamilton Labour Day Road Race | 10 miles | 3 | 58:05.0 |
| 1944 | Hamilton Round the Bay | 19 miles | 3 | 1:53:15 |
| | Berwick (Pennsylvania) | 9.3 miles | 3 | 50:05 |
| 1946 | Hamilton New Year's Day Race | 10 miles | 1 | 56:33 |
| | Waterdown Road Race | 6 miles | 1 | 32:04.4 |
| | Fergus Highland Games | 5 miles | 1 | 26:55 |
| | Hamilton Round the Bay | 19 miles | 1 | 1:54:28.0 |
| | Galt Road Race | 15 miles | 1 | 1:29:40.0 |
| | Berwick (Pennsylvania) | 9.3 miles | 2 | 48:50 |
| 1947 | Hamilton New Year's Day Race | 10 miles | 1 | 57:07 |

road racing

| year | competition | event | placing | result |
|------|-------------|-------|---------|--------|
| 1947 | Galt Road Race | 10 miles | 1 | 56:05 |
| | Port Colborne Road Race | 9 miles | 1 | 47:56 |
| | Hamilton Round the Bay | 19 miles | 3 | 1:57:37 |
| | Guelph Road Race | 15 miles | 2 | 1:22:06 |
| | Berwick (Pennsylvania) | 9.3 miles | 5 | 49:27 |
| 1948 | Hamilton New Year's Day Race | 10 miles | 1 | 58:24 |
| | Grimsby Road Race | 10 miles | 1 | 58:47 |
| | Fruitlands Road Race | 5.5 miles | 1 | 29:28 |
| | Hamilton Round the Bay | 19 miles | 3 | 1:53:12 |
| | Berwick (Pennsylvania) | 9.3 miles | 11 | |
| 1949 | Preston Road Race | 5 miles | 1 | 24:57 |
| | Berwick (Pennsylvania) | 9.3 miles | 11 | |
| 1950 | Hamilton New Year's Day Race | 10 miles | 2 | 56:06 |
| | Hamilton Firestone War Veterans' | 15 miles | 4 | 1:27:50 |
| | Syracuse Nugent Memorial | 14 miles | 2 | 1:15:58 |
| | Hamilton Round the Bay | 19 miles | 1 | 1:54:30 |
| | Guelph Road Race | 15 miles | 2 | 1:21:50 |
| | Berwick (Pennsylvania) | 9.3 miles | 5 | |
| 1951 | Hamilton New Year's Day Race | 10 miles | 5 | 57:00 |
| | Hamilton Firestone War Veterans' | 15 miles | 2 | 1:28:23 |
| | Dundas Road Race | 15 miles | 1 | 1:24:45 |

nr    Canadian record

*    Record time not accepted because mark set outside of Canada.

# FEDORUK, SYLVIA

"Syl"

| | |
|---|---|
| sport: | all-round |
| given name: | Fedoruk, Sylvia Olga |
| born: | Canora, Saskatchewan |
| | May 5, 1927 |
| height: | 1.70 m / 5'7" |
| weight: | . . . |

Upon graduation from high school, Sylvia Fedoruk was awarded the Hon. Paul Martin Medal for maintaining, for four consecutive years, the highest marks in her class and the highest athletic awards. At the University of Saskatchewan, the outstanding all-round athlete was a member of twelve intervarsity championship teams in the years 1946-47 to 1950-51. Competing in six sports, Fedoruk won titles in five. Hockey was the only sport where she failed to win a championship. She won five titles in basketball, two in athletics, three in volleyball, and two in golf.

At the 1947 Canadian Track and Field Championships, Fedoruk won four medals and was awarded with the T. Eaton Trophy, emblematic of the women's individual high point total at the championships. After graduating in 1951 with a Master's degree, Fedoruk continued to excel on basketball, softball and curling teams. She was with the 1952 Gradettes that made the finals of the Western Canada Basketball Playdowns. In 1954 and 1955, she played on teams that won the Western Canada Ladies' Softball Championships.

In 1960, the Western Canadian Ladies' Curling Championship team, of which she was a member, defeated Eastern Canada to win the first and only East-West Curling Championship. A year later she was a member of the rink that won the inaugural Canadian Ladies' Curling Championship. Sylvia Fedoruk's professional career has been even more notable. Professor Emeritus of Oncology and Chancellor of the University of Saskatchewan, the Honourable Sylvia Fedoruk was appointed Lieutenant Governor of the Province of Saskatchewan in 1989.

## INDUCTIONS

| | |
|---|---|
| 1976 | Saskatchewan Sports Hall of Fame  -  Member of the McKee Curling Team |
| 1984 | University of Saskatchewan Wall of Fame |
| 1986 | Canadian Curling Hall of Fame |
| 1987 | Saskatoon Sports Hall of Fame |
| 1989 | Saskatchewan Sports Hall of Fame  -  Member of Rambler Softball Team |

## AWARDS

| | |
|---|---|
| 1947 | T. Eaton Trophy  -  Senior Women's Individual High Point Total at the Dominion Track and Field Championships |
| 1949 | Spirit of Youth Trophy |
| 1949 | Governor General's Gold Medal |
| 1986 | Saskatchewan Order of Merit |
| 1986 | Officer, Order of Canada |

# RECORD

athletics

| year | competition | event | placing | result |
|------|-------------|-------|---------|--------|
| 1947 | Dominion Championships | javelin | 1 | 103 ft ¹/₂ in |
|      |             | softball throw | 1 | 186 ft 4¹/₂ in |
|      |             | shot put | 2 | |
|      |             | discus | 3 | |

curling

| year | competition | event | placing | result |
|------|-------------|-------|---------|--------|
| 1960 | Saskatchewan Championship | ladies | 1 | |
|      | East-West Canadian Final | ladies | 1 | |
| 1961 | Saskatchewan Championship | ladies | 1 | |
|      | Canadian Championship | ladies | 1 | 9-0 |
| 1962 | Saskatchewan Championship | ladies | 1 | |
|      | Canadian Championship | ladies | 2 | 8-1 |

softball

| year | competition | team | placing |
|------|-------------|------|---------|
| 1954 | Western Canadian Ladies Championship | Saskatoon Ramblers | 1 |
| 1955 | Western Canadian Ladies Championship | Regina Govins | 1 |

administrative/coaching

| year | position |
|------|----------|
| . . . | Coach, University of Saskatchewan Huskiette volleyball |
| . . . | Coach, University of Saskatchewan Huskiette curling |
| 1971-72 | President, Canadian Ladies' Curling Association |

# FESTERYGA, GEORGE

"Festy"

sport:      football
born:       Hamilton, Ontario
            July 31, 1926
height:     1.80 m / 5'11"
weight:     . . .
position:   quarterback, fullback, defence

In 1944, George Festeryga quarterbacked Hamilton Tech Institute to the city championship. In 1946, he was playing for the junior Hamilton Tigers of the Junior Big Four League. The club won the Eastern championship. A year later, Festeryga made the roster of the senior Hamilton Tigers of the IRFU - Big Four League. The team only won two games that year, and joined the weaker ORFU League for the 1948 season. Festeryga was used in various capacities in 1948 as the Tigers won the league title.

In 1949, George Festeryga joined the Montreal Alouettes. The club upset the Ottawa Roughriders in the conference final and went on to win the Grey Cup. A year later he was playing for the Saskatchewan Roughriders. The Roughies used Festeryga on defence. Towards the end of the season an attempt was made to use him at fullback. In his first game on offence Festeryga scored a touchdown. He also suffered a kidney injury and missed the rest of the season and the playoffs. Festeryga's stay in Regina lasted one season. He joined the Edmonton Eskimos in 1951 as a utility player. He played with the club for two years, retiring after the 1952 Grey Cup game.

In 1971, George Festeryga was named manager of the Sport Action Program. The program offered a variety of sports for hands-on participation by persons of all ages. It was sponsored by Fitness and Amateur Sport - Canada.

## RECORD

| scoring | | | regular season | | | playoffs | | | Grey Cup game | | |
|---|---|---|---|---|---|---|---|---|---|---|---|
| year | team | league | GP | TD | PTS | GP | TD | PTS | GP | TD | PTS |
| 1947 | Hamilton | IRFU | ... | | | | | | | | |
| 1948 | Hamilton | ORFU | ... | 0 | 0 | 3 | 1 | 5 | | | |
| 1949* | Montreal | IRFU | ... | | | 3 | 0 | 0 | 1 | 0 | 0 |

| scoring | | | regular season | | | playoffs | | | Grey Cup game | | |
|---|---|---|---|---|---|---|---|---|---|---|---|
| year | team | league | GP | TD | PTS | GP | TD | PTS | GP | TD | PTS |
| 1950 | Saskatchewan | WIFU | 10 | 1 | 5 | | | | | | |
| 1951 | Edmonton | WIFU | ... | 1 | 5 | 4 | 0 | 0 | | | |
| 1952 | Edmonton | WIFU | ... | | | 5 | | | 1 | 0 | 0 |

# GALANCHUK, KEN

| | |
|---|---|
| sport: | basketball |
| given name: | Galanchuk, Kenneth |
| born: | . . . |
| | . . . |
| height: | 1.85 m / 6'1" |
| weight: | . . . |
| position: | guard |

Ken Galanchuk first gained recognition as a basketball player during the 1959-60 basketball season when he led the Institute Prosvita Athletic Club (IPAC) to the Manitoba junior basketball title. For his outstanding play, Galanchuk was named to the Winnipeg league all-star team. The following season, while still with IPAC, Galanchuk also began to play for the University of Manitoba basketball team. In his rookie season, he led the university club in scoring with an average of 15.6 points per game. The following year, he was one of the stars as the IPAC senior team won the Manitoba title and finished second in the Western Canada Championship.

In the fall of 1962, Galanchuk was asked to try out for the national team and succeeded. The Canadian team at the time was the Lethbridge Nationals. As a result, Galanchuk put his legal studies on hold and moved to Alberta. With the national team, he competed at the 1962 seven-nation Philippines Invitational and at the 1963 Pan American Games in Brazil. With the Lethbridge Nationals, he won the 1963 Canadian basketball title. Galanchuk then returned to Winnipeg to complete his studies. At the same time, he rejoined the IPAC basketball team. Galanchuk almost repeated as national champion that year, as IPAC placed second in the nation. In 1967, Ken Galanchuk won the silver medal at the Canada Games while playing on the Manitoba team.

# RECORD

| year | competition | team | placing |
|------|-------------|------|---------|
| 1960 | Manitoba Junior Championships | IPAC | 1 |
| | Western Canada Junior Championships | IPAC | 2 |
| 1961 | Greater Winnipeg Jr. Basketball League | IPAC | 1 |
| 1962 | Manitoba Championships | IPAC | 1 |
| | Western Canada Championships | IPAC | 2 |
| | The Philippines Invitational | Canada | 2 |
| 1963 | Canadian Championships | Lethbridge Nationals | 1 |
| | Pan American Games | Canada | 6 |
| 1964 | Manitoba Championships | IPAC | 1 |
| | Canadian Championships | IPAC | 2 |
| 1967 | Canada Games | Manitoba | 2 |

# GARUIK, JOHN

"Milkman"
sport: football, wrestling, bowling
born: Pilot Butte, Saskatchewan
July 6, 1906
died: Regina, Saskatchewan
May 8, 1979
height: 1.68 m / 5'6"
weight: 100 kg / 220 lbs
position: lineman

While a member of the Regina Junior Tigers football club in 1929, John Garuik was asked to join the Regina Roughriders. His mother, though, was unimpressed and refused to grant him permission; times were difficult and she wanted her son working. Only after the Roughriders secured Garuik a job delivering milk for the Cooperative Creameries did his mother agree to let him join the team. Garuik's milk route included all of east Regina and he was soon referred to as the "Milkman" by teammates and fans alike.

John Garuik played with the Roughriders for 15 years. During that time he established himself as a dependable and versatile lineman. On and off the field he was a team leader. He inspired and motivated his teammates by his industrious work habits, spirited play, and jovial personality. For his efforts, he was named to the first Western Canada all-star team picked by sport writers in Western Canada in 1932.

Garuik's rookie season culminated with an appearance in the Grey Cup game; the Regina Roughriders lost 11-6 to Toronto's Balmy Beach. Garuik played in three more Grey Cup games, in 1931, 1932, and 1934. On all of these occasions, the Roughriders failed to win the Cup.

The stalwart lineman retired from competitive football after the 1943 season. His aging body was feeling the effects of the broken ribs, broken shoulders, and other injuries he sustained over time. Garuik nevertheless remained associated with the game. He was the Roughriders' defensive coach in 1943 and 1944, and later he worked as a part-time referee with the CFL.

John Garuik was also a fine wrestler. In the 1920s, he won the Canadian amateur junior wrestling championship in the heavyweight division. Subsequently, he wrestled as a professional until the late 1930s, developing a faithful following on the Prairies. During the winter months, Garuik enjoyed 10 pin bowling. He mastered the game sufficiently to play professionally for many years both in Canada and the United States.

INDUCTIONS

1991        Saskatchewan Roughrider Plaza of Honour

ALL-STAR SELECTIONS

1932        Western Canada All-Star Team

# GAWRYLUK, JOHNNY

| | |
|---|---|
| sport: | soccer |
| given name | Gawryluk, John Ronald |
| born: | Winnipeg, Manitoba |
| | April 25, 1939 |
| died | Winnipeg, Manitoba |
| | January 12, 1965 |
| height: | . . . |
| weight: | . . . |
| position: | goal |

Johnny Gawryluk's soccer career began in high school where he developed into an outstanding goalkeeper. While still in school, he was spotted by Army Navy Air Force (ANAF) Scottish of the Winnipeg National Soccer League. The club was impressed with his reflexes and terrific leaping ability, and he was promptly signed. Gawryluk did not disappoint club management and fans; he led his team to the Manitoba title in 1958. In the semi-final competition for the Dominion championship, Gawryluk was described as brilliant as the ANAF Scottish clobbered Montreal's Harrington 8-2. In the national final, the Winnipeg side could not muster any offence and lost 2-0 to the New Westminster Royals. The following year, ANAF Scottish repeated as Manitoba champions. Once again, New Westminster put a damper on their national championship aspirations by eliminating the Scottish in overtime in the Western Canada championship. With the exception of a fraction of a season when he kept goal for Germania, Gawryluk played all of his senior soccer with the ANAF Scottish.

Gawryluk's outstanding play resulted in numerous all-star selections. Commencing in 1958, he was often chosen to represent Winnipeg or Manitoba against touring teams from Europe. In 1960, he was named to Canada's national team for a tour of England, Scotland and the USSR. A high school teacher with a bright future ahead of him, and one of Canada's most outstanding soccer goalkeepers, Johnny Gawryluk passed away, a victim of leukemia, at the age of 25.

## GAZIUK, MURRAY

"Ukrainian Comet"
sport:          athletics
born:           Toronto, Ontario
                October 18, 1930
height:         1.78 m / 5'10"
weight:         77 kg / 170 lbs

Murray Gaziuk gained prominence in 1948 when he established three Canadian junior records for the half mile, and the United States junior record of 2:01.0 for the same distance. Refusing scholarships to American universities, Gaziuk enrolled at the University of Toronto where he starred on its cross country and track teams. He was an extremely versatile athlete, competing in the hurdles and the middle distance events. In 1950, Gaziuk won the Canadian Intercollegiate title in the 880 yards. One year later, he established a Canadian indoor record in the mile with a time of 4:19.4.

Murray Gaziuk placed second at the 1952 Olympic Trials in the 440-yard hurdles and just missed making the Olympic team. Two years later, he won the 440-yard hurdles at the national championships and represented Canada in the event at the Commonwealth Games, placing fifth in a time of 55.5 seconds. In his spare time Murray Gaziuk played basketball for a Ukrainian team competing in the YULNA.

RECORD

| year | competition | event | placing | result |
|------|-------------|-------|---------|--------|
| 1949 | Canadian Intercollegiate Championships | 880 y | 2 | 1:58.8 |
| | British Empire Games Trials | 440 y H | 3 | 55.3 |
| 1950 | Canadian Championships | 440 y H | 3 | 55.6 |
| | Canadian Intercollegiate Championships | 880 y | 1 | 2:02.5 |
| | Ontario Championships | 880 y | 1 | 2:05.9 |
| 1951 | U of T Indoor Championships | mile | 1 | 4:19.4 nir |
| | US National Indoor Championships | 1000 m | dnq | |
| 1952 | Ontario Olympic Trials | 440 y H | 1 | 58.0 |
| | Canadian Olympic Trials | 440 y H | 2 | 55.6 |
| 1954 | Ontario Championships | 440 y H | 1 | 57.3 |
| | Canadian Championships | 440 y H | 1 | 56.8 |
| | Commonwealth Games Trials | 440 y H | 2 | 56.6 |
| | Commonwealth Games | 440 y H | 5 | 55.5 |

nir    Canadian indoor record

# GERELA, ROY

| | |
|---|---|
| sport: | football |
| born: | Sarrail, Alberta |
| | April 2, 1948 |
| height: | 1.78 m / 5'10" |
| weight: | 84 kg / 185 lbs |
| position: | kicker |

Photo courtesy of the Pittsburgh Steelers

Roy Gerela was drafted by the Houston Oilers out of New Mexico State University in the fourth round of the 1969 college draft. While at the university, Gerela was used regularly as a defensive back and a punter. He began placekicking in only his senior year. In his first professional season, Gerela was used by Houston as a placekicker and a punter. In a game against Miami, he established a personal best and team record of five field goals. That same game he also added a convert to record a career-high 16 points. Also in his rookie season, Gerela kicked a career-long field goal of 50 yards. On punts, he averaged 40.4 yards.

Shortly before the start of the 1971 season, Gerela was claimed on waivers by the Pittsburgh Steelers. He immediately became an impact player. For five straight seasons he led the club in scoring. In 1972, he established club records of 119 points, 28 field goals, and kicked at least one field goal in each regular season game. His accomplishments that year were recognized by an All Pro selection. The following year Gerela scored a career-high 123 points to become the first Steeler ever to lead the league in scoring.

In 1974, Roy Gerela repeated as league scoring champion with 93 points. He also led the league for the third consecutive season in field goals. For the second time in his career, he was named All Pro and for the second time he played in the Pro Bowl. That season, Pittsburgh won the Super Bowl with Gerela contributing significantly to the success of the club. The following season concluded with Pittsburgh repeating as Super Bowl champions. Gerela contributed a career-high seven points in the January classic. Midway through the 1976 season, Gerela suffered calf and groin injuries which permanently affected his kicking. Nevertheless, he came back in 1978 to lead the Steelers in scoring. Pittsburgh once again won the Super Bowl that season, with Gerela establishing a Super Bowl record for most converts in a game with five.

In the summer of 1979, the Steelers released Roy Gerela, their all-time scoring leader with a record of 894 points. Shortly afterwards, he was signed as a free agent by the San Diego Chargers. He played in only three games for the Chargers before being once again released. In the summer of 1980, Gerela signed as a free agent with the St. Louis Cardinals but did not play any games for the team. He retired from the game as the league's 13th all-time scoring leader with 903 points. In the late 1980s, Gerela worked as a volunteer assistant specializing in placekicking with the coaching staff at Carnegie-Mellon University in Pittsburgh. Roy Gerela is the brother of football player Ted Gerela.

## INDUCTIONS

. . .    New Mexico State University Intercollegiate Athletic Hall of Fame

## ALL-STAR SELECTIONS

| 1972 | kicker | AFC |
| 1974 | kicker | AFC |

# RECORD

| year | team | league | regular season scoring | | | | | field goals | | | playoffs scoring | | | | | Super Bowl game scoring | | | | |
|---|---|---|---|---|---|---|---|---|---|---|---|---|---|---|---|---|---|---|---|---|
| | | | GP | TD | C | FG | PTS | ATT | GD | LK | GP | TD | C | FG | PTS | GP | TD | C | FG | PTS |
| 1969 | Houston | AFL | 14 | 0 | 29 | 19 | 86 | 40 | 19 | 50 | | | | | | | | | | |
| 1970 | Houston | NFL | 14 | 0 | 23 | 18 | 77 | 32 | 18 | | | | | | | | | | | |
| 1971 | Pittsburgh | NFL | 14 | 0 | 27 | 17 | 78 | 27 | 17 | | | | | | | | | | | |
| 1972 | Pittsburgh | NFL | 14 | 0 | 35 | 28 | 119 | 41 | 28 | | 2 | 0 | 3 | 3 | 12 | | | | | |
| 1973 | Pittsburgh | NFL | 14 | 0 | 36 | 29 | 123 | 43 | 29 | | 1 | 0 | 2 | 0 | 2 | | | | | |
| 1974* | Pittsburgh | NFL | 14 | 0 | 33 | 20 | 93 | 28 | 20 | | 2 | 0 | 5 | 3 | 14 | 1 | 0 | 2 | 0 | 2 |
| 1975* | Pittsburgh | NFL | 14 | 0 | 44 | 17 | 95 | 21 | 17 | | 2 | 0 | 5 | 1 | 8 | 1 | 0 | 1 | 2 | 7 |
| 1976 | Pittsburgh | NFL | 14 | 0 | 40 | 14 | 82 | 26 | 14 | | 1 | 0 | 3 | 2 | 9 | | | | | |
| 1977 | Pittsburgh | NFL | 14 | 0 | 34 | 9 | 61 | 14 | 9 | | 1 | 0 | 3 | 0 | 3 | | | | | |
| 1978* | Pittsburgh | NFL | 16 | 0 | 44 | 12 | 80 | 26 | 12 | | 2 | 0 | 7 | 4 | 19 | 1 | 0 | 5 | 0 | 5 |
| 1979 | San Diego | NFL | 3 | 0 | 6 | 1 | 9 | 7 | 1 | | | | | | | | | | | |

*Photo courtesy of the Canadian Football Hall of Fame and Museum*

# GERELA, TED

sport: football
born: Powell River, British Columbia
March 12, 1944
height: 1.78 m / 5'10"
weight: 93 kg / 205 lbs
position: kicker, running back

Ted Gerela joined the British Columbia Lions football club in 1967 after playing football with Washington State University. In his first year of professional football, the kicking specialist scored 77 points and was named the Outstanding Canadian Rookie in the Western Division. The following year, Gerela led the CFL in scoring with 117 points. Ninety of those points were accounted for by 30 field goals, an all-time professional record surpassing the record set by Peter Gogolak of the Buffalo Bills and equalled by Bruce Gosset of Los Angeles.

In 1969, Gerela placed second in scoring in the Western Division with 98 points. He was the only kicker in the league to make every convert that he attempted. The media began referring to him as a "mechanical genius" for his consistency. When Gerela retired from the Lions after the 1973 season, he was third on the list of the CFL's all-time field goal leaders with 123. He accomplished the feat in seven seasons. In 1969, Gerela was first used in a defensive capacity. He was a tough hitter, and put several players out of the game with his tackles. Later in his career, Gerela was also used as a running back, blocker and a kickoff return specialist. Gerela enjoyed the experiences but realized that his kicking suffered as a result. Ted Gerela is the brother of football player Roy Gerela.

## AWARDS

1967      Dr. Beattie Martin Trophy - CFL Western Division Outstanding Canadian Rookie
1968      Dave Dryburgh Memorial Trophy - CFL Western Division Scoring Leader

## RECORD

| scoring | | | regular season | | | | | | playoffs | | | | | | Grey Cup game | | | | | |
|---|---|---|---|---|---|---|---|---|---|---|---|---|---|---|---|---|---|---|---|---|
| year | team | league | GP | TD | C | FG | S | PTS | GP | TD | C | FG | S | PTS | GP | TD | C | FG | S | PTS |
| 1967 | British Columbia | CFL | ... | 0 | 21 | 16 | 8 | 77 | | | | | | | | | | | | |
| 1968 | British Columbia | CFL | ... | 0 | 16 | 30 | 9 | 115 | | | | | | | | | | | | |
| 1969 | British Columbia | CFL | ... | 0 | 17 | 22 | 15 | 98 | 1 | 0 | 3 | 0 | 0 | 3 | | | | | | |
| 1970 | British Columbia | CFL | ... | 0 | 29 | 22 | 12 | 107 | | | | | | | | | | | | |
| 1971 | British Columbia | CFL | ... | 0 | 7 | 12 | 0 | 43 | | | | | | | | | | | | |
| 1972 | British Columbia | CFL | ... | 0 | 25 | 19 | 6 | 88 | | | | | | | | | | | | |
| 1973 | British Columbia | CFL | 16 | 0 | 16 | 6 | 7 | 41 | | | | | | | | | | | | |

# GODYNYUK, ALEX

| | |
|---|---|
| sport: | hockey |
| born: | Kyiv, Ukraine |
| | January 27, 1970 |
| height: | 1.83 m / 6'0" |
| weight: | 94 kg / 207 lbs |
| position: | defense |
| shoots: | left |

*Card reproduced courtesy of O-Pee-Chee Co.*

Alexander Godynyuk joined the Kyiv Sokil hockey club of the USSR Top League at the age of 16. In his first season, Godynyuk played inspired hockey and was selected to represent the USSR at the European Junior Championship. Appearances on the USSR junior team continued, culminating with a world title at the 1989 World Junior Championship, and an all-star selection and the top defenseman award at the 1990 tournament.

The Toronto Maple Leafs were impressed by the strong and agile skater who handled and moved the puck well. As a result, the team took a chance and selected him in the sixth round, 155 overall, of the 1990 NHL Entry Draft. Godynyuk began the 1990-91 season with Kyiv. In late fall he arrived in Canada. He resumed his season playing for the Leafs and their farm team in Newmarket.

While with Kyiv, Godynyuk was referred to as the "actor" by his teammates, a result of his starring role in the made for TV movie *The Three*.

## AWARDS

| | |
|---|---|
| 1987 | Top Defenseman - 1987 European Junior Championship |
| 1990 | Top Defenseman - 1990 World Junior Championship |

## ALL-STAR SELECTIONS

| | | | |
|---|---|---|---|
| 1990 | defense | World Junior All-Stars | First Team |

# RECORD

| year | team | league | regular season GP | G | A | PTS | PIM | playoffs GP | G | A | PTS | PIM |
|---|---|---|---|---|---|---|---|---|---|---|---|---|
| 1989-90 | Kyiv | USSR | 37 | 3 | 2 | 5 | 31 | | | | | |
| 1990-91 | Kyiv | USSR | 19 | 3 | 1 | 4 | 20 | | | | | |
| | Toronto | NHL | 18 | 0 | 3 | 3 | 16 | | | | | |
| | Newmarket | AHL | 11 | 0 | 1 | 1 | 29 | | | | | |

international

| year | team | competition | GP | G | A | PTS | PIM | Place |
|---|---|---|---|---|---|---|---|---|
| 1987 | USSR | European Junior Championship | ... | | | | | 3 |
| 1988 | USSR | European U-18 Championship | ... | | | | | 3 |
| 1989 | USSR | World Junior Championship | 7 | 0 | 1 | 1 | 2 | 1 |
| 1990 | USSR | World Junior Championship | 7 | 3 | 2 | 5 | 4 | 2 |

# GORDIENKO, GEORGE

sport: professional wrestling
born: Winnipeg, Manitoba
January 7, 1928
height: 1.80 m / 5'11"
weight: 109 kg / 240 lbs

At age 12, George Gordienko decided to emulate his oldest brother by lifting weights. Three years later, he was introduced to amateur wrestling by the celebrated Prairie grappler Albert "Ole" Olsen, who needed a training partner. With his focus now on wrestling, the young Gordienko began working out with Olsen at the Winnipeg YMCA. At the time, he also had the opportunity to train with such notable champions as Steve Kozak and Jim Trifunov. In late 1945 or early 1946, Gordienko was spotted by American star professional wrestler Joe Pazandak. The American persuaded Gordienko to turn professional and train with him in Minneapolis under the management of Tony Stecher.

Thus began one of the most remarkable professional wrestling careers in history. George Gordienko quickly began to excel and gain international recognition. Within a year, the publication *The Ring* described him as a "wonder. . . with one of the most beautifully developed bodies. . ."[10] That same year, teenager Gordienko decided that while wrestling provided an income, he did not want to spend his life as a wrestler. He wanted to pursue something worthwhile and interesting. Before the year was out, while competing in San Francisco, Gordienko enrolled in art lessons.

Shortly thereafter, George Gordienko left wrestling and became involved in minor politics that had major repercussions: he was "Joe McCarthyed." The need to pay bills brought Gordienko back to the professional ring in 1953, but in Canada. His political involvement effectively closed the door to wrestling opportunities in the USA. After a tour of Australia, Gordienko meandered through the art centres of Europe settling in London, England, to pursue formal art training at the St. Martin's Art School. After a brief sojourn in Canada, Gordienko made Europe his home in 1956. The cultural and sporting ambience was more to his liking there.

George Gordienko was one of the top professional heavyweight wrestlers to come out of Canada. During his career, he was regarded as a genuine performer, a legitimate wrestler of remarkable skill and strength. Gordienko fought to win every match. His record attests to that reputation, since he won about 95 per cent of his fights. Gordienko fought on all continents aside from South America, gaining a huge following everywhere. His titles included the European version of the World Championship in 1964, the Commonwealth Championship in 1968, the Stampede International Tag title in 1972 and the Pacific Coast Championship, as Flash Gordon, in 1974.

After retiring from wrestling in 1975, George Gordienko pursued a successful career in art. He worked in Italy for seven years, and later on Vancouver Island. George Gordienko's brother Gordy was also a well-known athlete (boxing and wrestling).


INDUCTIONS

. . .     Calgary Stampede Wrestling Hall of Fame
. . .     Canadian Pro Wrestling Hall of Fame

# GREGOROVICH, ANDREW

| | |
|---|---|
| sport: | cycling |
| born: | Saskatoon, Saskatchewan |
| | July 18, 1935 |
| height: | 1.75 m / 5'9" |
| weight: | 67 kg / 147 lbs |

Andrew Gregorovich was in his early teens with very little cycling experience when he joined the Century Cycling Club of Hamilton. In a short period of time, he developed into a versatile cyclist who competed both on track and road; and in distances from one through 100 miles. At the 1951 Ontario dirt track championship, Gregorovich captured the one-mile event. A few weeks later, at the Canadian championship, he won the silver medal in the five-mile race. During the 10-mile race, Gregorovich crashed and was taken to a hospital with a broken backbone. The injury ended his racing career.

Andrew Gregorovich has authored numerous articles in English about Ukrainian athletes and sports in general. Most of the articles have appeared in *Trident Quarterly* and *Forum - A Ukrainian Review* which he has edited for many years.

## RECORD

| year | competition | event | placing |
|---|---|---|---|
| 1951 | Hamilton Road Race | 100 miles | 17 |
| | Ontario Championships | 1 mile | 1 |
| | Canadian Championships | 5 miles | 2 |
| | | 10 miles | dnf |

# GUZZELL, MIKE

| | |
|---|---|
| sport: | skiing |
| given name: | Gushul, Michael |
| born: | Fort William, Ontario |
| | (now Thunder Bay) |
| | October 8, 1912 |
| died: | Thunder Bay, Ontario |
| | June 22, 1993 |
| height: | 1.83 m / 6'0" |
| weight: | 93 kg  / 205 lbs |

Growing up, Mike Guzzell (the family changed the name from Gushul, to avoid possible internment as enemy aliens during World War I) competed in rural softball leagues, took part in track and field meets and skied on home-made barrel staves skiis.  In 1936, when the first Canadian Ski Championships were held in Fort William, Guzzell took part as a minor official.  In 1945, he spearheaded a group of enthusiasts to develop Mount Baldy into a new ski area.  Also in 1945, he organized and headed the first regional ski zone to be recognized by the Canadian Amateur Ski Association (CASI).  After serving for ten years as the technical chairman of CASI, Guzzell was elected president in 1959.

During the 1960 Olympics, Guzzell became the first Canadian official to assist in running Olympic ski competitions.  A year later he qualified and received the International Ski Federation (FIS) judge's badge and certificate, the first North American to do so.  He subsequently judged or officiated at many domestic and international ski events.  During the 1964 Olympics, for example, in addition to serving as manager of the Canadian ski team, he was an official judge.  He also conducted judging and officiating courses for aspiring Canadian ski officials. During the 1970s, Guzzell initiated a campaign to develop a nordic ski jumping facility in Thunder Bay.  The project was realized and "Big Thunder" soon became host to international competitions.

## INDUCTIONS

1982      Northwestern Ontario Sports Hall of Fame

## AWARDS

1985      Honourary Life Membership  -  Canadian Amateur Ski Association

# RECORD

| year | position |
|------|----------|
| 1945 | President, Lakehead Area Ski Zone |
| 1948-58 | Technical Chairman, Canadian Amateur Ski Association |
| 1959-... | President, Canadian Amateur Ski Association |
| 1960 | Official, Olympics |
| 1962 | Manager, Canadian Ski Team - European competition |
| 1964 | Manager, Canadian Ski Team - Olympic Games |
| 1964 | Judge, Olympic Games |
| 1968 | Manager, Canadian Ski Jumping Team - East European competition |
| 1968 | Judge, European ski circuit |

# GWOZDECKY, GEORGE

| | |
|---|---|
| sport: | hockey, soccer |
| born: | Lviv, Ukraine |
| | May 5, 1919 |
| height: | 1.88 m / 6'2" |
| weight: | 91 kg / 200 lbs |

Dr. George Gwozdecky settled in Port Arthur (now Thunder Bay) in the late 1940s. Immediately, he became involved with sport. In 1949, he organized, coached, and was president of a new entry into the Port Arthur Football Association, the Sicz Football Club. Although the club folded before completing its second season, Gwozdecky's personal commitment to sport did not waver. He was soon involved with other local clubs and associations. Gwozdecky was a doctor willing to donate his time to sport; as a result, his name was often associated with the position of club physician for many Lakehead area clubs. In that capacity, and concurrently serving as president, his hockey team, the Port Arthur Bearcats, won the Ahearne Trophy in Sweden in 1962. Some years later, he was with the Thunder Bay Marrs, the 1967 Memorial Cup finalists.

Dr. Gwozdecky's dedication to amateur sport and his knowledge of sports medicine resulted in his being named to the medical staff or as chief medical officer at various national and international competitions, including the Pan American Games and the Olympics. He was also a member of the Canadian Council of Sports Medicine. In the late 1980s, he served on an "Anti-doping" committee.

## INDUCTIONS

| | |
|---|---|
| 1988 | Northwestern Ontario Sports Hall of Fame |
| 1989 | Northwestern Ontario Sports Hall of Fame - member of the Port Arthur Bearcats |

## RECORD

| year | position |
|---|---|
| 1949-50 | President and Coach, Sicz, later Ukraina soccer club |
| 1952-54 | Club Physician, North Stars hockey club |
| 1953-54 | President, Lakehead Soccer Association |
| 1954-55 | Vice-President, Lakehead Tennis Club |
| 1958-62 | Club Physician, Port Arthur Bearcats hockey club |
| 1961-62 | President, Port Arthur Bearcats hockey club |
| 1963-... | President, Port Arthur Marrs hockey club |
| 1963-67 | Club Physician, Port Arthur Marrs hockey club |
| 1974 | Team Physician, Canadian Ski Jumping Team |
| 1974-85 | Chief Medical Officer, Big Thunder Ski Jumping Centre |
| 1976 | Chief Medical Officer, Canadian Olympic Team - Winter |
| 1978 | Chief Medical Officer, Canadian Figure Skating Championships |
| 1981 | Chief Medical Officer, Jeux Canada Games |
| 1983 | Team Physician, Canadian Pan American Games team |
| 1985- | Club Physician, Thunder Bay Twins hockey club |

# HAIDY, GORD

"Cowboy"

| | |
|---|---|
| sport: | hockey |
| given name: | Haidy, Gordon Adam |
| born: | Winnipeg, Manitoba |
| | April 11, 1928 |
| height: | 1.78 m / 5'10" |
| weight: | 92.5 kg / 204 lbs |
| position: | right wing |
| shoots: | left |

*Photo courtesy of the Windsor/Essex County Sports Hall of Fame and Museum*

In the Windsor-Detroit area, Gord Haidy was a hero for many years. He played his sports hard, giving everything he had. But as one of his softball managers observed, "He was wilder than a hawk." Haidy did things his way; some have speculated that this trait was career limiting. He had a good training camp with the Detroit Red Wings, and was offered a contract for $6,000. Haidy rejected the Wings' first offer and was promptly shipped to the minors for $4,000. The refusal to sign that contract likely kept Haidy out of the NHL. The Red Wings did not play him and the team twice rejected offers by the Chicago Black Hawks to purchase him.

Gord Haidy played in his one and only NHL game the year before when he was called up by Detroit from Indianapolis for the playoffs. He missed an opportunity to score a goal. Detroit general manager Jack Adams was furious and returned him to Indianapolis where Haidy helped the club win the championship of the AHL. Haidy played hockey through the mid-1960s, first for the Buffalo Bisons of the AHL, then for the Windsor Bulldogs, Chatham Maroons and Sarnia Rams of the OHA Sr. "A" loop. Haidy began his hockey career with the Windsor Spitfires of the IHL in 1945 and turned professional with Omaha of the USHL during the 1948-49 season.

Gord Haidy was also an outstanding softball pitcher. He threw five or six no-hitters and in one game struck out 18 batters. He played on teams in Detroit, Fort Wayne, Columbus, Sudbury and Windsor, winning the Canadian championship on three occasions.

# RECORD

| year | team | league | regular season | | | | | playoffs | | | | |
|------|------|--------|----|----|----|-----|-----|----|----|----|-----|-----|
| | | | GP | G | A | PTS | PIM | GP | G | A | PTS | PIM |
| 1945-46 | Windsor | IHL | 15 | 9 | 6 | 15 | 22 | | | | | |
| 1946-47 | Windsor | IHL | 26 | 31 | 25 | 56 | 35 | | | | | |
| 1947-48 | Windsor | IHL | 25 | 32 | 11 | 43 | 48 | | | | | |
| 1948-49 | Indianapolis | AHL | 48 | 14 | 10 | 24 | 51 | 2 | 0 | 0 | 0 | 0 |
| | Omaha | USHL | 6 | 3 | 4 | 7 | 0 | | | | | |
| 1949-50* | Indianapolis | AHL | 47 | 20 | 10 | 30 | 32 | 8 | 5 | 1 | 6 | 4 |
| | Detroit | NHL | | | | | | 1 | 0 | 0 | 0 | 0 |
| 1950-51 | Indianapolis | AHL | 59 | 26 | 18 | 44 | 40 | 3 | 0 | 0 | 0 | 0 |
| 1951-52 | suspended | | | | | | | | | | | |
| 1952-53 | New Westminster | WHL | 18 | 6 | 4 | 10 | 14 | | | | | |
| | Buffalo | AHL | 10 | 0 | 0 | 0 | 4 | | | | | |
| 1960-61 | Milwaukee | IHL | 14 | 5 | 6 | 11 | 8 | | | | | |
| 1963-64 | Windsor | IHL | 17 | 7 | 4 | 11 | 18 | | | | | |

# HAMELUCK, MIKE

| | |
|---|---|
| sport: | football |
| born: | Ottawa, Ontario |
| | August 27, 1955 |
| height: | 1.93 m / 6'4" |
| weight: | 113.5 kg / 250 lbs |
| position: | offensive centre |

*Photo courtesy of the Canadian Football Hall of Fame and Museum*

Mike Hameluck, a product of the Ottawa Junior Sooners football club, turned professional with the Montreal Alouettes during the 1978 season. He appeared in three games for the Alouettes that year. The following season, he played at the guard position and on special teams. Hameluck arrived at the 1980 training camp carrying an additional 20 pounds on his massive frame. The Alouettes at the time were in need of a starting centre and Hameluck was an obvious choice. He won the position, but conceded that he had a lot to learn about playing centre. Hameluck adjusted to the position well and was a starter with the Alouettes for two years. In 1982, Mike Hameluck was acquired by the Toronto Argonauts to fill a void at centre. He was with the club for three years and played an integral role in the successive appearance of the Argos in the Grey Cup game. The team came up short in 1982, but the following year it won the Cup.

Prior to the start of the 1985 season, the Argos traded Hameluck to Ottawa. He was released by the team before the completion of the schedule. In May of 1986, Hameluck was signed as a free agent by the Winnipeg Blue Bombers.

# HARDABURA, JASON

"Meat Loaf"

| | |
|---|---|
| sport: | gymnastics |
| born: | Toronto, Ontario |
| | September 12, 1975 |
| height: | 1.52 m / 5'0" |
| weight: | 41 kg / 90 lbs |

After viewing the gymnastics competition at the 1984 Olympics, Jason Hardabura decided to try the sport himself. He became hooked on it and was soon training regularly. His goal was to compete in the Olympic Games. In a short period of time, Hardabura began to dominate age group gymnastics in Canada. In 1988, he competed at his first national championships placing tenth in the 14-and-under division. A year later, he improved to second place. In 1990, Hardabura made his debut in the novice (14-18) division and placed third overall. He was the only first-year novice to win a medal. That same year, he gained his first international exposure when he competed at the Peter Vidmar International meet.

Jason Hardabura's long arms and legs made his routines appear very graceful. His technical work was described as "impeccable" by one sports writer. Unfortunately, his physique was also considered a liability. In 1990, Hardabura stood at 1.52 m (5'0") and weighed 41 kg (90 lbs). As a result, he lacked the size and strength to perform well on the pommel horse and in the vault. In 1990, Jason Hardabura was aware that his Olympic dream rested not only on his dedication to the sport, but also on how his body would develop.

## RECORD

| year | competition | event | placing |
|------|-------------|-------|---------|
| 1985 | Ontario Championships - Argo A | all-around | 1 |
| 1986 | Ontario Championships - Tyro A | all-around | 1 |
| 1987 | Ontario Championships - Tyro A | all-around | 1 |
| 1988 | Canadian Championships - Tyro A | all-around | 10 |
| 1989 | Canadian Championships - Tyro A | all-around | 2 |
| 1990 | Canadian Championships - Novice | all-around | 3 |
| | Peter Vidmar Invitational | all-around | 6 |
| | | bars | 1 |
| | | floor | 2 |
| | Alfa Invitational | all-around | 1 |
| 1991 | Canada Games | rings | 1 |
| | | team | 1 |
| | | parallel bars | 3 |
| | | all-around | 4 |

# HAWERCHUK, DALE

| | |
|---|---|
| sport: | hockey |
| born: | Toronto, Ontario |
| | April 4, 1963 |
| height: | 1.80 m / 5'11" |
| weight: | 84 kg / 185 lbs |
| position: | center |
| shoots: | left |

*Photo courtesy of the Winnipeg Jets*

Dale Hawerchuk's credentials going into the 1981 NHL Entry Draft were enviable.  In 1980 and once again in 1981, he captained the Cornwall Royals of the QMJHL to the Memorial Cup. In 1980, he won the league's Rookie of the Year Award.  The following year, because of his 81 goals and 102 assists, he won the league's player of the year award and the Canadian Major Junior Player of the Year award. At the draft, Hawerchuk was selected first overall by the Winnipeg Jets.

In his first year of professional hockey Hawerchuk did not disappoint. He had 45 goals and 58 assists, and became the youngest player to score 100 points. He established 17 team records and tied 5 others. He led the Jets to a 48-point single season improvement. For his efforts he was awarded the Calder Trophy. In subsequent seasons, Hawerchuk established himself as a consistent 40-goal scorer. He peaked during the 1984-85 season when he accumulated 53 goals and 77 assists for 130 points.

During the 1989-90 season, Hawerchuk started to complain about what he perceived to be a reduction in ice time. He asked to be traded. In June of 1990, the Jets dealt him to the Buffalo Sabres. Upon joining the Sabres, Hawerchuk told the press that he felt like a kid again. The new environment revitalized Hawerchuk and he responded by leading the Sabres in scoring.

During his career, Dale Hawerchuk had a number of opportunities to represent Canada in international competition. At the 1982 World Championship he won a bronze medal, and at the 1989 a silver. In 1987 and once again in 1991, Hawerchuk was selected to Team Canada which vied for the Canada Cup. On both occasions, Canada won the coveted Cup. A memorable experience was being on the ice during the dying seconds of the 1987 Canada Cup final, when Wayne Gretzky fed Mario Lemieux for the Cup winning goal.

## AWARDS

| | |
|---|---|
| 1980 | The Instructeurs Trophy  -  QMJHL Rookie of the Year |
| 1980 | Guy Lafleur Trophy  -  QMJHL Playoff MVP |
| 1980 | George Parsons Trophy  -  Memorial Cup Tournament Most Sportsmanlike Player |
| 1981 | Jean Beliveau Trophy  -  QMJHL Leading Scorer |
| 1981 | Michel Briere Trophy  -  QMJHL Player of the Year |
| 1981 | Stafford Smythe Memorial Trophy  -  Memorial Cup Tournament MVP |
| 1981 | CCM Trophy  -  Canadian Major Junior Player of the Year |
| 1982 | Calder Memorial Trophy  -  NHL Rookie of the Year |
| 1982 | Manitoba Ukrainian Sportsman of the Year (co-winner) |
| 1985 | Manitoba Ukrainian Sportsman of the Year |

## ALL-STAR SELECTIONS

| | | | |
|---|---|---|---|
| 1980 | left wing | Memorial Cup All-Star Team | |
| 1981 | center | Memorial Cup All-Star Team | |
| 1984-85 | center | NHL | Second Team |

RECORD

| year | team | league | regular season | | | | | playoffs | | | | |
|---|---|---|---|---|---|---|---|---|---|---|---|---|
| | | | GP | G | A | PTS | PIM | GP | G | A | PTS | PIM |
| 1981-82 | Winnipeg | NHL | 80 | 45 | 58 | 103 | 47 | 4 | 1 | 7 | 8 | 5 |
| 1982-83 | Winnipeg | NHL | 79 | 40 | 51 | 91 | 31 | 3 | 1 | 4 | 5 | 8 |
| 1983-84 | Winnipeg | NHL | 80 | 37 | 65 | 102 | 73 | 3 | 1 | 1 | 2 | 0 |
| 1984-85 | Winnipeg | NHL | 80 | 53 | 77 | 130 | 74 | 3 | 2 | 1 | 3 | 4 |
| 1985-86 | Winnipeg | NHL | 80 | 46 | 59 | 105 | 44 | 3 | 0 | 3 | 3 | 0 |
| 1986-87 | Winnipeg | NHL | 80 | 47 | 53 | 100 | 52 | 10 | 5 | 8 | 13 | 4 |
| 1987-88 | Winnipeg | NHL | 80 | 44 | 77 | 121 | 59 | 5 | 3 | 4 | 7 | 16 |
| 1988-89 | Winnipeg | NHL | 75 | 41 | 55 | 96 | 28 | | | | | |
| 1989-90 | Winnipeg | NHL | 79 | 26 | 55 | 81 | 60 | 7 | 3 | 5 | 8 | 2 |
| 1990-91 | Buffalo | NHL | 80 | 31 | 58 | 89 | 32 | 6 | 2 | 4 | 6 | 10 |

international

| year | team | competition | GP | G | A | PTS | PIM | Place |
|---|---|---|---|---|---|---|---|---|
| 1981 | Canada | World Junior Championship | 5 | 5 | 4 | 9 | 2 | 7 |
| 1982 | Canada | World Championship | 10 | 3 | 1 | 4 | 0 | 3 |
| 1986 | Canada | World Championship | 8 | 2 | 4 | 6 | 4 | 3 |
| 1987 | Canada | Canada Cup | 9 | 4 | 2 | 6 | 0 | 1 |
| 1989 | Canada | World Championship | 10 | 4 | 8 | 12 | 6 | 2 |
| 1991 | Canada | Canada Cup | 8 | 2 | 3 | 5 | 0 | 1 |

# HAWRYLAK, BILL

| | |
|---|---|
| sport: | football, bowling |
| given name: | Hawrylak, William S. |
| born: | Calgary, Alberta |
| | February 17, 1914 |
| height: | 1.91 m / 6'3" |
| weight: | 93 kg / 205 lbs |

An outstanding educator who has had a school named in his honour, Bill Hawrylak was also a dedicated sports administrator offering his services to bowling and football. During the 1939-40 academic year, he introduced high school bowling in Regina. In 1945, he was instrumental in organizing the Western Canada 5 Pin Bowling Association. In 1953, he organized the Canadian 5 Pin Bowling Association and the first Canadian 5 Pin Bowling Championships. Also in 1953, he was one of two men responsible for developing and introducing changes in the pin count in 5 pin bowling. The count was still in use at the time of writing. Hawrylak served as Secretary-Treasurer of the Western Canada Bowling Association for 28 years and was president on three occasions. He also served for 23 years as Secretary-Treasurer of the Canadian Bowling Association.

When Bill Hawrylak assumed the duties of Chief Statistician of the Western Interprovincial Football Union in 1950, he set up the format for recording game statistics. Four years later, the Interprovincial Rugby Football Union of Eastern Canada adopted the format. Eventually the two unions established the Canadian Football League. With some minor changes, Bill Hawrylak's format for recording statistics was used by the Canadian Football League at the time of writing.

## AWARDS

| | | |
|---|---|---|
| 1964 | Life Member - | Western Canada 5 Pin Bowling Association |
| 1973 | Life Member - | Canadian 5 Pin Bowling Association |
| 1977 | Life Member - | Saskatchewan 5 Pin Bowling Association |
| 1978 | Award of Merit - | Saskatchewan High School Athletic Association |

## RECORD

football

| year | position |
|---|---|
| 1950-67 | Chief Statistician, Western and Canadian Football Leagues |
| 1970-84 | Statistician, Saskatchewan Roughriders |
| 1975-82 | Secretary-Treasurer, Western Interprovincial Football Union |

bowling

| | |
|---|---|
| . . . | Secretary-Treasurer, Western Canada Bowling Association |
| . . . | President, Western Canada Bowling Association |
| 1953 | Organizer, 1st Canadian 5 Pin Bowling Championships |

# HEDGEWICK, MIKE

| | |
|---|---|
| sport: | football, lacrosse, athletics |
| given name: | Hatrycz, Michael |
| born: | Montreal, Quebec |
| | October 22, 1916 |
| height: | 1.70 m / 5'7" |
| weight: | 68 kg / 150 lbs |
| position: | halfback |

*Photo courtesy of the Windsor/Essex County Sports Hall of Fame and Museum*

While attending Windsor Vocational High School, Mike Hedgewick starred on the school's football, track, basketball and soccer teams. In his last two years, Hedgewick led the school to two city football championships and was a unanimous choice for the All-City Football Team. After graduating in 1936, he went to Sarnia to play with the Sarnia Imperials of the Ontario Rugby Football Union (ORFU).

Hedgewick's rookie season was spectacular. He led the league in scoring with 25 points on five touchdowns. He was named to the Eastern Canada Second All-Star team. The Imperials won the ORFU championship and advanced to the Grey Cup game. In the fall classic, Hedgewick contributed on offence and defence as the Imperials defeated the Ottawa Rough Riders 26-20 to win the Cup. Hedgewick ran back kickoffs, caught passes, and carried the ball from the backfield. He scored two touchdowns, both on lateral-run combination plays. His first touchdown run covered 42 yards. On defence, Hedgewick secured Sarnia's victory in the dying minutes of the game. With an Ottawa third down on the Sarnia 17-yard line, the Rough Riders gambled and went for the touchdown. Hedgewick streaked out of nowhere, went up high into the air and deflected the pass with his fingertips away from a waiting receiver in the end zone. In winning the Cup, Hedgewick became the first player in Canadian football history to go directly from high school football to a Grey Cup championship team.

Hedgewick played for the Imperials for three more seasons. Each year, the club won the ORFU title but failed to advance past the Eastern Canada final. While Hedgewick's scoring prowess dropped dramatically after his rookie season, he continued to electrify the fans with his offensive and defensive playmaking. The elusive fleet-footed Hedgewick was soon referred to by the media as a "streak of greased lighting."

In 1940, Hedgewick followed Imperials coach Art Massucci to Hamilton and the Tigers of the

Big Four League (IRFU).  A year later, the Big Four League suspended play and Hedgewick joined the Hamilton Wildcats of the ORFU.  He played with the Wildcats for two seasons before joining the war effort in 1943 when he enlisted in the Navy.  Hedgewick was stationed in Halifax where he played for a very strong Halifax Navy team.  Hedgewick, the team captain, ran, passed, and kicked the football.  In 1943, Halifax Navy was considered one of the finest football clubs in Canada.  A technicality kept the team from challenging for the Grey Cup.  Subsequently, Toronto Councillor Fred Hamilton tried to organize an exhibition charity game between Halifax and the Grey Cup champion Hamilton Flying Wildcats, but the Hamiltonians declined.  In 1943 and 1944, the *Halifax Chronicle* selected Hedgewick, who was playing some of his best football in years, as the Outstanding Football Sportsman of the Year.

While serving in the Navy, Hedgewick was given the opportunity to display his natural speed at track meets.  In 1944, he recorded the fastest times by a Canadian when he clocked 9.9 seconds in the 100-yard dash and 22.9 seconds in the 220.  The former result established a Canadian serviceman's record.

After demobilization, Hedgewick returned to Hamilton and played one season for the Tigers.  In 1946, he moved back to Windsor where he played for the Windsor Rockets of the ORFU for four seasons.  During that time he also served as an assistant coach of the Rockets.  In the years 1947 to 1950, Hedgewick played lacrosse for the Windsor Sterlings.  The club won the Canadian American Association title in the years 1947, 1948 and 1950.  In 1950, Mike Hedgewick turned to officiating.  He was the referee-in-chief of the Windsor Secondary School Association (1952-65).  He also refereed junior and senior ORFU games (1952-64).

## INDUCTIONS

| | |
|---|---|
| 1987 | Sarnia Lambton County Sports Hall of Fame |
| 1989 | Windsor-Essex County Sports Hall of Fame |

## AWARDS

| | |
|---|---|
| 1943 | Outstanding (Halifax) Football Sportsman of the Year |
| 1944 | Outstanding (Halifax) Football Sportsman of the Year |

## ALL-STAR SELECTIONS

| | | | |
|---|---|---|---|
| 1936 | fullback | Eastern Canada | Second Team |

# RECORD

| scoring | | | regular season | | | playoffs | | | Grey Cup game | | |
|---|---|---|---|---|---|---|---|---|---|---|---|
| year | team | league | GP | TD | PTS | GP | TD | PTS | GP | TD | PTS |
| 1936* | Sarnia | ORFU | 4 | 5 | 25 | 1 | 0 | 0 | 1 | 2 | 10 |
| 1937 | Sarnia | ORFU | ... | 0 | 0 | 2 | 2 | 10 | | | |
| 1938 | Sarnia | ORFU | 6 | 0 | 0 | 3 | 0 | 0 | | | |
| 1939 | Sarnia | ORFU | 6 | 1 | 5 | 3 | 1 | 5 | | | |
| 1940 | Hamilton | IRFU | 6 | 0 | 0 | | | | | | |
| 1941 | Hamilton | ORFU | 6 | 1 | 5 | 1 | 0 | 0 | | | |
| 1942 | Hamilton | ORFU | 10 | 0 | 0 | | | | | | |
| 1943 | Halifax | | 2 | 2 | 10 | | | | | | |
| 1944 | Halifax | AFFL | 1 | 1 | 5 | 2 | 0 | 0 | | | |
| 1945 | Hamilton | IRFU | 6 | 0 | 0 | | | | | | |
| 1946 | Windsor | ORFU | 9 | 2 | 10 | | | | | | |
| 1947 | Windsor | ORFU | ... | 0 | 0 | | | | | | |
| 1948 | Windsor | ORFU | ... | 0 | 0 | | | | | | |
| 1949 | Windsor | ORFU | ... | 0 | 0 | | | | | | |

*Photo courtesy of the Canadian Tour*

# HNATIUK, GLEN

| | |
|---|---|
| sport: | golf |
| given name: | Hnatiuk, Glen Anthony |
| born: | Selkirk, Manitoba |
| | May 15, 1965 |
| height: | 1.85 m / 6'1" |
| weight: | 70.5 kg / 180 lbs |

Growing up, Glen Hnatiuk could be found on a golf course almost daily during the summer months. If not, he would be at home watching his golfing heroes on television. In winter, he would play competitive hockey.

While still in high school, Hnatiuk developed into a steady golfer representing Manitoba at various junior events. Subsequently, he enrolled at the University of Southern Mississippi at Hattiesburg with a collegiate golf program on his mind. He returned to Canada in 1986 to win the Manitoba Amateur title, and in 1988 he achieved All-Metro Conference collegiate player status. Upon graduation, Hnatiuk joined the Pine Ridge Club in Winnipeg as an assistant pro.

In 1990, Glen Hnatiuk turned professional when he joined the Hogan Tour (later known as the Nike Tour). His first victory occurred in 1992 when he won the Mississippi Gulf Coast Classic.

## AWARDS

1987        Manitoba Ukrainian Sportsman of the Year

## RECORD

| year | event | placing |
|------|-------|---------|
| 1986 | Manitoba Amateur Championship | 1 |
| 1992 | Mississippi Gulf Coast Classic | 1 |

# HNATIW, PETE

sport:          curling
given name:     Hnatiw, Peter Leonard
born:           Fort William, Ontario
                (now Thunder Bay)
                November 3, 1932
height:         . . .
weight:         . . .

*Photo courtesy of the Northwestern Ontario Sports Hall of Fame*

Pete Hnatiw began to curl in the early 1950s. With time, his game improved steadily, but not spectacularly. In 1964, while playing second on the Ray Cousineau men's rink, Hnatiw won the zone playdowns and the right to represent the area in the Northwestern Ontario British

Consol playdowns. There the rink played to a fourth-place finish. Hnatiw would have to wait ten years before once again qualifying for the championship of Northwestern Ontario in 1974. This time around, Hnatiw was playing lead on the Bill Tetley rink. The foursome won the championship and advanced to the Northern Ontario Championship where it placed second.

In 1975, the Tetley rink, with Hnatiw playing lead, swept through the regional and provincial championships. Competing at the Canadian Macdonald Brier Championship, the foursome curled to a 9-2 record and the Canadian title. At the Air Canada Silver Broom World Championship in Perth, Scotland, the Tetley rink placed third.

For a number of years, Pete Hnatiw also competed successfully in mixed curling. On one occasion, his rink advanced to the regional playdowns. In addition, Hnatiw was a member of a rink that won the Canadian Trans-Canada Telephone Employees' Championship on four occasions.

## INDUCTIONS

1986     Northwestern Ontario Sports Hall of Fame - member of the 1975 Tetley Curling Rink

## RECORD

| year | competition | position | placing | result |
|------|-------------|----------|---------|--------|
| 1967 | Ontario Mixed Championship | second | 2 | |
| 1974 | Northern Ontario Championship | lead | 2 | |
| 1975 | Northern Ontario Championship | lead | 1 | |
| | Canadian Championship | lead | 1 | 9-2 |
| | World Championship | lead | 3 | |
| 1986 | Ontario Senior Championship | second | 2 | |

# HOMENUIK, TED

Photo courtesy of Golf Canada

"The Little Brown Man"

| | |
|---|---|
| sport: | golf |
| given name: | Homenuik, Theodore August |
| born: | Kamsack, Saskatchewan |
| | August 4, 1933 |
| height: | 1.65 m / 5'5" |
| weight: | 65 kg / 143 lbs |

When Ted Homenuik was not caddying, trimming the grass or looking for lost golf balls at the course across the street from the Homenuik home in Yorkton, Saskatchewan, he and one or more of his seven brothers would sneak in between foursomes and play a hole or two. The course, characterized by its sand greens, proved to be an excellent training ground for the young Homenuik. Later he recalled, "Sand greens are a great way to start this game. They develop accuracy and because they're small, there's a tendency to make the shots hold."[11]

Homenuik captured his first title in 1953: the Saskatchewan Junior Championship. A few years later, he moved to Manitoba and became a regular fixture on that province's golf courses. He competed prolifically, winning and placing in numerous events. On nine occasions he represented Manitoba in Willingdon Cup play, the interprovincial team championship. Twice he was runner-up in the Canadian Amateur Championship.

According to many observers, Ted Homenuik was the most talented of the Homenuik golfing brothers. Nevertheless, he did not pursue a professional career as brothers Wilf and Stan did. Upon being quizzed by a reporter as to this decision, Ted was both practical and philosophical in his reply. "I just don't like living out of a suitcase" he said, adding that for him golf was "only a game, not a way of life."[12]

## AWARDS

1961      Manitoba Athlete of the Year

## RECORD

| year | event | placing | result |
|---|---|---|---|
| 1953 | Saskatchewan Junior Championship | 1 | |
| | Saskatchewan Amateur Championship | 2 | |

| year | event | placing | result |
|---|---|---|---|
| 1953 | Canadian Junior Championship | 2 | |
| 1954 | Saskatchewan Junior Championship | 2 | |
| 1957 | Manitoba Amateur Championship | 2 | |
| | Canadian Amateur Championship | 2 | |
| | Willingdon Cup (team) | 4 | |
| 1958 | Manitoba Amateur Championship | 2 | |
| 1959 | Manitoba Amateur Championship | 2 | |
| 1961 | Manitoba Open | 2 | 216 |
| | Manitoba Amateur Championship | 1 | |
| | Canadian Amateur Championship | 2 | |
| | America's Cup (team) | 2 | |
| | Willingdon Cup (team) | 5 | 79-75-154 |
| 1962 | Willingdon Cup (team) | 3 | 71-73-144 |
| 1963 | Willingdon Cup (team) | 4 | |
| 1964 | Willingdon Cup (team) | 6 | 77-75-152 |
| 1965 | Willingdon Cup (team) | 3 | 71-79-150 |
| 1967 | Free Press Tournament of Champions | 1 | 71-74-145 |
| 1969 | Manitoba Amateur Championship | 1 | |
| 1971 | Manitoba Amateur Championship | 1 | |
| 1974 | Willingdon Cup (team) | 1 | 73-77-150 |

*Photo courtesy of Canada's Sports Hall of Fame*

# HOMENUIK, WILF

| | |
|---|---|
| sport: | golf |
| born: | Kamsack, Saskatchewan |
| | December 30, 1935 |
| height: | 1.70 m / 5'7" |
| weight: | 63.5 kg / 140 lbs |

Wilf Homenuik's initiation into the game of golf was no different from that of his six other brothers. He caddied, trimmed the grass, searched for lost golf balls and when an opportunity arose, would sneak in between foursomes and play a hole or two. He mastered the game quickly. Not yet in his teens, he was asked not to play in local tournaments. He was just too good and would embarrass the adults. "Stay away, son, this is a man's game," the adult golfers would say and for a while he took their advice. When he finally began to compete at the age of 15, he stunned the province's golf circuit with his dominance.

Twice runner-up for the Canadian Junior Championship, Wilf was optimistic that he would finally win it in 1956, the last year of his junior eligibility. To his disbelief, it was determined that he was overage and ineligible. An error in baptismal records caused the misunderstanding.

Two years later Homenuik turned professional. For many years, he competed on the Canadian, American, and Caribbean tours winning a number of tournaments. The winnings, though, did not come easily. While at times showing flashes of brilliance by setting numerous course records, Homenuik was also quite inconsistent. Pressure would affect him after a good round and his play would deteriorate. Fortunately, he was always able to bounce back, whether after a bad hole, round, or tournament.

On the Canadian Tour, Wilf Homenuik is best remembered for his respectable showing at the 1962 Canadian Open and for his two CPGA victories. At the 1962 Canadian Open, Homenuik scored a hole in one on the last round to finish tied for sixth overall and first among the Canadian golfers. His 1965 and 1971 CPGA victories established him as one of Canada's top golfers.

## RECORD

| year | event | placing | result |
|------|-------|---------|--------|
| 1951 | Saskatchewan Junior Championship | 2 | |
| 1952 | Saskatchewan Junior Championship | 2 | |
| 1953 | Saskatchewan Junior Championship | 2 | |
| | Saskatchewan Amateur Championship | 1 | |
| | Willingdon Cup (team) | 7 | |
| 1954 | Saskatchewan Junior Championship | 1 | |
| | Canadian Junior Championship | 2 | 154 |
| 1955 | Canadian Junior Championship | 2 | |
| 1956 | Manitoba Amateur Championship | 1 | |
| 1957 | Manitoba Amateur Championship | 1 | |
| 1958 | Willingdon Cup (team) | 4 | 78-76-154 |
| 1959 | Willingdon Cup (team) | 2 | 75-77-152 |
| 1961 | Manitoba Open | 1 | 211 |

| year | event | placing | result |
|------|-------|---------|--------|
| 1961 | Alberta Open | 1 | 211 |
| 1962 | McNaughton-Brooks Bursary | 2 | |
| | Canadian Open | 6 T | 70-69-75-71-285 |
| 1963 | McNaughton-Brooks Bursary | 1 T | 203 |
| | Canadian Open | 41 T | 73-76-69-75-293 |
| 1964 | Canadian Open | 51 T | 73-76-76-72-297 |
| 1965 | CPGA | 1 | 72-71-72-215 |
| | World Golf Classic | | 73-75-67-79-294 |
| | Peru Open | 1 | |
| | Puerto Rico Open | 4 | |
| | McNaughton-Brooks Bursary | 1 | 67-68-68-203 |
| 1966 | CPGA | 5 T | 65-74-72-211 |
| | Maracaibo Open | 7 T | 71-74-74-68-287 |
| | Panama Open | 1 | 283 |
| 1967 | Canadian Open | 58 T | 71-74-73-73-291 |
| 1969 | CPGA | 5 | 286 |
| | Canadian Open | 62 T | 76-72-77-70-295 |
| 1970 | CPGA | 3 T | 72-72-71-71-286 |
| | Sahara Invitational | 6 T | 69-68-69-75-281 |
| 1971 | CPGA | 1 | 65-68-67-73-273 |
| | Greater Greensboro Open | 7 T | |
| | Tallahassee Open | 7 T | 69-73-68-71-281 |
| | East Ridge Golf Classic | 1 | 73-67-72-70-282 |
| | Colonial Open | 5 T | 70-74-71-72-287 |
| | Canadian Open | | 73-73-72-74-292 |
| | World Cup (team) | 8 | 72-74-73-73-292 |
| 1972 | CPGA | 4 | 71-73-71-69-284 |
| | Byron Nelson Classic | 3 | |
| | Heritage Classic | | 75-69-76-73-293 |
| 1973 | Lake Michigan Classic | 1 | |
| 1974 | World Cup (team) | 12 | 72-70-74-74-290 |
| 1975 | Dauphin Pro-Am | 1 | |
| | CPGA | 4 T | 70-71-68-71-280 |

# HORDY, MIKE

| | |
|---|---|
| sport: | hockey |
| born: | Thunder Bay, Ontario |
| | October 10, 1956 |
| height: | 1.78 m / 5'10" |
| weight: | 81.5 kg / 180 lbs |
| position: | defense |
| shoots: | left |

*Photo courtesy of the New York Islanders*

Mike Hordy was drafted by the New York Islanders in the fifth round of the 1976 draft after having completed his junior tenure with the Sault Ste. Marie Greyhounds of the OHA. Hordy spent most of his career playing in the minor pro leagues, and was called up by the Islanders twice. In the minors, he played on three championship teams: the 1979 Fort Worth Texans, the 1982 Indianapolis Checkers, and the 1984 Maine Mariners. After he won the CHL title and was named to the first all-star team in 1982, Mike Hordy left for Europe to play with Zurich of the Swiss National League. He returned the following year and signed as a free agent with the New Jersey Devils. He finished his career with the Devils' affiliate, the Maine Mariners of the AHL.

## AWARDS

1978        Bob Gassoff Trophy  -  CHL Most Improved Defenseman

## ALL-STAR SELECTIONS

| | | | |
|---|---|---|---|
| 1978-79 | defense | CHL | Second Team |
| 1979-80 | defense | CHL | Second Team |
| 1980-81 | defense | CHL | Second Team |
| 1981-82 | defense | CHL | First Team |

| year | team | league | regular season | | | | | playoffs | | | | |
|------|------|--------|----|----|----|-----|-----|----|----|----|-----|-----|
| | | | GP | G | A | PTS | PIM | GP | G | A | PTS | PIM |
| 1976-77 | Muskegon | IHL | 77 | 16 | 45 | 61 | 38 | 7 | 2 | 4 | 6 | 2 |
| | Fort Worth | CHL | 2 | 0 | 0 | 0 | 5 | 3 | 0 | 0 | 0 | 0 |
| 1977-78* | Fort Worth | CHL | 76 | 14 | 35 | 49 | 87 | 14 | 2 | 9 | 11 | 15 |
| 1978-79 | NY Islanders | NHL | 2 | 0 | 0 | 0 | 0 | | | | | |
| | Fort Worth | CHL | 74 | 17 | 48 | 65 | 71 | 5 | 0 | 3 | 3 | 6 |
| 1979-80 | NY Islanders | NHL | 9 | 0 | 0 | 0 | 7 | | | | | |
| | Indianapolis | CHL | 64 | 4 | 32 | 36 | 43 | 7 | 0 | 4 | 4 | 2 |
| 1980-81 | Indianapolis | CHL | 70 | 10 | 48 | 58 | 103 | 5 | 1 | 3 | 4 | 6 |
| 1981-82* | Indianapolis | CHL | 79 | 17 | 49 | 66 | 86 | 10 | 4 | 6 | 10 | 15 |
| 1982-83 | Zurich | Swiss | 27 | 16 | 10 | 26 | 40 | | | | | |
| 1983-84* | Maine | AHL | 72 | 11 | 40 | 51 | 31 | 17 | 2 | 6 | 8 | 4 |
| 1984-85 | Maine | AHL | 68 | 1 | 18 | 19 | 46 | | | | | |

# HORECK, PETE

"Pistol Pete," "Horeck-cane"

| | |
|---|---|
| sport: | hockey |
| born: | Massey, Ontario |
| | June 15, 1923 |
| height: | 1.75 m / 5'9" |
| weight: | 71.5 kg / 158 lbs |
| position: | left wing |
| shoots: | left |

After playing minor pro hockey for a number of years, Pete Horeck broke into the NHL with the Chicago Black Hawks in the fall of 1944. In his rookie season, he scored 20 goals. Horeck duplicated the feat in his second season, and made the league's top ten scoring list. After a slow start to the 1946-47 campaign, Horeck was traded to Detroit. There the speedy and aggressive forward was used mostly in a penalty killing role. Horeck's constant hustle on the ice prompted his teammates to nickname him "Horeck-cane." During the 1948 playoffs, he led his team in scoring with ten points in ten games.

In August 1949, Horeck was traded to Boston. Much of his debut season with the Bruins was spent on the sidelines, a result of three serious injuries - a severe skate cut to his heel, a broken foot, and a shoulder separation. Midway through the following season, the Bruins partnered Horeck with Eddie Kryzanowski in a penalty killing role. The hustling twosome quickly turned the defensive role into an offensive threat. While the Bruins were shorthanded, the duo outscored the opposition by more than four goals to one. At season's end, Horeck announced his retirement from hockey - "After all these years, I've had enough."

The retirement, though, was short-lived. Pete Horeck joined the Black Hawks for the 1951-52 season, which proved to be his last in the NHL. Subsequently, he played minor pro hockey for a number of years.

## RECORD

| year | team | league | GP | G | A | PTS | PIM | GP | G | A | PTS | PIM |
|------|------|--------|----|---|---|-----|-----|----|---|---|-----|-----|
| | | | regular season | | | | | playoffs | | | | |
| 1941-42 | Atlantic City | EHL | 59 | 24 | 30 | 54 | 66 | 14 | 2 | 5 | 7 | 6 |
| 1942-43 | Cleveland/Providence | AHL | 59 | 25 | 20 | 45 | 58 | 4 | 1 | 1 | 2 | 2 |
| | Washington | AHL | 1 | 0 | 0 | 0 | 0 | | | | | |
| 1943-44 | Cleveland | AHL | 54 | 34 | 29 | 63 | 29 | 11 | 4 | 5 | 9 | 14 |
| 1944-45 | Chicago | NHL | 50 | 20 | 16 | 36 | 44 | | | | | |
| 1945-46 | Chicago | NHL | 50 | 20 | 21 | 41 | 34 | 4 | 0 | 0 | 0 | 2 |
| 1946-47 | Chicago | NHL | 18 | 4 | 6 | 10 | 12 | | | | | |
| | Detroit | NHL | 38 | 12 | 13 | 25 | 59 | 5 | 2 | 0 | 2 | 6 |
| 1947-48 | Detroit | NHL | 50 | 12 | 17 | 29 | 44 | 10 | 3 | 7 | 10 | 12 |
| 1948-49 | Detroit | NHL | 60 | 14 | 16 | 30 | 46 | 11 | 1 | 1 | 2 | 10 |
| 1949-50 | Boston | NHL | 34 | 5 | 5 | 10 | 22 | | | | | |
| 1950-51 | Boston | NHL | 66 | 10 | 13 | 23 | 57 | 4 | 0 | 0 | 0 | 13 |
| 1951-52 | Chicago | NHL | 60 | 9 | 11 | 20 | 22 | | | | | |
| 1952-53 | Sault Ste. Marie | NOHA | 19 | 4 | 8 | 12 | 22 | 3 | 0 | 1 | 1 | 7 |
| 1953-54 | Sudbury | NOHA | 12 | 3 | 5 | 8 | 25 | 11 | 2 | 4 | 6 | 18 |
| 1954-55 | Sudbury | NOHA | 38 | 18 | 18 | 36 | 42 | | | | | |
| 1955-56 | Sault Ste. Marie | NOHA | 36 | 12 | 24 | 36 | 30 | 7 | 2 | 1 | 3 | 22 |
| 1956-57 | Sault Ste. Marie | NOHA | 47 | 22 | 20 | 42 | 91 | 10 | 3 | 2 | 5 | 18 |
| 1957-58 | Louisville | IHL | 15 | 6 | 7 | 13 | 69 | | | | | |
| | Chatham | OHASr | 15 | 7 | 4 | 11 | 34 | | | | | |
| 1959-60 | Charlotte | EHL | 15 | 1 | 1 | 2 | 22 | | | | | |

| coaching record | | | regular season | | | | | playoffs | | | |
|------|------|--------|---|---|---|---|---------|---|---|---|---|
| year | team | league | G | W | L | T | Standing | G | W | L | T |
| 1958-59 | Charlotte | EHL | 64 | 24 | 38 | 2 | 6 | | | | |

# HOSPODAR, ED

"Box Car"

| | |
|---|---|
| sport: | hockey |
| born: | Bowling Green, Ohio, USA |
| | February 9, 1959 |
| height: | 1.88 m / 6'2" |
| weight: | 95.5 kg / 210 lbs |
| position: | defense, right wing |
| shoots: | right |

*Card reproduced courtesy of O-Pee-Chee Co.*

Ed Hospodar was two when his family settled in Toronto. He played Junior "B" hockey in Markham. In 1976, he joined the Ottawa 67's of the OMJHL. He played with the club for three years. During his tenure in Ottawa, a local reporter compared Hospodar's style of play to that of a runaway boxcar: he would not stop until he hit something. The sobriquet caught on and Ed Hospodar was soon known as the "Box Car."

In 1979, Hospodar was drafted in the second round, 34th overall, by the New York Rangers. In his rookie season, he played for the Rangers and their farm team, the New Haven Nighthawks of the AHL. Hospodar earned a regular starting position with the Rangers during the 1980-81 season. He responded by scoring a career-high 5 goals and 19 points. He also registered 214 penalty minutes. In the playoffs, Hospodar led all players with 93 penalty minutes, even though the Rangers did not advance to the Stanley Cup final. Hospodar played for one more season with the Rangers before being traded to the Hartford Whalers.

In Hartford, Hospodar was used as a utility player both on defense and right wing. After completing his second year with the Whalers, he was released and picked up as a free agent by the Philadelphia Flyers. His tenure with the Flyers did not last long. In November of 1985, Hospodar was traded to the Minnesota North Stars. A year later he was back with Philadelphia. Hospodar, who was selected by the Buffalo Sabres in the 1987 NHL waiver draft, ended his NHL career with the team at the end of the 1987-88 season.

## RECORD

| year | team | league | regular season | | | | | playoffs | | | | |
|------|------|--------|----|---|---|-----|-----|----|---|---|-----|-----|
| | | | GP | G | A | PTS | PIM | GP | G | A | PTS | PIM |
| 1979-80 | New Haven | AHL | 25 | 3 | 9 | 12 | 131 | 7 | 1 | 0 | 1 | 42 |
| | NY Rangers | NHL | 20 | 0 | 1 | 1 | 76 | 5 | 0 | 1 | 1 | 39 |

| | | | regular season | | | | | playoffs | | | | |
|---|---|---|---|---|---|---|---|---|---|---|---|---|
| year | team | league | GP | G | A | PTS | PIM | GP | G | A | PTS | PIM |
| 1980-81 | NY Rangers | NHL | 61 | 5 | 14 | 19 | 214 | 12 | 2 | 0 | 2 | 93 |
| 1981-82 | NY Rangers | NHL | 41 | 3 | 8 | 11 | 152 | | | | | |
| 1982-83 | Hartford | NHL | 72 | 1 | 9 | 10 | 199 | | | | | |
| 1983-84 | Hartford | NHL | 59 | 0 | 9 | 9 | 163 | | | | | |
| 1984-85 | Philadelphia | NHL | 50 | 3 | 4 | 7 | 130 | 18 | 1 | 1 | 2 | 69 |
| 1985-86 | Philadelphia | NHL | 17 | 3 | 1 | 4 | 55 | | | | | |
| | Minnesota | NHL | 43 | 0 | 2 | 2 | 91 | 2 | 0 | 0 | 0 | 2 |
| 1986-87 | Philadelphia | NHL | 45 | 2 | 2 | 4 | 136 | 5 | 0 | 0 | 0 | 2 |
| 1987-88 | Buffalo | NHL | 42 | 0 | 1 | 1 | 98 | | | | | |
| 1988-89 | Rochester | AHL | 5 | 0 | 0 | 0 | 10 | | | | | |

international

| year | team | competition | GP | G | A | PTS | PIM | Place |
|---|---|---|---|---|---|---|---|---|
| 1978 | USA | World Junior Championship | 6 | 3 | 4 | 7 | 10 | 5 |

# HOYDA, DAVE

| | |
|---|---|
| sport: | hockey |
| given name: | Hoyda, David Allan |
| born: | Edmonton, Alberta |
| | May 20, 1957 |
| height: | 1.85 m / 6'1" |
| weight: | 93 kg / 205 lbs |
| position: | left wing |
| shoots: | left |

*Card reproduced courtesy of O-Pee-Chee Co.*

Dave Hoyda's hockey career began in his home town of Edmonton where he played junior hockey for the Mets and the Oil Kings. Subsequently, he played for the Portland Winter Hawks of the WCHL. Hoyda played a strong and tough game. The Philadelphia Flyers, who at the time were known as the "Broad Street Bullies," were impressed by Hoyda's style and drafted him from the Portland Winter Hawks in the third round, 53rd overall, of the 1977 NHL Entry Draft. During the 1977-78 season, Hoyda played for the Flyers and for their farm club, the

Maine Mariners. The following year he played for the Flyers. In the summer of 1979, Hoyda was claimed by the Winnipeg Jets in the Expansion Draft. He only played sporadically for the Jets through two seasons.

RECORD

| year | team | league | regular season | | | | | playoffs | | | | |
|------|------|--------|----|----|----|-----|-----|----|----|----|-----|-----|
| | | | GP | G | A | PTS | PIM | GP | G | A | PTS | PIM |
| 1977-78 | Philadelphia | NHL | 41 | 1 | 3 | 4 | 119 | 9 | 0 | 0 | 0 | 17 |
| | Maine | AHL | 31 | 4 | 5 | 9 | 112 | | | | | |
| 1978-79 | Philadelphia | NHL | 67 | 3 | 13 | 16 | 138 | 3 | 0 | 0 | 0 | 0 |
| 1979-80 | Winnipeg | NHL | 15 | 1 | 1 | 2 | 35 | | | | | |
| | Tulsa | CHL | 32 | 11 | 6 | 17 | 89 | | | | | |
| 1980-81 | Winnipeg | NHL | 9 | 1 | 0 | 1 | 7 | | | | | |
| | Tulsa | CHL | 42 | 13 | 22 | 35 | 118 | | | | | |

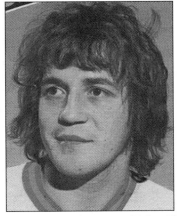

# HRECHKOSY, DAVE

"The Wrecker"

sport:          hockey
given name:     Hrechkosy, David John
born:           Winnipeg, Manitoba
                November 1, 1951
height:         1.88 m / 6'2"
weight:         98 kg / 216 lbs
position:       left wing
shoots:         left

*Card reproduced courtesy of O-Pee-Chee Co.*

Dave Hrechkosy had his start in organized hockey playing defense on the Blessed Virgin Mary Greek Orthodox Ukrainian Church hockey team in Winnipeg. By the time he graduated to the junior Winnipeg Jets, he had been moved to a forward position. Hrechkosy joined the minor pro circuit in 1971-72 playing with the New Haven of the EHL and Providence of the AHL. During the 1973-74 season he played for the Salt Lake Golden Eagles of the WHL. Towards the end of that campaign, Hrechkosy was called up to the NHL by the California Seals. A good skater and stickhandler, Hrechkosy could also mix it up when necessary. He had a reputation of being an extremely hard hitter, particularly in corners; hence the nickname "The Wrecker."

At the 1974 training camp, Hrechkosy earned a starting position with the California Seals. He played well in his rookie season, leading the team in goals scored with 29 and placing third in the balloting for the NHL Rookie of the Year. California responded by trading Hrechkosy to the St. Louis Blues in the spring of 1976. He played sporadically for the Blues, spending most of his time in the minor pro leagues. After retiring from the game in 1979, Dave Hrechkosy returned to Salt Lake City to do colour commentary on Golden Eagles broadcasts.

## RECORD

| year | team | league | regular season | | | | | playoffs | | | | |
|------|------|--------|----|----|----|-----|-----|----|----|----|-----|-----|
| | | | GP | G | A | PTS | PIM | GP | G | A | PTS | PIM |
| 1971-72 | New Haven | EHL | 75 | 31 | 34 | 65 | 66 | 7 | 4 | 5 | 9 | 16 |
| | Providence | AHL | 7 | 3 | 0 | 3 | 2 | | | | | |
| 1972-73 | Rochester | AHL | 70 | 15 | 24 | 39 | 48 | 4 | 0 | 2 | 2 | 8 |
| 1973-74 | Salt Lake City | WHL | 78 | 36 | 35 | 71 | 58 | 5 | 2 | 1 | 3 | 10 |
| | California | NHL | 2 | 0 | 0 | 0 | 0 | | | | | |
| 1974-75 | California | NHL | 72 | 29 | 14 | 43 | 25 | | | | | |
| 1975-76 | California | NHL | 38 | 9 | 5 | 14 | 14 | | | | | |
| | St. Louis | NHL | 13 | 3 | 3 | 6 | 0 | 3 | 1 | 0 | 1 | 2 |
| | Salt Lake City | CHL | 16 | 8 | 3 | 11 | 6 | | | | | |
| 1976-77 | St. Louis | NHL | 15 | 1 | 2 | 3 | 2 | | | | | |
| | Kansas City | CHL | 45 | 9 | 12 | 21 | 4 | 10 | 3 | 3 | 6 | 0 |
| 1977-78 | Salt Lake City | CHL | 55 | 5 | 12 | 17 | 11 | | | | | |
| 1978-79 | Saginaw | IHL | 2 | 0 | 2 | 2 | 0 | | | | | |
| | New Haven | AHL | 61 | 15 | 20 | 35 | 21 | 10 | 6 | 7 | 13 | 8 |
| 1979-80 | New Haven | AHL | 1 | 0 | 0 | 0 | 0 | | | | | |

# HRUDEY, KELLY

| | |
|---|---|
| sport: | hockey |
| given name: | Hrudey, Kelly Stephen |
| born: | Edmonton, Alberta |
| | January 13, 1961 |
| height: | 1.78 m / 5'10" |
| weight: | 81.5 kg / 180 lbs |
| position: | goal |
| shoots: | left |

*Photo courtesy of the Los Angeles Kings*

Kelly Hrudey was an underage junior playing for the Medicine Hat Tigers when the New York Islanders drafted him in the second round, 38th overall, in the 1980 NHL Entry Draft. He played for one more season with the Tigers before the Islanders assigned him to the Indianapolis Checkers of the IHL. Hrudey was with the Checkers for two years. In both years he was named to the league's first all-star team and was honoured with the Terry Sawchuk Trophy as the league's outstanding goaltender. In the second year he was also awarded with the league's MVP trophy.

Hrudey made the roster of the Islanders in the fall of 1983 as the club's third goalie. When the Islanders traded one of their goalies, Hrudey was given an opportunity to play regularly. His first full season was in 1984-85 when he appeared in 41 games, posting a 3.62 goals against average. In the playoffs against Philadelphia, Hrudey played superbly, allowing only 8 goals in 5 games for a 1.71 average. Unfortunately, the Islanders could not score and Hrudey won only one of those games. Two years later Hrudey played in one of the most memorable play-off games on record. The seventh and deciding game of the Stanley Cup semi-final ended in a 2-2 tie after regulation play. It took 68 minutes and 47 seconds of overtime for the Islanders to score and eliminate the Washington Capitals. Hrudey faced 75 shots and made 73 saves in the game.

In February of 1989, the Islanders traded Hrudey to the Los Angeles Kings. The trade had a positive impact on Hrudey's game: his goals against average for the remainder of the season decreased by a goal a game. During the 1989-90 season, his first complete with the Kings, Hrudey's average soared to an all time high of 4.07. The following year, the agile and acrobatic goaltender regained his form, winning 26 games and posting a 2.90 goals against average.

# AWARDS

| 1982 | Terry Sawchuk Trophy | - | CHL Top Goaltender |
| 1982 | Max McNab Trophy | - | CHL Playoff MVP |
| 1983 | Terry Sawchuk Trophy | - | CHL Top Goaltender |
| 1983 | Tommy Ivan Trophy | - | CHL MVP |

## ALL-STAR SELECTIONS

| 1981-82 | goal | CHL | First Team |
| 1982-83 | goal | CHL | First Team |

## RECORD

| | | | regular season | | | | | | | | playoffs | | | | | | | |
|---|---|---|---|---|---|---|---|---|---|---|---|---|---|---|---|---|---|---|
| year | team | league | GP | MIN | W | L | T | GA | AVE | SO | GP | MIN | W | L | T | GA | AVE | SO |
| 1980-81 | Indianapolis | CHL | | | | | | | | | 2 | 135 | | | | 8 | 3.56 | 0 |
| 1981-82 | Indianapolis | CHL | 51 | 3,033 | 27 | 19 | 4 | 149 | 2.95 | 1 | 13 | 842 | 11 | 2 | 0 | 34 | 2.42 | 1 |
| 1982-83 | Indianapolis | CHL | 47 | 2,744 | 26 | 17 | 1 | 139 | 3.04 | 2 | 10 | 637 | 7 | 3 | 0 | 28 | 2.64 | 0 |
| 1983-84 | NY Islanders | NHL | 12 | 535 | 7 | 2 | 0 | 28 | 3.14 | 0 | | | | | | | | |
| | Indianapolis | CHL | 6 | 370 | 3 | 2 | 1 | 21 | 3.40 | 0 | | | | | | | | |
| 1984-85 | NY Islanders | NHL | 41 | 2,335 | 19 | 17 | 3 | 141 | 3.62 | 2 | 5 | 281 | 1 | 3 | 0 | 8 | 1.71 | 0 |
| 1985-86 | NY Islanders | NHL | 45 | 2,563 | 19 | 15 | 8 | 137 | 3.21 | 1 | 2 | 120 | 0 | 2 | 0 | 6 | 3.00 | 0 |
| 1986-87 | NY Islanders | NHL | 46 | 2,634 | 21 | 15 | 7 | 145 | 3.30 | 0 | 14 | 842 | 7 | 7 | 0 | 38 | 2.71 | 0 |
| 1987-88 | NY Islanders | NHL | 47 | 2,751 | 22 | 17 | 5 | 153 | 3.34 | 3 | 6 | 381 | 2 | 4 | 0 | 23 | 3.62 | 0 |
| 1988-89 | NY Islanders | NHL | 50 | 2,800 | 18 | 24 | 3 | 183 | 3.92 | 0 | | | | | | | | |
| | Los Angeles | NHL | 16 | 974 | 10 | 4 | 2 | 47 | 2.90 | 1 | 10 | 566 | 4 | 6 | 0 | 35 | 3.71 | 0 |
| 1989-90 | Los Angeles | NHL | 52 | 2,860 | 22 | 21 | 6 | 194 | 4.07 | 2 | 9 | 539 | 4 | 4 | 0 | 39 | 4.34 | 0 |
| 1990-91 | Los Angeles | NHL | 47 | 2,730 | 26 | 13 | 6 | 132 | 2.90 | 3 | 12 | 798 | 6 | 6 | 0 | 37 | 2.78 | 0 |

### international

| year | team | competition | GP | MIN | W | L | T | GA | AVE | SO | Place |
|---|---|---|---|---|---|---|---|---|---|---|---|
| 1986 | Canada | World Championship | 5 | 299 | 2 | 3 | 0 | 22 | 4.41 | 0 | 3 |
| 1987 | Canada | Canada Cup | 0 | 0 | 0 | 0 | 0 | 0 | 0 | 0 | 1 |

# HRYB, TARAS

sport:       wrestling
born:       . . .

           . . .

height:       . . .
weight:       80 kg / 177 lbs

Taras Hryb was 12 years old, overweight, and generally disinterested in any athletic activity, when he first tried wrestling. He immediately took a liking to the sport, a liking which soon bordered on an obsession. Before too long, he was winning almost every event he entered. In 1968, he won the British Columbia high school championships. The following year, he won the first of three consecutive Canadian junior titles. He was also selected to represent Canada at the 1969 World Junior Wrestling Championships. Hryb placed third, becoming the first Canadian to ever win a medal at a World Wrestling Championship.

In the fall of 1969, Hryb enrolled in the University of British Columbia: "The only reason I went to UBC was to wrestle. . . The only thing I did at University was wrestle. I didn't take courses because I wanted to graduate, I took them so I could wrestle."[13] And wrestle he did, winning three interuniversity titles and three national titles. He represented Canada in all major international competitions, winning medals at the Pan American and Commonwealth Games. In fact, during the 1974 Commonwealth Games, Hryb wrestled with an injured knee cartilage and a rib separation. The 1972 Olympics were his dream. The 18-year-old made the Canadian team but lost both of his preliminary round bouts. "I psyched myself right out of the Olympics. I think they meant too much to me."[14]

## AWARDS

1970       Victoria Male Athlete of the Year

## RECORD

| year | competition | event | placing |
|------|-------------|-------|---------|
| 1969 | World Junior Championships | 180 lbs | 3 |
| 1970 | CIAU Championships | 177 lbs | 1 |

| year | competition | event | | placing |
|------|-------------|-------|---|---------|
| 1971 | CIAU Championships | 177 | lbs | 1 |
| | Canadian Championships | 180.5 | lbs | 1 |
| | Pan American Games | 82 | kg | 3 |
| 1972 | Canadian Championships | 180.5 | lbs | 1 |
| | Olympic Games | 82 | kg | |
| 1973 | CIAU Championships | 177 | lbs | 1 |
| | Canadian Championships | 180.5 | lbs | 1 |
| | World Student Games | | | |
| 1974 | Commonwealth Games | 82 | kg | 3 |

# HRYMNAK, STEVE

| | |
|---|---|
| sport: | hockey |
| given name: | Hrymnak, Stefan |
| born: | Port Arthur, Ontario (now Thunder Bay) March 3 1926 |
| height: | 1.80 m / 5'11" |
| weight: | 81 kg / 178 lbs |
| position: | defense |
| shoots: | left |

*Photo courtesy of the Northwestern Ontario Sports Hall of Fame*

Steve Hrymnak began his hockey career with the Lakehead Ukrainian Athletic Club Ukes in the fall of 1935. Later he played three seasons for the Port Arthur junior club. He missed one year of junior hockey when he was called into the Canadian Army and served in the armoured corp. That was the year in which Port Arthur won the Memorial Cup. Hrymnak played with the New York Rovers senior club in 1946-47 before turning professional in 1947 with New Haven. In the fall of 1950, he was purchased by the St. Louis Flyers and eventually became team captain before moving on to the Edmonton Flyers. Later he played with New Westminster and, from 1958 to 1963, with the Port Arthur Bearcats. In 1962, he captained the Bearcats to the Ahearne Cup in Sweden.

Hrymnak was a standout rushing defenseman and solid on the blue line. He was constantly aggressive, which sometimes resulted in mistakes particularly deep in opposition territory. As a result of his offensive abilities, he was frequently assigned to any of the forward positions. Players, coaches, and fans referred to him as the "Ukrainian handyman." Often Steve Hrymnak played injured, because of a sense of duty towards his club: "The sport's simply a job for me - and I think I work hard at it."[15] During his career, Hrymnak was called up twice to the NHL, once by Chicago, and the other time by Detroit.

## INDUCTIONS

1989    Northwestern Ontario Sports Hall of Fame  -  Member of the 1961-62 Bearcats

## RECORD

| year | team | league | regular season | | | | | playoffs | | | | |
|------|------|--------|----|---|---|-----|-----|----|---|---|-----|-----|
|      |      |        | GP | G | A | PTS | PIM | GP | G | A | PTS | PIM |
| 1946-47 | New York | EHL | 53 | 0 | 7 | 7 | 52 | 7 | 0 | 0 | 0 | 7 |
| 1947-48 | New Haven | AHL | 39 | 10 | 4 | 14 | 23 | 4 | 0 | 1 | 1 | 4 |
| 1948-49 | New Haven | AHL | 55 | 10 | 11 | 21 | 28 | | | | | |
| 1949-50 | New Haven | AHL | 70 | 13 | 17 | 30 | 28 | | | | | |
| 1950-51 | St. Louis | AHL | 57 | 11 | 11 | 22 | 32 | | | | | |
| 1951-52 | Chicago | NHL | 18 | 2 | 1 | 3 | 4 | | | | | |
|         | St. Louis | AHL | 48 | 14 | 36 | 50 | 19 | | | | | |
| 1952-53 | St. Louis | AHL | 64 | 14 | 27 | 41 | 31 | | | | | |
|         | Detroit | NHL | | | | | | 2 | 0 | 0 | 0 | 0 |
| 1953-54 | Edmonton | WHL | 69 | 13 | 17 | 30 | 41 | 13 | 3 | 4 | 7 | 5 |
| 1954-55* | Edmonton | WHL | 69 | 8 | 22 | 30 | 26 | 9 | 2 | 0 | 2 | 20 |
| 1955-56 | Edmonton | WHL | 69 | 8 | 17 | 25 | 26 | 3 | 0 | 0 | 0 | 0 |
| 1956-57 | New Westminster | WHL | 52 | 6 | 13 | 19 | 34 | | | | | |
| 1957-58 | New Westminster | WHL | 48 | 9 | 18 | 27 | 36 | 4 | 0 | 1 | 1 | 6 |

# HUBCHIK, WALTER

| | |
|---|---|
| sport: | curling |
| born: | Winnipeg, Manitoba |
| | May 25, 1923 |
| died: | Detroit, Michigan, USA |
| | July 2, 1991 |
| height: | 1.80 m / 5'11" |
| weight: | 79.5 kg / 175 lbs |

During the 1963 United States Curling Championship, the rink representing the State of Michigan consisted of expatriated Canadians, three of them childhood friends from Manitoba. Walter Hubchik, playing lead on the rink, was joined by the Slyziuk brothers, Mike (skip) and Ernest (second), all from Grandview, Manitoba, and Nelson Brown (third) of Southampton, Ontario. The Slyziuk rink completed the tournament with a 10 and 1 record which was identical to that of Wisconsin. In a tense playoff, Michigan came from behind to win 7-6 on the last rock of the tenth end. At the World Championship, the Slyziuk rink tied for second place with a 3-3 record. One of the American victories included the only defeat experienced by the eventual champion, E. Richardson of Canada.

Walter Hubchik began to curl in the 1940s in Grandview, Manitoba. After service with the Canadian Army during World War II, he settled in Windsor, Ontario. There he curled and also coached hockey. Subsequently, he moved to Detroit, United States, opened a business, and became a member of the Detroit Curling Club. In 1960, he joined his childhood friends, the Slyziuk brothers, on the Mike Slyziuk rink. Three years later they were national champions. Walter Hubchik curled for nearly 40 years. During that period, he represented Michigan at the United States Nationals on 11 occasions, three times as a skip of his own rink.

In the early 1950s, Walter Hubchik served as sports director of the Ukrainian Youth League of North America and in the years 1955-56 as its president.

INDUCTIONS

1978      Michigan Amateur Sports Hall of Fame

# RECORD

| year | competition | position | placing | result |
|------|-------------|----------|---------|--------|
| 1961 | United States Championship | lead | 3 | 8-3 |
| 1962 | United States Championship | lead | 2 | 8-3 |
| 1963 | United States Championship | lead | 1 | 10-1 |
|      | World Championship | lead | 2 (tied) | 3-3 |
| 1964 | United States Championship | lead | 2 (tied) | 8-3 |
| 1965 | United States Championship | second | 7 | 2-9 |
| 1966 | United States Championship | lead | 3 (tied) | 8-3 |
| 1967 | United States Championship | lead | 3 | 8-3 |
| 1968 | United States Championship | vice-skip | 3 | 8-3 |
| 1970 | United States Championship | skip | 4 | 6-5 |
| 1973 | United States Championship | skip | 6 | 4-7 |
| 1974 | United States Championship | skip | 5 | 7-4 |

# HUCUL, FRED

| | |
|---|---|
| sport: | hockey |
| given name: | Hucul, Frederick Albert |
| born: | Tubrose, Saskatchewan |
| | December 5, 1931 |
| height: | 1.80 m / 5'11" |
| weight: | 85 kg / 188 lbs |
| position: | defense |
| shoots: | left |

Fred Hucul, a rugged rearguard with the Moose Jaw Canucks, was called up by the Chicago Black Hawks late in the 1950-51 season. At the time, Hucul was the top scorer among defensemen in the Western junior loop, with 19 goals and 27 assists. He also had accumulated 165 penalty minutes. The following year, aside from being sidelined with a mysterious disorder which caused numbness in his legs, he had a good season with Chicago. Hucul played for two more years in the NHL before being farmed out in 1954. When the NHL expanded in 1967, Hucul was picked up by the St. Louis Blues. He was a steadying influence on the young team that year.

Hucul spent most of his minor pro hockey years with the Calgary Stampeders of the WHL. In 1957, he established a league record by scoring three unassisted goals in one game. For many years, he captained the team, and in the spring of 1963, he had the distinction of being both the captain and the coach of the club. During his days in Calgary, Fred Hucul built up his ranch in nearby Carolina. In the fall of 1968, he was named coach and general manager of the Kansas City Blues of the CHL. Fred Hucul is the brother of hockey player Sandy Hucul. In 1964, the two Hucul brothers were named to the WHL First All-star Team at the defense position.

## ALL-STAR SELECTIONS

| 1955-56 | defense | WHL | First Team |
| 1957-58 | defense | WHL | First Team (Prairie Division) |
| 1958-59 | defense | WHL | First Team (Prairie Division) |
| 1960-61 | defense | WHL | Second Team |
| 1961-62 | defense | WHL | Second Team |
| 1962-63 | defense | WHL | First Team |
| 1963-64 | defense | WHL | First Team |
| 1965-66 | defense | WHL | First Team |

## RECORD

| year | team | league | regular season | | | | | playoffs | | | | |
| | | | GP | G | A | PTS | PIM | GP | G | A | PTS | PIM |
|---|---|---|---|---|---|---|---|---|---|---|---|---|
| 1950-51 | Chicago | NHL | 3 | 1 | 0 | 1 | 2 | | | | | |
| 1951-52 | Chicago | NHL | 34 | 3 | 7 | 10 | 37 | | | | | |
| | St. Louis | AHL | 9 | 2 | 3 | 5 | 8 | | | | | |
| 1952-53 | Chicago | NHL | 57 | 5 | 7 | 12 | 25 | 6 | 1 | 0 | 1 | 10 |
| 1953-54 | Chicago | NHL | 27 | 0 | 3 | 3 | 19 | | | | | |
| | Calgary | WHL | 15 | 7 | 4 | 11 | 12 | | | | | |
| * | Quebec | QHL | 13 | 4 | 6 | 10 | 26 | 12 | 1 | 3 | 4 | 10 |
| 1954-55 | Calgary | WHL | 51 | 12 | 23 | 35 | 59 | | | | | |
| 1955-56 | Calgary | WHL | 70 | 21 | 38 | 59 | 85 | 8 | 1 | 4 | 5 | 19 |
| 1956-57 | Buffalo | AHL | 9 | 0 | 6 | 6 | 11 | | | | | |
| 1957-58 | Calgary | WHL | 61 | 18 | 40 | 58 | 51 | 14 | 1 | 4 | 5 | 27 |
| 1958-59 | Calgary | WHL | 64 | 7 | 36 | 43 | 61 | 8 | 1 | 0 | 1 | 9 |
| 1959-60 | Calgary | WHL | 66 | 7 | 46 | 53 | 32 | | | | | |
| 1960-61 | Calgary | WHL | 67 | 9 | 42 | 51 | 55 | 5 | 0 | 0 | 0 | 9 |
| 1961-62 | Calgary | WHL | 53 | 19 | 37 | 56 | 42 | 7 | 0 | 4 | 4 | 2 |
| 1962-63 | Calgary | WHL | 70 | 16 | 41 | 57 | 56 | | | | | |

| | | | regular season | | | | | playoffs | | | | |
|---|---|---|---|---|---|---|---|---|---|---|---|---|
| year | team | league | GP | G | A | PTS | PIM | GP | G | A | PTS | PIM |
| 1963-64 | Denver | WHL | 69 | 8 | 49 | 57 | 58 | 6 | 3 | 4 | 7 | 6 |
| 1964-65 | Victoria | WHL | 51 | 8 | 20 | 28 | 67 | 12 | 1 | 4 | 5 | 28 |
| 1965-66* | Victoria | WHL | 61 | 16 | 43 | 59 | 56 | 14 | 8 | 7 | 15 | 14 |
| | Tulsa | CPHL | 7 | 1 | 0 | 1 | 4 | | | | | |
| 1966-67 | Victoria | WHL | 13 | 3 | 6 | 9 | 12 | | | | | |
| 1967-68 | St. Louis | NHL | 43 | 2 | 13 | 15 | 30 | | | | | |
| 1968-69 | Kansas City | CHL | 2 | 0 | 1 | 1 | 0 | | | | | |

| coaching | | | regular season | | | | | playoffs | | | |
|---|---|---|---|---|---|---|---|---|---|---|---|
| year | team | league | G | W | L | T | standing | G | W | L | T |
| 1968-69 | Kansas City | CHL | 72 | 26 | 28 | 18 | 2 | | | | |
| 1969-70 | Kansas City | CHL | 72 | 24 | 37 | 11 | 7 | | | | |

# HUCUL, SANDY

| | |
|---|---|
| sport: | hockey |
| given name: | Hucul, Alexander Kenneth |
| born: | Eston, Saskatchewan |
| | December 5, 1933 |
| height: | 1.80 m / 5'11" |
| weight: | 79.5 kg / 175 lbs |
| position: | defense |
| shoots: | right |

For 18 seasons, Sandy Hucul played minor pro hockey in the Western Hockey League. When he retired in 1972, he was second on the all-time list of most regular season games played with 1,119, and fourth on the all-time list of penalty minutes with 1,330. He was a rugged defense-man who threw bone-crushing bodychecks. An opponent once described being at the receiving end of one: "He doesn't hit you and stop; he goes right through you and leaves you quivering."[16] Hucul also liked to mix it up. Most players, though, tried to avoid a two-fisted altercation with him.

Over time, Sandy Hucul developed into a team leader and served as team captain of the Victoria Maple Leafs in 1966-67, and the Phoenix Roadrunners between 1967 and 1970. In February of 1970, he took over the coaching duties with the last-place Roadrunners on an interim basis. Under his guidance, the club won 12, lost 9, and tied 4. At the end of the season, a teammate was appointed coach. Hucul was disappointed, but accepted the fact by signing on to play for yet another season.

When Hucul retired from the game in 1972, he was appointed coach of the Roadrunners. His task was a difficult one as the new World Hockey Association stripped him of all but nine players. Nevertheless, he led the club to back-to-back WHL championships. In 1974, Phoenix entered an expansion team into the WHA. Hucul was the club's coach. He led the team to a record of 78 wins, 66 loses and 14 ties in two seasons. Both years, Phoenix made it to the playoffs and in 1975 he was named the WHA Coach of the Year. His contract, though, was not renewed for the following year. Sandy Hucul is the brother of hockey player Fred Hucul.

## AWARDS

| 1968 | Hal Laycoe Cup - WHL Outstanding Defenseman |
|------|---------------------------------------------|
| 1972 | Hal Laycoe Cup - WHL Outstanding Defenseman |
| 1975 | Robert Schmertz Memorial Trophy - WHA Coach of the Year |
| 1975 | Arizona Coach of the Year |

## ALL-STAR SELECTIONS

| 1961-62 | defense | WHL | Second Team |
|---------|---------|-----|-------------|
| 1963-64 | defense | WHL | First Team |
| 1964-65 | defense | WHL | Second Team |
| 1965-66 | defense | WHL | Second Team |
| 1967-68 | defense | WHL | First Team |
| 1971-72 | defense | WHL | First Team |

## RECORD

| year | team | league | regular season | | | | | playoffs | | | | |
|------|------|--------|----|----|----|-----|-----|----|----|----|-----|-----|
| | | | GP | G | A | PTS | PIM | GP | G | A | PTS | PIM |
| 1954-55 | Calgary | WHL | 49 | 3 | 8 | 11 | 33 | 9 | 0 | 0 | 0 | 2 |
| 1955-56 | Calgary | WHL | 70 | 5 | 20 | 25 | 110 | 8 | 0 | 0 | 0 | 8 |
| 1956-57 | Calgary | WHL | 36 | 3 | 14 | 17 | 58 | | | | | |
| | Buffalo | AHL | 28 | 2 | 4 | 6 | 47 | | | | | |
| 1957-58 | Calgary | WHL | 62 | 4 | 21 | 25 | 100 | 14 | 1 | 4 | 5 | 26 |
| 1958-59 | Saskatoon | WHL | 63 | 4 | 16 | 20 | 41 | | | | | |
| 1959-60* | Vancouver | WHL | 67 | 6 | 20 | 26 | 62 | 11 | 1 | 3 | 4 | 4 |
| 1960-61 | Spokane | WHL | 62 | 6 | 24 | 30 | 83 | 4 | 2 | 1 | 3 | 4 |
| 1961-62 | Spokane | WHL | 61 | 6 | 21 | 27 | 100 | 6 | 0 | 4 | 4 | 15 |

| year | team | league | regular season | | | | | playoffs | | | | |
|---|---|---|---|---|---|---|---|---|---|---|---|---|
| | | | GP | G | A | PTS | PIM | GP | G | A | PTS | PIM |
| 1962-63 | Spokane | WHL | 68 | 7 | 24 | 31 | 85 | | | | | |
| 1963-64 | Denver | WHL | 66 | 7 | 23 | 30 | 85 | 6 | 1 | 2 | 3 | 10 |
| 1964-65 | Victoria | WHL | 70 | 4 | 26 | 30 | 106 | 11 | 1 | 2 | 3 | 20 |
| 1965-66* | Victoria | WHL | 68 | 5 | 22 | 27 | 92 | 14 | 1 | 4 | 5 | 28 |
| 1966-67 | Victoria | WHL | 69 | 1 | 27 | 28 | 87 | | | | | |
| 1967-68 | Phoenix | WHL | 71 | 6 | 26 | 32 | 67 | 4 | 0 | 0 | 0 | 2 |
| 1968-69 | Phoenix | WHL | 49 | 2 | 17 | 19 | 46 | | | | | |
| 1969-70 | Phoenix | WHL | 63 | 8 | 21 | 29 | 38 | | | | | |
| 1970-71 | Phoenix | WHL | 56 | 3 | 17 | 20 | 46 | | | | | |
| 1971-72 | Phoenix | WHL | 69 | 5 | 23 | 28 | 91 | | | | | |

coaching

| year | team | league | regular season | | | | | playoffs | | | |
|---|---|---|---|---|---|---|---|---|---|---|---|
| | | | G | W | L | T | standing | G | W | L | T |
| 1969-70 | Phoenix | WHL | 25 | 12 | 9 | 4 | 5 | | | | |
| 1972-73* | Phoenix | WHL | 72 | 37 | 26 | 9 | 1 | 10 | 8 | 2 | 0 |
| 1973-74* | Phoenix | WHL | 78 | 43 | 32 | 3 | 1 | 9 | 8 | 1 | 0 |
| 1974-75 | Phoenix | WHA | 78 | 39 | 31 | 8 | 4 | 5 | 1 | 4 | 0 |
| 1975-76 | Phoenix | WHA | 80 | 39 | 35 | 6 | 2 | 5 | 2 | 3 | 0 |
| 1977-78 | Phoenix | CHL | 27 | 4 | 20 | 3 | ** | | | | |

** team disbanded during season

# HUMENUIK, ROD

| | |
|---|---|
| sport: | football |
| born: | Detroit, Michigan, USA |
| | . . . |
| height: | 1.85 m / 6'1" |
| weight: | 106.5 kg / 235 lbs |
| position: | offensive guard |

*Photo courtesy of the Canadian Football Hall of Fame and Museum*

In the years 1956 to 1960, Rod Humenuik attended the University of Southern California

(USC) and played football for the Trojans at the offensive tackle position. In 1960, he graduated with a Master's degree and signed a contract with the Winnipeg Blue Bombers. He played with the Bombers for three years at the offensive guard position. In two of those years (1961 and 1962), the Bombers won the Grey Cup. While at Winnipeg, Humenuik qualified for his Canadian citizenship, which he obtained in 1961.

In 1966, Humenuik returned to USC as an assistant coach responsible for the offensive team. During his five-year tenure with the club, the USC Trojans participated in four consecutive Rose Bowl games and were crowned National Champions in 1967. Many future pro greats were coached by Humenuik at the time, among them Heisman Trophy winner O. J. Simpson. In 1971, Humenuik accepted the head coaching position at California State University, Northridge. The following year, he led the school to only its third winning season in history. The offence that Humenuik's team generated that year was awesome. It was ranked second in the nation with 5,004 total yards, or an average of 455 yards per game. It tallied 375 points or 34 points per game. These credentials resulted in Rod Humenuik's recruitment by the Toronto Argonauts in 1973 to coach the offensive line.

# HYNDUIK, OLLIE

"Pepper," "Jolly Ollie"
sport:          bowling, golf
born:           Winnipeg, Manitoba
                November 8, 1928
height:         1.60 m / 5'3"
weight:         68 kg / 150 lbs

Ollie Hynduik excelled in several sports. In 1945, she started competing in organized fastball. She played catcher with the St. Boniface Athletics, St. Vital Tigers, and the Canadian Ukrainian Athletic Club (CUAC) of Winnipeg. In 1953, she led CUAC to the provincial title.

In the early 1950s, Hynduik became interested in golf. She was taught the game at centre field of a baseball diamond hitting balls into the back stop. Neighbourhood friends such as Mike and Bill Pidlaski, Bill Ezinicki and Terry Sawchuk all had a hand in teaching her the basics. In 1960, Hynduik won the Manitoba Ladies' Championship. She had a second place finish in

1970. Hynduik represented Manitoba in the Canadian Ladies' Team Golf Championship nine times in the years 1961 to 1973, winning the championship trophy on one occasion. After moving to Ontario, Hynduik won the Canadian Ladies' Senior Team Championship in 1979.

Ollie Hynduik was also a championship bowler. In 1952, she bowled a perfect 450, and in 1954 a 440. Hynduik won numerous Winnipeg and Manitoba bowling titles. She held the Winnipeg high average bowling title in eight separate years with the highest at 256. In 1955, and once again in 1958, she won the Canadian singles titles. In 1959, she was a member of the Manitoba team that won the national team championship. Hynduik subsequently coached bowling. At the 1973 World Five Pin Championship, the Winnipeg team that she coached was victorious.

## INDUCTIONS

1990        Manitoba Sports Hall of Fame

## AWARDS

1973        Manitoba Order of the Buffalo Hunt
            (for coaching ladies team to World Five Pin Bowling Title)
1979        Ontario Achievement Award
            (for winning Canadian Sr. Ladies' Golf Team Championship)

## RECORD

| year | competition | division | placing |
|------|-------------|----------|---------|
| 1955 | Canadian 5 Pin Bowling Championship | singles | 1 |
| 1958 | Canadian 5 Pin Bowling Championship | singles | 1 |
| 1959 | Canadian 5 Pin Bowling Championship | team | 1 |
| 1960 | Manitoba Ladies' Golf Championship | singles | 1 |
| 1961 | Canadian Ladies' Golf Championship | team | 3 |
| 1964 | Canadian Ladies' Golf Championship | team | |
| 1970 | Canadian Ladies' Golf Championship | team | 6 |
| 1971 | Manitoba Ladies' Golf Championship | singles | 2 |
|      | Canadian Ladies' Golf Championship | team | 8 |
| 1972 | Manitoba Ladies' Golf Championship | singles | 3 |
| 1979 | Canadian Sr. Ladies' Golf Championship | team | 1 |
|      | Canadian Sr. Ladies' Golf Championship | singles | 4 |

# INGALDSON, FRED

sport:      basketball
born:       Pontiac, Michigan, USA
            September 2, 1932
height:     1.91 m / 6'3"
weight:     84 kg / 185 lbs
position:   guard, forward

In 1962, Dwayne Erickson of the *Winnipeg Free Press* wrote that Fred Ingaldson "was the finest piece of basketball machinery in Manitoba."[17] The compliment was certainly just. In 1952, Ingaldson won his first major championship - the Canadian junior basketball title. In the mid-1950s, while attending Montana State College, he broke the school's scoring record and was twice named the basketball team's most valuable player. Upon returning to Manitoba, he joined the local basketball league and was named rookie of the year.

Ingaldson then joined the Livingstons club of Tillsonburg, Ontario. With that club, he won the 1960 Canadian Basketball Championship. The victory qualified the club to represent Canada at the 1960 Olympics. Ingaldson gained personal recognition when he was named captain of the national team. Ingaldson's international career, in fact, began in 1959 when he competed at the Pan American Games. A year earlier, he declined a place on the national team to the world championship for personal reasons.

After the 1960 Olympics, Ingaldson returned to Winnipeg and joined the Carling club. He then brought most of the team over to the Institute Prosvita Athletic Club (IPAC) where he accepted the position of playing coach. He quickly moulded the team into one of the top basketball clubs in Canada. In 1964, he led the team to second place in the national championship. Ingaldson's outstanding play - he was the top scorer in the championship tournament - resulted in his being named to Canada's Olympic team once again. The Canadian side advanced to the Tokyo games after posting a 7-2 record at the Olympic qualifying tournament in Japan. Ingaldson was Canada's top scorer at the tournament. At the Olympic Games, the basketball team won 1 game and lost 8 to place 14th. A year later, Ingaldson toured South America with the national team.

On the court, Fred Ingaldson was an extremely aggressive player with an accurate shot. For a number of years, he was the run-away winner of the scoring title in the Winnipeg league.

Ingaldson also excelled on defence.

In addition, Fred Ingaldson was an outstanding soccer goalkeeper. For many years he tended goal for IPAC, the Kickers, and other clubs in the Winnipeg National Soccer League. He was a member of the 1955 IPAC team that won the Manitoba Championship. As a goalie, Ingaldson was aggressive and eccentric. Reporter Scotty Harper wrote that "Ingaldson likes to juggle the ball. When an opponent charges in on Ingaldson, he'll dangle the ball in the player's face, or juggle it around his body. He does everything with the ball but shove it down his pants."[18] In the fall, Ingaldson played football. A star end with the St. Vital Bulldogs of the Winnipeg Intermediate Football League, the "sure-handed receiver" was invited to the Winnipeg Blue Bomber camp for a tryout in 1956. However, a career in professional football did not materialize.

## AWARDS

1969      Manitoba Ukrainian Sportsman of the Year

## RECORD

basketball

| year | competition | team | placing |
|------|-------------|------|---------|
| 1952 | Canadian Junior Championship | | 1 |
| 1959 | Pan American Games | Canada | 5 |
| 1960 | Canadian Championship | Tillsonburg Livingstons | 1 |
| | Olympic Games | Canada | |
| 1962 | Manitoba Championship | IPAC | 1 |
| | Western Canada Championship | IPAC | 2 |
| 1963 | Canadian Championship | IPAC | 3 |
| 1964 | Manitoba Championship | IPAC | 1 |
| | Canadian Championship | IPAC | 2 |
| | Olympic Games | Canada | 14 |
| 1965 | Manitoba Championship | St. Andrews Dunlops | 1 |
| 1966 | Manitoba Championship | St. Andrews Dunlops | 1 |
| | Canadian Championship | St. Andrews Dunlops | 2 |
| 1967 | Canada Games | Manitoba | 2 |

# IVANOCHKO, SASHA

sport:          gymnastics
given name:  Ivanochko, Alexandra
born:          Windsor, Ontario
                October 12, 1970
height:         1.55 m / 5'1"
weight:        45.5 kg / 100 lbs

As a youngster, Sasha Ivanochko loved to dance; at age seven, she was enrolled in a ballet school. Although ballet was enjoyable, it somehow did not fulfil the high-energy desires of the young Ivanochko. On the advice of a teacher, she was evaluated at a school of gymnastics in 1979. The opinion of the committee was that Ivanochko had the potential to become a competitive gymnast. Soon afterwards, she joined the Xoces Eagles School of Gymnastics. Ivanochko was with the school and coach Dennis Fuhrman until the end of her career in 1987.

In a few short years, Ivanochko established herself as one of Canada's top gymnasts. Her career peaked in 1985 when she represented Canada at the World Championships. There she and her teammates placed ninth in the team competition. A hard worker during training sessions, Ivanochko was, unfortunately, apprehensive during competition, and this influenced her performances. In addition, three torn hamstring injuries took their toll. Her best routine was the floor exercise - clean, precise, and with good presentation. It was for her floor routine that she was named the Most Avant Garde gymnast at the 1982 Ontario-Quebec Invitational, and won the Floor Choreography award at the 1987 national championships. Upon retiring from gymnastics, Sasha Ivanochko returned to dance when she enrolled at the School of the Toronto Dance Theatre.

## RECORD

| year | competition | event | placing | result |
|------|-------------|-------|---------|--------|
| 1985 | US vs Canada | all-around | 1 | |
| | | parallel bars | 1 | |
| | | balance beam | 1 | |
| | | floor | 1 | |
| | Elite Canada | all-around | 11 | 69.22 |
| | Canadian Championships | all-around | 33 | |
| | World Trials | all-around | 7 | |

| year | competition | event | placing | result |
|------|------------|-------|---------|--------|
| 1985 | World Championships | team | 9 | 375.20 |
| | Taiwan International | all-around | 3 | |
| | | beam | 1 | |
| | | vault | 3 | |
| 1986 | Elite Canada | all-around | 4 | 72.92 |
| | | beam | 3 | |
| | Canadian Championships | all-around | 10 | 71.98 |
| | | beam | 14 | 17.54 |
| | | floor | 7 (tie) | 18.28 |
| | | uneven bars | 15 | 17.76 |
| | | vault | 8 (tie) | 18.40 |
| 1987 | Yugoslavian Invitational | all-around | 7 | 37.35 |
| | | beam | 6 | 18.60 |
| | | uneven bars | 6 | 18.40 |
| | | team | 2 | 75.25 |
| | Canadian Championships | all-around | 10 | 73.40 |
| | World Trials | all-around | 13 | 145.00 |

# IWANOCZKO, DALE

sport:      volleyball
born:       Selkirk, Manitoba
            September 13, 1968
height:     1.96 m / 6'5"
weight:     85 kg  / 187 lbs

*Photo courtesy of the Athlete Information Bureau*

Dale Iwanoczko was honoured with the Male Athlete of the Year award and the Governor-General's Award at his high school graduation in 1986. Iwanoczko was selected as his school's top athlete for having captained the volleyball team to the provincial title, for being named to the All-Manitoba High School Team, and for being selected the MVP at the provincial championship. That same year, he won the national title while competing for the Manitoba provincial juvenile team and was named MVP of the championship. In addition, Iwanoczko was named to Canada's national junior team. He competed with the team for two years, culminating his representation by participating at the 1987 World Junior Championships.

In the fall of 1986, he enrolled in the science program at the University of Manitoba and started playing on the school's volleyball team. It was a successful debut-year for Iwanoczko: he won the 1986-87 GPAC rookie of the year honours, and the team placed third at the CIAU championships. In the subsequent two seasons, the University of Manitoba won back-to-back silver medals at the championships while Iwanoczko was named to the First Team All-Canadian both seasons. In 1991, Dale Iwanoczko represented Canada at the World University and Pan American Games.

## AWARDS

| | |
|---|---|
| 1987 | Manitoba Sports Federation Youth Athlete |
| 1987 | Junior Player of the Year  -  Manitoba Volleyball Association |
| 1988 | Junior Player of the Year  -  Manitoba Volleyball Association |
| 1989 | Manitoba Ukrainian Sportsman of the Year (co-winner) |
| 1990 | CIAU Player of the Year |

## ALL-STAR SELECTIONS

| | | |
|---|---|---|
| 1988 | All-Canadian | First Team |
| 1989 | All-Canadian | First Team |
| 1990 | All-Canadian | First Team |
| 1991 | All-Canadian | First Team |

## RECORD

| year | competition | team | placing |
|---|---|---|---|
| 1985 | Canada Games | Manitoba | 2 |
| 1986 | Canadian Juvenile Championships | Manitoba | 1 |
| 1987 | Canada Games | Manitoba | 3 |
| | World Junior Championships | Canada | |
| | CIAU Championships | University of Manitoba | 3 |
| 1988 | Canadian Junior Championships | Manitoba | 1 |
| | CIAU Championships | University of Manitoba | 2 |
| 1989 | CIAU Championships | University of Manitoba | 2 |
| 1991 | World University Games | Canada | |
| | Pan American Games | Canada | |

# JAREMY, JOHN

| | |
|---|---|
| sport: | swimming |
| born: | Port Arthur, Ontario |
| | (now Thunder Bay) |
| | May 1, 1920 |
| height: | 1.73 m / 5'8" |
| weight: | 81.5 kg / 180 lbs |

John Jaremy began swimming competitively when he was 27 years old. A sore back, the result of his work in the mines in Timmins and as a steam fitter in Toronto, kept him from physical activity. Unfortunately, this lack of exercise started to show on his waistline. Swimming was something he could do to lose weight; it did not hurt, it was excellent exercise, and most of all, he enjoyed it. Exercise, though, soon turned into serious training. Jaremy realized that he had the potential to become a champion marathon swimmer, in a sport that was extremely popular at the time. He entered his first major competition in 1949: the Canadian National Exhibition 15-mile race. Forty-three swimmers started, but only three finished. Jaremy was pulled out of the cold water (13-16°C / 55-62°F), in fifth position among the non-finishers. For his efforts he pocketed $75.

In 1952, John Jaremy decided that he was going to swim Lake Ontario. He quit competing and began preparing for his quest. In winter, he trained at the old Central YMCA in Toronto, swimming three and one-half to four hours an evening. During the summer, he usually trained on Lake Wilcox, putting in 5 hours every night and 15 on weekends. In 1954, he watched Marilyn Bell become the first person to conquer Lake Ontario. Jaremy, though, was not ready yet.

At 5:47 a.m., on Sunday, July 22, 1956, John Jaremy entered Lake Ontario at Niagara-on-the-Lake. Doing a constant 58 strokes a minute crawl style, he covered 18 miles by 2:00 p.m. Towards evening, Jaremy ran into trouble. He became sick after eating and had to dog paddle for a few minutes. By 7:30 his stroke had little power. Soon water started seeping under his goggles and hurting his eyes. He got sick again, his legs did not respond, and he was starting to lose his balance in the water. By 1:30 a.m. on Monday, the strain was tremendous. Yet Jaremy never thought of giving up. With three miles to go, the choppy waves died down and the breeze subsided. Coach Pat Roach and the accompanying personnel and journalists started singing songs of encouragement. Only 400 yards from shore, Jaremy again ran into serious trouble: a swell carried him back 100 yards. He became disoriented and started zigzagging. Suddenly, small boats and cars on the shore started honking their horns. The encouragement roused Jaremy. In an all-out push, he covered the final distance. The first male to cross Lake Ontario, John Jaremy came ashore at 3:02 a.m., at Toronto's Eastern Gap, to a thunderous ovation from 7,000 well wishers.

In August of the same year, Jaremy was one of ten swimmers invited to compete in the Brading Cup Lake Ontario swim for $27,500 in prizes. The cold water of the lake defeated them all. In September, Jaremy went to Victoria, British Columbia, to challenge the Straights of Juan de Fuca. For a few days, rough waters kept him ashore. His sponsor, though, became tired of waiting; he wanted Jaremy in the water. The attempt failed as the rough water quickly drained Jaremy. John Jaremy's last major swim was a marathon organized by the city of Owen Sound in 1957 to celebrate its centennial.

## RECORD

| year | competition | event | placing | result |
|------|-------------|-------|---------|--------|
| 1949 | CNE | 15 miles | 8 | 6:40: * |
| 1950 | CNE | 15 miles | 8 | 10:05: 15 |
| 1952 | Atlantic City | | 8 | |
| 1956 | Brading Cup (across L. Ontario) | 32.5 miles | dnf | |
| 1957 | Owen Sound Marathon | | | |

\* pulled from the water after 6 hours and 40 minutes

# JAWORSKI, CHRISTINE

| | |
|---|---|
| sport: | arm wrestling, body building |
| given name: | Jaworski, Christine Mary |
| born: | Sudbury, Ontario |
| | December 5, 1962 |
| height: | 1.68 m / 5'6" |
| weight: | 66 kg / 145 lbs |

An outstanding all-round athlete, Christine Jaworski competed in track and field, soccer, volleyball, baseball, basketball, football, and bowling while attending primary and high school. She was honoured in grades 6, 7, and 8 with the All-Canadian Awards of Excellence. In grade 8, she also won the Northern Ontario age group discus championship.

Jaworski took up competitive arm wrestling in the early 1980s. She competed at her first national championship in 1982, placing second in the lightweight and third in the heavyweight division. The following year, in the lightweight division, she won the national title and placed second at the World Championships. Jaworski continued to dominate the sport of arm wrestling in Canada, winning two weight titles at the national championship in 1985. In 1986, she once again won the Canadian lightweight title and then proceeded to win three different world championships. The city of Sudbury recognized Jaworski's achievements and honoured her as its 1986 Athlete of the Year.

In 1986 and in 1987, Jaworski also competed with some success in body building. In 1986, she took some time out from training and competition to appear in the Sylvester Stallone movie *Over the Top*.

## AWARDS

1986        Sudbury Athlete of the Year

## RECORD

| year | competition | division | placing |
|------|-------------|----------|---------|
| 1982 | Canadian Armwrestling Championships | lightweight | 2 |
|      |             | heavyweight | 3 |
| 1983 | Canadian Armwrestling Championships | lightweight | 2 |
|      | World Armwrestling Championships | lightweight | 2 |
| 1984 | Canadian Armwrestling Championships | lightweight | 1 |
|      | World Armwrestling Championships | lightweight | 1 |
| 1985 | Canadian Armwrestling Championships | lightweight | 1 |
|      |             | heavyweight | 1 |
|      | World Armwrestling Championships |  | 2 |
| 1986 | Canadian Armwrestling Championships | lightweight | 1 |
|      | A.W.I. Worlds | lightweight | 1 |
|      | A.A.A. Worlds | lightweight | 1 |
|      | W.P.A.A. Worlds | lightweight | 1 |
|      | Northern Ontario Strong Man Competition |  | 2 |
| 1989 | A.W.I. Worlds |  | 3 |

# JUZDA, BILL

"The Beast," "The Fireman"

| | |
|---|---|
| sport: | hockey |
| given name: | Juzda, William |
| born: | Winnipeg, Manitoba |
| | October 29, 1920 |
| height: | 1.73 m / 5'8" |
| weight: | 92 kg / 203 lbs |
| position: | defense |
| shoots: | right |

In high school, Bill Juzda was a standout football halfback and the Manitoba junior shot put champion. Although he enjoyed the game of hockey at the time, he did not participate in the sport in an organized setting. He was a poor skater, and as a result, he preferred to play pick-up hockey. Juzda eventually played one season of junior hockey in Winnipeg before joining the Kenora Thistles. In Kenora, Juzda's skating improved dramatically as a result of intensive practising. The Thistles advanced to the Memorial Cup final in 1940, and Juzda was scouted and signed by the New York Rangers. A professional hockey career was not on his mind at the time; he believed that he had a better chance in football. Nevertheless, he did not want to let the opportunity slip away and decided to give professional hockey a try.

In the fall of 1940, the Rangers assigned Juzda to their farm team in New Haven. The following season, Juzda made the starting line-up of the Rangers. At the end of season, Juzda enlisted in the RCAF and served as a pilot in the Coastal Command for three years. During his military service, he played on the RCAF hockey team which was a finalist for the Allan Cup in 1943. Juzda rejoined the Rangers in 1945 and played for them until being traded to Toronto in 1948. During his tenure with the Leafs, he played on two Stanley Cup teams, in 1949 and 1951. When the Leafs made the Cup final in 1949, Juzda, on entering the dressing room, sighed "Ah well, another Stanley Cup."[19] It was his first.

After sitting on the bench for a good part of the 1951-52 season, Juzda asked the Leafs to release him but the team refused. He was put on waivers but no team picked him up. Subsequently, Juzda played for the Toronto affiliate at Pittsburgh before retiring from the Toronto organization in spring of 1953. That fall, he joined the senior Winnipeg Maroons and helped the team to two consecutive appearances in the Allan Cup final. Bill Juzda also coached hockey. In 1957, he led the Pine Fall Paper Kings to the Western Canada intermediate championship. In the years 1958-60, he worked behind the bench of St. Boniface Canadians of the Manitoba Junior League. In the early 1960s, Juzda returned to the Maroons as a coach and a part-time player. He was released in 1963 after leading the club to the Allan Cup final. In 1965, he briefly came out of retirement to play for the Warroad Lakers of the MIHL.

Bill Juzda was a solid rearguard, a naturally talented athlete. Les Lear, who was Juzda's football coach in Winnipeg and who went on to coach the Calgary Stampeders, called Juzda the greatest competitive athlete he had ever met. Juzda was also one of the strongest players in the NHL. His bodychecks were devastating. Bill Ezinicki referred to Juzda as a "guy who was capable of wrecking you." Tony Leswick labelled him "The Beast" after Juzda twisted his arm several times. Bill Juzda's hockey career, as an active player and a coach, lasted for more than 25 years. During that time period he was employed as a locomotive engineer by the Canadian Pacific Railway. The company gave him leaves of absence to pursue his hockey career.

## INDUCTIONS

| | |
|---|---|
| 1985 | Manitoba Hockey Hall of Fame |
| 1992 | Manitoba Sports Hall of Fame |

## AWARDS

| | |
|---|---|
| 1982 | Manitoba Ukrainian Sportsman of the Year (co-winner) |

## ALL-STAR SELECTIONS

| | | | |
|---|---|---|---|
| 1952-53 | defense | AHL | Second Team |

## RECORD

| year | team | league | regular season | | | | | playoffs | | | | |
|------|------|--------|----|---|---|-----|-----|----|---|---|-----|-----|
| | | | GP | G | A | PTS | PIM | GP | G | A | PTS | PIM |
| 1940-41 | NY Rangers | NHL | 5 | 0 | 0 | 0 | 2 | | | | | |
| | Philadelphia | AHL | 52 | 7 | 14 | 21 | 47 | | | | | |
| 1941-42 | NY Rangers | NHL | 45 | 4 | 8 | 12 | 29 | 6 | 0 | 1 | 1 | 4 |
| 1942-43 | Buffalo | AHL | 1 | 0 | 0 | 0 | 0 | | | | | |
| | Winnipeg | City | 13 | 3 | 3 | 6 | 8 | 17 | 1 | 3 | 4 | 28 |
| 1943-44 | Winnipeg | City | 3 | 0 | 0 | 0 | 4 | | | | | |
| 1944-45 | Dartmouth | City | 4 | 0 | 0 | 0 | 12 | 3 | 0 | 4 | 4 | 4 |
| 1945-46 | NY Rangers | NHL | 32 | 1 | 3 | 4 | 17 | | | | | |
| | Providence | AHL | 18 | 4 | 3 | 7 | 20 | 2 | 0 | 0 | 0 | 9 |
| 1946-47 | NY Rangers | NHL | 45 | 3 | 5 | 8 | 60 | | | | | |

| year | team | league | regular season | | | | | playoffs | | | | |
|---|---|---|---|---|---|---|---|---|---|---|---|---|
| | | | GP | G | A | PTS | PIM | GP | G | A | PTS | PIM |
| 1946-47 | New Haven | AHL | 16 | 2 | 4 | 6 | 20 | | | | | |
| 1947-48 | NY Rangers | NHL | 60 | 3 | 9 | 12 | 70 | 6 | 0 | 0 | 0 | 9 |
| 1948-49* | Toronto | NHL | 38 | 1 | 2 | 3 | 23 | 9 | 0 | 2 | 2 | 8 |
| | Pittsburgh | AHL | 7 | 0 | 3 | 3 | 4 | | | | | |
| 1949-50 | Toronto | NHL | 62 | 1 | 14 | 15 | 23 | 7 | 0 | 0 | 0 | 16 |
| 1950-51* | Toronto | NHL | 65 | 0 | 9 | 9 | 64 | 11 | 0 | 0 | 0 | 7 |
| 1951-52 | Toronto | NHL | 46 | 1 | 4 | 5 | 65 | 3 | 0 | 0 | 0 | 2 |
| 1952-53* | Pittsburgh | AHL | 59 | 1 | 15 | 16 | 108 | 10 | 0 | 1 | 1 | 11 |
| 1955-56 | Winnipeg | WHL | 3 | 0 | 1 | 1 | 4 | | | | | |

# KACHUR, ED

| | |
|---|---|
| sport: | hockey |
| given name: | Kachur, Edward Charles |
| born: | Fort William, Ontario |
| | (now Thunder Bay) |
| | April 22, 1934 |
| height: | 1.73 m / 5'8" |
| weight: | 77 kg / 170 lbs |
| position: | right wing |
| shoots: | right |

Eddie Kachur played professional hockey for almost 20 years. Of those years, less than two were spent in the NHL, but that did not discourage Kachur. He enjoyed the game immensely and saw no reason to make an early exit. A strong, bulky right winger, Kachur improved with age. Statistically, his best season was in 1967-68 when he led the AHL with 47 goals. Perpetually in motion, Kachur liked to be around the opposition's net looking for a pass or a rebound. As a result, he was constantly harassed with both legal and illegal tactics. The harassment often resulted in injuries which, especially in the later years, were difficult to mend. A series of operations to repair a cracked jaw and a badly damaged shoulder were painful, but did not keep him out of too many games.

Eddie Kachur played junior hockey with the Fort William Canadians. His professional career included play for the Black Hawks of the NHL and for minor pro teams in Shawinigan, Buffalo, Sault Ste. Marie, and Providence. During his career, Kachur played on three championship teams, the 1954 Cincinnati Mohawks, the 1955 Shawinigan Cataracts, and the 1963 Buffalo Bisons.

## ALL-STAR SELECTIONS

| | | | |
|---|---|---|---|
| 1955-56 | right wing | QHL | Second Team |
| 1960-61 | right wing | EPHL | First Team |
| 1967-68 | right wing | AHL | First Team |

## RECORD

| | | | regular season | | | | | playoffs | | | | |
|---|---|---|---|---|---|---|---|---|---|---|---|---|
| year | team | league | GP | G | A | PTS | PIM | GP | G | A | PTS | PIM |
| 1953-54* | Cincinnati | IHL | 63 | 32 | 26 | 58 | 61 | 11 | 2 | 2 | 4 | 2 |
| 1954-55* | Shawinigan Falls | QHL | 59 | 25 | 14 | 39 | 46 | 13 | 5 | 3 | 8 | 18 |
| 1955-56 | Shawinigan Falls | QHL | 64 | 31 | 34 | 65 | 91 | 11 | 6 | 5 | 11 | 16 |
| 1956-57 | Chicago | NHL | 34 | 5 | 7 | 12 | 21 | | | | | |
| | Shawinigan Falls | QHL | 32 | 12 | 12 | 24 | 12 | | | | | |
| 1957-58 | Chicago | NHL | 62 | 5 | 7 | 12 | 14 | | | | | |
| 1958-59 | Buffalo | AHL | 68 | 15 | 17 | 32 | 26 | 11 | 5 | 2 | 7 | 6 |
| 1959-60 | Buffalo | AHL | 57 | 19 | 10 | 29 | 10 | | | | | |
| 1960-61 | Sault Ste. Marie | EPHL | 70 | 38 | 43 | 81 | 71 | 12 | 3 | 6 | 9 | 16 |
| 1961-62 | Sault Ste. Marie | EPHL | 70 | 22 | 32 | 54 | 65 | | | | | |
| 1962-63* | Buffalo | AHL | 68 | 19 | 19 | 38 | 35 | 13 | 2 | 3 | 5 | 8 |
| 1963-64 | Buffalo | AHL | 64 | 13 | 14 | 27 | 10 | | | | | |
| 1964-65 | Providence | AHL | 41 | 16 | 7 | 23 | 16 | | | | | |
| | Los Angeles | WHL | 22 | 1 | 6 | 7 | 4 | | | | | |
| 1965-66 | Providence | AHL | 57 | 28 | 19 | 47 | 30 | | | | | |
| 1966-67 | Providence | AHL | 55 | 22 | 20 | 42 | 20 | | | | | |
| 1967-68 | Providence | AHL | 72 | 47 | 29 | 76 | 30 | 8 | 3 | 2 | 5 | 8 |
| 1968-69 | Providence | AHL | 71 | 26 | 26 | 52 | 24 | 9 | 1 | 4 | 5 | 6 |
| 1969-70 | Providence | AHL | 21 | 9 | 4 | 13 | 2 | | | | | |
| 1970-71 | Thunder Bay | USHL | 15 | 17 | 10 | 27 | 25 | | | | | |
| 1971-72 | Johnstown | EHL | 25 | 18 | 11 | 29 | 6 | | | | | |

# KALETA, ALEX

"Killer"

| | |
|---|---|
| sport: | hockey |
| given name: | Kaleta, Alexander |
| born: | Canmore, Alberta |
| | November 29, 1919 |
| died: | . . . |
| | July 9, 1987 |
| height: | 1.80 m / 5'11" |
| weight: | 79.5 kg / 175 lbs |
| position: | left wing |
| shoots: | left |

In the fall of 1940, Alex Kaleta transferred from the Regina Vic-Aces to the Lethbridge Maple Leafs of the Alberta Senior Hockey League. That season, the Lethbridge club won the Alberta-British Columbia Championship. The following year, the flamboyant speedster made his NHL debut with the Chicago Black Hawks.

Kaleta's career was interrupted in 1942, when he joined the army. He played for the Calgary Army Currie Barracks in the Alberta Services Senior Hockey League (ASSHL) for the next three years. The club won the league title in each of those years. During the 1942-43 season, Kaleta led the league in scoring and was named to the all-star team. The ASSHL teams were stocked with NHL players and, according to Kaleta, the calibre of play was just as high as in the professional leagues.

After the war, Kaleta returned to the Black Hawks. In 1948, he was traded to the Rangers. The New York fans took an immediate liking to him and jokingly named him "Killer" because he would never hurt an opposing player. After he was released by the Rangers in 1951, Alex Kaleta played for Saskatoon Quakers of the Pacific Coast League / Western Hockey League. He led the league with 57 assists during the 1952-53 season. His scoring touch continued into the playoffs, where he established a WHL playoff record with 14 assists and 23 points.

In hockey, the term "hat trick" refers to a player scoring three goals in a game. Allegedly, Alex Kaleta was in part responsible for the coining of the term. On one of Chicago Black Hawks' trips to Toronto, Kaleta was seen by Toronto clothier Sammy Taft eyeing a hat. The clothier offered Kaleta a challenge: score three goals in that evening's game and the hat is yours. Kaleta responded with three goals and the term entered hockey lexicon.

# ALL-STAR SELECTIONS

| 1942-43 | left wing | ASSHL | First Team |
| 1952-53 | center | WHL | Second Team |

## RECORD

| | | | regular season | | | | | playoffs | | | | |
| year | team | league | GP | G | A | PTS | PIM | GP | G | A | PTS | PIM |
| --- | --- | --- | --- | --- | --- | --- | --- | --- | --- | --- | --- | --- |
| 1941-42 | Chicago | NHL | 48 | 7 | 21 | 28 | 24 | 3 | 1 | 2 | 3 | 0 |
| 1942-43 | Calgary Army | ASSHL | 24 | 23 | 35 | 58 | 23 | 10 | 6 | 7 | 13 | 6 |
| 1943-44 | Calgary Army | ASSHL | 15 | 8 | 15 | 23 | 24 | 2 | 5 | 1 | 6 | 2 |
| 1944-45 | Calgary Army | ASSHL | 16 | 14 | 12 | 26 | 16 | 3 | 1 | 2 | 3 | 12 |
| 1945-46 | Chicago | NHL | 49 | 19 | 27 | 46 | 17 | 4 | 0 | 1 | 1 | 2 |
| 1946-47 | Chicago | NHL | 57 | 24 | 20 | 44 | 37 | | | | | |
| 1947-48 | Chicago | NHL | 52 | 10 | 16 | 26 | 40 | | | | | |
| 1948-49 | NY Rangers | NHL | 56 | 12 | 19 | 31 | 8 | | | | | |
| 1949-50 | NY Rangers | NHL | 67 | 17 | 14 | 31 | 40 | 10 | 0 | 3 | 3 | 0 |
| 1950-51 | NY Rangers | NHL | 58 | 3 | 4 | 7 | 26 | | | | | |
| | Hershey | AHL | 5 | 0 | 2 | 2 | 6 | | | | | |
| 1951-52* | Saskatoon | PCHL | 62 | 38 | 44 | 82 | 23 | 13 | 6 | 13 | 19 | 4 |
| 1952-53 | Saskatoon | WHL | 70 | 26 | 57 | 83 | 6 | 13 | 9 | 14 | 23 | 2 |
| 1953-54 | Saskatoon | WHL | 70 | 19 | 53 | 72 | 52 | 6 | 0 | 5 | 5 | 4 |
| 1954-55 | Saskatoon | WHL | 13 | 2 | 9 | 11 | 10 | | | | | |

# KAMINSKI, KEVIN

"Killer"

| sport: | hockey |
| born: | Churchbridge, Saskatchewan |
| | March 13, 1969 |
| height: | 1.75 m / 5'9" |
| weight: | 86 kg / 190 lbs |
| position: | centre |
| shoots: | left |

Kevin Kaminski was not yet two years old when he began skating. Hockey was a natural progression, and the youngster, often playing on teams coached by his father, developed into a star player. With time, his hockey skills outgrew his home town of 1,000 people and he left to pursue the game at the junior level with the Saskatoon Blades. Kaminski was a surprise selection in the third round (48th overall) of the 1987 NHL Entry Draft by the Minnesota North Stars as most scouts believed that he was too small to play in the big league. That fall, the junior age Kaminski failed to make the North Stars and was reassigned to the Blades where he played for two more seasons. The team was the 1989 Memorial Cup finalist losing the national championship game in overtime.

After turning professional, Kevin Kaminski spent much of his career in the minor pro leagues. The tough and aggressive forward led the IHL in penalties with 455 minutes during the 1990-91 season and 169 during the playoffs.

## RECORD

| year | team | league | regular season GP | G | A | PTS | PIM | playoffs GP | G | A | PTS | PIM |
|------|------|--------|-----|---|---|-----|-----|-----|---|---|-----|-----|
| 1988-89 | Minnesota | NHL | 1 | 0 | 0 | 0 | 0 | | | | | |
| 1989-90 | Quebec | NHL | 1 | 0 | 0 | 0 | 0 | | | | | |
| | Halifax | AHL | 19 | 3 | 4 | 7 | 128 | 2 | 0 | 0 | 0 | 5 |
| 1990-91 | Halifax | AHL | 7 | 1 | 0 | 1 | 44 | | | | | |
| | Fort Wayne | IHL | 56 | 9 | 15 | 24 | 455 | 19 | 4 | 2 | 6 | 169 |

# KARDASH, JIM

| | |
|---|---|
| sport: | football |
| born: | Brandon, Manitoba |
| | May 17, 1961 |
| height: | 1.96 m / 6'5" |
| weight: | 113.5 kg / 250 lbs |
| position: | guard, offensive tackle |

Jim Kardash played football with the University of Western Ontario Mustangs in the years 1980 to 1984. In those five years, the Mustangs won three provincial titles. In 1983, Kardash was selected in the fourth round of the CFL College Draft by the Montreal Concordes. He attended the Concordes' training camp, where he unsuccessfully sought a spot at the tight end position. Kardash returned to the Mustangs, where his superb play was recognized with an All-

Canadian selection at tight end.

Kardash tried out with the Concordes once again in 1984 but failed to make the club and was released. In the summer of 1986, Kardash was signed as a free agent by the Toronto Argonauts. He dressed for a total of four games that season as a back-up offensive lineman. The following year, Kardash became an Argo regular, playing solidly on the offensive line. The season culminated with Kardash's first appearance in a Grey Cup game, albeit in a losing cause. In 1991, the Argos with Jim Kardash won the Grey Cup.

## KARPUK, PETE

| | |
|---|---|
| sport: | football, baseball |
| born: | Toronto, Ontario |
| | . . ., 1926 |
| died: | Toronto, Ontario |
| | . . ., 1985 |
| height: | 1.80 m / 5'11" |
| weight: | 75 kg / 165 lbs |
| bats: | right |
| throws: | right |

Pete Karpuk was a flashy and versatile athlete whose career was marred by controversies. He was an outstanding shortstop, pitcher, and hitter with the Ottawa Nationals of the Border Baseball League. In 1949, he won 8 games, lost 1, and posted a 2.32 ERA. He also batted a respectable .332. For his efforts, he was named league MVP, only one vote short of a unanimous decision. That year, the speedy halfback also scored a career-high four touchdowns while playing for the Ottawa Rough Riders football club. For a number of years, Karpuk juggled a baseball and a football career.

Karpuk played in three Grey Cup games, of which the first two were most memorable. During the 1948 game, he suffered a momentary loss of concentration and fumbled a lateral. The play was offside and a horn was sounded to indicate the infraction, but not to stop the play. Karpuk and all the other Ottawa players believed the play was dead and milled about. A Calgary player picked the ball up and ran it for the game-winning touchdown. In 1951, Karpuk redeemed himself when he powered the Rough Riders to the Grey Cup. He nullified the opposition's kicking game with incredible runbacks, caught passes with ease, and scored the winning touchdown as the Rough Riders won the Grey Cup 21-14. He was the "hero of the day," according to the journalists who covered the game.

Towards the end of the 1953 season, Karpuk was "fired" by Ottawa for indifference and disobeying coach Clem Crowe. The Rough Riders, though, did not release him, and he took the Ottawa club, the IRFU, and the CRU to court. The matter was resolved out of court in August of 1954, when Karpuk dropped his legal proceedings after Ottawa released him on waivers. He was picked up by Toronto and traded within days to the Hamilton Tiger-Cats. With Hamilton he played on defence and also saw action on punt and missed field goal returns. In 1955, Karpuk was back with the Rough Riders; however, the following year, he was cut by Ottawa for breaking training camp curfew. He was subsequently picked up by Montreal where he played as a safety back. After retiring from football, Karpuk worked as a golf pro.

Pete Karpuk is one of a very few professional football players whose name is synonymous with a play and, subsequently, with a rule. In a game against Toronto on November 3, 1951, with a play in motion, Karpuk (then playing for Ottawa) left the bench, charged onto the field, and tackled an opposing player who was heading for a sure touchdown. The "play" became known as the "Karpuk play," and the rule to prevent it from recurring was coined the "Karpuk rule."

## AWARDS

1949          Border Baseball League MVP

## ALL-STAR SELECTIONS

1949          shortstop          Border Baseball League          First Team

## RECORD

baseball

| | | | batting | | | | | | | pitching | | | | |
|---|---|---|---|---|---|---|---|---|---|---|---|---|---|---|
| year | team | league | GP | AB | R | H | HR | RBI | AVG | GP | IP | W | L | ERA |
| 1947 | Ottawa | Border | 44 | 152 | 25 | 42 | 1 | 13 | .276 | 14 | 81 | 5 | 6 | 4.22 |
| 1948 | Ottawa | Border | 110 | 430 | 79 | 162 | 1 | 33 | .252 | | | | | |
| 1949 | Ottawa | Border | 123 | 515 | 113 | 171 | 8 | 61 | .332 | 11 | 66 | 8 | 1 | 2.32 |
| 1950 | Ottawa | Border | 117 | 492 | 111 | 163 | 3 | 47 | .331 | | | | | |
| 1951 | Ottawa | International | 13 | 41 | 4 | 8 | 0 | 6 | .196 | | | | | |

football

| | | | scoring | | | | | | | | | |
|---|---|---|---|---|---|---|---|---|---|---|---|---|
| | | | regular season | | | playoffs | | | Grey Cup game | | | |
| year | team | league | GP | TD | PTS | GP | TD | PTS | GP | TD | PTS | |
| 1948 | Ottawa | IRFU | 8 | 2 | 10 | 3 | 0 | 0 | 1 | 0 | 0 | |
| 1949 | Ottawa | IRFU | 10 | 4 | 20 | 2 | 0 | 0 | | | | |
| 1950 | Ottawa | IRFU | 5 | 1 | 5 | | | | | | | |
| 1951* | Ottawa | IRFU | 12 | 2 | 10 | 3 | 2 | 10 | 1 | 1 | 5 | |

football      scoring

| | | | regular season | | | playoffs | | | Grey Cup game | | |
|---|---|---|---|---|---|---|---|---|---|---|---|
| year | team | league | GP | TD | PTS | GP | TD | PTS | GP | TD | PTS |
| 1952 | Ottawa | IRFU | 12 | 1 | 5 | | | | | | |
| 1953 | Ottawa | IRFU | ... | 0 | 0 | | | | | | |
| 1954 | Hamilton | IRFU | 14 | 1 | 5 | 2 | 1 | 5 | | | |
| 1955 | Ottawa | IRFU | ... | 0 | 0 | | | | | | |
| 1956 | Montreal | IRFU | ... | 0 | 0 | 2 | 0 | 0 | 0 | 0 | 0 |
| 1957 | Montreal | IRFU | 14 | 1 | 6 | 3 | 0 | 0 | | | |

regular season

| | | | | interception returns | | | | | punt returns | | | | |
|---|---|---|---|---|---|---|---|---|---|---|---|---|---|
| year | team | league | GP | NO | YDS | AVE | LG | TD | NO | YDS | AVE | LG | TD |
| 1954 | Hamilton | IRFU | 14 | 4 | 120 | 30.0 | 85 | 1 | 35 | 247 | 7.1 | 25 | 0 |
| 1955 | Ottawa | IRFU | ... | 3 | 101 | 33.7 | 49 | 0 | 7 | 51 | 7.3 | 11 | 0 |
| 1956 | Montreal | IRFU | ... | 1 | 5 | 5.0 | 5 | 0 | 44 | 256 | 5.8 | 20 | 0 |
| 1957 | Montreal | IRFU | 14 | | | | | | 57 | 307 | 5.4 | 17 | 0 |

# KASSIAN, DENNIS

| | |
|---|---|
| sport: | hockey |
| born: | Vegreville, Alberta |
| | July 14, 1941 |
| height: | 1.80 m / 5'11" |
| weight: | 77 kg / 170 lbs |
| position: | left wing |
| shoots: | left |

Dennis Kassian was signed by the Edmonton Flyers of the WHL shortly after helping the junior Edmonton Oil Kings to the Memorial Cup final in 1961. In the fall, he was assigned to Edmonton's affiliate in Sudbury. In the next eight years, Kassian played for seven minor pro teams. Kassian expressed his disappointment about not making it to the NHL in 1968, but readily admitted that a poor attitude may have had something to do with it. The 27-year-old went on to say ". . . I finally got serious when I realized how quickly the years were going by."[20]

Dennis Kassian's game did improve after that self-assessment. He helped Buffalo Bisons capture the AHL championship in 1969-70 and the following year he scored a career-high 35 goals while playing for Salt Lake Golden Eagles of the WHL. While an NHL career did elude him, in 1972 Dennis Kassian made the roster of the Alberta Oilers of the fledgling World Hockey Association.

## RECORD

| | | | regular season | | | | | playoffs | | | | |
|---|---|---|---|---|---|---|---|---|---|---|---|---|
| year | team | league | GP | G | A | PTS | PIM | GP | G | A | PTS | PIM |
| 1960-61 | Edmonton | WHL | 1 | 0 | 0 | 0 | 0 | | | | | |
| 1961-62 | Sudbury | EPHL | 59 | 12 | 10 | 22 | 22 | 5 | 3 | 1 | 4 | 2 |
| 1962-63 | St. Louis | EPHL | 32 | 20 | 20 | 40 | 42 | | | | | |
| | Edmonton | WHL | 15 | 3 | 8 | 11 | 8 | | | | | |
| 1963-64 | Cincinnati | CPHL | 45 | 12 | 18 | 30 | 16 | | | | | |
| 1964-65 | Memphis | CPHL | 70 | 18 | 32 | 50 | 61 | | | | | |
| 1965-66 | Pittsburgh | AHL | 61 | 0 | 8 | 8 | 12 | | | | | |
| 1966-67 | Buffalo | AHL | 61 | 12 | 18 | 30 | 30 | | | | | |
| 1967-68 | Buffalo | AHL | 71 | 29 | 33 | 62 | 65 | 5 | 4 | 3 | 7 | 2 |
| 1968-69 | Buffalo | AHL | 71 | 29 | 34 | 63 | 37 | 1 | 1 | 2 | | 4 |
| 1969-70* | Buffalo | AHL | 72 | 29 | 31 | 60 | 48 | 7 | 3 | 10 | | |
| 1970-71 | Salt Lake City | WHL | 70 | 35 | 26 | 61 | 61 | | | | | |
| 1971-72 | Salt Lake City | WHL | 72 | 22 | 20 | 42 | 39 | | | | | |
| 1972-73 | Alberta | WHA | 50 | 6 | 7 | 13 | 14 | | | | | |
| 1973-74 | Winston-Salem | SHL | 64 | 25 | 40 | 65 | 51 | | | | | |

# KASSIAN, ED

| | |
|---|---|
| sport: | hockey |
| given name: | Kassian, Edward Lawrence |
| born: | Vegreville, Alberta |
| | . . . |
| height: | 1.83 m / 6'0" |
| weight: | 86 kg / 190 lbs |
| position: | left wing |
| shoots: | left |

Ed Kassian played junior hockey for the Prince Albert Mintos gaining an all-star berth during the 1952-53 season. The following year, his service was secured by the Vancouver Canucks of the WHL.

In October 1954, Kassian joined the Penticton Vees of the Okanagan Senior Hockey League. The team had won the Allan Cup the previous season and thus gained the right to represent Canada at the 1955 World Championship. Kassian adjusted well to his new teammates, scoring 14 times in his first 25 league games. At 21, the youngest member of the Vees brought to the team a new style of rugged and hustling hockey.

Ed Kassian played well in exhibition games at Berlin and Prague prior to the World Championship. Unfortunately, as a result of food poisoning, he was sidelined for the World Championship tournament that the Penticton Vees won. Nevertheless, Ed Kassian was awarded with two medals: for participating and winning the championship.

## RECORD

| year | team | league | GP | G | A | PTS | PIM | GP | G | A | PTS | PIM |
|------|------|--------|----|----|----|-----|-----|----|----|----|-----|-----|
| | | | regular season | | | | | playoffs | | | | |
| 1952-53 | Saskatoon | WHL | 3 | 1 | 2 | 3 | 0 | | | | | |
| 1953-54 | Vancouver/New | | | | | | | | | | | |
| | Westminster | WHL | 61 | 4 | 6 | 10 | 16 | | | | | |

international

| year | team | competition | GP | G | A | PTS | PIM | Place |
|------|------|-------------|----|----|----|-----|-----|-------|
| 1955 | Penticton | World Championship | 0 | 0 | 0 | 0 | 0 | 1 |

# KASZYCKI, MIKE

"Kaz"

| | |
|---|---|
| sport: | hockey |
| born: | Milton, Ontario |
| | February 27, 1956 |
| height: | 1.75 m / 5'9" |
| weight: | 86 kg / 190 lbs |
| position: | center |
| shoots: | left |

*Card reproduced courtesy of O-Pee-Chee Co.*

In his last year of junior hockey, while playing for the Sault Ste. Marie Greyhounds, Mike

Kaszycki established an OHA Jr. "A" record for most points in a season with 170. He also had a league-leading 119 assists. At the end of the season, the New York Islanders made him their second choice, 32nd overall, in the 1976 NHL Entry Draft. Kaszycki failed to make the cut at his first professional training camp and was assigned to Fort Worth of the CHL, where he played well and finished the season second in the league scoring race.

Kaszycki made his NHL debut during the 1977-78 season. His play was inconsistent and his goal production was below expectations. Although disappointed, the Islanders were patient with him. They kept him on for another year, hoping that his scoring touch would return. During the 1979-80 season, the Islanders traded him to Washington. Two months later, Washington traded him to Toronto. While he was with the Leafs, Kaszycki again had problems finding the net and spent most of the time in minors.

During the 1981-82 season, while playing for the New Brunswick Hawks of the AHL, Kaszycki came within one point of establishing a league record for most points in a season. His 118 points and 82 assists were nevertheless league-leading. He also paced New Brunswick to the league championship with a playoff-leading 13 assists and 21 points. Mike Kaszycki's newly found scoring prowess, though, failed to impress big league coaches and he finished his career in the minors.

## AWARDS

| 1976 | Eddie Powers Scoring Trophy - OHL Scoring Leader |
| 1982 | John B. Sollenberger Trophy - AHL Scoring Leader |
| 1982 | Les Cunningham Plaque - AHL MVP |
| 1982 | Fred Hunt Memorial Award - AHL Sportsmanship |
| 1982 | Tim Horton Trophy - AHL Outstanding Canadian |

## ALL-STAR SELECTIONS

| 1981-82 | center | AHL | First Team |
| 1983-84 | center | AHL | Second Team |

## RECORD

| year | team | league | regular season | | | | | playoffs | | | | |
|------|------|--------|----|---|---|-----|-----|----|---|---|-----|-----|
| | | | GP | G | A | PTS | PIM | GP | G | A | PTS | PIM |
| 1976-77 | Fort Worth | CHL | 76 | 32 | 55 | 87 | 50 | 6 | 3 | 3 | 6 | 10 |
| 1977-78 | NY Islanders | NHL | 58 | 13 | 29 | 42 | 24 | 7 | 1 | 3 | 4 | 4 |
| | Rochester | AHL | 6 | 4 | 2 | 6 | 2 | | | | | |

| | | | regular season | | | | | playoffs | | | | |
|---|---|---|---|---|---|---|---|---|---|---|---|---|
| year | team | league | GP | G | A | PTS | PIM | GP | G | A | PTS | PIM |
| 1978-79 | NY Islanders | NHL | 71 | 16 | 18 | 34 | 37 | 10 | 1 | 3 | 4 | 4 |
| 1979-80 | NY Islanders | NHL | 16 | 1 | 4 | 5 | 15 | | | | | |
| | Washington | NHL | 28 | 7 | 10 | 17 | 10 | | | | | |
| | Toronto | NHL | 25 | 4 | 4 | 8 | 10 | 2 | 0 | 0 | 0 | 2 |
| 1980-81 | Toronto | NHL | 6 | 0 | 2 | 2 | 2 | | | | | |
| | Dallas | CHL | 42 | 15 | 21 | 36 | 42 | 6 | 2 | 2 | 4 | 9 |
| 1981-82* | New Brunswick | AHL | 80 | 36 | 82 | 118 | 67 | 15 | 8 | 13 | 21 | 17 |
| 1982-83 | Toronto | NHL | 22 | 1 | 13 | 14 | 10 | | | | | |
| | St. Catharines | AHL | 56 | 26 | 42 | 68 | 30 | | | | | |
| 1983-84 | St. Catharines | AHL | 72 | 39 | 81 | 110 | 51 | 5 | 1 | 1 | 2 | 7 |
| 1984-85 | Moncton | AHL | 30 | 9 | 15 | 24 | 8 | | | | | |

# KATAN, JOHN

"Honest John," "Palermo Panther," "Calgary Eyeopener"

sport: wrestling, professional wrestling

born: Chernivtsi, Ukraine
July 12, 1901

died: Brantford, Ontario
March 9, 1968

height: 1.85 m / 6'1"

weight: 109 kg / 240 lbs

John Katan was four years old when his family immigrated to Canada and settled in Lethbridge, Alberta. When he turned 17, Katan started to work in the local coal mine. Katan's incredible strength was evident even then; one day he managed to shovel 58,000 pounds of coal in an eight-hour shift. This was a Western Canada record that earned him $28.13 and a turkey. In his spare time, Katan trained and wrestled with the mine's sports club. Competing as an amateur for three years, Katan never lost once. He entered the ring on 150 occasions; he won the middleweight, light-heavyweight and heavyweight championships of Western Canada.

John Katan fought his first professional fight on July 1, 1928, at Milk River, Alberta. Five thousand nine hundred and eighty-five professional bouts and 21 years later, in London, he stepped out of the ring for the last time. During his career, he was regarded as a genuine performer, a wrestler who was out to win every match. His record attests to that reputation, since he won about 90 per cent of his fights.

In 1940, in New Zealand, Katan won the British Empire heavyweight title by defeating reigning champion Earl McCready of Canada. Katan had previously challenged McCready for the title, drawing once and losing three times. During the next few years, Katan lost and regained the title three times before losing it for the final time to Whipper Billy Watson in 1945. On one occasion, he won the title by using his best hold: the standing, upside down toe-hold. The hold immobilized McCready for seven minutes, and he fell to the floor unconscious.

For many years, John Katan was considered Canada's top heavyweight. He was a big attraction and travelled widely; particularly memorable were his three trips to Australia and New Zealand. During one of those trips, Canada declared war on Japan. Katan decided to return to Canada, and while on the liner, he trained officers in hand-to-hand combat. Once in Canada, he and some of his wrestler colleagues visited military bases and entertained the troops by staging bouts. He also found time to coach promising Olympic wrestlers and to train the Hamilton Police force in hand-to-hand combat.

In 1947, Katan bought out two wrestling franchises in Hamilton and began a successful career in promoting wrestling events in that city. For two years, he ran the business while wrestling. The workload was more than he bargained for, and in 1949, he retired from competitive wrestling to concentrate fully on the business. John Katan stopped promoting wrestling in 1958, when he bought the Ava Golf Club in Brantford. He operated the club for many years.

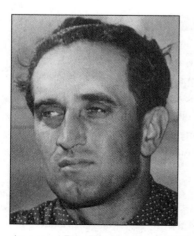

# KEPRON, ROY

| | |
|---|---|
| sport: | athletics, golf |
| born: | Winnipeg, Manitoba |
| | August 17, 1918 |
| height: | 1.78 m / 5'10" |
| weight: | 81.5 kg / 180 lbs |

As a teen, Roy Kepron excelled in golf and track and field. He placed second at the Manitoba junior golf championship in 1934. At the 1936 Canadian junior track and field championships, he won three events - the shot put, discus, and triple jump - and placed second in the long jump. That same year, at the Canadian senior track and field championships, he placed third in three events. After these successes, Kepron gave up golf and track and field in favour of gymnastics. He did not enter competition in gymnastics, though. In 1939, he joined the Canadian armed forces, eventually becoming a Flying Officer and instructor.

In 1944, Kepron started to play golf again. His first tournament victory occurred in 1949 when he won the Clear Lake Golf Championship. He would win this tournament on two other occasions. In addition, Kepron won the Western Manitoba Open, the Kenora Open, and the North Eastern Open three times. In 1951, he reached the quarter-finals of the Canadian Amateur Championship. Two years later, he won the Manitoba Amateur Championship. He won the right to represent Manitoba in Willingdon Cup play for the Canadian team championship three times. Roy Kepron had a booming and accurate tee shot, but had to work hard on the rest of his game.

## RECORD

athletics

| year | competition | event | placing | result |
|------|-------------|-------|---------|--------|
| 1935 | Manitoba Championships | javelin | 3 | |
| 1936 | Winnipeg Track Meet | discus | 1 | 141 ft 3 in njr |
| | Canadian Junior Championships | discus | 1 | 101 ft 3¼ in |
| | | shot | 1 | 40 ft 4¾ in |
| | | triple jump | 1 | 38 ft 9½ in |
| | | long jump | 2 | |
| | Canadian Championships | shot | 3 | |
| | | discus | 3 | |
| | | javelin | 3 | |

njr    Canadian Junior Record

golf

| year | event | placing |
|------|-------|---------|
| 1934 | Manitoba Junior Championship | 2 |
| 1949 | Clear Lake Championship | 1 |
| 1950 | Clear Lake Championship | 1 |
| 1951 | Canadian Amateur Championship | quarter-finals |
| | Willingdon Cup (team) | 3 |
| 1952 | Manitoba Amateur Championship | 2 |
| | Manitoba Open | 3 |

golf

| year | event | placing |
|------|-------|---------|
| 1953 | Manitoba Amateur Championship | 1 |
|      | Western Manitoba Open | 1 |
|      | Willingdon Cup (team) | 4 |
|      | Clear Lake Championship | 1 |
| 1954 | Kenora Open | 1 |
|      | Willingdon Cup (team) | 4 |

# KINASEWICH, GENE

| | |
|--|--|
| sport: | hockey |
| given name: | Kinasewich, Eugene |
| born: | Edmonton, Alberta |
| | August 4, 1941 |
| height: | 1.72 m / 5'8" |
| weight: | 75 kg / 165 lbs |
| position: | center |
| shoots: | left |

Photo courtesy of Harvard University Athletic Department

Gene Kinasewich was a promising hockey player when he enrolled at Harvard University on an academic scholarship in 1960. Kinasewich wanted to play hockey for the school but was ruled ineligible by the Ivy League; it was argued that he made money playing junior "A" hockey for the Edmonton Oil Kings and, more important, that he was recruited for the purpose of playing hockey. Kinasewich, though, was more interested in an education: "It was hard for me to think of staying four years in college without hockey, but it would have been ridiculous to pass up a Harvard education."[21] The following year, Kinasewich's case was reviewed and he was deemed eligible.

Gene Kinasewich responded by single-handedly turning the fortunes of Harvard around and leading it to the 1962 and 1963 Ivy League championships, as well as the university's first Eastern Collegiate Athletic Conference championship in 1963. In the ECAC championship final, Kinasewich scored three goals, including the game winner in sudden-death overtime, to secure Harvard a 4-3 victory over Boston College.

After graduating magna cum laude in 1964, Kinasewich was retained by the university in an academic capacity and as an assistant coach of its hockey team. In August of 1969, Kinasewich left Harvard and took over as president of the Western Hockey League. At 27, he was the youngest executive in hockey. During his reign as president, he was a great advocate of collegiate hockey and a proponent of more American-born players in the NHL. He resigned from the post in April of 1971.

## INDUCTIONS

1991        Harvard Varsity Club Hall of Fame

## AWARDS

1963        Most Valuable Player in Tournament  -  ECAC Division 1
1964        Bingham Award  -  Harvard Athlete of the Year

## ALL-STAR SELECTIONS

1961-62     center     All-Ivy
            center     All-ECAC
1962-63     center     All-ECAC
1963-64     center     All-Ivy
            center     All-ECAC

## RECORD

| year | team | league | GP | G | A | PTS | PIM |
|------|------|--------|----|----|----|-----|-----|
| 1961-62 | Harvard | ECAC | 27 | 20 | 20 | 40 | |
| 1962-63 | Harvard | ECAC | 24 | 18 | 14 | 32 | |
| 1963-64 | Harvard | ECAC | 24 | 23 | 16 | 39 | |

# KINASEWICH, RAY

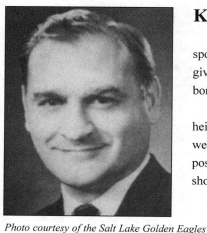

| | |
|---|---|
| sport: | hockey |
| given name: | Kinasewich, Raymond |
| born: | Smokey Lake, Alberta |
| | September 12, 1933 |
| height: | 1.75 m / 5'9" |
| weight: | 81.5 kg / 180 lbs |
| position: | right wing |
| shoots: | right |

*Photo courtesy of the Salt Lake Golden Eagles*

Ray Kinasewich played junior hockey with the Edmonton Oil Kings. He subsequently played minor pro hockey for more than ten seasons in the WHL and the AHL. Twice, he gained all-star berths in the WHL, and in 1964 he helped the Cleveland Barons win the AHL championship.

In November of 1965, Kinasewich returned to the Edmonton Oil Kings where he replaced Bill Warwick as the club's coach. His first season behind the Oil King bench culminated with the club's winning the Memorial Cup, emblematic of the Canadian junior championship. Kinasewich, who was calm and understanding with the young players, was credited with moulding them into a championship team.

Subsequently, Kinasewich coached the Houston Apollos. In July 1969, he was named coach and general manager of the new WHL entry, the Salt Lake Golden Eagles. The club managed to win only 15 games in its inaugural season. Kinasewich was not behind the bench the following year; citing family health problems, he resigned during the summer. In 1972, Kinasewich was named coach of the Edmonton entry into the WHA, a league that had just formed. The Alberta Oilers won 38 games in their debut season, but did not make the playoffs. The following year, Kinasewich was appointed player personnel director with the Oilers. He held the position for a number of seasons.

In 1984, Ray Kinasewich helped organize a trip to the Soviet Union for the Edmonton Old Timers hockey club, a team that he was playing with. Included in the itinerary was a game in Kyiv.

# ALL-STAR SELECTIONS

| 1956-57 | right wing | WHL | First Team (Coast Division) |
| 1957-58 | right wing | WHL | Second Team (Coast Division) |

## RECORD

| year | team | league | regular season | | | | | playoffs | | | | |
|------|------|--------|----|----|----|-----|-----|----|----|----|-----|-----|
| | | | GP | G | A | PTS | PIM | GP | G | A | PTS | PIM |
| 1953-54 | Edmonton | WHL | 1 | 0 | 0 | 0 | 0 | | | | | |
| 1954-55 | Edmonton | WHL | 3 | 0 | 1 | 1 | 0 | | | | | |
| 1955-56 | Edmonton | WHL | 68 | 16 | 17 | 33 | 41 | 3 | 0 | 0 | 0 | 4 |
| 1956-57 | Seattle | WHL | 70 | 44 | 38 | 82 | 62 | 6 | 1 | 2 | 3 | 17 |
| 1957-58 | Seattle | WHL | 70 | 42 | 26 | 68 | 40 | 9 | 5 | 5 | 10 | 10 |
| 1958-59 | Edmonton | WHL | 63 | 15 | 32 | 47 | 40 | 3 | 0 | 0 | 0 | 2 |
| 1959-60 | Hershey | AHL | 72 | 24 | 28 | 52 | 20 | | | | | |
| 1960-61 | Hershey | AHL | 67 | 31 | 24 | 55 | 34 | 8 | 4 | 4 | 8 | 0 |
| 1961-62 | Hershey | AHL | 69 | 10 | 25 | 35 | 34 | 7 | 2 | 1 | 3 | 0 |
| 1962-63 | Edmonton | WHL | 68 | 25 | 32 | 57 | 24 | 3 | 0 | 2 | 2 | 0 |
| 1963-64* | Cleveland | AHL | 72 | 28 | 30 | 58 | 46 | 9 | 5 | 8 | 13 | 10 |
| 1964-65 | Seattle | WHL | 61 | 10 | 25 | 35 | 26 | 7 | 1 | 0 | 1 | 6 |

coaching

| year | team | league | regular season | | | | | playoffs | | | |
|------|------|--------|----|----|----|----|----------|------|----|----|----|
| | | | G | W | L | T | Standing | G | W | L | T |
| 1967-68 | Houston | CHL | 70 | 28 | 31 | 11 | 4 | | | | |
| 1969-70 | Salt Lake City | WHL | 72 | 15 | 43 | 14 | 7 | | | | |
| 1972-73 | Alberta | WHA | 78 | 38 | 37 | 3 | 4 | 1** | 0 | 1 | 0 |

** tie breaker

# KINDRACHUK, OREST

"The Little O"

| | |
|---|---|
| sport: | hockey |
| born: | Nanton, Alberta |
| | September 14, 1950 |
| height: | 1.78 m / 5'10" |
| weight: | 79.5 kg / 175 lbs |
| position: | center |
| shoots: | left |

Photo courtesy of the Philadelphia Flyers

Orest Kindrachuk played junior hockey with the Saskatoon Blades. He then enrolled at the University of Saskatchewan to pursue a degree in optometry. Upon entering university, he quit playing hockey; as a result, he was bypassed in the 1970 NHL Entry Draft. In 1971, he was signed as a free agent by the Philadelphia Flyers. He spent two years in the minors, with San Diego and Richmond, before getting a regular job with the Flyers.

In his rookie season, as the team's fourth center, Kindrachuk impressed the coaching staff with his composed play and forechecking skills. As a result, he was given the opportunity to prove himself during power plays and short-handed situations. Kindrachuk quickly adapted to the dual role and was used in that capacity in his five years with the Flyers. This defined role also took a lot of pressure off Kindrachuk. Not a natural or prolific scorer, he was able to concentrate on the special teams rather than on goal production.

In his rookie year, he also helped the Flyers win the first of two consecutive Stanley Cups.

After the 1977-78 season, Kindrachuk was traded to the struggling Pittsburgh Penguins. The trade was a tremendous shock to Kindrachuk. Nevertheless, he reported to training camp with a positive attitude. After only a few weeks of camp, his teammates elected him captain, even though he had never played a regular season game for the team. His hard work, dedication, and leadership skills resulted in Pittsburgh experiencing a single-season improvement of 17 points. When the Penguins released Kindrachuk in 1981, he signed with the Washington Capitals, with whom he finished his NHL career.

| year | team | league | regular season | | | | | playoffs | | | | |
|------|------|--------|-----|-----|-----|-----|-----|-----|-----|-----|-----|-----|
| | | | GP | G | A | PTS | PIM | GP | G | A | PTS | PIM |
| 1971-72 | San Diego | WHL | 61 | 18 | 36 | 54 | 71 | 4 | 1 | 1 | 2 | 0 |
| 1972-73 | Philadelphia | NHL | 2 | 0 | 0 | 0 | 0 | | | | | |
| | Richmond | AHL | 72 | 35 | 51 | 86 | 133 | 3 | 0 | 1 | 1 | 10 |
| 1973-74* | Philadelphia | NHL | 71 | 11 | 30 | 41 | 85 | 17 | 5 | 4 | 9 | 17 |
| 1974-75* | Philadelphia | NHL | 60 | 10 | 21 | 31 | 72 | 14 | 0 | 2 | 2 | 12 |
| 1975-76 | Philadelphia | NHL | 76 | 26 | 49 | 75 | 101 | 16 | 4 | 7 | 11 | 4 |
| 1976-77 | Philadelphia | NHL | 78 | 15 | 36 | 51 | 79 | 10 | 2 | 1 | 3 | 0 |
| 1977-78 | Philadelphia | NHL | 73 | 17 | 45 | 62 | 128 | 12 | 5 | 5 | 10 | 13 |
| 1978-79 | Pittsburgh | NHL | 79 | 18 | 42 | 60 | 84 | 7 | 4 | 1 | 5 | 7 |
| 1979-80 | Pittsburgh | NHL | 52 | 17 | 29 | 46 | 63 | | | | | |
| 1980-81 | Pittsburgh | NHL | 13 | 3 | 9 | 12 | 34 | | | | | |
| 1981-82 | Washington | NHL | 4 | 1 | 0 | 1 | 2 | | | | | |

# KINDY, ANNA

| | |
|------|------|
| sport: | freestyle skiing |
| born: | Montreal, Quebec |
| | August 14, 1962 |
| height: | 1.72 m / 5'8" |
| weight: | 60 kg / 133 lbs |

Anna Kindy began skiing at the age of six in the Eastern Townships near Montreal. When the family moved to Calgary, ski resorts in the Rocky Mountains became a frequent destination. In 1989, Kindy began to compete in the moguls discipline of freestyle skiing. A year later, she was named to the national team. A strong showing at the 1991 World Championships at Lake Placid pre-qualified Kindy to the 1992 Canadian Olympic team. Shortly afterwards, she suffered a major setback when she seriously injured her right knee. Major surgery and rehabilitation affected her preparations for the Olympics. Kindy, though, would not let the injury keep her out of the Olympic Games; she struggled, but trained with determination. In Albertville, with her knee held in a brace, Kindy skied to an 18th place finish. Dr. Anna Kindy, a general practitioner, stayed in shape during the summer by playing basketball, cycling and scuba diving.

## RECORD

| year | competition | event | placing | result |
|------|-------------|-------|---------|--------|
| 1990 | WC Tignes, France | moguls | 13 | |
| 1991 | WC Blackcomb, Canada | moguls | 13 | |
| | World Championships | moguls | 13 | |
| | WC Skole, Ukraine | moguls | 14 | |
| 1992 | WC Blackcomb, Canada | moguls | 20 | |
| | Olympic Games | moguls | 18 | 14.75 |

# KLUKAY, JOE

"Duke of Paducah"

| | |
|---|---|
| sport: | hockey |
| born: | Sault Ste. Marie, Ontario |
| | November 6, 1922 |
| height: | 1.83 m / 6'0" |
| weight: | 79.5 kg / 175 lbs |
| position: | left wing |
| shoots: | left |

Joe Klukay played juvenile and junior B hockey in his home town of Sault Ste. Marie. In the early 1940s, his Junior B Rapids team won the Northern Ontario championship. During competition for the Ontario championship, which the Rapids lost, Klukay was noticed by the manager of the Stratford junior A team. He joined Stratford the following season, and his NHL rights were acquired by Toronto. During the 1943 playoffs, the Leafs called him up for one game. Shortly afterwards, Klukay entered the Navy; he served for two years and for a time played hockey for HMCS *Cornwallis*. Upon demobilization in 1945, Klukay was assigned to the Leafs' affiliate in Pittsburgh.

In the fall of 1946, Klukay cracked the starting line-up of Toronto and was with the club when it won the Stanley Cup at season's end. Through the next four years, Klukay played consistent hockey for a club studded with stars. During that time, the Leafs won three more Stanley Cups. Klukay, in addition to his regular shifts, was used by the Leafs to kill penalties. He was a strong skater, with effortlessly smooth and easy strides. Men who knew the game referred to Klukay and other skaters with that style as "river" players, those who learned to skate on the open expanses of a river. It is not known, though, whether Klukay had his skating start on a river.

After a dismal 1951-52 season during which he scored only four goals, the Leafs sold him to the Boston Bruins. Klukay's career was rejuvenated in Boston; he scored a career-high 20 goals and 37 points during the 1953-54 season. Ten games into the following season, the Leafs reacquired him in a trade. Joe Klukay played out his professional career with Pittsburgh. Afterwards, he played senior hockey with the Windsor Bulldogs and contributed to the club's Allan Cup victory in 1963.

## RECORD

| year | team | league | regular season | | | | | playoffs | | | | |
|------|------|--------|----|----|----|-----|-----|----|----|----|-----|-----|
| | | | GP | G | A | PTS | PIM | GP | G | A | PTS | PIM |
| 1942-43 | Toronto | NHL | | | | | | 1 | 0 | 0 | 0 | 0 |
| 1945-46 | Pittsburgh | AHL | 57 | 26 | 23 | 49 | 20 | 6 | 4 | 1 | 5 | 2 |
| 1946-47* | Toronto | NHL | 55 | 9 | 20 | 29 | 12 | 11 | 1 | 0 | 1 | 0 |
| 1947-48* | Toronto | NHL | 59 | 15 | 15 | 30 | 28 | 9 | 1 | 1 | 2 | 2 |
| 1948-49* | Toronto | NHL | 45 | 11 | 10 | 21 | 11 | 9 | 2 | 3 | 5 | 4 |
| 1949-50 | Toronto | NHL | 70 | 15 | 16 | 31 | 19 | 7 | 3 | 0 | 3 | 4 |
| 1950-51* | Toronto | NHL | 70 | 14 | 16 | 30 | 16 | 11 | 4 | 3 | 7 | 0 |
| 1951-52 | Toronto | NHL | 43 | 4 | 8 | 12 | 6 | 4 | 1 | 1 | 2 | 0 |
| 1952-53 | Boston | NHL | 70 | 13 | 16 | 29 | 20 | 11 | 1 | 2 | 3 | 9 |
| 1953-54 | Boston | NHL | 70 | 20 | 17 | 37 | 27 | 4 | 0 | 0 | 0 | 0 |
| 1954-55 | Boston | NHL | 10 | 0 | 0 | 0 | 4 | | | | | |
| | Toronto | NHL | 56 | 8 | 8 | 16 | 44 | 4 | 0 | 0 | 0 | 4 |
| 1955-56 | Toronto | NHL | 18 | 0 | 1 | 1 | 2 | | | | | |
| | Pittsburgh | AHL | 47 | 24 | 26 | 50 | 40 | 4 | 4 | 1 | 5 | 8 |

# KLYMKIW, JULIAN

sport: hockey

born: Brooklands, Manitoba
July 16, 1933

height: 1.80 m / 5'11"

weight: 81.5 kg / 180 lbs

position: goal

shoots: right

Julian Klymkiw began skating at the age of four. He played junior hockey for the Brandon Wheat Kings. In 1953, the Detroit Red Wings sent Klymkiw for seasoning to the Troy Bruins of the IHL. The following year, he was back in Brandon. During the next three seasons, Klymkiw played for the Marquete Sentinel of the NMHOL, the Soo Indians of the NOHA, and the Winnipeg Warriors of the WHL. He would return to Winnipeg for the summers and play soccer for United Weston.

Klymkiw joined the Detroit Red Wings at the start of the 1958-59 season as the club's backup goalie and assistant trainer. He managed to play part of one game, albeit not for his side. The Rangers arrived in Detroit without a backup goaltender and when their starter got hurt, the team co-opted Klymkiw. In June of 1959, Klymkiw suffered a double fracture of his right leg playing soccer. The injury terminated his hopes of playing in the NHL.

In the fall of 1961, Klymkiw made a comeback when he joined the Winnipeg Maroons. In the spring of 1963, the club was a finalist for the Allan Cup. The following year, the Maroons won the Allan Cup. Klymkiw played for the Maroons for one more season before joining the Manitoba NHL Old Timers in 1966 for six years.

Klymkiw's association with hockey has also included work as a trainer with Canada's national team in 1964-65. He did public relations work for Team Canada, which the WHA put together to challenge the Soviets in 1974. In the years 1975 to 1977, Julian Klymkiw served on the Board of Directors of the Winnipeg Jets of the WHA.

| year | team | league | regular season | | | | | | | | playoffs | | | | | | | |
|---|---|---|---|---|---|---|---|---|---|---|---|---|---|---|---|---|---|---|
| | | | GP | MIN | W | L | T | GA | AVE | SO | GP | MIN | W | L | T | GA | AVG | SO |
| 1953-54 | Troy | IHL | 57 | 3,420 | | | | 239 | 4.19 | 1 | | | | | | | | |
| 1956-57 | Winnipeg | WHL | 4 | 240 | 2 | 2 | 0 | 20 | 5.00 | 0 | | | | | | | | |
| | Sault Ste. Marie | NOHA | 33 | 1,980 | | | | 133 | 4.03 | 1 | | | | | | | | |
| 1957-58 | Winnipeg | WHL | 3 | 180 | 0 | 2 | 1 | 8 | 2.67 | 0 | | | | | | | | |
| 1958-59 | NY Rangers | NHL | 1 | 19 | 0 | 0 | 0 | 2 | 6.32 | 0 | | | | | | | | |

# KLYSH, MYRON

"Maestro"

| | |
|---|---|
| sport: | volleyball |
| born: | Winnipeg, Manitoba |
| | December 17, 1965 |
| height: | 1.92 m / 6'4" |
| weight: | 81.5 kg / 180 lbs |

In 1982, while playing volleyball for the provincial runner-up Fort Richmond Collegiate of Winnipeg, Myron Klysh was named to Manitoba's all-star team. A year later, Klysh won the Canadian juvenile championship while competing with the Manitoba Bisons, and was selected to the championship all-star team. He was also named to Canada's junior volleyball team with which he would see action through 1985.

In the years 1984 to 1988, Myron Klysh starred on the University of Manitoba Bisons. The club never placed lower than third in the nation during those years, and won national titles in 1984 and 1985. During those two championship seasons, the club posted back-to-back undefeated seasons.

In 1988, in what was undoubtedly his personal best season, Klysh captained the Bisons to a second-place finish in the nation. He was named to the CIAU championship tournament all-star team, the CIAU second all-star team, and was selected MVP at the University of Manitoba and Sherbrooke tournaments. He was also honoured with the Manitoba Ukrainian Sportsman of the Year award and the University of Manitoba Athlete of the Year award.

Klysh also toured Central America with Athletes in Action that year. In the fall, Klysh was named to Canada's national volleyball team, with which he saw action through May of 1989.

A chartered accountant, Myron Klysh won the Canadian volleyball championship in 1990 playing for Winnipeg Free Kick.

## AWARDS

| | |
|---|---|
| 1988 | University of Manitoba Athlete of the Year |
| 1988 | Manitoba Ukrainian Sportsman of the Year |

## ALL-STAR SELECTIONS

| | |
|---|---|
| 1988 | All-Canadian Second Team |
| 1988 | CIAU Championships Tournament All-Star |

## RECORD

| year | competition | team | placing |
|---|---|---|---|
| 1983 | Canadian Juvenile Championship | | 1 |
| | vs England and Scotland | Canada | |
| 1984 | CIAU Championships | University of Manitoba | 1 |
| | Pacific Rim Championships (Jr) | Canada | 5 |
| 1985 | CIAU Championships | University of Manitoba | 1 |
| 1986 | CIAU Championships | University of Manitoba | 2 |
| 1987 | CIAU Championships | University of Manitoba | 3 |
| 1988 | CIAU Championships | University of Manitoba | 2 |
| | Haarlem Christmas Tournament | Canada | 5 |
| 1989 | Apeldoorn Tournament | Canada | 3 |
| 1990 | Canadian Championships | Free Kick | 1 |

# KOBELKA, KENDRA

sport:      skiing
born:       Lynn Lake, Manitoba
            May 1, 1967
height:     1.60 m / 5'3"
weight:     65 kg / 143 lbs

*Photo courtesy of the Athlete Information Bureau*

Kendra Kobelka began to ski at age eleven, after her family moved from Manitoba to Revelstoke, British Columbia. All her new friends and classmates skied and Kobelka quickly joined in this, the most popular winter pastime of her new small home town in the Rockies. Within one year she was competing, and at age 16 she represented Canada at the Junior World Ski Championships placing 24th in the downhill.

An outgoing and fun-loving individual, Kobelka was named to the national team in 1987. For a number of years, she competed on the Nor-Am, FIS and the World Cup circuits with varying degrees of success in all the alpine skiing disciplines. Nevertheless, Kobelka preferred the downhill and the super giant slalom events. In 1990, she became the pace-setter of the national women's downhill team, after a personal best eighth-place finish at a World Cup event at Santa Caterina, Italy. Later that year, at the inaugural Pan American Winter Games in Las Lenas, Argentina, Kobelka won a gold medal in the downhill and a silver in the super giant slalom. In early 1991, Kobelka was seriously hurt when she crashed during the final training run at the World Alpine Ski Championship in Saalbach, Austria. She failed to fully regain her form and retired from competitive skiing the following year.

At the conclusion of the 1988-89 World Cup ski season, Kobelka was ranked 20th in the super giant slalom, 30th in the downhill and 47th overall. A year later, her ranking in the downhill improved to 14th, while her overall placing dropped to 56th.

## RECORD

| year | competition | event | placing | result |
|------|-------------|-------|---------|--------|
| 1984 | World Junior Championships | downhill | 24 | 1:18.27 |
|      | WC Puy St. Vincent, France | downhill | 63 | 1.32.92 |
|      | WC Davos, Switzerland | super G | 75 | 1.59.69 |

| year | competition | event | placing | result |
|------|-------------|-------|---------|--------|
| 1984 | WC  Santa Caterina, Italy | giant slalom | 87 | 2:51.83 |
|      |             | downhill | 68 | 1:31.64 |
| 1985 | US Championships | downhill | 16 | 1:42.93 |
|      | Canadian Championships | slalom | 11 | 1:34.18 |
|      |             | giant slalom | 27 | 2:33.72 |
|      |             | downhill | 7 | 1:28.11 |
|      |             | super G | dnf |  |
|      | WC Banff, Canada | downhill | dnf |  |
|      |             | super G | 44 | 1:30.44 |
| 1986 | Canadian Championships | downhill | 12 | 1:16.08 |
|      |             | super G | 13 | 1:25.43 |
| 1987 | Canadian Championships | downhill | 5 | 1:34.45 |
|      | WC Leukerbad, Switzerland | super G | 44 | 1:36.07 |
| 1988 | WC Zinal, Switzerland | downhill | dnf |  |
|      |             | downhill | 27 | 1:56.08 |
|      | WC Bad Gastien, Austria | downhill | dnf |  |
|      | Canadian Championships | downhill | 4 | 1:20.70 |
|      |             | super G | 8 | 1:23.76 |
|      |             | giant slalom | 9 | 2:37.99 |
|      | WC Rossland, Canada | downhill | 23 | 1:45.92 |
|      |             | super G | dnf |  |
|      | WC Schladming, Austria | super G | 56 | 1:32.03 |
|      | WC Les Menuires, France | giant slalom | dnf |  |
|      | WC Val d'Isere, France | downhill | 46 | 1:15.27 |
|      | WC Altenmarkt, Austria | downhill | 9 | 1:36.66 |
| 1989 | WC Schwazenberg, Austria | giant slalom | dnf |  |
|      | WC Grindelwald, Switzerland | downhill | 36 | 1:59.98 |
|      |             | downhill | 25 | 1:59.22 |
|      | WC Tignes, France | downhill | 27 | 1:23.06 |
|      |             | super G | 48 | 1:21.47 |
|      | World Championships | downhill | 17 | 1:49.02 |
|      | WC Lake Louise, Canada | downhill | 22 | 1:45.24 |
|      |             | downhill | dnf |  |
|      | WC Steamboat Springs, USA | downhill | 29 | 1:29.01 |
|      |             | super G | 7 | 1:19.52 |
|      | Canadian Championships | super G | 1 | 1:23.37 |
|      |             | giant slalom | 3 | 2:27.21 |
|      |             | slalom | 10 | 1:38.44 |
|      | WC Panorama, Canada | downhill | 27 | 1:40.46 |
|      |             | downhill | 18 | 1:36.67 |

| year | competition | event | placing | result |
|------|-------------|-------|---------|--------|
| 1990 | WC Haus, Austria | downhill | 26 | 1:39.95 |
| | WC Santa Caterina, Italy | downhill | 8 | 1:29.09 |
| | WC Veysonnaz, Switzerland | downhill | 23 | 1:19.29 |
| | | downhill | 10 | 1:18.78 |
| | WC Are, Sweden | super G | 41 | 59.05 |
| | Pan American Games | downhill | 1 | 1:41.21 |
| | | super G | 2 | 1:09.54 |
| | | giant slalom | 11 | 2:12.07 |

# KOHUT, MERON

| | |
|---|---|
| sport: | wrestling |
| born: | . . . |
| | . . . |
| height: | . . . |
| weight: | 48 kg / 105 lbs |

Meron Kohut began wrestling while attending Kirkland Lake Collegiate and Vocational Institute. He quickly became a star performer winning the Northern Ontario and District high school championship in the years 1967 to 1970 and placing second at the Ontario high school championship in 1970.

In 1971, nineteen-year-old Kohut won the Ontario and Canadian titles in the 105.5 pound weight class. Victory at the national championship assured him of a trip to Cali, Colombia, for the 1971 Pan American Games. There, Meron Kohut failed to advance to the medal round.

## RECORD

| year | competition | event | placing |
|------|-------------|-------|---------|
| 1971 | Ontario Championships | 105.5 lbs | 1 |
| | Canadian Championships | 105.5 lbs | 1 |
| | Pan American Games | light flyweight | |

# KOLASKI, PETER

| | |
|---|---|
| sport: | boxing |
| born: | Brethour, Ontario |
| | July 19, 1924 |
| height: | 1.80 m / 5'11" |
| weight: | 67 kg / 147 lbs |

In 1941, Peter Kolaski came to Toronto to enlist in the army. He was rejected from service because of an ankle injury. Dejected, Kolaski decided to remain in Toronto. Later that year, Kolaski and a friend went to an amateur boxing match at Toronto's Massey Hall. Kolaski was immediately captivated by the art of boxing. He also told his friend that he was unimpressed by the two boxers that just fought, adding that he could "lick these guys any day of the week." A short while later he joined the Elmgrove Club and began to train after work and on week-ends.

In September of 1944, Kolaski registered as an amateur and fought his first bout. He scored a technical knockout (TKO) over his opponent in the third round. Over the next four years, Kolaski fought more than 50 amateur bouts, and developed into one of the finest welterweights in Canada. Promoters were eager to have him on their card and he was featured in the main event at least 25 times. This was, of course, at a time when a good amateur boxer could easily draw a crowd of 2,000 to 3,000 fans.

In the ring, Peter Kolaski was a very effective but not a pretty boxer. He readily took hits if he knew that he could exploit the situation for a counterattack. His most dependable weapon was his deadly right hand. Although amateur records from that time period do not exist, Kolaski won well over half of his fights, was never knocked out, and went down only on three occasions. A broken knuckle forced him to retire from the ring in 1948. In subsequent years, he continued his association with boxing by coaching and training youngsters at the Elmgrove and the Classic clubs.

## INDUCTIONS

1988     Canadian Boxing Hall of Fame

# KONIHOWSKI, JOHN

| | |
|---|---|
| sport: | athletics, football |
| given name: | Konihowski, John William |
| born: | Moose Jaw, Saskatchewan |
| | January 6, 1950 |
| height: | 1.91 m / 6'3" |
| weight: | 84 kg / 185 lbs |

*Photo courtesy of the Canadian Football Hall of Fame and Museum*

John Konihowski entered Bringham Young University on an athletic scholarship with five national age group triple jump titles to his credit. In addition, he held Saskatchewan high school records in the triple jump, long jump, and high hurdles. At the 1967 Canadian Juvenile championships, he won the triple jump; the winning distance was sixth best by a Canadian of any age that year. In 1968, Konihowski won the national junior title and in 1970, the Canadian title. He also established the Canadian indoor record in the triple jump when he traversed 49 feet and 10 inches.

In 1972, Konihowski established a Canadian indoor record for the 300 metres in a time of 34.7. In the summer, he won the Canadian 400-metre hurdles title after running the event for only a few months. "I was No. 1 in Canada in the 400-metre hurdles then and assumed I'd be going to Munich [for the Olympics]. I was three-tenths of a second off the qualifying time but that wouldn't have been a problem. However, they said they simply couldn't afford to send me. I couldn't accept that reason. I was totally disillusioned."[22]

In 1971, Konihowski had enrolled at the University of Saskatchewan to continue his education. To keep in shape for track, he decided to try out for the football team, but was cut. Konihowski's disenchantment with track after the 1972 Canadian championships resulted in renewed interest in football. He made the team in the fall of 1972 and saw some action. The following year he started at the wide receiver position. At the end of the season he gained All-Canadian honours. Konihowski was drafted by the Calgary Stampeders but was cut after training camp. He then joined the Edmonton Eskimos and played with them briefly, dropping the only pass thrown to him. In 1975, Konihowski became a starter with the Eskimos, catching 45 passes for 828 yards and eight touchdowns. The effort earned him a nomination for the Schenley Most Outstanding Canadian Award.

John Konihowski was with the Eskimos for seven years, but injuries hampered his career. He missed a good part of three seasons and often played hurt. Konihowski also missed two Grey Cup games because of injuries. Nevertheless, he did play in three and was a member of a championship team on two occasions. Prior to the start of the 1981 season, Konihowski was traded to the Winnipeg Blue Bombers. He saw limited action during two seasons with the Bombers.

John Konihowski's infatuation with track was not completely shattered by the decision which kept him from competing at the 1972 Olympics. His marriage to Diane Jones, Canada's top pentathlete, played a significant role in his continued pursuit of track. The two trained together and coached each other. Konihowski had a hand in coaching his wife to the gold medal at the 1978 Commonwealth Games. Eligibility rules pertaining to professional athletes prevented him from representing Canada in international competition, though. As a result, he competed primarily on the indoor circuit.

## INDUCTIONS

. . .        University of Saskatchewan Wall of Fame

## ALL-STAR SELECTIONS

1973        wide receiver        All-Canadian

## RECORD

athletics - field

| year | competition | event | placing | result |
|------|-------------|-------|---------|--------|
| 1967 | Canadian Juvenile Championships | triple jump | 1 | 48 ft 5³/₄ in |
| 1968 | Canadian Junior Championships | triple jump | 1 | 48 ft 5¹/₂ in |
|      | Canada Games | triple jump | 3 | 14.50 m |
| 1969 | Provo, Utah | triple jump | 1 | 49 ft 1³/₄ in |
|      | Canadian Championships | triple jump | 2 | 48 ft 7 in |
| 1970 | Canadian Championships | triple jump | 1 | 49 ft 1¹/₂ in |
|      | Commonwealth Games Trials | triple jump | 2 | 48 ft 6 in |
|      | Winnipeg | triple jump | 1 | 50 ft 4³/₄ in |

athletics - track

| year | competition | event | placing | result |
|------|-------------|-------|---------|--------|
| 1970 | Canadian Junior Championships | 110 m H | 2 | 14.7 |
| 1972 | . . . | 300 m | | 34.7 nir |

athletics - track

| year | competition | event | placing | result |
|------|-------------|-------|---------|--------|
| 1972 | Canadian Championships | 400 m H | 1 | 51.9 |
| 1973 | Tri-Province Meet | 110 m H | 1 | 14.8 |
| 1974 | Canadian Indoor Championships | 50 m H | 1 | 6.97 |
| 1976 | Canadian Indoor Championships | 50 m H | 5 | 7.1 |
| | | 400 m | 5 | 49.8 |
| 1981 | Canadian Indoor Championships | 50 m H | 5 | 7.03 |
| 1982 | Canadian Indoor Championships | 50 m H | 6 | 7.16 |
| | | 4 x 200 m | 1 | 1:28.88 |

football

pass receiving

| | | | regular season | | | | | | playoffs | | | | | | Grey Cup game | | | | | |
|------|------|--------|----|----|-----|------|----|----|----|----|-----|------|----|----|----|----|-----|------|----|----|
| year | team | league | GP | NO | YDS | AVE | LG | TD | GP | NO | YDS | AVE | LG | TD | GP | NO | YDS | AVE | LG | TD |
| 1974 | Edmonton | CFL | 4 | 0 | 0 | 0.0 | 0 | 0 | | | | | | | | | | | | |
| 1975* | Edmonton | CFL | 16 | 45 | 828 | 18.4 | 80 | 8 | 1 | 6 | 72 | 12.0 | | 1 | 1 | 3 | 26 | 8.7 | | 0 |
| 1976 | Edmonton | CFL | 7 | 13 | 170 | 13.1 | 43 | 0 | | | | | | | | | | | | |
| 1977 | Edmonton | CFL | 10 | 21 | 368 | 17.5 | 47 | 2 | 1 | 4 | 87 | 21.8 | 37 | 0 | 1 | 1 | 11 | 11.0 | 11 | 0 |
| 1978* | Edmonton | CFL | 7 | 2 | 75 | 37.5 | 64 | 0 | 1 | 0 | 0 | 0.0 | 0 | 0 | 0 | 0 | 0 | 0.0 | 0 | 0 |
| 1979* | Edmonton | CFL | 16 | 30 | 490 | 16.3 | 52 | 4 | 1 | 2 | 54 | 27.0 | 32 | 1 | 1 | 0 | 0 | 0.0 | 0 | 0 |
| 1980* | Edmonton | CFL | 5 | 2 | 17 | 8.5 | 9 | 0 | 0 | 0 | 0 | 0.0 | 0 | 0 | 0 | 0 | 0 | 0.0 | 0 | 0 |
| 1981 | Winnipeg | CFL | 14 | 20 | 254 | 12.7 | 24 | 0 | | | | | | | | | | | | |
| 1982 | Winnipeg | CFL | 16 | 3 | 30 | 10.0 | 22 | 0 | 2 | 0 | 0 | 0.0 | 0 | 0 | | | | | | |

scoring

| | | | regular season | | | playoffs | | | Grey Cup game | | |
|------|------|--------|----|----|-----|----|----|-----|----|----|-----|
| year | team | league | GP | TD | PTS | GP | TD | PTS | GP | TD | PTS |
| 1974 | Edmonton | CFL | 4 | 0 | 0 | | | | | | |
| 1975* | Edmonton | CFL | 16 | 8 | 48 | 1 | 1 | 6 | 1 | 0 | 0 |
| 1976 | Edmonton | CFL | 7 | 0 | 0 | | | | | | |
| 1977 | Edmonton | CFL | 10 | 2 | 12 | 1 | 0 | 0 | 1 | 0 | 0 |
| 1978* | Edmonton | CFL | 7 | 0 | 0 | 1 | 0 | 0 | 0 | 0 | 0 |
| 1979* | Edmonton | CFL | 16 | 4 | 24 | 1 | 1 | 6 | 1 | 0 | 0 |
| 1980* | Edmonton | CFL | 5 | 0 | 0 | 0 | 0 | 0 | 0 | 0 | 0 |
| 1981 | Winnipeg | CFL | 14 | 0 | 0 | | | | | | |
| 1982 | Winnipeg | CFL | 16 | 0 | 0 | 2 | 0 | 0 | | | |

# KORCHAK, BUD

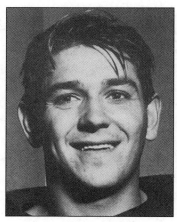

| | |
|---|---|
| sport: | football |
| given name: | Korchak, Borden |
| born: | Winnipeg, Manitoba |
| | August 15, 1927 |
| height: | 1.78 m / 5'10" |
| weight: | 86 kg / 190 lbs |
| position: | flying wing, placekicker |

*Photo courtesy of the Western Canada Pictorial Index*

Bud Korchak was recruited by the Winnipeg Blue Bombers from the St. John's junior football team in 1949. During his first four seasons with Winnipeg, Korchak was primarily used as a receiver at the flying wing position. He was the club's fastest player and also possessed amazing leaping abilities and sure hands. The latter two skills were in part cultivated by simultaneously playing soccer at the goalkeeper position. Korchak's most productive season pass receiving was in 1951, when he scored a career-high seven touchdowns. That season he was named for the first time to a WIFU all-star team.

In 1951, Korchak began placekicking after the regular kicker was released. Once again Korchak's soccer skills came through: he was able to kick 50-yard field goals and send kickoffs 75 yards. As placekicking became popular, Korchak's workload increased, and by 1953, he led the WIFU in scoring with 66 points. In post-season play, he established a league record for most converts in a playoff game with seven, most converts in the playoffs with 19, and most games scoring points with six. The following season, Korchak lost his kicking touch and was used sparingly. In 1955, the Bombers re-signed Korchak but he did not dress for any of the games. In September, the club released him. After being waived by WIFU clubs, Korchak was acquired by the Montreal Alouettes. The move rejuvenated his game and he scored 60 points, third best in the league. Korchak did not last long in Montreal. Part-way through the 1956 season, he was traded to Ottawa. Bud Korchak finished his professional career with the Calgary Stampeders a year later.

Football was still in his blood and upon returning to Winnipeg, Korchak joined the St. James Rams of the Manitoba Intermediate Football Conference in the capacity of kicker and co-coach. Later he coached the Rams of the Winnipeg Senior Football league.

Bud Korchak was also an all-star soccer goalkeeper. He played for United Weston, with which he won the Manitoba championship, and later with O'Kum Inn Bred.  In 1951 and 1952, he played for the Manitoba All-stars against touring English teams.

## AWARDS

1953    Dave Dryburgh Memorial Trophy  -  Leading Scorer Western Division

## ALL-STAR SELECTIONS

| 1951 | flying wing | WIFU | Second Team |
| 1952 | flying wing | WIFU | First Team |
| 1953 | flying wing | WIFU | First Team |

## RECORD

| scoring | | | regular season | | | | | | playoffs | | | | | | Grey Cup game | | | | | |
|---|---|---|---|---|---|---|---|---|---|---|---|---|---|---|---|---|---|---|---|---|
| year | team | league | GP | TD | C | FG | S | PTS | GP | TD | C | FG | S | PTS | GP | TD | C | FG | S | PTS |
| 1949 | Winnipeg | WIFU | ... | | | | | | | | | | | | | | | | | |
| 1950 | Winnipeg | WIFU | ... | 2 | 1 | 0 | 1 | 12 | 3 | 1 | 0 | 0 | 0 | 5 | 0 | 0 | 0 | 0 | 0 | 0 |
| 1951 | Winnipeg | WIFU | ... | 7 | 0 | 0 | 0 | 35 | 1 | 0 | 0 | 0 | 0 | 0 | | | | | | |
| 1952 | Winnipeg | WIFU | ... | 4 | 34 | 4 | 3 | 69 | 3 | 0 | 0 | 0 | 0 | 0 | | | | | | |
| 1953 | Winnipeg | WIFU | ... | 1 | 29 | 9 | 5 | 66 | 6 | 0 | 19 | 0 | 2 | 21 | 1 | 0 | 1 | 0 | 0 | 1 |
| 1954 | Winnipeg | WIFU | ... | 0 | 12 | 4 | 4 | 28 | 2 | 0 | 0 | 0 | 0 | 0 | | | | | | |
| 1955 | Winnipeg | WIFU | 0 | 0 | 0 | 0 | 0 | 0 | | | | | | | | | | | | |
| | Montreal | IRFU | ... | 0 | 49 | 3 | 2 | 60 | 1 | 0 | 5 | 1 | 0 | 8 | 1 | 0 | 3 | 0 | 1 | 4 |
| 1956 | Mont/Ottawa | IRFU | 11 | 0 | 31 | 4 | 2 | 45 | 1 | 0 | 3 | 0 | 0 | 3 | | | | | | |
| 1957 | Calgary | WIFU | 16 | 0 | 8 | 1 | 0 | 11 | 2 | 0 | 1 | 1 | 0 | 4 | | | | | | |

# KORNEY, MIKE

| | |
|---|---|
| sport: | hockey |
| born: | Dauphin, Manitoba |
| | September 15, 1953 |
| height: | 1.91 m / 6'3" |
| weight: | 88.5 kg / 195 lbs |
| position: | right wing |
| shoots: | right |

*Card reproduced courtesy of O-Pee-Chee Co.*

For Mike Korney, a big, strong and aggressive winger, the 1973-74 season was one to remember. He made his NHL debut that year with the Detroit Red Wings. He also played for the Detroit affiliate, London Lions of the British League, Virginia of the AHL, and Port Huron of the IHL. During the next two seasons, Korney played for the Red Wings and in the minors. In 1977, he was traded to Philadelphia by Detroit. Failing to make the team, he was signed as a free agent by St. Louis in the summer of 1978. In the fall he was traded to Montreal. Two days later, he was claimed by the New York Rangers in the NHL Waiver Draft. Mike Korney ended his NHL career with the Rangers.

## RECORD

| year | team | league | regular season | | | | | playoffs | | | | |
|---|---|---|---|---|---|---|---|---|---|---|---|---|
| | | | GP | G | A | PTS | PIM | GP | G | A | PTS | PIM |
| 1973-74 | Detroit | NHL | 2 | 0 | 0 | 0 | 0 | | | | | |
| | London | British | 31 | 15 | 10 | 25 | 33 | | | | | |
| | Virginia | AHL | 19 | 1 | 1 | 2 | 15 | | | | | |
| | Port Huron | IHL | 7 | 1 | 0 | 1 | 9 | | | | | |
| 1974-75 | Detroit | NHL | 30 | 8 | 2 | 10 | 18 | | | | | |
| | Virginia | AHL | 2 | 0 | 0 | 0 | 0 | | | | | |
| | Providence | AHL | 3 | 1 | 0 | 1 | 0 | | | | | |
| | Springfield | AHL | 1 | 0 | 0 | 0 | 0 | | | | | |
| | Hampton | SHL | 13 | 0 | 1 | 1 | 35 | | | | | |
| 1975-76 | Detroit | NHL | 27 | 1 | 7 | 8 | 23 | | | | | |
| | New Haven | AHL | 21 | 8 | 9 | 17 | 31 | | | | | |
| | Oklahoma City | CHL | 18 | 8 | 6 | 14 | 20 | 4 | 0 | 0 | 0 | 2 |
| 1976-77* | Kansas City | CHL | 74 | 17 | 24 | 41 | 82 | 10 | 1 | 6 | 7 | 13 |

| year | team | league | regular season | | | | | playoffs | | | | |
| --- | --- | --- | --- | --- | --- | --- | --- | --- | --- | --- | --- | --- |
| | | | GP | G | A | PTS | PIM | GP | G | A | PTS | PIM |
| 1977-78 | Maine | AHL | 15 | 2 | 4 | 6 | 20 | | | | | |
| | Milwaukee | IHL | 3 | 0 | 0 | 0 | 2 | | | | | |
| | Salt Lake City | CHL | 54 | 12 | 8 | 20 | 75 | 6 | 2 | 4 | 6 | 6 |
| 1978-79 | NY Rangers | NHL | 18 | 0 | 1 | 1 | 18 | | | | | |
| | New Haven | AHL | 5 | 1 | 3 | 4 | 0 | | | | | |
| | Tulsa | CHL | 11 | 0 | 9 | 9 | 36 | | | | | |
| 1979-80 | Syracuse | AHL | 73 | 11 | 16 | 27 | 87 | 4 | 1 | 2 | 3 | 18 |

# KOROLL, CLIFF

| | |
| --- | --- |
| sport: | hockey |
| given name: | Koroll, Clifford Eugene |
| born: | Canora, Saskatchewan |
| | October 1, 1946 |
| height: | 1.83 m / 6'0" |
| weight: | 88.5 kg / 195 lbs |
| position: | right wing |
| shoots: | right |

In the 1960s, a number of Canadian hockey players, among them Cliff Koroll, opted to forgo the Canadian junior hockey program by enrolling at American universities. Koroll enrolled at the University of Denver where he quickly became a standout on the school's hockey team. In his senior year, he led Denver to the NCAA American collegiate hockey title. The following year Koroll tried out with the Chicago Black Hawks. He failed to make the Hawks and was assigned to their farm club in Dallas. The team won the CHL championship.

Cliff Koroll won a regular starting position with the Black Hawks at the 1969 training camp. He played with the club for 11 years, amassing 208 goals and 254 assists during the regular season. Statistically, his best season was in 1972-73 when he registered 33 goals and 24 assists. In each of those 11 years, the Hawks qualified for post-season play. Twice the Hawks made it to the Stanley Cup final but in both instances they went down in defeat. Koroll contributed in the playoffs with 19 goals and 29 assists. Upon retiring as a player in 1980, Koroll served as an assistant coach with the Black Hawks for a number of years.

1968      right wing      NCAA      First Team

## RECORD

| | | | regular season | | | | | playoffs | | | | |
|---|---|---|---|---|---|---|---|---|---|---|---|---|
| year | team | league | GP | G | A | PTS | PIM | GP | G | A | PTS | PIM |
| 1968-69* | Dallas | CHL | 67 | 28 | 34 | 62 | 50 | 11 | 2 | 8 | 10 | 15 |
| 1969-70 | Chicago | NHL | 73 | 18 | 19 | 37 | 44 | 8 | 1 | 4 | 5 | 9 |
| 1970-71 | Chicago | NHL | 72 | 16 | 34 | 50 | 85 | 18 | 7 | 9 | 16 | 18 |
| 1971-72 | Chicago | NHL | 76 | 22 | 23 | 45 | 51 | 8 | 0 | 0 | 0 | 11 |
| 1972-73 | Chicago | NHL | 77 | 33 | 24 | 57 | 38 | 16 | 4 | 6 | 10 | 6 |
| 1973-74 | Chicago | NHL | 78 | 21 | 25 | 46 | 32 | 11 | 2 | 5 | 7 | 13 |
| 1974-75 | Chicago | NHL | 80 | 27 | 32 | 59 | 27 | 8 | 3 | 5 | 8 | 8 |
| 1975-76 | Chicago | NHL | 80 | 25 | 33 | 58 | 29 | 4 | 1 | 0 | 1 | 0 |
| 1976-77 | Chicago | NHL | 80 | 15 | 26 | 41 | 8 | 2 | 0 | 0 | 0 | 0 |
| 1977-78 | Chicago | NHL | 73 | 16 | 15 | 31 | 19 | 4 | 1 | 0 | 1 | 0 |
| 1978-79 | Chicago | NHL | 78 | 12 | 19 | 31 | 20 | 4 | 0 | 0 | 0 | 20 |
| 1979-80 | Chicago | NHL | 47 | 3 | 4 | 7 | 6 | 2 | 0 | 0 | 0 | 2 |

*Photo courtesy of the Athlete Information Bureau*

# KOSTIUK, AL

sport:      volleyball
born:       Flin Flon, Manitoba
            October 1, 1955
height:     1.98 m / 6'6"
weight:     95.5 kg / 210 lbs

While living in British Columbia, Al Kostiuk was selected to that province's volleyball team for the 1975 Canada Games. The team won the gold medal. That same year Kostiuk represented Canada at the Pan American Games. It was his first major international experience with the national team. In the next four years, Kostiuk continued to play on the national team, representing Canada at the World University Games, the World Cup, and the World Championships. One of the tallest members of Canada's team at the time, Kostiuk used his height advantage to excel at the center blocker position. While a student of physical education at the University of Calgary, Al Kostiuk also competed for the university team. After retiring from the national team, Kostiuk pursued a professional volleyball career in Italy.

## RECORD

| year | competition | team | placing |
|------|-------------|------|---------|
| 1975 | Canada Games | British Columbia | 1 |
|      | Pan American Games | Canada | 5 |
| 1977 | World University Games | Canada | 13 |
|      | World Cup | Canada | 12 |
| 1978 | World Championships | Canada | 20 |
| 1979 | Pan American Games | Canada | |

# KOWCINAK, DICK

| | |
|---|---|
| sport: | hockey |
| given name: | Kowcinak, Richard |
| born: | Winnipeg, Manitoba |
| | May 25, 1917 |
| height: | 1.70 m / 5'7" |
| weight: | 61 kg / 135 lbs |
| position: | center |
| shoots: | left |

*Photo courtesy of the Manitoba Hockey Hall of Fame*

Dick Kowcinak began his hockey career with the East Kildonan midgets, coached by Mike Kryschuk. In 1935 he joined the Winnipeg Monarchs. The club won the national junior title in 1937, and Kowcinak was the top scorer in the championship series. The media credited Kowcinak for securing the championship for Winnipeg, referring to him as a "bundle of dynamite" who may one day prove to be the "mighty atom of the NHL." Hockey broadcaster Stew

McPherson described Kowcinak and his linemates Alf Pike and Johnny McCreedy as "the greatest line, bar none, I've ever seen."[23]

An NHL career, though, did not materialize. Kowcinak had an offer to tryout with the Boston Bruins but turned it down. He also rejected Conn Smythe's offer of a contract with the Toronto Maple Leafs. Possibly Kowcinak's decision not to play in the NHL had to do with his size: he weighed only 135 pounds. Although he was extremely enthusiastic, hard working, and talented, Kowcinak realized that his body would be brutally punished by the big skaters and a long career in hockey would be out of the question.

For the 1937-38 season, Kowcinak joined the Trail Smoke Eaters of the East Kootenay League. The club won the Allan Cup that spring and the right to represent Canada at the 1939 World Championship. In Switzerland the Smoke Eaters were undefeated, winning the world title. In the spring of 1940, Kowcinak was once again on an Allan Cup winning team, this time with the Kirkland Lake Blue Devils senior club. Because of World War II, the World Championship was cancelled. Kowcinak then moved on to play for the Sydney Millionaires, Indianapolis Capitals, Detroit Auto Club, and the Sarnia Sailors.

## AWARDS

| | |
|---|---|
| 1948 | George Wilkinson Memorial Trophy - IHL Scoring Leader |
| 1950 | George Wilkinson Memorial Trophy - IHL Scoring Leader |
| 1950 | James Gatschene Memorial Trophy - IHL MVP |

## ALL-STAR SELECTIONS

| | | | | |
|---|---|---|---|---|
| 1949 | center | IHL | Second Team |
| 1950 | center | IHL | First Team |

## RECORD

| | | | regular season | | | | | playoffs | | | | |
|---|---|---|---|---|---|---|---|---|---|---|---|---|
| year | team | league | GP | G | A | PTS | PIM | GP | G | A | PTS | PIM |
| 1937-38 | Trail | EKL | 36 | 26 | 9 | 35 | | | | | | |
| 1938-39 | Trail | EKL | ... | | | | | | | | | |
| 1939-40 | Kirkland Lake | NOSL | ... | | | | | | | | | |
| 1940-41* | Sydney | CBHL | ... | 19 | 24 | 43 | | 0 | 0 | 0 | 0 | 0 |
| 1943-44 | Indianapolis | AHL | 31 | 10 | 12 | 22 | 4 | 5 | 0 | 2 | 2 | 2 |
| 1944-45 | Indianapolis | AHL | 53 | 18 | 35 | 53 | 13 | 5 | 2 | 3 | 5 | 2 |
| 1945-46 | St. Louis | AHL | 57 | 9 | 30 | 39 | 19 | | | | | |

| | | | regular season | | | | | playoffs | | | | |
|---|---|---|---|---|---|---|---|---|---|---|---|---|
| year | team | league | GP | G | A | PTS | PIM | GP | G | A | PTS | PIM |
| 1947-48 | Detroit | IHL | 30 | 25 | 42 | 67 | 18 | | | | | |
| 1948-49 | Detroit | IHL | 30 | 17 | 32 | 49 | 4 | 6 | 5 | 3 | 8 | 4 |
| 1949-50 | Sarnia | IHL | 38 | 25 | 58 | 83 | 18 | 10 | 5 | 7 | 12 | 12 |
| 1950-51 | Sarnia | IHL | 47 | 12 | 50 | 62 | 43 | 3 | 0 | 0 | 0 | 0 |

international

| year | team | competition | GP | G | A | PTS | PIM | Place |
|---|---|---|---|---|---|---|---|---|
| 1939 | Trail | World Championship | ... | | | | | 1 |

# KOZAK, DON

"Kozy," "Star Trek"

| | |
|---|---|
| sport: | hockey |
| given name: | Kozak, Donald |
| born: | Saskatoon, Saskatchewan February 2, 1952 |
| height: | 1.75 m / 5'9" |
| weight: | 83.5 kg / 184 lbs |
| position: | right wing |
| shoots: | right |

*Photo courtesy of the Vancouver Canucks*

Don Kozak began playing hockey at the age of seven; at the time, he was a goalie. After a while, he became tired of being scored upon, and wanted to score goals himself. As a result, he was moved to a forward position. Kozak quickly developed into a fine goal scorer. He progressed through the junior ranks, playing for Saskatoon, Swift Current and Edmonton. In his last two years of junior hockey he netted 60 and 55 goals respectively. He was the Los Angeles Kings' first round selection, 20th overall, in the 1972 NHL Entry Draft.

Don Kozak played all out on every occasion. He was an aggressive player and a hustler with tremendous desire. He tried to be everywhere on the ice, and as a result his positional play and backchecking suffered. With time, he became more disciplined and settled down to a more controlled style of play. Kozak spent six seasons with Los Angeles before moving to the Vancouver Canucks. In June of 1979, he was picked up by the Hartford Whalers in the NHL Expansion Draft but did not play any games for the club. Kozak finished his hockey career in the minors.

## RECORD

| year | team | league | regular season | | | | | playoffs | | | | |
|------|------|--------|----|----|----|-----|-----|----|---|---|-----|-----|
| | | | GP | G | A | PTS | PIM | GP | G | A | PTS | PIM |
| 1972-73 | Los Angeles | NHL | 72 | 14 | 6 | 20 | 104 | | | | | |
| 1973-74 | Los Angeles | NHL | 76 | 21 | 14 | 35 | 54 | 5 | 0 | 0 | 0 | 33 |
| 1974-75 | Los Angeles | NHL | 77 | 16 | 15 | 31 | 64 | 3 | 1 | 1 | 2 | 7 |
| 1975-76 | Los Angeles | NHL | 62 | 20 | 24 | 44 | 94 | 9 | 1 | 0 | 1 | 12 |
| 1976-77 | Los Angeles | NHL | 79 | 15 | 17 | 32 | 89 | 9 | 4 | 1 | 5 | 17 |
| 1977-78 | Los Angeles | NHL | 43 | 8 | 5 | 13 | 45 | | | | | |
| | Springfield | AHL | 71 | 4 | 5 | 0 | | | | | | |
| 1978-79 | Vancouver | NHL | 28 | 2 | 5 | 7 | 30 | 3 | 1 | 0 | 1 | 0 |
| | Tulsa | CHL | 29 | 15 | 10 | 25 | 44 | | | | | |
| | Dallas | CHL | 7 | 2 | 4 | 6 | 9 | | | | | |
| 1979-80 | Cincinnati | CHL | 33 | 10 | 7 | 17 | 68 | | | | | |
| | Springfield | AHL | 51 | 9 | 17 | 26 | 48 | | | | | |
| 1980-81 | Binghamton | AHL | 41 | 5 | 10 | 15 | 37 | | | | | |

# KOZAK, DOROTHY

"Dot"

sport: athletics
born: Winnipeg, Manitoba
April 17, 1932
height: 1.73 m / 5'8"
weight: 51 kg / 112 lbs

In her youth, Dorothy "Dot" Kozak was an outstanding all-round athlete. She ran, jumped, and competed on CUAC softball teams. At the 1951 Manitoba Track and Field Championships, she won three gold medals and a silver. In 1952, she ran the 100 yards in 11.2 seconds, just two-tenths of a second off the Canadian record. At the national championships, she was disqualified in the 100-metre final for jumping the gun. In the 200 metres she did not make the final. In 1953, Kozak recorded the fastest time by a Canadian woman in the 220-yard dash when she covered the distance in 25.5 seconds.

Dot Kozak represented Canada at the 1954 Commonwealth Games. In the 100-yard dash she was eliminated in a qualifying heat. With the 4x110-yard relay team she won a bronze medal in a Canadian record time of 47.8 seconds. At the 1956 Olympic Trials, Kozak qualified for the Games in the long jump and the 4x100-metre relay. Shortly before the departure of the Canadian team to Melbourne, an Olympic training meet was held. In the long jump qualifying round, Kozak jumped 18 feet 5³/₄ inches to establish a new Canadian record, 2³/₄ inches better than the previous record. In the final, contested the following day, she improved the record to 18 feet 6 inches (5.625 m). The latter mark, though, was not ratified; the first was, and it stood for seven years. Kozak was also a member of the team that established a Canadian record in the 4x100-metre relay with a time of 47.2 seconds.

At the Olympic Games, Kozak failed to jump 5.68 metres in the qualifying round and did not make the long jump final. In the 4x100-metre relay, Dorothy Kozak ran the third leg for Canada. She received the baton with a 10-metre deficit and could not make up the distance. The Canadian foursome placed fifth in the semi-finals and did not advance, but their time of 46.6 seconds was the fastest ever by a Canadian relay team. The record, though, was not ratified because it was established outside of Canada. After the Olympics, Kozak remained in Australia for a year and a half. Upon returning to Canada she participated in the 1958 Commonwealth Games trials. She failed to make the team, and retired from track and field.

## RECORD

athletics - track

| year | competition | event | placing | result | |
|------|-------------|-------|---------|--------|---|
| 1951 | Manitoba Championships | 75 y | 1 | 9.2 | |
| | | 100 y | 1 | 11.6 | |
| 1952 | Manitoba Relays | 100 y | 1 | 11.2 | |
| | Winnipeg Championships | 100 y | 1 | 11.6 | |
| | Canadian Championships | 100 m | dsq | | |
| | | 200 m | dnq | | |
| 1953 | CNE Track Meet | 100 y | 1 | 11.5 | |
| | | 220 y | 1 | 25.5 | |
| 1954 | Commonwealth Games Trials | 100 y | 3 | 11.8 | |
| | Commonwealth Games | 100 y | 7 H | 11.2 | |
| | | 4 x 110 y | 3 | 47.8 | nr |
| 1955 | CNE Track Meet | 100 y | 2 | 11.2 | |
| | Calgary | 220 y | 1 | 25.6 | |
| 1956 | Olympic Trials | 100 m | 4 | | |
| | | 200 m | 4 | | |
| | Olympic Training Meet | 100 m | 2 | | |

athletics - track

| year | competition | event | placing | result | |
|------|-------------|-------|---------|--------|---|
| 1956 | Olympic Training Meet | 4 x 100 m | 1 | 47.2 | nr |
| | Olympic Games | 4 x 100 m | 5 H | 46.6 | |

athletics - field

| 1951 | Manitoba Championships | high jump | 1 | 4 ft 3 in | |
|------|------------------------|-----------|---|-----------|---|
| 1952 | Winnipeg Championships | long jump | 1 | 15 ft 10 in | |
| 1955 | Calgary | long jump | 1 | 18 ft 0½ in | |
| 1956 | Olympic Training Meet | long jump | qr | 18 ft 5¾ in | nr |
| | | long jump | 1 | 18 ft 6 in | |
| | Olympic Games | long jump | qr | 5.50 m | |

nr    Canadian Record

qr    qualifying round

# KOZAK, LES

| | |
|---|---|
| sport: | hockey |
| given name: | Kozak, Leslie Paul |
| born: | Yorkton, Saskatchewan |
| | October 28, 1940 |
| height: | 1.83 m / 6'0" |
| weight: | 84 kg / 185 lbs |
| position: | left wing |
| shoots: | left |

*Photo courtesy of the St. Michael's College School Archives*

Les Kozak played junior hockey for Toronto St. Michael's College of the OHA. In 1959, he was selected in a "draft" to augment the Kitchener-Waterloo Dutchmen club, which was to represent Canada at the upcoming Olympic Games. The opportunity to play at the Olympics, though, never materialized.

Kozak joined the Toronto Maple Leafs during the 1961-62 season, playing 12 games before being reassigned to the Rochester Americans of the AHL for more seasoning. There he sustained a skull fracture after sliding into the boards. Surgery was required, and a silver plate was inserted in his skull. The injury ended his professional hockey career. As a result, Kozak shifted his energies to complete his undergraduate degree in chemistry. Subsequently, he obtained a Ph.D. in bio-chemistry. Some years later, he was named deputy director of the Jackson Laboratory at Bar Harbour, Maine, an international centre specializing in the study of genetic diseases.

RECORD

| year | team | league | regular season | | | | | playoffs | | | | |
|------|------|--------|----|----|----|-----|-----|----|----|----|-----|-----|
| | | | GP | G | A | PTS | PIM | GP | G | A | PTS | PIM |
| 1961-62 | Toronto | NHL | 12 | 1 | 0 | 1 | 2 | | | | | |
| | Rochester | AHL | 45 | 14 | 9 | 23 | 31 | | | | | |

## KOZAK, PAUL

| | |
|---|---|
| sport: | hockey |
| born: | Hammond, Indiana, USA |
| | June 29, 1910 |
| died: | Kimberley, British Columbia |
| | November 1, 1953 |
| height: | 1.80 m / 5'11" |
| weight: | 81.5 kg / 180 lbs |
| position: | defense |
| shoots: | left |

Paul Kozak was two years old when his family immigrated to Canada and settled in Canmore, Alberta. There he played minor and junior hockey, and began working in a coal mine. In May 1931, Kozak moved to Kimberley, British Columbia, and secured a job at a local mine. He joined the Kimberley Dynamiters hockey club upon its formation in the fall of 1931. The team, comprised primarily of miners, quickly became a contender, winning the Allan Cup in 1936 and the right to represent Canada at the 1937 World Championship.

In London, England, the Dynamiters swept their opposition by winning nine straight games to take the World Championship title. During the tournament, the Canadians outscored their opponents 60-4. Kozak, while playing steady on defense, contributed at least two goals and an assist to the tally (game records not fully complete).

Paul Kozak was a rugged defenseman who commanded the respect of opposing forwards. He played a clean game and was respected for his all-round good sportsmanship. During the Dynamiters' championship era, Kozak received an extraordinary amount of ice time, a result of the coach's use of only three blue-liners. In February 1938, the big Dynamiter suffered a severely broken ankle which effectively terminated his hockey career.

Paul Kozak passed away suddenly in 1953. To recognize and celebrate his sporting accomplishments, the Kimberley Loyal Order of Moose presented the Paul Kozak Memorial Trophy to the Western International Hockey League in 1956. The award was to annually recognize the league's most valuable defenseman.

RECORD

international

| year | team | competition | GP | G | A | PTS | PIM | Place |
|------|------|-------------|-----|---|---|-----|-----|-------|
| 1937 | Kimberley | World Championship | ... | | | | | 1 |

# KOZAK, STEVE

"Little Giant"

| | |
|---|---|
| sport: | wrestling, professional wrestling |
| born: | . . ., Ukraine |
| | . . ., 1915 |
| died: | Vancouver, British Columbia |
| | July 14, 1975 |
| height: | 1.68 m / 5'6" |
| weight: | 98 kg / 215 lbs |

Steve Kozak was 15 years old when he started wrestling at the Winnipeg YMCA. After winning numerous amateur titles, Kozak turned professional in the mid-1940s. Competing in the junior heavyweight division, he quickly established himself as a prominent wrestler on the Prairies. By 1946, he was defeating the likes of Tommy "The Colorado Comet" Bradley and Abe "King Kong" Cashey, thus setting the stage for a world title challenge.

Misfortune struck Steve Kozak during the title bout with reigning champion Ken Fenalon. After a thrilling start, Kozak's head connected with a ring post leaving him somewhat dazed.

Fenalon took advantage of this and pinned the challenger. Nevertheless, Kozak proved to be a worthy challenger and a rematch was set. On March 20, 1947, Steve Kozak defeated Ken Fenalon to capture the World Junior Heavyweight Championship. The bout was 51 minutes old when Kozak applied a headlock to Fenalon and thrice slammed him to the canvas. The world champion was then straddled and his shoulders pinned to the ground for a three count.

A year later, Kozak challenged World Heavyweight Champion Sandor Szabo (a full-fledged heavyweight at more than 225 pounds) to a match. Fighting in front of a home crowd, Kozak twice had Szabo on the mat for the count, but each time the champion managed to break free. Szabo ended the bout by flipping Kozak and breaking the challenger's collarbone. The injury had lasting implications - Kozak never fully recovered his upper body strength.

In 1950, Kozak was suspended after failing to appear for a match. Money was apparently at stake. In defiance of the suspension, Kozak set up his own promotion company. The venture failed and Kozak retired to concentrate on his restaurant business. Two years later, for a brief period of time, he was able to resurrect his promotion business. In 1955, Kozak made up with the local promoter and once again began appearing on his card. The comeback though was short-lived.

Known as the "Little Giant," Steve Kozak packed 215 pounds (98 kg) into a 5 foot 6 inch (168 cm) frame. His chest measured 52 inches while his waist was 34. Kozak used his incredible strength and his favourite hold - the crushing headlock - to systemically defeat his opponents. He lost only four times during a career that included about 200 fights. Steve Kozak was considered a genuine wrestler, not a showman. This endeared him to wrestling fans and resulted in a large following. Often, Steve Kozak would visit Winnipeg Veterans' Hospital and hand out tickets to his matches.

# KOZYRA, TARAS

sport:      broomball, administrator
born:      Bilawyncij, Ukraine
           September 26, 1941
height:     1.75 m / 5'9"
weight:    77 kg  / 170 lbs

During the late 1950s, Taras Kozyra was one of Lakehead's most outstanding high school athletes. He primarily competed in middle distance track and cross country events. In 1959, he was selected to attend the Junior Olympics Training camp. In 1961, while attending Lakehead University, Kozyra began seriously competing in broomball. He played and coached broomball through 1984. Some of the teams he was associated with were the Port Arthur Prosvita, the Film Factory, and the Hodden Avenue Hotel. In 1975, at the World Broomball championship, his team lost the championship final game in sudden-death overtime.

In the years 1978 to 1982, Kozyra served as General Manager of the 1981 Jeux Canada Games, a two-week spectacular of summer sports. He eventually led a staff of 60 people overseeing 200 committees, 1,000 officials, 3,000 athletes and 5,000 volunteers. At the conclusion of the games, Kozyra was hired by the federal government's Secretary of State for Fitness and Amateur Sport to write a comprehensive manual on the Canada Games. The 1,500 page final draft was submitted in June 1982. In 1987, Taras Kozyra was elected to the Ontario Provincial Legislature. He served for one term.

## AWARDS

1971     Most Valuable Player - Thunder Bay Broomball League

## RECORD

administration

| year | position |
| --- | --- |
| 1967 | Official, Pan American Games - track and field |
| 1968 | Official, Canadian Olympic Track and Field trials |
| 1978-82 | General Manager, 1981 Jeux Canada Summer Games |

# KRAMCHYNSKY-NELSON, EILEEN

| | |
|---|---|
| sport: | volleyball |
| nee: | Kramchynsky, Eileen |
| born: | Saskatoon, Saskatchewan |
| | May 30, 1966 |
| height: | 1.83 m / 6'1" |
| weight: | 72 kg / 158 lbs |

*Photo courtesy of the Athlete Information Bureau*

While in her early teens, Eileen Kramchynsky starred on volleyball teams that vied for national age group championships. In 1984, she was named to Canada's national junior team. Kramchynsky lasted with the team for only a year. Coaches with the national senior team were impressed with her skills and her sense for the game. She was asked to join the senior club in 1985. Primarily used as a middle blocker, Kramchynsky's tenure with the national squad lasted through 1988 and included competition at most major international events. After Canada failed to qualify for the 1988 Olympics, she retired from the national team.

Eileen Kramchynsky joined a professional volleyball team in Stuttgart, West Germany, for the 1988-89 season. The club won the championship. The following two seasons she played in Salzburg, Austria, pacing her club to two second-place finishes. Eileen Kramchynsky-Nelson rejoined the national team in May of 1990.

## AWARDS

1984    Saskatchewan Volleyball Athlete of the Year

## RECORD

| year | competition | team | placing |
|---|---|---|---|
| 1983 | Canada Games | Saskatchewan | 8 |
| 1985 | Canada Cup | Canada | 2 |
| 1986 | World Championships | Canada | 15 |
| | Canada Cup | Canada | 4 |
| 1987 | Savaria Cup | Canada | 7 |
| | Liberation Cup | Canada | 3 |

| year | competition | team | placing |
|------|-------------|------|---------|
| 1987 | World University Games | Canada | 7 |
| | Pan American Games | Canada | 5 |
| | Canada Cup | Canada | 5 |
| | NORCECA Championships | Canada | 3 |
| 1988 | Bremen Cup | Canada | 6 |
| | Canada Cup | Canada | 4 |
| 1990 | Goodwill Games | Canada | 7 |
| | World Championships | Canada | 14 |
| 1991 | Pan American Games | Canada | |

# KRUSHELNYSKI, MIKE

"Krusher"

| | |
|---|---|
| sport: | hockey |
| given name: | Krushelnyski, Michael |
| born: | Montreal, Quebec |
| | April 27, 1960 |
| height: | 1.88 m / 6'2" |
| weight: | 90.5 kg / 200 lbs |
| position: | center |
| shoots: | left |

Photo courtesy of the Los Angeles Kings

Mike Krushelnyski began to play organized hockey for the fun of it at the age of 11. Seven years later, while playing with the junior Montreal Canadiens, Krushelnyski was selected by the Boston Bruins as an underage junior in the 1979 NHL Entry Draft. He was picked in the sixth round, 120th overall. Krushelnyski played one more season of junior hockey before being assigned to the minors for seasoning. During the 1981-82 season, he made his NHL debut when the Bruins called him up for a few games. The following year, he won a regular starting position with Boston. In his rookie season, he was second best among rookies in the plus/minus department with a plus 38, and fifth in scoring with 65 points. He also led all rookies in scoring during the playoffs with 14 points in 17 games.

In the summer of 1984, Krushelnyski was traded by the Bruins to the Stanley Cup champions, the Edmonton Oilers. The move to a winning team did wonders for Krushelnyski; in his first year there, he responded with a career-high 43 goals and 45 assists. He added 13 points in the playoffs as the Oilers repeated as Cup champions. Krushelnyski won two more Stanley Cups with Edmonton before he was sent to Los Angeles on August 8, 1988, in a blockbuster trade that included Wayne Gretzky. Krushelnyski barely had time to settle in Los Angeles; in November of 1990, he was traded to the Toronto Maple Leafs.

Although a natural center, Krushelnyski played effectively at the left wing position. A deceptive player with quick acceleration, long reach, and good puck sense, Mike Krushelnyski established himself as a solid all-purpose player over the years.

## RECORD

| year | team | league | regular season | | | | | playoffs | | | | |
|------|------|--------|----|----|----|-----|-----|----|----|----|-----|-----|
|      |      |        | GP | G | A | PTS | PIM | GP | G | A | PTS | PIM |
| 1980-81 | Springfield | AHL | 80 | 25 | 28 | 53 | 47 | 7 | 1 | 1 | 2 | 29 |
| 1981-82 | Boston | NHL | 17 | 3 | 3 | 6 | 2 | 1 | 0 | 0 | 0 | 2 |
|  | Erie | AHL | 62 | 31 | 52 | 83 | 44 |  |  |  |  |  |
| 1982-83 | Boston | NHL | 79 | 23 | 42 | 65 | 43 | 17 | 8 | 6 | 14 | 12 |
| 1983-84 | Boston | NHL | 66 | 25 | 20 | 45 | 55 | 2 | 0 | 0 | 0 | 0 |
| 1984-85* | Edmonton | NHL | 80 | 43 | 45 | 88 | 60 | 18 | 5 | 8 | 13 | 22 |
| 1985-86 | Edmonton | NHL | 54 | 16 | 24 | 40 | 22 | 10 | 4 | 5 | 9 | 16 |
| 1986-87* | Edmonton | NHL | 80 | 16 | 35 | 51 | 67 | 21 | 3 | 4 | 7 | 18 |
| 1987-88* | Edmonton | NHL | 76 | 20 | 27 | 47 | 64 | 19 | 4 | 6 | 10 | 12 |
| 1988-89 | Los Angeles | NHL | 78 | 26 | 36 | 62 | 110 | 11 | 1 | 4 | 5 | 4 |
| 1989-90 | Los Angeles | NHL | 63 | 16 | 25 | 41 | 50 | 10 | 1 | 3 | 4 | 12 |
| 1990-91 | Los Angeles | NHL | 15 | 1 | 5 | 6 | 10 |  |  |  |  |  |
|  | Toronto | NHL | 59 | 17 | 22 | 39 | 48 |  |  |  |  |  |

# KRYSCHUK, MIKE

sport:          hockey
born:           Cooks Creek, Manitoba
                December 26, 1910
height:         1.65 m / 5'5"
weight:         62.5 kg / 138 lbs

Growing up, Mike Kryschuk was an avid athlete, playing baseball in the summer and hockey in winter. In 1930, he decided to try his hand at coaching hockey and immediately became attached to the job. In the next five years, he coached East Kildonan teams at the midget and juvenile levels. Five players from Kryschuk's 1934-35 juvenile team - Pete Langelle, Alf Pike, Terry Reardon, Walter Stanowski, and John McCreedy - went on to play professional hockey, and Dick Kowcinak won the World title in 1939. Kryschuk moved to Alberta in the summer of 1935, where he became playing coach of the McLeod Antics. The club won the Foothills intermediate championship that season. The following year, he coached the Bellevue Bulldogs of the Crows Nest League in Alberta.

Kryschuk returned to Manitoba, and assumed the coaching duties of the St. Boniface Seals junior hockey club for the 1937-38 season. The team played well, advancing to the Memorial Cup. In the final game, played at the Toronto Maple Leaf Gardens, Kryschuk's Seals won the Canadian title by defeating the Oshawa Generals 7-1. The game was played in front of 15,617 fans, the largest crowd ever to witness a hockey game in Canada. The Seals were honoured that year as the outstanding sports club in all of Canada.

Mike Kryschuk returned to Alberta to coach the Coleman Canadians of the Alberta Big Seven League. The next season, he was once again coaching in Winnipeg. His Elmwood Maple Leafs lost out in the final of the Manitoba junior championship. That same year, he was the associate coach of the Treherne Indians which won the Manitoba intermediate title. In 1941, Kryschuk coached the Canadian Ukrainian Athletic Club Blues junior hockey team.

Mike Kryschuk enlisted in the army in 1942. He was the playing coach of the Royal Canadian Signals of the Eastern Canada Military League while stationed in Kingston. After deployment to England, Kryschuk played and coached the RCCS Signals, which were competing in the Military League. The team placed second to Conn Smythe's Battery in 1943. Upon returning to Manitoba, Kryschuk coached the Winnipeg Monarchs to an undefeated season which culminated with the 1948 Manitoba midget championship. Mike Kryschuk retired from coaching after that season.

ALL-STAR SELECTIONS

1938    coach   MHL Jr  (North Division)
1940    coach   MHL Jr  (North Division)

INDUCTIONS

1985    Manitoba Hockey Players Foundation Hall of Fame

# KUCHARCHUK-ANDRUCHIW, JULIA

sport:      volleyball
nee:        Kucharchuk, Julia
born:       Horsham, England
            September 8, 1950
height:     1.73 m / 5'8"
weight:     66 kg  / 145 lbs

Julia Kucharchuk began playing volleyball for the Ukrainian Youth Association (SUM) club of Toronto in 1965. She led the club to two second-place finishes at the national junior championships, and a third at a national championship. She also led the club to seven consecutive Association of Ukrainian Sport Clubs of North America (USCAK) inter-club championships, and was named the tournament's outstanding female competitor on six occasions. In addition, over a number of years Kucharchuk coached men's and women's volleyball teams at SUM. In 1976, after 11 years, she left the association's volleyball program.

During those eleven years, Kucharchuk did not limit herself to competing and coaching with SUM. In 1967, she represented Ontario at the Canada Games winning a gold medal. In the years 1971-74, she was a member of Canada's national team. With the Canadian squad, she competed at the 1971 Pan American Games in Colombia and at the 1973 World

Championships in Uruguay. The team also toured Japan, China and North America. Between the years 1968-73, Kucharchuk competed for the University of Toronto. The team was virtually undefeated, winning five consecutive Ontario-Quebec University Athletic Association championships with Kucharchuk's gaining numerous all-star berths.

In 1975, Julia Kucharchuk-Andruchiw began coaching women's varsity volleyball at the University of Toronto. She guided the team for 13 seasons. Her most successful year was 1985, when the club placed second at the Ontario University championships. In 1979, Kucharchuk-Andruchiw took time out to coach Ontario's team to a fourth place finish at the Canada Games.

## RECORD

competitive

| year | competition | team | placing |
|------|-------------|------|---------|
| 1967 | Canada Games | Ontario | 1 |
| 1968 | Canadian Junior Championships | Ukrainian Youth SUM | 2 |
| 1969 | Canadian Junior Championships | Ukrainian Youth SUM | 2 |
| 1970 | Canadian Championships | Ukrainian Youth SUM | 3 |
| 1971 | Pan American Games | Canada | 5 |
| 1973 | World Championships | Canada | |
| 1978 | Canadian Championships | Metro Globals | 2 |

coaching

| year | competition | team | placing |
|------|-------------|------|---------|
| 1979 | Canada Games | Ontario | 4 |
| 1985 | OUAA Championships | University of Toronto | 2 |
| 1986 | OUAA Championships | University of Toronto | 3 |
| 1987 | OUAA Championships | University of Toronto | 4 |

# KULKA, GLENN

| | |
|---|---|
| sport: | football, professional wrestling |
| born: | Edmonton, Alberta |
| | March 3, 1964 |
| height: | 1.91 m / 6'3" |
| weight: | 113.5 kg / 250 lbs |
| position: | defensive end |

Glenn Kulka was signed as a free agent by the Edmonton Eskimos in 1986, after having played collegiate football with Bakersfield College. Injuries prevented Kulka from playing with the Eskimos, and after he sat out 11 games, the team released him. Kulka was acquired by the Montreal Alouettes and he finished the season with them. When the club folded in June of 1987, Kulka was selected by Saskatchewan in the Alouettes Dispersal Draft and was promptly traded to the Toronto Argonauts.

During the 1987 season, Kulka was credited with ten quarterback sacks, three of which occurred in one game. He also scooped up two fumbles. The following year, the hard-hitting and highly energized Kulka recorded eleven quarterback sacks, knocked down two passes, and collected two fumbles. For his efforts, he was named to the All-Eastern All-Star team. Prior to the start of the 1990 season, Kulka signed as a free agent with Ottawa Rough Riders.

Glen Kulka also wrestled professionally and played hockey for the Medicine Hat Tigers.

### ALL-STAR SELECTIONS

| | | | |
|---|---|---|---|
| 1988 | defensive end | CFL | All-Eastern |

# KURYLUK, MERVIN

| | |
|---|---|
| sport: | hockey |
| born: | Yorkton, Saskatchewan |
| | August 10, 1937 |
| height: | 1.80 m / 5'11" |
| weight: | 84 kg / 185 lbs |
| position: | left wing |
| shoots: | left |

A journeyman left winger, Mervin Kuryluk played for about ten years in the minor pro ranks. He scored 95 goals and added 125 assists while playing four seasons in the EPHL. Those numbers made him the sixth-highest all-time goal scorer in league history, and eighth in the assist department. Kuryluk's one brief appearance in the NHL occurred during the 1962 Stanley Cup playoffs.

## RECORD

| year | team | league | regular season | | | | | playoffs | | | | |
|---|---|---|---|---|---|---|---|---|---|---|---|---|
| | | | GP | G | A | PTS | PIM | GP | G | A | PTS | PIM |
| 1956-57 | Calgary | WHL | 4 | 1 | 0 | 1 | 0 | 3 | 0 | 1 | 1 | 2 |
| 1957-58 | Calgary | WHL | 59 | 12 | 16 | 28 | 44 | 14 | 1 | 3 | 4 | 10 |
| 1958-59 | Saskatoon | WHL | 59 | 15 | 33 | 48 | 34 | | | | | |
| 1959-60 | Calgary | WHL | 22 | 5 | 9 | 14 | 16 | | | | | |
| | Sault Ste. Marie | EPHL | 45 | 15 | 26 | 41 | 40 | | | | | |
| 1960-61 | Sault Ste. Marie | EPHL | 69 | 22 | 20 | 42 | 84 | 12 | 4 | 7 | 11 | 13 |
| 1961-62 | Sault Ste. Marie | EPHL | 65 | 36 | 26 | 62 | 130 | | | | | |
| | Chicago | NHL | | | | | | 2 | 0 | 0 | 0 | 0 |
| 1962-63 | St. Louis | EPHL | 61 | 22 | 53 | 75 | 60 | | | | | |
| 1963-64 | Buffalo | AHL | 72 | 14 | 25 | 39 | 45 | | | | | |
| 1964-65 | St. Louis | CHL | 58 | 9 | 31 | 40 | 66 | | | | | |
| | Los Angeles | WHL | 14 | 0 | 1 | 1 | 8 | | | | | |
| | Buffalo | AHL | 1 | 1 | 0 | 1 | 0 | | | | | |

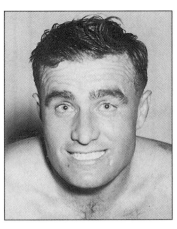

# KUSYJ, GEORGE

| | |
|---|---|
| sport: | wrestling |
| given name: | Klymach, Yuri |
| born: | Pisky, Ukraine |
| | March 29, 1913 |
| height: | 1.80 m / 5'11" |
| weight: | 77-91 kg / 170-200 lbs |

In Ukraine, George Kusyj was an outstanding all-round athlete. He competed in soccer, track and field, weight lifting and wrestling. He also worked as a sports director in Stanislaw. World War II interrupted his sports career. During the war, he spent time in a Soviet concentration camp and for three years worked in a forced labour camp in Germany. After hostilities ceased, Kusyj wound up in a displaced persons camp. Immediately, he began training with the Berkut Sports Club and was soon competing in weight lifting and wrestling. In 1947, and again the following year, Kusyj won the Southern Germany wrestling title.

Kusyj immigrated to Canada in 1948. He settled in St. Catharines where he joined the local YMCA. Kusyj not only wrestled out of the club, but he spent much time coaching younger club members. Although Kusyj won a number of Canadian titles, the disappointments of what could have happened remained. In 1956, he won the Olympic trials. His Olympic dream was shattered, though, when the selection committee overlooked him, citing lack of funds. He did manage to make it to the 1954 Commonwealth Games. The day he arrived, disaster struck. In a friendly warmup match, he severely strained ligaments in his right arm. As a result, he was unable to compete.

## RECORD

| year | competition | event | placing |
|---|---|---|---|
| 1949 | Canadian Championships | 191 lbs | 2 |
| 1951 | Canadian Championships | 174 lbs | 1 |
| 1952 | Olympic Trials | 174 lbs | 3 |
| 1953 | Canadian Championships | 191 lbs | 1 |
| 1954 | Commonwealth Game Trials | | 1 |
| | Commonwealth Games | | dnc |
| 1956 | Canadian Championships | 174 lbs | 1 |
| 1957 | Canadian Championships | 191 lbs | 3 |

# KUZYK, KEN

"Kooz"

| | |
|---|---|
| sport: | hockey |
| given name: | Kuzyk, Kenneth Michael |
| born: | Toronto, Ontario |
| | August 11, 1953 |
| height: | 1.85 m / 6'1" |
| weight: | 88.5 kg / 195 lbs |
| position: | right wing |
| shoots: | right |

Ken Kuzyk combined hockey with an education when he enrolled at Boston University in 1972 on a hockey scholarship. He made his professional debut during the 1976-77 season with the Salt Lake Golden Eagles of the CHL. In the same season, he was called up by the Cleveland Barons and made his NHL debut with the team. The following year, Kuzyk played for four teams. When the Barons merged with the Minnesota North Stars after the 1978-79 season, Kuzyk did not make the team, was put on the Stars' reserve list, and was assigned to the minors. In the fall of 1981, Kuzyk joined the Krefeld Ice Hockey Club in West Germany. After returning to North America, Kuzyk played briefly with the farm team of the New York Rangers at Tulsa before retiring to coach university hockey.

## AWARDS

1977        Rookie of the Year  -  CHL

## ALL-STAR SELECTIONS

1976-77      right wing      CHL      Second Team

## RECORD

| year | team | league | regular season | | | | | playoffs | | | | |
|---|---|---|---|---|---|---|---|---|---|---|---|---|
| | | | GP | G | A | PTS | PIM | GP | G | A | PTS | PIM |
| 1976-77 | Cleveland | NHL | 13 | 0 | 5 | 5 | 2 | | | | | |
| | Salt Lake City | CHL | 62 | 33 | 27 | 60 | 10 | | | | | |
| 1977-78 | Cleveland | NHL | 28 | 5 | 4 | 9 | 6 | | | | | |
| | Phoenix | CHL | 17 | 10 | 11 | 21 | 2 | | | | | |
| | Salt Lake City | CHL | 14 | 4 | 8 | 12 | 0 | 6 | 1 | 0 | 1 | 0 |

| year | team | league | regular season | | | | | playoffs | | | | |
| --- | --- | --- | --- | --- | --- | --- | --- | --- | --- | --- | --- | --- |
| | | | GP | G | A | PTS | PIM | GP | G | A | PTS | PIM |
| 1977-78 | Binghamton | AHL | 14 | 1 | 1 | 2 | 2 | | | | | |
| 1978-79 | Tulsa | CHL | 74 | 31 | 32 | 63 | 22 | | | | | |
| 1979-80 | Oklahoma City | CHL | 41 | 10 | 12 | 22 | 11 | | | | | |
| | Cincinnati | CHL | 17 | 3 | 7 | 10 | 0 | | | | | |

# KWASNYCIA, DON

| | |
| --- | --- |
| sport: | shooting |
| given name: | Kwasnycia, Bohdan |
| born: | Toronto, Ontario |
| | April 30, 1952 |
| height: | 1.93 m / 6'4" |
| weight: | 106 kg / 233 lbs |

*Photo courtesy of the Athlete Information Bureau*

While in his teens, Don Kwasnycia worked on a trap and skeet shooting range which was located near his home. There he had the opportunity of seeing some of Canada's finest shooters in action, to witness shooting demonstrations, and to discuss the sport with his co-workers and club members. One day, Kwasnycia tried skeet shooting and did fairly well. His co-workers believed that Kwasnycia had a natural gift for the sport. His size allowed him to handle the gun with ease. His eye-hand coordination and concentration allowed him to track and shoot the targets, which at times travel at an excess of 160 km/h (100 mph).

Within months of his initiation into skeet shooting, Kwasnycia shot his first perfect round. He was soon competing at the national level. Kwasnycia enjoyed much success as a trap shooter in Canada. He won the national title on a number of occasions and established four individual Canadian records. He also represented Canada at World Championships and the Pan American, Commonwealth, and Olympic Games. His results in international competition were somewhat disappointing. Sometimes he succumbed to pressure, and as a result, his shooting was inconsistent. Nevertheless, he succeeded in winning team medals at the Pan American and Commonwealth Games.

# RECORD

| year | competition | event | placing | result | |
|------|-------------|-------|---------|--------|---|
| 1976 | Olympic Trials | skeet | 13 | 359/600 | |
| 1977 | Canadian Championships | skeet | 1 | 385/400 | nr |
| | European Grand Prix | skeet | 7 | 192/200 | |
| | World Championships | skeet | | 183/200 | |
| 1978 | Commonwealth Games | skeet | 4 | 189/200 | |
| | Canadian Championships | skeet | 1 | 378/400 | |
| | World Championships | skeet | | 179/200 | |
| 1979 | Pan American Games | skeet | 7 | 189/200 | |
| | | team skeet | 4 | | |
| | Canadian Championships | skeet | 5 | 350/400 | |
| | U.S. Int'l Championships | skeet | 2 | 394/400 | nr |
| 1980 | Canadian Championships | skeet | 1 | 291/300 | |
| | Olympic Trials | skeet | 3 | 192/200 | |
| | Grand Prix Von Lippe | skeet | 3 | 192/200 | |
| | | team skeet | 1 | 434 | nr |
| 1981 | Canadian Championships | skeet | 1 | 293/300 | nr |
| | World Championships | skeet | 71 | 177 | |
| | | team skeet | 15 | 535 | |
| 1982 | Canadian Championships | skeet | 3 | 255/300 | |
| | World Championships | skeet | 62 tie | 140/150 | |
| 1985 | Canadian Championships | skeet | 1 | 294/300 | nr |
| | World Championships | skeet | 38 | 188 | |
| | | team skeet | 14 | 419 | |
| 1986 | Commonwealth Games Trials | skeet | 1 | 291/300 | |
| | Commonwealth Games | skeet | 9 | 190/200 | |
| | | team skeet | 2 | 193 | |
| 1987 | Pan American Games | skeet | 10 | | |
| | | team skeet | 3 | | |
| 1988 | Olympic Games | skeet | 25 tie | 144/150 | |
| 1989 | Canadian Championships | skeet | 2 ** | 292/300 | |

nr     Canadian record

**     top Canadian

# LAKUSIAK, GENE

sport:          football
given name:     Lakusiak, Eugene Gregory
born:           Winnipeg, Manitoba
                June 1, 1942
height:         1.85 m / 6'1"
weight:         95.5 kg / 210 lbs
position:       defensive back

*Card reproduced courtesy of O-Pee-Chee Co.*

Gene Lakusiak played collegiate football at the University of Tulsa. He returned to Canada to play with the Ottawa Rough Riders of the CFL in 1967. Prior to the start of the 1968 season, Lakusiak was traded to the Winnipeg Blue Bombers. He was with the club until his retirement in 1974. Lakusiak arrived in Winnipeg as a running back. In his first year with the team, he averaged 4.6 yards per carry. With time, Lakusiak's role changed and he became a defensive specialist. In 1972, and once again in 1973, he was named to the CFL All-Western All-Star team at the defensive back position. In the latter year, he was Winnipeg's nominee for the Schenley Most Outstanding Canadian Award. Lakusiak was also an effective kicker. In 1973, he averaged 56.4 yards on kickoffs.

## AWARDS

1973        Manitoba Ukrainian Sportsman of the Year

## ALL-STAR SELECTIONS

1972        defensive back     CFL     All-Western
1973        defensive back     CFL     All-Western

# LAKUSTA, KEN

| | |
|---|---|
| sport: | boxing |
| born: | Two Hills, Alberta |
| | . . . |
| height: | 1.85 m / 6'1" |
| weight: | 97.5 kg / 215 lbs |

Ken Lakusta was attracted to boxing by an advertisement for a "Tough Guy" tournament offering $2,500 in prize money. Even though he had no boxing experience, Lakusta entered the event. The 24-year-old was of the opinion that his physical fitness, and experience acquired in gaining a black belt in karate and the world number one ranking in kick boxing (heavyweight division) would keep him in contention. Lakusta not only won the tournament but thus embarked on a professional boxing career.

A journeyman boxer, Ken Lakusta held the Canadian heavyweight boxing title on two occasions. In 1986, he defeated Conroy Nelson in 12 rounds to win the vacant title, only to lose it six months later to Olympian Willie deWit. In 1989, after coming out of a short-lived retirement, Lakusta was once again matched in a title bout. He lost in a controversial narrow decision to Tony Morrison. The decision was successfully appealed by Lakusta's management with the Canadian Professional Boxing Federation, and a rematch was ordered. Lakusta won the rematch, and the Canadian title, with a controversial, although, unanimous decision.

Ken Lakusta challenged for the Commonwealth title in 1983, but was knocked out in the tenth round by Trevor Berbick. One of Lakusta's most memorable fights was against George "Punchin' Preacher" Foreman, whom he wobbled with a powerful overhand right. Unfortunately, Lakusta could not exploit the situation to his advantage and was himself sent down to the canvas seconds later.

## RECORD

| year | opponent | result | round |
|---|---|---|---|
| 1979 | Frank Terry | KO | 1 |
| 1980 | Ron Rousselle | KO by | 2 |
| | Ron Harry | KO | 1 |

| year | opponent | result | round | |
|------|----------|--------|-------|---|
| 1980 | Johnny Jackson | W | 4 | |
| | Craig Henderson | W | 4 | |
| | Jim Flair | TKO | 1 | |
| | Mike Bennet | KO | 1 | |
| | Craig Henderson | TKO | 4 | |
| | Mike Gans | L | 6 | |
| 1981 | Jimmy Anthony | TKO | 2 | |
| | Gaston Berube | TKO | 3 | |
| | Jerry Hunter | W | 6 | |
| | Roddy MacDonald | KO by | 6 | |
| | Ron Rousselle | KO | 1 | |
| 1982 | Leroy James | W | 10 | |
| 1983 | Harvey Steichan | TKO | 9 | |
| | Mark Lee | L | 10 | |
| | Trevor Berbick | KO by | 10 | + |
| 1984 | Stefan Tangstadt | L | 8 | |
| | Frank Bruno | KO by | 2 | |
| 1985 | Frank Askew | TKO | 2 | |
| | Mark Wills | KO by | 4 | |
| 1986 | Conroy Nelson | W | 12 | ++ |
| | Willie deWit | L | 12 | ++ |
| 1989 | Tony Morrison | L | 12 | ++ |
| 1990 | Tony Morrison | W | 12 | ++ |
| | George Foreman | KO by | 3 | |

+    Canadian and Commonwealth Professional Championship

++   Canadian Professional Championship

# LANDY, FRANK

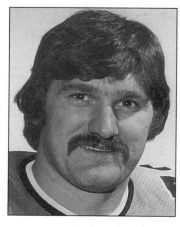

| | |
|---|---|
| sport: | football |
| born: | Fort William |
| | (now Thunder Bay) |
| | May 24, 1950 |
| height: | 1.91 m / 6'3" |
| weight: | 106.5 kg / 235 lbs |
| position: | defensive tackle |

Frank Landy was introduced to the game of football by his father Pete Landy (Landiak), who for a number of years played the game for the Lakehead Ukrainian Athletic Club Ukes. Frank Landy started in organized football with the Fort William minor football league. While in high school, he excelled at the game and was offered an athletic scholarship by North Dakota University. Landy accepted the offer, and played at the defensive tackle position on the football team in the years 1969-72. In 1971, he co-captained the team, was its MVP, and was honoured as the NCAA All Conference tackle. While at North Dakota University, Landy majored in physical education.

After completing his collegiate career, Landy signed with the Saskatchewan Roughriders. While playing for the team, Landy broke his ankle, which limited his mobility somewhat. The Roughies then traded him to the British Columbia Lions. He played some of his best football on the coast, and was named to the CFL All-Western All-Star team in 1977. Subsequently, Landy played for the Toronto Argonauts. During his football career, Landy was often referred to as the "comic laureate of the locker room." His humour eased tension in the dressing room before games or at halftime.

Frank Landy returned to Vancouver after retiring from the game, and became the hospitality manager at BC Place Stadium.

## INDUCTIONS

| | |
|---|---|
| 1986 | Northwestern Ontario Sports Hall of Fame |

## ALL-STAR SELECTIONS

| | | | |
|---|---|---|---|
| 1977 | defensive tackle | CFL | All-Western |

# LANGELLE, PETE

"Snake Hips"

| | |
|---|---|
| sport: | hockey |
| given name: | Landiak, Peter |
| born: | Winnipeg, Manitoba |
| | November 4, 1917 |
| height: | 1.78 m / 5'10" |
| weight: | 77 kg / 170 lbs |
| position: | center |
| shoots: | left |

Pete Landiak began his hockey career with the East Kildonan juvenile team which was coached by Mike Kryschuk. Some years later, while playing junior hockey, he was placed on a line with two French-Canadians. As a result, he changed his name to Langelle. In 1937, he was a member of the Canadian Junior Championship Winnipeg Monarchs team. During his junior days, Langelle was described as a "flashy skater and a tricky stick handler." Toronto Maple Leafs' general manager Conn Smythe called Langelle "one of the greatest prospects" after the center was signed to a contract.

An outstanding professional career did not materialize for Langelle. Perhaps World War II took away those seasons when he may have peaked. Nevertheless, Langelle made a name for himself by scoring the winning goal in the 1942 Stanley Cup final. The series was one of the most outstanding on record. The Leafs lost the first three games before coming back to tie the series at three apiece. In the seventh and deciding game, the score was tied 1-1 when Langelle banged in a rebound behind the Detroit goalie. The initial shot was fired by Johnny McCreedy, a teammate of Langelle's with East Kildonan. The goal and game were the last in the NHL for Langelle. Soon after, he left for the service.

During the war, Langelle served with the RCAF. He was the pilot originally credited with shooting-up the staff car carrying German Field Marshall Erwin Rommel. Later it was determined that the car was that of another German general. When hostilities ceased, Langelle played in the Canadian Services Hockey League in England. Upon returning to Canada, Pete Langelle was assigned to the Leafs' farm team in Pittsburgh where he played for five years.

INDUCTIONS

1985        Manitoba Hockey Hall of Fame

# RECORD

| year | team | league | regular season GP | G | A | PTS | PIM | playoffs GP | G | A | PTS | PIM |
|------|------|--------|----|----|----|-----|-----|----|----|----|-----|-----|
| 1937-38 | Syracuse | AHL | 48 | 4 | 14 | 18 | 8 | 8 | 5 | 4 | 9 | 2 |
| 1938-39 | Toronto | NHL | 2 | 1 | 0 | 1 | 0 | 11 | 1 | 2 | 3 | 2 |
| | Syracuse | AHL | 51 | 10 | 13 | 23 | 8 | | | | | |
| 1939-40 | Toronto | NHL | 39 | 7 | 14 | 21 | 2 | 10 | 0 | 3 | 3 | 0 |
| 1940-41 | Toronto | NHL | 47 | 4 | 15 | 19 | 0 | 7 | 1 | 1 | 2 | 0 |
| 1941-42* | Toronto | NHL | 48 | 10 | 22 | 32 | 9 | 13 | 3 | 3 | 6 | 2 |
| 1946-47 | Pittsburgh | AHL | 64 | 20 | 30 | 50 | 4 | 12 | 4 | 7 | 11 | 2 |
| 1947-48 | Pittsburgh | AHL | 67 | 21 | 37 | 58 | 8 | 2 | 0 | 0 | 0 | 0 |
| 1948-49 | Pittsburgh | AHL | 68 | 10 | 26 | 36 | 13 | | | | | |
| 1949-50 | Pittsburgh | AHL | 47 | 8 | 15 | 23 | 7 | | | | | |
| 1950-51 | Pittsburgh | AHL | 47 | 4 | 10 | 14 | 0 | 8 | 1 | 3 | 4 | 2 |
| 1951-52* | St. John | MMHL | 72 | 16 | 18 | 34 | 35 | 15 | 1 | 3 | 4 | 2 |

# LASHUK, MIKE

sport: football
born: Edmonton, Alberta
December 9, 1938
height: 1.85 m / 6'1"
weight: 90.5 kg / 200 lbs
position: corner linebacker, full back

*Photo courtesy of the Canadian Football Hall of Fame and Museum*

In his teens, Mike Lashuk was an outstanding all-round athlete. He won the Edmonton high school shot put title, played hockey with the Jr. "A" Edmonton Oil Kings, and played football in the Alberta Junior Football League. At age 18, with two years of junior eligibility remaining, Lashuk made the roster of the Edmonton Eskimos. When the season ended, he was named the winner of the Dr. Beattie Martin Trophy, awarded annually to the rookie of the year in the Western Conference.

Lashuk played with the Eskimos for seven seasons. He was a muscular fullback and corner linebacker whose career was plagued by injuries. Nevertheless, in 1961, and once again in 1962, Lashuk was the Eskimos' nominee for the Schenley Most Outstanding Canadian Award. In the spring of 1964, Lashuk informed the Eskimos that he was no longer interested in playing and retired from the game.

While playing for the Eskimos, Lashuk attended the University of Alberta and also played varsity football. Upon graduation, he embarked on a teaching career. After retiring from football, he enrolled at Southern Illinois University where he obtained a Master of Education degree. Subsequently, he joined the faculty of the University of Calgary where he taught and coached the varsity football team. In 1975, Mike Lashuk led the University of Calgary Dinosaurs to the College Bowl final.

## AWARDS

1957      Dr. Beattie Martin Trophy - Outstanding Canadian Rookie in the Western Division

## RECORD

| scoring | | | regular season | | | playoffs | | | Grey Cup game | | |
|---------|------|--------|----|----|-----|----|----|-----|----|----|-----|
| year | team | league | GP | TD | PTS | GP | TD | PTS | GP | TD | PTS |
| 1957 | Edmonton | WRFU | ... | 2 | 10 | 0 | 0 | 0 | | | |
| 1958 | Edmonton | CFL | ... | | | 5 | 0 | 0 | | | |
| 1959 | Edmonton | CFL | ... | | | 4 | 0 | 0 | | | |
| 1960 | Edmonton | CFL | ... | | | | | | 1 | 0 | 0 |
| 1961 | Edmonton | CFL | ... | | | | | | | | |
| 1962 | Edmonton | CFL | ... | | | | | | | | |
| 1963 | Edmonton | CFL | ... | | | | | | | | |

# LESCHYSHYN, CURTIS

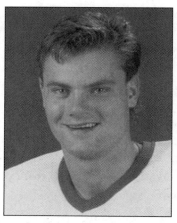

| | |
|---|---|
| sport: | hockey |
| born: | Thompson, Manitoba |
| | September 21, 1969 |
| height: | 1.85 m / 6'1" |
| weight: | 93 kg / 205 lbs |
| position: | defense |
| shoots: | left |

*Photo courtesy of the Quebec Nordiques*

After a successful junior career with the Saskatoon Blades, Curtis Leschyshyn was selected by the Quebec Nordiques in the first round, third overall, of the 1988 NHL Entry Draft. That fall, he earned a starting position with Quebec. During his rookie season, Leschyshyn was one of the few bright spots on a team that had a dismal record. The following year, Leschyshyn had a poor start. While Quebec faltered and missed the playoffs, Leschyshyn finished the season strongly. As a result, he was named to Canada's team for the 1990 World Championship.

In February of 1990, Leschyshyn suffered a serious knee injury which required surgery. He missed the remainder of the season. A strong defensive defenseman, Leschyshyn developed a reputation in the NHL for being tough in front of his team's net.

## RECORD

| year | team | league | regular season | | | | | playoffs | | | | |
|---|---|---|---|---|---|---|---|---|---|---|---|---|
| | | | GP | G | A | PTS | PIM | GP | G | A | PTS | PIM |
| 1988-89 | Quebec | NHL | 71 | 4 | 9 | 13 | 71 | | | | | |
| 1989-90 | Quebec | NHL | 68 | 2 | 6 | 8 | 44 | | | | | |
| 1990-91 | Quebec | NHL | 55 | 3 | 7 | 10 | 49 | | | | | |

international

| year | team | competition | GP | G | A | PTS | PIM | Place |
|---|---|---|---|---|---|---|---|---|
| 1990 | Canada | World Championship | 9 | 0 | 0 | 0 | 4 | 4 |

# LESUK, BILL

sport:          hockey
given name:     Lesuk, William Anton
born:           Moose Jaw, Saskatchewan
                November 1, 1946
height:         1.75 m / 5'9"
weight:         85 kg  / 187 lbs
position:       left wing
shoots:         left

*Card reproduced courtesy of O-Pee-Chee Co.*

In the years 1964-67, Bill Lesuk played junior hockey for the Weyburn Red Wings. In February 1966, the Detroit Red Wings traded his NHL rights to the Boston Bruins. Lesuk spent the 1967-68 season, his first in professional hockey, skating for the Oklahoma Blazers of the CHL, a Boston farm team. The following two seasons, Lesuk continued to play in the minor leagues, making only brief appearances with the parent club. During the 1970 Stanley Cup playoffs, which the Bruins won, Lesuk appeared in two games. That summer, he was selected by the Philadelphia Flyers in an intra-league draft.

The Flyers employed Lesuk as a forechecker; his job was to keep opposing players from scoring. This defensive assignment gave Lesuk an opportunity to play regularly in the NHL. Foreckecking often created good scoring opportunities, and Lesuk responded by recording a career-high 19 goals in his first year with the Flyers. In January of 1972, the Flyers traded Lesuk to the Los Angeles Kings. Subsequently, the Kings sold him to the Washington Capitals. Prior to the start of the 1975-76 season, Lesuk jumped to the rival WHA when he signed with the Winnipeg Jets. Lesuk played with the Jets for five years. On three occasions, the club won the league championship Avco Cup. In 1979, the WHA folded and the Winnipeg Jets and Bill Lesuk were absorbed by the NHL. At the end of Winnipeg's inaugural season in the NHL, he retired as an active player.

The Winnipeg Jets respected Bill Lesuk's hockey knowledge and retained him within their organization in a scouting capacity. Later, he was promoted to director of scouting, a position that he continued to hold through the end of 1990-91 season.

| year | team | league | regular season | | | | | playoffs | | | | |
|---|---|---|---|---|---|---|---|---|---|---|---|---|
| | | | GP | G | A | PTS | PIM | GP | G | A | PTS | PIM |
| 1967-68 | Oklahoma City | CPHL | 67 | 14 | 10 | 24 | 53 | | | | | |
| 1968-69 | Boston | NHL | 5 | 0 | 1 | 1 | 0 | 1 | 0 | 0 | 0 | 0 |
| | Oklahoma City | CHL | 64 | 17 | 30 | 47 | 46 | 12 | 0 | 4 | 4 | 8 |
| 1969-70* | Boston | NHL | 3 | 0 | 0 | 0 | 0 | 2 | 0 | 0 | 0 | 0 |
| | Hershey | AHL | 70 | 20 | 20 | 40 | 82 | 7 | 5 | 4 | 9 | 10 |
| 1970-71 | Philadelphia | NHL | 78 | 17 | 19 | 36 | 81 | 4 | 1 | 0 | 1 | 8 |
| 1971-72 | Philadelphia | NHL | 45 | 7 | 6 | 13 | 31 | | | | | |
| | Los Angeles | NHL | 27 | 4 | 10 | 14 | 14 | | | | | |
| 1972-73 | Los Angeles | NHL | 67 | 6 | 14 | 20 | 90 | | | | | |
| 1973-74 | Los Angeles | NHL | 35 | 2 | 1 | 3 | 32 | 2 | 0 | 0 | 0 | 4 |
| 1974-75 | Washington | NHL | 79 | 8 | 11 | 19 | 77 | | | | | |
| 1975-76* | Winnipeg | WHA | 81 | 15 | 21 | 36 | 92 | 13 | 2 | 2 | 4 | 8 |
| 1976-77 | Winnipeg | WHA | 78 | 14 | 27 | 41 | 85 | 18 | 2 | 1 | 3 | 22 |
| 1977-78* | Winnipeg | WHA | 80 | 9 | 18 | 27 | 48 | 9 | 2 | 5 | 7 | 12 |
| 1978-79* | Winnipeg | WHA | 79 | 17 | 15 | 32 | 44 | 10 | 1 | 3 | 4 | 6 |
| 1979-80 | Winnipeg | NHL | 49 | 0 | 1 | 1 | 43 | | | | | |

# LESWICK, JACK

| | |
|---|---|
| sport: | hockey |
| born: | Saskatoon, Saskatchewan |
| | January 1, 1910 |
| died: | Winnipeg, Manitoba |
| | July ?, 1934 |
| height: | 1.68 m / 5'6" |
| weight: | 70 kg / 155 lbs |
| position: | forward |
| shoots: | right |

Jack Leswick began his hockey career with the Drumheller Miners. His first professional contract was with the Duluth Hornets. Leswick played minor pro hockey for a number of years before breaking into the NHL with the Chicago Black Hawks in 1933. He played in the big league only that one season.

In the summer, Leswick was traded by Chicago to Cleveland of the International League. Two weeks after the trade, Leswick was found dead in the Red River in Winnipeg. Leswick's family believed the cause of death was murder because his body was stripped of valuables. The city police and the provincial coroner, however, ruled that the 24-year-old Leswick drowned accidentally, and that foul play was not involved. Jack Leswick was the older brother of hockey players Peter and Tony Leswick.

RECORD

| year | team | league | regular season | | | | | playoffs | | | | |
|------|------|--------|----|----|----|-----|-----|----|----|----|-----|-----|
|      |      |        | GP | G  | A  | PTS | PIM | GP | G  | A  | PTS | PIM |
| 1929-30 | Duluth | AHA | 9  | 1  | 1  | 2  | 6  | 3 | 0 | 0 | 0 | 4 |
| 1930-31 | Duluth | AHA | 41 | 22 | 9  | 31 | 27 | 4 | 0 | 1 | 1 | 4 |
| 1931-32 | Duluth | AHA | 35 | 9  | 7  | 16 | 36 | 8 | 0 | 5 | 5 | 4 |
| 1932-33 | Wichita | AHA | 41 | 22 | 18 | 40 | 76 |   |   |   |   |   |
| 1933-34 | Chicago | NHL | 47 | 1  | 7  | 8  | 16 |   |   |   |   |   |
|         | Kansas City | AHA | 8 | 1 | 5 | 6 | 14 |   |   |   |   |   |

# LESWICK, PETER

| | |
|---|---|
| sport: | hockey |
| born: | Saskatoon, Saskatchewan |
| | July 12, 1918 |
| height: | 1.68 m / 5'6" |
| weight: | 66 kg / 145 lbs |
| position: | right wing |
| shoots: | right |

During the 1935-36 season, Peter Leswick played his last year of junior hockey for the Saskatoon Wesleys. The club won the Western Canada championship and was the Dominion - Memorial Cup finalist. Leswick turned professional with the New York Americans of the NHL in the fall and was immediately assigned to New Haven of the AHL. That year, he played one game for the Americans. Leswick then went to play for Spokane and Seattle of the Pacific Coast League before heading to the midwest and playing for Kansas and Fort Worth of the American Hockey Association. In the years 1942-44, he served in the armed forces. Leswick started the 1944-45 season with the Boston Bruins but was assigned to Indianapolis, where he played for two seasons.

In the fall of 1946, Leswick was purchased by the Cleveland Barons of the AHL. Leswick fit in well and quickly became a team favourite. A fast and tricky skater, he gained numerous all-star berths and in 1948-49 was the leading Cleveland scorer. In his spare time, Leswick developed an interest in race horses and, with time, he became an owner of a few. Peter Leswick is the brother of hockey players Tony and the late Jack Leswick.

## ALL-STAR SELECTIONS

| 1941-42 | right wing | AHA | First Team |
| 1944-45 | right wing | AHL | Second Team |
| 1945-46 | right wing | AHL | First Team |
| 1946-47 | right wing | AHL | Second Team |
| 1947-48 | right wing | AHL | First Team |
| 1948-49 | right wing | AHL | First Team |
| 1949-50 | right wing | AHL | First Team |

## RECORD

| year | team | league | regular season | | | | | playoffs | | | | |
| | | | GP | G | A | PTS | PIM | GP | G | A | PTS | PIM |
|---|---|---|---|---|---|---|---|---|---|---|---|---|
| 1936-37 | NY Americans | NHL | 1 | 1 | 0 | 1 | 0 | | | | | |
| | New Haven | AHL | 21 | 4 | 3 | 7 | 0 | | | | | |
| 1937-38* | Seattle | PCHL | 42 | 20 | 10 | 30 | 22 | 4 | 0 | 0 | 0 | 2 |
| 1938-39 | Kansas City | AHA | 25 | 12 | 13 | 25 | 10 | | | | | |
| | Spokane | PCHL | 20 | 7 | 3 | 10 | 9 | | | | | |
| 1939-40 | Kansas City | AHA | 45 | 14 | 18 | 32 | 17 | | | | | |
| 1940-41 | Kansas City | AHA | 45 | 14 | 22 | 36 | 16 | 8 | 2 | 4 | 6 | 0 |
| 1941-42 | Fort Worth | AHA | 50 | 35 | 30 | 65 | 17 | 5 | 1 | 4 | 5 | 2 |
| 1944-45 | Boston | NHL | 2 | 0 | 0 | 0 | 0 | | | | | |
| | Indianapolis | AHL | 53 | 29 | 39 | 68 | 12 | 3 | 1 | 0 | 1 | 0 |
| 1945-46 | Indianapolis | AHL | 61 | 29 | 52 | 81 | 10 | 5 | 1 | 1 | 2 | 0 |
| 1946-47 | Cleveland | AHL | 64 | 32 | 41 | 73 | 35 | 4 | 1 | 1 | 2 | 0 |
| 1947-48* | Cleveland | AHL | 59 | 36 | 40 | 76 | 8 | 6 | 2 | 4 | 6 | 2 |
| 1948-49 | Cleveland | AHL | 68 | 44 | 35 | 79 | 10 | 5 | 0 | 2 | 2 | 0 |
| 1949-50 | Cleveland | AHL | 64 | 36 | 50 | 86 | 18 | 9 | 2 | 2 | 4 | 0 |
| 1950-51 | Seattle | PCHL | 49 | 14 | 21 | 35 | 6 | | | | | |
| | Buffalo | AHL | 11 | 6 | 5 | 11 | 0 | | | | | |
| 1951-52 | Halifax | MMHL | 70 | 32 | 36 | 68 | 6 | 9 | 3 | 4 | 7 | 4 |

# LESWICK, TONY

"Tough Tony"

sport:          hockey
born:           Humboldt, Saskatchewan
                March 17, 1923
height:         1.68 m / 5'6"
weight:         72.5 kg / 160 lbs
position:       left wing
shoots:         right

In 1945, the New York Rangers signed Tony Leswick, a versatile hockey player and a one-time Saskatchewan diving champion, to a contract. The scrappy and dynamic Leswick, who had just been demobilized from the Royal Canadian Navy, made an immediate impact on the Rangers. He had a hard and accurate shot which made him the club's scoring leader in just his second year. More importantly, Leswick liked to mix it up and fire up the team. Even though he was small in stature, he feared no one, as a result of his better-than-average boxing skills. "Tough Tony," as he was soon known in New York, was in part instrumental in turning the fortunes of the Rangers around.

Leswick's specialty, though, was shadowing opposing players. Gordie Howe and Rocket Richard could not keep him off their backs. In one game, Richard got two penalties for blowing up at Leswick. When the game ended, Richard charged at Leswick and the two fought it out. The two continued to feud for many years. Once when Leswick had a penalty, he so confused the time keeper that he was let back on to the ice before the penalty expired. A tireless skater, he was also used in short-handed situations.

In 1951, Leswick was traded to the Detroit Red Wings. With this club he won three Stanley Cups, the most memorable in 1954. That year, the final series against Montreal was tied at three games a piece with the seventh and deciding game going into overtime. Leswick scored the winner. After the 1955 Cup final, he was picked up by Chicago, where he played for a year before finishing his NHL career with the Red Wings.

Subsequently, Tony Leswick coached the Edmonton Flyers before going into the hotel business. He came out of retirement in the fall of 1963 to coach Indianapolis, a new entry in the CPHL. Tony Leswick is the brother of hockey players Peter and the late Jack Leswick.

## INDUCTIONS

1989        Saskatoon Sports Hall of Fame

## ALL-STAR SELECTIONS

| 1949-50 | left wing  | NHL | Second Team |
| 1956-57 | right wing | WHL | Second Team (Coast Division) |

## RECORD

| year | team | league | regular season | | | | | playoffs | | | | |
|---|---|---|---|---|---|---|---|---|---|---|---|---|
| | | | GP | G | A | PTS | PIM | GP | G | A | PTS | PIM |
| 1942-43 | Cleveland | AHL | 52 | 14 | 26 | 40 | 43 | | | | | |
| 1945-46 | NY Rangers | NHL | 50 | 15 | 9 | 24 | 26 | | | | | |
| 1946-47 | NY Rangers | NHL | 59 | 27 | 14 | 41 | 51 | | | | | |
| 1947-48 | NY Rangers | NHL | 60 | 24 | 16 | 40 | 76 | 6 | 3 | 2 | 5 | 8 |
| 1948-49 | NY Rangers | NHL | 60 | 13 | 14 | 27 | 70 | | | | | |
| 1949-50 | NY Rangers | NHL | 69 | 19 | 25 | 44 | 85 | 12 | 2 | 4 | 6 | 12 |
| 1950-51 | NY Rangers | NHL | 70 | 15 | 11 | 26 | 112 | | | | | |
| 1951-52* | Detroit | NHL | 70 | 9 | 10 | 19 | 93 | 8 | 3 | 1 | 4 | 22 |
| 1952-53 | Detroit | NHL | 70 | 15 | 12 | 27 | 87 | 6 | 1 | 0 | 1 | 11 |
| 1953-54* | Detroit | NHL | 70 | 6 | 18 | 24 | 90 | 12 | 3 | 1 | 4 | 18 |
| 1954-55* | Detroit | NHL | 70 | 10 | 17 | 27 | 137 | 11 | 1 | 2 | 3 | 20 |
| 1955-56 | Chicago | NHL | 70 | 11 | 11 | 22 | 71 | | | | | |
| 1956-57 | Edmonton | WHL | 60 | 22 | 31 | 53 | 107 | 8 | 2 | 1 | 3 | 6 |
| 1957-58 | Detroit | NHL | 22 | 1 | 2 | 3 | 2 | 4 | 0 | 0 | 0 | 0 |
| | Edmonton | WHL | 42 | 10 | 15 | 25 | 46 | | | | | |
| 1958-59 | Edmonton | WHL | 36 | 3 | 13 | 16 | 27 | | | | | |
| 1959-60* | Vancouver | WHL | 9 | 3 | 6 | 9 | 0 | 11 | 0 | 1 | 1 | 0 |

coaching

| year | team | league | regular season | | | | | playoffs | | | |
|---|---|---|---|---|---|---|---|---|---|---|---|
| | | | G | W | L | T | Standing | G | W | L | T |
| 1958-59 | Edmonton | WHL | 64 | 33 | 28 | 3 | 2 | 3 | 0 | 3 | 0 |
| 1963-64 | Cincinnati | CPHL | 72 | 12 | 53 | 12 | 5 | | | | |

# LEWICKI, DANNY

| | |
|---|---|
| sport: | hockey |
| given name: | Lewicki, Daniel |
| born: | Fort William, Ontario |
| | (now Thunder Bay) |
| | March 12, 1931 |
| height: | 1.75 m / 5'9" |
| weight: | 75 kg / 165 lbs |
| position: | left wing |
| shoots: | left |

*Photo courtesy of the Northwestern Ontario Sports Hall of Fame*

During Danny Lewicki's childhood, the outdoor rinks of Fort William were home in the winter months. Every spare moment he had, he would play hockey. On weekends, he would be out for eight to ten hours a day. "I can still remember crying all the way home, it was so cold. But I went back the next day."[24] Lewicki began to play organized hockey a few years later, at age 11, with the Fort William East End's. He then played for the Fort William Columbus Club. In the spring of 1948, Lewicki was picked up as a replacement by the Port Arthur Bruins who were in the race for the Memorial Cup. Lewicki led the Bruins in scoring as they won the Cup.

One minute after Lewicki turned 16, the NHL's required age for negotiations, he was claimed by the Providence Reds of the AHL. It was a blow to the Toronto Maple Leafs, who had helped in his development through one of their scouts. Leafs' managing director Conn Smythe wanted Lewicki badly and swung a deal for him. Although the terms of the deal were not released, at the time it was the second largest cash deal negotiated by the Leafs. Lewicki was then assigned to the junior Marlboros. Instead, he went to play for Stratford. In 1949-50, he finally joined the Marlies. When the team was eliminated from post-season play, he was picked up by the senior Toronto Marlboros who needed reinforcements in their bid for the Allan Cup. Lewicki was the top Marlboro scorer as the club won the Cup.

In the fall of 1950, Lewicki made his NHL debut. He was well on his way to a 20-goal season, and was a strong candidate for the Calder Trophy, when tragedy struck. At an open practice, a school boy threw a paper clip on the ice. Lewicki's skate caught it, he went down with a knee injury, and missed twelve games. He came back to help the Leafs win the Stanley Cup, establishing a record which still stands; he is the first and only hockey player to have won the Memorial Cup, the Allan Cup, and the Stanley Cup while still of junior age.

In the next three seasons, Lewicki fell into disfavour with Smythe and saw less ice time. In

1955, he was sold to New York. The move rejuvenated his career. He had his finest season yet, scoring 29 goals and assisting on 24, he was named to the NHL's second all-star team, and was runner-up for the Lady Byng Trophy. The New York hockey writers selected him the club's MVP. In the summer of 1958, Lewicki was acquired by Montreal. After failing to make the team, he was picked up by Chicago where he finished his NHL career. Subsequently, he played for three years with Quebec Aces of the AHL before retiring in 1963. In the mid-1960s, Lewicki coached junior hockey in Hamilton and Toronto. He rejected an offer to coach a minor pro team in Memphis.

## INDUCTIONS

1989        Northwestern Ontario Sports Hall of Fame

## AWARDS

1954        Outstanding Ukrainian Professional Athlete - UYLNA

## ALL-STAR SELECTIONS

| 1953-54 | center | AHL | Second Team |
| 1954-55 | left wing | NHL | Second Team |

## RECORD

| year | team | league | regular season | | | | | playoffs | | | | |
|------|------|--------|----|----|----|-----|-----|----|----|----|-----|-----|
|      |      |        | GP | G | A | PTS | PIM | GP | G | A | PTS | PIM |
| 1950-51* | Toronto | NHL | 61 | 16 | 18 | 34 | 26 | 9 | 0 | 0 | 0 | 0 |
| 1951-52 | Toronto | NHL | 51 | 4 | 9 | 13 | 26 | | | | | |
|  | Pittsburgh | AHL | 6 | 3 | 4 | 7 | 6 | | | | | |
| 1952-53 | Toronto | NHL | 4 | 1 | 3 | 4 | 2 | | | | | |
| * | Pittsburgh | AHL | 56 | 19 | 42 | 61 | 27 | 10 | 6 | 4 | 10 | 12 |
| 1953-54 | Toronto | NHL | 7 | 0 | 1 | 1 | 12 | | | | | |
|  | Pittsburgh | AHL | 60 | 36 | 45 | 81 | 19 | 5 | 0 | 2 | 2 | 16 |
| 1954-55 | NY Rangers | NHL | 70 | 29 | 24 | 53 | 8 | | | | | |
| 1955-56 | NY Rangers | NHL | 70 | 18 | 27 | 45 | 26 | 5 | 0 | 3 | 3 | 0 |
| 1956-57 | NY Rangers | NHL | 70 | 18 | 20 | 38 | 47 | 5 | 0 | 1 | 1 | 2 |
| 1957-58 | NY Rangers | NHL | 70 | 11 | 19 | 30 | 26 | 6 | 0 | 0 | 0 | 6 |
| 1958-59 | Chicago | NHL | 58 | 8 | 14 | 22 | 4 | 3 | 0 | 0 | 0 | 0 |
| 1959-60 | Buffalo | AHL | 62 | 14 | 41 | 55 | 56 | | | | | |
| 1960-61 | Quebec | AHL | 67 | 18 | 25 | 43 | 42 | | | | | |

| year | team | league | regular season | | | | | playoffs | | | | |
|------|------|--------|-----|-----|-----|-----|-----|-----|-----|-----|-----|-----|
| | | | GP | G | A | PTS | PIM | GP | G | A | PTS | PIM |
| 1961-62 | Quebec | AHL | 65 | 27 | 28 | 55 | 18 | | | | | |
| 1962-63 | Quebec | AHL | 64 | 23 | 25 | 48 | 30 | | | | | |

# LOZINSKI, LARRY

| | |
|---|---|
| sport: | hockey |
| given name: | Lozinski, Larry Peter |
| born: | Hudson Bay, Saskatchewan |
| | March 11, 1958 |
| height: | 1.80 m / 5'11" |
| weight: | 79.5 kg / 175 lbs |
| position: | goal |
| shoots: | right |

Larry Lozinski was selected 219th in the 1978 NHL Entry Draft by the Detroit Red Wings. In his first season of professional hockey, he played for Kansas of the CHL. The following season, he played for Kalamazoo of the International Hockey League. He led the IHL in shutouts with five. For his efforts he was named to the first all-star team and awarded the James Norris Trophy which honoured the league's top goaltender. In the fall of 1980, Larry Lozinski cracked the line-up of the Red Wings. He played with the Wings only that one season, posting a 4.32 average.

## AWARDS

1980      James Norris Trophy  -  IHL Top Goaltender

## ALL-STAR SELECTIONS

1979-80      goal      IHL      First Team

## RECORD

| year | team | league | regular season | | | | | | | | playoffs | | | | | | | |
|------|------|--------|-----|-----|-----|-----|-----|-----|-----|-----|-----|-----|-----|-----|-----|-----|-----|
| | | | GP | MIN | W | L | T | GA | AVE | SO | GP | MIN | W | L | T | GA | AVE | SO |
| 1978-79 | Kansas City | CHL | 13 | 688 | 4 | 6 | 1 | 45 | 3.92 | 0 | 10 | 597 | | | | 24 | 2.41 | 1 |
| 1979-80* | Kalamazoo | IHL | 69 | 4,000 | | | | 232 | 3.48 | 5 | | | | | | | | |
| 1980-81 | Detroit | NHL | 30 | 1,459 | 6 | 11 | 7 | 105 | 4.32 | 0 | | | | | | | | |

| year | team | league | GP | MIN | W | L | T | GA | AVE | SO | GP | MIN | W | L | T | GA | AVE | SO |
|------|------|--------|----|-----|---|---|---|----|-----|----|----|-----|---|---|---|----|-----|----|
| | | | | | | | | | | | | playoffs | | | | | | |
| 1980-81 | Adirondack | AHL | 16 | 789 | 4 | 9 | 1 | 53 | 4.03 | 0 | | | | | | | | |
| 1981-82 | Adirondack | AHL | 55 | 3,205 | 25 | 23 | 4 | 175 | 3.27 | 1 | 5 | 280 | | | | 22 | 4.71 | 0 |
| 1982-83 | Adirondack | AHL | 32 | 1,709 | | | | 128 | 4.49 | 3 | 6 | 390 | | | | 22 | 3.38 | 0 |
| | Kalamazoo | IHL | 12 | 674 | | | | 51 | 4.54 | 0 | | | | | | | | |

# LUKOWICH, BERNIE

| | |
|---|---|
| sport: | hockey |
| given name: | Lukowich, Bernard Joseph |
| born: | North Battleford, Saskatchewan |
| | March 18, 1952 |
| height: | 1.83 m / 6'0" |
| weight: | 86 kg / 190 lbs |
| position: | right wing |
| shoots: | right |

Bernie Lukowich broke into the NHL with the Pittsburgh Penguins during the 1973-74 season, a year after being drafted out of the New Westminster Bruins. He spent the following season in the minor pro ranks. In January of 1975, Lukowich was traded by Pittsburgh to the St. Louis Blues. During the off-season, he jumped to the Calgary Cowboys of the WHA but only saw spot duty. He finished his hockey career playing in the minors. Bernie Lukowich is the cousin of curler Ed Lukowich and hockey player Morris Lukowich.

## RECORD

| year | team | league | GP | G | A | PTS | PIM | GP | G | A | PTS | PIM |
|------|------|--------|----|---|---|-----|-----|----|---|---|-----|-----|
| | | | regular season | | | | | playoffs | | | | |
| 1972-73 | Hershey | AHL | 69 | 22 | 24 | 46 | 64 | | | | | |
| 1973-74 | Pittsburgh | NHL | 53 | 9 | 10 | 19 | 32 | | | | | |
| | Hershey | AHL | 17 | 4 | 5 | 9 | 12 | | | | | |
| 1974-75 | St. Louis | NHL | 26 | 4 | 5 | 9 | 2 | 2 | 0 | 0 | 0 | 0 |
| | Denver | CHL | 7 | 6 | 6 | 12 | 8 | | | | | |
| | Hershey | AHL | 27 | 9 | 14 | 23 | 53 | | | | | |
| 1975-76 | Calgary | WHA | 15 | 5 | 2 | 7 | 18 | | | | | |
| | Providence | AHL | 64 | 21 | 17 | 38 | 62 | | | | | |
| 1976-77 | Calgary | WHA | 6 | 0 | 1 | 1 | 0 | | | | | |
| | Hershey | AHL | 37 | 15 | 18 | 33 | 18 | 6 | 1 | 1 | 2 | 4 |

# LUKOWICH, ED

"Fast Eddy"

| | |
|---|---|
| sport: | curling |
| given name: | Lukowich, Edward Richard |
| born: | North Battleford Saskatchewan |
| | March 3, 1946 |
| height: | 1.75 m / 5'9" |
| weight: | 79.5 kg / 175 lbs |

Photo courtesy of the Athlete Information Bureau

Ed Lukowich began curling at the age of six. At first, throwing a few rocks was a reward for helping his father operate a two-sheet natural curling rink in the farming village of Speers. In a short period of time, curling became a passion. While in high school, Ed curled third on a rink skipped by brother Mike. The rink, representing Speers School, advanced to the Saskatchewan Junior Championship on three occasions. In 1962, the rink won the Saskatchewan title and then captured the Canadian Championship.

For a period of time after leaving the junior ranks, Ed Lukowich played third on a rink that was skipped by his brother Mike. Playing lead on that rink was their father Joseph. The Lukowich team placed second at the Saskatchewan Championship in 1966. While attending the University of Saskatchewan, Ed Lukowich curled for the school, winning three Western Intercollegiate Curling Championships.

A few lean years followed before Ed Lukowich savoured major victories again. Competing out of Calgary, he won the Alberta title and the Brier - Canadian Championship - in 1978. At the World Championship, the Lukowich rink had a successful round robin tournament but was eliminated by a team from Norway in a sudden-death playoff. Lukowich returned to the national championship on a number of occasions, but failed to capture the title again until 1986. At the World Championship that year, the Lukowich rink did not play well in the qualifying round and was fortunate to advance to the playoffs. The foursome rallied in the playoffs and won the world title.

A natural all-round athlete, Lukowich excelled in a number of sports. In his twenties, he played semi-professional baseball for the Saskatoon Commodores. He also played good hockey. Many observers wondered why he did not try out for the National Hockey League.

In 1987, Ed Lukowich won the Olympic curling trials and became the first curler to win over $100,000 in cash bonspiels in a season. The following year, Lukowich went to the Calgary Olympics as a heavy favourite to win the gold medal. Unfortunately, the team's playmaking was not up to par and they had to settle for the bronze medal. Ed Lukowich is the brother of hockey player Morris Lukowich and the cousin of hockey player Bernie Lukowich.

## INDUCTIONS

. . .       University of Saskatchewan Wall of Fame

## AWARDS

1986       Scott-Mamini Trophy  -  Calgary Athlete of the Year

## ALL-STAR SELECTIONS

1983       skip       Brier
1986       skip       Brier

## RECORD

| year | competition | position | placing | result |
| --- | --- | --- | --- | --- |
| 1961 | Saskatchewan Junior Championship | third | 4 | |
| 1962 | Saskatchewan Junior Championship | third | 1 | |
| | Canadian Junior Championship | third | 1 | 10-1 |
| 1963 | Northern Saskatchewan Jr. Championship | third | 1 | |
| 1966 | Saskatchewan Championship | third | 2 | |
| 1978 | Alberta Championship | skip | 1 | |
| | Canadian Championship | skip | 1 | 9-2 |
| | World Championship | skip | 3 | |
| 1983 | Alberta Championship | skip | 1 | 10-1 |
| | Canadian Championship | skip | 2 | 10-2 |
| 1984 | Alberta Championship | skip | 1 | 8-3 |
| | Canadian Championship | skip | 3 | 8-4 |
| 1986 | Alberta Championship | skip | 1 | 9-2 |
| | Canadian Championship | skip | 1 | 10-2 |
| | World Championship | skip | 1 | 9-3 |
| 1987 | Olympic Trials | skip | 1 | 7-3 |
| 1988 | Olympic Games | skip | 3 | |

# LUKOWICH, MORRIS

"Luke"

| | |
|---|---|
| sport: | hockey |
| born: | Speers, Saskatchewan |
| | June 1, 1956 |
| height: | 1.73 m / 5'8" |
| weight: | 77 kg / 170 lbs |
| position: | left wing |
| shoots: | left |

*Photo courtesy of the Winnipeg Jets*

Growing up in Speers, Saskatchewan, Morris Lukowich would spend the winter months skating down a country road to a patch of ice known as the town rink. There he and his friends would chase the puck for hours on end. In the summer, he passed the time playing baseball. Hockey was his passion, though, and he left all other sports behind when he signed with the junior Medicine Hat Tigers. In his final year with the Tigers, he registered 142 points and helped establish a league record for most points by a line with 477.

In 1976, Morris Lukowich was selected in the third round of the NHL Entry Draft by the Pittsburgh Penguins. The Penguins, though, showed little interest in Lukowich, and he opted for the Houston Aeros of the WHA who drafted him in the first round. Lukowich sat out part of his rookie season with injuries. Even so, he managed to score 27 goals. In the summer of 1978, when the Houston franchise folded, Lukowich was sold to the Winnipeg Jets. The move disappointed him and he wanted out. Eventually, he overcame the turmoil within and settled down to score a career-high 65 goals. His shooting accuracy of 23.4 per cent was fourth best in the WHA. In the playoffs, Lukowich contributed greatly as Winnipeg won the WHA championship.

During the summer of 1979, the WHA folded. The Winnipeg Jets were one of four clubs accepted as expansion franchises by the NHL. Each club, though, could only protect two goalies and two skaters from their previous year's roster. One of the players the Jets protected was Morris Lukowich. He was the heart and soul of the club and management did not want to lose him. Lukowich responded to the honour by leading the club in its first trying years. On two occasions, he was Winnipeg's player of the year and he represented the Jets twice at all-star games. During the 1980-81 season, he served as captain. In February of 1985, Lukowich was traded to the Boston Bruins. He finished his NHL career with the Los Angeles Kings. Morris Lukowich is the brother of curler Ed Lukowich and the cousin of hockey player Bernie Lukowich.

# AWARDS

1979        Manitoba Ukrainian Sportsman of the Year

## ALL-STAR SELECTIONS

1979       left wing     WHA     Second Team

## RECORD

| year | team | league | regular season | | | | | playoffs | | | | |
|------|------|--------|-----|-----|-----|-----|-----|-----|-----|-----|-----|-----|
| | | | GP | G | A | PTS | PIM | GP | G | A | PTS | PIM |
| 1976-77 | Houston | WHA | 62 | 27 | 18 | 45 | 67 | 11 | 6 | 4 | 10 | 19 |
| 1977-78 | Houston | WHA | 80 | 40 | 35 | 75 | 131 | 6 | 1 | 2 | 3 | 17 |
| 1978-79* | Winnipeg | WHA | 80 | 65 | 34 | 99 | 119 | 10 | 8 | 7 | 15 | 21 |
| 1979-80 | Winnipeg | NHL | 78 | 35 | 39 | 74 | 77 | | | | | |
| 1980-81 | Winnipeg | NHL | 80 | 33 | 34 | 67 | 90 | | | | | |
| 1981-82 | Winnipeg | NHL | 77 | 43 | 49 | 92 | 102 | 4 | 0 | 2 | 2 | 16 |
| 1982-83 | Winnipeg | NHL | 69 | 22 | 21 | 43 | 67 | | | | | |
| 1983-84 | Winnipeg | NHL | 80 | 30 | 25 | 55 | 71 | 3 | 0 | 0 | 0 | 0 |
| 1984-85 | Winnipeg | NHL | 47 | 5 | 9 | 14 | 31 | | | | | |
| | Boston | NHL | 22 | 5 | 8 | 13 | 21 | 1 | 0 | 0 | 0 | 0 |
| 1985-86 | Boston | NHL | 14 | 1 | 4 | 5 | 10 | | | | | |
| | Los Angeles | NHL | 55 | 11 | 9 | 20 | 51 | | | | | |
| 1986-87 | Los Angeles | NHL | 60 | 14 | 21 | 35 | 64 | 3 | 0 | 0 | 0 | 8 |

international

| year | team | competition | GP | G | A | PTS | PIM | Place |
|------|------|-------------|-----|-----|-----|-----|-----|-------|
| 1981 | Canada | World Championship | 8 | 2 | 1 | 3 | 4 | 4 |

# LUPUL, GARY

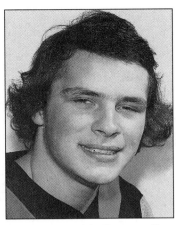

Photo courtesy of the Vancouver Canucks

"Loopy"

| | |
|---|---|
| sport: | hockey |
| given name: | Lupul, Gary John |
| born: | Powell River, British Columbia |
| | April 4, 1959 |
| height: | 1.75 m / 5'9" |
| weight: | 78 kg / 172 lbs |
| position: | center |
| shoots: | left |

In the summer of 1979, Gary Lupul's hockey career appeared to have stalled. He just had completed his last year of junior hockey scoring 53 goals and 54 assists. Those numbers should have impressed most professional teams, but they did not; scouts were concerned about his health. In 1977, he tore ligaments in his left knee, and in 1978, he injured an ankle while working in a logging camp. The Vancouver Canucks, though, took a chance and signed Lupul as a free agent in September of 1979.

In his seven seasons with the Canucks, Lupul established himself as a dynamic and inspiring hockey player. Fans took an immediate liking to him, shouting "Loop" whenever he was on the ice.

## RECORD

| | | | regular season | | | | | playoffs | | | | |
|---|---|---|---|---|---|---|---|---|---|---|---|---|
| year | team | league | GP | G | A | PTS | PIM | GP | G | A | PTS | PIM |
| 1979-80 | Vancouver | NHL | 51 | 9 | 11 | 20 | 24 | 4 | 1 | 0 | 1 | 0 |
| | Dallas | CHL | 26 | 9 | 15 | 24 | 4 | | | | | |
| 1980-81 | Vancouver | NHL | 7 | 0 | 2 | 2 | 2 | | | | | |
| | Dallas | CHL | 53 | 25 | 32 | 57 | 27 | 6 | 4 | 1 | 5 | 5 |
| 1981-82 | Vancouver | NHL | 41 | 10 | 7 | 17 | 26 | 10 | 2 | 3 | 5 | 4 |
| | Dallas | CHL | 31 | 22 | 17 | 39 | 76 | | | | | |
| 1982-83 | Vancouver | NHL | 40 | 18 | 10 | 28 | 46 | 4 | 1 | 3 | 4 | 0 |
| | Fredericton | AHL | 35 | 16 | 26 | 42 | 48 | | | | | |
| 1983-84 | Vancouver | NHL | 69 | 17 | 27 | 44 | 51 | 4 | 0 | 1 | 1 | 7 |
| 1984-85 | Vancouver | NHL | 66 | 12 | 17 | 29 | 82 | | | | | |
| 1985-86 | Vancouver | NHL | 19 | 4 | 1 | 5 | 12 | 3 | 0 | 0 | 0 | 0 |
| | Fredericton | AHL | 43 | 13 | 22 | 35 | 76 | 3 | 2 | 0 | 2 | 4 |

| year | team | competition | GP | G | A | PTS | PIM | Place |
|------|------|-------------|----|----|----|-----|-----|-------|
| 1979 | New Westminster | World Junior Championship | 5 | 2 | 1 | 3 | 0 | 5 |

# LYSIAK, TOM

"The Bomb"

| | |
|---|---|
| sport: | hockey |
| given name: | Lysiak, Thomas James |
| born: | High Prairie, Alberta |
| | April 22, 1953 |
| height: | 1.85 m / 6'1" |
| weight: | 88.5 kg / 195 lbs |
| position: | center |
| shoots: | left |

*Card reproduced courtesy of O-Pee-Chee Co.*

For Tom Lysiak, hockey became a passion the day he saw his first game at the age of six. His parents, though, did not share their son's preoccupation with the game. His father considered it a waste of time; his mother tolerated it, but also thought that one's time could be spent more productively.

When Tom Lysiak became eligible for the NHL Entry Draft, he had some impressive statistics to market his cause. In his last two years of junior hockey, while playing for the Medicine Hat Tigers, he was the WCHL scoring champion with 143 and 154 points respectively. He led the league in assists with 97 and 96. He also tied the league record with 10 points in a single game. In the 1973 draft, he was picked in the first round. The Atlanta Flames made him their first choice, second overall.

Tom Lysiak joined the Flames at a time when the team was struggling. He generated much needed offence, and the club started to improve its position in the standings. In his rookie year, he led the club in scoring and was the top rookie scorer in the league. In voting for the Calder Trophy, he lost out to defenseman Denis Potvin. Over the next decade, Lysiak established himself as a colourful and consistent performer. He enjoyed doing fancy things with the puck, passing it from behind his back or between his legs.

In March 1979, Lysiak was traded to the Chicago Black Hawks. He had a number of good seasons there, peaking with a career-high 32 goals during the 1981-82 campaign. After a disappointing 1985-86 season in which he scored only two goals, Tom Lysiak retired from the game.

## AWARDS

| 1972 | Bob Brownridge Memorial Trophy - WCHL Scoring Leader |
| 1973 | Bob Brownridge Memorial Trophy - WCHL Scoring Leader |

## RECORD

| | | | regular season | | | | | playoffs | | | | |
|---|---|---|---|---|---|---|---|---|---|---|---|---|
| year | team | league | GP | G | A | PTS | PIM | GP | G | A | PTS | PIM |
| 1973-74 | Atlanta | NHL | 77 | 19 | 45 | 64 | 54 | 4 | 0 | 2 | 2 | 0 |
| 1974-75 | Atlanta | NHL | 77 | 25 | 52 | 77 | 73 | | | | | |
| 1975-76 | Atlanta | NHL | 80 | 31 | 51 | 82 | 60 | 2 | 0 | 0 | 0 | 2 |
| 1976-77 | Atlanta | NHL | 79 | 30 | 51 | 81 | 52 | 3 | 1 | 3 | 4 | 8 |
| 1977-78 | Atlanta | NHL | 80 | 27 | 42 | 69 | 54 | 2 | 1 | 0 | 1 | 2 |
| 1978-79 | Atlanta | NHL | 52 | 23 | 35 | 58 | 36 | | | | | |
| | Chicago | NHL | 14 | 0 | 10 | 10 | 14 | 4 | 0 | 0 | 0 | 2 |
| 1979-80 | Chicago | NHL | 77 | 26 | 43 | 69 | 31 | 7 | 4 | 4 | 8 | 0 |
| 1980-81 | Chicago | NHL | 72 | 21 | 55 | 76 | 20 | 3 | 0 | 3 | 3 | 0 |
| 1981-82 | Chicago | NHL | 71 | 32 | 50 | 82 | 84 | 15 | 6 | 9 | 15 | 13 |
| 1982-83 | Chicago | NHL | 61 | 23 | 38 | 61 | 27 | 13 | 6 | 7 | 13 | 8 |
| 1983-84 | Chicago | NHL | 54 | 17 | 30 | 47 | 35 | 5 | 1 | 1 | 2 | 2 |
| 1984-85 | Chicago | NHL | 74 | 16 | 30 | 46 | 13 | 15 | 4 | 8 | 12 | 10 |
| 1985-86 | Chicago | NHL | 51 | 2 | 19 | 21 | 14 | 3 | 2 | 1 | 3 | 2 |

international

| year | team | competition | GP | G | A | PTS | PIM | Place |
|---|---|---|---|---|---|---|---|---|
| 1978 | Canada | World Championship | 7 | 1 | 1 | 2 | 4 | 3 |

# MAICH, BILL

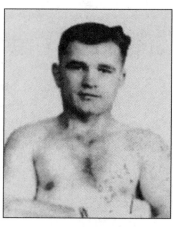

"One Punch"

| | |
|---|---|
| sport: | boxing |
| given name: | Maich, William |
| born: | Fort William, Ontario |
| | (now Thunder Bay) |
| | June 19, 1910 |
| height: | 1.83 m / 6'0" |
| weight: | 84-95.5 kg / 185-210 lbs |

Bill Maich was 11 years old when he quit school to help his family make ends meet. He worked on the family farm and sold newspapers on a street corner in nearby Brantford. In his free time, he pursued baseball and hockey with the hope of making it to the professional leagues. He had a dream - he wanted to be someone special. He was also tired of selling newspapers and working on the farm.

One day a teammate brought a pair of boxing gloves to the baseball diamond. Maich was hooked. At 15 or 16, he began training diligently at the Brantford Armouries. The Dufferin Rifles Regiment provided the enthusiastic youth with access to its facilities and let him spar with older military pugilists. At 17, Maich fought his first fight and won. It was a start of a career that included some 100 fights, both amateur and professional. In the 70 fights that have been documented, Maich knocked out about 80 per cent of his opponents while never being knocked out himself. His punching power was legendary. He was nicknamed Bill "One Punch" Maich and was compared to the great Gene Tunney. He was described as the "Brantford Hercules" or the "Jack Dempsey of Canada." Circumstances and choices though precluded Bill Maich from fully realizing his boxing potential.

Bill Maich's boxing prowess quickly became respected and feared. Only experienced veterans would venture into the ring with him. Very early in his career, in fact when he was still only 17, Maich fought his first national champion - Cutts Carere, and lost. In 1930, he finally defeated a Canadian Heavyweight Champion (Phil Lightheart), albeit in a non-title bout. At the 1932 Olympic Trials, boxing was not on Maich's mind - his father had died less than two weeks earlier. Nevertheless, Bill Maich fought well, advancing to the final only to lose in a decision. In 1933, he won the Canadian Amateur Heavyweight title by knocking out Tony Evans in 87 seconds of the first round. The following year, it took him less time - 55 seconds - and one punch to dispose of his opponent in the final of the national championship. The victory also qualified him to represent Canada at the British Empire Games (forerunner of the

Commonwealth Games) in London, England. At the Games, Maich was eliminated in a semi-final bout by eventual gold medallist H. P. Floyd of England. In the consolation final, Maich lost to Lord David Hamilton of Scotland.

To gain more experience and exposure, upon returning from Europe, Maich began fighting in the United States. In early 1935, he defeated Stanley Evans, the United States Amateur Heavyweight Champion in a unanimous decision to win the North American Heavyweight Championship. In the past year, Evans had fought heavyweight legend Joe Louis three times, defeating him twice. It seemed that Maich was destined for even greater successes. It was not to be. He had a falling out with his management team. It appeared that expenses were unfailingly greater than the purse, regardless of the sum. As a result, Maich semi-retired from boxing.

In August 1937, Maich fought George Leslie for the vacant Canadian Professional Heavyweight Championship. The pre-fight favourite Leslie was knocked out a mere 77 seconds into the bout. After the fight, 27-year-old Bill Maich retired his gloves permanently. Pounding an opponent in a boxing ring was not compatible with his new found interest in religion. Bill Maich's brothers Joe (wrestling) and Don (boxing) were also well-known athletes.

## INDUCTIONS

1977      Canadian Boxing Hall of Fame
1984      The Brantford and Area Sports Hall of Recognition

## RECORD

| year | opponent | result | round |
|------|----------|--------|-------|
| 1928 | A. Chinnery | W | 3 |
| | Alex Cushenan | KO | 3 |
| | Cutts Carere | L | 3 |
| 1929 | Al Pitcher | L | 3 |
| | Cutts Carere | L | 3 |
| 1930 | Cutts Carere | W | 4 |
| | Tony Sayloski | L | 3 |
| | W. Skimming | L | 3 |
| | Phil Lightheart | L | |
| | Phil Lightheart | L | |
| | Phil Lightheart | L | |
| | Phil Lightheart | L | |
| | Phil Lightheart | L | |
| 1931 | Phil Lightheart | W | |

| year | opponent | result | round |
|------|----------|--------|-------|
| 1932 | Bill Brown | KO | 2 + |
|      | George Maughn | L | 3 + |
| 1933 | Tony Sayloski | W | 3 |
|      | George Hees | KO | 1 |
|      | George Hees | KO | 2 |
|      | Stan Duke | KO | 2 |
|      | Jake Allen | KO | 1 |
|      | Tony Evans | KO | 1 ++ |
| 1934 | Steve Neri | KO | 1 ++ |
|      | Walter Potter | W | 5 |
|      | H. P. Floyd | L | 2 +++ |
|      | Lord David Hamilton | L | 3 +++ |
|      | Beb Baxter | KO | 3 |
| 1935 | Stanley Evans | W | |
| 1936 | George Leslie | KO | 2 |
|      | Marv Linton | dsq | |
| 1937 | George Leslie | KO | 1 ++++ |

+     Canadian Amateur Championship / Olympic Trials

++    Canadian Amateur Championship

+++   British Empire Games

++++ Canadian Professional Championship

# MAICH, JOE

sport:        wrestling

given name:  Maich, Joseph

born:        Fort William, Ontario
                 (now Thunder Bay)
                 . . ., 1916

height:      . . .

weight:     . . .

Joe Maich was fourteen years old when he started wrestling. In a short period of time, he was able to harness his natural athletic ability and body strength into competitive form. His first competitions were as an amateur. As his skills developed, he began delving into professional wrestling. Competing concurrently in amateur and professional wrestling during the Great Depression appeared acceptable.

Eventually, Joe Maich turned professional. During a career that finally ended in 1952, Maich competed against some of the finest wrestlers on the continent. At first, he fought in the middleweight division. Subsequently, he moved up to the heavyweight.

Upon retirement from the ring, Joe Maich became a wrestling promoter. For 27 years, he organized events throughout southern Ontario. Joe Maich's brothers Bill and Don were also well-known athletes.

INDUCTIONS

1984      The Brantford and Area Sports Hall of Recognition

# MAKOHON, JEFF

| | |
|---|---|
| sport: | golf |
| born: | Saskatoon, Saskatchewan |
| | September 24, 1970 |
| height: | 1.73 m / 5'8" |
| weight: | 67 kg / 148 lbs |

Jeff Makohon broke into national prominence in 1987 when he became the first golfer ever to capture two provincial junior championships in one year. In addition, he was the only Canadian golfer to qualify for the U.S. Junior Open. Makohon capped the year off by winning the Canadian Juvenile Championship. Two years later, Jeff Makohon established two more firsts: he became the first Saskatchewan golfer to win the Canadian Junior Championship, and also became the first golfer to win three Saskatchewan junior titles.

Academically inclined, Jeff Makohon was the 1988, 1989, and 1990 recipient of both the Canadian Golf Foundation Academic Scholarship and the Saskatchewan Golf Association

Academic and Golf Excellence Scholarship. Upon graduating from high school, Makohon enrolled at Rice University in Houston, Texas, and represented the school at NCAA Division 1 golf tournaments.

## AWARDS

| | |
|---|---|
| 1989 | Saskatchewan Male Athlete of the Year |
| 1989 | Canadian Male Junior Golfer of the Year |

## RECORD

| year | event | placing | result |
|---|---|---|---|
| 1987 | Alberta Junior Championship | 1 | 214 |
| | Saskatchewan Junior Championship | 1 | 212 |
| | Canadian Juvenile Championship | 1 | 303 |
| 1988 | Saskatchewan Junior Championship | 1 | 214 |
| | United States Junior Qualifying | 1 | 148 |
| | United States Junior Open | 11 | 147 |
| 1989 | Saskatchewan Junior Championship | 1 | 222 |
| | Canadian Junior Championship | 1 | 306 |

# MALAR, JOANNE

| | |
|---|---|
| sport: | swimming |
| born: | Hamilton, Ontario |
| | October 30, 1975 |
| height: | 1.70 m / 5'7" |
| weight: | 55 kg / 120 lbs |

Joanne Malar was three years old when her father tried to enrol her in a local swim club. Membership was denied for the club did not accept swimmers under the age of seven. Malar's father nevertheless persisted suggesting that the three-year-old prove herself. After swimming lengths in four different strokes - freestyle, backstroke, breaststroke and butterfly - the young

Malar was accepted. Over the years, Malar developed her swimming skills establishing her first provincial record at age ten. She also began to excel in other sports - basketball, tennis, volleyball, gymnastics and cross country running.

In grade nine, Joanne Malar opted to concentrate on swimming. At age 14, she became a member of the national team and competed at the 1990 Commonwealth Games. The youngest athlete in any event, she made the final of both the 200 and 400-metre individual medleys (IM). The following year, she won five medals - four silver and a bronze - at the Pan American Games. At the 1992 Olympics, Joanne Malar placed 11th in the 400-metre IM.

## RECORD

| year | competition | event | placing | result |
|------|-------------|-------|---------|--------|
| 1989 | Commonwealth Games Trials | 200 m IM | 2 | 2:20.16 |
| 1990 | Commonwealth Games | 200 m IM | 5 | 2:18.51 |
|      |             | 400 m IM | 6 | 4:52.35 |
|      |             | 200 m breaststroke | 9 | 2:38.45 |
|      | Canadian Championships | 200 m backstroke | 1 | 2:17.20 |
|      |             | 200 m IM | 2 | 2:18.60 |
|      |             | 400 m IM | 3 | 4:52.81 |
| 1991 | Pan American Games | 200 m IM | 2 | 2:19.14 |
|      |             | 400 m IM | 2 | 4:51.27 |
|      |             | 200 m backstroke | 3 | 2:16.36 |
|      |             | 4 x 100 m freestyle | 2 | 3:52.29 |
|      |             | 4 x 200 m freestyle | 2 | 8:21.62 |
| 1992 | Olympic Trials | 200 m IM | 3 | 2:17.92 |
|      |             | 400 m IM | 2 | 4:49.26 |
|      |             | 200 m backstroke | 3 | 2:17.92 |
|      | Olympic Games | 400 m IM | 11 | 4:48.52 |

# MALARCHUK, CLINT

"Mallard"

sport:      hockey
born:       Grande Prairie, Alberta
            May 1, 1961
height:     1.78 m / 5'10"
weight:     78 kg / 172 lbs
position:   goal
shoots:     left

*Photo courtesy of the Buffalo Sabres*

Clint Malarchuk grew up working on a dairy farm. He enjoyed riding horses, and referred to himself as a cowboy; rodeos were part of his background. Hockey, though, was Malarchuk's yearning and ambition. His father and older brother both played goal, and the young Clint decided to follow in their footsteps. He quickly developed into a top prospect and was soon playing junior hockey with Fort Saskatchewan. Malarchuk then played for the Portland Winter Hawks of the WHL from where he was drafted by the Quebec Nordiques, 74th overall, in the 1981 NHL Entry Draft.

Malarchuk spent his first three years of professional hockey tending goal for the Quebec farm team at Fredericton. He made only a handful of appearances with the Nordiques in those years. In the fall of 1985, Malarchuk earned a regular position on the Nordique roster, playing 46 games and registering a 3.21 goals against average. In the summer of 1987, Malarchuk was traded to the Washington Capitals. The trade pleased him; although he had enjoyed playing for the Nordiques, he had difficulty adjusting to life in Quebec City.

Malarchuk played with the Capitals for a season and a half before being traded to the Buffalo Sabres. Shortly after joining the Sabres, Malarchuk experienced a life-threatening injury. In heated action in front of the goal, a skate cut him on the neck. His jugular was cut into and a neck muscle torn. Only the quick response of trainers and doctors prevented Malarchuk from bleeding to death.

## AWARDS

1983     Harry "Hap" Holmes Memorial Award - AHL Lowest Goals Against

# RECORD

| year | team | league | GP | MIN | W | L | T | GA | AVE | SO | GP | MIN | W | L | T | GA | AVE | SO |
|------|------|--------|----|-----|---|---|---|----|-----|----|----|-----|---|---|---|----|-----|----|
| | | | | | | | regular season | | | | | | playoffs | | | | | |
| 1981-82 | Quebec | NHL | 2 | 120 | 0 | 1 | 1 | 14 | 7.00 | 0 | | | | | | | | |
| | Fredericton | AHL | 51 | 2,906 | 15 | 34 | 2 | 247 | 5.10 | 0 | | | | | | | | |
| 1982-83 | Quebec | NHL | 15 | 900 | 8 | 5 | 2 | 71 | 4.73 | 0 | | | | | | | | |
| | Fredericton | AHL | 25 | 1,506 | 14 | 6 | 5 | 78 | 3.11 | 0 | | | | | | | | |
| 1983-84 | Quebec | NHL | 23 | 1,215 | 10 | 9 | 2 | 80 | 3.95 | 0 | | | | | | | | |
| | Fredericton | AHL | 11 | 663 | 5 | 5 | 1 | 40 | 3.62 | 0 | | | | | | | | |
| 1984-85 | Fredericton | AHL | 56 | 3,347 | 26 | 25 | 4 | 198 | 3.55 | 2 | 6 | 379 | 2 | 4 | 0 | 20 | 3.17 | 0 |
| 1985-86 | Quebec | NHL | 46 | 2,657 | 26 | 12 | 4 | 142 | 3.21 | 4 | 3 | 143 | 0 | 2 | 0 | 11 | 4.62 | 0 |
| 1986-87 | Quebec | NHL | 54 | 3,092 | 18 | 26 | 9 | 175 | 3.40 | 1 | 3 | 140 | 0 | 2 | 0 | 8 | 3.43 | 0 |
| 1987-88 | Washington | NHL | 54 | 2,926 | 24 | 20 | 4 | 154 | 3.16 | 4 | 4 | 193 | 0 | 2 | 0 | 15 | 4.66 | 0 |
| 1988-89 | Washington | NHL | 42 | 2,428 | 16 | 18 | 7 | 141 | 3.48 | 1 | | | | | | | | |
| | Buffalo | NHL | 7 | 326 | 3 | 1 | 1 | 13 | 2.39 | 1 | 1 | 59 | 0 | 1 | 0 | 5 | 5.08 | 0 |
| 1989-90 | Buffalo | NHL | 29 | 1,596 | 14 | 11 | 2 | 89 | 3.35 | 0 | | | | | | | | |
| 1990-91 | Buffalo | NHL | 37 | 2,131 | 12 | 14 | 10 | 119 | 3.35 | 1 | 4 | 246 | 2 | 2 | 0 | 17 | 4.15 | 0 |

# MALINOSKY, JOHN

| | |
|---|---|
| sport: | football |
| born: | Fernie, British Columbia |
| | May 8, 1955 |
| height: | 1.96 m / 6'5" |
| weight: | 118 kg / 260 lbs |
| position: | offensive guard, tackle |

*Photo courtesy of the Canadian Football Hall of Fame and Museum*

A product of the Michigan State University football program, John Malinosky was the Calgary Stampeders' Territorial Exemption in the 1977 CFL College Draft. He played with the Stampeders in 1978. The following year, Malinosky was traded to the Winnipeg Blue Bombers. He was with the club for one year. The Toronto Argonauts acquired Malinosky prior to the start of the 1980 season. He played for five years with the Argonauts. In 1982, and once again in 1983, Malinosky played in the Grey Cup game. He was on the victorious side in the latter year. In 1984, the big offensive tackle was selected to the Eastern all-star team.

The Toronto Argonauts dealt Malinosky to the Hamilton Tiger-Cats in May of 1985. That year, the Tiger-Cats advanced to the Grey Cup final but lost the game to British Columbia. In 1986, Hamilton once again advanced to the Cup final winning the East-West classic against the Edmonton Eskimos. Malinosky played one more season with the Tiger-Cats before retiring from the game.

ALL-STAR SELECTIONS

1984      offensive tackle      CFL      All-Eastern

# MANCHUK, BILL

| | |
|---|---|
| sport: | football |
| born: | Edmonton, Alberta |
| | January 9, 1947 |
| height: | 1.88 m / 6'2" |
| weight: | 96 kg / 212 lbs |
| position: | defensive back |

Bill Manchuk played varsity football at Idaho State University and the University of Alberta. In 1971, he was selected by the Saskatchewan Roughriders in the first round, eighth overall, in the CFL College Draft. Manchuk played with the Roughriders for ten seasons. In 1976, the defensive back was named to the CFL's Western all-star team. That same year, he played in his first Grey Cup game. In 1980, Manchuk was traded to the Edmonton Eskimos. He played in the 1981 and 1982 Grey Cup games with the Eskimos, winning the Cup on both occasions. Bill Manchuk retired from the game after the 1982 season.

ALL-STAR SELECTIONS

1976      defensive back      CFL      All-Western

# MARKS, VICTOR

*Photo courtesy of the Canadian Football Hall of Fame and Museum*

| | |
|---|---|
| sport: | football |
| given name: | Marks, Victor Peter |
| born: | Melita, Manitoba |
| | December 7, 1933 |
| height: | 1.78 m / 5'10" |
| weight: | 93 kg / 205 lbs |
| position: | fullback |

Playing in only his first year of organized football, Victor Marks led the Fort William Redskins to the 1955 Dominion intermediate football final. In the championship game against the Peterborough Orfuns, Marks was one of the most outstanding players on the field, albeit in a losing cause. He scored Fort William's lone touchdown. The following year, the powerful fullback joined the Saskatchewan Roughriders. Marks played with the Roughriders for five seasons.

Victor Marks was also a talented hockey player. After arriving at the Lakehead in 1951, he played for the junior Fort William Columbus Canadians from 1951 to 1954, and for the senior Port Arthur Bearcats in 1955-56.

# MARUK, BARRY

*Photo courtesy of the Brampton Excelsiors*

"Paco"

| | |
|---|---|
| sport: | lacrosse |
| born: | Toronto, Ontario |
| | July 4, 1957 |
| height: | 1.73 m / 5'8" |
| weight: | 72.5 kg / 160 lbs |
| position: | goal |

In the years 1975 to 1978, Barry Maruk tended goal for the Rexdale Warriors Jr. "A" lacrosse team.  In his final year with the Warriors, Maruk was second in club scoring with 86 points, all on assists, in 29 games.  The tally established a league record for a goaltender.  During the winter, Maruk broke his leg playing hockey.  The injury prevented him from attending the 1979 training camp of the Brampton Excelsiors who had earlier made him their number one draft pick.  Barry Maruk joined the club part way through the season and immediately became an impact player.  The Excelsiors qualified for the playoffs, where they battled with the Peterborough Red Oaks for the Eastern Canada championship.  Brampton lost, but Maruk's brilliant play was recognized when the Red Oaks requested that he be their standby goaltender at the competition for the Mann Cup, emblematic of senior lacrosse supremacy in Canada. Maruk, though, was not called to play.

In 1980, the Excelsiors played inconsistent lacrosse all season, just barely qualifying for the playoffs.  In the opening playoff series, behind the superb goaltending of Maruk, the Excelsiors upset the first place Brooklin Redmen.  The club then won the Eastern Canada championship and the right to vie for the Mann Cup by defeating Peterborough.  In the best-of-seven series for the national title, the New Westminster Salmonbellies were completely frustrated by Maruk.  He performed brilliantly, stopping shots, intercepting breakaway passes, and setting up goals.  The Excelsiors won the Mann Cup in five games, and Maruk was awarded the championship's MVP trophy.  Brampton coach John McCauley exclaimed, "He's the best goalie ever to play in Brampton."[25]

The following year, Maruk led the league in scoring by a goaltender.  The Excelsiors once again vied for the Mann Cup, but lost the championship final in four straight games to New Westminster.

Barry Maruk played lacrosse with the Brampton Excelsiors through the 1990 season.  In those years, neither the Excelsiors nor Maruk were able to attain the high level of play which saw them win the Canadian championship in 1980 and place second in 1981.  Maruk, though, continued to play well; his assist totals were constantly high.  In 1991, Maruk played for the Brantford Warriors and the Vancouver Burrards.  Barry Maruk is the brother of hockey player Dennis Maruk.

## AWARDS

1980       Mike Kelly Memorial Award  -  CLA Mann Cup MVP


## ALL-STAR SELECTIONS

1991       goal       NLL       First Team

# RECORD

| year | team | league | regular season | | | | | playoffs | | | | |
|---|---|---|---|---|---|---|---|---|---|---|---|---|
| | | | GP | G | A | PTS | PIM | GP | G | A | PTS | PIM |
| 1979 | Brampton | OLA | 2 | 0 | 4 | 4 | 0 | 8 | 0 | 13 | 13 | 0 |
| 1980* | Brampton | OLA | 15 | 2 | 29 | 31 | 17 | 8 | 0 | 14 | 14 | 0 |
| 1981 | Brampton | OLA | 24 | 3 | 43 | 46 | 12 | 12 | 0 | 31 | 31 | 8 |
| 1982 | Brampton | OLA | 21 | 0 | 38 | 38 | 14 | | | | | |
| 1983 | Brampton | OLA | 21 | 1 | 43 | 44 | 14 | | | | | |
| 1984 | Brampton | OLA | 21 | 0 | 35 | 35 | 6 | 4 | 0 | 2 | 2 | 0 |
| 1985 | Brampton | OLA | 17 | 0 | 30 | 30 | 4 | 4 | 0 | 5 | 5 | 0 |
| 1986 | Brampton | OLA | 11 | 0 | 6 | 6 | 4 | 3 | 0 | 0 | 0 | 0 |
| 1987 | Brampton | | | | | | | | | | | |
| 1988 | Brampton | OLA | 14 | 0 | 11 | 11 | 6 | 4 | 0 | 4 | 4 | 2 |
| 1989 | Brampton | OLA | 14 | 0 | 16 | 16 | 10 | 4 | 0 | 4 | 4 | 4 |
| 1990 | Brampton | OLA | 9 | 0 | 4 | 4 | 21 | 4 | 0 | 5 | 5 | 0 |
| 1991 | Brantford | NLL | 13 | 0 | 15 | 15 | 10 | | | | | |
| | Vancouver | WLA | 6 | 0 | 6 | 6 | 0 | | | | | |

# MARUK, DENNIS

| | |
|---|---|
| sport: | hockey |
| given name: | Maruk, Dennis John |
| born: | Toronto, Ontario |
| | November 17, 1955 |
| height: | 1.73 m / 5'8" |
| weight: | 79.5 kg / 175 lbs |
| position: | center |
| shoots: | left |

In his last season of junior hockey, Dennis Maruk established an OHA Jr. "A" record for most points in a season, with 145 on 66 goals and 79 assists. That same year, he won the Red Tilson Trophy as the league's MVP. Based on these credentials, Maruk expected to be selected early in the 1975 NHL draft. He was overlooked, though, until the second round, when the California Golden Seals made him their second pick, 21st overall. The Seals, like the other

NHL teams, were impressed with his skills but concerned about his size. He was but 5'8" (1.73 m), and weighed only 165 lbs (75 kg). His physique appeared so unsuited for hockey that he was once even denied entrance at the player door of the Montreal Forum.

Maruk proved his detractors wrong; in his rookie year, he scored 30 goals and established an NHL record for most short-handed goals by a rookie with five. The Seals and Maruk moved to Cleveland at the end of the season. After two years, the financially strapped franchise merged with Minnesota. Two games into the 1978-79 season, the North Stars traded Maruk to the inept Washington Capitals. Maruk responded with 31 goals. The following year, he underwent knee surgery and missed more than half of the season.

During the 1980-81 season, Dennis Maruk scored 50 goals. The following year, he became only the seventh player in league history to net 60 goals. After the 1982-83 season, in which he scored 31 goals, Maruk was traded back to the Minnesota North Stars. He played for six seasons with Minnesota before retiring from the game as a result of a shattered knee cap which did not want to heal.

During his 14-year NHL career, the teams that Maruk played on made the playoffs only four times. Being a star on these also-ran teams, he was recruited at the end of the regular season to represent Canada at the world championships winning bronze medals in 1978 and 1983. An extremely hard working center, Maruk was also very quick and shifty. He had a habit of always going for the puck. Once in scoring position, Maruk used his quick release and accuracy to their full advantage. Because of his size, he was often the victim of intimidation. He learned how to fight back, stood up to the bullies, and developed a reputation for ferocity.

Dennis Maruk also excelled in lacrosse and is the brother of lacrosse player Barry Maruk.

## AWARDS

| 1973 | Hap Emms Rookie Award  -  OHA |
| 1975 | Albert "Red" Tilson Memorial Trophy  -  OHA MVP |

## RECORD

| year | team | league | regular season | | | | | playoffs | | | | |
|------|------|--------|----|----|----|-----|-----|----|----|----|-----|-----|
| | | | GP | G | A | PTS | PIM | GP | G | A | PTS | PIM |
| 1975-76 | California | NHL | 80 | 30 | 32 | 62 | 44 | | | | | |
| 1976-77 | Cleveland | NHL | 80 | 28 | 50 | 78 | 68 | | | | | |
| 1977-78 | Cleveland | NHL | 76 | 36 | 35 | 71 | 50 | | | | | |
| 1978-79 | Minnesota | NHL | 2 | 0 | 0 | 0 | 0 | | | | | |
| | Washington | NHL | 76 | 31 | 59 | 90 | 71 | | | | | |

| | | | regular season | | | | | playoffs | | | | |
|---|---|---|---|---|---|---|---|---|---|---|---|---|
| year | team | league | GP | G | A | PTS | PIM | GP | G | A | PTS | PIM |
| 1979-80 | Washington | NHL | 27 | 10 | 17 | 27 | 8 | | | | | |
| 1980-81 | Washington | NHL | 80 | 50 | 47 | 97 | 87 | | | | | |
| 1981-82 | Washington | NHL | 80 | 60 | 76 | 136 | 128 | | | | | |
| 1982-83 | Washington | NHL | 80 | 31 | 50 | 81 | 71 | 4 | 1 | 1 | 2 | 2 |
| 1983-84 | Minnesota | NHL | 71 | 17 | 43 | 60 | 42 | 16 | 5 | 5 | 10 | 8 |
| 1984-85 | Minnesota | NHL | 71 | 19 | 41 | 60 | 56 | 9 | 4 | 7 | 11 | 12 |
| 1985-86 | Minnesota | NHL | 70 | 21 | 37 | 58 | 67 | 5 | 4 | 9 | 13 | 4 |
| 1986-87 | Minnesota | NHL | 67 | 16 | 30 | 46 | 52 | | | | | |
| 1987-88 | Minnesota | NHL | 22 | 7 | 4 | 11 | 15 | | | | | |
| 1988-89 | Minnesota | NHL | 6 | 0 | 1 | 1 | 2 | | | | | |
| | Kalamazoo | IHL | 5 | 1 | 5 | 6 | 4 | | | | | |

international

| year | team | competition | GP | G | A | PTS | PIM | Place |
|---|---|---|---|---|---|---|---|---|
| 1978 | Canada | World Championship | 10 | 6 | 1 | 7 | 2 | 3 |
| 1979 | Canada | World Championship | 7 | 1 | 1 | 2 | 2 | 4 |
| 1981 | Canada | World Championship | 8 | 5 | 3 | 8 | 6 | 4 |
| 1983 | Canada | World Championship | 10 | 4 | 3 | 7 | 4 | 3 |

# MASNICK, PAUL

| | |
|---|---|
| sport: | hockey |
| given name: | Masnick, Paul Andrew |
| born: | Regina, Saskatchewan |
| | April 14, 1931 |
| height: | 1.75 m / 5'9" |
| weight: | 75 kg / 165 lbs |
| position: | center |
| shoots: | right |

*Photo courtesy of the Hockey Hall of Fame*

During the 1949-50 season, his last in junior hockey, Paul Masnick led the Regina Pats to the Western Canada Junior Hockey Championship and a berth in the Memorial Cup final. Masnick was the team's big shooter with 43 goals and 44 assists in 40 games. In the fall of

1950, he joined the Montreal Canadiens. Masnick's misfortune was that his play appeared to be average on the star-studded team. In addition, he was a relatively poor passer on a team that was known for its passing game. At training camp, management judged Masnick to be the team's fourth or fifth center. As a result, he spent much time commuting to the farm clubs. During the 1951-52 season, Montreal did not know what to do with Masnick, so they kept him until a call came from the Buffalo Bisons urgently requesting a replacement for an injured player. Masnick, who was not doing anything, was sent to Buffalo. When the injured player returned, Buffalo returned Masnick to Montreal with a request not to send him back.

In Montreal, Masnick was given the post of "hockey player without portfolio;" that is, he picked up a cheque for not playing. Montreal finally swung a deal, and Masnick was sent to Cincinnati, a New York Rangers affiliate that was going nowhere. Masnick, a strong defensive center, turned Cincinnati's season around with his hustle and spirit. The club made the playoffs, and in the opening round they met the Buffalo Bisons. Masnick's revenge was sweet; he was instrumental in leading Cincinnati to victory. Suddenly Masnick's service was desired by the Canadiens who were in the midst of a playoff series. He returned just in time to score a game-winning goal against Boston in the second overtime period. Montreal, though, lost the series.

Masnick spent most of the following two seasons with the Canadiens and was a member of the 1953 Stanley Cup team. In November of 1954, he was traded to Chicago. A month later, he was back in Montreal. Subsequently, Masnick played for two seasons in the minor pro leagues before being bought by Toronto in 1957. The 1957-58 season with the Leafs was his last in the NHL. Paul Masnick finished his career playing for minor pro teams in Winnipeg, Saskatoon, St. Paul and Victoria.

## RECORD

| year | team | league | regular season | | | | | playoffs | | | | |
|------|------|--------|----|----|----|-----|-----|----|----|----|-----|-----|
| | | | GP | G | A | PTS | PIM | GP | G | A | PTS | PIM |
| 1950-51 | Montreal | NHL | 43 | 4 | 1 | 5 | 14 | 11 | 2 | 1 | 3 | 4 |
| | Cincinnati | AHL | 19 | 5 | 7 | 12 | 15 | | | | | |
| 1951-52 | Montreal | NHL | 15 | 1 | 2 | 3 | 2 | 6 | 1 | 0 | 1 | 12 |
| | Cincinnati | AHL | 31 | 8 | 20 | 28 | 23 | 7 | 0 | 4 | 4 | 4 |
| 1952-53* | Montreal | NHL | 53 | 5 | 7 | 12 | 44 | 6 | 1 | 0 | 1 | 7 |
| | Montreal | QSHL | 10 | 6 | 6 | 12 | 10 | | | | | |
| 1953-54 | Montreal | NHL | 50 | 5 | 21 | 26 | 57 | 10 | 0 | 4 | 4 | 4 |
| | Montreal | QSHL | 14 | 3 | 14 | 17 | 9 | | | | | |
| 1954-55 | Montreal | NHL | 11 | 0 | 0 | 0 | 0 | | | | | |
| | Chicago | NHL | 11 | 1 | 0 | 1 | 8 | | | | | |
| | Montreal | NHL | 8 | 0 | 1 | 1 | 0 | | | | | |

| | | | regular season | | | | | playoffs | | | | |
|---|---|---|---|---|---|---|---|---|---|---|---|---|
| year | team | league | GP | G | A | PTS | PIM | GP | G | A | PTS | PIM |
| 1954-55 | Montreal | QHL | 27 | 10 | 13 | 23 | 14 | 14 | 2 | 9 | 11 | 14 |
| 1955-56* | Winnipeg | WHL | 62 | 29 | 39 | 68 | 37 | 14 | 11 | 9 | 20 | 14 |
| 1956-57 | Rochester | AHL | 64 | 24 | 38 | 62 | 46 | 10 | 5 | 5 | 10 | 17 |
| 1957-58 | Toronto | NHL | 41 | 2 | 9 | 11 | 14 | | | | | |
| 1958-59 | Saskatoon | WHL | 64 | 24 | 51 | 75 | 48 | | | | | |
| 1959-60 | Winnipeg/Victoria | WHL | 68 | 16 | 29 | 45 | 16 | 11 | 2 | 5 | 7 | 2 |
| 1960-61 | Victoria | WHL | 11 | 0 | 0 | 0 | 16 | | | | | |
| * | St. Paul | IHL | 30 | 12 | 23 | 35 | 20 | 9 | 5 | 4 | 9 | 7 |
| 1961-62 | St. Paul | IHL | 60 | 31 | 59 | 90 | 34 | 11 | 2 | 6 | 8 | 12 |
| 1962-63 | St. Paul | IHL | 31 | 11 | 21 | 32 | 4 | | | | | |

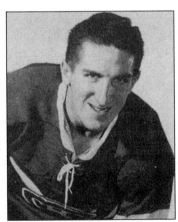

*Photo courtesy of the Hockey Hall of Fame*

# MAZUR, EDDIE

"Spider"

| | |
|---|---|
| sport: | hockey |
| given name: | Mazur, Edward Joseph |
| born: | Winnipeg, Manitoba |
| | July 25, 1929 |
| height: | 1.88 m / 6'2" |
| weight: | 84.5 kg / 186 lbs |
| position: | left wing |
| shoots: | left |

Eddie Mazur played junior hockey with the Winnipeg Monarchs, a Toronto Maple Leafs affiliate. In September of 1948, he turned professional with Dallas of the USHL, a Montreal farm team. The Leafs were most upset with this tampering and filed a protest. The matter was resolved when Montreal paid Toronto $2,000 to get Mazur's rights. Mazur made a number of appearances with the Canadiens, spending much time in the minors. His most memorable year was at the end of the 1952-53 season when he was called up for the playoffs. Mazur contributed two goals and two assists as Montreal won the Stanley Cup.

A tall and lanky athlete, Mazur was nicknamed the "Spider" because it appeared that he had many extra arms when he stickhandled up the ice. In May of 1956, he was sold to the Chicago Black Hawks. He briefly appeared with Chicago that season before completing his hockey career in the mid-1960s with stints in the AHL and WHL.

## INDUCTIONS

1985        Manitoba Hockey Hall of Fame

## ALL-STAR SELECTIONS

| 1949-50 | left wing | PCHL | Second Team |
|---------|-----------|------|-------------|
| 1950-51 | left wing | PCHL | Second Team |
| 1956-57 | left wing | AHL  | Second Team |
| 1958-59 | left wing | AHL  | Second Team |

## RECORD

| year | team | league | regular season | | | | | playoffs | | | | |
|------|------|--------|----|----|----|-----|-----|----|----|----|-----|-----|
|      |      |        | GP | G  | A  | PTS | PIM | GP | G  | A  | PTS | PIM |
| 1948-49  | Dallas     | USHL | 66 | 10 | 20 | 30 | 48 | 4  | 1 | 1  | 2  | 0  |
| 1949-50  | Victoria   | PCHL | 65 | 33 | 26 | 59 | 17 |    |   |    |    |    |
| 1950-51* | Victoria   | PCHL | 70 | 43 | 30 | 73 | 41 | 12 | 4 | 6  | 10 | 8  |
|          | Montreal   | NHL  |    |    |    |    |    | 2  | 0 | 0  | 0  | 0  |
| 1951-52  | Buffalo    | AHL  | 60 | 19 | 18 | 37 | 55 | 1  | 0 | 1  | 1  | 2  |
|          | Montreal   | NHL  |    |    |    |    |    | 5  | 2 | 0  | 2  | 4  |
| 1952-53  | Victoria   | WHL  | 51 | 20 | 18 | 38 | 54 |    |   |    |    |    |
| *        | Montreal   | NHL  |    |    |    |    |    | 7  | 2 | 2  | 4  | 11 |
| 1953-54  | Montreal   | NHL  | 67 | 7  | 14 | 21 | 95 | 11 | 0 | 3  | 3  | 7  |
| 1954-55  | Montreal   | NHL  | 25 | 1  | 5  | 6  | 21 |    |   |    |    |    |
|          | Montreal   | QHL  | 19 | 4  | 8  | 12 | 16 | 14 | 8 | 5  | 13 | 27 |
| 1955-56* | Winnipeg   | WHL  | 70 | 34 | 30 | 64 | 72 | 14 | 6 | 11 | 17 | 16 |
| 1956-57  | Chicago    | NHL  | 15 | 0  | 1  | 1  | 4  |    |   |    |    |    |
|          | Rochester  | AHL  | 47 | 24 | 40 | 64 | 90 | 10 | 3 | 9  | 12 | 18 |
| 1957-58  | Rochester  | AHL  | 59 | 22 | 25 | 47 | 67 |    |   |    |    |    |
| 1958-59  | Cleveland  | AHL  | 70 | 34 | 44 | 78 | 54 | 7  | 2 | 2  | 4  | 8  |
| 1959-60  | Cleveland  | AHL  | 61 | 29 | 24 | 53 | 79 | 7  | 2 | 4  | 6  | 24 |
| 1960-61  | Cleveland  | AHL  | 72 | 30 | 39 | 69 | 73 | 4  | 1 | 0  | 1  | 17 |
| 1961-62  | Cleveland  | AHL  | 70 | 24 | 24 | 48 | 44 | 6  | 0 | 0  | 0  | 4  |
| 1962-63  | Providence | AHL  | 72 | 18 | 33 | 51 | 72 | 4  | 1 | 0  | 1  | 8  |
| 1963-64  | Providence | AHL  | 64 | 23 | 33 | 56 | 56 | 3  | 1 | 4  | 5  | 6  |
| 1964-65  | Victoria   | WHL  | 62 | 16 | 30 | 46 | 97 | 11 | 1 | 0  | 1  | 6  |

# MELESCHUK, OREST

"Big O"

| | |
|---|---|
| sport: | curling |
| born: | St. Boniface, Manitoba |
| | April 11, 1940 |
| height: | . . . |
| weight: | . . . |

*Photo courtesy of the Western Pictorial Index*

Orest Meleschuk began curling in high school. His first success was winning the Inter-City High School Curling Championship. In 1962, while attending United College, he won the University of Manitoba Bonspiel. Over the years he won numerous bonspiels, among them the Kenora Invitational in 1968, the Boissevain Invitational in 1971, and the Sudbury Superspiel in 1976. Meleschuk won the Labatt's Grand Aggregate Award in 1982. The award was presented to the rink that amassed the most wins in the Free Press Trophy and the Sir J. Eaton Trophy competitions. The flamboyant Meleschuk also won the Free Press Trophy that year.

In 1972, Orest Meleschuk and his rink (composed of Dave Romano, at third; John Hanesiak, at second; and Pat Hailley, at lead) won the British Consols Trophy, emblematic of the Manitoba curling championship. Competing at the Brier, the Canadian championship, Meleschuk swept away all opposition to win the title and the right to represent Canada at the World Curling Championship. In Garmisch-Partenkirchen, Germany, Orest Meleschuk played through the round robin without suffering a defeat. In the semi-finals, he defeated Alex Torrance of Scotland 8-3.

The final against 21-year-old Robert Labonte of the United States is still one of the most talked about curling games on record. At the completion of the fourth end, Meleschuk's rink was down 5-1 to the American foursome. After six ends, Meleschuk was losing 7-3. Two points in the seventh and two in the eighth had the game tied up at seven. Labonte scored two in the ninth to take a 9-7 lead. In the tenth end, it appeared that the Americans had the game won. Unfortunately, they began to celebrate prematurely. Labonte, in joy, started jumping but fell kicking one of the Canadian stones. A measure was taken. The kicked stone was now good for points, and the game was declared tied at nine. In an extra end, Meleschuk made one of the greatest clutch shots in international curling. He landed a shot in the four-foot behind two guards. Curling last, Labonte could not counter Meleschuk's shot. The game and the world title were for Orest Meleschuk to savour.

In 1989, Meleschuk returned to the Brier. He placed fourth in the round robin competition and did not advance to the playoffs. Orest Meleschuk's rink included his son Sean.

## INDUCTIONS

1985        Manitoba Sports Hall of Fame  -  Member of the 1972 Orest Meleschuk Rink
1991        Manitoba Curling Hall of Fame and Museum  -  Member of the 1972 Orest Meleschuk Rink

## AWARDS

1972        Manitoba Ukrainian Sportsman of the Year

## RECORD

| year | competition | position | placing | result |
|------|-------------|----------|---------|--------|
| 1972 | Manitoba Championship | skip | 1 | |
| | Canadian Championship | skip | 1 | 9-1 |
| | World Championship | skip | 1 | 9-0 |
| 1989 | Manitoba Championship | skip | 1 | |
| | Canadian Championship | skip | 4 | 7-4 |

# MELNYK, GERRY

| | |
|---|---|
| sport: | hockey |
| given name: | Melnyk, Michael Gerald |
| born: | Edmonton, Alberta |
| | September 16, 1934 |
| height: | 1.78 m / 5'10" |
| weight: | 81.5 kg / 180 lbs |
| position: | center |
| shoots: | right |

Gerry Melnyk played junior hockey with the Edmonton Oil Kings, a Detroit Red Wing affiliate.  He then spent six seasons with Detroit's farm team the Edmonton Flyers, making one brief appearance with the Red Wings during the 1956 playoffs.  In the fall of 1959, he made the roster of the Red Wings and was with the team for two seasons before being traded to Chicago. Melnyk played one year for the Black Hawks before being farmed out.  In the minors, during the 1962-63 season, the soft-spoken Melnyk showed amazing versatility by playing every position but goal.  Although he lacked speed, Melnyk was a talented player with desire.

Gerry Melnyk was drafted by the St. Louis Blues in the 1967 Expansion Draft.  The following year, he moved to the Philadelphia Flyers.  During training camp, Melnyk experienced breathing problems.  He was diagnosed having a "coronary artery inefficiency," and on doctors' recommendation retired from the game.  The Flyers kept Melnyk in their organization and named him scout for Alberta and British Columbia.  Melnyk responded by convincing the Flyers to draft Bobby Clarke and to sign free agent Orest Kindrachuk.  Subsequently, Melnyk was named chief scout for the Flyers and served in that capacity for more than twenty years.  In addition, at the end 1981-82 season, Gerry Melnyk saw some coaching duties with the Portland Mariners, an affiliate of the Flyers.

## ALL-STAR SELECTIONS

| 1958-59 | center | WHL | Second Team (Prairie Division) |
| 1966-67 | center | CHL | Second Team |

## RECORD

| year | team | league | regular season | | | | | playoffs | | | | |
|------|------|--------|----|----|----|-----|-----|----|----|----|-----|-----|
| | | | GP | G | A | PTS | PIM | GP | G | A | PTS | PIM |
| 1952-53 | Edmonton | WHL | | | | | | 2 | 0 | 1 | 1 | 0 |
| 1953-54 | Edmonton | WHL | 3 | 1 | 1 | 2 | 0 | | | | | |
| 1954-55* | Edmonton | WHL | 69 | 14 | 29 | 43 | 24 | 9 | 2 | 8 | 10 | 0 |
| 1955-56 | Edmonton | WHL | 70 | 37 | 50 | 87 | 37 | 3 | 1 | 3 | 4 | 2 |
| | Detroit | NHL | | | | | | 6 | 0 | 0 | 0 | 0 |
| 1956-57 | Edmonton | WHL | 60 | 21 | 44 | 65 | 26 | 8 | 5 | 3 | 8 | 2 |
| 1957-58 | Edmonton | WHL | 50 | 22 | 40 | 62 | 19 | | | | | |
| 1958-59 | Edmonton | WHL | 64 | 30 | 37 | 67 | 8 | 3 | 0 | 1 | 1 | 2 |
| 1959-60 | Detroit | NHL | 63 | 10 | 10 | 20 | 12 | 6 | 3 | 0 | 3 | 0 |
| 1960-61 | Detroit | NHL | 70 | 9 | 16 | 25 | 2 | 11 | 1 | 0 | 1 | 2 |
| 1961-62 | Chicago | NHL | 63 | 5 | 16 | 21 | 6 | 7 | 0 | 0 | 0 | 2 |
| 1962-63* | Buffalo | AHL | 72 | 14 | 36 | 50 | 20 | 13 | 6 | 7 | 13 | 4 |
| 1963-64 | Buffalo | AHL | 70 | 11 | 34 | 45 | 0 | | | | | |
| | St. Louis | CPHL | | | | | | 6 | 1 | 4 | 5 | 2 |

| | | | regular season | | | | | playoffs | | | | |
|---|---|---|---|---|---|---|---|---|---|---|---|---|
| year | team | league | GP | G | A | PTS | PIM | GP | G | A | PTS | PIM |
| 1964-65 | Buffalo | AHL | 72 | 22 | 47 | 69 | 12 | 9 | 1 | 4 | 5 | 2 |
| | Chicago | NHL | | | | | | 6 | 0 | 0 | 0 | 0 |
| 1965-66 | Buffalo | AHL | 69 | 18 | 61 | 79 | 10 | | | | | |
| 1966-67 | St. Louis | CHL | 67 | 24 | 47 | 71 | 12 | | | | | |
| 1967-68 | St. Louis | NHL | 73 | 15 | 35 | 50 | 14 | 17 | 2 | 6 | 8 | 2 |

# MELNYK, LARRY

| | |
|---|---|
| sport: | hockey |
| given name: | Melnyk, Lawrence Joseph |
| born: | New Westminster, British Columbia |
| | February 21, 1960 |
| height: | 1.83 m / 6'0" |
| weight: | 88.5 kg / 195 lbs |
| position: | defense |
| shoots: | left |

*Photo courtesy of the Vancouver Canucks*

Larry Melnyk was drafted as an underage junior by the Boston Bruins in the fourth round of the 1979 NHL Entry Draft. The next season, he completed his junior tenure with the New Westminster Bruins. Melnyk made his NHL debut during the 1980-81 season with Boston. He spent three seasons playing with Boston and its minor league affiliates. In March of 1983, Melnyk was traded by Boston to the Edmonton Oilers. He played in six playoff games as Edmonton won the Stanley Cup. League rules, though, prevented his name from appearing on the Cup.

The following year, Larry Melnyk contributed to the success of the Oilers during the regular season and the playoffs. The team repeated as Cup champions, and this time Melnyk was officially listed as a Stanley Cup winner. Melnyk, a hard checking stay-at-home defenseman, did not fit in with the free-wheeling Oilers, and in 1985 he was traded to the New York Rangers. Two years later, he was playing for the Vancouver Canucks. Larry Melnyk's NHL career concluded at the end of the 1989-90 season.

# RECORD

| year | team | league | regular season GP | G | A | PTS | PIM | playoffs GP | G | A | PTS | PIM |
|------|------|--------|------|---|---|-----|-----|------|---|---|-----|-----|
| 1980-81 | Boston | NHL | 26 | 0 | 4 | 4 | 39 | | | | | |
| | Springfield | AHL | 47 | 1 | 10 | 11 | 109 | 1 | 0 | 0 | 0 | 0 |
| 1981-82 | Boston | NHL | 48 | 0 | 8 | 8 | 84 | 11 | 0 | 3 | 3 | 40 |
| | Erie | AHL | 10 | 0 | 3 | 3 | 36 | | | | | |
| 1982-83 | Boston | NHL | 1 | 0 | 0 | 0 | 0 | 11 | 0 | 0 | 0 | 9 |
| | Baltimore | AHL | 72 | 2 | 24 | 26 | 215 | | | | | |
| 1983-84 | Hershey | AHL | 50 | 0 | 18 | 18 | 156 | | | | | |
| | Moncton | AHL | 14 | 0 | 3 | 3 | 17 | | | | | |
| * | Edmonton | NHL | | | | | | 6 | 0 | 1 | 1 | 0 |
| 1984-85* | Edmonton | NHL | 28 | 0 | 11 | 11 | 25 | 12 | 1 | 3 | 4 | 26 |
| | Nova Scotia | AHL | 37 | 2 | 10 | 12 | 97 | | | | | |
| 1985-86 | Edmonton | NHL | 6 | 2 | 3 | 5 | 11 | | | | | |
| | NY Rangers | NHL | 46 | 1 | 8 | 9 | 65 | 16 | 1 | 2 | 3 | 46 |
| | Nova Scotia | AHL | 19 | 2 | 8 | 10 | 72 | | | | | |
| 1986-87 | NY Rangers | NHL | 73 | 3 | 12 | 15 | 182 | 6 | 0 | 0 | 0 | 4 |
| 1987-88 | NY Rangers | NHL | 14 | 0 | 1 | 1 | 34 | | | | | |
| | Vancouver | NHL | 49 | 2 | 3 | 5 | 73 | | | | | |
| 1988-89 | Vancouver | NHL | 74 | 3 | 11 | 14 | 82 | 4 | 0 | 0 | 0 | 2 |
| 1989-90 | Vancouver | NHL | 67 | 0 | 2 | 2 | 91 | | | | | |

international

| year | team | competition | GP | G | A | PTS | PIM | Place |
|------|------|-------------|----|---|---|-----|-----|-------|
| 1979 | New Westminster | World Junior Championship | 5 | 1 | 1 | 2 | 2 | 5 |

# MICHALUK, ART

sport:        hockey
given name:   Michaluk, Arthur
born:         Canmore, Alberta
              May 4, 1923
height:       1.83 m / 6'0"
weight:       82.5 kg / 182 lbs
position:     defense
shoots:       right

During World War II, Art Michaluk served in the armed forces and played hockey for the Calgary Army Currie Barracks of the ASSHL.  Michaluk was with the club when it won the league championship in 1943.  Subsequently, he played for the Air Force team.  Once hostilities ceased, Michaluk signed with the Calgary Stampeders of the Western Canada Senior Hockey League.  The club won the Allan Cup in 1946.  Midway through the 1947-48 season, Michaluk joined the Providence Reds of the AHL.  He also made a brief appearance with the Chicago Black Hawks of the NHL.  In the fall of 1948, Michaluk had a very successful training camp with the Black Hawks, but the owner of the Reds wanted him back in Providence and paid Chicago a substantial amount for his services.

Michaluk quickly became one of the Reds' most popular players.  He played a rugged game and threw bruising bodychecks.  At the same time, he was very cool under pressure, did not panic, and stayed out of the penalty box.  He was known as the "silent one," hardly ever speaking unless spoken to.  In the fall of 1952, the Reds agreed to Michaluk's request to be near his expecting wife and their four children in Canmore, and loaned him to the Calgary Stampeders of the WHL.  The loan eventually became permanent.  Michaluk had a number of good seasons with Calgary; he was named to a string of all-star teams and led the club to the 1954 playoff championship trophy.  At the conclusion of the 1954-55 season, Michaluk quit hockey and joined the Calgary police force.  In the fall of 1955, he was talked out of retirement and juggled full-time police work with hockey.  Art Michaluk is the brother of hockey player John Michaluk.

## ALL-STAR SELECTIONS

| | | | |
|---|---|---|---|
| 1952-53 | defense | WHL | First Team |
| 1953-54 | defense | WHL | Second Team |
| 1954-55 | defense | WHL | Second Team |

| 1955-56 | defense | WHL | First Team |
| 1956-57 | defense | WHL | First Team (Prairie Division) |

## RECORD

| | | | regular season | | | | | playoffs | | | | |
|---|---|---|---|---|---|---|---|---|---|---|---|---|
| year | team | league | GP | G | A | PTS | PIM | GP | G | A | PTS | PIM |
| 1947-48 | Chicago | NHL | 5 | 0 | 0 | 0 | 0 | | | | | |
| | Providence | AHL | 40 | 6 | 10 | 16 | 32 | 5 | 1 | 2 | 3 | 2 |
| 1948-49* | Providence | AHL | 65 | 4 | 17 | 21 | 55 | 11 | 1 | 3 | 4 | 6 |
| 1949-50 | Providence | AHL | 67 | 7 | 20 | 27 | 32 | 4 | 1 | 2 | 3 | 2 |
| 1950-51 | Providence | AHL | 70 | 13 | 21 | 34 | 34 | | | | | |
| 1951-52 | Providence | AHL | 62 | 3 | 15 | 18 | 41 | 15 | 0 | 5 | 5 | 8 |
| 1952-53 | Calgary | WHL | 70 | 10 | 26 | 36 | 22 | 5 | 0 | 2 | 2 | 8 |
| 1953-54* | Calgary | WHL | 68 | 7 | 26 | 33 | 20 | 18 | 1 | 7 | 8 | 8 |
| 1954-55 | Calgary | WHL | 70 | 8 | 22 | 30 | 24 | 9 | 0 | 7 | 7 | 10 |
| 1955-56 | Calgary | WHL | 54 | 3 | 14 | 17 | 28 | 8 | 0 | 2 | 2 | 6 |
| 1956-57 | Calgary | WHL | 51 | 2 | 12 | 14 | 15 | 3 | 0 | 2 | 2 | 2 |
| 1957-58 | Calgary | WHL | 17 | 3 | 15 | 18 | 2 | 14 | 0 | 3 | 3 | 6 |

# MICHALUK, JOHN

| | |
|---|---|
| sport: | hockey |
| given name: | Michaluk, John Jr. |
| born: | Canmore, Alberta |
| | November 2, 1928 |
| height: | 1.78 m / 5'10" |
| weight: | 70 kg / 155 lbs |
| position: | forward |
| shoots: | left |

John Michaluk literally followed his brother Art from one hockey team to another. Before turning professional, they both played with the Calgary Stampeders. From there, John followed Art to Providence and later back to Calgary. The two brothers also made very brief appearances with the Chicago Black Hawks, although at separate times.

# RECORD

| year | team | league | regular season | | | | | playoffs | | | | |
|------|------|--------|------|------|------|------|------|------|------|------|------|------|
| | | | GP | G | A | PTS | PIM | GP | G | A | PTS | PIM |
| 1950-51 | Chicago | NHL | 1 | 0 | 0 | 0 | 0 | | | | | |
| | Milwaukee | USHL | 56 | 13 | 11 | 24 | 41 | | | | | |
| 1951-52 | Providence | AHL | 46 | 13 | 12 | 25 | 16 | 3 | 0 | 1 | 1 | 0 |
| 1952-53 | Providence | AHL | 18 | 1 | 3 | 4 | 6 | | | | | |
| | Quebec | QSHL | 22 | 3 | 3 | 6 | 17 | 21 | 0 | 2 | 2 | 5 |
| 1953-54* | Calgary | WHL | 66 | 7 | 9 | 16 | 8 | 18 | 2 | 7 | 9 | 8 |
| 1954-55 | Calgary | WHL | 14 | 3 | 4 | 7 | 2 | 9 | 0 | 0 | 0 | 2 |

# MICHALUK, JOHN

| | |
|------|------|
| sport: | football |
| born: | Hamilton, Ontario |
| | September 14, 1942 |
| height: | 1.83 m / 6'0" |
| weight: | 95.5 kg / 210 lbs |
| position: | linebacker |

*Photo courtesy of the Canadian Football Hall of Fame and Museum*

As a youngster, John Michaluk sold programs at Hamilton Tiger-Cats football games. In his teens, he quarterbacked Hamilton's Central High School and the Burlington Braves football teams. He then attended Kent State University on a football scholarship. In 1966, Michaluk graduated with a degree in business administration and a wealth of football experience. That year, he returned to the stadium where he sold programs as a member of the Hamilton Tiger-Cats. Michaluk was with the club for four seasons, winning the Grey Cup in 1967. He played at the linebacker position with an intensity that earned him the distinction of cracking more helmets than any other Tiger-Cat.

Upon retiring from the Tiger-Cats in 1969, Michaluk expanded his banking interests, which he had been juggling with football since 1966. Football, though, was still in his blood, and when in 1971 he was asked to become a part of the Tiger-Cats' radio broadcast team, he quickly agreed. Initially, Michaluk handled the post-game phone-in show. Subsequently, he became a colour commentator and then the play-by-play announcer. Following a 1992 Hamilton Tiger-Cat Football Club change in ownership, John Michaluk was named the team's new President and Chief Executive Officer.

# MICHAYLUK, DAVE

"Boris"

| | |
|---|---|
| sport: | hockey |
| given name: | Michayluk, David |
| born: | Wakaw, Saskatchewan |
| | May 18, 1962 |
| height: | 1.78 m / 5'10" |
| weight: | 81.5 kg / 180 lbs |
| position: | right wing |
| shoots: | left |

After an outstanding rookie season with the Regina Pats, during which he registered 133 points, Dave Michayluk was selected 85th overall by the Philadelphia Flyers in the 1981 Entry Draft. Michayluk spent most of the 1981-82 season back in Regina, scoring 172 points during the regular season and a league-leading 40 points during the playoffs. He also made his NHL debut that year, but it lasted just one game. During the 1982-83 season, he played with the Flyers and Maine of the AHL. Michayluk was not a fast skater, a handicap which probably kept him out of the NHL. Despite his lack of speed, he was an excellent playmaker and penalty killer.

Michayluk spent the 1983-84 season with Springfield of the AHL. He split the 1984-85 season between Hershey of the AHL and Kalamazoo of the IHL. That season, he scored 101 points and began a string of seven consecutive 100 point seasons. In the summer of 1985, Michayluk was signed as a free agent by the Edmonton Oilers and assigned to Nova Scotia of the AHL. After a few games, he was sent to the Muskegon Lumberjacks of the IHL. He performed steadily for the Lumberjacks, scoring a league-leading 56 goals during the 1987-88 season; a year later he led the league in points with 122.

### AWARDS

1981        Stewart "Butch" Paul Memorial Trophy  -  WHL Top Rookie

| 1989 | Leo Lamoreau Memorial Trophy  -  IHL Top Scorer |
|------|--------------------------------------------------|
| 1989 | James Gatschene Memorial Trophy  -  IHL MVP |
| 1989 | N.R. Poile Memorial Trophy  -  IHL Playoff MVP |

## ALL-STAR SELECTIONS

| 1985 | right wing | IHL | Second Team |
|------|-----------|-----|-------------|
| 1987 | right wing | IHL | First Team |
| 1988 | right wing | IHL | First Team |
| 1989 | right wing | IHL | First Team |
| 1990 | right wing | IHL | First Team |

## RECORD

| year | team | league | regular season | | | | | playoffs | | | | |
|------|------|--------|----|----|----|-----|-----|----|----|----|-----|-----|
| | | | GP | G | A | PTS | PIM | GP | G | A | PTS | PIM |
| 1981-82 | Philadelphia | NHL | 1 | 0 | 0 | 0 | 0 | | | | | |
| 1982-83 | Philadelphia | NHL | 13 | 2 | 6 | 8 | 8 | | | | | |
| | Maine | AHL | 69 | 32 | 40 | 72 | 16 | 8 | 0 | 2 | 2 | 0 |
| 1983-84 | Springfield | AHL | 79 | 18 | 44 | 62 | 37 | 4 | 0 | 0 | 0 | 2 |
| 1984-85 | Hershey | AHL | 3 | 0 | 2 | 2 | 2 | | | | | |
| | Kalamazoo | IHL | 82 | 66 | 33 | 99 | 49 | 11 | 7 | 7 | 14 | 0 |
| 1985-86 | Nova Scotia | AHL | 3 | 0 | 1 | 1 | 0 | | | | | |
| | Muskegon | IHL | 77 | 52 | 52 | 104 | 73 | 14 | 6 | 9 | 15 | 12 |
| 1986-87 | Muskegon | IHL | 82 | 47 | 53 | 100 | 29 | 15 | 2 | 14 | 16 | 8 |
| 1987-88 | Muskegon | IHL | 81 | 56 | 81 | 137 | 46 | 6 | 2 | 0 | 2 | 18 |
| 1988-89* | Muskegon | IHL | 80 | 50 | 72 | 122 | 84 | 13 | 9 | 12 | 21 | 24 |
| 1989-90 | Muskegon | IHL | 79 | 51 | 51 | 102 | 80 | 15 | 8 | 14 | 22 | 10 |
| 1990-91 | Muskegon | IHL | 83 | 40 | 62 | 102 | 116 | 5 | 2 | 2 | 4 | 4 |

# MICKOSKI, NICK

"Broadway Nick"

| | |
|---|---|
| sport: | hockey, golf |
| given name: | Mickoski, Nicholas |
| born: | Winnipeg, Manitoba |
| | December 7, 1927 |
| height: | 1.85 m / 6'1" |
| weight: | 87.5 kg / 193 lbs |
| position: | left wing |
| shoots: | left |

Nick Mickoski will probably be best remembered for the goal he did not score. During the 1950 playoffs, the Stanley Cup final series was tied at three games a piece with the seventh and deciding game in its second overtime period. Mickoski received a pass from a Chicago teammate and walked in on Detroit goalie Harry Lumley. Mickoski's shot whistled right by Lumley, hit the post, and bounced out. Detroit eventually won the game and the Stanley Cup.

After a junior career that included play for the Canadian Ukrainian Athletic Club, St. James Canadians and the Stratford Kroehlers, Mickoski joined the senior New York Rovers. In 1947, he turned professional with the Rangers organization and was farmed out to New Haven for the season. The following year, he gained a starting position with the Rangers. In his seventh year with the club he was traded to Chicago. Eventually he played for Detroit and Boston. After his NHL career ended, Mickoski played for Providence and Cincinnati of the American League before moving on to the San Francisco Seals of the Western Hockey League. Midway through the 1963-64 season, Mickoski was named playing coach of the Seals. He led the club to the WHL championship that year. Starting in the fall of 1966, he was playing coach of the Grand Falls Cataracts of the Newfoundland Senior Hockey League for three seasons.

Nick Mickoski later coached the Winnipeg Junior Jets for three seasons. He preached a strong-skating, close-checking positional brand of hockey. His workouts were tough; he was of the opinion that a little bit of sweat would do no harm. When the World Hockey Association came into existence, he was instrumental in the formation of the Winnipeg Jets and luring Bobby Hull to the team. Mickoski was the Jets' first coach and subsequently co-coached the team with Hull until the end of the 1974 season.

An avid golfer during the summer months, Mickoski was the top amateur at the 1962 Manitoba Open and won the Manitoba Amateur Championship in 1966. In 1969, he won the Northeastern Open and the Free Press Tournament of Champions. In 1963, 1966, and 1967, Nick Mickoski represented Manitoba in Willingdon Cup play for the Canadian interprovincial amateur championship. Manitoba placed fourth, sixth, and fifth in the respective years. In 1983, he won the provincial senior title.

# INDUCTIONS

1985      Manitoba Hockey Hall of Fame

# AWARDS

1967      Manitoba Ukrainian Sportsman of the Year
1984      Manitoba Ukrainian Sportsman of the Year

# ALL-STAR SELECTIONS

1962-63    left wing    WHL    First Team

# RECORD

| year | team | league | regular season | | | | | playoffs | | | | |
|------|------|--------|-----|-----|-----|-----|-----|-----|-----|-----|-----|-----|
| | | | GP | G | A | PTS | PIM | GP | G | A | PTS | PIM |
| 1944-45 | Providence | AHL | 6 | 0 | 0 | 0 | 5 | | | | | |
| 1945-46 | New York | EHL | 25 | 6 | 8 | 14 | 8 | | | | | |
| 1946-47 | New York | EHL | 10 | 9 | 16 | 25 | 10 | | | | | |
| 1947-48 | New Haven | AHL | 22 | 11 | 16 | 27 | 4 | 4 | 2 | 1 | 3 | 2 |
| | NY Rangers | NHL | | | | | | 2 | 0 | 1 | 1 | 0 |
| 1948-49 | NY Rangers | NHL | 54 | 13 | 9 | 22 | 20 | | | | | |
| 1949-50 | NY Rangers | NHL | 45 | 10 | 10 | 20 | 10 | 12 | 1 | 5 | 6 | 2 |
| | New Haven | AHL | 23 | 12 | 17 | 29 | 7 | | | | | |
| 1950-51 | NY Rangers | NHL | 64 | 20 | 15 | 35 | 12 | | | | | |
| 1951-52 | NY Rangers | NHL | 43 | 7 | 13 | 20 | 20 | | | | | |
| | Cincinnati | AHL | 22 | 11 | 10 | 21 | 15 | 5 | 2 | 3 | 5 | 4 |
| 1952-53 | NY Rangers | NHL | 70 | 19 | 16 | 35 | 39 | | | | | |
| 1953-54 | NY Rangers | NHL | 68 | 19 | 16 | 35 | 22 | | | | | |
| 1954-55 | NY Rangers | NHL | 18 | 0 | 14 | 14 | 6 | | | | | |
| | Chicago | NHL | 52 | 10 | 19 | 29 | 42 | | | | | |
| 1955-56 | Chicago | NHL | 70 | 19 | 20 | 39 | 52 | | | | | |
| 1956-57 | Chicago | NHL | 70 | 16 | 20 | 36 | 24 | | | | | |
| 1957-58 | Chicago | NHL | 28 | 5 | 6 | 11 | 20 | | | | | |
| | Detroit | NHL | 37 | 8 | 12 | 20 | 30 | 4 | 0 | 0 | 0 | 4 |
| 1958-59 | Detroit | NHL | 66 | 11 | 15 | 26 | 20 | | | | | |
| 1959-60 | Boston | NHL | 18 | 1 | 0 | 1 | 2 | | | | | |
| | Providence | AHL | 48 | 29 | 22 | 51 | 6 | 5 | 2 | 5 | 7 | 4 |
| 1960-61 | Winnipeg | WHL | 69 | 25 | 24 | 49 | 16 | | | | | |

| year | team | league | regular season | | | | | playoffs | | | | |
|------|------|--------|----|----|----|-----|-----|----|----|----|-----|-----|
| | | | GP | G | A | PTS | PIM | GP | G | A | PTS | PIM |
| 1961-62 | San Francisco | WHL | 70 | 31 | 48 | 79 | 24 | 2 | 1 | 1 | 2 | 0 |
| 1962-63* | San Francisco | WHL | 68 | 41 | 54 | 95 | 10 | 17 | 5 | 17 | 22 | 6 |
| 1963-64* | San Francisco | WHL | 68 | 20 | 37 | 57 | 28 | 11 | 2 | 10 | 12 | 4 |
| 1964-65 | San Francisco | WHL | 60 | 13 | 33 | 46 | 24 | | | | | |

# MIHAYCHUK, MANOLY

sport: athletics
born: Bridok, Ukraine
    . . ., 1894
died: Arbaka, Manitoba
    May 17, 1967
height: . . .
weight: . . .

Manoly Mihaychuk was one of the first, if not the first, Canadian of Ukrainian descent to compete in an officially sanctioned sport event, when he placed third in the pole vault at a Manitoba versus North Dakota Intervarsity track meet in 1914. According to the *Kalendar Ukrainskoho Holosu - 1915*, Mihaychuk also won a Canadian title in a "jumping" event. Unfortunately, this latter result could not be independently verified.

After embarking on a career in dentistry, Dr. Mihaychuk became an active proponent of organized sport for Ukrainian youth. In 1923, he organized a Ukrainian Track and Field Day. The primary objective of the meet was to determine the athletic proficiency of Ukrainian youth. It was hoped that the better athletes would form the nucleus of a Ukrainian athletic club. The plan never materialized. A year later, Dr. Mihaychuk lectured at a four-week course for Ukrainian teachers on the historical development of Ukrainian sport and physical education.

## RECORD

| year | competition | event | placing | result |
|------|-------------|-------|---------|--------|
| 1914 | Manitoba vs North Dakota | pole vault | 3 | |

# MITRUK, CHRISTOPHER

sport:          trampoline
given name:     Mitruk, Christopher Frederick William
born:           Etobicoke, Ontario
                March 1, 1974
height:         1.80 m / 5'11"
weight:         66 kg / 145 lbs

When Christopher Mitruk was young, many believed that he would follow in his father's footsteps and become one of Canada's top gymnasts. In 1985, he finished 26th in his age group at the Canadian gymnastic championships. That same year, he placed 13th at the national trampoline championships. It was then that he decided to forgo gymnastics to concentrate on the trampoline.

The years of gymnastics training and his natural athletic ability were the building blocks that quickly established Mitruk as a dominant force on the trampoline. At the 1986 national trampoline championships, Mitruk finished first in his age group. A year later, he repeated as national champion and also won first prize at both the North American Invitational and the Harbour Front World Cup. In 1989, competing in the senior category, Mitruk placed second in the national championships and second at the North American Invitational. Christopher Mitruk is the son of gymnast Stephen Mitruk and the brother of gymnast Terry Mitruk.

## RECORD

| year | competition | placing |
|------|-------------|---------|
| 1985 | Canadian Championships - Junior | 13 |
| 1986 | Canadian Championships - Junior | 1 |
| 1987 | Canadian Championships - Junior | 1 |
|      | North American Invitational - Junior | 1 |
|      | Harbour Front World Cup - Junior | 1 |
| 1988 | Canadian Championships - Junior | 1 |
|      | North American Invitational | 1 |
|      | Harbour Front World Cup | 1 |
| 1989 | Canadian Championships | 2 |
|      | North American Invitational | 2 |

| year | competition | placing |
|------|-------------|---------|
| 1989 | Harbour Front Invitational | 7 |
| 1990 | World Championships | 21 |
| 1992 | World Championships | 15 |

# MITRUK, STEVE

| | |
|---|---|
| sport: | gymnastics |
| given name: | Mitruk, Stephen Frederick |
| born: | Hamilton, Ontario |
| | January 17, 1947 |
| height: | 1.78 m / 5'10" |
| weight: | 75 kg / 165 lbs |

In the years 1966 through 1976, Steve Mitruk was one of the top male gymnasts in Canada. He had numerous top-three finishes at the Canadian championships. At the 1967 Canada Games, Mitruk won five gold and two silver medals. Mitruk's international experience included competition at two Olympics - Mexico in 1968 and Munich in 1972, two World Championships, two World University Games, two World Cups, and the 1971 Pan American Games. While competing at the university level, Mitruk became the first athlete to be honoured with the OUAA Gymnast of the Year Award for five consecutive years.

A very talented natural athlete, Steve Mitruk was a quick learner of elements and routines. His best successes were on the pommel horse, an apparatus that he enjoyed performing on.

In 1975, Steve Mitruk began coaching with the Mississauga Gymnastics Club. After retiring from competitive gymnastics in 1976, Mitruk continued to coach. In 1978, he founded the Burlington Boys Gymnastics Club. He designed the club's gymnastic facilities and served as the club's head coach and president through 1986. The following year, Mitruk returned to coach at McMaster University. He had previously coached the club in 1977-78. Benefiting from the many years of experience gained as an athlete and coach, Mitruk began judging gymnastics at the national level in 1976 and trampoline in 1985. In the years 1980-88, he served on the Ontario men's gymnastics technical committee. A high school teacher, Stephen Mitruk is the father of gymnast Terry Mitruk and trampolinist Christopher Mitruk.

# INDUCTIONS

| | |
|---|---|
| 1986 | McMaster University Hall of Fame |

# AWARDS

| | |
|---|---|
| 1969 | OUAA Gymnast of the Year |
| 1970 | OUAA Gymnast of the Year |
| 1971 | OUAA Gymnast of the Year |
| 1972 | Ivor Wynne Trophy  -  McMaster University Athlete of the Year |
| 1972 | OUAA Gymnast of the Year |
| 1973 | OUAA Gymnast of the Year |

# RECORD

| year | competition | event | placing |
|---|---|---|---|
| 1966 | Canadian Junior Championships | all-around | 3 |
| 1967 | Canada Games | all-around | 1 |
| | | pommel | 1 |
| | | floor | 3 |
| | | parallel bars | 3 |
| | | horizontal bars | 1 |
| 1969 | Copa de las Americas | all-around | 18 |
| 1968 | Olympic Games | | |
| 1970 | Canadian Championships | pommel | 3 |
| | World Championships | | |
| | World Student Games | | |
| 1971 | Pan American Games | all-around | 16 |
| | | team | 3 |
| 1972 | Olympic Games | all-around | 97 |
| 1973 | World Student Games | | |
| 1974 | World Championships | | |
| 1975 | World Cup | | |
| 1976 | Olympic Trials | | |

# MITRUK, TERRY

sport:            gymnastics
given name:       Mitruk, Terry Stephen
born:             Hamilton, Ontario
                  March 25, 1968
height:           1.75 m / 5'9"
weight:           70 kg  / 155 lbs

Terry Mitruk began practising gymnastics under the guidance of his father in 1978. Ten years later, while competing for McMaster University, Mitruk was still coached by his father. He was an extremely hard worker during training but did not have luck on his side while competing. There was always some minor glitch in each routine. This may have been caused by apprehension, since Mitruk was always very concerned with whether a particular routine would work out.

Terry Mitruk had some success at the national championships. He was better known, though, for his performances on the inter-collegiate circuit. His best results were on the high bar, pommel horse, and in the vault. In his spare time, Mitruk coached recreational gymnastics and judged trampoline competitions. Terry Mitruk is the son of gymnast Stephen Mitruk and the brother of Christopher Mitruk who competes on the trampoline.

## AWARDS

| 1988 | Gymnastics MVP | - | McMaster University |
| 1989 | Gymnastics MVP | - | McMaster University |

## RECORD

| year | competition | event | placing |
|------|-------------|-------|---------|
| 1986 | Ontario Games | all-around | 1 |
|      |             | vault | 1 |
|      |             | parallel bars | 1 |
|      |             | high bar | 1 |

| year | competition | event | placing |
|------|-------------|-------|---------|
| 1987 | Canadian Championships | all-around | 27 |
|      |             | team | 1 |
|      | Canada Games | team | 1 |
|      |             | rings | 6 |
|      |             | parallel bar | 4 |
| 1988 | Canadian Championships | all-around | 23 |
|      |             | team | 1 |
|      | University National Cup | all-around | 10 |
| 1989 | Canadian Championships | all-around | 18 |
|      | University National Cup | all-around | 8 |
|      |             | high bar | 2 |

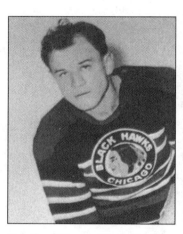

# MOSIENKO, BILL

"Mosi," "Mozie"

| | |
|---|---|
| sport: | hockey |
| given name: | Mosienko, William |
| born: | Winnipeg, Manitoba |
| | November 2, 1921 |
| height: | 1.73 m / 5'8" |
| weight: | 72.5 kg / 160 lbs |
| position: | right wing |
| shoots: | right |

For the Chicago Black Hawks and the New York Rangers, the final game of the season on March 23, 1952, could not have come sooner. The two clubs were out of the playoffs, with Chicago at the basement of the league. Five minutes into the third period, Chicago was down 6-2. Then the Gus Bodnar line came on to the ice.

Bodnar won the draw and passed the puck to his right winger Bill Mosienko. Mosienko gathered speed, stepped around all-star defenseman Hy Buller and fired a low wrist shot to the right side of the net. It went in. The time was 6:09. Bodnar once again won the face-off and passed the puck to Mosienko who neatly outflanked Buller and had goalie Lorne Anderson all to himself. Once again, a low shot to the right side found its mark. The time was 6:20. After the goal, the Chicago coach wanted to remove the Bodnar line but in the last second decided to keep the threesome on. Bodnar once again won the face-off, but this time he passed to his left winger George Gee. Mosienko, who was streaking in towards goal, was spotted by Gee who laid him a perfect pass. Mosienko pulled Anderson out of the net and fired the puck over him into the right corner of the net. The time was 6:30. Three goals in 21 seconds: a record that may never be broken.

Bill Mosienko started his organized hockey career with the Sherburn club in Winnipeg. He moved up to the junior ranks in 1939 with the Winnipeg Monarchs. With three years of junior eligibility still remaining, Mosienko joined the Chicago Black Hawks. He was farmed out by Chicago to Providence and Kansas City. During the 1941-42 season, he was finally called up by Chicago, albeit just for twelve games. He scored two goals and assisted on another two in his first NHL game. The following year, he played only two games for the Hawks.

Mosienko's first complete season was in 1943-44, when he scored 32 goals and assisted on 38 to establish a record for most points by a rookie in a 50-game season. The following year, he tallied for 54 points and did not receive one penalty. For his efforts, he was awarded the Lady Byng Trophy as the most gentlemanly player of the year. During his NHL career, Mosienko had a grand total of 121 minutes in penalties, which averages out to less than nine minutes per season. He was an extremely fast and elusive skater. In 1953, when he was in his thirties, he was voted the fastest skater in the league by sportscasters and sports writers.

After retiring from the Black Hawks, Mosienko and fellow Winnipeger and ex-Ranger Alf Pike launched the Winnipeg Warriors minor pro team. The Warriors, with Mosienko in their line-up, won the Edinburgh Trophy in their first year of existence. Mosienko finally hung up his skates in the spring of 1959; his bruised body was tired. During the 1959-60 season, Mosienko replaced Pike as Warrior coach when the latter was offered a position in the NHL. At the end of the 1960-61 season, Mosienko resigned. In subsequent years, Bill Mosienko did not distance himself from hockey. He served on the Board of Directors of the Manitoba Hockey Players Association and was a governor of Hockey Canada.

## INDUCTIONS

| 1965 | Hockey Hall of Fame |
| 1980 | Manitoba Sports Hall of Fame |

## AWARDS

| 1945 | Lady Byng Trophy  -  NHL Most Gentlemanly Player |
| 1956 | Ches McCance Trophy  -  Manitoba Athlete of the Year |
| 1980 | Manitoba Ukrainian Sportsman of the Year |
| 1990 | Manitoba Ukrainian Sportsman of the Past 25 Years |

# ALL-STAR SELECTIONS

| 1944-45 | right wing | NHL | Second Team |
| 1945-46 | right wing | NHL | Second Team |
| 1956-57 | right wing | WHL | First Team (Prairie Division) |
| 1957-58 | right wing | WHL | First Team (Prairie Division) |
| 1958-59 | right wing | WHL | First Team (Prairie Division) |

# RECORD

| year | team | league | regular season GP | G | A | PTS | PIM | playoffs GP | G | A | PTS | PIM |
|------|------|--------|-----|-----|-----|-----|-----|-----|-----|-----|-----|-----|
| 1940-41 | Providence | AHL | 36 | 14 | 19 | 33 | 8 | | | | | |
| | Kansas City | AHA | 7 | 2 | 2 | 4 | 0 | 8 | 4 | 1 | 5 | 2 |
| 1941-42 | Chicago | NHL | 12 | 6 | 8 | 14 | 4 | 3 | 2 | 0 | 2 | 0 |
| | Kansas City | AHA | 33 | 12 | 19 | 31 | 9 | | | | | |
| 1942-43 | Chicago | NHL | 2 | 2 | 0 | 2 | 0 | | | | | |
| | Quebec | QSHL | 8 | 5 | 3 | 8 | 2 | 4 | 2 | 2 | 4 | 2 |
| 1943-44 | Chicago | NHL | 50 | 32 | 38 | 70 | 10 | 8 | 2 | 2 | 4 | 6 |
| 1944-45 | Chicago | NHL | 50 | 28 | 26 | 54 | 0 | | | | | |
| 1945-46 | Chicago | NHL | 40 | 18 | 30 | 48 | 12 | 4 | 2 | 0 | 2 | 2 |
| 1946-47 | Chicago | NHL | 59 | 25 | 27 | 52 | 2 | | | | | |
| 1947-48 | Chicago | NHL | 40 | 16 | 9 | 25 | 0 | | | | | |
| 1948-49 | Chicago | NHL | 60 | 17 | 25 | 42 | 6 | | | | | |
| 1949-50 | Chicago | NHL | 69 | 18 | 28 | 46 | 10 | | | | | |
| 1950-51 | Chicago | NHL | 65 | 21 | 15 | 36 | 18 | | | | | |
| 1951-52 | Chicago | NHL | 70 | 31 | 22 | 53 | 10 | | | | | |
| 1952-53 | Chicago | NHL | 65 | 17 | 20 | 37 | 8 | 7 | 4 | 2 | 6 | 7 |
| 1953-54 | Chicago | NHL | 65 | 15 | 19 | 34 | 17 | | | | | |
| 1954-55 | Chicago | NHL | 64 | 12 | 15 | 27 | 24 | | | | | |
| 1955-56* | Winnipeg | WHL | 64 | 22 | 23 | 45 | 37 | 14 | 6 | 12 | 18 | 4 |
| 1956-57 | Winnipeg | WHL | 61 | 27 | 26 | 53 | 25 | | | | | |
| 1957-58 | Winnipeg | WHL | 65 | 38 | 36 | 74 | 43 | 7 | 1 | 0 | 1 | 6 |
| 1958-59 | Winnipeg | WHL | 63 | 42 | 46 | 88 | 55 | 7 | 1 | 3 | 4 | 10 |

coaching record

| year | team | league | regular season G | W | L | T | Standing | playoffs G | W | L | T |
|------|------|--------|-----|-----|-----|-----|----------|-----|-----|-----|-----|
| 1959-60 | Winnipeg | WHL | 70 | 25 | 42 | 3 | 6 | | | | |
| 1960-61 | Winnipeg | WHL | 70 | 21 | 45 | 4 | 8 | | | | |

# MOTOCH, GEORGE

| | |
|---|---|
| sport: | football |
| born: | . . . |
| | February 23, 1947 |
| height: | 1.88 m / 6'2" |
| weight: | 111 kg / 245 lbs |

While attending Bemidji State University in the years 1966-70, George Motoch started at the guard position on the school's football team. In 1970, he had a tryout with the Winnipeg Blue Bombers but did not catch on. Motoch's desire to be associated with the game of football resulted in his accepting the coaching job with the juvenile Winnipeg Hawkeyes in 1971. In his first year, he led the club to a record of 11 wins and 1 loss. The season culminated with the Hawkeyes winning the Canadian "Little Grey Cup" championship. The following year, the Hawkeyes posted an identical record. They once again won the Little Grey Cup and Motoch was honoured as the coach of the year.

In 1973, Motoch coached the offensive line of the junior Hawkeyes. At the end of the season, he left full-time coaching due to increasing business commitments. Motoch returned to football in 1981 when he accepted the head coaching position with the junior Winnipeg Hawkeyes. He immediately made the club competitive, and that same year it won the first of three consecutive provincial titles.

In 1982, George Motoch was a scout for the Montreal Concordes covering universities in western Canada and North Dakota. The following year, he declined an offer to guest coach with the Concordes, opting for a position coaching the defensive line of the Winnipeg Blue Bombers and scouting for the team. In 1984, Motoch continued working with the defensive line and scouting. He also became the club's Co-ordinator of Amateur Football Development. He served in that capacity through 1987.

## AWARDS

| | |
|---|---|
| 1983 | Manitoba Coaches Association Award |
| 1987 | Outstanding Amateur Coach |

# MULARCHYK, ED

| | |
|---|---|
| sport: | football |
| born: | Windsor, Ontario |
| | December 14, 1933 |
| died: | Windsor, Ontario |
| | May 5, 1992 |
| height: | 1.88 m / 6'2" |
| weight: | 104 kg / 230 lbs |
| position: | end |

Ed Mularchyk played junior football with the Windsor AKO under coach Al Newman in the years 1952 to 1954. Each year, the club reached the national final, and in 1952 and 1954 it won the Dominion junior championship. In 1955, Mularchyk joined the Ottawa Roughriders. At season's end, his fine play earned him the Gruen Trophy as the outstanding Canadian rookie in the East. Mularchyk played for Ottawa for another season before returning to Windsor where he played for the Jets of a cross border league. When Mularchyk enrolled at the University of Western Ontario in 1959, he joined the school's varsity team with which he played for two years. Western won the national championship in his first year there, and Mularchyk's fine play was recognized with an all-star selection. Upon graduation, Mularchyk set up an ophthalmological practice in Windsor.

During the winter of 1954-55 and 1955-56, Ed Mularchyk played for St. Vladimir's basketball team in Windsor. He was one of the club's top playmakers and leading scorers. In April of 1955, Mularchyk's consistent shooting contributed to St. Vladimir's winning the Ontario Church Basketball Association championship.

## AWARDS

1955    Gruen Trophy - IRFU Outstanding Canadian Rookie in East

# MUZYKA, ALEX

"Muzz"

| | |
|---|---|
| sport: | football |
| born: | Hamilton, Ontario |
| | December 8, 1928 |
| height: | 1.80 m / 5'11" |
| weight: | 111 kg / 245 lbs |
| position: | tackle, guard |

*Photo courtesy of the Canadian Football Hall of Fame and Museum*

Alex Muzyka joined the Hamilton Tigers of the ORFU in 1948. He scored one touchdown that season. The Tigers qualified for the playoffs and defeated the Toronto Beaches Indians to win the ORFU title. In the Eastern Canada final, the Tigers were whipped by the Ottawa Rough Riders. Muzyka played with the Tigers one more year. In 1950, the Hamilton Tigers of the ORFU and the Hamilton Wildcats of the IRFU amalgamated to form the Hamilton Tiger-Cats. The team was to play in the IRFU "Big Four" league. Muzyka was with the new team through the 1956 season.

One of Alex Muzyka's most exciting moments in sport was winning the Grey Cup in 1953. It was the hard-hitting Muzyka's only appearance in the fall classic.

Over the years, Alex Muzyka maintained his interest in football. He was one of the organizers of the Hamilton Minor Football Association and served as its secretary-treasurer for 30 years. For a number of years he was on the executive of the Hamilton Tiger-Cat Alumni Association. He also represented the sport of football on the Hamilton Sports Council and served on the council's executive as vice-president.

# NAGURSKI, BRONKO

| | |
|---|---|
| sport: | football, professional wrestling |
| given name: | Nagurski, Bronislaw |
| born: | Rainy River, Ontario |
| | November 3, 1908 |
| died: | International Falls, Minnesota, USA |
| | January 7, 1990 |
| height: | 1.88 m / 6'2" |
| weight: | 104 kg / 230 lbs |

He is a symbol of brute strength, raw power, and unyielding determination. He is a legend immortalized by his opponents, teammates, and all those who had the fortune of seeing him play. Football great Red Grange perhaps best described this giant: "When it comes to the greatest football player ever, it's no contest, it's the Bronk". And in 1969, when the Football Writers Association of America picked an all-time All-American team, Bronko Nagurski was selected at the tackle position.

Bronko Nagurski was born in Rainy River, Ontario. When he was four, the Nagurski family moved across the Rainy River to International Falls, Minnesota. While in high school, Nagurski was one of the most recruited athletes in the country. He chose to attend the University of Minnesota; in his first year (1927) he played tackle, and the following year he played fullback as well. In his final year, Nagurski was on the field for most of the game. He rushed for 259 yards on 61 carries and scored three touchdowns. On defence, from his left tackle position, Nagurski stymied opposing offences. When the 1929 All-American team was selected, Nagurski became the first and so far only player in history to be selected to two different positions on the same All-American team. Coach Dr. C. Spears not only agreed with the selection, but proudly stated that Nagurski is the "most versatile player of all time. He could be All-American at any position."

In 1930, Nagurski signed with the Chicago Bears of the NFL. His strength, power, and determination on the field were feared. On runs from the  backfield he would he drop his massive shoulders, bring in his neck by tightening the muscles in his size 19 neck, and drive with his powerful legs. He never bothered to run around defenders; he ran right through them. It usually took two, sometimes three or four, defenders to bring him down. Opposing coaches spent hours perfecting ways to stop Nagurski. On the eve of the 1933 NFL title game, coach Steve Owens of the Giants was asked by a reporter how his team was going to stop Nagurski. Owens calmly replied: "With a shotgun, as he comes out of the dressing room."

In 1932, Nagurski began wrestling professionally. His appearances, although very lucrative, were sporadic because of his commitment to football. Nagurski was well aware that he had a very large following in wrestling, and that promoters considered him one of the top drawing cards of the 1930s. As a result, his decision to retire from football, after failing to reach an agreement with the Bears ($500 kept them apart), coincided with the start of a full-time wrestling career.

In June of 1937, Bronko Nagurski won the World Heavyweight Wrestling title by pinning Dean Detton, the world champion, in 46 minutes. In November of 1938, he lost the title to Jimmy Londos. The championship was regained in an upset decision over Lou Thesz in June of 1939, and held until March of 1940, when Nagurski was defeated by Ray Steele. A year later, almost to a day, Nagurski overpowered Steele to recapture the world title. His final championship reign was short-lived, as three months later he lost to Sandor Szabo. Nevertheless, Nagurski continued to wrestle through the 1950s, only taking time off in 1943 to rejoin the Chicago Bears. The club was experiencing a manpower shortage due to the war effort and had lured Nagurski out of retirement. That season, Nagurski primarily played at the tackle position. Bronko Nagurski is the father of football player Bronko Nagurski, Jr.

## INDUCTIONS

| | |
|---|---|
| 1951 | National Football Hall of Fame |
| 1951 | College Football Hall of Fame |
| 1963 | Pro Football Hall of Fame - Charter Enshrinee |
| . . . | Major League Football Hall of Fame |

## ALL-STAR SELECTIONS

| | | |
|---|---|---|
| 1929 | fullback (offense) | All-American |
| 1929 | tackle (defense) | All-American |
| 1932 | fullback | All NFL |
| 1933 | fullback | All NFL |
| 1934 | fullback | All NFL |

## RECORD

football

| | | | scoring | | | rushing | | | | pass receiving | | | |
|---|---|---|---|---|---|---|---|---|---|---|---|---|---|
| year | team | league | GP | TD | PTS | N0 | YDS | AVE | TD | NO | YDS | AVE | TD |
| 1930 | Chicago | NFL | (records not kept) | | | | | | | | | | |
| 1931 | Chicago | NFL | (records not kept) | | | | | | | | | | |
| 1932* | Chicago | NFL | ... | 4 | 24 | 111 | 496 | 4.5 | 4 | 6 | 67 | 11.2 | 0 |

football

| year | team | league | scoring | | | rushing | | | | pass receiving | | | |
|------|------|--------|----|----|-----|-----|-----|-----|----|----|-----|------|----|
| | | | GP | TD | PTS | N0 | YDS | AVE | TD | NO | YDS | AVE | TD |
| 1933* | Chicago | NFL | ... | 1 | 7 | 128 | 533 | 4.2 | 1 | 1 | 23 | 23.0 | 0 |
| 1934x | Chicago | NFL | ... | 0 | 0 | 123 | 586 | 4.8 | 0 | 3 | 32 | 10.7 | 0 |
| 1935x | Chicago | NFL | ... | 1 | 6 | 50 | 170 | 3.4 | 1 | 0 | 0 | 0.0 | 0 |
| 1936 | Chicago | NFL | ... | 3 | 19 | 122 | 529 | 4.3 | 3 | 1 | 12 | 12.0 | 0 |
| 1937 | Chicago | NFL | ... | 1 | 6 | 73 | 343 | 4.7 | 1 | 0 | 0 | 0.0 | 0 |
| 1943* | Chicago | NFL | 8 | 1 | 6 | 16 | 84 | 5.3 | 1 | 0 | 0 | 0.0 | 0 |

x Discrepancies exist between statistical sources for these two years. Some claim that in 1934 Nagurski scored 7 touchdowns; while in 1935, some claim that he rushed only 37 times for a total of 137 yards.

# NAGURSKI Jr., BRONKO

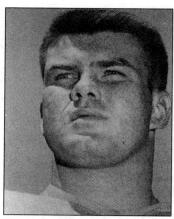

| | |
|---|---|
| sport: | football |
| born: | Minneapolis, Minnesota, USA |
| | . . . |
| height: | 1.85 m / 6'1" |
| weight: | 107.5 kg / 237 lbs |
| position: | offensive tackle |

*Photo courtesy of the Canadian Football Hall of Fame and Museum*

Bronko Nagurski Jr., the son of one of the greatest football players ever, followed in the footsteps of his father by also pursuing a career in football. Nagurski Jr. attended Notre Dame University and played football with the Fighting Irish. He performed superbly in his last year with the club and was chosen to play in the All-American Bowl Game and the East-West Shrine Game.

Bronko Nagurski Jr. joined the Hamilton Tiger-Cats of the CFL in 1959 and immediately became embroiled in a political controversy. According to the league's import rule, clubs had to report the citizenship of signed players. At the time the Tiger-Cats signed Nagurski Jr., they included him among their Canadian players. Concurrently, Nagurski Jr. applied for and was granted Canadian citizenship. In parliament the opposition questioned why Nagurski Jr. got his citizenship papers "in a hurry," implying that it was because the responsible Minister was from Hamilton and had an attachment to the football club. The Hon. Madam Fairclough replied that Nagurski Jr. qualified because his father was a Canadian.

After the controversy subsided, Bronko Nagurski Jr. became a regular starter at the offensive tackle position with the Tiger-Cats. His game was strong and aggressive in the seven seasons he played. Three times he was named to the Eastern Conference all-star team and twice to the league all-star team. During his years with the team, the Tiger-Cats played in six Grey Cup games but failed to win even once.

ALL-STAR SELECTIONS

| 1962 | offensive tackle | CFL | All-Eastern |
|------|------------------|-----|-------------|
|      | offensive tackle | CFL |             |
| 1964 | offensive tackle | CFL | All-Eastern |
| 1965 | offensive tackle | CFL | All-Eastern |
|      | offensive tackle | CFL |             |

# NESTERENKO, ERIC

| sport: | hockey |
|--------|--------|
| given name: | Nesterenko, Eric Paul |
| born: | Flin Flon, Manitoba |
|       | October 31, 1933 |
| height: | 1.88 m / 6'2" |
| weight: | 89.5 kg / 197 lbs |
| position: | right wing |
| shoots: | right |

Eric Nesterenko grew up across the street from a rink in Flin Flon, Manitoba. It is not surprising, therefore, that he started playing hockey at the early age of four. Many years later Nesterenko reminisced: "We never had any gear. I used to wrap *Life* magazines around my legs. We didn't have organized hockey like they have now. All our games were pickup, a never-ending game. Maybe there would be three kids to a team, then there would be fifteen, and the game would go on. Nobody kept score. It was a pure kind of play."[26]

In 1950, Nesterenko joined the Toronto Marlboros Jr. "A" club of the OHA. After two successful seasons, he signed a contract with the Toronto Maple Leafs in 1952. In 1956, Nesterenko was sold by the Leafs to the Chicago Black Hawks. He also enrolled at university that year. In the fall, while the Black Hawks were preparing for the season opener, Nesterenko was studying. Eventually, Chicago lured him out of "retirement," agreeing that his studies would supersede hockey. He was allowed to miss practices and to fly in for games. This preferential treatment upset many of the Chicago players, but impressed the media, who started to admire his profound thinking and intellect. In 1960, Nesterenko decided to pursue a football career. He failed to make the Toronto Argos and returned to hockey.

A free-wheeling and tireless skater, Nesterenko was also an excellent stickhandler. In his era, he was rated as the best defensive forward in the league. A tenacious checker, he was used extensively in a penalty killing role and to shadow opposing stars. During the 1964-65 season, he established an NHL record of six shorthanded goals.

Eric Nesterenko spent 21 seasons playing professional hockey for the Toronto Maple Leafs, the Chicago Black Hawks, and the Chicago Cougars. He rejected an offer to coach the Cougars of the WHA opting for a coaching position in Lausanne, Switzerland. Upon returning to Canada, he coached the Trail Smoke Eaters. Subsequently, Eric Nesterenko became a ski instructor.

## INDUCTIONS

1990        Manitoba Hockey Hall of Fame

## RECORD

| year | team | league | regular season | | | | | playoffs | | | | |
|------|------|--------|-----|-----|-----|-----|-----|-----|-----|-----|-----|-----|
| | | | GP | G | A | PTS | PIM | GP | G | A | PTS | PIM |
| 1951-52 | Toronto | NHL | 1 | 0 | 0 | 0 | 0 | | | | | |
| 1952-53 | Toronto | NHL | 35 | 10 | 6 | 16 | 27 | | | | | |
| 1953-54 | Toronto | NHL | 68 | 14 | 9 | 23 | 70 | 5 | 0 | 1 | 1 | 9 |
| 1954-55 | Toronto | NHL | 62 | 15 | 15 | 30 | 99 | 4 | 0 | 1 | 1 | 6 |
| 1955-56 | Toronto | NHL | 40 | 4 | 6 | 10 | 65 | | | | | |
| | Winnipeg | WHL | 20 | 8 | 6 | 14 | 27 | 14 | 3 | 7 | 10 | 22 |
| 1956-57 | Chicago | NHL | 24 | 8 | 15 | 23 | 32 | | | | | |
| 1957-58 | Chicago | NHL | 70 | 20 | 18 | 38 | 104 | | | | | |
| 1958-59 | Chicago | NHL | 70 | 16 | 18 | 34 | 81 | 6 | 2 | 2 | 4 | 8 |
| 1959-60 | Chicago | NHL | 61 | 13 | 23 | 36 | 71 | 4 | 0 | 0 | 0 | 2 |
| 1960-61* | Chicago | NHL | 68 | 19 | 19 | 38 | 125 | 11 | 2 | 3 | 5 | 6 |
| 1961-62 | Chicago | NHL | 68 | 15 | 14 | 29 | 97 | 12 | 0 | 5 | 5 | 22 |

| year | team | league | regular season | | | | | playoffs | | | | |
|------|------|--------|----|----|----|-----|-----|----|----|----|-----|-----|
| | | | GP | G | A | PTS | PIM | GP | G | A | PTS | PIM |
| 1962-63 | Chicago | NHL | 67 | 12 | 15 | 27 | 103 | 6 | 2 | 3 | 5 | 8 |
| 1963-64 | Chicago | NHL | 70 | 7 | 19 | 26 | 93 | 7 | 2 | 1 | 3 | 8 |
| 1964-65 | Chicago | NHL | 56 | 14 | 16 | 30 | 63 | 14 | 2 | 2 | 4 | 16 |
| 1965-66 | Chicago | NHL | 67 | 15 | 25 | 40 | 58 | 6 | 1 | 0 | 1 | 4 |
| 1966-67 | Chicago | NHL | 68 | 14 | 23 | 37 | 38 | 6 | 1 | 2 | 3 | 2 |
| 1967-68 | Chicago | NHL | 71 | 11 | 25 | 36 | 37 | 10 | 0 | 1 | 1 | 2 |
| 1968-69 | Chicago | NHL | 72 | 15 | 17 | 32 | 29 | | | | | |
| 1969-70 | Chicago | NHL | 67 | 16 | 18 | 34 | 26 | 7 | 1 | 2 | 3 | 4 |
| 1970-71 | Chicago | NHL | 76 | 8 | 15 | 23 | 28 | 18 | 0 | 1 | 1 | 19 |
| 1971-72 | Chicago | NHL | 38 | 4 | 8 | 12 | 27 | 8 | 0 | 0 | 0 | 11 |
| 1973-74 | Chicago | WHA | 29 | 2 | 5 | 7 | 8 | | | | | |

# NEWMAN, BERNIE

| | |
|------|------|
| sport: | gymnastics |
| born: | Windsor, Ontario |
| | August 4, 1914 |
| height: | . . . |
| weight: | . . . |

Bernie Newman (the family had anglicized the surname from Novoselsky) began coaching gymnastics while teaching secondary school in Windsor, and he quickly established himself as one of Canada's finest coaches. Among his proteges were four-time national women's champion Ernestine Russel and the 1954 Canadian junior athlete of the year, Ed Gagnier. During his career, Newman coached more than 170 individual titlists. At the 1955 Pan American Games, Newman coached and managed the Canadian gymnastics team. The following year, he was appointed coach of the Olympic team. Both Russel and Gagnier were on the team. While preparing Russel for the 1958 World Championships in Moscow, Newman spent endless hours studying movies of Soviet gymnasts. He concluded that Russel's success depended on altering her style to that preferred by East European judges. She placed fourth in the vault, her best placing in a major international competition. After the championships, Newman and Russell spent their free time wandering through Moscow and handing out Canadian nickels and chewing gum to Soviet children. When the authorities discovered this "cultural exchange," they ordered the two out of the country within 12 hours.

In 1959, Bernie Newman coached the Canadian gymnastics team at the Pan American Games in Chicago. That same year, he was elected to the Ontario Legislature by the constituents of the Windsor-Walkerville riding. He held the seat for 28 years. In 1980, he served as a patron of the Free Olympiad.

RECORD

coaching

| year | competition |
|------|-------------|
| 1955 | Pan American Games |
| 1956 | Olympic Games |
| 1958 | World Championships |
| 1959 | Pan American Games |

administrative

| 1955-56 | AAU of Canada - Gymnastics, National Chairman |
|---------|---------------------------------------------|

# NYKOLUK, DANNY

| sport: | football |
|--------|----------|
| born: | Scarborough, Ontario |
| | June 16, 1934 |
| height: | 1.91 m / 6'3" |
| weight: | 111 kg / 245 lbs |
| position: | offensive tackle |

*Photo courtesy of the Canadian Football Hall of Fame and Museum*

When the Modern Era (1945-73) All Argo Team was selected, Danny Nykoluk was the obvious choice for the offensive tackle position. It was a fitting tribute to a man who played in more games with the club than anyone in history. Over a span of 16 seasons, he appeared in a total of 204 league and 16 playoff games.

Danny Nykoluk began to play football while attending Scarborough Collegiate Institute. In 1954, he played for Balmy Beach of the ORFU. A year later, he joined the Argos. A serious elbow injury forced Nykoluk to sit out the 1956 season. When he returned to action in 1957, he became recognized as one of the game's most punishing tackles and an excellent pass blocker. Nykoluk, though, was not a flashy player and did not get the acknowledgement he may have deserved.

In the latter years of his career, past the age when football players retire, Nykoluk continued to excel. It was then that he was honoured with his only all-star selections. He was also named captain of the team that affectionately revered him as the "Old Fossil." In 1970, at the age of 36, Nykoluk decided to retire. At the last home game of the season, promoted as the Danny Nykoluk Day, the Argo players presented him with an automobile. The team then retired his number 60 jersey.

In 1971, Nykoluk joined the York University Yeomen Football Club as a line coach. He also did an Argo post-game radio show. Late in October, Argo coach Leo Cahill asked Nykoluk to come out of retirement. The team had a number of injured players and the coach was looking for someone with experience for the playoffs. Nykoluk readily agreed. He played with youthful vigour as the Argos advanced to the Grey Cup game. In 16 years of football, it was Nykoluk's first trip to the fall classic. The Argos lost the game and Danny Nykoluk once again retired.

Danny Nykoluk is the brother of hockey player and coach Mike Nykoluk.


ALL-STAR SELECTIONS

| 1967 | offensive tackle | CFL All-Eastern |
| 1969 | offensive tackle | CFL All-Eastern |

# NYKOLUK, MIKE

"Big Bear"

| | |
|---|---|
| sport: | hockey |
| given name: | Nykoluk, Michael |
| born: | Toronto, Ontario |
| | December 11, 1934 |
| height: | 1.80 m / 5'11" |
| weight: | 96 kg / 212 lbs |
| position: | right wing |
| shoots: | right |

Captain Mike Nykoluk's junior hockey career ended on a high note when he led the Toronto Marlboros to the Memorial Cup championship in 1955. The following year Nykoluk refined his hockey skills with Winnipeg of the WHL and Rochester of the AHL. He was called up by the Toronto Maple Leafs during the 1956-57 season, appearing in 32 games. The following year, Nykoluk once again was playing for Rochester. In 1958, he was traded to the Hershey Bears. He played 14 seasons with Hershey, twice being named to the AHL all-star teams. In 1967, he won the Les Cunningham Plaque as the league's MVP. When Nykoluk hung up his skates for good in 1972, the Hershey Bears honoured him by retiring his number. When the AHL celebrated its 50th anniversary during the 1986-87 season, Mike Nykoluk was named to the league's 50 Year All-Star Team.

In the fall of 1972, Fred Shero, coach of the Philadelphia Flyers, hired Nykoluk as an assistant coach. Nykoluk thus became the first assistant coach in NHL history. Under Shero and Nykoluk the Flyers won two Stanley Cups. When Shero left for the New York Rangers in 1978, Nykoluk followed. In 1979, Harold Ballard offered Nykoluk the position of head coach with the Leafs but Nykoluk declined, believing that the Rangers would eventually offer him their top coaching job. When that failed to materialize, Nykoluk quit the Rangers and joined his brother's construction company. He also signed to do commentary on Leafs' radio broadcasts. In January of 1981, the Leafs fired their coach. Nykoluk was offered the position again and he accepted.

Mike Nykoluk led the Leafs during turbulent times. The club was trading players on a regular basis, the general manager was changed, and numerous players were injured. Even for the easy-going coach, the uncertainties made the job difficult. Nykoluk tried to improve morale by applying his easy-going manner to coaching. He often suggested that a team that is relaxed and which is enjoying itself plays better. Nykoluk was also a coach who stressed a "system" of play. It was a way of doing things in various situations. Nykoluk's system was not sophisticated and he argued that even pee-wee coaches could apply it; all that was required was drilling. Fundamentally, Nykoluk was concerned with ways of bringing the puck out of his team's zone and forechecking.

Under Mike Nykoluk, the Leafs gained a playoff berth twice. On both occasions they were eliminated from further play in the opening round. At the conclusion of the 1983-84 season, Nykoluk was released by the Leafs. Mike Nykoluk is the brother of football player Danny Nykoluk.

## AWARDS

| 1963 | AHL Best Defensive Forward |
| 1967 | Les Cunningham Plaque - AHL MVP |

## ALL-STAR SELECTIONS

| 1966-67 | center | AHL | Second Team |
| 1967-68 | center | AHL | First Team |

## RECORD

| year | team | league | regular season | | | | | playoffs | | | | |
|------|------|--------|----|---|---|-----|-----|----|---|---|-----|-----|
| | | | GP | G | A | PTS | PIM | GP | G | A | PTS | PIM |
| 1955-56* | Winnipeg | WHL | 70 | 10 | 25 | 35 | 18 | 14 | 10 | 12 | 22 | 7 |
| 1956-57 | Toronto | NHL | 32 | 3 | 1 | 4 | 20 | | | | | |
| | Rochester | AHL | 28 | 9 | 13 | 22 | 30 | 9 | 3 | 2 | 5 | 4 |
| 1957-58 | Rochester | AHL | 69 | 14 | 37 | 51 | 45 | | | | | |
| 1958-59* | Hershey | AHL | 66 | 15 | 38 | 53 | 60 | 13 | 5 | 4 | 9 | 15 |
| 1959-60 | Hershey | AHL | 71 | 13 | 32 | 45 | 55 | | | | | |
| 1960-61 | Hershey | AHL | 71 | 10 | 24 | 34 | 14 | 8 | 1 | 5 | 6 | 0 |
| 1961-62 | Hershey | AHL | 59 | 4 | 20 | 24 | 13 | 7 | 1 | 2 | 3 | 12 |
| 1962-63 | Hershey | AHL | 72 | 7 | 36 | 43 | 21 | 15 | 1 | 9 | 10 | 2 |
| 1963-64 | Hershey | AHL | 72 | 9 | 63 | 72 | 39 | 6 | 1 | 3 | 4 | 0 |
| 1964-65 | Hershey | AHL | 71 | 11 | 55 | 66 | 29 | 15 | 2 | 11 | 13 | 6 |
| 1965-66 | Hershey | AHL | 67 | 10 | 53 | 63 | 14 | 3 | 0 | 1 | 1 | 0 |
| 1966-67 | Hershey | AHL | 72 | 16 | 68 | 84 | 26 | 5 | 0 | 4 | 4 | 4 |
| 1967-68 | Hershey | AHL | 72 | 19 | 66 | 85 | 30 | 5 | 2 | 6 | 8 | 0 |
| 1968-69* | Hershey | AHL | 74 | 15 | 55 | 70 | 14 | 11 | 0 | 8 | 8 | 0 |
| 1969-70 | Hershey | AHL | 72 | 16 | 57 | 73 | 12 | 7 | 0 | 2 | 2 | 2 |
| 1970-71 | Hershey | AHL | 71 | 14 | 39 | 53 | 33 | 4 | 0 | 3 | 3 | 0 |
| 1971-72 | Hershey | AHL | 62 | 13 | 30 | 43 | 20 | 4 | 0 | 2 | 2 | 4 |

coaching record

| year | team | league | regular season | | | | | playoffs | | | |
|------|------|--------|---|---|---|---|----------|---|---|---|---|
| | | | G | W | L | T | Standing | G | W | L | T |
| 1980-81 | Toronto | NHL | 40 | 15 | 15 | 10 | 5 | 3 | 0 | 3 | 0 |
| 1981-82 | Toronto | NHL | 80 | 20 | 44 | 16 | 5 | | | | |
| 1982-83 | Toronto | NHL | 80 | 28 | 40 | 12 | 3 | 4 | 1 | 3 | 0 |
| 1983-84 | Toronto | NHL | 80 | 26 | 45 | 9 | 5 | | | | |

# OGRODNICK, JOHN

| | |
|--|--|
| sport: | hockey |
| given name: | Ogrodnick, John Alexander |
| born: | Ottawa, Ontario |
| | June 20, 1959 |
| height: | 1.83 m / 6'0" |
| weight: | 93 kg / 205 lbs |
| position: | left wing |
| shoots: | left |

John Ogrodnick began to play hockey at the Canadian Forces Base at Cold Lake where his father was stationed. At first he played defense, but at age twelve he was moved to left wing because he was considered too small for blue line duties. In the fall of 1976, he joined the Maple Leaf Bruins, a tier II club in British Columbia. Subsequently, he played junior hockey with the New Westminster Bruins. At the conclusion of the 1977-78 season, his first full year with the club, Ogrodnick was named co-winner of the league's Rookie of the Year Award. Collectively, the Bruins won the Memorial Cup that year. In the summer of 1979, Ogrodnick was chosen by the Detroit Red Wings in the NHL Entry Draft. He was taken in the fourth round, 66th overall.

Ogrodnick started his professional rookie season in the minors. He worked extremely hard and was soon called up by the Red Wings. He was with the team for almost eight seasons, and often led the team in goals and scoring. In 1984-85, he established a club record for most points by a left winger in one season. He was seventh best in the league with 105 points, on 55 goals and 50 assists. For his efforts, he was named to the NHL first all-star team. While a member of the Wings, Ogrodnick also made five appearances in the NHL All-Star Game.

In January of 1987, Ogrodnick was traded to the Quebec Nordiques. He was disappointed at his being traded and played poorly for the rest of the regular season. In the playoffs, Ogrodnick redeemed himself with 9 goals in 13 games. In the summer of that year, Ogrodnick's family informed him that they would not be returning to Quebec City. Ogrodnick informed the Nordiques that if they did not trade him, he would retire. His wish was granted; he was dealt to the New York Rangers.

## AWARDS

1978      Stewart "Butch" Paul Memorial Trophy - WHL Top Rookie
1981      Stu Evans Trophy - Most Sportsmanlike Red Wing

## ALL-STAR SELECTIONS

1984-85    left wing    NHL    First Team

## RECORD

| | | | regular season | | | | | playoffs | | | | |
|---|---|---|---|---|---|---|---|---|---|---|---|---|
| year | team | league | GP | G | A | PTS | PIM | GP | G | A | PTS | PIM |
| 1979-80 | Detroit | NHL | 41 | 8 | 24 | 32 | 8 | | | | | |
| | Adirondack | AHL | 39 | 13 | 20 | 33 | 21 | | | | | |
| 1980-81 | Detroit | NHL | 80 | 35 | 35 | 70 | 14 | | | | | |
| 1981-82 | Detroit | NHL | 80 | 28 | 26 | 54 | 28 | | | | | |
| 1982-83 | Detroit | NHL | 80 | 41 | 44 | 85 | 30 | | | | | |
| 1983-84 | Detroit | NHL | 64 | 42 | 36 | 78 | 14 | 4 | 0 | 0 | 0 | 0 |
| 1984-85 | Detroit | NHL | 79 | 55 | 50 | 105 | 30 | 3 | 1 | 1 | 2 | 0 |
| 1985-86 | Detroit | NHL | 76 | 38 | 32 | 70 | 18 | | | | | |
| 1986-87 | Detroit | NHL | 39 | 12 | 28 | 40 | 6 | | | | | |
| | Quebec | NHL | 32 | 11 | 16 | 27 | 4 | 13 | 9 | 4 | 13 | 6 |
| 1987-88 | NY Rangers | NHL | 64 | 22 | 32 | 54 | 16 | | | | | |
| 1988-89 | NY Rangers | NHL | 60 | 13 | 29 | 42 | 14 | 3 | 2 | 0 | 2 | 0 |
| | Denver | IHL | 3 | 2 | 0 | 2 | 0 | | | | | |
| 1989-90 | NY Rangers | NHL | 80 | 43 | 31 | 74 | 44 | 10 | 6 | 3 | 9 | 0 |
| 1990-91 | NY Rangers | NHL | 79 | 31 | 23 | 54 | 10 | 4 | 0 | 0 | 0 | 0 |

international

| year | team | competition | GP | G | A | PTS | PIM | Place |
|---|---|---|---|---|---|---|---|---|
| 1979 | New Westminster | World Junior Championship | 5 | 3 | 0 | 3 | 4 | 5 |
| 1981 | Canada | World Championship | 8 | 3 | 2 | 5 | 0 | 4 |

# OLENSKY, HARRY

| | |
|---|---|
| sport: | dog sledding |
| given name: | Ulianytskyi, Hryhorii |
| born: | Vilshanka, Ukraine |
| | . . . |
| height: | . . . |
| weight: | . . . |

Harry Olensky arrived in Canada in the early 1900s. He lived in Winnipeg for a few years before settling in The Pas in 1912. In the 1920s, Olensky, who by then was the owner-operator of the Avenue Hotel in The Pas, became interested in dog sled racing.

In 1926, Olensky entered a team in the inaugural Saskatchewan Dog Derby Championship run out of Prince Albert. The 160-mile event, contested over four days, was considered the unofficial championship of Northern Canada. Prime Minister W. L. McKenzie King donated a silver trophy, worth approximately $1,500, which was to be presented to the winner. Olensky finished the race in third place.

In 1927, Olensky once again entered a team in the Saskatchewan Derby. He started the race with eight dogs. On the second day the wiry musher lost one dog to a stomach disorder and another to a leg injury. Olensky nevertheless pressed on, slowly leaving his opponents behind. By the end of the third day he had a lead of more than an hour but was down to four dogs. Olensky and his team of dogs managed to hold on to the overall lead in the fourth leg and win the championship in a time of 16 hours, 58 minutes, and 49 seconds. Among those whom Olensky defeated was the acknowledged world champion, Emile St. Godard.

## RECORD

| year | competition | placing | result |
|---|---|---|---|
| 1926 | Saskatchewan Dog Derby | 3 | 17:03:17 |
| 1927 | Saskatchewan Dog Derby | 1 | 16:58:49 |
| 1928 | The Pas Dog Derby | dnf | |

# OLESCHUK, BILL

| | |
|---|---|
| sport: | hockey |
| given name: | Oleschuk, William Stephen |
| born: | Edmonton, Alberta |
| | July 20, 1955 |
| height: | 1.91 m / 6'3" |
| weight: | 88 kg / 194 lbs |
| position: | goal |
| shoots: | left |

Bill Oleschuk was selected 110th overall in the 1975 NHL Entry Draft by the Kansas City Scouts. The club assigned him to the minors to gain experience. In 1976, the Scouts franchise was transferred to Colorado and renamed the Rockies. Oleschuk had a good training camp with the Rockies but did not get a starting or a backup position with the team. He spent the 1977-78 season living out of a suitcase, playing for five teams in four leagues. Oleschuk described the experience as nightmarish; it was depressing and it hurt his game. The following season, Oleschuk made it as a backup goalie with the Rockies. He played in half of the struggling team's games, posting a respectable goals against average of 3.85. A year later, the personable and quiet goaltender played only a handful of games for the Rockies. He spent most of the season in the minors where, a few years later, he finished his professional career.

## RECORD

| | | | regular season | | | | | | | | playoffs | | | | | | | |
|---|---|---|---|---|---|---|---|---|---|---|---|---|---|---|---|---|---|---|
| year | team | league | GP | MIN | W | L | T | GA | AVE | SO | GP | MIN | W | L | T | GA | AVE | SO |
| 1975-76 | Kansas City | NHL | 1 | 60 | 0 | 1 | 0 | 4 | 4.00 | 0 | | | | | | | | |
| | Port Huron | IHL | 44 | 2,417 | | | | 145 | 3.60 | 0 | 9 | 443 | | | | 24 | 3.25 | 0 |
| 1976-77 | Baltimore | SHL | 30 | 1,780 | | | | 97 | 3.27 | 1 | | | | | | | | |
| | Oklahoma City | CHL | 3 | 159 | | | | 15 | 5.66 | 0 | | | | | | | | |
| 1977-78 | Colorado | NHL | 2 | 100 | 0 | 2 | 0 | 9 | 5.40 | 0 | | | | | | | | |
| | Phoenix | CHL | 9 | 549 | 2 | 6 | 1 | 45 | 4.92 | 0 | | | | | | | | |
| | Hampton | AHL | 11 | 616 | 1 | 9 | 1 | 40 | 3.90 | 0 | | | | | | | | |
| | Philadelphia | AHL | 2 | 65 | 0 | 1 | 0 | 9 | 8.30 | 0 | | | | | | | | |
| | Flint | IHL | 13 | 702 | | | | 57 | 4.87 | 0 | 4 | 204 | | | | 10 | 2.94 | 0 |
| 1978-79 | Colorado | NHL | 40 | 2,118 | 6 | 19 | 8 | 136 | 3.85 | 1 | | | | | | | | |
| 1979-80 | Colorado | NHL | 12 | 557 | 1 | 6 | 2 | 39 | 4.20 | 0 | | | | | | | | |
| | Fort Worth | CHL | 43 | 2,478 | 24 | 14 | 5 | 134 | 3.24 | 1 | 2 | 72 | 1 | 1 | 0 | 8 | 6.67 | 0 |
| 1980-81 | Fort Worth | CHL | 36 | 2,054 | 10 | 22 | 1 | 122 | 3.56 | 0 | 5 | 300 | | | | 14 | 2.80 | 0 |

| year | team | league | GP | MIN | W | L | T | GA | AVE | SO | GP | MIN | W | L | T | GA | AVE | SO |
|------|------|--------|----|----|----|----|----|----|------|----|----|-----|---|---|---|----|-----|-----|
| 1981-82 | Dallas | CHL | 7 | 322 | 2 | 4 | 0 | 26 | 4.84 | 0 | | | | | | | | |
| 1982-83 | Preoria | IHL | 19 | 1,448 | | | | 147 | 6.09 | 1 | | | | | | | | |
| 1983-84 | Fort Wayne | IHL | 1 | 60 | | | | 7 | 7.00 | 0 | | | | | | | | |

# OLINEK, GAYLE

| | |
|--|--|
| sport: | athletics, body building |
| given name: | Olinekova, Gayle |
| born: | Toronto, Ontario |
| | . . ., 1953 |
| height: | 1.68 m / 5'6" |
| weight: | 56.5 kg / 125 lbs |

*Photo courtesy of the Ontario Track & Field Association*

At age 15, Gayle Olinek competed in her first real track meet. She did well, breaking the Toronto girls' high school record in the 440 yards by ten seconds. Olinek ran the race wearing sweat pants. This was not because of self-confidence, but rather to cover her source of embarrassment - her enormously muscular legs. Within eight months those legs carried her to a place on Canada's track team. And in 1981, *Sports Illustrated* featured Gayle Olinek in an article titled the "Greatest Legs to Ever Stride the Earth."

Olinek's track career, though, was marred by disappointments. Upon being named to the national team, Olinek undertook a training regiment that totally drained her, and she contracted mononucleosis. After a two-year recovery, Olinek returned to the track with a second-place finish in the 800 metres at the 1971 Pan American Games Trials. The selection committee overlooked her and sent the third place finisher to the Games instead. In 1972, just three weeks before the Olympic trials, while doing wind sprints, Olinek collided with a little girl who ran out on the track. Olinek suffered whiplash and a fractured skull. Nevertheless, she entered the trials, but failed to secure an Olympic berth. In 1973, during a Canada - USSR meet, she severely damaged her hamstring; doctors told her that she would never run again. Never one to give up, Olinek set out to make a comeback. By 1974, she was running world class times again. In 1976, her Olympic hopes were once again shattered when she fell ill just prior to the trials.

In August of that year, while jogging, she met her future husband Michael Grandi. After a five minute chat, Grandi declared: "You could be one of the world's greatest marathon runners." In January of the next year, Olinek ran her first marathon and won. In the next four years, the disappointments of track were replaced by stellar performances in the marathon. Twice she broke the Canadian record, and twice she established Canadian unofficial records. Even so, her infatuation with Olympic track continued and she attempted to make a comeback in 1980. The boycott ruined that dream. In addition to track and the marathon, Gayle Olinek competed in body building. She also authored two best-selling books, *Go For It!* and *Legs*.

## RECORD

| year | competition | event | placing | result | |
|------|-------------|-------|---------|--------|---|
| 1969 | Canadian Junior Championships | 400 m | 1 | 55.5 | njr |
| | | 800 m | 2 | 2:13.4 | |
| | Canadian Championships | 400 m | 1 | 55.8 | |
| | | 800 m | 4 | 2:10.0 | |
| | Canada Games | 400 m | 1 | 56.6 | |
| | | 800 m | 2 | 2:11.4 | |
| 1970 | Canadian Championships | 400 m | 3 | 56.8 | |
| | | 800 m | 6 | 2:13.5 | |
| | Commonwealth Games Trials | 400 m | 6 | 56.2 | |
| | | 800 m | 10 | 2:11.9 | |
| 1971 | Pan American Games Trials | 800 m | 2 | 2:07.2 | |
| 1972 | Canada vs US | 800 m | 3 | 2:07.3 | |
| 1974 | Zurich International Meet | 800 m | 1 | 2:06.22 | |
| 1975 | Canadian Championships | 1,500 m | 6 | 4:21.0 | |
| 1976 | Olympic Trials | 800 m | 7 | 2:15.43 | |
| | | 1,500 m | 9 | 4:44.9 | |
| | Martin Luther King Games | 1,500 m | 3 | | |
| 1977 | Greater Miami Marathon | marathon | 1 | 3:29:00 | |
| | Fort Myers Marathon | marathon | 1 | 3:18:30 | |
| | Boston Marathon | marathon | 4 | 2:56:55 | cb |
| 1978 | Boston Marathon | marathon | 10 | 2:53:25 | cb |
| 1979 | New Orleans Classic | marathon | 1 | 2:38:12 | nr |
| | Boston Marathon | marathon | 9 | 2:47:30 | |
| | Women's International Marathon Championship | marathon | 6 | 2:44:04 | |
| | Fiesta Bowl Marathon | marathon | 1 | 2:36:12 | nr |
| 1980 | New Orleans' Mardi Gras Classic Marathon | marathon | | 2:35:12 | |
| | Pepsi/UCLA Invitational | 1,500 m | | 4:29.2 | |

| year | competition | event | placing | result |
|------|-------------|-------|---------|--------|
| 1980 | New York Marathon | marathon | 9 | 2:41:33 |
| njr | Canadian junior record | | | |
| nr | Canadian record | | | |
| cb | Canadian best | | | |

# ONESCHUK, STEVE

| | |
|---|---|
| sport: | football |
| born: | St. Catharines, Ontario |
| | November 22, 1930 |
| height: | 1.78 m / 5'10" |
| weight: | 81.5 kg / 180 lbs |
| position: | half back, kicker |

Steve Oneschuk was a versatile athlete in his teens; he played high school basketball and football and also played organized lacrosse. In 1948, Oneschuk was a member of the St. Catharines Athletics lacrosse club, a finalist for the Minto Cup (emblematic of the national junior lacrosse championship). In 1949 and 1950, he played with the senior Athletics. In the years 1951-54, Oneschuk attended the University of Toronto, where he earned a degree in physical education and competed on the school's basketball and football teams.

In 1951, Oneschuk led the Ontario intercollegiate football league in rushing with 385 yards, an average of 6.4 yards per carry. His play was recognized when he was named to the Ontario All-Star team. It was the first of four consecutive appearances on the all-star team. In 1951, Oneschuk was also named to the Second All-Eastern Canadian Press Team. He was the only university player selected. In his last season with Toronto, Oneschuk was awarded the Johnny Copps Trophy as the most valuable player on the team. During the winter months, Oneschuk played basketball for the university and for the Ukrainian Sports Club Trident.

Oneschuk moved to Hamilton in 1955 to pursue a teaching career and to play professional football with the Hamilton Tiger-Cats. He was with the team from 1955 to 1960. During those years, he was used as a corner linebacker, fullback, and kicker. In 1956, Oneschuk was named captain of the Tiger-Cats. He responded by more than doubling his point production from the previous year.  A year later, he led the team in scoring with 60 points; he added 18 points in the playoffs and 2 in the Grey Cup game, which the Tiger-Cats won.  He played in two more Grey Cup games (which Hamilton did not win).  During his career with the Tiger-Cats, Steve Oneschuk was recognized as one of the best Canadian players in the league.  The Toronto *Globe and Mail* recognized him with five consecutive selections to the Eastern Canadian All-Star team.  In 1961, he coached the Tiger-Cats' backfield.

### INDUCTIONS

1988        University of Toronto Sports Hall of Fame

### RECORD

| scoring | | | regular season | | | | | | playoffs | | | | | | Grey Cup game | | | | | |
|---|---|---|---|---|---|---|---|---|---|---|---|---|---|---|---|---|---|---|---|---|
| year | team | league | GP | TD | C | FG | S | PTS | GP | TD | C | FG | S | PTS | GP | TD | C | FG | S | PTS |
| 1955 | Hamilton | IRFU | ... | 2 | 1 | 4 | 0 | 23 | 1 | 0 | 0 | 1 | 0 | 3 | | | | | | |
| 1956 | Hamilton | IRFU | 14 | 1 | 42 | 1 | 2 | 53 | 3 | 0 | 12 | 1 | 1 | 16 | | | | | | |
| 1957* | Hamilton | IRFU | 14 | 1 | 22 | 9 | 5 | 60 | 2 | 0 | 6 | 4 | 0 | 18 | 1 | 0 | 2 | 0 | 0 | 2 |
| 1958 | Hamilton | CFL | 8 | 0 | 12 | 0 | 0 | 12 | 2 | 0 | 7 | 1 | 0 | 10 | 1 | 0 | 4 | 0 | 0 | 4 |
| 1959 | Hamilton | CFL | ... | 0 | 26 | 3 | 4 | 39 | 2 | 0 | 3 | 1 | 2 | 8 | 1 | 0 | 0 | 2 | 0 | 6 |
| 1960 | Hamilton | CFL | 1 | 0 | 1 | 1 | 0 | 4 | | | | | | | | | | | | |

| rushing | | | regular season | | | | | |
|---|---|---|---|---|---|---|---|---|
| year | team | league | GP | NO | YDS | AVE | LG | TD |
| 1955 | Hamilton | IRFU | ... | 41 | 233 | 5.7 | 30 | 2 |

# ONULIAK, ALBERT

"Ab"

sport:      baseball
born:       Fort William, Ontario
            (now Thunder Bay)
            November 10, 1930
died:       Fort William, Ontario
            September 17, 1956
height:     1.80 m / 5'11"
weight:     75 kg  / 165 lbs

At the age of two, Ab Onuliak lost sight in one eye.  An active individual, he did not let this disability keep him from participating in sport and becoming one of the Lakehead area's most promising athletes. In his teens, Onuliak competed in baseball, basketball, football, and hockey, winning many area age group championships. Baseball soon became his forte, and by the age of 18, he was making headlines in the local papers. As a rookie righthand pitcher playing for the Fort William Lumbermen of the Lakehead Senior Baseball League, he set a Lakehead record by striking out 20 batters and allowing but one hit in a game. A few days later, he pitched a no-hitter.

This prowess on the mound led Onuliak to the Jack Rossiter Baseball School in Cocoa Beach, Florida, in 1952. A year later, he was signed by the Washington Senators of the American League and assigned to their farm team, the Orlando Senators of the Class D circuit. In 1952, he posted a 10 win, 10 loss record and was given an outstanding chance of going all the way to the majors. This opportunity began to materialize before the start of the 1953 season, when Onuliak was offered a spot with the Senators' AAA team as final preparation for the big league.

Unfortunately, Ab Onuliak would never have the opportunity to play major league baseball. Shortly after the Senators made him the offer, Onuliak fell ill. As a result, he retired from the Senators organization and returned to Fort William, where he played ball for a few seasons. In 1956, one of Lakehead's most promising athletes passed away at the age of 25.

## INDUCTIONS

1988        Northwestern Ontario Sports Hall of Fame

## RECORD

| year | team | league | batting | | | | | | | pitching | |
|------|------|--------|---------|-----|---|---|----|-----|------|----------|---|
|      |      |        | GP | AB | R | H | HR | RBI | AVG | W | L |
| 1949 | Fort William Lumbermen | Lakehead | ... | | | | | | | 5 | 2 |
| 1950 | Port Arthur Navy | Lakehead | ... | 36 | 4 | 9 | | 17 | .250 | | |
| 1951 | Orlando Senators | Florida | ... | | | | | | | 10 | 10 |
| 1952 | Orlando Senators | Florida | ... | | | | | | | | |
| 1953 | Port Arthur Red Sox | Lakehead | ... | | | | | | | | |
| 1954 | Port Arthur Red Sox | Lakehead | ... | | | | | | | | |

# ORYSZCZYN, EUGENE

sport:       gymnastics
born:       Lviv, Ukraine
              October 14, 1914
height:     1.68 m / 5'6"
weight:    66 kg  / 146 lbs

Eugene Oryszczyn's association with gymnastics began in his home town of Lviv at the rather late age of 15. He took a liking to the sport and in no time excelled at it. From 1930 to 1939, while competing for the Sokil club, he won numerous titles, among them the 1938 all-around championship of Western Ukraine. World War II put Oryszczyn's gymnastic career on hold. In 1939, while working for the Ukrainian resistance movement, he was arrested by the KGB and sentenced to ten years in a labour camp at Vorkuta, Komi ASSR. An agreement between the Polish government in exile and Stalin landed him in the Polish army which was integrated into the Red Army.

After the war, Oryszczyn settled in Poland. A career in law did not materialize. His pre-war law degree was not valid in the new Poland. In addition, not being a member of the communist party, he was excluded from this work. As a result, he enrolled at a physical education institute in Warsaw. In 1948, he began coaching. In 1952, he became a national level judge and two years later an international judge. While in Poland, Oryszczyn coached a number of clubs, the head coaching position at the Wlokniarz sport club being the most significant. Among those training under his direction were Helena Racoczy, the 1950 all-around world champion, and the bronze medallist in the all-around competition and uneven bars at the 1954 World Championships; and Jerzy Solarz, a 1952 Olympic and 1954 World Championship team member.

In 1960, Oryszczyn arrived in Canada. A year later, he took over the head coaching position of the Etobicoke Jaycees Gymnastics Club. He held the position through 1975. In 1961, Oryszczyn judged at his first Canadian National Championships. Subsequently, he judged at every national championship through the year 1990. In addition, Oryszczyn judged at the World Championships, World Cups, World Student Games, Commonwealth Games, Pan American Games, and the Olympics.

Eugene Oryszczyn also served in various administrative capacities on the Ontario Men's Technical Committee and the National Judging Committee, and also assisted in writing judging manuals. During his years in Canada, Eugene Oryszczyn's commitment to gymnastics was total, even though he held a full-time job and often had to pay his own way to serve his sport.

In 1980, Eugene Oryszczyn was honoured as the Canadian Amateur Sports Official of the Year. And in 1993, for his steadfast work as a judge, the International Gymnastics Federation (FIG) named Oryszczyn the inaugural recipient of the "Honourary Judge of the FIG" award.

Eugene Oryszczyn was also an advocate of organized sport for Ukrainian youth. In the years 1961-67 he held clinics for members of the Ukrainian Youth Association (SUM), at which youngsters were introduced to various sports. During the summer, he attended camps and advocated sport. He also organized and coordinated massive group drills. The more memorable performances were at the unveiling of monuments of Ukrainian poet Taras Shevchenko in Winnipeg in 1961 and Washington in 1964; and at Expo '67 in Montreal. Some of the drill performances included more than 800 participants.

## AWARDS

| 1977 | Ontario Gymnastics Federation Recognition Award |
| 1980 | Canadian Amateur Sports Official of the Year |
| 1984 | Canadian Gymnastics Federation Life Membership |
| 1985 | Krakow Gymnastics Federation Recognition Award (Poland) |
| 1992 | Canada 125 Medal |
| 1993 | Honourary Judge of the FIG |

## RECORD

officiating

| year | competition |
|------|-------------|
| 1955 | World Youth Festival |
| 1957 | World Youth Festival |
| 1958 | World Championships |
| 1970 | World Championships |
| 1972 | Olympic Games |
| 1974 | World Championships |
| 1975 | Pan American Games |
| 1976 | Olympic Games |
| 1978 | World Championships |
|      | Commonwealth Games |
| 1979 | World Championships |

officiating

| year | competition |
|------|-------------|
| 1979 | World Student Games |
| 1980 | Olympic Games |
|      | World Cup |
| 1981 | World Championships |
|      | World Student Games |
| 1982 | Commonwealth Games |
| 1983 | World Championships |
| 1984 | Olympic Games |

coaching

| year | competition |
|------|-------------|
| 1958 | Poland vs USSR |
|      | Poland vs Czechoslovakia |
| 1977 | Ontario Juniors vs Poland |

administrative

| year | competition | |
|------|-------------|---|
| 1959 | European Championships | meet director |

# OSBORNE, MARK

"Ozzie"

| | |
|---|---|
| sport: | hockey |
| given name: | Osborne, Mark Anatole |
| born: | Toronto, Ontario |
| | August 13, 1961 |
| height: | 1.88 m / 6'2" |
| weight: | 93 kg / 205 lbs |
| position: | left wing |
| shoots: | left |

*Photo courtesy of the Toronto Maple Leafs*

While playing junior hockey, Mark Osborne seriously injured his hip. As a result, most professional clubs were reluctant to draft him. The Detroit Red Wings decided to take a chance by selecting him as an underage junior in the 1980 NHL Entry Draft. After the draft, Osborne played one more year of junior hockey with the Niagara Falls Flyers. He also appeared in the playoffs for the Adirondack Red Wings as they won the AHL championship.

Osborne made the roster of the Detroit Red Wings during the 1981 training camp. That year he led the club in scoring with 26 goals and 41 assists. After two seasons with Detroit he was traded to the New York Rangers. In 1987, the Toronto Maple Leafs acquired him in a trade. With the Leafs he scored a career-high 73 points during the 1989-90 season. His stay in Toronto was also short lived; in the fall of 1990 he was dealt to the Winnipeg Jets. Mark Osborne, a strong grinder who hit anything that moved on the ice, was particularly tough in the corners.

## RECORD

| year | team | league | regular season | | | | | playoffs | | | | |
|------|------|--------|----|----|----|-----|-----|----|----|----|-----|-----|
| | | | GP | G | A | PTS | PIM | GP | G | A | PTS | PIM |
| 1980-81* | Adirondack | AHL | | | | | | 13 | 2 | 3 | 5 | 2 |
| 1981-82 | Detroit | NHL | 80 | 26 | 41 | 67 | 61 | | | | | |
| 1982-83 | Detroit | NHL | 80 | 19 | 24 | 43 | 83 | | | | | |
| 1983-84 | NY Rangers | NHL | 73 | 23 | 28 | 51 | 88 | 5 | 0 | 1 | 1 | 7 |
| 1984-85 | NY Rangers | NHL | 23 | 4 | 4 | 8 | 33 | 3 | 0 | 0 | 0 | 4 |
| 1985-86 | NY Rangers | NHL | 62 | 16 | 24 | 40 | 80 | 15 | 2 | 3 | 5 | 26 |
| 1986-87 | NY Rangers | NHL | 58 | 17 | 15 | 32 | 101 | | | | | |
| | Toronto | NHL | 16 | 5 | 10 | 15 | 12 | 9 | 1 | 3 | 4 | 6 |
| 1987-88 | Toronto | NHL | 79 | 23 | 37 | 60 | 102 | 6 | 1 | 3 | 4 | 16 |
| 1988-89 | Toronto | NHL | 75 | 16 | 30 | 46 | 112 | | | | | |
| 1989-90 | Toronto | NHL | 78 | 23 | 50 | 73 | 91 | 5 | 2 | 3 | 5 | 12 |
| 1990-91 | Toronto | NHL | 18 | 3 | 3 | 6 | 4 | | | | | |
| | Winnipeg | NHL | 37 | 8 | 8 | 16 | 59 | | | | | |

# OSTAPCHUK, BILL

| | |
|---|---|
| sport: | figure skating |
| given name: | Ostapchuk, William |
| born: | Toronto, Ontario |
| | December 8, 1932 |
| height: | 1.78 m / 5'10" |
| weight: | 75 kg / 165 lbs |

More often than not, children follow one or both parents into sport. In William Ostapchuk's case it was the opposite. He became interested in figure skating because both of his daughters skated. He became involved at the club level to help those who were working with his children. Some 25 years later, in 1990, he was elected President of the Canadian Figure Skating Association (CFSA). His platform included the same grass roots philosophy that got him involved in figure skating: "New volunteers must be encouraged to get involved so as to spread the workload and bring new vitality to our activities." It is believed, that when Ostapchuk assumed the presidency of the CFSA, it was the largest figure skating association in the world with close to 17,000 paid members belonging to 1,400 clubs.

Over the years, Ostapchuk served on most committees of Canadian Figure Skating Association. In 1968, partly because of his accounting background, he became interested in competition accounting (tabulation of results). By 1970, he redesigned the accounting and judges' forms used for competition. They were first used in Canada and in the 1980s adopted by the International Skating Union. He became the first Chairman of the National Accounts Committee and strove to develop and promote volunteer involment in accounting. He developed a training program and wrote a manual which was still in use at the time of writing. His experience resulted in Ostapchuk serving as chief accountant at one World and seven Canadian championships. Bill Ostapchuk is the father of figure skater and coach Cathy Ostapchuk-Mackowski.

## AWARDS

1988     Honourary Membership - Brant Figure Skating Club

administrative

| year | position |
|------|----------|
| 1964-65 | Director, Brant Figure Skating Club |
| 1966 | Vice President, Brant Figure Skating Club |
| 1967-69 | Director, Western Ontario Section, CFSA |
| 1973-82 | Chairman, Accounts Committee, CFSA |
| 1981-86 | Director, CFSA |
| 1982-86 | Chairman, Finance Committee, CFSA |
| 1986-88 | Chairman, Marketing Committee, CFSA |
| 1986-90 | Vice President, CFSA |
| 1988-90 | Chairman, International Team Committee, CFSA |
| 1990- | President, CFSA |

## OSTAPCHUK-MACKOWSKI, CATHY

| | |
|---|---|
| sport: | figure skating |
| nee: | Ostapchuk, Cathy |
| born: | Toronto, Ontario |
| | August 21, 1958 |
| height: | 1.52 m / 5'0" |
| weight: | 54.5 kg / 100 lbs |

At age 11, Cathy Ostapchuk competed in her first Canadian Championships, albeit as a novice. She was, at the time, one of the youngest to ever compete, and placed in the top five. Some time later, at the junior level, she had consistent results at the Central Canadian and Canadian Championships. In 1975, she competed in the Canadian Senior Championships for the first time, placing fifth. The result guaranteed her a spot on the national team. She represented Canada at two international competitions in Europe, placing third at the Grand Prix de Paris.

Upon retiring from competitive skating, Ostapchuk became a professional figure skating coach, first in upstate New York and later in Ontario. She has coached figures, free skating, and dance. In addition, in the early 1980s, Ostapchuk-Mackowski became involved in coaching precision skating. Her teams have won numerous medals at provincial and Canadian Precision Skating Championships. In 1988, the Kitchener-Waterloo precision team that she coached was invited to partake in the Closing Ceremonies of the Calgary Olympics. As a result, Mackowski assisted with the training and choreography of the skating portion of the Closing Ceremonies. Cathy Ostapchuk-Mackowski is the daughter of figure skating administrator William Ostapchuk.

## RECORD

| year | competition | placing |
|------|-------------|---------|
| 1971 | Ontario Winter Games | 2 |
| 1972 | Canadian Junior Championships | 3 |
| 1973 | Canadian Junior Championships | 7 |
| 1974 | Canadian Junior Championships | 3 |
| 1975 | Canadian Championships | 5 |
|      | Grand Prix de Paris | 3 |
|      | Neblehorn Trophy | 5 |
| 1976 | Canadian Championships | 7 |
| 1977 | Canadian Championships | 9 |

coaching

| year | club |
|------|------|
| 1977-79 | Genesee Figure Skating Club, Rochester, USA |
| 1977-79 | Syracuse Figure Skating Club, Syracuse, USA |
| 1980-87 | Brant Figure Skating Club, Brantford, Ontario |
| 1981- | Kitchener-Waterloo Figure Skating Club, Kitchener, Ontario |

administrative

| year | position |
|------|----------|
| 1986-90 | Coaching Member, CFSA National Precision Committee |

# OWCHAR, DENNIS

| | |
|---|---|
| sport: | hockey |
| born: | Dryden, Ontario |
| | March 28, 1953 |
| height: | 1.80 m / 5'11" |
| weight: | 86 kg / 190 lbs |
| position: | defense |
| shoots: | right |

*Photo courtesy of the Northwestern Ontario Sports Hall of Fame*

During the 1972-73 season Dennis Owchar played junior hockey for the Toronto Marlboros. The club won the Memorial Cup. He was then drafted by the Pittsburgh Penguins in the fourth round of the 1973 amateur draft. Pittsburgh assigned Owchar to the Hershey Bears for seasoning. That year Hershey won the AHL championship. In the next two years, Owchar played for both Pittsburgh and Hershey. During the 1974-75 season he went back and forth twelve times. Eventually Owchar made Pittsburgh his home, but he was soon traded to the Colorado Rockies with whom he finished his NHL career. In the 1980s, Owchar joined the Thunder Bay Twins. With the club he won the 1984 Allan Cup.

Early in his professional career, Owchar's game was inconsistent. The constant shuttling and the pressure to produce resulted in many careless errors. With time the shuttling decreased. Owchar settled down and the errors diminished. During his career, Owchar was best known for his crushing bodychecks. Numerous players were caught with their heads down at mid-ice by Owchar's shoulder. After levelling Buffalo star Rick Martin three times in one period, Owchar told him to keep his head up, quipping "or you'll make a star out of me."

## RECORD

| year | team | league | regular season | | | | | playoffs | | | | |
| | | | GP | G | A | PTS | PIM | GP | G | A | PTS | PIM |
|---|---|---|---|---|---|---|---|---|---|---|---|---|
| 1973-74* | Hershey | AHL | 74 | 16 | 17 | 33 | 51 | 14 | 1 | 5 | 6 | 14 |
| 1974-75 | Pittsburgh | NHL | 46 | 6 | 11 | 17 | 67 | 6 | 0 | 1 | 1 | 4 |
| | Hershey | AHL | 24 | 3 | 14 | 17 | 31 | 4 | 0 | 1 | 1 | 0 |
| 1975-76 | Pittsburgh | NHL | 54 | 5 | 12 | 17 | 19 | 2 | 0 | 0 | 0 | 2 |
| | Hershey | AHL | 7 | 5 | 1 | 6 | 13 | | | | | |
| 1976-77 | Pittsburgh | NHL | 46 | 5 | 18 | 23 | 37 | | | | | |
| 1977-78 | Pittsburgh | NHL | 22 | 2 | 8 | 10 | 23 | | | | | |

| | | | regular season | | | | | playoffs | | | | |
|---|---|---|---|---|---|---|---|---|---|---|---|---|
| year | team | league | GP | G | A | PTS | PIM | GP | G | A | PTS | PIM |
| 1977-78 | Colorado | NHL | 60 | 8 | 23 | 31 | 25 | 2 | 1 | 0 | 1 | 2 |
| 1978-79 | Colorado | NHL | 50 | 3 | 13 | 16 | 27 | | | | | |
| 1979-80 | Colorado | NHL | 10 | 1 | 0 | 1 | 2 | | | | | |
| | New Haven | AHL | 40 | 6 | 27 | 33 | 26 | | | | | |
| 1980-81 | New Haven | AHL | 57 | 2 | 16 | 18 | 67 | 4 | 0 | 0 | 0 | 5 |

international

| year | team | competition | GP | G | A | PTS | PIM | Place |
|---|---|---|---|---|---|---|---|---|
| 1979 | Canada | Izvestia Cup | 3 | 0 | 1 | 1 | 4 | 5 |

# PANASIUK, BOB

"Snake," "Panny"

| | |
|---|---|
| sport: | golf |
| born: | Windsor, Ontario |
| | October 20, 1941 |
| height: | 1.83 m / 6'0" |
| weight: | 79.5 kg / 175 lbs |

*Photo courtesy of the Windsor/Essex County Sports Hall of Fame and Museum*

Bob Panasiuk was born into a golfing family. His mother Virginia was one of the Windsor area's outstanding golfers. In his youth, his father Nick was a noted local golfer who eventually became the owner of the Hydeaway Golf Club near Windsor. In addition to overseeing the golf club, Nick Panasiuk taught golf. He instructed, among others, junior golf champions Bob Panasiuk, Audrey Bendick and Joye McAvoy. The development of son Bob though was Nick Panasiuk's main ambition for many years.

It is not surprising, therefore, that Bob Panasiuk began to hit golf balls at a very early age. People who remember him from those days will swear that they never saw him do anything else but play golf. At 15 years, 8 months and 20 days, Panasiuk became the youngest ever to play in a PGA Tour event when he teed off (and made the cut) at the 1957 Canadian Open. At 16, Panasiuk won two major titles, the Ontario and Canadian Junior Championships. A year later, he won the Ontario Amateur Championship. At 19, he turned professional. At the time, many believed that Panasiuk could hold his own on the American tour.

Panasiuk though did not find success in the United States. As a result, he opted for the Canadian tour. Although the prize money was not great when compared to that in the USA, neither were the expenses or the competition. Remarked Panasiuk: "I don't play golf just to say I'm a professional golfer. It's my business. I made over $20,000 last year [1974] because I know where to play. And I knew where I could win. . . Listen, there's not a guy in Canada who can play the big tour. . . Who wants to be missing cuts and going home Monday mornings when you could be winning the Manitoba Open - At least here you're a winner."[27]

Opting for the Canadian tour did not in any way weaken Panasiuk's game. In 1974, which undoubtedly was his best year, he averaged an incredible 69.6 strokes per round. He won three tournaments while his defence of a third consecutive CPGA title fell short by just two strokes. He was also named Canada's top golfer.

AWARDS

1974        CPGA - Golf Canada Tournament Player of the Year

## RECORD

| year | event | placing | result |
|---|---|---|---|
| 1956 | Ontario Junior Championship | 2 | |
| | Canadian Open (as an amateur) | | 71-74-75-76-296 |
| 1958 | Ontario Junior Championship | 1 | 77-67-144 |
| | Canadian Junior Championship | 1 | 76-77-153 |
| 1959 | Ontario Amateur Championship | 1 | |
| | Willingdon Cup (team) | 5 | 80-72-152 |
| 1961 | McNaughton-Brooks Bursary | 1 | |
| | Canadian Open | 35 T | 74-72-69-69-284 |
| 1962 | Ontario Open | 6 T | 70-75-72-73-290 |
| | Canadian Open | 2 T | 77-76-68-69-290 |
| 1963 | Canadian Open | 2 T | 72-72-72-74-290 |
| 1964 | US Open | | 72-78-78-73-301 |
| | Canadian Open | 4 T | 73-77-74-72-296 |
| | Ontario Open | 2 | 211 |
| 1965 | Ontario Open | 2 | 212 |
| 1968 | CPGA | 4 T | 282 |
| 1969 | Canadian Open | | 74-71-70-74-289 |
| | CPGA | 6 | 287 |

| year | event | placing | result |
|------|-------|---------|--------|
| 1970 | CPGA | 5 | 72-70-70-75-287 |
| 1972 | CPGA | 1 | 64-67-75-73-279 |
|      | Canadian Open | | 70-70-73-70-283 |
|      | World Cup (team) | 17 T | 75-75-87-237 |
| 1973 | CPGA | 1 | 65-68-70-69-272 |
|      | World Cup (team) | 27 | 81-79-73-73-306 |
| 1974 | CPGA | 2 | 64-69-71-69-273 |
|      | Alberta Open | 1 | 206 |
|      | Quebec Open | 1 | |
|      | Saskatchewan Open | 1 | |
|      | World Cup (team) | | |
| 1975 | Atlantic Open | 1 | |
|      | Alberta Open | 1 | 209 |
|      | CPGA | 5 T | 72-71-69-69-281 |
| 1988 | Titusville - CPGA mini tour | 1 | |

# PATRICK, JAMES

"Jeep"

| | |
|--|--|
| sport: | hockey |
| born: | Winnipeg, Manitoba |
| | June 14, 1963 |
| height: | 1.88 m / 6'2" |
| weight: | 84 kg / 185 lbs |
| position: | defense |
| shoots: | right |

*Photo courtesy of the Canadian Amateur Hockey Association*

James Patrick began to play hockey at the age of four. He was an average player until about the age of 16. He then began to refine his skills while playing for Notre Dame College (high school) in Wilcox, Saskatchewan. In 1980, he led the school to the national championship. Patrick then proceeded to play one season for the Prince Albert Raiders of the SJHL with whom he won the Centennial Cup in the spring of 1981. He was named the outstanding player at the Centennial Cup tournament. That summer he was drafted by the New York Rangers as an underage junior in the first round, ninth overall.

Rather than return to Prince Albert in the fall of 1981, Patrick opted for hockey and an education at the University of North Dakota. In his first year there, he led the university to the NCAA championship and was named rookie of the year in the WCHA. In his second year, he led the team with 48 points and was named to the first team All-American. He took time out from college hockey to represent Canada at the 1982 World Junior Championship. The Canadians won the gold medal, the first since the inception of the tournament. A year later he was co-captain of the team that won the bronze medal at the tournament.

Upon completing university in 1983, Patrick helped Canada to a third place finish at the World Championship. He then turned down a reported offer of more than $500,000 (US) to join the Rangers. He chose instead to spend the 1983-84 season with Canada's Olympic team. At the 1984 Olympics the Canadian team placed fourth. The failure to win a medal was a major disappointment for Patrick who was the team's defensive and spiritual leader. Some years later, in 1987, Patrick once again wore the colours of his country. He was a member of Team Canada that won the Canada Cup.

James Patrick joined the New York Rangers immediately after the 1984 Olympics. He quickly proved to be a steady and reliable blueliner. He played good defensive positional hockey while often switching into an offensive mode to lead rushes up the ice. An exceptional skater and passer, Patrick also possessed a powerful low shot from the point. James Patrick is the son of football player Steve Patrick and the brother of hockey player Steve Patrick, Jr.

## AWARDS

| 1981 | Chapstick Player of the Year - Top Canadian Tier II Junior |
| 1981 | Outstanding Player - Centennial Cup Tournament |

## ALL-STAR SELECTIONS

| 1982 | NCAA Championship All-Tournament Team |
| 1982-83 | All-American NCAA West |

## RECORD

| year | team | league | regular season | | | | | playoffs | | | | |
| | | | GP | G | A | PTS | PIM | GP | G | A | PTS | PIM |
| --- | --- | --- | --- | --- | --- | --- | --- | --- | --- | --- | --- | --- |
| 1983-84 | Olympic Team | | 63 | 7 | 24 | 31 | 52 | | | | | |
| | NY Rangers | NHL | 12 | 1 | 7 | 8 | 2 | 5 | 0 | 3 | 3 | 2 |
| 1984-85 | NY Rangers | NHL | 75 | 8 | 28 | 36 | 71 | 3 | 0 | 0 | 0 | 4 |

| year | team | league | regular season GP | G | A | PTS | PIM | playoffs GP | G | A | PTS | PIM |
|------|------|--------|-------------------|---|---|-----|-----|-------------|---|---|-----|-----|
| 1985-86 | NY Rangers | NHL | 75 | 14 | 29 | 43 | 88 | 16 | 1 | 5 | 6 | 34 |
| 1986-87 | NY Rangers | NHL | 78 | 10 | 45 | 55 | 62 | 6 | 1 | 2 | 3 | 2 |
| 1987-88 | NY Rangers | NHL | 70 | 17 | 45 | 62 | 52 | | | | | |
| 1988-89 | NY Rangers | NHL | 68 | 11 | 36 | 47 | 41 | 4 | 0 | 1 | 1 | 2 |
| 1989-90 | NY Rangers | NHL | 73 | 14 | 43 | 57 | 50 | 10 | 3 | 8 | 11 | 0 |
| 1990-91 | NY Rangers | NHL | 74 | 10 | 49 | 59 | 58 | 6 | 0 | 0 | 0 | 6 |

international

| year | team | competition | GP | G | A | PTS | PIM | Place |
|------|------|-------------|----|---|---|-----|-----|-------|
| 1982 | Canada | World Junior Championship | 7 | 0 | 3 | 3 | 6 | 1 |
| 1983 | Canada | World Junior Championship | 7 | 0 | 2 | 2 | 4 | 3 |
| 1983 | Canada | World Championship | 9 | 1 | 1 | 2 | 10 | 3 |
| 1984 | Canada | Olympic Games | 7 | 0 | 3 | 3 | 4 | 4 |
| 1987 | Canada | World Championship | 8 | 0 | 1 | 1 | 2 | 4 |
| 1987 | Canada | Canada Cup | 6 | 0 | 1 | 1 | 2 | 1 |
| 1989 | Canada | World Championship | 10 | 2 | 2 | 4 | 8 | 2 |

# PATRICK, STEVE

| | |
|--|--|
| sport: | football |
| born: | Glenella, Manitoba |
| | March 24, 1932 |
| height: | 1.83 m / 6'0" |
| weight: | 115 kg / 253 lbs |
| position: | tackle |

*Photo courtesy of the Canadian Football Hall of Fame and Museum*

Steve Patrick played junior football with the Winnipeg Light Infantry club in the years 1950 and 1951. His talents were quickly noticed and in 1952, the twenty-year-old made the roster of the Winnipeg Blue Bombers. He was with the club for thirteen years, always playing first string. Patrick began his rookie season playing both on offence and defence. Midway through the year his workload was reduced to that on defence and for the remainder of his career he started on defence, playing nose guard, middle guard or tackle.

Steve Patrick was a bruising tackle who was very difficult to contain. Within a few years he gained recognition as one of the league's finest defensive players. In 1957, he was the team's nominee for the Schenley Outstanding Lineman Award and two years later for the Schenley Most Outstanding Canadian Award. In 1957, Patrick was named to the all-Canadian team. The following year, he was chosen as one of the top twelve Canadian players in the CFL by the *Weekend Magazine*. The latter recognition was accorded to him for five consecutive years.

Steve Patrick played in six Grey Cup games, winning on four occasions. He was the captain of the team that won the 1962 Cup in most unfavourable playing conditions. The game, which has gone down in history as the "Fog Bowl," had to be called with nine minutes remaining because of thick fog. The players could not see each other on the field. The game was completed the following day.

In the early 1950s, Patrick wrestled during the off-season to pick up a few extra dollars. Eventually he started an insurance business. In 1962, he was elected to the Manitoba Legislature. Through his retirement from football in 1964, Patrick juggled responsibilities as a member of the legislature, a businessman and a professional football player. In 1982, Patrick was named as one of twelve All-time great Blue Bombers of the One Half Century and in 1988, he was inducted into the Manitoba Sports Hall of Fame. Steve Patrick is the father of hockey players James Patrick and Steve Patrick, Jr.

## INDUCTIONS

1988      Manitoba Sports Hall of Fame

## AWARDS

1959      Tommy Lumsden Trophy  -  Winnipeg's Most Valuable Canadian

## ALL-STAR SELECTIONS

| 1958 | middle guard | WIFU | All-Western |
|------|--------------|------|-------------|
| 1959 | middle guard | WIFU | All-Western |

# PATRICK Jr., STEVE

| | |
|---|---|
| sport: | hockey |
| given name: | Patrick, Stephen Gary |
| born: | Winnipeg, Manitoba |
| | February 4, 1964 |
| height: | 1.93 m / 6'4" |
| weight: | 93.5 kg / 206 lbs |
| position: | right wing |
| shoots: | right |

*Photo courtesy of the Buffalo Sabres*

Steve Patrick Jr. was drafted from the Brandon Wheat Kings by the Buffalo Sabres as an under-age junior in the first round, 20th overall, of the 1980 NHL Entry Draft. He spent the 1980-81 season playing for Brandon and Buffalo. He played the next three seasons with Buffalo and the Rochester Americans of the AHL. The assignments to the minor league disheartened Patrick, and when he failed to report to Rochester in February of 1983 he was suspended. Patrick was subsequently reinstated and eventually traded to the New York Rangers. The Rangers then dealt him to the Quebec Nordiques.

Disappointed in the way his hockey career was progressing, Steve Patrick came to the conclusion that hockey was no longer fun. With one year to go in a lucrative contract, he retired from the game in the fall of 1986. Steve Patrick Jr. is the son of football player Steve Patrick and the brother of hockey player James Patrick.

## RECORD

| year | team | league | regular season | | | | | playoffs | | | | |
|---|---|---|---|---|---|---|---|---|---|---|---|---|
| | | | GP | G | A | PTS | PIM | GP | G | A | PTS | PIM |
| 1980-81 | Buffalo | NHL | 30 | 1 | 7 | 8 | 25 | 5 | 0 | 1 | 1 | 6 |
| 1981-82 | Buffalo | NHL | 41 | 8 | 8 | 16 | 64 | | | | | |
| | Rochester | AHL | 38 | 11 | 9 | 20 | 15 | 5 | 3 | 2 | 5 | 12 |
| 1982-83 | Buffalo | NHL | 56 | 9 | 13 | 22 | 26 | 2 | 0 | 0 | 0 | 0 |
| 1983-84 | Buffalo | NHL | 11 | 1 | 4 | 5 | 6 | 1 | 0 | 0 | 0 | 0 |
| | Rochester | AHL | 30 | 8 | 14 | 22 | 33 | 13 | 2 | 1 | 3 | 18 |
| 1984-85 | Buffalo | NHL | 14 | 2 | 2 | 4 | 4 | | | | | |
| | NY Rangers | NHL | 43 | 11 | 18 | 29 | 63 | | | | | |
| 1985-86 | NY Rangers | NHL | 28 | 4 | 3 | 7 | 37 | | | | | |
| | Quebec | NHL | 27 | 4 | 13 | 17 | 17 | 3 | 0 | 0 | 0 | 0 |

# PATTEN, STEPHAN

| | |
|---|---|
| sport: | athletics |
| born: | Montreal, Quebec |
| | March 8, 1973 |
| height: | 1.78 m / 5'10" |
| weight: | 68 kg / 150 lbs |

Stephan Patten was a high school student competing in track, cross-country, and road racing when he had his first taste of international competition. After winning the Ontario high school cross-country championship at the junior level, St. Michael's College of Toronto was invited to represent Canada at the biannual World High School Cross-Country Championships in France. At the championship, which was dominated by runners from Morocco and Nigeria, Stephan Patten placed 77th and his St. Michael's team placed tenth. After returning to Canada, Patten suffered a serious knee injury.

## RECORD

| year | competition | event | placing | result |
|---|---|---|---|---|
| 1988 | McQuaid Cross-Country Invitational | 3 m | 5 | 17:05 |
| | Brampton 10 K | 10 km | | 39:50.6 |
| | Sharkey's 5 K | 5 km | | 18:09 |
| 1990 | World I.S.F. Cross-Country Championships | | 77 | |
| | | team | 10 | |

# PECHALUK, FRED

| | |
|---|---|
| sport: | bowling |
| born: | Toronto, Ontario |
| | February 23, 1917 |
| height: | 1.70 m / 5'7" |
| weight: | 75 kg / 165 lbs |

After 36 years of bowling, Fred Pechaluk retired from the sport after the 1977-78 season because of a knee injury. His career included 7,148 games played in 8 leagues and a life-time average of 251. His highest league average was 279 bowled in the Willowdale Men's Major League during the 1964-65 season.

Fred Pechaluk competed at two national championships. In 1953, his team lost by a mere 43 points. Pechaluk returned to the championship in 1959. His ten game average of 266 helped his side to victory in a men's team record score of 12,686 points.

Over the years Pechaluk also contributed to the growth of bowling through administrative work. He held various posts with most of the bowling leagues he was associated with. In 1964, he co-founded the York West 5 Pin Bowlers' Association and served as its president for fourteen years. He also served as assistant secretary of the Canadian Bowling Association (CBA) for three years.

In 1936, representing the Ukrainian Softball League of Toronto, Pechaluk won the 220-yard dash at the Ukrainian Youth League of North America's first Ukrainian Olympiad in Philadelphia. In 1939 and 1940, Fred Pechaluk was the manager of the Toronto Ukrainian Ladies' Softball team that won the Toronto Ladies' Church League championship.

## INDUCTIONS

1988      Ontario Five Pin Bowling Association Hall of Fame

## RECORD

| year | competition | division | placing |
|---|---|---|---|
| 1953 | Canadian 5 Pin Bowling Championship | team | 2 |
| 1959 | Canadian 5 Pin Bowling Championship | team | 1 |

# PELYK, MIKE

| | |
|---|---|
| sport: | hockey |
| born: | Toronto, Ontario |
| | September 29, 1947 |
| height: | 1.83 m / 6'0" |
| weight: | 86 kg / 190 lbs |
| position: | defense |
| shoots: | left |

*Card reproduced courtesy of O-Pee-Chee Co.*

Mike Pelyk began his junior hockey career with York Steel, which advanced to the Ontario Junior "B" finals in 1965-66. The following season, he earned a starting position with the Toronto Marlboros. The club won the Memorial Cup that year. In the fall of 1967, with one year of junior eligibility remaining, Pelyk was invited to attend the Toronto Maple Leafs' training camp. He impressed the Leafs' brass and was offered a contract. At the time, Pelyk was unsure whether he wanted to pursue a hockey career or to finish university. He decided to do both: play hockey and go to school part time. He succeeded doing both: playing hockey in the NHL and obtaining an MBA.

Pelyk began the 1967-68 season playing for Tulsa of the CHL. Towards the end of the season he was called up by the Leafs. For the next six years, Pelyk saw regular action on the Leafs blue line. At first he performed well, but with time his play became inconsistent and he fell into disfavour with the Leafs' management. When Red Kelly took over the club in 1973, Pelyk's career was rejuvenated and he scored a career-high 12 goals and 19 assists. After that season, Pelyk defected to the WHA after signing a lucrative five-year contract with the Cincinnati Stingers.

As the Stingers were still one year from commencing operations, Mike Pelyk was loaned for the season to the Vancouver Blazers. There, he played good hockey, scoring more than forty points. In the fall of 1975, Pelyk suited up with the Stingers. He played with them for only one year and was released from his contract. Pelyk resigned with Toronto and in the next two seasons saw action with the Leafs and in the minor leagues with Dallas and Tulsa.

| year | team | league | regular season | | | | | playoffs | | | | |
|---|---|---|---|---|---|---|---|---|---|---|---|---|
| | | | GP | G | A | PTS | PIM | GP | G | A | PTS | PIM |
| 1967-68 | Toronto | NHL | 24 | 0 | 3 | 3 | 55 | | | | | |
| | Tulsa | CHL | 47 | 0 | 16 | 16 | 131 | | | | | |
| 1968-69 | Toronto | NHL | 65 | 3 | 9 | 12 | 146 | 4 | 0 | 0 | 0 | 8 |
| 1969-70 | Toronto | NHL | 35 | 1 | 3 | 4 | 37 | | | | | |
| 1970-71 | Toronto | NHL | 73 | 5 | 21 | 26 | 54 | 6 | 0 | 0 | 0 | 10 |
| 1971-72 | Toronto | NHL | 46 | 1 | 4 | 5 | 44 | 5 | 0 | 0 | 0 | 8 |
| 1972-73 | Toronto | NHL | 72 | 3 | 16 | 19 | 118 | | | | | |
| 1973-74 | Toronto | NHL | 71 | 12 | 19 | 31 | 94 | 4 | 0 | 0 | 0 | 4 |
| 1974-75 | Vancouver | WHA | 75 | 14 | 26 | 40 | 121 | | | | | |
| 1975-76 | Cincinnati | WHA | 75 | 10 | 23 | 33 | 117 | | | | | |
| 1976-77 | Toronto | NHL | 13 | 0 | 2 | 2 | 4 | 9 | 0 | 2 | 2 | 4 |
| | Dallas | CHL | 62 | 9 | 26 | 35 | 73 | | | | | |
| 1977-78 | Toronto | NHL | 41 | 1 | 11 | 12 | 14 | 12 | 0 | 1 | 1 | 7 |
| | Tulsa | CHL | 32 | 2 | 12 | 14 | 35 | | | | | |

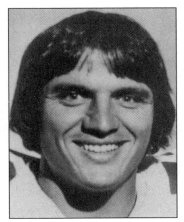

# PIASKOSKI, JIM

"Pia"

| | |
|---|---|
| sport: | football |
| born: | . . . |
| | September 10, 1948 |
| height: | 1.91 m / 6'3" |
| weight: | 106.5 kg / 235 lbs |
| position: | defensive end |

*Photo courtesy of the Canadian Football Hall of Fame and Museum*

Jim Piaskoski began his football career with the Sudbury Spartans of the Northern Football Conference. Subsequently, he played football with Eastern Michigan University before returning to the Spartans in 1971. The following year, Piaskoski joined the Ottawa Rough Riders and earned a starting spot with the club's defensive front four at the end position. Piaskoski and his colleagues were quickly recognized as the best front four in the nation. Their main objective was to destroy opposing quarterbacks, and their prime mental attribute was the total hatred for the enemy. In recognition of their all-out play, they were labelled "Capital Punishment."

Piaskoski played with Ottawa for eleven seasons. During that time, he was a member of two Grey Cup championship teams, in 1973 and 1976. In 1977, he was named to the All-Eastern All-Star team and was the Rough Riders' nominee for the Schenley Most Outstanding Defensive Player Award. Jim Piaskoski was a fast and strong defensive end who had a reputation as a tough hitter.

ALL-STAR SELECTIONS

1977      defensive end      CFL      All-Eastern

## PIDSOSNY, STEVE

| | |
|---|---|
| sport: | speed skating |
| given name: | Pidsosny, Slawko Stephen |
| born: | Clermont Oise, France |
| | March 22, 1940 |
| height: | . . . |
| weight: | . . . |

When Steve Pidsosny became editor of the Canadian Amateur Speed Skating Association's (CASSA) *The Racer*, he made the publication bilingual. He wrote all the articles in both official languages. This was a first for *The Racer*, the longest-publishing newspaper by a sports governing body in Canada. Knowledge of three languages also helped Pidsosny in some of the other administrative functions that he has held with the CASSA. He often served as a bilingual announcer at various competitions, including the 1988 Olympic Games. Knowledge of Ukrainian helped him deal with Soviet and other East European officials. While Vice President of Advanced Programmes of CASSA in the 1980s, Pidsosny was in control of all facets of the national team (which competes internationally). During his tenure, Canadian speed skating reached new international heights, mainly as a result of Gaetan Boucher's strong performances.

RECORD

| year | position |
|------|----------|
| 1976-78 | Editor, *The Racer*, Canadian Amateur Speed Skating Association (CASSA) publication |
| 1978-80 | Vice President (Administration), CASSA |
| | President, Saskatchewan Amateur Speed Skating Association |
| 1980-88 | Vice President (Advanced Programmes), CASSA |
| 1984 | CASSA representative, Olympic Games |
| 1985 | CASSA representative, World Speed Skating Championships |
| | CASSA representative, World Sprint Speed Skating Championships |
| 1986 | CASSA representative, World Sprint Speed Skating Championships |
| 1988 | CASSA delegate, Olympic Games |
| | Bilingual announcer, Olympic Games - Speed Skating Oval |

# PIDZARKO-MORE, CHRIS

| | |
|------|----------|
| sport: | curling |
| nee: | Pidzarko, Christine |
| born: | Winnipeg, Manitoba |
| | February 19, 1954 |
| height: | 1.57 m / 5'2" |
| weight: | 52 kg / 115 lbs |

*Photo courtesy of the Western Canada Pictorial Index*

Chris Pidzarko-More's first major curling success occurred in 1969 when she skipped her Manitoba rink, which included her twin sister Cathy, to the Canada Games gold medal. Since then, Pidzarko-More has been a member of rinks which have represented Manitoba at eight Canadian championships - three junior, one mixed, and four women's. In 1972, and once again in 1974, she skipped rinks to the Canadian junior titles. In 1978, playing third on a rink skipped by sister Cathy, Chris won her first women's title. She won her second Canadian championship in 1984 when she played third on the Connie Laliberte rink. That rink went on to win the World Championship.

The victory assured Pidzarko-More a spot in Canadian curling history as she became the first female curler to win the Canadian junior, Canadian, and World championships.

Chris Pidzarko-More has also done well as a skip. In 1979, and in 1989, she led her rink to the Manitoba titles and the playoff round of the Canadian Championship.


## INDUCTIONS

1984    Manitoba Sports Hall of Fame  -  member of the 1984 Connie Laliberte Rink
1988    Canadian Curling Hall of Fame


## RECORD

| year | competition | position | placing | result |
|------|-------------|----------|---------|--------|
| 1971 | Canada Games | skip | 1 | |
| 1972 | Manitoba Junior Championship | skip | 1 | |
| | Canadian Junior Championship | skip | 1 | 7-0 |
| 1973 | Manitoba Junior Championship | skip | 1 | |
| | Canadian Junior Championship | skip | 2 | 7-2 |
| 1974 | Manitoba Junior Championship | skip | 1 | |
| | Canadian Junior Championship | skip | 1 | 8-1 |
| 1978 | Manitoba Championship | third | 1 | |
| | Canadian Championship | third | 1 | 7-3 |
| 1979 | Manitoba Championship | skip | 1 | |
| | Canadian Championship | skip | 2 | 9-4 |
| 1984 | Manitoba Championship | third | 1 | 8-2 |
| | Canadian Championship | third | 1 | 9-2 |
| | World Championship | third | 1 | 10-2 |
| 1988 | Olympic Trials | skip | | 2-5 |
| 1989 | Manitoba Championship | skip | 1 | 8-3 |
| | Canadian Championship | skip | 2 | 8-4 |

# PIDZARKO-SHAW, CATHY

sport:       curling

nee:        Pidzarko, Cathy

born:       Winnipeg, Manitoba

              February 19, 1954

height:     . . .

weight:    . . .

*Photo courtesy of the Western Canada Pictorial Index*

Cathy Pidzarko-Shaw's early curling career is almost identical to that of her twin sister Chris. For a number of years Cathy played third on a rink which was skipped by Chris. The rink won the 1969 Canada Games gold medal, three Manitoba junior titles in the years 1972-74, and the 1972 and 1974 Canadian Junior Championships. A few years later, the sisters exchanged positions with Cathy assuming duties of skip. In 1978, this new-look Pidzarko rink won the Manitoba and Canadian curling championships.

Since that victory, Pidzarko-Shaw has called many cities home. In each new locale, she would seek out a curling club and put together a foursome. In very little time she would mould that foursome into a competitive team. The success of those teams is a testament to her knowledge of the game and her great skipping skills. In 1980, she skipped her Yellowknife team to the Yukon and Territories title and a 5-5 record at the Canadian Championship. Two years later, she skipped her Edmonton rink to the Alberta title and a spot in the playoffs at the Canadian Championship. In 1988, curling out of Ontario, Cathy Pidzarko-Shaw was unsuccessful in her bid to make the Olympic curling team.

## RECORD

| year | competition | position | placing | result |
|------|-------------|----------|---------|--------|
| 1971 | Canada Games | third | 1 | |
| 1972 | Manitoba Junior Championship | third | 1 | |
| | Canadian Junior Championship | third | 1 | 7-0 |
| 1973 | Manitoba Junior Championship | third | 1 | |
| | Canadian Junior Championship | third | 2 | 7-2 |
| 1974 | Manitoba Junior Championship | third | 1 | |
| | Canadian Junior Championship | third | 1 | 8-1 |
| 1978 | Manitoba Championship | skip | 1 | |

| year | competition | position | placing | result |
|---|---|---|---|---|
| 1978 | Canadian Championship | skip | 1 | 7-3 |
| 1980 | Yukon & Territories Championship | skip | 1 | |
| | Canadian Championship | skip | 6 | 5-5 |
| 1982 | Alberta Championship | skip | 1 | 7-3 |
| | Canadian Championship | skip | 5 | 7-4 |
| 1983 | Alberta Championship | skip | 1 | 8-3 |
| | Canadian Championship | skip | 2 | 8-4 |
| 1988 | Olympic Trials | | | |

# PODBORSKI, STEVE

| | |
|---|---|
| sport: | skiing |
| given name: | Podborski, Stephen Gregory |
| born: | Toronto, Ontario |
| | July 25, 1957 |
| height: | 1.74 m / 5'9" |
| weight: | 72 kg / 158 lbs |

*Photo courtesy of Canada's Sports Hall of Fame*

Steve Podborski learned to ski when he was two and a half years old. At the age of ten he was racing in the juvenile interclub Nancy Greene League. At 13, he competed at his first age group nationals, and at 16 he was invited to try out for Canada's national alpine team. No one expected him to make the team. Podborski, though, shocked everyone, including himself, when he won all five downhill runs. He made the team, and at age 17 took part in his first World Cup race. The European press was soon referring to Podborski and his teammates as the "Crazy Canucks" or the "Kamikaze Kids." Podborski later reminisced: "At first, we went right by the limits and off the edge. You eventually found out how far you can go and then start pushing for it. Sure, you get a little ragged - that's really a neat feeling - looking for those horizons. But crazy isn't the way to put it. . ."[28] Initially, Podborski competed in all three alpine disciplines - the slalom, giant slalom, and the downhill. His preference was the downhill and his first victory on the World Cup circuit came in that event in 1979 at Morzine-Avoriaz, France.

A few weeks later, just a month before the 1980 Olympic Games, Podborski took an awful spill while pushing himself to the limit on the legendary Hahnenkamm course in Kitzbuhel, Austria. His helmet broke through a retaining fence. He later told the press, "I knew I was going extremely well because I was completely out of control."[29] In Europe, this is what legends are made of. Podborski recovered fully from the crash and went on to win the Olympic bronze medal in the downhill. After the completion of the 1980 season, while testing new skis, Podborski fell and severely damaged his knee. That same knee had been reconstructed in 1976 after a fall tore his ligaments. Once again, surgery was followed by physiotherapy and hard training.

Podborski began the 1980-81 season with a strong third-place finish at Val d'Isere. As his knee held up, Podborski became more confident and determined than ever to win. A third and a tenth place finish were followed by three consecutive victories: on the extremely fast St. Moritz course, Garmish-Partenkirchen, and the Hahnenkamm at Kitzbuhel, where he was mobbed by the fans and media after the race. Podborski was at the top of the skiing world. The World Cup downhill title was within his grasp. Unfortunately, it was not to be in 1980-81. Before the season ended, Podborski was in a serious car accident. His performance in the final two races of the season was not up to par. He placed second in the overall World Cup title race but was ranked number one in the world.

During the 1981-82 season, Podborski had three first and two second-place finishes on the World Cup circuit. He also had two fourth-place finishes which were good for points. When the season concluded, Steve Podborski became the first non-European to be crowned with the World Cup Downhill Championship.

Steve Podborski competed for another two years with varying success but was unable to duplicate the results of the previous years. In the latter part of the 1980s, Podborski was involved with Toronto's bid for the 1996 Olympics.

## INDUCTIONS

1985    Canadian Olympic Hall of Fame
1987    Canada's Sports Hall of Fame

## AWARDS

1980    Ontario Amateur Athlete of the Year
1981    Ontario Amateur Athlete of the Year
1981    Norton Crowe Award  -  Canadian Amateur Male Athlete of the Year
1981    John Semmelink Trophy  -  Canadian Ski Association

| 1981 | *Ski Racing's* Canadian Alpine Skier of the Year |
|------|--------------------------------------------------|
| 1982 | Norton Crowe Award - Canadian Amateur Male Athlete of the Year |
| 1982 | Officer, Order of Canada |
| 1982 | *Ski Racing's* Canadian Alpine Skier of the Year |
| 1984 | *Ski Racing's* Canadian Alpine Skier of the Year |

## RECORD

| year | competition | event | placing | result |
|------|-------------|-------|---------|--------|
| 1974 | WC Val d'Isere | downhill | 31 | 2:09.57 |
|      | WC St. Moritz | downhill | 23 | 1:59.57 |
| 1975 | WC Garmisch-Partenkirchen | downhill | dnf | |
|      | WC Wengen | downhill | dnf | |
|      | WC Kitzbuhel | downhill | 36 | 2:10.15 |
|      | WC Innsbruck | downhill | 19 | 1:59.20 |
|      | WC Chamonix | downhill | 15 | 2:07.67 |
|      | WC Jackson Hole | downhill | 18 | 2:00.84 |
|      | WC Val d'Isere | downhill | 10 | 2:07.28 |
|      | WC Madonna di Campiglio | downhill | 16 | 1:42.85 |
|      | WC Schladming | downhill | 26 | 2:05.37 |
| 1976 | WC Wengen | downhill | 11 | 2:10.38 |
|      | WC Wengen | downhill | 8 | 2:44.87 |
|      | WC Morzine-Avoriaz | downhill | 20 | 1:57.27 |
|      | WC Cortina | downhil | 16 | |
|      | WC Val d'Isere | giant slalom | 36 | |
|      | WC Val Gardena | downhill | 18 | 2:08.37 |
|      | WC Val Gardena | downhill | 27 | 2:12.48 |
| 1977 | Canadian Championships | giant slalom | 3 | |
|      |  | slalom | 1 | |
|      | WC Garmisch-Partenkirchen | downhill | 42 | 2:09.14 |
|      |  | giant slalom | dnf | |
|      | WC Kitzbuhel | downhill | 32 | 2:17.53 |
|      | WC Wengen | downhill | 31 | 2:41.66 |
|      | WC Morzine-Avoriaz | downhill | 31 | 1:50.05 |
|      | WC Heavenly Valley | downhill | 13 | 1:39.94 |
|      | WC Heavenly Valley | downhill | 36 | 1:58.21 |
|      | WC Val d'Isere | downhill | 21 | 2:10.51 |
|      | WC Val Gardena | downhill | 14 | 2:05.26 |
|      | WC Cortina d'Ampezzo | downhill | 19 | 1:53.15 |
|      | WC Ebnat | giant slalom | 30 | |

| year | competition | event | placing | result |
|------|-------------|-------|---------|--------|
| 1977 | WC St. Anton | slalom | dnf | |
| | WC Sun Valley | slalom | dnf | |
| 1978 | WC Kitzbuhel | downhill | 10 | 2:07.81 |
| | | downhill | 14 | 2:09.43 |
| | World Championships | downhill | 7 | 2:04.98 |
| | WC Les Houches | downhill | 20 | 2:10.72 |
| | WC Laax | downhill | 4 | 1:58.71 |
| | WC Laax | downhill | 6 | 1:57.07 |
| | WC Schladming | downhill | 9 | 1:32.75 |
| | WC Val Gardena | downhill | 10 | 2:13.73 |
| 1979 | Canadian Championships | downhill | 7 | |
| | | slalom | 11 | |
| | WC Morzine-Avoriaz | downhill | 1 | 1:43.97 |
| | WC Crans-Montana | downhill | 7 | 2:00.24 |
| | WC Kitzbuhel | downhill | 8 | 2:06.01 |
| | WC Villars | downhill | 38 | 1:48.87 |
| | WC Lake Placid | downhill | 8 | 1:44.17 |
| | WC Val d'Isere | downhill | dnf | |
| | WC Val Gardena | downhill | 45 | 2:08.69 |
| 1980 | WC Pra Loup | downhill | dnf | |
| | WC Kitzbuhel | downhill | dnf | |
| | WC Wengen | downhill | 8 | 2:32.20 |
| | | downhill | 3 | 2:30.66 |
| | Olympic Games | downhill | 3 | 1:46.62 |
| | WC Lake Louise | downhill | 4 | 1:51.76 |
| | Canadian Championships | downhill | 2 | 1:48.14 |
| | WC Saalbach | giant slalom | 44 | 2:46.23 |
| | | slalom | dnf | |
| | WC Arber Osthang | giant slalom | 32 | 2:14.16 |
| | WC Val d'Isere | downhill | 3 | 2:00.71 |
| | WC Val Gardena | downhill | 3 | 2:02.00 |
| | | downhill | 10 | 1:54.26 |
| | WC St. Moritz | downhill | 1 | 1:54.31 |
| 1981 | WC Garmisch-Partenkirchen | downhill | 1 | 1:55.48 |
| | WC Kitzbuhel | downhill | 1 | 2:03.76 |
| | WC Wengen | downhill | 3 | 2:28.46 |
| | WC St. Anton | downhill | 3 | 2:00.15 |
| | Canadian Championships | downhill | 7 | 1:38.07 |
| | FIS | downhill | 2 | 1:37.26 |

| year | competition | event | placing | result |
|------|------------|-------|---------|--------|
| 1981 | WC Aspen | downhill | 10 | 1:54.35 |
| | | downhill | 2 | 1:52.49 |
| | WC Val d'Isere | downhill | 4 | 2:05.70 |
| | WC Val Gardena | downhill | 4 | 2:07.91 |
| | WC Crans-Montana | downhill | 1 | 2:09.22 |
| 1982 | WC Kitzbuhel | downhill | 2 | 1:57.89 |
| | | downhill | 1 | 1:57.24 |
| | WC Wengen | downhill | 11 | 2:06.41 |
| | World Championships | downhill | 9 | 1:56.78 |
| | WC Garmisch-Partenkirchen | downhill | 1 | 1:50.52 |
| | WC Whistler | downhill | 2 | 2:15.53 |
| | WC Aspen | downhill | 14 | 1:48.84 |
| | | downhill | 14 | 1:48.67 |
| | WC Pontresina | downhill | 12 | 1:44.12 |
| | WC Val Gardena | downhill | 24 | 2:12.81 |
| | | downhill | 17 | 2:12.21 |
| 1983 | WC Val d'Isere | downhill | dnf | |
| | | downhill | 34 | 2:02.31 |
| | WC Kitzbuhel | downhill | 2 | 2:06.79 |
| | | downhill | 9 | 2:03.20 |
| | WC Sarajevo | downhill | 2 | 1:49.02 |
| | WC St. Anton | downhill | 4 | 2:05.08 |
| | Canadian Championships | downhill | 1 | 1:50.64 |
| | WC Schladming | downhill | 3 | 1:58.90 |
| | WC Val d'Isere | downhill | 7 | 2:02.14 |
| | WC Val Gardena | downhill | 3 | 1:57.79 |
| 1984 | WC Laax | downhill | 17 | 1:58.40 |
| | WC Wengen | downhill | 20 | 2:12.56 |
| | WC Kitzbuhel | downhill | 20 | 2:04.52 |
| | WC Garmisch-Partenkirchen | downhill | 1 | 1:56.95 |
| | WC Cortina d'Ampezzo | downhill | 6 | 1:53.59 |
| | Olympic Games | downhill | 8 | 1:46.59 |
| | Canadian Championships | downhill | 1 | 1:54.94 |
| | WC Aspen | downhill | 8 | 1:50.31 |
| | WC Whistler | downhill | 5 | 2:03.73 |

# PODDUBNY, WALT

| | |
|---|---|
| sport: | hockey |
| given name: | Poddubny, Walter Michael |
| born: | Thunder Bay, Ontario |
| | February 14, 1960 |
| height: | 1.85 m / 6'1" |
| weight: | 70 kg / 205 lbs |
| position: | center |
| shoots: | left |

*Photo courtesy of the New Jersey Devils*

As a fifteen-year-old, Walt Poddubny enjoyed sports but did not excel, in part because of his size: he stood 1.85 m (5'10") and weighed 70 kg (230 lbs). At seventeen, Poddubny grew two inches, lost thirty pounds, and started to lift weights. He made the football team that fall and in winter was asked to join the Fort William Canadians junior hockey team. He also played baseball and was offered a scholarship by Kansas University. Poddubny decided to pursue hockey and in the next two years he played on four junior teams: the Brandon Wheat Kings, Thunder Bay DeGagne Buccaneers, Kitchener Rangers, and Kingston Canadians. In 1980, he was the fourth choice of the Edmonton Oilers and 90th overall in the NHL Entry Draft.

Poddubny's first year of professional hockey was spent in the minors. The following year, he made his NHL debut with the Oilers, spent more time in the minors, and was traded to the Toronto Maple Leafs late in the season. In his first season with the Leafs and his first full year in the NHL, Poddubny broke the club record for goals by a rookie with 28. He also had the best plus/minus record on the team. The next two seasons were disappointing as Poddubny nursed injury after injury. When he took the club to salary arbitration twice and won twice, Leafs' management decided that he was expandable.

The New York Rangers acquired Poddubny prior to the start of the 1986-87 season. Rangers' general manager Phil Esposito, who saw a little bit of himself in Poddubny, told his new skater to be creative on the ice. Poddubny responded by scoring a team-leading 40 goals. The following season, Poddubny tallied 38 goals and a career-high 88 points. During the summer he was traded to the Quebec Nordiques, with whom he played a season before being traded to the New Jersey Devils. The 1989-90 season with the Devils was frustrating; first he injured his back and then tore a knee ligament.

| year | team | league | regular season | | | | | playoffs | | | | |
|------|------|--------|-----|-----|-----|-----|-----|-----|-----|-----|-----|-----|
| | | | GP | G | A | PTS | PIM | GP | G | A | PTS | PIM |
| 1980-81 | Milwaukee | IHL | 5 | 4 | 2 | 6 | 4 | | | | | |
| | Wichita | CHL | 70 | 21 | 29 | 50 | 207 | 11 | 1 | 6 | 7 | 26 |
| 1981-82 | Edmonton | NHL | 4 | 0 | 0 | 0 | 0 | | | | | |
| | Toronto | NHL | 11 | 3 | 4 | 7 | 8 | | | | | |
| | Wichita | CHL | 60 | 35 | 46 | 81 | 79 | | | | | |
| 1982-83 | Toronto | NHL | 72 | 28 | 31 | 59 | 71 | 4 | 3 | 1 | 4 | 0 |
| 1983-84 | Toronto | NHL | 38 | 11 | 14 | 25 | 48 | | | | | |
| 1984-85 | Toronto | NHL | 32 | 5 | 15 | 20 | 26 | | | | | |
| | St. Catharines | AHL | 8 | 5 | 7 | 12 | 10 | | | | | |
| 1985-86 | Toronto | NHL | 33 | 12 | 22 | 34 | 25 | 9 | 4 | 1 | 5 | 4 |
| | St. Catharines | AHL | 37 | 28 | 27 | 55 | 52 | | | | | |
| 1986-87 | NY Rangers | NHL | 75 | 40 | 47 | 87 | 49 | 6 | 0 | 0 | 0 | 8 |
| 1987-88 | NY Rangers | NHL | 77 | 38 | 50 | 88 | 76 | | | | | |
| 1988-89 | Quebec | NHL | 72 | 38 | 37 | 75 | 107 | | | | | |
| 1989-90 | New Jersey | NHL | 33 | 4 | 10 | 14 | 28 | | | | | |
| | Utica | AHL | 2 | 1 | 2 | 3 | 0 | | | | | |
| 1990-91 | New Jersey | NHL | 14 | 4 | 6 | 10 | 10 | | | | | |

# POLIS, GREG

| | |
|---|---|
| sport: | hockey |
| given name: | Polis, Gregory Linn |
| born: | Westlock, Alberta |
| | August 8, 1950 |
| height: | 1.83 m / 6'0" |
| weight: | 88.5 kg / 195 lbs |
| position: | left wing |
| shoots: | left |

After scoring more than 200 points in two seasons with the junior Estevan Bruins of the WCHL, Greg Polis was selected by the Pittsburgh Penguins in the first round, seventh overall, of the 1970 NHL Entry Draft. Polis made the team immediately and overcame a bout with mononucleosis to have a relatively successful rookie season. The following year, he notched 30 goals and added 19 assists for 49 points; it was to be his most productive NHL season. During the 1972-73 season, Polis appeared in the NHL All-Star Game. He scored two goals and was named NHL All-Star Game MVP.

The Penguins traded Polis to the St. Louis Blues in January of 1974. He barely had time to settle in before the New York Rangers acquired him in a trade prior to the start of the 1974-75 season. In New York, Polis played left wing on a line centered by Walt Tkaczuk for a number of years. In January of 1979, Polis was claimed on waivers by the Washington Capitals, with whom he finished his NHL career.

## RECORD

| year | team | league | regular season | | | | | playoffs | | | | |
|------|------|--------|-----|-----|-----|-----|-----|-----|-----|-----|-----|-----|
| | | | GP | G | A | PTS | PIM | GP | G | A | PTS | PIM |
| 1970-71 | Pittsburgh | NHL | 61 | 18 | 15 | 33 | 40 | | | | | |
| 1971-72 | Pittsburgh | NHL | 76 | 30 | 19 | 49 | 38 | 4 | 0 | 2 | 2 | 0 |
| 1972-73 | Pittsburgh | NHL | 78 | 26 | 23 | 49 | 36 | | | | | |
| 1973-74 | Pittsburgh | NHL | 41 | 14 | 13 | 27 | 32 | | | | | |
| | St. Louis | NHL | 37 | 8 | 12 | 20 | 24 | | | | | |
| 1974-75 | NY Rangers | NHL | 76 | 26 | 15 | 41 | 55 | 3 | 0 | 0 | 0 | 6 |
| 1975-76 | NY Rangers | NHL | 79 | 15 | 21 | 36 | 77 | | | | | |
| 1976-77 | NY Rangers | NHL | 77 | 16 | 23 | 39 | 44 | | | | | |
| 1977-78 | NY Rangers | NHL | 37 | 7 | 16 | 23 | 12 | | | | | |
| 1978-79 | NY Rangers | NHL | 6 | 1 | 1 | 2 | 8 | | | | | |
| | Washington | NHL | 19 | 12 | 6 | 18 | 6 | | | | | |
| | New Haven | AHL | 10 | 3 | 3 | 6 | 0 | | | | | |
| 1979-80 | Washington | NHL | 28 | 1 | 5 | 6 | 19 | | | | | |
| | Hershey | AHL | 9 | 0 | 2 | 2 | 2 | | | | | |
| 1980-81 | Hershey | AHL | 2 | 1 | 0 | 1 | 5 | | | | | |

# POLONICH, DENNIS

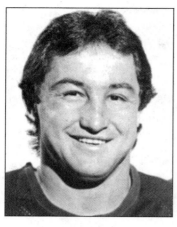

"Polo"

sport:          hockey

given name:     Polonich, Dennis Daniel

born:           Foam Lake, Saskatchewan

                December 4, 1953

height:         1.68 m / 5'6"

weight:         77 kg / 170 lbs

position:       center

shoots:         right

Dennis Polonich grew up working on his parents' farm in Saskatchewan. He played junior hockey with the Flin Flon Bombers of the WCHL. In 1973, he was drafted in the eighth round of the NHL Entry Draft by the Detroit Red Wings. The Wings farmed Polonich out to their affiliate, the London Lions of England. The Red Wings were impressed with his play and the following season they brought him back to North America. He spent most of the year with Virginia of the AHL but also saw limited action with the Wings.

During the 1975-76 season, Polonich got a chance to play regularly with the Wings. Unfortunately, a shoulder separation forced him to sit out part of that season. The following year he was named team captain. Polonich responded by registering his best offensive numbers: 18 goals and 28 assists for 46 points. During the 1978-79 season, Polonich was a victim of a brutal stick swinging attack and suffered severe facial injuries: "The incident caused me a lot of pain - headaches, problems with my nose and other injuries to my face."[30] Polonich sued the perpetrator of the attack, and won.

Dennis Polonich was one of the smallest players to ever play professional hockey. Like most small players, he was tough, tenacious, and willing to mix it up. In 390 NHL games played over eight seasons he accumulated 1,242 penalty minutes and was often referred to as "Dennis the Menace." Polonich, though, believed that it was his toughness and all out play that got him a chance to play in the NHL. Penalties were a price that one had to pay.

Dennis Polonich enjoyed the game of hockey immensely. As a result, he accepted demotions to the minors as part of the game. During his career he made a number of trips to the Wings' farm club at Adirondack. His last appearance in the NHL was during the 1982-83 season. He played minor pro hockey for a number of years before retiring part way through the 1986-87 season.

RECORD

| year | team | league | regular season | | | | | playoffs | | | | |
|---|---|---|---|---|---|---|---|---|---|---|---|---|
| | | | GP | G | A | PTS | PIM | GP | G | A | PTS | PIM |
| 1973-74 | London | British | 67 | 17 | 43 | 60 | 57 | | | | | |
| 1974-75 | Detroit | NHL | 4 | 0 | 0 | 0 | 0 | | | | | |
| | Virginia | AHL | 60 | 14 | 20 | 34 | 194 | 5 | 0 | 2 | 2 | 30 |
| 1975-76 | Detroit | NHL | 57 | 11 | 12 | 23 | 302 | | | | | |
| | Kalamazoo | IHL | 5 | 1 | 8 | 9 | 32 | | | | | |
| 1976-77 | Detroit | NHL | 79 | 18 | 28 | 46 | 274 | | | | | |
| 1977-78 | Detroit | NHL | 79 | 16 | 19 | 35 | 254 | 7 | 1 | 0 | 1 | 19 |
| 1978-79 | Detroit | NHL | 62 | 10 | 12 | 22 | 208 | | | | | |
| 1979-80 | Detroit | NHL | 66 | 2 | 8 | 10 | 127 | | | | | |
| 1980-81 | Detroit | NHL | 32 | 2 | 2 | 4 | 77 | | | | | |
| * | Adirondack | AHL | 40 | 16 | 13 | 29 | 99 | 14 | 9 | 5 | 14 | 95 |
| 1981-82 | Adirondack | AHL | 80 | 30 | 26 | 56 | 202 | 5 | 2 | 2 | 4 | 0 |
| 1982-83 | Detroit | NHL | 11 | 0 | 1 | 1 | 0 | | | | | |
| | Adirondack | AHL | 61 | 18 | 22 | 40 | 128 | 6 | 2 | 2 | 4 | 10 |
| 1983-84 | Adirondack | AHL | 66 | 14 | 26 | 40 | 122 | | | | | |
| 1984-85 | Adirondack | AHL | 53 | 18 | 17 | 35 | 153 | | | | | |
| 1985-86* | Muskegon | IHL | 78 | 32 | 36 | 68 | 222 | 14 | 8 | 10 | 18 | 36 |
| 1986-87 | Muskegon | IHL | 22 | 2 | 9 | 11 | 24 | | | | | |

# PRUSKI, STEVE

sport: football
given name: Pruski, Stephen Albert
born: St. Catharines, Ontario
January 20, 1924
height: 1.83 m / 6'0"
weight: 106.5 kg / 235 lbs
position: centre

Steve Pruski began his football career in 1940 with the Western Technical School team in Toronto. The following year, he enlisted with the RCAF. In 1944, Pruski was transferred to the Navy's Fleet Air Arm. While he was stationed in Toronto, his athletic prowess was recognized by the Navy and he was assigned to the Sports Locker Department, where his duties included instructing physical training classes and co-ordinating a sports program at the Toronto Naval Station. He served in that capacity through 1946, when he obtained an honourable discharge. While in uniform, Pruski participated in inter-service sports, such as basketball, football, and hockey, and won the inter-service Canadian championships in football and basketball.

In 1945, Steve Pruski made the starting roster of the Toronto Argonaut Football Club at the snap (centre) position. The club completed the regular schedule tied for first place in the Eastern Conference. The club then swept through the playoffs and humiliated Winnipeg 35-0 to win the Grey Cup. Pruski was on the field for most of the Grey Cup game. During the next two seasons, Pruski saw limited action with the Argos, while the team continued to dominate the playoffs and won the Grey Cup on both occasions. In 1948, Pruski sustained a back injury, and remained with the club as an assistant trainer through the end of the season.

In 1949, Steve Pruski joined the Balmy Beach Football Club as a playing line coach. The team won the ORFU championship in 1950. Later he played and coached with the Parkdale Intermediate "A" Football Club, winning the ORFU intermediate championship. In 1954, Pruski sustained another back injury and sat out the season. He attempted a comeback the following year with the Edmonton Eskimos, but had to return to Toronto for personal reasons.

Subsequently, Steve Pruski coached and managed football, hockey, bowling and baseball teams for various age groups. From 1969 to 1983, he was a member of Mohawk College's Athletic Department.

## PRYCHUN, DARIA

| | |
|---|---|
| sport: | figure skating |
| born: | . . . |
| | . . . |
| height: | . . . |
| weight: | . . . |

Daria Prychun began skating at age two and a half. By seven she was an accomplished skater, a result of what her coach called "natural good coordination." She won titles both as a solo performer and in the pairs competition. In 1970, she placed second in the junior ladies' competition and teamed up with R. Uuemae to win the novice title in the pairs at the Canadian Championships. That same year she won a gold medal in the ladies' competition at the Canada Winter Games. At the 1972 Canadian Championships, Prychun placed fourth. A short time later, she was a last-minute replacement for a skater unable to compete in the World Championships because of an injury. Daria Prychun skated with poise and little visible nervousness to place 15th.

### RECORD

| year | competition | placing |
|------|-------------|---------|
| 1970 | Canadian Junior Championships | 2 |
| 1971 | Canadian Junior Championships  (pairs) | 2 |
|      | Canada Winter Games | 1 |
|      | Canada Winter Games (pairs) | 2 |
| 1972 | Canadian Junior Championships  (pairs) | 2 |
|      | Canadian Championships | 4 |
|      | World Championships | 15 |
| 1973 | Canadian Championships | 7 |
| 1974 | Canadian Championships | 3 |
|      | Prague Skate | |

# PRYSTAI, METRO

"Marvellous Metro," "Meatball"

| | |
|---|---|
| sport: | hockey |
| born: | Yorkton, Saskatchewan |
| | November 7, 1927 |
| height: | 1.75 m / 5'9" |
| weight: | 77 kg  / 170 lbs |
| position: | center |
| shoots: | left |

*Photo courtesy of the Saskatchewan Sports Hall of Fame and Museum*

Metro Prystai began playing the game of hockey at age seven on a pair of crude skates made by his father. They were old boots to which old blades were attached. The skates, though, did not hamper the boy's desire to play the game. He eagerly received his early training while attending Burke Public School and the Ukrainian St. Joseph's College in Yorkton.

In 1944, Prystai joined the Moose Jaw Canucks junior hockey team. He almost single-handedly led the team to three provincial championships, two Western Canada championships, and two Memorial Cup finals (which the Canucks lost on both occasion to St. Michael's College of Toronto). He led the Saskatchewan Junior Hockey League in scoring during the 1945-46 and 1946-47 seasons. He was also voted the league's MVP in those two seasons. The Yorkton native was the most talked about amateur hockey player in the country at the time. The Saskatchewan media referred to him as "a hockey brilliant," "Metro the Great," or "the Marvellous One."

In 1947, with one year of junior eligibility remaining, Prystai joined the Chicago Black Hawks. He played in the NHL for eleven seasons, and was traded back and forth by Chicago and Detroit. Prystai was shifty on his skates and was a natural goal scorer. His most productive season was in 1949-50 when he placed seventh in the NHL scoring race with 29 goals and 22 assists. While in Detroit, he helped the club to six first-place finishes. Prystai was twice a member of Stanley Cup championship teams, on both occasions with Detroit. For a while he played on a line with Ted Lindsay and Gordie Howe, a memorable experience for him. In 1957, Detroit farmed out Prystai to Edmonton. After breaking his leg for the third time within a year, he announced his retirement in 1959.

In the fall of 1959, Prystai accepted the position of coach and manager of the Omaha Knights of the IHL. His tenure with the club lasted only a few months. He was fired half-way through the season, partly on account of a record that included only 8 wins in 42 starts. The following season, he signed with the Moose Jaw Junior Canucks of the SJHL. He was with the team for three years, and in 1961-62 led them to the Saskatchewan title. He also coached the Melville Millionaires for two seasons. In the summer, Metro Prystai would play and coach baseball. He coached the senior Yorkton Cardinals for a number of years.

INDUCTIONS

1989        Saskatchewan Sports Hall of Fame

AWARDS

1946        Wes Champ Memorial Trophy  -  SJHL Most Valuable Player
1947        Wes Champ Memorial Trophy  -  SJHL Most Valuable Player
1953        Stu Evans Trophy  -  Most Sportsmanlike Red Wing

# RECORD

| year | team | league | regular season | | | | | playoffs | | | | |
|------|------|--------|------|------|------|------|------|------|------|------|------|------|
| | | | GP | G | A | PTS | PIM | GP | G | A | PTS | PIM |
| 1947-48 | Chicago | NHL | 54 | 7 | 11 | 18 | 25 | | | | | |
| 1948-49 | Chicago | NHL | 59 | 12 | 7 | 19 | 19 | | | | | |
| 1949-50 | Chicago | NHL | 65 | 29 | 22 | 51 | 31 | | | | | |
| 1950-51 | Detroit | NHL | 62 | 20 | 17 | 37 | 27 | 3 | 1 | 0 | 1 | 0 |
| 1951-52* | Detroit | NHL | 69 | 21 | 22 | 43 | 16 | 8 | 2 | 5 | 7 | 0 |
| 1952-53 | Detroit | NHL | 70 | 16 | 34 | 50 | 12 | 6 | 4 | 4 | 8 | 2 |
| 1953-54* | Detroit | NHL | 70 | 12 | 15 | 27 | 26 | 12 | 2 | 3 | 5 | 0 |
| 1954-55 | Detroit | NHL | 12 | 2 | 3 | 5 | 9 | | | | | |
| | Chicago | NHL | 57 | 11 | 13 | 24 | 28 | | | | | |
| 1955-56 | Chicago | NHL | 8 | 1 | 3 | 4 | 8 | | | | | |
| | Detroit | NHL | 63 | 12 | 16 | 28 | 10 | 9 | 1 | 2 | 3 | 6 |
| 1956-57 | Detroit | NHL | 70 | 7 | 15 | 22 | 16 | 5 | 2 | 0 | 2 | 0 |
| 1957-58 | Detroit | NHL | 15 | 1 | 1 | 2 | 4 | | | | | |
| | Edmonton | WHL | 21 | 13 | 14 | 27 | 6 | | | | | |
| 1958-59 | Edmonton | WHL | 4 | 1 | 0 | 1 | 4 | | | | | |

# RATUSHNY, DAN

| | |
|------|------|
| sport: | hockey |
| born: | Windsor, Ontario |
| | October 29, 1970 |
| height: | 1.85 m / 6'1" |
| weight: | 93 kg / 205 lbs |
| position: | defense |
| shoots: | right |

While in high school, Dan Ratushny competed in lacrosse, baseball, soccer, football, and hockey. Hockey, though, was the sport he excelled in. While playing junior hockey with the Nepean Raiders in 1987-88, he was named to the COJHL all-star team and was the MVP during the league's all-star game. Opting to combine an education with a hockey career, Ratushny enrolled at Cornell University in the United States the following year. He quickly gained respect of his teammates and coaches with his inspirational play and was named to the league's All-Rookie team, and team co-captain for the 1990-91 season.

In 1989, Ratushny was named to the Canadian team which vied for the Spengler Cup. The Canadians finished in second place. The following year, Ratushny was selected to represent Canada at the World Junior Hockey Championship and was named the team's co-captain. The team was victorious, and Ratushny gained personal recognition when he was selected as the top defenseman on the Canadian side.

A second-round draft pick of the Winnipeg Jets in 1989, Dan Ratushny joined the Canadian national team for the 1991-92 season. With this team, he won the silver medal at the 1992 Albertville Olympics. The high intensity, hard hitting and tough defenseman finished the season playing in Europe. Dan Ratushny is the brother of hockey player Kim Ratushny.

## ALL-STAR SELECTIONS

1989-90    defense    All-American    Second Team

## RECORD

| | | | regular season | | | | | playoffs | | | | |
|---|---|---|---|---|---|---|---|---|---|---|---|---|
| year | team | league | GP | G | A | PTS | PIM | GP | G | A | PTS | PIM |
| 1988-89 | Canada | | 2 | 0 | 0 | 0 | 2 | | | | | |
| 1991-92 | Canada | | 50 | 5 | 13 | 18 | 59 | | | | | |

international

| year | team | competition | GP | G | A | PTS | PIM | Place |
|---|---|---|---|---|---|---|---|---|
| 1989 | Canada | Spengler Cup | | | | | | 2 |
| 1990 | Canada | World Junior Championship | 7 | 2 | 2 | 4 | 4 | 1 |
| 1992 | Canada | Olympic Games | 8 | 0 | 0 | 0 | 4 | 2 |

# RATUSHNY, KIM

| | |
|---|---|
| sport: | hockey |
| born: | Ottawa, Ontario |
| | June 24, 1969 |
| height: | 1.68 m / 5'6" |
| weight: | 63.5 kg / 140 lbs |
| position: | forward |
| shoots: | left |

Kim Ratushny was ten years old when she began playing organized house league hockey. In the fall of 1984, she joined the Ottawa-Nepean Raiders. She played for the team and was its co-captain for four years. During that time, the Raiders won the Ontario Midget A championship in 1986 and the Intermediate A championship in 1988. The team was coached by her father Ed Ratushny. Kim Ratushny also competed at the Ontario Winter Games, winning a bronze medal in 1985 and a silver in 1987. She was named to the Games' all-star team on both occasions.

In the fall of 1988, Ratushny joined Cornell University's "Big Red" team. She was an immediate standout, winning the Rookie of the Year award and being named to the Ivy League all-star team. In 1990, she was selected to the Canadian team for the inaugural Women's World Ice Hockey Championship. Playing in front of home-town fans in Ottawa, Kim Ratushny and her teammates won the gold medal. Kim Ratushny is the sister of hockey player Dan Ratushny.

## AWARDS

1989        Rookie of the Year  -  Ivy League

## ALL-STAR SELECTIONS

| 1988-89 | forward | Ivy League | First Team |
|---|---|---|---|
| 1989-90 | forward | Ivy League | First Team |

## RECORD

| | | | regular season | | | | | playoffs | | | | |
|---|---|---|---|---|---|---|---|---|---|---|---|---|
| year | team | league | GP | G | A | PTS | PIM | GP | G | A | PTS | PIM |
| 1988-89 | Cornell | Ivy | 23 | 14 | 16 | 30 | | | | | | |
| 1989-90 | Cornell | Ivy | ... | 16 | 14 | 30 | | | | | | |

international

| year | team | competition | GP | G | A | PTS | PIM | Place |
|------|------|-------------|----|----|----|-----|-----|-------|
| 1990 | Canada | World Championship | 5 | 1 | 4 | 5 | 0 | 1 |

# RIZAK, GENE

| | |
|--|--|
| sport: | basketball |
| given name: | Rizak, Eugene |
| born: | Windsor, Ontario |
| | August 27, 1938 |
| height: | 1.78 m / 5'10" |
| weight: | 63.5 kg / 140 lbs |

Gene Rizak started to play organized basketball in elementary school. In high school he was an all-star. When he enrolled at Windsor's Assumption College he brought with him great expectations for the varsity basketball team. Rizak did not disappoint. In his second year, he led the Ontario-Quebec Athletic Association (OQAA) in scoring as Assumption College won the Ontario Intercollegiate basketball championship. He also set an Ontario record of 44 points in a varsity game and a North American record of hitting 26 of 29 free throws in one game. He repeated as the league-leading scorer in 1960-61. Playing for the IGA Grocers in Vancouver, Rizak was a member of three consecutive Canadian basketball championship teams commencing in 1965. In 1967, he was a member of Canada's national team at the Pan American Games. The team finished in eighth place with a 0-8 record.

Upon being appointed to the faculty of the University of Regina in 1970, Gene Rizak assumed the coaching duties of the university basketball team. He held the position for ten years. In the early 1980s, Rizak redirected his energies to sports research. His two main areas of interest were the role of the Canadian high school coach and the differences in the world-wide sport delivery systems within the educational system. He lectured on the latter subject in Eastern and Western Europe and in China. He also penned the textbook *Basketball: A Text for Teachers and Coaches in Elementary and Junior High Schools*, a booklet *Slam Duck's Skills and Drills*, and numerous academic papers and articles.

AWARDS

1965        Art Willoughby Trophy  -  Vancouver Men's Rookie

RECORD

| year | team |
|---|---|
| 1957-60 | Assumption College |
| 1960-61 | McMaster University |
| 1961-62 | Tillsonburg Livingstons |
| | London Fredericksons |
| 1962-64 | Montreal Yvon Coutu Huskies |
| 1964-65 | University of British Columbia |
| 1965-68 | IGA Grocers |
| 1967 | Canada  -  Pan American Games |

administrative

| year | position |
|---|---|
| 1970 | Board of Directors - member, Basketball Saskatchewan Inc. |
| 1971-74 | Board of Directors - Vice-President, Basketball Saskatchewan Inc. |
| 1974-78 | Board of Directors - member, Basketball Saskatchewan Inc. |
| 1975-77 | Director of Athletics, University of Regina |
| 1975-76 | Basketball Committee member, Western Canada Games |
| 1980-81 | Board of Directors - member, Basketball Saskatchewan Inc. |
| 1984-88 | Member, Sasksport Research Trust Fund Committee |

# ROMANCHYCH, LARRY

| | |
|---|---|
| sport: | hockey |
| given name: | Romanchych, Larry Brian |
| born: | Vancouver, British Columbia |
| | September 7, 1949 |
| height: | 1.85 m / 6'1" |
| weight: | 81.5 kg / 180 lbs |
| position: | right wing |
| shoots: | right |

*Card reproduced courtesy of O-Pee-Chee Co.*

Larry Romanchych began playing organized hockey at fourteen.  In the fall of 1967, he made the roster of the junior Brandon Wheat Kings. The following season he played for the Western Canada junior champions, the Flin Flon Bombers. At the 1969 NHL Entry Draft, Romanchych was selected in the second round, 24th overall, by the Chicago Black Hawks. Aside from a brief appearance with Chicago during the 1970-71 season, Romanchych spent his first three years of professional hockey gaining experience with the Hawks' farm team at Dallas. In the summer of 1972, he was picked up in the NHL Expansion Draft by the Atlanta Flames.

Romanchych earned a regular spot on the team and in its first year was the club's second leading scorer. In all, Romanchych played for five seasons with the Flames. A strong and quick skater, he was known for his hard slapshot. An unfortunate knee injury early in his career hampered his mobility, though, and with every passing year it caused more aggravation. In 1977, the Philadelphia Flyers picked him up as a free agent. He was assigned to the Flyers' farm team the Maine Mariners of the AHL. In the playoffs, he was the team's top goal scorer as the Mariners battled to win the championship of the AHL. At the conclusion of the playoffs, Romanchych retired. The pain in the knee was just too great to continue playing.

## RECORD

| year | team | league | regular season | | | | | playoffs | | | | |
|------|------|--------|------|------|------|------|------|------|------|------|------|------|
| | | | GP | G | A | PTS | PIM | GP | G | A | PTS | PIM |
| 1969-70 | Dallas | CHL | 57 | 21 | 12 | 33 | 38 | | | | | |
| 1970-71 | Chicago | NHL | 10 | 0 | 2 | 2 | 2 | | | | | |
| | Dallas | CHL | 65 | 18 | 34 | 52 | 26 | 10 | 2 | 4 | 6 | 4 |
| 1971-72* | Dallas | CHL | 60 | 21 | 23 | 44 | 31 | 12 | 3 | 4 | 7 | 28 |
| 1972-73 | Atlanta | NHL | 70 | 18 | 30 | 48 | 39 | | | | | |
| 1973-74 | Atlanta | NHL | 73 | 22 | 29 | 51 | 33 | | | | | |
| 1974-75 | Atlanta | NHL | 53 | 8 | 12 | 20 | 16 | 4 | 2 | 2 | 4 | 4 |
| 1975-76 | Atlanta | NHL | 67 | 16 | 19 | 35 | 8 | 2 | 0 | 0 | 0 | 0 |
| 1976-77 | Atlanta | NHL | 25 | 4 | 5 | 9 | 4 | 1 | 0 | 0 | 0 | 0 |
| | Tulsa | CHL | 37 | 20 | 28 | 48 | 18 | | | | | |
| 1977-78* | Maine | AHL | 79 | 17 | 34 | 51 | 23 | 12 | 8 | 4 | 12 | 6 |

# ROMANIUK, ALEX

"Chief"

| | |
|---|---|
| sport: | wrestling, football |
| born: | Edmonton, Alberta |
| | August 4, 1927 |
| died: | Edmonton, Alberta |
| | December 22, 1988 |
| height: | 1.83 m / 6'0" |
| weight: | 86 kg / 190 lbs |

Alex Romaniuk started to wrestle while in primary school. In high school he was undefeated. He continued to wrestle in university, winning three consecutive Western Canada titles. At the same time, he also played varsity football. In 1949, he made the roster of the Edmonton Eskimos at the guard position. After graduation, Romaniuk became an active boxing and wrestling coach and official. He coached the Alberta team at the 1954 Commonwealth Games boxing trials, and his protege, Wilf Greaves, won a gold medal at the Games. In 1966, Romaniuk was named coach of Canada's wrestling team to the Commonwealth Games. Interestingly, he also officiated at the Games.

As one of the world's most respected wrestling officials, Romaniuk was, in the late 1960s, only one of sixteen world officials classified as 1 - CHO, the highest category bestowed by the World Amateur Wrestling Federation (FILA). During his career, Romaniuk officiated at numerious national and international events, including the Canadian and World Championships, Olympic, Commonwealth and Pan American Games. While often paying all expenses personally to serve the sport at these events, Romaniuk was just as dedicated to his profession. A school principal for more than twenty years, he declined, for example, an invitation to officiate at the 1972 Olympic Games because the wrestling competition coincided with the opening of the school year.

In 1970, Romanuik brought the World Wrestling Championships to Edmonton; they were an overwhelming success. The championships had barely concluded when Romaniuk was named chairman of a committee seeking to bring the 1978 Commonwealth Games to Edmonton. Once Edmonton was named the host city, Romaniuk became involved in the organizational preparation of the Games. For his instrumental role in bringing the Commonwealth Games to Edmonton, the city named a street in his honour. In addition, Alex Romaniuk authored *Countdown '76*, a five-year sports development plan, and co-authored a wrestling manual with Dr. A. W. Taylor.

# INDUCTIONS

| 1974 | Alberta Sports Hall of Fame |
| 1976 | Edmonton Boxing and Wrestling Hall of Fame |
| 1981 | Canadian Amateur Sports Hall of Fame |
| 1985 | Edmonton Sports Hall of Fame |

# AWARDS

| 1969 | Presidents Award - Alberta Amateur Athletic Union |
| 1970 | Certificate of Merit - Canadian Amateur Wrestling Association |
| 1970 | Medal of Honor and Statute of Honor - United States Amateur Athletic Association |
| 1972 | Diploma of Honour - International Amateur Wrestling Association (FILA) |
| 1972 | Olympic Gold Star Award - International Amateur Wrestling Association (FILA) |
| 1972 | Certificate of Honour - Maccabiah Games |
| 1975 | Edmonton Sportsman of the Year |

# RECORD

wrestling

| year | competition | event | placing |
|------|-------------|-------|---------|
| 1949 | WCIAU Championships | 165 lbs | 1 |
| 1950 | WCIAU Championships | 165 lbs | 1 |
| 1951 | WCIAU Championship | 165 lbs | 1 |

coaching

| 1952-58 | University of Alberta - wrestling |
| 1954 | Alberta boxing team - Commonwealth Games Trials |
| 1966 | Canadian wrestling team - Commonwealth Games |

officiating

| year | competition |
|------|-------------|
| 1965 | World Championships |
| 1966 | Commonwealth Games |
| 1967 | Pan American Games |
|      | World Championships |
| 1968 | Olympic Games |
| 1969 | World Championships |
| 1970 | Commonwealth Games |
| 1971 | World Junior Championships |
|      | World Championships |
| 1973 | Maccabiah Games - Mat Chairman and Chief Clinician |

administrative

| year | position |
|------|----------|
| 1960-66 | President, Edmonton Amateur Wrestling Association |

| 1962-67 | Executive Member, Edmonton Oil Kings Jr. Hockey Club |
| 1964 | President, Canadian Wrestling Championships |
| 1966 | President, Canadian Wrestling Championships |
| 1969-73 | President, Canadian Amateur Wrestling Association |
| 1970 | President, World Wrestling Championships |
| 1970-72 | Chairman, 1978 Commonwealth Games Bid Committee |
| 1972-78 | Venue Chairman, 1978 Commonwealth Games |
| 1978-80 | President, Sports Alberta |

# ROMANIUK, JOHN

| sport: | gymnastics |
| born: | Ottawa, Ontario |
| | May 11, 1964 |
| height: | 1.73 m / 5'8" |
| weight: | 68 kg / 150 lbs |

John Romaniuk was seven years old in 1971 when he started training with the Ottawa Gymnastics Club under the guidance of coach Jerry Mills. He was soon winning various medals and ribbons at provincial age group championships, culminating with the all-around Ontario boys' championship in 1977. In 1978, Romaniuk transferred to the Olympians Gymnastics Club. Under the watchful eye of coach Darryl Howe, Romaniuk made his international debut and appeared at his first Canadian championships. In 1982, Romaniuk enrolled at the University of Calgary. He represented the university in competition for four years, gaining an All-Canadian selection in each of the years.

Romaniuk was a good all-round gymnast. His best performances were on the high bar, the weakest on the pommel horse.

In 1983, Romaniuk placed third in the all-around competition at the Canadian Championships. The following year he won the Canadian all-around junior championship and was named to the national team. He was with the team for four years, representing Canada at meets in Brazil and Romania. He retired from the sport in 1988.

## RECORD

| year | competition | event | placing |
|------|-------------|-------|---------|
| 1983 | Canadian Championships | all-around | 3 |
| 1984 | Canadian Junior Championships | all-around | 1 |
| | Brazil Cup II | team | 3 |

# ROMANIUK, RUSS

| | |
|---|---|
| sport: | hockey |
| given name: | Romaniuk, Russell |
| born: | Winnipeg, Manitoba |
| | June 9, 1970 |
| height: | 1.83 m / 6'0" |
| weight: | 84.0 kg / 185 lbs |
| position: | left wing |
| shoots: | left |

*Card reproduced courtesy of O-Pee-Chee Co.*

Russ Romaniuk played minor hockey with the St. Boniface Saints from age 11 to 16. With the exception of the first year, the Saints won the city and/or provincial titles in each of the years.

In 1987, Romaniuk moved up to the junior level scoring 50 goals in 38 games while playing for St. Boniface of the MJHL. He won the league's rookie of the year honours and was named to the all-star team. In the 1988 NHL Entry Draft, he was selected by the Winnipeg Jets in the second round, 31st overall. Opting to combine an education with a hockey career, Romaniuk enrolled at the University of North Dakota on a full scholarship. He played collegiate hockey for three years gaining a First Team all-star selection in 1990-91.

Russ Romaniuk, a tenacious checker known for his intensity, saw limited action with Canada's national team in 1988-89.

## RECORD

| | | | regular season | | | | | playoffs | | | | |
|------|------|--------|-----|-----|-----|-----|-----|-----|-----|-----|-----|-----|
| year | team | league | GP | G | A | PTS | PIM | GP | G | A | PTS | PIM |
| 1988-89 | Canada | | 3 | 1 | 0 | 1 | 0 | | | | | |

# RUFF, LINDY

| | |
|---|---|
| sport: | hockey |
| given name: | Ruff, Lindy Cameron |
| born: | Warburg, Alberta |
| | February 17, 1960 |
| height: | 1.88 m / 6'2" |
| weight: | 86 kg / 190 lbs |
| position: | defense, left wing |
| shoots: | left |

*Photo courtesy of the Buffalo Sabres*

Lindy Ruff was drafted from the Lethbridge Broncos by the Buffalo Sabres as an underage junior in the second round of the 1979 Entry Draft. He spent almost ten seasons with the Sabres prior to being traded to the New York Rangers in March of 1989. Ruff, who was given assignments on defense and left wing, was a defensively-oriented player even when playing on the wing. He played disciplined positional hockey, making sure that his movements would not give opposing teams scoring opportunities. This was quite the feat since he was a tough and hard-hitting athlete who liked to go into corners and battle for the puck. He also liked to mix it up.

During his career Ruff was never considered an offensive threat. His best goal production was during the 1985-86 season when he netted 20. Nevertheless, he was considered a team leader. He worked extremely hard and he showed the way by example. Lindy Ruff was the brother of Brent Ruff, an outstanding junior hockey player with the Swift Current Broncos who died at the age of 16, when the Bronco team bus left the road during a blizzard.

## RECORD

| year | team | league | regular season | | | | | playoffs | | | | |
|---|---|---|---|---|---|---|---|---|---|---|---|---|
| | | | GP | G | A | PTS | PIM | GP | G | A | PTS | PIM |
| 1979-80 | Buffalo | NHL | 63 | 5 | 14 | 19 | 38 | 8 | 1 | 1 | 2 | 19 |
| 1980-81 | Buffalo | NHL | 65 | 8 | 18 | 26 | 121 | 6 | 3 | 1 | 4 | 23 |
| 1981-82 | Buffalo | NHL | 79 | 16 | 32 | 48 | 194 | 4 | 0 | 0 | 0 | 28 |
| 1982-83 | Buffalo | NHL | 60 | 12 | 17 | 29 | 130 | 10 | 4 | 2 | 6 | 47 |
| 1983-84 | Buffalo | NHL | 58 | 14 | 31 | 45 | 101 | 3 | 1 | 0 | 1 | 9 |
| 1984-85 | Buffalo | NHL | 39 | 13 | 11 | 24 | 45 | 5 | 2 | 4 | 6 | 15 |
| 1985-86 | Buffalo | NHL | 54 | 20 | 12 | 32 | 158 | | | | | |

| | | | regular season | | | | | playoffs | | | | |
|---|---|---|---|---|---|---|---|---|---|---|---|---|
| year | team | league | GP | G | A | PTS | PIM | GP | G | A | PTS | PIM |
| 1986-87 | Buffalo | NHL | 50 | 6 | 14 | 20 | 74 | | | | | |
| 1987-88 | Buffalo | NHL | 77 | 2 | 23 | 25 | 179 | 6 | 0 | 2 | 2 | 23 |
| 1988-89 | Buffalo | NHL | 63 | 6 | 11 | 17 | 86 | | | | | |
| | NY Rangers | NHL | 13 | 0 | 5 | 5 | 31 | 2 | 0 | 0 | 0 | 17 |
| 1989-90 | NY Rangers | NHL | 56 | 3 | 6 | 9 | 80 | 8 | 0 | 3 | 3 | 12 |
| 1990-91 | NY Rangers | NHL | 14 | 0 | 1 | 1 | 27 | | | | | |

# RUSEDSKI, GREG

| | |
|---|---|
| sport: | tennis |
| born: | Montreal, Quebec |
| | September 6, 1973 |
| height: | 1.91 m / 6'3" |
| weight: | 72.5 kg / 160 lbs |

*Photo courtesy of Chris Guly and the Ukrainian Weekly*

Greg Rusedski started to compete in tennis at the national level early in his teens. His first major success was winning the Canadian under-14 title. Subsequently, he won numerous other national age group titles, culminating with the under-18 singles crown at the 1990 Philips Junior Nationals. The tall left-hander, with a blistering serve and with good topspin forehands and backhands, finished the year ranked tenth in Canada and a member of the Sunshine Cup and Davis Cup teams.

In 1991, Rusedski decided that an appearance at Wimbledon would be a good way to end his junior career. He played there three years earlier as a 14-year-old in the doubles event without success. At the 1991 Wimbledon, Rusedski fought his way to the semi-finals of the junior singles, losing in a tie-breaker 6-4, 7-6 (7-4) to American Michael Joyce on the prestigious Court 1. In doubles play, Rusedski was paired with Moroccan Karim Alami. The tandem defeated Andrei Medvedev of the USSR and John-Laffnie de Jager of South Africa to win the pairs title.

| year | competition | event | placing |
|------|-------------|-------|---------|
| 1989 | Junior National | under-16 singles | 2 |
| 1990 | Philips Junior Nationals | under-18 singles | 1 |
|      |             | under-18 doubles | 2 |
| 1991 | Wimbledon | junior singles | SF |
|      |           | junior pairs | 1 |

Year End World Rankings:

1989 (1103), 1990 (679), 1991 (603), 1992 (158).

# RYHORCHUK, IVAN

"Buddah," "Kubi"

| | |
|---|---|
| sport: | bowling |
| given name: | Ryhorchuk, Ivan Barry |
| born: | Melfort, Saskatchewan |
| | February 18, 1958 |
| height: | 1.83 m / 6'0" |
| weight: | 136 kg / 300 lbs |

In 1977, Ivan Ryhorchuk was finally old enough to enter the Carling O'Keefe Bowling Championship in Saskatchewan. He won the provincial title with a record of 11 victories and 4 losses. At the Canadian and World Championships held in Niagara Falls that year, Ryhorchuk won 12 games and lost only 2 to win both titles. He averaged 272 with a best score of 344 and a worst of 205. The average was significantly higher than the 168 he bowled in Saskatchewan. His performance at the concurrent championships was extraordinary, considering that it was only his fourth year of bowling and his first at the senior level.

In 1981, Ryhorchuk won the Saskatchewan Team Classic. At the Canadian Championship, Ryhorchuk and his teammates placed third. In 1987, he retired from competitive bowling. Ivan Ryhorchuk has also coached bowling and has served on the executive of the Melfort Five Pin Bowling Association.

| year | competition | placing |
|------|-------------|---------|
| 1977 | Saskatchewan 5 Pin Championship | 1 |
|      | Canadian 5 Pin Championship | 1 |
|      | World 5 Pin Championship | 1 |
| 1981 | Saskatchewan Team Classic | 1 |
|      | Canadian 5 Pin Championship | 3 |

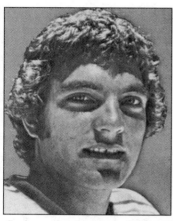

# SACHARUK, LARRY

"Satch"

| | |
|--|--|
| sport: | hockey |
| given name: | Sacharuk, Lawrence |
| born: | Saskatoon, Saskatchewan |
| | September 16, 1952 |
| height: | 1.83 m / 6'0" |
| weight: | 91 kg / 200 lbs |
| position: | defenseman |
| shoots: | right |

*Card reproduced courtesy of O-Pee-Chee Co.*

During the 1971-72 season, Larry Sacharuk established a Western Canada Junior Hockey League record for most goals by a defenseman when he scored 50 times while playing for the Saskatoon Blades. The dangerous and gifted offensive defenseman was noticed by NHL scouts and he was selected in the second round of the 1972 NHL Entry Draft, 21st overall, by the New York Rangers. Sacharuk's rookie season in the NHL was just a few games old when he suffered a freak injury. To work his way back into shape, the Rangers assigned him to the Providence Reds of the AHL. The following season, Sacharuk split between the Rangers and the Reds. He played 42 games for the Reds, scoring 27 goals to break a 24-year-old AHL record for goals by a defenseman. For his accomplishment he was named Minor Pro Player of the Year by *Hockey News*.

Prior to the start of the 1974 season, Sacharuk was traded to the St. Louis Blues. There, the free-skating defenseman, who loved to rush up the ice, was given an opportunity to play the whole season. Sacharuk responded by scoring 20 goals, only the seventh defenseman in NHL history to achieve that total.  He scored half of the goals on powerplays with hard and accurate slapshots.  In September of 1975, Sacharuk was traded back to New York.  The Rangers used Sacharuk sparingly, calling him up whenever necessary from the AHL.  He finished his hockey career in Europe.

AWARDS

| 1974 | *Hockey News* Minor Pro Player of the Year |

RECORD

| year | team | league | regular season | | | | | playoffs | | | | |
|------|------|--------|----|---|---|-----|-----|----|---|---|-----|-----|
|      |      |        | GP | G | A | PTS | PIM | GP | G | A | PTS | PIM |
| 1972-73 | NY Rangers | NHL | 8 | 1 | 0 | 1 | 0 | | | | | |
|         | Providence | AHL | 64 | 14 | 35 | 49 | 42 | 4 | 0 | 1 | 1 | 0 |
| 1973-74 | NY Rangers | NHL | 23 | 2 | 4 | 6 | 4 | | | | | |
|         | Providence | AHL | 42 | 27 | 35 | 62 | 26 | 15 | 1 | 14 | 15 | 4 |
| 1974-75 | St. Louis | NHL | 76 | 20 | 22 | 42 | 24 | 2 | 1 | 1 | 2 | 2 |
| 1975-76 | NY Rangers | NHL | 42 | 6 | 7 | 13 | 14 | | | | | |
| 1976-77 | NY Rangers | NHL | 2 | 0 | 0 | 0 | 0 | | | | | |
|         | New Haven | AHL | 55 | 23 | 31 | 54 | 18 | | | | | |
| 1977-78 | New Haven | AHL | 72 | 19 | 37 | 56 | 12 | 11 | 0 | 5 | 5 | 0 |
| 1978-79 | Indianapolis | WHA | 15 | 2 | 9 | 11 | 25 | | | | | |
| 1979-80 | Birmingham | CHL | 80 | 11 | 29 | 40 | 28 | 4 | 0 | 0 | 0 | 0 |

# SADOWICK-YAKUBOWICH, JOYCE

| sport: | athletics |
|--------|-----------|
| nee: | Sadowick, Joyce Louise |
| born: | Toronto, Ontario |
|       | May 29, 1953 |
| height: | 1.70 m / 5'7" |
| weight: | 57 kg  / 126 lbs |

*Photo courtesy of the Ontario Track & Field Association*

Joyce Yakubowich, nee Sadowick, was one of Canada's finest sprinters in the 1970s.  Her career ended prematurely in 1978, a result of a blood disorder. In the span of two months in 1970, a 17-year-old Sadowick ran her first competitive track race, established a new Canadian high school record in the 400 metres of 54.7 seconds, and made her international debut winning a bronze medal in the 4x100-metre relay at the 1970 Commonwealth Games in a national record time of 44.6. The following year she ran the 100 yards in 10.7, the fastest time by a Canadian that year. In 1972, Sadowick won the Olympic Trials in the 200 and 400 metres, but was named to the team only in the latter event. At the Olympics, she did not advance past the qualifying heats. A year later, Sadowick represented Canada at the World University Games. She placed fifth in the 400 metres in a time of 53.5.

Nineteen seventy-five proved to be one of the most successful years in the career of Joyce Sadowick-Yakubowich. She won the national championship in the 200 metres and was named to the Canadian team for the Pan American Games. In the 400-metre final at the Games, she ran a blistering 51.62, more than a second faster than her previous best time, to win the gold medal and establish a Canadian and a Pan American Games record. On the winner's podium she wept openly during the playing of *O Canada*. "Something just stirs you deep inside. I guess I'm pretty nationalistic."[31] Yakubowich also won a gold medal in the 4x400-metre relay and a bronze in the 4x100-metre relay. Both relay teams also established national records. At the end of the year, Joyce Yakubowich was honoured by the Canadian Track and Field Association with the Dr. Phillip Edwards Memorial Shield as the outstanding Canadian athlete in track.

Shortly after returning from the Pan American Games, Yakubowich was struck by a blood disorder. She lost her endurance and constantly felt fatigued. Yakubowich, though, did not want to give up track. She was one of the world's top sprinters and was expected to do well at the 1976 Olympics in the 400 metres and the two relays. As a result, she trained valiantly. At the Olympics, Yakubowich ran a slow 55.02 in the 400 metres and did not advance past the preliminary round. As a member of Canada's 4x400-metre relay team, she ran a solid lap in the event final which prevented the Canadian foursome from losing too much ground to the rest of the field. She was too sick two days later to run in the 4x100-metre relay and asked to be replaced. Joyce Sadowick-Yakubowich's last major success on the track was winning the national title in the 400 metres in 1977.


INDUCTIONS

. . .        Simon Fraser University Sports Hall of Fame

# AWARDS

| | |
|---|---|
| 1975 | Victoria Female Athlete of the Year |
| 1975 | British Columbia Athlete of the Year |
| 1975 | Dr. Phillip Edwards Memorial Shield - Outstanding Canadian Track Athlete |

# RECORD

| year | competition | event | placing | result | |
|---|---|---|---|---|---|
| 1970 | BC High School Championships | 200 m | 1 | 24.1 | |
| | | 400 m | 1 | 55.0 | |
| | British Columbia Championships | 100 m | 2 | 11.8 | |
| | Canadian Championships | 4 x 400 m | 1 | 3:48.2 | nr |
| | Commonwealth Games | 400 m | 6 H | 55.2 | |
| | | 4 x 100 m | 3 | 44.6 | nr |
| 1971 | Eugene, Oregon | 100 y | 1 | 10.7 | |
| | Pan American Games | 400 m | 6 | 54.8 | |
| | | 4 x 100 m | 4 | 46.1 | |
| | | 4 x 400 m | 4 | 3:41.2 | |
| | Holland | 4 x 200 m | 1 | 1:39.6 | nr |
| 1972 | Canada vs US | 200 m | 3 | 24.2 | |
| | Champaign, Illinois | 4 x 440 y | 2 | 3:41.2 | nr |
| | Canadian Championships | 200 m | 1 | 24.1 | |
| | | 400 m | 1 | 54.1 | |
| | | 4 x 400 m | 1 | 3:43.7 | nr |
| | Sittart, Holland | 400 m | 1 | 53.6 | nr |
| | Olympic Games | 400 m | 5 H | 54.4 | |
| 1973 | World University Games | 200 m | 5 SF | 24.02 | |
| | | 400 m | 5 | 54.02 | |
| | Pan Pacific Games | 200 m | 1 | 23.2 | |
| | | 400 m | 3 | 54.0 | |
| | | 4 x 100 m | 2 | 45.3 | |
| 1975 | Canadian Championships | 200 m | 1 | 23.5 | |
| | Pan American Games | 200 m | 6 | 23.34 | |
| | | 400 m | 1 | 51.62 | nr @ |
| | | 4 x 100 m | 3 | 43.68 | nr |
| | | 4 x 400 m | 1 | 3:30.36 | nr |
| 1976 | Olympic Trials | 200 m | 2 | 24.45 | |
| | Olympic Games | 400 m | 7 H | 55.02 | |
| | | 4 x 400 m | 8 | 3:28.91 | nr |

| year | competition | event | placing | result |
|------|-------------|-------|---------|--------|
| 1977 | Pacific Conference Games | 400 m | 4 | 54.44 |
|      | Canadian Championships | 400 m | 1 | 55.86 |
| nr   | Canadian record | | | |
| @    | Pan American Games record | | | |

# SAGANIUK, ROCKY

| | |
|---|---|
| sport: | hockey |
| given name: | Saganiuk, Rocky Ray |
| born: | Myrnam, Alberta |
| | October 15, 1957 |
| height: | 1.73 m / 5'8" |
| weight: | 84 kg / 185 lbs |
| position: | right wing |
| shoots: | right |

*Card reproduced courtesy of O-Pee-Chee Co.*

Rocky Saganiuk's junior hockey career began with the Taber Golden Suns. The following year he played for three teams: the Golden Suns, Kamloops Chiefs and the Lethbridge Broncos. In his final year of junior hockey, while playing for the Broncos, he scored 60 goals and added 48 assists. He also amassed 203 penalty minutes. Saganiuk was drafted from Lethbridge by the Toronto Maple Leafs in the second round, 29th overall, of the 1977 NHL Entry Draft.

Saganiuk spent his first season of professional hockey playing in the minors with the Dallas Black Hawks of the CHL. During the 1978-79 season, he made his NHL debut but could not earn a regular spot with the Leafs. He spent most of the year playing with the New Brunswick Hawks of the AHL. He led the league in goals with 47, was named to the first all-star team, and was honoured with the Les Cunnigham Plaque as the league's MVP. The following season, the speedy right winger, became a Leafs regular. He responded by scoring 24 goals.

Saganiuk was with the Leafs for two more seasons. Although he dressed for most of the games, the Leafs did not play him regularly. In August of 1983, he was traded to the Pittsburgh Penguins. His NHL career came to an end that season after he suffered a back injury.

Saganiuk tried to make a comeback with St. Catharines of the AHL the following year but was unsuccessful. The urge to play hockey, though, was overpowering, and he joined the Flamboro Motts Clamatoes of the less physically demanding Ontario Senior League. In January of 1988, Saganiuk accepted a coaching position with the Scottish hockey team Ayr Bruins. The following year Rocky Saganiuk led his team to the United Kingdom's final four tournament.

## AWARDS

| 1979 | Les Cunnigham Plaque - AHL MVP |
| 1991 | British Ice Hockey Writers' Association Coach of the Year |

## ALL-STAR SELECTIONS

1978-79    right wing    AHL    First Team

## RECORD

| year | team | league | regular season | | | | | playoffs | | | | |
|------|------|--------|----|----|----|-----|-----|----|----|----|-----|-----|
| | | | GP | G | A | PTS | PIM | GP | G | A | PTS | PIM |
| 1977-78 | Dallas | CHL | 42 | 16 | 13 | 29 | 71 | | | | | |
| 1978-79 | Toronto | NHL | 16 | 3 | 5 | 8 | 9 | 3 | 1 | 0 | 1 | 5 |
| | New Brunswick | AHL | 62 | 47 | 29 | 76 | 91 | | | | | |
| 1979-80 | Toronto | NHL | 75 | 24 | 23 | 47 | 52 | 3 | 0 | 0 | 0 | 10 |
| 1980-81 | Toronto | NHL | 71 | 12 | 18 | 30 | 52 | | | | | |
| 1981-82 | Toronto | NHL | 65 | 17 | 16 | 33 | 49 | | | | | |
| 1982-83 | Toronto | NHL | 3 | 0 | 0 | 0 | 2 | | | | | |
| | St. Catharines | AHL | 61 | 26 | 23 | 49 | 83 | | | | | |
| 1983-84 | Pittsburgh | NHL | 29 | 1 | 3 | 4 | 37 | | | | | |
| | Baltimore | AHL | 5 | 1 | 1 | 2 | 0 | | | | | |
| 1984-85 | St. Catharines | AHL | 4 | 1 | 1 | 2 | 11 | | | | | |

# SAMOLENKO, GEORGE

sport:      hockey
born:       Edenwold, Saskatchewan
            December 20, 1930
height:     . . .
weight:     . . .
position:   right wing
shoots:     . . .

During the 1954-55 season, George Samolenko played for the Paisley Pirates of Scotland in the British League. His rookie year in the league was impressive as he placed sixth in scoring with 122 points and was named to the "B" all-star team. The next year he returned to Canada to play for the Kingston Tinkers, a Sr. "B" team. Samolenko signed with the Whitby Dunlops for the 1956-57 season. He led the team in points and played a key role as the Dunlops won the Allan Cup, emblematic of Canadian senior hockey supremacy. The victory entitled the Dunlops to represent Canada at the 1958 World Championship.

In Oslo, Canada won the World Championship. The Dunlops performed flawlessly, winning every game they played. Samolenko contributed with two goals and three assists. Whitby repeated as Allan Cup champions in 1959, but declined the chance to represent Canada at the 1960 Olympics. A number of Whitby players, among them the line of Attrersley, Etcher, and Samolenko were invited to augment the Kitchener-Waterloo Dutchmen, the team selected to represent Canada. Samolenko performed well at Squaw Valley, scoring eight goals in seven games. Canada, though, was upset by the Americans and the team had to settle for a silver medal.

## ALL-STAR SELECTIONS

1954-55      forward      British League      "B" Team

## RECORD

| | | | regular season | | | | | playoffs | | | | |
|---|---|---|---|---|---|---|---|---|---|---|---|---|
| year | team | league | GP | G | A | PTS | PIM | GP | G | A | PTS | PIM |
| 1954-55 | Paisley | British | 62 | 65 | 57 | 122 | | | | | | |
| 1957-58 | Whitby | OHA Sr. | | 15 | 25 | 40 | | | | | | |

international

| year | team | competition | GP | G | A | PTS | PIM | Place |
|------|------|-------------|----|----|----|-----|-----|-------|
| 1958 | Whitby | World Championship | 7 | 2 | 3 | 5 | | 1 |
| 1960 | Canada | Olympic Games | 7 | 8 | 4 | 12 | 0 | 2 |

Photo courtesy of Swim Canada

# SAWCHUK, BILL

| | |
|---|---|
| sport: | swimming |
| given name: | Sawchuk, William |
| born: | Roblin, Manitoba |
| | January 8, 1959 |
| height: | 1.83 m / 6'0" |
| weight: | 78.5 kg / 173 lbs |

Bill Sawchuk began swimming competitively in 1973 with the Thunder Bay Thunderbolts Swim Club. Two years later, he was named to the national team. At the 1975 Pan American Games, his first major international competition, Sawchuk won the bronze medal in the 200-metre individual medley. Sawchuk remained with the national team through 1982. In 1976, he captured his first national title when he won the 200-metre freestyle event. At the Olympic trials that year the versatile swimmer qualified for three individual events. His best performance at the Olympics was a ninth-place finish in the 400-metre individual medley.

At the 1977 Canadian Championships, Sawchuk established a national record in winning the 200-metre freestyle in a time of 1:53.66. The following year at the Commonwealth Games, Bill Sawchuk won seven medals, the most by one individual in the history of the Games. In individual competition his medal-take included silver in the 100-metre freestyle and the 200-metre individual medley, and bronze in the 400-metre individual medley and the 100-metre butterfly. In the relay events, he won gold in the 4x100-metre freestyle and in the 4x100-metre medley; both relay gold medals were won in Commonwealth Games record times. He also won a silver in the 4x200-metre freestyle relay.

Bill Sawchuk established Canadian short course records in the 100-metre freestyle, 200-metre butterfly, and 400-metre individual medley at the 1979 Winter Nationals. In 1980, at the peak of his career, Sawchuk once again qualified for the Olympic team. The boycott prevented him from competing. After the Olympics, Sawchuk competed sporadically. He retired in 1982, never realizing his goal of winning an individual gold medal in a major international competition. Subsequently, he accepted a coaching position with the Hyack Swim Club in New Westminster. In 1987, he co-managed the Canadian Pan Pacific Games swim team.

## INDUCTIONS

| | |
|---|---|
| 1986 | Aquatic Hall of Fame of Canada |
| 1990 | Northwestern Ontario Sports Hall of Fame |
| 1991 | Ontario Aquatic Hall of Fame |

## AWARDS

| | |
|---|---|
| 1976 | Outstanding Citizen of the City of Thunder Bay |
| 1977 | Thunder Bay Male Athlete of the Year |
| 1978 | Thunder Bay Male Athlete of the Year |
| 1980 | Southeastern Conference Swimmer of the Year |

## RECORD

| year | competition | event | placing | result |
|---|---|---|---|---|
| 1975 | Pan American Games | 200 m IM | 3 | 2:11.63 |
| | Canadian Championships | 200 m IM | 4 | 2:13.49 |
| | | 400 m IM | 7 | 4:55.12 |
| 1976 | Canadian Championships | 100 m butterfly | 10 | 58.45 |
| | | 50 m freestyle | 5 | 25.02 |
| | | 100 m freestyle | 2 | 53.35 |
| | | 200 m freestyle | 1 | 1:54.12 |
| | | 400 m freestyle | 2 | 4:03.79 |
| | | 1,500 m freestyle | 3 | 15:52.09 |
| | | 200 m IM | 1 | 2:08.37 |
| | | 400 m IM | 3 | 4:34.37 |
| | Olympic Games | 200 m freestyle | H | 1:54.07 |
| | | 400 m freestyle | H | 4:02.18 |
| | | 400 m IM | 9 | 4:32.65 |
| 1977 | Canadian Championships | 100 m butterfly | 6 | 57.66 |
| | | 50 m freestyle | 7 | 24.91 |
| | | 100 m freestyle | 2 | 52.41 |

| year | competition | event | placing | result | |
|------|-------------|-------|---------|--------|---|
| 1977 | Canadian Championships | 200 m freestyle | 1 | 1:53.66 | nr |
| | | 400 m freestyle | 3 | 3:59.67 | |
| | | 200 m IM | 2 | 2:05.41 | |
| | | 400 m IM | 1 | 4:32.29 | |
| 1978 | Commonwealth Games | 100 m butterfly | 3 | 56.37 | |
| | | 100 m freestyle | 2 | 52.81 | |
| | | 200 m IM | 2 | 2:05.61 | |
| | | 400 m IM | 3 | 4:27.99 | |
| | | 4 x 100 m freestyle | 1 | 3:27.94 | cr |
| | | 4 x 100 m medley | 1 | 3:49.76 | cgr |
| | | 4 x 200 m freestyle | 2 | 7:36.58 | |
| | World Championships | 100 m freestyle | H | 53.20 | |
| | | 200 m freestyle | H | 1:55.02 | |
| | | 200 m IM | 5 | 2:06.65 | |
| | | 400 m IM | 8 | 4:33.25 | |
| 1979 | Canadian Championships | 200 m butterfly | 1 | 2:02.54 | |
| | | 400 m IM | 1 | 4:30.48 | |
| | Pan American Games | 100 m freestyle | 4 | 52.93 | |
| | | 200 m freestyle | 6 | 1:53.86 | |
| | | 200 m butterfly | 3 | 2:02.93 | |
| | | 200 m IM | 4 | 2:07.51 | |
| | | 400 m IM | 2 | 4:30.21 | |
| | | 4 x 100 m freestyle | 2 | 3:29.64 | |
| | | 4 x 100 m medley | 2 | 3:50.02 | |
| | | 4 x 200 m freestyle | 3 | 7:39.27 | |
| 1980 | US Championships | 200 m IM | 4 | 2:05.59 | |
| | Olympic Trials | 50 m freestyle | 2 | 23.93 | |
| | | 100 m freestyle | 3 | 52.16 | |
| | | 100 m butterfly | 2 | 55.59 | |
| | | 200 m butterfly | 3 | 2:01.83 | |
| | | 100 m breast | 7 | 1:07.46 | |
| | | 200 m IM | 3 | 2:04.83 | |
| 1981 | Canadian Championships | 100 m freestyle | 1 | 52.10 | |
| | | 200 m freestyle | 4 | 1:54.38 | |

nr   Canadian record

cr   Commonwealth record

cgr   Commonwealth Games record

# SAWCHUK, TERRY

"Uke," "Ukey"

| | |
|---|---|
| sport: | hockey |
| given name: | Sawchuk, Terrance Gordon |
| born: | Winnipeg, Manitoba |
| | December 28, 1929 |
| died: | New York, New York, USA |
| | May 31, 1970 |
| height: | 1.83 m / 6'0" |
| weight: | 88.5 kg / 195 lbs |
| position: | goal |
| shoots: | left |

Terry Sawchuk was one of professional hockey's most brilliant performers and tragic figures. He played more games and recorded more shutouts than any goaltender in history. His life, though, was marred by injuries, illnesses, accidents, family crises, and emotional breakdowns.

Terry Sawchuk was introduced to the art of tending goal by his older brother Mike, who was an aspiring hockey goaltender. Mike, though, never had the opportunity to see his protege develop; he died when Terry was ten years old. Two years later, Terry was scouted by the Detroit Red Wings and placed on a Detroit-sponsored midget team. At 15, he was playing junior hockey with the Winnipeg Rangers. The Wings were so impressed with him that they soon transferred him to their Junior "A" team in Galt, Ontario. A year later he was playing junior hockey for the Windsor Spitfires.

At 17, Sawchuk signed his first professional contract and was assigned to Omaha of the USHL. He led the league in shutouts, had the lowest goals against average, and was named the league's outstanding rookie. Sawchuk returned to Winnipeg for the summer and played first base for the Elmwood Giants of the Mandak (Manitoba-North Dakota) Baseball League. Professional baseball's Pirates and Cardinals were impressed with his league-leading batting average of .376 and offered him tryouts. Sawchuk declined, opting to pursue hockey. In the fall he reported to Indianapolis of the AHL. At season's end, he won that league's rookie of the year honours as well.

In the fall of 1950, the Red Wings made Sawchuk their number one goaltender. In his first season, Sawchuk played all 70 games for Detroit, recording 11 shutouts and posting a 1.99 goals against average. At the end of the season he was awarded with the Calder Trophy and named to the first all-star team. The following year Sawchuk improved his average to 1.90 and recorded 12 shutouts, helping Detroit to place first in the league standings. He repeated his first team all-star selection and won the Vezina Trophy. During the playoffs, Sawchuk performed brilliantly, putting on a display that may never be repeated. Detroit swept the playoffs in eight straight games, during which Sawchuk surrendered a mere five goals and recorded four shutouts. During the next three seasons, Sawchuk's goals against average did not exceed 1.96. Twice more he won the Vezina Trophy, and twice more he had his name engraved on the Stanley Cup.

Terry Sawchuk was an innovative goaltender. He came to the Red Wings in 1950 with a unique style of play: he played in a crouch. The style, he claimed, gave him a better chance to see the puck on screen shots. It also gave him better balance. Detroit boss Jack Adams tried to get Sawchuk to change his style to the traditional upright. Adams, though, gave up on the idea after witnessing some of Sawchuk's spectacular goaltending. Hockey pundit Trent Frayne thus described the goalie's style: "In action, Sawchuk was one of the most acrobatic goaltenders. Someone once wrote that he didn't move so much as he exploded into a kind of desperate epileptic action; down the glove, up the arm, over the stick, up the leg pad - all in such incredibly swift succession that he resembled a human pinwheel."[32]

In the summer of 1955, Sawchuk was traded to the hapless Boston Bruins. The trade stunned and upset him. Nevertheless, Sawchuk pulled himself together and played well on a team which had trouble scoring goals. His spirits, though, did not improve. In his second season with Boston, Sawchuk was stricken with mononucleosis and hospitalized for two weeks. After returning to the ice, Sawchuk played poorly and the Boston media became very critical of him. Sawchuk responded to the pressure by quitting the Bruins and hockey. Back home in Detroit, his doctor announced, "Mr. Sawchuk is on the verge of a complete nervous breakdown."[33]

The breakdown was another calamity in a tragic life. At ten, he badly damaged his right elbow playing football. Because his parents forbade him to play the game, he hid the injury from them and doctors. The arm healed poorly and was two inches shorter than his left. In the early 1950s, the arm was operated on three times, with 60 chips being removed on one occasion. While playing in Omaha, he caught a stick on his eyeball; doctors feared that he would lose the eye but miraculous surgery saved it. In 1954, a tie rod broke in the steering of a car he was driving and he smashed into a tree. The steering wheel crushed Sawchuk's chest.

For most of his adult life Sawchuk walked in a stoop. The pain of straightening out was unbearable. In 1966, his left side went numb. He was successfully operated on for herniated discs. Over the years his playing weight fluctuated between a low of 162 pounds and a high of 228. He did not sleep well, he did not eat well, and his nervous system was highly strung out.

In the summer of 1957, Sawchuk's rights were traded back to Detroit and the Wings talked him into playing hockey again. He played with them for seven seasons. The brilliance of the early years, though, was gone. In 1964, the Wings left Sawchuk unprotected and he was drafted by the Toronto Maple Leafs. At the time, Toronto general manager and coach George "Punch" Imlach was criticized for obtaining the 35-year-old Sawchuk to share goaltending duties with a 40-year-old Johnny Bower. Some suggested that Imlach was running a home for the aged rather than a hockey team. Sawchuk and Bower dispelled all the critics by winning the Vezina Trophy in their first year together. Two seasons later, the twosome led the Maple Leafs to an unexpected Stanley Cup. In the deciding game against Montreal, Sawchuk made 41 saves as the Leafs won 3-1.

That summer, the Leafs left Sawchuk unprotected and he was picked up by the Los Angeles Kings in the NHL Expansion Draft. A year later, Sawchuk was traded to Detroit. He barely had time to settle down before he was traded to the New York Rangers. There, his career came to a tragic end. After an altercation with his roommate and teammate, Sawchuk ended up in a hospital. He died of a pulmonary embolism on May 31, 1970. District Attorney William Cahn ruled the death "senseless and completely accidental."

Terry Sawchuk's death ended one of the most brilliant careers in professional hockey. His record of 103 shutouts in 971 regular season NHL games played in 21 seasons will likely never be matched.

## INDUCTIONS

| | |
|---|---|
| 1971 | Hockey Hall of Fame |
| 1975 | Canada's Sports Hall of Fame |
| 1982 | Manitoba Sports Hall of Fame |
| 1985 | Manitoba Hockey Hall of Fame |

## AWARDS

| | |
|---|---|
| 1947-48 | USHL Outstanding Rookie |
| 1948-49 | Dudley "Red" Garrett Memorial Trophy - AHL Top Rookie |
| 1950-51 | Calder Memorial Trophy - NHL Rookie of the Year |
| 1951-52 | Vezina Trophy - NHL Top Goaltender |
| 1952-53 | Vezina Trophy - NHL Top Goaltender |
| 1954-55 | Vezina Trophy - NHL Top Goaltender |
| 1955-56 | E. Dufresne Trophy - Outstanding Boston Player in Home Games |
| 1964-65 | Vezina Trophy - NHL Top Goaltender |
| 1971 | Lester Patrick Trophy - NHL (for Contributions to American Hockey) |

# ALL-STAR SELECTIONS

| | | | |
|---|---|---|---|
| 1947-48 | goal | USHL | Second Team |
| 1949-50 | goal | AHL | First Team |
| 1950-51 | goal | NHL | First Team |
| 1951-52 | goal | NHL | First Team |
| 1952-53 | goal | NHL | First Team |
| 1953-54 | goal | NHL | Second Team |
| 1954-55 | goal | NHL | Second Team |
| 1958-59 | goal | NHL | Second Team |
| 1962-63 | goal | NHL | Second Team |

# RECORD

| year | team | league | regular season | | | | | | | | playoffs | | | | | | | |
|---|---|---|---|---|---|---|---|---|---|---|---|---|---|---|---|---|---|---|
| | | | GP | MIN | W | L | T | GA | AVE | SO | GP | MIN | W | L | T | GA | AVE | SO |
| 1947-48 | Omaha | USHL | 54 | 3,248 | 30 | 18 | 5 | 174 | 3.21 | 4 | 3 | 180 | 1 | 2 | 0 | 9 | 3.00 | 0 |
| 1948-49 | Indianapolis | AHL | 67 | 4,020 | | | | 205 | 3.06 | 2 | 2 | 120 | 0 | 2 | 0 | 9 | 4.50 | 0 |
| 1949-50 | Detroit | NHL | 7 | 420 | 4 | 3 | 0 | 16 | 2.29 | 1 | | | | | | | | |
| * | Indianapolis | AHL | 61 | 3,660 | 31 | 20 | 10 | 188 | 3.08 | 3 | 8 | 480 | 8 | 0 | 0 | 12 | 1.50 | 0 |
| 1950-51 | Detroit | NHL | 70 | 4,200 | 44 | 13 | 13 | 139 | 1.99 | 11 | 6 | 463 | 2 | 4 | 0 | 13 | 1.68 | 1 |
| 1951-52* | Detroit | NHL | 70 | 4,200 | 44 | 14 | 12 | 133 | 1.90 | 12 | 8 | 480 | 8 | 0 | 0 | 5 | 0.63 | 4 |
| 1952-53 | Detroit | NHL | 63 | 3,780 | 32 | 15 | 16 | 120 | 1.90 | 9 | 6 | 372 | 2 | 4 | 0 | 21 | 3.39 | 1 |
| 1953-54* | Detroit | NHL | 67 | 4,000 | 35 | 19 | 13 | 129 | 1.94 | 12 | 12 | 751 | 8 | 4 | 0 | 20 | 1.60 | 2 |
| 1954-55* | Detroit | NHL | 68 | 4,040 | 40 | 17 | 11 | 132 | 1.96 | 12 | 11 | 660 | 8 | 3 | 0 | 26 | 2.36 | 1 |
| 1955-56 | Boston | NHL | 68 | 4,080 | 22 | 33 | 13 | 181 | 2.66 | 9 | | | | | | | | |
| 1956-57 | Boston | NHL | 34 | 2,040 | 18 | 10 | 6 | 81 | 2.38 | 2 | | | | | | | | |
| 1957-58 | Detroit | NHL | 70 | 4,200 | 29 | 29 | 12 | 207 | 2.96 | 3 | 4 | 252 | 0 | 4 | 0 | 19 | 4.52 | 0 |
| 1958-59 | Detroit | NHL | 67 | 4,020 | 23 | 36 | 8 | 209 | 3.12 | 5 | | | | | | | | |
| 1959-60 | Detroit | NHL | 58 | 3,480 | 24 | 20 | 14 | 156 | 2.69 | 5 | 6 | 405 | 2 | 4 | 0 | 20 | 2.96 | 0 |
| 1960-61 | Detroit | NHL | 37 | 2,150 | 12 | 16 | 8 | 113 | 3.17 | 2 | 8 | 465 | 5 | 3 | 0 | 18 | 2.32 | 1 |
| 1961-62 | Detroit | NHL | 43 | 2,580 | 14 | 21 | 8 | 143 | 3.33 | 5 | | | | | | | | |
| 1962-63 | Detroit | NHL | 48 | 2,775 | 23 | 16 | 7 | 119 | 2.57 | 3 | 11 | 660 | 5 | 6 | 0 | 36 | 3.27 | 0 |
| 1963-64 | Detroit | NHL | 53 | 3,140 | 24 | 20 | 7 | 138 | 2.64 | 5 | 13 | 677 | 6 | 5 | 0 | 31 | 2.75 | 1 |
| 1964-65 | Toronto | NHL | 36 | 2,160 | 17 | 13 | 6 | 92 | 2.56 | 1 | 1 | 60 | 0 | 1 | 0 | 3 | 3.00 | 0 |
| 1965-66 | Toronto | NHL | 27 | 1,521 | 10 | 11 | 4 | 80 | 3.16 | 1 | 2 | 120 | 0 | 2 | 0 | 6 | 3.00 | 0 |
| 1966-67* | Toronto | NHL | 28 | 1,409 | 15 | 5 | 4 | 66 | 2.81 | 2 | 10 | 565 | 6 | 4 | 0 | 25 | 2.65 | 0 |
| 1967-68 | Los Angeles | NHL | 36 | 1,936 | 11 | 14 | 6 | 99 | 3.07 | 2 | 5 | 280 | 2 | 3 | 0 | 18 | 3.86 | 1 |
| 1968-69 | Detroit | NHL | 13 | 641 | 3 | 4 | 3 | 28 | 2.62 | 0 | | | | | | | | |
| 1969-70 | NY Rangers | NHL | 8 | 412 | 3 | 1 | 2 | 20 | 2.91 | 1 | 3 | 80 | 0 | 1 | 0 | 6 | 4.50 | 0 |

# SAWULA, LORNE

| | |
|---|---|
| sport: | volleyball |
| born: | Edmonton, Alberta |
| | February 19, 1947 |
| height: | 1.78 m / 5'11" |
| weight: | 96 kg / 211 lbs |

*Photo courtesy of the Athlete Information Bureau*

In the years 1964-69, Lorne Sawula starred on the University of Alberta volleyball team, and in each of the years he was named to the Western Conference collegiate all-star team. On the basis of his strong play, he was selected to the Alberta team for the 1967 Canada Games. When Sawula's collegiate playing eligibility expired, he embarked on a coaching career with the men's team at the University of Alberta. Some years later, he defended his Ph.D. thesis, *The National Physical Fitness Act of Canada, 1943-1954*, at the university.

Lorne Sawula coached the Dalhousie University women's team in the years 1973-75. The club won successive Atlantic Conference titles. He then coached at the University of British Columbia, leading the men's team to the 1976 CIAU championship, and later at the University of Ottawa, leading the women's team to a second-place finish at the 1980 national championship. During that time period, Sawula also performed various administrative functions, most notably holding down the post of technical director of the Canadian Volleyball Association.

In May of 1982, Lorne Sawula was appointed head coach of Canada's national women's volleyball team. The appointment was not only based on his impressive collegiate coaching record, but also on his international experience, which included duties as assistant coach of the national women's team in 1974 and 1975, and head coach of the national junior team in 1976.

Sawula's seven-year tenure with the national team brought about a new era in women's volleyball in Canada. The club partook in more international tournaments and major championships than ever before. It was a well-moulded group that played with poise and determination. The club's standings improved: the fourth-place finish at the 1983 World University Games was a best ever by a Canadian team, while the eighth-place finish at the 1984 Olympics equalled a Canadian best. In the spring of 1989, Sawula retired from coaching to become the High-Performance Director of men's and women's national teams.

Over the years, Lorne Sawula served in numerous capacities with the Federation Internationale de Volleyball (FIVB). He was the chairman of the FIVB sub-committee on recreational volleyball, a member of the FIVB technical committee and coaches' commission, and an FIVB instructor. In addition, he authored most of the coaching manuals used in Canada in the 1980s.

## RECORD

competitive

| year | competition | team | placing |
|------|-------------|------|---------|
| 1967 | Canada Games | Alberta | |

coaching

| year | competition | capacity | team | placing |
|------|-------------|----------|------|---------|
| 1974 | World Championships | assistant coach | Canada | 11 |
| 1976 | CIAU Championships | coach | U of BC (men) | 1 |
| | NORCECA Jr Championships | coach | Canada | 3 |
| 1977 | CIAU Championships | coach | U of BC (men) | 2 |
| 1981 | CIAU Championships | coach | U of Ottawa | 3 |
| 1982 | World Championships | coach | Canada | 11 |
| 1983 | World University Games | coach | Canada | 4 |
| | NORCECA Championships | coach | Canada | 3 |
| | Pan American Games | coach | Canada | 5 |
| 1984 | Olympic Games | coach | Canada | 8 |
| 1985 | World University Games | coach | Canada | 6 |
| | NORCECA Championships | coach | Canada | 3 |
| 1986 | World Championships | coach | Canada | 15 |
| | Canada Cup | coach | Canada | 4 |
| 1987 | World University Games | coach | Canada | 7 |
| | Pan American Games | coach | Canada | 5 |
| 1988 | Bremen Cup | coach | Canada | 6 |
| | Canada Cup | coach | Canada | 4 |

administrative

| year | position |
|------|----------|
| 1977-82 | Technical Director - Canadian Volleyball Association |
| 1981 | Technical Chairman - World University Games |
| 1989- | High-Performance Director - Canadian Volleyball Association |

# SEMENKO, DAVE

| | |
|---|---|
| sport: | hockey |
| given name: | Semenko, David |
| born: | Winnipeg, Manitoba |
| | July 22, 1957 |
| height: | 1.91 m / 6'3" |
| weight: | 97.5 kg / 215 lbs |
| position: | left wing |
| shoots: | left |

*Card reproduced courtesy of O-Pee-Chee Co.*

For eight seasons, Dave Semenko was hockey's best-known enforcer. He was strong, tough, and always pumped up. Former Edmonton Oilers assistant coach Billy Harris referred to him as "our John Wayne." Former Vancouver Canucks coach Harry Neale also went to the big screen to describe Semenko: "In the movie *Missouri Breaks*, Marlon Brando rode around the edge of trouble. He was The Regulator. That's Semenko." His presence on the ice was respected; his duty was to protect Wayne Gretzky.

Dave Semenko played junior hockey for Brandon Wheat Kings, from where he was drafted by the Minnesota North Stars of the NHL and the Houston Aeros of the WHA. He did not play for either team; the Aeros traded his rights to the Edmonton Oilers, with whom he signed in November of 1978. Semenko played with the Oilers for nine seasons, two in the WHA and seven in the NHL. Twice he won the Stanley Cup with the Oilers. Semenko amazed his critics and fans during 1984 playoffs. Playing regular shifts on a line centered by Wayne Gretzky, he scored five goals and added five assists as the Oilers skated to their first Stanley Cup championship.

Semenko's first hockey fight occurred at age 17 when he was playing for Brandon. He didn't do too badly, but the experience jolted him into realizing that violence was also a part of hockey, and that weaker teammates had to be protected. He put on twenty pounds and started taking boxing lessons. In no time he developed into one of hockey's hardest punchers and toughest players. His fighting reputation was second to none, and when organizers of a 1983 charity boxing bout were seeking an opponent for former world heavyweight champion Muhammad Ali, Dave Semenko was selected.

A few games into the 1986-87 season, the Oilers traded Semenko to the Hartford Whalers. He was disappointed to leave Edmonton but happy to earn his pay in American dollars since he was experiencing financial problems. At season's end, Semenko refused the terms of a new

Hartford contract, deciding to try his luck in the waiver draft. The Toronto Maple Leafs, in need of an enforcer, acquired Semenko. The veteran winger, though, abstained from the physical game and as a result saw little ice time. Frustrated, he walked out on the Leafs and hockey, unannounced, prior to the conclusion of the season. The game was no longer fun.

## RECORD

| year | team | league | regular season | | | | | playoffs | | | | |
|------|------|--------|-----|-----|-----|-----|-----|-----|-----|-----|-----|-----|
| | | | GP | G | A | PTS | PIM | GP | G | A | PTS | PIM |
| 1977-78 | Edmonton | WHA | 65 | 6 | 6 | 12 | 140 | 5 | 0 | 0 | 0 | 8 |
| 1978-79 | Edmonton | WHA | 77 | 10 | 14 | 24 | 158 | 11 | 4 | 2 | 6 | 29 |
| 1979-80 | Edmonton | NHL | 67 | 6 | 7 | 13 | 135 | 3 | 0 | 0 | 0 | 2 |
| 1980-81 | Edmonton | NHL | 58 | 11 | 8 | 19 | 80 | 8 | 0 | 0 | 0 | 5 |
| | Wichita | CHL | 14 | 1 | 2 | 3 | 40 | | | | | |
| 1981-82 | Edmonton | NHL | 59 | 12 | 12 | 24 | 194 | 4 | 0 | 0 | 0 | 2 |
| 1982-83 | Edmonton | NHL | 75 | 12 | 15 | 27 | 141 | 15 | 1 | 1 | 2 | 69 |
| 1983-84* | Edmonton | NHL | 52 | 6 | 11 | 17 | 118 | 19 | 5 | 5 | 10 | 44 |
| 1984-85* | Edmonton | NHL | 69 | 6 | 12 | 18 | 172 | 14 | 0 | 0 | 0 | 39 |
| 1985-86 | Edmonton | NHL | 69 | 6 | 12 | 18 | 141 | 6 | 0 | 0 | 0 | 32 |
| 1986-87 | Edmonton | NHL | 5 | 0 | 0 | 0 | 0 | | | | | |
| | Hartford | NHL | 51 | 4 | 8 | 12 | 87 | 4 | 0 | 0 | 0 | 15 |
| 1987-88 | Toronto | NHL | 70 | 2 | 3 | 5 | 107 | | | | | |

# SEMOTIUK, DARWIN

| | |
|------|------|
| sport: | basketball, football |
| given name: | Semotiuk, Darwin Michael |
| born: | Edmonton, Alberta |
| | February 6, 1945 |
| height: | 1.83 m / 6'0" |
| weight: | 82 k g / 180 lbs |

*Photo courtesy of Intercollegiate Athletics Program, The University of Western Ontario*

While attending the University of Alberta in the years 1963-67, Darwin Semotiuk starred on the school's basketball and football teams. He played at the guard position on the basketball team for five years and was captain of the team for three. He played on the football team for four years, at both the wide receiver and defensive back positions. He captained the football team for two years. In 1965, Darwin Semotiuk was named to Canada's national basketball team with which he competed for a year. In his last year at the University of Alberta, he was named the institution's most outstanding athlete.

During the 1967-68 academic year, Semotiuk taught at the University of Manitoba and was the head coach of the school's basketball team. He also played basketball for St. Andrews Dunlops, a powerhouse in the Winnipeg senior league. Semotiuk then enrolled at Ohio State University to pursue a Ph.D. His thesis was titled *The Development of a Theoretical Framework for Analyzing the Role of National Government Involvement in Sport and Physical Education and its Application to Canada*. Upon graduation, Semotiuk joined the Faculty of Physical Education at the University of Western Ontario and immediately became involved in coaching. He was named assistant football coach responsible for the defensive secondary and special teams. That year the University of Western Ontario Mustangs won the national title.

In 1975, Darwin Semotiuk was named head coach of the Mustangs. He held the position for nine years. During Semotiuk's tenure, the Mustangs had an impressive record of 71 wins, 23 loses, and 1 tie for a winning percentage of .750. The team won the Yates Cup - emblematic of the Ontario championship - six times, and the National Championship twice. Semotiuk also gained personal recognition when he was named CIAU Football Coach of the year in 1976. Two years later, he coached the Canadian College All-Star Team against Team USA in the Can-Am Bowl in Tampa, Florida. The Canadian squad lost the game 22-7.

In 1982, Darwin Semotiuk was named Chairman of Intercollegiate Athletics at the university. In addition, he has held numerous other internal and external administrative positions. Of note was his involvement in the city of London's bid for the 1991 Pan American Games and the 1994 Commonwealth Games. He was Chef de Mission of Canada's team at the 1989 World Winter Universiade. Darwin Semotiuk has also authored five books, contributed chapters to fifteen others, and written more than 100 sport related papers and technical reports.

INDUCTIONS

1986      Vanier Cup Honour Roll

AWARDS

1967      University of Alberta Most Outstanding Athlete
1976      OUAA Football Coach of the Year

| 1976 | Frank Tindall Award - CIAU Football Coach of the Year |
|---|---|
| 1977 | Award for Outstanding Contribution in the Development of Amateur Football in Ontario - Ontario Amateur Football Association |
| 1978 | Award for Outstanding Contribution to Coaching Development - Alberta Amateur Football Association |
| 1978 | Outstanding Young Canadian Award of Recognition - Canada Jaycees |
| 1981 | OUAA Football Coach of the Year |
| 1985 | John McManus Award - OUAA |

## RECORD

coaching

| year | team | W | L | T | highlight |
|---|---|---|---|---|---|
| 1975 | University of Western Ontario Mustangs | 4 | 5 | 0 | |
| 1976 | University of Western Ontario Mustangs | 9 | 2 | 0 | Canadian Championship |
| 1977 | University of Western Ontario Mustangs | 11 | 1 | 0 | Canadian Championship |
| 1978 | University of Western Ontario Mustangs | 8 | 2 | 0 | |
| 1979 | University of Western Ontario Mustangs | 9 | 2 | 0 | Yates Cup |
| 1980 | University of Western Ontario Mustangs | 8 | 3 | 0 | Yates Cup |
| 1981 | University of Western Ontario Mustangs | 10 | 1 | 0 | Yates Cup |
| 1982 | University of Western Ontario Mustangs | 9 | 3 | 0 | Yates Cup |
| 1983 | University of Western Ontario Mustangs | 3 | 4 | 1 | |

administrative

| year | position |
|---|---|
| 1974-76 | Chairman, History of Sport and Physical Activity Committee, The Canadian Association for Health Physical Education and Recreation |
| 1980-81 | Vice-President, Canadian University Football Coaches Association |
| 1981-83 | President, Canadian University Football Coaches Association |
| 1982- | Chairman, Intercollegiate Athletics |
| 1984-85 | Executive Member and Vice-Chairman, 1991 London Pan American Games Bid Committee |
| 1985-87 | Vice-Chairman - Sports and Venues, 1994 London Commonwealth Games Bid Committee |
| 1988-90 | Co-editor, Journal of Comparative Physical Education and Sport |
| 1989 | Chef de Mission - Canadian team, World University Games |

# SEREDIUK, RUMMY

sport:        wrestling
born:         Calgary, Alberta
                September 16, 1931
height:      1.74 m / 5'9"
weight:     61 kg / 135 lbs

*Photo courtesy of the Alberta Sports Hall of Fame & Museum*

Rummy Serediuk started to wrestle in 1950 while in his late teens. In 1956, Serediuk captured the first of six Alberta titles which he would win in a span of seven years. He only failed to win a title in 1959. Serediuk retired from competitive wrestling in 1963 to concentrate on coaching. By that time he had been coaching the Calgary Boys Club for eight years. Subsequently, Serediuk coached at the University of Calgary and the Southern Alberta Institute of Technology.

For many years Rummy Serediuk held administrative positions with the Calgary and Alberta wrestling associations and with wrestling officials' associations. Serediuk also contributed to the sport of wrestling as a referee. In 1963, he began officiating at the provincial level. In 1970, he officiated at his first national championship, and in 1977 in his first international competition. Besides wrestling, Rummy Serediuk coached a rugby team and worked on the executive of the Alberta Baton Twirling Association.

For his contribution to the sport of wrestling, Rummy Serediuk was inducted into the Alberta Sports Hall of Fame in 1978 in the Builder category.

## INDUCTIONS

1978      Alberta Sports Hall of Fame

## AWARDS

1977      Alberta Wrestling Administrator of the Year
1978      Canadian Amateur Wrestling Association Contributor of the Year

# RECORD

**coaching**

| | |
|---|---|
| 1955-67 | Calgary Boys Club |
| 1968-69 | University of Calgary |
| 1969-85 | Southern Alberta Institute of Technology |

**administrative**

| year | position |
|---|---|
| 1969-70 | President, Calgary Amateur Wrestling Association |
| 1971-72 | Vice-President, Alberta Wrestling Officials' Association |
| 1973-77 | Secretary/Treasurer Calgary Amateur Wrestling Association |
| 1975-77 | Treasurer, Alberta Baton Twirling Association |
| 1976-79 | Treasurer, Alberta Wrestling Association |
| 1978 | President, Calgary Wrestling Officials' Association |

# SERWETNYK, CARRIE

| | |
|---|---|
| sport: | soccer |
| born: | Hamilton, Ontario |
| | July 17, 1965 |
| height: | 1.60 m / 5'3" |
| weight: | 54 kg / 120 lbs |
| position: | striker |

*Photo courtesy of the Canadian Soccer Association*

Carrie Serwetnyk has been generally acknowledged as a trailblazer for Canadian women in soccer. Most of the trailblazing occurred outside of Canada, though, for when Serwetnyk was at the peak of her career, women's soccer in Canada was still in its infancy. She did, never-theless, provide Canadians with exposure to her skills whenever she returned to Canada to play on its fledgling national team or for the Ontario team.

Serwetnyk developed her soccer skills playing for Clarkson-Sheridan of the Peel-Halton Soccer Association. In 1983, she led the club to the Ontario title and a berth in the national final.  In 1984, Serwetnyk enrolled at the University of North Carolina on an athletic scholarship and won a starting position on the star studded three-time defending NCAA champion Lady Tar Heels soccer team.  With Serwetnyk leading the attack, the Tar Heels qualified for the NCAA final for four consecutive seasons, winning in 1984, 1986 and 1987.  While the club lost the championship final in 1985, Serwetnyk led the team in scoring during that year and was voted its offensive MVP.

In 1989 and 1990, Serwetnyk played in the top women's league in France and helped her club to the national final.  In 1992, the diminutive striker became the first Canadian woman to enter the ranks of professional soccer when she signed for one season with Fujita Tendai of the Japan Women's Football League (JWFL) for a reported $100,000 (US).  She scored 14 of her team's 19 goals, was named to the all-star team, and honoured with the league's Fighting Spirit Award.

Carrie Serwetnyk played 19 times for Canada.  Appearances in international matches included the Taiwan Cup (1987), FIFA International Tournament in China (1988) and the CONCACAF zone World Cup Qualifying tournament in Haiti (1991).  She also played for Ontario, leading the side to the 1986 and 1987 national championships.

## AWARDS

1992        Fighting Spirit Award  -  JWFL

## ALL-STAR SELECTIONS

1992        striker        JWFL        First Team

## RECORD

competitive

| year | team |
|------|------|
| 1984-87 | University of North Carolina  -  Chapel Hill, USA |
| 1989-90 | Jeunesse Sportive Femminine  -  Poissy, France |
| 1992 | Fujita Tendai  -  Japan |

international

| year | team | competition | GP | G | Place |
|------|------|-------------|-----|---|-------|
| 1987 | Canada | Taiwan Cup | ... | | |
| 1988 | Canada | FIFA International | ... | | |
| 1991 | Canada | World Cup Qualifying | ... | | |

# SHABAGA, MIKE

"Quicksilver"

| | |
|---|---|
| sport: | hockey |
| born: | Rosthern, Saskatchewan |
| | August 19, 1922 |
| height: | 1.70 m / 5'7" |
| weight: | 68 kg / 150 lbs |
| position: | left wing |
| shoots: | left |

Mike Shabaga played junior hockey for the Saskatoon Quakers. In 1942, he was a member of the Quaker team which won the Saskatchewan Senior League championship. Thereafter he played minor pro hockey for teams in Buffalo, Cleveland, Hershey, Philadelphia, and Owen Sound. Upon regaining his amateur status in 1947, Shabaga rejoined the Saskatchewan Quakers. In 1951, he settled in Trail and began playing for the local Smoke Eaters. When the Penticton Vees were named to represent Canada at the 1955 World Championship, the club augmented its roster by securing the service of Mike Shabaga, an outstanding stickhandler and playmaker.

At the World Championship in Germany, Shabaga did not disappoint. His best performance was undoubtedly against the Soviet Union in the deciding game of the championship. He scored Canada's first goal and added another en route to a 5-0 Canadian victory. The Penticton team was undefeated in eight starts as it won the world title for Canada that year.

Subsequently, Mike Shabaga took up coaching hockey. In 1959, he coached the Vancouver Carlings to the Coy Cup, emblematic of the BCAHA senior "A" championship. In the 1960s, he coached Swift Current of the WHL.

## INDUCTIONS

1990        Saskatoon Sports Hall of Fame

## RECORD

| year | team | league | regular season | | | | | playoffs | | | | |
|---|---|---|---|---|---|---|---|---|---|---|---|---|
| | | | GP | G | A | PTS | PIM | GP | G | A | PTS | PIM |
| 1942-43 | Cleveland | AHL | 21 | 3 | 4 | 7 | 12 | | | | | |
| 1943-44 | Cleveland | AHL | 36 | 10 | 12 | 22 | 4 | 11 | 2 | 0 | 2 | 0 |

| year | team | league | regular season | | | | | playoffs | | | | |
|------|------|--------|----|---|----|-----|-----|----|---|---|-----|-----|
| | | | GP | G | A | PTS | PIM | GP | G | A | PTS | PIM |
| 1944-45 | Cleveland/Hershey | AHL | 54 | 9 | 19 | 28 | 9 | | | | | |
| | Hershey | AHL | | | | | | 11 | 5 | 4 | 9 | 0 |
| 1945-46 | Hershey/Buffalo | AHL | 15 | 5 | 6 | 11 | 2 | | | | | |
| * | Buffalo | AHL | | | | | | 5 | 0 | 0 | 0 | 0 |
| | Dallas | USHL | 38 | 13 | 28 | 41 | 6 | | | | | |

international

| year | team | competition | GP | G | A | PTS | PIM | Place |
|------|------|-------------|----|---|---|-----|-----|-------|
| 1955 | Penticton | World Championship | 8 | 7 | 3 | 10 | 0 | 1 |

# SHACK, EDDIE

"The Entertainer"

| | |
|---|---|
| sport: | hockey |
| born: | Sudbury, Ontario |
| | February 11, 1937 |
| height: | 1.85 m / 6'1" |
| weight: | 91 kg / 200 lbs |
| position: | right wing |
| shoots: | left |

At the age of 13, Eddie Shack had no time for school or to play with kids his age. He did find time, though, to obtain a driver's licence, and he worked at a number of jobs. Eddie's father became concerned that his son was not associating with his peers and forced him to sign up with a bantam hockey team. Shack's speed, size, and determination made him an instant star and the following year he joined the junior Guelph Biltmores. He played with the club for five seasons, from 1952-53 to 1956-57.

Eddie Shack's first season of professional hockey was with Providence of the AHL in 1957-58. The following year he broke into the NHL with the New York Rangers. Shack's tenure in New York was not particularly memorable. The Rangers were playing poor hockey and Shack had his differences with the coach and management. At one team meeting the players were invited to vent their frustrations without anything being held against them. Shack spoke his mind and was promptly assigned to the farm team.

In November 1960, Shack was traded to the Toronto Maple Leafs. He played with the Leafs to the end of the 1966-67 season. During that time the club won four Stanley Cups. Eddie Shack's most memorable contribution was scoring the Stanley Cup winning goal in the 1963 series.

Eddie Shack was one of hockey's most colourful and entertaining personalities. His style of play inspired his teammates and roused fans. He was known as the "Entertainer" and every shift on the ice was a theatrical experience. "Clear the track, here comes Shack!" was a cry that was heard in hockey arenas throughout North America. Jack Sullivan of the Canadian Press wrote: "Shack is a big gangling, awkward skater who doesn't know anything else except to go at full speed when he gets the puck. His legs are wide apart, as if he has hoops between them, and when he is hit he goes down with great flamboyancy. If he lands head first, it's 10 to 1 his nose will hit the ice first, because it's one of the most prominent things about him."[34] In the book *After the Applause* by Colleen and Gordie Howe and Charles Wilkins, Shack was thus described: "He was hockey's version of a (barely) guided missile - reckless speed, fiery enthusiasm, explosion on contact."[35]

In May of 1967, the Leafs traded Shack to the Boston Bruins. He then played for the Los Angeles Kings, Buffalo Sabres, and Pittsburgh Penguins before returning to Toronto in 1973 to finish his career with the Leafs at the conclusion of the 1974-75 season.

Throughout his hockey career, Eddie Shack was quite a business entrepreneur. He sold hats and Christmas trees, he advertised autos and grocery stores, and he spoke at banquets. In 1970, Shack and three other partners purchased a farm northwest of Toronto and began building a golf course. In June of 1972, the Vaughan Valley Golf Course was opened to the public. Some years later Shack opened the nine-hole River Oaks Golf Course in Oakville.

## INDUCTIONS

1966        Sudbury Sports Hall of Fame

## AWARDS

1962        NHL All-Star Game MVP

## RECORD

| | | | regular season | | | | | playoffs | | | | |
|---|---|---|---|---|---|---|---|---|---|---|---|---|
| year | team | league | GP | G | A | PTS | PIM | GP | G | A | PTS | PIM |
| 1957-58 | Providence | AHL | 35 | 16 | 18 | 34 | 98 | | | | | |
| 1958-59 | NY Rangers | NHL | 67 | 7 | 14 | 21 | 109 | | | | | |

| year | team | league | regular season GP | G | A | PTS | PIM | playoffs GP | G | A | PTS | PIM |
|---|---|---|---|---|---|---|---|---|---|---|---|---|
| 1959-60 | NY Rangers | NHL | 62 | 8 | 10 | 18 | 110 | | | | | |
| | Springfield | AHL | 9 | 3 | 4 | 7 | 10 | | | | | |
| 1960-61 | NY Rangers | NHL | 12 | 1 | 2 | 3 | 17 | | | | | |
| | Toronto | NHL | 55 | 14 | 14 | 28 | 90 | 4 | 0 | 0 | 0 | 2 |
| 1961-62* | Toronto | NHL | 44 | 7 | 14 | 21 | 62 | 9 | 0 | 0 | 0 | 18 |
| 1962-63* | Toronto | NHL | 63 | 16 | 9 | 25 | 97 | 10 | 2 | 1 | 3 | 11 |
| 1963-64* | Toronto | NHL | 64 | 11 | 10 | 21 | 128 | 13 | 0 | 1 | 1 | 25 |
| 1964-65 | Toronto | NHL | 67 | 5 | 9 | 14 | 68 | 5 | 1 | 0 | 1 | 8 |
| 1965-66 | Toronto | NHL | 63 | 26 | 17 | 43 | 88 | 4 | 2 | 1 | 3 | 33 |
| | Rochester | AHL | 8 | 3 | 4 | 7 | 12 | | | | | |
| 1966-67* | Toronto | NHL | 63 | 11 | 14 | 25 | 58 | 8 | 0 | 0 | 0 | 8 |
| 1967-68 | Boston | NHL | 70 | 23 | 19 | 42 | 107 | 4 | 0 | 1 | 1 | 6 |
| 1968-69 | Boston | NHL | 50 | 11 | 11 | 22 | 74 | 9 | 0 | 2 | 2 | 23 |
| 1969-70 | Los Angeles | NHL | 73 | 22 | 12 | 34 | 113 | | | | | |
| 1970-71 | Los Angeles | NHL | 11 | 2 | 2 | 4 | 8 | | | | | |
| | Buffalo | NHL | 56 | 25 | 17 | 42 | 93 | | | | | |
| 1971-72 | Buffalo | NHL | 50 | 11 | 14 | 25 | 34 | | | | | |
| | Pittsburgh | NHL | 18 | 5 | 9 | 14 | 12 | 4 | 0 | 1 | 1 | 15 |
| 1972-73 | Pittsburgh | NHL | 74 | 25 | 20 | 45 | 84 | | | | | |
| 1973-74 | Toronto | NHL | 59 | 7 | 8 | 15 | 74 | 4 | 1 | 0 | 1 | 2 |
| 1974-75 | Toronto | NHL | 26 | 2 | 1 | 3 | 11 | | | | | |
| | Oklahoma City | CHL | 8 | 3 | 4 | 7 | 10 | | | | | |

# SHALEY, JOHN

| | |
|---|---|
| sport: | baseball |
| born: | Winnipeg, Manitoba |
| | May 13, 1908 |
| height: | 1.80 m / 5'11" |
| weight: | 78 kg / 172 lbs |

John Shaley began his baseball career with the Columbus Club juvenile team of Winnipeg. In the spring of 1926, he transferred to the first team fielded by the fledgling Canadian Ukrainian Athletic Club (CUAC). Shaley pitched for the CUAC Blues for 14 years, advancing from the juvenile to the senior ranks.

In 1941, Shaley was appointed coach of the CUAC senior girls' softball team. He gained much experience in helping guide the team to the 1941, 1942, and 1947 Manitoba senior championships. In 1949, the team was reorganized and Shaley was appointed its manager. He held that position through 1973 when the local senior baseball league folded. With nowhere to play, the CUAC Blues followed suit.

During Shaley's tenure at the helm, the club won the 1953 Manitoba championship and then ran up an unprecedented string of 17 consecutive provincial titles between 1957 and 1973. In 1957, the Blues won the Western Canada Championship, the first team from Manitoba to attain the honour. In 1965, the team won the inaugural Canadian Championship. Jubilant Shaley told the press that "this has to be the best of all the championships we have won."

During the winter months Shaley participated in the CUAC house league bowling program. In the fall of 1947, he organized a junior girls' basketball team and led it to the provincial final during its first year of operation. The following season the team moved to the senior ranks. Its undefeated regular season was capped with the 1949 Manitoba Championship. The club defended the title in 1950. John Shaley also served as president of the Canadian Ukrainian Athletic Club in the years 1943-45, 1957-64 and 1967-92.

In 1991, John Shaley and his brother Stan were inducted into the Softball Canada Hall of Fame. They thus became the first Canadians of Ukrainian descent to be inducted into a hall of fame for their work with a Ukrainian community sports club.


INDUCTIONS

1991     Softball Canada Hall of Fame
1992     Manitoba Sports Hall of Fame  -  member 1965 CUAC softball team (manager)


AWARDS

1992     Manitoba Ukrainian Sportsman of the Year

# SHALEY, STAN

| | |
|---|---|
| sport: | baseball |
| born: | Winnipeg, Manitoba |
| | April 20, 1910 |
| died: | Winnipeg, Manitoba |
| | July 13, 1984 |
| height: | 1.80 m / 5'11" |
| weight: | 81.5 kg / 180 lbs |

Commencing in 1935, Stan Shaley played with the intermediate and senior Canadian Ukrainian Athletic Club (CUAC) baseball teams at the first base position. In 1936 and 1937, he played in Regina. The following two years he played with the Lake Shore Mines AAA baseball team of Kirkland Lake - the 1938 EOBA, TBL and Ennis Cup Champions. Shaley returned to the CUAC in 1940 as a playing assistant manager. In 1941, he was named playing manager of the senior club. That year the team won its first Manitoba Championship. The following year Shaley reverted back to his playing role and hit a team leading .460 as the Blues repeated as champions. In 1943, Shaley was once again named playing manager. Under his guidance CUAC won the 1943, 1944, 1946, 1947, 1950, 1952, and 1954 Manitoba Championships.

Stan Shaley played and managed the senior men's team through the end of the 1958 season. Shortly thereafter the league ceased operations. With nowhere to play, the men's team folded. In 1961, Stan Shaley joined the CUAC senior girls' team, which was managed by his brother John, in the capacity of a coach. He was with the club through the end of the 1973 season when the women's senior baseball league folded. In each of those years the team won the provincial championship and in 1965 it won the inaugural Canadian Championship.

In 1991, Stan Shaley and his brother John were inducted into the Softball Canada Hall of Fame. They thus became the first Canadians of Ukrainian descent to be inducted into a hall of fame for their work with a Ukrainian community sports club.

## INDUCTIONS

| | |
|---|---|
| 1967 | American Espirito Sports Fraternity |
| 1991 | Softball Canada Hall of Fame |
| 1992 | Manitoba Sports Hall of Fame - Member 1965 CUAC Softball Team (Coach) |

1965     Order of the Buffalo Hunt - Province of Manitoba

# SHEWCHUK, JACK

| | |
|---|---|
| sport: | hockey |
| given name: | Shewchuk, John Michael |
| born: | Brantford, Ontario |
| | June 19, 1917 |
| died: | . . . |
| | May 15, 1989 |
| height: | 1.85 m / 6'1" |
| weight: | 86 kg / 190 lbs |
| position: | defense |
| shoots: | left |

Jack Shewchuk began his hockey career with the Copper Cliff Juniors. His first season of professional hockey was in 1937-38 with the Providence Reds of the AHL. The following year, he once again played for the Reds but was called up for a couple of games by the Boston Bruins. Shewchuk gained a starting position with the Bruins in 1939-40. In the subsequent two seasons, he played for both the Bruins and Hershey Bears of the AHL. In 1943, Shewchuk joined the Canadian Army. Upon being discharged he returned to Boston and played one more season for the Bruins.

After his NHL career ended, Shewchuk played for Hershey and the St. Louis Flyers. The husky defenseman was the Flyers' captain and a major inspiration to the club. He played a hard-hitting driving brand of hockey. Always on the hustle, Shewchuk would constantly shout words of encouragement to his teammates. Eventually Jack Shewchuk's hockey career returned to his home town of Brantford. He was the playing coach of the Brantford Redmen Sr. "A" team during the 1951-52 season. Later he coached the Brantford Sr. "B" team.

INDUCTIONS

1984     The Brantford and Area Sports Hall of Recognition

# RECORD

| year | team | league | regular season | | | | | playoffs | | | | |
|------|------|--------|-----|-----|-----|-----|-----|-----|-----|-----|-----|-----|
| | | | GP | G | A | PTS | PIM | GP | G | A | PTS | PIM |
| 1937-38* | Providence | AHL | 42 | 4 | 3 | 7 | 69 | 7 | 0 | 0 | 0 | 8 |
| 1938-39 | Boston | NHL | 3 | 0 | 0 | 0 | 2 | | | | | |
| | Providence | AHL | 46 | 8 | 17 | 25 | 72 | 5 | 1 | 1 | 2 | 8 |
| 1939-40 | Boston | NHL | 47 | 2 | 4 | 6 | 55 | 6 | 0 | 0 | 0 | 0 |
| 1940-41 | Boston | NHL | 20 | 2 | 2 | 4 | 8 | | | | | |
| | Hershey | AHL | 31 | 1 | 5 | 6 | 22 | 9 | 0 | 0 | 0 | 2 |
| 1941-42 | Boston | NHL | 22 | 2 | 0 | 2 | 14 | 5 | 0 | 1 | 1 | 7 |
| | Hershey | AHL | 34 | 1 | 9 | 10 | 28 | | | | | |
| 1942-43 | Boston | NHL | 48 | 2 | 6 | 8 | 50 | 9 | 0 | 0 | 0 | 12 |
| 1944-45 | Boston | NHL | 47 | 1 | 7 | 8 | 31 | | | | | |
| 1945-46 | Hershey | AHL | 55 | 3 | 15 | 18 | 79 | 3 | 0 | 1 | 1 | 2 |
| 1946-47 | St. Louis | AHL | 51 | 1 | 9 | 10 | 34 | | | | | |
| 1947-48 | St. Louis | AHL | 65 | 1 | 12 | 13 | 58 | | | | | |

# SHEWCHUK, STEPHANIE

| | |
|------|------|
| sport: | swimming |
| born: | Montreal, Quebec |
| | May 25, 1974 |
| height: | 1.70 m / 5'7" |
| weight: | 60 kg / 132 lbs |

Stephanie Shewchuk started to swim competitively at the age of seven. Her progress was meteoric. In 1987, she established Canadian 11 to 12-year-old age group short course records in the 400-metre freestyle (4:23.93) and the 800-metre freestyle (8:55.85). In establishing the 800-metre record, she became the first Canadian girl to swim the distance in less than nine minutes. Two years later, Shewchuk broke the national 13 to 14-year-old age group record in the 1,500 metres with a time of 16:38.11. At fourteen, the highly touted swimmer was named to Canada's 1992 Olympic Games development team.

In 1989, Shewchuk represented Canada at the Pan Pacific Games. The following year she was named to the national team competing on the World Cup circuit in Europe. At about that time her results started to slump. Competitive and outside pressures were taking their toll on the young swimmer. She switched swim clubs by moving to Toronto; the move did not help and she returned to Montreal with a changed perspective on the sport. From now on she would swim and compete for fun.

## RECORD

| year | competition | event | placing | result |
|------|-------------|-------|---------|--------|
| 1987 | Canadian Summer Championships | 800 m freestyle | 21 | 9:22.50 |
| 1988 | Canadian Winter Championships | 1,500 m freestyle | 9 | 17:29.93 |
| 1989 | Canadian Summer Championships | 400 m freestyle | 6 | 4:22.99 |
| | | 800 m freestyle | 5 | 8:56.43 |
| | | 1,500 m freestyle | 2 | 16:49.64 |
| | Pan Pacific Championship | 800 m freestyle | 13 | 8:55.52 |
| | | 1,500 m freestyle | 8 | 16:50.84 |
| | Commonwealth Games Trials | 800 m freestyle | 3 | 8:52.81 |
| 1990 | WC Gothenburg, Sweden | 400 m freestyle | 1 | 4:22.07 |
| | | 800 m freestyle | 3 | 8:58.32 |
| | WC Florence, Italy | 800 m freestyle | 3 | 8:41.45 |
| | WC Leicester, England | 400 m IM | 3 | 4:59.33 |
| | Canadian Winter Championships | 400 m freestyle | 9 | 4:19.04 |
| | | 800 m freestyle | 1 | 8:43.87 |
| | | 1,500 m freestyle | 1 | 16:32.20 |
| | Canadian Summer Championships | 800 m freestyle | 6 | 8:52.75 |
| | | 1,500 m freestyle | 4 | 16:55.47 |
| 1991 | Canadian Winter Championships | 800 m freestyle | 1 | 8:44.17 |
| | | 1,500 m freestyle | 1 | 16:39.78 |
| | Canadian Summer Championships | 800 m freestyle | 10 | 9:00.32 |
| | | 1,500 m freestyle | 9 | 17:10.77 |
| | WC Montreal, Canada | 400 m freestyle | 6 | 4:18.81 |

# SHIBICKY, ALEX

| | |
|---|---|
| sport: | hockey |
| born: | Winnipeg, Manitoba |
| | May 19, 1914 |
| height: | 1.83 m / 6'0" |
| weight: | 81.5 kg / 180 lbs |
| position: | right wing |
| shoots: | right |

Alex Shibicky first gained prominence in the fall of 1933 when he was selected to the Winnipeg All-Star team which toured Eastern Canada. During the 1934-35 season, Shibicky played with the New York Crescents. The following year he was called up by the New York Rangers. Shibicky played his entire NHL career with the Rangers. He scored a career-high 24 goals during the 1938-39 season. The following year he savoured champagne from the Stanley Cup. During World War II, Shibicky served in the Canadian armed forces. While stationed in Ottawa, he played for the Ottawa Engineers and Ottawa Commandos of the QSHL. During the 1942-43 season, the Commandos won the Allan Cup.

After the war, Shibicky returned to the Rangers for one more season before playing out his career with the New Haven Ramblers the following year. In the fall of 1947, he assumed the coaching duties with the New Westminster Royals. He held the position for two seasons. Shibicky then coached the Flin Flon Bombers of the SJHL for four seasons before returning to New Westminster for the 1953-54 campaign. Shibicky also coached the Kelowna Packers of the Okanagan League in 1954-55 and the Indianapolis Chiefs of the IHL in 1960-61.

Alex Shibicky was a strong skater with a hard shot. His one weakness was that he held on to the puck too long. Many glorious scoring opportunities were missed because he hesitated before shooting.

## INDUCTIONS

1986        Manitoba Hockey Hall of Fame

## ALL-STAR SELECTIONS

1934-35     right wing      EHL     First Team

# RECORD

| year | team | league | regular season | | | | | playoffs | | | | |
|------|------|--------|----|----|----|-----|-----|----|----|----|-----|-----|
| | | | GP | G | A | PTS | PIM | GP | G | A | PTS | PIM |
| 1934-35 | New York | EHL | 21 | 16 | 9 | 25 | 31 | 8 | 8 | 1 | 9 | 4 |
| 1935-36 | NY Rangers | NHL | 18 | 4 | 2 | 6 | 6 | | | | | |
| | Philadelphia | CAHL | 28 | 16 | 6 | 22 | 26 | | | | | |
| 1936-37 | NY Rangers | NHL | 47 | 14 | 8 | 22 | 30 | 9 | 1 | 4 | 5 | 0 |
| 1937-38 | NY Rangers | NHL | 48 | 17 | 18 | 35 | 26 | 3 | 2 | 0 | 2 | 2 |
| 1938-39 | NY Rangers | NHL | 48 | 24 | 9 | 33 | 24 | 7 | 3 | 1 | 4 | 2 |
| 1939-40* | NY Rangers | NHL | 44 | 11 | 21 | 32 | 33 | 11 | 2 | 5 | 7 | 4 |
| 1940-41 | NY Rangers | NHL | 41 | 10 | 14 | 24 | 14 | 3 | 1 | 0 | 1 | 2 |
| 1941-42 | NY Rangers | NHL | 45 | 20 | 14 | 34 | 16 | 6 | 3 | 2 | 5 | 2 |
| 1942-43 | Ottawa Engineers | QSHL | 9 | 9 | 13 | 22 | 6 | | | | | |
| * | Ottawa Commandos | QSHL | 18 | 15 | 7 | 22 | 25 | 22 | 18 | 18 | 36 | 14 |
| 1943-44 | Ottawa Commandos | QSHL | 10 | 6 | 6 | 12 | 6 | | | | | |
| 1944-45 | Ottawa Engineers | City | 4 | 3 | 5 | 8 | 0 | 5 | 8 | 3 | 11 | 4 |
| 1945-46 | NY Rangers | NHL | 33 | 10 | 5 | 15 | 12 | | | | | |
| | Providence | AHL | 18 | 7 | 12 | 19 | 4 | 1 | 0 | 0 | 0 | 0 |
| 1946-47 | New Haven | AHL | 53 | 20 | 12 | 32 | 28 | 3 | 0 | 2 | 2 | 0 |

coaching record

| year | team | league | regular season | | | | | playoffs | | | |
|------|------|--------|----|----|----|---|----------|----|----|----|----|
| | | | G | W | L | T | Standing | G | W | L | T |
| 1948-49 | New Westminster | WHL | 70 | 39 | 26 | 5 | 1 | 12 | 8 | 4 | 0 |
| 1953-54 | New Westminster | WHL | 70 | 28 | 34 | 8 | 6 | | | | |

# SHISHKA, STEVEN

| | |
|------|------|
| sport: | football |
| born: | Brody, Ukraine |
| | May 1, 1915 |
| height: | 1.73 m / 5'8" |
| weight: | 77 kg / 170 lbs |
| position: | halfback |

In 1935, Steven Shishka (who later changed his surname to Martin) was playing for the

Winnipeg Deer Lodge rugby-football club when it won the provincial and the Western Canada junior championships. The following year, after an unsuccessful tryout with the Winnipeg Blue Bombers, he once again played junior football, winning the provincial title with the Winnipeg Victorias. In 1937, the short but powerful halfback made the roster of the Blue Bombers. The club won the Western Conference playoffs, but lost the Grey Cup game to the Argos by one point.

After the 1937 football season, Shishka/Martin enrolled at Loyola University in Los Angeles. A veteran of both junior and senior hockey in Manitoba, he joined the school's team on defense. Loyola won the Pacific Coast University League championship in 1938 and 1939. During the 1941-42 season, Martin played minor pro hockey with the Los Angeles Monarchs of the Pacific Coast League. At that time, his sports career was cut short by military service. After returning from the war, Martin pursued a career in law and did not go back to sports.

*Photo courtesy of the Canadian Forces Sports Hall of Fame*

# SHWALUK, BILL

| | |
|---|---|
| sport: | weightlifting |
| born: | Fort William, Ontario |
| | (now Thunder Bay) |
| | . . . |
| height: | 1.75 m / 5'9" |
| weight: | 104.5 kg / 230 lbs |

Bill Shwaluk wanted to become a professional hockey player. To make the dream a reality, he took up weight training at the age of 14. A hockey career, though, did not materialize. In 1955, he enlisted with the RCAF. The following year he witnessed the Ontario Open weightlifting competition. Convinced that he could do better than the winner, Shwaluk embarked on a training regiment. A year later, he entered the same contest and placed third. En route, he established a new Canadian record of 280 pounds in the military press portion of the competition. Shwaluk won the Canadian heavyweight championship in 1959, lifting a total of 930 pounds. In the process, he tied the national record of 370 pounds in the clean and jerk. At the 1959 Pan American Games, Shwaluk placed fourth with lifts of 279.5 pounds in the press, 330.5 pounds in the clean and jerk, and 242.5 pounds in the snatch for a total of 870.5 pounds.

At the 1960 Quebec Championships, Shwaluk broke the Canadian record in the clean and jerk when he hoisted 378 pounds. A month later at the Canadian Championships he improved the mark to 381 pounds. At the 1960 Rome Olympics, Shwaluk and his 230-pound frame looked greatly undernourished compared to some of the other athletes who were tipping the scale at more than 300 pounds. He managed only a 14th-place finish with lifts 297.5 pounds in the press, 259.5 pounds in the snatch, and 352.5 pounds in the clean and jerk for a total of 909.5 pounds.

After the Olympics, Shwaluk retired from competitive weightlifting. While stationed at CFS Val d'Or he organized a weightlifting club and trained the group. In 1968, Shwaluk was posted to CFSE HQ AFCENT in Holland. There he volunteered to coach a local Dutch weightlifting club. In a very short time he made the club into a contender. In 1969, and once again in 1970, the club won the South Holland Championship and two of Shwaluk's lifters represented Holland at the 1972 Olympics.

## INDUCTIONS

1971        Canadian Forces Sports Hall of Fame

## RECORD

| year | competition | event | placing | result | |
|------|-------------|-------|---------|--------|--|
| 1957 | Ontario Open | heavyweight | 3 | | |
| 1958 | Ontario Open | heavyweight | 1 | | |
| 1959 | Ontario Open | heavyweight | 1 | 910 | lbs |
| | Canadian Championships | heavyweight | 1 | 930 | lbs |
| | Pan American Games | heavyweight | 4 | 870 $^{1}/_{2}$ | lbs |
| 1960 | Ontario Championships | heavyweight | | 1,030 | lbs |
| | Canadian Championships | heavyweight | 2 | 955 | lbs |
| | North American Championships | heavyweight | 2 | | |
| | Olympic Games | heavyweight | 14 | 909 $^{1}/_{4}$ | lbs |

# SKOCEN, OLEKSANDER

"Lenio"

| | |
|---|---|
| sport: | soccer |
| born: | Lviv, Ukraine |
| | July 28, 1918 |
| height: | 1.78 m / 5'10" |
| weight: | 74 kg / 163 lbs |
| position: | forward |

Oleksander Skocen started to play organized soccer at the age of ten. He quickly developed a sense for the game and at age 17 made his debut with the premier SA Ukraina team in his home town of Lviv. Skocen rapidly adjusted to the more advanced level of play and was soon considered a star. He was extremely dangerous in the offensive zone, easily able to convert passes into goals.

After the occupation of Western Ukraine by the USSR in the fall of 1939, Skocen was instructed to report to the Moscow Dynamo soccer club. He attended the training camp but did not see any action as he had to report for military service in Lviv. Subsequently, he was assigned to Kyiv and made available to the Dynamo Kyiv soccer team. He played for it during the 1940-41 season. After the German invasion of the USSR, Skocen returned to Western Ukraine, playing soccer in Lviv and later in Kolomyia. In 1944, before the advancing front, he moved to Slovakia where he played for a team in Zilina.

After the cessation of hostilities, Skocen helped establish, and played for, Ukrainian soccer teams at displaced persons camps in Salzburg, Austria, and Ulm, West Germany. In August of 1948, he made his debut with l'O.G.C. Nice of the French First Division. He was a regular with the club for two seasons.

Oleksander Skocen arrived in Canada in 1950 and was immediately signed by SA Ukraina - Edmonton in the capacity of playing coach. The following year, he joined SA Ukraina - Toronto also as a playing coach. Part way through the season, Skocen helped found the Ukrainian Canadian Athletic Club Trident and was named its coach. In 1952, Skocen led the team to the championship of the Second Division of the National Soccer League. The following year, the Tridents played in the first division and Skocen was awarded the Holland Trophy for his sportsmanship and gentlemanly conduct. He retired from the game at the conclusion of the 1954 season.

Oleksander Skocen continued his association with soccer as a coach, referee, and a sport journalist and radio commentator. In 1956, he was named coach of the Ontario all-star team that competed against touring European teams. Subsequently, he coached senior SA Ukraina and Tridents soccer teams. He also served on various executives of the Association of Ukrainian Sport Clubs of North America (USCAK). Skocen's autobiography *With Soccer into the World* appeared in 1985.

## RECORD

competitive

| year | team |
| --- | --- |
| 1935-39 | SA Ukraina - Lviv, Ukraine |
| 1940 | Dynamo Moskva - Moscow, Russia |
| 1940-41 | Dynamo Kyiv - Kyiv, Ukraine |
| 1942 | SA Ukraina - Lviv, Ukraine |
| 1943 | USA Dovbush - Kolomyia, Ukraine |
| 1944 | SC Zilina - Zilina, Slovakia |
| 1945 | SC Ukraina - Salzburg, Austria |
| 1946-47 | SC Ukraina - Ulm, Germany |
| 1948-50 | l'O.G.C. Nice - Nice, France |
| 1950 | SA Ukraina - Edmonton |
| 1951 | SA Ukraina - Toronto |
| 1952-54 | USC Trident - Toronto |

coaching

| | |
| --- | --- |
| 1943 | USA Dovbush - Kolomyia, Ukraine |
| 1944 | SC Zilina - Zilina, Slovakia |
| 1950 | SA Ukraina - Edmonton |
| 1951 | SA Ukraina - Toronto |
| 1952-54 | USC Trident - Toronto |
| 1956-57 | SA Ukraina - Toronto |
| 1960 | USC Trident - Toronto |
| 1963-65 | SA Ukraina - Toronto |

# SLIPCHUK, MICHAEL

| sport: | figure skating |
| --- | --- |
| born: | Edmonton, Alberta |
| | March 19, 1966 |
| height: | 1.67 m / 5'6" |
| weight: | 64 kg / 142 lbs |

*Photo courtesy of Gerard Chataigneau and the Canadian Figure Skating Association*

Michael Slipchuk took up figure skating to improve his hockey skills. Three years later, he quit playing hockey to fully concentrate on figure skating. Another three years later Slipchuk won his first major title, the gold medal at the 1983 Canada Winter Games. As a junior, Slipchuk had a first and a fifth-place finish at the Canadian Junior Championships. He also partook in his first international competition, placing a respectable tenth in Prague.

At the 1987 Canadian Championships, Slipchuk, now competing at the senior level, dazzled the crowd in the short program with moves that included Ukrainian dance steps performed to traditional Ukrainian dance music. It was, no doubt, a result of the many years he danced with Ukrainian troupes in Edmonton. In the long program he performed an animated routine, which included his first triple jump in competition. He placed third, behind two future World Champions, Brian Orser and Kurt Browning. Nineteen eighty-eight was a year of disappointment for Slipchuk when he managed only a fourth-place finish at the Canadian Championships and as a result nullified his Olympic hopes. Slipchuk came back the following year to place second at the Canadian Championships and ninth at the Worlds. In 1990 and 1991 he had third-place finishes at the nationals.

At the 1992 Canadian Championship, with defending Canadian and World champion Kurt Browning on the sidelines, Slipchuk won the gold medal. His victory was extraordinary considering that during the original program he suffered from a serious nose bleed. Prior to the free-skating final, Slipchuk had to have his nose frozen and a blood vessel cauterized. In the final, he skated well landing two triple axels in the same program for the first time in his career. In total, he landed seven triple jumps to score 5.7s and 5.8s in the technical judging and 5.8s and 5.9s in the artistic.

| year | competition | placing |
|------|-------------|---------|
| 1983 | Canada Winter Games | 1 |
| 1985 | Canadian Junior Championships | 5 |
|      | Skate Prague | 10 |
| 1986 | Canadian Junior Championships | 1 |
|      | Skate Vienna | 1 |
|      | Skate Canada | 6 |
| 1987 | Canadian Championships | 3 |
|      | World Championships | 20 |
|      | St. Gervais | 3 |
| 1988 | Canadian Championships | 4 |
|      | Skate America | 6 |
|      | Grand Prix de Paris | 3 |
| 1989 | Canadian Championships | 2 |
|      | World Championships | 9 |
|      | Skate Electric Invitational | 5 |
|      | Skate Canada | 4 |
| 1990 | Canadian Championships | 3 |
|      | World Championships | 11 |
|      | Goodwill Games | 8 |
| 1991 | Canadian Championships | 3 |
|      | World Championships | 8 |
| 1992 | Canadian Championships | 1 |
|      | Olympic Games | 9 |

# SLYZIUK, ERNEST

"Mighty Mite"

| | |
|--|--|
| sport: | curling |
| born: | Venlaw, Manitoba |
| | March 12, 1920 |
| height: | 1.60 m / 5'3" |
| weight: | 61 kg / 135 lbs |

Ernest Slyziuk's curling career was almost identical to that of his brother Mike. For many years they played on the same team and twice they won the United States Curling Championship.

At the 1963 United States Championship, Ernie Slyziuk, playing second, was joined by his brother Mike (skip) and childhood friend Walter Hubchik (lead), all from Grandview, Manitoba and Nelson Brown (third) of Southampton, Ontario. The Slyziuk rink completed the tournament with a 10 and 1 record which was identical to that of Wisconsin. In a tense play-off, Michigan came from behind to win 7-6 on the last rock of the tenth end. At the World Championship, the Slyziuk rink tied for second place with a 3-3 record. One of the American victories included the only defeat experienced by the eventual champion, E. Richardson of Canada.

Ernie Slyziuk began curling in 1944 in Windsor, Ontario. That same year, while serving with the Canadian Army, he won the Military Softball Championship of Canada. In 1950, he moved across the river to Detroit, United States, to pursue a better job. Slyziuk immediately joined the Detroit Curling Club out of which he competed for 33 years. In the years 1979 to 1981, he also served as club president. For his many years of active involvement with the club, he was honoured with a life membership in 1986.

Ernie Slyziuk's first major curling success was in 1958 when he won the United States Championship playing second on the Douglas Fisk rink. Five years later, playing on a rink skipped by his brother Mike, he once again won the national title. Ernie Slyziuk represented the State of Michigan at the United States nationals on eleven occasions. Detroit-born boxer Ed Chyz, the 1946 United States National Golden Glove champion in the bantamweight division, is the cousin of Ernie Slyziuk.

## RECORD

| year | competition | position | placing | result |
|------|-------------|----------|---------|--------|
| 1958 | United States Championship | second | 1 | 8-1 |
| 1960 | United States Championship | second | 3 | 6-3 |
| 1961 | United States Championship | second | 3 | 8-3 |
| 1962 | United States Championship | second | 2 | 8-3 |
| 1963 | United States Championship | second | 1 | 10-1 |
|      | World Championship | second | 2 (tied) | 3-3 |
| 1964 | United States Championship | second | 2 (tied) | 8-3 |
| 1966 | United States Championship | second | 3 (tied) | 8-3 |
| 1967 | United States Championship | second | 3 | 8-3 |
| 1968 | United States Championship | second | 3 | 8-3 |
| 1970 | United States Championship | vice-skip | 4 | 6-5 |

# SLYZIUK, MICHAEL

sport:       curling
born:        Gilbert Plains, Manitoba
             September 18, 1918
height:      1.65 m / 5'5"
weight:      70.5 kg / 155 lbs

During the 1963 United States Curling Championship, the rink representing the State of Michigan consisted of expatriated Canadians, three of them childhood friends from Manitoba. Mike Slyziuk, the skip of the rink, was joined by his brother Ernest (second) and Walter Hubchik (lead), all from Grandview, Manitoba and Nelson Brown (third) of Southampton, Ontario. Mike Slyziuk skipped the Michigan rink to a 10 and 1 record which was identical to that of Wisconsin. In a tense playoff, Slyziuk came from behind to win 7-6 on the last rock of the tenth end. At the World Championship, the Slyziuk rink tied for second place with a 3-3 record. One of the American victories included the only defeat experienced by the eventual champion, E. Richardson of Canada.

Mike Slyziuk began to curl in the 1940s in Grandview, Manitoba. After serving with the Canadian Army during World War II, he settled in Windsor, Ontario. In 1948, he moved across the river to Detroit, United States, to pursue a better job and to curl. Slyziuk immediately joined the Detroit Curling Club out of which he competed for 22 years. In the years 1969 and 1970, he also served as club president. For his many years of active involvement with the club, he was elected to an honourary membership in 1982.

Mike Slyziuk's first major curling success was in 1958 when he won the United States Championship playing vice-skip on the Douglas Fisk rink. Five years later he skipped his own rink to the national title. Mike Slyziuk represented the State of Michigan at the United States nationals on ten occasions, never placing lower than third. Mike Slyziuk is the cousin of Detroit-born boxer Ed Chyz, the 1946 United States National Golden Glove champion in the bantamweight division.

## INDUCTIONS

1979       Michigan Amateur Sports Hall of Fame

1990      United States Curling Hall of Fame

## AWARDS

1966      Top skip at the United States Championship

## RECORD

| year | competition | position | placing | result |
|------|-------------|----------|---------|--------|
| 1958 | United States Championship | vice-skip | 1 | 8-1 |
| 1960 | United States Championship | skip | 3 | 6-3 |
| 1961 | United States Championship | skip | 3 | 8-3 |
| 1962 | United States Championship | skip | 2 | 8-3 |
| 1963 | United States Championship | skip | 1 | 10-1 |
| | World Championship | skip | 2 (tied) | 3-3 |
| 1964 | United States Championship | skip | 2 (tied) | 8-3 |
| 1966 | United States Championship | skip | 3 (tied) | 8-3 |
| 1967 | United States Championship | skip | 3 | 8-3 |
| 1968 | United States Championship | skip | 3 | 8-3 |

Photo courtesy of the Vancouver Canucks

# SMYL, STAN

"Steamer"

| | |
|---|---|
| sport: | hockey |
| given name: | Smyl, Stanley Philip |
| born: | Glendon, Alberta |
| | January 28, 1958 |
| height: | 1.73 m / 5'8" |
| weight: | 86 kg / 190 lbs |
| position: | right wing |
| shoots: | right |

Stan Smyl's earliest memories are of his father's clearing trees to make fields on the family farm. Smyl followed his father's hard work ethic throughout his life. He grew up playing a lot of hockey, and at sixteen he left home to play junior "B" hockey for the Bellingham

Blazers. Towards the end of the season he joined the New Westminster Bruins of the WCHL. At the time, the Bruins were Canada's premier junior team and Smyl's contribution to the club's success is noteworthy. With the team he played in four Memorial Cup Tournaments, the first and only player to achieve that feat. The Bruins won the national championship on two occasions, in 1977 and in 1978.

After completing his junior tenure, Smyl was selected by the Vancouver Canucks in the third round, 40th overall, of the 1978 NHL Entry Draft. Most hockey experts predicted that Smyl would not make it in the NHL: "too small," they insisted. Smyl proved them wrong. With the exception of three games that he played in a minor pro league during his rookie season, Smyl's complete 13-year professional career was with the Vancouver Canucks. When Smyl retired from the game after the 1990-91 season, he was the club's all-time scoring leader. The Canucks honoured Smyl and his accomplishments by retiring his number 12 jersey in 1991.

Stan Smyl was an extremely hard working and tenacious winger. He enjoyed tangling with larger players and beating them for the puck. He was particularly fearless in the corners; on open ice, he was a skilled playmaker. Smyl was also a natural leader. His inspirational play, combined with his nine goals and nine assists, was instrumental in leading the Canucks to an unexpected appearance in the 1982 Stanley Cup final. For his leadership he was named captain the following season, a position he held through the end of the 1989-90 season. During his career, Smyl was nominated three times for the Bill Masterson Trophy which recognizes perseverance, sportsmanship, and dedication to the game of hockey.

## AWARDS

1978       Stafford Smythe Memorial Trophy - Memorial Cup Tournament MVP

## ALL-STAR SELECTIONS

1978       right wing       Memorial Cup All-Star Team

## RECORD

| | | | regular season | | | | | playoffs | | | | |
|---|---|---|---|---|---|---|---|---|---|---|---|---|
| year | team | league | GP | G | A | PTS | PIM | GP | G | A | PTS | PIM |
| 1978-79 | Vancouver | NHL | 62 | 14 | 24 | 38 | 89 | 2 | 1 | 1 | 2 | 0 |
| | Dallas | CHL | 3 | 1 | 1 | 2 | 9 | | | | | |
| 1979-80 | Vancouver | NHL | 77 | 31 | 47 | 78 | 204 | 4 | 0 | 2 | 2 | 14 |
| 1980-81 | Vancouver | NHL | 80 | 25 | 38 | 63 | 171 | 3 | 1 | 2 | 3 | 0 |
| 1981-82 | Vancouver | NHL | 80 | 34 | 44 | 78 | 144 | 17 | 9 | 9 | 18 | 25 |
| 1982-83 | Vancouver | NHL | 74 | 38 | 50 | 88 | 114 | 4 | 3 | 2 | 5 | 12 |

| | | | regular season | | | | | playoffs | | | | |
|---|---|---|---|---|---|---|---|---|---|---|---|---|
| year | team | league | GP | G | A | PTS | PIM | GP | G | A | PTS | PIM |
| 1983-84 | Vancouver | NHL | 80 | 24 | 43 | 67 | 136 | 4 | 2 | 1 | 3 | 4 |
| 1984-85 | Vancouver | NHL | 80 | 27 | 37 | 64 | 100 | | | | | |
| 1985-86 | Vancouver | NHL | 73 | 27 | 35 | 62 | 144 | | | | | |
| 1986-87 | Vancouver | NHL | 66 | 20 | 23 | 43 | 84 | | | | | |
| 1987-88 | Vancouver | NHL | 57 | 12 | 25 | 37 | 110 | | | | | |
| 1988-89 | Vancouver | NHL | 75 | 7 | 18 | 25 | 102 | 7 | 0 | 0 | 0 | 9 |
| 1989-90 | Vancouver | NHL | 47 | 1 | 15 | 16 | 71 | | | | | |
| 1990-91 | Vancouver | NHL | 45 | 2 | 12 | 14 | 87 | | | | | |

international

| year | team | competition | GP | G | A | PTS | PIM | Place |
|---|---|---|---|---|---|---|---|---|
| 1978 | Canada | World Junior Championship | 6 | 1 | 1 | 2 | 6 | 3 |
| 1985 | Canada | World Championship | 10 | 1 | 1 | 2 | 6 | 2 |

# SOBCHUK, DENNIS

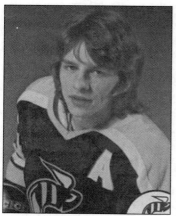

| | |
|---|---|
| sport: | hockey |
| given name: | Sobchuk, Dennis James |
| born: | Lang, Saskatchewan |
| | January 12, 1954 |
| height: | 1.88 m / 6'2" |
| weight: | 81.5 kg / 180 lbs |
| position: | center |
| shoots: | left |

*Card reproduced courtesy of O-Pee-Chee Co.*

Dennis Sobchuk was one of junior hockey's most prolific snipers while playing for the Regina Pats of the WCHL in the early 1970s. In three seasons he scored 191 goals and added 225 assists for 416 points. After completing his first season with the Pats, Sobchuk signed a million-dollar ten-year deal with the Cincinnati Stingers of the WHA. As a formality, the Philadelphia Flyers drafted Sobchuk in the 1974 NHL Entry Draft.

Sobchuk joined the ranks of the professionals in the fall of 1974 in style. Not yet having played a professional game, Sobchuk was named as an alternate to the WHA team which would face the Soviets.  He partook in the training camp, gaining much experience.  For the duration of the 1974-75 season, the Stingers lent Sobchuk to the Phoenix Roadrunners.  He made his debut in Cincinnati the following year.  Described as the "franchise," he had two good seasons with the Stingers but failed to live up to expectations.  Half-way through his third season with the Stingers, he was acquired by the Oilers.

When the WHA folded, Sobchuk's NHL rights were reclaimed by Philadelphia and then trad- ed to Detroit.  Sobchuk, who was riddled with injuries, did not play well for the Wings.  He had trouble adjusting to the NHL, and as a result, he was released by the club.  For a short time, he played in Europe before returning to Canada to take up farming.  In 1982, Glen Sather talked him out of retirement and Sobchuk signed with Moncton.  When the team benched him, he headed to Europe to play in Austria.  Upon his return, he was signed as a free agent by the Quebec Nordiques.  Dennis Sobchuk is the brother of hockey player Gene Sobchuk.

## AWARDS

| 1972 | Stewart "Butch" Paul Memorial Trophy  -  WCHL top rookie |
| 1973 | MVP Trophy  -  WCHL |

## RECORD

| | | | regular season | | | | | playoffs | | | | |
| --- | --- | --- | --- | --- | --- | --- | --- | --- | --- | --- | --- | --- |
| year | team | league | GP | G | A | PTS | PIM | GP | G | A | PTS | PIM |
| 1974-75 | Phoenix | WHA | 38 | 32 | 45 | 77 | 36 | 5 | 4 | 1 | 5 | 2 |
| 1975-76 | Cincinnati | WHA | 79 | 32 | 40 | 72 | 74 | | | | | |
| 1976-77 | Cincinnati | WHA | 81 | 44 | 52 | 96 | 38 | 3 | 0 | 1 | 1 | 2 |
| 1977-78 | Cincinnati | WHA | 23 | 5 | 9 | 14 | 22 | | | | | |
| | Edmonton | WHA | 13 | 6 | 3 | 9 | 4 | 5 | 1 | 0 | 1 | 4 |
| 1978-79 | Edmonton | WHA | 74 | 26 | 37 | 63 | 31 | 12 | 6 | 6 | 12 | 4 |
| 1979-80 | Detroit | NHL | 33 | 4 | 6 | 10 | 0 | | | | | |
| | Adirondack | AHL | 15 | 6 | 4 | 10 | 6 | 4 | 0 | 1 | 1 | 0 |
| 1980-81 | Birmingham | CHL | 5 | 1 | 3 | 4 | 0 | | | | | |
| 1982-83 | Quebec | NHL | 2 | 1 | 0 | 1 | 12 | | | | | |
| | Fredericton | AHL | 29 | 12 | 17 | 29 | 2 | 12 | 8 | 4 | 12 | 10 |
| | Moncton | AHL | 20 | 5 | 12 | 17 | 0 | | | | | |

international

| year | team | competition | GP | G | A | PTS | PIM | Place |
| --- | --- | --- | --- | --- | --- | --- | --- | --- |
| 1977 | Cincinnati | Rude Pravo Cup | 4 | 0 | 1 | 1 | | 3 |

# SOBCHUK, GENE

| | |
|---|---|
| sport: | hockey |
| given name: | Sobchuk, Eugene |
| born: | Lang, Saskatchewan |
| | February 19, 1951 |
| height: | 1.75 m / 5'9" |
| weight: | 72.5 kg / 160 lbs |
| position: | left wing |
| shoots: | left |

Gene Sobchuk played his junior hockey for the Weyburn Red Wings and the Regina Pats of the WCHL. In the 1971 NHL Entry Draft, he was selected by the New York Rangers in the ninth round, 109th overall. At the time, there was no room for Sobchuk in the big league and he played for the Des Moines Oak Leafs of the IHL before joining Rochester of the AHL. During the 1973-74 season, he played in what was to be his only NHL game with the Vancouver Canucks. Sobchuk then jumped to the rival WHA. During the 1975-76 season, he played with the Cincinnati Stingers. The center of his line was his brother Dennis Sobchuk.

## RECORD

| | | | regular season | | | | | playoffs | | | | |
|---|---|---|---|---|---|---|---|---|---|---|---|---|
| year | team | league | GP | G | A | PTS | PIM | GP | G | A | PTS | PIM |
| 1971-72 | Des Moines | IHL | 56 | 16 | 18 | 34 | 16 | | | | | |
| 1972-73 | Rochester | AHL | 58 | 22 | 16 | 38 | 29 | 6 | 1 | 4 | 5 | 4 |
| 1973-74 | Vancouver | NHL | 1 | 0 | 0 | 0 | 0 | | | | | |
| | Seattle | WHL | 55 | 15 | 19 | 34 | 30 | | | | | |
| | Virginia | AHL | 18 | 12 | 5 | 17 | 14 | | | | | |
| 1974-75 | Phoenix | WHA | 3 | 1 | 0 | 1 | 2 | | | | | |
| | Tulsa | CHL | 73 | 35 | 28 | 63 | 65 | 2 | 1 | 0 | 1 | 2 |
| 1975-76 | Cincinnati | WHA | 78 | 24 | 19 | 43 | 37 | | | | | |
| 1976-77 | Oklahoma City | CHL | 29 | 4 | 11 | 15 | 6 | | | | | |
| | Springfield | AHL | 3 | 1 | 0 | 1 | 0 | | | | | |
| 1977-78 | Hampton | AHL | 37 | 3 | 5 | 8 | 2 | | | | | |

# SOPINKA, JOHN

| | |
|---|---|
| sport: | football |
| born: | Broderick, Saskatchewan |
| | March 19, 1933 |
| height: | 1.80 m / 5'11" |
| weight: | 79 kg / 174 lbs |
| position: | halfback |

*Photo courtesy of the Canadian Football Hall of Fame and Museum*

In his teens, John Sopinka played football for the junior Hamilton Tiger-Cats. The club advanced to and won the "Little Grey Cup" final in 1951. The following year, Sopinka enrolled at Queen's University. He played at the halfback position on the school's football team. In 1953, Sopinka transferred to the University of Toronto. He also played at the halfback position with Toronto. Sopinka played an instrumental role in the 1954 national intercollegiate championship victory by the Varsity Blues.

In the fall of 1955, Sopinka made the roster of the Toronto Argonauts. He also commenced law studies that fall. For the next three years, Sopinka juggled a football career and law school. Sopinka was with the Argos for two seasons. He captained the Argos defensive team and also played on offence at the halfback position. In a surprise move, John Sopinka was cut by the Argos in September of 1957. He was immediately claimed by the Montreal Alouettes. Montreal used Sopinka in a defensive capacity and as a punt return specialist. Attending school in Toronto and competing in Montreal proved to be too difficult, and Sopinka retired after the 1957 season. During the next two seasons, while employed with Fasken Robertson, Sopinka coached the Varsity Blues intermediate football team and acted as a scout for the Toronto Argonauts.

In the early 1980s, Sopinka chaired the Ontario Task Force on Equal Opportunity in Athletics and was the author of its report *Can I Play?* In 1988, John Sopinka was named to the Supreme Court of Canada.

## RECORD

| scoring | | | regular season | | | | | | playoffs | | | | | | Grey Cup game | | | | |
|---|---|---|---|---|---|---|---|---|---|---|---|---|---|---|---|---|---|---|---|
| year | team | league | GP | TD | C | FG | S | PTS | GP | TD | C | FG | S | PTS | GP | TD | C | FG | S PTS |
| 1955 | Toronto | IRFU | 12 | 2 | 0 | 0 | 0 | 10 | 2 | 0 | 0 | 0 | 0 | 0 | | | | | |

| scoring | | | regular season | | | | | | playoffs | | | | | | Grey Cup game | | | | | |
|---|---|---|---|---|---|---|---|---|---|---|---|---|---|---|---|---|---|---|---|---|
| year | team | league | GP | TD | C | FG | S | PTS | GP | TD | C | FG | S | PTS | GP | TD | C | FG | S | PTS |
| 1956 | Toronto | IRFU | ... | 0 | 0 | 0 | 0 | 0 | | | | | | | | | | | | |
| 1957 | Montreal | IRFU | ... | 0 | 0 | 0 | 0 | 0 | | | | | | | | | | | | |

| regular season | | | | pass receiving | | | | | interception returns | | | | | punt returns | | | | |
|---|---|---|---|---|---|---|---|---|---|---|---|---|---|---|---|---|---|---|
| year | team | league | GP | NO | YDS | AVE | LG | TD | NO | YDS | AVE | LG | TD | NO | YDS | AVE | LG | TD |
| 1955 | Toronto | IRFU | 12 | 4 | 71 | 17.8 | 23 | 1 | 2 | 0 | 0.0 | 0 | 0 | | | | | 1 |
| 1956 | Toronto | IRFU | ... | 4 | 45 | 11.3 | 16 | 0 | 4 | 5 | 1.3 | 5 | 0 | 1 | 0 | 0 | 0 | 0 |
| 1957 | Montreal | IRFU | ... | 0 | 0 | 0.0 | 0 | 0 | 0 | 0 | 0.0 | 0 | 0 | 14 | 71 | 5.1 | 8 | 0 |

# STANOWSKI, WALLY

"The Whirling Dervish"

| | |
|---|---|
| sport: | hockey |
| given name: | Stanowski, Walter Peter |
| born: | Winnipeg, Manitoba |
| | April 28, 1919 |
| height: | 1.80m / 5'11" |
| weight: | 81.5 kg / 180 lbs |
| position: | defense |
| shoots: | left |

In 1938, the St. Boniface Seals won the Memorial Cup, emblematic of junior hockey suprema-cy in Canada. The Seals were led by Wally Stanowski, a free-skating defenseman who led spectacular rushes up the ice. Stanowski, who at the time was on the New York Americans protected list, impressed Toronto Maple Leafs' general manager Conn Smythe, and he negoti-ated a deal to bring the defenseman to Toronto. Stanowski spent one year in the minors before gaining a regular starting position with the Leafs in the fall of 1939. In his first game, he broke an ankle and was forced to sit out twenty games.

The following season, with his ankle fully healed, Stanowski played some of his best hockey. He added much colour to the game with his patented rushes up the ice. The fans and the media took an immediate liking to his style of play and he was soon known as "The Whirling Dervish." He also scored 7 goals and added 14 assists. At the conclusion of the schedule, he was named to the league's First All-Star Team. During the 1941-42 season, Stanowski re-injured his ankle after stepping on a glove during a fight. The injury once again forced him to miss part of the season. He came back in time for the Stanley Cup playoffs, which the Leafs won.

In the summer of 1942, Stanowski joined the war effort. He served in the armed forces for two years. Upon discharge, he rejoined the Leafs part-way into the 1944-45 season. He helped the club to a third-place finish and an upset Stanley Cup victory. Stanowski won two more Stanley Cups with the Leafs, in 1947 and 1948. After the 1948 Cup final, the Leafs traded Stanowski to the New York Rangers. He finished his NHL career with the Rangers in 1951.

## INDUCTIONS

1985          Manitoba Hockey Hall of Fame

## ALL-STAR SELECTIONS

1940-41     defense     NHL     First Team

## RECORD

| year | team | league | regular season | | | | | playoffs | | | | |
|------|------|--------|----|----|----|-----|-----|----|----|----|-----|-----|
| | | | GP | G | A | PTS | PIM | GP | G | A | PTS | PIM |
| 1938-39 | Syracuse | AHL | 54 | 1 | 16 | 17 | 8 | 3 | 0 | 2 | 2 | 0 |
| 1939-40 | Toronto | NHL | 27 | 2 | 7 | 9 | 11 | 10 | 1 | 0 | 1 | 2 |
| | Providence | AHL | 8 | 0 | 3 | 3 | 6 | | | | | |
| 1940-41 | Toronto | NHL | 47 | 7 | 14 | 21 | 35 | 7 | 0 | 3 | 3 | 2 |
| 1941-42* | Toronto | NHL | 24 | 1 | 7 | 8 | 10 | 13 | 2 | 8 | 10 | 2 |
| 1944-45* | Toronto | NHL | 34 | 2 | 9 | 11 | 16 | 13 | 0 | 1 | 1 | 5 |
| 1945-46 | Toronto | NHL | 45 | 3 | 10 | 13 | 10 | | | | | |
| 1946-47* | Toronto | NHL | 51 | 3 | 16 | 19 | 12 | 8 | 0 | 0 | 0 | 0 |
| 1947-48* | Toronto | NHL | 54 | 2 | 11 | 13 | 12 | 9 | 0 | 2 | 2 | 2 |
| 1948-49 | NY Rangers | NHL | 60 | 1 | 8 | 9 | 16 | | | | | |
| 1949-50 | NY Rangers | NHL | 37 | 1 | 1 | 2 | 10 | | | | | |
| 1950-51 | NY Rangers | NHL | 49 | 1 | 5 | 6 | 28 | | | | | |
| | Cincinnati | AHL | 7 | 0 | 0 | 0 | 2 | | | | | |
| 1951-52 | Cincinnati | AHL | 33 | 0 | 11 | 11 | 42 | | | | | |

# STASIUK, Most Rev. PETER

| | |
|---|---|
| sport: | hockey |
| born: | Roblin, Manitoba |
| | July 16, 1943 |
| height: | . . . |
| weight: | . . . |

As a youth, Peter Stasiuk enjoyed playing hockey. In 1967, he was ordained into the priest-hood. Shortly thereafter, he returned to his home town of Roblin to assume teaching and parish duties. In 1969, father Stasiuk began coaching hockey. He coached in Roblin from 1969 to 1975, and then for two years in Saskatchewan. Subsequently, he returned to Roblin where he coached from 1981 to 1983. He also served as president of the Roblin Minor Hockey Association.

Father Stasiuk's juvenile teams consistently won league championships. In 1971, the juvenile B team placed second at the Manitoba Championships and a year later the midget B team also placed second. At the junior B level, he led the Roblin team to the league title in 1975. Over the years, father Stasiuk witnessed a number of his players advance into the professional ranks.

In May 1993, in Melbourne, Australia, father Peter Stasiuk was installed Bishop of Ukrainian Catholics of Australia, New Zealand and Oceania.

## INDUCTIONS

1986      Roblin Ice Hockey Hall of Fame

# STASIUK, VIC

"Yogi"

| | |
|---|---|
| sport: | hockey |
| given name: | Stasiuk, Victor John |
| born: | Lethbridge, Alberta |
| | May 23, 1929 |
| height: | 1.85 m / 6'1" |
| weight: | 84 kg / 185 lbs |
| position: | left wing |
| shoots: | left |

*Photo courtesy of the Philadelphia Flyers*

Vic Stasiuk played his junior hockey for the Lethbridge Maple Leafs and the Wetaskiwin Canadians. He turned professional during the 1948-49 season with the Chicago Black Hawks' affiliate Kansas City of the USHL. The following year, he played for both Chicago and Kansas City before being traded in late 1950 to the Detroit Red Wings. In 1955, he helped Detroit win the Stanley Cup by scoring five goals and assisting on three during the playoffs. That summer he was traded to Boston. A year later Boston acquired Johnny Bucyk; Stasiuk was placed on a line with Bucyk and Bronco Horvath. The high-scoring threesome was soon known as the "Uke Line." Horvath, who was not of Ukrainian descent, called himself an "adopted Ukrainian."

Stasiuk played his best hockey with the Red Wings and later with the Boston Bruins, in spite of major problems with his legs. He was an intimidating left winger who was not afraid to use his body. He was not a natural but he worked hard at the game. Stasiuk once gave himself "a mediocre rating in talent, but a high score for effort and desire."[36]

After spending more than five seasons with Boston, Stasiuk was traded back to Detroit where he finished his NHL career in the spring of 1963. That summer, the Red Wings named Stasiuk playing coach of the Pittsburgh Hornets of the AHL. For the 1965-66 season he was demoted to Memphis of the CPHL and later fired. In April of 1966, Stasiuk had a blood clot removed from his leg just in time to save his life. Doctors ordered him to stop playing hockey.

Shortly afterwards, Stasiuk became involved with the future Philadelphia Flyers in a scouting capacity. He also coached the Jersey Devils of the EHL and later the Quebec Aces of the AHL. He was at the helm of the Aces for two seasons and both times he led them to the AHL Calder Cup final. In 1969, Stasiuk was named coach of the Flyers. Difference of opinion with a number of players resulted in his being replaced at the end of the 1970-71 season, even though the club made the playoffs. He headed back to his farm in Lethbridge.

In November of 1971, Stasiuk was once again behind the bench, replacing the fired coach of the California Golden Seals. The club did not make the playoffs. The following year, Vic Stasiuk coached the Vancouver Canucks. Once again he could not lead the team to a post-season berth. Stasiuk then moved to the St. Louis Blues as an assistant coach. Midway through the 1973-74 season he was named coach and general manager of the Denver Spurs of the WHL.

## AWARDS

1958-59    E. Dufresne Trophy  -  Outstanding Boston Player in Home Games
1967-68    Louis Pieri Memorial Award  -  AHL Outstanding Coach

## ALL-STAR SELECTIONS

1952-53    right wing    WHL    First Team

## RECORD

| year | team | league | regular season | | | | | playoffs | | | | |
|---|---|---|---|---|---|---|---|---|---|---|---|---|
| | | | GP | G | A | PTS | PIM | GP | G | A | PTS | PIM |
| 1948-49 | Kansas City | USHL | 66 | 7 | 13 | 20 | 56 | 2 | 0 | 0 | 0 | 0 |
| 1949-50 | Chicago | NHL | 17 | 1 | 1 | 2 | 2 | | | | | |
| | Kansas City | USHL | 39 | 10 | 13 | 23 | 27 | | | | | |
| 1950-51 | Chicago | NHL | 20 | 5 | 3 | 8 | 6 | | | | | |
| | Detroit | NHL | 50 | 3 | 10 | 13 | 12 | 7 | 0 | 2 | 2 | 0 |
| 1951-52 | Detroit | NHL | 58 | 5 | 9 | 14 | 19 | | | | | |
| | Indianapolis | AHL | 8 | 7 | 1 | 8 | 6 | | | | | |
| 1952-53 | Detroit | NHL | 3 | 0 | 0 | 0 | 0 | | | | | |
| | Edmonton | WHL | 48 | 37 | 43 | 80 | 71 | | | | | |
| 1953-54 | Detroit | NHL | 42 | 5 | 2 | 7 | 4 | | | | | |
| | Edmonton | WHL | 21 | 6 | 12 | 18 | 37 | 13 | 2 | 6 | 8 | 23 |
| 1954-55* | Detroit | NHL | 59 | 8 | 11 | 19 | 67 | 11 | 5 | 3 | 8 | 6 |
| | Edmonton | WHL | 11 | 7 | 6 | 13 | 32 | | | | | |
| 1955-56 | Boston | NHL | 59 | 19 | 18 | 37 | 118 | | | | | |
| 1956-57 | Boston | NHL | 64 | 24 | 16 | 40 | 69 | 10 | 2 | 1 | 3 | 2 |
| 1957-58 | Boston | NHL | 70 | 21 | 35 | 56 | 55 | 12 | 0 | 5 | 5 | 13 |
| 1958-59 | Boston | NHL | 70 | 27 | 33 | 60 | 63 | 7 | 4 | 2 | 6 | 11 |
| 1959-60 | Boston | NHL | 69 | 29 | 39 | 68 | 121 | | | | | |
| 1960-61 | Boston | NHL | 46 | 5 | 25 | 30 | 35 | | | | | |
| | Detroit | NHL | 23 | 10 | 13 | 23 | 16 | 11 | 2 | 5 | 7 | 4 |
| 1961-62 | Detroit | NHL | 59 | 15 | 28 | 43 | 45 | | | | | |

| year | team | league | regular season | | | | | playoffs | | | | |
|---|---|---|---|---|---|---|---|---|---|---|---|---|
| | | | GP | G | A | PTS | PIM | GP | G | A | PTS | PIM |
| 1962-63 | Detroit | NHL | 36 | 6 | 11 | 17 | 37 | 11 | 3 | 0 | 3 | 4 |
| | Pittsburgh | AHL | 22 | 9 | 20 | 29 | 24 | | | | | |
| 1963-64 | Pittsburgh | AHL | 42 | 10 | 10 | 20 | 32 | 5 | 0 | 0 | 0 | 4 |
| 1964-65 | Pittsburgh | AHL | 63 | 14 | 21 | 35 | 58 | 3 | 0 | 0 | 0 | 0 |
| 1965-66 | Memphis | CPHL | 25 | 9 | 3 | 12 | 14 | | | | | |

coaching record

| year | team | league | regular season | | | | | playoffs | | | |
|---|---|---|---|---|---|---|---|---|---|---|---|
| | | | G | W | L | T | Standing | G | W | L | T |
| 1963-64 | Pittsburgh | AHL | 72 | 40 | 29 | 3 | 1 | 5 | 1 | 4 | 0 |
| 1964-65 | Pittsburgh | AHL | 72 | 29 | 36 | 7 | 3 | 4 | 1 | 3 | 0 |
| 1965-66 | Memphis | CHL | 70 | 25 | 33 | 12 | 6 | | | | |
| 1967-68 | Quebec | AHL | 72 | 33 | 28 | 11 | 2 | 15 | 8 | 7 | 0 |
| 1968-69 | Quebec | AHL | 74 | 26 | 34 | 14 | 3 | 15 | 7 | 8 | 0 |
| 1969-70 | Philadelphia | NHL | 76 | 17 | 35 | 24 | 5 | | | | |
| 1970-71 | Philadelphia | NHL | 78 | 28 | 33 | 17 | 3 | 4 | 0 | 4 | 0 |
| 1971-72 | California | NHL | 75 | 21 | 38 | 16 | 6 | | | | |
| 1972-73 | Vancouver | NHL | 78 | 22 | 47 | 9 | 7 | | | | |

# STECKIW, OSTAP

| | |
|---|---|
| sport: | soccer |
| born: | Lviv, Ukraine |
| | March 13, 1924 |
| height: | 1.75 m / 5'9" |
| weight: | 69 kg / 152 lbs |
| position: | right half back |

Ostap Steckiw began kicking a soccer ball around almost as soon as he could walk. At twelve he was playing goal for the junior SA Ukraina team of Lviv. Subsequently, he was moved to the half back position. The German occupation of Lviv in 1941 resulted in the suspension of most sport activities. A year later, when the Germans allowed the soccer clubs to resume their operations, Steckiw was named to the senior SA Ukraina squad. He played with the team for two seasons. After the war, Steckiw resumed his soccer career with SA Ukraina of Salzburg. There he made an immediate impact and was recruited by FC Phonix of Karlsruhe of the Suddeutschen Oberliga. Steckiw then transferred to the FC Sporting Club of Charleroi, Belgium.

In the fall of 1948, Ostap Steckiw signed a professional contract with the FC Nice. He later played for the faltering Valenciennes club, which he is credited with reviving, and subsequently for Olympique Lyonnais. During his career in France, Steckiw was often described by the local media as a soccer wizard, and in 1951 he was named to the Northern France Selects for a match against Sweden.

In 1952, Steckiw arrived in Canada and joined the SA Ukraina soccer club in Toronto. Towards the end of the season, he was named the club's playing coach. The following year, SA Ukraina won the first of three consecutive National League championships under Steckiw's guidance. In 1956, Steckiw played for the Ukrainian American Sports Club (UASC) of Rochester. The club advanced to the semi-finals of the American championship. In 1957, UASC won the Eastern US championship and advanced to the final of the US championship. That series concluded, Steckiw joined the Canadian national team in the preliminary round of the 1958 World Cup playdowns. Canada defeated the United States twice, 5-1 and 3-2, with Steckiw scoring the winning goal on a free kick in the latter match. Against Mexico, Canada lost twice and was eliminated from further play.

Upon returning to Canada, Steckiw was signed by SA Ukraina of Montreal. That fall, SA Ukraina won the Canadian championship, becoming the first Ukrainian club to win a Canadian title. In addition to his demanding playing schedule, Steckiw also coached the USC Trident soccer team of Toronto during the 1956 and 1957 seasons. In 1958, Steckiw returned to SA Ukraina of Toronto as a playing coach. He was with the club through the 1960 season. In 1961, he joined SC Roma of Toronto as a playing coach. He led Roma to the 1961 and 1964 National League titles. At the end of the 1964 season, he retired as an active player. In 1965, Steckiw returned to SA Ukraina as a coach and guided the club to the league title that year. He coached SA Ukraina for a number of seasons.

Ostap Steckiw was one of the most exciting half backs to play soccer in Canada during the 1950s. Often referred to as the "General," Steckiw had the ability to control the tempo of the game. He was named to numerous city and provincial all-star teams.

## RECORD

competitive

| year | team |
|---|---|
| 1942-44 | SA Ukraina - Lviv, Ukraine |
| 1946-47 | SA Ukraina - Salzburg, Austria |

competitive

| year | team |
|---|---|
| 1947-48 | FC Phonix  -  Karlsruhe, Germany |
| 1948 | FC Sporting Club  -  Charleroi, Belgium |
| 1948-50 | FC Nice  -  Nice, France |
| 1950 | USVA Valenciennes  -  Valenciennes, France |
| 1951-52 | Olympique Lyonnais  -  Lyon, France |
| 1952-55 | SA Ukraina  -  Toronto |
| 1956-57 | Ukrainian American Sports Club  -  Rochester, USA |
| 1957 | SA Ukraina  -  Montreal |
| 1958-60 | SA Ukraina  -  Toronto |
| 1961-64 | FC Roma  -  Toronto |

international

| year | team | competition | GP | G | Place |
|---|---|---|---|---|---|
| 1957 | Canada | World Cup Qualifying | 4 | 1 | eliminated |

coaching

| year | team | league | W | L | T | Place |
|---|---|---|---|---|---|---|
| 1952 | SA Ukraina | NL | 5 | 6 | 3 | 5 |
| 1953 | SA Ukraina | NL | 11 | 2 | 3 | 1 |
| 1954 | SA Ukraina | NL | 13 | 2 | 4 | 1 |
| 1955 | SA Ukraina | NL | 11 | 2 | 5 | 1 |
| 1956 | USC Trident | NL | 12 | 7 | 5 | 4 |
| 1957 | USC Trident | NL | 12 | 12 | 3 | 6 |
| 1958 | SA Ukraina | NL | 16 | 7 | 5 | 5 |
| 1959 | SA Ukraina | NL | 14 | 7 | 5 | 3 |
| 1960 | SA Ukraina | NL | 12 | 10 | 4 | 6 |
| 1961 | FC Roma | NL | 14 | 2 | 4 | 1 |
| 1962 | FC Roma | ECPSL | ... | | | 3 |
| 1963 | FC Roma | ECPSL | ... | | | 3 |
| 1964 | FC Roma | ECPSL | ... | | | 1 |
| 1965 | SA Ukraina | NL | 15 | 3 | 4 | 1 |
| 1966 | SA Ukraina | NL | 17 | 4 | 5 | 3 |
| 1967 | SA Ukraina | NL | 8 | 8 | 2 | 6 |
| 1968 | SA Ukraina | NL | 11 | 1 | 6 | 2 |
| 1973 | SA Ukraina | NL | 9 | 15 | 5 | 10 |
| 1974 | SA Ukraina | NL | 6 | 24 | 5 | 14 |
| 1975 | SA Ukraina | NL | 5 | 18 | 7 | 9 |
| 1976 | SA Ukraina | NL | 7 | 5 | 0 | 4 |
| 1977 | SA Ukraina | NL | 4 | 13 | 4 | 9 |

# STEFANIUK, PETER

"Big Pete"

| | |
|---|---|
| sport: | volleyball |
| given name: | Stefaniuk, Peter John |
| born: | Toronto, Ontario |
| | April 28, 1953 |
| height: | 2.06 m / 6'9" |
| weight: | 97.5 kg / 215 lbs |

Peter Stefaniuk began playing volleyball at 14 with the Ukrainian Youth Association (SUM) team of Toronto. He was with the team when it won the gold medal at the 1971 Ontario Games. Subsequently, Stefaniuk played for the Ukrainian Volleyball Club and later for SA Ukraina. In 1975, he captained SA Ukraina to the provincial and national championships.

While studying physical education at York University during the winter of 1972-73, Peter Stefaniuk played volleyball for the school. Although the team lost in the CIAU national final, Stefaniuk's play during that year was impressive and he was asked to try out for the national team. He made the team in 1973, and that year he helped the Canadian squad win a bronze medal at the NORCECA Zonal Championships. It was the first medal ever won by a Canadian men's volleyball team in international competition.

In 1975, "Big Pete" Stefaniuk decided to forgo amateur volleyball and try out for the Los Angeles Stars volleyball team of the fledgling professional International Volleyball Association (IVA). Stefaniuk, a draft choice of the Stars, won a starting position at training camp. Over the season he developed into an impact player and helped the team advance to the inaugural IVA championship. The following year the Stars experienced financial difficulties, and Stefaniuk was traded to the El Paso-Juarez Sol where he finished the season. In the play-offs, the Sol were eliminated by San Diego. During the off-season, Peter Stefaniuk signed as a free agent with Tucson Sky. The club played poorly, and with a few matches remaining in the season, Stefaniuk was released, only to be signed that same day by the Santa Barbara Spikers. His new club qualified for the playoffs but lost in the semi-finals.

Peter Stefaniuk was an outstanding all-round volleyball player. For a number of years he was ranked consistently in the top three in spiking and blocking percentages, stuffed blocking, and service aces in the IVA. He was also credited with introducing to volleyball the concept of double blocking the middle attack combinations. Among the factors that contributed to

Stefaniuk's success on the courts was his height (six feet nine inches), his surprising agility, and his sense for the game.

During the 1978 season, Peter Stefaniuk played a prominent role in the Spikers' most successful season, which included 28 wins and 8 losses. The club carried the momentum into the playoffs and won the IVA championship, defeating the Tucson Sky in the playoff final. Stefaniuk gained personal recognition when he was named to the league's All Pro all-star team. The following year Santa Barbara once again advanced to the league playoff final, but lost to the Sky. During the off-season, the Spikers changed ownership and Stefaniuk was asked to take a pay cut. Instead, he signed with the Albuquerque Lazers for the 1980 season as a playing assistant coach. The league, though, suspended operations midway through the season. Prior to the suspension of play, Stefaniuk was once again named to the All Pro team.

Peter Stefaniuk's involvement with volleyball has also included coaching men's varsity teams at the University of Toronto, George Brown College, and Ryerson Polytechnical Institute, and the women's team at Ryerson. In addition, Stefaniuk taught the game for some ten summers at the Al Scates Volleyball Camp in the United States. He also co-authored a number of articles that appeared in *Coaching Volleyball*, the official publication of the American Volleyball Coaches' Association. Peter Stefaniuk is the brother of volleyball player Halya Stefaniuk, and the two had the distinction of being the only brother and sister that played concurrently on the Canadian national volleyball teams.

## ALL-STAR SELECTIONS

| | | |
|---|---|---|
| 1978 | IVA | All Pro |
| 1979 | IVA | All Pro |
| 1980 | IVA | All Pro |

## RECORD

| year | competition | team | placing |
|---|---|---|---|
| 1971 | Ontario Games | Ukrainian Youth Association (SUM) | 1 |
| | Canada Games | Ontario | 2 |
| 1973 | CIAU Championships | York University | 2 |
| | NORCECA Zonal Championship | Canada | 3 |
| 1975 | Canadian Championships | SA Ukraina | 1 |
| | IVA | Los Angeles Stars | 1 |
| 1976 | IVA | Los Angeles Stars | |
| | | El Paso-Juarez Sol | 4 |
| 1977 | IVA | Tucson Sky | |

| year | competition | team | placing |
|------|-------------|------|---------|
| 1977 | IVA | Santa Barbara Spikers | 4 |
| 1978 | IVA | Santa Barbara Spikers | 1 |
| 1979 | IVA | Santa Barbara Spikers | 2 |
| 1980 | IVA | Albuquerque Lazers | |
| 1989 | US National Championships | Chicago K. Allen | 1 |

# STELMACH, NATALIE

"Stormy Stelmach"

sport:          snooker
given name:  Stelmach, Natalie Anne Marie
born:           Sudbury, Ontario
                 September 13, 1959
height:         1.65 m / 5'5"
weight:         72.5 kg / 160 lbs

Natalie Stelmach began to dominate the sport of snooker in Canada in 1976 when she won the national championship. The victory was the first of her six consecutive Canadian titles. In 1978 and 1979, she was a finalist at the World Championships. She won the World title in the mixed pair event in 1981. For her accomplishments, she was honoured by the city of Sudbury that year as its Athlete of the Year. Stelmach has also entered the record books as the first woman in the world to achieve a century break - she scored 109 points consecutively without missing a shot.

Her expertise and knowledge of the game provided Natalie Stelmach with an occupational opportunity. She became the owner operator of Varsity Billiards in Sudbury. Snooker, though, is not the only game in which she participates; Stelmach is also an avid golfer: "The two sports have a lot in common," she wrote, "for example, timing, eye contact and putting the ball in the hole."

## AWARDS

1981      Sudbury Athlete of the Year

| year | competition | placing |
|------|-------------|---------|
| 1976 | Canadian Snooker Championship | 1 |
|      | Canadian National Exhibition Championship | 1 |
| 1977 | Canadian Snooker Championship | 1 |
|      | Canadian National Exhibition Championship | 1 |
| 1978 | Canadian Snooker Championship | 1 |
|      | Canadian National Exhibition Championship | 1 |
|      | World Snooker Championship | finalist |
| 1979 | Canadian Snooker Championship | 1 |
|      | World Snooker Championship | finalist |
| 1980 | Canadian Snooker Championship | 1 |
| 1981 | Canadian Snooker Championship | 1 |
|      | World Snooker Championship (mix pairs) | 1 |
| 1989 | Canadian Snooker Championship | finalist |

# SYRNYK, RAY

| | |
|---|---|
| sport: | football |
| given name: | Syrnyk, Raymond Nicholas |
| born: | Buchanan, Saskatchewan |
| | August 25, 1933 |
| died: | Mt. Slesse, British Columbia |
| | December 9, 1956 |
| height: | 1.80 m / 5'11" |
| weight: | 97.5 kg / 215 lbs |
| position: | corner linebacker, guard |

*Photo courtesy of the Canadian Football Hall of Fame and Museum*

Ray Syrnyk arrived in Saskatoon in 1949 to pursue his grade 11 education at Nutena Collegiate. Saskatoon was selected by his father because of its Ukrainian Petro Mohyla Institute student residence. During his five years in residence at the Institute, Syrnyk completed high school and enrolled in the University of Saskatchewan's geology program.

In the fall of 1950, Syrnyk played high school football with Nutena. The following year, he tried out and made the roster of the Saskatoon Hilltops junior football club at the offensive guard position. Syrnyk rapidly matured into an outstanding athlete and team leader. In his last year of junior eligibility, Syrnyk captained the Saskatoon Hilltops to the 1953 Dominion junior football title.

In 1954, Syrnyk joined the Saskatchewan Roughriders and showed great promise at the guard position. Midway through the following season, the rugged guard injured his leg and was side-lined. Syrnyk recovered fully to start the 1956 season, alternating between the offensive guard and corner linebacker positions. His game improved immensely and he nearly made the all-star team.

At season's end, Syrnyk decided to go to the all-star game as a spectator. He was discouraged from attending by a teammate who suggested that the following year Syrnyk would go for free as a player. Syrnyk nevertheless went to the game. On the return trip from Vancouver, the Trans-Canada Airline plane on which he was flying ran into severe turbulence over the Rocky Mountains and smashed into Mount Slesse, killing all passengers. Perishing with Ray Syrnyk were three teammates and nearly 60 additional passengers and crew.

# TANASICHUK, HAL

"Happy Hal"

| | |
|---|---|
| sport: | curling |
| born: | Clanwilliam, Manitoba |
| | March 19, 1938 |
| height: | 1.78 m / 5'10" |
| weight: | 81.5 kg / 180 lbs |

*Photo courtesy of the Western Canada Pictorial Index*

Hal Tanasichuk began curling in the late 1960s. In 1976, he curled his Civic Caledonia rink to the Manitoba Mixed Curling Championship. At the national championship, his foursome posted a 7-4 record. Playing third on the team was his wife Rose. A year later the rink once again won the Manitoba mixed title. Thereafter, on a record of 10 wins and 1 loss, Tanasichuk won the Canadian Mixed Curling Championship. In 1986, he once again skipped his rink to the Manitoba mixed title. At the Canadian championship, the Deer Lodge foursome did not fare well.

Although most noted for his success in mixed curling, Hal Tanasichuk did not restrict himself to that format. He also skipped many competitive rinks in the men's division.

AWARDS

1977        Manitoba Ukrainian Sportsman of the Year

RECORD

| year | competition | position | placing | result |
|------|-------------|----------|---------|--------|
| 1976 | Manitoba Mixed Championship | skip | 1 | |
|      | Canadian Mixed Championship | skip | | 7-4 |
| 1977 | Manitoba Mixed Championship | skip | 1 | |
|      | Canadian Mixed Championship | skip | 1 | 10-1 |
| 1986 | Manitoba Mixed Championship | skip | 1 | |
|      | Canadian Mixed Championship | skip | | 6-5 |

# TATARCHUK, HANK

| | |
|---|---|
| sport: | basketball, administrator |
| given name: | Tatarchuk, Waldmar Eli |
| born: | Vegreville, Alberta |
| | August 2, 1930 |
| height: | 1.80 m / 5'11" |
| weight: | 80 kg / 176 lbs |

When Hank Tatarchuk began coaching basketball at the Royal Military College during the 1963-64 season, he never imagined that the insight he would gain into the various coaching and administrative aspects of the game over the next ten years would vault him to the position of Director of Basketball Competition at the Montreal Olympics. Subsequently, his expertise would be solicited by two non-Canadian Olympic organizing committees. He served as Vice-

President of Sports at the 1984 Los Angeles Games, and as a consultant to the 1988 Seoul Games. Coaching and lecturing in physical education at the university level provided Tatarchuk with an insight into student athletes and an appreciation of university sports. As a result, he also served in various capacities at the Universiades - World University Games.

In the years 1951 to 1979, Hank Tatarchuk served in the Royal Canadian Air Force and the Canadian Forces as a squadron leader and a physical training specialist.

## AWARDS

| 1976 | Diploma - Games of the XXI Olympiad, Montreal |
| 1977 | Award of Merit - National Association of Basketball Coaches of Canada |

## RECORD

coaching

| year | team | capacity | league |
|------|------|----------|--------|
| 1963-67 | Royal Military College | head coach | OSSLA |
| 1967-68 | University of Alberta | assistant coach | WCIAA |
| 1968-71 | University of Manitoba | associate coach | WCIAA |
| 1971-73 | Carleton University | associate coach | OUAA |
| 1973-78 | University of Ottawa | associate coach | OUAA |
| 1979-83 | University of Alberta | associate coach | CWUAA |

administration

| year | position |
|------|----------|
| 1961-63 | Secretary-Treasurer, Quebec Branch Amateur Athletic Union of Canada |
| 1967 | Official - Basketball, Pan American Games - Winnipeg |
| 1974-76 | Director of Competition - Basketball, 1976 Olympics - Montreal |
| 1981-83 | Vice-President - Sports, 1983 World University Games - Edmonton |
| 1983-84 | Vice-President - Sports, 1984 Olympic Games - Los Angeles |
| 1985 | Technical Commission, World University Games |
| 1987 | Technical Commission, World University Games |
| 1985-88 | Consultant - Sport, Seoul Olympic Organizing Committee |
| 1991 | Assistant to the President, Technical Commission, World University Games |
| 1993 | Director of Sports and Venues, 1993 World University Games - Buffalo |

# TKACZUK, WALT

| | |
|---|---|
| sport: | hockey |
| given name: | Tkaczuk, Walter Robert |
| born: | Emsdetten, Germany |
| | September 29, 1947 |
| height: | 1.83 m / 6'0" |
| weight: | 86 kg / 190 lbs |
| position: | center |
| shoots: | left |

*Card reproduced courtesy of O-Pee-Chee Co.*

Walt Tkaczuk was initiated into the game of hockey at age seven in the town of South Porcupine, Ontario, where his family immigrated after World War II. Unfortunately for the youngster, he spent most of the time on the bench. This upset Tkaczuk and he vowed that it would never happen again. To improve his skills, he got a job cleaning the ice at the local rink for eight cents an hour and permission to practise from six o'clock in the morning until the start of classes. In no time, Tkaczuk developed into a star midget player and was picked up by the New York Rangers for their junior team in Kitchener. During the summer, Tkaczuk would return to South Porcupine and work in the mines with his father: "I carried sticks of dynamite, lit the fuses and then ran to get away."[37] When the Rangers found out about this dangerous activity, they talked him out of it.

In Kitchener, Tkaczuk was the star of the team, and in his last year of junior hockey was honoured with the OHA MVP award. He turned professional with the Buffalo Bisons but after five games and nine points, Bisons' coach Shero told the Rangers that Tkaczuk should be in New York. Tkaczuk moved to New York and spent thirteen seasons with the Rangers.

Walt Tkaczuk played a tough physical game of hockey which did not include fighting. He was a player known not for his finesse but for his strength. He would eagerly go into corners to get the puck, would rarely get knocked off his skates, and liked to take the shortest route possible to a destination. If that included going through an opposing player, so be it. In the early 1970s, Rangers coach Francis concluded that Tkaczuk was a gifted checker. As a result, he had Tkaczuk center a checking line with wingers Dave Balon and Bill Fairbairn. For their tenacious checking and penalty killing they were soon named the "Bulldog Line." During the 1972 Stanley Cup final, Tkaczuk shadowed Boston's scoring machine Phil Esposito. In six games Esposito did not score one goal. The Rangers, though, lost the series.

1968       Albert "Red" Tilson Memorial Trophy - OHA MVP

## RECORD

| year | team | league | regular season | | | | | playoffs | | | | |
|------|------|--------|----|----|----|-----|-----|----|----|----|-----|-----|
| | | | GP | G | A | PTS | PIM | GP | G | A | PTS | PIM |
| 1967-68 | NY Rangers | NHL | 2 | 0 | 0 | 0 | 0 | | | | | |
| 1968-69 | NY Rangers | NHL | 71 | 12 | 24 | 36 | 28 | 4 | 0 | 1 | 1 | 6 |
| | Buffalo | AHL | 5 | 2 | 7 | 9 | 9 | | | | | |
| 1969-70 | NY Rangers | NHL | 76 | 27 | 50 | 77 | 38 | 6 | 2 | 1 | 3 | 17 |
| 1970-71 | NY Rangers | NHL | 77 | 26 | 49 | 75 | 48 | 13 | 1 | 5 | 6 | 14 |
| 1971-72 | NY Rangers | NHL | 76 | 24 | 42 | 66 | 65 | 16 | 4 | 6 | 10 | 35 |
| 1972-73 | NY Rangers | NHL | 76 | 27 | 39 | 66 | 59 | 10 | 7 | 2 | 9 | 8 |
| 1973-74 | NY Rangers | NHL | 71 | 21 | 42 | 63 | 58 | 13 | 0 | 5 | 5 | 22 |
| 1974-75 | NY Rangers | NHL | 62 | 11 | 25 | 36 | 34 | 3 | 1 | 2 | 3 | 5 |
| 1975-76 | NY Rangers | NHL | 79 | 8 | 28 | 36 | 56 | | | | | |
| 1976-77 | NY Rangers | NHL | 80 | 12 | 38 | 50 | 38 | | | | | |
| 1977-78 | NY Rangers | NHL | 80 | 26 | 40 | 66 | 30 | 3 | 0 | 2 | 2 | 0 |
| 1978-79 | NY Rangers | NHL | 77 | 15 | 27 | 42 | 38 | 18 | 4 | 7 | 11 | 10 |
| 1979-80 | NY Rangers | NHL | 76 | 12 | 25 | 37 | 36 | 7 | 0 | 1 | 1 | 2 |
| 1980-81 | NY Rangers | NHL | 43 | 6 | 22 | 28 | 28 | | | | | |

# TUROW, THOMAS

sport:           baseball, administrator
given name:   Turiw, Yakim
born:          . . ., Ukraine
               September 6, 1908
height:        . . .
weight:        . . .

Thomas (Tim) Turow was four years old when his family immigrated to Canada and settled in

Preston, Ontario. By the age of ten, he was an avid sports fan and at the age 15 began competing. Six decades later, Tim Turow was acknowledged locally as a sport legend.

Over the years, Turow competed in baseball, bowling, football hockey and softball. In 1928, he captained the Preston baseball team to the Inter County championship. He played softball with ten consecutive championship teams, staring in 1932. He captained the 1928 and 1929 Galt Junior Ontario Rugby Football team and in 1930 and 1931 he played for the Kitchener senior team. In 1948, he won the Ontario singles bowling title. Years later, the modest Turow commented: "I was never much good at sports, but I got through with determination and desire to play. . ."

In 1935, Turow became involved in sports administration when he spearheaded the formation of the Preston Minor Baseball Association. He joined the executive of the Inter County Baseball Association in 1943 and became its president ten years later. In 1947, Turow became an executive member of the Ontario Baseball Association, and once again rising through the ranks, assumed its presidency in 1954. He remained involved with the OBA through the early 1990s.

In 1973, Tim Turow was presented with an award recognizing his 50 years of involvement in sport. The following year, the award became the Tim Turow Award presented annually to the Cambridge Athlete of the Year.

AWARDS

1993        Volunteer of the Year  -  Ontario Baseball Association

# TYZUK, BORIS

sport:          volleyball
born:           Winnipeg, Manitoba
                January 17, 1952
height:         1.88 m / 6'2"
weight:         . . .

Boris Tyzuk enrolled at the University of Winnipeg with outstanding high school credentials.

He was the school's athlete of the year and also the recipient of the Governor-General's Award. While at university, Tyzuk excelled in volleyball and in 1971 was named to Manitoba's team for the Canada Winter Games. The Manitoba squad won the gold medal. Two years later, Tyzuk was selected to represent Canada in volleyball at the World University Games in Moscow.

In 1976, while attending Oxford University in England on a Rhodes Scholarship, Boris Tyzuk trained and competed on the school's rowing team. Upon returning to Canada, Tyzuk enrolled in law school and assumed administrative duties with the Manitoba Volleyball Association. After completing his studies, Tyzuk moved to Vancouver where he held the post of director of the British Columbia Volleyball Association.

## AWARDS

1974  Manitoba Ukrainian Sportsman of the Year

## RECORD

competitive

| year | competition | team | placing |
|------|-------------|------|---------|
| 1971 | Canada Games | Manitoba | 1 |
| 1973 | World University Games | Canada | 16 |

administrative

| year | position |
|------|----------|
| 1978-79 | Vice-president, Manitoba Volleyball Association |
| 1984-85 | Director, British Columbia Volleyball Association |

# UPHAM, JOHN

| | |
|---|---|
| sport: | baseball |
| given name: | Upham, John Leslie |
| born: | Windsor, Ontario |
| | December 29, 1941 |
| height: | 1.83 m / 6'0" |
| weight: | 81.5 kg / 180 lbs |
| bats: | left |
| throws: | left |

*Photo courtesy of the Windsor/Essex County Sports Hall of Fame and Museum*

John Upham began playing organized baseball at the age of ten in Windsor. Two years later he was playing in the Babe Ruth League in Detroit. By the age of 18, he played up through Class D of the Detroit Amateur Baseball League and twice won the United States Amateur Baseball Federation championship, competing for Lindquist Insurance. A strong pitcher, Upham impressed major league scouts.

In the summer of 1959, Upham signed a professional contract with the Philadelphia Phillies of the National League. The Phillies decided to exploit Upham's great speed, natural hitting ability, and good defence by converting him to an outfielder. The following season, he made his professional debut in the minor loop with Tampa of the Florida State League. Playing in Bakersfield of the California League in 1961, Upham gained much attention when he hit .356 and was named best center fielder on the Class C professional circuit. Moving up to the International League the following season, Upham suffered a serious leg injury. While the injury did not terminate his career, it severely restricted his potential and "rudely jolted his meteoric rise in professional baseball."[38]

John Upham made his comeback in 1963 playing for Little Rock of the Texas League. His game improved progressively, and in 1966, after hitting .288 and pitching to a 3-3 record, he was drafted out of the Philadelphia organization by the Chicago Cubs. In 1967 and 1968, John Upham saw limited action in the National League with the Cubs, playing in the outfield and pitching. At the end of the 1968 season, Upham retired from the game after re-injuring his arm. He returned to Windsor and pursued a teaching career.

While teaching, John Upham maintained his interest in the game of baseball. He managed and coached numerous teams. In 1982, he managed the Windsor Chiefs to the Canadian Senior Baseball Championship. For five years (three as a coach and two as manager), he was associated with Canada's National Youth team. In addition, John Upham coached baseball's Team Canada at the 1988 Olympics, was the team's assistant coach at the 1991 Pan American Games, and was named pitching and third base coach of the team preparing for the 1992 Olympiad.

## RECORD

| year | team | league | batting | | | | | | | | pitching | |
|------|------|--------|----|-----|-----|-----|----|-----|------|---|---|
| | | | GP | AB | R | H | HR | RBI | AVG | W | L |
| 1960 | Tampa | Florida | 133 | 477 | 83 | 132 | 0 | 38 | .277 | | |
| 1961 | Bakersfield | California | 129 | 491 | 107 | 175 | 3 | 63 | .356 | | |
| 1962 | Buffalo | International | | | | | | | | | |
| 1963 | Little Rock | International | 121 | 432 | 42 | 110 | 0 | 24 | .255 | | |
| 1964 | Little Rock | International | 11 | 30 | 4 | 8 | 0 | 2 | .267 | | |
| 1965 | Eugene | Northwest | 107 | 342 | 49 | 94 | 0 | 35 | .275 | | |
| 1966 | Dallas-Fort Worth | Texas | 124 | 419 | 45 | 119 | 0 | 25 | .284 | 3 | 3 |
| 1967 | Chicago | National | 8 | 3 | 1 | 2 | 0 | 0 | .667 | 0 | 1 |
| | Tacoma | Pacific Coast | 3 | 1 | 0 | 0 | 0 | 0 | .000 | | |
| 1968 | Chicago | National | 13 | 10 | 0 | 2 | 0 | 0 | .200 | 0 | 1 |
| | Tacoma | Pacific Coast | | | | | | | .385 | | |

managing

| year | team | event | place |
|------|------|-------|-------|
| 1981 | Ontario | Canada Games | 1 |
| 1982 | Windsor Chiefs | Canadian Championship | 1 |
| 1985 | Ontario | Canada Games | 1 |
| 1989 | Canada | World Junior Championship | dnq |

# VEITCH, DARREN

| | |
|---|---|
| sport: | hockey |
| given name: | Veitch, Darren William |
| born: | Saskatoon, Saskatchewan |
| | April 24, 1960 |
| height: | 1.80 m / 5'11" |
| weight: | 88.5 kg / 195 lbs |
| position: | defense |
| shoots: | right |

*Photo courtesy of the Washington Capitals*

While playing junior hockey with the Regina Pats during the 1979-80 season, Darren Veitch established three club records for a defenseman: he scored 29 goals and added 93 assists for a total of 122 points. That summer the Washington Capitals made him their first choice (fifth overall) in the NHL Entry Draft. Veitch spent more than five seasons in the Washington organization, playing for the Capitals and in the minor leagues. The quiet and laidback player never performed at the level that the Capitals expected from such a high draft pick. At times he was inconsistent, and early in his career he had a tendency for giving the puck away.

In part, Darren Veitch's inconsistent play was the result of injuries which plagued him throughout his career. At the start of the 1982-83 season, Veitch fractured his collarbone in three places. He barely returned to the line-up before he broke it again. A year later, his ribs were broken. Veitch's knees were bad and he had to wear braces which allowed him to skate but restricted his mobility.

The Detroit Red Wings acquired Veitch in a trade in March of 1986. The trade rejuvenated Veitch's career. The club used him on regular shifts and on the power play. Veitch responded with a career-high 13 goals, 45 assists and 58 points, best among Red Wings defensemen. The following year, Veitch's production fell, and in June of 1988 he was traded to the Toronto Maple Leafs. Over the next three seasons, Veitch saw only spotted duty with the club.

An avid golfer, Darren Veitch won the 1980 Carling O'Keefe Open Golf Championship in Regina with a 54 hole total of 214.

# ALL-STAR SELECTIONS

1990        defense    AHL    Second Team

## RECORD

| year | team | league | regular season | | | | | playoffs | | | | |
|------|------|--------|----|----|----|-----|-----|----|----|----|-----|-----|
| | | | GP | G | A | PTS | PIM | GP | G | A | PTS | PIM |
| 1980-81 | Washington | NHL | 59 | 4 | 21 | 25 | 46 | | | | | |
| | Hershey | AHL | 26 | 6 | 22 | 28 | 12 | 10 | 6 | 3 | 9 | 15 |
| 1981-82 | Washington | NHL | 67 | 9 | 44 | 53 | 54 | | | | | |
| | Hershey | AHL | 10 | 5 | 10 | 15 | 16 | | | | | |
| 1982-83 | Washington | NHL | 10 | 0 | 8 | 8 | 0 | | | | | |
| | Hershey | AHL | 5 | 0 | 1 | 1 | 2 | | | | | |
| 1983-84 | Washington | NHL | 46 | 6 | 18 | 24 | 17 | 5 | 0 | 1 | 1 | 15 |
| | Hershey | AHL | 11 | 1 | 6 | 7 | 4 | | | | | |
| 1984-85 | Washington | NHL | 75 | 3 | 18 | 21 | 37 | 5 | 0 | 1 | 1 | 4 |
| 1985-86 | Washington | NHL | 62 | 3 | 9 | 12 | 27 | | | | | |
| | Detroit | NHL | 13 | 0 | 5 | 5 | 2 | | | | | |
| 1986-87 | Detroit | NHL | 77 | 13 | 45 | 58 | 52 | 12 | 3 | 4 | 7 | 8 |
| 1987-88 | Detroit | NHL | 63 | 7 | 33 | 40 | 45 | 11 | 1 | 5 | 6 | 6 |
| 1988-89 | Toronto | NHL | 37 | 3 | 7 | 10 | 16 | | | | | |
| | Newmarket | AHL | 33 | 5 | 19 | 24 | 29 | 5 | 0 | 4 | 4 | 4 |
| 1989-90 | Newmarket | AHL | 78 | 13 | 54 | 67 | 30 | | | | | |
| 1990-91 | Toronto | NHL | 2 | 0 | 1 | 1 | 0 | | | | | |
| | Newmarket | AHL | 56 | 7 | 28 | 35 | 26 | | | | | |
| *       | Peoria | IHL | 18 | 2 | 14 | 16 | 10 | 19 | 4 | 12 | 16 | 10 |

# WASNIE, NICK

sport:          hockey
given name:     Wasnie, Nicholas
born:           Selkirk, Manitoba
                January 28, 1905
died:           Brainerd, Minnesota, USA
                May 26, 1991
height:         1.78 m / 5'10"
weight:         79 kg  / 174 lbs
position:       right wing
shoots:         right

A product of the Selkirk minor hockey system, Nick Wasnie played amateur hockey with the Coleman Tigers of the Crow's Nest Pass League in Alberta. The high-scoring defenseman joined the minor pro Winnipeg Maroons during the 1925-26 season. It was a year of major adjustments for Wasnie as he was assigned to a forward position. Wasnie missed a good portion of the following season as a result of a broken collar bone. He nevertheless played impressively and was invited to try out for the Chicago Black Hawks of the NHL in the fall of 1927. Wasnie made the team, but played only sporadically. He was then lent to the Quebec Beavers of the Canadian American Hockey League. When the Black Hawks released Wasnie prior to the start of the 1928-29 season, he signed with Newark of the CAHL.

In 1929, Wasnie joined the Montreal Canadiens, playing right wing on a line that included center Howie Morenz and left wing Aurel Joliat. That season Morenz had his finest scoring year ever with 40 goals in 44 games. It was Wasnie's most productive year also: he netted 12 goals. In the playoffs, Wasnie added two goals and two assists to help the Canadiens win the Stanley Cup. The following year, Wasnie played on a weaker line and his point production fell significantly. In the playoffs, Wasnie, who was elusive around the net, scored four goals in four games as the Canadiens defended the Cup.

Prior to the start of the 1932-33 season, the Canadiens lent Wasnie to the New York Americans. A few days before the conclusion of the schedule, the Canadiens announced that Wasnie had been traded to the Ottawa Senators but was to finish the season with the Americans. At the Senators' training camp in the fall of 1933 Wasnie injured his groin. He returned for the opening game of the regular schedule, but suffered another injury which forced him to miss the first part of the season. That year, the Ottawa club continued to play poorly in front of few fans. When the season ended, the club was transferred to St. Louis. Wasnie finished his NHL career with the St. Louis Eagles. Subsequently, he played minor pro hockey for a number of seasons.

# INDUCTIONS

1986        Manitoba Hockey Hall of Fame

## ALL-STAR SELECTIONS

1934-35    right wing    CHL        First Team
1936-37    right wing    AHA        First Team

## RECORD

| | | | regular season | | | | | playoffs | | | | |
|---|---|---|---|---|---|---|---|---|---|---|---|---|
| year | team | league | GP | G | A | PTS | PIM | GP | G | A | PTS | PIM |
| 1926-27 | Winnipeg | AHL | 21 | 7 | 3 | 10 | 33 | | | | | |
| 1927-28 | Chicago | NHL | 14 | 1 | 0 | 1 | 22 | | | | | |
| | Quebec | CAHL | 22 | 8 | 3 | 11 | 32 | 6 | 3 | 0 | 3 | 18 |
| 1928-29 | Newark | CAHL | 40 | 14 | 6 | 20 | 76 | | | | | |
| 1929-30* | Montreal | NHL | 44 | 12 | 11 | 23 | 64 | 6 | 2 | 2 | 4 | 12 |
| 1930-31* | Montreal | NHL | 44 | 9 | 2 | 11 | 26 | 4 | 4 | 1 | 5 | 8 |
| 1931-32 | Montreal | NHL | 48 | 10 | 2 | 12 | 16 | 4 | 0 | 0 | 0 | 0 |
| 1932-33 | NY Americans | NHL | 48 | 11 | 12 | 23 | 36 | | | | | |
| 1933-34 | Ottawa | NHL | 37 | 11 | 6 | 17 | 10 | | | | | |
| 1934-35 | St. Louis | NHL | 13 | 3 | 1 | 4 | 2 | | | | | |
| | Minneapolis | CHL | 33 | 16 | 19 | 35 | 32 | 5 | 2 | 3 | 5 | 4 |
| 1935-36 | Pittsburgh | IHL | 60 | 17 | 25 | 42 | 60 | | | | | |
| 1936-37 | Kansas City | AHA | 46 | 18 | 19 | 37 | 52 | 3 | 0 | 1 | 1 | 0 |
| 1937-38 | Kansas City | AHA | 45 | 9 | 12 | 21 | 14 | | | | | |
| 1938-39 | Kansas City | AHA | 48 | 34 | 27 | 61 | 19 | | | | | |
| 1939-40 | Kansas City | AHA | 48 | 18 | 21 | 39 | 36 | | | | | |

# WASZCZUK, HENRY

| | |
|---|---|
| sport: | football, fishing |
| born: | Oshawa, Ontario |
| | August 26, 1950 |
| height: | 1.83 m / 6'0" |
| weight: | 105.5 kg / 235 lbs |
| position: | centre |

*Photo courtesy of the Canadian Football Hall of Fame and Museum*

Henry Waszczuk was a standout football player for Kent State University. In 1975, he was named to the All-Mid-American Conference All-Star team, the All-Mid-American Conference All-Academic team, and was given an honourable mention as an All-American. He joined the Hamilton Tiger-Cats in 1975; the club made him a protected draft choice in the college draft. Waszczuk was named the team's starting centre in 1977. He held the position through retirement in 1984. During his career, Waszczuk was generally considered the lightest centre in the league. Weight, though, was not much of a drawback. He utilized speed, agility, and deceit to stop linemen who outweighed him by more than 30 pounds. His effectiveness at the position was recognized by three nominations for the Schenley Most Outstanding Offensive Lineman Award and four all-star selections.

After losing the Grey Cup final to Winnipeg in 1984, Henry Waszczuk retired from football to pursue a business career. His greatest regret was never winning the Grey Cup. Years later he stated, "I wanted a Grey Cup ring, I wanted it bad. I'd do anything for it."[39] In 1986, he contemplated a comeback, even meeting with the Ti-Cat management, but eventually he changed his mind. Ironically, the Tiger-Cats won the Cup that year.

Fishing became Henry Waszczuk's preoccupation and business after retiring from football. He teamed up with Italo Labignan to operate Canadian Sportsfishing Productions. The duo produced the very popular "Canadian Sports Fishing" show for television which has had air time in Canada, the United States, and Europe. The show featured the best fishing spots in Canada, whether in southern Ontario or in the wilds of the Northwest Territories. Waszczuk has also co-authored four books on fishing, and has written columns for newspapers and magazines.

1989      City of Oshawa Sports Hall of Fame

## ALL-STAR SELECTIONS

| | | | |
|---|---|---|---|
| 1980 | centre | CFL | All-Eastern |
| 1981 | centre | CFL | All-Eastern |
| 1982 | centre | CFL | All-Eastern |
| 1984 | centre | CFL | All-Eastern |

# WAWRYSHYN, EVELYN

"Ev," "Evie"

| | |
|---|---|
| sport: | baseball, hockey |
| given name: | Wawryshyn, Evelyn Florence |
| born: | Tyndall, Manitoba |
| | November 11, 1924 |
| height: | 1.63 m / 5'4" |
| weight: | 61 kg / 135 lbs |
| bats: | right |
| throws: | right |

An outstanding all-round athlete, Evelyn Wawryshyn excelled in just about every sport that she tried. With very little previous softball experience, Wawryshyn cracked the starting line-up at the shortstop position of the powerful senior CUAC Blues in 1945. Her hitting, fielding, and base stealing were exceptional, and she was named the club's MVP that year. Winnipeg sport columnist Tony Allan wrote: "If Evelyn Wawryshyn, the CUAC Blues, had been born a boy, she might be worth $50,000 in today's baseball market, and the stands would be filled with major league scouts." The following summer, after winning the Manitoba Ladies' Basketball Championship with the Flin Flon Doodlebugs, Wawryshyn decided to forgo a teaching career when she signed a contract with Kenosha Comets of the All-American Girls Professional Baseball League.

In her first two seasons in the professional loop, she was used sparingly by the Comets and later by the Muskegon Lassies. With the Lassies, though, she won the league pennant in 1947. The following year, Wawryshyn became a regular starter with the Springfield Sallies at the second base position. She finished the year fifth in the AAGPBL batting race, stole 66 bases and played steady defence all season to earn a berth on the third all-star team. The following year Wawryshyn was the most-sought after player after the Springfield franchise collapsed. She was picked up by the Fort Wayne Daisies. Of the three years she spent with the Daisies, 1950 was the most memorable; she hit .311, batted in 50 runs, stole 65 bases, and was named to the first all-star team. In 1989, Wawryshyn was recognized as a member of the Fort Wayne Daisies and the All-American Girls Professional Baseball League at the Baseball Hall of Fame at Cooperstown, New York.

In addition to her prowess on the baseball diamond, Wawryshyn was one of Canada's top female hockey players. She began playing hockey with boys' teams at the age of ten. At the age of fifteen she temporarily hung up her skates. Ten years later, when the Winnipeg Girls' Hockey League was organized, Wawryshyn signed up with the Doodlebugs. Averaging more than four goals a game and scoring more than three quarters of her team's goals, Wawryshyn led her side to the 1950 Manitoba Championship. Afterwards she was selected to the Winnipeg All-Star team. She led that team to the Western Canada Championship by scoring eight goals as the All-Stars swept Moose Jaw in a best-of-three playoff. The All-Stars then faced the Port Arthur Bombers for the national title. In a two-game total-goal series, Wawryshyn scored six goals as the All-Stars captured the Lady Bessborough Trophy, emblematic of the Dominion Championship.

An avid golfer, Evelyn Wawryshyn Litwin Moroz scored a hole-in-one at the Kildonan Golf Course in 1987.

## INDUCTIONS

1992        Manitoba Sports Hall of Fame

## ALL-STAR SELECTIONS

| 1948 | second base | AAGPBL | Third Team |
| 1949 | second base | AAGPBL | Second Team |
| 1950 | second base | AAGPBL | First Team |

## RECORD

| year | team | league | GP | AB | R | H | HR | RBI | AVG |
|------|------|--------|----|----|---|---|----|-----|-----|
| 1945 | CUAC Blues | Winnipeg | | 41 | | 16 | 5 | | .390 |
| 1946 | Kenosha Comets/ | | | | | | | | |
| | Muskegon Lassies | AAGPBL | 73 | 235 | 29 | 51 | 0 | 18 | .217 |

| year | team | league | GP | AB | R | H | HR | RBI | AVG |
|------|------|--------|----|----|----|----|----|-----|-----|
| 1947 | Muskegon Lassies | AAGPBL | 36 | 93 | 10 | 22 | 0 | 7 | .237 |
| 1948 | Springfield Sallies | AAGPBL | 118 | 435 | 58 | 114 | 0 | 30 | .262 |
| 1949 | Fort Wayne Daisies | AAGPBL | 109 | 391 | 47 | 98 | 0 | 34 | .251 |
| 1950 | Fort Wayne Daisies | AAGPBL | 104 | 399 | 71 | 124 | 1 | 50 | .311 |
| 1951 | Fort Wayne Daisies | AAGPBL | 104 | 390 | 60 | 108 | 0 | 54 | .277 |

# WELYHORSKYJ, MYROSLAW

| | |
|---|---|
| sport: | fishing, administration |
| born: | Serafyntsi, Ukraine |
| | January 14, 1920 |
| height: | . . . |
| weight: | . . . |

Voluntarism was the trademark of Myroslaw Welyhorskyj's leisure time. Much of it centred on sport, outdoor recreation and conservation.

While attending high school in Stanyslaviv (today Ivano-Frankivsk), Welyhorskyj participated in various sports. In the years 1938-40, he attended Lviv Pedagogical Institute and represented the school in decathlon, volleyball and shooting. Subsequently, while pursuing medical studies, he led the track and field arm of the Lviv Ukrainian Students' Sports Club. In 1944, before the advancing Soviet front, he moved to Bratislava, Slovakia. There, his horses and wagon were commandeered by the Germans, and he was assigned to a forced labour camp.

At the end of the war, Welyhorskyj settled at the displaced persons camp in Fuessen, West Germany, and immediately became involved with the camp's Sports Club Kalyna (Guelder-Rose). In June 1946, the Fuessen camp was closed, and Welyhorskyj and its other inhabitants were moved to the Jager-Kaserne camp (population 3,000) in Mittenwald. There, Welyhorskyj became a member of the camp council, secretary of the Sports Club Levy (Lions), founder and first president of the Ukrainian YMCA-YWCA, physical education instructor at the camp's high school, member of the Ukrainian Council for Physical Education in (West) Germany and chef de mission of the Ukrainian track and field team at the 1948 Displaced

Persons Olympics.

In November 1948, a month after arriving in Canada, Welyhorskyj was elected president of the fledgling SA Ukraina (Toronto). He also began editing the sports section of the weekly *Homin Ukrainy - Ukrainian Echo,* and was national chairman of the Ukrainian Youth Association's (SUM) sports program.

Myroslaw Welyhorskyj moved to Espanola in 1951, holding various jobs before establishing himself as a laboratory supervisor at a paper mill. He also became active in community activities. These included: Director and Vice President of the Espanola Game and Fish Protection Association, Co-founder and President of the Espanola Ski Club, Co-founder and Director of the Espanola Junior Game and Fish Protection Association, Chief Hunter Safety Education Instructor, Chairman of the Espanola Handgun Club, Chairman of the Espanola Winter Carnival, Chairman of the Lang Lake Association on Fish Planning, District Commissioner of Boy Scouts, etc.

In the 1960s, Myroslaw Welyhorskyj began warning the community about the environmental threat of acid rain. He thus embarked on a crusade promoting environmental protection and conservation. In the 1980s, he surveyed and analyzed water samples from local lakes and provided the results to government. He built and promoted fish hatcheries, helped replenish depleted pickerel and trout stocks, monitored the rehabilitation of the Spanish River. For many years he provided technical and inspirational leadership for a project to restore walleye fishing in seven northern Ontario lakes that had been damaged by acid rain. The project was a success and at least five other northern Ontario communities established similar projects. For this work, Myroslaw Welyhorskyj was honoured in 1991 by Governor General Ramon Hnatyshyn with the Recreational Fishery Award.

## AWARDS

| | |
|---|---|
| 1979 | Sportsman of the Year - Espanola Fish and Game Protection Association |
| 1989 | Sportsman of the Year - Espanola Fish and Game Protection Association |
| 1991 | Governor General's Recreational Fishery Award |

# WERBENIUK, BILL

"Big Bill"

| | |
|---|---|
| sport: | snooker |
| born: | . . . |
| | January 14, 1947 |
| height: | . . . |
| weight: | 127 kg / 280 lbs |

*Photo courtesy of the World Professional Billiards & Snooker Association*

Bill Werbeniuk moved to England in 1973 to compete on the United Kingdom professional snooker circuit. There he saw his fortunes soar as he climbed to eighth in the world rankings. Four times he reached the quarter-finals of the Embassy World Professional Snooker Championship. Werbeniuk also represented Canada in the World Cup of Snooker. He was a member of teams that reached the finals on four different occasions, winning once in 1982.

In the late 1980s, to combat a hereditary nervous disorder, Werbeniuk was instructed to drink beer in large quantities (upwards of 40 pints a day). His heartbeat increased substantially from the alcohol, and to counter the effects he was prescribed a beta-blocker drug. This substance, though, was considered "performance enhancing" by the governing body of snooker, and he was fined and banned from competition in 1988. Werbeniuk was reinstated in 1989 and returned to competition in 1990. In his first comeback match, it was reported that he drank 28 pints of lager, ten of which were double strength and eight double whiskies. "It is unfair that I have to get totally drunk in order to compete,"[40] Werbeniuk retorted after the match.

# WERENICH, ED

"The Wrench"

| | |
|---|---|
| sport: | curling |
| given name: | Werenich, Edward |
| born: | Benito, Manitoba |
| | June 23, 1947 |
| height: | 1.70 m / 5'7" |
| weight: | 88.5 kg / 195 lbs |

*Photo courtesy of Andrew Gregorovich*

Ed Werenich was one of Canada's most dominant curlers in the 1970s and 80s. A native of Manitoba, Werenich decided to call southern Ontario home after coming to Toronto to study in 1968. His first major curling success came in 1973, when he won the provincial title while playing second on the Paul Savage rink. Werenich continued to experience success with the Savage rink for some years, winning two more provincial titles.

In the early 1980s, Ed Werenich assumed the skipping duties of the rink while Paul Savage was assigned to the third position. The shuffle of personnel seemed to click immediately and the rink won the 1981 provincial title. Two years later, the "Dream Team," as Werenich and company were called, emerged victorious at the provincial and national championships. Winning the Brier - the Canadian Championship - was Werenich's most thrilling moment in sport. He celebrated by partying for three weeks straight, only taking time out to represent Canada at the World Championship, which he also won.

One of Ed Werenich's greatest ambitions was to compete at the 1988 Calgary Winter Olympics. Unfortunately, he failed to qualify. Some observers believe that the events leading up to and during the Olympic Trials were perhaps the most unfortunate in Werenich's career. A number of curlers, among them Werenich, voiced their displeasure with the format of the trials. In addition, a few months before the trials, Curl Canada, the governing body of curling in Canada, decided that all curlers wishing to try out had to meet certain weight and fitness requirements. Werenich was told to lose nine kilograms (20 lbs). In addition, he had to be prepared to do a required number of sit-ups, push-ups, and other exercises. Werenich, although upset with the weight and physical fitness requirement and the short notice, nevertheless managed to pass the physical. Unfortunately, his loss of weight threw his game off balance. He no longer had a feel for the draw weight and failed to qualify. Disillusioned, Werenich began thinking that he would never again curl at the elite level.

It would be a number of years before Ed Werenich would regain his draw weight and confidence.  In the spring of 1990, he captured his second Brier and was named to the championship all-star team.  A few weeks later he won his second World Championship.

A fireman by profession, Ed Werenich has been the Firefighter Curling Champion of Canada on many occasions.

## INDUCTIONS

1988        Canadian Curling Hall of Fame

## AWARDS

1983        Dick Ellis Memorial Trophy  -  Canada's Outstanding Team of the Year

## ALL-STAR SELECTIONS

1990        skip        Brier

## RECORD

| year | competition | position | placing | result |
|------|-------------|----------|---------|--------|
| 1973 | Ontario Championship | second | 1 | |
| | Canadian Championship | second | | 6-4 |
| 1974 | Ontario Championship | second | 1 | |
| | Canadian Championship | second | | 6-4 |
| 1977 | Ontario Championship | third | 1 | |
| | Canadian Championship | third | | 8-3 |
| 1981 | Ontario Championship | skip | 1 | |
| | Canadian Championship | skip | | 7-5 |
| 1983 | Ontario Championship | skip | 1 | |
| | Canadian Championship | skip | 1 | 12-1 |
| | World Championship | skip | 1 | |
| 1984 | Ontario Championship | skip | 1 | |
| | Canadian Championship | skip | 2 | 10-5 |
| 1987 | Olympic Trials | third | | |
| 1988 | Ontario Championship | third | 1 | |
| | Canadian Championship | third | 3 | 8-4 |
| 1990 | Ontario Championship | skip | 1 | 10-1 |
| | Canadian Championship | skip | 1 | 11-1 |
| | World Championship | skip | 1 | 9-2 |

# WILK, LUCIE

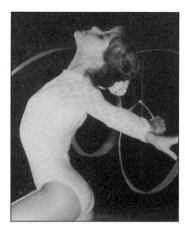

| | |
|---|---|
| sport: | rhythmic gymnastics |
| born: | Toronto, Ontario |
| | June 11, 1972 |
| height: | . . . |
| weight: | . . . |

Lucie Wilk was nine years old in 1981 when her parents enrolled her in the rhythmic gymnastics program at the Seneca Sports Club. Under the guidance of Liliana Dimitrova and Linda Thompson, Wilk quickly developed into a premier gymnast. In 1983, she won the overall title at the Junior-Elite provincial championships. Two years later she placed fifth at the national championships and was selected to represent Canada at the Lahti International Gymnastics meet in Finland. There she placed 15th. In February 1986, Wilk won the overall title at the National Selections Meet. She set her sights on the Seoul Olympics. A serious and unfortunate injury a few months later terminated her gymnastics career.

## RECORD

| year | competition | event | placing |
|---|---|---|---|
| 1983 | Junior Elite Provincial Chmp | all-around | 1 |
| 1985 | Canadian Championship | all-around | 5 |
| | Lahti International (Finland) | all-around | 15 |
| 1986 | National Selection Meet | all-around | 1 |

# WITIUK, STEVE

| | |
|---|---|
| sport: | hockey |
| born: | Winnipeg, Manitoba |
| | January 8, 1929 |
| height: | 1.70 m / 5'7" |
| weight: | 75 kg / 165 lbs |
| position: | right wing |
| shoots: | right |

Steve Witiuk played junior hockey with the Winnipeg Black Hawks. The small but tough winger played professional hockey for almost twenty years. Except for part of one season that he played in the NHL, Witiuk's professional career was in the minor leagues. For six seasons he was with Calgary of the WHL. There he played on the team's most productive line which was responsible for 80 per cent of the goal output. Witiuk was very injury-prone.

## RECORD

| | | | regular season | | | | | playoffs | | | | |
|---|---|---|---|---|---|---|---|---|---|---|---|---|
| year | team | league | GP | G | A | PTS | PIM | GP | G | A | PTS | PIM |
| 1951-52 | Chicago | NHL | 33 | 3 | 8 | 11 | 14 | | | | | |
| | St. Louis | AHL | 14 | 5 | 2 | 7 | 11 | | | | | |
| 1952-53 | Calgary | WHL | 60 | 21 | 20 | 41 | 66 | 1 | 0 | 0 | 0 | 0 |
| 1953-54* | Calgary | WHL | 69 | 19 | 36 | 55 | 52 | 18 | 3 | 6 | 9 | 20 |
| 1954-55 | Calgary | WHL | 60 | 26 | 37 | 63 | 61 | 9 | 5 | 2 | 7 | 14 |
| 1955-56 | Calgary | WHL | 66 | 30 | 34 | 64 | 76 | 8 | 5 | 6 | 11 | 12 |
| 1956-57 | Calgary | WHL | 47 | 17 | 18 | 35 | 55 | | | | | |
| 1957-58 | Calgary/Winnipeg | WHL | 65 | 27 | 46 | 73 | 43 | | | | | |
| | Winnipeg | WHL | | | | | | 7 | 0 | 2 | 2 | 2 |
| 1958-59 | Winnipeg | WHL | 62 | 12 | 33 | 45 | 43 | 6 | 1 | 4 | 5 | 2 |
| 1959-60 | Winnipeg | WHL | 62 | 20 | 27 | 47 | 40 | | | | | |
| 1960-61 | Spokane | WHL | 67 | 28 | 24 | 52 | 79 | 4 | 0 | 1 | 1 | 4 |
| 1961-62 | Spokane | WHL | 64 | 26 | 40 | 66 | 49 | 16 | 4 | 9 | 13 | 34 |
| 1962-63 | Spokane | WHL | 66 | 21 | 33 | 54 | 96 | | | | | |
| 1963-64 | Denver | WHL | 70 | 25 | 28 | 53 | 62 | 4 | 0 | 0 | 0 | 10 |
| 1964-65 | Victoria | WHL | 56 | 11 | 21 | 32 | 37 | 11 | 2 | 2 | 4 | 16 |
| 1965-66* | Victoria | WHL | 72 | 6 | 16 | 22 | 47 | 3 | 0 | 0 | 0 | 0 |
| 1966-67 | Victoria | WHL | 59 | 5 | 10 | 15 | 34 | | | | | |

| year | team | league | regular season | | | | | playoffs | | | | |
|------|------|--------|------|-----|-----|-----|-----|------|-----|-----|-----|-----|
| | | | GP | G | A | PTS | PIM | GP | G | A | PTS | PIM |
| 1967-68 | Spokane | WHL | 41 | 20 | 34 | 54 | 57 | | | | | |

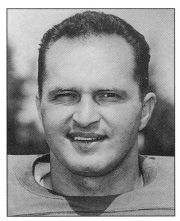

# WLASIUK, GENE

| | |
|---|---|
| sport: | football |
| born: | . . . |
| | . . . |
| height: | 1.73 m / 5'8" |
| weight: | . . . |
| position: | halfback, defensive back |

*Photo courtesy of the Saskatchewan Sports Hall of Fame and Museum*

In 1955, Gene Wlasiuk played with the Winnipeg Rods football club which won the Canadian Junior Football Championship. He saw some action with the Winnipeg Blue Bombers before signing with the Saskatchewan Roughriders in 1959. The Roughriders used the versatile Wlasiuk on offence, defence, and on special teams. On offence, Wlasiuk played sparingly at the halfback position. On defence, he played regularly at the defensive back position, accounting for 27 interceptions in nine seasons.

Gene Wlasiuk's specialty was returning punts. According to Roughrider historians Bob Calder and Garry Andrews, Gene Wlasiuk and Jim Copeland "formed the best punt return combination in the league in the early sixties."[41] The diminutive Wlasiuk was extremely elusive, avoiding would-be tacklers by going underneath them. By the time he retired from the game after the 1967 season, Wlasiuk accumulated 3,333 yards on punt returns. The yardage established a CFL record.

Gene Wlasiuk played in his first Grey Cup game with the Saskatchewan Roughriders in 1966. The Roughriders won the contest, the club's first Grey Cup championship. Overcome by emotion, Wlasiuk wept in the corner of the dressing room after the game. Wlasiuk and the Roughriders returned to the Grey Cup game the following season but came up short. The game was Wlasiuk's last.

| regular season | | | | interception returns | | | | | punt returns | | | | | |
| year | team | league | GP | NO | YDS | AVE | LG | TD | NO | YDS | AVE | LG | TD |
|------|------|--------|-----|-----|-----|-----|-----|-----|-----|-----|-----|-----|-----|
| 1958 | Winnipeg | CFL | ... | | | | | | 59 | 298 | 5.0 | | |
| 1959 | Saskatchewan | CFL | ... | 3 | | | | | 47 | 322 | 6.9 | | |
| 1960 | Saskatchewan | CFL | ... | 4 | | | | | 60 | 334 | 5.6 | | |
| 1961 | Saskatchewan | CFL | ... | 5 | 59 | 11.8 | | | 40 | 407 | 10.2 | | |
| 1962 | Saskatchewan | CFL | ... | 4 | 73 | 18.3 | | | 55 | 325 | 5.9 | | |
| 1963 | Saskatchewan | CFL | ... | 5 | 80 | 16.6 | | | 51 | 307 | 6.0 | | |
| 1964 | Saskatchewan | CFL | ... | 1 | | | | | 78 | 528 | 6.7 | | |
| 1965 | Saskatchewan | CFL | ... | 2 | 10 | 5.0 | | | 84 | 486 | 5.8 | 22 | 0 |
| 1966* | Saskatchewan | CFL | ... | 3 | 25 | 8.3 | | | 79 | 326 | 4.1 | | |
| 1967 | Saskatchewan | CFL | ... | 0 | 0 | 0.0 | 0 | 0 | 0 | 0 | 0.0 | 0 | 0 |

| Grey Cup game | | | | interception returns | | | | | punt returns | | | | | |
| year | team | league | GP | NO | YDS | AVE | LG | TD | NO | YDS | AVE | LG | TD |
|------|------|--------|-----|-----|-----|-----|-----|-----|-----|-----|-----|-----|-----|
| 1966* | Saskatchewan | CFL | 1 | | | | | 0 | 8 | 34 | 4.3 | 11 | 0 |

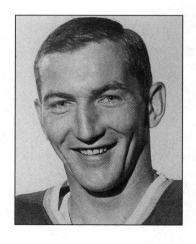

# WOYTOWICH, BOB

"Augie"

| | |
|---|---|
| sport: | hockey |
| given name: | Woytowich, Robert Ivan |
| born: | Winnipeg, Manitoba |
| | August 18, 1941 |
| died: | Winnipeg, Manitoba |
| | July 30, 1988 |
| height: | 1.80 m / 5'11" |
| weight: | 88.5 kg / 195 lbs |
| position: | defense |
| shoots: | right |

After completing his junior hockey tenure with the Winnipeg Rangers, Bob Woytowich turned professional in 1962 with the New York Rangers farm club, the Sudbury Wolves of the EPHL. In the summer of 1964, he was drafted by the Boston Bruins. Woytowich began the new season in the minors with the Hershey Bears. He was called up by the Bruins midway through the year and remained with the club through the 1967 Expansion Draft, where he was selected by the Minnesota North Stars. The fledgling club named Woytowich its first captain.

Prior to the start of the 1968-69 season, Woytowich was traded to the Pittsburgh Penguins. There the fans took an immediate liking to the defenseman with the long stick and effective poke checks, and organized the "Bob Woytowich Polish Army" fan club. Woytowich explained that he was not of Polish descent but that did not matter. "Bob Woytowich Polish Army" banners appeared regularly at the Pittsburgh arena and a dedicated cheering section urged him on. After sitting on the bench for most of the 1971-72 season, Woytowich was traded to the Los Angeles Kings. In the summer of 1972, the Winnipeg Jets made Woytowich an offer he could not refuse and he jumped to the newly organized rival World Hockey Association.

Bob Woytowich played for the Jets for more than two seasons. In December of 1974, he was sold to the Indianapolis Racers. Subsequently, Woytowich coached Mohawk Valley of the NAHL.

## INDUCTIONS

1989          Manitoba Hockey Hall of Fame

## ALL-STAR SELECTIONS

1963-64      defense      CPHL      First Team

## RECORD

| year | team | league | regular season | | | | | playoffs | | | | |
|------|------|--------|------|------|------|------|------|------|------|------|------|------|
| | | | GP | G | A | PTS | PIM | GP | G | A | PTS | PIM |
| 1960-61 | Seattle | WHL | 2 | 0 | 0 | 0 | 0 | | | | | |
| 1962-63 | Sudbury | EPHL | 71 | 17 | 27 | 44 | 69 | 8 | 0 | 3 | 3 | 0 |
| 1963-64 | St. Paul | CPHL | 68 | 9 | 31 | 40 | 101 | 11 | 2 | 4 | 6 | 8 |
| 1964-65 | Boston | NHL | 21 | 2 | 10 | 12 | 16 | | | | | |
| | Hershey | AHL | 48 | 5 | 21 | 26 | 56 | | | | | |
| 1965-66 | Boston | NHL | 68 | 2 | 17 | 19 | 75 | | | | | |
| 1966-67 | Boston | NHL | 64 | 2 | 7 | 9 | 43 | | | | | |
| 1967-68 | Minnesota | NHL | 66 | 4 | 17 | 21 | 63 | 14 | 0 | 1 | 1 | 18 |
| 1968-69 | Pittsburgh | NHL | 71 | 9 | 20 | 29 | 62 | | | | | |
| 1969-70 | Pittsburgh | NHL | 68 | 8 | 25 | 33 | 49 | 10 | 1 | 2 | 3 | 2 |
| 1970-71 | Pittsburgh | NHL | 78 | 4 | 22 | 26 | 30 | | | | | |
| 1971-72 | Pittsburgh | NHL | 31 | 1 | 4 | 5 | 8 | | | | | |

| year | team | league | regular season | | | | | playoffs | | | | |
|---|---|---|---|---|---|---|---|---|---|---|---|---|
| | | | GP | G | A | PTS | PIM | GP | G | A | PTS | PIM |
| 1971-72 | Los Angeles | NHL | 36 | 0 | 4 | 4 | 6 | | | | | |
| 1972-73 | Winnipeg | WHA | 62 | 2 | 4 | 6 | 47 | 14 | 1 | 1 | 2 | 4 |
| 1973-74 | Winnipeg | WHA | 72 | 6 | 28 | 34 | 43 | 4 | 0 | 0 | 0 | 0 |
| 1974-75 | Winnipeg | WHA | 24 | 0 | 4 | 4 | 8 | | | | | |
| | Indianapolis | WHA | 42 | 0 | 8 | 8 | 28 | | | | | |
| 1975-76 | Indianapolis | WHA | 42 | 1 | 7 | 8 | 14 | | | | | |
| 1976-77 | Mohawk Valley | NAHL | 37 | 0 | 10 | 10 | 4 | | | | | |

# WOZNESENSKY, LYALL

"Woz," "The Woztusi"

sport: football
born: Melville, Saskatchewan
April 4, 1953
height: 2.01 m / 6'7"
weight: 109 kg / 240 lbs
position: defensive end

Photo courtesy of the Canadian Football Hall of Fame and Museum

Lyall Woznesensky joined the Winnipeg Blue Bombers football club in 1977 after playing collegiate football at Simon Fraser University. He was one of two varsity players whom Winnipeg protected in the Territorial Exemptions prior to that year's draft. In his first season with the Bombers, Woznesensky was named the club's rookie of the year and was the club's nominee for the Schenley Rookie Award. In 1979, Woznesensky was traded to the Calgary Stampeders where he gained a reputation as one of the best pass rushers in the league. He used his massive frame to neutralize the passing game of opponents.

In 1980, Woznesensky signed with the Hamilton Tiger-Cats. The team had a successful season and advanced to the Grey Cup game. Woznesensky, though, was released by Hamilton at the end of the year. He signed as a free agent with the Saskatchewan Roughriders in 1981. He had an excellent season, registering 13 quarterback sacks and being named to the CFL All-Western All-star team. He was also nominated for the Schenley Most Outstanding Canadian Award. During the 1983 season, Woznesensky played for the Toronto Argonauts and the

Montreal Concordes. He ended his career in 1984 with the Calgary Stampeders. That year he was once again nominated for the Schenley Most Outstanding Canadian Award.

AWARDS

1978      Manitoba Ukrainian Sportsman of the Year

ALL-STAR SELECTIONS

1981      defensive end    CFL   All-Western

# WUSYK, BILL

| | |
|---|---|
| sport: | football |
| given name: | Wusyk, William |
| born: | Calgary, Alberta |
| | April 18, 1918 |
| died: | Calgary, Alberta |
| | December 8, 1975 |
| height: | 1.73 m / 5'8" |
| weight: | 90.5 kg / 200 lbs |
| position: | quarterback, halfback, flying wing |

In 1935, when Bill Wusyk was 17 years old, he joined a newly organized football team, the Calgary Bronks. A stand-out at the quarterback position with Technical High, Wusyk jumped at the opportunity to play senior level football with the Bronks. The first few years, he played infrequently; he lacked experience and was somewhat underweight. By the 1938 season, Wusyk put on some weight and matured into a fine all-round athlete. He played regularly at the flying wing and quarterback positions. When not handling the ball, Wusyk was used effectively as a blocker. He was also a capable defensive player. Wusyk played with the Bronks through the completion of the 1940 season. At that time, the club suspended operations because of World War II.

During the war, Bill Wusyk volunteered for active service in the Air Force and Army but was rejected. He even travelled to Vancouver to enlist in the Navy, only to be rejected again. Dejected, he returned to Calgary where he worked in the steel industry and coached junior football teams.

After the cessation of hostilities in 1945, Bill Wusyk and a number of other football players brought senior football back to the city when they organized the Calgary Stampeders. The team played only a few games that fall since there was no regular schedule. The following year, when a full schedule was restored, Bill Wusyk led the WIFU in scoring with 32 points. All the points were scored by kicking, and the media began referring to his toe as being "educated." That year, Wusyk was a near-unanimous selection to the Western All-star team at the flying wing position. He was also the inaugural winner of the Jeff Nicklin Memorial Trophy, awarded to the player in the WIFU judged most valuable to his team.

In 1948, the Calgary Stampeders recorded an undefeated season. When the team arrived in Toronto for the Grey Cup game, Calgary fans revelled through downtown Toronto on saddle horses and chuck wagons. The spontaneous pageantry led to the official organization of parades in the future. Roused by their fans, the Stampeders won the Grey Cup. Wusyk, though, did not play in the game. He was kept on the sidelines by a revised league rule, which reduced the number of players eligible to dress for the game. Nevertheless, for Wusyk the championship was the culmination of a 13-year career. He finally was a member of a Grey Cup team. He was also the only player of the original 1935 Bronks still with the team. After the game, Wusyk retired from football.

Bill Wusyk was also a fine baseball player. In 1935, while playing at the catcher position, he helped a Calgary team win the Alberta junior title. Wusyk also enjoyed curling and golf, which he pursued avidly after retiring from football.

## AWARDS

1946        Jeff Nicklin Memorial Trophy

## ALL-STAR SELECTIONS

1946        flying wing          WIFU

## RECORD

| scoring | | | regular season | | | | | | playoffs | | | | | | Grey Cup game | | | | | |
|---|---|---|---|---|---|---|---|---|---|---|---|---|---|---|---|---|---|---|---|---|
| year | team | league | GP | TD | C | FG | S | PTS | GP | TD | C | FG | S | PTS | GP | TD | C | FG | S | PTS |
| 1936 | Calgary | WIFU | ... | | | | | | | | | | | | | | | | | |
| 1937 | Calgary | WIFU | ... | | | | | | | | | | | | | | | | | |
| 1938 | Calgary | WIFU | ... | | | | | | | | | | | | | | | | | |
| 1939 | Calgary | WIFU | ... | | | | | | 2 | 0 | 0 | 0 | 0 | 0 | | | | | | |
| 1940 | Calgary | WIFU | 8 | 2 | 0 | 0 | 1 | 11 | | | | | | | | | | | | |

| year | team | league | GP | TD | C | FG | S | PTS | GP | TD | C | FG | S | PTS | GP | TD | C | FG | S | PTS |
|---|---|---|---|---|---|---|---|---|---|---|---|---|---|---|---|---|---|---|---|---|
| | | | regular season | | | | | | playoffs | | | | | | Grey Cup game | | | | | |
| 1945 | Calgary | WIFU | 1 | 0 | 0 | 0 | 0 | 0 | 3 | 0 | 0 | 0 | 0 | 0 | | | | | | |
| 1946 | Calgary | WIFU | 8 | 0 | 4 | 8 | 4 | 32 | 2 | 0 | 2 | 1 | 0 | 5 | | | | | | |
| 1947 | Calgary | WIFU | 8 | 0 | 8 | 4 | 1 | 21 | 3 | 0 | 2 | 3 | 0 | 11 | | | | | | |
| 1948* | Calgary | WIFU | ... | 0 | 12 | 0 | 0 | 12 | 2 | 0 | 0 | 0 | 0 | 0 | 0 | 0 | 0 | 0 | 0 | 0 |

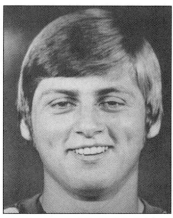

# WYROZUB, RANDY

| | |
|---|---|
| sport: | hockey |
| given name: | Wyrozub, William Randall |
| born: | Lacombe, Alberta |
| | April 8, 1950 |
| height: | 1.80 m / 5'11" |
| weight: | 77 kg / 170 lbs |
| position: | center |
| shoots: | left |

*Photo courtesy of the Buffalo Sabres*

The Buffalo Sabres drafted Randy Wyrozub from the Edmonton Oil Kings in the fourth round, 43rd overall, of the 1970 NHL Entry Draft. Wyrozub's rookie season included play for the Sabres and an assignment to Salt Lake City of the WHL. He also missed part of the season because of an eye injury and a fractured collarbone. Wyrozub played with the Buffalo organization for four seasons. During that time, he made only 100 appearances in a Buffalo uniform, spending much time in the minors. In the summer of 1984, he was selected by the Washington Capitals in the NHL Expansion Draft. Once again he ended up playing in the minors. The following year the stocky, hard-hitting Wyrozub jumped to the Indianapolis Racers of the WHA.

## RECORD

| year | team | league | GP | G | A | PTS | PIM | GP | G | A | PTS | PIM |
|---|---|---|---|---|---|---|---|---|---|---|---|---|
| | | | regular season | | | | | playoffs | | | | |
| 1970-71 | Buffalo | NHL | 16 | 2 | 2 | 4 | 6 | | | | | |
| | Salt Lake City | WHL | 23 | 7 | 4 | 11 | 2 | | | | | |
| 1971-72 | Buffalo | NHL | 34 | 3 | 4 | 7 | 0 | | | | | |

| | | | regular season | | | | | playoffs | | | | |
|---|---|---|---|---|---|---|---|---|---|---|---|---|
| year | team | league | GP | G | A | PTS | PIM | GP | G | A | PTS | PIM |
| 1971-72 | Cincinnati | AHL | 35 | 14 | 14 | 28 | 10 | | | | | |
| 1972-73 | Buffalo | NHL | 45 | 3 | 3 | 6 | 4 | | | | | |
| 1973-74 | Buffalo | NHL | 5 | 0 | 1 | 1 | 0 | | | | | |
| | Cincinnati | AHL | 69 | 22 | 35 | 57 | 17 | 5 | 0 | 3 | 3 | 0 |
| 1974-75 | Richmond | AHL | 71 | 21 | 32 | 53 | 31 | 7 | 2 | 3 | 5 | 6 |
| 1975-76 | Indianapolis | WHA | 55 | 11 | 14 | 25 | 8 | | | | | |
| | Mohawk Valley | NAHL | 11 | 6 | 7 | 13 | 0 | 4 | 1 | 2 | 3 | 5 |
| 1976-77 | Mohawk Valley | NAHL | 73 | 26 | 57 | 83 | 18 | 5 | 4 | 2 | 6 | 2 |
| 1977-78 | San Francisco | PHL | 42 | 27 | 33 | 60 | 12 | | | | | |
| 1978-79 | Tuscon | PHL | 29 | 15 | 20 | 35 | 0 | | | | | |
| | Erie | EHL | 19 | 6 | 10 | 16 | 6 | | | | | |

# YAKIWCHUK, ALANNA

sport: athletics
born: Winnipeg, Manitoba
April 17, 1965
height: 1.68 m / 5'6"
weight: 55 kg / 120 lbs

After working for two years as the Technical Director of the Manitoba Five Pin Bowling Federation, Alanna Yakiwchuk returned to school in 1988 to pursue a Bachelor of Education degree and to train seriously for the 400-metre sprint. Results were immediate. She established Manitoba records in the 400 metres and was named to represent Canada at the first Francophone Games in Morocco. She qualified for the semi-finals but became extremely ill the next day with food poisoning. The following year, she won the 400 metres at a tri-country meet with a personal best of 53.63. At the 1991 Pan American Games, Alanna Yakiwchuk's 55.61 was not fast enough to qualify her for the final. A year later, she lowered her personal best in the 400 metres to 52.67 seconds.

# AWARDS

1989       Athletics Manitoba - Female Sprint Athlete of the Year

## ALL-STAR SELECTIONS

1989       All-Canadian
1990       All-Canadian

## RECORD

| year | competition | event | placing | result |
|------|-------------|-------|---------|--------|
| 1988 | Canadian Indoor Championships | 400 m | 7 | 56.90 |
|      | Canadian Championships | 400 m | 10 | 56.33 |
| 1989 | CIAU Indoor Championships | 300 m | 2 | 38.92 |
|      | Canadian Indoor Championships | 400 m | 2 | 54.98 |
|      | Canadian Championships | 400 m | 7 | 55.8 |
|      | National Sprint Camp, Utah | 400 m | 4 | 53.93 |
|      | Francophone Games | 400 m | | |
| 1990 | CIAU Indoor Championships | 300 m | 1 | 38.16 |
|      | Canadian Championships | 200 m | 5 | 24.64 |
|      |  | 400 m | 3 | 54.26 |
|      | Canada vs GDR and GBR | 400 m | 1 | 53.63 |
| 1991 | Canadian Championships | 200 m | 7 | 24.59 |
|      |  | 400 m | 8 | 56.07 |
|      | Pan American Games | 400 m | 6 SF | 55.61 |
| 1992 | Utah | 400 m | | 52.67 |
|      | Canadian Championships | 400 m | 2 | 53.81 |

# YAREMCHUK, GARY

"Weasel"

| | |
|---|---|
| sport: | hockey |
| born: | Edmonton, Alberta |
| | August 15, 1961 |
| height: | 1.83 m / 6'0" |
| weight: | 83 kg / 183 lbs |
| position: | center |
| shoots: | left |

After a junior career that included play for Fort Saskatchewan and the Portland Winter Hawks, Gary Yaremchuk was selected by the Toronto Maple Leafs in the second round, 24th overall, of the 1981 NHL Entry Draft. He was with the Toronto organization for four years but saw only limited action; most of the time was spent playing minor pro hockey in the farm system. In the summer of 1985, he was signed as a free agent by the Detroit Red Wings and promptly farmed out to the Adirondack Red Wings. The following year, Gary Yaremchuk took his hockey skills to Finland and played a number of seasons there. Gary Yaremchuk is the brother of hockey player Ken Yaremchuk.

## RECORD

| year | team | league | regular season | | | | | playoffs | | | | |
|---|---|---|---|---|---|---|---|---|---|---|---|---|
| | | | GP | G | A | PTS | PIM | GP | G | A | PTS | PIM |
| 1981-82 | Toronto | NHL | 18 | 0 | 3 | 3 | 10 | | | | | |
| | Cincinnati | AHL | 53 | 21 | 35 | 56 | 101 | 4 | 0 | 2 | 2 | 4 |
| 1982-83 | Toronto | NHL | 3 | 0 | 0 | 0 | 2 | | | | | |
| | St.Catharines | AHL | 61 | 17 | 28 | 45 | 72 | | | | | |
| 1983-84 | Toronto | NHL | 1 | 0 | 0 | 0 | 0 | | | | | |
| | St. Catharines | AHL | 73 | 24 | 37 | 61 | 64 | 7 | 5 | 1 | 6 | 2 |
| 1984-85 | Toronto | NHL | 12 | 1 | 1 | 2 | 16 | | | | | |
| | St. Catharines | AHL | 66 | 17 | 47 | 64 | 75 | | | | | |
| 1985-86* | Adirondack | AHL | 60 | 12 | 32 | 44 | 90 | 1 | 1 | 0 | 1 | 0 |
| 1986-87 | Jokerit | Finnish | 20 | 7 | 21 | 28 | 116 | | | | | |
| 1987-88 | Karpat | Finnish | 36 | 16 | 27 | 43 | 92 | | | | | |
| 1988-89 | Kookoo | Finnish | 44 | 12 | 27 | 39 | 50 | | | | | |
| 1989-90 | Kookoo | Finnish | 42 | 16 | 19 | 35 | 81 | | | | | |

# YAREMCHUK, KEN

| | |
|---|---|
| sport: | hockey |
| born: | Edmonton, Alberta |
| | January 1, 1964 |
| height: | 1.80 m / 5'11" |
| weight: | 84 kg / 185 lbs |
| position: | center |
| shoots: | right |

*Photo courtesy of the Toronto Maple Leafs*

Ken Yaremchuk was a highly touted junior when he played for the Portland Winter Hawks of the WHL. During three seasons he scored 165 goals and added 287 assists. For his efforts he was honoured with two all-star selections. The Chicago Black Hawks selected Yaremchuk as an underage junior in the first round, seventh overall, of the 1982 NHL Entry Draft. Yaremchuk played with Chicago for three seasons but lacked the offensive spark of his junior days. In addition, the speedy and clever center had problems with positional play, particularly when he did not have the puck. In the summer of 1987, the Blackhawks traded him to the Toronto Maple Leafs.

Yaremchuk made sporadic appearances with the Leafs during the 1987-88 season. The following year, the Leafs gave Yaremchuk a choice of reporting to their farm team or playing for Canada's 1988 Olympic team. Yaremchuk chose the Olympic program. The Canadian team placed fourth at the Calgary Games. After the Olympics, Yaremchuk returned to the Toronto organization. He saw action with both the Leafs and their farm club at Newmarket. Subsequently, he played in Italy and Switzerland. Ken Yaremchuk is the brother of hockey player Gary Yaremchuk.

## ALL-STAR SELECTIONS

1983      center   Memorial Cup All-Star Team

## RECORD

| | | | regular season | | | | | playoffs | | | | |
|---|---|---|---|---|---|---|---|---|---|---|---|---|
| year | team | league | GP | G | A | PTS | PIM | GP | G | A | PTS | PIM |
| 1983-84 | Chicago | NHL | 47 | 6 | 7 | 13 | 19 | 1 | 0 | 0 | 0 | 0 |
| 1984-85 | Chicago | NHL | 63 | 10 | 16 | 26 | 16 | 15 | 5 | 5 | 10 | 37 |

| | | | regular season | | | | | playoffs | | | | |
|---|---|---|---|---|---|---|---|---|---|---|---|---|
| year | team | league | GP | G | A | PTS | PIM | GP | G | A | PTS | PIM |
| 1984-85 | Milwaukee | IHL | 7 | 4 | 6 | 10 | 9 | | | | | |
| 1985-86 | Chicago | NHL | 78 | 14 | 20 | 34 | 43 | 3 | 1 | 1 | 2 | 2 |
| 1986-87 | Toronto | NHL | 20 | 3 | 8 | 11 | 16 | 6 | 0 | 0 | 0 | 0 |
| | Newmarket | AHL | 14 | 2 | 4 | 6 | 21 | | | | | |
| 1987-88 | Toronto | NHL | 16 | 2 | 5 | 7 | 10 | 6 | 0 | 2 | 2 | 10 |
| | Olympic Team | | 38 | 15 | 18 | 33 | 63 | | | | | |
| 1988-89 | Toronto | NHL | 11 | 1 | 0 | 1 | 2 | | | | | |
| | Newmarket | AHL | 55 | 25 | 33 | 58 | 145 | 5 | 7 | 7 | 14 | 12 |
| 1989-90 | Asiago | Italian | 34 | 37 | 76 | 113 | 32 | | | | | |
| 1990-91 | Zug | Swiss | 26 | 17 | 14 | 31 | | | | | | |

international

| year | team | competition | GP | G | A | PTS | PIM | Place |
|---|---|---|---|---|---|---|---|---|
| 1988 | Canada | Olympic Games | 8 | 3 | 3 | 6 | 2 | 4 |

# ZADUK, PETE

"Punchin' Pete"

| | |
|---|---|
| sport: | boxing |
| born: | Guelph, Ontario |
| | April 9, 1928 |
| height: | . . . |
| weight: | 66 kg / 145 lbs |

Pete Zaduk started to box in his teens. As an amateur lightweight, he appeared in 55 bouts and lost only four. At 19 years of age, Zaduk turned professional, competing as a welterweight. He developed into an extremely hard puncher and won many of his bouts by knockouts. Zaduk's fighting prowess was admired by boxing fans, and promoters were eager to have him on their card. Pete Zaduk's brothers Bill and Mike were also well-known boxers.

## INDUCTIONS

1975    Canadian Boxing Hall of Fame

# ZAKALUZNY, WALTER

sport: soccer
given name: Zakaluzny, Wolodymyr
born: Przemysl, Poland
May 2, 1925
height: 1.75 m / 5'9"
weight: 77 kg / 170 lbs
position: forward, half back

Walter Zakaluzny began his soccer career in Przemysl with the Ukrainian junior Sian club in the late 1930s. World War II put a hold on his sport aspirations. After the war, Zakaluzny resumed his career with the FC Phonix of Karlsruhe of the Suddeutschen Oberliga and with the Ukrainian club Dnister, which operated out of the Zuffenhausen Displaced Persons Camp. In 1948, he was named to the Ukrainian soccer team for the Displaced Persons Olympics. After a round robin tournament, Ukraine was tied with Poland and Latvia for top spot. A round robin final was then played, and Ukraine won both its games and the gold medal. Zakaluzny scored three of Ukraine's ten goals in the final. One of the goals was scored using a spectacular over-the-head scissors kick.

After the DP Olympics, Zakaluzny played with the DP club Sitch Regensburg. The coach of the German team Jahn Regensburg was impressed with Zakaluzny's game and signed him to a contract. Subsequently, Zakaluzny played with Shwaben Augsburg in the German Oberliga.

In 1951, Zakaluzny arrived in Canada and joined the SA Ukraina soccer team. He was with the club when it won three consecutive National League championships commencing in 1953. In 1956, Zakaluzny played for the Ukrainian American Sports Club (UASC) of Rochester. The club advanced to the semi-finals of the American championship. In 1957, UASC won the Eastern US championship and advanced to the final of the US championship. That series concluded, Zakaluzny joined the Canadian national team in the preliminary round of the 1958 World Cup playdowns. Canada defeated the United States twice, 5-1 and 3-2. Against Mexico, Canada lost twice and was eliminated from further play. In 1958, Zakaluzny returned to SA Ukraina before transferring to SA Ukraina of Montreal for the 1960 season. He retired as an active player after completing the 1961 season with UASC of Rochester.

Walter Zakaluzny was an intense and fearless forward who eagerly challenged opponents for the possession of the soccer ball. One of his recognized specialties was heading the ball. In winter Zakaluzny played competitive volleyball and table tennis.

For many years, Walter Zakaluzny coached and managed SA Ukraina junior teams. In 1965, he was elected to the executive of the Sport Association Ukraina. He held various administrative positions through 1991.

## RECORD

competitive

| year | team |
| --- | --- |
| 1947 | FC Phonix - Karlsruhe, Germany |
| | Dnister - Zuffenhausen, Germany |
| 1948 | Sitch - Regensburg, Germany |
| 1949-50 | FC Jahn - Regensburg, Germany |
| 1950-51 | Shwaben - Augsburg, Germany |
| 1951-55 | SA Ukraina - Toronto |
| 1955-56 | Ukrainian American Sports Club - Rochester, USA |
| 1956-57 | Hellas - Toronto |
| 1958-59 | SA Ukraina - Toronto |
| 1960 | SA Ukraina - Montreal |
| 1961 | Ukrainian American Sports Club - Rochester, USA |

international

| year | team | competition | GP | G | Place |
| --- | --- | --- | --- | --- | --- |
| 1957 | Canada | World Cup Qualifying | 4 | 0 | eliminated |

# ZAMICK, VICTOR

"Chick"

| | |
| --- | --- |
| sport: | hockey |
| born: | Winnipeg, Manitoba |
| | August 16, 1926 |
| height: | 1.73 m / 5'8" |
| weight: | 63.5 kg / 140 lbs |
| position: | centre |
| shoots: | left |

Victor "Chick" Zamick was one of Canada's greatest exports to England. He was the first player in English hockey to score 500 goals and one of only two to surpass the 1,000 goal plateau. Zamick's Canadian hockey roots, though, are less than inspiring; nothing suggested that he would become a perennial all-star. In Winnipeg, Zamick played for the Canadian Ukrainian Athletic Club. Later he played junior hockey in St. Catharines.

Chick Zamick's arrival in England in 1947 can at best be described as accidental. Phil Drackett, editor of *Ice Hockey World*, recounted it in his book *Flashing Blades - The Story of British Ice Hockey*: "During the off-season, 'Sandy' Archer, back in Winnipeg to replace the weak links in his Nottingham side, had recruited some useful-looking men including a centre of excellent repute. However, forty-eight hours before the party was due to leave for England, the centreman pulled out. Archer, at his wit's end, grabbed the first player he could find, a skinny, undersized and undernourished Ukrainian youngster called Victor Zamick. 'I thought I was crazy to take a chance on him. I was sure he would be a failure,' Archer was to say later. Nottingham officials who met the boat thought Archer was crazy too. At first they did not realize that this ill-at-ease youngster was one of their new players. When they were told they nearly collapsed of shock."[42]

In his first season with the Nottingham Panthers of the English National League, Chick Zamick dispelled all preconceived notions about his hockey ability. He led the league in scoring with 124 points in 56 games and was voted *Ice Hockey World* Most Popular Player. In subsequent years, Zamick proved that he was not a one-season phenomenon. Five times he was the league scoring champion. His scoring prowess peaked in 1954-55 when he netted 94 goals and assisted on 75 others for a league-leading total of 169 points. Zamick became the first player in British hockey to score 500 goals, and two seasons later, he became the first player in the world to score 600 goals in senior hockey.

Hockey scribe Andy O'Brien wrote in 1956 that Chick Zamick is a "spurt player - not too fast, but highly deceptive with a shift from either foot. He has good balance and neat balance. His shot isn't hard but accurate and, like all great scorers, he gets it away with minimum waste of time."[43]

In 1951, Zamick led Nottingham to their first English League championship. In 1955, he helped Nottingham win the international Ahearne Cup. The following year, as a playing coach, he guided Nottingham to the British title. In 1958, Zamick assumed the duties of playing coach with Servette Geneva. In his first season, the team captured the Swiss Cup. Zamick remained with the club for two more years before returning to Britain where he played for the Altrincham Aces and subsequently for the Wembley Lions. After retiring as a player, Chick Zamick coached Nottingham for a number of years. Chick Zamick's brothers Paul and Joe and cousin Ted Semeniuk played briefly with Nottingham during that era.

# INDUCTIONS

| 1951 | British Ice Hockey Hall of Fame |

# AWARDS

| 1949 | Player of the Year, English National League |
| 1949 | Nottingham Sportsman of the Year |
| 1951 | Nottingham Sportsman of the Year |

# ALL-STAR SELECTIONS

| 1947-48 | centre | English League | "B" Team |
| 1948-49 | centre | English League | "A" Team |
| 1949-50 | centre | English League | "B" Team |
| 1950-51 | centre | English League | "A" Team |
| 1951-52 | centre | English League | "A" Team |
| 1952-53 | centre | English League | "A" Team |
| 1953-54 | centre | English League | "B" Team |
| 1954-55 | centre | British League | "A" Team |
| 1955-56 | centre | British League | "A" Team |
| 1957-58 | centre | British League | "A" Team |

# RECORD

| year | team | league | GP | G | A | PTS | PIM |
|------|------|--------|-----|-----|-----|-----|-----|
| 1947-48 | Nottingham | English | 56 | 65 | 59 | 124 | 8 |
| 1948-49 | Nottingham | English | 56 | 80 | 54 | 134 | 22 |
| 1949-50 | Nottingham | English | 70 | 87 | 61 | 148 | 26 |
| 1950-51* | Nottingham | English | 58 | 78 | 61 | 139 | 34 |
| 1951-52 | Nottingham | English | 41 | 47 | 51 | 98 | 22 |
| 1952-53 | Nottingham | English | 60 | 74 | 57 | 131 | 20 |
| 1953-54* | Nottingham | English | 57 | 69 | 55 | 124 | 12 |
| 1954-55 | Nottingham | British | 62 | 94 | 75 | 169 | 16 |
| 1955-56* | Nottingham | British | 56 | 62 | 73 | 135 | 12 |
| 1956-57 | Nottingham | British | 53 | 50 | 53 | 103 | 9 |
| 1957-58 | Nottingham | British | 55 | 72 | 46 | 118 | 11 |
| 1958-59* | Geneva | Swiss | ... | | | | |
| 1959-60 | Geneva | Swiss | ... | | | | |
| 1960-61 | Geneva | Swiss | ... | | | | |
| 1961-62 | Altrincham | British | 4 | 9 | 7 | 16 | |
| 1963-64 | Wembley | British | 11 | 19 | 12 | 31 | 0 |

# ZUBKEWYCH, MORRIS

sport:       football
born:        . . .
             July 4, 1951
height:      1.93 m / 6'4"
weight:      113.5 kg / 250 lbs
position:    centre, defensive tackle

Morris Zubkewych first gained prominence while attending Toronto's Humberside Collegiate. He was an all-star middle linebacker on the school's championship football team, played basketball, and was the city champion in the discus and the shot put events. Zubkewych then enrolled at Simon Fraser University. He was a versatile starter on the school's football team, seeing action at the defensive tackle and end as well as offensive tackle and centre positions. In 1974, the Toronto Argonauts selected Zubkewych in the CFL Territorial Exemption Draft. At training camp that spring, Zubkewych won the starting assignment at the centre position. He had a good rookie year. After spending the off-season lifting weights to gain bulk, Zubkewych suffered a severely broken leg during a scrimmage. He sat out the 1975 season. After a winter-long rehabilitation program, Zubkewych returned to the Argos, but saw limited action. After retiring from football, Morris Zubkewych pursued a career in chiropractic medicine in Toronto.

# ZUKE, MIKE

"Zuker"
sport:        hockey
given name:   Zuke, Michael
born:         Sault Ste. Marie, Ontario
              April 16, 1954
height:       1.83 m / 6'0"
weight:       81.5 kg / 180 lbs
position:     center
shoots:       right

Mike Zuke played junior hockey with the Sault Ste. Marie Greyhounds during the 1971-72 season.  The following year he opted to combine an education with hockey and he enrolled in the business administration program at Michigan Tech.  In his rookie collegiate year, he was named Freshman of the Year in the WCHA.  Twice he was selected to the first team All-American West.  In 1976, at the conclusion of his last season of collegiate hockey, he was named the league's most valuable player.

Mike Zuke was drafted by the St. Louis Blues in the fifth round of the 1974 draft.  He decided to delay turning professional until after he finished his studies in 1976.  Zuke began his professional career playing for the Indianapolis Racers and the Edmonton Oilers of the WHA before signing with the Blues in September of 1978.  He was with the Blues for five seasons before being picked up by the Hartford Whalers in the 1983 NHL Waiver Draft.

Mike Zuke was an imaginative center with a good shot and excellent stickhandling abilities.  He was also good at faceoffs.  While with the Blues, Zuke was used extensively to kill penalties.  He quickly gained a reputation as one of the league's most effective penalty killers.  A tenacious forechecker, he was constantly hustling to neutralize powerplays.  During the 1978-79 season, the Blues penalty killing team, which included Zuke, was the most effective in the league with an 84.8 per cent success rate.

## RECORD

| year | team | league | regular season | | | | | playoffs | | | | |
|---|---|---|---|---|---|---|---|---|---|---|---|---|
| | | | GP | G | A | PTS | PIM | GP | G | A | PTS | PIM |
| 1976-77 | Indianapolis | WHA | 15 | 3 | 4 | 7 | 2 | | | | | |
| | Mohawk Valley | NAHL | 48 | 42 | 29 | 71 | 33 | | | | | |
| 1977-78 | Edmonton | WHA | 71 | 23 | 34 | 57 | 47 | 5 | 2 | 3 | 5 | 0 |
| 1978-79 | St. Louis | NHL | 34 | 9 | 17 | 26 | 18 | | | | | |
| | Salt Lake City | CHL | 29 | 9 | 13 | 22 | 4 | | | | | |
| 1979-80 | St. Louis | NHL | 69 | 22 | 42 | 64 | 30 | 3 | 0 | 0 | 0 | 2 |
| 1980-81 | St. Louis | NHL | 74 | 24 | 44 | 68 | 57 | 11 | 4 | 5 | 9 | 4 |
| 1981-82 | St. Louis | NHL | 76 | 13 | 40 | 53 | 41 | 8 | 1 | 1 | 2 | 2 |
| 1982-83 | St. Louis | NHL | 43 | 8 | 16 | 24 | 14 | 4 | 1 | 0 | 1 | 4 |
| | Salt Lake City | CHL | 13 | 7 | 8 | 15 | 0 | | | | | |
| 1983-84 | Hartford | NHL | 75 | 6 | 23 | 29 | 36 | | | | | |
| 1984-85 | Hartford | NHL | 67 | 4 | 12 | 16 | 12 | | | | | |
| 1985-86 | Hartford | NHL | 17 | 0 | 2 | 2 | 12 | | | | | |

# APPENDICES

# Appendix I

## NATIONAL AND PROVINCIAL CLUB CHAMPIONS

### NATIONAL

| | | | |
|---|---|---|---|
| 1957 | SA Ukraina, Montreal | soccer | (M) |
| 1965 | Canadian Ukrainian Athletic Club, Winnipeg | softball | (F) |
| 1975 | SA Ukraina, Toronto | volleyball | (M) |

Junior

| | | | |
|---|---|---|---|
| 1952 | Institute Prosvita Athletic Club, Winnipeg | soccer | (M) |
| 1965 | Ukrainian Youth Association Plast, Toronto | volleyball | (F) |
| 1966 | Ukrainian Youth Association Plast, Toronto | volleyball | (F) |

### PROVINCIAL

#### MANITOBA

| | | | |
|---|---|---|---|
| 1938 | Canadian Ukrainian Athletic Club, Winnipeg | softball | (F) |
| 1941 | Canadian Ukrainian Athletic Club, Winnipeg | softball | (F) |
| | Canadian Ukrainian Athletic Club, Winnipeg | baseball | (M) |
| 1942 | Canadian Ukrainian Athletic Club, Winnipeg | softball | (F) |
| | Canadian Ukrainian Athletic Club, Winnipeg | baseball | (M) |
| 1943 | Canadian Ukrainian Athletic Club, Winnipeg | baseball | (M) |
| 1944 | Canadian Ukrainian Athletic Club, Winnipeg | baseball | (M) |
| 1946 | Canadian Ukrainian Athletic Club, Winnipeg | baseball | (M) |
| 1947 | Canadian Ukrainian Athletic Club, Winnipeg | softball | (F) |
| | Canadian Ukrainian Athletic Club, Winnipeg | baseball | (M) |
| 1949 | Canadian Ukrainian Athletic Club, Winnipeg | basketball | (F) |
| 1950 | Canadian Ukrainian Athletic Club, Winnipeg | basketball | (F) |
| | Canadian Ukrainian Athletic Club, Winnipeg | baseball | (M) |
| 1952 | Ukrainian Canadian Veterans Branch 141, Winnipeg | fastball | (M) |
| | Canadian Ukrainian Athletic Club, Winnipeg | baseball | (M) |
| 1953 | Canadian Ukrainian Athletic Club, Winnipeg | softball | (F) |

| | | | |
|---|---|---|---|
| | Ukrainian Canadian Veterans Branch 141, Winnipeg | fastball | (M) |
| 1954 | Institute Prosvita Athletic Club, Winnipeg | soccer | (M) |
| | Canadian Ukrainian Athletic Club, Winnipeg | baseball | (M) |
| 1955 | Institute Prosvita Athletic Club, Winnipeg | soccer | (M) |
| 1957 | Canadian Ukrainian Athletic Club, Winnipeg | softball | (F) |
| 1958 | Canadian Ukrainian Athletic Club, Winnipeg | softball | (F) |
| 1959 | Canadian Ukrainian Athletic Club, Winnipeg | softball | (F) |
| 1960 | Canadian Ukrainian Athletic Club, Winnipeg | softball | (F) |
| 1961 | Canadian Ukrainian Athletic Club, Winnipeg | softball | (F) |
| 1962 | Canadian Ukrainian Athletic Club, Winnipeg | softball | (F) |
| | Institute Prosvita Athletic Club , Winnipeg | basketball | (M) |
| 1963 | Canadian Ukrainian Athletic Club, Winnipeg | softball | (F) |
| | Institute Prosvita Athletic Club, Winnipeg | basketball | (M) |
| 1964 | Canadian Ukrainian Athletic Club, Winnipeg | softball | (F) |
| | Institute Prosvita Athletic Club, Winnipeg | basketball | (M) |
| 1965 | Canadian Ukrainian Athletic Club, Winnipeg | softball | (F) |
| 1966 | Canadian Ukrainian Athletic Club, Winnipeg | softball | (F) |
| | Institute Prosvita Athletic Club, Winnipeg | volleyball | (M) |
| 1967 | Canadian Ukrainian Athletic Club, Winnipeg | softball | (F) |
| 1968 | Canadian Ukrainian Athletic Club, Winnipeg | softball | (F) |
| 1969 | Canadian Ukrainian Athletic Club, Winnipeg | softball | (F) |
| 1970 | Canadian Ukrainian Athletic Club, Winnipeg | softball | (F) |
| 1971 | Canadian Ukrainian Athletic Club, Winnipeg | softball | (F) |
| 1972 | Canadian Ukrainian Athletic Club, Winnipeg | softball | (F) |
| 1973 | Canadian Ukrainian Athletic Club, Winnipeg | softball | (F) |

Junior

| | | | |
|---|---|---|---|
| 1952 | Institute Prosvita Athletic Club, Winnipeg | soccer | (M) |
| 1959 | Institute Prosvita Athletic Club, Winnipeg | basketball | (M) |
| 1960 | Institute Prosvita Athletic Club, Winnipeg | basketball | (M) |
| 1964 | Institute Prosvita Athletic Club, Winnipeg | basketball | (M) |
| 1965 | Institute Prosvita Athletic Club, Winnipeg | basketball | (M) |

## ONTARIO

| | | | |
|---|---|---|---|
| 1954 | USC Trident, Toronto | basketball | (M) |
| 1970 | Ukrainian Youth Association (SUM), Toronto | volleyball | (F) |
| 1972 | Ukrainian Youth Association (SUM), Toronto | volleyball | (F) |
| 1973 | Ukrainian Volleyball Club, Toronto | volleyball | (M) |
| 1974 | SA Ukraina, Toronto | volleyball | (M) |

| 1975 | SA Ukraina, Toronto | volleyball | (M) |

## Intermediate

| 1950 | SA Ukraina, Toronto | volleyball | (M) |
| 1957 | Ukrainian Youth Association (SUM), Toronto | volleyball | (M) |

## Junior

| 1957 | SA Ukraina, Toronto | volleyball | (M) |
| 1965 | Ukrainian Youth Association Plast, Toronto | volleyball | (F) |
| 1966 | Ukrainian Youth Association Plast, Toronto | volleyball | (F) |
| 1968 | Ukrainian Youth Association (SUM), Toronto | volleyball | (F) |
| 1969 | Ukrainian Youth Association (SUM), Toronto | volleyball | (F) |
| 1970 | Ukrainian Youth Association (SUM), Toronto | volleyball | (F) |
| 1973 | Ukrainian Youth Association (SUM), Toronto | volleyball | (F) |
|  | Ukrainian Youth Association (SUM), Toronto | volleyball | (M) |

# QUEBEC

| 1955 | SA Ukraina, Montreal | soccer | (M) |
| 1957 | SA Ukraina, Montreal | soccer | (M) |
| 1969 | SA Ukraina, Montreal | soccer | (M) |
| 1972 | SA Ukraina, Montreal | soccer | (M) |
| 1979 | SA Ukraina, Montreal | soccer | (M) |

## Junior

| 1962 | SA Ukraina, Montreal | soccer | (M) |
| 1967 | SA Ukraina, Montreal | soccer | (M) |

F - Female
M - Male

# Appendix II

## OLYMPIC, COMMONWEALTH, FRANCOPHONE AND PAN AMERICAN GAMES TEAM MEMBERS

### OLYMPIC GAMES

**athletes**

| | |
|---|---|
| Alexiuk, Ed | Montreal 1976 |
| Bossy, George | Helsinki 1952, Melbourne 1956 |
| Boychuk, Andy | Mexico City 1968 |
| Burak, Ron | Montreal 1976 |
| Chambul, Borys | Montreal 1976, Moscow 1980 |
| Charalambij, Ivan | Montreal 1976 |
| Dacyshyn, John | Tokyo 1964 |
| Danyluk, Terry | Los Angeles 1984 |
| Diachun, Jennifer | Mexico City 1968, Munich 1972 |
| Domansky, Don | Mexico City 1968, Montreal 1976 |
| Drayton, Jerome | Mexico City 1968, Montreal 1976 |
| Fedorick, Walter | London 1948 |
| Harbluk, W. | Garmisch-Partenkirchen 1940 |
| Hryb, Taras | Munich 1972 |
| Humeniuk, Marianne | Tokyo 1964 |
| Ingaldson, Fred | Rome 1960, Tokyo 1964 |
| Kindy, Anna | Albertville 1992 |
| Kobelka, Kendra | Albertville 1992 |
| Kozak, Dorothy | Melbourne 1956 |
| Kwasnycia, Don | Moscow 1980, Seoul 1988 |
| Lukowich, Ed | Calgary 1988 |
| Malar, Joanne | Barcelona 1992 |
| Mitruk, Steve | Mexico City 1968, Munich 1972 |
| Patrick, James | Sarajevo 1984 |
| Podborski, Steve | Lake Placid 1980, Sarajevo 1984 |
| Ratushny, Dan | Albertville 1992 |
| Sadowick-Yakubowich, Joyce | Munich 1972, Montreal 1976 |
| Samolenko, George | Squaw Valley 1960 |

| | |
|---|---|
| Sawchuk, Bill | Montreal 1976, Moscow 1980 |
| Shwaluk, Bill | Rome 1960 |
| Slipchuk, Michael | Albertville 1992 |
| Yaremchuk, Ken | Calgary 1988 |

**team personnel**

| | |
|---|---|
| Guzzell, Mike | Innsbruck 1964 |
| Gwozdecky, George | Innsbruck 1976 |
| Newman, Bernard | Melbourne 1956 |
| Sawula, Lorne | Los Angeles 1984 |
| Upham, John | Seoul 1988, Barcelona 1992 |

**officials, judges and referees**

| | |
|---|---|
| Eurchuk, Mike | Montreal 1976 |
| Guzzell, Mike | Squaw Valley 1960, Innsbruck 1964 |
| Oryszczyn, Eugene | Munich 1972, Montreal 1976, Moscow 1980, Los Angeles 1984 |
| Romaniuk, Alex | Mexico City 1968 |

**organizing committee**

| | |
|---|---|
| Tatarchuk, Hank | Montreal 1976, Los Angeles 1984, Seoul 1988 |

Note:     1940 Games cancelled due to war
              Moscow 1980 Games boycotted by Canada

# BRITISH EMPIRE / COMMONWEALTH GAMES

**athletes**

| | |
|---|---|
| Andrusyshyn, Zenon | 1966 |
| Boychuk, Andy | 1966, 1970 |
| Chambul, Borys | 1978 |
| Chambul, Lubomyr | 1982, 1986 |
| Chepesuik, Mike | 1930 |
| Czich, John | 1978 |
| Dacyshyn, Anna | 1990 |
| Domansky, Don | 1966, 1970 |
| Drayton, Jerome | 1970, 1974, 1978 |
| Fedko, Alex | 1966 |
| Fedorick, Walter | 1950 |

| | |
|---|---|
| Gaziuk, Murray | 1954 |
| Hryb, Taras | 1974 |
| Kozak, Dorothy | 1954 |
| Kusyj, George | 1954 |
| Kwasnycia, Don | 1978, 1986 |
| Maich, Bill | 1934 |
| Malar, Joanne | 1990 |
| Sadowick-Yakubowich, Joyce | 1970 |
| Sawchuk, Bill | 1978 |

**team personnel**

| | |
|---|---|
| Romaniuk, Alex | 1966 |

**officials, judges and referees**

| | |
|---|---|
| Eurchuk, Mike | 1978, 1982 |
| Oryszczyn, Eugene | 1978, 1982 |
| Romaniuk, Alex | 1970 |

**organizing committee**

| | |
|---|---|
| Romaniuk, Alex | 1978 |

# PAN AMERICAN GAMES

**athletes**

| | |
|---|---|
| Alexiuk, Ed | 1975 |
| Baydock, Donna | 1979 |
| Bossy, Don | 1967 |
| Boychuk, Andy | 1967 |
| Boychuk, Chris | 1987 |
| Chambul, Borys | 1979 |
| Danyluk, Terry | 1983 |
| Diachun, Jennifer | 1971 |
| Domansky, Don | 1967, 1975 |
| Eliashevsky, Christine | 1967 |
| Galanchuk, Ken | 1963 |
| Hryb, Taras | 1971 |
| Ingaldson, Fred | 1959 |
| Iwanoczko, Dale | 1991 |
| Kobelka, Kendra | 1990 |

| | |
|---|---|
| Kohut, Meron | 1971 |
| Kostiuk, Al | 1975 |
| Kramchynsky, Eileen | 1987, 1991 |
| Kucharchuk, Julia | 1971 |
| Kwasnycia, Don | 1979, 1987 |
| Malar, Joanne | 1991 |
| Mitruk, Steve | 1971 |
| Rizak, Gene | 1967 |
| Rosocha, Walter | 1967 |
| Sadowick-Yakubowich, Joyce | 1971, 1975 |
| Sawchuk, Bill | 1975, 1979 |
| Shwaluk, Bill | 1959 |
| Yakiwchuk, Alanna | 1991 |

**team personnel**

| | |
|---|---|
| Burchuk, Mike | 1991 |
| Gwozdecky, George | 1983 |
| Newman, Bernard | 1955, 1959 |
| Sawula, Lorne | 1983, 1987 |
| Upham, John | 1991 |

**officials, judges and referees**

| | |
|---|---|
| Eurchuk, Mike | 1975, 1979 |
| Oryszczyn, Eugene | 1975 |
| Romaniuk, Alex | 1967 |
| Tatarchuk, Hank | 1967 |

# FRANCOPHONE GAMES

**athletes**

| | |
|---|---|
| Yakiwchuk, Alanna | 1989 |

# Appendix III

# HALLS OF FAME INDUCTEES

## CANADA'S SPORTS HALL OF FAME
Toronto, Ontario

Inductees through 1992

athletes
| | |
|---|---|
| Drayton, Jerome | track and field |
| Podborski, Steve | skiing |
| Sawchuk, Terry | hockey |

## CANADIAN OLYMPIC HALL OF FAME*
Montreal, Quebec

Inductees through 1992

athletes
| | |
|---|---|
| Podborski, Steve | skiing |

* formerly known as the Canadian Amateur Sports Hall of Fame

## ALBERTA SPORTS HALL OF FAME
Calgary, Alberta

Inductees through 1992

builders
| | |
|---|---|
| Eurchuk, Mike | wrestling |
| Romaniuk, Alex | wrestling |
| Serediuk, Rummy | wrestling |

# MANITOBA SPORTS HALL OF FAME

Winnipeg, Manitoba

Inductees through 1992

athletes

| | |
|---|---|
| Broda, Turk | hockey |
| Hynduik, Ollie | bowling |
| Juzda, Bill | hockey |
| Mosienko, Bill | hockey |
| Patrick, Steve | football |
| Sawchuk, Terry | hockey |
| Wawryshyn-Moroz, Evelyn | softball |

teams

1965 Canadian Ukrainian Athletic Club "Blues" softball team
1972 Meleschuk Curling Rink  (Meleschuk, Orest)


# NORTHWESTERN ONTARIO SPORTS HALL OF FAME

Thunder Bay, Ontario

Inductees through 1991

athletes

| | |
|---|---|
| Bodnar, Gus | hockey |
| Domansky, Don | track and field |
| Landy, Frank | football |
| Lewicki, Danny | hockey |
| Onuliak, Ab | baseball |
| Sawchuk, Bill | swimming |

builders

| | |
|---|---|
| Baryluk, Mitch | basketball |
| Guzzel, Mike | skiing |
| Gwozdecky, George | all-round |

teams

1975 Tetley Curling Rink  (Hnatiw, Pete)

# SASKATCHEWAN SPORTS HALL OF FAME
Regina, Saskatchewan

athletes
| | |
|---|---|
| Bower, Johnny | hockey |
| Prystai, Metro | hockey |

teams
1960 and 1961 McKee Curling Team  (Fedoruk, Sylvia)


# MICHIGAN AMATEUR SPORTS HALL OF FAME

athletes
| | |
|---|---|
| Slyziuk, Mike | curling |


# THE BRANTFORD AND AREA SPORTS HALL OF RECOGNITION
Brantford, Ontario

Inductees through  1992

athletes
| | |
|---|---|
| Maich, Bill | boxing |
| Maich, Joe | wrestling |
| Shewchuk, Jack | hockey |


# CITY OF OSHAWA SPORTS HALL OF FAME
Oshawa, Ontario

Inductees through  1992

athletes
| | |
|---|---|
| Waszczuk, Henry | football |

# ROBLIN ICE HOCKEY HALL OF FAME

Roblin, Manitoba

builders
Stasiuk, Most Rev. Peter          hockey


# SASKATOON SPORTS HALL OF FAME

Saskatoon, Saskatchewan

Inductees through 1992

athletes
Leswick, Tony          hockey
Shabaga, Mike          hockey


# SUDBURY SPORTS HALL OF FAME

Sudbury, Ontario

athletes
Shack, Eddie          hockey


# WINDSOR/ESSEX COUNTY SPORTS HALL OF FAME

Windsor, Ontario

Inductees through  1992

athletes
Delaney, Al          boxing
Hedgewick, Mike          football

builders
Newman, Bernie          gymnastics

# AQUATIC HALL OF FAME OF CANADA

Winnipeg, Manitoba

Inductees through 1992

athletes
Sawchuk, Bill                          swimming


# CANADIAN BOXING HALL OF FAME

Toronto, Ontario

Inductees through 1990

athletes
Kolaski, Peter
Maich, Bill
Zaduk, Pete


# CURLING HALL OF FAME

Baie d'Urfe, Quebec

Inductees through 1991

athletes
Pidzarko-More, Chris
Werenich, Ed

builders
Fedoruk, Sylvia

## CANADIAN FOOTBALL HALL OF FAME
Hamilton, Ontario

Inductees through 1992

athletes
Evanshen, Terry


## HOCKEY HALL OF FAME
Toronto, Ontario

Inductees through 1991

athletes
Bossy, Mike
Bower, Johnny
Broda, Turk
Bucyk, Johnny
Mosienko, Bill
Sawchuk, Terry


## CANADIAN ROAD RUNNING HALL OF FAME
no permanent home

athletes
Drayton, Jerome


## SOFTBALL CANADA HALL OF FAME
no permanent home

Inductees through 1991

builders
Shaley, John
Shaley, Stan

# CANADIAN FORCES SPORTS HALL OF FAME
Ottawa, Ontario

Inductees through 1991

athletes
Czich, John                badminton
Shwaluk, William           weightlifting


# UNITED STATES CURLING HALL OF FAME
Northbrook, Illinois, USA

athletes
Slyziuk, Ernie
Slyziuk, Mike


# PRO FOOTBALL HALL OF FAME
Canton, Ohio, USA

Inductees through 1990

athletes
Nagurski, Bronko


# NATIONAL FOOTBALL HALL OF FAME
Kings Mills, Ohio, USA

Inductees through 1990

athletes
Nagurski, Bronko

# MAJOR LEAGUE FOOTBALL HALL OF FAME
Los Angeles, California, USA

Inductees through 1990

athletes
Nagurski, Bronko


# MANITOBA CURLING HALL OF FAME AND MUSEUM
Winnipeg, Manitoba

Inductees through 1991

Teams
1972 Meleschuk Curling Rink  (Meleschuk, Orest)


# MANITOBA HOCKEY HALL OF FAME
Winnipeg, Manitoba

Inductees through 1992

athletes
Cooper, Joe
Ezinicki, Bill
Juzda, Bill
Langelle, Pete
Mazur, Ed
Mickoski, Nick
Nesterenko, Eric
Sawchuk, Terry
Shibicky, Alex
Stanowski, Wally
Wasnie, Nick
Woytowich, Bob

## ONTARIO AQUATIC HALL OF FAME

no permanent home

Inductees through 1992

athletes
Sawchuk, Bill                          swimming


## ONTARIO 5 PIN BOWLING HALL OF FAME

no permanent home

Inductees through 1988

athletes
Pechaluk, Fred


## STAMPEDE WRESTLING HALL OF FAME

no permanent home

Inductees through 1990

athletes
Gordienko, George


## UNIVERSITY OF GUELPH SPORTS HALL OF FAME

Guelph, Ontario

athletes
Chepesuik, Mike                        wrestling

# UNIVERSITY OF SASKATCHEWAN WALL OF FAME

Saskatoon, Saskatchewan

athletes

| | |
|---|---|
| Fedoruk, Sylvia | curling |
| Konihowski, John | football |
| Lukowich, Ed | curling |

# UNIVERSITY OF TORONTO SPORTS HALL OF FAME

Toronto, Ontario

Inductees through 1991

athletes

| | |
|---|---|
| Oneschuk, Steve | football |

# HARVARD VARSITY CLUB HALL OF FAME

Boston, Massachusetts, USA

Inductees through 1991

athletes

| | |
|---|---|
| Kinasewich, Gene | hockey |

# NEW MEXICO STATE UNIVERSITY INTERCOLLEGIATE ATHLETIC HALL OF FAME

Las Cruces, New Mexico, USA

athletes

| | |
|---|---|
| Gerela, Roy | football |

# Appendix IV

## MANITOBA UKRAINIAN SPORTSMAN
## OF THE YEAR HONOUREES

Sponsored by the St. Nicholas Men's Club, Winnipeg
Honours outstanding sportsman of Ukrainian descent from Manitoba

| 1965 | To all Ukrainian Sportsmen | | | |
|------|------|------|------|------|
| 1966-67 | Mickoski, Nick | athlete | - | hockey |
| 1967-68 | Chernecki, Wayne | athlete | - | hockey |
| 1968-69 | Ingaldson, Fred | athlete | - | basketball |
| 1969-70 | Hrycaiko, Dennis | coach | - | football |
| 1970-71 | Krucik, David | athlete | - | golf |
| 1971-72 | Meleschuk, Orest | athlete | - | curling |
| 1972-73 | Lakusiak, Gene | athlete | - | football |
| 1973-74 | Tyzuk, Boris | athlete | - | volleyball |
| 1974-75 | Tesluk, Norm | athlete | - | hockey |
| 1975-76 | Poleschuk, Matt | athlete | - | golf |
| 1976-77 | Tanasichuk, Hal | athlete | - | curling |
| 1977-78 | Woznesensky, Lyall | athlete | - | football |
| 1978-79 | Lukowich, Morris | athlete | - | hockey |
| 1979-80 | Mosienko, Bill | athlete | - | hockey |
| 1980-81 | Burtnyk, Kerry | athlete | - | curling |
| 1981-82 | Juzda, Bill | athlete | - | hockey |
| | Hawerchuk, Dale | athlete | - | hockey |
| 1982-83 | Burchuk, Mike | coach | - | volleyball |
| 1983-84 | Mickoski, Nick | athlete | - | hockey |
| 1984-85 | Hawerchuk, Dale | athlete | - | hockey |
| 1985-86 | Trakalo, Dale | athlete | - | hockey |
| 1986-87 | Hnatiuk, Glen | athlete | - | golf |
| 1987-88 | Klysh, Myron | athlete | - | volleyball |
| 1988-89 | Budy, Tim | athlete | - | hockey |
| | Iwanoczko, Dale | athlete | - | volleyball |
| 1989-90* | no winner | | | |
| 1990-91 | Stetch, David | athlete | - | hockey |
| 1991-92 | Shaley, John | manager | - | softball |

\*   In 1990, to celebrate the 25th anniversary of the award, hockey player Bill Mosienko was
honoured as the "Athlete of the Past 25 Years, 1965 - 1990."

# Appendix V

## WORLD WAR II
## ARMED SERVICES HONOUR ROLL

Athletes, coaches and administrators profiled in this work who enlisted for military service during World War II. This is by no means an exhaustive list.

Bower, Johnny
Broda, Turk
Cooper, Joe
Copot, Murray
Delaney, Al
Dyzandra, Paul
Ezinicki, Bill
Hedgewick, Mike
Hrymnak, Steve
Hubchik, Walter
Juzda, Bill
Kaleta, Alex
Kepron, Roy
Klukay, Joe
Kryschuk, Mike
Langelle, Pete
Leswick, Peter
Leswick, Tony
Michaluk, Art
Oryszczyn, Eugene   (Poland)
Pruski, Steve
Shewchuk, Jack
Shibicky, Alex
Shishka, Steve
Slyziuk, Ernest
Slyziuk, Michael
Stanowski, Wally

Athletes who volunteered or were drafted for service but did not serve.

Kolaski, Pete
Nagurski, Bronko  (USA)
Wusyk, Bill

# Appendix VI

## HOST SITES

Canadian host sites of major sport events which were organized or co-organized by Ukrainians.

### Free Olympiad

| | |
|---|---|
| 1980 | Toronto |
| 1984 | Toronto |

### Ukrainian Youth League of North America
### Sports Rally

| | |
|---|---|
| 1950 | Toronto |
| 1953 | Toronto |

### Ukrainian Sports Federation of USA and Canada (USCAK)
### Inter-club Championship

| | |
|---|---|
| 1957 | Toronto, volleyball |
| 1960 | Toronto, track and field |
| 1961 | Acton, track and field |
| | Toronto, volleyball |
| 1962 | Acton, track and field |
| 1963 | Toronto, volleyball |
| 1965 | Mt. Blanc, skiing |
| | Grafton, track and field |
| 1966 | Mt. Blanc, skiing |
| 1967 | St. Jovite, skiing |
| 1968 | Grafton, track and field |
| 1969 | Grafton, track and field |
| | Toronto, chess |
| | Toronto, volleyball |
| 1971 | Grafton, track and field |
| 1975 | Toronto, chess |
| 1978 | Toronto, chess |
| | Toronto, track and field |
| 1979 | St. Catharines, volleyball |
| 1983 | Toronto, chess |
| 1990 | Toronto, chess |
| | Toronto, volleyball |

# Appendix VII

# A NOTE ON THE STATISTICAL DATA

The statistics presented reflect the style of data accumulation particular to each sport and league. As a result, inconsistencies exist. In addition, statistical compilation of sporting results over time has undergone major revisions. Revisions have also occurred in the interpretation of criteria by which records are verified.

For example, prior to World War II, records established in track and field events were not officially accepted if set on Sunday. Prior to 1954, a record established by a Canadian outside of Canada was not considered a Canadian record. On the other hand, foreigners could set Canadian records. This resulted in the establishment of a two tier record system: "Canadian Open" records could be set by any athlete on Canadian soil while only Canadian born or British subjects residing in Canada for at least three months could set a "Canadian Native" record.

Records that have not been officially accepted are called "Canadian Best" (CB).

The reader will notice, no doubt, the usage of both imperial and metric measurements. Through most of Canada's history, imperial measurements were used in sport and daily life. Metrication began in the mid-1960s. For example, from 1878 to 1966 (with Olympic years generally being the exception), Canadian Track and Field Championships were conducted over imperial distances of 100, 220, 440, and 880 yards, and one, three, five and ten miles. Results of field events were recorded in imperial measurements. In 1967, metrication was introduced, and races were now held over distances of 100, 200, 400, 800, 1,500, 3,000, 5,000 and 10,000 metres. Results of field events were now recorded in metric.

To avoid confusion, the data have been provided in the form given at the time of competition. Conversion factors are found in Appendix VIII.

An asterisk (*) indicates that the athlete won the league championship in the particular year, i.e. Grey Cup, Stanley Cup, etc.

# Appendix VIII

## MEASURES, WEIGHTS AND TEMPERATURE

**LENGTH**

| Imperial Unit | Equivalent | Metric Equivalent |
|---|---|---|
| 1 inch | | 2.54 centimetres |
| 1 foot | 12 inches | 30.48 centimetres |
| 1 yard | 36 inches; 3 feet | 0.91 metres |
| 1 mile | 5,280 feet | 1.6 kilometres |

| Metric Unit | Equivalent | Imperial Equivalent |
|---|---|---|
| 1 centimetre | 0.01 metre | 0.39 inch |
| 1 metre | 100 centimetres | 1.09 yards; 3.28 feet; 39.37 inches |
| 1 kilometre | 1,000 metres | 0.62 mile |

**WEIGHT** (for ordinary commodities)

| Imperial Unit | Equivalent | Metric Equivalent |
|---|---|---|
| 1 ounce | | 28.35 grams |
| 1 pound | 16 ounces | 0.45 kilogram |
| 1 ton (short) | 2,000 pounds | 907.18 kilograms |

| Metric Unit | Equivalent | Imperial Equivalent |
|---|---|---|
| 1 gram | | 0.035 ounce |
| 1 kilogram | 1,000 grams | 2.2 pounds |
| 1 ton (metric) | 1,000 kilograms | 1.1 ton (short) |

**CAPACITY** (liquid)

| Imperial Unit | Equivalent | Metric Equivalent |
|---|---|---|
| 1 pint | 20 ounces | 0.57 litre |
| 1 quart | 2 pints; 40 ounces | 1.14 litres |
| 1 gallon | 4 quarts | 4.55 litres |

| Metric Unit | Equivalent | Imperial Equivalent |
|---|---|---|
| 1 litre | | 0.88 quart |

## AREA

| Imperial Unit | Equivalent | Metric Equivalent |
| --- | --- | --- |
| 1 acre | 43,560 sq. feet | 0.4 hectare; 4,047 sq. metres |

| Metric Unit | Equivalent | Imperial Equivalent |
| --- | --- | --- |
| 1 hectare | 10,000 sq. metres | 2.47 acres |

## TEMPERATURE

| | |
| --- | --- |
| 32 degrees Fahrenheit | 0 degrees Celsius (or Centigrade) |
| 212 degrees Fahrenheit | 100 degrees Celsius (or Centigrade) |

# Appendix IX

## ABBREVIATIONS AND GLOSSARY OF UKRAINIAN TERMS

### ABBREVIATIONS

#### LEAGUES, ASSOCIATIONS, GOVERNING BODIES

| | | |
|---|---|---|
| AAGPBL | - | All-American Girls Professional Baseball League |
| AAUofC | - | Amateur Athletic Union of Canada |
| ACHL | - | Atlantic Coast Hockey League |
| AFC | - | American Football Conference |
| AFFL | - | Armed Forces Football League |
| AFL | - | American Football League |
| AHA | - | American Hockey Association |
| AHL | - | American Hockey League |
| AJHL | - | Alberta Junior Hockey League |
| AL | - | American League |
| APA | - | Athletic Patriotic Association |
| ASSHL | - | Alberta Services Senior Hockey League |
| BCAHA | - | British Columbia Amateur Hockey Association |
| BCJHL | - | British Columbia Junior Hockey League |
| CAHA | - | Canadian Amateur Hockey Association |
| CAHL | - | Canadian-American Hockey League |
| CASA | - | Canadian Amateur Ski Association |
| CASSA | - | Canadian Amateur Speed Skating Association |
| CBHL | - | Cape Breton Hockey League |
| CFL | - | Canadian Football League |
| CFSA | - | Canadian Figure Skating Association |
| CHL | - | Central Hockey League |
| CIAU | - | Canadian Interuniversity Athletic Union |
| CLA | - | Canadian Lacrosse Association |
| COA | - | Canadian Olympic Association |
| CPGA | - | Canadian Professional Golfers' Association |
| CRU | - | Canadian Rugby Union |
| CVA | - | Canadian Volleyball Association |
| ECPSL | - | Eastern Canada Professional Soccer League |

| | | |
|---|---|---|
| EHL | - | Eastern Hockey League |
| EKL | - | East Kootenay League |
| EPHL | - | Eastern Pro Hockey League |
| FIFA | - | International Federation of Soccer Associations |
| | | (French: *Federation Internationale de Football Association*) |
| FIG | - | World Gymnastics Federation |
| | | (French: *Federation Internationale de Gymnastique*) |
| FILA | - | World Amateur Wrestling Federation |
| | | (French: *Federation Internationale de Lute Amateur*) |
| FIS | - | International Ski Federation (French: *Federation Internationale de Ski*) |
| FISU | - | International University Sports Federation |
| | | (French: *Federation Internationale du Sport Universitaire*) |
| IAHL | - | International American Hockey League |
| IHL | - | International Hockey League |
| IOC | - | International Olympic Committee |
| IRFU | - | Interprovincial Rugby Football Union |
| IVA | - | International Volleyball Association |
| JWFL | - | Japan Women's Football League |
| MHL Sr. | - | Manitoba Hockey League (Senior) |
| MJHL | - | Manitoba Junior Hockey League |
| MMHL | - | Maritime Major Hockey League |
| MOAHL | - | Mainline-Okanagan Amateur Hockey League |
| NAHL | - | North American Hockey League |
| NAIA | - | National Association of Inter-Collegiate Athletics |
| NASL | - | North American Soccer League |
| NBSHL | - | New Brunswick Senior Hockey League |
| NCAA | - | National Collegiate Athletic Association |
| NFL | - | National Football League |
| NHA | - | National Hockey Association |
| NHL | - | National Hockey League |
| NL | - | National League |
| NLL | - | National Lacrosse League |
| NORCECA | - | North Central America and Caribbean Zone |
| OHA | - | Ontario Hockey Association |
| OHL | - | Ontario Hockey League |
| OLA | - | Ontario Lacrosse Association |
| OMJHL | - | Ontario Major Junior Hockey League |
| ORFU | - | Ontario Rugby Football Union |
| OSHL | - | Okanagan Senior Hockey League |
| OUAA | - | Ontario Universities Athletic Association |

| | | |
|---|---|---|
| OVA | - | Ontario Volleyball Association |
| PCHL | - | Pacific Coast Hockey League |
| PGA | - | Professional Golfers' Association |
| QHL | - | Quebec Hockey League |
| QJHL | - | Quebec Junior Hockey League |
| QSAHL | - | Quebec Senior Amateur Hockey League |
| RCGA | - | Royal Canadian Golf Association |
| SHL | - | Southern Hockey League |
| SJHL | - | Saskatchewan Junior Hockey League |
| SSHL | - | Saskatchewan Senior Hockey League |
| TBJHL | - | Thunder Bay Junior Hockey League |
| USFL | - | United States Football League |
| USHL | - | United States Hockey League |
| WCHA | - | Western Collegiate Hockey Association |
| WCHL | - | Western Canada Hockey League |
| WIFU | - | Western Interprovincial Football Union |
| WHA | - | World Hockey Association |
| WHL | - | Western Hockey League |
| WLA | - | Western Lacrosse Association |

## TERMS

| | | |
|---|---|---|
| A | - | assists |
| AB | - | at bats |
| AC | - | athletic club |
| ATT | - | attempts |
| AVE | - | average |
| C | - | converts |
| C-1 | - | canoe singles |
| C-2 | - | canoe doubles |
| C-4 | - | canoe fours |
| CB | - | Canadian Best |
| dnc | - | did not compete |
| dnf | - | did not finish |
| dnq | - | did not qualify |
| dsq | - | disqualified |
| ERA | - | earned run average |
| FC | - | football club |
| FG | - | field goals |
| ft | - | feet |
| G | - | goals |

| GA | - | goals against |
| GD | - | good |
| GP | - | games played |
| H | - | heat |
| H | - | hits |
| HR | - | home runs |
| IM | - | individual medley |
| in | - | inches |
| IP | - | innings pitched |
| Jr | - | junior |
| kg | - | kilograms |
| km/h | - | kilometres per hour |
| KO | - | knockout |
| L | - | lost |
| lbs | - | pounds |
| LG | - | longest |
| m | - | metres |
| MIN | - | minutes |
| mph | - | miles per hour |
| MVP | - | most valuable player |
| nir | - | Canadian indoor record |
| NO | - | number |
| nr | - | Canadian record |
| PIM | - | penalties in minutes |
| PTS | - | points |
| QF | - | quarter-final |
| qr | - | qualifying round |
| R | - | runs |
| RBI | - | runs batted in |
| S | - | singles |
| SA | - | sports association |
| SC | - | sports club |
| SF | - | semi-final |
| SO | - | shutouts |
| Sr | - | senior |
| T | - | ties, tied |
| TD | - | touchdowns |
| TKO | - | technical knockout |
| USA | - | Ukrainian Sport Association |
| W | - | wins |

| | | |
|---|---|---|
| W | - | won by decision (boxing) |
| WC | - | World Cup |
| wr | - | world record |
| y, YDS | - | yards |
| " | - | inches |
| ' | - | feet |
| ° | - | degrees |

**NON-SPORT**

| | | |
|---|---|---|
| ANAF | - | Army, Navy, Air Force |
| ASSR | - | Autonomous Soviet Socialist Republic |
| CBC | - | Canadian Broadcasting Corporation |
| CNE | - | Canadian National Exhibition |
| CNR | - | Canadian National Railway |
| CPR | - | Canadian Pacific Railway |
| DP | - | displaced person |
| Dr. | - | Doctor |
| HMCS | - | His (Her) Majesty's Canadian Ship |
| Hon. | - | Honourable |
| KGB | - | Committee of State Security (Russian: *Komitet Gosudarstvennoy Bezopasnosti*) |
| MA | - | Master of Arts (Latin: *Magister Artium*) |
| MBA | - | Master of Business Administration |
| MD | - | Doctor of Medicine (Latin: *Medicinae Doctor*) |
| MLA | - | Member of Legislative Assembly |
| MP | - | Member of Parliament |
| MPP | - | Member of Provincial Parliament |
| Ph.D. | - | Doctor of Philosophy (Latin: *Philosophiae Doctor*) |
| Q.C. | - | Queen's Counsel |
| RCAF | - | Royal Canadian Air Force |
| RCCS | - | Royal Canadian Corps of Signals |
| RCMP | - | Royal Canadian Mounted Police |
| RCN | - | Royal Canadian Navy |
| Rev. | - | Reverend |
| Rt. Hon. | - | Right Honourable |
| USA | - | United States of America |
| USSR | - | Union of Soviet Socialist Republics |
| YMCA | - | Young Men's Christian Association |
| YMHA | - | Young Men's Hebrew Association |
| YWCA | - | Young Women's Christian Association |

## UKRAINIAN CLUBS, ORGANIZATIONS, ASSOCIATIONS

| | | |
|---|---|---|
| AUUC | - | Association of United Ukrainian Canadians |
| BUAC | - | Brooklands Ukrainian Athletic Club |
| CUAC | - | Canadian Ukrainian Athletic Club |
| IPAC | - | Institute Prosvita Athletic Club |
| KUAC | - | Kenora Ukrainian Athletic Club |
| UCC | - | Ukrainian Canadian Committee (1943-1989) |
| | | Ukrainian Canadian Congress (1989-  ) |
| UCSA | - | Ukrainian Canadian Servicemen's Association |
| ULFTA | - | Ukrainian Labour-Farmer Temple Association |
| UNF | - | Ukrainian National Federation |
| UNYF | - | Ukrainian National Youth Federation |
| UVC | - | Ukrainian Volleyball Club |
| UYLNA | - | Ukrainian Youth League of North America |
| WBA | - | Workingmen's Benevolent Association |
| WCFU | - | World Congress of Free Ukrainians |

## UKRAINIAN ABBREVIATIONS AND ACRONYMS USUALLY NOT TRANSLATED

| | | |
|---|---|---|
| KLK | - | Carpathian Ski Club |
| ODUM | - | Ukrainian National Democratic League |
| SUM | - | Ukrainian Youth Association of Canada |
| SUMK | - | Canadian Ukrainian Youth Association |
| USCAK | - | Association of Ukrainian Sport Clubs of North America, subsequently replaced by Ukrainian Sports Federation of USA and Canada |

# GLOSSARY OF UKRAINIAN TERMS

| | | |
|---|---|---|
| Berkut | - | golden eagle |
| Dnipro | - | largest river in Ukraine (also Dnieper) |
| Hetman | - | head of the Cossack state and supreme military commander |
| Kozaks | - | Cossacks |
| Lviv | - | city in Western Ukraine |
| Lysiachyj Bih | - | fox run |
| Orlyk or Orlick | - | Pylyp Orlyk (1672-1742), Cossack leader and hetman in exile |
| Sitch or Sicz | - | central fortress of the Cossacks (1552-1775) |
| Skala | - | rock, crag or large mass of stone |
| Sokil | - | falcon |
| Strila | - | arrow |
| Ukraina | - | Ukraine |
| Vedmedyky | - | teddy bears |

# NOTES

## INTRODUCTION

1.   Nancy Howell and Maxwell Howell, *Sports and Games in Canadian Life: 1700 to Present* (Toronto: Macmillan of Canada, 1969) introduction.

2.   A. Lunn, *The History of Skiing* (London: Oxford University Press, 1927) p. 3.

3.   Bruce Kidd, "The Workers' Sports Movement in Canada, 1924-40: the Radical Immigrants' Alternative," *Polyphony* Vol.7, No.1 (Spring/Summer, 1985): p. 80.

4.   Volodymyr Kubijovyc, *Encyclopedia of Ukraine: Volume 1* (Toronto: University of Toronto Press, 1984): p. 344.

5.   W. L. Morton, *Manitoba: A History* (Toronto: University of Toronto Press, 1967) p. 312.

6.   Michael Marunchak, *The Ukrainian Canadians: A History* (Winnipeg: Ukrainian Academy of Arts and Science - UVAN, 1982) pp. 121 & 186.

7.   In an effort to promote Ukrainian language education on Ukrainian ethnographical lands of the Austro-Hungarian Empire, the *Ridna Shkola* (Native Language School) Society was established in Lviv in 1881. Subsequently, many Ukrainian language schools in Europe, Australia, and North and South America bore the name *Ridna Shkola*.

8.   Mykhailo Kumka, *Pochatky Rukhanky Sered Ukraintsiv u Vinnipehu* (Winnipeg: Biblioteka Ukrainskoi Shkoly v Kanadi, 1925) p. 3.

9.   Henry Roxborough, *One Hundred-Not Out: The Story of Nineteenth-Century Canadian Sport* (Toronto: Ryerson Press, 1966) pp. 155-57.

10.   Morris K. Mott, "Manly Sports and Manitobans, Settlement Days to World War I," Ph.D. dissertation, Queen's University, 1980, p. 190.

11.   Morton, p. 309.

12.   Levko Rohatyn, "Ukrainian Sports Activity in the Sudbury Region," *Polyphony* Vol.7 No. 1 (Spring/Summer, 1985): p. 73.

13.   Gerald Redmond, *Sports and Ethnic Groups in Canada* (Calgary: CAHPER, 1978): p. 42.

14.   Jim Tester, ed., *Sport Pioneers - A History of the Finnish-Canadian Amateur Sports Federation 1906-1986* (Sudbury: Alerts AC Historical Committee, c.1986) pp. 7 & 9.

15.   During an eight-month period (May - December, 1918) of Ukraine's short-lived independence (1918-20), Hetman Pavlo Skoropadsky served as the head of the Ukrainian state.

16.   Letters Patent of the Ukrainian Boy Scouts and Sporting 'Sitch' Association of Canada, issued December 3, 1924 by A. Copp, Secretary of State, Canada.

17.   Vasyl Dyky, "Viiskovi vpravy Sichei Ameryky i Kanady v rotsi 1927," *Kalendar Kanadiiskoho Ukraintsia* (Winnipeg) 1928: pp. 189-192. Also see Kumka, op. cit., pp. 11-17.

18.   Dyky, p. 190.

19. *IX ULFTA National Convention Report* (Winnipeg, 1928) p. 28.

20. Kidd, p. 81.

21. "Two Years Since the Canadian Workers' Sports Movement Began," *The Young Worker* (Toronto) February, 1928: p. 3.

22. "Youth from Fascist Clubs Won for WSA," *The Young Worker* (Toronto) October 20, 1931: p. 6.

23. Kidd, p. 85.

24. *XVI ULFTA National Convention Report* (Winnipeg, 1937) p. 64.

25. Dr. Martin Chepesiuk, Personal Interview, Toronto, Ontario, December 7, 1988.

26. Slaw Rebchuk and John Shaley, Personal Interview, Winnipeg, Manitoba, August 4, 1989; see also Mott, for a discussion of the role of Anglo-Canadian protestant churches in sport in Winnipeg during the early twentieth century.

27. "Kanadiisko-Ukrainskyi Sportovyi Klub," *Almanakh Klenovyi Lystok* (Winnipeg) 1929: p. 70.

28. *The Port Arthur News-Chronicle* September 24, 1936.

29. Michael Starr, Personal Interview, Oshawa, Ontario, July 5, 1990.

30. *CUAC 1941 Year Book* (Winnipeg, 1941), p. 13.

31. *The Port Arthur News-Chronicle* September 24, 1936.

32. Michael Starr, op. cit.

33. *The Fort William Daily Times-Journal* March 8, 1939: p. 12.

34. M. Mihaychuk, "Sportovyi Den Ukrainskykh gimnastiv u Vinipehu," *Ukrainskyi Holos* (Winnipeg) September 12, 1923.

35. "An Interview with Dr. Elias Wachna," *Polyphony* Vol.7, No.1 (Spring/Summer, 1985): p. 127.

36. Marunchak, p. 444.

37. Kumka, p. 16.

38. Marunchak, p. 558.

39. See B. Panchuk, ed., *Royal Canadian Legion Memorial Souvenir Book 1 - Ukrainian Branches* (Montreal: Ukrainian Canadian Veterans' Association, 1986) pp. 128-29 & 171.

40. The following discussion on post-World War II sport in Canada is primarily based on newspaper clippings compiled by Jaroslaw Chorostil, Wolodymyr Ihnatowycz, Ostap Steckiw, and the author.

41. K. W. Sokolyk, "Vedmedyky - Volleyball Champions," *Polyphony* Vol.10 (1988): pp. 243-44.

42. Christine Tomkiw, "Upon Returning to Toronto from Vancouver," Unpublished Recollection, (1965).

43. *CUAC 50th Anniversary and Re-Union Banquet Programme - 1926-1976* (Winnipeg, 1976) p. 6.

44. Paul Kulchisky, Personal Interview, Toronto, Ontario, 1988.

45. J. Chorostil and R. Kostiuk, *"Ukraina" Sport Association - Toronto* (Toronto: SA Ukraina - Toronto, 1983) p. 137.

46. "Kanadiisko-Ukrainskyi Sportovyi Klub," *Almanakh Klenovyi Lystok, 1929* (Winnipeg) 1929: p. 70.

47. *Novyi Shliakh* (Winnipeg) November 11, 1950: p. 7.

48. Karlo Mulkewytch, "Vid Redakcii i Vydavnytstva," *Sportowi Wisti* (Toronto) May 12, 1954: p. 1.

49. Chorostil and Kostiuk, p. 54.

50. Jennifer Diachun-Palmer, Personal Interview, Speyside, Ontario, April 30, 1991.

51. M. Czuboka, *Ukrainian Canadian, Eh?* (Winnipeg: Communigraphics Printers Aid Group, 1983) p. 170.

52. See Jaroslaw Pryszlak, *Two Idealistic Brothers* (Montreal: Ukrainian-American "Freedom" Foundation, 1990) pp. 229-240.

53. See *Nash Sport* (Newark, N.J., 1991): pp. 3-9; *Sportyvna Hazeta* (Kyiv) March 22, 1990: p. 2; May 7, 1991: p. 1; September 5, 1991; September 20, 1991: p. 2; and *Homin Ukrainy* (Toronto) July 3, 1991: p. 13.

54. George Tatomyr, *Beyond the Uke Line: Ukrainians in the National Hockey League* (Trenton: City Print, 1990) p. 7.

55. Tony Unitas, "Peter Kolaski: The Fighting Uke," *Canadian Boxing News* (1988): p. 7.

56. R. Harney, "Homo Ludens and Ethnicity," *Polyphony*, Vol.7, No.1 (Spring/Summer, 1985): p. 1.

57. Studs Terkel, *Working* (New York: Pantheon Books, 1972) p. 383.

58. C. and G. Howe and C. Wilkins, *After the Applause* (Toronto: McClelland & Stewart Inc., 1989) p. 17.

59. Harney, p. 1.

60. David Blaikie, *Boston: The Canadian Story* (Ottawa: Seneca House Books, 1984) p. 157.

61. Mordecai Richler, *Notes on an Endangered Species and Others* (New York: A. Knopf, Inc., 1974) p. 171.

62. "Y. Kusyj Zdobuv Pershist Kanady," *Homin Ukrainy* (Toronto) October 13, 1956: p. 6.

63. Joyce Yakubowich, Speech at the inaugural Canadian Ukrainian Sports Hall of Fame dinner, August 12, 1992.

64. Cleve Dheensaw, *Island of Champions: A Sporting History of Vancouver Island* (Victoria: Orca Book Publishers, 1988) p. 262.

65. George Gross, "Canucks Back on the Glory Trail," *The Toronto Sun* May 27, 1986: World Cup insert, p. 62.

66. Harney, p. 3.

67. One athlete wrote the author in 1988: "My mother and father were born in 1881 and 1873, respectively, in Horodenka, Austria. As a result of decisions after the 1914-18 war, Austria was considerably reduced in size. Horodenka is now in Ukraine, USSR. Look at me: born in 1913 in Moose Jaw, Saskatchewan. What does that make me?" In some cases, individuals changed their surnames, whether to forever rid of the immigrant label, or to simplify a difficult name to spell. Or take the case of Mike Guzzell, whose parents at the suggestion of a sympathetic policeman changed their surname, to avoid possible interment as enemy aliens during World War I. And there is the case of hockey legend Wayne Gretzky. His paternal grandparents and father, for example, spoke Ukrainian at home, but seemingly did not relate to Ukrainian roots.

## CLUBS, LEAGUES AND TEAMS

1.  *Militant Youth* (Winnipeg) October, 1931: p. 11 and June, 1932: p. 9.
2.  *Hamilton Spectator*, October 12, 1956.
3.  Lubomyr Luciuk, *Ukrainians in the Making - Their Kingston Story* (Kingston: Limestone Press, 1980) p. 114.
4.  "Sportovomu T-vu 'Ukraina' - Montreal - Slava," *Vilne Slovo* (Toronto) September 28, 1957: p. 12.
5.  *SA Ukraina Montreal 25 Anniversary Booklet, 1949-1974* (Montreal: SA Ukraina, 1974) p. 5.
6.  "Refuse Junior Club Entry Because of Lack of Ice," *The Fort William Daily Times-Journal* November 18, 1936.
7.  "Riotous Scene is Witnessed," *The Fort William Daily Times-Journal* March 8, 1939: p. 12.
8.  *The Port Arthur News-Chronicle* August 2, 1951.
9.  Michael Pawlyshyn, "The Sports Parade," *Ukrainian Life* (Scranton) October, 1940: p. 14.
10. J. Chorostil and R. Kostiuk, *"Ukraina" Sport Association - Toronto* (Toronto: Kiev Printers Ltd., 1983) p. 292.
11. "Red Sport Column," *The Young Worker* (Toronto) June, 1925: p. 4.
12. "Red Sport Column," *The Young Worker* (Toronto) April, 1925: p. 2.
13. See Bruce Kidd, "The Workers' Sports Movement in Canada, 1924-40: The Radical Immigrants' Alternative," *Polyphony* Vol. 7 No. 1 (Spring/Summer, 1985).
14. "Sport Note," *The Young Worker* (Toronto) November, 1928: p. 3.
15. "Sports Notes," *Ukrainian Life* (Scranton, PA) May, 1940.
16. "An Interview with Dr. Elias Wachna," *Polyphony* Vol. No. 1 (1985): p. 127.
17. "Sports Notes," *Ukrainian Trend* (New York, NY) Winter, 1952: p. 37.
18. "Kanadiisko-Ukrainskyi Sportovyi Klub," *Almanakh Klenovyi Lystok, 1929* (Winnipeg) 1929: p. 70.
19. *CUAC 1941 Year Book* (Winnipeg) 1941: p. 70.
20. "Fifty Year History of C.U.A.C. Sport," *CUAC 50th Anniversary and Re-Union Banquet Programme - 1926-1976* (Winnipeg) 1976: p. 3.
21. *ibid.* p. 9.
22. *CUAC 1946 Year Book* (Winnipeg) 1946: p. 39.
23. "Centralized Recreation Authority Backed," *Winnipeg Free Press* November 23, 1972: p. 3.
24. Slaw Rebchuk and John Shaley, Personal Interview, Winnipeg, Manitoba, August 4, 1989.
25. *CUAC 1951 Year Book* (Winnipeg) 1951: p. 7.

# THE ATHLETES, COACHES AND ADMINISTRATORS

1. Tom Lobaugh, "Beverley Launches Coaching Career," *The Hockey News*, October 3, 1980: p. 31.
2. "Book Reviews," *The Alpine Journal* Vol. 91, No. 335 (1986): p. 259.
3. Earl McRae, "A Hockey Star Owes a Lot of People," *Canadian Magazine* January 20, 1973: p. 13.
4. George Pachovsky, "Borys Chambul: The King of Canadian Discus Throwers," *Ontario Athletics* (c.1979/80): p. 12.
5. Michael Czuboka, *Ukrainian Canadian, Eh?* (Winnipeg: Communigraphics, 1983) p. 140.
6. Tony Techko, "The Rise and Fall of Al Delaney," *Windsor This Month* November, 1980: p. 18.
7. Paul Vasey, "The days of wine and roses."
8. *The Hockey News* October 6, 1948: p. 13.
9. David Blackie, *Boston: The Canadian Story* (Ottawa: Seneca House Books, 1984) p. 173.
10. *The Ring* June 1947.
11. Ed Dearden, "The Homenuiks of Saskatchewan," *Golf Canada* August, 1972: p. 10.
12. ibid. p. 10.
13. Glynn A. Leyshon, *Of Mats and Men* (London: Sports Dynamic, 1984): p. 72.
14. ibid. p. 72.
15. George Carson, "Steve Hrymnak One Big Reason for Lofty Perch of Flyers," *The Hockey News* January 10, 1953: p. 12.
16. Doug McConnell, "A Long-time WHL All-Star Hucul Turns to Coaching with Faith and Hope," *Hockey Pictorial* May, 1973: p. 61.
17. Dwayne Erickson, "Buffs Sweep to Cage Title," *Winnipeg Free Press* March 20, 1962: p. 23.
18. Scotty Harper, *Winnipeg Free Press* October 24, 1956: p. 19.
19. Bob Hesketh, "Back to his Engine," *The Hockey News* September, 1952: p. 11.
20. Charley Barton, "Kassian says NHL Snub Won't Stop Him," *The Hockey News* October 19, 1968: p. 15.
21. Duncan Barnes, "Harvard Recruits a Hockey Player - Or Does It?," *Sports Illustrated* March 19, 1963: p. 58.
22. Jim Proudfoot, "Konihowskis Still Share Dream of Winning Medals for Canada," *The Toronto Star* November 24, 1979: p. D2.
23. *Winnipeg Free Press* July 13, 1970.
24. Jim Mason, "Ex-Forts Remember Early Days Here," *The Chronicle-Journal* (Thunder Bay), February 11, 1987: p. 13.
25. Gary Mugford, "Mann Cup famine ends, Excels triumph," *The Guardian* (Brampton) September 10, 1980: p. 51.
26. Studs Terkel, *Working* (New York: Pantheon Books, 1972): p. 381.
27. Roy MacGregor, "Almost Dead Solid Perfect," *The Canadian* October 11, 1975: p. 16.

28. Gerald Donaldson, "Apres Ski," *The Financial Post Moneywise Magazine* (Toronto) October 1986: p. 26.

29. John Barber, "Fear of Flying," *Today*: p. 14.

30. George Tatomyr, *Beyond the Uke Line* (Trenton, City Print: 1990) p. 115.

31. Cleve Dheensaw, *Island of Champions: A Sporting History of Vancouver Island* (Victoria: Orca Book Publishers, 1988) p. 263.

32. Trent Frayne, *Famous Hockey Players* (New York: Dodd, Mead and Co.: 1973) p. 153.

33. ibid. p. 150.

34. Jack Sullivan, "Shack Leafs' Answer to Bill Ezinicki?" *Winnipeg Free Press* Nov. 18, 1961.

35. Colleen and Gordie Howe and Charles Wilkins, *After the Applause* (Toronto: McClelland & Stewart Inc., 1989) p. 20.

36. Margaret Scott, "I'll Survive the Disappointments and Carry On," *Hockey World* October 1972: p. 55.

37. Randy Schultz, "Yesterday's Heroes," *Hockey Digest* January 1986: p. 74.

38. Tony Techko, notes on John Upham.

39. Rex MacLeod, "Once a tough Ticat, now a leader of fishermen," *The Toronto Star* July 28, 1987: p. B2.

40. "Sobering Return for Bill Werbeniuk," *The Toronto Star* January 23, 1990: p. S1.

41. B. Calder and G. Andrews, *Rider Pride* (Saskatoon: Western Producers Prairie Books, 1984) p. 112.

42. Phil Drackett, *Flashing Blades - The Story of British Ice Hockey* (Wiltshire: The Crowood Press, 1987) p. 107.

43. Andy O'Brien, "England's Own Rocket Richard," *Weekend Magazine* Vol. 6 No. 11, 1956: p. 47.

# BIBLIOGRAPHY

**English Language**

**Books**

Allen, George. *Pro Football's 100 Greatest Players*. Indianapolis: Bobbs-Merrill Company, Inc., 1982.

Baran, Theodore, ed. *Jubilee Book: 75th Anniversary of the St. George's Ukrainian Catholic Parish, Saskatoon*. Yorkton: The Parish Editorial Committee of St. George's Cathedral Parish in Saskatoon, 1987.

Batten, Jack. *The Leafs in Autumn*. Toronto: Macmillan Co. of Canada, 1975.

Blaikie, David. *Boston: The Canadian Story*. Ottawa: Seneca House Books, 1984.

Boyle, Mickey. *Ninety Years of Golf*. Regina: Saskatchewan Golf Association, 1987.

Bower, Johnny. *How to Play Hockey*. Toronto: Coca-Cola, 1966.

Bratton, Robert. *Canadian Volleyball: A History to 1967*. Vanier: Canadian Volleyball Association, 1972.

Bucyk, John. *Hockey is my Blood*. Toronto: Pagurian Press Limited, 1972.

Burgess, A. and Palmer, J. *Everest Canada: The Ultimate Challenge*. Toronto: Stoddart Publishing, 1983.

Calder, B. and Andrews, G. *Rider Pride: The Story of Canada's Best-Loved Football Team*. Saskatoon: Western Producers Prairie Books, 1984.

Chalk, Ocania. *Pioneers of Black Sport*. New York: Dodd, Mead and Co., 1975.

Coleman, Charles L. *The Trail of the Stanley Cup*. Sherbrooke: Progressive Publications, 1969.

Cosentino, Frank. *Canadian Football: Grey Cup Years*. Toronto: Musson Book Co. Ltd., 1969.

Cosentino, F. and Howell, M. *A History of Physical Education in Canada*. Don Mills: General Publishing Co. Ltd., 1971.

Czuboka, Michael. *Ukrainian Canadian, Eh?* Winnipeg: Communigraphics Printers Aid Group, 1983.

Daley, Arthur. *Pro Football's Hall of Fame*. New York: Grosset & Dunlap, 1969.

Dheensaw, Cleve. *Island of Champions: A Sporting History of Vancouver Island*. Victoria: Orca Book Publishers, 1988.

Dryden, K. and MacGregor, R. *Home Game*. Toronto: McClelland & Stewart Inc., 1989.

Ferguson, Bob. *Who's Who in Canadian Sport*. Toronto: Summerhill Press, 1985.

Fischler, Stan. *Hockey's 100*. Toronto: Stoddart Publishing, 1984.

Frayne, Trent. *Famous Hockey Players*. New York: Dodd, Mead and Co., 1973.

Gitler, Ira. *Ice Hockey A to Z*. New York: Lothrop, Lee and Shepard Co., 1978.

Hershfield, Leible. *The Jewish Athlete: A Nostalgic View*. 1980.

Howell, M. and Howell, R. *History of Sports in Canada*. Champagne: Stipes Publishing Co., 1981.

Howell, N. and Howell, M. *Sports and Games in Canadian Life: 1700 to the Present*. Toronto: Macmillan of Canada, 1969.

Johnson, C. Fred. *Book of Champions of the Canadian Canoe Association, 1900-1984*. Ottawa: Canadian Canoe Association, 1988.

Jones, Terry. *Canadian Pro Football '84*. Markham: PaperJacks Ltd., 1984.

Kavanaugh, L.V. *History of Golf in Canada*. Toronto: Fitzhenry and Whiteside, 1973.

Kearney, Jim. *Champions: A British Columbia Sports Album*. Vancouver: Douglas and McIntyre Ltd., 1985.

Leah, Vince. *Manitoba Hockey: A History*. Winnipeg: Manitoba Hockey Players' Foundation, Inc., 1970.

Leyshon, Glynn A. *Of Mats and Men*. London: Sports Dynamic, 1984.

Liss, Howard. *Hockey's Greatest Allstars*. New York: Hawthorn Books, Inc., 1972.

Luciuk, Lubomyr. *Ukrainians in the Making: Their Kingston Story*. Kingston: Limestone Press, 1980.

Lysenko, Vera. *Men in Sheepskin Coats*. Toronto: Ryerson Press, 1947.

McAuley, Jim. *The Ottawa Sports Book*. Burnstown: General Store Publishing House, 1987.

McNabb, Fred. *Sports History of St. Catharines*. St. Catharines: Advance Printing, 1969.

McNulty, B. and Radcliffe, T. *Canadian Athletics 1839-1992*. Self-published, 1992.

Marunchak, Michael H. *The Ukrainian Canadians: A History*. Winnipeg: Ukrainian Academy of Arts and Science, 1982.

Melady, John. *Overtime, Overdue: The Bill Barilko Story*. Trenton: City Print, 1988.

Morrow, D. and Keyes, M. *A Concise History of Sports in Canada*. Toronto: Oxford University Press, 1987.

Olney, Ross. *Super Champions of Ice Hockey*. New York: Clarion Books, 1982.

Panchuk, Bohdan, ed. *Royal Canadian Legion Memorial Souvenir Book 1: Ukrainian Branches*. Montreal: Ukrainian Canadian Veterans' Association, 1986.

Redmond, Gerald. *The Sporting Scots of Nineteenth-Century Canada*. Toronto: Associated University Press, 1982.

Redmond, Gerald, ed. *Edmonton '78*. Edmonton: Executive Sport Publication Ltd., 1978.

Richler, Mordecai. *Notes on an Endangered Species and Others*. New York: A. Knopf, Inc., 1974.

Roxborough, Henry. *One Hundred-Not Out: The History of Nineteenth-Century Canadian Sports*. Toronto: Ryerson Press, 1966.

Sodernberg, Paul, Washington, Helen and Press, Cattel, Jaques, eds. *The Big Book of Halls of Fame in the United States and Canada*. New York: R. R. Bowker Co., 1977.

Sonmor, Jean. *Burned by the Rock: Inside the World of Men's Championship Curling*. Toronto: Macmillan Canada, 1991.

Sullivan, Jack. *The Grey Cup Story*. Toronto: Pagurian Press Limited, 1970.

Tatomyr, George. *Beyond the Uke Line: Ukrainians in the National Hockey League*. Trenton: City Print, 1990.

Terkel, Studs. *Working*. New York: Pantheon Books, 1972.

Tester, Jim, ed. *Sports Pioneers: A History of the Finnish-Canadian Amateur Sports Federation 1906 - 1986*. Sudbury: Alerts AC Historical Committee, c.1986.

Thom, Douglas J. *The Hockey Bibliography*. Toronto: OISE, 1978.

Treat, Roger. *Encyclopedia of Football: 15th Revised Edition*. South Brunswick & New York: A.S. Barnes and Co., Inc.

Wallechinsky, David. *The Complete Book of the Olympics*. New York: Viking Penguin Inc., 1988.

Wynnyckyj, Iroida, ed. *Milestones - A History of the Ukrainian Catholic Church of the Transfiguration, Kitchener, Ontario, 1926-86*. Kitchener: Ukrainian Catholic Church of the Transfiguration, 1987.

Young, Scott. *War on Ice: Canada in International Hockey*. Toronto: McClelland and Stewart, 1976.

Yuzik, Paul. *Ukrainians in Manitoba*. Toronto: University of Toronto Press, 1953.

Zinkewych, Osyp. *Ukrainian Olympic Champions*. Baltimore: V. Symonenko Smoloskyp Publishers, 1984.


**Memorial Books, Media Guides and Year Books**

American Hockey League. *American Hockey League Media Guide*. 1981/82-1988/89.

Canadian Amateur Hockey Association. *Canada's National Junior Team 1990 Media Guide*.

Canadian Amateur Hockey Association. *1990 Women's World Ice Hockey Championship*.

Canadian Football League. *Facts Figures and Records. 1987- .*

Canadian Interuniversity Athletic Union. *Canadian Team Guide: 1987 Summer Universiade*.

Canadian Interuniversity Athletic Union. *Canadian Team Handbook: 1991 Summer Universiade*.

Canadian Olympic Association. *Canadian Team Handbook: Olympic Games Canada 88*.

Canadian Olympic Association. *Canadian Team Handbook: Olympic Winter Games Canada 88*.

Canadian Olympic Association. *1987 Pan American Games*.

Canadian Olympic Association. *Canadian Team Handbook: XI Pan American Games*.

Canadian Ukrainian Athletic Club. *CUAC Year Book*. Winnipeg, 1940-51.

Canadian Ukrainian Athletic Club. *CUAC 50th Anniversary and Re-Union Banquet Programme: 1926-1976*. Winnipeg.

Commonwealth Games Association of Canada. *Canadian Team Handbook: XIV Commonwealth Games*.

Free Olympiad Organizing Committee. *1980 Free Olympiad*. Toronto.

Free Olympiad Organizing Committee. *Free Olympiad 1984*. Toronto.

International Ice Hockey Federation. *International Hockey Guide*. Helsinki, 1978/79 - 1981/82.

Manitoba Curling Association. *Manitoba Curling Association Centennial: 1888-1988*.

Manitoba Curling Association. *Yearbook 1989*.

Manitoba Ladies Curling Association. *1988-89 Yearbook*.

National Hockey League. *NHL Press and Radio Guide*. 1945-82.

National Hockey League. *NHL Guide and Official NHL Record Book*. 1982/83.

National Hockey League. *NHL Official Guide and Record Book*. 1983/84- .

Ontario Track and Field Association. *1991 Athletics Annual*.

Royal Canadian Legion. *Track and Field Annual*. 1963-69.

Sporting News. *National Football Guide*. 1970-80

Sporting News. *Hockey Register*. 1974- .

University of Western Ontario. *Western Mustang Football 1990*.


## Dissertations

Mott, Morris K. *Manly Sports and Manitobans: Settlement Days to World War I*. Ph.D. dissertation, Queen's University, 1980.


## Newspapers

*The Fort William Daily Times-Journal*, 1936-48.

*Hamilton Spectator*, 1948-59.

*Ontario Reformer* (Oshawa), 1922-26.

*Oshawa Daily Reformer*, 1926-27.

*Oshawa Daily Times*, 1927-32, 1940.

*The Port Arthur News-Chronicle*, 1949-53.

*Sudbury Daily Star*, 1950-55, 1969-75.

*Winnipeg Free Press*, 1935-73.

*The Young Worker* (Toronto), 1924-36.


## Periodicals

*Branch 141 Newsletter* (Winnipeg), 1946-88.

*Forum* (Scranton), 1967- .

*Goal: The National Hockey League Magazine* (New York), 1980-92.

*Hockey News* (Toronto), 1947- .

*Horizon* (Chicago), 1957-71.

*Maple Leaf Garden Hockey Magazine* (Toronto), 1967-73.

Multicultural History Society of Ontario. *Polyphony*, Vol. 7 No.1, (Toronto, Spring/Summer

1985) & Vol.10, (Toronto, 1988).

*Ontario Athletics* (Toronto), December 1980- .

*Opinion* (Winnipeg), 1946-65.

Redmond, Gerald. *Sports and Ethnic Groups in Canada*. Calgary: CAHPER, 1978.

*St. John's Institute Newsletter* (Edmonton), 1966-83.

*Student* (Toronto, Edmonton, Toronto), 1968- .

*Swim* (Toronto), 1974-83.

*Swim Canada* (Toronto), 1983- .

*The Unitas Boxing Weekly* (Toronto), 1974-78.

*Track and Field News* (Los Altos), 1966- .

*Trident* (Chicago), 1960-62.

*Ukrainian Canadian* (Toronto), 1947- .

*Ukrainian Canadian Review* (Winnipeg), 1941-44.

*Ukrainian Life* (Scranton), 1940-42.

*Ukrainian Trend* (New York), 1941-69.

*Youth Speaks* (Winnipeg), 1949-54.


## Ukrainian Language

### Books

Chorostil, Jaroslaw. *Boritesia - Poborete: Ohliad Dialnosty ST "Ukraina" v Toronti za Roky 1948-1949*. Toronto: SA Ukraina, 1950.

Chorostil, J. and Kostiuk, R. *"Ukraina" Sport Association - Toronto*. Toronto: Kiev Printers Ltd., 1983.

Davydowych, Maria, ed. *Smoloskyp Osvity i Zhyttia: Zolotyi Uvilei T-va "Prosvita" imeny T. Shevchenka v Montreali-Point St. Charles*. Montreal: Prosvita, 1963.

Didiuk, Wasyl, ed. *A Historical Outline of the Ukrainian Canadian Congress Toronto-Branch*. Toronto: Ukrainian Canadian Congress Toronto-Branch, c.1992.

Figol, M., ed. *25 Rokiv SUM Kanady 1948-1973*. Toronto: SUM, 1973.

Kinach, M. and Oschypko, H., eds. *Jubilee Book: Ukrainian Youth Association "SUM" of Quebec*. Montreal: SUM, 1980.

Knysh, Zynovy, ed. *Na Shliakhu do Natsionalnoi Yednosty: Piadesiat Rokiv Pratsi Ukrainskoho Natsionalnoho Obiednnania Kanady, 1932-1982*. Toronto: Ukrainian National Federation of Canada, 1982.

Kosikowsky, Oleksa. *My Windsor Reminiscences*. Hamtramck: 1974.

Kumka, M. *Pochatky Rukhanky Sered Ukraintsiv u Vinnipehu*. Winnipeg: Biblioteka Ukrainskoi Shkoly v Kanadi, 1925.

Kuzmowych, Olha, ed. *Almanac of KLK: Ukrainian-American Sports Club*. New York: KLK, 1989.

Marunchak, Michael, ed. *Biographical Dictionary of the History of Ukrainian Canadians*. Winnipeg: Ukrainian Academy of Arts and Science, 1986.

Marunchak, Michael, ed. *Horodenshchyna: A Collection of Historical Data and Memoirs*. Winnipeg: Shevchenko Scientific Society, 1978.

Mostenko, Stepan. *Lehka Atletyka v Istorii Olimpiiskykh Ihor*. Toronto: Ukrainian Toiler Publishing Co., 1952.

Pryszlak, Jaroslaw. *Two Idealistic Brothers*. Montreal: Ukrainian-American "Freedom" Foundation, 1990.

Skocen, Oleksander. *With Soccer into the World: Memoirs*. Toronto: Basilian Press, 1985.

Vicking, . *Fundamentals of Sport Shooting*. Saskatoon: New Pathways, 1939.

Woycenko, Olha. *Annals of Ukrainian Life in Canada*, Vol. 1-6. Winnipeg: Trident, 1963.

Woycenko, Olha, ed. *Ukrainians in Kenora: Prosvita Jubilee Book 1915-1965*. Kenora: Prosvita, 1965.

**Memorial Books, Media Guides and Year Books**

Boretsky, Metodij, ed. *Ukrainian Sports Olympiad in Philadelphia, May 28-30, 1988: Results Summary*. Philadelphia: Ukrainian Olympiad Committee, 1989.

Kucil, R. and Twardowsky, O., eds. *U 25 Richia Ukrainskoi Sportovoi Tsentrali Ameryky i Kanady*. Ukrainian Sports Association of USA and Canada, 1980.

Lushycky, Alexander. *Ukrainian Olympiad and Youth Rally*. Philadelphia: Ukrainian Olympiad Committee, 1988.

Mohyla Ukrainian Institute. *Kameniari*. Saskatoon, 1919.

Ukrainian National Federation. *Trydsiaty-Littia Ukrainskoho Natsionalnoho Obiednania v Hamiltoni, 1935-1965*.

Ukrainian Youth Association Plast. *XI Lehkoatletychni Pershosti Ukrainskoi Sportovoi Tsentrali Ameryky i Kanady*. Toronto, 1969.

**Newspapers and Periodicals**

*Homin Ukrainy* (Toronto), 1948- .

*Militant Youth* (Winnipeg), 1930-32.

*Nash Sport* (Newark), 1962- .

*Novyi Shliakh* (Edmonton, Saskatoon, Winnipeg, Toronto), 1930- .

*Oko* (Montreal), 1979-85.

*Sport* (Toronto), 1955-56.

*Sportowi Wisti* (Toronto), 1954.

*Svit Molodi* (Winnipeg), 1927-30.

*Ukrainian News* (Edmonton), 1988- .

*Ukrainskyi Holos* (Winnipeg), 1919- .

*Vilne Slovo* (Toronto), 1956-78.
*Yunak* (Toronto), 1966-84.


**Archival Deposits**

**Archives of Ontario**
Fred Kazor Papers   (F 1405 Series 56, UKR: 0076)
Helen Mozewsky Papers   (F 1405 Series 56, UKR: 0095)
Wasyl Rukulak Papers   (F 1405 Series 56, UKR: 0086)
Ihor Szkrumelak Papers   (F 1405 Series 56, UKR: 0006)
Dr. Elias Wachna Papers   (F 1405 Series 56, UKR: 0080)
Peter Werbowecki Papers   (F 1405 Series 56, UKR: 0119)


**National Archives of Canada**
Walter J. Bossy Papers (MG 30, C72)
Ukrainian National Youth Federation Collection (MG 28, V8)

# CROSS REFERENCE

PART 1:  THE CLUBS, LEAGUES AND TEAMS

PART 2:  THE ATHLETES, COACHES AND ADMINISTRATORS

# SURVEYED
# SPORTS CLUBS, LEAGUES AND TEAMS
(by city)

**BROOKLANDS**
Brooklands Ukrainian Athletic Club

**CALGARY**
Red Aces

**EDMONTON**
Canadian Sports Association Ukraina (*see* Ukrainian Sports Association *Ukraina*)
*Karpaty* (*see* Ukrainian Sports Association *Ukraina*)
Lions
Taras Shevchenko Institute *Shevs*
Ukrainian Sports Association *Sitch*
Ukrainian Sports Association *Ukraina*
Ukrainian Sports Association *Ukraina*
Ukrainian Sports Club of Edmonton (*see* Ukrainian Sports Association *Ukraina*)

**HAMILTON**
St. Vladimir Softball Team
Sports Association *Ukraina* (*see* Ukrainian Sports Club *Dnipro*)
Ukrainian Sport Club *Dnipro*
Ukrainian Vets

**KENORA**
Kenora Ukrainian Athletic Club

**KINGSTON**
Ukrainian Sports Club of Kingston

**KIRKLAND LAKE**
Ukrainian Sport Association *Dnipro*

**KITCHENER**
Ukrainian Catholic Church of the Transfiguration Hockey Team

**LETHBRIDGE**
Ukrainian Sports Association *Orlyk*

**LONDON, ENGLAND**
Ukrainian Canadian Servicemen's Association

**MONTREAL**
Sport Association *Ukraina*
Ukrainian National Athletic Club
Ukrainian Sports Club *Dnipro* (*see* Sport Association *Ukraina*)
Ukrainian Youth Association (SUM)

**MOOSE JAW**
Ukrainian National Youth Federation

**OSHAWA**
Dnipro (*see* Ukrainian Youth Association SUM)
St. George's
St. John's
Sports Association *Ukraina* c.1960s
Tridents
*Ukraina* c.1980s (*see* Tridents)
Ukrainian Athletic Club
Ukrainian Nationals (*see* Ukrainian Athletic Club)
Ukrainian Sitch (*see* Ukrainian Athletic Club)
Ukrainian Sports Association *Strila*
Ukrainian Youth Association (SUM)
Young Ukrainian Nationals

**ST. CATHARINES**
Ukrainian Sports Club Trident

**SASKATOON**
St. George's Softball Team
Sports Tournament
Ukrainian Sports Club

**SHANDRO**
Shandro Basketball Team

**SUDBURY**
Ukrainian Soccer Club Tridents
Ukrainian Sports Club Lions
Ukrainian Sports Club *Sitch*

**THUNDER BAY** (Port Arthur and Fort William)
Football Club *Sicz*
Lakehead Ukrainian Athletic Club
Ukrainian Football Club (*see* Football Club *Sicz*)

**TORONTO**
Association of United Ukrainian Canadians (*see* Ukrainian Labour-Farmer Temple Association)
Canadian Ukrainian Youth Association (SUMK) (*see* St. Vladimir)
Carpathian Ski Club
St. Josaphat's
St. Vladimir's
Sport Association *Ukraina*
Ukrainian Basketball League
Ukrainian Canadian Athletic Club Trident (*see* Ukrainian Sport Club Trident)
Ukrainian-Canadian Girls Slo-Pitch League
Ukrainian Labour-Farmer Temple Association
Ukrainian National Democratic League (ODUM) (*see* St. Vladimir)
Ukrainian Nationals (*see* Ukrainian Sport Club Trident)
Ukrainian Orienteering Club *Lysiachyj Bih*
Ukrainian Slo-Pitch Softball League
Ukrainian Softball League
Ukrainian Sports Club Trident
Ukrainian Tennis Club *Lviv*
Ukrainian Volleyball Club Toronto
Ukrainian Volleyball League
Ukrainian Youth Association *Plast*
Ukrainian Youth Association (SUM)
Ukrainian Youth Soccer Association
University Settlement Ukrainians
*Vedmedyky* (*see* Ukrainian Youth Association *Plast*)

**VANCOUVER**
Ukrainian Sports Club *Berkut*
Ukrainian Sports Club *Sokil*

## WINDSOR
Canadian Ukrainian Youth Association (SUMK) - St. Vladimir
St. Vladimir (*see* Canadian Ukrainian Youth Association - SUMK)
Sport Association Ukraine
Ukrainian Nationals
Ukrainian Sports Association *Sitch* (*see* Sport Association Ukraine)

## WINNIPEG
Canadian Ukrainian Athletic Club
Canadian Ukrainian Football Club
Institute Prosvita Athletic Club
Institute Prosvita Ukrainians (see Institute Prosvita Athletic Club)
Sts. Peter and Paul
Sts. Vladimir and Olga
Trident Golf Club
Ukrainian Canadian Veterans Branch 141
Ukrainian Chess Club
Ukrainian Diamond Ball League
Ukrainian Sports Club (*see* Canadian Ukrainian Football Club)
Ukrainian Students' Club *Kozaks*
Ukrainian Tennis Club
Winnipeg *Ukraina*

## YORKTON
St. Joseph's College

# OTHER CLUBS, LEAGUES AND TEAMS

In addition to the sports clubs surveyed, others clubs, leagues and teams existed or were reported to have existed. Unfortunately, lack of information has precluded a presentation of their histories in this work. For the record, they are listed below. This is by no means an exhaustive list.

| City | Known Name | Known Year(s) of Operation |
|------|-----------|---------------------------|
| Brantford | Ukrainian Youth Section Sport (ULFTA) | 1931 |
| Calgary | Prosvita softball team | 1931 |
| Detroit | Adanacs* | 1928 |
| Edmonton | Canadian Ukrainian Athletic Club | 1935 |
| Edmonton | *Skob* | 1951 |
| Espanola | Ukrainian Nationalists (?) (UNYF) | 1939 |
| Westfort ** | *Sitch* | 1911-12 |
| Halifax | Ukrainian Chess Club (?) | 1952 |
| Hamilton | Sports Club *Dnipro* | 1964-65 |
| Kingston | Ukrainian Sporting *Sitch* Association | 1946 |
| Kirkland Lake | Tridents (UNYF) | 1937 |
| Modelfarm | St. Mary's Church Softball Club | 1930s |
| Montreal | Prosvita Youth Sports Club | 1939-40 |
| Montreal | Ukrainian Sporting *Sitch* Association | 1925 |
| Mundare | Sts. Peter and Paul's Church Sports Club | |
| Preston | SUMK | 1935 |
| St. Catharines | Sport Association *Kyiv* | 1949 |
| St. Catharines | Ukrainian Volleyball Club Dynamo | 1978 |
| Sudbury | Ukrainians | 1952 |
| Sudbury | St. Mary's Church Softball Club | 1950s |
| Toronto | Ukrainian Floor Hockey League | 1977 |
| Toronto | Ukrainian Touch Football League | 1980s |
| Windsor | Ukrainian Sports Club | 1955-56 |
| Winnipeg | Blessed Virgin Mary Church hockey club | 1954-56 |
| Winnipeg | *Chayka* | 1969-70 |
| Winnipeg | Dynamo (ULFTA) | 1952 |
| Winnipeg | St. Nicholas Church softball teams | 1944 |
| Winnipeg | Ukrainian Chess Club - Winnipeg | 1956 |
| Winnipeg | Ukrainian Catholic Hockey League | 1960-61 |
| Winnipeg | Ukrainian Tigers | 1962 |

\* Team made up of expatriated Ukrainians from Manitoba. Adanacs is Canada backwards.
\*\* Now Thunder Bay.

# PROFILED ATHLETES, COACHES AND ADMINISTRATORS

## ADMINISTRATORS/COACHES

Achtymichuk, Gene
Baryluk, Mitch
Baydock, Donna
Beverley, Nick
Bezruchka, Stephen
Bodnar, Gus
Bossy, Leo
Boytchuk, William
Broda, Turk
Bucyk, Johnny
Bunka, George
Burchuk, Mike
Chumak, Valentin
Copot, Murray
Danychuk, Bill
Daski, Mike
Eurchuk, Mike
Fedoruk, Sylvia
Festeryga, George
Guzzell, Mike
Gwozdecky, George
Hawrylak, Bill
Hucul, Fred
Hucul, Sandy
Humenuik, Rod
Katan, John
Kinasewich, Gene
Kinasewich, Ray
Klymkiw, Julian
Kozyra, Taras
Kryschuk, Mike
Kucharchuk-Andruchiw, Julia
Lashuk, Mike

Leswick, Tony
Mackowski, Cathy
Maich, Joe
Melnyk, Gerry
Michaluk, John
Mickoski, Nick
Mitruk, Steve
Mosienko, Bill
Motoch, George
Muzyka, Alex
Newman, Bernie
Nykoluk, Mike
Oryszczyn, Eugene
Ostapchuk, Bill
Ostapchuk-Mackowski, Cathy
Pidsosny, Steve
Prystai, Metro
Rizak, Gene
Romaniuk, Alex
Saganiuk, Rocky
Sawula, Lorne
Semotiuk, Darwin
Serediuk, Rummy
Shaley, John
Shaley, Stan
Shibicky, Alex
Shwaluk, Bill
Skocen, Oleksander
Stasiuk, Most Rev. Peter
Stasiuk, Vic
Steckiw, Ostap
Tatarchuk, Hank
Turow, Thomas
Tyzuk, Boris

Upham, John
Welyhorskyj, Myroslaw
Zamick, Victor

**ALL-ROUND**
Fedoruk, Sylvia

**ARM WRESTLING**
Jaworski, Christine

**ATHLETICS**
Andrusyshyn, Zenon
Boychuk, Andy
Chambul, Borys
Chambul, Lubomyr
Chumak, Valentin
Domansky, Don
Drayton, Jerome
Fedorick, Walter
Fedoruk, Sylvia
Gaziuk, Murray
Hedgewick, Mike
Kepron, Roy
Konihowski, John
Kozak, Dorothy
Mihaychuk, Manoly
Olinek, Gayle
Patten, Stephan
Sadowick-Yakubowich, Joyce
Yakiwchuk, Alanna

**BADMINTON**
Czich, John

**BASEBALL**
Karpuk, Pete
Onuliak, Albert
Shaley, John
Shaley, Stan
Turow, Thomas

Upham, John
Wawryshyn, Evelyn

**BASKETBALL**
Baryluk, Mitch
Dacyshyn, John
Galanchuk, Ken
Ingaldson, Fred
Rizak, Gene
Semotiuk, Darwin
Tatarchuk, Hank

**BODY BUILDING**
Jaworski, Christine
Olinek, Gayle

**BOWLING**
Garuik, John
Hawrylak, Bill
Hynduik, Ollie
Pechaluk, Fred
Ryhorchuk, Ivan
Turow, Thomas

**BOXING**
Delaney, Al
Dyzandra, Paul
Kolaski, Peter
Lakusta, Ken
Maich, Bill
Zaduk, Pete

**BROOMBALL**
Kozyra, Taras

**CANOEING**
Bossy, Dan
Bossy, Don
Bossy, George
Bossy, Leo

Charalambij, Ivan

## CURLING
Burtnyk, Kerry
Fedoruk, Sylvia
Hnatiw, Pete
Hubchik, Walter
Lukowich, Ed
Meleschuk, Orest
Pidzarko-More, Chris
Pidzarko-Shaw, Cathy
Slyziuk, Ernest
Slyziuk, Michael
Tanasichuk, Hal
Werenich, Ed

## CYCLING
Gregorovich, Andrew

## DIVING
Dacyshyn, Anna

## DOG SLEDDING
Olensky, Harry

## FIGURE SKATING
Ostapchuk, Bill
Ostapchuk-Mackowski, Cathy
Prychun, Daria
Slipchuk, Michael

## FISHING
Waszczuk, Henry
Welyhorskyj, Myroslaw

## FOOTBALL
Ambrosie, Randy
Andrusyshyn, Zenon
Bahnuik, Don
Bossy, George

Boyko, Bruce
Chepesuik, Mike
Cherkas, Ron
Chomyc, Lance
Chorney, Terris
Cyncar, Marco
Danychuk, Bill
Evanshen, Terry
Festeryga, George
Garuik, John
Gerela, Roy
Gerela, Ted
Hameluck, Mike
Hawrylak, Bill
Hedgewick, Mike
Humenuik, Rod
Kardash, Jim
Karpuk, Pete
Konihowski, John
Korchak, Bud
Kulka, Glenn
Lakusiak, Gene
Landy, Frank
Lashuk, Mike
Malinosky, John
Manchuk, Bill
Marks, Victor
Michaluk, John
Motoch, George
Mularchyk, Ed
Muzyka, Alex
Nagurski, Bronko
Nagurski Jr., Bronko
Nykoluk, Danny
Oneschuk, Steve
Patrick, Steve
Piaskoski, Jim
Pruski, Steve
Romaniuk, Alex
Semotiuk, Darwin

Shishka, Steven
Sopinka, John
Syrnyk, Ray
Waszczuk, Henry
Wlasiuk, Gene
Woznesensky, Lyall
Wusyk, Bill
Zubkewych, Morris

## GOLF
Baluik, Stan
Ezinicki, Bill
Hnatiuk, Glen
Homenuik, Ted
Homenuik, Wilf
Hynduik, Ollie
Kepron, Roy
Makohon, Jeff
Mickoski, Nick
Panasiuk, Bob

## GYMNASTICS
Baraniuk, Chris
Borowik, Alexandra
Diachun, Jennifer
Hardabura, Jason
Ivanochko, Sasha
Mitruk, Steve
Mitruk, Terry
Newman, Bernie
Oryszczyn, Eugene
Romaniuk, John

## HOCKEY
Achtymichuk, Gene
Andreychuk, Dave
Baby, John
Babych, Dave
Babych, Wayne
Balon, Dave

Baluik, Stan
Barilko, Bill
Bellows, Brian
Berehowsky, Drake
Beverley, Nick
Black, Stephen
Bodnar, Gus
Boimistruck, Fred
Bolonchuk, Larry
Bossy, Leo
Bossy, Mike
Bower, Johnny
Boyko, Darren
Broda, Turk
Bucyk, Johnny
Bucyk, Randy
Budy, Tim
Burega, Bill
Busniuk, Mike
Busniuk, Ron
Chorney, Marc
Chychrun, Jeff
Chyzowski, Dave
Cooper, Joe
Copot, Murray
Daneyko, Ken
Daski, Mike
Derlago, Bill
Diduck, Gerald
Diduck, Judy
Dorohoy, Eddie
Elynuik, Pat
Ezinicki, Bill
Federko, Bernie
Godynyuk, Alex
Gwozdecky, George
Haidy, Gord
Hawerchuk, Dale
Hordy, Mike
Horeck, Pete

Hospodar, Ed
Hoyda, Dave
Hrechkosy, Dave
Hrudey, Kelly
Hrymnak, Steve
Hucul, Fred
Hucul, Sandy
Juzda, Bill
Kachur, Ed
Kaleta, Alex
Kaminski, Kevin
Kassian, Dennis
Kassian, Ed
Kaszycki, Mike
Kinasewich, Gene
Kinasewich, Ray
Kindrachuk, Orest
Klukay, Joe
Klymkiw, Julian
Korney, Mike
Koroll, Cliff
Kowcinak, Dick
Kozak, Don
Kozak, Les
Kozak, Paul
Krushelnyski, Mike
Kryschuk, Mike
Kuryluk, Mervin
Kuzyk, Ken
Langelle, Pete
Leschyshyn, Curtis
Lesuk, Bill
Leswick, Jack
Leswick, Peter
Leswick, Tony
Lewicki, Danny
Lozinski, Larry
Lukowich, Bernie
Lukowich, Morris
Lupul, Gary

Lysiak, Tom
Malarchuk, Clint
Maruk, Dennis
Masnick, Paul
Mazur, Eddie
Melnyk, Gerry
Melnyk, Larry
Michaluk, Art
Michaluk, John
Michayluk, Dave
Mickoski, Nick
Mosienko, Bill
Nesterenko, Eric
Nykoluk, Mike
Ogrodnick, John
Oleschuk, Bill
Osborne, Mark
Owchar, Dennis
Patrick, James
Patrick Jr., Steve
Pelyk, Mike
Poddubny, Walt
Polis, Greg
Polonich, Dennis
Prystai, Metro
Ratushny, Dan
Ratushny, Kim
Romanchych, Larry
Romaniuk, Russ
Ruff, Lindy
Sacharuk, Larry
Saganiuk, Rocky
Samolenko, George
Sawchuk, Terry
Semenko, Dave
Shabaga, Mike
Shack, Eddie
Shewchuk, Jack
Shibicky, Alex
Smyl, Stan

Sobchuk, Dennis
Sobchuk, Gene
Stanowski, Wally
Stasiuk, Most Rev. Peter
Stasiuk, Vic
Tkaczuk, Walt
Veitch, Darren
Wasnie, Nick
Wawryshyn, Evelyn
Witiuk, Steve
Woytowich, Bob
Wyrozub, Randy
Yaremchuk, Gary
Yaremchuk, Ken
Zamick, Victor
Zuke, Mike

## LACROSSE
Hedgewick, Mike
Maruk, Barry

## MOUNTAINEERING
Bezruchka, Stephen

## RHYTHMIC GYMNASTICS
Wilk, Lucie

## RINGETTE
Diduck, Judy

## SHOOTING
Kwasnycia, Don

## SKIING
Guzzell, Mike
Kindy, Anna
Kobelka, Kendra
Podborski, Steve

## SNOOKER
Stelmach, Natalie
Werbeniuk, Bill

## SOCCER
Bereza, Myron
Boytchuk, William
Gawryluk, Johnny
Gwozdecky, George
Serwetnyk, Carrie
Skocen, Oleksander
Steckiw, Ostap
Zakaluzny, Walter

## SPEED SKATING
Pidsosny, Steve

## SWIMMING
Fedko, Alex
Jaremy, John
Malar, Joanne
Sawchuk, Bill
Shewchuk, Stephanie

## TENNIS
Rusedski, Greg

## TRAMPOLINE
Mitruk, Christopher

## VOLLEYBALL
Alexiuk, Ed
Baydock, Donna
Burchuk, Mike
Danyluk, Terry
Eliashevsky, Christine
Iwanoczko, Dale
Klysh, Myron
Kostiuk, Al
Kramchynsky-Nelson, Eileen

Kucharchuk-Andruchiw, Julia
Sawula, Lorne
Stefaniuk, Peter
Tyzuk, Boris

**WEIGHTLIFTING**
Shwaluk, Bill

**WRESTLING**
Bilinski, Mike
Bunka, George
Chepesuik, Mike
Demchuk, John

Eurchuk, Mike
Garuik, John
Gordienko, George
Hryb, Taras
Katan, John
Kohut, Meron
Kozak, Steve
Kulka, Glenn
Kusyj, George
Maich, Joe
Nagurski, Bronko
Romaniuk, Alex
Serediuk, Rummy

# OTHER ATHLETES

In addition to the athletes, coaches and administrators profiled, a number of other individuals have either competed or coached in the professional ranks, represented Canada in amateur or professional competitions, or distinguished themselves in Canadian sport. Unfortunately, lack of information has precluded a presentation of their profiles in this work. For the record, they are listed below. This is by no means an exhaustive list.

| | |
|---|---|
| Bala, Ray | bowling |
| Bossy, Igor | football |
| Boychuk, Chris | handball |
| Burak, Ron | rowing |
| Daneliuk, Luki | football |
| Diachuk, Ed | hockey |
| Harbluk, W. | hockey |
| Humeniuk, Marianne | swimming |
| Kozak, Tiger | football |
| Kuzyk, Gary | football |
| Mendyk, Dennis | football |
| Rosocha, Walter | volleyball |
| Semenko, Mel | football |
| Shastel, Mary | baseball |
| Skerlton, Luba | bowling |
| Slobodian, Pete | hockey |
| Stanko, Andrew | volleyball |
| Stefaniuk, Halya | volleyball |
| Stochansky, Walter | volleyball |
| Vancha, Andy | bowling |
| Wolkowski, Stan | football |
| Wozney, Rich | football |
| Yakimischuk, Orest | football |
| Yakymyk, Mike | football |

# INDEX - PART I

## GENERAL

# INDEX - PART II

## PERSONAL NAMES

(Bold indicates main entry)

Bidiak, Taras, 173, 183, 185, 186

Bilak, Yaroslaw, 241

Bilinski, Mike, **332**

Bilinsky, Stephen, 294

Bilinsky, Stephen, 255

Bilynskyj, Dr. Volodymyr, 272

Bilous, M., 108

Bilous, V., 164

Black, Stephen, **333**

Blaschuk, Jim, 75

Blazenko, Peter, 237

Bobersky, Ivan, 34

Bobyn, Patrick, 127

Bochna, Bohdan, 283

Bodnar, Gus, **334**, 620, 805

Bodnar, William, 146

Boguski, Ed, 210, 212, 213

Boimistruck, Fred, **336**

Bolonchuk, Larry, **337**

Borecky, W., 175, 176, 177

Boretsky, W., 242

Borowik, Alexandra, **338**

Borowyk, Michael, 269

Borshuk, Alex, *see* Delaney, Al

Borys, B., 139

Borzov, Valery, 50

Bossy, Dan, **340**

Bossy, Don, **341**, 802

Bossy, George, **342**, 800

Bossy, Igor, 852

Bossy, Leo, **344**

Bossy, Michael, 26, **344**, 809

Bossy, Volodymyr, 26, 297

Bouchard, Grace, 264

Boukailo, Oleh, 285

Bower, Johnny, **347**, 706, 806, 809, 815

Boychuk, Andy, **351**, 800, 801, 802

Boychuk, Chris, 802, 852

Boyko, Bruce, **353**

Boyko, Darren, **354**

Boyko, Dr., 217

Boytchuk, Stephen, 161

Boytchuk, William, 161, 172, 173, 175, 176, 177, 188, **355**

Bradawaski, Laurie, 264, 265

Bratkiw, Hryhoriy, 70

Brezdenj, Taras, 77

Broadbent, Ed, 51

Broda, Turk, **357**, 805, 809, 815

Brygadyr-Wrubelsky, Mykhailo, 188

Bubela, Peter, 244

Buchanan, Cammie, 98

Buchatsky, J., 95, 100

Buchatsky, O., 95

Bucyk, Johnny, 53, **359,** 809

Bucyk, Randy, **362**

Budka, Bishop, 297

Budko, Gregory, 213

Budy, Tim, **363**, 814

Budyk, Nestor, 293

Bukata, W., 175

Bukatyj, M., 270

Bukojemsky, Steve, 155, 156

Buniak, Peter, *see* Drayton, Jerome

Bunka, George, **364**

Burak, Ron, 800, 852

Burchowych, Joe, 115, 122

Burchuk, Mike, **365**, 803, 814

Burdz, P., 270

Burega, Bill, **367**

Burke, Sean, 170

Burtnyk, Kerry, **368**, 814

Busniuk, Mike, **369**

Busniuk, Ron, **370**

Bychynsky, Zyhmont, 293

Byhold, B., 282


Cahill, Chris, 74

Campbell, Doug, 97

Cap, W., 95, 97

Cap, Wasyl, 272

Derbish, Lida, 192

Derkach, 270

Derlago, Bill, **406**

Derzhko, Oleksander, 161

Dezman, Paul, 68, 71

Diachuk, Ed, 852

Diachun, Jennifer, 47, 56, **407**, 800, 802

Diak, Walter, 204

Didiuk, Wasyl, 87

Diduck, Gerald, **410**

Diduck, Judy, **411**

Dmytriw, Hryhoriy, 71

Dmytryshyn, Harry, 295

Dnieper, Robert, 215

Dobby, Roy, 116

Dobby, Steven, 116

Dobush, Peter, 29

Dolhun, Sam, 275, 277, 278, 279

Dolishny, Hryhoriy, 115

Domansky, Don, **412**, 800, 801, 802, 805

Dorohoy, Eddie, **415**

Doros, Peter, 159, 204

Dorosh, Osyp, 244

Dowhaluk, Leonid, 170, 174, 178, 179, 183

Dowhanyk, Lesia, 258, 259, 274

Dowhosza, John, 146

Drach, Z. 217

Drake, Bill, 98, 101

Drakich, Eli, 234

Drayton, Jerome, 50, 54, **417**, 800, 801, 804, 809

Drebotij, L., 269

Drozda, Stan, 275

Drunewych, Lucy, 156, 157, 158, 216, 217, 218

Duda, Zenon, 98, 100, 101, 222, 225

Duguid, Betty, 265

Dulak, Bohdan, 119, 120, 121

Dwornyk, M., 67

Dyczkowsky, Jerry, 183, 187, 188

Dyczkowsky, Lev, 165, 168, 181

Dyczkowsky, W., 168

Dyk, Joseph,  247

Dyma, Dr. Boryslaw,  289, 292

Dyrda, Harry,  127

Dyrda, Rev. Marko,  71

Dyzandra, Paul,  **420**, 815

Dzera, Victor,  178, 179, 181, 183, 184, 185

Dzerowych, Roman,  216, 218

Dziuba, P.,  109

Dzurman, Bill,  202


Eleniak, Wasyl,  22

Eliashevsky, Christine,  41, 225, 226, **421**, 802

Eliashevsky, John,  180

Eliashevsky, Lida,  225, 226

Elynuik, Pat,  **422**

Eurchuk, Mike,  **423**, 800, 801, 804

Evanshen, Terry,  **426**, 809

Ewaskiw, William,  272, 286

Ezinicki, Bill,  **428**, 490, 501, 811, 815


Faryna, Mykhailo,  288

Fedak, Mstyslaw "Misty,"  180

Federko, Bernie,  **430**

Fedko, Alex,  **432**, 801

Fedori, Zeon,  145

Fedorick, Walter,  **434**, 800, 801

Fedoruk, Mike,  237

Fedoruk, Hon. Sylvia,  55, **437**, 806, 808, 813

Fedoryshyn, John,  125

Fedun, Alex,  291

Fedun, Paul,  206

Feeney, Joseph,  101, 102

Fenkanyn, Steve,  244

Fenyn, Yaroslaw,  188

Festeryga, George,  **440**

Figol, Myron,  109

Fil, A.,  185

Fil, B.,  187

Flynn, Dennis,  201

Fodchuk, Boris "Bo,"  58

Formensky, Peter,  70

Franchi, Harry,  151

Haras, Orysia,  216

Harasym, Jean,  189, 204, 207, 209

Harasymchuk, Rev. T.,  100

Harasymovych, S.,  110

Harbluk, W.,  800, 852

Harbuzinski, Wolodymyr,  78

Hardabura, Jason,  **458**

Harrow, William,  272

Hawerchuk, Dale,  **459**, 814

Hawrylak, Bill,  **461**

Hawryliw, Rev. Konstantin,  286

Hawryluk, John,  253, 254

Hawryshko, M.,  282

Hedgewick, Mike,  **463**, 807, 815

Heindl, Ron,  275

Hentosh, Dmytro,  120

Hercia, Peter,  122

Hewak, R.,  75

Hewryk, Ivan,  269

Hextall, Heather,  265

Hilderman, Jim,  275

Hirniak, W.,  109

Hirnyj, Walter,  138, 139, 143

Hirshfield, Leible,  21

Hlady, Eugene,  145

Hluszok, Zenon,  282, 283, 284, 286

Hlynka, Anthony (Antin),  71

Hnatiuk, Glen,  **465**, 814

Hnatiw, Mykola,  269

Hnatiw, Pete,  **466**, 805

Hnatowich, F.,  254

Hoffman, Abigail,  55

Hohel, F.,  284

Holick, Mel,  180, 219, 220

Holinsky, O.,  25, 53

Holowczynski, Ihor,  294

Homenuik, Ted,  **468**

Homenuik, Wilf,  **469**

Horban, M.,  216

Horbow, Alex,  147, 148, 149, 151

Hordy, Mike, **472**

Horeck, Pete, **473**

Horobiowskyj, Osyp, 102

Horochowskyj, Lesia, 190

Horsky, A., 177, 178

Horyn-Sergio, Darka, 184, 185

Hoshowatiuk, G., 154, 155

Hospodar, Ed, **475**

Howell, Maxwell, 21

Howell, Nancy, 21

Hoyda, Dave, **476**

Hrab, M., 87

Hrabowych, Roman, 294

Hradoway, Mike, 249

Hraynyk, John, 124

Hrechkosy, Dave, **477**

Hrineky, J., 283

Hrudey, Kelley, **479**

Hryb, Taras, **481**, 800, 802

Hrycaiko, Dennis, 814

Hrycak, P., 110

Hrycyn, Myron, 102

Hrymnak, Steve, 146, **482**, 815

Hubchik, Walter, **484**, 815

Hucul, Fred, **485**

Hucul, Sandy, **487**

Huculak, Dr. Paul, 288, 289, 292

Huffmann, Dick, 292

Hul, Borys, 157, 172, 174, 175, 178, 179, 180, 184, 188, 223

Humeniuk, Donna, 106

Humeniuk, George, 202

Humeniuk, Marianne, 800, 852

Humenuik, Rod, **489**

Huminilowycz, S., 212

Hunt, Johnny, 278

Hupaliwsky, R., 109

Hynduik, Ollie, **490**, 805


Ihnatowych, Ivan, 173, 174, 175

Ihnatowycz, George, 180, 184

Kozak, Paul,  56, **545**

Kozak, Steve,  450, **546**

Kozak, Tiger,  852

Kozemchuk, Terry,  137

Kozoriz, John,  286

Kozoris, R.,  241

Kozub, P.,  100

Kozulak, M.,  101

Kozyra, Taras,  **548**

Kramchynsky-Nelson, Eileen,  **549**, 803

Krauss, George,  136

Krawchenko, Bohdan,  73

Kril,  67

Krill, Bernie,  275

Krucik, David,  814

Krushelnyski, Mike,  **550**

Krutish, Joe,  275

Kryschuk, Mike,  252, **552**, 815

Kryskiw, P.,  193

Krywonis, Yaroslaw,  179, 219, 220, 222, 228, 229

Kucharchuk-Andruchiw, Julia,  41, 50, 232, 233, 234, **553**, 803

Kucharsky, Evhenia,  283

Kucharsky, Ivan,  108

Kucharsky, Wasyl,  283, 284, 286

Kuchkuda, O.,  209

Kuchma, E.,  75

Kuchma, V.,  75

Kukulowicz, Aggie,  261

Kulba, J.,  95

Kulchisky, Paul,  41, 48, 199, 202

Kulchycky, B.,  272

Kuliak, A.,  241

Kulka, Glenn,  **555**

Kulyk, Dmytro,  165, 168

Kulyk, Lucien (Luka),  106, 108

Kumka, Mykhailo,  34

Kurdyak, Vic,  209, 210

Kurok, Ihor,  235

Kuryluk, Mervin,  **556**

Kuryluk, T.,  230

Kushper, Ihor,  180

Kussy, Ben,  281, 285

Kusyj, George,  54, 55, 125, **557**, 802

Kutic, Mike,  105

Kuz, Walter,  196, 197, 222, 223, 224, 225, 226

Kuzik, Bill,  255

Kuzik, Mike,  255

Kuzmyn, Roman,  232, 233, 234

Kuzyk, Gary,  852

Kuzyk, Ken,  **558**

Kwasnycia, Don,  **559**, 800, 802, 803

Kwong, Normie,  57

Kyrylo, W.,  73


Lakusiak, Gene,  **561**, 814

Lakusta, Ken,  **562**

Landy, Frank,  **564**, 805

Langelle, Pete,  253, **565**, 811, 815

Larmour, Dennis,  74

Laschuk, Steve,  117

Lashuk, Mike,  **566**

Latezek, John,  74

Lawryshyn, Slavko,  222

Lazerri, Tony,  57

Leah, Vince,  252

Leluk, Nicholas,  51

Lenko, Roman,  182

Leschyshyn, Curtis,  **568**

Lesiuk, Walter,  142

Leskiw, John,  244

Leslie, Michael,  247

Lesuk, Bill,  **569**

Leswick, Jack,  **570**

Leswick, Pete,  **571**, 815

Leswick, Tony,  501, **573**, 807, 815

Levinsky, E.,  258

Lewicki, Danny,  **575**, 805

Lewicki, Walter,  268

Lewitski, Marta,  190, 192, 201

Lidow, Nick,  139

Lipkin, Harvey,  279
Little, Frankie,  264
Lotocky, Ihor,  180
Lowry, Ron,  198
Loyowsky, Yaroslaw,  183
Lozinski, Karl,  83
Lozinski, Larry,  **577**
Lubinsky, Emile,  235
Lubinsky, W.,  139
Luciw, Fred,  244
Lucki, Lou,  290, 291
Luszczyk, P.,  286
Lushczyk, P.,  282
Luchkovich, Michael,  71
Luciw, Fred,  244
Lucyk, Dr. Michael,  205
Lucyk, Dr. S.,  208
Luczkiw, John,  166
Lukowich, Bernie,  **578**
Lukowich, Ed,  **579**, 800, 813
Lukowich, Morris,  **581**, 814
Lunn, A.,  21
Lupiniak, A.,  182
Lupul, Gary,  **583**
Lykhach, Vera,  235
Lysak, Harry,  124
Lysak, Orest,  177, 215
Lysiak, Tom,  **584**
Lysko, Mykhailo,  70

MacAuley, James,  98, 100, 102
McCallion, Hazel,  201
McCallum, S.,  251, 253
McCulla, Bill,  195
McFarlane, Helen,  265
Mackevych, Semen,  161, 207, 215
Mackowski, Cathy,  *see* Ostapchuk-Mackowski, Cathy
McMullan, Dave,  275
McVicar, John,  102
Magur, Bill,  140

Maich, Bill, **586**, 802, 806, 808

Maich, Joe, **588**, 806

Majors, W. L., 293

Makohon, Jeff, **589**

Maksymiv, Onufriy, 208

Maksymiv, Roman, 235

Malanczyj, Vera, 196, 197, 198, 225, 226, 227

Malaniuk, Mykhailo, 77

Malar, Joanne, **590**, 800, 802, 803

Malarchuk, Clint, **592**

Malawy, Frank, 115

Malinosky, John, **593**

Maluha, 139

Maluzynsky, Rev. Taras, 285

Mamalyga, Roman, 202

Manastyrsky, Peter, 285, 286

Manchuk, Bill, **594**

Mancini, John, 74

Manson, Bill, 252

Maraschuk, J., 75

Marchenkowsky, Walter, 244

Marko, Walter, 208, 215

Marks, Victor, **595**

Marples, David, 73

Martin, Diane, 265

Martin, H., 254, 263

Martin, Sammy, 98

Martiniuk, Fedir, 125

Maruk, Barry, **595**

Maruk, Dennis, **597**

Marunchak, Moe, 135

Masarick, S., 29

Masiewich, John, 114

Masina, Ujeko, 141

Maslak, Bill, 250

Masnick, Paul, **599**

Matheson, Jack, 292

Mauthe, Harold, 257, 258, 259

Maxwell, Sylvia, 252

Maykut, D., 115

Maziar, Stephen, 154, 155, 216

Mazur, Ed, **601**, 811

Medwidskyj, Dr. Walter, 235

Melaschenko, O., 213

Meleschuk, Orest, **603**, 805, 811, 814

Melnycky, Peter, 294

Melnyk, D., 177, 215

Melnyk, Gerry, **604**

Melnyk, John, 127, 129, 130

Melnyk, Larry, **606**

Melnyk, O., 270

Melnyk, R., 218

Melnyk, Steve, 292

Melnyk, Wasyl, 83

Melnyk, W., 289

Memrick, J., 249

Mendyk, Dennis, 852

Metelsky, Dennis, 236

Metelsky, M., 236

Methodius, Brother, 69

Michaluk, Art, **608**, 815

Michaluk, John (hockey), **609**

Michaluk, John (football), **610**

Michayluk, Dave, **611**

Mickoski, Nick, **613**, 811, 814

Mihay, Vic, 195

Mihaychuk, Dr. Manoly, 34, 53, **615**

Mikhailovitch, Pera, 107

Millar, M., 204

Minerch, Anne, 252

Mirus, John, 253, 268

Miskie, John, 268

Mitruk, Christopher, **616**

Mitruk, Stephen, **617**, 800, 803

Mitruk, Terry, **619**

Mlynczyk, Eugene, 197, 198

Mocherniak, Ivan, 161

Monson, W., 253, 254

Moroz (nee Shumsky), Iryna, 95, 165, 176

Moroz, Jaroslaw, 216, 228

Moroz, John, 63, 247, 248, 268

Moroz, Roman, 233

Morris, Bill, 194

Morton, W., 25

Mosienko, Bill, 286, 334, **620**, 805, 809, 814

Mosienko, Harry, 253

Mosienko, Jim, 286

Moskal, Mike, 272

Moskal, Myron, 186, 187, 188

Moski, Frank, 274, 275, 276, 278

Motoch, George, **623**

Mularchyk, Ed, 243, **624**

Mulkewytch, Karlo, 37, 46, 52, 188

Mulyk, Todd, 74

Murmylyk, William, 43

Mushey, John, 268

Mushie, Herb, 81

Muzychenko, Mykhailo, 272

Muzychka, 215

Muzychka, Mykhailo, 234

Muzyka, Alex, **625**

Mykytyn, Stephen, 254, 256, 268

Myndiuk, Bohdan, 181


Nagurski, Bronko, 53, **626**, 810, 811, 815

Nagurski Jr., Bronko, **628**

Nasadiuk, G., 172, 174

Nathan, Bert, 102

Nazarko, Bohdan, 177, 178, 179, 184

Neilson, John, 102

Nesterenko, Eric, 54, **629**, 811

Netchuk, Alex, 29

Newman, Bernard, 51, **631**, 801, 803, 807

Nimchuk, Sandy, 190, 201

Nimylowych, Bill, 244

Nitchuk, Alex, 257

Nitchuk, John, 250, 252, 253, 256, 257, 258

Noha, Mike, 103, 170

Nosyk, Bob, 202

Nykoluk, Danny, **632**

Parubchak, Rosie,  192

Parubchak, Yurko,  47

Pasiak, Harry,  194

Pasichniak, Ted,  129, 130

Patraniuk, Pete,  144

Patrick, James,  **655**, 800

Patrick, Michael,  246

Patrick, Nicholas,  246

Patrick, Steve,  **657**, 805

Patrick Jr., Steve,  **659**

Patten, Stephan,  **660**

Pauk, Vera,  194

Pavlenchuk, George,  124

Pavliw, O.,  210

Pawlak, William,  203

Pawliuk, Stephen,  188

Pawluski, Barton,  74

Pawlychko-Skocen, Marika,  180, 233, 234

Pechaluk, Fred,  204, **661**, 812

Pechaluk, Gus,  204

Pecuh, I.,  284

Peepre, Sass,  196

Peiluk, Joe,  194

Pelech, Rev. Michael,  127

Pelech, Rev. O.,  289

Pelyk, Mike,  **662**

Penner, Orval,  151

Pereyma, O.,  124

Perun, I.,  115

Pesclovitch, William,  292

Petrow, Peter,  286, 287

Petrow, W.,  286

Petrucha, Mykola,  137

Petruk, Nick,  243

Petrychkovych, Fedir,  73

Petryshyn, Mike,  122

Petryshyn, Onufriy,  188

Philipovich, Billy,  29

Piaskoski, Jim,  **663**

Pidhirnyj, Ihor,  285

Shack, Eddie,  54, **718**, 807

Shaley, John,  58, 252, 253, 254, 256, 257, 258, 259, 260, 262, 263, 264, 265, 266, 268, **720**,
   809, 814

Shaley, Nick,  63, 247, 249, 252, 253, 254, 256, 268

Shaley, Stan,  58, 252, 253, 254, 256, 258, 259, 260, 263, 265, 268, **722**, 809

Shandro, Andrew,  133

Shapka, Anatol,  102, 168

Sharko, Walter,  129

Shastel, Mary,  255, 273, 852

Shaver, Rev. J.M.,  29

Shebunchak, Dr. Bohdan,  49

Shelenkoff, Boris,  122, 124

Shero, Doris,  255, 258

Shestokowsky, Alex,  124

Shewchuk, Jack,  **723**, 806, 815

Shewchuk, Stephanie,  **724**

Shibicky, Alex,  **726**, 811, 815

Shishka, Steven,  **727**, 815

Shklarenko, Bohdan,  235

Shmahun, Nykola,  77

Shmotolocha, Mykhailo,  172, 188

Shneider, Joseph,  102

Shugan, Bill,  81

Shumsky, Iryna,  *see* Moroz, Iryna

Shwaluk, Bill,  **728**, 801, 803, 810

Shwetz, Wolodymyr,  67

Shymko, Yuri,  50, 201

Sidney, Ken,  198

Sikevych, L.,  292

Sikorski, Paul,  249

Sim, Jack,  102

Simenik, Met,  291

Simpson, William,  56, 171

Skerlton, Luba,  852

Sklar, J.,  95

Skocen, Oleksander,  22, 37, 71, 72, 167, 168, 172, 173, 174, 177, 207, 209, 210, 213, **730**

Skocen, Wolodymyr,  179

Skoropadsky, Danylo,  165

Skoropadsky, Hetman Pavlo,  26, 165

Slipchuk, Michael,  74, **732**, 801

Slipetz, Eugene, 254
Slivinski, Albert, 30, 144, 145
Slobodian, Pete, 852
Slywynskyj, Alex, 196
Slyziuk, Ernest, **733**, 810, 815
Slyziuk, Michael, **735**, 806, 810, 815
Smerkal, I., 284
Smigelski, Ernie, 208, 209
Smith, Charles, 115
Smith, Frank, 80
Smith, William, 203
Smyl, Stan, **736**
Snylyk, Zenon, 98, 102
Sobchuk, Dennis, **738**
Sobchuk, Gene, **740**
Sochaniwsky, Alex, 186, 229
Sochaniwsky, M., 174
Sohuyko, Stephen, 167
Sokolyk, K.W., 50
Sokolyk, Yaroslaw, 162
Solarz, Ed, 275
Soliljak, Nick, 64
Solomon, John, 289
Soltys brothers, 242
Sopinka, John, 58, **741**
Sorbey, Wayne, 263
Sorokiwsky, Borys, 169
Sorokowski, B., 75
Spolsky, Evhen, 37
Sribnyj, Mike, 282, 286
Stanko, Andrew, 41, 180, 214, 219, 228, 852
Stanko, Orest, 180
Stanowski, Wally, **742**, 811, 815
Starr, Anne, 114, 120
Starr, Hon. Michael, 30, 114, 117, 118, 119, 120, 122
Stasiuk, B., 75
Stasiuk, Mike, 80
Stasiuk, Most Rev. Peter, **744**, 807
Stasiuk, S., 75
Stasiuk, Vic, 333, 337, 360, **745**

Tanasichuk, Hal, **754**, 814

Tarnawskyj, Maria, 225, 226

Tatarchuk, Hank, **755**, 801, 803

Tatarsky, George, 158

Tatarsky, Zenon, 228

Tatomyr, George, 22

Taylor, Barney, 147

Telepchuk, Stephen, 77

Teodorovych-Suk, Ivan, 163, 166, 170, 175, 176, 177, 181

Terlecki, Y., 216

Terry, Martin, 281

Tesluk, Norm, 814

Tester, Jim, 21

Tkaczuk, Walt, 316, **757**

Tolan, Eddie, 57

Tomiuk, Ihor, 108

Tomiuk, Dr. Sviatoslav, 108

Tomkiw, Christine, 39, 225, 226

Tomko, I., 101

Topolnicki, Marko, 205

Trach, L., 241

Trakalo, Dale, 814

Trofymovych, M., 164

Trutiak, M., 172

Tsar, Mykhailo, 210, 215

Tseyko, Ivan, 108

Tully, Joyce, 265

Turenko, Roman, 202

Turow, Thomas, **758**

Turyk, Walter, 77

Turylo, Walter, 199, 202

Tymchyshyn, Ivan, 67, 69

Tymochko, Myron, 190, 199, 201, 202

Tyzuk, Boris, **759**, 814


Ukrainitz, W., 75

Ulliot, 255

Unitas, Tony, 53

Upham, John, **761**, 801, 803

Urick, Nettie, 145

Wlasiuk, Gene,  **777**

Wolkowski, F.,  80

Wolkowski, Stan,  80, 852

Woloshansky, Paul,  237

Woloshinski, Myroslaw,  *see* Wilson, Sonny

Wolycka, Chrystyna,  224

Woodlands, Rita,  264

Worobetz, Mykhailo,  269, 272

Worobetz, Hon. Stephen,  129, 131

Worsley, Lorne "Gump,"  99

Woycyshyn, P.,  87, 88

Woytowich, Bob,  **778**, 811

Woznesensky, Lyall,  **780**, 814

Wozney, Rich,  852

Wrigley, Philip,  255

Wrzesnewskyj, Borys,  186

Wrzesnewskyj, Roman,  269

Wusyk, Bill,  **781**, 815

Wynnyckyj, Ostap,  171, 175

Wynnyckyj, Roman,  235

Wyrozub, Randy,  **783**


Yacashyn, B.,  75

Yakimischuk, Orest,  852

Yakiwchuk, Alanna,  **784**, 803

Yakubowich, Joyce,  *see* Sadowick-Yakubowich, Joyce

Yakymiv, Stephen,  235

Yakymyk, Mike,  852

Yanick, S.,  104

Yanush, John,  246

Yarema, Stephen,  161

Yaremchuk, Gary,  **786**

Yaremchuk, Ken,  **787**, 801

Yaremko, Hon. John,  15, 172

Yaremko, Mike,  272, 273

Yaremy, George,  89

Yaremy, Michael,  89

Yellow, P.,  159

Yemchuk, Morris,  144, 147

Yemchuk, N.,  146, 147

# INDEX - PART III


## UKRAINIAN
## SPORTS CLUBS, LEAGUES AND TEAMS

For the listing of clubs, leagues and teams, please see Table of Contents, pages 11-13.